LEGAL ETHICS IN THE PRACTICE OF LAW

Third Edition

Richard Zitrin
Adjunct Professor of Law
University of California, Hastings College of Law

Carol M. Langford
Adjunct Professor of Law
University of San Francisco School of Law

Nina W. Tarr
Professor of Law
University of Illinois College of Law

ISBN#: 0-8205-7034-6

Library of Congress Cataloging-in-Publication Data

Legal ethics in the practice of law / by Richard Zitrin, Carol M. Langford, Nina W. Tarr.
— 3rd ed.

p. cm.

Includes index.

ISBN 0-8205-7034-6 (hard cover)

1. Legal ethics — United States. I. Langford, Carol M. (Carol Mae), 1958-II. Tarr, Nina
W., 1952-III. Title.

KF306.Z57 2006

174'.30973—dc22

2006035389
CIP

This publication is designed to provide accurate and authoritative information in regard to the subject matter covered. It is sold with the understanding that the publisher is not engaged in rendering legal, accounting, or other professional services. If legal advice or other expert assistance is required, the services of a competent professional should be sought.

LexisNexis and the Knowledge Burst logo are trademarks of Reed Elsevier Properties Inc, used under license. Matthew Bender is a registered trademark of Matthew Bender Properties Inc.

Editorial Offices
744 Broad Street, Newark, NJ 07102 (973) 820-2000
201 Mission St., San Francisco, CA 94105-1831 (415) 908-3200
701 East Water Street, Charlottesville, VA 22902-7587 (434) 972-7600
www.lexis.com

(Pub. 03083)

To Jesse, Gabriel, and Maya —RZ

To Gregory and Nicholas —CML

To Michaela, Alex, and Stuart
Who help me keep my values straight —NWT

ACKNOWLEDGMENTS

Compiling the third edition of this book has been an exciting and challenging experience. Between the last edition and this there have been not just one but several sea changes in the world of legal ethics. We could not have kept up with these changes in a successful third edition without the help of many people, and we are indebted to each of them. Ethics professors Kathleen Clark, Monroe Freedman, Peter Joy, Drew Kershen, Rory Little, Judith Maute, and especially Bob Kuehn of the University of Alabama, have provided valuable comments over the years. Richard Heafy, our colleague at the University of San Francisco, has provided a constant and invaluable stream of new cases and articles that has helped keep us on our toes. Rob Waring, another USF colleague, developed film excerpts for each of our problems — a valuable teaching tool that we will pass on to those using this book. Maggie Moses has provided constant behind-the-scenes support vital to sustaining our work on each of our editions. Research assistants Mark Hsen Wu Chu, Manoj Gorantla Govindaiah, Kimbery B. Janas, Kenneth Wang, and Maureen Kay Wurfel all put their inventive minds to work. Patricia Estergard, Brenda Faul, and Angela Martin each provided valuable administrative assistance, and the University of Illinois College of Law Faculty Research Funds and the Stuart N. Greenberger Fund helped support Professor Tarr and her research assistants.

At the same time, we are reminded of those whose help was invaluable during our preparation of the first and second editions. Claude Piller, researcher extraordinaire, gave both inspiration and perspiration to both of those earlier efforts, combing the archives and the Internet for the most interesting potential new readings. Jane Nydorf was our rock for these earlier editions, unsparingly giving us her tireless and ever-cheerful help. Bob D'Arcy read every word of the first two editions and provided consistent editorial wisdom. For the second edition, both William M. Balin and Victoria Zitrin combined skilled drafting and creativity to help mold and modify existing problems and create new ones, and Waqar Hasib made certain that every reading was accounted for and properly cited.

We again thank those who helped us the first time around: Elona Baum, the law firm of Carroll, Burdick & McDonough, Peter Cling, Joan Cortez, Nancy Castor, Ralph Francis, Diane Gamlowski, Ted Gest, Michael Hartmann, Terry Inghroff, Steve Kassirer, Janet Loduca, Joe Levin, Peter McGaw, Laurie Robertson, Tracy Swann, Arthur Zitrin, Charlotte Zitrin, and Elizabeth Zitrin. Our friends and colleagues at USF, especially Professor (and former dean) Jay Folberg and former associate dean Linda Clardy, and at UC Hastings, especially Professor (and former academic dean) Leo Martinez, have always supported our efforts. Thank you.

We would like to single out for thanks our friends at LexisNexis, particularly our wonderful editors, Ally VonHockman and Pali Chheda, and again thank Lee Freudberg, who as director of law school publications for the Michie Company years ago, was among the first to have the vision to see the value of a book such as this. Finally, we are forever grateful to the hundreds of students at the University of California's Hastings campus, the University of San Francisco, and the University of Illinois, who over the last 28 years have tested both our materials and our teaching methods, and who consistently challenge us and help to make us wiser teachers and better lawyers.

Richard Zitrin
Carol M. Langford
Nina W. Tarr

October 2006

PREFACE TO THE THIRD EDITION

The first part of our Introduction, which follows on page 1, serves to explain the practice-oriented, "real world," problem-driven approach of this book. It also outlines both our approach to the discipline of legal ethics and the book's organizational structure. The purpose of this Preface is to give those with some familiarity with our first two editions a brief overview of what has changed — both in the world of legal ethics and, especially, in this volume.

In both instances, the changes have been substantial. The ABA adopted a wholesale revision to its Model Rules of Professional Conduct in 2002 and 2003, and the ALI's Restatement of the Law Governing Lawyers was finalized. More recently, Sarbanes-Oxley and new SEC regulations have changed the way corporate counsel deal with their clients, especially in the area of confidentiality. Corporate scandals, among them the Enron debacle, the WorldCom implosion, and, new as we go to press, the malfeasance involved in HP's "pretexting," implicated lawyers as well as corporate higher-ups. The explosion of high-tech advances continues at a faster pace than ever before.

In this Third Edition, we have tried to be responsive to these changes, while keeping intact the core of what seemed to work well in previous editions. Throughout, we have maintained our predisposition for accessible, readable materials that still satisfy necessary academic rigor.

Without exception, every Problem (for we continue to divide the book by Problems rather than Chapters) is changed from the last edition, and while several have mostly nips, tucks, and updates of citations, many required more substantial revision. We have excerpted several dozen new articles and cases that were published since our last edition, but we have maintained the last edition's structure and, we're glad to report, avoided significantly lengthening the text. (We have not, however, removed readings merely because they are older; some readings continue to have both resonance and importance.)

Among the most important new material we have added are:

- A new problem and readings on lawyering in a multi-cultural world;
- Extensive readings describing and analyzing Sarbanes-Oxley and the related SEC regulations;
- Readings on Enron and related corporate scandals, noting the themes common among these scandals;
- Continued focus on the responsibilities of the government lawyer, and extensive analysis of the Bybee "torture memorandum";
- Newly updated readings on technology, including the latest on e-mail confidentiality and how lawyers may get "clients" — and thus a conflicts of interest — from their own websites;
- Increasing and more pervasive discussion of the significance of race and gender issues as they affect the practice of law and legal ethics;
- Updated readings reflecting the evolution of conflicts of interest law, especially as it relates to disqualification, law firm imputation, and screening;

- Pervasively, an updated analysis where the new ABA rule modifications have changed the standards of ethical practice.

We hope you, both professors and students, find the changes useful and enjoyable. Anyone with questions or comments can reach us at zitrinr@usfca.edu, langford@usfca.edu, and ntarr@law.uiuc.edu. We look forward to hearing from you.

Richard Zitrin
Carol M. Langford
Nina W. Tarr

October 15, 2006

SUMMARY TABLE OF CONTENTS

TABLE OF CONTENTS

Page

INTRODUCTION

A. A PRACTICING LAWYER'S APPROACH TO ETHICS

Imagine yourself two or three years from now practicing law. You're an associate in a law firm, working hard for your clients and trying to impress the partners that one day you should make partner yourself. But a problem comes up in a matter you are handling for one of the firm's largest clients. It seems that either you or your secretary miscalculated by a day the deadline to file your opposition to a summary judgment motion. You've got the pleadings done and they're good, but you're a day late and the motions judge is a stickler on deadlines. You're in a panic, thinking about losing your job and how you'd make your student loan payments, not to mention the payments on the sports sedan you treated yourself to when you passed the bar. You confide in a fellow associate who was a couple of years ahead of you at law school, and she tells you, "Look, here's what you can do. Just turn the postage meter back a day, backdate the date on your opposition and mail it out this morning. Sometimes the postal service rejects backdated mail, but usually if you get it in the mail early enough, they don't. It'll probably get you off the hook, and no one will know the difference."

You walk away from the conversation feeling confused and upset. You know that turning back the postage meter is not the right thing to do, yet it seems so easy, and the ethics of the situation raised little concern with your more experienced friend, whose sense of "right" and "wrong" you have always admired. You feel enormous pressure, not just for yourself, but to protect your client's case. You know your law school ethics teacher would have cited you a rule — probably several — that your conduct would violate. You also recall how your supervising partner always talks about "whatever it takes to get the job done." You consider whether turning back the postage meter may be a situation of "no harm, no foul," since no one will be the wiser. You don't know how to resolve your dilemma, and you're not sure how fully your ethics course prepared you to deal with this situation.

Law schools teach students legal ethics in many different ways. Some schools, including many that title their courses "professional responsibility," focus on lecturing on the formal rules that govern that responsibility. They believe that a thorough knowledge of the black-letter "law of lawyering" provides the best law school curriculum.

Our focus is a little different. We ask this question: What is the role of a law school — or of a legal ethics text — if not to prepare students for the "real world"? We do not underestimate the importance of the rules, codes, opinions, and decisional law that articulate the underlying basic precepts of legal ethics. But the goal of this volume is considerably broader than just teaching these precepts. It is to help you prepare for the ethical dilemmas you will certainly

1

face as a practicing lawyer. We want to explore not just the traditional principles of legal ethics, but *how* these principles are used, how they interact, indeed how they conflict, in the real world practice of law. We also want to examine the relationship between these ethical principles and other important issues concerning the conduct of attorneys: Legal malpractice and related torts; bar discipline; court sanctions; and contempt, among others.

No ethical precepts conflict more frequently or graphically than two presented in our brief opening hypothetical — the competent, diligent, and thorough advocacy of a client's interests vs. the obligation to be truthful in one's words and deeds. And it would be naïve for us to ignore one more element of the equation — the practical and economic consequences of doing things by the book when doing it that way could jeopardize your job. After all, if you do not get that summary judgment opposition filed, the consequences to the client, and to your future at your firm, could be dire.

Accordingly, the focus of this book will be on the problem areas, ethical dilemmas rather than bright line tests, conflicts among ethical principles rather than resolution, and recognition of these dilemmas, rather than concrete solutions. There is an excellent reason for this approach. While some ethical issues can be answered simply and concretely, many of the day-to-day issues confronting practicing lawyers are far more subtle. As we will see throughout this volume, these are issues on which reasonable minds — including those of thoughtful ethics experts — often differ. Experience has shown us that while most lawyers learn the rules of ethics well enough to pass a short-answer ethics bar exam, too many simply aren't able to recognize ethical dilemmas in their own practices until it's too late.

The lawyer who learns to recognize ethical problems early is halfway to a solution. If you are able to recognize the warning signs, consider the dilemma you face and articulate the issues to yourself, finding a response to the situation becomes much easier. This will be the case whether you practice estate planning, criminal defense, civil litigation, transactional contract work, or public interest law.

Many of the most interesting ethical "grey areas," the issues that create dilemmas and conflict over ethical principles, arise because of tension between black letter rules of legal ethics and society's sense of right and wrong. Some ethical principles, including those that justify why the clearly guilty criminal defendant should be zealously represented, and why that defendant's confidences must be strictly protected, have their genesis in our Constitution. That document is a major source of the strong precepts of loyal and devoted advocacy for our clients, right or wrong, that have long been a fundamental part of our ethical rules. We will examine the tension between these rules and other important principles of our society: The obligation to tell the truth; the duty of fairness; the avoidance of racial, ethnic, and gender bias; the duty not to allow others to use our legal skills for their own illegal ends; the increasing significance of our multi-cultural society; and the obligation not to allow harm to come to others by virtue of our conduct, even if it means "blowing the whistle" on a client.

We will examine these issues in the context of the rules of legal ethics. In that analysis, however, we will not attempt to define morality any more than the rules of ethics could successfully legislate it. Rather, we hope that you will take your own sense of personal morality and analyze it in light of the principles of legal ethics that you learn here, in a way that helps you to develop a deeper understanding of yourself as an ethical lawyer.

You may wonder what we mean by the term "ethics" in the context of the practice of law. We believe that there is no one single answer to this complex question. Some commentators believe that legal ethics refers to "the law of lawyering," or the formal body of rules and opinions and cases that govern our behavior. Others agree with us that an understanding of legal ethics involves more — the consideration of both individual and group morality. A lawyer evaluating this moral component might ask questions like "How do I want to live my life as a practitioner?" and "What do I think the legal profession should be, and what is my role in that profession?" A group moral component has been defined by some as a law firm ethic, culture, or attitude. We hope that our own answer to the question of what "legal ethics" means will be more fully defined throughout the course of this book.

B.   A BRIEF WORD ABOUT THE ORGANIZATION OF THIS BOOK

This book adopts a problem-driven approach. The primary divisions in the syllabus are *problems*, not chapters; these problems are real world examples of the situations that face practicing lawyers every day. We have tried to keep the problems simple, believing that a "blank canvas" without too much detail will allow for the broadest possible analysis. The problems deal with many important black letter principles of legal ethics, which are amplified through the cases, ethics opinions, scholarly articles, and numerous colloquial readings which follow each problem. But we have also tried to infuse these problems with an element of reality, recognizing as practicing lawyers that from time to time, lawyers will consider the practical as well as the ethical consequences of their behavior.

We follow each problem with a series of readings, most of which are directly relevant to the problem, but some of which concern other related issues. Many of the readings are cases, excerpts of law review articles, or formal ethics opinions. But many of the readings are more colloquial — accounts from legal periodicals, newspaper accounts from the popular press, or our own discussion and analysis, which we often find is the most efficient way to express or stitch together several important ideas. Certain readings provide more black letter law analysis, while others, including many sections that we have written ourselves, are more important for making the ethical principles more accessible and easier to grasp, or for providing a strong dose of practicality. *We consider all these readings to be of equal importance. You will not get the full significance or flavor of this text by reading only the excerpted readings.* When we teach with these materials, we prefer to have our students lead discussions on each of the problems. The analysis of each problem will be more complete and informative if it includes a review of the readings which follow and a discussion of what ethical rules apply. These rules can be found in a supplementary volume. We discuss the formation and organization of these rules later in this Introduction. But no discussion of a problem is complete if it stops there. Discussing the rules provides a framework and a foundation, a beginning but not the end result.

We suggest that as you read a problem and the readings which follow it, you consider the following questions: (1) What conduct described in the problem either does or might violate a formal ethical rule?; (2) What conduct appears to violate some other obligation of a lawyer?; (3) Might the conduct result in civil liability for the lawyer or law firm?; (4) Is there tension or conflict between competing interests or rules of conduct, and if so, in what respect?; (5) How do you feel a lawyer *should* be acting in these circumstances, and why?; (6) Is there a tension or conflict between what you feel a lawyer *should* do in this situation and what the black letter rules seem to say a lawyer *must* do?; and (7) What practical considerations may be difficult to ignore in determining how a lawyer may behave in these circumstances? This is not a definitive list, but rather one we recommend to give you a sense of how to take a full, well-rounded approach to these issues.

The readings that follow each problem are organized by sub-headings, and have been edited by us specifically for this book. We have provided our own text before each reading, and after most of the readings we conclude with a *Notes* section that reflects some of our own thoughts. In addition, under many sub-headings, the text consists entirely of our own thoughts or analysis of a particular issue. Each outside reading is clearly demarcated with its author and title; in doing the editing, we have generally eliminated footnotes and citations without further reference.

We end the material on each problem with a list of several supplemental readings, which we briefly describe. Often, we use this section to point you to interesting readings that either were less adaptable to brief excerpting, concerned very narrow or collateral issues, or developed concepts somewhat more challenging or difficult to grasp. These readings are for those who are particularly interested in the subject matter raised and wish further resources. Since we prefer to teach these materials by using two student discussion leaders for each problem, the students often use these supplemental readings as further source materials for their analysis of the problem.

C.   THE RULES AND STANDARDS OF OUR PROFESSION

The Early Days. Before the ABA established its Canons of Ethics in 1908, there were no uniform rules of professional conduct. The principal guidance to the legal profession came from common law edicts setting forth a lawyer's duties, such as to advocate zealously for one's client and to maintain a client's confidences. These early standards were statements of principle with little if any disciplinary enforcement. Early guidance also came from treatises such as Baltimore lawyer David Hoffman's 1836 volume, *A Course of Legal Study,* that included "Fifty Resolutions" which he believed reflected the values important to attorneys of his time. In 1854 came Judge George Sharswood's *A Compend of Lectures on the Aims and Duties of the Profession of Law,* the publication of his lectures on the profession at the University of Pennsylvania.

The first ethical code originated in Alabama in 1887, based in part on Sharswood's precepts. In 1908, the ABA issued its first ethical principles, in the form of 32 Canons of Professional Ethics. But the ABA of 1908 was a far cry from the ABA today, exclusionary in membership and more interested in protecting those lawyers who represented large monied interests than the millions who formed the constituency for populist politicians of the time. The stimulus for the ABA's Canons came not so much from a desire to control lawyer conduct as from a speech critical of the profession given at Harvard in 1905 by the country's number one populist, President Theodore Roosevelt. Henry St. George Tucker, a wealthy Virginia lawyer, was then president of the ABA. Tucker was a political opponent of Roosevelt, and took personally the President's criticism of corporate lawyers who made their living advising clients on ways to evade regulatory control. Tucker formed a committee to draft rules of conduct. Perhaps not surprisingly, the resulting Canons reflected more closely the concerns of wealthy "gentlemen" practitioners than they did the views of the President.

Of the original 32 Canons, some clearly set a moral tone while others provided more specific regulatory principles. In reality, the former may have been designed primarily to regulate what powerful Philadelphia lawyer Henry Drinker called "Russian Jew boys" and other riff-raff who had become lawyers from "up out of the gutter." Drinker personified the elitism of the bar of the early twentieth century. He felt threatened by the idea that lawyers would lose professional status through creeping diversity, and so took matters into his own hands. As Chair of the ABA Committee on Professional Ethics for over a decade, he became a leading advocate of the Pennsylvania Preceptor Plan, a program designed to keep the bar clean by forbidding membership to lawyers from different ethnic backgrounds and lower social strata.

The early Canons addressed issues such as advertising and fee arrangements, but not because these were seen as purely ethical concerns. Their purpose was largely to control the conduct of sole practitioners and non-corporate lawyers who had to hustle for business, unlike Drinker and his colleagues, whose client base emanated from their social and Big Business connections. This helped to ensure that the balance of power in the profession would remain securely entrenched in the hands of those who held it throughout most of the nineteenth century.

The ABA Model Code. Over the first half of this century, the ABA Canons were expanded and improved on, finally increasing in number to 47. But not until 1964, when then ABA President and future Supreme Court Justice Lewis F. Powell formed a committee to develop a new set of standards, did the ABA even begin to modernize its approach. The result of Powell's initiative was the passage of the Model Code of Professional Responsibility in 1969. The Model Code began its life successfully. Although membership in the ABA is entirely voluntary, within a few years most states adopted the Code, in whole or in part, for their own rules of professional conduct. Unlike the Canons, the Code had a clear and detailed structure: Nine Canons, in effect chapters, each embodying a very broad general principle, and within each Canon, a series of Disciplinary Rules (DRs) and Ethical Considerations (ECs). The Preamble explains the function of the different elements of the Code:

> The Canons are statements of axiomatic norms, expressing in general terms the standards of professional conduct expected of

lawyers in their relationships with the public, with the legal system, and with the legal profession. They embody the general concepts from which the Ethical Considerations and the Disciplinary Rules are derived.

The Ethical Considerations are aspirational in character and represent the objectives toward which every member of the profession should strive. . . .

The Disciplinary Rules, unlike the Ethical Considerations, are mandatory in character. The Disciplinary Rules state the minimum level of conduct below which no lawyer can fall without being subject to disciplinary action. . . .

The ABA Model Rules. Despite the success of the Code, some lawyers felt that the ABA had not progressed enough in articulating a modern set of standards. They argued for an approach along the lines adopted by the American Law Institute in forming its restatements of law, with black letter rules followed by annotated comments. In 1977, only eight years after passage of the Code, the ABA formed another rules commission, this time led by noted Kansas City attorney Robert J. Kutak, with Yale Professor Geoffrey Hazard, Jr. acting as Reporter, or chief of staff to the Commission. Popularly known as the Kutak Commission, this group set out to develop standards that better reflected the modern practice of law. Unlike the committee which drafted the Code, much of the Kutak Commission's work occurred in the light of public scrutiny, and the Commission provided drafts of its rules for criticism and debate to the public as well as to lawyers.

The Kutak Commission published three drafts of its work in progress, in 1980 and 1981, and its 1982 submission to the ABA House of Delegates. True to its mission, the Commission recommended significant changes in certain traditional ethical precepts. Perhaps the most controversial was the idea that lawyers who see their clients doing harm to the public should have broad powers to abrogate attorney-client confidentiality where it is necessary for public protection. "Whistleblowing" provisions were drafted into both the rule on confidentiality and the rule describing the obligations of corporate counsel. While supported by much of the public, these provisions were excoriated by the majority of lawyers, especially trial lawyers and corporate counsel. By the time the ABA House of Delegates passed the Model Rules of Professional Conduct in August, 1983, these provisions had been removed. Indeed, one of the introductory paragraphs describing the scope of the Rules specifically warns against second-guessing lawyers who, because of confidentiality, decide *not* to disclose information.

The ABA Model Rules are divided into brief black letter rules and longer Comment sections. According to the introduction, the purpose of the Comments is to explain and interpret: "The Comments are intended as guides to interpretation, but the text of each Rule is authoritative." Tables were provided that cross-referenced the sections of the Rules with their Code counterparts. These tables proved necessary, because many states, having so recently adopted the Model Code, were reluctant to adopt a new set of Rules based on a wholly different organizational scheme. By 1994, however, the District of Columbia and all but six states had adopted some form of the Model

Rules as their own rules of conduct. Five states, Illinois, New York, North Carolina, Oregon, and Virginia, base their rules on both the Model Code and Model Rules.[1] And one state, California, which had never adopted the Model Code, also chose not to adopt the Model Rules, preferring instead to revise its own system of codification in 1989.

"Ethics 2000," and the New ABA Model Rules. In the late 1990s, the ABA undertook yet another revision of the rules. It began as a modest effort to modify the ABA Model Rules with a few nips and tucks, and to harmonize them with the American Law Institute's (ALI) new Restatement of the Law Governing Lawyers. By 2000, it was clear that the ABA "Ethics 2000" Commission, or "E2K," as it became known, had taken on a full-scale revision of the rules. Unlike the Kutak Commission, Ethics 2000 did not seek a new rules structure but revisions with the same rule and comment organization as the current Model Rules. Many rules were changed little, while others were substantially modified. The commission conducted widespread public hearings and consulted an extensive advisory council in an effort to get as many divergent views as possible. The result was a complete revision of the ABA Model Rules, passed by the House of Delegates in 2002 and 2003. As we go to press with this edition, about half the states have formally adopted their own versions of these new rules.

The ALI Restatement, and the MDP Commission. Meanwhile, the ALI, which had begun to create its Restatement of lawyering in 1986, continued to revise that document throughout the 1990s. This and E2K's efforts were joined by those of the ABA's Commission on Multidisciplinary Practice (MDP Commission), which in 1999 and again in 2000 recommended changes to the rules governing lawyers who practice with accountants and other non-legal professionals.

By the millennium, the efforts of the MDP commission and the ALI had became increasingly political processes — perhaps not surprising in light of the history of rules-making from 1908 on. The MDP Commission, while proposing needed and perhaps inevitable reforms, met overwhelming resistance from those in the ABA who were afraid to yield on the issue of lawyers' monopoly of legal services.[2] The ABA's House of Delegates soundly rejected the MDP Commission's proposals more than once.

The ALI was racked by political disputes from within. Criticizing the politicization of the Restatement, as exemplified by an incident in which insurance industry lawyers overtly lobbied for votes, one of the ALI's 3,000 members, Georgetown professor Sherman L. Cohn, wrote in 1997 that if the ALI had ever been considered "an objective, disinterested body [of lawyers that] struggled for a restatement of the law based upon their own consciousness of what the law is, . . . it is clearly not true today."[3]

---

[1] *See* American Bar Association & Bureau of National Affairs, *Lawyer's Manual of Professional Conduct* 1:3-1:4 (rev. 1999).

[2] We discuss this issue at some length in Chapter 13.

[3] Sherman L. Cohn, *The Organization Client: Attorney-Client Privilege and the No-Contact Rule*, 10 GEO. J. LEGAL ETHICS 739, 789 (1997).

Nevertheless, the ALI navigated through its issues and approved the Restatement, Third, of the Law Governing Lawyers[4] before the new Model Rules were completed. At the same time however, its politicization, coupled with the fact that its purpose (unlike the ABA's) was not to create a work that would actually become the officially approved ethical standard in any jurisdiction, make it, at least in our judgment, significantly less important than the ABA Model Rules. Despite its rocky road to completion, however, the Restatement has garnered a good measure of general acceptance as a significant source document among both academics and courts.

Sources of Guidance Beyond the Rules. Neither the ABA's nor the individual states' rules of ethics stand alone. The ABA Standing Committee on Ethics and Professional Responsibility drafts opinions on ethical issues. So too do the ethics committees of most states and several local bars. These opinions supplement and explain the rules in their respective jurisdictions. In addition, there are other sources of ethical guidance provided by both the ABA and other organizations. In the late 1970s, the ABA developed Standards Relating to the Administration of Criminal Justice for both prosecutors and defense lawyers. The Standards do not have the same authority as the ABA Model Code or Rules themselves, but are useful guidelines which have often been relied on by state and federal courts when evaluating the conduct of the criminal bar. The ABA's Model Code of Judicial Conduct, revised in 2004, is now in the process of being adopted by most states and federal courts.

Numerous voluntary associations of lawyers have also created their own ethical guidelines. In addition to the ALI, the Federal Bar Association, for example, an organization made up of lawyers practicing federal law, issued its Model Rules of Professional Conduct for Federal Lawyers in 1990. The American Trial Lawyers Foundation, concerned by provisions in the ABA's proposed Model Rules, published the American Lawyer's Code of Conduct (ALCC) in 1982, and has significantly revised that Code since. Other special practice organizations, from national district attorneys and criminal defense groups, to associations of labor lawyers, patent attorneys, and so on, draft their own ethical codes. These, though not binding in individual states, provide important guidance from thoughtful colleagues who are engaged in a similar practice.

READINGS

The Way It Was. As we will do throughout the course of this book, we now present readings that we find relevant to our discussion above. Our first is an excerpt from Jerold S. Auerbach's fascinating 1976 book on the history of lawyers in America. We focus on the period before America's entry into the First World War, the time when the ABA's first Canons of Ethics were taking

---

[4] There is no Restatement Second or First. The "Third" refers to the fact that the ALI is in its third edition of Restatements. This is the *first* ALI ethics codification, one of the indications of the increasing importance of ethics in the legal world in the last generation.

shape. There are many more interesting stories in this book, which is still in print and recommended to anyone interested in American legal history.

JEROLD S. AUERBACH, UNEQUAL JUSTICE: LAWYERS AND SOCIAL CHANGE IN MODERN AMERICA
(1976)[5]

The bar association movement was a characteristic feature of the decades surrounding 1900. . . . [T]he American Bar Association, organized in 1878, had more diffuse purposes: To promote the administration of justice, to advance jurisprudence, to uphold professional honor, and to encourage social intercourse among lawyers. But the ABA exuded the genial tone of a social club, set by its predominantly Southern members who came to Saratoga Springs each year to escape the summer heat. The "benefit of the waters," one member declared, rivaled in importance the professional business of the association. Simeon Baldwin, the moving spirit behind the association, labored to confine membership "to leading men or those of high promise. . . ." Local associations often were similarly exclusive. The Boston Bar Association seemed to exist solely for the benefit of State Street and Federal Street lawyers. The Chicago Bar Association, founded (in the words of one of its presidents) to bring "the better and the best elements of the profession together," charged high admission fees and annual dues to achieve its purpose. The strongest pillars of the Association of the Bar of the City of New York were Yale, Harvard, and Protestantism. . . .

Bar associations did venture timidly into the shallower waters of law reform, but they usually skirted the dangerous shoals of substantive change. In 1912 ABA president Stephen Gregory declared that professional associations were "the chief instrumentality of constructive legal reform." Rarely, however, did their concern extend to such problems as the provision of legal services. At best, they preoccupied themselves with the most technical, professional aspects of legal issues — for example, the ethical proprieties of contingent fees rather than the social and individual cost of lives broken in industrial accidents. The result was that law reform served as "a banner of rectitude waved in the public eye," a shield to deflect public criticism. . . .

During the second decade of the twentieth century the American Bar Association began to assert itself aggressively as a professional protective organization. Its purpose was twofold: To preserve its own exclusiveness (and the status that accompanied its preservation) and to exert professional leverage upon the political process. Two prewar episodes provided a test of its strength and scope: The admission of black lawyers and the nomination of Louis D. Brandeis to the Supreme Court.

In 1912 the executive committee of the American Bar Association unknowingly admitted three black lawyers to membership. Informed of its carelessness, it quickly passed a resolution rescinding the admission and — "since the settled practice of the Association has been to elect only white men as members" — referring the matter for determination by the entire association. Attorney General George W. Wickersham protested (one of the contested

---

members, a Harvard law school graduate, was his assistant in the Department of Justice) — not from any commitment to racial equality but from disgust with procedural irregularities that violated association by-laws. He was assured by the association's secretary that the recision resolution had been adopted only with "a sincere purpose to do what seemed . . . to be right and just. . . ." And he was sternly chastised for his "discourteous and dogmatic" criticism, a display of pique unbecoming an association member. But Moorfield Storey, a past president of the bar association and the first president of the National Association for the Advancement of Colored People, was incensed. "It is a monstrous thing," he complained, "that we should undertake to draw a color line in the Bar Association." Storey repudiated the notion that blacks were excluded by association policy, although he conceded that none had ever been admitted. The association was in a quandary. Claiming to be a national organization, it functioned as a restricted social club. The admission of blacks, in the words of its membership chairman, posed "a question of keeping pure the Anglo-Saxon race." A compromise resolution precluded future associational miscegenation. Prodded by Storey, members permitted the three duly elected black lawyers to remain but provided that all future applicants must identify themselves by race. The association thereby committed itself to lily-white membership for the next half-century. It had elevated racism above professionalism.

Professionalism converged with politics in the Brandeis donnybrook. The first of several dramatic twentieth-century Court nomination controversies, it brought into sharp focus the public implications of professional parochialism. More was at stake than a judicial seat, although a place on the Supreme Court was hardly inconsequential at a time when the judiciary was praised or blamed as the most reliable defender of vested property interests against public regulation. On the surface the division seemed clear. Brandeis' opponents, drawn largely from State Street law firms and from the American Bar Association, could plausibly see the Boston people's attorney as a threat to their restricted professional world. They spoke of the law as a bulwark of private property; Brandeis, who would not have disagreed, had often used it as an instrument of social change to make property owners more responsible to the public. They devoted their careers to counseling private interests; Brandeis committed much of his to public service. Their law was a "brooding omnipresence"; his was shaped by contemporary social needs. They defined themselves as counselors to corporations; Brandeis, an opponent claimed, "acts the part of a judge toward his clients instead of being his clients' lawyer." They were Protestant; he was the first Jewish nominee to the Supreme Court.

These differences masked some striking similarities between Brandeis and his critics: His commitment to efficiency and order; his application of business values to the operation of his law firm; his admiration for the great New York firms; his fear of radical challenges to American institutions; and his insistence that only lawyers were competent to criticize and remedy defects in the administration of law and justice. But the differences were crucial. They determined that the challenge to Brandeis would cut across every major professional concern of the day: Ethnicity; the social functions of law; the role of lawyers; and standards of professional character, conduct, and ethics. As "an outsider, successful, and a Jew," Brandeis was suspect. His confirmation fight was a symbolic crusade, pitting the newest defenders of the established professional order against the outsider who was especially dangerous because he shared so many of their attributes yet put them to such different use. It was precisely because Brandeis' credentials were so impeccable — a brilliant record at Harvard Law School and a lucrative corporate practice — that the opposition to his appointment was so revealing.

. . . .

Brandeis' opponents staked their claim on the ground of ethics and character. Moorfield Storey . . . testified to Brandeis' reputation as "an able lawyer, very energetic, ruthless in the attainment of his objects, not scrupulous in the methods he adopts, and not to be trusted." . . . Dipping his pen in vitriol, [former President and future Chief Justice William Howard Taft] dispatched letter after letter of calumny to friends and family, berating Brandeis for his ethics, politics, and religion.

By resting their public opposition on ethical and character defects, opponents of the nomination avoided a direct confrontation on the grounds of religion or reform. Storey, for example, vigorously denied that criticism of Brandeis was attributable to anti-Semitism or to politics. Lawyers, he insisted, objected to Brandeis solely "on the ground of his character." But "character" already had become a term of art in the legal profession, applied unerringly to those lawyers — and only to those — whose religion, national origin, or politics threatened the professional status quo. Certainly it is impossible to know (and unnecessary to establish) what distressed his opponents more: His Jewishness, his public service, his successful practice, his outspoken opposition to corporate arrogance, his social approach to legal problems, or his judgments upon the justness of a client's case. Success aside, these traits made Brandeis a professional outsider — reason enough to contest his nomination.

NOTES

Brandeis, of course, made it to the Court, albeit by the slimmest of margins. What about the attitude of the early bar associations, including the ABA? Does it surprise you? Remember the times in which this exclusionary, elitist conduct occurred: The Jim Crow segregated South, mass immigration in the North that threatened the established white Protestant order, and the exponential growth of trade unions and the workers' rights movement. Perhaps this history shows that lawyers are products of their times, and have as much difficulty as anyone else in rising above them. Think about the state of the legal profession today. Are the same circumstances true, or is it possible for legal institutions to stake out a higher moral ground? If institutions can't do it, can individual lawyers?

SUPPLEMENTAL READINGS

1. One of the deans of legal ethics, Prof. Monroe Freedman of Hofstra, long a member of the ALI, has written a stinging indictment of the ALI Restatement's drafting process, *Caveat Lector: Conflicts of Interest of ALI Members in Drafting the Restatements*, 26 Hofstra L. Rev. 641 (1998).

2. There are several valuable e-newsletters available, including *Ethics and Lawyering Today*, published roughly once a month by William Freivogel (see No. 5 below) and Lucian Pera, a Tennessee practitioner and member of the Ethics 2000 commission. Their goal is a practical approach to ethics, brief and to-the-point summaries of new cases and opinions and an alert on breaking issues. Subscriptions and other information are available at *www.ethicsandlawyering.com*. The national lawyer defense firm Hinshaw & Culbertson produces several e-newsletters, including "Lawyers for the Profession" and "Lawyers' Professional Liability Update" both of which help keep other attorney conduct lawyers up to date. Hinshaw's research site at *www.hinshawculbertson.com/knowledge/knowledge.aspx* links to both "alerts" and newsletters.

3. Our other supplemental readings for this introduction are all websites with valuable information on legal ethics. We begin by referencing the website of the ABA's Center for Professional Responsibility, *www.abanet.org/cpr/home.html*. Other websites of particular value in researching and evaluating legal ethics issues include the following:

4. *www.legalethics.com*, a site maintained by cyberethics experts Peter Krakaur and Prof. David Hricik, posts ethics information including a large library of state ethics opinions, information on Internet ethics and other cyberspace issues, as well as links to other information. The site covers far more than ethics and technology, and also emphasizes ethics and legal malpractice avoidance. David Hricik has his own home page at *www.hricik.com* that features risk management and intellectual property issues and contains a nice, straightforward series of links to state ethics sources.

5. Freivogel on Conflicts at *www.freivogelonconflicts.com* is quite an extraordinary site, chock full of summaries of a huge number of conflicts of interest cases, a similarly extensive and easy-to-navigate table of contents, and a "what's new" section that gives recent updates. Attorney William Frievogel, long involved in ethics and malpractice avoidance issues, maintains the site, which is designed as a "practical online guide to conflicts of interest for lawyers with sophisticated business and litigation practices." It's straightforward enough, though, for any researcher to understand, breaking conflicts of interest issues into about three dozen separate categories.

6. Cornell University's *www.law.cornell.edu/ethics* is perhaps the most complete research library of information on legal ethics on the web, maintained by Cornell ethics professor Roger Cramton and others.

7. *legalethicsforum.com* is as of this writing perhaps the most significant ethics blog: A group of about ten law school ethics professors from across the country lead a vigorous and dynamic discussion on a wide variety of current issues.

8. *findlaw.com/01topics/14ethics/index.html:* The ethics portion of the Findlaw site also provides excellent research and library sources.

Chapter 1

INITIAL REFLECTIONS ON ETHICS, MORALITY, AND JUSTICE IN AN ADVERSARY SYSTEM

READINGS

1. Some Initial Reflections, and Some Thoughts From Abe Lincoln. We are about to embark on a journey thorough the practice of law — one that quite naturally begins with the formation of a special relationship between lawyer and client. In our adversary system of justice, it is that special relationship that has long been given primacy in defining our behavior as lawyers. But before we begin our analysis and discussion of that relationship, we want to take note of what we believe to be the central ethical question which drives modern American jurisprudential thinking. It is this — how do we balance two conflicting considerations: First, our strong Anglo-American tradition of advocacy, where the client's needs are considered paramount and lawyers serve as the willing tools of their clients; and second, our obligations to the system of justice, and a society of laws in which we all work and live? Put another way, how do we reconcile our roles as ethical, professionally responsible attorneys, acting loyally, perhaps even zealously, on our clients' behalves, with our private selves, human beings with strongly held beliefs of personal morality?

Indeed, it is precisely this issue which is most often raised in disapproval by those outside the profession. There, the tenor of the inquiry may be more along the lines of "How can you in good conscience act the way you do?" Or, more bluntly, "Why do lawyers seem so morally bankrupt? Why are they such jerks?"

We will return to these questions, and the tension between the goals of a client-oriented adversary system and a society-based system of morality, on more than one occasion in these pages. Like a diamond — or perhaps more apt, Rubic's cube — it is an issue that has many facets, and appears to look quite different depending on the perspective that we have at the time.

We begin with the perspective of perhaps the one American lawyer whose public image remains almost completely untarnished — Abraham Lincoln.

ABRAHAM LINCOLN, NOTES OF A LAW LECTURE
(July 1, 1850)[1]

Discourage litigation. Persuade your neighbors to compromise whenever you can. Point out to them how the nominal winner is often the real loser — in fees, expenses and waste of time. As a peacemaker, the lawyer has a superior opportunity of being a good man. Never stir up litigation. A worse man can scarcely be found than one who does this.

. . . .

There is a vague popular belief that lawyers are necessarily dishonest. . . . [T]he impression is common, almost universal. Let no young man choosing the law for a calling for a moment yield to the popular belief. Resolve to be honest at all events; and if in your own judgment you cannot be an honest lawyer, resolve to be honest without being a lawyer. Choose some other occupation, rather than one in the choosing of which you do in advance, consent to be a knave.

2. The Duty of Advocacy and Defending the Guilty. In 1840 in England, a man named Courvoisier was accused of murdering Lord William Russell. He had the good fortune to have as his attorney one of the leading barristers of his day, Charles Phillips. In his wonderful 1973 treatise *The Conscience of a Lawyer*, Professor David Mellinkoff describes Phillips' zealous defense of Courvoisier, who nevertheless was convicted and sentenced to death. During the course of the case, Courvoisier had confessed his guilt to his lawyer, putting Phillips in the unenviable position of having to decide whether to advocate on behalf of a guilty man. When he chose to do so, he gained little but disapprobation, as Prof. Mellinkoff tells us in these excerpts.

DAVID MELLINKOFF, THE CONSCIENCE OF A LAWYER
(1973)[2]

[I]n the same Monday morning newspapers carrying the story of Courvoisier's conviction and the first accounts of his confession of guilt, the word was out that before Charles Phillips spoke to the jury Courvoisier had confessed his guilt to his counsel. Of all the confessions of Courvoisier, this one was to have the most lasting effects, surviving Courvoisier's making peace with man and God, clouding the remaining years of Charles Phillips, following Phillips into the final estimate of his contemporaries, stirring controversy over the role of Courvoisier's counsel and counsel in general, and ultimately influencing the ethical canons of lawyers in England, America, and wherever the Anglo-American system of legal representation has taken hold.

. . . .

Without bothering for the moment with the details of exactly what it was that Phillips had said to the jury, some immediately struck out at the fundamental horror, as repellant to Victorian London as to many today:

---

[1] These "notes" have been quoted in many sources, including several books on legal quotations, among them *2000 Famous Legal Quotations* by M. Frances McNamara (1967) and *The Oxford Book of Legal Quotations* (1993), and in collections of Lincoln's writings, including Volume 2 of *The Collected Works of Abraham Lincoln*, edited by Roy P. Basler.

[2] Copyright © 1973. Reprinted with permission of the West Publishing Corporation.

Phillips had been trying to persuade a jury to acquit a man he knew was guilty.

"One of the Profession" summed up the public's outrage in a letter to *The Times*:

> Sir, — After reading the eloquent and impassioned address of Mr. C. Phillips in defence of Courvoisier, a doubt suggested itself to my mind whether a profession in which a man employs his talent 'to screen the guilty, and to varnish crime', can be considered honorable.
>
> The culprit had avowed his guilt, and in the course of his speech Mr. Phillips stated to the jury 'that the prisoner was accused of murdering a member of the admirable Russell family, and the only son of the deceased victim he was proud to call his friend.' . . .
>
> I seek not to impeach Mr. Phillips' character, which, from report, I believe to be of a high order, nor that of counsel in general pursuing the same line of conduct. They may be, and possibly are, 'all honourable men,' but . . . I am simple enough to consider that he who defends the guilty, knowing him to be so, forgets alike honour and honesty, and is false to God and man!
>
> If my friend is to protect the butcher of my sleeping parent, though conscious of his guilt, Lord save me from my friends.
>
> . . . .

A legal periodical *The Jurist* tackled the "grave and difficult question" raised by Courvoisier's case. It editorialized that the customary rule of the English bar requiring counsel to defend regardless of his opinion as to guilt or innocence is "inconsistent with the laws of morality, since it amounts to neither more nor less than that a man is bound to deceive, if it be for the interest of his client." To Lord Erskine's argument that "[i]f the advocate refuses to defend, he assumes the character of the judge; nay, he assumes it before the hour of judgment . . . .", *The Jurist* replied that in the unlikely event that no lawyer would take a man's case, he would have himself to thank for it that "the evidence . . . on his own shewing, was so strong as to afford irresistible inference of his guilt." "We contend," *The Jurist* bluntly concluded, "that if an accused person be really guilty, he has no moral right to any defence."

The Bishop of London brought the moral issue (in "what had occurred on a late most melancholy and remarkable occasion") onto the floor of the House of Lords. He presented a petition from "the inhabitants of London" asking that the legislation of 1836 giving prisoner's counsel a right to address the jury be now reconsidered, as being "a principle of exceedingly questionable propriety." Without attacking the profession as such, it was, the Bishop said, a "question that really concerned the character of the community at large." He found himself unable to reconcile some "passages of God's word . . . with the propriety of any man taking a reward to prove that to be otherwise which the accused himself had distinctly confessed."

In the Lords when the Bishop of London spoke was Charles Phillips' friend Lord Brougham, who two decades earlier in the same chamber had successfully defended Queen Caroline against a charge of adultery, and in doing so had pulled out the last stop in speaking of the zeal a lawyer must bring to his client's cause:

> . . . If once a barrister is to be allowed to refuse a brief, and to say he will not defend a man because he is in the wrong, many will be found who will refuse to defend men, not on account of the case, but because they are weak men, under the pressure of unpopularity, against whom power has set its mark, because they are the victims of oppression, or are about to be made so. . . .

The argument between the Bishop of London and Lord Brougham has been continued in a thousand forums since, and has not ended. It renewed not only the fundamental questioning of the morality of the profession of law, but even more basic questions of the purpose of the system of justice.

. . . .

[Both David Hoffman and George Sharswood addressed the issue which faced Charles Phillips. Hoffman, writing four years before Courvoisier's case, questioned the very representation itself.]

. . . While not naming "Hoffman's Resolutions" as a source of misapprehended duty, Judge Sharswood went straight to the point of Hoffman's dudgeon over lawyers who "screen such foul offenders from merited penalties." He stated plainly that even a guilty man "has a constitutional right to a trial according to law . . . It is not to be termed screening the guilty from punishment, for the advocate to exert all his ability, learning, and ingenuity in such a defense, even if he should be perfectly assured in his own mind of the actual guilt of the prisoner." . . .

> Nothing seems plainer than the proposition, that a person accused of a crime is to be tried and convicted, if convicted at all, *upon evidence*, and *whether guilty or not guilty*, if the evidence is insufficient to convict him, he has a *legal right* to be acquitted. The tribunal that convicts without sufficient evidence may decide according to the fact; but the next jury, acting on the same principle, may condemn an innocent man. . . . And what offence to truth or morality does his advocate commit in discharging that duty to the best of his learning and ability? What apology can he make for throwing up his brief? The truth he cannot disclose; the law seals his lips as to what has been communicated to him in confidence by his client. He has no alternative, then, but to perform his duty. It is his duty, however, as an advocate merely, as Baron Parke has well expressed it, to use ALL FAIR ARGUMENTS ARISING ON THE EVIDENCE. Beyond that, he is not bound to go in any case; in a case in which he is satisfied in his own mind of the guilt of the accused, he is not justified in going.

3. Should Legal Ethics Ignore Social Morality? Both Lord Brougham and Judge Sharswood rose to Charles Phillips' defense by arguing that Phillips did the ethical thing. But what does this conduct say about the *morality* of being a lawyer? Prof. Mellinkoff himself asks this larger question. Do we as lawyers have the luxury of answering it? Should a lawyer consider the morality as well as the ethics of his or her conduct? Should morality ever determine the issue?

The debate about defending the known guilty party has continued to the present day, to the extent that the question most often asked of lawyers by non-lawyers is "How can you justify representing someone you're convinced is guilty?" Many cases in recent years — the Menendez brothers, the New York City policemen who shot the unarmed Amadeo Diallo, Timothy McVeigh, and, most compellingly, O.J. Simpson — have made it clear that this issue continues to resonate with the American public, and with lawyers and legal scholars as well. We will focus on it specifically in Problem 14.

Meanwhile, read one modern journalist's view of the relationship of legal ethics to morality.

RICHARD COHEN, A ROLLING ETHIC GATHERS NO MOSS
Washington Post Magazine (May 1, 1988) [3]

I asked a lawyer, an eminent and well-respected one, what he would do if he discovered that the murder suspect he was defending was guilty. Without pausing, he gave his answer. He would make sure his client did not take the stand to testify. That would ensure that the defendant would not commit perjury. Other than that, the lawyer would give the murderer the best defense possible. It was, the lawyer said, the ethical thing to do.

Notice the use of the word "ethical." It's a powerful word, much in vogue nowadays if only because every profession has its code of ethics. But notice, too, how it obscures all sorts of moral questions. Take the case of the lawyer with a guilty client on his hands. He said, as most lawyers would, that it was not his obligation to determine guilt or innocence. That was the jury's job. It was his obligation to provide the best defense possible.

Yes, but the client is a killer and the lawyer knows it. A jury verdict of innocence would not change that fact. Nor would it change the fact that a murderer had gone free, possibly to murder again. If the killer did kill again, would the lawyer hold himself morally responsible? Not likely. Instead, he would say he did the ethically proper thing. . . .

My own profession is not averse to braying its ethical obligations whenever challenged. Journalists maintain they have an ethical obligation to protect their sources. They say this whenever someone who has been skewered in the press demands to know the source of the charges. The right to face your accused is basic under law, but not in journalism. We have an ethical obligation to shield those who give us information. As for our moral obligation, well, we almost never consider it. The word "ethics" stops us cold.

Until relatively recently, doctors and lawyers were ethically proscribed from advertising. This was a serious injunction, and violators could lose their livelihood. Did that ethical prohibition have anything to do with morality? Nope. In fact, what it did was ensure that fees remained high — reflecting a school of ethical thought that holds that what's good for me is ethical.

Niccolo Machiavelli, the great Florentine thinker whose name the French came to use as a synonym for immorality, is the father of modern ethics. Writing in the late 15th and early 16th century from a Florence that was being buffeted by every regional war, that was a constant pawn in the struggles between the church, France and the Holy Roman Empire, Machiavelli yearned for a leader who could rescue his poor city-state. Such a man — a prince — would have to be both ruthless and cynically realistic. He would have to understand the base nature of man. It might be immoral to slaughter your enemies, as Cesare Borgia, a ruthless leader in Machiavelli's time, had done, but if in the long run such policies resulted in stability and peace, then ethically, according to Machiavelli, they were permissible. Morality would be considered but could be disregarded; ethics would replace it.

But at least Machiavelli — a poet, novelist, romantic and, ultimately, religious man — knew the meaning and importance of morality. He knew right from wrong. The end might justify the means, but he recognized that the means nevertheless might be immoral. The concept of morality still had meaning. Not so with the contemporary professional. To him, everything comes down to ethics, usually an ethical code. If something is permitted, it's right — and how dare anyone question.

Probably in the long run it's best that lawyers defend anyone in need of a defense. Their ethical code makes sense. It has a utility. Ultimately, it serves society's interests. The same is probably true for journalists. (If you think I'm going to also pardon lobbyists, you're wrong.) But these ethical codes (sometimes merely oral traditions) are too often cited as if nothing more need be — or could be — said, as if they replaced individual morality or, if you will, character. For instance, Lloyd Cutler, a Washington lawyer of such eminence that there is no one more eminent, defended his role as a lobbyist for the makers of dangerous all-terrain vehicles by saying, "It's the duty of a lawyer to represent anyone for whom a responsible argument could be made." In other words, since it's ethical, how dare anyone question his morality.

Erich Segal, author of the goopy novel *Love Story*, wrote that being in love means never having to say you're sorry. Wrong. People in love are forever apologizing. Having a code of ethics means never having to say you're sorry.

NOTES

Is it as simple as Cohen states, that lawyers ignore the moral in choosing the ethical? Would some lawyers at least consider morality before deciding to do what their profession requires? Might some lawyers even argue that defending the guilty person is not only ethical, but also has a moral justification? For example, suppose a lawyer argued that while *truth* might not be served, *justice*, including forcing the state to meet its heavy burden of proof, would indeed be served by defending the guilty. What is your reaction to this justification? Can you think of others?

4. "Moral Costs." In the courtrooms and legislatures of 1990s America, a morality play was staged in the national political theater. The subject was the dangerous and addictive properties of tobacco smoke, and the efforts made by the tobacco industry both to adjust nicotine levels and to prevent public disclosure of the industry's own highly damaging scientific studies. Lawyers, of course, were central members of the cast. The tobacco company lawyers' efforts to hide behind the shield that all clients should be afforded zealous representation sounded increasingly tenuous and hollow. Still, as late as 1992, tobacco lawyers had a perfect record of protecting the industry from outside scrutiny. The only chink in the armor was a series of disclosures made in a single New Jersey federal court case that was reversed on appeal.[4]

By 1998, however, with the settlement of lawsuits brought by states' attorneys general and the release by Congress of 39,000 formerly secret documents, it became clear that lawyers were directly involved in the tobacco industry's attempt to cover up what it knew about the dangers of its product. Some lawyers went even farther: The Council on Tobacco Research (CTR), supposedly an organization for scientific study, turned out to be a repository of damaging information for which confidentiality was claimed, and maintained, because the CTR was largely run by *lawyers*, not scientists. On some level, the American public — and, on this occasion at least, the governments in Washington and almost every state — seemed to be insisting on more: A moral imperative to lawyer conduct.

Years earlier, in 1980, Gerald Postema wrote a particularly thoughtful article about the interrelationship between a lawyer's ethical conduct and the moral imperative of that lawyer's actions. We excerpt some of his thoughts here.

GERALD POSTEMA, MORAL RESPONSIBILITY IN PROFESSIONAL ETHICS
55 New York University Law Review 63 (1980)[5]

The requirements of professional ethics can sometimes move some distance from the concerns of private or ordinary morality, a phenomenon we might call *moral distance*. . . .

Morality seems to require not only that one be able to apply moral principles properly to one's own or another's conduct, but also that one be able to appreciate the moral costs of one's actions, perhaps even when those actions are unintentional. By "moral costs" I mean those features of one's action and its consequences touching on important concerns, interests, and needs of others that, in the absence of specific justification, would provide substantial if not conclusive moral reasons against performing it.

. . . .

Since the lawyer often acts as an extension of the legal and moral personality of the client, the lawyer is under great temptation to refuse to accept responsibility for his professional actions and their consequences. Moreover, except when his beliefs coincide with those of his client, he lives with a recurring dilemma: He must engage in activities, make arguments, and present positions which he himself does not endorse or embrace. The lawyer's integrity is put into question by the mere exercise of the duties of his profession.

To preserve his integrity, the lawyer must carefully distance himself from his activities. Publicly, he may sharply distinguish statements or arguments

---

[4] *Haines v. Liggett Group, Inc.*, 140 F.R.D. 681 (D.N.J. 1992), *rev'd* 975 F.2d 81 (3rd Cir. 1992).

[5] Copyright © 1980. Reprinted by permission.

he makes for the client and statements on which he stakes his professional honor. The danger in this strategy is that a curious two-stage distancing may result. First, the lawyer distances himself from the argument: It is not his argument, but that of his client. His job is to construct the arguments; the task of evaluating and believing them is left to others. Second, after detaching himself from the argument, he is increasingly tempted to identify with this stance of detachment. What first offers itself as a device for distancing oneself from personally unacceptable positions becomes a defining feature of one's professional self-concept. This, in turn, encourages an uncritical, uncommitted state of mind, or worse, a deep moral skepticism. When such detachment is defined as a professional ideal, as it is by the standard conception, the lawyer is even more apt to adopt these attitudes.

. . . .

Consider first the personal costs the lawyer must pay to act in this detached manner. . . . In a large portion of his daily experience, in which he is acting regularly in the moral arena, he is alienated from his own moral feelings and attitudes and indeed from his moral personality as a whole. Moreover, in light of the strong pressures for role identification, it is not unlikely that the explicit and conscious adoption of the minimal identification strategy involves a substantial element of self-deception.

The social costs of cutting off professional deliberation and action from their sources in ordinary moral experience are even more troubling. . . .

[M]ost importantly, when professional action is estranged from ordinary moral experience, the lawyer's sensitivity to the moral costs in both ordinary and extraordinary situations tends to atrophy. The ideal of neutrality permits, indeed requires, that the lawyer regard his professional activities and their consequences from the point of view of the uninvolved spectator. One may abstractly regret that the injury is done, but this regret is analogous to the regret one feels as a spectator . . . ; one is in no way personally impli-cated. . . . This has troubling consequences: Without a proper appreciation of the moral costs of one's actions one cannot make effective use of the faculty of practical judgment. In fact, a proper perspective of the moral costs of one's action has both intrinsic and instrumental value. The instrumental value lies in the added safeguard that important moral dilemmas will receive appropri-ate reflection. As Bernard Williams argued, "only those who are reluctant or disinclined to do the morally disagreeable when it is really necessary have much chance of not doing it when it is not necessary. . . ."

. . . .

Finally, the moral detachment of the lawyer adversely affects the quality of the lawyer-client relationship. Unable to draw from the responses and relations of ordinary experience, the lawyer is capable of relating to the client only as a client. He puts his moral faculties of reason, argument, and persuasion wholly at the service of the client, but simultaneously disengages his moral personality. He views himself not as a moral actor but as a legal technician. In addition, he is barred from recognizing the client's moral personality. The moral responsibilities of the client are simply of no interest to him. Thus, paradoxically, the combination of partisanship and neutrality jeopardizes client autonomy and mutual respect (two publicly stated objectives of the standard conception), and yields instead a curious kind of impersonal relationship. . . .

The unavoidable social costs of the standard conception of professional legal behavior argue strongly for a radical rethinking of the lawyer's role. One alternative . . . is to recognize the unavoidable discontinuities in the moral landscape and to bridge them with a unified conception of moral personality. Achieving any sort of bridge, however, requires that lawyers significantly alter the way they view their own activities. Each lawyer must have a conception of the role that allows him to serve the important functions of that role in the legal and political system while integrating his own sense of moral responsibility into the role itself. Such a conception must improve upon the current one by allowing a broader scope of engaged moral judgment in day-to-day professional activities while encouraging a keener sense of personal responsibility for the consequences of these activities.

NOTES

In the years since the tobacco lawsuits, we have seen both the Enron scandal and government regulations — especially the Sarbanes-Oxley Act, about which more later in this volume — that have been regarded by some as in part an effort to legislate lawyer morality by requiring attorneys in certain regulatory situations to candidly disclose the conduct of their clients. As you think about these initial readings, and throughout the course of the book, give some thought to whether morality can, or should, be legislated, and how.

5. Some Further Thoughts on Ethics and Morality. As you evaluate the problems that focus on the lawyer-client relationship, and again as you move through the problems that discuss the balance between client advocacy and a lawyer's other duties, we think it is useful to keep Gerald Postema's perspective in mind. The issues he raises — whether lawyers must take into account the "moral costs" of their actions; whether lawyers who distance their professional activities from their personal morality are guilty of self-deception or, even worse, moral atrophy; and finally, whether there should be a "bridge" between a lawyer's legal role and moral beliefs, creating a "unified conception of moral personality" — will recur in different contexts throughout this volume. Consider also how the public may feel about these issues. After all, the public criticism of lawyers has rested on the foundation that in zealously (arguably overzealously) representing their clients, lawyers fail to meet the needs of society. But when a member of the public changes hats and becomes a client, the likelihood is that that same individual will want, and even insist on, that same narrowly focused, zealous representation.

Consider too how you view yourself as a prospective attorney. Is there a gulf between your vision of an ethical, professionally responsible lawyer and a moral citizen of the world, or do these two ideas merge in your mind? Should legal ethics be defined in terms of the four corners of legal representation, or as part of a larger canvas, in which the needs of society are considered? Finally, should "ethics" be determined by defining what the written rules permit a lawyer to "get away with" or by defining "the ethical lawyer" as one who meets a different standard based in part on moral responsibility?

We don't presume to tell anyone how to answer these questions; the issues they raise are far too personal. But permit us to throw in our "two cents" before we move on.

Practicing lawyers understand full well that clients retain us to meet *their* needs, not our own or those of society. Most of the time, they couldn't care less what "society" or "the public" thinks is the proper way for us to act, or the ethical thing for us to do. Most clients are members of the public who expect *lawyers in the abstract* to be fair-minded and evenhanded, but want *their own* lawyer to do whatever it takes to win.

A few years ago, a student, while leading a class discussion on a problem that now appears in this book, said that to act in a particular way would be immoral and wrong, but it would be "ethical." When we asked what she meant, she said that the conduct was clearly wrong, even repugnant, but applying the rules of ethics, she could "get away with it." Should "ethical" be defined by what one may "get away with"? Or is a better definition one attorney commenting on another: "You know, there goes a really 'ethical' lawyer?" Many lawyers adopt the first conception: "Here's how we have to do it in order to stay out of trouble." Ethics opinions, as valuable as they are, foster this view by concentrating on conduct which can be sanctioned by suspension or disbarment, rather than on what is the "right" thing for an "ethical" lawyer to do.

When we asked our student what path she would take, the morally "right" course or the technically "ethical" one, she became confused. She looked at her personal morality as so distinct from what she had learned about the rules of ethics that she had never truly considered the two concepts together. As a result, she was unable to give us a practical answer to the question we find most important — "What would *you* do if this happens to *you*?"

As practicing lawyers *and* ethics teachers and advisors, we have sympathy for Professor Postema's basic thesis; lawyers who separate their professional obligations from their personal morality will too often find themselves in the same quandary that faced our student. Should lawyers then try to merge their legal and moral selves? The rules of ethics themselves do appear to have a strong moral component. But thoughtful lawyers, practitioners, and ethicists alike disagree widely on whether their legal ethics and morality systems should be merged, or even commingled.

One way to look at the body of work we call "legal ethics" is to integrate, even internalize, it along with one's own personal morality. It's as if one's sense of what is moral expands to absorb and include one's sense of what is "ethical." How then do you deal with the dilemmas faced every day in the practice of law? What do you do about revealing your knowledge of the body buried in the mine shaft (a question we'll examine in detail in Problem 4)? The desire to inform a distraught family is pitted against the duty and promise to the client to keep the information confidential. Are you stuck in the same place as our student, between what is moral and what is ethical? Perhaps these issues can be viewed as *moral dilemmas*, a term with which we are all familiar. Evaluating the situation as an integrated person, with professional ethics and personal morality absorbed into one integrated belief system, may not help to come up with the *right* answer, but it may make it easier to find *an* answer.

6. "Is There a Collective or Institutional Ethic Beyond the Ethics of the Individual?" This is the question asked by investment banker Bowen "Buzz" McCoy in the next article. McCoy tells us about his own compelling experience in a situation literally involving life or death, and the lessons he learned about the development of individual and group ethics.

BOWEN H. McCOY, THE PARABLE OF THE SADHU
Harvard Business Review (September-October 1983)[6]

Last year, as the first participant in the new six-month sabbatical program that Morgan Stanley has adopted, I enjoyed a rare opportunity to collect my thoughts as well as do some traveling. I spent the first three months in Nepal, walking 600 miles through 200 villages in the Himalayas and climbing some 120,000 vertical feet. On the trip my sole Western companion was an anthropologist who shed light on the cultural patterns of the villages we passed through.

During the Nepal hike, something occurred that had a powerful impact on my thinking about corporate ethics. Although some might argue that the experience has no relevance to business, it was a situation in which a basic ethical dilemma suddenly intruded into the lives of a group of individuals. How the group responded I think holds a lesson for all organizations no matter how defined.

The Sadhu

The Nepal experience was more rugged and adventuresome than I had anticipated. . . . My friend Stephen, the anthropologist, and I were halfway through the 60-day Himalayan part of the trip when we reached the high point, an 18,000-foot pass over a crest that we'd have to traverse to reach to the village of Muklinath, an ancient holy place for pilgrims.

Six years earlier I had suffered pulmonary edema, an acute form of altitude sickness, at 16,500 feet in the vicinity of Everest base camp, so we were understandably concerned about what would happen at 18,000 feet. Moreover, the Himalayas were having their wettest spring in 20 years; hip-deep powder and ice had already driven us off one ridge. If we failed to cross the pass, I feared that the last half of our "once in a lifetime" trip would be ruined.

The night before we would try the pass, we camped at a hut at 14,500 feet. In the photos taken at that camp, my face appears wan. The last village we'd passed through was a sturdy two-day walk below us, and I was tired.

During the late afternoon, four backpackers from New Zealand joined us, and we spent most of the night awake, anticipating the climb. Below we could see the fires of two other parties, which turned out to be two Swiss couples and a Japanese hiking club.

---

[6] Copyright © 1983. Reprinted by permission.

To get over the steep part of the climb before the sun melted the steps cut in the ice, we departed at 3:30 A.M. The New Zealanders left first, followed by Stephen and myself, our porters and Sherpas, and then the Swiss. The Japanese lingered in their camp. The sky was clear, and we were confident that no spring storm would erupt that day to close the pass.

At 15,500 feet, it looked to me as if Stephen was shuffling and staggering a bit, which are symptoms of altitude sickness . . . . I felt strong, my adrenaline was flowing, but I was very concerned about my ultimate ability to get across. A couple of our porters were also suffering from the height, and Pasang, our Sherpa sirdar (leader) was worried.

Just after daybreak, while we rested at 15,500 feet, one of the New Zealanders, who had gone ahead, came staggering down toward us with a body slung across his shoulders. He dumped the almost naked, barefoot body of an Indian holy man — a sadhu — at my feet. He had found the pilgrim lying on the ice, shivering and suffering from hypothermia. I cradled the sadhu's head and laid him out on the rocks. The New Zealander was angry. He wanted to get across the pass before the bright sun melted the snow. He said, "Look, I've done what I can. You have porters and Sherpa guides. You care for him. We're going on!" He turned and went back up the mountain to join his friends.

I took a carotid pulse and found that the sadhu was still alive. We figured he had probably visited the holy shrines at Muklinath and was on his way home. It was fruitless to question why he had chosen this desperately high route instead of the safe, heavily traveled caravan route through the Kali Gandaki gorge. Or why he was almost naked and with no shoes, or how long he had been lying in the pass. The answers weren't going to solve our problem.

Stephen and the four Swiss began stripping off outer clothing and opening their packs. The sadhu was soon clothed from head to foot. He was not able to walk, but he was very much alive. I looked down the mountain and spotted below the Japanese climbers marching up with a horse.

Without a great deal of thought, I told Stephen and Pasang that I was concerned about withstanding the heights to come and wanted to get over the pass. I took off after several of our porters who had gone ahead.

On the steep part of the ascent where, if the ice steps had given way, I would have slid down about 3,000 feet, I felt vertigo. I stopped for a breather, allowing the Swiss to catch up with me. I inquired about the sadhu and Stephen. They said that the sadhu was fine and that Stephen was just behind. I set off again for the summit.

Stephen arrived at the summit an hour after I did. Still exhilarated by victory, I ran down the snow slope to congratulate him. He was suffering from altitude sickness, walking 15 steps, then stopping, walking 15 steps, then stopping. Pasang accompanied him all the way up. When I reached them, Stephen glared at me and said: "How do you feel about contributing to the death of a fellow man?"

I did not fully comprehend what he meant.

"Is the sadhu dead?" I inquired.

"No," replied Stephen, "but he surely will be!"

After I had gone, and the Swiss had departed not long after, Stephen had remained with the sadhu. When the Japanese had arrived, Stephen had asked to use their horse to transport the sadhu down to the hut. They had refused. He had then asked Pasang to have a group of our porters carry the sadhu. Pasang had resisted the idea, saying that the porters would have to exert all their energy to get themselves over the pass. He had thought they could not carry a man down 1,000 feet to the hut, reclimb the slope, and get across safely before the snow melted. Pasang had pressed Stephen not to delay any longer.

The Sherpas had carried the sadhu down to a rock in the sun at about 15,000 feet and had pointed out the hut another 500 feet below. The Japanese had given him food and drink. When they had last seen him he was listlessly throwing rocks at the Japanese party's dog, which had frightened him.

We do not know if the sadhu lived or died.

For many of the following days and evenings Stephen and I discussed and debated our behavior toward the sadhu. Stephen is a committed Quaker with deep moral vision. He said, "I feel that what happened with the sadhu is a good example of the breakdown between the individual ethic and the corporate ethic. No one person was willing to assume ultimate responsibility for the sadhu. Each was willing to do his bit just so long as it was not too inconvenient. When it got to be a bother, everyone just passed the buck to someone else and took off . . . ."

I defended the larger group, saying, "Look, we all cared. We all stopped and gave aid and comfort. Everyone did his bit. The New Zealander carried him down below the snow line. I took his pulse and suggested we treat him for hypothermia. You and the Swiss gave him clothing and got him warmed up. The Japanese gave him food and water. The Sherpas carried him down to the sun and pointed out the easy trail toward the hut. He was well enough to throw rocks at a dog. What more could we do?"

"You have just described the typical affluent Westerner's response to a problem. Throwing money — in this case food and sweaters — at it, but not solving the fundamentals!" Stephen retorted.

"What would satisfy you?" I said. "Here we are, a group of New Zealanders, Swiss, Americans, and Japanese who have never met before and who are at the apex of one of the most powerful experiences of our lives. Some years the pass is so bad no one gets over it. What right does an almost naked pilgrim who chooses the wrong trail have to disrupt our lives? Even the Sherpas had no interest in risking the trip to help him beyond a certain point."

Stephen calmly rebutted, "I wonder what the Sherpas would have done if the sadhu had been a well-dressed Nepali, or what the Japanese would have done if the sadhu had been a well-dressed Asian, or what you would have done, Buzz, if the sadhu had been a well-dressed Western woman?"

"Where, in your opinion," I asked instead, "is the limit of our responsibility in a situation like this?" . . .

Stephen said, "As individual Christians or people with a Western ethical tradition, we can fulfill our obligations in such a situation only if (1) the sadhu dies in our care, (2) the sadhu demonstrates to us that he could undertake the two-day walk down to the village, or (3) we carry the sadhu for two days down to the village and convince someone there to care for him."

The Individual vs. The Group Ethic

Despite my arguments, I felt and continue to feel guilt about the sadhu. I had literally walked through a classic moral dilemma without fully thinking through the consequences. My excuses for my actions include a high adrenaline flow, a superordinate goal, and a once-in-a-lifetime opportunity — factors in the usual corporate situation, especially when one is under stress.

Real moral dilemmas are ambiguous, and many of us hike through them, unaware that they exist. When, usually after the fact, someone makes an issue of them, we tend to resent his or her bringing it up. Often, when the full import of what we have done (or not done) falls on us, we dig into a defensive position. . . .

Among the many questions that occur to me when pondering my experience are: What are the practical limits of moral imagination and vision? Is there a collective or institutional ethic beyond the ethics of the individual? At what level of effort or commitment can one discharge one's ethical responsibilities?

Not every ethical dilemma has a right solution. Reasonable people often disagree; otherwise there would be no dilemma. In a business context, however, it is essential that managers agree on a process for dealing with dilemmas.

The sadhu experience offers an interesting parallel to business situations. An immediate response was mandatory. Failure to act was a decision in itself. Up on the mountain we could not resign and submit our résumés to a headhunter. In contrast to philosophy, business involves action and implementation — getting things done. Managers must come up with answers to problems based on what they see . . . .

One of our problems was that as a group we had no process for developing a consensus. We had no sense of purpose or plan. The difficulties of dealing with the sadhu were so complex that no one person could handle it. Because it did not have a set of preconditions that could guide its action to an acceptable resolution, the group reacted instinctively as individuals. The cross-cultural nature of the group added a further layer of complexity. We had no leader with whom we could all identify and in whose purpose we believed. Only Stephen was willing to take charge, but he could not gain adequate support to care for the sadhu.

. . . .

The word "ethics" turns off many and confuses more. Yet the notions of shared values and an agreed-on process for dealing with adversity and change — what many people mean when they talk about corporate culture — seem to be at the heart of the ethical issue. People who are in touch with their own core beliefs and the beliefs of others and are sustained by them can be more comfortable living on the cutting edge. At times, taking a tough line or a decisive stand in a muddle of ambiguity is the only ethical thing to do. If a manager is indecisive and spends time trying to figure out the "good" thing to do, the enterprise may be lost. . . .

What would have happened had Stephen and I carried the sadhu for two days back to the village and become involved with the villagers in his care? In four trips to Nepal my most interesting experiences occurred in 1975 when I lived in a Sherpa home in the Khumbu for five days recovering from altitude sickness. The high point of Stephen's trip was an invitation to participate in a family funeral ceremony in Manang. Neither experience had to do with climbing the high passes of the Himalayas. Why were we so reluctant to try the lower path, the ambiguous trail? Perhaps because we did not have a leader who could reveal the greater purpose of the trip to us.

Why didn't Stephen with his moral vision opt to take the sadhu under his personal care? The answer is because, in part, Stephen was hard-stressed physically himself, and because, in part, without some support system that involved our involuntary and episodic community on the mountain, it was beyond his individual capacity to do so. . . .

That is the lesson of the sadhu. In a complex corporate situation, the individual requires and deserves the support of the group. If people cannot find such support from their organization, they don't know how to act. If such support is forthcoming, a person has a stake in the success of the group, and can add much to the process of establishing and maintaining a corporate culture. . . .

For each of us the sadhu lives. Should we stop what we are doing and comfort him, or should we keep trudging up toward the high pass? Should I pause to help the derelict I pass on the street each night as I walk by the Yale Club en route to Grand Central Station? Am I his brother? What is the nature of our responsibility if we consider ourselves to be ethical persons? Perhaps it is to change the values of the group so that it can, with all its resources, take the other road.

NOTES

McCoy learned a valuable lesson about corporate ethics from his experience. Can the lesson be applied with equal force to the legal profession? What about the idea that even a highly moral individual, like McCoy's friend Stephen, is unlikely to be able to fulfill his perceived moral obligations without some support from the larger group? Is developing such a "group culture" important to finding ways to "do the right thing," or is this merely an excuse for our personal failures? Finally, what about the sadhu? How certain could McCoy and Stephen be that bringing the holy man down to the village was truly what the sadhu wished?

7. Ethics and Cultural Differences. The story of the sadhu also illustrates that culture has a significant impact on our sense of morality and ethics. As you read the materials in this text, you will find opportunities to examine how cultural norms impact the decisions that lawyers make. Consider your own opportunity to develop a deeper understanding of how your own culture affects your approach to the problems in this book and those in the "real world" practice of law.

There is a tendency in most of us to assume that we have "mainstream American" values, but are any of us sure what those are? Take two recent examples — the Justice Department's so-called "torture memos" — which we'll discuss at length later in this volume — and the use of on-line servers and browsers to track information. As to the first, did the memos from the Justice Department's Office of Legal Counsel "violate values key to our national identity" and "distort . . . laws to permit governmental conduct that is fundamentally un-American," as Yale Law School Dean Harold Koh, argued?[7] Or are they acts of patriotism, made necessary in these perilous times, justified by a fight aginst a new kind of enemy, and an interpretation of laws permitted by the government's lawyers, as Attorney General — and former White House counsel — Alberto Gonzales has claimed?

How one views the torture memos may relate to the background and culture of the observer as well as what the observer understands about what it means to be an "American" or a patriot. For example, do you think there is a national consensus on whether American soldiers should engage in torture? Or is it more complicated than "yes or "no"? Do you see a clear verdict, as Dean Koh implies, that Justice Department lawyers stepped over a moral boundary? What about lawyers representing private entities or individuals? Does it matter if the private entity is doing business in a country with very different standards of morality or ethics? Or extremely different standards, such as terrorist organizations?

Our second example is the Chinese government's request to Yahoo for communications from Shi Tao, a Chinese journalist for the newspaper *Contemporary Business News*. After Yahoo complied, presumably after consulting its attorneys, Shi Tao was sentenced to ten years in prison for "illegally providing state secrets abroad" based on the information Yahoo turned over. One recent commentator observed that on the one hand, it is understandable that while Yahoo "may have a moral obligation to criticize the practices of the host state [it is] not directly liable for the human rights violations of the state . . . ." But on the other hand, "the lawyer should be candid to her client about the economic, political, and moral effects of the client's actions when following a local law that may violate human rights."[8]

8. When the Individual Alone Chooses to Act. As we will see later in this volume, lawyers are focusing more and more frequently on the idea of a group or law firm culture as an important component of ethical behavior. In the following story, however, one aspiring lawyer chose to act with little, if any, support from the others around him.

---

[7] Harold Hongiu Koh, *Can the President be Torturer in Chief?*, 81 IND. L.J. 1145, 1165, 1166 (2006).

[8] James Heffernan, Note, *An American in Beijing: An Attorney's Ethical Considerations Abroad with a Client*, 19 GEO. J. LEGAL ETHICS 721, 728 (2006).

MIKE COMEAUX, BAR EXAM: HE SAVED A LIFE, GOT NO EXTRA TIME
The Los Angeles Daily News (February 26, 1993) [9]

While others kept taking their state bar exam, one aspiring lawyer put aside his papers to give cardiopulmonary resuscitation to a stricken test-taker until paramedics arrived — and then was refused extra time to finish the test, officials said.

More than 6,000 people were taking the timed, three-hour test — to qualify to be lawyers — in the Pasadena Convention Center on Tuesday when a 50-year-old man taking the exam suffered a seizure, officials said yesterday.

Witnesses said only a handful dared to interrupt their test to help the man, who survived the seizure.

But four witnesses and a state bar official confirmed that one of the test-takers administered CPR to the victim until paramedics arrived.

Jerome Braun, the state bar's senior executive for admissions, said that the incident did not reflect poorly on the legal profession.

"I don't think lawyers are that hard-hearted as a group," Braun said.

He said the test supervisor acted properly by refusing to give the good Samaritan extra time to make up for the minutes lost giving CPR.

"If he or she asked for additional time, additional time probably would not be given because under those circumstances we could not determine how much people were affected by the situation," Braun said.

"The fairest way of all is to deal with the situation after the exam," he said. "That could be done by a post-exam analysis of scores, and if appropriate to do so by making such adjustments as seem necessary." . . .

Other would-be lawyers present — who will learn in May whether they passed the bar exam — said they were sobered by their own reactions to the incident and the refusal of bar officials to grant extra time for the hero to complete his test.

At least one paramedic was taking the test when the man had the seizure, a witness said.

"A man sitting behind me was a paramedic, and he really felt the need to go to the assistance of this person, but he knew if he did that he risked blowing the entire exam," said Kim Enriquez of Ojai. "He really felt bad about that."

"It really upset me, but I had to keep taking the test," Enriquez said. "It made me feel like a real cold person."

Enriquez said that she compared notes with others and discovered many with similar feelings.

The seizure was heard by many, although not all, of the people in the room, said Mark Smith of La Verne, who also was taking the exam.

"All of a sudden you heard a loud groan or a scream," Smith said. "You could hear a commotion at the back (of the convention hall). A lot of proctors went to the back."

He said that the pressure to continue taking the test uninterrupted was enormous.

"We're so pressed for time that even 10 or 15 minutes makes a difference here," Smith said. "One or two missed issues could be the difference between passing and failing."

Two others taking the test — a 30-year-old West Los Angeles woman who was taking the test for the second time, and a 28-year-old Los Angeles woman — declined to give their names, fearing retribution by bar officials.

"If these people aren't willing to give an extra 30 minutes to someone who gave CPR and saved someone's life, can you imagine what they'd do to us for bad-mouthing them?" the West Los Angeles woman said.

. . . .

Braun said the state bar officials administering the exam are trained in CPR and first aid. If the good Samaritan had not rushed to the victim's aid, one of the proctors could have aided him, he said. . . .

The incident occurred during a performance exam, which required reading about a legal case and writing an analysis of the legal points involved.

A decision to adjust the good Samaritan's score will be made by a 19-person committee of bar examiners, consisting of 10 lawyers and nine lay people, Braun said.

"The person may pass the exam as given, so we may have to do nothing."

NOTES

The good Samaritan in this story chose to act as he did despite the lack of support from the group, and despite the personal risk involved. The spokesperson for the State Bar, arguably the entity which should lead the way in creating an ethical environment for lawyers, seems to make the case that what the good Samaritan did was not that significant. He notes not only that the proctors acted properly, but defends those who did not respond, arguing that the proctors themselves were CPR trained and would have assisted the man with the seizure.

What would have happened if the entire room full of exam-takers had stopped and organized a concerted effort to help the distressed man? Would this have caused the State Bar to take a more sympathetic position? Would it have protected the risk-taker, by making it more difficult not to extend the time of everyone in the room? While the answers to these questions are unknown, the good news is that despite his interruption, the good Samaritan passed the bar exam and is now a practicing lawyer.

9. Going the Whole Nine Yards. You do not have to be an extraordinary lawyer in order to accomplish extraordinary things. Any lawyer willing to infuse his or her lawyering with humanity — or morality, if you will — can achieve this. In a moment, we will read about the extraordinary achievements of one such lawyer on behalf of his client. First, though, we hear from a lawyer of the authors' acquaintance: "I represent people, not cases. If I just stopped after the case was over, I'd be leaving my client out in the cold. It goes back to the old days when I did criminal defense work. Clients came to me with more than just their criminal case. Their families were on welfare, or they'd lose their job if they couldn't make bail. There are drug problems which affect whole families. I'd spend time with mothers, girlfriends, aunts, and uncles. One time, my client came to court with her three-year-old child, and the judge rolled her up into jail on some technicality. We got her out on a writ, but I couldn't leave the child there, so I took her with me.

"You've got to go the whole nine yards for your clients. If you don't, you're really not meeting their needs. I had a poor client with a big products liability case. She had almost no clothes and had never been in a courthouse, so we went out and bought her a whole wardrobe for trial. When we won big, we gave her financial advice even though we're not financial advisors. Common sense stuff, like put money in trust for the kids, and buy a nice home but pay in cash so you don't have monthly payments. Otherwise, the money could have been gone in a year. If that was risky for us to do, so be it.

"I don't want to take over their lives or force them to do something they don't want, but I never want to abandon my clients at the courthouse door. I guess that means getting emotionally involved in your clients' lives, something which I remember professors in law school telling me not to do: 'You're a lawyer, not a social worker.' But that's a price I'll gladly pay to try to help the *person*, not just the case."

Does this philosophy make sense, or is it asking for trouble? Read the following article about an attorney who went "the whole nine yards."

DAVID MARGOLICK, AT THE BAR
The New York Times (February 19, 1993) [10]

Ask Julius Burger to describe what his lawyer did for him, and he responds as best a 95-year-old man, the victim of two strokes, can. His eyes water, and as he reaches for an elusive encomium he pounds his cane on the floor in frustration. Finally, the mot juste wends its way through the damaged neurological maze.

"Everything!" he exclaims. "Everything!"

Through tax tips and testamentary tricks, probate lawyers spend their days helping people die in peace. But Ronald Pohl, a probate lawyer at Rothfield & Pohl in Manhattan, did more for Mr. Burger than tidy up his estate. He gave him new life by giving him back his music.

When the two first met in April 1990, Mr. Burger, once an assistant conductor of the Metropolitan Opera, was a new widower, grieving and depressed. He was planning for his own death and told Mr. Pohl his posthumous wishes: To turn what he had managed to save — earnings from his days as a conductor in Europe and America along with German war reparations — into scholarships for young Israeli musicians whose careers, he hoped, would never know a Holocaust. Mr. Burger, a Jew, had been an assistant conductor at the Berlin Staatsoper before World War II when he was stripped of his job by the Nazis and forced to flee.

---

[10] Copyright © 1993 by The New York Times Company. Reprinted by permission.

As Mr. Burger shared his memories, he also disclosed a dream. Tucked away in the closets and desk drawers of his apartment in Elmhurst, Queens, he told Mr. Pohl, were sheafs of his own, almost entirely unperformed musical compositions, sonatas, symphonic fragments and songs, most of them also refugees from his incinerated Europe. Among them was a cello concerto; after the war he had dedicated its second movement to his mother, whom the Germans shot on her way to Auschwitz. How nice it would be, he said, to hear it performed before he died.

Exit Mr. Pohl, lawyer; enter Mr. Pohl, impresario. Persuading musicians to perform something new, he quickly learned, was an arduous task, far more complicated than devising trusts or writing codicils but ever so much more rewarding.

Mr. Pohl's first task was to determine whether Mr. Burger's music was any good. He turned to Maya Reiser, an Israeli cellist, who went to Mr. Burger's home and, with Mr. Burger accompanying her on the piano, performed the piece. Suddenly, music that had been imprisoned on paper for decades filled the room. Mr. Burger wept. Mr. Pohl resolved to have the concerto performed by a full orchestra, and quickly, because in 1990 Mr. Burger had suffered two nearly fatal strokes.

. . . .

In March 1991, Mr. Pohl persuaded the Orchestra of St. Luke's to perform the cello concerto, along with four other compositions, at a concert to be held that June. Mr. Pohl booked Alice Tully Hall at Lincoln Center, found a conductor, prepared the programs, had the music copied, hired a publicist and arranged for a digital recording.

The concert got rave reviews, and it was repeated in Israel and New York. Tomorrow night the New York Virtuoso Singers will play his "Miserere," a composition for chorus and organ, at St. Peter's Church on Lexington Avenue at 54th Street in Manhattan.

"My goal has been to have Julius hear all of his music before he dies, and by enough people so that it could last on its own merits," Mr. Pohl said. "We're close to accomplishing that."

Besides being a lawyer and impresario, Mr. Pohl has played grandson, too. He and his wife, Diane, have invited Mr. Burger to a family seder as well as to outings at the New York Botanical Garden. When Mr. Burger dined with his niece at the Palm Court, Mr. Pohl secretly arranged to have a violinist serenade them with a Burger arrangement of a Dvorak melody. Mr. Pohl secured a new housekeeper and physical therapist for Mr. Burger, and helped him buy new glasses, new dentures, a new hearing aid and a new suit. He has done much of the work free because, like most of those who spend any time with Mr. Burger, he has come to love him.

With Mr. Pohl's help, Mr. Burger also bought a new stereo. Now he can play recordings of his music, including his cello concerto. As the mournful, Hebraic sounds of its second movement filled his apartment recently, Mr. Burger listened silently, rocking, and then began crying anew. . . . .

SUPPLEMENTAL READINGS

1. Phillip B. Heymann & Lance Liebman, *The Social Responsibilities of Lawyers* (1988). We will refer several times to this excellent soft-cover work, which contains a series of interesting case studies on significant ethical and moral dilemmas that face practicing lawyers in today's society.

2. The battle over Lord Brougham, referred to in David Mellinkoff's piece, continues to this day, almost two centuries later. Did Brougham truly set the standard of defending a client regardless of guilt or innocence? Not necessarily, say ethics professors Bruce A. Green and Fred Zacharias. In their article, *Reconceptualizing Advocacy Ethics*, 74 Geo. Wash. L. Rev. 1 (2005), these two well-known ethics professors claim that Brougham repudiated his statement in Queen Carolyn's case. Poppycock, says one of the deans of legal ethics, Monroe Freedman, who in his brief piece *Henry Lord Brougham, Written by Himself*, 19 Geo. J. Legal Ethics 1213 (2006), argues that Brougham actually reiterated his position even more strongly.

3. W. Bradley Wendel has written important article, *Public Values and Professional Responsibility*, 75 Notre Dame L. Rev. 1 (1999). Prof. Wendel attacks the "regulatory model" of legal ethics as one which does less to regulate than to instruct lawyers in how to avoid blame. Wendel insists on moral accountability in lawyering and a "values centered" method of teaching the discipline while at the same time recognizing that there is more than one set of acceptable moral values.

4. Howard Lesnick, *Being a Lawyer: Individual Choice and Responsibility in the Practice of Law* (1992). This interesting volume raises many issues similar to those in this chapter. Included among them are discussions of the lawyer as advocate, the autonomy of clients and the related issues of attorney detachment and paternalism, and the meaning of a legal education.

5. Darlene Ricker, "Judgment Daze," (ABA) *Student Lawyer* (February 1994). This lawyer and legal writer has written a valuable piece about what students can and should do when confronted with ethical dilemmas in the law offices where they work.

6. Jeffrey M. Lipshaw, *Law as Rationalization: Getting Beyond Reason to Business Ethics*, 37 U. Tol. L. Rev 959 (2006) examines how law, ethics, economics, and philosophy interrelate when lawyers advise clients and make decisions. The author distinguishes between a lawyer's moral choices when the law is neutral (such as a tobacco company buying a fast food chain) and others when it is not, such as representing a corporation that is doing risk assessment on products known to be faulty.

7. Richard Wasserstrom, *Lawyers as Professionals: Some Moral Issues*, 5 Human Rights 1 (1975). This ground-breaking analysis of what the author calls the "role-differentiated morality" of lawyers is an important reading on lawyer professionalism and morality.

8. Fred C. Zacharias, *Coercing Cients: Can Lawyer Gatekeeper Rules Work?*, 47 B.C. L. Rev 455 (2006). The article's abstract describes it well: "Recent federal regulations and amendments to the Model Rules of Professional Conduct — most of which have responded to lawyer involvement in corporate scandals — rest on the assumption that lawyers have a role to play in forcing clients to act legally, morally, or appropriately. Lawyers are distinctive, perhaps even unique among professionals, in that they are sometimes legally authorized to force clients into obeying the lawyers' advice. This Article reviews the rules that empower lawyers in this way, with a focus on the corporate context."

9. Marvin E. Frankel, *The Search for Truth: An Umpireal View*, 123 U. Pa. L. Rev. 1031 (1975), and Monroe Freedman, *Judge Frankel's Search for Truth*, 123 U. Pa. L. Rev. 1060 (1975). A debate between two of the most articulate thinkers on these issues. Judge Frankel argues that the legal system pays too little attention to the truth, and Professor Freedman replies that our justice system, in context, must govern the lawyer's professional obligation, even if that sometimes results in the "subordination" and "distortion" of truth.

10. Since the advocacy debate was subjected to renewed scrutiny in the 1970s, a vast number of law review articles and studies have expanded on and modified these ideas. Among the most interesting are: Stephen Gillers, *Can a Good Lawyer Be a Bad Person?*, 84 Mich. L. Rev. 1011 (1986); Theodore J. Schneyer, *Moral Philosophy's Standard Misconception of Legal Ethics*, 1984 Wis. L. Rev. 1529; William H. Simon, *Ethical Discretion in Lawyering*, 101 Harv. L. Rev. 1083 (1988), and Simon's *The Ideology of Advocacy: Procedural Justice and Professional Ethics*, 1978 Wis. L. Rev. 29.

PART ONE
THE LAWYER-CLIENT RELATIONSHIP

"[My client has] made his decisions consciously, temperately, and not in the heat of passion, but based on his true and sincere and honest beliefs about what is right for him. I stand with him 100 percent."

—Ronald Lee Deere's public defender, refusing to abide by a court order that would have forced him to act against his client's wishes, 1991

Chapter 2

UNDERTAKING A CASE

PROBLEM 1

What standards must a lawyer meet in order to take a case? Does a presumption of competence come with admission to the bar? If not, what more is required? How much depends on the kind of case the lawyer is asked to undertake? Think about these questions as you read Problem 1.

Hanging Out Your Shingle

I. Arthur Hunnicut has been practicing law for eight years, emphasizing advice and incorporation of small businesses. Long-time client Ann Wilson consults Arthur about her son, whose leg was severely injured in a train collision apparently caused by a switching error or malfunction. She wants Arthur to represent her son in a suit against the railroad for damages.

Hunnicut is inexperienced in personal injury cases, though he believes he has done enough business litigation to be generally competent to handle the case. But he has two concerns: First, he has never presented medical evidence before at trial; and second, he knows almost nothing about the workings of railroads.

Hunnicut has two old law school friends, Fred and Mary. Both are, in his opinion, top-notch personal injury attorneys, and he knows that Mary has been plaintiff's counsel in more than one train accident case. Hunnicut also knows that Mary would refuse to pay him a "referral fee" if he sends the case to her because she considers the practice "unethical."

QUESTIONS

1. Would it be unethical of Arthur to keep the case? Even if he felt Fred and Mary could perform better than he?

2. Can Arthur justify taking the case by pointing out that Ms. Wilson told him: "I know this isn't right up your alley, but I really trust your judgment and ability?"

3. If Arthur refers out the case, can he accept a fee? Would it make a difference if he remained associated with the new counsel? What if it were only a "paper" association? Can he choose Fred instead of Mary because of Mary's unwillingness to split fees? Even if he believes Mary is better qualified than Fred?

II. You have recently been admitted to the Bar and have just rented space from Hunnicut to open your own practice. After a few weeks waiting for the phone to ring, you get calls from two prospective clients. One is an old friend who wants you to incorporate his small boutique, "Sprouts and Peacock

Feathers." Another is a referral from an attorney acquaintance — a domestic relations case involving two children, a house, and a few other assets. In law school you took classes in both corporations and domestic relations law, but this would be your first experience of actual practice in those areas. Arthur has said, however, "I'll point you in the right direction on the incorporation."

QUESTIONS

1. Should you take the incorporation matter? Should you take on the marital dissolution? Are there any differences between the two?

2. Because you are just starting your practice, your hourly fee will be lower than what Arthur charges his clients. You expect the incorporation will take between 15 to 25 hours. A more experienced attorney would expect to spend roughly 10 hours. It is not possible for you to estimate how long the domestic relations case will take. If you take either matter, how should you bill your client? How should you document your fee arrangement?

3. If you decide to take these cases, are you obliged to tell your clients that you have no experience in these kinds of matters? If so, what should you tell them?

READINGS

1. Competence and the "Right" Lawyer. What should a client look for in a lawyer? How does a person find the right lawyer for the job? The author of the following article claims that it is difficult for the average member of the public to find a qualified lawyer, and that the legal system has not adequately addressed this problem.

As you read this article, consider the following questions. What constitutes competence? Every lawyer has a first case; does inexperience with a particular type of matter necessarily render an attorney incompetent to handle the matter? Is it enough that the attorney studied the subject in law school? Or that the attorney can consult a more experienced colleague? What other criteria should be considered?

Suppose a lawyer is competent, but perhaps not as talented as the lawyer next door. Must the matter be referred to the "better" lawyer? If so, is there ever a point where an attorney can undertake any representation? Or are there circumstances in which an attorney is ethically obliged to refer a matter to a specialist?

What if a lawyer is competent, but does not have the staff or other resources adequate to handle a complex matter? May the lawyer still take the case? What if the lawyer hires paralegal assistants and contract attorneys?

Finally, how do ethical rules deal with the issue of competence? How do ethical standards of "competence" compare with the public's notion of what this term means?

MARTIN L. HAINES, INSIDE THE COURTS: FINDING THE RIGHT LAWYER — THE PROBLEM
131 New Jersey Law Journal (July 20, 1992)[1]

Imagine this: Louisa P., while a passenger in a car involved in an accident, is badly injured. She speaks to a friend who tells her she should consult a lawyer. The friend, a political candidate at the time, recommends Samuel T., the lawyer conducting her campaign. Samuel T. has been admitted to the bar for one year, practices alone, has yet to try a case and is politically active in the hope of attracting business. Louisa P., unaware of these circumstances and favorably impressed with Samuel's personality, retains him. He undertakes negotiations with the responsible insurance carrier and receives an immediate offer to settle Louisa's claim for $25,000. That seems like a lot of money to Samuel, as it does to Louisa even after a substantial attorney's fee is deducted; on Samuel's advice she settles her claim for the proffered amount. Seasoned attorneys would not have accepted less than $100,000 for Louisa's injuries.

While this story is not true, it is one easily imagined. It underlines two points: (1) the importance of representation by a qualified lawyer, and (2) the difficulty of finding one.

How does an unsophisticated member of the public, needing a lawyer, find one qualified for a particular assignment? The legal profession provides little help — a significant problem.

Our system of law honors a myth: That anyone who passes a bar examination is equipped to provide legal services to all comers in all matters, however complex. Nothing, except the after-the-fact threat of discipline, prevents the brand new solo practitioner from tackling, for example, the world's biggest antitrust case, with or without previous exposure to antitrust law.

. . . .

Clients who have been harmed by an incompetent performance can sue their lawyers, a prospect that imposes its own discipline.

. . . [H]owever, it is an after-the-fact threat. Such threats affect the case-acceptance decisions of lawyers — decisions over which clients have little control.

With these concerns in mind, how does a person needing a lawyer find the right one? Speak to a friend, as in the case of Louisa P.? Ask the trash collector? Talk to a judge, another lawyer, a court employee, a bar association, a senator? Call a lawyer referral service? Respond to lawyer advertising? Few people know whom to ask or where to look and have little means with which to assess the value of any information they do obtain.

Most of the sources suggested are of little value. Speaking to a friend is not likely to be much better than speaking to the trash collector. Judges resist requests; they, properly, won't discriminate. Prospective clients are reluctant to ask one lawyer to recommend another — for fear of offending. Lawyers who are asked may suggest themselves or their firms. Court employees have particular allegiances. So do senators.

---

[1] Copyright © 1992 by American Lawyer Media, L.P. Reprinted by permission.

Bar association referral services do not assess competence; they accept the word of attorneys themselves when establishing areas of expertise. Who has the competence to disagree? Who has the authority?

Advertisements — permitted, optimistically, as a way to lower fees through competition — are not reliable conveyors of competence; they are completely self-serving.

A few well-connected people can find the right lawyers. They are the business executives able to call on their counterparts for advice; the officers and employees of organizations with house counsel; professionals with access to colleagues having lawyer-retaining experience; and others with like connections. Some unions retain counsel for all members, thus providing a presumed source of competent representation. It is society, however, not the legal system, that has provided the means of selection for these privileged few, while ignoring most of the rest.

Law firms offer a partial solution to the competence problem. In them, seasoned practitioners are available to supervise and instruct young associates. Nothing requires such supervision, however, and firms, too often concentrating on billable hours, may ignore the obligation. Firms are of little help to the lawyer going it alone. Today, more and more new lawyers, of which there are a great many, are doing just that — because they can't find firm employment.

A handful of dedicated law firms employ new attorneys who spend all of their time in *pro bono* activities. Proper supervision may assure competence. The programs themselves are entitled to high praise. More are needed.

"Inns of Court," hands-on teaching institutions run by local bar associations, provide highly qualified lawyer instructors for inexperienced attorneys. A number of associations sponsor them. Their services are of great value.

The [New Jersey] State Bar Association, recognizing the problem of competence, has responded with an excellent program. It provides a network of experienced lawyers ready to answer the questions of their inexperienced colleagues. No charge is involved. This is a welcome reaction to the problem, but, necessarily, one that provides only a partial solution. Answering questions helps; it is a far cry from hands-on experience. New lawyers do not always know what questions to ask; many will not ask at all.

. . . .

The fact is that any lawyer-seeking lay person, unsophisticated and lacking the right connections, has great difficulty in finding the right one. And the further fact is that the legal system has done very little to address that circumstance.

The problem is basic. It affects the public impression of lawyers and of the legal system itself, the ethics system, and the practice of malpractice. It affects access to the courts, the adequacy of education before and after admission to the bar, specialization practices, lawyer referral practices, lawyer obligations to prospective clients and other lawyers, lawyer to lawyer relations, and firm versus solo practice. Most of all, it affects, negatively, the vast public need for competent legal service.

Our system's inadequate response to the general public's quest for a competent lawyer invites a court-lawyer-public dialogue. Solutions must be considered and developed.

2. Malpractice and the Wrong Client. A skill just as important as being able to attract and take on good clients is the ability to assess which clients are to be avoided. This skill, which takes some lawyers a lifetime to develop, is crucial for new lawyers who are driven by the need to earn fees to support themselves and their families and pay off law school loans. Consider the following advice from an insurance claims director who oversees the defense of legal malpractice claims.

KATJA KUNZKE, THE HAZARD: FAILURE TO SCREEN CASES, in *Why Bad Things Happen to Good Lawyers, a Symposium*
ABA Journal (March 1998)[2]

One of the best things lawyers can do to reduce their legal malpractice exposure is screen cases and clients in efforts to avoid, or at least be aware of, the ones that present the greatest risks for producing malpractice claims.

Certainly, lawyers must screen cases to make sure that they have sufficient time and resources to give to the matters they take on. But effective screening also seeks to identify three major risk factors: Expectations, communication and control.

Expectations. In a way, all malpractice claims are the result of unmet expectations, some reasonable and some not. If the expectations that clients have for their matters and for the lawyers they retain cannot be adjusted to attainable levels, a high malpractice claim risk exists.

If the lawyer discovers that the client wants an outcome that the legal system does not provide or that cannot be achieved under the circumstances, the lawyer must seriously consider rejecting the representation.

Motives play an important role in creating expectations. A client motivated by greed, vengeance or some lofty sentiment will expect you to further that motive, and that expectation should be discerned as early in the representation as possible.

. . . .

Communication. Effective communication between lawyer and client is critical to keeping expectations in line. But some clients require special handling to assure accurate communication and avoid unmet expectations.

[C]lients who communicate an unwillingness to understand their matters should be avoided. If a client shows no respect for your need to spend adequate preparation time or sufficient money to assure proper representation, warning bells should go off.

Control. Beware of the client who wields too much control. The evidence of this is lawyer switching, avoidable delays, insistence on knowing everything or doing parts of the lawyer's job, telling the lawyer how to do his or her job,

---

balking at retainers or fees, impatience, or simple refusal to comprehend the lawyer's cautions about associated risks and costs.

Equally as dangerous are clients who cannot control themselves. A client's personal history of serious drinking or drug problems, employment terminations or criminal activity may evidence self-denial, dishonesty or an entitlement perspective that places a lawyer in the position of being the next logical target of the client's destructive tendencies.

NOTES

While Kunzke emphasizes discovery of these problems "early in the representation," the best and most sophisticated attorneys are those who develop ways of divining these difficulties *before* representation begins. It is much easier to walk away from a case or client before committing than after the case starts. As you will see in Problem 13 on cross-cultural lawyering, good lawyers develop sophisticated insights about whether potential clients are difficult and problematic or just "different" — for cultural, disability, or many other reasons. In those instances, the question becomes whether the lawyer can bridge the cultural (or other) barriers and effectively represent the client.

3. Competence and Law School Education. Is it really necessary that lawyers attend three years of law school before they are allowed to take a bar exam? Until the 1920s most lawyers apprenticed themselves to other attorneys, studied the law as they worked for their mentors, and then took the law exams. Christopher T. Cunniffe, a 1996 Harvard law school graduate, reports that a major impetus for a mandatory three-year law school education was the report to the ABA by a committee chaired by Elihu Root in 1921 that cited the need to protect the public from incompetent and unscrupulous lawyers.[3] Other commentators have noted, however, that the desire to rid the profession of "unscrupulous" lawyers was often a veiled attempt to justify the exclusion of those of non-Northern European stock from the profession. If law students were required to complete legal education at an accredited law school before being allowed to take a bar exam, then the profession could maintain its ethnic singularity.

However the current practice of requiring lawyers to attend law schools before they are allowed to take the bar exam does not answer the question "Why three years?" Consider the following article by a well-respected appellate justice criticizing the three-year curriculum. As you read Judge Posner's article, consider what is being offered at your school and whether it prepares you to do the legal work you want to do. Do you think that law faculty should be hired and rewarded for interdisciplinary scholarship or for training law students to practice law?

---

[3] *The Case for Alternative Third-Year Programs*, 61 ALB. L. REV. 85 (1997).

RICHARD POSNER, LAW SCHOOL SHOULD BE TWO YEARS, NOT THREE
Harvard Law Record (January, 16, 1998)[4]

In this article I will be discussing . . . the dissatisfaction of many lawyers and judges, and some law professors with the changing character of legal scholarship and more broadly, with the growing estrangement between academia and law practice. This estrangement is nicely captured in the following statement by a professor at the Yale Law School. "Law professors are not paid to train lawyers, but to study the law and teach their students what they happen to discover."

[This] would be ameliorated by the deregulation of legal education and practice which I believe would lead to a two-year J.D. on the model of the two-year M.B.A. awarded by business schools, and would lead indirectly to a slight reduction in the pressure on young lawyers to recoup their investment in legal education by working ridiculously long hours. . . .

The deteriorating in the working conditions of lawyers is a product in part of the increased competitiveness of the legal service industry. That increased competitiveness is part of an economy-wide movement toward greater competitiveness in service industries ranging from medical care to funerals, . . . helped along by a relaxation of regulatory controls, notably over the pricing and advertising of legal services and over the provision of substitute services by accountants, trust officers, paralegals and others. Since the tendency of competition is to transform producer surplus into consumer surplus, it is no surprise that one effect of the competitive revolution in legal services has been to make lawyers work harder.

Turning now to the changing character of legal scholarship, . . . [b]eginning in the early 1960s, developments in economics, in political theory, in philosophy more generally in history and even in literary criticism presented increasing opportunities to analyze law using the tools of other disciplines. . . . [W]hen I became a law teacher I quickly became confirmed in the view that I had already formed that economic analysis of law was a lot more interesting than doctrinal analysis. Many others of my wave and subsequent waves of new law teachers had the same reactions, though the external discipline that fascinated them was not always economics. Eventually these people came to occupy positions of influence in academic law and began recasting legal scholarship in their image.

So, to summarize, law is becoming more like a business at the same time that law school is becoming less like a business school and more like a graduate department in the humanities and social science. The practice and the academy are indeed drifting apart. What if anything is to be done?

I want to consider what law schools can do about the drift, since there is very little law firms, subject as they are to intense competitive pressures, can do about it. I think that what law schools can do is to recognize that the public regulation of legal education, as a result of which lawyers cannot (with unimportant exceptions) be admitted to the bar without three years of

---

residential study at a law school, is anachronistic, and to press for deregulation. The elite law schools at least can do this without grave jeopardy to their existences. They could attract more students to a shorter course of instruction, and many of their students would voluntarily elect a third year at such a school, though not perhaps until a later point in their career. And with the captive-audience character of the third year removed, those students who did stay (or come back) for a third year would be eager and attentive.

The main benefit of the abolition of a third-year requirement, however, would accrue to the students who decided not to stay for a third year. The shorter the course of instruction is, the lower the cost of law school to the students and hence less intense the pressure to work killing hours in order to pay off one's student loans. The student who obtained a J.D. (or call it an LL.B. and limit the J.D. to the three-year graduates, if you want) from an elite law school after completing the program that I have outlined would have saved himself as much as $100,000 — $20,000 in tuition for the third year and $80,000 in foregone income in that year (less, of course, after taxes, but still considerable). In an age of specialization is this so clearly an inferior alternative in the present system that it should be banned by the state?

NOTES

Should practical training be required in law school curricula, or is the traditional third year of advanced seminars the better route? Should the the third year of law school be reserved for practical training in simulation courses and clinics?

Would it be better to have an apprentice program like Canada and England? Cunniffe criticizes clinical programs as being too expensive and not practical enough. He would like to see law students actually work in outside firms, government law offices or legal assistance programs.

Others would counter Cunniffe with the argument that lawyer competence is a process that begins with simulation courses and is improved with closely supervised clinical programs where students can take the time to reflect on their work, which is often difficult once students leave school. Is the "real world" the only way for a lawyer to gain competence? If so, what does that mean for the lawyer's first client?

Should there be a competency requirement in our law schools which, in addition to the usual course requirements for graduation, must be met before a new attorney may practice? If so, what should the requirement be? For example, should all students be required to pass an examination for oral advocacy skills? What if a student wants to be a transactional lawyer who will never go to court? Or should bar examinations suffice? In some states, the bar examination now includes a "practical" or "performance" component.[5] But such examinations, in written form, still focus on analytical ability.

4. Law School Clinics. Should the mission of law school clinics be skills training or service to under-represented populations? Are these goals

---

[5] Our best estimate, as of Spring 2006, is that 29 states require a "skills" exam such as the Multi-State Peformance test.

inconsistent? Some see law students as a potential source of staffing for underfunded and overloaded legal services programs, law offices and clinics that take low-fee clients, as well as public defenders' offices and others who serve the needs of the poor or under-represented. Some argue that, in accordance with the aspirational goals of the profession that lawyers donate time and effort to pro bono causes, law schools should *require* every student to give time to such programs. (We'll look further at this issue in the last problem of this volume.)

The following news article, reporting a student protest over possible loss of a clinic for AIDS sufferers, highlights the tension between traditionalists, who believe that law school should teach students how to "think like a lawyer," and proponents of clinical curricula. The debate between proponents of these two methodologies has gone on for years in the academic community. Although the following article dates from 1989, the tension at many schools continues today and is often even more intense. The American Bar Association includes in its law school accreditation standards that "(a) a law school shall require each student receive substantial instruction in: . . . (4) other professional skills generally regarded as necessary for effective and responsible participation in the profession; . . . and (b) a law school shall offer substantial opportunities for live-client or other real-life experiences . . . ." However, the ABA Accreditation Standards have not been interpreted to require live client experiences, nor must a law school provide opportunities for *every* student. This leaves law schools under little compulsion to require meaningful experiential programs.

CONSTANCE L. HAYS, STUDENTS PROTEST POSSIBLE CLOSING OF LEGAL CLINIC
The New York Times (April 16, 1989)[6]

Students at Columbia University Law School are protesting what they fear may be the closing of a popular clinic that offers legal help to victims of AIDS discrimination and practical experience for credit to the students who represent them.

. . . .

At the heart of the dispute is a larger debate between advocates of such practical studies in the education of a lawyer and traditionalists, who believe the clinics detract from the school's academic image.

On Thursday, about 200 students occupied part of the law school's main building, alternately chanting and studying.

No Decision on Clinic

"One-two-three-four, do not shut the clinic door!" the students chanted, clutching heavy textbooks with titles like "Gratuitous Transfers." They also sang a student-written song called "A Kinder, Gentler Law School."

. . . .

---

[6] Copyright © 1989 by The New York Times Company. Reprinted by permission.

University officials said afterward that no decision had been made about the future of the clinic or the instructor who teaches it. The instructor, Mark Barnes, does not have tenure and students said it was unclear whether his contract would be renewed. . . . .

Mr. Barnes refused to comment on his status. He added that he thought Columbia ought to continue the clinic whether he remained there or not. "This law school and every other institution in New York has a responsibility and an obligation to the community in this epidemic," he said. "It is disturbing that a law school like Columbia would close down this clinic in the middle of the crisis."

Students who sign up for the clinic, which was started last September, receive course credits while they represent clients who charge they have been discriminated against in housing, health care and employment because they have AIDS or because others believe they may have AIDS. The clients usually cannot afford a lawyer. The students may settle the disputes out of court or appear with the clients at hearings before the state Human Rights Commission.

Debate Among Faculty

. . . .

The students' fears about the clinic's future were prompted by what they say has been a split among faculty members about the value of clinical studies in the education of law students, long the subject of debate at the 1,000-student law school. The students say traditionalists on the faculty, less than enamored of clinics, have now gained the upper hand in the debate.

"There's a real tension between a group of faculty members who believe a legal education at Columbia should be more academic, and others who think there's a lot to be said for learning what lawyers do," said Robert Spinna, a third-year student who recently took a community-development clinic.

Dean [Barbara A.] Black denied that the faculty was divided. "I know of nothing that can be described as a split in the faculty at all," she said in an interview Friday.

Similar clinics are offered at other schools. Perhaps the most well-known is at the City University of New York's law school, where a six-year-old program is dedicated to producing public-interest lawyers. But that emphasis on clinical studies has been questioned recently within the legal-education circles; only 30 percent of CUNY graduates passed the July 1987 bar exam, less than half the average statewide.

NOTES

In July 1998, the Louisiana Supreme Court enacted new regulations that severely tightened the rules for student legal clinics at the state's law schools. While the regulations applied across the board, many argued that the restrictions were in response to the actions of the Tulane Environmental Law

Clinic, which had aggressively challenged the building of a several hundred-million-dollar plant on environmental grounds. Louisiana Governor Mike Foster, a supporter of the plant, had taken a strong stand against the clinic, calling the participants "a bunch of outlaws."

As it happened, the annual January meeting of the Association of American Law Schools (AALS) was held in New Orleans in 1999. Several hundred law school professors, clinical and non-clinical alike, marched to the Louisiana Supreme Court and held a protest rally, where Deborah Rhode, noted Stanford law school professor, ethics teacher and writer, and then president of AALS, told the crowd that the Louisiana court's decision was "a blatant infringement on academic freedom" as well as an assault on social justice.

The Supreme Court was not moved; it upheld its restrictive clinic rules.

This is hardly the only recent example of the politicization of the work of law school clinics. In 2003, the University of North Dakota School of Law Civil Rights Project was threatened by a state legislator after it filed a suit against a municipality challenging a display of the 10 commandments on public property. The lawmaker suggested that the clinic and its students were out of control and needed to be "reined in." But the state Attorney General sided with the law school, noting that the clinic's representation need not reflect either the school's or the state's own positions on the issue, and that lawyers have an ethical duty to accept all kinds of cases, even unpopular ones.

5. Law Firm "Mentoring." What if lawyers and law firms, rather than law schools, were to bear the responsibility for training new lawyers? The author of the following article discusses the decline in the traditional role of senior lawyers as "mentors" in the wake of increased billing pressures, to the particular detriment of female and minority attorneys. As you read this article, ask how the decline of "mentoring" affects the issues of competence raised in Problem 1.

MARCIA CHAMBERS, SUA SPONTE
The National Law Journal (February 1, 1993)[7]

The law lives by symbols. And one of the law's most enduring symbols is the image of the mentor, the teacher, the person who serves as a young attorney's guide in learning the law and how to practice it.

Mentors have had a long and distinguished tradition, in part because they originally served as the primary teachers of law students. Before the proliferation of organized law schools, mentors usually were practicing lawyers, teaching student apprentices in the law firm setting. This relationship still exists in some states.

As most lawyers know, the ideal mentor functions on many levels: Showing young attorneys how to behave with clients and opposing counsel, judges and colleagues; imparting his or her own sense of style and humor, discussing strategy so that a case or stubborn deal is brought to a conclusion with finesse; showing by example the moral and ethical subtleties of the legal profession.

---

[7] Reprinted with the permission of The National Law Journal. Copyright © 1993 by The New York Law Publishing Company.

But what happens as the explosive growth of law firms loosens the bonds between senior lawyers and their charges, leaving junior lawyers without mentors to help them negotiate between advocacy and unprofessional conduct? And what if the associate is a woman, or a black, or a Hispanic or an Asian? How does the mentor fare with these groups, the very groups law schools are recruiting in greater numbers than ever before?

Louise A. LaMothe, the new head of the powerful, 65,000-member litigation section of the American Bar Association — and only the second woman ever to hold that post — is concerned about the training of young lawyers. She was the first woman partner at Irell & Manella in Los Angeles, where she spent the majority of her career, and is now a partner at Riordan & McKinzie. She has served on the Board of Visitors of her law school at Stanford University, and most recently she worked with Secretary of State Warren Christopher when he chaired a blue-ribbon commission that investigated the Los Angeles Police Department.

Her specialty is complex business litigation. In the course of her career she has seen many junior lawyers leave the profession or show a strong dissatisfaction with their work. She believes that the reason, particularly for women, is the decline in mentoring at law firms:

"This decline has occurred just as women and minority lawyers began entering the profession in ever-increasing numbers. . . . They have been left to fend for themselves, with predictable results — law firms have been unable to contain the hemorrhaging of these young lawyers from the associate ranks."

. . . .

Ms. LaMothe recalls her own experience 20 years ago. Her first real mentor, Prentice Marshall, was a man with whom she never practiced and who did not work in her city. She met Mr. Marshall in 1972 at the National Institute for Trial Advocacy. He gave her an opportunity the next year to teach at NITA as his assistant and took an interest in her career. He is now a federal district senior judge in Illinois. . . .

Ms. LaMothe counts herself lucky for having a mentor and for being in the position to be one. As she sees it, mentoring has fallen to the sidelines for several reasons:

• In the absence of business growth, senior lawyers tend to hoard work rather than to delegate it to younger lawyers and train them on the way.

• As clients demand more, they want partners to do the work, not junior associates. Some clients refuse to pay for the associate's work, and indirectly for their training.

• The pressure to clock billable hours is intense, and thus the time spent in non-billable activities, including mentoring, has decreased.

• With decreasing institutional loyalty, some partners view associates as dispensable workers instead of colleagues and future partners. They may delegate, but it is to get the work done rather than to train in the process.

• Female partners and associates with families do not have the luxury of staying late to socialize at the office. . . .

Generally, women lawyers have difficulty in finding mentors among the senior male partners, even though they are usually the only ones available. Ms. LaMothe outlines the reasons why: Some male lawyers refuse to be mentors to women because they worry about romantic involvement or about sexual harassment charges, or they fear that co-workers or spouses will believe they have ulterior motives.

. . . .

Minority attorneys also report serious problems in finding mentors. Many say they are perceived as not competent. That makes finding a mentor difficult because often there are very few minority partners. Minority lawyers often complain that they get no mentoring because they cannot identify with any senior lawyer in the firm.

The problems are not limited to minorities or women. [But] Ms. LaMothe feels that junior lawyers, particularly women and minorities, should think hard before accepting a job at a firm. She says they should study the hiring and firing practices regarding women and minorities. And she suggests they choose a firm not on the basis of the highest starting salary, but on what kind of training the associate will get.

"Higher salaries encourage firms to expect young associates to perform at 100 percent efficiency and with no allowance for learning time. There is no such thing as a free lunch — high starting salaries drive the firm's overhead, and all lawyers have to work harder so the partners will make the same profits as before."

The moral: You may have to give up something to get what you need. Ms. LaMothe knows that well. She left Irell & Manella for Riordan & McKinzie, a smaller Los Angeles firm, where she will have greater responsibility for management and for crafting the values of the litigation group. As for mentoring, she says, "It is one of the most satisfying aspects of my professional life."

6. Legal "Internships" After Graduation, and Continuing Education. What if lawyers, like physicians, were required to serve a "residency" after passing the bar examination and before actual practice? Canada and England have long had extensive mandatory "apprenticeship" programs. At least two states, New Jersey and Pennsylvania, attempted to implement such a program, but both have abandoned the effort. In 1989, a California State Bar consortium on competence recommended just such a program. Among the proposals, which the consortium's chairman acknowledged were "hotter than a firestorm," were: "internships" of up to 600 hours, supervised by law schools, and taken either during school or as a post-graduate course; "residencies" of two years which would limit new lawyers to practice under defined programs; and a bar exam that would test practical skills. The first two ideas, facing objections from both young lawyers' associations and local bars, never got off the ground. The third is now part of the rigorous California bar examination testing requirements. However, there is no oral component to the exam.

Thirteen states now require new graduates to complete a "basic skills course" within twelve months of being admitted to the bar as part of a Continuing Legal Education program. In Illinois, which started its require-ment in 2005, for example, the planned courses will cover topics such as local court rules, government agency filing requirements, drafting pleadings, practice techniques, procedures under the Illinois Professional Responsibility Code, client communications, trust accounts, and record keeping, among other practice-based topics. Do such Basic Skills programs in the first year after law school make sense? If you were designing the requirements for such a program, what would you include?

Are new graduates the only ones who need to improve their competence and skills? Should education and training stop once a lawyer graduates from law school and is admitted to the bar? Does more experience equate with more competence or should experienced lawyers be required to improve their skills as well as their knowledge of the law? At least 41 states have adopted some form of mandatory continuing legal education ("MCLE") for practicing lawyers. What courses do you think should be required for experienced lawyers? Should such requirements be uniform for all lawyers, or should it depend on the nature of their practice?

7. Competence and Negligence. How is competence measured after the fact? Every jurisdiction has ethical rules that make competence a requirement. The ABA Model Code devotes the entire Canon 6 to the issue. The Model Rules specifically address both competence (Rule 1.1) and diligence (Rule 1.3). Nevertheless, it is generally true that only egregious examples of incompetent lawyering result in attorney discipline. For example, in 2003, the Supreme Court of South Dakota disbarred a lawyer who practiced out of her home with no computer, no staff, an outdated library, one bank account for both her practice and her personal finances, and no malpractice insurance. By the time of her disbarment she had six previous complaints with more pending. Several judges testified that she was "not competent." Among the conclusions of the court:

> • Laprath does not understand how to commence an action, venue an action, give notice prior to hearing, or appeal administrative matters;

> • Laprath is unable to diagnose and analyze even the most common legal problem and solve it within applicable rules;

> • Laprath's written documents are error laden, poorly written, illogical or incomprehensible;

> • Laprath's oral communication is poor. She fails to lay the proper foundation for evidence, objections are not made or are inappropriate, and evidence is presented in a disjointed, rambling fashion; and

> • Laprath is chronically late in filing documents and court appearances.[8]

But should matters descend to this extreme level before disbarring an incompetent lawyer?

What standards should courts use in disbarring or otherwise disciplining lawyers for incompetence? The court in *People ex rel. Goldberg v. Gordon*, 199 Colo. 296, 607 P.2d 995, 998 (1980), made an impassioned statement that the "license to practice law is a proclamation to the public that . . . the lawyer

---

[8] *In re Laprath*, 67 N.W.2d 41 (S.D. 2003).

will perform the basic legal tasks undertaken, competently, ethically, and in accordance with the highest standards of professional conduct." But the court in fact disciplined the lawyer for "lack of minimal professional competence," a very low threshold that Arthur Hunnicut would undoubtedly meet, and nowhere close to the "highest standards" mentioned by the court. Should the bar be set higher? Should lawyers be required to have more than "minimal professional competence" in order to avoid discipline?

Even cases that discipline lawyers purely on competence grounds recognize the difficulty in applying what many see more as a negligence standard. Thus, in *Office of Disciplinary Counsel v. Henry*, 664 S.W.2d 62, 64 (Tenn. 1983), the Tennessee Supreme Court disciplined a lawyer for "mishandling four cases in a relatively short period of time," but noted: "There are problems inherent in using disciplinary proceedings to punish an attorney for the incompetent handling of a client's affairs, or for negligence, and it is not in every malpractice case that disciplinary action should or would be ordered."

If competence is indeed addressed more frequently in legal malpractice cases than in disciplinary matters, should we improve the way those cases are handled in order to provide the assurance of competent representation? The author of the following article believes so.

MANUEL R. RAMOS, LEGAL MALPRACTICE: REFORMING LAWYERS AND LAW PROFESSORS
70 Tulane Law Review 2583 (1996)[9]

In a Reebok ad shown during the 1993 Super Bowl, viewers were reminded that on a " 'perfect planet' there would be no lawyers." However, in our most imperfect world, there will always be lawyers. Both the number of lawyers and the incidents of legal malpractice will continue to increase. Getting rid of the ineffective systems of lawyer or judicial self-regulation and putting greater pressure on the existing criminal and consumer justice system to do more comprise only part of the answer. What about the breach of ethical and competency standards by lawyers that do not rise to the level of violations of criminal or consumer protection statues? What about aggrieved clients who have been damaged?

In theory, many, including lawyers, would agree with the former Dean of the Harvard Law School, James Vorenberg, that legal malpractice claims and lawsuits put pressure on lawyers to maintain high professional standards. Even the ABA, in its McKay Report, acknowledged that legal malpractice litigation is an option for aggrieved clients but that only those with large claims would find lawyers willing to take on the delays and expenses involved with litigating against other lawyers. Many scholars also complain that legal malpractice is not an effective form of lawyer regulation.

Legal malpractice, despite its current shortcomings, is still, by far, the predominant way in which lawyers are regulated. For instance, while insurance carriers, and lawyers, through their insurance premiums, spent $4 billion a year to resolve legal malpractice claims and lawsuits, only $100 million is spent collectively by all jurisdictions to discipline lawyers. Both figures may

---

[9] Copyright © Tulane University 1996. Reprinted by permission.

be higher today, but it is unlikely that the proportion or the 2.4% comparison of the disciplinary funding compared to legal malpractice funding has changed. The $100 million being spent on lawyer discipline could be better spent on hiring more white collar prosecutors or strengthening consumer protection sections in district attorneys' offices to keep an eye on lawyers. These prosecutors would be better paid, more competent, and more highly motivated than any discipline counsel.

Similarly, the $4 billion per year spent on legal malpractice, like other forms of tort compensation, could be better structured to favor the aggrieved clients. Many smaller claims, usually those under $100,000, fall through the cracks because clients are too unsophisticated to pursue the claims with insurance companies. Plaintiffs' lawyers do not find claims under $100,000 to be cost effective. Insurance companies seemingly do not mind paying for exorbitant defense fees that erode policy limits. [10]

The presentation of data by insurance companies dilutes the numbers with a high percentage of dismissed claims where a claimant is probably not even represented by counsel. Without distinguishing claims from lawsuits, the "ABA Study based on early 1980s insurance data found that almost 70% of claims were disposed of for $1,000 or less."

However, the high percentage of claims that result in either zero or small payments contrasts with the high percentage of lawsuits that are settled for significantly higher sums. Those insurance claims that eventually mature into lawsuits handled by plaintiffs' lawyers tend to be successful, but the majority of claims remain claims and are easily disposed of by insurance companies. Add to these unsuccessful insurance claims the significant number of potential claims against uninsured and underinsured lawyers that are never paid by an insurance carrier, and the existing tort system of compensating aggrieved clients looks like a pyramid with the overwhelming majority of aggrieved clients left uncompensated.

Even those at the top of the pyramid, the clients or nonclients who receive compensation from the existing $4 billion annual fund of insurance monies, are second in line, taking their share only after the plaintiff and defense attorneys are paid their compensation. For instance, between 1981 and 1993, according to reported Florida legal malpractice insurance data, a total of $119,503,041 was paid for indemnity and defense costs by insurance carriers: 48.7%, if one assumes a one-third contingency fee, went to the client, 20.9% went to the client's lawyer, and 30.4% went to defense costs, or mostly attorneys' fees. In 1993, insurance carriers in California paid $109,678,279 for indemnity and defense costs; assuming the same one-third contingency fee for plaintiffs' lawyers, claimants or plaintiffs received 45.6%, plaintiffs' lawyers obtained 22.8%, and defense lawyers took 31.6%. Extrapolate from the more current California figures, and the $4 billion annual cost to insurance carriers roughly means that only $1.824 billion is received by aggrieved clients. . . . Clearly, something is wrong when the plaintiff and defense lawyers end up getting more than the aggrieved client.

---

10 [88] All legal malpractice policies now have "eroding" policy limits. For instance, it would not be unusual on a $300,000 policy for it to be reduced to $200,000 after defense costs through trial.

Litigation vis-à-vis the traditional tort system, however, is basically the only game in town. Legal malpractice litigation suffers from the same shortcomings that any other type of tort-based compensation system has when clients must pay plaintiffs' attorneys on a contingency fee basis and insurance carriers must pay defense lawyers at an hourly rate.

The inherent conflicts found in any disciplinary system for lawyers and by lawyers make that model a nonstarter. Regulation by the existing tort system of legal malpractice offers greater potential. There are highly motivated actors. The aggrieved client wants justice, but obviously is looking for some type of compensation. Moreover, there is the plaintiff's legal malpractice lawyer, who, after sifting through hundreds of cases, acts as the gatekeeper and takes the best ones against insured lawyers for a contingency. . . .

Where the motivation, however, breaks down in legal malpractice litigation is on the defense side. As a former defense lawyer, I am convinced that there is no motivation to settle the case early. "Complicated" legal malpractice files "justify" even more time and attorneys' fees. The "case within a case" defense attorney's mentality is to settle as late as possible and wring out, on an hourly fee basis, the greatest amount possible per case. Indeed as seen in the Florida and California data, in legal malpractice cases, defense lawyers actually get more than plaintiffs' lawyers.

Insurance carriers, who should be highly motivated to save costs by quickly evaluating and settling "bad" cases early, instead defer to defense counsel to set the budgets. Insurers focus on marketing their policies; claims handling is almost an afterthought, especially when costs are simply passed through premiums to the insured lawyers.

Only recently have legal malpractice insurance carriers become receptive to contingency fees and flat fees by defense counsel. For instance, Richard Bush, a prominent Florida legal malpractice defense lawyer, is now paid on a "bulk" flat or contingency fee basis by legal malpractice insurance carriers looking to settle cases early and reduce defense costs. These carriers have finally discovered that hourly fees, and not contingency fees, are major obstacles to tort reform.

[Ramos then recommends mandatory malpractice insurance as a way of assuring that aggrieved clients get compensated and that complaints against lawyers would be more efficiently handled. His section on malpractice claims as being the best way to monitor lawyer competency concludes with the following:]

Despite its problems, legal malpractice litigation continues to be the overwhelming way in which the legal profession regulates itself. There is nothing else, particularly the lawyer or judicial disciplinary systems, that even comes close. So, why not just improve the handling of legal malpractice claims and lawsuits?

NOTES

While clients may waive confidentiality and certain conflicts of interest, almost every jurisdiction holds that clients cannot waive their own attorney's competence.[11] Is malpractice litigation really the best way to assure lawyer competence, as Prof. Ramos asserts? Or does the disciplinary system work well enough, at least in most jurisdictions? Can the disciplinary system be improved to better regulate the practice of law? And if the profession truly relies on malpractice insurance to protect clients, can lawyers be forced to buy insurance[12] and can insurance companies be required to provide it even to "high risk" attorneys? Finally, there may be many ethical situations where malpractice simply won't apply. How will those situations be addressed if not through discipline?

Malpractice claims don't arise only between clients and their attorneys; we will address some other situations in greater detail in Problem 3. It is possible that a lawyer could be sued for negligent referral. Assuming that Arthur Hunnicut knows of a qualified specialist, is he obligated to refer the case to that lawyer? What circumstances, if any, are there in which a general practitioner has a duty to refer a matter to a specialist? If the client refuses the lawyer's referral to a specialist, may the original lawyer perform the services without assistance?

Horne v. Peckham, 97 Cal. App. 3d 404, 414, 158 Cal. Rptr. 714, 720 (1979), took a strong stand on this question by upholding a trial court's use of a form jury instruction that said:

> It is the duty of an attorney who is a general practitioner to refer his client to a specialist or recommend the assistance of a specialist if under the circumstances a reasonably careful and skillful practitioner would do so.

> If he fails to perform that duty and undertakes to perform professional services without the aid of a specialist, it is his further duty to have the knowledge and skill ordinarily used by specialists in good standing in the same or similar locality and under the same circumstances.

> A failure to perform any such duty is negligence.

While violation of rules of professional conduct does not automatically create a cause of action for malpractice, a breach of such a rule may be evidence of a failure to meet a standard of care. Frequently these days ethics "experts" are being called on to opine whether an attorney accused of malpractice met or failed to meet the standard of care. Is there really a distinction between malpractice and a breach of one's ethical duties?

8. Fiduciary Duty. When a lawyer agrees to take a client's case, that lawyer takes on a fiduciary responsibility to the client. Like "competence," the term "fiduciary duty" (sometimes referred to in the plural as "duties") has both an ethical and negligence usage; like "competence," the meaning of the term "fiduciary duty" is much the same whether it describes a professional standard of conduct or a negligence standard of care. But unlike "competence," the term "fiduciary duty" is not itself mentioned in specific ethics rules. Rather, these

---

[11] Ironically, the clear incompetence of criminal defense attorneys may not result in reversal. See the article by Bruce Shapiro, described further in the Supplemental Readings, which details this phenomenon.

[12] Currently, only Oregon requires lawyers to carry malpractice insurance.

rules are found under the term's component parts, among them: Diligence, loyalty, candor to the client, a duty to keep the client informed, and a duty to maintain inviolate a client's confidences. Together, however, the concept of fiduciary duty is still larger than the sum of its parts. It is that duty which a lawyer owes to each client, by virtue of the lawyer's special position of trust over the client's affairs. It requires the lawyer to place the client's cause above the lawyer's own individual interests, and always to act on the client's behalf in the utmost good faith. Here is how the California Supreme Court has long evaluated the fiduciary relationship in matters of lawyer discipline:

> The relationship between an attorney and client is a fiduciary relationship of the very highest character. All dealings between an attorney and his client that are beneficial to the attorney will be closely scrutinized with the utmost strictness for any unfairness.[13]

In most jurisdictions, a lawyer's fiduciary duty to a client begins only after the attorney-client relationship is established, not before.[14] Not only does the fiduciary duty apply to the attorney's handling of the client's legal affairs, it also applies to any business dealings the lawyer may have with the client, another issue we'll examine more closely in Problem 3.

9. Referral Fees. There are rules governing fee arrangements for referrals, but do they work? Are there circumstances in which a referring attorney might end up in conflict with the client? Read the following article. Despite the rules, debate persists whether referral fees are ethical. There are good arguments on both sides of the issue. While the following article by one of the deans of legal ethics was written some years ago — and discusses the old ABA Code rather than ABA Model Rule 1.5 on fee-splitting — the principles are still on point today.

GEOFFREY C. HAZARD, JR., REALITIES OF REFERRAL FEES HERE TO STAY
The National Law Journal (November 16, 1987)[15]

Although referral-fee practice is well-known within the profession, its ethical implications are not commonly confronted. Strictly speaking, a referral fee is a fee charged by a lawyer for sending a client to another lawyer. Such a fee is not authorized by the rules of legal ethics, and by implication is prohibited. The rules require that all fees be reasonable, or at least not unreasonable. (See ABA Model Rules of Professional Conduct Rule 1.5; Code of Professional Responsibility DR 2-107.) A referral fee amounts to a fee for not taking a case, and that is virtually unreasonable per se.

The objection to referral fees is similar to the objection to "kickbacks" paid by surgeons to doctors practicing general medicine who refer surgical cases to them. If the professional who makes the referral cannot himself competently perform the necessary professional service, ethical tradition requires him

---

[13] *Hunniecutt v. State Bar of California*, 44 Cal. 3d 362, 372, 243 Cal. Rptr. 699 (1988), quoting *Clancy v. State Bar*, 71 Cal. 2d 140, 146, 77 Cal. Rptr. 657, 454 P.2d 329 (1969).

[14] *See, e.g., In re Marriage of Pagano*, 154 Ill. 2d 174, 607 N.E.2d 1242, 1247 (1993).

[15] Reprinted with the permission of The National Law Journal. Copyright © 1987 by The New York Law Publishing Company.

simply to forward the case to one who can. He should not exploit his knowledge about competent specialists to collect a fee from a client who happens to have come his way.

. . . .

The situation is as follows: When a personal-injury or wrongful-death case involving potentially large recovery comes into the office of a practitioner who is not a specialist in such matters, the practitioner signs the client on a standard contingent-fee agreement. The contingent fee usually is a third of any recovery by judgment or settlement . . . . An arrangement then is made between the lawyers that the referring lawyer will receive one-third of any fee that is realized.

The specialist lawyer takes over all significant tasks vis-à-vis the prospective defendants — gathering evidence, conducting discovery, retaining necessary experts and trying the case if settlement negotiations fail. Usually, the specialist also bears the entrepreneurial risk involved in the time and effort committed and the "up front" money for investigation, experts, exhibits and so forth.

The referring lawyer may or may not do much beyond acting as a go-between. The lawyer performs a service for the client in identifying the trial specialist, and performs a service for the trial specialist by referring only those cases that involve potentially large damages. That lawyer also may perform important "hand-holding" services — such as keeping the client advised of developments and consulting about settlement offers. But are his services worth one-third of a third? . . . .

Other Services

If the referral fee clearly were being earned, presumably the referring lawyer's contribution to the representation openly would be explained and justified to the client. But such is often not done. In practice, the client may be told simply that another lawyer will be involved, and that the overall fee will be the same.

Directly, or by implication, the client understands that the referring lawyer will get a share of the fee. But the client usually will not be told the size of that share. Lawyers understandably fear that clients would feel exploited if they knew the referring lawyer will get 10 percent of a $100,000 settlement for what may be at most a few hours' work.

Arrangement Permitted

The rules of professional ethics, in effect, permit such an arrangement. DR 2-107 of the ABA Code of Professional Responsibility identifies the transaction not as a "referral fee" but as a "division of fees." It permits the arrangement [but] requires that the division between referring lawyer and specialist be "in proportion to the services performed and responsibility assumed by each." This provision is ambiguous. One of the two factors to which it refers, "services performed," is quantifiable in terms of time and value. The other factor, "responsibility assumed," could be quantified by correlating it with "services performed." On the other hand, "responsibility assumed" can be regarded as an independent intangible, like a laying on of hands.

. . . . [R]eferring lawyers assume they should get a share of the fee. After all, they have steered the client to a lawyer who can bring out the full potential value of the claim. And if the originating lawyer did not get a substantial share of the contingent fee, he might be tempted to handle some cases he should not.

This temptation — which is strongest in cases of intermediate damages potential, say $25,000 up to $100,000 — poses the crucial ethical issue. . . . The originating lawyer could keep the case and get the full contingent fee, but his skill and trial threat are likely to be inadequate to realize the claim's full value. Allowing him a "division of fee" for referring the case to a specialist eliminates this temptation. Of course, the originating lawyer thereby can get a real windfall, especially in cases with large damages potential.

SUPPLEMENTAL READINGS

1. Scott Turow, "Why Competence Isn't Enough," 17 *Student Lawyer* 46 (Dec. 1988). The author of this article, a well-known attorney-turned-novelist, subscribes to the school of thought that advocates more practical training in law school.

2. Russell G. Pearce, *Teaching Ethics Seriously: Legal Ethics as the Most Important Subject in Law School*, 29 Loy. U. Chi. L.J. 719 (Summer 1998). Prof. Pearce bemoans the state of the ethical conduct of today's lawyers. He advocates more active involvement of law schools, including that they take teaching legal ethics more seriously. His solution is to require a three-credit first semester course, at least one advanced upperclass course, and "pervasive" ethics teaching in all other classes.

3. Robert MacCrate, *Yesterday, Today, and Tomorrow; Building the Continuum of Legal Education and Professional Development*, 10 Clin. L. Rev. 805 (2004). The principal author of the "MacCrate report" on increasing the practical aspects of legal education discusses ways to update continuing legal education requirements at various schools and continues his recommendation to shift legal education from content-focused to outcome-focused instruction in order to ensure more competent and capable graduates.

4. Michelle Craven & Michael Pitman, *To the Best of One's Ability: A Guide to Effective Lawyering*, 14 Geo. J. Legal Ethics 983 (2001), offers a comparison between competence and negligence and examines many ethical issues surrounding both. The authors focus on the varying approaches taken by different state bars to protect clients from inadequate legal representation, and eventually conclude that all rules must be written to protect client interests.

5. Robert Kehr, *Lawyer Error: Malpractice, Fiduciary Breach, Or Disciplinable Offense?*, 29 W. St. U. L. Rev. 235 (2002), speaks about the fiduciary duty of competence. Kehr contrasts negligence and fiduciary duty breaches as torts. He argues that the difference is most apparent in the contrast in remedies: In negligence, remedies serve to make whole those adversely affected by conduct falling below minimum standards; in breaches of fiduciary duties remedies are used to assist those injured by acts that go beyond simple negligence.

6. *Strickland v. Washington*, 466 U.S. 668, 104 S. Ct. 2052 (1984), and *Kimmelman v. Morrison*, 477 U.S. 365, 106 S. Ct. 2574 (1986), are the two leading United States Supreme Court cases which define competence of counsel in criminal cases, in terms of what a criminal defendant must show in order to gain a reversal of a conviction or sentence based on the conduct of counsel. Contrast these cases with *New Jersey v. Davis*, 116 N.J. 341, 561 A.2d 1082 (1989), which takes a broader view of attorney incompetence in criminal cases.

7. Bruce Shapiro, "Sleeping Lawyer Syndrome; Murder Case in Texas, During Which the Defendant's Lawyer Was Observed Sleeping," *The Nation*, April 7, 1997. Not all courts hold that a criminal defense attorney must be competent, perhaps most often when that attorney is representing a murder defendant at court expense. This article details the 7-2 decision of the Texas Court of Criminal Appeals sustaining George McFarland's conviction despite McFarland's trial counsel reportedly sleeping though much of the trial. The court reasoned that McFarland's second trial counsel may have had a tactical reason for letting his co-counsel sleep. This and other chilling tales of sleeping defense counsel are discussed in the article.

PROBLEM 2

Does a lawyer have an obligation to represent every person who walks in the door? Can law firms pick and choose their clients based on their personal preferences, or do they have an obligation from time to time to accept representation of those whom they disagree with or even find repugnant? Can a law firm reject representing such a client merely on a cost/benefit analysis? Finally, what about the law firm's associates? Should they have any say on the kinds of cases or clients the firm takes? After all, they will do the bulk of the day-to-day work. The general ethical guidelines which address these questions can be difficult to apply in practice, as the John law firm of University City finds out.

Must We Take This Case?

John, John, John & Badou is a fast-growing 40-lawyer firm in University City, fourth largest city in the state, and home of the largest campus of State University. Senior partner Mitchell John has, since founding the firm 15 years before, tried to change its image from a small town law office to a full-service firm which can compete for clients with the firms in the state's largest cities.

In order to improve its image, the law firm has done a substantial amount of public interest work, including pro bono work in the area of civil liberties. This, the partners believe, gives the firm an enhanced reputation in the state's legal community, and increases the firm's attractiveness to the best law students in the state, and even students from the big eastern schools.

Mitchell John's younger brother Dean John heads up the pro bono and civil liberties effort. He spends a majority of his time, both paid and unpaid, on first amendment issues, and often works as a volunteer attorney with local civil liberties agencies. Dean chairs a bar association committee on free speech issues.

The biggest news story of the year in this college town has been the University's attempt to dismiss Professor of History Ernestine Hemp. Almost from her arrival at SU several years before, Hemp created controversy by lecturing on what she called "Euro-ism," her theme that Protestants of European ancestry are, on average, superior in abilities and morals to other groups, especially blacks and Jews. The controversy was largely limited to the academic community until the publication, two years ago, of her second book, *The Myth of the Holocaust*. This book claims that the vast majority of events surrounding the extermination of six million Jews and others never took place. Hemp's book blames "Jewish propagandists and self-victimizers." She also implies that the American enslavement of blacks was "largely the fault of black Africans themselves." As Hemp's book gained more notoriety and she began to attract more publicity for her off-campus speeches, SU instituted proceedings to dismiss her for cause from her tenured professorship.

Dean John has a close working relationship with the local university teachers' union, and has frequently represented its members. One day, he gets a call from Wilfred Allen, President of the union. "Dean," says Allen, "we need your help with Professor Hemp. You know we always turn to you for the tough ones. You did a helluva job three years ago with Laurence Jerrold, and the issue is really the same: academic freedom. We want you to take Hemp's case, and we're hoping you'll scale down your fee like you did for Jerrold."

"Wilfred," says Dean, "I'm going to have to think about this one and get back to you. I've got to discuss it with my partners."

At the partnership meeting, the following issues are raised:

• Chief law firm recruiter Andrea Badou points out that unlike typical free speech and public interest litigation, this case could substantially hurt recruitment among top law students.

• Mitchell John argues that his brother's political aspirations — Dean plans to run for Congress in the next election — could be seriously damaged by his association with "extremist views" like those of Prof. Hemp, even if Dean is acting only as her attorney. "By advocating the academic freedom of a racist," argues Mitchell, "Dean will be arguing for the end of his political career even before it begins."

• Managing partner Tom John argues that taking the case will cost the firm clients. He expresses particular concern about two of the firm's largest clients, Burt & Jonah's, a nationally known confection company which has taken strong stands against ethnic and racial bias, and Pathways, the largest regional pharmaceutical chain, privately owned by two Jewish families.

Partner Alice Arnold points out, however, that three years ago, Dean John successfully represented Professor Jerrold in an appeal of his dismissal as head of the SU African Studies Department. Jerrold had written a number of papers which argued that African-Americans were superior to whites, and claimed that people with a high level of melanin pigment in their skin (primarily those of African ancestry) are more intelligent and physically stronger than others. "That's no less racist than this," says Arnold, and, echoing the union President, asks, "doesn't this case raise precisely the same issues as the Jerrold case?"

"Maybe," says Mitchell, "but Dean wasn't about to run for Congress then."

"Yes, and Jerrold didn't directly attack a particular ethnic group in a way that would cost us clients," Tom John points out.

"Besides," notes Andrea Badou, "you know our diversity goals and how important we decided they are. Representing Jerrold didn't hurt us attracting minority associates; since Jerrold himself is black, the free speech issues somehow seemed clearer. But with Hemp," Badou continues, "what do we say to racial and ethnic minority students? And what about our negotiations to formalize our association with that minority-run firm in Capital City?"

"Wait a minute, Andrea" says Dean John, "are you seriously arguing that because Jerrold is African-American, he's less racist than Hemp?"

"No," replies Badou, "I'm simply saying that representing him didn't have the cost to the firm — or to you — that representing Hemp would have."

Finally, the partners ask the advice of the firm's two Jewish and two African-American partners. One of the Jewish partners strongly objects to taking the case, noting that he had many relatives who died in the Holocaust. But the other Jewish partner and both black partners say they would support Dean if he chose to take the case.

QUESTIONS

1. Are the objections voiced by the firm's partners cumulatively sufficient to cause the John law firm to decline to take Hemp's case? Are any of the objections sufficient, in and of themselves, to reject the case?

2. What if it were acknowledged that Dean John and the John law firm are clearly the best lawyer and law firm in the area to handle this case? Does that increase their obligation?

3. What is the significance of the fact that although Dean and the law firm are not on retainer to the teachers' union, they have a close working relationship with the union and that Wilfred Allen's expectation is that the firm is available to assist?

4. If the issues in the Hemp and Jerrold cases are truly the same, can the firm justify turning down Hemp after having represented Jerrold, solely for the reasons articulated here?

5. What if you were an associate at this firm and personally felt strongly opposed to working on Hemp's behalf? Should the partners solicit the opinions of associates? If the firm does take the case and you are asked to work on it, should you have the right to refuse?

READINGS

1. Ethical Rules and Their Limited Utility. It has long been said that "One of the highest services the lawyer can render to society is to appear in court on behalf of clients whose causes are in disfavor with the general public."[1] But when is a lawyer ethically obligated to accept employment? Strong aspirational statements exist in both the ABA Model Code and the Model Rules[2] but there is nothing in either the Code or the Rules that requires a lawyer to accept unpopular cases.

Some states, however, appear to be more explicit in mandating that their attorneys accept unpopular causes. California has perhaps the strongest such statement, stating it is "the duty" of every attorney "never to reject, for any consideration personal to himself or herself, the cause of the defenseless or the oppressed." Calif. Bus. & Prof. Code § 6068(h).

But how successfully can states legislate this kind of rule? What if a lawyer's personal feelings interfere with the lawyer's duty to be a vigorous advocate? What if undertaking a case would have serious financial considerations for the law firm? On the other hand, can we realistically expect lawyers always to "believe" in their clients' causes in order to vigorously represent those clients?

Ethical issues often are not easily resolved by general rules. Consider how you would apply these rules to guide you in your practice. Can such rules truly

---

[1] *Professional Responsibility: Report of the Joint Conference*, 44 A.B.A. J. 1159, 1216 (1958).

[2] The Code, Ethical Consideration 2-27, states strongly that "a lawyer should not decline representation because a client or a cause is unpopular or community reaction is adverse," while Paragraph 6 of the Preamble of the Model Rules and Model Rule 6.1 both have language encouraging lawyers to provide access and representation to those who have economic and social barriers that prevent them from hiring a lawyer.

give rise to a duty? Or should they merely be aspirational? And how would they affect you as a working member of a small, mid-sized, or large law firm?

2. Two Famous Lawyers and an Infamous Client. Consider the following article, in which two of the country's best-known lawyers, a noted professor of legal ethics and a famous trial attorney, square off in a debate about representing an undesirable client.

DAVID MARGOLICK, AT THE BAR; THE DEMJANJUK EPISODE
The New York Times (October 15, 1993)[3]

Representing the unpopular person or cause is not always easy or kind. . . .

So vilified was Abraham Sofaer of Hughes, Hubbard & Reed when he took as a client Col. Muammar el Qaddafi, the Libyan leader, that he was quickly forced to drop him. And Yoram Sheftel, John Demjanjuk's Israeli counsel, one of those lawyers who find vilification invigorating, nearly lost an eye when acid was thrown in his face.

Michael Tigar of Austin, Tex., suffered no such physical abuse upon becoming American counsel for Mr. Demjanjuk, the man the Justice Department had accused of being Ivan the Terrible of Treblinka, accessory to the murder of 850,000 Jews. But Mr. Tigar did not escape unattacked. Indeed, it was one of the grand middle-aged men of legal ethics who attacked him, in print.

Writing in August [1993] in the weekly publication *Legal Times,* Monroe Freedman of Hofstra Law School conceded that Mr. Demjanjuk, as much as anyone else, was entitled to a good lawyer. And, he related, until he was bested in an ethics debate 25 years ago, he would have defended Mr. Tigar's decision to be that man. Mr. Freedman, after all, was counsel to Rabbi Bernard Bergman, the infamous nursing home owner once dubbed "the meanest man in New York."

The debate Mr. Freedman mentioned was held after a group of law students, led by Ralph Nader, picketed the Washington megafirm of Wilmer, Cutler & Pickering for representing General Motors in an air pollution case. Mr. Freedman defended the firm's conduct; even large corporations were entitled to a defense. But then his rival, whom he at first left tantalizingly unidentified in his article, convinced him that in picking clients, morality mattered.

General Motors could surely find someone else to defend it, his opponent declared. The man said the Wilmer lawyers should be asking themselves two questions: "Is this really the kind of client to which I want to dedicate my training, my knowledge, my skills?" And, "Did I go to law school to help a client that harms other human beings by polluting the atmosphere with poisonous gases?"

Mr. Freedman, for one, was convinced. All lawyers, he maintained in the *Legal Times* article, should bear a "burden of public justification" for the work they undertake. This was certainly true for anyone representing Mr. Demjanjuk; the same Israeli court that cleared him of the Treblinka charges, Mr.

Freedman asserted, concluded that he had been a mass murderer a few miles down the road.

"And so I now ask my victorious opponent in that long-ago debate, Mike Tigar: Is John Demjanjuk the kind of client to whom you want to dedicate your training, your knowledge, your extraordinary skills?" Mr. Freedman wrote, "Did you go to law school to help a client who has committed mass murder of other human beings with poisonous gases? Of course, someone should, and will, represent him. But why you, old friend?"

Mr. Tigar, who said in an interview that he had spent a large part of his career "involved in things that disturb people" and who is representing Mr. Demjanjuk without charge, quickly responded. "All of Monroe Freedman's statements about me are wrong, except two," he wrote in Legal Times a few weeks later. "We are — or were — old friends. And I do represent John Demjanjuk." The rest, he contended, was false, defamatory and wrongheaded.

Mr. Freedman, he maintained, had his facts wrong: the Israeli Supreme Court never found conclusively that Mr. Demjanjuk had engaged in any killing at all. Having misrepresented the case, he continued, Mr. Freedman misrepresented what Mr. Tigar had said at their debate (held 23 years ago rather than 25, he noted), then accused him of violating a principle he had never espoused — all while claiming to be his friend.

Worse, he went on, by placing a "burden of justification" on counsel, Mr. Freedman had invented a new and "pernicious" ethical requirement. Mr. Tigar explained his decision to represent Mr. Demjanjuk: He was, he said, striving to hold the United States Government to its own principles, surely a fitting way to honor the victims of the Holocaust. But no lawyer should have to so explain; as if Atticus Finch didn't have it bad enough, must he justify himself publicly to the citizens of Maycomb?

Mr. Freedman, pummeled from other directions for his views — various writers described them as "worse than absurd," "impertinent" and "dangerous," while a fellow law professor speculated that "Joe McCarthy would be proud of you" — quickly made nice. Mr. Tigar's spirited and convincing self-defense, he argued in what is, at least for now, the fight's final salvo, proved how vital it is for lawyers to explain what they do. It also demonstrated why he remained "proud to call Mike Tigar my friend."

A lawyer's code may sometimes require him to represent a given client. But must he like the client too? The same Israeli court that freed Mr. Demjanjuk made clear its belief that he had been a death camp guard and had perjured himself to hide that role. But neither that nor anything else that Mr. Tigar has heard has shaken his affection for Mr. Demjanjuk, whom he met in an Israeli jail cell last January.

"I came away with enormous respect for him," Mr. Tigar said. "I credit his version of where he was and what he did."

3. The Courageous Stand of Anthony Griffin. The consequences of representing an undesirable client can go far beyond a debate between old friends played out in legal periodicals. Anthony Griffin is a Texas civil rights lawyer who in 1993 agreed through the A.C.L.U. to represent the grand dragon of the Texas Knights of the Ku Klux Klan against the efforts of Texas to obtain the Klan's membership list. Griffin is African-American, and was at that time Chief Counsel to the Texas branch of the NAACP. He made it clear that he found his new client personally repugnant. But, he told the *New York Times* in 1993, "people forget." Texas's arguments were the same as those "always used against every organization 'We' do not like. It was used against the N.A.A.C.P., . . . the Black Panther Party." Indeed, Griffin based his defense of the Klan on the case which first established an organization's right to privacy of its information, Alabama's attempt to get the membership lists of the NAACP. *N.A.A.C.P. v. Alabama*, 357 U.S. 449 (1958).

Most of Griffin's NAACP colleagues strongly disagreed with him, and believed that he could not represent both the Klansman and the NAACP. Griffin was soon discharged from his NAACP post, and as the Klan litigation proceeded, the NAACP filed an amicus brief supporting the State of Texas and opposing the applicability of *N.A.A.C.P v. Alabama.*

Eventually, however, Griffin and his Klansman client prevailed both in and out of court. In June 1994, the Texas Supreme Court sided with Griffin on First Amendment grounds. Griffin himself received the first annual William Brennan Award for upholding freedom of expression. Perhaps more important, Griffin felt he had regained his reputation in the black community. When he addressed a Texas NAACP meeting after his dismissal, few in the audience would look at him in the beginning, he told writer Nat Hentoff, but by the end "200 people lined up to tell me, 'Now we understand, and we will tell others!'" And though he was dismissed as Texas NAACP general counsel, he took on a reverse discrimination case for its sister organization, the NAACP Legal Defense Fund.

No redemption is unanimous, of course, and not everyone was persuaded that Anthony Griffin did the right thing. Harvard professor David Wilkins, who has written extensively and thoughtfully on law and the African American experience, and whose writings we will get to later in this volume, has argued that it made an important difference that Griffin, a black lawyer, was acting against the group he was identified with — and thus owed an obligation to.

But from the beginning, Griffin maintained that he was doing the right thing. "In our role as lawyers, we're not God," he told the *New York Times.* "If lawyers backed off because someone is unpopular or hated, then our whole system of justice would just fall apart."

Years after the event, Griffin told criminal defense lawyer Amy Porter that he strongly disagreed with the criticism that because he is black he should not have taken the Klan's case. Porter wrote that Griffin believes that "'saddling black attorneys' with Wilkins' obligation thesis does a disservice to those who confront racism in the courts and in their practice daily. To limit black attorneys' client choices would paralyze their ability to practice."[4]

Griffin explained to Porter why he did not believe his representation of the Klan conflicted with his representation of the NAACP. Simply put, not all his clients like his other clients. Griffin noted that while he was representing the

---

[4] Amy Porter, *Representing the Reprehensible and Identity Conflicts in Legal Representation,* 14 TEMP. POL. & CIV. RTS. L. REV. 143 (2004).

Klan, he was also representing several black student organizations as well as participating on behalf of the NAACP Legal Defense Fund in the important case of *Hopwood v. State of Texas*.[5]

4. Representing the Unpopular in a Post-9/11 World. The post 9/11 world has brought us lawyers representing accused terrorists whose cases have come under important appellate scrutiny regarding their basic rights, including their very right to counsel; *unaccused* detainees at Guantanamo who have never been charged but for whom representation is both difficult and unpopular; and one lawyer, Lynne Stewart, who was convicted in 2005 of several felonies for disclosures she made after post-conviction visits to her client, the "blind sheikh," Omar Abdel Rahman, convicted of being the leader of a terrorist organization that masterminded the 1993 bombing of the World Trade Center.

Many analysts argue that Stewart would never have been charged, much less convicted, had the events of September 11, 2001 not occurred. These analysts would also argue that her conviction was fueled by restrictive changes in government policy that were applied unduly harshly. But that doesn't change the wide disapprobation that the public had towards Stewart's representation. And those unaccused, Griffin-like lawyers who have taken on cases for "terrorists" have suffered similar disapprobation. Clearly the stakes have been raised when it comes to representing the unpopular client.

Some law firms have gone so far as to conceal their involvement in unpopular causes. This had happened well before 9/11; *The American Lawyer*'s Alison Frankel found a wide disparity in how firms dealt with representation on perhaps the most difficult and emotionally charged issue of its time — abortion.[6] One Boston firm which represented several dozen protestors associated with Operation Rescue emphasized the First Amendment nature of its representation and took the position that recruitment concerns would not color its judgment about what cases to take. At the other extreme was a Chicago firm which handled a "hot potato" case by filing its briefs "anonymously," omitting the firm's name. Can the business of law be incompatible with a law firm's ethics? What if law firm recruitment is directly affected? Is keeping the firm's name off the brief a proper solution, or does it simply beg the question?

5. Law Firm Associates, Credit Suisse, and the Decision to Take a Case. Usually, a law firm's partners, or simply its "new business committee," have authority to accept or reject a new case or client. But who should have this authority when a firm considers taking on a highly controversial matter? Should associates ever be asked their opinions? If they are not, how do they handle working for what to them may be reprehensible causes or unsavory clients? After all, it is the associates, not the partners who landed the client, who will do the bulk of the day-to-day work on most cases. Consider the different responses of associates and their firms in the Credit Suisse and other Holocaust reparations cases.

Credit Suisse and other Swiss banks were accused in a class action case of denying payments to the survivors of Holocaust victims. Credit Suisse in

---

[5] 78 F.3d 932 (5th Cir. 1996).

[6] *Handling the Abortion Hot Potato*, AM. LAW.Jan./Feb. 1990.

particular had been widely accused of stealing gold belonging to those who died in concentration camps. In early 1997, Washington D.C.'s Wilmer, Cutler & Pickering and New York's Cravath, Swaine & Moore were asked to represent Credit Suisse.

Despite the horrific implications of the allegations against Credit Suisse, Wilmer, Cutler accepted Credit Suisse as a client in the routine manner: The firm's "new business" committee approved it, and the new client then simply appeared on the periodic "new business" memo the firm circulates to all its lawyers. There was no indication that the firm's new business committee contacted all the firm's partners, much less its associates, for their input or to consider their opinions.

Cravath, Swaine & Moore, on the other hand, took pains to claim that its role would be advisory only. Cravath has about a thousand employees, about a third of whom are Jewish. Although the firm insisted that it was simply providing strategic advice to help the bank determine its proper course of conduct, twelve associates challenged the decision in a written memorandum. The partner in charge of the representation admitted that these objectors "felt very strongly that the bank acted improperly in some of the vilest acts in memory and should not be represented," but overruled the associates' objections.

It is impossible to know what motivated Cravath and Wilmer, Cutler to take on Credit Suisse. Everyone, Credit Suisse no less than the worst criminal defendant, is entitled to representation. However, unlike the typical criminal defendant, the Swiss banks can and will pay whatever they must to get the best possible counsel. But, unlike the typical criminal defense attorney, an associate in a large firm is not likely to be given a say in deciding what clients the firm will represent.

However, another Washington D.C. law firm took an approach very different from that of Wilmer, Cutler. Arent, Fox, Kintner, Plotkin & Kahn was asked to represent one of the European insurance companies accused of wrongfully denying life insurance claims of relatives of people who had died in the Holocaust. The plaintiffs charged that when they tried to collect on the policies, the companies denied their claims for reasons such as not having original policies or proper death certificates, impossibilities given the realities of the death camps. Instead of approving the client, the Arent, Fox partners held a firm-wide meeting open to *all* who wanted to attend. After a vigorous debate at the meeting, the firm's management committee unanimously turned down the case.

What is remarkable about Arent, Fox's inclusive decisionmaking is that it occurred in an environment in which large law firms have become big businesses first and associations of professionals second. The economics of large modern American law firms virtually require a conscious decision to focus on the bottom line first, not the feelings of associates, no matter how strong. Profitability is an important law firm issue — one that involves competition among law firms, not just money.

6. Happy, Healthy, and Ethical? Recently, salaries for first year associates at some large law firms in "hot" legal marketplaces have skyrocketed to over $150,000 per year, more than the salaries of many of the judges who will decide the motions they have drafted. Do these enormous salaries for associates give the firms that employ them *carte blanche* to force them to work on any case for any client, no matter how personally repugnant?

The culture of wealth among big firms, an issue we will revisit later in this volume, has been soundly criticized by many, including one former big firm partner whose article appears below. University of St. Thomas associate dean Patrick Schiltz clearly believes that decisions such as those made by Wilmer, Cutler and Cravath, Swaine & Moore are movitvated by a "big firm culture" that pays homage to little beyond the bottom line. As you read this article, consider whether associates' soaring incomes make it easier for them to compromise their moral beliefs. And what about Dean Schiltz? Does he over-state the problem or correctly evaluate the dangers of this culture to the future health and happiness — and ethics — of today's law students?

PATRICK J. SCHILTZ, ON BEING A HAPPY, HEALTHY AND ETHICAL MEMBER OF AN UNHAPPY, UNHEALTHY, AND UNETHICAL PROFESSION
52 Vanderbilt Law Review 871 (1999)[7]

Dear Law Student:

I have good news and bad news. The bad news is that the profession that you are about to enter is one of the most unhappy and unhealthy on the face of the earth — and, in the view of many, one of the most unethical. The good news is that you can join this profession and still be happy, healthy, and ethical. I am writing to tell you how.

I. *The Well-Being of Lawyers*

If one looks hard enough, one can scratch up some information about the health and happiness of attorneys. And this information — although rather sparse and, in some cases, of limited value — strongly suggests that lawyers are in remarkably poor health and quite unhappy.

Lawyers seem to be among the most depressed people in America. In 1990, researchers affiliated with Johns Hopkins University studied the prevalence of major depressive disorder ("MDD") across 104 occupations. They discovered that, although only about 3% to 5% of the general population suffers from MDD, the prevalence of MDD exceeds 10% in five occupations [including] lawyers. . . . The researchers did not know whether lawyers were depressed because "persons at high risk for major depressive disorder" are attracted to the legal profession or because practicing law "causes or precipitates depression." They just know that, whatever the reason, lawyers were depressed.

. . . .

Depression is not the only emotional impairment that seems to be more prevalent among lawyers than among the general population. [A 1996] Washington study found indicia of anxiety, social alienation and isolation,

---

[7] Copyright © 1999 by Vanderbilt Law Review, Vanderbilt University School of Law. Reprinted by permission.

obsessive-compulsiveness, paranoid ideation, interpersonal sensitivity, phobic anxiety, and hostility in "alarming" rates among lawyers — rates many times the national norms.

Lawyers appear to be prodigious drinkers. . . . One researcher conservatively estimated that 15% of lawyers are alcoholics. The study of Washington lawyers found that 18% were "problem drinkers," a percentage "almost twice the approximately 10 percent alcohol abuse and/or dependency prevalence rates estimated for adults in the United States."

. . . .

The extremely limited information that is available indicates that the physical health of lawyers may not be much better than their emotional health. . . . In sum, attorneys seem to be an unhealthy lot.

People who are this unhealthy — people who suffer from depression, anxiety, alcoholism, drug abuse, divorce, and suicide to this extent — are almost by definition unhappy. It should not be surprising, then, that lawyers are indeed unhappy, nor should it be surprising that the source of their unhappiness seems to be the one thing that they have in common: their work as lawyers. "Work satisfaction affects life satisfaction." Almost a century ago, Russian playwright Maxim Gorky wrote: "When work is a pleasure, life is a joy! When work is a duty, life is slavery." If Gorky was right, then life for many lawyers is "slavery," as "job dissatisfaction among lawyers is widespread, profound and growing worse."

II. *Explaining the Poor Health and Unhappiness of Laywers*

Why are lawyers so unhealthy and unhappy? Why do so many lawyers, in the words of Judge Laurence Silberman, "hate what the practice of law has become"? Lawyers give many reasons. They complain about the commercialization of the legal profession — about the fact that practicing law has become less of a profession and more of a business. They complain about the increased pressure to attract and retain clients in a ferociously competitive marketplace. They complain about having to work in an adversarial environment "in which aggression, selfishness, hostility, suspiciousness, and cynicism are widespread." They complain about not having control over their lives and about being at the mercy of judges and clients. They complain about a lack of civility among lawyers. They complain about a lack of collegiality and loyalty among their partners. And they complain about their poor public image. Mostly, though, they complain about the hours. . . . Lawyers are complaining with increasing vehemence about "living to work, rather than working to live" — about being " 'asked not to *dedicate*, but to *sacrifice* their lives to the firm.' "

III. *The Ethics of Lawyers*

At this point, I should say a few words about ethics. I hesitate to do so. . . . I realize that, by raising the topic of ethics, I risk making your eyes glaze over. . . . [L]aw students do not think that they will become unethical lawyers. Students think of unethical lawyers as the sleazeballs who chase ambulances (think Danny DeVito in *The Rainmaker*) or run insurance scams (think Bill Murray in *Wild Things*) or destroy evidence (think Al Pacino's crew in *The Devil's Advocate*). Students have a hard time identifying with these lawyers. When students think of life after graduation, they see themselves sitting on the 27th floor of some skyscraper in a freshly pressed dark suit (blue, black, or gray) with a starched blouse or shirt (white or light blue) doing sophisticated legal work for sophisticated clients. Students imagine — wrongly — that such lawyers do not have to worry much about ethics, except, perhaps, when the occasional conflict of interest question arises.

If you think this — if you think that you will not have any trouble practicing law ethically — you are wrong. Dead wrong. In fact, particularly if you go to work for a big firm, you will probably begin to practice law unethically in at least some respects within your first year or two in practice. This happens to most young lawyers in big firms. It happened to me, and it will happen to you, unless you do something about it.

A. Practicing Law Ethically

Let's first be clear on what I mean by practicing law ethically. I mean three things.

First, you generally have to comply with the formal disciplinary rules . . . . In many other ways, subtle or blatant, you will be encouraged to think that conduct that does not violate the rules is "ethical," while conduct that does violate the rules is "unethical."

I don't have anything against the formal rules. Often, they are all that stands between an unethical lawyer and a vulnerable client. You should learn them and follow them. But you should also understand that the formal rules represent nothing more than "the lowest common denominator of conduct that a highly self-interested group will tolerate." For many lawyers, "[e]thics is a matter of steering, if necessary, just clear of the few unambiguous prohibitions found in rules governing lawyers." But complying with the formal rules will not make you an ethical lawyer, any more than complying with the criminal law will make you an ethical person. Many of the sleaziest lawyers you will encounter will be absolutely scrupulous in their compliance with the formal rules. In fact, they will be only too happy to tell you just that. Complying with the rules is usually a necessary, but never a sufficient, part of being an ethical lawyer.

The second thing you must do to be an ethical lawyer is to act ethically in your work, even when you aren't required to do so by any rule. To a substantial extent, "bar ethical rules have lost touch with ordinary moral institutions." To practice law ethically you must practice law consistently with those institutions. For the most part, this is not complicated. Being an ethical lawyer is not much different from being an ethical doctor or mail carrier or gas station attendant. Indeed, long before you applied to law school, your parents had probably taught you all that you need to know to practice law ethically. You should treat others as you want them to treat you. Be honest and fair. Show respect and compassion. Keep your promises. Here is a good rule of thumb: If you would be ashamed if your parents or spouse or children knew what you were doing, then you should not do it.

The third thing you must do to be an ethical lawyer is to live an ethical life. . . . [B]eing admitted to the bar does not absolve you of your responsibilities outside of work — to your family, to your friends, to your community, and, if you're a person of faith, to your God. To practice law ethically, you must meet those responsibilities, which means that you must a balanced life. If you become a workaholic lawyer, you will be unhealthy, probably unhappy, and, I would argue, unethical.

B. Big Firm Culture

It is hard to practice law ethically. Complying with the formal rules is the easy part. The rules are not very specific, and they don't demand very much. . . . [B]y and large, you will have no trouble complying with the rules; indeed, you are unlikely to give the rules much thought.

Acting as an ethical lawyer in the broader, non-formalistic sense is far more difficult. . . . To understand why, you need to understand what it is that you will do every day as a lawyer. Most of a lawyer's working life is filled with the mundane.

Because practicing law ethically will depend primarily upon the hundreds of little things that you will do almost unthinkingly every day, it will not depend much upon your thinking. You are going to be busy. The days will fly by. When you are on the phone negotiating a deal or when you are at your computer drafting a brief or when you are filling out your time sheet at the end of the day, you are not going to have time to reflect on each of your actions. You are going to have to act almost instinctively.

What this means, then, is that you will not practice law ethically — you *cannot* practice law ethically — unless acting ethically is *habitual* for you. You have to be in the habit of being honest. You have to be in the habit of being fair. You have to be in the habit of being compassionate. These qualities have to be deeply ingrained in you, so that you can't turn them on and off — so that acting honorably is not something you have to *decide* to do — so that when you are at work, making the thousands of phone calls you will make and writing the thousands of letters you will write and dealing with the thousands of people with whom you will deal, you will *automatically* apply the same values in the workplace that you apply outside of work, when you are with family and friends.

Here is the problem, though: After you start practicing law, nothing is likely to influence you more than "the culture or house norms of the agency, department, or firm" in which you work. If you are going into private practice — particularly private practice in a big firm — you are going to be immersed in a culture that is hostile to the values you now have. The system does not *want* you to apply the same values in the workplace that you do outside of work (unless you're rapaciously greedy outside of work); it wants you to replace those values with the system's values. The system is obsessed with money, and it wants you to be, too. The system wants you — it *needs* you — to play the game.

. . . .

[Y]ou will absorb big firm culture — a culture of long hours of toil inside the office and short hours of conspicuous consumption outside the office. You will work among lawyers who will talk about money constantly and who will be intensely curious about how much money other lawyers are making. If you want to get some sense of this, leave your tax return on the photocopier glass sometime. (At least one hapless lawyer seems to do this every spring at most firms.) Every lawyer in the firm will know how much money you made last year in about fifteen minutes, and every lawyer who joins the firm during the next quarter century will hear the story of your tax return.

Big firm culture also reflects the many ways in which lawyers who are winning the game broadcast their success. . . . When lawyers speak with envy or admiration about other lawyers, they do not mention a lawyer's devotion to family or public service, or a lawyer's innate sense of fairness, or even a lawyer's skill at trying cases or closing deals, nearly as much as they mention a lawyer's billable hours, or stable of clients, or annual income.

It is very difficult for a young lawyer immersed in this culture day after day to maintain the values she had as a law student. Slowly, almost imperceptibly, young lawyers change. They begin to admire things they did not admire before, be ashamed of things they were not ashamed of before, find it impossible to live without things they lived without before. . . . [A]bsorbing the values of big firm culture will also push a lawyer away from practicing law ethically in the narrower sense of being honest and fair and compassionate.

. . . .

[N]either big firms nor big firm lawyers are all alike. But what you need to understand is that they they *becoming* more alike. One of the most consistent findings of the social scientists involved in a recent ABA study of the ethics of big firm litigators was that the cultures of individual firms are weakening, leaving a "void of guidance to junior lawyers." This void, in turn, is being "filled by other powerful systemic or environmental influences," especially influences from outside the firm. In other words, the distinctive cultures of individual big firms are influencing young lawyers less and less, while a generic big firm culture is influencing young lawyers more and more. That is why, no matter which big firm you join, there is a good chance that working at the firm will make you unhealthy, an even better chance it will make you unhappy, and an almost 100% chance that it will make you unethical. . . .

IV. *On Being a Happy, Healthy, and Ethical Lawyer*

This is the best advice I can give you: Right now, while you are still in law school, make the commitment — not just in your head, but in your heart — that, although you are willing to work hard and you would like to make a comfortable living, you are not going to let money dominate your life to the exclusion of all else. And don't just structure your life around this negative; embrace a positive. *Believe* in something — *care* about something — so that when the culture of greed presses in on you from all sides, there will be something inside of you pushing back. Make the decision now that *you* will be the one who defines success for you — not your classmates, not big law firms, not clients of big law firms, not the *National Law Journal*. You will be a happier, healthier, and more ethical attorney as a result.

NOTES

Are large law firms more justified in demanding associates' compliance with their choice of clients because they pay higher salaries? Can a firm justify its decision to take on a client like Credit Suisse because it has to meet the higher payrolls resulting from the higher salaries it pays? Even though Schiltz does not directly mention the lack of control over the selection of clients or cases as a major factor leading to associates' unhappiness with their jobs, many associates certainly feel they have the worst of both worlds: No power to decide whom they represent, but the clear expectation that they will summon all the zeal necessary to further the interests of clients they may find repugnant.

7. Appointments by the Court. What are a lawyer's obligations to accept representation when requested to do so by a court? ABA Model Rule 6.2 requires a lawyer to accept appointment unless there is good cause to withdraw, such as the representation would result in a violation of the rules or other law; the representation would impose an unreasonable financial burden on the lawyer; or the client or the cause is "so repugnant to the lawyer as to be likely to impair the client-lawyer relationship or the lawyer's ability to represent the client."

Are there clients so repugnant that the lawyer simply cannot be a zealous advocate? What if the John law firm and Dean John were appointed by a court to represent Professor Hemp, or John Demjanjuk, or the grand dragon of the Ku Klux Klan? Or the convicted sheikh represented by Lynne Stewart? Could the firm successfully argue that the repugnance of these individuals is so great that the attorney-client relationship would be impaired? The comment to Rule 6.2 notes that a lawyer's freedom to select clients is "limited," and that all lawyers are required to accept "a fair share of unpopular matters or indigent or unpopular clients."

Could the law firm successfully argue that representation of these individuals would create an "unreasonable financial burden" because two major clients might leave? Or would it first have to show that the clients will in fact leave? And what constitutes an *unreasonable* financial burden? What if the firm's biggest "rainmaker" states that he will resign and take his book of business elsewhere?

In England, barristers, the bar's trial attorneys, don't have their choice of clients at all. They operate under what Professor David Mellinkoff has called the "taxi-cab" rule, meaning that if a client requests the barrister, the barrister can no more decline employment than a cab driver can decline a fare. "The rule is explicit," says Mellinkoff in *The Conscience of a Lawyer*. "Personal predilections" are not considered, and the rule "exists on paper and in practice." Could you envision such a rule in the United States?

There has been some stateside support for this view. The Ninth Circuit once noted that the bar's duty to represent indigents upon court order is "an ancient tradition of the legal profession" that dates back to the fifteenth century. In requiring a lawyer to represent an indigent criminal defendant without compensation, the court said: "An applicant for admission to practice law may justly be deemed to be aware of the traditions of the profession which he is joining, and to know that one of these traditions is that a lawyer is an officer of the court obligated to represent indigents for little or no compensation upon court order. Thus the lawyer has consented to, and assumed, this obligation and when he is called upon to fulfill it, he cannot contend that it is a 'taking of his services.'"[8]

Many studies have shown that this "ancient tradition" doesn't work well on a purely voluntary basis. This can result in attorney shortages of the most compelling kind. In 1988, for example, in his column in the *Texas Bar Journal*, James B. Sales, then President of the Texas bar, pleaded with Texas attorneys to represent indigent death row inmates. Sales used all the persuasive tools of his trade to convince his fellow attorneys. He began by citing Texas Canon 2-27, which says, "A lawyer should not decline representation because a client or a cause is unpopular or community reaction is adverse." He cited Canon 2-29: "When a lawyer is . . . requested by a bar association to undertake representation of a person unable to obtain counsel . . . he should not seek to be excused from undertaking representation except for compelling reasons." He pointed out the enormous number of pending death sentences in the state, and the fact that only 25 of the 370 Texas law firms with over 20 lawyers had agreed to take such a case. Tellingly, he wrote that death penalty attorneys had to be recruited from other states to handle the volume of Texas appeals. "In the context of the magnitude and importance of the problem," he wrote, "a seven percent participation is . . . morally, ethically, and legally unacceptable." He included with his message a post card for law firms to fill out volunteering for the program, saying that participants "answer the highest calling of our noble profession when you involve yourself in this program."

"Perhaps," wrote Texas's Sales, "irrepressible optimism misguides my perception." Unfortunately, in this respect he was correct, as his plea failed to solve the lawyer shortage. But does that mean that courts have the power to conscript attorneys involuntarily into free legal service?

8. Mr. Mallard Goes to Washington. Consider the plight of a young Iowa bankruptcy lawyer who was "asked" by the federal District Court to take on, without compensation, a civil rights case on behalf of a group of prisoners.

LINDA GREENHOUSE, THE LAW; CAN LAWYERS BE FORCED TO REPRESENT THE POOR?
The New York Times (March 3, 1989)[9]

WASHINGTON, March 2 — When a Federal District Court in Iowa asked a young member of its bar to handle a civil rights suit on behalf of two state prisoners, the lawyer, John E. Mallard, assumed he was free to decline.

He was wrong, at least according to the United States Court of Appeals for the Eighth Circuit, which interprets a 97-year-old Federal law as giving

---

[8] *United States v. Dillon*, 346 F.2d 633, 635 (9th Cir. 1965).

[9] Copyright © 1989 by The New York Times Company. Reprinted by permission.

district judges in its seven Midwestern states the power to assign lawyers to represent indigent civil litigants without compensation.

Two years later Mr. Mallard's refusal to donate his time has set off waves far beyond Fairfield, Iowa, a town of 9,500 people where he practices corporate and securities law with a three-member firm.

The 34-year-old lawyer argued his appeal before the United States Supreme Court this week. At a moment of heightened debate throughout the legal profession over how to address the legal needs of the poor, *Mallard v. United States District Court* presents the Justices with a vehicle for shaping the mandatory public service concept now taking root in bar associations and Federal and state courts.

Bar Associations Divided

The case has divided bar associations around the country, highlighting the lack of consensus within the profession as to whether lawyers should be required to devote a certain number of hours each year to those who cannot afford legal representation.

The Association of the Bar of the City of New York filed a brief urging the Supreme Court to view the duty of lawyers to donate their services "for the public good" — lawyers use the Latin phrase pro bono publico — as an obligation that comes with the power and privilege of bar membership.

The State Bar of California, by contrast, warned that "to compel unwilling attorneys to render uncompensated services" promised "incompetent representation" and might well be unconstitutional. "A solution to the unmet legal needs of the least among us cannot rest solely on the backs of private attorneys," the California bar's brief said.

The American Bar Association, which has been split for years over the issue of donated services, did not file a brief.

In the hourlong argument on Tuesday, the Justices appeared intensely interested in the case and troubled by the implications of the arguments.

Challenging Question

Responding to Mr. Mallard's assertion that Federal judges might request but not order a lawyer to donate services on a civil case, Justice Sandra Day O'Connor asked:

"What if every lawyer in the district is like you? What if they all say, 'No, we just don't want to do it' " Referring to her own days of law practice in Arizona, Justice O'Connor said, "In my day it would have been unthinkable to tell the judge that I wouldn't do it."

Mr. Mallard said the prospect of an indigent litigant being left unrepresented, while troubling, was highly unlikely. "As a practical matter," he said, lawyers who had continuing relationships with Federal judges would be unlikely to refuse.

In his own case, he said, he had almost no Federal court experience and little desire to develop any. A Federal civil rights case, with multiple plaintiffs and defendants, was outside his expertise. His counteroffer to help an unrepresented person with a bankruptcy case or other financial matter was refused, he said.

The Federal court in Iowa has one of the country's most active civil pro bono programs. All attorneys admitted to practice before the court, who have appeared as counsel in a non-bankruptcy case in the last five years, are held available for assignment. Lawyers are reimbursed for their expenses but do not receive a fee.

At the simplest level, Mr. Mallard's case requires the Supreme Court to interpret a Federal statute, Section 1915(d) of Title 28 of the United States Code. The law, which dates to 1892, provides that a Federal court in a civil case "may request an attorney to represent" a person "unable to employ counsel." There is confusion among the lower Federal courts on what this language means.

Mr. Mallard urged the Court to interpret the law according to its "plain meaning."

Perception of Justice

"Request does not mean require," he said, noting that in other statutes, including the Criminal Justice Act, which provides lawyers for indigent criminal defendants, Congress was unambiguous about authorizing mandatory appointments. (The criminal program does not pose a pro bono issue, however, since lawyers are assigned to criminal defendants as a matter of constitutional right and are paid from $40 to $75 an hour from Federal funds.)

But even if the Court agrees with Mr. Mallard on the statutory language, the case does not necessarily end there. Gordon E. Allen, a Deputy Attorney General of Iowa, who argued on behalf of the district court, said a judge could require a lawyer to take such a case as "an expression of the inherent power of the court." He added, "What is at stake today is really the perception of justice."

Several Justices appeared interested in that approach, which has formed the basis for some mandatory programs of donated services at the state level. In New York, where the issue is under study by a special committee appointed by Chief Judge Sol Wachtler of the State Court of Appeals, the State Supreme Court in Westchester County has invoked its "inherent power" to require lawyers to handle divorce cases for the poor without compensation. . . .

Making his first Supreme Court appearance, Mr. Mallard, a graduate of Harvard College and Vanderbilt University Law School, turned in a capable if stilted performance. He started by referring, in formal Supreme Court style, to "the petitioner."

"That's you, is that right?" Justice O'Connor asked. Yes, Mr. Mallard said, and switched to the first person for the rest of his argument.

He did so well, in fact, that Justice John Paul Stevens was openly skeptical of his argument that he was "not competent" to handle the civil rights case. "Before this case came up, how many cases had you had in this Court?" Justice

Stevens asked. "Did you think you were competent to come here? You must have. You picked yourself."

<hr>

NOTES

Mr. Mallard was so effective before the United States Supreme Court that he won his case, by a 5-4 vote, on precisely the basis he argued — that "request" meant just that, and not, as Justice Stevens argued in dissent, "respectfully command."[10] Nevertheless, since the district court did not rely on its "inherent authority" in making the appointment, the Supreme Court expressly declined to answer the larger question before it: Does a court have the inherent power to order a lawyer to serve without compensation?

SUPPLEMENTAL READINGS

1. David Mellinkoff, *The Conscience of a Lawyer* (1973). Professor Mellinkoff's study of an 1840 English case, excerpted briefly in the Introduction, remains a compelling treatise. Mellinkoff describes the struggle of barrister Charles Phillips in deciding whether he could continue to defend a man he knew to be guilty. This issue may be clear to the criminal defense lawyers of today, but in its time had many parallels to the questions raised in Problem 2.

2. Philip B. Heymann & Lance Leibmann, "California Rural Legal Assistance," in *The Social Responsibilities of Lawyers: Case Studies* 22-48 (Part II (A)) (1988). This article discusses a successful approach to providing legal services to indigent clients in rural areas.

3. Amy Porter, *Representing the Reprehensible and Identity Conflicts in Legal Representation*, 14 Temp. Pol. & Civ. Rts. L. Rev. 143 (2004). This article, referred to in section 3, above, contains a thorough review of the Griffin-Wilkins and Tigar-Freedman discussions on reprehensible clients, as well as a series of models to describe how lawyers approach — and should approach — these issues.

4. There are a large number of interesting articles about representation of clients despite moral opposition. In her thoughtful piece on morality-centered thinking, *Justice, and the Challenge of Moral Pluralism*, 90 Minn. L. Rev. 389 (2005), Professor Katherine Kruse argues that lawyers should be permitted to evaluate their own "moral conflicts of interest" in deciding whether or not to represent a client, even if they are "the last lawyer in town." Larry Cunningham, *Can a Catholic Lawyer Represent a Minor Seeking a Judicial Bypass for an Abortion? A Moral and Canon Law Analysis*, 44 J. Cath. Leg. Stud. 379 (2005), argues that pursuant to Catholic moral values and Canon law, a Catholic lawyer should not represent a minor seeking an abortion.

5. Many, many articles have been written about the Lynne Stewart case. This one, Alissa Clare, *Note: Current Development 2004-2005: We Should Have Gone to Med School: In the Wake of Lynne Stewart, Lawyers Face Hard Time for Defending Terrorists,* 18 Geo. J. Legal Ethics 651 (2004-05), is particularly

<hr>

[10] *Mallard v. United States District Court*, 490 U.S. 296, 109 S. Ct. 1814 (1989).

compelling because of the chilling effect the author believes the Stewart case will have on lawyers representing alleged terrorists or other unpopular criminal defendants.

6. Charles W. Wolfram, "Selecting Clients: Are You Free to Choose?," *Trial*, January 1998, p. 21. Wolfram criticizes a decision by the Massachusetts Commission on Discrimination for sanctioning a female divorce lawyer who only handled women's cases. The lawyer rejected a male potential client who had been the homemaker and secondary bread winner to his physician wife. Prof. Wolfram argues that the lawyer had a constitutional right to limit her practice to representing women, since she did so on political and moral grounds.

7. Carrie Johnson, "Arent Fox Rejects a Client," *Legal Times*, April 14, 1997, p. 14. This article describes in greater detail the decisionmaking process at Arent, Fox that led it to reject the case of one of the European insurers that had been denying claims of relatives of Holocaust victims.

8. *Yarbrough v. Superior Court*, 39 Cal. 3d 197, 216 Cal. Rptr. 425 (1985). Yarbrough was a prisoner convicted of murder and then sued civilly for wrongful death arising from the murder. The California Supreme Court reaffirmed its previous view that indigent prisoners are entitled to access to the courts, including appointment of counsel in appropriate cases. But the court declined to affirm the appellate court's view that counsel could be appointed without compensation. Rather, as in *Mallard*, the *Yarbrough* court consciously avoided the issue.

9. *Madden v. Township of Delran*, 126 N.J. 591, 601 A.2d 211 (1992). New Jersey's highest court strongly criticized a system which does not require local governments to provide counsel to all defendants other than by relying on the bar. Nevertheless, the court upheld the right of the town of Delran to appoint a lawyer to represent an indigent defendant on a driving-while-intoxicated charge without compensating the attorney. Interestingly, after the attorney's law firm submitted a bill, had it denied, and brought suit, the town paid the bill. The law firm refused payment in order to bring the issue before the state Supreme Court, which commended the firm for acting in "the best traditions of the bar."

PROBLEM 3

Getting a new client can be much more complicated than just meeting someone with a legal problem in your office and opening a new file. It's possible for lawyers to get new clients without knowing it. On other occasions, the issue of whether the lawyer has taken on a new client is at best ambiguous. Increasingly, there are issues about what duties the lawyer may owe to non-clients. And once it is clearly understood that the lawyer does have a new client, there remain many issues about how the lawyer is retained. Is the fee reasonable? Is it appropriate for the representation? How is the *scope* of representation defined? To what extent may the lawyer be paid in stock, stock options, or the rights to the client's life story?

Getting a new client is one of the most exciting moments of a case. But it is also a moment filled with ethical traps for the unwary. This problem explores those pitfalls.

Getting a Client and Getting Paid

I. Alice Tennant is the junior partner at the small real estate law firm Land, Lord & Tennant. Her practice has emphasized real property law for seven years. At the request of the local realty board, she gives a speech to a group of business people on negotiating commercial real property leases. There is a cocktail reception after the speech.

Olive Martini, an old college friend, comes up to Alice and tells her how much she enjoyed the speech. Olive also tells Alice that she is intending to start a furniture business and is in the process of negotiating a lease. Olive explains that she is concerned because the lease states that the landlord is not responsible for any water or plumbing leaks from any of the residential units above the commercial unit. She tells Alice that when she inspected the premises, she noted numerous water spots in the ceiling and along the walls. She asks Alice how she can protect herself.

"Look," Alice tells Olive, "you really ought to call me at my office on Monday to discuss this further. But whatever else you do, make sure you're not underinsured. Come in to see me next week and we'll discuss the lease in more detail."

Olive, however, satisfied with the information she has already gotten, never makes an appointment with the lawyer. A month later, Alice notices an announcement for the opening of Olive's business and assumes Olive went ahead and signed the lease.

QUESTIONS

1. Was there an attorney-client relationship between Alice and Olive?

2. When Olive asked for advice was Tennant's reply appropriate? If not, how should she have replied?

3. Should Alice have done anything when Olive did not make an appointment?

4. Suppose a few months later, the plumbing in one of the residential units above Olive's shop bursts, and water floods the store causing extensive

damage to the furniture. Assume the insurance company denies Olive's claim, arguing that because she had prior knowledge of the leaks, her loss was not covered. Can Olive sue Tennant for malpractice? Might the lawsuit be successful?

II. Jeremiah Hamilton is an experienced and well-known business entrepreneur. Three years ago, Joan Goebel represented him in the purchase of a small business. Now Hamilton is back with a new matter — the purchase of a boat marina in Ocean City. The marina berths boats, rents boats and jet skis, and has a bar and restaurant.

Jerry and Joan meet in Joan's office, where Jerry tells Joan that he only wants Joan to deal with the marina purchase itself. Jerry says that he will take care of the transfer of the bar's liquor license, and obtaining necessary title to the boats, jet skis and the like. "I probably know more about that stuff than you do anyway," he says.

Joan and Jerry sign a brief fee agreement, part of which looks like this: "3. Services to be rendered: Lawyer shall represent Client in a matter regarding: *Purchase of Handleby's Boat Marina, Ocean City.*"

Since Jerry is short on cash, he proposes that that Joan be paid only $50 per hour, one-quarter her ordinary rate, in return for receiving a 10% interest in the closely-held corporation being formed to own the Marina. Jerry will own the other 90% of the stock. Later, Jerry further suggests that instead of the $50 per hour portion of the fee, he is willing to pay Joan a contingency fee of 25% for every dollar below $3 million he saves on the marina's sales price, including the extras. Joan is tempted, thinking that she can negotiate a better price. Pushed by Jerry, she finally agrees.

The marina deal closes a few months later, at $2.7 million, and Goebel, who has spent only 60 hours on the case, is feeling very good about her fee/stock arrangement.

QUESTIONS

1. Is it appropriate for Goebel to negotiate for the stock she agreed to take in lieu of her ordinary fees?

2. Is the contingency fee charged by Goebel ethical? Even given her per-hour recovery for 60 hours of work, and the fact she is also getting stock?

3. Suppose that the liquor license transfers without a hitch, and Hamilton assures Goebel that he obtained all the necessary UCC-1 forms for the boats and jet skis. Three months after close, however, Jerry is contacted by Carlo DiCredit, who says that he holds a $112,000 promissory note from the marina's previous owner, that the note is now due, and that it is secured by Department of Motor Vehicles "pink slips," which manifest title to the marina's boats and jet skis. Jerry, who didn't know that the boats and skis even had pink slips, calls Joan in a rage. Meanwhile, he is refusing to pay Goebel her $75,000 contingency fee or issue her stock.

What was the scope of Goebel's representation? Is *she* responsible for what happened with the boats and jet skis? Is she liable for malpractice? If so, what could she have done to avoid this? Finally, will she ever see her fees or her stock?

READINGS

1. When Does the Attorney-Client Relationship Begin? Sometimes, lawyers can find themselves representing a client without even knowing it. When representation begins — and what the scope of that representation is — are not bright line tests, but they are particularly important issues. Their importance comes from the fact that the existence of an attorney-client relationship is usually the trigger for a lawyer's fiduciary duty.

Courts and ethics authorities take a variety of approaches in determining when someone becomes a client. But most agree with the Iowa Supreme Court that neither a retainer nor a formal agreement is required to establish the attorney-client relationship. *Kurtenbach v. TeKippe*, 260 N.W.2d 53, 56 (Iowa 1977). Many courts and experts believe that the attorney-client relationship may be inferred by the conduct of the lawyer, including what one commentator has called "casually rendered advice."[1] In *Kurtenbach*, the Iowa Supreme Court developed the following test to examine the existence of a lawyer-client relationship: (1) Did the client seek advice from the lawyer? (2) Was it within the lawyer's area of competence? and (3) Did the lawyer, either directly or implicitly, agree to give the requested advice? The reasonable expectations and reliance of the putative client are important to courts evaluating this issue. One Massachusetts case, *DeVaux v. American Home Assurance Company*, 387 Mass. 814, 444 N.E.2d 355 (1983), held that an attorney-client relationship could result from the client talking to the lawyer's secretary:

The plaintiff claims that the attorney placed his secretary in a position where prospective clients might reasonably believe that she had the authority to establish an attorney-client relationship. There is a question of fact for the jury whether the attorney permitted [this], thereby creating the appearance of authority. *Id.* at 819, 358.

Not all courts have gone this far. But the use of contract law concepts, including detrimental reliance, reasonable belief, and express and implied agreement, is common in most jurisdictions.[2] What do these contract principles say about Tennant's casual conversation with her old college chum?

Just as importantly, what is the significance of these standards in determining malpractice liability? If a lawyer can get a client almost without knowing it, what if the lawyer doesn't perform the services the client expects — even if those services are no more than making a phone call or citing a single legal principle or case? The *Togstad* case described in the Supplemental Readings sets perhaps the highest known malpractice benchmark. But it is clear that once "clienthood" is conferred on the Olive Martinis of the world — and many states look to the reasonable belief of the putative client as evidence — the lawyer who fails to perform competently will be liable for malpractice.

2. Client "for Purposes of Confidentiality"? If Olive Martini had simply asked her old friend Alice some questions and Alice had declined to answer,

---

[1] Ronald I. Friedman, *The Creation of the Attorney-Client Relationship: An Emerging View*, 22 CAL. W. L. REV. 209, 220 (1986). Friedman warns against giving advice "at cocktail parties, in building corridors, over the backyard fence. . . ."

[2] *See, e.g., Miller v. Metzinger*, 91 Cal. App. 3d 31, 154 Cal. Rptr. 22 (1979).

would the lawyer have any responsibility to Olive if Olive discussed confidential information about her situation? Does a lawyer in such circumstances have any duty to hold the prospective client's communication confidential, even if she never becomes a client? We will address extensively the issue of confidentiality in the next three problems. Suffice it to say here that the almost universally accepted answer is "yes." Yet until recently, with the approval of the Restatement (Third) of the Law Governing Lawyers, section 15, and ABA Model Rule 1.18, new in 2002, the rules and regulations were less than clear.

If a lawyer has to maintain confidentiality even of a non-or prospective client, issues relating to conflicts of interest may also have to be addressed. After all, if the lawyer cannot reveal a confidence, even of a non-client, that confidence will be significant in evaluating whether the lawyer may represent someone against that non-client if the confidence comes into play.[3] Few published cases have dealt directly with this issue. Under the interesting facts of *Flatt v. Superior Court*, 9 Cal. 4th 275, 36 Cal. Rptr. 2d 537, 885 P.2d 950 (1994), the California Supreme Court held that where a prospective client spoke to a lawyer about suing his own former lawyer and that former lawyer turned out to be a *current* client of the firm the prospective client consulted, the consulted lawyer had to maintain the prospective client's confidential communications, but did *not* have to tell the prospective client about the pending statute of limitations because of her firm's duty to its current client.

3. Getting a Client Online. Increasingly, law firms have used the Internet to attract potential clients to their websites, and sometimes to sign them up as new clients of the firm. Later in this volume we will look at the risks of inadvertent disclosures caused by technology and take a closer look at solicitation using the web, but here we consider how a website might impact developing an attorney client relationship..

MICHAEL OREY, SEEKING CLIENTS, LAWYERS FIND THEM ON THE NET
The Wall Street Journal (June 21, 2000)[4]

Type the keyword "Ritalin" into a personal computer's search engine, and what might you find? Among other things, a solicitation to join a potential class-action lawsuit.

It's on a Web site with the no-holds-barred name of ritalinfraud.com sponsored by the Dallas plaintiffs' law firm Waters & Kraus. Its target: Swiss manufacturer Novartis AG, maker of the drug for hyperactivity and attention-deficit disorder. The site suggests that Web surfers join a suit filed last month in state court in Brownsville, Texas, alleging that Novartis failed to adequately disclose Ritalin's side effects. Novartis denies the allegation and is fighting the suit.

As Americans flock to the Internet to investigate nearly every problem of modern life, lawyers are greeting them with invitations to sue someone. Skeptics of the plaintiffs' bar might call this development online ambulance

---

[3] We will address issues of conflicts of interest in substantial detail in Problems 7 through 11.

[4] Copyright © 2000 by Wall Street Journal. Reprinted with permission.

chasing. Legal-ethics experts, however, say that like old-fashioned advertising on billboards or in the Yellow Pages, Web solicitation is, in most cases, constitutionally protected speech. . . .

Dan Bryson, a construction lawyer in Raleigh, N.C., recently set up syntheticstucco.com because he was swamped by phone calls from people who wanted information on what to do about rot in their homes that they blame on artificial stucco siding. The site offers text, graphics and Web links for such consumers. It also has a section titled "Should you file a lawsuit?" and offers an in-depth questionnaire for visitors to fill out if they think they have a claim against a siding producer. "In this day and age," says Mr. Bryson, people with a problem are "going to go to their computer and type in 'synthetic stucco' and 'lawyer' or 'attorney.' "

When Paul Anderson, an Oakton, Va. homeowner, did just that, he arrived at Mr. Bryson's site and invited the attorney to meet a group of unhappy consumers in the Washington, D.C. area. Mr. Bryson walked away with 21 clients and has filed suit on their behalf against two synthetic stucco manufacturers.

. . . .

As more law firms of all kinds discover the power of the Web, sites seeking plaintiffs proliferate, many with descriptive Web addresses — securitiesfraud.com, justiceseekers.com, diveinjury.com. But Thomas Hargett, a partner at Maddox Koeller Hargett & Caruso, says a catchy name isn't what attracts surfers. His firm . . . has a Web site called investorprotection.com. . . . Once at the investorprotection.com site, visitors can call up explanations of various forms of broker misconduct. They can also click on "grade your broker," which walks them through a series of questions about their broker's practices. A visitor who answers "yes" to any of the questions is then invited to fill out an e-mail form with details of a possible legal claim. Clicking on "investor protection kit" brings up the same form.

Mr. Hargett says his firm invested more than $25,000 to get the site up and running during its first year, as well as more than 1,000 attorney work hours. The payoff, though, has been huge. "We have been retained by a significant number of new clients — and large clients — through our Web site," he says, although he won't provide specifics.

. . . .

Defense lawyers aren't happy about online marketing. Stephen Gillers, a legal-ethics expert at New York University Law School, says he has been contacted by two defense counsels wondering if they could challenge plaintiffs' attorneys who recruited clients on the Web.

But Prof. Gillers says legal advertising — even when it targets specific groups of alleged victims — has been deemed by courts to be "protected commercial speech." That conclusion should hold, whether the advertising is done on or off the Web, he adds.

Lawyers operating online do need to observe state rules on solicitation. A state, for example, may require a notice that, even in contingent fee cases, plaintiffs are responsible for expenses. But even though online solicitation crosses borders, Prof. Gillers says lawyers should be safe if they follow the rules in the state in which they are admitted to the bar.

Monroe Freedman, a legal ethics specialist at Hofstra University School of Law in Hempstead, N.Y., says that the Web informs "consumers of their rights and that there are lawyers to represent them." It is, Prof. Freedman says, "capitalism at its best."

4. Consumers or Clients? What Duties Are Owed When Representation is Limited? Website "advertisements" are replete with problems. While ethics professors Gillers and Freedman conclude that the websites described in the article don't engage in unethical solicitation, they were not asked at what point a website visitor might become a client. To what extent does filling out and e-mailing a "grade your broker" form give someone the belief that he or she has become the firm's client? To what extent does asking for an "investor protection kit" lead consumers to the conclusion that they are being given legal advice by the firm? To what extent does the consumer who fills out these forms provide confidential information and thus become a "client for purposes of confidentiality"? And how is the law firm to know which of these situations has occurred?

One interesting twist on law firm websites are a number of "self-help" sites that charge money to "assist" clients — if they *are* clients — in resolving their legal claims. Among the sites are those calling themselves MyClaim.com and SelfSettle.com. On one such site, the computer walks the consumer through the writing of a demand letter in a personal injury case, complete with attached supporting information, creating what the site calls a "Settlement Demand Package (SDP)." This SDP, trumpets the site, "will forcefully inform the [insurance claims] adjuster that you know what you're doing and that this may be his or her last chance to settle without getting attorneys involved."

But if attorneys *are* involved running such sites, have they taken on clients to whom they owe fiduciary duties — including the duty of competence — and who may sue them in the event of professional negligence? One lawyer who owns and operates such a website describes his site as providing "unbundled" services, a term increasingly used by those involved in delivery of legal services to the poor and those of modest means. "Unbundling" refers to legal services that cover part of a client's needs but are rendered in combination with non-lawyer resources, generally without the lawyer formally appearing in the proceedings. The website's owner also claims that none of his site's consumers are clients, just transitory users of forms and information. What do you think? Under traditional definitions of "client," such as the *Kurtenbach* standard, is it reasonable to conclude that these consumers are indeed clients? If they are, what duties are they owed? What standards of care need to be met to reach a level of competent representation?

A related issue concerns "ghost writing" pleadings for *pro se* litigants. This is not an uncommon procedure; it might occur, for example, when a prospective client arrives on the lawyer's doorstep with a claim whose statute of limitations is about to run. One federal district court recently criticized lawyers who accepted a flat fee for drafting a *pro se* employment discrimination complaint for a group of plaintiffs. Not only did the judge find this conduct ethically objectionable, but also questioned whether the lawyers had violated Fed. R.

Civ. Proc. 11, which requires that pleadings be "nonfrivolous" and presented only after a "reasonable inquiry" has been conducted into the facts and law.[5]

Although the court did not discipline these lawyers, many saw this case as putting counsel on notice of the dangers of ghost-writing pleadings. One issue that perturbed the judge was that the lawyers did not make their ghost writing known to the court, in accordance with the holdings of several state ethics opinions. But Fordham ethics professor Bruce Green, who serves as Co-Chair of the ABA Litigation Section's ethics committee, commented that while the court might understandably be "annoyed" with the lawyers' failure to disclose, "requir[ing] lawyers who provide drafting assistance to sign the pleading, enter an appearance on that party's behalf, or refrain from providing any assistance whatsoever" forces them into an all-or-nothing situation that does not serve those who need legal assistance.

There is no question that "unbundling" is a more acceptable practice than it was even a few years ago, especially when it relates to poor or otherwise unrepresented persons. Recent changes in the ethics rules of some states have explicitly allowed for unbundling in such situations as preparing papers but not going to court. Several states — six and counting as of mid-2006 — have formalized their rules, especially their versions of ABA Model Rule 1.2, to account for unbundling. Colorado, Florida, Maine, New Mexico, Utah, and Wyoming specifically provide for "limited representation" on certain issues but not others, and Virginia has a proposed change pending in its Supreme Court. Utah specifically uses the term "unbundling." Wyoming's rules include an approved notice and consent form for limited representation.

What of the potential malpractice consequences of a partial representation? In *Laremont-Lopez*, the ghost-writing case, the plaintiffs, who paid for drafting the complaint, seem clearly to have been clients, albeit with a "limited scope of representation."[6] What level of competence should be required of these lawyers? Should the standard of care be lower because of the limited representation, or should it be the same as if the lawyers had put their names on the complaint? What are counsel's fiduciary duties to the plaintiffs? *Must* they investigate the claim, if not under Rule 11, then to protect themselves from malpractice liability? What of the good Samaratan lawyer who drafts a complaint *pro bono* in order to preserve an individual's claim? Has this lawyer taken on a client? Can such a lawyer avoid taking on fiduciary responsibilities?

A number of cases in various jurisdictions have addressed the issue of whether attorneys may owe duties of care to third parties who are, unarguably, *not* their clients. The issue has come up most frequently in cases involving the beneficiaries of a will who want to file a malpractice suit against the lawyer who drafted the will for the decedent. The leading early case is *Lucas v. Hamm*, 56 Cal. 2d 583, 15 Cal. Rptr. 821 (1961), which upheld the beneficiaries' right to sue. Since that case, a growing number of jurisdictions have taken an increasingly liberal view of the ability of intended beneficiaries to sue for malpractice.

---

[5] *Laremont-Lopez v. Southeastern Tidewater Opportunity Project*, 968 F. Supp. 1075 (E.D. Va. 1997), *aff'd*, 172 F.3d 44 (4th Cir. 1999). We will examine Rule 11 in detail in Problem 16.

[6] We discuss this concept further in Section 5 below.

Traditionally, privity of contract had been required in order to maintain an action against a lawyer. This requirement has eroded substantially in the last twenty years. Some more recent cases have waived the privity requirement not only to permit the beneficiary to maintain a negligence action, but a contract action as well.[7]

5. Fee Agreements. Many states do not require written fee contracts between lawyers and their clients. The ABA's Ethics 2000 Commission has given written fee contracts a strong endorsement. The new ABA rules require written contingency fee contracts with written client consents, though the ABA declined to follow the Commission's recommendation on requiring *all* fee contracts to be written. But even where ethics rules don't currently require it, the advantages of such agreements are great for both lawyer and client, while the disadvantages are substantial. It is hard to imagine many circumstances where some written memorialization of the fee arrangements is not a good idea. Such memorializations protect the client, by putting the understandings in writing and by clarifying ambiguous points, and also protect the lawyer, since in most jurisdictions, ambiguities in the agreement — and most "swearing contests" between lawyer and client — are likely to be resolved against the attorney.

Such agreements do not have to be complex. Often a simple "engagement letter" can suffice, a "Dear Client" missive which sets forth the agreement and asks for a signature acknowledgement in reply. But the agreement should clearly state the rate or other manner of compensation, the way in which the costs of suit are to be handled, and the *scope of the representation.*

By "scope of representation," we mean a clear delineation of which tasks are being performed by the attorney, and which are not. The lawyer's most important job in a fee agreement may be to clearly define this scope. This is as — if not more — important as a clear description of the fee itself. For instance, is the lawyer handling the incorporation responsible only for the incorporating documents, or for holding a first meeting of shareholders as well? Will the lawyer be considered general counsel? And how is the term "general counsel" defined? What services are covered, and which are subject to special arrangements?

When these matters are set out from the beginning, the parties — lawyer and client alike — have the clearest possible understanding of the lawyer's role. Without this, the lawyer's expectations about what legal services will be performed may differ materially from the client's expectations about what legal services have been promised. Fees are usually simply a matter of money. But a misunderstanding about the limits of the engagement can affect the entire case itself, leading to ill will at a minimum and a malpractice suit and even discipline at worst.

Since many states follow the general principle that for malpractice purposes, the reasonable expectations of the client are at least relevant to determining the duties of the lawyer, a clearly defined scope of representation becomes crucial. Even where that scope of representation may appear to be clearly narrow, the lawyer may still have duties to at least inform the client of other

---

[7] *See, e.g., Leyba v. Whitley,* 907 P.2d 172 (N.M. 1995).

remedies in other forums. In *Nichols v. Keller*, 15 Cal. App. 4th 1672, 19 Cal. Rptr. 2d 601 (1993), a lawyer retained to file a workers' compensation claim for Nichols failed to advise Nichols that Nichols might also have a third-party personal injury claim. When the statute of limitations ran on the third-party claim, Nichols sued for malpractice. The lawyer won a summary judgment motion in the trial court, but the court of appeals reversed. The higher court held that the lawyer was in a far better position to know of another remedy available to the client and thus had a duty to tell the client about that: "Generally speaking, a workers' compensation attorney should be able to limit the retention to the compensation claim . . . . However, even when a retention is expressly limited, the attorney may still have a duty to alert the client to legal problems that are reasonably apparent, even though they fall outside the scope of the retention."

There are several other issues that a good fee agreement should address. First, are people other than the client involved? If a third party is paying the fee (even if it's a parent paying for a child) the lawyer would be well-advised to specify who the client is, and who it is not. Most states' ethics codes have strong regulations about ensuring the independent professional judgment of the lawyer. The ABA Model Rules have affirmed this important concept in three separate places. Comment 10 to MR 1.7 says that "A lawyer may be paid from a source other than the client, if the client is informed of that fact and consents and the arrangement does not compromise the lawyer's duty of loyalty to the client." MR 1.8(f) explicitly requires that accepting compensation from another can only be done when "there is no interference with the lawyer's independence of professional judgment or with the client-lawyer relationship." Were that not enough, MR 5.4(c) is even broader: "A lawyer shall not permit a person who recommends, employs, or pays the lawyer to render legal services for another to direct or regulate the lawyer's professional judgment in rendering such legal services." An organized crime kingpin may buy a lawyer's services and try to influence the defense of his lieutenant, but it is clearly unethical for the lawyer to go along.

What about other provisions a lawyer might want in an engagement agreement? May counsel require mandatory arbitration of any fee dispute? How about mandatory arbitration of any malpractice claim? States differ on these issues, and conflicting viewpoints exist even within states. The development of the law on these matters — and how to apply the law to principles of legal ethics — is very much in flux. So, too, is the legality of "retaining liens," or the ability of the lawyer to "lien," or retain, possession of the client's file until paid. We discuss these more fully in Problem 9.

There is broader consensus on the validity of fee agreement provisions that forbid the client from settling the case without the lawyer's permission, or to settle only if it is understood that the lawyer will get paid what he or she "would have" gotten paid had only the client followed counsel's advice. Most states agree with this language from Nebraska Advisory Opinion 95-1 (1995): "[T]he client may not be asked to agree to . . . surrender the right to settle litigation that the lawyer may wish to continue." Citing a 1916 Minnesota case, the opinion concludes that "a contractual provision removing a client's ability to compromise, settle or negotiate his own claim would be void as against public policy."

One final point about fee agreements: They should be set forth in a language understood by both attorney and client. That language is usually English, but can be Spanish, Korean, Arabic, or dozens of other languages. The one language that should be avoided is "legalese." Fee agreements, as well as other communications with the client, should be written in terms the client can clearly understand.

6. Contingency Fees. Are contingency fees necessary to provide litigants access to the courts? Or is the contingency fee largely responsible for creating conflicts of interest between clients and their lawyers, as so-called "tort reformers" claim? While they have now been around for some time, contingency fees are still a relatively new form of payment. Most European countries forbid such fees, while Great Britain has only permitted them since 1995. Indeed, allowing such fees requires an exception to the long-standing ethical precept that in order to maintain independent professional judgment on behalf of the client, a lawyer must not acquire a proprietary interest in the client's case.[8]

It is clear why a lawyer is generally prohibited from having a "proprietary interest" in the client's case. It can be harder to advise the client objectively when the lawyer has a "piece of the action." And yet, this is clearly what happens with contingency fees. Were this not enough, modern fee arrangements might have lawyers receiving hybrid contingency fees, such as a reduced hourly sum plus a smaller contingency in the event of a substantial recovery, or a combination of contingency and statutory fees, in which the attorney gets the greater of the two. These hybrid fees put even more pressure on the lawyer's ability to maintain independent professional judgment, especially since the more complicated the fee arrangement, the harder it will be, particularly for unsophisticated clients, to understand it clearly.

"Structured settlements" are used increasingly in larger personal injury claims. Such settlements usually involve the purchase of an annuity by the paying party, such as an insurance company, which allows the plaintiff to be paid periodically over a term of years. There can be advantages to an annuity for plaintiffs who are minors and need protection of their settlement funds, or who have serious, permanent injuries, such as paralysis, which require continual ongoing medical care, that the periodic payments could be "structured" to cover.

But in a "structured settlement," how does the lawyer get paid? Lawyers are not generally happy to accept their fees in small payments over time. Recognizing this, defendants and insurance companies will often offer a substantial portion of the settlement in "up front" money, to cover the payment of those fees. But is this method fair to the client? Does such a proposal create an overt conflict between lawyer and client, making it even more difficult than in the ordinary fee situation to exercise *independent* judgment on behalf of the client? Here's what one California ethics opinion had to say on the subject.

---

[8] *See* MR 1.8(j) and DR 5-103(A), which specifically exempt certain contingency fees.

CALIF. FORMAL OPINION 1994-135
(1994)

Take for example, a wheelchair-bound Client who wants the substantial structured annuity allocated in such a way as to provide the cost of living, care and human assistance on an ongoing annual basis to last for Client's lifetime. Here, the structure most advantageous to Client is likely to involve an initial payment of only a small percentage of the total, far less than Attorney's fee. Yet if Attorney insists on payment of the entirety of her fees before Client receives anything, the fees could eat up not only the entire downpayment but the first several years of structured annuity as well. This would defeat the very purpose behind Client's desire for such a settlement.

In such a circumstance, Attorney would have to alter her receipt of fees to avoid an unconscionable result. This is true even if the fee agreement permits her receipt of fees in their entirety in advance of payment to Client. This is the case not only because of rule 4-200 [governing reasonable fees], but because Attorney's ongoing fiduciary duty to Client prohibits Attorney from collecting her fees in a way that defeats the very purpose of Client's willingness to settle.

NOTES

There are other issues that arise with contingency fees that can have important financial implications. For example, how costs are computed in relation to the fees can have a substantial effect on the client's recovery. If costs are deducted from the gross amount awarded, before fees are computed, they come out of both the client's and the lawyer's shares of the recovery. But if *fees* are computed first, the costs wind up coming from the *client's* portion of the recovery alone. In *Baker v. Whitaker*, 887 S.W.2d 664 (Mo. App. 1994), a client agreed to pay a percentage of "amounts paid to me." When the client got a $1 million settlement, the existence of $200,000 in medical costs meant that how this phrase was interpreted — and whether the lawyer computed the fee as a percentage of the gross of $1 million or the net of $800,000 — had a substantial financial impact. The *Baker* court remanded the case, but strongly suggested the contract should be construed against the lawyer drafting the agreement.

Why, given all the potential problems, do all of our jurisdictions allow contingency fees in personal injury and other similar cases? The biggest argument in favor is access: The ability to go to court for those who don't have the money to fund litigation, but who have a legitimate complaint against someone, often an adversary with far more power and money. It is a valid argument, and though tort reformers argue that it opens the courts' floodgates to frivolous litigation, contingency fee lawyers don't get paid unless the client does, giving attorneys a disincentive for filing unreasonable cases. A second important reason to allow contingency fees is that, despite the lawyer having a "proprietary interest" in the client's case, that interest is closely aligned with the client's interest. The more money the lawyer can recover for the client, the more the lawyer gets paid. Finally, proponents argue that even if the lawyer gets more than an average hourly fee with a favorable outcome, the lawyer has assumed from the client most of the risks of the costs of litigation.[9] On balance, given the importance of access and that few cases are sure things, contingency fees seem necessary, but they do place an added burden on lawyers' shoulders to make sure their judgment is exercised in the client's best interests, not their own.

7. Excessive Fees? Every jurisdiction in the country has an ethical rule which prohibits excessive or unreasonable fees. Most rules, like ABA Model Rule 1.5, which states that "A lawyer shall not make an agreement for, charge, or collect an unreasonable fee or an unreasonable amount for expenses," is accompanied by a laundry list of factors to be considered in determining whether the fee in question is "excessive" or "reasonable." But these are just words until they are applied. Since state bars and other lawyer regulatory agencies have only rarely imposed discipline for charging an excessive fee, the most frequent forum for discussing the reasonableness of fees is either a request for fees or a lawsuit arising from a fee dispute. How do courts interpret the reasonableness of a fee? The answer, not surprisingly, is "It depends." Here are two very different views from courts at opposite ends of the country.

BROBECK, PHLEGER & HARRISON v. TELEX CORP.
602 F.2d 866 (9th Cir.), cert. denied, 444 U.S. 981 (1979)

PER CURIAM:

This is a diversity action in which the plaintiff, the San Francisco law firm of Brobeck, Phleger & Harrison ("Brobeck"), sued the Telex Corporation ("Telex") to recover $1,000,000 in attorney's fees. Telex had engaged Brobeck on a contingency fee basis to prepare a petition for certiorari after the Tenth Circuit reversed a $259.5 million judgment in Telex's favor against International Business Machines Corporation ("IBM") and affirmed an $18.5 million counterclaim judgment for IBM against Telex. Brobeck prepared and filed the petition, and after Telex entered a "wash settlement" with IBM in which both parties released their claims against the other, Brobeck sent Telex a bill for $1,000,000, that it claimed Telex owed it under their written contingency fee agreement. When Telex refused to pay, Brobeck brought this action. Both parties filed motions for summary judgment. The district Court granted Brobeck's motion, awarding Brobeck $1,000,000 plus interest. Telex now appeals. . . .

Having had reversed one of the largest antitrust judgments in history, Telex officials decided to press the Tenth Circuit's decision to the United States Supreme Court. To maximize Telex's chances for having its petition for certiorari granted, they decided to search for the best available lawyer. They compiled a list of the preeminent antitrust and Supreme Court lawyers in the country, and Roger Wheeler, Telex's Chairman of the Board, settled on Moses Lasky of the Brobeck firm as the best possibility.

---

[9] Tort reformers also disagree, claiming that too often, such as when liability is clear in a personal injury case, "contingency" fees are hardly contingent at all. They also argue that while there may be incentives for lawyers to work hard in "big" cases, there are disincentives for hard work and solid preparation in cases of lower value. *See, e.g.*, Lester Brickman, *Contingent Fees Without Contingencies: Hamlet Without the Prince of Denmark?*, 37 UCLA L. REV. 29 (1989).

[Eventually, the following fee agreement between Lasky and Telex was signed.]

MEMORANDUM

1. Retainer of $25,000.00 to be paid. If Writ of Certiorari is denied and no settlement has been effected in excess of the Counterclaim, then the $25,000.00 retainer shall be the total fee paid; provided, however, that. . . .

3. Once a Petition for Writ of Certiorari has been filed with the Clerk of the United States Supreme Court then Brobeck will be entitled to the payment of an additional fee in the event of a recovery by Telex from IBM by way of settlement or judgment of its claims against IBM; and, such additional fee will be five percent (5%) of the first $100,000,000.00 gross of such recovery, undiminished by any recovery by IBM on its counterclaims or cross-claims. The maximum contingent fee to be paid is $5,000,000.00, provided that if recovery by Telex from IBM is less than $40,000,000.00 gross, the five percent (5%) shall be based on the net recovery, i.e., the recovery after deducting the credit to IBM by virtue of IBM's recovery on counterclaims or cross-claims, but the contingent fee shall not then be less than $1,000,000.00.

. . . .

[Telex president] Jatras signed Lasky's proposed agreement, and on February 28 returned it to Lasky with a letter and a check for $25,000 as the agreed retainer. To "clarify" his thinking on the operation of the fee agreement, Jatras attached a set of hypothetical examples to the letter. This "attachment" stated the amount of the fee that would be paid to Brobeck assuming judgment or settlements in eight different amounts. In the first hypothetical, which assumed a settlement of $18.5 million and a counterclaim judgment of $18.5 million, Jatras listed a "net recovery" by Telex of "$0" and a Brobeck contingency fee of "$0."

Lasky received the letter and attachment on March 3. Later that same day he replied: "Your attachment of examples of our compensation in various contingencies is correct, it being understood that the first example is applicable only to a situation where the petition for certiorari has been denied, as stated in paragraph 1 of the memorandum."

No Telex official responded to Lasky's letter. . . .

Lasky, as agreed, prepared the petition for certiorari and filed it in July 1975 . . . .

[A Telex settlement] meeting was held on September 5. Lasky told the assembled Telex officials that the chances that the petition for certiorari would be granted were very good. Wheeler, however, was concerned that if the petition for certiorari was denied, the outstanding counterclaim judgment would threaten Telex with bankruptcy. Wheeler informed Lasky that Telex was seriously considering the possibility of a "wash settlement" in which neither side would recover anything and each would release their claims against the other. Lasky responded that in the event of such a settlement he would be entitled to a fee of $1,000,000.

. . . .

On October 2 IBM officials . . . contacted Telex and the parties agreed that IBM would release its counterclaim judgment against Telex in exchange for Telex's dismissal of its petition for certiorari. On October 3, at the request of Wheeler and Jatras, Lasky had the petition for certiorari withdrawn. Thereafter, he sent a bill to Telex for $1,000,000.

. . . .

Telex contends that the $1 million fee was so excessive as to render the contract unenforceable. Alternatively, it argues that unconscionability depends on the contract's reasonableness, a question of fact that should be submitted to the jury.

Preliminarily, we note that whether a contract is fair or works an unconscionable hardship is determined with reference to the time when the contract was made and cannot be resolved by hindsight.

There is no dispute about the facts leading to Telex's engagement of the Brobeck firm. Telex was an enterprise threatened with bankruptcy. It had won one of the largest money judgments in history, but that judgment had been reversed in its entirety by the Tenth Circuit. In order to maximize its chances of gaining review by the United States Supreme Court, it sought to hire the most experienced and capable lawyer it could possibly find. After compiling a list of highly qualified lawyers, it settled on Lasky as the most able. Lasky was interested but wanted to bill Telex on an hourly basis. After Telex insisted on a contingent fee arrangement, Lasky made it clear that he would consent to such an arrangement only if he would receive a sizable contingent fee in the event of success.

In these circumstances, the contract between Telex and Brobeck was not so unconscionable that "no man in his senses and not under a delusion would make on the one hand, and as no honest and fair man would accept on the other." This is not a case where one party took advantage of another's ignorance, exerted superior bargaining power, or disguised unfair terms in small print. Rather, Telex, a multi-million [dollar] corporation, represented by able counsel, sought to secure the best attorney it could find to prepare its petition for certiorari, insisting on a contingent fee contract. Brobeck fulfilled its obligation to gain a stay of judgment and to prepare and file the petition for certiorari. Although the minimum fee was clearly high, Telex received substantial value from Brobeck's services. For, as Telex acknowledged, Brobeck's petition provided Telex with the leverage to secure a discharge of its counterclaim judgment, thereby saving it from possible bankruptcy in the event the Supreme Court denied its petition for certiorari. We conclude that such a contract was not unconscionable.

NOTES

What do you think of Lasky's response to Telex president Jatras' note on hypothetical fee situations? By saying the hypothetical was "correct," was Lasky misleading Jatras? Or was Lasky's explanation of what he meant by "correct" sufficient? What obligations should counsel have to make their fee agreements clear and unambiguous? On whom should the burden of an ambiguous agreement fall? Lest you think lawyers are given complete *carte blanche* by courts, read this next case. Can you reconcile *Brobeck* and the *Fordham* decision, below, or do they appear to be inconsistent?

IN RE FORDHAM
668 N.W.2d 816 (Mass. 1996)

This is an appeal from the Board of Bar Overseers' (board's) dismissal of a petition for discipline filed by bar counsel against attorney Laurence S. Fordham. On March 11, 1992, bar counsel served Fordham with a petition for discipline alleging that Fordham had charged a clearly excessive fee . . . for defending Timothy Clark (Timothy) in the District Court against a charge that he operated a motor vehicle while under the influence of intoxicating liquor. . . .

After five days of hearings, and with "serious reservations," the hearing committee concluded that Fordham's fee was not substantially in excess of a reasonable fee and that, therefore, the committee recommended against bar discipline. Bar counsel appealed from that determination to the board. By a vote of six to five, with one abstention, the board accepted the recommendation of the hearing committee. . . . We conclude . . . that the board erred in dismissing bar counsel's petition for discipline. We direct a judgment ordering public censure be entered in the county court.

We summarize the hearing committee's findings. On March 4, 1989, the Acton police department arrested Timothy, then twenty-one years old, and charged him with OUI, operating a motor vehicle after suspension, speeding, and operating an unregistered motor vehicle. At the time of the arrest, the police discovered a partially full quart of vodka in the vehicle. After failing a field sobriety test, Timothy was taken to the Acton police station where he submitted to two breathalyzer tests which registered.10 and.12 respectively.

Subsequent to Timothy's arraignment, he and his father, Laurence Clark (Clark) consulted with three lawyers, who offered to represent Timothy for fees between $3,000 and $10,000. Shortly after the arrest, Clark went to Fordham's home to service an alarm system which he had installed several years before. While there, Clark discussed Timothy's arrest with Fordham's wife who invited Clark to discuss the case with Fordham. Fordham then met with Clark and Timothy.

At this meeting, Timothy described the incidents leading to his arrest and the charges against him. Fordham, whom the hearing committee described as a "very experienced senior trial attorney with impressive credentials," told Clark and Timothy that he had never represented a client in a driving while under the influence case or in any criminal matter, and he had never tried a case in the District Court. The hearing committee found that "Fordham explained that although he lacked experience in this area, he was a knowledgeable and hard-working attorney and that he believed he could competently represent Timothy." Fordham described himself as 'efficient and economic in the use of [his] time.' . . .

"Towards the end of the meeting, Fordham told the Clarks that he worked on [a] time charge basis and that he billed monthly. . . . He also told the

Clarks that he would engage others in his firm to prepare the case. Clark had indicated that he would pay Timothy's legal fees." After the meeting, Clark hired Fordham to represent Timothy. [Fordham won an innovative motion to suppress the blood alcohol results obtained by a breathalyzer. Then he gained acquittal for Clark at trial before a judge sitting without a jury.]

. . . .

Fordham sent the following bills to Clark [totalling] $50,022.25, reflecting 227 hours of billed time, 153 hours of which were expended by Fordham and seventy-four of which were his associates' time. Clark did not pay the first two bills when they became due and expressed to Fordham his concern about their amount. Clark paid Fordham $10,000 on June 20, 1989. At that time, Fordham assured Clark that most of the work had been completed "other than taking [the case] to trial." Clark did not make any subsequent payments. . . .

Bar counsel and Fordham have stipulated that all the work billed by Fordham was actually done and that Fordham and his associates spent the time they claim to have spent. They also have stipulated that Fordham acted conscientiously, diligently, and in good faith in representing Timothy and in his billing in this case.

. . . The board noted that "[a]lthough none of the experts who testified at the disciplinary hearing had ever heard of a fee in excess of $15,000 for a first-offense OUI case, the hearing committee found that [Clark] had entered into the transaction with open eyes after interviewing other lawyers with more experience in such matters."

In reviewing the hearing committee's and the board's analysis of the various factors, as appearing in DR 2-106(B), which are to be considered for a determination as to whether a fee is clearly excessive, . . . we are persuaded that [the fee was] clearly excessive.

The first factor listed in DR 2-106(B) requires examining "[t]he time and labor required, the novelty and difficulty of the questions involved, and the skill requisite to perform the legal service properly." Although the hearing committee determined that Fordham "spent a large number of hours on [the] matter, in essence learning from scratch what others . . . already know," [t]he hearing committee reasoned that even if the number of hours Fordham "spent [were] wholly out of proportion" to the number of hours that a lawyer with experience in the trying of OUI cases would require, the committee was not required to conclude that the fee based on time spent was "clearly excessive." . . . We disagree.

Four witnesses testified before the hearing committee as experts on OUI cases. One of the experts, testifying on behalf of bar counsel, opined that "the amount of time spent in this case is clearly excessive." He testified that there were no unusual circumstances in the OUI charge against Timothy and that it was a "standard operating under the influence case." The witness did agree that Fordham's argument for suppression of the breathalyzer test results, which was successful, was novel and would have justified additional time and labor. He also acknowledged that the acquittal was a good result; even with the suppression of the breathalyzer tests, he testified, the chances of an acquittal would have been "[n]ot likely at a bench trial." . . . A second expert, testifying on behalf of bar counsel, expressed his belief that the issues presented in this case were not particularly difficult, nor novel, . . . [H]e did recognize, however, that the theory that Fordham utilized to suppress the breathalyzer tests was impressive and one of which he had previously never heard. Nonetheless, the witness concluded that "clearly there is no way that [he] could justify these kind of hours to do this kind of work." . . .

An expert called by Fordham testified that the facts of Timothy's case presented a challenge and that without the suppression of the breathalyzer test results it would have been "an almost impossible situation in terms of prevailing on the trier of fact." He further stated that, based on the particulars in Timothy's case, he believed that Fordham's hours were not excessive . . . . The fourth expert witness, called by Fordham, testified [similarly]. . . .

Based on the testimony of the four experts, the number of hours devoted to Timothy's OUI case by Fordham and his associates was substantially in excess of the hours that a prudent experienced lawyer would have spent. According to the evidence, the number of hours spent was several times the amount of time any of the witnesses had ever spent on a similar case. We are not unmindful of the novel and successful motion to suppress the breathalyzer test results, but that effort cannot justify a $50,000 fee in a type of case in which the usual fee is less than one-third of that amount.

The board determined that "[b]ecause [Fordham] had never tried an OUI case or appeared in the district court, [Fordham] spent over 200 hours preparing the case, in part to educate himself in the relevant substantive law and court procedures." Fordham's inexperience in criminal defense work and OUI cases in particular cannot justify the extraordinarily high fee. It cannot be that an inexperienced lawyer is entitled to charge three or four times as much as an experienced lawyer for the same service. A client "should not be expected to pay for the education of a lawyer when he spends excessive amounts of time on tasks which, with reasonable experience, become matters of routine."

. . . .

DR 2-106(B) provides that the third factor to be considered in ascertaining the reasonableness of a fee is its comparability to "[t]he fee customarily charged in the locality for similar legal services." [Bar counsel's expert witnesses testified that fees ran from as little as $1,000 to as much as $15,000 but never more.]

[N]othing contained within the disciplinary rule nor within any pertinent case law indicates in any manner that a clearly excessive fee does not warrant discipline whenever the time spent during the representation was spent in good faith. The fact that this court has not previously had occasion to discipline an attorney in the circumstances of this case does not suggest that the imposition of discipline in this case offends due process. . . .

In charging a clearly excessive fee, Fordham departed substantially from the obligation of professional responsibility that he owed to his client. . . . Accordingly, a judgment is to be entered in the county court imposing a public censure.

NOTES

Does it matter that Lasky's fee was contingent and Fordham's fee hourly? (Note that contingency fees are almost universally prohibited in criminal cases.) What other factors distinguish these two cases? Consider these two other recent decisions.

In *Raymark Industries, Inc. v. Butera, Beausang, Cohen & Brennan*, 1997 U.S. Dist. Lexis 19070 (E.D. Pa. 1997), *aff'd*, 193 F.3d 210 (3d Cir. 1999), client Raymark retained attorney Beausang and his law firm for a $1 million non-refundable retainer. Ten weeks later, Raymark terminated the relationship effective immediately, and sued to have the fee returned. The Court denied the recovery, stating, "This case is not about overreaching attorneys who took unfair advantage of an unsophisticated client. . . . Ten weeks into the relationship, Raymark abruptly fired Defendants. . . . In our legal system, a client is free to terminate its attorney at any time. . . . But Raymark's decision . . . had a $1 million price tag — a price set by Raymark, not Defendants."

Very different results can occur when trial juries make the decisions and individuals rather than sophisticated corporations are the clients. In November 1999, Houston's Piro & Lilly suffered a $6.3 million award against them and in favor of their client, the ex-wife of a billionaire who had challenged her prenuptial contract. The lawyers had charged a contingency fee that the client claimed was unconscionably excessive. The client's new lawyer claimed that "you can put the entire client file in two file boxes," and that the fee charged gave Piro $47,379 per hour for his 67 hours of billed time, while his partner received $8,079 per hour. The lawyers argued that the great result they had obtained for their client more than justified their fees, an argument not unlike Lasky and Fordham's claims.[10]

Should the sophistication of the client clearly be a factor underlying all of these decisions? What about using the standard in the community as a barometer for determining excessive fees? Is this reasonable, or could it lead to unjust results if all lawyers in the locality charge what most people would consider unfair?[11]

Finally, under the category of "nothing lasts forever," a Washington State appeals court ruled that where a law firm's fee, set in 1972, for helping two entrepreneurs develop a shopping mall was discounted initially in return for 5% of the cash distribution from the mall in perpetuity, resulting in the original approximate $8,000 fee blossoming into a total of $380,000, the fee was unreasonable. The court took the position that a fee contract, generally evaluated at the time it is made, could be reevaluated in the face of subsequent altered circumstances such as these.[12]

---

[10] *See* Margaret Cronin Fisk, *Two Texas Lawyers Hit with $6.3M Overcharging Verdict*, Nat'l L.J., Dec. 6, 1999.

[11] Note that using the community standard has its limits. In *Goldfarb v. Virginia State Bar*, 421 U.S. 773, 95 S. Ct. 2004 (1975) the Supreme Court held that a bar association could not set minimum fees without violating the Sherman Anti-Trust Act. California has eliminated the community standard factor entirely from its fee-evaluation rule. Cal. Rule of Prof'l Conduct 4-200.

[12] *Holmes v. Loveless*, 94 P.3d 338 (Wash. App. 2004).

8. Must Reasonable Fees Be Proportional to a Case's Dollar Value?
What fees may a court deem "reasonable" when measured against the amount of the client's recovery? *City of Riverside v. Rivera*, 477 U.S. 561, 106 S. Ct. 2686 (1986), concerned allegations against the city of Riverside, California that police officers unlawfully entered people's homes and committed other violations of the Bill of Rights, and also engaged in racial and ethnic slurs against the mostly Latino plaintiffs. A sharply divided Supreme Court held that the amount of attorneys' fees awarded in a civil rights action need not be proportional to the monetary recovery awarded the plaintiffs. A federal district court had ordered payment of almost $250,000 in legal fees in a case where the plaintiffs' recovery was only $33,350. Justice Brennan, writing for the Court, said that barring such fee recoveries would substantially diminish the incentive of lawyers to take on civil rights cases.[13]

The dissents of both Chief Justice Burger and Justice Rehnquist, however, found both the fee and the amount of time spent flatly unreasonable. Rehnquist noted that the two plaintiffs' lawyers spent almost 2,000 hours on a case in which the jury awarded a mere $13,300 in damages for the violation of plaintiffs' federal constitutional rights. Analogizing to a lawyer who charges a client $25,000 to protect title to "Blackacre," a piece of real property worth only $10,000, the future Chief Justice found the fee award unreasonable per se.

Justice Powell provided the swing vote. He did not agree with Brennan's broad thesis or his interpretation of precedent. He did acknowledge, however, that "the court may consider the vindication of constitutional rights in addition to the amount of damages," and noted that the district court had "made an explicit finding that the 'public interest' had been served by the jury's verdict." But he also remarked in a footnote that a private damage award which benefits the public interest "probably will be the rare case."

The point of *Riverside v. Rivera* appears to be that a determination of the reasonableness of a lawyer's fee need not turn solely on the *economic* benefit received by the lawyer's clients, but it must be tied to *some* benefit, in this case to the public interest. Under these circumstances, is Rehnquist's analogy to Blackacre apt? Or does he miss the point that there are issues broader than "mere" economic recovery? Would the lawyer in Rehnquist's analogy be clearly charging an excessive fee if the client had said "I don't care what it costs to quiet title to Blackacre; it's a family dispute, and if I lose it, I'll never get it back. I know it's only worth $10,000 on the open market, but it's worth $1,000,000 to me?"

What about the opposite situation? By this we mean circumstances in which injunctive or other equitable relief is not in issue, but a lawyer, knowing that a case is not likely to be financially viable, nevertheless undertakes the representation. Take, for example, a small business dispute over the payment of $10,000, where there is no provision for the payment of attorneys' fees and the lawyer will charge between $7,500 and $15,000 to perform the work. Do lawyers owe any duties to their prospective clients to warn them that such

---

[13] Brennan had made a similar argument in dissent two months earlier. In *Evans v. Jeff D.*, 475 U.S. 717, 106 S. Ct. 1531 (1986), he questioned the propriety of offering plaintiffs a settlement which granted them relief conditioned on a waiver of attorneys' fees.

cases are likely to result in only one winner — the lawyer? Is undertaking such a case at least arguably a breach of fiduciary duty, in that the client's interests are subordinated to the lawyer's fee?

In *In re Taxman Clothing Co.*, 49 F.3d 54 (7th Cir. 1995), counsel for a bankruptcy trustee was denied fees when the court determined that his pursuit of the bankruptcy estate's claims cost more than the probable revenue to the estate. Even if the lawyer had not intentionally acted merely to generate work for himself, to plunge ahead without adequately evaluating the financial viability of the claims breached the lawyer's fiduciary duty.

9. Business Relationships, "IPOs," and Lawyer-Client "Deals." Agreements for the payment of fees are hardly the only financial circumstances which can create conflicts between lawyer and client. According to the *National Law Journal*, one of the frequent complaints about high-powered entertainment lawyers is that they "don additional hats as business or personal managers, lenders or investors." The suspicion is that they "risk . . . placing their personal or financial interests above those of their clients." Because a lawyer has a fiduciary relationship with the client — one in which the client should be entitled to repose trust — all business transactions between lawyers and their clients should be closely scrutinized.

While it's clear that entering into a real estate partnership with a client or lending or borrowing a client's money is a business transaction, what if the client assigns the lawyer the rights to her life story in return for representation? The ABA Model Rules address this issue in the conflict rules rather than under fee arrangements. Does this organization of the Rules make sense to you? Where does the interest of the lawyer lie in that circumstance — to get the client off, or to have the rights to a best-selling book? Are these interests consistent or inconsistent? Read the following article.

GARY TAYLOR, DID LITERARY DEAL RAISE CONFLICT?
The National Law Journal (June 10, 1991)[14]

A literary-rights contract between a Texas lawyer and a female client condemned to die looms as a central issue in a federal judge's decision to overturn the conviction, and it raises new questions about conflict of interest.

The case centers on the 1985 representation of Betty Lou Beets by E. Ray Andrews, a sole practitioner in Athens, Texas, where the trial occurred. Ms. Beets was sentenced to the death penalty after being convicted of murder-for-hire in the death of her fifth husband, Dallas Fire Department Capt. Jimmy Don Beets, who had been reported missing after a 1983 boating mishap.

The discovery of his body in a fake wishing well outside her mobile home — plus the discovery of Ms. Beets' fourth husband's body buried nearby — attracted worldwide media attention and prompted her arrest. Mr. Andrews became her attorney, accepting literary and media rights in place of a fee, according to Asst. Attorney General Bill Zaplac.

. . . .

---

[14] Reprinted with the permission of The National Law Journal. Copyright © 1991 by The New York Law Publishing Company.

Typical death-penalty conflict complaints feature situations in which an attorney somehow ended up representing a witness as well as the defendant. In this case, the attorney himself should have been the witness, according to the May 9 decision by U.S. District Judge Robert M. Parker of Tyler. *Beets v. Collins*, CA 6:90 CV 575 (E.D. Texas).

Robert L. McGlasson, director of the Texas Appellate Practice & Educational Resource Center in Austin . . . charges that Mr. Andrews should have withdrawn as Ms. Beets' attorney because he learned information important enough to make him "the best witness she could have had." The contract, however, prevented withdrawal, Mr. McGlasson speculates.

During a visit to Mr. Andrews' office before the body was found, Ms. Beets disclosed she was unaware of a $110,000 insurance policy due her upon her husband's demise. Mr. McGlasson argues that her ignorance of the opportunity to profit from her husband's death would undercut an element crucial to a capital conviction — a monetary motive.

Says Mr. Andrews, "I don't feel like there was a conflict of interest," but he concedes that the contract was his idea. He says that Ms. Beets filed a grievance with the State Bar of Texas about a year ago, but "it was dismissed in five minutes."

He adds: "I don't think I would have been a significant witness. I worked my butt off and got it reversed once for nothing. But promises and bad publicity is my reward. I tried the case as hard as I could. I didn't create the facts. I'm satisfied with the job I did."

. . . .

New rules that took effect in Texas last year tighten up the prohibitions against literary contracts between lawyers and clients, says Dawn Miller, senior assistant general counsel with the state bar. They now prohibit such agreements until after the attorney has completed the term of employment.

. . . .

"The question is ineffective assistance of counsel, and we feel Mr. Andrews did everything he could," says Mr. Zaplac. "I can't say he was motivated by anything other than a desire to get her acquitted."

Mr. McGlasson, however, charges that the literary-rights contract violates ethical codes.

George Kendall, associate counsel with the NAACP Legal Defense and Educational Fund Inc., agrees, saying that the case once again illustrates the problems that can occur when attorneys trade legal services for literary rights to their clients' experiences.

. . . .

NOTES

One of the problems in evaluating the responsibilities of lawyers who enter business relationships with clients is the issue of when an attorney's fiduciary duty begins. In many states, while the attorney's fiduciary duty exists from the moment the lawyer has a client (as we saw earlier in discussing the *Kurtenbach* case), the contract for fees is considered an "arms-length transaction" in which the lawyer is free to negotiate as any businessperson would — at arm's length. While this view may make some sense from the point of view of the lawyer, it would appear to endanger unsophisticated clients who may be seeking representation for the first time.

This accusation is one that has often been hurled at Silicon Valley law firms that invest in their start-up clients. Firms such as Wilson, Sonsini, Goodrich & Rosati and the Venture Law Group have earned well-deserved reputations both as entrepreneurs and lawyers. So long as their investment is made at the inception of the relationship, they would argue that they owe no fiduciary duty at the time that investment is agreed to. Lawyers still have to meet the requirements of their state's rules on engaging in business transactions with a client. But when a start-up with a great idea, a great product, but no money comes to a big, powerful law firm, the start-up's principals may feel they have little choice but to accede to the firm's demands.

Investing in clients is an increasingly common occurrence, no longer limited to a few parts of the country. It is clear that, if one properly follows all the safeguards involved in doing business with clients, the practice is presumptively ethical. But are there so many pitfalls along the road that prudence, if not ethics, should make law firms forbear from this practice? Read the following article.

JONATHAN RINGEL, INVESTING IN CLIENTS: SUNNY GAINS, BUT OTHERS SEE ETHICS CLOUD
Fulton County Daily Report (Feb. 7, 2000)[15]

Atlanta law firms are discovering what their counterparts in Silicon Valley have known for years — investing in clients may be the best idea since the billable hour.

The practice, which has helped Internet start-ups raise capital and save legal fees, also has raised tricky ethics questions. . . . Some see conflicts of interest when lawyers who own a piece of their clients give advice that will directly affect the value of the lawyers' investment. Others say stock ownership, when limited, doesn't enhance a lawyer's temptation for misconduct.

Atlanta Firms Jump In

As legal ethicists debate, Atlanta firms are getting into the act. The most active client-investors appear to be in the technology area. Intellectual property boutique Needle & Rosenberg has invested in 12 biotechnology and dot-com clients. A two-year-old firm called The Red Hot Law Group has opened an adjacent mentoring program for start-up clients who pay for their legal services with warrants allowing the law firm to own 5 percent of the company.

Big firms are interested too. Powell, Goldstein, Frazer & Murphy is starting its own private equity fund to invest in potential high-growth clients, as well as non-clients. "We see opportunities that are attractive," says Richard H.

---

[15] Copyright © 2000, American Lawyer Media, L.P.

Miller, the PoGo partner who heads the firm's high-growth group called Eagle Partners. "We want to be able to take advantage of that."

Not New in Silicon Valley

Silicon Valley firms have been investing in their clients for 30 years, says Craig W. Johnson, chairman of the Venture Law Group in Menlo Park, Calif.

"The only reason this is interesting now is because the returns have been astronomical," says Johnson. For example, Johnson notes, the firm invested $30,000 in Yahoo! while helping the Internet giant go public. Yahoo! is worth more than $90 billion today.

Asked how the firm did, Johnson says only, "We sold too early."

The American Bar Journal recently reported that Securities and Exchange Commission records show Johnson's firm took stock in 17 of its clients that made initial public offerings in 1999. The firm's investment in six of those clients had a value of more than $1 million each at the end of the first day of trading.

Thirty grand is the typical investment for a $5 million financing, Johnson says, and the firm doesn't take stock in lieu of fees. If the firm takes a larger position in a company, Johnson adds, it doesn't represent the company in legal matters but just acts as its business adviser.

Lawyers say limiting a firm's investment in clients is key to avoiding ethics problems. But Andrew L. Kaufman, who teaches professional responsibility at Harvard Law School, is uncomfortable with the prospect that a lawyer's advice might affect the value of his or her investment. "As a lawyer you might be thinking to give cautious advice," he says. "As an entrepreneur, you might be more of a risk taker."

Stanford Law School legal ethics professor William H. Simon takes a different view. He says ethics fears surrounding lawyers investing in their clients are "unwarranted," although he acknowledges that lawyers obviously should not compromise their legal responsibility because they are too invested in the value of the company. He points out, in the interest of full disclosure, that his wife practices law at a Silicon Valley firm that invests in its clients.

Simon says a lawyer can be just as tempted to bend rules to keep its client afloat when the client's demise will mean the end of a major source of legal fees as it is to protect a stock investment. "You don't want the lawyer to compromise her ethics because she's too invested in the success" of her client, whether the client represents too much of a lawyer's client base or stock portfolio, he says. For that reason, Simon suggests that firms investing in their clients have, at the most, no more than 5 percent of a client's stock.

Harvard's Kaufman disagrees that the ethics problems presented by investments are the same as those related to fees. When lawyers are paid in cash, he says, as opposed to in stock, "what you get isn't determined by the advice you give."

Where to Draw the Line

Gregory J. Kirsch, a partner in Atlanta IP boutique Needle & Rosenberg, ponders the gray line surrounding the ethics of equity and concludes, "I don't think there's any magic formula on what you can and cannot do." For the past few years, the firm has accepted stock in lieu of fees from 10 biotech and two Internet clients, he says. Kirsch, who has worked only with the Internet clients, says if he's just helping a client file a patent claim, he has no problems taking stock. But if the same client then asks him to render an opinion on whether a proposed activity would infringe on someone else's patent, he'd likely send the client to another firm. Worried more about an appearance of conflict than an actual one, Kirsch says, "We might be a little biased."

A Potential Problem

W. Pitts Carr, a shareholder lawsuit expert at Atlanta's Carr, Tabb & Freeman, says he sees nothing wrong with lawyers owning stock in corporations and representing those corporations in litigation or writing their contracts.

Carr does suggest a potential problem, even if he adds he's never seen it happen. If lawyers approve press releases or Securities and Exchange Commission disclosures, he says, "to me that would be a rock-solid conflict of interest" since those disclosures will have a direct effect on investors' valuation of the company.

That scenario doesn't both Evelyn A. Ashley, founder of the Red Hot Law Group, which has two public securities lawyers. "If you have the highest standard, that's not something that's going to enter your mind," she says. When preparing documents for public companies, "We don't say, 'My God, how is that going to affect my investment?'"

NOTES

The foregoing article addresses only some of the troubling issues involved in investing in clients. Malpractice insurers are increasingly worried about the practice, often requiring that law firm investment in the client not exceed five percent. Even then, some malpractice carriers are uncomfortable, as they are with the related practice — also increasingly prevalent — of members of a company's outside law firm sitting on the company's board of directors. "It's clear that an outside lawyer who is also a director is much more likely to be sued for malpractice," Robert E. O'Malley told *Legal Times* a few years ago. O'Malley is vice chairman of ALAS, or, more formally, Attorneys' Liability Assurance Society, Inc., one of the country's largest malpractice insurers. "If there are two alternative courses of action before the board, and one of them would produce a big fee for the lawyer's firm while the other would not, it is difficult to imagine how the lawyer/director could offer disinterested advice," said O'Malley.

Even Wilson, Sonsini general counsel Donald Bradley acknowledges that "there is no no-risk way" to invest in a client.[16] Bradley points out that individual Wilson, Sonsini lawyers are not allowed to invest in clients and a separate investment corporation makes the investment, rather than the firm

---

[16] Remarks of Donald Bradley, Annual Ethics Symposium of the State Bar of California's Committee on Professional Responsibility and Conduct, June 2000.

itself. But the effect of this separation is questionable: The separate corporation's list of shareholders is virtually identical to the list of the law firm's shareholder attorneys.

Some of the troubling issues are relatively subtle and sophisticated in nature. For instance, Joseph F. Troy, a California attorney who has written and spoken often about investing in clients, believes that an independent third party should be brought in to evaluate the transaction, though he acknowledges that no rule of professional conduct requires this. Other issues include the inherent tension about how the value of the shares will be negotiated, when and under what conditions stock options will vest, and to what extent stock issuance can be the sole, or principal, means of compensation.

There is also an important distinction between accepting stock or options from a start-up with little cash, and the practice of some firms of making ongoing investments in ongoing clients. Start-ups have little power to fight off the entreaties of the firms that they hire to do their initial public offerings (or IPOs). But they also have little to lose, and little cash with which to hire counsel. Ongoing investing, however, seems to be more directly about making money with little justification from a client-needs point of view. Should ethics rules make any distinctions in what kinds of law firm investments are appropriate?

SUPPLEMENTAL READINGS

1. *Togstad v. Vesely, Otto, Miller & Keefe*, 291 N.W.2d 686 (Minn. 1980). In this action for legal malpractice, the court found an attorney-client relationship existed and that malpractice arose from an office visit, where the attorney advised that he did not think the client had a case, but would discuss it with his partner. The lawyer failed to contact the client again, and the client did not consult another lawyer until a year later. This case may provide the broadest definition of attorney-client tort liability, since the lawyer made it clear he had not agreed to take the case in question.

2. The number of non-clients to whom lawyers owe duties seems ever-increasing. A good recent summary of the duties to non-clients is an article by Jay M. Feinman, *Attorney Liability to Nonclients*, 31 Tort & Ins. L.J. 735 (1996). Prof. Feinman discusses several important derivative liability issues, including duties to primary and intended beneficiaries, negligent misrepresentation, duties to third party beneficiaries, and parties' reliance on the attorney's statements, and then discusses different ways to cohesively approach these theories.

3. Other cases not cited in Section 4 above that have addressed the issue of third party beneficiaries, particularly in the estate planning context, include *Trask v. Butler*, 123 Wash. 2d 835, 872 P.2d 1084 (1994); *Pizel v. Zuspann*, 247 Kan. 54, 795 P.2d 42 (1990); *Hale v. Groce*, 304 Ore. 281, 744 P.2d 1289 (1987); *Lorraine v. Grover, Ciment, Weinstein & Stauber, P.A.*, 467 So. 2d 315 (Fla. 1985); and *Guy v. Liederbach*, 501 Pa. 47, 459 A.2d 744 (1983).

4. Rachel Brill and Rochelle Sparko, *Limited Legal Services and Conflicts of Interest: Unbundling in the Public Interest*, 16 Georgetown J. Legal Ethics 553 (2003), is a valuable article that engages in an extensive discussion of the effect of unbundled legal services on representation of the limited-scope client and other prospective clients.

5. *White v. McBride*, 937 S.W.2d 796 (Tenn. Sup. 1996), concerned a lawyer who had a contingency fee contract with a husband to get one-third of the amount recovered from his wife's estate. The facts of the case are complicated, but the holding is significant: Not only did the court find the contingency fee contract excessive and unenforceable, but also denied the lawyer's claim for *quantum meruit* fees. Interestingly, the court did not find that contingency fees in probate cases were invalid *per se*, but rather that here, the percentage was clearly excessive, especially given that there was little if any contingency about the husband eventually receiving funds. The court's holding on *quantum meruit* fees reversed previous case law on public policy grounds: "To permit an attorney to fall back on the theory of quantum meruit when he unsuccessfully fails to collect a clearly excessive fee does absolutely nothing to promote ethical behavior."

6. Tort reformers have written many articles attacking contingency fees and suggesting, at a minimum, that percentages should be substantially curtailed where the risk of no recovery is small. Perhaps the most prolific tort reformer is Lester Brickman of Cardozo Law School. In addition to the 1989 article cited above in Section 5, the following are of interest: Brickman, *A Massachusetts Debacle: Gagnon v. Shoblom*, 12 Cardozo L. Rev. 1417 (1991), analyzes a case in which liability was sufficiently clear and the damages so catastrophic that the trial court limited the lawyer's contingency percentage though the Massachusetts high court reinstated the fee award; and Brickman, Michael Horowitz & Jeffrey O'Connell, "Rethinking Contingency Fees," Manhattan Institute Monograph No. 1 (1994), which proposes a comprehensive "reform" plan that includes lowering contingency fee rates and other ideas that formed the basis for the 1998 California tort reform initiative which was eventually defeated in a close vote.

7. Court cases and ethics opinions differ substantially from state to state as to whether and under what circumstances an attorney may take and keep an advance retainer. Some jurisdictions distinguish an advance fee, which even if termed non-refundable may be refunded if the lawyer doesn't do the work, and a "true" retainer, payable in advance to secure a particular lawyer's availability on behalf of a client. "True" retainers are of particular value in highly specialized fields where few lawyers with expertise are available. *Baranowski v. State Bar*, 24 Cal. 3d 158, 154 Cal. Rptr. 752 (1979), discusses the distinction between these two types of retainers. *Federal Savings & Loan Ins. Corp. v. Angell, Holmes & Lea*, 838 F.2d 395 (9th Cir. 1988), holds that even where the fee agreement between the lawyers and the S&L provided that the retainer was earned upon receipt, this was *not* binding on the S&L's eventual receiver, who could terminate the lawyers and insist on a refund of the unearned fees. In *Jacobson v. Sassower*, 66 N.Y.2d 991 (1985), the New York Court of Appeals refused to allow a discharged lawyer to keep the unearned portion of a retainer since the notice to the client about what is meant by "non-refundable" was not entirely clear and should be construed against the lawyer.

8. A great deal has been written about taking stock for legal services. Though there have been some law review studies, most of the best articles have been in the colloquial legal press. Two of these are Debra Baker, "Who Wants to Be a Millionaire?", *ABA Journal*, February 2000, and "From the Epicenter: A Discussion of Clients, Culture, and Competition," a roundtable "special report" on "dot.com practices" published by *Legal Times*, October 4, 1999.

9. ABA Formal Opinion 00-418 (July 7, 2000) concludes that lawyers may acquire ownership interests in their clients either by obtaining stock in lieu of fees or by developing investment opportunities, and that "no inherent conflict of interest" exists. While the opinion warns about possible conflicts and the need to comply with ABA Rules 1.8(a) regarding business transactions and 2.1 regarding independent professional judgment, the opinion is an affirmation of the legitimacy of such arrangements.

10. ABA Formal Opinion 98-410 (February 27, 1998) addresses the issue of serving in the dual capacity of officer or director of a corporation and counsel to the corporation. The opinion warns that the lawyer must make clear to the corporation from the outset the differences between the two roles, that some matters discussed with the lawyer in the role as director may not be confidential, and that conflicts of interest can and do occur. Nevertheless, the opinion states that this dual role is not prohibited.

Chapter 3

COMMUNICATION AND CONFIDENTIALITY

PROBLEM 4

Confidentiality is a vitally important aspect of the attorney-client relationship. The nature and extent of that confidentiality can create difficult issues for the attorney confronted by conflicting obligations — to the legal system and society as a whole. The dilemma of Roger Earl, the attorney in the following problem, is complicated by the fact that physical evidence — both the fruits and instrumentalities of crimes — is involved.

Roger Earl Receives Some Evidence

Roger Earl is a well-known criminal defense lawyer. One afternoon four individuals consult him.

Adams, whose murder trial is to begin the next week, comes into Earl's office and says, "I was lying when I told you I didn't kill my wife. I did it, and here's the gun I used. I don't know what to do with it; I only know that I don't want the DA to get hold of it." Adams then places the gun on Earl's desk.

Then Baker comes in. She informs Earl that the money she took in the robbery for which Earl is defending her is buried in a plastic bag in the woods behind her home. She specifies the location. Earl knows that the prosecution's case against Baker is weak unless the DA can produce the money. The case is scheduled for trial in three weeks.

By now Earl is inundated with work; the last thing he needs is a new client. But Carlton, whom Earl has never met, barges in, and before Earl can say he is too busy, Carlton blurts out: "I just killed my partner. I used this gun. I don't want the gun found, and I don't want to get caught. I am prepared to pay for your advice, and if I am arrested I want you to represent me." Carlton then places the gun on Earl's desk.

While contemplating the events of the day, Earl gets a phone call from Dunn, a longstanding client. Dunn informs Earl that he has been organizing "the heist of the decade," a burglary of the Philadelphia mint. He also tells Earl that the burglary will occur the following Wednesday. He wants to retain Earl in advance in case anything goes wrong.

QUESTIONS

1. What should Earl do in Adams' case? Specifically, consider the following:

    a.   How should Earl advise him?

    b.   Should Earl inform authorities of the existence of the physical evidence?

c. What, if anything, should Earl do with the physical evidence? What about fingerprints, serial numbers, etc.?

d. To what extent is the communication confidential?

e. May Earl continue to represent Adams?

f. How, if at all, does Baker's case differ from Adams'?

2. How are Carlton's and Dunn's situations different from Adams'? Are their communications as confidential as Adams'? Does it matter whether Earl takes on Carlton as a client? Does it matter that Dunn has long been Earl's client?

3. Examine the hypotheticals in Professor Zacharias's article in Section 10 below. Pick three of the hypotheticals and decide what you would do if confronted by such a situation.

READINGS

1. Mr. Garrow, His Lawyers, and Two Buried Bodies. Consider the circumstances confronting lawyers Francis R. Belge and Frank Armani. In this case, there was physical evidence — bodies, the victims of murders committed by their client. The following article describes the terrible dilemma these lawyers faced, and the gruesome decision they made. Following the article are excerpts from the opinions of two courts — the first ruling on Belge's criminal indictment, the second upholding that ruling. Last is a newspaper synopsis of the New York State Bar Association's ethics committee's opinion on whether Belge's conduct was ethical. Are the trial court's conclusions correct? What about the appellate court's distinctions between the evidence rule of "privilege" and the ethics rule of "confidentiality"? Are the appellate court and the ethics committee in essential agreement or disagreement?

Does protection of the client's interests result in abandonment of "human standards of decency"? Are the client's interests and fundamental notions of justice mutually exclusive?

SLAYER'S LAWYERS KEPT SECRET OF 2 MORE KILLINGS
The New York Times (June 20, 1974)[1]

Lake Pleasant, N.Y., June 19 — Two lawyers for a man on trial here for murder did not disclose for six months that they had seen the bodies of two other people killed by their client because, they said, they were bound by the confidentiality of a lawyer-client relationship.

The court-appointed attorneys said today that their client had told them where to find the bodies of two missing women. They photographed the bodies, they said, but did not report the discoveries to authorities searching for the murder victims.

The lawyers also said they had kept their discovery from the father of one of the women, who had visited them in the hope that they could shed some light on the disappearance of his 20-year-old daughter.

---

[1] Copyright © 1974 by The New York Times Company. Reprinted by permission.

"The information was so privileged — I was bound by my lawyers' oath to keep it confidential after I found the bodies," said Francis Belge, one of the two lawyers representing Robert Garrow. Mr. Garrow, a 38-year-old mechanic for a Syracuse bakery, is accused of fatally stabbing Philip Domblewski, an 18-year-old Schenectady student who was camping in the Adirondacks last July.

From what his lawyers said in a news conference today, as well as from what Mr. Garrow has — sometimes incoherently — blurted out in court, the defendant may be connected to at least four murders.

Mr. Belge and his associate on the case, Frank Armani, told of the secret they had kept at a news conference in this Adirondack village. They indicated that they could come forth now, released from their obligation by Mr. Garrow's own testimony yesterday. . . .

The Police Chief of Syracuse . . . said he would ask the Onondaga District Attorney to bring obstruction of justice charges against the lawyers. . . .

According to Mr. Belge, Mr. Garrow told him of raping and killing a woman in an abandoned mine shaft near Mineville, NY. The lawyer said this information was provided by Mr. Garrow a few weeks after the suspect was wounded and captured last Aug. 9 following a manhunt involving 200 state troopers and others.

Some three weeks later Mr. Belge said, he discovered the body of Susan Petz, a 20-year-old woman from Skokie, Ill. She had been missing since July 20, when the body of her camping companion, Daniel Porter, a Harvard student, was found near Weavertown.

"We passed the shaft 10 times before I found it with a flashlight at twilight," Mr. Belge said. "Frank lowered me into the shaft by my feet and I took pictures."

The finding of Miss Petz's body was reported to the state police four months later by two children who had been playing in the mine.

Meanwhile, Mr. Belge said, Miss Petz's father visited him because his client, Mr. Garrow, had been unofficially linked to killings in the area.

"I spent many, many sleepless nights [over] my ability to reveal the information, especially after Mr. Petz came in from Chicago and talked to me," Mr. Belge said.

The lawyer found the second body at the end of September. He said that while Mr. Garrow provided a rough diagram locating Miss Petz's body, in the second instance he gave only a general description of an area in Syracuse near Syracuse University.

There, in Oakwood cemetery, Mr. Belge said, he found the body of Alicia Hauck, a 16-year-old high school girl who disappeared from her home in Syracuse nearly two months earlier, on July 11.

Concern for Parents

Miss Hauck's body was ultimately found and reported by a Syracuse University student on December 1. In the intervening months, her father, the owner of a bowling alley in Syracuse, and the police were treating the case as that of a runaway and were advertising pleas for the girl to come home.

"We both, knowing how the parents must feel, wanted to advise them where the bodies were," Mr. Belge said. "But since it was a privileged communication, we could not reveal any information that was given to us in confidence."

Both lawyers had apparently felt the weight of the confidence they honored until today. "Death is difficult enough to accept," Mr. Armani said, "but worrying and wondering, it'll drive you insane."

Two Obligations Seen

Prof. David Mellinkoff of the University of California at Los Angeles' Law School, the author of a book, "The Conscience of a Lawyer," and a specialist in matters of legal ethics and confidentiality, said after being told of the case that in general the lawyers seemed to be under two conflicting obligations.

On one hand, he said, a lawyer is committed to keeping his clients' confessions of a completed crime in confidence. On the other, the lawyer cannot hide physical evidence, such as a weapon, or in this case, bodies, from the prosecution.

PEOPLE v. BELGE
83 Misc. 2d 186, 372 N.Y.S.2d 798 (1975)

[D]iscovery [of the bodies] was not disclosed to the authorities, but became public during the trial of Mr. Garrow in June of 1974, when to affirmatively establish the defense of insanity, these three other murders were brought before the jury by the defense in the Hamilton County trial. Public indignation reached the fever pitch; statements were made by the District Attorney of Onondaga County relative to the situation and he caused the Grand Jury of Onondaga County, then sitting, to conduct a thorough investigation. As a result of this investigation Frank Armani was No Billed by the Grand Jury but Indictment No. 75-55 was returned as against Francis R. Belge, Esq., accusing him of having violated § 4200(l) of the Public Health Law, which, in essence, requires that a decent burial be accorded the dead, and § 4143 of the Public Health Law, which, in essence, requires anyone knowing of the death of a person without medical attendance, [sic] to report the same to the proper authorities. Defense counsel moves for a dismissal of the Indictment on the grounds that a confidential, privileged communication existed between him and Mr. Garrow, which should excuse the attorney from making full disclosure to the authorities.

The National Association of Criminal Defense Lawyers, as Amicus Curiae, citing *Times Publishing Co. v. Williams*, 222 So. 2d 470, 475 (Fla. App. 1970) succinctly state the issue in the following language:

If this indictment stands,

"The attorney-client privilege will be effectively destroyed. No defendant will be able to freely discuss the facts of his case with his attorney. No attorney will be able to listen to those facts without being faced with the Hobson's choice of violating the law or violating his professional code of Ethics."

. . . .

In the most recent issue of the New York State Bar Journal (June 1975) there is an article by Jack B. Weinstein, entitled "Educating Ethical Lawyers." In a sub-caption to this article is the following language which is pertinent:

"The most difficult ethical dilemmas result from the frequent conflicts between the obligation to one's client and those to the legal system and to society. It is in this area that legal education has its greatest responsibility, and can have its greatest effects."

. . . .

Our system of criminal justice is an adversary system and the interests of the state are not absolute, or even paramount. . . .

A trial is in part a search for truth, but it is only partly a search for truth.

. . . .

The effectiveness of counsel is only as great as the confidentiality of its client-attorney relationship. If the lawyer cannot get all the facts about the case, he can only give his client half of a defense. This, [sic] of necessity involves the client telling his attorney everything remotely connected with the crime.

Apparently, in the instant case, after analyzing all the evidence, and after hearing of the bizarre episodes in the life of their client, they decided that the only possibility of salvation was a defense of insanity. For the client to disclose not only everything about this particular crime but also everything about other crimes which might have a bearing upon his defense, requires the strictest confidence in, and on the part of, the attorney.

When the facts of the other homicides became public, as a result of the defendant's testimony to substantiate his claim of insanity, "Members of the public were shocked at the apparent callousness of these lawyers, whose conduct was seen as typifying the unhealthy lack of concern of most lawyers with the public interest and with simple decency." A hue and cry went up from the press and other news media suggesting that the attorneys should be found guilty of such crimes as obstruction of justice or becoming an accomplice after the fact. From a layman's standpoint, this certainly was a logical conclusion. However, the constitution of the United States of America attempts to preserve the dignity of the individual and to do that guarantees him the services of an attorney who will bring to the bar and to the bench every conceivable protection from the inroads of the state against such rights as are vested in the constitution for one accused of crime. Among those substantial constitutional rights is that a defendant does not have to incriminate himself. His attorneys were bound to uphold that concept and maintain what has been called a sacred trust of confidentiality.

. . . In this type situation the Court must balance the rights of the individual against the rights of society as a whole. There is no question that Attorney Belge's failure to bring to the attention of the authorities the whereabouts of Alicia Hauck when he first verified it, prevented bringing

Garrow to the immediate bar of justice for this particular murder. This was in a sense, obstruction of justice. This duty, I am sure, loomed large in the mind of Attorney Belge. However, against this was the Fifth Amendment right of his client, Garrow, not to incriminate himself. . . .

It is the decision of this Court that Francis R. Belge conducted himself as an officer of the Court with all the zeal at his command to protect the constitutional rights of his client. Both on the grounds of a privileged communication and in the interests of justice the Indictment is dismissed.

PEOPLE v. BELGE
376 N.Y.S.2d 771, 50 A.D.2d 1038 (1975)

. . . We believe that an attorney must protect his client's interests, but also must observe basic human standards of decency, having due regard to the need that the legal system accord justice to the interests of society and its individual members.

We write to emphasize our serious concern regarding the consequences which emanate from a claim of an absolute attorney-client privilege. Because the only question presented, briefed and argued on this appeal was a legal one with respect to the sufficiency of the indictments, we limit our determination to that issue and do not reach the ethical questions underlying this case. *Order Affirmed.*

TOM GOLDSTEIN, BAR UPHOLDS LAWYER WHO WITHHELD KNOWLEDGE OF CLIENT'S PRIOR CRIMES
The New York Times (March 2, 1978)[2]

More than four years ago, a Syracuse mechanic charged with a homicide told his lawyer that he had killed two other people as well. The lawyer discovered the bodies and photographed them. He later destroyed the photographs. For six months, he did not disclose the whereabouts of the bodies to the police, who were seeking clues in the two unsolved murders or to the father of one of the victims who had come to him seeking help in finding his missing daughter.

Then, in plea-bargaining negotiations with a prosecutor, the lawyer suggested that, in return for lenient treatment of his client, he was in a position to provide information about two unsolved murders.

Did this lawyer uphold the highest tradition of his profession, or should he be punished for acting unethically?

In an opinion released last week, the committee on professional ethics of the New York State Bar Association found that, because of the lawyer-client privilege, the lawyer, Francis R. Belge of Syracuse, had behaved properly.

"The relationship between lawyer and client is in many respects like that between priest and penitent," the committee said. "Both lawyer and priest are bound by the bond of silence." . . .

In only one aspect did the committee express misgivings about Mr. Belge's behavior. Before taking photographs, he had moved parts of one of the bodies, which had been dismembered, to bring it within range of his camera.

---

[2] Copyright © 1978 by The New York Times Company. Reprinted by permission.

"Such conduct should be avoided to prevent even the appearance that there might have been an intent to tamper with or suppress evidence," the committee said.

The committee had completed its report late in 1974, but it said it did not release it until now because it wanted all other legal proceedings against Mr. Belge to be completed.

Mr. Belge, with another court-appointed lawyer, Frank Armani, represented Robert Garrow. . . . Mr. Garrow was convicted and is now serving a sentence of life in prison. After the trial, Mr. Belge was indicted and charged with violating the public health law by failing to provide a decent burial to the dead and by failing to report the death of a person. The charges were ultimately dismissed.

. . . .

"Proper representation of a client calls for full disclosure by the client to his lawyer of all possibly relevant facts, even though such facts may be the client's commission of prior crimes," the committee said.

"To encourage full disclosure, the client must be assured of confidentiality," the committee continued. "Frequently, clients have a disposition to withhold information from lawyers. If the client suggests that his confidences will not be adequately protected or in some way be used against him, he will be far more likely to withhold information which he believes may be to his detriment or which he does not want generally known."

"The client who withholds information from his lawyer runs a substantial risk of not being accorded his full legal rights. At the same time, the lawyer from whom such information is withheld may well be required to assert, in complete good faith and with no violation" of the lawyers' code of ethics, "totally meritless" or frivolous claims or defenses to which his client has no legal right.

"Thus, the interests served by the strict rule of confidentiality are far broader than merely those of the client, but include the interests of the public generally and of effective judicial administration."

NOTES

The New York State Bar Association concludes that "a strict rule of confidentiality" best serves the client's interests as well as the interests of the public and the judicial system. Do you agree? It is noteworthy that at least one study has shown that even a rule of confidentiality won't assure truthful disclosure by a client. It is common knowledge among public defenders that clients withhold from them more information than from paid attorneys because they see the public defenders as part of the system rather than as advocates. As few as a third of criminal clients are aware of confidentiality rules.

If you had never been to law school, what would you do if someone gave you a gun that had been used in a crime? Or told you the location of a body? How would you have acted when confronted with the dilemma faced by Messrs. Belge and Armani?

2. Future and "Continuing" Crimes and the ABA Model Rules. Two cases decided within six weeks of each other in the late 1990s brought the buried bodies case back to mind. In one, another case from Onondaga County, NY, the trial judge cited *Belge* in holding that a lawyer could not be compelled to testify before a grand jury about the whereabouts of a client who had disappeared with her child in violation of a custody order. The court concluded that even if a crime had been committed it could not be deemed a "continuing" one, and upheld the attorney-client privilege.[3]

The Texas Court of Criminal Appeals came to a very different result under facts not that dissimilar from the Garrow case.[4] Babysitter Cathy Lynn Henderson admitted to her lawyer, Nona Byington, that she had kidnapped and killed a three-month-old baby boy. Henderson eventually drew two maps indicating the boy's location, and gave them to her lawyer. The local grand jury subpoenaed the maps, and the trial court, ruling that kidnapping was a continuing crime, compelled Byington to produce them. Texas law enforcement officers used the maps to locate the body of the boy. Byington's motion to suppress the maps and the evidence gained from them — the baby's body and evidence of a fatal blow to his head — was denied. Henderson's death sentence was upheld by the appeals court, which noted that "the attorney-client privilege was legitimately required to yield to the strong public policy interest of protecting a child from death or serious bodily injury." Yet there was no real issue about the child still being alive; Henderson had admitted to police that the boy had died, but claimed it was the result of an accidental fall.

As we mentioned in our Introduction, the Kutak Commission, charged with drafting the ABA Model Rules eventually approved in 1983, had proposed broad exceptions to the rule of confidentiality when a lawyer learns of the client's intent to commit a crime. The ABA House of Delegates did not accept this approach, however, and by the time the rules were passed, both MR 1.6, and MR 1.13, relating to corporations, had become even more protective of attorney-client confidentiality than under the old Code. Not until the Ethics 2000 Commission rules were approved in 2002 and 2003 did the ABA swing back towards Kutak's intent of broader exceptions to confidentiality. In mid-2006, states were still in the process of deciding whether to adopt these broader changes — and if so, which — with about half the states having decided and, not surprisingly, coming to different conclusions.

3. *In re Ryder.* Is there a difference between active concealment of evidence versus simply not disclosing information? Read *In re Ryder,* which follows. How does Ryder's conduct differ from that of Belge? As you read this decision, 40 years old but still oft-cited, consider how it might guide Earl in deciding what to do with his clients' evidence.

---

[3] *In re Grand Jury Investigation*, 175 Misc. 2d 398, 669 N.Y.S.2d 179 (1998).

[4] *Henderson v. State*, 962 S.W.2d 544 (Tex. Crim. App. 1997).

IN RE RYDER
263 F. Supp. 360 (E.D. Va. 1967),
aff'd, 381 F.2d 713 (4th Cir. 1967) (per curiam)

This proceeding was instituted to determine whether Richard R. Ryder should be removed from the roll of attorneys qualified to practice before this court. Ryder was admitted to this bar in 1953. He formerly served five years as an Assistant United States Attorney. He has an active trial practice, including both civil and criminal cases.

In proceedings of this kind the charges must be sustained by clear and convincing proof, the misconduct must be fraudulent, intentional, and the result of improper motives. We conclude that these strict requirements have been satisfied. Ryder took possession of stolen money and a sawed-off shotgun, knowing that the money had been stolen and that the gun had been used in an armed robbery. He intended to retain this property pending his client's trial unless the government discovered it. He intended by his possession to destroy the chain of evidence that linked the contraband to his client and to prevent its use to establish his client's guilt.

On August 24, 1966 a man armed with a sawed-off shotgun robbed the Varina Branch of the Bank of Virginia of $7,583. Included in the currency taken were $10 bills known as "bait money," the serial numbers of which had been recorded.

On August 24, 1966 Charles Richard Cook rented safety deposit box 14 at a branch of the Richmond National Bank. Later in the day Cook was interviewed at his home by agents of the Federal Bureau of Investigation, who obtained $348 from him. Cook telephoned Ryder, who had represented him in civil litigation. Ryder came to the house and advised the agents that he represented Cook. He said that if Cook were not to be placed under arrest, he intended to take him to his office for an interview. The agents left. Cook insisted to Ryder that he had not robbed the bank. He told Ryder that he had won the money, which the agents had taken from him, in a crap game. At this time Ryder believed Cook.

Later that afternoon Ryder telephoned one of the agents and asked whether any of the bills obtained from Cook had been identified as part of the money taken in the bank robbery. The agent told him that some bills had been identified. The next morning, Saturday, August 27, 1966, Ryder conferred with Cook again. . . .

That afternoon Ryder telephoned a former officer of the Richmond Bar Association to discuss his course of action. He had known this attorney for many years and respected his judgment. The lawyer was at home and had no library available to him when Ryder telephoned. In their casual conversation Ryder told what he knew about the case, omitting names. He explained that he thought he would take the money from Cook's safety deposit box and place it in a box in his own name. This, he believed, would prevent Cook from attempting to dispose of the money. The lawyers thought that eventually F.B.I. agents would locate the money and that since it was in Ryder's possession, he could claim a privilege and thus effectively exclude it from evidence. This would prevent the government from linking Ryder's client with the bait money and would also destroy any presumption of guilt that might exist arising out of the client's exclusive possession of the evidence.

. . . .

Ryder took the power of attorney which Cook had signed to the Richmond National Bank. He rented box 13 in his name with his office address, presented the power of attorney, entered Cook's box, took both boxes into a booth, where he found a bag of money and a sawed-off shotgun in Cook's box. . . . He transferred the contents of Cook's box to his own and returned the boxes to the vault. He left the bank, and neither he nor Cook returned.

Ryder testified that he had some slight hesitation about the propriety of what he was doing.

. . . .

On September 7, 1966 Cook was indicted for robbing the Varina Branch of the Bank of Virginia. On September 12, 1966 F.B.I. agents procured search warrants for Cook's and Ryder's safety deposit boxes in the Richmond National Bank. They found Cook's box empty. In Ryder's box they discovered $5,920 of the $7,583 taken in the bank robbery and the sawed-off shotgun used in the robbery. . . .

On October 14, 1966 the three judges of this court removed Ryder as an attorney for Cook [and] suspended him from practice before the court until further order. . . .

At the outset, we reject the suggestion that Ryder did not know the money which he transferred from Cook's box to his was stolen. We also find that Ryder was not motivated solely by certain expectation the government would discover the contents of his lockbox. . . . He also recognized that discovery was not inevitable. His intention in this event, we find, was to assist Cook by keeping the stolen money and the shotgun concealed in his lockbox until after the trial. . . .

We reject the argument that Ryder's conduct was no more than the exercise of the attorney-client privilege. The fact that Cook had not been arrested or indicted at the time Ryder took possession of the gun and money is immaterial. Cook was Ryder's client and was entitled to the protection of the lawyer-client privilege.

Regardless of Cook's status, however, Ryder's conduct was not encompassed by the attorney-client privilege. . . .

The essentials of the privilege have been stated in 8 Wigmore, Evidence § 2292 (McNaughton Rev. 1961):

> "(1) Where legal advice of any kind is sought (2) from a professional legal adviser in his capacity as such, (3) the communications relating to that purpose, (4) made in confidence (5) by the client, (6) are at his instance permanently protected (7) from disclosure by himself or by the legal adviser, (8) except the protection be waived."

It was Ryder, not his client, who took the initiative in transferring the incriminating possession of the stolen money and the shotgun from Cook. Ryder's conduct went far beyond the receipt and retention of a confidential communication from his client.

. . . .

Ryder, an experienced criminal attorney, recognized and acted upon the fact that the gun and money were subject to seizure while in the possession of Cook.

[The court then quotes Justice Cardozo in *Clark v. United States*, 289 U.S. 1, 15, 53 S. Ct. 465, 469, (1993):]

". . . . The privilege takes flight if the relation is abused. A client who consults an attorney for advice that will serve him in the commission of a fraud will have no help from the law. He must let the truth be told."

Securities & Exchange Comm. v. Harrison, 80 F. Supp. 226, 230 (D.D.C. 1948), describes the privilege and its limitations:

"That privilege has long been recognized as a very proper and necessary one. . . . This privilege has, however, never been intended to be, and should not be, a cloak or shield for the perpetration of a crime or fraudulent wrong doing."

. . . .

In helping Cook to conceal the shotgun and stolen money, Ryder acted without the bounds of law. He allowed the office of attorney to be used in violation of law. The scheme which he devised was a deceptive, legalistic subterfuge — rightfully denounced by the [Virginia ethics rules] as chicane.

Ryder also . . . intended that his actions should remove from Cook exclusive possession of stolen money, and thus destroy an evidentiary presumption. His service in taking possession of the shotgun and money, with the intention of retaining them until after the trial, unless discovered by the government, merits the "stern and just condemnation" the canon prescribes.

. . . .

Ryder's action is not justified because he thought he was acting in the best interests of his client. To allow the individual lawyer's belief to determine the standards of professional conduct will in time reduce the ethics of the profession to the practices of the most unscrupulous.

. . . .

There is much to be said, however, for mitigation of the discipline to be imposed. Ryder intended to return the bank's money after his client was tried. He consulted reputable persons before and after he placed the property in his lockbox, although he did not precisely follow their advice. Were it not for these facts, we would deem proper his permanent exclusion from practice before this court. In view of the mitigating circumstances, he will be suspended from practice in this court for eighteen months.

4. The *Meredith* Case. *Ryder* involved a lawyer's active participation in the secretion of evidence. What is the difference between active participation and passive participation? Can a lawyer advise a client to destroy evidence as long as the lawyer does not participate in the act of destruction? Can counsel hint at such destruction in the context of explaining the law? What about physical alteration of evidence? Or removal from its original location?

The following case — again, older but oft-cited — addresses some of these issues.

PEOPLE v. MEREDITH
29 Cal. 3d 682, 175 Cal. Rptr. 612, 631 P.2d 46 (1981)

Defendants Frank Earl Scott and Michael Meredith appeal from convictions for the first degree murder and first degree robbery of David Wade. Meredith's conviction rests on eyewitness testimony that he shot and killed Wade. Scott's conviction, however, depends on the theory that Scott conspired with Meredith and a third defendant, Jacqueline Otis, to bring about the killing and robbery. To support the theory of conspiracy the prosecution sought to show the place where the victim's wallet was found, and, in the course of the case this piece of evidence became crucial. The admissibility of that evidence comprises the principal issue on this appeal.

At trial the prosecution called Steven Frick, who testified that he observed the victim's partially burnt wallet in a trash can behind Scott's residence. . . . Frick served as a defense investigator. Scott himself had told his former counsel that he had taken the victim's wallet, divided the money with Meredith, attempted to burn the wallet, and finally put it in the trash can. At counsel's request, Frick then retrieved the wallet from the trash can. Counsel examined the wallet and then turned it over to the police.

The defense acknowledges that the wallet itself was properly admitted into evidence. The prosecution in turn acknowledges that the attorney-client privilege protected the conversations between Scott, his former counsel, and counsel's investigator. . . . The issue before us, consequently, focuses upon a narrow point: Whether under the circumstances of this case Frick's observation of the location of the wallet, the product of a privileged communication, finds protection under the attorney-client privilege.

This issue, one of first impression in California, presents the court with competing policy considerations. On the one hand, to deny protection to observations arising from confidential communications might chill free and open communication between attorney and client and might also inhibit counsel's investigation of his client's case. On the other hand, we cannot extend the attorney-client privilege so far that it renders evidence immune from discovery and admission merely because the defense seizes it first.

Balancing these considerations, we conclude that an observation by defense counsel or his investigator, which is the product of a privileged communication, may not be admitted unless the defense by altering or removing physical evidence has precluded the prosecution from making that same observation. In the present case the defense investigator, by removing the wallet, frustrated any possibility that the police might later discover it in the trash can. The conduct of the defense thus precluded the prosecution from ascertaining the crucial fact of the location of the wallet. Under these circumstances, the prosecution was entitled to present evidence to show the location of the wallet in the trash can.

. . . .

We now recount the evidence relating to Wade's wallet, basing our account primarily on the testimony of James Schenk, Scott's first appointed attorney. . . . Scott told Schenk . . . that he picked up the wallet, put it in the paper bag, . . . and then tried to burn the wallet in his kitchen sink. He took the partially burned wallet, Scott told Schenk, placed it in a plastic bag, and threw it in a burn barrel behind his house.

Schenk, without further consulting Scott, retained Investigator Stephen Frick and sent Frick to find the wallet. Frick found it in the location described by Scott and brought it to Schenk. After examining the wallet and determining that it contained credit cards with Wade's name, Schenk turned the wallet and its contents over to Detective Payne, investigating officer in the case. Schenk told Payne only that, to the best of his knowledge, the wallet had belonged to Wade.

The prosecution subpoenaed Attorney Schenk and Investigator Frick to testify at the preliminary hearing. When questioned at that hearing, Schenk said that he received the wallet from Frick but refused to answer further questions on the ground that he learned about the wallet through a privileged communication. Eventually, however, the magistrate threatened Schenk with contempt if he did not respond "yes" or "no" when asked whether his contact with his client led to disclosure of the wallet's location. Schenk then replied "yes," and revealed on further questioning that this contact was the sole source of his information as to the wallet's location.

At the preliminary hearing[,] . . . [o]ver objections by counsel, Frick testified that he found the wallet in a garbage can behind Scott's residence.

. . . .

The fundamental purpose of the attorney-client privilege is, of course, to encourage full and open communication between client and attorney. . . .

Judicial decisions have recognized that the implementation of these important policies may require that the privilege extend not only to the initial communication between client and attorney but also to any information which the attorney or his investigator may subsequently acquire as a direct result of that communication. In a venerable decision involving facts analogous to those in the instant case, the Supreme Court of West Virginia held that the trial court erred in admitting an attorney's testimony as to the location of a pistol which he had discovered as the result of a privileged communication from his client. That the attorney had observed the pistol, the court pointed out, did not nullify the privilege: "All that the said attorney knew about this pistol, or where it was to be found, he knew only from the communications which had been made to him by his client confidentially and professionally, as counsel in this case. And it ought therefore, to have been entirely excluded from the jury. It may be, that in this particular case this evidence tended to the promotion of right and justice, but as was well said in *Pearce v. Pearce,* 11 Jar. 52, in page 55, and 2 De Gex & Smale 25-27: 'Truth like all other good things may be loved unwisely, may be pursued too keenly, may cost too much.'" (*State of West Virginia v. Douglass* (1882) 20 W.Va. 770, 783.)

. . . [T]he attorney-client privilege is not strictly limited to communications, but extends to protect observations made as a consequence of protected communications. We turn therefore to the question whether that privilege encompasses a case in which the defense, by removing or altering evidence, interferes with the prosecution's opportunity to discover that evidence.

. . . .

When defense counsel alters or removes physical evidence, he necessarily deprives the prosecution of the opportunity to observe that evidence in its original condition or location. As the Attorney General points out, to bar admission of testimony concerning the original condition and location of the evidence in such a case permits the defense in effect to "destroy" critical information; it is as if, he explains, the wallet in this case bore a tag bearing the words "located in the trash can by Scott's residence," and the defense, by taking the wallet, destroyed this tag. To extend the attorney-client privilege to a case in which the defense removed evidence might encourage defense counsel to race the police to seize critical evidence. (See *In re Ryder* (E.D.Va. 1967) 263 F. Supp. 360, 369. . . .)

We therefore conclude that whenever defense counsel removes or alters evidence, the statutory privilege does not bar revelation of the original location or condition of the evidence in question. We thus view the defense decision to remove evidence as a tactical choice. If defense counsel leaves the evidence where he discovers it, his observations derived from privileged communications are insulated from revelation. If, however, counsel chooses to remove evidence to examine or test it, the original location and condition of that evidence loses the protection of the privilege. Applying this analysis to the present case, we hold that the trial court did not err in admitting the investigator's testimony concerning the location of the wallet.

NOTES

Consider these questions about these two leading cases. If attorney Ryder's conduct was so egregious, why was he able to escape with only an 18-month suspension? If the state agreed in *Meredith* that defendant Scott's conversations with his former counsel and investigator were protected, then why were both required to testify at Scott's preliminary hearing? And why did the Supreme Court refer to this testimony? Since the preliminary hearing testimony was used to tie the wallet to Scott, why did the defense acknowledge that the wallet was admissible evidence? Finally, how much is *Meredith* about confidentiality and how much about the evidentiary, or testimonial, rule of attorney-client privilege?

5. The Criminal Defense Lawyer's View. Read the following excerpt from an article expressing a criminal defense counsel's view of the ethics of discovery in criminal cases. The author, applying *Ryder, Meredith,* and other authorities, makes a distinction between fruits or instrumentalities, on the one hand, and other types of evidence obtained through defense investigations. Do you agree with the author's interpretation?

MILTON J. SILVERMAN, FUNDAMENTALS OF CRIME SCENE INVESTIGATION: WHAT CAN A LAWYER DO?

California Attorneys for Criminal Justice Forum
(October/November/December 1983)[5]

Prosecutorial Discovery

When the district attorney figured I must have found something, he filed a motion to give him anything and everything that was removed from the scene by the defense team.

After spending a good five hours on my hands and knees looking at rugs and plywood and getting wet and cold and hungry and having to pay about $1,000 — what with the carpenter's bill and the criminalist and investigator and the graphics man — to hand it all over to the guys that are trying to convict my client of first degree murder, you would think they would at least offer to pay half the bill. . . .

But instead, they looked sore and huffed and puffed — as if the defense team were a bunch of criminals. They muttered about "withholding evidence" from "law enforcement." (The guys that left for sludge what we spent hours getting.) They murmured menacingly about search warrants and didn't seem to see the humor when I threatened to file a counter motion demanding that they put the wall back together in one piece so I could get the trajectory off of it. . . .

The prosecution needed the evidence, it said, to "reconstruct" what happened. It sure did. At various times, I heard that the rifle had jammed, that the defendant had been hiding behind the door, that there was a fight and even that the defendant had carefully *placed* the various cartridge cases around the room, presumably to throw the police off. (Why else would there be *three* cartridge cases on the far side of the room and only *two* holes on the floor?)

After arguing the issue in Superior Court, the judge told me to give them the floor, the waterbed and a few other things. I told the judge I wouldn't do it unless they promised to keep the guy with the ballpeen hammer away from it.

I took a writ to the Court of Appeal. It denied without opinion. Then, on that fateful day, I sadly handed over the fruits of our labor to the prosecution. They proudly brought it into the trial and displayed it with a bunch of coathangers running through it to show the "trajectory."

Something is very, very wrong here, something that threatens the heart of the advocacy system in America. . . .

Effective Assistance of Counsel

The defendant is entitled to effective assistance of counsel. Isn't that what *Powell v. Alabama* ((1932) 287 U.S. 45) said?

---

[5] Copyright © 1983. Reprinted by permission.

The California Supreme Court in 1979 in *People v. Pope* . . . said that ". . . a *substantial portion* of the obligation counsel owes is not directly concerned with the trial but involves *investigation* and advice at *pre-trial* and post-trial stages." (Emphasis added). . . . The *Pope* Court mentioned the minimum standards established by the American Bar Association for defense counsel. Things like counsel's "diligence and active *participation* in the *full* and *effective preparation* of his client's case" were mentioned. . . .

When the court tells me to do my job requires "active participation," I figure they said it that way so I won't get the idea I can sit in my chair at the office and wait for the police to tell me what the case is all about. When they say my job is to "carefully investigate" the facts, I get the idea I'm supposed to do something more than read the arrest reports while eating a cheeseburger and helping my daughter with her homework.

. . . .

Looking at Supreme Court decisions since *Pope,* it becomes clear *Pope* meant what it said. In *In re Hall* ((1981) 30 Cal. 3d 408), the Court granted *habeas* relief to a young man convicted of first degree murder. The Court found . . . the "most blatant" violation of the lawyer's obligation to be the turning over of information to the police for further investigation. "This practice," the Court said, "was fraught with the danger of violating the attorney client privilege. . . ." (Ibid at 408).

That's exactly what the Superior Court forced me to do when it ordered that I turn over the floor to the prosecution.

. . . .

There is a very narrow exception to this rule, and this relates — as I will show — to the duty of the defense lawyer to surrender contraband or *fruits* or *instrumentalities* of the crime.

In re Ryder (1967) 263 F. Supp 360, was a federal case; it was cited in the subsequent California case of *People v. Lee* (1970) 3 Cal. App. 3d 514.

In *Lee,* the defendant was charged with attempted murder. It appeared that the head injuries suffered by the victim might have been caused by someone kicking her in the head. Blood on a pair of the defendant's shoes was found to be of the same type as the victim's and the shoes appeared to have the same sole pattern as that of a bloody footprint found at the crime scene. The shoes, hidden by the defendant, were delivered to the Public Defender's Office by the defendant's wife and were turned over to a municipal judge when private counsel was appointed to represent the defendant. The district attorney subsequently obtained the shoes through a search warrant. They were introduced in evidence over defendant's objection.

The Court of Appeal held that no illegality was involved in the district attorney obtaining the defendant's shoes, and testimony from representatives of the Public Defender's Office in that connection was not protected under the attorney-client privilege.

. . . .

In each of these situations the "thing" or "things" that were in dispute were fruits or instrumentalities of the crime. In *Lee,* it was the shoes that were used to kick in the head of the victim. In *Ryder* the "loot" from the holdup.

. . . .

People v. Meredith

By far the most important case on the duty of the defense counsel to turn over evidence to the prosecution is *People v. Meredith*. Two points are critical in the *Meredith* case. First, the article involved is virtually the same as in *Ryder*, except that instead of being loot it is the container which carries the loot — a wallet. This is most properly characterized as a "fruit."

Second, the [California] Supreme Court stressed, at least six times, that the controlling question is whether the defense, by altering or removing the evidence, has *interfered with the prosecution's opportunity to discover the evidence.* . . .

Analyzing these cases together and harmonizing them, I think the following is and should be the law:

First, that the defense counsel has the obligation to surrender contraband, fruits or instrumentalities of the crime which he has taken into his possession (and by this I mean any member of his team has taken it into his possession). In the case involving the floor, none of the things seized were fruits, instrumentalities or contraband.

Let me explain the difference by using the *Lee* case as an example. That's the case where the victim was kicked in the head by a shoe. Let's say that instead of the shoe being the issue, it is a *shoe print.* Let's say that this crime occurs in an open field, and the police secure it, do their investigation and release the scene. When the defense does its investigation, the defense lawyer notes that there is a shoe print in the ground. He makes a cast of it and has the ground cut out so that the print can be preserved. Can the prosecution then demand the evidence? Will the defense lawyer be required to turn it over?

If the answer is yes, then the effective assistance of counsel protection of the constitution is meaningless. The defense counsel cannot be told on the one hand that his job is to zealously determine the *facts* in the case and acquire *evidence,* and on the other that the fruit of his labor must be turned over to the prosecution on demand. . . .

NOTES

Is Silverman accepting and distinguishing *Meredith*? If so, does his distinction — that is, between fruits and instrumentalities and "mere" evidence — make sense?

6. *Tarasoff,* its Progeny, and its Consequences. In 1976, the California Supreme Court decided the case of *Tarasoff v. Regents of the Univ. of California*, 17 Cal. 3d 425, 551 P.2d 334 (1976). *Tarasoff* was a wrongful death case filed by the family of a woman who was killed by a University of California psychiatric patient after the patient had made direct threats on the woman's life to his therapist. The court upheld the family's right to sue the university, established an exception to the patient-psychotherapist privilege, and created a legal duty to warn potential victims when a patient presents a serious danger of violence.

Tarasoff quickly caused an enormous stir in both legal and medical circles, and has since become standard fare in law school texts on both ethics and torts. Psychiatrists argued that it could mark the end of psychiatry as they knew it, since patients would no longer be willing to disclose their true feelings in therapy, similar reasoning to that used by the New York State Bar Association in refusing to discipline attorney Francis Belge. For their part, lawyers worried that the *Tarasoff* standard would be applied to them, thus eroding the attorney-client relationship.

But the *Tarasoff* case presented an issue of civil liability and evidentiary privilege, and did not directly address a therapist's ethical duties. Years later, the case has seemed to have little practical effect on the attorney-client relationship, while psychiatrists continue to practice without much visible change in the treatment of their patients.

Yet some psychiatrists — and some lawyers — now keep fewer records of their clients' confidences. One who still kept records was the psychiatrist in the highly publicized Menendez case in Los Angeles. That physician kept notes and tapes describing what both Eric and Lyle Menendez told him about killing their parents. The doctor also claimed that the brothers had threatened violence to others — including the doctor himself and his family. These threats became the focus of debate after the District Attorney got a search warrant to seize the psychiatrist's files and tapes in what was called a *"Tarasoff* raid." In a pre-trial proceeding, the California appellate court held that the evidence seized could be used at trial. *Menendez v. Superior Court*, 7 Cal. App. 4th 147, 279 Cal. Rptr. 521 (1991). The doctor's tapes and notes then became a principal focus in the explosive Menendez trial.

Tarasoff raises more questions than it answers. How much guidance does the case provide, since it is rooted in civil liability issues, not ethical ones? The concept of evidentiary privilege is considerably more narrow than that of a confidential communication. "Privilege" only protects an in-court revelation; confidentiality applies at all times and in all circumstances. What does that mean about how confidentiality (and the ability or duty to warn) and evidentiary privilege at trial should or could interact?

Should attorneys have a *Tarasoff* duty to warn? Why or why not? How, if at all, do attorneys' obligations differ from those of psychiatrists? Every jurisdiction has rules that provide exceptions where confidentiality may be waived, but interestingly, there was *no* disclosure exception at all under California law when *Tarasoff* was decided. Does this mean that in these unusual circumstances the ethics rules are irrelevant to the analysis of duty? Finally, how should ethics rules and tort principles interrelate on such issues?

7. Balancing the Duty to Warn: Pulling the Trigger vs. Jumping the Gun. At the least, most would argue that a lawyer should persuade the client not to act wrongly or violently. But is this always wise? What if that conversation spurs the client to violence? On the other hand, perhaps a bit of remonstration would persuade the lawyer that no real danger of violence exists. David McLaughlin, who filed the complaint excerpted below, would certainly argue this view. He made remarks to his lawyer which could have been construed as a threat to kill a judge who had ruled against him. The attorney elected to inform authorities, and McLaughlin found himself on trial. McLaughlin told the jury he was "just letting off steam," when he threatened to get his 9mm semiautomatic pistol and shoot the judge. The jury, several of whom acknowledged having made angry statements they later regretted, found McLaughlin not guilty. McLaughlin's next court case was his suit against his former lawyer for violating the attorney-client confidential relationship.

What would you have done if you were in this attorney's shoes? Is the lawyer "between a rock and a hard place" in deciding the right course of action? How do you determine when the threat is idle, and when a judge could end up dead? What standards should you apply? How sure must you be? Finally, must the propriety of the attorney's conduct in such a case always be judged in hindsight?

David McLaughlin
Plaintiff In Pro Per

SUPERIOR COURT OF THE STATE OF CALIFORNIA
IN AND FOR THE COUNTY OF MARIN
DAVID MCLAUGHLIN, Plaintiff,
vs. JAMES T. PROCTOR, and DOES 1-10, Defendants, No. 147546

COMPLAINT FOR MALPRACTICE AND BREACH OF ATTORNEY-CLIENT PRIVILEGE AND FALSE STATEMENT TO POLICE OFFICER

Plaintiff alleges:

. . . .

During or about July 1984, plaintiff retained and employed defendant JAMES PROCTOR to represent plaintiff as plaintiff's attorney at law in his litigation of McLAUGHLIN vs. WALDO POINT HARBOR. . . .

By such attorney client relationship between plaintiff and defendant JAMES T. PROCTOR, all communications between attorney and client made in the course of the relationship were to have been confidential and privileged.

Defendant, at all times herein, was authorized and had a duty to claim and invoke the attorney client privilege on behalf of plaintiff, as set forth in Evidence Code § 955, if at any time any confidential communication was sought to be disclosed by another party.

On or about September 11th, 1989 defendant failed to claim the attorney client privilege on behalf of plaintiff when questioned by Marin County deputy sheriff J. CARROL concerning events of that date.

Instead, defendant volunteered confidential information as to plaintiff's psychiatric history, mental state, and medication which had been prescribed to plaintiff and revealed to defendant in the course of the attorney client relationship.

Defendant also revealed confidential statements made by plaintiff concerning Marin County Judge [X] and also further statements concerning Judge

[Y] which defendant claimed that plaintiff made in 1982. Defendant told deputy CARROL that plaintiff had threatened both Judge [X] and Judge [Y].

Defendant was at that time under no Court order to disclose the above stated confidential information to deputy CARROL. No prima facie showing that a crime was about to be committed had been established in a Court of law. Furthermore, defendant had made no attempt to call plaintiff at home on that date to determine if a crime was about to be committed.

At a later date, January 1990, a trial of the alleged threat to Judge [X] determined in fact that no crime was committed by plaintiff.

As a proximate result of defendant's failure to claim the attorney client privilege on behalf of plaintiff on that date, the information provided to deputy CARROL was used to issue a warrant for plaintiff's arrest with bail set at $500,000.

Two newspapers reported the arrest of plaintiff and the details of his psychiatric history, medication and mental state in prominent fashion. Plaintiff was incarcerated for a period of 17 (seventeen) days because such high amount of bail was beyond his means.

Had defendant not provided such details of plaintiff's mental state, medication, and psychiatric history, bail would not have been set so high and plaintiff would have been released earlier.

In the alternative, had defendant not revealed the confidential statement concerning Judge [X], no arrest warrant would have issued, and plaintiff would not have been injured.

As a result, plaintiff has suffered humiliation and damage to his reputation, great pain of mind, mental anguish, distress to his well being, and loss of good will in the community, all in the sum of $200,000.

. . . .

WHEREFORE, plaintiff prays judgment against defendants, and each of them, as follows:

1. For damages in the sum of $600,000.

2. For punitive damages in the amount of $400,000.

3. For costs of the suit herein incurred.

4. For such other relief as the court may deem proper.

David McLaughlin
Plaintiff In Pro Per

NOTES

Mr. McLaughlin, whatever his background and history may have been, makes some interesting points. Did his attorney jump the gun by failing to do enough to make sure the situation was as dangerous as he thought? Did this lawyer unnecessarily violate his client's confidence? Should he have at least discussed the matter with his client first?

8. A Second Look at "Clients for Purposes of Confidentiality." Can such clients exist? In a word, yes. After all, if it were otherwise, how could a prospective client ever interview a lawyer, disclose facts about the case, and dare not accept that lawyer as counsel? A confidential relationship is formed even when the lawyer does not want to take a case but just listens, such as when Nevada attorney Samuel Bull was approached by a criminal defendant in a jail where he had gone to speak to his own client.[6] A communication to a secretary has also been held to be confidential, even if the prospective client has yet to see the lawyer.[7] Whether a lawyer considers the individual imparting the confidences a client with a very limited scope of representation or a non-client who is a "client for purposes of confidentiality only" may, practically speaking, be of little moment. The analysis is similar to the cases in Problem 3 concerning the inception of the attorney-client relationship.[8] Thus, according to one California court, when the lawyer affirmatively states in advance that he is *not* willing to represent the prospective client, the client can no longer have an expectation of confidentiality, and the subsequent statements are neither confidential nor privileged.[9]

Interestingly, while the ethical requirements of confidentiality may be broader than the privilege in most instances, it can occasionally work the other way around. In *Purcell v. District Attorney for Suffolk District*, 424 Mass. 109, 676 N.E.2d 436 (1997), attorney Purcell was consulted by a client named Tyree about an eviction. After hearing Tyree threaten to burn down his building and deciding the threat was serious, Purcell informed the Boston police. When police went to Tyree's apartment, they found incendiary devices and other evidence of a planned arson. Tyree was charged with attempted arson. His first trial ended in a hung jury. Purcell had been subpoenaed to testify, but successfully quashed his subpoena. At the retrial, however, the judge ordered Purcell to testify. Purcell then filed his own appellate action to quash.

The Massachusetts Supreme Court agreed with Purcell. They noted that even though Purcell was justified in breaking his duty of *confidentiality before* the arson because of the potential danger to others, that did not break the attorney-client *privilege after* the fact. The court acknowledged the existence of a "crime fraud exception" to the privilege — that a client who uses an attorney's representation to further a crime or fraud loses the right to claim the privilege. But here, the lawyer was consulted about an eviction case, and none of Purcell's advice related to Tyree's planned crime.[10]

---

[6] *Todd v. State of Nevada*, 931 P.2d 721 (Nev. 1997), reversing and remanding Todd's sentencing. Incredibly, Bull turned over to the judge Todd's handwritten notes explaining his claim for police brutality, together with Bull's own assessment that Todd should be sentenced heavily. One wonders whether Bull received any discipline.

[7] *Commonwealth v. Mrozek*, 657 A.2d 997 (Pa. Super. 1995). When Mrozek called, the lawyer was meeting with other clients, and despite Mrozek's entreaties, the secretary was unable to interrupt the lawyer until Mrozek said "Honey, I don't think you understand. I've just committed a homicide." That message finally got the lawyer on the phone but was suppressed on appeal as confidential.

[8] In fact, *Todd* cites both the *DeVaux* and *Kurtenbach* cases we discussed in Problem 3.

[9] *People v. Gionis*, 9 Cal. 4th 1196, 40 Cal. Rptr. 2d 456 (1995).

[10] If the concern is the harm that may befall the public in anticipation of a dangerous event, this decision makes sense. It is interesting and ironic that California law was, counterintuitively, exactly the reverse until a *confidentiality* exception was approved in 2003 harmonizing it with a pre-existing *privilege* exception. *See* Calif. Evid. Code § 956.5, and Bus. & Prof. Code § 6068(e) as amended.

9. Confidentiality and Moral Imperative. What should a lawyer do with knowledge that a client has AIDS? Can the lawyer disclose that fact on the basis of danger to others? Read the following digest of an opinion by the Delaware Bar Association Professional Ethics Committee. Do you agree with this opinion? Are you comfortable that the Delaware Bar draws a distinction between a lawyer's ethical requirements and a "moral code"? How far should the ethical obligation to keep confidences extend in the face of what many would consider a moral imperative? Should there be a "moral compulsion" exception in the ethics rules?

DELAWARE BAR ASSOCIATION PROFESSIONAL ETHICS COMMITTEE, OPINION 1988-2
as digested in ABA/BNA's Lawyers' Manual on Professional Conduct, Vol. 5, No. 12 (1989), Ethics Opinions p. 901:2203[11]

The lawyer's client has revealed that he has acquired immune deficiency syndrome. The woman with whom the client has lived for the last six months is a client of the lawyer's partner. This medical information was revealed to the lawyer in the course of representing the client, and the client has asked the lawyer not to reveal this to anyone. The lawyer is uncertain if the client has told the woman, but inquires whether he may properly disclose this fact to her if the client has not and does not choose to reveal it himself.

Rule 1.6 provides, in pertinent part, that a lawyer may not reveal information learned during the course of a representation unless the client has consented or unless it is necessary "to prevent the client from committing a criminal act that the lawyer believes is likely to result in imminent death or substantial bodily harm."

There is no Delaware statute that clearly makes criminal the transmission of AIDS to an unknown victim. Moreover, here it is not at all certain that the client will actually transmit AIDS to the woman with whom he lives, and therefore, the likelihood of imminent death or substantial bodily harm is less than in the situation where the client informs his lawyer that he intends to commit murder. Furthermore, under existing Delaware laws, the lawyer is not faced with a certain risk of civil or criminal liability if he maintains silence. Delaware law presently imposes no duty to warn a potential victim that AIDS may be contracted.

According to the letter of the ethics rules, the lawyer must maintain silence if his client requires it. But the lawyer may appropriately confront his client and under any moral code should do so. He should also point out the potential dangers in not disclosing. For example, it is not a crime, under current law, to fail to make disclosure, but a test case could be made. A prosecutor might argue that the client's conduct constitutes reckless endangering under 11 Del.C. 603 or 604. Also the lawyer should point out that there may be possible civil liability to the woman for failure to warn although existing law imposes no such obligation.

If, following confrontation with the client, the client still refuses to disclose his condition to the woman, then the lawyer's duty is non-disclosure. If the

---

[11] Copyright © 1990 by The American Bar Association/The Bureau of National Affairs, Inc. Reprinted by permission.

lawyer's moral code is such that he cannot abide by this duty, he may be pressed to the point of civil disobedience because obeying the letter of the law may require him to sacrifice more of his principles than he can bear. If so, the lawyer should inform his client of the decision to disclose and then be prepared to accept discipline if he cannot convince the disciplinary authorities to read a "moral compulsion" exception to the letter of Rule 1.6.

10. A Terrorist Exception to Confidentiality? In the aftermath of September 11, 2001, the United States government implemented the USA PATRIOT Act, and by the end of October 2001 the federal Bureau of Prisons (BOP) had adopted a new rule permitting the monitoring of otherwise confidential attorney-client communications.

The new rule authorized the Attorney General to order the BOP to monitor these communications when law enforcement had reasonable suspicion to believe that a prisoner was using attorney-client communications to facilitate acts of terrorism. Monitoring did not require judicial approval, and the Attorney General was given authority to review claims of privilege. The rule required the AG to set up a separate team to investigate and monitor attorney-client communications. Although the team was to act separately from the office of the Attorney General and generally disclose material to law enforcement only by court order, communications could be disclosed without court approval if the team concluded that acts of violence were imminent.[12]

The government justified these measures on grounds of national security, noting that the AG would only monitor where "inmates who have been involved in terrorist activities will pass messages through their attorneys for the purpose of continuing terrorist activities."[13] Others saw the rule as direct interference with the attorney-client confidential relationship, claiming that the government's reliance on the crime fraud exception to the attorney-client *privilege* should not justify a preemptive interference with lawyer-client *confidentiality*.

The National Association of Criminal Defense Counsel (NACDL) took a strong position against the rule, claiming that it prevented *any* conversations between lawyers and their prisoner clients, at least where the BOP had given the required written notification of monitoring. Some NACDL leaders argued that lawyers should refuse even to represent such prisoners. (The NACDL also argued that no lawyer should represent detainees in Guantanamo and thereby tacitly sanction the lack of due process afforded those detainees.)

Other government agencies also were accused of "spying" on lawyers and their terrorism-related clients. In New York City, Legal Aid lawyers appointed to represent detainees came up with a novel Fourth Amendment argument to protect *the lawyers' rights* to an attorney-client privilege, and seemed to gain some acceptance from the court.

---

[12] It was largely this rule and attendant BOP regulations that resulted in the criminal prosecution of attorney Lynne Stewart, referred to in Problem 2.

[13] *Prevention of Acts of Violence and Terrorism*, 66 Fed. Reg. at 55,064 (Oct. 31, 2001), as quoted in Avidan Y. Cover, *A Rule Unfit for All Seasons: Monitoring Attorney-Client Communications Violates Privilege and the Sixth Amendment*, 87 CORNELL L. REV. 1233, 1236 (2002).

JOHN CAHER, LAWYERS' SUIT PROCEEDS OVER TAPING OF CONVERSATIONS WITH CLIENTS
New York Law Journal (June 26, 2006) [14]

Legal Aid lawyers claiming the government violated their rights by secretly recording attorney-client communications with 9/11 detainees won a major battle last week when a federal judge permitted the bulk of the action to proceed. The case is unusual in that it centers on the rights and privileges of lawyers operating behind the attorney-client shield, rather than the rights of the clients.

Eastern District of New York Judge Nina Gershon rejected nearly all of the arguments for dismissal, including qualified immunity, and said the attorneys raised a viable complaint under both the Wiretap Act and the Fourth Amendment. She dismissed a Fifth Amendment claim alleging violations of substantive due process rights, but only because that claim arose from the same alleged injuries and seeks the same remedy as the Fourth Amendment claim.

"The oldest privilege for confidential communications recognized by law, the attorney-client privilege, is intended to encourage full and frank communications between attorneys and their clients and thereby promote broader public interests in the observations of laws and the administration of justice," Judge Gershon wrote in Lonegan v. Hasty, 04-CV-2743. "That an individual is held in connection with an investigation of terrorist acts does not render that individual — or his or her attorney — ineligible for the protections of the Fourth Amendment."

Gershon's 36-page opinion and order is rooted in the terrorist attacks of Sept. 11, 2001, and the nation's response. In the aftermath, 84 individuals were arrested on immigration charges and detained at the Metropolitan Detention Center [MDC] in Brooklyn. None was ever charged with terrorist activity and most were simply deported.

Between Oct. 23, 2001, and Dec. 31, 2001, lawyers with the Legal Aid Society of New York conducted about 30 interviews with detainees. Officers at the MDC assured the lawyers that the meetings were not being taped. However, an investigation connected to another case led to the discovery of 308 videotapes proving that authorities had recorded meetings between attorneys and their clients.

A probe by the Justice Department's Office of the Inspector General found that meetings between attorneys and their clients were routinely recorded, despite the assurances the plaintiffs claim they were given by officials at the MDC.

. . . .

Gershon termed "misplaced" the defendant's reliance on cases holding that a convicted prisoner does not have a reasonable expectation of privacy within a prison cell. She observed that the plaintiffs in this case are defense attorneys, not convicted criminals, and that the interviews took place in an area designated for attorney-client communications, not in a cell.

---

[14] Copyright © 2006 by the New York Law Journal. Reprinted with permission.

. . . .

Gershon's decision came just days after attorneys for defense lawyer Lynne Stewart filed a memo seeking information on whether Stewart was subject to the National Security Agency eavesdropping program.

Stewart was convicted last year for helping her client, Sheik Omar Abdel Rahman, communicate with a terror organization. Her attorney, Joshua Dratel, this week filed papers raising concerns that his trial strategy and other privileged communication were essentially leaked to the prosecution through the government's wiretapping program. Meanwhile, Stewart awaits sentencing. . . .

NOTES

There are many issues related to the PATRIOT Act and other anti-terrorism measures, but here, we focus on the following questions: Should national security ever trump the attorney-client confidential relationship? Is the distinction between the privilege and confidentiality still viable when national security is at stake? Or should it remain inappropriate for the AG — the prosecuting arm of the government — to make the decision about when that security is at issue? Would advance court approval help protect attorney-client confidentiality, or would requiring that protection simply be too slow in light of the threat of terrorism?

11. Other Possible Exceptions to Confidentiality. The author of the following law review excerpt poses hypothetical exceptions to a strict rule of confidentiality. As the author states, the article raises more questions than it answers. As you read these hypotheticals, consider the possible consequences of each.

FRED C. ZACHARIAS, RETHINKING CONFIDENTIALITY
74 Iowa Law Review 351 (1989)[15]

[I]n extreme situations calling for intervention, strict confidentiality rules often reduce lawyers' ability and desire to act.

Allowing lawyers some leeway to reveal client information would not destroy our legal order. Other well-developed legal systems circumscribe confidentiality more narrowly than we. Their continued viability suggests that our system, too, would survive limited exceptions.

At root, whether to adopt exceptions is a balance of countervailing costs and benefits. But the balance inevitably depends on facts. Only by determining how well strict confidentiality serves its intended purposes, and how much exceptions would undermine those goals, can code drafters put the normative question into proper perspective.

This Article's theoretical analysis and the data it presents are a first step toward providing that perspective. The Article unashamedly raises more questions than it answers. It is intended as a bridge to further study, and to show that empirical analysis of confidentiality rules is possible. . . .

---

[15] Copyright © 1989. Reprinted by permission.

Appendix — Hypotheticals

1. A client tells a lawyer the location of a "missing child" or kidnapping victim. The client is not implicated in the person's disappearance, but does not want the lawyer to disclose the information because the client "doesn't want to get involved." The client will not accept the lawyer's assurance that the lawyer could act without naming the client.[16]

2. An attorney obtains information from a client that would prove that another person falsely accused of a crime, is innocent. The attorney could reveal the information without implicating the client in the crime. The client refuses to disclose the information voluntarily.[17]

3. In a civil suit involving a serious automobile accident, the plaintiff is examined by defendant's doctor. The doctor discovers a life threatening aneurism. Although the aneurism was probably caused by the accident, plaintiff's own physician has not discovered it. The condition is curable, but if defendant's lawyer does not reveal the danger — against the client's wishes — plaintiff may die.[18]

4. The general counsel to a firm that produces a metal alloy used in the manufacture of airplanes learns of a company study that suggests that in some high-altitude flight patterns the alloy might weaken and cause a plane to explode. The alloy does, however, meet the minimum safety standards set by the government. The lawyer urges the Board of Directors to recall the alloy or at a minimum to inform users of its potential danger. The Board decides that the study is too inconclusive to warrant action in light of the dire financial consequences of disclosure to the company.[19]

5. From information given by and conversations with a client, an attorney becomes convinced that the client is mentally imbalanced, out of control, and will injure someone in the near future. The client has, however, not expressed any specific intention to commit a crime. [Footnote citing *Tarasoff* omitted.]

6. X negotiates directly with Y and agrees to buy Y's house. Y agrees to provide "owner financing," subject to the contingency that X supply certain information concerning X's ability to pay. The only role X's attorney is to play in the transaction is to write the final sale contract and preside over the

---

[16] [278] In Subin, *supra* note 26, at 1103-04, Professor Subin discusses the even more dramatic situation in which the kidnap victim may die if the lawyer does not act promptly.

Numerous interesting "disclosure" situations beyond this Article's scope arise when a lawyer represents a client who is or may become a criminal defendant. . . . At one time or another, most criminal lawyers must consider whether to tell the authorities about (1) the whereabouts of a client who has skipped bail, (2) the possibility that the client has committed perjury, see *Nix v. Whiteside,* 475 U.S. 157 (1986) and authorities cited therein, and (3) client admissions or information that might lead to the discovery of additional evidence or crimes.

[17] [279] Cases have arisen in which lawyers learn from a criminal client that he or she, rather than the accused, has committed a crime. The courts uniformly have held that these communications are privileged and confidential. . . .

[18] [280] *Spaulding v. Zimmerman,* 263 Minn. 346, 116 N.W.2d 704 (1962), discussed in G. Hazard, Jr. & W. Hodes, *supra* note 105, at 114; Luban, *The Adversary System Excuse* in D. Luban, *supra* note 25, at 83, 115.

[19] [281] The position of the CPR on various manifestations of this hypothetical is discussed in Ferren, *The Corporate Lawyer's Obligation to the Public Interest,* 33 Bus. Law. 1253 (1978).

closing. Right before the closing, X's attorney learns from X's accountant that the financing information X supplied to Y contained inaccurate information. If any fraud was committed, it occurred before the attorney became involved.[20]

7. A client fortuitously receives an undeserved payment from the government (e.g., a duplicate welfare check or tax refund) and deposits it in a savings account. The client then contacts his/her attorney who advises the client to return the money. The client refuses.[21]

. . . .

10. A lawyer for a political organization learns that the client is secretly a Nazi front.

11. There are rumors that a former Vice President who resigned after pleading nolo contendere to tax evasion charges plans to run for public office again. He publishes a book in which he asserts that he at all times protested his innocence of any wrongdoing to his attorney. The attorney remembers that, in fact, the Vice President admitted accepting graft.[22]

12. President Nixon announces publicly that the Watergate tapes show he knew nothing about any potentially illegal activities. Nixon's lawyer listens to the tapes and urges Nixon to disclose its contents "in the national interest." Nixon refuses and tells the press that he will not disclose anything about them because of his "duty to protect the presidency."

13. A car manufacturer knows that the placement of the gas tank on its compact car will cause the vehicle to burst into flames in 5% of rear end collisions. Its accountants determine that moving the gas tank will cost more than the company would have to pay in tort liability for injuries caused by the car's design. The company's attorney concludes that the company would not violate any criminal statute by continuing to produce the car, but nevertheless urges recall and redesign of the "defect." The company declines.[23]

. . . .

SUPPLEMENTAL READINGS

1. *Spaulding v. Zimmerman*, 263 Minn. 346, 116 N.W.2d 704 (1961), is a case as unique — and as important — as the buried bodies case. This case, the basis for Prof. Zacharias' third hypothetical, sets forth the balancing of confidentiality against public policy in the most dramatic possible fashion.

2. *State v. Olwell*, 64 Wash. 2d 828, 394 P.2d 681 (1964). This case set forth a balancing test between the prosecution's right to introduce evidence, here a knife, and the lawyer's obligation to protect the source of the evidence. The knife was allowed into evidence, though the Washington Supreme Court

---

[20] [283]Callan and David discuss a variant of this hypothetical in Callan & David, *supra* note 26, at 388-89. In a similar securities context, the Securities and Exchange Commission has taken the position that attorneys aware of proxy misinformation must disclose. See *S.E.C. v. National Student Mktg. Corp.*, 457 F. Supp. 682, 713 (D.D.C. 1978). The S.E.C. rule has fostered much debate.

[21] [284]Arguably, this scenario too involves an ongoing fraud. See *supra* note 283.

[22] [285] See *Agnew v. State,* 51 Md. App. 614, 649-56, 446 A.2d 425, 44-54 [sic] (1982).

[23] [286] See generally D. Luban, *supra* note 25 (discussing the Ford Pinto case).

reversed the lawyer's contempt citation, citing the attorney-client relationship and noting that the lawyer was entitled to hold the evidence for a reasonable period for testing purposes.

3. *State v. Green,* 493 So. 2d 1178 (La. 1986). After shooting someone, the defendant met with an attorney to discuss how he might turn himself in. On his way to the police station, the defendant collected several items from his car and left them in the attorney's care. Rummaging through the items, the attorney found the gun involved in the shooting. The attorney turned the gun over to the authorities and then resigned from the case. In the subsequent murder trial appeal, the Louisiana Supreme Court ruled that the gun could be admitted into evidence, but barred the lawyer's testimony on attorney-client privilege grounds.

4. John Randall Trahan, *A First Step Toward Resolution of the Physical Evidence Dilemma:* State v. Green, 48 La. L. Rev. 1019 (1988). This article analyzes the Louisiana Supreme Court's reasoning in *State v. Green,* and also reviews how different jurisdictions and courts have handled the "physical evidence dilemma."

5. Jennifer Hodgkins, *Note: Attorney Compelled to Produce Kidnapper's Maps to Location of Baby's Body: Attorney-Client Privilege Yields to Policy Interests Embodied in State Ethical Rules of Confidentiality,* 29 Tex. Tech. L. Rev. 885 (1998) is a thorough, well-written review of the *Henderson* case discussed in Section 2 above, the disapprobation and other pressures directed at the defense lawyer, and the ethical, public policy, and political decisions made by the court.

6. Monroe Freedman, "Where the Bodies Are Buried: The Adversary System and the Obligation of Confidentiality," 10 Criminal Law Bulletin, October 1975, at 979. One of the leading thinkers on this issue concludes that the obligation of the attorney to the client and to the system of justice prevents the attorney from divulging information contrary to the client's interests.

7. Gerald Uelmen, "The Disappearing Knife," *San Jose Mercury News*, April 28, 1996, page 1C. Prof. Uelmen, a former law school dean, an expert on ethics in criminal defense, and part of the O.J. Simpson defense team, was in charge of deciding what to do with the knife discovered by the Simpson defense team that was eventually turned over to the judge. This article tells the true story of the knife and the ethical dilemma Prof. Uelmen faced.

8. John M. Burman, *Lawyers and Domestic Violence: Raising the Standard of Practice*, 9 Mich. J. Gender & L. 207 (2003), proposes that when it comes to issues of domestic violence, a lawyer should disclose. Burman reviews *Tarasoff* and surveys the status of the law in all 51 jurisdictions after the Ethics 2000 changes.

9. *In re Goebel*, 703 N.E.2d 1045 (Ind. 1998), is another case involving almost unique facts. Goebel, under physical threat from his indicted client, gave that client information about another client of the firm, whose husband was a witness against Goebel's client. The information — an envelope that had been returned by the Postal Service due to a wrong address — contained a similar address from which the client deduced the correct address. The client in fact tracked down the witness and killed him. The lawyer could have revealed to the authorities the client's threat to himself and to the witness, but did not. Nevertheless, despite the breach of confidentiality and the obvious conflict of interest between the firm's clients, Goebel was punished with only a reprimand.

PROBLEM 5

In this chapter, we look at confidences from both ends of the spectrum. For Problem 4, we looked at when ordinarily protected confidential information must — or at least *may* — be revealed. Here, we examine the inopportune and unwise disclosure of confidences that otherwise would clearly be protected. We also examine the effects on confidentiality when an attorney consults another lawyer to obtain assistance in the first attorney's representation of a client. (We will discuss inadvertent disclosures of confidences in Problem 6.)

What may a lawyer say about a client? What is permissible to reveal and what is "talking out of school"? If a confidence is revealed, either deliberately or unwisely, may opposing counsel use the information? What if circumstances make it difficult to engage in confidential communications at all? What limits are there, if any, on using the confidential information given by a consult*ing* lawyer to a consult*ed* attorney? May the consulting lawyer define such limits? Are there some matters, like a client's identity or whereabouts, that a lawyer *must* reveal because they don't rise to the level of confidential information? Consider the following scenarios involving three lawyers in Oil City.

When Does a Lawyer Talk Too Much?

I. Attorney Matt Gold has a general practice in Oil City. He represents Anthony Verdi in a bitter divorce case. Discovery has been extensive, centering on the value of Verdi's business, and Gold has been having a lot of difficulty getting Verdi's cooperation. Verdi is an emotional sort, and argues about producing documents for far more time than he spends looking for them. In the last few weeks, he has called Gold at home several times to complain about his handling of the case.

Every Thursday afternoon, Matt joins Bruno Bianco and Joan Silver, good friends from their days together as associates, for a couple of hours of what they call "happy hour shop talk." Lately, Gold has taken to telling stories about Verdi, whom he's dubbed "the client from Hell." Last Thursday, Gold told his friends how Verdi called him at home at 10:30 p.m. and started yelling about Gold's having produced a document which was clearly discoverable. "This guy is such a pain in the keister," said Matt. "He's driving me nuts, and he's unpleasant on his best days. And he insists on telling me how to run the case. Besides," adds Matt, "I'm not so sure he's telling me the truth anyway about what his business is worth."

QUESTIONS

1. Is this reasonable discourse between friends or the improper revelation of the confidences or secrets of a client? Would it make a difference if Gold referred to a "client from Hell" without revealing his actual identity?

2. Suppose that Gold and opposing counsel Nancy Russo agree to talk settlement. Gold and Russo have been friends for years, and have opposed each other several times before. "Nancy," says Matt, "I'm going to make you a good offer here. My guy is a real pain in the neck and harder than hell to control, and I'm sure your client's just as bad, from what Tony tells me. So

let's come up with the best solution we can and then try to figure out how to get our clients to go along." Would such a conversation violate any confidences or secrets?

II. Samantha Redfern is a family law practitioner currently representing Serge Popnik, the owner of a chain of high-end men's clothing stores, in a contested divorce proceeding. Redfern learns from Popnik that he has hidden some assets, arguably community property or joint marital property, through questionable transfers to relatives. Redfern is concerned about certain tax aspects of Popnik's dealings. She calls tax attorney James T. McGuire for advice. Redfern has met McGuire a few times and knows his reputation, but not his list of clients. Redfern meets with McGuire. In order to ask McGuire for his thoughts on solutions for Popnik's tax problems, she discloses to McGuire some of the confidential information that Popnik revealed to her.

QUESTIONS

1. May Redfern reveal Popnik's confidential information to McGuire without letting her client know? What if it is necessary to reveal most of Popnik's secrets in order to get adequate advice from McGuire? Does Redfern need an advance promise or guarantee of confidentiality from McGuire before discussing Popnik's case with him? Or should she have taken steps to conceal Popnik's identity, and spoken to McGuire only "hypothetically"?

2. Suppose that two weeks after Redfern's chat with McGuire, Mrs. Popnik's attorney calls McGuire to hire him as a expert consultant in the divorce. May McGuire accept the engagement? If McGuire works for Mrs. Popnik, may he disclose the information he learned from Redfern about Mr. Popnik? Must he? Would it matter if McGuire had no idea of the identity of Redfern's client?

III. David Grey is an Oil City general practitioner. One of his oldest clients is Armand Varady, a businessman who owns the city's only Hungarian restaurant. Early one morning, Varady is arrested for driving under the influence. After he is released on his promise to appear, Varady meets with Grey and makes a confession. "David, I got to tell you, Varady is not my real name. See, 15 years ago I got in trouble in Ohio, and I ran away from a work furlough house before I served my whole sentence. Armand Varady is the name of my cousin in Cleveland who died back in '77. But if I give my real name, everything I've accomplished here, my business, my family, is for nothing." After Varady leaves, Grey sits down to think about what to do.

QUESTIONS

1. Does Grey have an obligation to the court to reveal Varady's true identity, or at least the fact his client is using a false name?

2. Instead, must Grey protect Varady's confidence at all costs?

READINGS

1. Do "Loose Lips Sink Ships"? In dealing realistically with the confidences of a client, how tight-lipped must an attorney be? Confidences are generally considered to include not only information conveyed directly by the client, but *all* information regarding the representation, whatever the source. *See* ABA Model Rule 1.6, Comment 3.[1] In many states, and under the old ABA Model Code, "confidences," learned from the client, are distinguished from "secrets," potentially embarrassing or detrimental information learned during the course of the representation, but a lawyer is charged with protecting both from disclosure.

Consider the actions of the criminal defense lawyer in the highly publicized Polly Klaas case. On October 1, 1993, 12-year-old Polly Klaas was abducted from her bedroom in the small, semi-rural town of Petaluma, California. Two months later, her body was found in a wooded area 50 miles north of her home. Polly's case attracted enormous national media attention, and an 8,000-member volunteer army that circulated millions of flyers nationwide. Her memorial service was attended by 2,000 people, and was broadcast live on CNN. Her father, Marc Klaas, became a national spokesperson for parents of child victims.

Parolee Richard Allen Davis, was arrested and charged with Polly's abduction and killing. The police reported that Davis had confessed to the crime and led them to the girl's body.

Public Defender Marteen Miller was appointed to represent Davis. After the arraignment, Miller held a sidewalk press conference in an atmosphere of intense media attention. Miller told the press Davis had admitted abducting and strangling Polly while under the influence of drugs and alcohol. Miller also said that Davis was not using his drugged state as an excuse and quoted Davis as saying, "I am responsible for this and I deserve any punishment I get." Miller said that Davis "just doesn't care about his fate" and might plead guilty.

Miller's press interview provoked considerable controversy. Some legal experts were concerned that Miller's statements laid the groundwork for an inevitable appeal, and others called for his removal. Dennis Riordan, whose clients have included "Onion Field" defendant Gregory Powell and San Quentin Six prisoner Johnny Spain, told the *National Law Journal* he was stunned that Mr. Miller "would apparently walk out of the interview with his client and announce what his client had said." Other lawyers were more tolerant. Davis was "already on the bus to the gas chamber," Oakland defense attorney Lincoln Mintz told the *National Law Journal*.

What do you think? Were Miller's public remarks ethical? Or did they improperly disclose client confidences? If confidential material was disclosed, does it matter whether the remarks helped or hurt Davis? The Davis case also raises another question: Would it be ethical for a defendant's trial lawyer, seeing no viable defense, to purposely create error by revealing confidences, thus jeopardizing a conviction and possibly postponing the client's execution date?

In practice, the revelation of attorney-client confidences may be far more common than most attorneys would like to think. Nevertheless, most ethical rules are broadly prohibitive of such revelations, and most courts adopt a strict "loose lips sink ships" attitude.

---

[1] Pre-2002 ABA Model Rule Comment 5.

Writing in 2004, Professor Abbe Smith, co-director of Georgetown's Criminal Justice Clinic, decries the words of another loose-lipped lawyer, quoted in the 2003 documentary "Capturing the Friedmans," and then sets forth her outspoken philosophy as a "confidentiality absolutist."

ABBE SMITH, TELLING STORIES AND KEEPING SECRETS
8 UDC Law Review 255 (2004)[2]

I. *A Storyteller and Confidentiality Absolutist*

In the course of writing this article, I saw the documentary Capturing the Friedmans, a powerful and disturbing film about . . . the father Arnold Friedman and the youngest son Jesse . . . charged with multiple counts of child sexual abuse. Although both Arnold and Jesse pleaded guilty, the charges seem questionable at best. . . .

For me, one of the most distressing things about the film was the appearance of Jesse's lawyer, Peter Panaro. . . . Clearly not among those lawyers who believe there is a professional obligation to preserve client confidences and secrets in the broadest sense, Panaro feels free to talk about everything from his revulsion toward Jesse's father to his belief that Jesse must have been guilty. . . .

Worse is Panaro's account of Jesse's tearful "confession." . . . In the film, Jesse denies his lawyer's account, and clearly did not give Panaro permission to say such a thing. The lawyer's conduct in the film is appallingly unethical.

. . . .

There is a growing concern, in clinical legal education and elsewhere, about telling client stories, mostly because of the potential exploitation of clients and, secondarily, because it encroaches on client confidentiality. . . .

I confess that I can sometimes be glib about this. I have even been known to refer to the "Good Story Exception" to confidentiality. . . . Of course, this is a narrowly drawn exception: If the story is run-of-the-mill, workaday, or otherwise not very compelling, the exception would not apply. This exception is in keeping with the increasing call for lawyers to violate client confidences in furtherance of the greater social good. But does protecting innocent human life necessarily have more social value than a really good story well told?

Glibness aside, how . . . can I — someone who makes her living by talking to judges and juries, clients and witnesses, students and fellows — accommodate a professional requirement to keep my mouth shut? Odd combination though it is, I believe in both telling stories and keeping secrets. I believe that doing both is what good lawyers do. As much as I love a good story — and I love it absolutely — I am equally committed to keeping a secret and keeping it absolutely.

Lawyers who believe that the ethical duty to protect client confidences is inviolable, no matter the social cost, are "confidentiality absolutists." To these lawyers — and I am one — client trust is sacrosanct; all other values must give way to the principle of maintaining client trust and confidence.

---

[2] Copyright © 2004 by University of District of Columbia Law Review. Reprinted by permission.

. . . .

Confidentiality absolutists believe that attorney-client confidentiality, unlike doctor-patient confidentiality and/or psychotherapist-client confidentiality, is inviolate. In this regard, it is more like priest-penitent confidentiality. It is not that attorneys, like priests, are stand-ins for God, but that confidences shared in a lawyer's office, police office, or jail cell should be treated as if they were shared in the confessional.

The concept of confidentiality has a long history dating back (ignominiously) to ancient Rome, where slaves were prohibited by law from revealing their master's secrets, and (not so ignominiously) attorneys were not allowed to give testimony against clients. The attorney-client privilege was first recognized in England in the late sixteenth century, and provided the basis for the ethical duty of confidentiality in the common law and in various professional codes. The ethical obligation of client confidentiality was recognized in the United States at least by the middle of the nineteenth century. Under the Field Code of Procedure, adopted in 1848 in New York, lawyers were required to "maintain inviolate the confidence and at every peril to himself, to preserve the secrets of . . . clients." Under the influential 1887 Alabama Code of Ethics, the first formally adopted body of ethical rules, lawyers had "not only a legal duty to maintain the client's confidences under the attorney-client privilege, but . . . an absolute duty to maintain the secrets and confidences of the client at all costs as a matter of professional ethics." The ABA's Canons of Professional Ethics, adopted in 1908, expressly protected clients' "secrets or confidences" in Canon 6.

. . . . Trust between lawyer and client has been called the "cornerstone of the adversary system and effective assistance of counsel." Just as the Bill of Rights protects individual freedom, lawyers who maintain client confidences protect individual privacy, dignity, and autonomy.

. . . .

II. *The Hard Cases*

There are always hard cases. Law practice wouldn't be nearly as interesting if there weren't hard cases raising difficult moral dilemmas. For me, the hard cases are (1) the hypothetical client who confesses to a murder for which the wrong man is about to be executed; (2) the real-life client who confides in his lawyer about judicial corruption; and (3) corporate clients who confide in lawyers about wrongful and/or criminal conduct that will likely pose danger to others . . . .

A. *The Wrong Inmate About to be Executed*

I became a criminal lawyer because, among other reasons, I wanted to help make sure that no innocent people (at least on my watch) are convicted and imprisoned or put to death. My commitment to this goal — and my life-long opposition to the death penalty — make the "execution of the wrong man" hypothetical especially difficult for me. It would be painful if I ever had to confront this situation in the flesh.

Still, if a client came to me and revealed that he had committed a crime for which an innocent man had been sent to death row, [i]f the client refused, . . . resisted all entreaties, and I were forced to conclude that he could not be moved, I would leave him be and keep his trust. It would not be easy, but I would manage it. In the aftermath, I would do what I could not to take it all on myself — though I imagine I would feel aggrieved and guilt-ridden.

In order to soothe my guilty conscience, I would likely point out that there is no guarantee, if I divulge such a confidence, that it would have any effect on the fate of the wrongly convicted man. The criminal justice system is deeply flawed, and this would be just one more wrongful conviction and punishment. . . .

B. *Judicial Corruption*

In 1992, Douglas Schafer, a lawyer in Tacoma, Washington, had a conversation with a client named William Hamilton. Hamilton told Schafer that Grant Anderson, who was about to become a Superior Court judge, was going to engage in improprieties as the trustee of a decedent's estate. Soon afterward, Hamilton bought a bowling alley owned by the estate at a below-market price, and, at around the same time, gave Judge Anderson a Cadillac. Hamilton shared this information with Schafer, who, outraged by such blatant judicial corruption, disclosed it to the authorities. Schafer's disclosure had impact. In 1999, in response to the information Schafer conveyed, the Washington Supreme Court removed Judge Anderson from the bench for "a pattern of dishonest behavior unbecoming a judge."

In 2003, attorney Schafer . . . was suspended from law practice for six months for the "willful, unnecessary and repeated violation of his ethical duty not to betray his client's trust." The ruling by the Washington Supreme Court prompted outcry on the order of "no good deed goes unpunished."

This is a hard case for me because, to my mind, there is no greater problem in our justice system than judicial corruption. Judicial corruption strikes at the heart of our system of justice. . . .

When judges are found to have engaged in corrupt conduct — whether as judges or lawyers — they ought to be brought down, and brought down hard.

Still, whatever Schafer's motive, I have no problem with his being disciplined. Schafer should not have divulged his client's confidences, no matter what sort of shenanigans his client was involved in. As Professor Steven Lubet remarked about the Schafer case, "The public has a lot of trouble understanding that lawyers keep secrets for guilty people, but it is important for the functioning of the legal system." . . .

It is important to remember that the client confidences Shafer divulged put his client in jeopardy as well as a corrupt judge. Hamilton's insider deal with his Cadillac quid pro quo was surely not lawful.

C. *Corporate Clients*

A number of legal scholars distinguish between corporate lawyers and criminal defense lawyers when it comes to confidentiality. I am sympathetic to this view and wish I could agree that a principled line can be drawn. Corporate clients are wealthy and bent on becoming wealthier. The dignity and autonomy interests of corporations and their CEO's are less compelling to me than those of individual criminal defendants. . . .

On the other hand, there is a compelling argument that lawyers ought to balance their professional obligations more heavily on the side of the public interest in a corporate context. Corporations are powerful entities. They can do real harm, whether we are talking about product safety, environmental hazards, tax evasion, or fraud. The traditional concern about individual rights is not an effective rejoinder to the claim that confidentiality has been used to shield organizational misconduct.

Still, I believe that lawyers can use their powers of persuasion and more [in the] long tradition of the corporate lawyer as "wise counselor." Corporations . . . choose their counsel based on many attributes, including the lawyer's value system. This is all the more reason for these lawyers to engage in moral as well as legal counseling with their clients. They should do everything they can to get these clients to do the right thing.

Conclusion

. . . [I]n the end, I don't have much faith in lawyers . . . exercising their own moral discretion about whether to disclose client confidences. I don't want to give lawyers the authority to determine when it is in the public interest to divulge confidences, even if they were allowed to do so only under limited circumstances, such as "where necessary to avoid 'substantial injustice.' ". . .

But, I do believe in the power of lawyer storytelling. I believe that a lawyer's gifts as a storyteller are helpful not only at dinner parties but in courtroom advocacy and client counseling. Ironically, it turns out that telling stories and keeping secrets go quite nicely together. But don't tell anyone.

NOTES

Professor Smith raises a series of issues we'll address later on in this volume, from the innocent man on death row[3] to an examination of corporate confidentiality in the new millennium.[4] Smith's "absolutist" perspective raises several interesting questions, among them: Should lawyers ever be complicit, even by their silence, in the death of an innocent person? Is there a point where "the interests of justice" must trump lawyer-client confidentiality to avoid the corruption of the judicial system? Are corporate entities entitled to the same principles of confidentiality that arose as an *individual* right?

The timing of this article — and many others focusing renewed scrutiny on confidentiality — is hardly coincidental. In 2002 and 2003, the ABA modified two important rules — MRs 1.6 and 1.13 in order to create several exceptions to strict confidentiality. Many if not most observers attributed some of these modifications, especially to Rule 1.13, to the fallout over Enron and

---

[3] *See* Problem 15.

[4] *See* Problem 25 and elsewhere.

similar scandals, and the effect of the so-called Sarbanes-Oxley legislation which, coupled with new SEC regulations addressing the duties of attorneys confronted by wrongdoing on the part of their "issuer" clients, materially increased the scope of attorney whistleblowing.[5]

2. Lawyer-to-Lawyer Consultations, Client Confidences, and an ABA Opinion. Lawyers frequently consult with other lawyers to get specific advice or ideas on how to handle difficult or unfamiliar situations. In fact, as we learned in Problem 1, sometimes a lawyer *must* consult with an attorney more knowledgeable about the subject of the representation in order to take on the case. However, if the consulting attorney discloses client confidences to the consulted attorney, does the information lose its confidentiality? If so, what steps may, or must, the consulting attorney take to protect the client's secrets?

On the other hand, what must the *consulted* attorney consider before giving advice? Is there information the consulted attorney should obtain before agreeing to the consultation? May the consulted attorney use the information received to the detriment of the client of the consulting attorney?

The ABA Standing Committee on Ethics and Professional Responsibility addressed these questions in Formal Opinion 98-411. The opinion concluded that without express client authorization for the consultation, the consulting attorney had only limited authority to disclose client information. Client secrets could best be protected by asking the consulted attorney anonymous or hypothetical questions. However, the opinion warned that if the consulted attorney could decipher either the client's identity or the specific case from the facts given, the consulting attorney would have violated the client's confidences under Model Rule 1.6.

The opinion suggested that the consulting attorney give the client full disclosure and obtain the client's authorization before consulting with another attorney. The opinion also recommended that the consulting attorney avoid consulting with anyone who might represent an adverse party, and get advance assurances of confidentiality from the consultant before proceeding.

On the other hand, the opinion concludes that the mere act of consulting does not give the *consulted* attorney any duty to the client of the *consulting* attorney. The opinion cautions that the consulted lawyer may take on a duty to protect the new client's confidences either by expressly agreeing to do so, or whenever a reasonable attorney would know the information received was intended to be confidential. But absent any express or implied agreement of confidentiality, the consulted attorney could use the client's information or disclose it to third persons.

Cautioning that giving advice could compromise the consulted lawyer's loyalty to existing clients, the opinion suggests that the consulted attorney get as much information about the consulting attorney's case and client as possible in order to do a thorough conflicts check (something we'll address at length in Problem 10.) Additionally, the opinion recommends that the consulted attorney ask the consulting attorney to waive any conflicts of interest,

---

[5] We'll return at some length to Sarbanes-Oxley and other new corporate whistleblowing standards in Problem 25.

or have the consulting lawyer's client agree to an ethical screen (another subject we discuss in Problem 10.)

Formal Opinion 98-411 raises at least as many questions as it attempts to answer. It has been the subject of considerable debate and substantial criticism. The following is a rather thorough critique of the opinion by two ethics professors at Southern Methodist University, who use the article as an opportunity to pay homage to a mentor, Professor Walter Steele, who they appreciated for both his healthy skepticism and his quick wit.

FREDERICK C. MOSS & WILLIAM J. BRIDGE, "CAN WE TALK?": A "STEELE-Y" ANALYSIS OF ABA OPINION 411
52 SMU Law Review 683 (1999)[6]

[In this article, the authors refer to the attorney who asks for advice as "Ting" (from consul*ting*) and the lawyer who gives the advice as "Ted" (from consul*ted*).]

[W]e . . . conclude that the Opinion may well contain . . . more noise than practical consequence. . . . Its main tactic is to establish, if only by repetition, that a client-lawyer relationship does not arise between the consulting lawyer's client and the consulted lawyer. Thus, if a consulted lawyer makes no promise, he is free of any ethical obligation to the consulting lawyer's client.

Dodging Consultations for the Lawyer's Benefit

At the outset, the Opinion limits the scope of its discussion, [dividing] legal consultations into two basic categories: Consultations for the benefit of the lawyer and those for the benefit of the client. The first category includes consultations by lawyers who represent clients when the lawyers have questions concerning the lawyers' ethical duties vis-à-vis the client. . . . This consultation is not to benefit the client, but rather the lawyer. The Opinion, in its own words, "does not necessarily apply to or discuss all of the ethical issues" concerning lawyer-benefit consultations. "Not necessarily" is hedging language obscuring any assistance in this important kind of consulting. . . .

The Opinion either applies or it does not; it appears not.

The Rules of "Engagement:" Whither Opinion 97-407?

The remaining category of legal consultations are those for the benefit of the client. Here, a lawyer seeks ethical or legal advice or information that will assist in the representation of a client.

The Committee further limits the scope of Opinion 98-411 by distinguishing consultations where there is an intent to engage the consulted lawyer's services from those where there is no intent to engage. We "suspicion"[7] that the reason for excluding formally engaged legal experts is because the Committee wanted to limit the reach of Opinion 97-407. Opinion 97-407 addresses the ethical duties of lawyers hired as either consulting or testifying legal experts.

---

[6] Copyright © 1999 by SMU Law Review. Used by permission. All rights reserved.

[7] [21] As Walter would say.

At first blush, Opinion 98-411 seems contrary to Opinion 97-407. Opinion 97-407 takes the position that a lawyer hired to be a non-testifying consulting expert has a client-lawyer relationship with the consulting lawyer's client. This conclusion of Opinion 97-407 has the potential to include every lawyer consulted by another lawyer, no matter how briefly or informally. Clearly, the Committee seeks to avoid this result. Its objective is to keep informal legal consultations as free as possible from ethical restricts that might discourage a lawyer from seeking advice from another lawyer. To do this the Committee . . . tamed Opinion 97-407 by resorting to "engagement." But, as Walter might say, "that ol' dog won't hunt."

First, . . . [a]s the Committee itself recognizes in Opinion 97-407, whether a client-lawyer relationship arises is a matter of law beyond the scope of the rules of ethics. Legally, it is clear that the formation of that relationship does not depend upon a formal retention agreement or any other single criterion. . . .

Second, the Opinion seems to say that its conclusions hold no matter how much client information is communicated to Ted or how much work Ted does, as long as Ted is not "engaged." Is the Committee saying that, even when he learns sensitive, confidential details of Ting's case and consults at length with Ting's client, Ted cannot be the client's lawyer simply because there is no formal retainer?

That is not to say that Opinion 98-411 might not be perfectly correct in other respects. The Opinion envisions what we call the "quickie consult." The "quickie consult" occurs when a lawyer calls a colleague at another firm or a former law professor to pose a hypothetical situation. . . . The question might grow from a real cases, but contains no identifying information. Opinion 98-411 plainly sees no client-lawyer relationship between the answerer and the questioner's client. That seems beyond dispute. . . .

. . . .

The Middle Ground: Ethical Swampland?

The Opinion identifies a broad middle ground between the "quickie consult" and the formal engagement. Ting may reveal varying amounts of confidential client information, ranging from merely identifying the client to imparting detailed case information and privileged communications to Ted, even though not engaged.

The Opinion recognizes that in these middle cases, even without a client-lawyer relationship, things can get ethically tricky. Information Ting learns as a result of her representation is confidential under Rule 1.6. Knowing that lawyers who consult others on legal questions often must reveal Rule 1.6 information . . . the Opinion explores the territory of "impliedly authorized" disclosures.

Ting's Implied Authority: Can She Talk?

The Opinion first seems to create a hitherto unknown exception to the duty of confidentiality . . . "if it is public knowledge [for example] that a lawyer represents a particular criminal defendant, the defense lawyer may reveal that fact in a consultation without violating Rule 1.6, although disclosure of other facts not publicly known may be a violation." This seems to say that information learned in the course of representing a client is not covered by Rule 1.6 if it is publicly known. Whoa, Bubba. The Rule contains no such exception. A lawyer is not free to disclose client information just because it is public knowledge.

Eschewing the easy out by saying that all disclosures to Ted for the benefit of Ting's client are impliedly authorized under Rule 1.6(a) "in order to carry out the representation," the Opinion limits Ting's implied authority to disclose [and] notes that the unauthorized disclosure of privileged information might amount to a waiver of the privilege. . . .

We are left to guess exactly how the client is protected by her "reasonable expectation" of confidentiality. The Opinion declares that, absent a promise, Ted has no obligation to keep the information confidential. . . . We find this analysis as leaky as a bad bait bucket.

Sounds as if the Committee wants to make sure that Ted is a tough fish to hook. That same hook poses great danger to Ting.

The Almost Ethics-Free Zone

As for the consultation which becomes "un-anonymous" when Ted later learns enough from other sources to connect the dots, the Committee rejects what it calls a "springing" duty of confidentiality under Rule 1.6. Its reasoning is as circular as it seems. The only reason no duty arises later is because there was no duty before. No client-lawyer relationship exists, and therefore there is no duty. If Ted has not promised confidentiality, there is no duty. The fact that Ted later links Ting's information to an identified client is irrelevant. . . .

The Committee's solution to the problem of the consultation that later becomes "un-anonymous" is, of course, prevention: The Opinion advises Ted to learn who Ting's client is and to check for conflicts before consulting. Again, curious advice, when Ted is not forming a client-lawyer relationship with that person, and when the Committee elsewhere endorses the hypothetical consultation.

NOTES

As the preceding article makes abundantly clear, there are many unanswered questions — and unsatisfying answers — about lawyer-to-lawyer consultations. Some authorities posit that a client's confidences are protected so long as the consulting attorney seeks advice for the benefit of the client. Others are concerned that if lawyers must take such elaborate precautions to protect their respective clients (and guard against malpractice claims), will they simply take a pass on seeking advice, even when their lack of expertise or knowledge puts them at a disadvantage?

3. Other Forms of Lawyer-to-Lawyer Consultations. Do similar problems arise when a client replaces one attorney with another? May the old attorney disclose to the new attorney the client secrets he or she gained during the representation? Analyst Marla B. Rubin[8] believes that in general the old attorney may not divulge the client's secrets to the new lawyer, unless the client will benefit by such a disclosure.

Another important issue — referred to in the beginning of the Moss-Bridge article — is the circumstance in which Attorney A wants to consult Lawyer B not for the benefit of A's client, but for the protection of the *attorney*. For instance, attorney A may have become privy to information about a client's possible future crime, or may be worried about an emerging conflict of interest. Here, the attorney wants to consult with a lawyer to protect the *attorney's own* rights, not the client's. Even though the need for such lawyer-to-lawyer help seems obvious, ethical rules had traditionally not dealt with this issue, until the recent amendment to Model Rule 1.6, subsection (b)(4), added language authorizing attorneys to "reveal information relating to the representation of a client to secure legal advice about the lawyer's compliance with the Rules." This goes a long way towards enabling lawyers to get appropriate advice before making decisions — possibly ill-advised or ill-considered ones — on their clients' behalf.

4. "MDPs," "Unbundling," and Confidentiality. Many consumers would like to see "one stop shopping" for legal and other related services. At the high, monied end, such services are generally called "multidisciplinary practices," or "MDPs"; for the poor, the move towards one-stop shopping is often called "unbundling." Whether for big corporations or the poor, multidisciplinary services raise a host of ethical issues, including how confidentiality can be maintained when non-lawyers become involved. We'll revisit the issue of multidisciplinary practice in the last chapter of this volume, but meanwhile, this article provides food for thought.

STACY L. BRUSTIN, LEGAL SERVICES PROVISION THROUGH MULTIDISCIPLINARY PRACTICE — ENCOURAGING HOLISTIC ADVOCACY WHILE PROTECTING ETHICAL INTERESTS
73 University of Colorado Law Review 787 (2002)[9]

Barbara Davis has three kids [and] receives public assistance to support herself and her three children. She attends a job training program sponsored by a community college and is three courses away from receiving her certification in child development. She hopes to find a job and get off of public assistance within a year. The program is full time, five days a week.

Ms. Davis found out about the job training program from her case manager at The Community Center, a neighborhood organization located a few blocks from her apartment. Ms. Davis first went to The Community Center to get medical care for her kids. She could make an appointment with a doctor rather than waiting for hours as she had done in other clinics and emergency rooms.

---

[8] Marla B. Rubin, *Not Unless It Would Be to Their Benefit: Can You Disclose Clients' Confidences to New Counsel?*, in LAW FIRM PARTNERSHIP AND BENEFITS REPORT 10 (Oct. 1997).

[9] Copyright © 2002 by the University of Colorado Law Review. Reprinted by permission.

As a patient of the medical clinic, she was entitled to use all of the services offered at The Community Center. She obtained two large bags of food once a month. She selected clothes and shoes from the second-hand clothing donations available on site, and she met with a caseworker. She expressed concerns to the caseworker about the difficulties her son, Michael, was having in school. She had requested that the school evaluate him to see if he had some type of learning problem, but school officials did not respond to her request. The caseworker sent her upstairs to make an appointment with someone in the legal clinic. She met with a lawyer at The Community Center who handles special education cases and the lawyer has been advocating on her behalf with the school system. . . .

Multiservice organizations such as The Community Center provide holistic, one-stop shopping to clients who face problems that require a multidisciplinary solution. Clients at these organizations are often struggling financially as well as emotionally. Rather than going from one non-profit agency to another in search of medical, legal, or social work services, they are able to access the services they need in one convenient location. The service providers working with these clients communicate with one another and thereby ensure quality, coordinated care. . . .

The recent push to expand the rules regarding multidisciplinary practice (MDP) is often associated with the "Big Five" accounting firms. These firms are interested in offering a package of services, including legal services, to customers in the United States, and they have vigorously advocated for rules changes. While the impetus for change has come from the heights of the corporate business world, the ramifications of such changes on legal services practice for those living in poverty are significant

. . . .

The first major effort to change the prohibitions against MDPs took place in the early 1980s. The Kutak Commission of the American Bar Association, which drafted the original ABA Model Rules of Professional Conduct, recommended that the ABA adopt a version of Rule 5.4 that would allow a variety of business arrangements between lawyers and nonlawyers. In 1983, the ABA House of Delegates rejected this proposal and adopted the current version of Model Rule 5.4 banning partnerships.

In 1998, [s]purred by fears that the world's largest accounting firms were providing legal services and engaging in the unauthorized practice of law, the ABA created the Commission on Multidisciplinary Practice to make recommendations about whether and how such multidisciplinary enterprises should be regulated. During a two-year period, the Commission held public hearings throughout the United States. . . .

Proponents of MDP argue that such practice reflects the changing marketplace and global economy. It is increasingly difficult for corporations to distinguish between "legal" issues and "business" issues. The accounting firms argue that clients should have one-stop shopping available to them and that MDPs are essential to permit efficient and effective integration, coordination, and delivery of services.

One can find small firm lawyers and solo practitioners aligned on both sides of the MDP debate. Those in favor of MDPs argue that multidisciplinary practice offers convenience to clients and may be the key to the economic survival of small practices. They worry that financial planners, accountants, and alternative dispute resolution professionals are increasingly attracting clients away from the services of attorneys. Other small firm lawyers and solo practitioners, however, express fears that . . . large companies and franchises will offer a multitude of services, including legal services, and small practices will not be able to compete.

There is further concern that non-lawyers in MDPs might be compelled by law or subpoena to divulge information that a lawyer would be prohibited from divulging. Clients who are the victims of domestic violence or elder abuse, for example, might disclose the situation to an attorney believing that the information will remain confidential. A social worker partnering with the attorney in an MDP might discover such information and be obligated by state statute to report the information. Others voice concern that MDP will erode the attorney-client privilege. Once information is disclosed to other professionals, the client may no longer be able to claim the attorney-client privilege (although other privileges may apply, i.e. doctor-patient, clergy-parishioner, social worker- or psychologist-patient) or the exception for agents of the attorney.

Opponents also fear that the independence lawyers have to make judgments and devise strategies for their cases will be compromised by the involvement of other professionals. Some believe that the sharing of fees, for example, may allow the bottom line to control, rather than concern for clients. . . .

After two years of public hearings and investigation, the Commission recommended, in its July 2000 report, that the ABA revise the Model Rules of Professional Conduct to allow lawyers and nonlawyers to engage in limited forms of multidisciplinary practice. Once again, however, the ABA rejected the proposal. The ABA House of Delegates urged jurisdictions around the country to resist the move toward MDP and to revise their ethical rules so as to "preserve the core values of the legal profession."

5. How Far Does Confidentiality Extend? Must lawyers reveal either their clients' whereabouts or their clients' identities? Read the following article about Barry P. Wilson, a lawyer imprisoned for contempt for refusing to answer to a grand jury concerning one of his clients. Do you agree with the court's contempt ruling? Did the lawyer properly rely on his duty to maintain confidences, or did he simply go too far?

TRACY BRETON, MORAL DECISION SENDS LAWYER INTO U.S. PRISON
The National Law Journal (September 30, 1985) [10]

For nearly four months, Boston lawyer Barry P. Wilson has been an inmate at the federal prison camp in Danbury, Conn.

He isn't there because he committed any crime. He reported there on May 30 because he had refused to answer questions before a federal grand jury in Providence, R.I. The grand jury has been investigating the alleged role of

---

[10] Copyright © 1985 by Tracy Breton. Reprinted by permission.

his client, whose whereabouts are unknown, in a drug smuggling venture in which 8,785 pounds of marijuana worth $8 million were seized in 1982.

Mr. Wilson, a sole practitioner who specializes in criminal defense work, was found in contempt Jan. 25 by U.S. District Senior Judge Raymond J. Pettine of Providence. Six days later, Judge Pettine imposed an open-ended sentence in which he ordered Mr. Wilson to remain incarcerated until he answered the questions before the grand jury, or until the grand jury's term expires on Oct. 27.

. . . .

When he reported to the prison in Danbury at the end of May, he was assigned for three weeks to the medium security prison, where his job was to pick up cigarette butts from the prison grounds. When space opened up for him in the minimum security camp, he was assigned the bunk bed formerly occupied by the Rev. Sun Myung Moon.

. . . .

While the 35-year-old attorney . . . performs his routine tasks at the prison, the legal debate over his incarceration rages.

He steadfastly maintains, for instance, that his decision to go to jail was a "moral" one.

Mr. Wilson argues that the government can get the information it seeks about his client, Alan Tucker, through means other than subpoenaing him. He also claims that if he were to abide by the grand jury subpoena and answer its questions, it would violate the attorney-client privilege and weaken the criminal defense bar in general.

In a brief submitted to the 1st Circuit, one of Mr. Wilson's lawyers, Carol A. Donovan, asserted: "The government's attempt to use Mr. Wilson, a criminal defense attorney, as a source for information to facilitate his client's prosecution, is not an isolated incident due to peculiar or unusual circumstances.

"It is an instance of what has become a rather routine invasion of the attorney-client relationship pursuant to a well-considered and deliberate law enforcement strategy, . . ." said Ms. Donovan. . . .

Mr. Wilson was first subpoenaed to appear before the federal grand jury on Aug. 18, 1982 — just nine days after 221 bales of Colombian marijuana were seized on a 46-foot sloop off the coast of Watch Hill, R.I., by a Coast Guard crew acting under the direction of a joint federal, state and local narcotics task force.

Three men arrested on the sloop, "Fiesta," and on a high-speed motor boat that attempted to rendezvous with it near shore, were convicted in connection with the drug-smuggling scheme by a federal court jury in December 1982 and sentenced to jail. One of the three defendants, Frank Termini, was represented by Mr. Wilson at trial.

. . . .

Mr. Tucker, whom Mr. Wilson has acknowledged representing during the spring of 1982 in a "landlord-tenant" matter, is very much a target of the [grand jury] probe, [U.S. Attorney Lincoln C. Almond of Rhode Island] said.

Alan Tucker, said Mr. Almond in [a] memorandum, is being sought because he "has been identified . . . as the individual who rented . . . safehouses from which marijuana, once smuggled ashore in Rhode Island, would be packaged for distribution," Mr. Almond charged. . . .

Mr. Wilson was brought into the investigation, Mr. Almond said, because when Mr. Tucker rented the home he provided Mr. Wilson's name as one of two references. The realtor called Mr. Wilson, who told the realtor that he knew Mr. Tucker as "an investment broker" and could vouch for his ability to meet his financial obligations as they became due.

Authorities have not been able to locate Mr. Tucker since the sloop Fiesta was seized back in August 1982. A Honda sedan with Hawaii plates that he drove could not be traced, and the New York home address and phone number Mr. Tucker had given to the realtor turned out to be fictitious. . . .

Mr. Almond said that in all, the investigation of the Fiesta scheme "uncovered 22 fictitious corporations and 32 vehicles listed to fictitious persons and addresses, all of which were linked to the smuggling operation."

Because Mr. Wilson had represented to the realtor that "he knew the Tucker family for some time and that they were a reputable family," and because the other reference Mr. Tucker gave the realtor turned out to be a fictitious person, Mr. Wilson's testimony is needed by the grand jury to continue its probe, prosecutors asserted. "What else can we do to find out who Alan Tucker is?" asked Asst. U.S. Attorney James H. Leavey.

Mr. Wilson, at his hearing before Judge Pettine, said, "I don't believe I'm above the law." But, he also told the judge, he also understands his "role as a lawyer" to mean that "when a person hires me, that a certain bond . . . trust has been established. . . ."

Judge Pettine, in sentencing Mr. Wilson, said he recognized the attorney was refusing to answer the grand jury's questions "because of moral convictions."

But, he added, Mr. Wilson must accept the consequences of choosing "to openly disobey" what he feels is "unjust law."

NOTES

Almost 20 years after this article was written, there remains substantial disagreement on whether a client's whereabouts are privileged against disclosure, even when sought by a court. "Neither the ABA Code, the Model Rules, nor the ABA Defense Function Standards contain a specific rule directly answering the question when — or whether — an attorney is permitted or required to divulge a client's address or whereabouts," writes Professor John Burkoff in the September 2005 edition of his *Criminal Defense Ethics: Law and Liability* (see supplemental readings). Burkoff notes that the ABA and Association of American Trial Lawyers (ATLA) have published ethics opinions that come to opposite conclusions.

Some case examples: In *Commonwealth v. Maguigan*, 511 A.2d 1327 (Pa. 1986), the Court held that an attorney had to disclose his client's location because the client had violated a court order. On the other hand, the New Jersey Supreme Court has held that an attorney could not be held in contempt for failing to disclose his client's whereabouts to a grand jury investigating the client. In *In re Joseph Nackson, on Contempt*, 555 A.2d 1101 (N.J. 1989), the client had consulted with Nackson about a fugitive warrant. The Court reasoned that an attorney should not be made to disclose information received from the client that concerned the continuing aspects or effects of past criminal conduct.

However, where an attorney does more than merely withhold client information, the attorney will likely get into trouble. Consider the case of attorney Dennis Sieg, who aided his client in avoiding three traffic citations by helping the client represent to the court that the client was really his brother. *In re Disciplinary Proceedings of Sieg*, 515 N.W.2d 694, 183 Wis. 2d 704 (1994). Sieg found out that his client had forged a letter ostensibly from the client's brother that said the brother consented to having the tickets on his record. Knowing it could further incriminate the client, Sieg then denied having known about the letter when the police requested a copy. He also failed to disclose his client's true identity to the court when he discovered it. Sieg was suspended for 60 days.

Professor Burkoff's monograph contains an extensive list of cases and secondary authorities decided in both directions.

6. Is a Client's Identity Confidential? As the previous section shows, there is a close relationship between whereabouts and identity. Read the following article by noted ethics professor Charles W. Wolfram, discussing when a client's identity is protected by the attorney-client privilege.

CHARLES W. WOLFRAM, HIDE AND SECRETS: THE BOUNDARIES OF PRIVILEGE
Legal Times (April 3, 1989) [11]

Most lawyers fulfill with enthusiasm the duty of keeping client information secret. They know that what might hurt a client should not be bruited about.

. . . .

Does the [attorney-client] privilege cover the name of a client, one who killed a pedestrian in a hit-and-run accident? If it does, does it also provide tactical advantages? For example, can a lawyer keep the client's name secret if he tries to plea-bargain with the police and prosecutor — attempting to cut a deal for the anonymous client but leaving a safe, protected route of retreat if he cannot? Can he hold the name secret if the personal-injury lawyer for the surviving relatives of the victim, learning of the plea bargaining, tries to subpoena the defense lawyer to force him to reveal the name?

In Florida last October, tentative answers to these questions emerged, then disappeared. The first answer came in *Baltes v. Doe* when West Palm Beach lawyer Barry E. Krischer persuaded state Circuit Judge Timothy P. Poulton to reject such a subpoena. Instead, Poulton entered a protective order against any attempt to coerce Krischer into giving up his client's name. But the

---

[11] Copyright © 1989. Reprinted by permission of Legal Times.

parents of the 28-year-old victim, Mark Baltes, persisted. . . . At stake was a $5 million wrongful-death suit . . . .

Krischer's moves had been careful and elaborate. Copying the procedure successfully employed by a California lawyer in *Baird v. Koerner,* 279 F.2d 623 (9th Cir. 1960), Krischer first went to a second lawyer, Scott N. Richardson. . . . Allegedly without mentioning the name of the secret client, Krischer filled Richardson in on the facts that he had learned and asked Richardson to open plea talks. Knowing that the Balteses would have to be involved in any plea arrangement, the prosecutor eventually notified [the Baltes'] lawyer Farish. Richardson's efforts foundered when the Balteses would not agree to an anonymous plea. But Farish still had no name — although he now knew who did.

Farish had little else to go on beyond some tantalizing details. Baltes, an electrician, was killed as he staggered into a road — drunk, as a post-mortem blood test would show — during the night of March 9, 1986. The driver never paused and was gone from the scene before anyone could identify the car. Pieces of the car left on the road by the force of the collision and paint chips from Baltes' skull indicated that the hit-and-run vehicle was a 1984 or 1985 white Buick Riviera. A search of auto records and interviews led nowhere. A reward offer brought only false leads.

All that changed dramatically on Election Eve 1988, when the local Florida prosecutor, with whom Richardson had been negotiating and who was up for reelection, publicly announced a sleuthing breakthrough — the driver was a local car salesman named William D. Morser. State Police established that a chip from the [Morser] car matched the chip from young Baltes' skull.

In February, Morser pleaded no contest to the criminal charges against him and was sentenced. . . . The Baltes' civil suit has been reinvigorated. . . . Judge Poulton's October order protecting Morser's name under the attorney-client privilege had been widely reported. Less widely reported was that, before Morser stepped forward and after lawyer Krischer appeared on a local talk show, Poulton rescinded his protective order to rethink the issue. Shortly thereafter, once Morser's name became public, the question whether the attorney-client privilege applies to a client's name became moot in the Baltes litigation. But the issue remains very much alive in legal circles.

The question of the confidentiality of a client's name actually rarely arises, but for many lawyers the issue seems to evoke strong protective instincts. . . . Several courts . . . have held that a client's identity is never protected by the privilege. Those courts reason that the privilege safeguards only client communications and that a name is not a communication but a fact, just like the fact that a client has red hair or a facial tattoo.

A few other courts, following one of the lines of reasoning in *Koerner,* protect client identity as privileged in some instances under a concept that seems to misapply the self-incrimination protection: Identity is protected if revealing it would supply the "last link" of evidence necessary to convict the client of a crime. But self-incrimination is irrelevant because the client's lawyer, and not the client, is the subject of compulsion. The last-link theory is also problematic because its application depends on the incriminating force of other evidence in the case — a consideration that has nothing to do with confidentiality of the original communication.

Courts agree that the purpose of the attorney-client privilege is to encourage clients to provide information to their lawyers that, in the absence of the privilege, lawyers would not as likely learn. On that basis, the response of most courts is that clients need no encouragement to reveal their name to their attorney. Indeed, in most instances, the first thing a lawyer learns about a client is the client's identity. The secrets follow.

Yet to conclude that client identity is never privileged might be too facile. While the analysis of the majority of courts is sound as far as it goes, it does not follow that confidential client communications will never be put at risk by forcing a lawyer to reveal a client's identity. Such a risk might have been what motivated the court in *Koerner*. The lawyer there had sent the Internal Revenue Service a letter with a large check, explaining that the check was to pay past-due taxes owed by an anonymous client. The government convened a grand jury and sought to compel the lawyer to identify the delinquent taxpayer. In the circumstances, revealing the client's name might also have revealed a confidential communication — the client's statement admitting owing overdue taxes.

But even with a reworked *Koerner* test, two problems remain. In both *Koerner* and *Baltes*, the risk of disclosure was self-inflicted because the web of incriminating evidence was self-constructed. The clients were exposed to no risk until their lawyers tried to have the cake of negotiating with the government while enjoying the culinary pleasure of asserting the privilege.

NOTES

Do you agree with Professor Wolfram that clients rarely expect confidentiality when they disclose their identities to lawyers? What about his assertion that "self-incrimination is irrelevant"? Interestingly, Wolfram's article discusses the boundaries of *privilege,* focusing on the evidentiary rather than the ethical issue. But when a lawyer's conduct is evaluated by ethical standards, many states, through their ethics committees, have held that a client's identity may well be *confidential*. For example, several recent state bar opinions hold that lawyers cannot reveal their clients' identities to banks when their law firms seek loans based on receivables owed by the clients. *See, e.g.*, Arizona Opinion 92-4 (1992); Maryland Opinions 91-54 (1991), 93-8 (1993); Michigan Opinion RI-77 (1991); Texas Opinion 479 (1991).

Other cases and opinions discuss circumstances closer to those of Armand Varady. Several discuss the lawyer's dual responsibilities of protecting the confidentiality of a client's identity on the one hand while avoiding misrepresentations to the court on the other. Sometimes, navigating between these two duties can be like walking a tightrope. When a lawyer appears in court for a client, is referring to the client by an alias protecting the client's identity or a misrepresentation? Or perhaps both?

Among the several cases and ethics opinions with varying views of this tightrope is *State v. Casby*, 348 N.W.2d 736 (Minn. 1984). There a client gave police a relative's name, and the lawyer used that false name during plea negotiations with the prosecutor. The lawyer herself was convicted of misdemeanor misconduct, and also disciplined. But in *D'Alessio v. Gilberg*, 617 N.Y.S.2d 484, 205 A.D.2d 8 (N.Y. App. Div. 1994), the court held that an attorney could not be compelled to reveal the name of a client who had consulted with the attorney regarding his possible past commission of a crime, where the crime was already committed, there was no possibility of further criminal acts if the individual was not identified, and the disclosure would expose the client to possible criminal prosecution. On almost the same facts as *Casby*, North Carolina Opinion 33 (1987) holds that a lawyer *cannot* reveal a client's identity if it will hurt the client (such as by revealing a prior record), until it comes time for the client to testify falsely at trial. The reality is that lawyers may find themselves between a rock and a hard place — either revealing a confidence or facing contempt. There are few safe harbors for those confronted with this dilemma.

7. Death and Taxes. There are two other areas where an attorney's refusal to disclose client information can be nettlesome for even the most savvy lawyer: The client's death and the receipt of large sums of cash from the client. In one of the controversies swirling around President Clinton during his incumbency, special prosecutor Kenneth Starr investigated allegations that presidential aides had lied about Hillary Clinton's role in the firing of seven employees of the White House travel office. One of the people Starr wanted to question was White House counsel Vincent Foster. Foster consulted with another attorney, James Hamilton, who took three pages of notes. Nine days later, before Starr could question him, Foster killed himself. Starr then sought Hamilton's notes, claiming that the attorney-client privilege does not extend beyond a client's death. In a case named for Hamilton's law firm, the matter went all the way to the United States Supreme Court. Read the following.

SWIDLER & BERLIN v. UNITED STATES
524 U.S. 899 (1998)

CHIEF JUSTICE REHNQUIST delivered the opinion of the court.

The Court of Appeals thought that the risk of posthumous revelation, when confined to the criminal context, would have little to no chilling effect on client communication, but that the costs of protecting communications after death were high. . . . We granted certiorari, and we now reverse.

 . . . .

The Independent Counsel . . . argues that the exception reflects a policy judgment that the interest in settling estates outweighs any posthumous interest in confidentiality. He then reasons by analogy that in criminal proceedings, the interest in determining whether a crime has been committed should trump client confidentiality, particularly since the financial interests of the estate are not at stake.

 . . . [T]he premise of his analogy is incorrect, since cases consistently recognize that the rationale for the testamentary exception is that it furthers the client's intent. There is no reason to suppose as a general matter that grand jury testimony about confidential communications furthers the client's intent.

Despite the scholarly criticism, we think there are weighty reasons that counsel in favor of posthumous application [of the privilege]. Knowing that communications will remain confidential even after death encourages the client to communicate fully and frankly with counsel. . . . Clients may be concerned about reputation, civil liability, or possible harm to friends or family. Posthumous disclosure of such communications may be as feared as disclosure during the client's lifetime. . . .

The Independent Counsel assumes, incorrectly we believe, that the privilege is analogous to the Fifth Amendment's protection against self-incrimination. But as suggested above, the privilege serves much broader purposes. Clients consult attorneys for a wide variety of reasons, [beyond] possible criminal liability.

This is true of disclosure before and after the client's death. Without assurance of the privilege's posthumous application, the client may very well not have made disclosures to his attorney at all, so the loss of evidence is more apparent than real. In the case at hand, it seems quite plausible that Foster, perhaps already contemplating suicide, may not have sought legal advice from Hamilton if he had not been assured the conversation was privileged.

[T]here is no case authority for the proposition that the privilege applies differently in criminal and civil cases. . . . In any event, a client may not know at the time he discloses information to his attorney, whether it will later be relevant to a civil or a criminal matter, let alone whether it will be of substantial importance.

. . . .

The judgment of the Court of Appeals is *Reversed*.

NOTES

While this is the United States Supreme Court speaking, since both ethical and evidentiary rules are a state-by-state affair, courts are not unanimous in their agreement with *Swidler*. *Wesp v. Everson*, 33 P.3d 191 (Colo. 2001), is consistent with *Swidler* in holding that the privilege survives death in a case where a woman was suing her deceased step father's estate for sexual abuse. On the other hand, a California court in *HLC Properties, Ltd., v. Superior Court,* 35 Cal. 4th 54, 105 P.3d 560, 24 Cal. Rptr. 3d 199 (2005), held that the attorney client privilege passes to the personal representative and when that person has discharged all duties, the privilege terminates

Although death doesn't destroy an attorney's duty to keep a client's secrets, it is another matter to conceal a client's death. For example, New Jersey explicitly forbids lawyers from concealing personal injury clients' deaths in order to get better settlements.[12] In other instances courts have held that there is no duty to reveal the death of a client or a witness.[13]

---

[12] *See* Eleanor Barrett, *Concealing Client's Death Gets Lawyer Suspended*, American Law Media online services (July 9, 1999).

[13] See *People v. Jones*, 44 N.Y.2d 76, 404 N.Y.S.2d 85, 375 N.E.2d 41 (1978), which we excerpt in Problem 18.

Businesses that receive $10,000 or more in cash must report these transactions to the Internal Revenue Service. This requirement applies to lawyers. Filling out the required Form 8300 presents problems for criminal defense attorneys, since the transfer of large amounts of cash is frequently a signal to prosecutors and police that the person paying the money may be dealing in drugs or other contraband. The form requires the recipient to list not only the amount of money received, but also identifying information about the payer. In *United States v. Gertner & Newman*, 873 F. Supp. 729 (D. Mass. 1995), a federal district court held that an attorney *could refuse* to provide the identifying information on the form when the person paying was a current client with a pending case. On the other hand, *United States v. Blackman*, 72 F.3d 1418 (9th Cir. 1995) required an attorney to disclose the client information where there was no ongoing investigation, the information would not incriminate the client, and the information constituted corporate records that had no 5th Amendment protection. It is hard to know whether the *Blackman* court would have reached a different conclusion if, as in *Gertner & Newman*, there was an ongoing investigation or a pending criminal case against the client.

8. Confidentiality and Problems at Guantánamo. Finally, the problems confronting lawyers representing Guantánamo detainees form an excellent case study for what confidentiality is all about. The reading below excerpts a brief prepared by Philadelphia ethics guru Lawrence J. Fox on behalf of lawyers suing the government because of restrictions on their ability to maintain a viable confidential relationship with their clients.[14] The brief touches on a number of "real world" practical consequences when confidentiality cannot easily be maintained.

BRIEF OF AMICI PROFESSORS OF ETHICS AND LAWYERS PRACTICING IN THE PROFESSIONAL RESPONSIBILITY FIELD, CENTER FOR CONSTITUTIONAL RIGHTS v. BUSH
Case No. 06-cv-313 (S.D.N.Y.) (July 13, 2006)

Lawyers at the Center for Constitutional Rights and affiliated lawyers represent a number of foreign nationals detained at Guantanamo and considered "enemy combatants" by the United States government, [and] their next friends, primarily family members of the detainees. The NSA program of electronic eavesdropping raises serious ethical issues for these lawyers, who have both an ethical obligation to communicate with their clients and other individuals concerning these cases and an ethical obligation to ensure the confidentiality of those communications. The criteria announced by government officials for targets of the NSA eavesdropping program are so open-ended that they would include many, if not all, of those clients, family members and others these lawyers must contact. . . .

---

[14] We must note that two of this volume's authors were signatories on the brief.

A. The Fiduciary Obligation to Assure Confidentiality

Lawyers are fiduciaries of their clients. Lawyers' fiduciary obligations to their clients were originally recognized in the common law, and now they are codified in the rules of professional ethics. One of these fiduciary obligations requires lawyers to protect the confidentiality of their clients' information. This fiduciary obligation is recognized in three distinct doctrines of law: The lawyer's ethical duty of confidentiality; the evidentiary privilege for attorney-client communications; and the evidentiary privilege for attorney work-product. Analysis of these three doctrines demonstrates that the law has been robust in protecting the confidentiality of client information.

1. The Duty of Confidentiality

The first aspect of the lawyer's fiduciary obligation is the duty to ensure the confidentiality of information learned in the course of a representation. The confidentiality obligation is two-fold, consisting of both a prohibition and an affirmative duty. First, it prohibits the lawyer from disclosing confidential information about the client without client consent. . . . Second, the confidentiality obligation imposes on lawyers an affirmative duty to take steps to ensure the secrecy of client information. When communicating with clients or in pursuit of a client case, the lawyer must ensure that the communication is private, whether the communication is in person, on paper or electronic. No client matters are discussed in public locations, such as elevators or courthouse corridors, where they can be overheard. "A lawyer must act competently to safeguard information relating to the representation of a client against inadvertent or unauthorized disclosure. . . ." ABA MR 1.6, cmt. 16 (2005).

Client information must be kept away from prying eyes and ears. Client files must be kept secure. Lawyers must instruct and supervise their employees to preserve confidentiality. A lawyer must take reasonable steps so that law-office personnel properly handle confidential client information with care. . . .

2. Attorney Client Privilege

The rules of evidence recognize clients need to consult lawyers in confidence, and those rules provide virtually absolute bar on discovery of confidential lawyer-client communications that are for purpose of seeking or providing legal advice. To ensure that such communications will be covered by the privilege, the lawyer must make sure that only the lawyer and the client are privy to the communication. The attendance of a client's accountant [or child] at a meeting between the lawyer and client can destroy the privilege.

Similarly, written communications are treated with special care. All confidential client information must be acquired, stored, retrieved, and transmitted under systems that are reasonably designed and managed to maintain confidentiality, and therefore it is up to lawyers to take necessary affirmative steps to put those systems in place. Lawyers are also obliged to label written communications with an appropriate description. Copies are not sent to anyone whose knowledge of the information would waive the privilege. . . .

Electronic communications also must be protected to maintain the privilege. Telephone conversations are not conducted in public places or with individuals on the line who could break the privilege. Faxes are sent with appropriate identification of their privileged content. And bar associations have spent endless hours debating (and largely resolving) to what extent lawyers may employ e-mail and cell phones when communicating with clients consistent with maintaining the privilege.[15]

Finally, lawyers are bound to resist — to the greatest extent legally permissible — the attempts by others to access privileged information. Lawyers are required to refuse to testify, to argue that their refusal is consistent with the privilege and, if the lawyer is subject to an adverse decision on the issue, to seek if at all possible appellate review, including suffering a possible contempt citation to force a further adjudication of the privilege claim.

3. The Attorney Work Product Privilege

Evidence law also protects the confidentiality of client information through the attorney work product privilege. This doctrine applies to all work undertaken by or at the direction and control of the lawyer either in anticipation of or in actual litigation, as these lawyers here are so engaged. . . . The work product privilege is intended to preserve a zone of privacy in which a lawyer or other representatives of a party can prepare and develop legal theories and strategy "with an eye toward litigation," free from intrusion by their adversaries. *Hickman v. Taylor*, 329 U.S. 495, 510-511 (1947).

But the privilege is only available, and the ability to prevent the review of the lawyer's work product will only succeed, if, again, the lawyer takes the precautions to ensure the confidentiality of the work product. . . . This requires the lawyer to conduct these activities in a careful manner. No one participates who is not essential to the task. All who participate are required to maintain confidentiality.

B. The Public Policy Foundation

Why do the legal profession and courts go to such great lengths to maintain confidentiality and the privileges? Because courts have determined that " 'full and frank communication between attorneys and their clients . . . promote[s] the] broader public interests in the observance of law and the administration of justice.' " *Swidler & Berlin v. United States*, 524 U.S. 399, 403 (1998) (quoting *Upjohn Co. v. United States*, 449 U.S. 383, 389, 101 S. Ct. 677, 682, 66 L. Ed. 2d 584 (1981)). We must encourage our clients to trust us and share their innermost secrets with us. Otherwise [i]f we do not know what our clients did or what they plan to do, we cannot provide them with the legal advice they require. . . .

For this reason, a lawyer who knows that his or her conversations are subject to surveillance, even if the surveillance were by someone other than an adversary, has no choice. "Given the objectives of the attorney-client

---

[15] [We will look at this debate in Problem 6. Eds.]

privilege, a communication must be made in circumstances reasonably indicating that it will be learned only by the lawyer, client, or another privileged person. The circumstances must indicate that the communicating persons reasonably believed that the communication would be confidential." Restatement (Third) of the Law Governing Lawyers § 71 (2000). . . .

For example, if a lawyer thinks there might be a listening device in a room, the lawyer should meet with the client elsewhere. If telephone calls are being monitored, the lawyer should not use the telephone. If the lawyer has reason to believe that emails are being reviewed or mail read by persons other than the client, the lawyer must find an alternative confidential means of communication. Even if the client is at some distance, the lawyer must take appropriate precautions and, if necessary, only communicate face-to-face.

What is described here is not simply a best practice, one that is recommended if at all possible. Rather it is an obligation. Lawyers have an uncompromising duty to be competent. Model Rules of Prof'l Conduct R. 1.1 (2005). This includes a duty to . . . assure the client that the fact-gathering process remains confidential and protected from inadvertent disclosure or waiver. The lawyer must protect not only information gathered but the sources of the information, *i.e.* witnesses the lawyer has interviewed or sources the lawyer has consulted.

Lawyers also have a duty to communicate with their clients. Model Rules of Prof'l Conduct R. 1.4 (2005). Without such communication the lawyer cannot know the client's lawful goals and concerns, nor can the client learn the results of the lawyer's diligent work and the advice the lawyer must provide the client. And, again, the two-way communication process must be kept confidential or the lawyer will be in breach of the duty of confidentiality owed to the client.

C. The Effect of Surveillance Here

It is easy to understand how a threat of surveillance could compromise and undermine the ability to represent the client in a profound way when the lawyer resides near next friends, witnesses and others. Avoiding telephone calls and e-mail exchange would force all communications — not just those with the client — to be carefully planned and scheduled with follow-up communication and spur of the moment inspiration or inquiry giving way to an obligation to engage in the stilted and time-consuming task of rescheduling yet another meeting. Cutting off electronic communication in this scenario does not just place a burden on the lawyer-client relationship[;] it erodes the relationship in a fundamental way.

This is particularly so given the fact that we live in a world where otherwise instantaneous conversations — with clients not incarcerated, witnesses and other sources — on a whim or a breakthrough are the norm. When lawyers are forced to deviate from that norm, the result is a dramatically unbalanced playing field. An adversary with all the power and resources of the government is free, without any fear of surveillance, to take advantage of every form of modern electronic communication — telephone, facsimile, e-mail and the internet. . . .

If the situation is virtually impossible when the individuals with whom the lawyer must communicate are geographically close and easily accessible so that the lawyer has the capability to work around the surveillance, it is truly impossible to conjure how much more difficult it would be for a lawyer, required by a real threat of surveillance, to avoid traditional methods in dealing with clients and their next friends, potential witnesses and other sources of information who reside across the seas. Just the act of making appointments, if subject to surveillance, invades the attorney-work product privilege, reveals confidential information and perhaps, in and of itself, discloses attorney-client privileged information as well. A fortiari, no substantive conversation can take place if it is possibly subject to surveillance. . . .

The burden this places on the lawyer-client relationship is without precedent and in effect destroys the relationship entirely. Government surveillance of electronic communications [means that these lawyers] cannot do their job and their clients cannot have effective representation when 6,000 miles, huge expense and two or more airplane flights, a train and a taxicab ride, separate the lawyer from his or her clients and others who must be contacted. Simply posing the required follow-up question becomes an expensive multi-week ordeal. . . . And heaven forefend that the contacted individual — like every other individual in the history of the modern world — forgets to tell the lawyer something and needs to communicate yet again.

SUPPLEMENTAL READINGS

1. *Suburban Sew'n Sweep, Inc. v. Swiss-Bernina, Inc.*, 91 F.R.D. 254 (N.D. Ill. 1981). Plaintiff in this case obtained documents that defendants had discarded in a trash dumpster. All parties agreed that the documents were covered by the attorney-client privilege *and* that the defendants intended that they remain confidential. Nonetheless, using analogies to Fourth Amendment abandoned property cases and disclosure in the presence of bystanders or eavesdroppers, the court permitted the evidence.

2. *Commonwealth v. Chmiel*, 889 A.2d 501 (Pa. 2005) held that the fee arrangement between a client and attorney is not privileged. The case involved a murder trial in which the prosecutor attempted to prove that part of the motivation for the murder was the defendant's need for money to pay a prior attorney's fee. The Supreme Court of Pennsylvania rejected defendant's arguments that his attorney-client privilege had been violated when his former attorney testified about their fee arrangement. See also *In re Nassau County Grand Jury Subpoena Duces Tecum*, 4 N.Y.3d 665 (2005), which also held that identity and fees were not protected by the attorney-client privilege.

3. Clark D. Cunningham, *How to Explain Confidentiality?*, 9 Clinical L. Rev. 579 (2003), Professor Cunningham's article is best captured in this quote from the article:

One of the most critical, yet inadequately explored, issues in lawyer client communication is the problem of explaining confidentiality, especially exceptions which permit or require the lawyer to disclose confidential information. Failure to disclose these exceptions results in misrepresentation to the client (e.g. "everything you tell me is confidential"), yet an accurate and complete explanation of the exceptions may inhibit the very trust that the right of confidentiality is intended to create. This article reports on the use of simulated interviews in the classroom to model an empirical approach to analyzing this problem that can be applied to law school clinics.

4. John S. Dzienkowski & Robert J. Peroni, *Multidisciplinary Practice and the American Legal Profession: A Market Approach to Regulating the Delivery of Legal Services in the Twenty-first Century*, 69 Fordham L. Rev. 83 (2000), advocates for the value of MDPs.

5. John Burkoff, *Criminal Defense Ethics: Law and Liability* (September 2005 edition), Chapter 5, and especially section 5.13, contains an extensive review of case law and secondary opinions on the propriety of revealing a client's whereabouts, and the reasoning of some courts in dealing with the issue on a case-by-case basis.

6. *In re Marriage of Decker*, 204 Ill. App. 3d 566, 562 N.E.2d 1000 (1990). In a domestic relations case, the husband's attorney was properly held in contempt for refusing to obey the trial court's order that she disclose her client's whereabouts and his intent to abscond with his child.

7. *In re Burns*, 536 N.E.2d 1206 (Ohio 1988), and *Cesena v. DuPage County*, 582 N.E.2d 177 (Ill. 1991), are two recent cases which address the issue of the confidentiality of a client's identity when it would affect that client's status in criminal matters.

8. For a lengthy and thorough analysis of the *Nackson* and *Maguigan* cases and an attorney's duty to inform the courts as to a fugitive client's whereabouts, see Shelly Hillyer, *The Attorney-Client Privilege, Ethical Rules of Confidentiality and Other Arguments Bearing on Disclosure of a Fugitive Client's Whereabouts*, 68 Temple L. Rev. 307 (Spring 1995).

9. For an analysis of a case that required an attorney to disclose information on IRS Form 8300 as to one client but not as to a second, see Ronald K. Vaske, *Uncertain Attorney-Client Privilege Provides No Assurance: The Form 8300 Dilemma in* United States v. Sindel, 29 Creighton L. Rev. 1323 (April 1996). The court conducted an *in camera* hearing and held that the attorney could not provide the information regarding "Mrs. Jane Doe" without disclosing the subject matter of confidential client communications, and therefore the attorney had to keep the information secret. On the other hand, the same was not true of her husband. Since the basis of the court's distinction between the two clients was never disclosed on the record, Vaske questions whether the decision provides any guidance to other attorneys faced with the same situation. Another question, of course, is just how secret was the wife's information if the attorney had to disclose her husband's identity to the authorities.

PROBLEM 6

Cell phones, e-mail, faxes and voicemail, websites with chat rooms and hypertext links, integrated work servers, and wireless Internet. What do these common technological advances have to do with practicing law? Plenty, when you consider that the majority of lawyers utilize most, if not all, of these technologies in their practices. Not only do all have an effect on the way we practice law, they can also have a significant effect on the confidentiality and security of our communications with our clients. When you toss in mobile scanners, computer-to-computer faxing, cellular voice mail, even the latest in online courier services, confidentiality and security issues become even more important.

This problem discusses attorney-client relations — especially confidentiality and privilege issues — when viewed through the prism of modern technology. This is one area where even the law is moving quickly. By the time you read this — a minimum of months, as we move from writing to printing to publishing — things will have changed already.

Technology + Confidentiality = Trouble

I. Frank Tecchi is a newly-minted partner who's considered a rising star by his law firm. Tecchi grew up in the electronic age, and he loves it. He's always the first in his firm to have the latest in cellular technology, "smart phones" and other hand-held computers, cordless and infrared interfaces, and Wi-Fi equipment. Many of his clients are young start-ups and dot.coms whose executives feel the same way. It's not surprising, then, that many of Frank's communications with his clients occur by cell phone and portable e-mail. As often as not, documents are transmitted by computer-to-computer facsimiles direct from his firm's work server, or even downloaded from a secure area on Frank's state-of-the-art website.

QUESTIONS

1. Tecchi has given little thought to the possible dangers of these communications, but the issue hasn't escaped the notice of the firm's managing partner, Jeanette Glanville. Glanville, worried about breaches of confidentiality, asks Tecchi to evaluate three issues:

- Must the firm's e-mails to its clients be encrypted to ensure confidentiality? What about e-mails from a PDA, BlackBerry, or smart phone? Or from a coffee shop with an unsecured wireless connection?

- Are cellular phone transmissions confidential, or does the ease with which they can be intercepted make them open to all who may be listening?

- The website's "clients only" area requires each client to have an individual "username" and password, but is that sufficient security to allow clients to download information left for them by Tecchi, and to ensure that no client can access another client's area?

Glanville makes it clear that she is concerned about both ethical requirements and possible waiver of the attorney-client privilege, as well as potential malpractice liability. Evaluate Tecchi's communications in light of Glanville's concerns.

II. Susan Browning and her client were exchanging drafts of a contract. They decided to send opposing counsel Russ Bluestone the latest draft of their proposed contract by e-mail. When Bluestone opened the proposed contract, he turned on a feature of the word processing software that displayed the text of all "embedded data," including previous drafts exchanged between Browning and her client, and all of the comments that Browning and her client exchanged, some of which dealt with their strategy in redrafting the contract.

QUESTIONS

1. May Bluestone read the edits and comments in the document? *Must* he? What other obligations, if any, does he have?

2. What difference would it make if Bluestone had received the document with the edits, "tracked changes," and comments already displayed in the text without him having to do anything other than open the document?

3. If Browning realizes her mistake later the same day and calls Bluestone to ask him to delete the document without looking at the embedded data, does that change Bluestone's obligations? How?

4. What if Bluestone had received a fax transmission from Browning discussing strategy that was clearly directed to her client, but was mistakenly sent to Bluestone's office? Should he read it? Why (or why not)?

5. What difference would it make, if any, if the fax transmission was accompanied by a cover sheet that stated, at the bottom:

CONFIDENTIAL!

THE INFORMATION CONTAINED IN THIS FACSIMILE TRANSMISSION IS CONFIDENTIAL, AND MAY ALSO CONTAIN PRIVILEGED ATTORNEY-CLIENT OR WORK PRODUCT INFORMATION, AS WELL AS CLIENT CONFIDENCES AND SECRETS. IF YOU ARE NOT THE INTENDED RECIPIENT, OR AUTHORIZED TO RECEIVE IT FOR THE ADDRESSEE, DO NOT READ, COPY, DISTRIBUTE, OR USE IT. IF YOU HAVE RECEIVED THIS FACSIMILE IN ERROR, PLEASE NOTIFY US BY TELEPHONE, AND RETURN THE FACSIMILE BY MAIL. WE WILL GLADLY REIMBURSE YOU FOR ANY COSTS YOU INCUR. OUR PHONE, FAX NUMBER, AND ADDRESS ARE ALL SET FORTH ABOVE. THANK YOU.

READINGS

1. How Safe Is E-Mail? The explosion in the use of e-mail came late to the legal profession. Once it came, it was soon followed by a spate of ethics opinions about whether e-mail communications with clients were sufficiently secure to be deemed confidential. Most of the early opinions — those in 1994 through 1996 — determined they were not.

Iowa's Board of Professional Responsibility made this call twice in the space of a few months.[1] First, Iowa Opinion 95-30 concluded that in order for e-mails containing "sensitive material" to meet the ethical standard of confidentiality, they must be encrypted, or coded in a special way like wartime messages, to prevent anyone but the intended recipient from reading them. Opinion 95-30, which also covered webpages and Internet advertising, received a great deal of publicity, enough so that a few months later, the Board reconsidered its position. But its second opinion, 96-1, adhered to the idea that e-mails with sensitive material were not sufficiently secure. This opinion offered more alternatives: Get the client's consent to the communication, or in the alternative, encrypt, create a password firewall, or otherwise ensure security. Other states with early opinions, including Colorado and North and South Carolina, also concluded that encryption was necessary.

Many experts in "cyberlaw" disagreed, arguing that e-mail was no less secure than the U.S. mail or overnight couriers (all of which reserve the right to open packages sent through their services). Others pointed out that the federal Electronic Communications Privacy Act (ECPA) made it a felony to intercept an e-mail, just like it is for "snail mail," and argued that it requires no technological know-how to take a letter out of a mailbox or mailroom, a much easier task than stealing an e-mail.

By 1997, the tide had turned in favor of the confidentiality of e-mails. A few states, including Illinois and New Jersey, declined to require encryption, and then South Carolina and Iowa[2] reversed themselves. To explain the trend, we reprint an excerpt from the South Carolina opinion here.

SOUTH CAROLINA ADVISORY ETHICS OPINION 97-08
(June 1997)

Facts: The South Carolina Bar Technology Committee has requested that Advisory Opinion 94-27 be re-examined in light of the current state of technology.

Questions: May confidential client communications be transmitted via electronic mail (e-mail)?

Summary: There exists a reasonable expectation of privacy when sending confidential information through electronic mail (whether direct link, commercial service, or Internet). Use of electronic mail will not affect the confidentiality of client communications under South Carolina Rule of Professional Conduct 1.6.

Opinion: The duty to maintain client confidences under Rule 1.6 implies the duty to use methods of communication that provide reasonable assurance that information will be and remain confidential. This duty was implicated in Advisory Opinion 94-27, when this Committee stated:

> It is the opinion of this committee that unless certainty can be obtained regarding the confidentiality of communications via electronic media, that representation of a client, or communication with

---

[1] Iowa Opinions 95-30 (May 16, 1996) and 96-1 (August 29, 1996).

[2] Iowa Opinion 97-01 (September 18, 1997).

a client, via electronic media, may violate Rule 1.6, absent an express waiver by the client.

This opinion is correct in that an attorney must have some certainty or reasonable expectation that a means of communication will remain confidential. Since Opinion 94-27 was issued, the use of e-mail has become commonplace, and there now exists a reasonable level of "certainty" and expectation that such communications may be regarded as confidential, created by improvements in technology and changes in the law.

There are essentially three means by which e-mail is transmitted by computer: Private networks, semi-private networks, and the Internet.

. . . .

In addressing the issue of whether information transmitted via e-mail through any of the above-described networks is confidential, it is helpful to examine the confidentiality of other media used in client communications. It is beyond argument that confidential communications may be transmitted via land-based telephone, United States Mail, private carrier, express mail, and even facsimile. . . .

The confidentiality of e-mail communications should not be compromised through the use of private networks. A law firm's network transmitting information through a private, land-based telephone line to a client's private network does not risk interception or any other waiver of the confidence any more than a telephone call or facsimile transmission would.

Likewise, e-mail transmissions via commercial networks or the Internet maintain confidentiality. While there exists a potential for communications to be intercepted, albeit illegally, from a commercial network mailbox or an Internet "router," the Committee does not believe such a potential makes an expectation of privacy unreasonable. The same potential exists for the illegal interception of regular mail. . . .

[A] finding of confidentiality and privilege of such communications should not end the analysis. An attorney owes a client a duty of reasonable care in keeping information confidential. There exists information that a prudent attorney would be hesitant to discuss by facsimile, telephone, or regular mail. A lawyer should discuss with a client such options as encryption in order to safeguard against even inadvertent disclosure of sensitive or privileged information when using e-mail.

NOTES

Since these opinions, technology has advanced considerably — high-speed e-mail and Internet access have become the norm, and wireless connections are widespread. It is unclear whether the majority view accepting e-mail confidentiality would be sustained if ethics committees considered such issues as e-mails from handhelds and BlackBerrys, or from unsecured coffee shop connections.

2. E-Mails and Malpractice. As we have pointed out before, ethical violations and malpractice are far from identical, and while the existence of the former may be some evidence of the latter, an ethical violation — even where it occurs — is insufficient in and of itself to prove malpractice. Here, however, the question seems to be the reverse: Can a malpractice action be maintained even where the attorney has acted entirely ethically? Another, perhaps more central question is why the authors of ethics opinions seem nervous enough to add caveats.

Perhaps the explanation lies with the increasing use of e-mail attachments. Attachments can be used to send drafts of sensitive documents or briefs, or memos detailing case strategy. Nevertheless, the Attorneys' Liability Assurance Society, or ALAS, which insures many larger firms, has taken the position that attorneys need not encrypt e-mail in order for their clients to have an expectation of privacy. No communication is perfect, argues William Freivogel, one of ALAS's principal spokespersons. Even in face-to-face communications, "many people read lips," he told Wendy R. Leibowitz of the *National Law Journal* in 1997.

3. Telephone Tag. If e-mails are deemed safe, even though few of us understand how they get from the sender to the recipient, why are phone calls seen by many as a more difficult issue? The answer has to do with both law and technology — and ultimately, the reasonable expectations of the participants in the phone call. Telephones provide an excellent example of how changing technology results in changes in reasonable expectations, as the following excerpted article, by a law professor who has developed an expertise in ethics and technology, explains.

DAVID HRICIK, LAWYERS WORRY TOO MUCH ABOUT TRANSMITTING CLIENT CONFIDENCES BY INTERNET E-MAIL
11 Georgetown Journal of Legal Ethics 459 (1998)[3]

The legal protections afforded land-based phone calls are strong. Such calls are subject to Fourth Amendment protection against unreasonable search and seizure. In addition, the Federal Wiretap Act protects land-based telephone calls, making interception of an oral phone call a crime. Finally, federal law provides a civil damage remedy for any person whose oral communication is intercepted, disclosed, or intentionally used in violation of federal law, and illegally intercepted oral communications may not be admitted as evidence even if they are not privileged.

Despite the actual risk of misdirection or interception, discussion of client confidences during land-based telephone calls does not violate the duty of confidentiality — even though phones are easily tapped. The required expectation of confidentiality need *not* be absolute. It only needs to be a *reasonable* expectation. . . .

Confidentiality and Cordless Telephone Calls

The objective facts regarding the ease with which cordless phone calls (not cellular phones — *cordless* phones) may be intercepted vary dramatically from

---

[3] Copyright © 1998 by David Hricik. Reprinted by permission.

those underlying land-based phone calls; the current legal rules governing interception do not.

As a factual matter, the broadcast of a cordless telephone call can far more readily be intentionally intercepted or inadvertently overheard than a land-based call. "Inadvertent interceptions have occurred frequently with cordless phones, which transmit on a normal FM frequency within radio range. Using a cordless phone is like operating a radio station and broadcasting your message. Anyone within range could receive the communication."

. . . Merely because people know that the cordless broadcast might be intercepted does not mean they do not expect the land-line based transmission of their call to be protected. The critical issue, then, is whether the fact that a cordless phone *broadcasts* the conversation over FM radio frequencies destroys any objective expectation of confidentiality.

The legal protection afforded to the broadcast portion of a cordless phone call has, since 1994, been identical to a land-based phone. [T]he 1994 amendments to ECPA § 2512(A) protect cordless telephone broadcasts as a matter of federal law in the same manner as land-based telephone calls. However, the criminalization of interception "does not, of course, make it technologically more difficult for someone to intercept" or inadvertently receive them. Thus, although it is now illegal to intercept cordless broadcasts, it is still more common for inadvertent interception to occur, and such unintended interception can occur through devices which are legal and common for the general public to own — namely, other cordless phones, FM radios, and baby monitors.

Consequently, whether a lawyer should use a cordless phone to discuss confidential information — even though privilege is almost certainly not waived and any interception or subsequent disclosure or use of the message would be unlawful — probably depends on whether the disclosure of the transmitted information would likely be detrimental to a client. . . .

Confidentiality and Cellular Telephone Communications

The interception on a police scanner of a call between House Speaker Newt Gringrich and others made it known to all that cellular phone broadcasts can be intercepted. However, in the three years preceding 1997, the Federal Communications Commission (FCC) received a total of five complaints of invasions of cellular privacy.

Despite their wide-spread use, cellular phones have been legal to use in the United States only since 1982. Like cordless phones, cellular phones *broadcast* conversations over the airwaves to receiving stations which then transmit the calls over land-based phone lines. . . .

While cordless phones may still be intercepted or inadvertently overheard through common household appliances, the "same is not true for cellular phones, however. While they use part of the spectrum for transmission, they do not transmit within a range or frequency capable of inadvertent interception by commercial users of the air waves or listeners." Since April 1994, it has been illegal to market the scanners that can intercept cellular communications in the United States. . . .

Nonetheless, it is still lawful to own a scanner sold before 1994, and other scanners can be purchased by the general public that can be modified to monitor cellular phone frequencies by someone with some particular skills, even though it is illegal to do so. . . . Further, it is not unusual for someone using a cellular phone to overhear portions of another party's cellular phone call (although the newer digital cellular phones appear to lessen that likelihood). In addition, the *range* of a cellular broadcast is generally much greater than the range of a typical cordless phone. . . .

Sensitive communication over a cellular phone, still, may be overheard. While most lawyer-client conversations could safely take place on a cellular phone, because interception could cause no harm, some information may be so sensitive that it should not be transmitted by cellular phone. Consequently, disclosure of identifiable confidential information that would likely be detrimental to the client should be avoided during cellular phone calls, absent client consent or the use of technology that is particularly difficult to intercept.

NOTES

If both cellular and cordless phone communications are now protected by both state and federal law, why does Professor Hricik hedge in his conclusions about how freely lawyers and their clients may speak on these phones? Perhaps it's because of the rapidly changing technology. For instance, although calls made from digital cell phones are supposed to be far more difficult to intercept than analog calls, a method of changing a flip phone into a digital receiver was posted on the Internet. Office voice mail accessed by cell phone can be overheard, and cellular voice mail is doubly vulnerable. As security and "hacker" technologies leapfrog past each other, it's understandable why commentators are cautious.

The biggest issue may not be ethics-by-the-book or even malpractice. Until 1997, ALAS warned that any radio-transmitted phone calls except relatively safe digital calls were dangerous enough to raise malpractice concerns. By the Spring of 1997, in light of the new federal and state protections, including criminal penalties for interception, ALAS had changed its position, adopting the view that no loss of privilege or malpractice claim would occur by using any of these phones.[4]

As a major insurer, of course, ALAS itself has an interest in having both e-mail and radio-transmitted communications immune from being a source of malpractice claims. But the caution expressed by Hricik, like the caveats expressed at the end of the ABA's e-mail opinion, may have their greatest significance in simple practical terms: When an attorney *can* be overheard, legally or illegally, talking on a cell phone or in a restaurant or elevator, that lawyer had better be careful what's said. The walls have ears; so do the airwaves.

4. The Problem with Websites. The author of the following article is Senior Vice President of the Texas Lawyers' Insurance Exchange. The article

---

[4] *See* William Freivogel, *Cellular and Cordless Telephones, Privilege, Confidentiality and Liability,* VIII ALAS Loss Prevention Journal, (1997).

was written from the perspective of malpractice issues in Texas, but it is applicable elsewhere — a valuable treatment of a wide variety of issues relating to attorney websites.

JETT HANNA, ATTORNEY LIABILITY FOR INTERNET RELATED ACTIVITY: AN EARLY ANALYSIS
tlie.org / intermal / internet.htm, reprinted in Spring 2000 ABA Legal Malpractice Conference Program Materials (New York, Apr. 6-7, 2000)[5]

Current Online Legal Services

There is a long history of animosity between "self-help" publishers and the organized bar. With suits against Quicken Family Lawyer and Nolo Press for software packages, that animosity continued.

A number of form and kit services are now operating on the web, such as Nolo Press at *www.nolo.com* and US Legal Forms at *www.uslegalforms.com*. Nolo's site simply functions as an order point, while US Legal Forms actually lets you download forms immediately. What is truly an innovation is a number of sites now offering kits and forms that are clearly lawyers or law firms. . . .

The home page of Richard S. Granat, a Maryland attorney, at *www.granat.com*, illustrates one of the primary innovations in marketing that the Internet makes possible. On the front page, there is a link that says "self help divorce form kits." That link takes you to a listing of divorce kits available in not only Maryland, but other states as well, from *www.divorcelawinfo.com*, which Granat's home page discloses is an "affiliated site." Granat's home page also states that the only legal services his firm performs is to assist pro se parties. Document drafting services are available if the consumer (client?) cannot fill out the forms in the kits offered. Email and phone consultations are available at a fixed rate of $30 per phone call. For more complicated matters, the Granat home page states that a referral will be made to another attorney. Mediation services can also be arranged.

        . . . .

LegalAdviceLine, at *www.legaladviceline.com*, plans to offer certain kinds of legal documents in all 50 states, as they intend to employ associate attorneys in every state. In Maryland, they already offer divorce, estate planning, guardianship, child support, custody, name change, adoption and power of attorney document generation online for immediate downloading. The service is combined with a $30 per phone call consultation option. As of this writing, it appears that *www.mylawyer.com* tends to offer similar services, and is looking for persons interested in being "telephone attorneys." . . .

[T]he Atlanta law firm of Alston & Bird has moved their database systems to a web based system that allows for easier programming of database driven applications. The firm has also created Internet based extranet systems that allow them to exchange documents with clients easily — client centered extranets. One of the partners at the firm describes the system as "a shared filing cabinet." It is not hard to imagine how having a secure system

---

connecting with repeat clients could lead to great efficiencies in providing legal services.

It is unlikely that all legal services will be provided on the Internet in the near future, but certainly significant aspects of law practice can be transferred to the web or other software efficiently. The web can be your paralegal. It is very easy to create a web site that takes information from a client and then generates a document utilizing the client's responses. Imagine clients simply logging on to your website, answering the questionnaire you used to have to fill out with them during an appointment, and generating legal documents for them instantly. . . .

Liability for Kits and Forms

There is no law directly on point in Texas regarding liability for "kits" or "forms" of which I am aware. In the past, kits and forms were generally printed as books. In all cases found in Texas, there has been no finding of liability for providing a defective book to someone.

The new cyberworld of kits and forms may lead to different results, however. The way in which Texas has defined legal services with regard to publications indicates that failure to warn someone that a kit or form is not a substitute for representation by an attorney could lead to liability. . . .

If a lawyer providing a kit or form with instructions is rendering legal advice, do all of the characteristics of an attorney client relationship attach to the situation? That would certainly appear [to be] the case. . . . A "client" who has chosen a kit may not be choosing the right kit, and thus providing the kit or form may not be part of "competent and diligent" representation. . . . The possibility of imposition of liability on an attorney for a defective kit or form that is either prepared by or recommended by the attorney thus seems high.

Mistakes by the Client

Clients will make mistakes when filling out forms or providing information to attorneys. When they do, they may claim that the attorney should have investigated the situation further and realized the client's mistake.

If clients are filling out forms to create automated legal documents, review of the document by an attorney or paralegal may avoid problems. For example, legal descriptions on deeds might be something that should be reviewed by a professional. Other types of information that are simply misspelled or omitted, however, are probably going to be a problem regardless of whether the information is gathered automatically or not. It is possible to force a web page user to respond to a particular question, but situations in which a blank answer is acceptable or where multiple responses might be appropriate could be overlooked.

. . . .

Confidentiality

One of the basic foundations of the attorney client relationship is confidentiality. Recent events have demonstrated that some of the best web sites have had significant security problems. In one case, a hacker appears to have stolen a large list of credit cards from an online merchant and distributed them to a large number of people. . . .

Security must be analyzed on several levels. Secure transmission for the client to the attorney's web server is required. Secure transmission of the legal document is required. Any information about the client that remains on the attorney's web server or on the attorney's computer system needs to be secure from hacking. While the ABA opinion on e-mail encryption may be a basis for arguing that client interactions with a secure web site are entitled to similar presumptions of privacy, the security issues for a web site and secure storage of client information are more complex than those of e-mail security.

Conflicts of Interest

Automated generation of legal documents creates some significant conflict of interest questions. . . . Consider the following scenario: Husband and wife decide to generate wills online, each working separately with the same automated system. The husband leaves his share to his girlfriend, while the unsuspecting wife leaves her share to her husband. . . .

Conclusion

The Internet will definitely give attorneys new ways to practice their profession. When lawyers utilize the Internet, it is critical that attorneys review basic ethical rules and malpractice avoidance procedures, and consider what new questions may surface. Undoubtedly new ethical rules and opinions will be issued and malpractice cases will suggest additional cautions for attorneys to consider. Even lawyers who do not utilize the Internet themselves may have clients, partners, associates or employees who use the Internet to perform their duties, and should stay abreast of the changing nature of ethical and malpractice issues associated with Internet use.

NOTES

Note the concern that underlines much of Hanna's discussion — the fine line between providing information and giving advice, an issue we've already examined in Problem 3. Another issue familiar from Problem 3 is the importance of defining the scope of representation. Hanna makes a significant point in this regard: Texas specifically forbids lawyers from making the scope of representation so narrow as to preclude competent representation. Think about how this might affect some of the issues, such as ghost-writing pleadings, that we discussed in Problem 3.

5. A Few More Internet Issues. Hanna's article covers a lot of territory, but by no means exhausts all the ethical or malpractice issues of cyberspace. Consider these:

Networks, Hard Drives, and Work Servers. Many law firms, even small ones, have computer networks, and DSL and wireless connections, which are direct portals to the Internet. Many networks operate in a way that requires the computers to remain on, and the networks open. This means that remote access to a law firm's computer network is often available around the clock.

This access, of course, is extremely desirable. It enables lawyers to "tele-commute," working from home while using files located at the office — in the firm's computer system. It allows them to draft emergency pleadings to be filed in New York while they are in trial in Texas, to communicate with their branch offices in Anchorage and Salt Lake City from a skybox at Giants Stadium, and to send files to their clients all across the country while sitting in an airport lounge in Philadelphia. But with access comes risk. The fact that ethics opinions are moving in the direction of viewing more new technology as "ethical" does not inoculate a law firm from malpractice if its security systems fail.

While firewalls and passwords generally protect law firm work servers, the non-law firm portals at airports, hotels, and coffee shops may be far less secure. Computer hackers still seem to have too easy a time breaking through many firewalls, breaking down passwords, and accessing computer networks. Once the computer hard drive or network server is accessed, confidential client information is jeopardized. Even files that have been deleted, including those that have been emptied from the "recycle bin," may be recoverable. They will still exist on the hard disk if they are located on a part of the disk that has not actually been overwritten by another file.[6]

As you can imagine, law firms have begun to store and backup files electronically. After Hurricane Katrina, most of the country became aware of how easily both primary and back-up data can be lost if they are stored in the same location so off-site legal storage companies are doing a booming business providing electronic storage in addition to keeping physical files.

Cookies. Most people know by now that when talking cyberspeak, "cookies" doesn't refer to Oreos or chocolate chip, but to the little text files placed on your computer when you access a new web site. These files help speed up access time and can be used to identify you (or, more accurately, your computer) when you re-access the site at a later date. But in the wrong hands, your hard drive could be used to trace where your computer has traveled on the net. Depending on the travel, this could result in the discovery of confidential information.

Fewer people are aware of the claim that many websites keep "surveillance cookies," or cookies that archive private information about their visitors. A Texas lawsuit filed early in 2000 against Yahoo! makes this contention. If these claims are true, "surveillance cookies" could further endanger the ability of lawyers to use the net to garner confidential information or do confidential research free of any privacy concerns.

Legal Briefing Services. These concerns may be of particular significance for those lawyers and (mostly small) firms who have taken to using research

---

[6] In addition to hackers, hard disks can become the focus of discovery battles. In that arena, there is a reasonable argument to be made that, like garbage, a deleted file has been abandoned, and if the law firm does not do the equivalent of "shredding," the file is still subject to discovery. This creates the possibility that opposing counsel could be permitted to bring in a computer expert to attempt to recover these files.

and briefing services to alleviate some of their workload. This work is usually done by licensed attorneys, though whether the lawyers are admitted to practice in the particular state where the work will be used is open to serious question. More significantly, these services, including research, memoranda, and even briefs ready for filing with a court, don't consider either the attorney who hires them or the end-user — the attorney's client — to be their own client. Accordingly, they generally do not perform conflict of interest checks. At least theoretically, these briefing services could be writing the papers filed on both sides of the same case.

Websites and Disclaimers. Law firm websites often contain disclaimers that the information contained there is not intended as legal advice, and does not result in the formation of an attorney-client relationship. But just saying this doesn't necessarily make it so. First, in order to be effective, the disclaimers have to be both complete and accurate. Second, if they are placed anywhere other than on the home page, a visitor may not see the disclaimer until after a fair amount of site exploration. Third, once the visitor does encounter the disclaimer, the guest should at least be required to "click" on a button accepting the disclaimer before proceeding. Fourth, disclaimers that state, for example, that the firm is not giving legal advice are unlikely to override the actual receipt of legal advice. And finally, if the website provides hypertext links to other locations over which it has no control, inaccuracies at those linked sites may be attributable to the law firm. In other words, disclaimers may say whatever they say, but the true test will be what information was imparted to a prospective client, under what circumstances, and with what expectations.

Chat Rooms and Solicitation. Of course, the Internet doesn't only provide opportunities for law firm websites, but for a myriad of consumer-based and -run sites. Sites for victims of mass torts, plane crashes, or defective products are venues for opportunistic lawyers to lurk and troll in real-time chat rooms for new clients. We discuss this further in Problem 30 on solicitation. As we await further developments, the California bar has weighed in with an ethics opinion that although participating in a chat room does not necessarily constitute solicitation, it may run afoul of the rules that prevent solicitation "transmitted in any manner which involves intrusion, coercion, duress, compulsion, intimidation, threats, or vexatious or harassing conduct," or "which is delivered to a potential client whom the member knows or should reasonably know is in such a physical, emotional, or mental state that he or she would not be expected to exercise reasonable judgment. . . ."[7] Seller beware.

6. "Metadata," Embedded Data, and Two New York State Opinions. The term "metadata," as used by "techies," generally means proprietary information not intended ever to be seen by the software's "end-user," here the law firm. As used by lawyers and ethics opinions to describe legal documents, however, the term has been given a much broader use — any hidden data from previous edits of a brief or other document, comments and drafting notes that may not be part of the final document itself, or templates that could be from the same or another case. When it comes to confidentiality,

---

[7] California Formal Opinion Number 2004-166 (2004).

the implications from transmitting and reviewing this hidden or embedded data are huge.

The New York State Bar Association was in the vanguard of developing ethics opinions about "metadata." First, in late 2001, Opinion 749 (12/14/01) determined that information "that the sender has not intentionally made available" to others could not ethically be examined by the receiving lawyer. The opinion makes it clear that any disclosure of metadata is "unknowing and unwilling, rather than inadvertent or careless," and noted:

> In the "inadvertent" and "unauthorized" disclosure decisions, the public policy interest in encouraging more careful conduct had to be balanced against the public policy in favor of confidentiality. No such balance need be struck here because it is a deliberate act by the receiving lawyer, not carelessness on the part of the sending lawyer, that would lead to the disclosure of client confidences and secrets.

Then, in late 2004, N.Y.S. Bar Assoc. Opinion 782 (12/8/04) looked again at the ethical requirements for the lawyer *sending* the hidden data. This time using the term "metadata," the ethics body stated:

> When a lawyer sends a document by e-mail, as with any other type of communication, a lawyer must exercise reasonable care to ensure that he or she does not inadvertently disclose his or her client's confidential information. What constitutes reasonable care will vary with the circumstances, including the subject matter of the document, whether the document was based on a "template" used in another matter for another client, whether there have been multiple drafts of the document with comments from multiple sources, whether the client has commented on the document, and the identity of the intended recipients of the document. Reasonable care may, in some circumstances, call for the lawyer to stay abreast of technological advances and the potential risks in transmission. . . .

While this later opinion reiterated that "lawyer-recipients also have an obligation not to exploit an inadvertent or unauthorized transmission of client confidences or secrets," this more recent opinion seems to raise the bar for the sending lawyer. Opinion 782 thus seems somewhat at odds with Opinion 749 as to the basis for the receiving lawyer's unethical conduct. Nevertheless, the later opinion cites the earlier one with approval. Thus, at least in New York, both the receiving and the sending lawyer have responsibilities, the former not to look, and the latter not to transmit. These responsibilities may overlap and depending on the facts, *both* lawyers may be seen as failing in their obligations.

In an article not yet published at the time of this writing, Professor Hricik, the ethics-tech expert, lends support to this dual duty concept: "A lawyer who transmits a document knowing that it contains embedded client confidences violates the duty of confidentiality."[8] But Hricik nevertheless concludes that the transmission of embedded data is "inadvertent," and that the lawyer

---

[8] David Hricik, *I Can Tell When You're Telling Lies: Ethics and Embedded Confidential Information,* __ J. LEGAL PROF. __ (Forthcoming 2006).

receiving and tempted to examine it may not do so if "the recipient should know that the transmission was inadvertent."

7. Inadvertent Disclosure. The reality is that issues of electronic transmission, which go back little more than a decide, are still so new that we must all take care to await — and monitor — further developments. Ethics opinions are important, and thoughtful techno-ethics updates from those in the know are vital to set the table for discussion, but they do not substitute for binding authority. For that, we turn to a review of what case law exists on inadvertent disclosure, an increasingly important and heavily-litigated subject.

To review just some of the issues: What should a lawyer do with confidential information that is inadvertently disclosed by the opposing side? Does it make a difference whether the disclosure is completely accidental, the result of imprudence, or intentionally leaked by a disgruntled employee? Does it matter whether the lawyer who receives the information is aware of its confidentiality? What about notice to the disclosing lawyer? Is there a difference between transmission of *confidential* information vs. *privileged* data?

One of the earliest opinions to directly address the issue of inadvertent disclosure is excerpted below.

AEROJET-GENERAL CORP. v. TRANSPORT INDEMNITY INSURANCE
18 Cal. App. 4th 996, 22 Cal. Rptr. 2d 862 (1993)

Sometime between July 1988 and August 1989, . . . [Attorney Scott] DeVries received a packet of documents concerning the Aerojet litigation from David Strode, an Aerojet employee. . . .

According to DeVries, the only item he was interested in was a memorandum revealing the existence of a witness, Warren Michaels. Michaels was a Sacramento-based independent insurance adjustor who investigated a prior industrial accident at the Aerojet facility. The memorandum by an attorney with Bronson, Bronson & McKinnon (Bronson), opposing counsel herein, described an interview with Michaels and contained the attorney's assessment of Michaels' "witness potential" in the litigation. DeVries initially contacted Michaels by telephone and spoke with him about the case. When the stay was lifted and discovery resumed, DeVries took Michaels' deposition.

Curiosity developed about how DeVries had learned of Michaels' existence because his name had not been divulged during the discovery process. . . . DeVries revealed that he learned of Michaels from a document that had originated from the Bronson firm, which represented a number of the defendant insurers. . . .

Almost a year later, Bronson searched its records to find the document naming Michaels. At this point it was discovered that the memorandum naming Michaels was part of a larger packet of documents that had presumably been sent to Bronson's client, Crum & Forster, the parent corporation for the insurers represented by Bronson. . . .

When deposed in connection with respondents' motion for sanctions, DeVries acknowledged that he had no reason to believe that Bronson or their clients had consented to the disclosure of the documents. Nevertheless, he reviewed them, and did not immediately notify any opposing counsel, the special discovery master, or the trial court that he had received them. . . . He kept the documents for a period of "weeks to months" on his desk or credenza, and did not put them in the Aerojet case file. The documents were ultimately destroyed "during a routine housecleaning."

. . . .

The [trial court's] sanction order was not based on DeVries' failure to advise opposing counsel of his receipt of the documents, but for his failure to do so in a timely fashion. It recites that the documents given to DeVries were "undeniably a privileged communication between opposing counsel and his client detailing pretrial and trial strategies." Furthermore, "neither the Bronson office nor Crum & Forster had knowledge of or had consented to Aerojet's possession of these documents." The court summarized the conduct that it found to be "unethical and in bad faith . . . . Upon receipt of the documents, Mr. DeVries failed to contact opposing counsel. Mr. DeVries failed to investigate how his client obtained the documents. Mr. DeVries failed to tell his partners he had received the documents from Aerojet. Mr. DeVries looked at the documents and used the information contained therein to his own advantage. Finally, Mr. DeVries destroyed the documents."

. . . It was further ordered that Warren Michaels be precluded from testifying during any phase of the trial. . . .

. . . DeVries did not violate any laws, statutory or decisional, or any rules of court or rules of professional conduct in the manner by which he obtained the subject information. It is undisputed that DeVries is free of any wrongdoing in his initial receipt of the documents.

The issue concerns the duty of an attorney who, without misconduct or fault, obtains or learns of a confidential communication (Evid. Code § 952) among opposing counsel, or between opposing counsel and opposing counsel's client. Assuming there to be such a duty, it becomes more difficult to define when the confidential communication reveals a relevant and potentially helpful witness, such as occurred here, regardless of whether the witness should have been revealed through discovery. There is no State Bar rule of professional conduct, no rule of court nor any statute specially addressing this situation and mandating or defining any duty under such circumstances.

In response to respondents' argument that DeVries should not even have read the documents at issue, which they support with an American Bar Association ethics opinion, we note that this complex litigation involves hundreds of insurance policies and parties, numerous law firms, scores of individual attorneys and a great number of documents. The files were voluminous — the attorneys were swamped with pleadings, correspondence, discovery and other documents. Their job entailed careful review and cataloguing of the documents coming across their desks, and one cannot identify, let alone analyze, many of these documents until they have been reviewed. . . . Given the number of attorneys and documents involved in this case, DeVries cannot be faulted for examining this memorandum.

. . . .

The attorney-client privilege is a shield against deliberate intrusion; it is not an insurer against inadvertent disclosure. Further, not all information that passes privately between attorney and client is entitled to remain confidential in the literal sense. The most obvious example is information that is required to be disclosed in response to discovery, such as the identification of potential witnesses. Consequently, whether the existence and identity of a witness or other nonprivileged information is revealed through formal discovery or inadvertence, the end result is the same: The opposing party is entitled to the use of that witness or information. This fundamental concept was lost in the skirmish below.

"The attorney-client privilege only protects disclosure of communications; it does not protect disclosure of the underlying facts upon which the communications are based. . . ."

If the underlying information which respondents sought to prevent plaintiffs from using is not privileged, and if such information was revealed to plaintiffs' counsel through no fault or misconduct of his own, plaintiffs and their counsel were entitled to use it. . . . In the instant case, the existence of witness Warren Michaels was not privileged. Michaels was not unknown to Aerojet in the literal sense — he had previously adjusted a workers' compensation claim by an Aerojet employee, and he had knowledge relevant to the litigation. . . .

We think that the manner in which DeVries obtained the information in this case — through documents inadvertently transmitted to his client — is irrelevant to resolution of the issue. Assuming no question of waiver, the problem would be no different if DeVries had obtained the same information from someone who overheard respondents discussing the matter in a restaurant or a courthouse corridor, or if it had been mistakenly sent to him through the mail or by facsimile transmission. Once he had acquired the information in a manner that was not due to his own fault or wrongdoing, he cannot purge it from his mind. Indeed, his professional obligation demands that he utilize his knowledge about the case on his client's behalf.

. . . In the absence of any clear statutory, regulatory or decisional authority imposing a duty of immediate disclosure of the inadvertent receipt of privileged information, we conclude the sanction order cannot stand.

NOTES

What do you think of the assertion in *Aerojet* that it doesn't matter whether witness Michaels' name was revealed during discovery or from inadvertently disclosed confidential communications, since "the end result is the same"? Does this "end result" analysis justify all lawyers' use of all material no matter how it is obtained?

What of the court's final assertion that how DeVries obtained the witness' name is "irrelevant"? The court argues that had the information come by mail or by fax, DeVries could still use it, and indeed *must* use it. But most confidential faxes come with cover-sheet notices that the fax is a lawyer-client confidential communication. Would a lawyer receiving such a fax have as legitimate a justification for reading it as DeVries had to read the Bronson memo? Wouldn't such a lawyer know the fax was intended to be confidential? Is this argument of the court pure dicta, since DeVries did not know the memo was confidential as he read it? Finally, how does that dicta square with the court's earlier reasoning that DeVries was blameless because he didn't know what he was reading?

8. The ABA's Changing View. The ABA opinion referred to in passing by the *Aerojet* court is ABA Formal Opinion 92-368 (November 10, 1992). That opinion comes to a very different conclusion than *Aerojet*, or at least *Aerojet's* dicta. It holds that when a lawyer receives information which appears confidential and not intended for that lawyer, the recipient should *not* look at the materials, but rather should notify the sending attorney and abide by that attorney's further instructions. The opinion says that a lawyer's zeal in pursuing the client's cause must be tempered by "doing the right thing." But the ABA cites little direct authority in support of this proposition. The opinion does offer an analogy between inadvertent disclosures of confidences and inadvertent *waivers* of the evidentiary privilege.

The ABA ethics committee's willingness to reach a do-the-right-thing conclusion squares with the views of many ethics experts and commentators — that lawyers who use information they know is not meant for them provide a sad commentary on the state of the profession and its lack of comity. But for years, there was a dearth of hard authority supporting this position. It was clear that many attorneys closer to the reality of the daily practice of law are more sanguine about the profession's rougher edges. These lawyers might ask whether we really expect a Scott DeVries *not* to look at all the material he received. Or, for that matter, can we really expect Russ Bluestone *not* to read the entire electronic file, and to use the information it provides?

In 2005, in Formal Opinion 05-437, the ABA withdrew Formal Opinion 92-368 to be consistent with the 2002 version of Model Rule 4.4, which only requires notification to the opposing, inadvertently disclosing party. Neither Rule 4.4 nor Opinion 05-437 require that the receiving lawyer will forego looking at the document.

Nevertheless, put yourself in the shoes of the lawyer whose secretary pushes speedfax button 11 instead of button 12 and sends the message to the opposition instead of the client. A lawyer of our acquaintance tells us this story:

> It was my first year as an associate for a large urban law firm. I was the junior person on a massive litigation matter, and the senior partner told me to send a letter to certain defense counsel and not to others. I wasn't sure exactly who he meant, so I asked him again. But he got impatient and said it too quickly, then stalked off. I was afraid he'd think I wasn't smart enough, but I guess I was still confused. The letter was about defense strategy. I sent it out, but I sent it to one lawyer who wasn't part of the strategy, whose client we were pointing the finger at. I admit it; it was a big mistake. When the partner found out, he was livid. He was a powerful partner and I knew I would be finished at that firm, but a friend of mine in the

mailroom figured out a way to blame it on a messenger who had just quit.

I look at inadvertent disclosure this way: If you left your purse in the subway, wouldn't you hope someone would return it? If you found someone's purse in the subway, would you take all the money or give it back? I see it as "There but for the grace of God go I."

This argument is persuasive, but is it enough to convince you? Or do you still feel not only that you must look inside the purse, but *use* what you find there?

9. *WPS* and Notice to Opposing Counsel. In 1999, a different district of the California Court of Appeals than the *Aerojet* court decided what has become known as the "WPS" (appropriately pronounced "Whoops") case.[9] WPS's lawyer received boxes of trial exhibits from the State Compensation Insurance Fund's lawyer, including litigation summaries that were clearly marked in bold capital letters at the top "Attorney-Client Communication/ Attorney Work Product," and "Do Not Circulate or Duplicate." The word "CONFIDENTIAL" appeared around the perimeter of each page. Despite this, WPS's attorney showed the documents to his expert, who in turn gave them to another lawyer who was involved in a separate case against the Fund. The trial court determined that the documents were privileged and should have been returned by WPS's lawyer. Relying substantially on ABA Opinion 92-368, the court sanctioned WPS's lawyer $6,000.

The appeals court agreed that the documents were privileged, and held that their inadvertent disclosure did not waive any privilege:

The conclusion we reach is fundamentally based on the importance which the attorney-client privilege holds in the jurisprudence of this state. Without it, full disclosure by clients to their counsel would not occur, with the result that the ends of justice would not be properly served. We believe a client should not enter the attorney-client relationship fearful that an inadvertent error by its counsel could result in the waiver of privileged information or the retention of privileged information by an adversary who might abuse and dissemi- nate the information with impunity. In addition, it has long been recognized that " '[a]n attorney has an obligation not only to protect his client's interests, but also to respect the legitimate interests of fellow members of the bar, the judiciary, and the administration of justice.' "

Despite this language, the appeals court reversed the sanctions against the attorney, noting that California, whose rules are not based on either the ABA's Model Rules or Model Code, does not generally rely on American Bar Associa- tion opinions. More significantly, however, the *WPS* court set forth guidelines to be followed in future instances of inadvertent disclosure. First, the lawyer should examine the materials without reading them to ascertain whether they are privileged and if they are, refrain from further examination. Second, the recipient should notify the sender that the privileged material was received.

---

[9] *State Compensation Insurance Fund v. WPS Inc.*, 70 Cal. App. 4th 644, 82 Cal. Rptr. 2d 799 (1999).

Third, the sending and receiving lawyers should meet and confer to resolve what to do with the material, or in the absence of an agreement, seek guidance from the court.

At least one knowledgeable California ethics authority, Ellen Peck, who served as both a State Bar Court judge and principal staff to California's ethics and rules revision bodies, believes that *WPS* and *Aerojet* are easily reconciled with each other. *WPS*, in Peck's view, explains what to do with the receipt of what is "patently attorney-client privileged or confidential information or is clearly marked [as such]," while *Aerojet* deals with information that is not privileged or confidential.[10] But is it so clear that *Aerojet* involves discovery that both sides agreed is not privileged or confidential? And how does the recipient attorney know whether material is "patently" privileged merely because of its label? The label may raise a presumption or at least provide notice, but the issue of privilege and confidentiality is often in substantial disagreement between the parties. Besides, facsimile cover sheets and e-mails with confidentiality admonitions are routinely used for non-confidential purposes — including dinner reservations, requests for tee times, and, in our experience, communications to opposing counsel.

One final issue raised by *WPS*: How can the recipient attorney comply with the court's first requirement, to refrain from examining the materials, and then knowledgeably attempt to resolve the issue with the other side — or, indeed, test the claim of privilege itself? Peck leaves it to the recipient attorney to "analyze the content of the document and the circumstances of its release to determine whether you have one of three independent grounds for usage of the information. . . ." Clearly, this is necessary, as she puts it, to fulfill "your duties of competence and loyalty to your client." But if a lawyer must make this analysis later, what sense does it make to refrain from doing this when the document is first received?

One thing the *WPS* case makes clear is the necessity in California of notice to opposing counsel. As of this writing, *Rico v. Mitsubishi Motors Corp.*[11] is pending before the California Supreme Court. There, a lawyer was disqualified after obtaining confidential documents, about which he did not alert opposing counsel. Although the attorney felt it would be disadvantageous to his client to disclose, the appeals court would have none of that idea post-*WPS*. It is unclear whether the state Supreme Court will permit use of the materials or whether the disqualification will stand. But it seems unlikely that the Supreme Court's opinion in *Rico* will absolve the lawyer for his failure to tell opposing counsel about what he had seen. That issue, at least, appears to be moving strongly, across the country, in the direction of disclosure.

Since *WPS*, there has been strong criticism directed at lack of notice to opposing counsel. As discussed above, the ABA included among its "Ethics 2000" amendments a new provision, Rule 4.4(b), which states:

> (b) A lawyer who receives a document relating to the representation of the lawyer's client and knows or reasonably should know that the document was inadvertently sent shall promptly notify the sender.

---

[10] *Walking the Ethics Tightrope: What to Do About Inadvertent Disclosure*, 14 LAWYERS' MUTUAL INSURANCE CO. BULLETIN 1 (1999).

[11] *Rico v. Mitsubishi Motors Corp.*, 116 Cal. App. 4th 51, 10 Cal. Rptr. 3d 601, *hearing granted*, 91 P.3d 162 (2004).

10. If the Current Trend Continues. It is easy to discern a clear trend favoring notice to the other side. But what about whether, after notice, the receiving lawyer may still take advantage of the inadvertently disclosed information? And what are the risks of that lawyer being disqualified? Some see a trend towards the inadvertently disclosed material *not* constituting a waiver of the attorney-client privilege. Even though the basic principles of privilege and waiver have not changed too much since Wigmore's day, the increased use of technology, especially the routine and heavy use of facsimile transmissions, plays a clear part in this trend to relax strict application of Wigmore, and is often mentioned in court and ethics committee opinions as a reason not to hold inadvertent disclosures to be waivers of the privilege. A few examples follow.

After discussing older, stricter authorities, including Wigmore on Evidence and Wright & Graham on Federal Practice & Procedure,[12] one federal judge wrote the following:

> A disadvantage of this traditional approach is that it divests the client of the opportunity to protect communications he or she intended to maintain confidential. The privilege for confidential communications can be lost if papers are in a car that is stolen, a briefcase that is lost, a letter that is misdelivered, or in a facsimile that is mis-sent. This approach takes from the client the ability to control when his or her privilege is waived, and is inconsistent with the Supreme Court's admonition that courts should apply the privilege to ensure a client remains free from apprehension that consultations with a legal advisor will be disclosed.

Berg Electronics, Inc. v. Molex, Inc., 875 F. Supp. 261, 262 (D. Del. 1995).

The court reached this determination even though Berg had argued that much of what Molex claimed to be privileged was not. Rather than allowing the inadvertent disclosure to resolve the issue, the court only required that Molex produce a privilege log, in the same manner as would occur in ordinary discovery.

In *Van Hull v. Marriott Courtyard*, 63 F. Supp. 2d 840 (N.D. Ohio 1999), the judge went beyond holding that inadvertent disclosure did not waive the privilege and required return of the document in question.[13] He warned that "willful or deliberate noncompliance" with the order to return the document would result in "the customary sanctions" *and* "may lead to dismissal with prejudice of the plaintiff's complaint and an award of attorneys' fees and costs."

Even stiffer medicine was meted out in a Florida state court opinion:

---

[12] More precisely, JOHN H. WIGMORE, EVIDENCE, § 2325, at 633, and CHARLES ALAN WRIGHT & KENNETH W. GRAHAM, JR., FEDERAL PRACTICE AND PROCEDURE § 5726, at 543, n.75, the latter stating that inadvertence can only be claimed if the holder "did not bother to look at [the documents] before turning them over," and even then, "it is difficult to see why courts should come to his rescue when he realizes he should have been more careful."

[13] The same result occurred in Maine. *See Corey v. Norman, Hanson & Detroy*, 742 A.2d 933 (Me. 1999).

The receipt of privileged documents is grounds for disqualification of the attorney receiving the documents based on the unfair tactical advantage such disclosure provides. Moreover, contrary to plaintiffs' argument, on certiorari review a movant is "not required to demonstrate specific prejudice in order to justify disqualification."

While recognizing that disqualification of a party's chosen counsel is an extraordinary remedy and should be resorted to sparingly, we believe the prudent course in this case is to disqualify counsel. . . . [P]erceptions are of the utmost importance. Thus, how much of an advantage, if any, one party may gain over another we cannot measure. However, the possibility that such an advantage did accrue warrants resort to this drastic remedy for the sake of the appearance of justice, if not justice itself, and the public's interest in the integrity of the judicial process.[14]

While the overall trend is to relax the rules on waiver, *perhaps* to be more forgiving of those who disclose and *possibly* to be harsher to those who read what is disclosed, the debate about this issue is not only far from over, it is just beginning. After all, the fact that there is no privilege waiver does not necessarily lead to a complete bar against receiving counsel using any of the material. And when a court rules that disqualification of counsel is an appropriate remedy even without a showing of prejudice, one suspects that the fight over inadvertent disclosures may not even have peaked. *Aerojet* and similar opinions continue to make sense to many, particularly those who argue that the burden should not be on the innocent recipient of information to figure out what is truly confidential.

Moreover, the recent trend since *Aerojet* is hardly uniform. For example, in another 1998 case, the Texas Supreme Court refused to disqualify a lawyer who received *purloined* documents taken by his own client from the opposing party.[15] And although the facts are unusual, a unanimous 1995 Washington Supreme Court declined to disqualify state deputy attorneys general in a physician disciplinary case, even though an administrative law judge had held that these lawyers had violated their ethical duties by not revealing an errant fax. The court reasoned that the doctor had not shown prejudice.[16]

While the debate on notifying opposing counsel may be nearing a consensus, what a lawyer may actually do with the obtained material — and whether and under what circumstances the lawyer may be disqualified — remain largely open questions that are not likely to be resolved any time soon. Until the California Supreme Court issues its opinion in *Rico* and several other state courts have chimed in with their own written opinions, the debate will continue.

---

[14] *ABAMAR Housing and Development, Inc. v. Lisa Daly Lady Decor, Inc.*, 724 So. 2d 572, 573-74 (Fla. App. 1998).

[15] *In re Meador*, 968 S.W.2d 346 (Tex. 1998). The court cited ABA Opinion 94-382, which analyzes *intentional* disclosures and follows Opinion 92-368.

[16] *Sherman v. State of Washington*, 128 Wash. 2d 164, 905 P.2d 355 (1995).

SUPPLEMENTAL READINGS

1. Since this is an extremely fluid and shifting area of the law, we recommend that you begin any research by looking at the ABA Legal Technology Resource Center Website, available at www.abanet.org/tech/ltrc/home.html.

2. Several law review articles — though their number remains surprisingly few in the past decade — do an excellent job covering the new territory of cyberethics. Here are a few of particular note. Catherine J. Lanctot, *Attorney-Client Relationships in Cyberspace: The Peril and the Promise*, 49 Duke L.J. 147 (1999), is a scholarly treatment that also points out how using the telephone for confidential communications was treated with considerable caution by lawyers when it first arrived on the scene — much like the wariness about the Internet today. J. Clayton Athey, then a third year law student at Georgetown, wrote an excellent comment for his school's law journal, *The Ethics of Attorney Web Sites: Updating the Model Rules to Better Deal with Emerging Technologies*, 13 Georgetown J. Leg. Ethics 499 (2000). Joseph W. Rand, *What Would Learned Hand Do?: Adapting to Technological Change and Protecting the Attorney-Client Privilege on the Internet*, 66 Brooklyn L. Rev. 361 (2000), explains that lawyers take the wrong approach when they assume e-mail encryption is not a viable option and that by doing so, they misunderstand the fundamentals of technology. Peter R. Jarvis & Bradley F. Tellam, *Competence and Confidentiality in the Context of Cellular Telephone, Cordless Telephone, and E-Mail Communications*, 33 Willamette L. Rev. 467 (1997), is a thorough discussion of ethics, confidentiality, and these communication mechanisms. Finally, Oklahoma law professor Drew L. Kershen has written a valuable article on websites, *Professional Legal Organizations of the Internet: Websites and Ethics*, 4 Drake J. Agric. L. 141 (1999).

3. Several more colloquial articles are worthy of mention for their practical value: Stephen Masciocchi, "E-Mail Confidential," 24 *(ABA) Law Practice* No. 7, at 42 (1998); Richard Zitrin and Carol M. Langford, "A Tale of Two Faxes and Other Stories of Modern Legal Practice," "The Moral Compass" column, *law.com,* April 25, 2000, reprinted in the *New Jersey Law Journal*, May 8, 2000 and *Texas Lawyer*, May 22, 2000; and Wendy R. Leibowitz's series of articles on lawyers and technology in the *National Law Journal,* including three in August 1997.

4. J.T. Westermeier, *Ethics and the Internet*, 17 Geo. J. Legal Ethics 267 (2003), offers a comprehensive look at ethical issues surrounding metadata, chat rooms, websites, and website links by examining varying state opinions and focusing on confidentiality and inadvertent disclosure.

5. Andrew M. Pearlman, *Untangling Ethics Theory from Attorney Conduct Rules: The Case of Inadvertent Disclosures*, 13 Geo. Mason L. Rev. 767 (2005), gives a comprehensive overview of the ethical issues surrounding inadvertent disclosure, and offers both practical and normative ideas on the ethical consequences of an attorney's receipt and choice to read or to not to read inadvertently disclosed materials.

6. Michael Lewis' "Attack of the Masked Cyberdudes!," *New York Times Magazine* (July 15, 2001). The best-selling author tells the incredible story of Marcus Arnold, who, using a "pseudonym on top of a pseudonym," became the highest-rated legal expert on AskMe.com, a heavily-trafficked Internet "knowledge exchange," despite the facts that he wasn't an attorney and was, in fact, only 15 years old.

7. David Hricik, *I Can Tell When You're Telling Lies: Ethics and Embedded Confidential Information*, __ J. Legal Prof. __ (Forthcoming 2006), cited in the Readings above, is a valuable up-to-the-minute review of embedded data, its confidentiality, transmission, and use, and the duties that impact the lawyers who transmit and receive that information.

8. In *Competent Computing: A Lawyer's Ethical Duty to Safeguard the Confidentiality and Integrity of Client Information Stored on Computers and Computer Networks*, 19 Geo. J. Legal Ethics 629 (2006), John D. Comerford promotes the approach taken by a recent Arizona ethics opinion for safeguarding electronic client information. Ariz. Formal Opin. 05-04 (2005) states that attorneys who do not possess the expertise necessary to safeguard their systems are "ethically required to retain an expert consultant who does have such competence." Comerford notes that the ABA's position is less stringent, but argues that the Arizona approach should serve as a model for both the ABA and other state bars to protect the confidentiality and integrity of electronically stored client information.

9. In the quickly-moving world of electronic ethics, Audrey Rogers' 1995 article is already "old," but it provides an important — and at the time, much needed — review of the traditional and new tests of attorney-client privilege waivers and their ramifications in light of the modern reality of frequent inadvertent disclosures. *New Insights on Waiver and the Inadvertent Disclosure of Privileged Materials: Attorney Responsibility as the Governing Precept*, 47 Florida L. Rev. 159 (1995).

Chapter 4

LOYALTIES AND CONFLICTS OF INTEREST

PROBLEM 7

This chapter focuses on another critical aspect of the lawyer-client relationship — the duty of loyalty. In the previous chapter, we discussed an important corollary of that duty: Preserving the client's confidences and secrets. The loyalty lawyers owe their clients is sometimes referred to as "undivided" loyalty. This means that lawyers must serve their clients' needs without interference or impairment from any other interests. Such "conflicts of interest" can arise in a number of circumstances.

Problem 7 illustrates several of those circumstances. Few lawyers, of course, represent only one client at a time. Potential conflicts of interest can arise when the lawyer represents multiple parties in the same matter, or whenever the interests of other clients might compromise the lawyer's loyalty and judgment on behalf of the client.

But conflicting loyalties involving one lawyer and two separate clients are just the tip of an increasingly complex iceberg. In the following several problems we'll get beneath the surface of this iceberg. For instance, lawyers' duties of loyalty may be affected by their own legal fees, how they invest their money, who they know, even what positions they have taken in other cases. Their loyalty may not be impaired because of their representation of other clients, but their relationship to witnesses or duties to non-clients who have an interest in the outcome of their work. Conflicts of interest also are increasingly difficult to evaluate when the client is an entity, such as a corporation or partnership, which speaks through its principal constituents.

There are three other significant issues to be discussed in this chapter. First, there is an important distinction to be made between conflicts of interest involving concurrent representations or successive ones (that is, one current and one former representation.) Second, we will examine whether and to what extent all conflicts must be "imputed" to all members of a lawyer's firm. This is particularly important given the modern-day mobility of lawyers moving "laterally" from one firm to another. For example, the question must be asked whether, for purposes of conflicts of interest, when lawyers change firms they bring with them all of their former firm's client base, even if they never worked for those clients. Third, throughout this chapter we will examine what remedies are available where a lawyer or law firm's loyalty may be impaired. Among the remedies we discuss in Problem 10 are exempting law firms from some imputed conflicts because of the nature of the relationship between former and current representations, and the possibility of "screening" the "tainted" lawyer from any knowledge of the current case. The most obvious remedy is the willingness of all affected clients to waive any conflicts of interest, an issue we discuss in this Problem.

Returning then to Problem 7, examine each of the following scenarios. It is important for lawyers always to be vigilant in looking for actual and, less obvious, but of equal importance, *potential* conflicts of interest, and to recognize these conflicts early in representation. Once the client is clearly identified — not always an easy issue, but one we explore at length in later problems — the lawyer should consider two related issues: Whether conflicts of interest exist; and whether it is possible to represent more than one client even where conflicts exist, if the clients give their informed consent.

When Are Two Clients Too Many?

I. Sam and Irma Hammond want to dissolve their marriage. They believe that they can do it on a friendly basis. Both trust Margaret Healy, a lawyer who has done work for both of them before. The Hammonds tell Healy that they have sat down and discussed it seriously, and that they have agreed on child custody, how much child support would be paid, and how the property should be divided. Neither one wants to consult another lawyer. "We trust you, Margaret," says Irma. "All two lawyers would do is argue with each other and add to the expense."

QUESTIONS

1. May Healy represent both parties? If so, should she place any conditions on her representation?

2. What can and/or should Healy say to the Hammonds about matters told to her in confidence by one or the other? What if one party knows information which that party does not want to disclose to the other?

3. Assume that the child support money Mr. Hammond is prepared to pay his wife is 50% higher than the local court's guidelines for such payments. Should Healy inform the parties of this fact? Should Healy advise Sam to pay less? If Healy does, what are her duties to Irma? What happens if the Hammonds don't know that Sam's pension is jointly owned, or community property, which means that under the law of their state it should be shared between them? Should Healy tell them or remain silent?

4. What happens if both parties fail to agree on a complete settlement?

II. Tyler Plevin is an experienced attorney who specializes in representing small businesses and their owners. He has represented Tom Quan and Emerald and Joe Huen, the owners of Quan Huen Graphics, for many years, both regarding their business partnership and on other matters. One day, Tom Quan calls Tyler and says, "Since Joe Huen's death, Emerald and I have decided that she should sell her interest in the business to the company. We've discussed the terms of the sale and we've worked it all out. We're each 50% owners now, so it shouldn't be too complicated. We want you to draft the papers."

QUESTIONS

1. May Plevin draw up the papers on behalf of both parties? Does the size of the company matter? Or the direct involvement of each principal? What other considerations might make a difference?

2. Does Plevin have a duty to inform both Tom and Emerald that there may be a conflict of interest? If so, what must he say?

III. Faye Stern represents Ted and Esther Vandiver. They are plaintiffs in a personal injury action against a taxicab company and the driver of another car for injuries sustained in a traffic accident while they were passengers in the taxi. Mr. Vandiver suffered a broken arm, while Mrs. Vandiver sustained a severe spine injury, requiring surgery and long-term rehabilitation.

QUESTIONS

1. Do Mr. and Mrs. Vandiver have common or conflicting interests? What if there is no possibility that one spouse would sue the other? Are there still possible conflicts?

2. What happens if just before trial, the defendant offers what Stern believes to be a good settlement, but the Vandivers can't agree on what to do?

3. Suppose the stress of the litigation takes its toll on the Vandivers, and they file for divorce. How will this affect Stern's representation of the couple?

IV. Arturo Ziegler represents brothers Joe and Billy Brown on robbery charges. They tell Ziegler, "We totally trust each other, and we're afraid that two lawyers might drive us apart."

QUESTIONS

1. May Ziegler represent both brothers? What if Billy is accused of merely driving the getaway car, while Joe is accused of pulling a gun on the store owner?

2. Assume that during plea negotiations, the DA offers to drop charges against Billy, but only if Joe will plead guilty. How does this affect Arturo's representation?

READINGS

1. Conflicts of Interest. Any time a lawyer or law firm acts on behalf of more than one individual whose interests are intertwined — be it in litigation, a business transaction, or family, estate and probate matters — the danger of a conflict of interest exists. That is true when there is more than one client in the same litigation (adverse or not) or more than one client in the same negotiation or enterprise, or simply when more than one client seeks the attorney's advice. In many situations this conflict will not manifest itself. But it is usually difficult, and often impossible, to predict at the outset which matters will go smoothly and which will not.

Although every state's ethical rules preclude a lawyer from representing conflicting interests, these general rules are rarely definitive about the subtleties of such conflicts. It is easy enough to spot an actual conflict — a lawyer or law firm representing opposite sides in the same litigation matter — but how do lawyers identify "potential" conflicts of interest? ABA Model Rule 1.7 moves away from the term "conflict of interest" in favor of a discussion of when a lawyer's ability to represent a client "may be materially limited" by the lawyer's other responsibilities.[1] This concept, focusing on the lawyer's unimpaired loyalty to each client, makes sense. But what does "materially limited" mean?

Consider the following two brief articles, both about lawyers — one nationally known, one not — who didn't see a potential conflict of interest and found themselves criticized for it.

ANDREW BLUM, LOCKERBIE LAWYER ADVISES LIBYA
The National Law Journal (November 29, 1993)[2]

F. Lee Bailey, who has represented Patty Hearst, the Boston Strangler and other famous clients, traveled to Libya in August and was paid to advise that nation on procedures and options in turning over two suspects in the Pan Am 103 bombing, The National Law Journal has learned.

Mr. Bailey's trip made him the latest in a line of lawyers the Libyans have either contacted or asked to represent them in the aftermath of the Lockerbie bombing. But in Mr. Bailey's case, his New York law firm also represents five clients in the civil litigation.

Although Mr. Bailey said he saw no conflict of interest, at least one client wondered otherwise, and officials of Pan Am families' groups criticized him both for the trip and for not telling his clients about it. Word of his trip surfaced among the families in recent weeks.

. . . .

Mr. Bailey went to Libya under a Treasury Department license required for Americans who do business with, travel to, or accept payments from Libya. Mr. Bailey declined to say how much the Libyans had paid him but said Treasury officials had a full accounting of his fees. . . .

In an interview from Florida, where he is in a trial, Mr. Bailey said he went to Libya to advise "upper-level" members of the government "as to what the comparative options would be for surrendering the two [suspected] bombers in the Pan Am 103 case."

Libya intelligence agents Abdel Basset Ali Al-Megrahi and Lamen Khalifa Fhimah have been indicted in both the United States and Scotland on charges that they planted and detonated the bomb that killed 270 people in 1988. . . .

Mr. Bailey said his advice included information on U.S. and other justice systems, and whether surrender in a particular country could lead to a resolution of all the criminal charges. While ruling out representing the suspects, Mr. Bailey said he saw no conflict in advising the Libyans on "what the means of surrender should be. The families would be in favor of that. The purpose of my going there was to facilitate their return to somewhere."

. . . .

Mr. Bailey said he was prepared to inform clients of his trip but did not because the visit did not become public. He added that he was mindful of not

---

[1] One of the authors of this volume has even suggested, not entirely facetiously, that there is no real difference between "actual" and "potential" conflicts of interest.

[2] Reprinted with the permission of The National Law Journal. Copyright © 1993 by The New York Law Publishing Company.

working for the suspects, though: "With my position in the aviation community, representing anyone indicted in the bombing would not go down well with most of my colleagues."

. . . .

Elizabeth Phillips, former president of Victims of Pan Am 103, said none of the families Mr. Bailey represents "would want to have him represent Libya. It's our understanding our State Department represents us in these matters."

. . . .

A sobbing [client] said she was "uptight" and declined to talk further. Another victim family member was upset with Mr. Bailey: "I'm finding it difficult to believe he would do something that would jeopardize the victims he represents.

"But I just don't know why he didn't contact us to ask how we felt before he went," the relative said, noting that because Mr. Bailey was paid, it "sounds like it's a conflict somewhere there."

. . . .

LAWRENCE A. DUBIN, ETHICS
The National Law Journal (November 29, 1993)[3]

In early 1989, Vickie McMillen retained Clark Frame to represent her in a divorce action. Ms. McMillen was a 52 percent owner of a mobile-home company named Markwoods. Mr. Frame was a member of the Morgantown, W. Va., law firm Wilson, Frame and Metheney.

In the latter part of 1988, Mr. Frame's partner, Wesley Metheney, had filed a civil action on behalf of a personal injury client against Markwoods.

Both of these cases, which were handled by the same law firm, progressed on the court docket during 1989. When a motion for summary judgment was filed on behalf of Markwoods in the personal injury case, a lawyer at Wilson, Frame and Metheney first noticed the law firm was representing both Ms. McMillen in her divorce case, and the personal injury client against Markwoods. The lawyers realized Ms. McMillen would be an adverse witness against their personal injury client.

Upon researching the ethical ramifications of their actions, the lawyers concluded that no conflict of interest existed because only Markwoods had been sued, and not Ms. McMillen individually. Hence, no disclosure to or consent from either Ms. McMillen or their personal injury client was necessary.

Ms. McMillen became disturbed when she later learned about the situation, which she felt amounted to a conflict of interest. She unsuccessfully attempted to disqualify her law firm in the personal injury case against her company.

Once that case was settled, she discharged her law firm in the divorce proceedings and then filed a grievance against Clark Frame. Formal misconduct proceedings were initiated against Mr. Frame charging that he had

---

[3] Reprinted with the permission of The National Law Journal. Copyright © 1993 by The New York Law Publishing Company.

violated West Virginia Rule of Professional Conduct 1.7, which states: "(a) lawyer shall not represent a client if the representation of that client will be directly adverse to another client," in the absence of proper consent.

Clark Frame argued that this rule was not applicable because no direct adversarial relationship existed between the personal injury plaintiff and Ms. McMillen. The Supreme Court of Appeals of West Virginia disagreed with this contention, finding that the personal injury plaintiff's interest was directly adverse to Ms. McMillen's interest "in her capacity as a majority shareholder, corporate officer, and manager of Markwoods."

Further, the court determined that Rule 1.7 is always applicable when a lawyer is placed in a position in which the representation of one client compels the lawyer to cross-examine another current client.

Mr. Frame further argued that no client had suffered any negative consequences as a result of the simultaneous representation of the personal injury client and Ms. McMillen. The court responded by pointing out that a violation of Rule 1.7 does not require proof that a client suffered any damages.

The court affirmed the hearing panel's recommendation that Mr. Frame be reprimanded for his acts of misconduct.

NOTES

Was attorney Frame correct, because there was no "direct adversarial relationship"? One judge dissented from the discipline order on these grounds, also pointing out that it was really the corporation's insurance carrier who would have to pay the claim. On the other hand, the language of Rule 1.7(b) seems quite broad, certainly broad enough to encompass more than literally direct adversity.

And what of the conduct of F. Lee Bailey? Are you persuaded that there is no conflict between representing the families of victims of the crash, and advising the Libyan government about the terms of surrender of the alleged perpetrators? Is advising Libya insufficient to amount to a "lawyer's responsibilities to another client or to a third person"? What of Bailey's comments expressing concern about how his colleagues (as opposed to his clients) would feel about his Libyan connection?

Interestingly, in April 1994, the *National Law Journal* provided a postscript to Bailey's possible conflict when it obtained documents through a Freedom of Information Act request. The paper learned that Bailey's State Department request for a travel license to Libya was *not* to consult with the government, but rather because he had been "requested to take on the defense" of the two accused. When confronted with this, however, Bailey claimed that he ultimately never met with the defendants, and argued he had no conflict with his civil clients. Indeed, he remained on as counsel for all his Lockerbie victim families.

2. Representing Multiple Clients and Getting Informed Consent. Are there some situations in which multiple clients not only can but should have the same lawyer, because of convenience, economy, or trust? Are some of the hypothetical scenarios set forth in this problem appropriate for a single lawyer to handle? Both subsections of Model Rule 1.7 allow for representation if the lawyer "reasonably believes" it is workable, and if the client consents. But are clients well advised to give this consent? And what is it they are really consenting to?

For example, don't clients expect their lawyers to protect every confidence, even if they are co-represented? Is it asking for trouble to allow such parties to tell their lawyer confidences which are withheld from the other party? Read the analysis in the following article.

RICHARD A. ZITRIN, RISKY BUSINESS . . . REPRESENTING MULTIPLE INTERESTS
[Cal. State Bar] Ethics Hotliner, Vol. I, No. 1 (Winter 1992-1993)[4]

A San Francisco attorney represents the driver-husband and passenger-wife in a simple auto accident. Now the couple is divorcing, and it's not amicable. A small Los Angeles law firm has represented an International Union and several of its Southern California locals for years; now there's a dispute between the international and one of the locals that may lead to litigation. A Riverside lawyer negotiates a contract for the sale of a business between two of his biggest clients; a year later they're accusing each other of negotiating in bad faith.

By the time these lawyers — composites based on real cases — sought help out of their conflict of interest dilemmas, it was too late.

Indeed, where a lawyer's loyalty to a particular client is any way impaired by that attorney's other loyalties or interests, withdrawal — and the loss of a valued client — may be the least that can happen. At worst is the possibility [of] a malpractice lawsuit or even potential discipline. . . .

Recognizing the Problem

The everyday practice of most firms, large and small, is replete with potential conflicts of interest. Careful practitioners must learn to spot these situations and anticipate potential problems before they occur. I advise lawyers who consult me to follow these rules:

First, think not of conflicts of interest, but of *potential* conflicts. Look at any representation situation from the point of view that there *is* — or could be — a conflict of interest, rather than from the perspective that there's not.

Second, think beyond "conflicts"; think in terms of *"impaired loyalty."* This phrase, taken from rule 1.7 of the American Bar Association Model Rules of Professional Conduct, suggests the lawyer ask not "Do I have a conflict of interest?" or even "Do I have a potential conflict?" The question becomes "Is there *any* way — through my representation or *anything else* — in which my loyalty to Client may be impaired?"

Third, remember that, although in perhaps 99 of 100 cases a conflict will never ripen, it is impossible to predict with certainty *which* case is the 100th.

The only way to protect the interest of all clients — and the law firm itself — is if preventive measures are undertaken at the inception of representation, and in *all* 100 cases.

There are many situations in which multiple clients not only can but should have the same lawyer. . . . But situations where the lawyer's ability to represent a client is impaired should trigger a full explanation to the client(s). A disclosure of divided loyalties will rarely, if ever, be meaningful if it merely recites the existence of the problem. At a minimum, the lawyer must also advise the client of "the actual and reasonably foreseeable adverse consequences." (Rule 3-310(A)(1), California Rules of Professional Conduct.)

[These suggestions may help:]

(1) memorialize all communications, not just the clients' consents;

(2) specifically address what happens to attorney-client confidences in the multiple representation situation;

(3) spell out specific ramifications of multiple representation in an "if/then" format; and

(4) specifically address the ground rules of what will happen in the event a conflict arises, including withdrawal.

One point — too often overlooked — which should always be a part of any disclosure is how client confidentiality will be treated. Clients have come to expect that lawyers will strictly protect every confidence, and they will still expect it, even if they are co-plaintiffs in a personal injury case, or both sides in a contract negotiation, or the parties to an "uncontested" dissolution. But allowing such parties to tell their mutual lawyer anything which can be held in confidence vis-à-vis the other party inevitably asks for trouble. It is almost impossible to maintain, for example, "his" secrets as against "her," and "hers" as against "him," with the parties feeling mistrust, knowing that the lawyer may know something they don't. This may doom efforts to cooperate before they've begun. The best solution is to agree — in advance — that, among multiple clients, there shall be no confidences. Should the client insist on blurting out a "confidence," however, the lawyer may be required to withdraw.

Explaining the multiple representation from an "if this happens, then here's what happens next" point of view may make the ramifications clearer to the client. The if/then approach is also valuable in explaining confidences, and in delineating when the lawyer must withdraw from representation.

One final point: client consent can't cure conflicts in every — or even most — situations. The lawyer should adopt the standards suggested by rule 1.7 of the American Bar Association Model Rules of Professional Conduct: agree to conflict waivers only where the clients' consents, viewed objectively, are reasonable; and make certain no consent is obtained where the lawyer is unable to make full disclosure.

These suggestions for preventive, anticipatory communications are neither new, nor particularly sophisticated, nor difficult to carry out. But the dangers of ignoring such communications can be severe. The rewards are ample: clients who are more efficiently served with quality legal help, and lawyers who are free to serve the needs of all their clients without fear of the consequences.

NOTES

Is the approach taken in the previous article really workable? How effective can such client consents really be? For example, suppose the clients agree that anything one client tells the lawyer will be told to the other client. Suppose further that some time down the road, one client inadvertently discloses something that he or she doesn't want the other party to know, and tells the lawyer that notwithstanding their prior agreement, the lawyer may not reveal it. May the lawyer simply rely on the earlier consent and tell the other party? Or may the client now revoke the earlier consent? If the client can't change his or her mind, does that mean that right at the beginning of the case, the client has consented to a permanent waiver of a fundamental part of the lawyer-client relationship — confidentiality. But if the client *may* change the agreement, how effective was that agreement in the first place?

3. Confidentiality and Joint Representation. Those relatively few authorities that have directly addressed the issue are not unanimous that waiving confidentiality is necessarily a part of a waiver of conflicts of interest. Take, for example, the common occurrence of one lawyer representing both husband and wife in estate planning matters. As in some of our problem's examples, it is understandable that many couples will want one attorney handling the affairs of both spouses. But one can easily imagine situations in which one spouse is hiding something — money, perhaps, or a secret relationship — from the other. Should a waiver of confidences be necessary for joint representation?

Opinions go both ways. No, says Florida Ethics Opinion 95-4 (May 1997). The facts posited are that "Husband, Wife, and Lawyer have always shared all relevant asset and financial information," but there was never an understanding about whether or not the lawyer would maintain separate confidences. When the husband reveals that he has executed a codicil in favor of a woman with whom he has had an extra-marital affair, the lawyer is precluded from revealing either the affair or the codicil to the wife. The lawyer, according to the opinion, can only withdraw from representing both parties, citing a conflict of interest. The drawbacks to the lawyer's taking such a course may seem obvious. (How would you feel if you were the wife and *your* lawyer withheld this information?) Indeed, the opinion acknowledges that while a prior agreement about confidences is "not ethically required," such an understanding might have avoided the situation that occurred. And there is certainly the possibility that, from the point of view of civil liability, the wife could maintain a cause of action for professional negligence and breach of fiduciary duty based on the lawyer's failure to inform her of highly significant matters relating to the representation.

On the other hand, in *A. v. B. v. Hill Wallack*, 158 N.J. 51, 726 A.2d 924 (1999), the New Jersey Supreme Court faced an unusual fact pattern involving the Hill Wallack law firm, which represented both husband and wife in estate planning matters. The lawyers wanted to reveal their knowledge of the existence of the husband's illegitimate child to the wife, even though there was no explicit agreement between them to waive confidentiality. They reasoned that this information was significant to the wife's estate planning, as part of what she devised to the husband could eventually go to the illegitimate child. The Supreme Court reversed the appellate court and agreed that the law firm could tell the wife, relying in part on the unusually broad exceptions to confidentiality contained in New Jersey's version of Model Rule 1.6. Also, however, in an interesting conflicts of interest twist, the law firm had learned of the illegitimate child when it represented the child's mother in a paternity action against the husband without being aware of the conflict (and without the husband raising it). When the firm learned of the conflict, they withdrew as counsel to the mother, but felt obligated to reveal the existence of the child to the husband's wife. The court used the fact that the lawyers had not learned of the child from the husband as one reason to permit that circumstance to be disclosed to the wife.

Should there be at least a presumption of a waiver of confidentiality? The Restatement Third of the Law Governing Lawyers, § 60, describes sharing confidentiality between clients is "normal and typically expected." But D.C. Legal Ethics Opinion No. 296 (2000) disagrees, at least in part: The lawyer has the duty to inform the clients of how confidentiality will be dealt with, and absent that, confidentiality is presumed.

4. Adequate Disclosure, Reasonable Consent, and "Unwaivable" Conflicts. Is it realistic to expect attorneys to go through the kind of analysis and disclosure suggested above in the "Risky Business" article each time more than one party is involved, even where there is no direct conflict? The article says that consent should only be permitted "where the clients' consents, viewed objectively, are reasonable." But can this objective view be obtained without an objective individual, such as outside counsel? And what about the admonition that "no consent is obtained where the lawyer is unable to make full disclosure." There are many situations in which it may be impossible to make completely full disclosure, for to do so might reveal confidences or secrets of one of the prospective clients that are the very cause of the potential conflict.

Posit this situation, which we have used for many years in our continuing education seminars for lawyers. Joan Black, a potential client, comes in to see you. She has been harassed continually at her job for the past three years, ever since her new supervisor, Tom Nemo, arrived. The harassment has included suggestive remarks and asides sent through E-mail, and offensive notes placed on her desk in Nemo's handwriting. You believe she has an excellent case, with unusually good documentation.

After Joan meets with you, she calls you to say that, upon discussing it with her husband and family, she has decided not to file suit. "It's just too emotionally expensive," she tells you. "I found a comparable job at another company, and I just want to put all this behind me."

Two months later, Dora Brown comes in to see you. She discusses a sexual harassment case, and you soon realize that it too relates to Nemo. Unfortunately, Dora doesn't have any of the documentation that Joan had. "I was disgusted," she tells you, "so I threw it away." After Dora leaves, you call Joan and ask whether she would be willing to be a witness and have her documentation used. "No!" she tells you emphatically. "I put all that behind me and that's where I want it to stay." Can you take Dora's case?

Though they recognize that they can't reveal what former client Joan told them, most lawyers still believe at first that they can take Dora's new case. After all, they reason, they are no worse off than any other lawyer who doesn't know about Joan or her documentation. But doesn't the inability to reveal what Joan told you — evidence which would now be extremely helpful to Dora — interfere with how zealously you can represent Dora? For example, how would you know to subpoena Joan and her documents except from her confidential communications? Finally, the Catch-22: how effective would Dora's waiver of conflict be, since you can't tell Dora what it is that you know but can't use, for to do so would violate Joan's trust?[5]

The language of the Comment to ABA Rule 1.7, paragraph (8), is illuminating: Where "the lawyer's ability to recommend or advocate all possible positions that each [client] might take because of the lawyer's duty of loyalty to the others," consent may be impossible, since "[t]he conflict in effect forecloses alternatives that would otherwise be available to the client."

5. Multiple Conflicts and Billy Joel. In the Fall of 1992, singer Billy Joel filed a malpractice lawsuit against his lawyers, the high-profile New York law firm of Grubman, Indursky & Schindler. The suit rocked both the entertainment world and the entertainment law community. The issues presented by the Billy Joel suit reprise many of the conflict of interest issues we have raised for this problem. Read the following article.

JEFFREY JOLSON-COLBURN, JOEL SUIT HAS MUSIC LAWYERS DEEPLY DIVIDED
The Hollywood Reporter (October 14, 1992)[6]

The legal slugfest between pop singer Billy Joel and his former attorney has brought to a head the highly charged conflict-of-interest issue that is bitterly dividing major music industry attorneys.

"Some attorneys have forgotten what they learned in law school about ethics," said prominent music lawyer Don Engel. He referred to the increasingly common practice of counsel representing multiple sides in a negotiation. "The sleaze factor is getting worse in the industry," he believes.

To the alarm of some observers, a number of powerful attorneys have increasingly become the wheeling-dealing superagents of the music business. Like the biggest Hollywood film agencies, these lawyers often package deals while collecting from all parties involved, sometimes representing a label, artist and manager simultaneously.

"The ethics in the music business are between weak and none, and hopefully this suit will be able to do something about that," said Joel's attorney, Leonard Marks, after filing the $90 million suit against Allen Grubman.

---

[5] A similar situation occurred in *Selby v. Revlon Consumer Products*, 6 F. Supp. 577 (N.D. Tex. 1997). There a lawyer had represented two plaintiffs in a sexual harassment case. One client dropped out. The lawyer continued to represent the other client, and set his former client's deposition. The district court agreed with the former client that the lawyer was barred from taking the deposition.

[6] Copyright © 1992 by The Hollywood Reporter. Reprinted by permission.

A survey of the industry's most powerful lawyers revealed a deep rift, even in the ranks of those who benefit most from representing multiple sides in a deal. The attorneys are violently torn on whether this is an acceptable practice or not. Some said it's all right, assuming clients sign a waiver, while others dismiss it as unethical and a clear conflict of interest.

Nonetheless, it has become quite commonplace in the industry and observers said the Joel suit against Grubman is shining a bright light into this dark region of horse-trading and incestuous backroom bedfellowing.

In the current case, Joel says Grubman was representing his label, CBS Records (now Sony), at the same time he represented Joel. The suit says Grubman never informed Joel of this, never explained the potential conflict nor had him sign a conflict-of-interest waiver. Grubman's reply to the suit says that there was no conflict of interest as Joel "handsomely benefitted" from Grubman's good relations with CBS and that CBS did not formally retain Grubman until well after Joel's recording contract was signed.

Whatever the merits of this particular case, it has brought the issue to the forefront. Most major attorneys agreed that a waiver could be sufficient in certain friendly negotiations. But they differed widely in their views of the ethics of multilateral practice.

"It is an obvious conflict of interest and it's gotten worse in the last few years," said attorney Owen Sloane, whose clients include Elton John, Kenny Rogers, Frank Zappa and Motown. "In negotiations, every single point is adverse. Either you are violating record company confidences or you are not getting the best deal for the artist."

"Some of the present people are so caught up in the sleaze, they can't change it," said Engel, who has represented Luther Vandross, Clint Black and Boston in their fights against their labels. "They are cutting corners and are in danger of being caught."

On the other side of the coin, most attorneys in the music industry viewed the present standards as acceptable.

Bert Fields, a key industry attorney whose clients include Michael Jackson as well as Allen Grubman in the Billy Joel suit, said, "It's the client's choice. If full disclosure is made and the client wants to go forward, then there is no problem and you get a written waiver to protect yourself."

Noting he was speaking in the abstract and not about the Joel case, where he states there is no conflict of interest, Fields added that "99 percent of the time a client wants to go ahead with a certain lawyer because he has terrific contacts at the label. If you get income from a label, it's all right to them because they believe they can get a better deal from someone connected. The client says, 'I realize you may be influenced, but I'll take that risk.' That is nothing unethical."

Other attorneys pointed out that a lawyer's strong ties to a label only increased the conflict-of-interest potential for a young band.

"If a lawyer is paid every year from a label, the attorney may worry that pushing too hard on a deal will hurt, and that's a conflict," said Don Passman, who represents Janet Jackson and Quincy Jones, among others. "You have to take conflict of interest on a case-by-case basis, but generally, it's being done too much by some people and we need to pull back from it a little bit."

"Who's going to turn down millions a year because of a little conflict of interest?" asked Engel.

. . . .

"Even more insidious and pervasive is when artist attorneys do not represent the label, but are looking to the labels as a future source of business," Sloane observed. "Even though they don't represent the label, they make a sweetheart deal because they want the label to know they are their type of lawyer, so they get referrals and otherwise benefit from the largesse of the record companies."

Veteran industry attorney Jay Cooper explained that "it's hard for young lawyers to get in the business. It takes years to get the contacts and the power, so there are fewer law firms handling more artists and companies. The business has been becoming somewhat incestuous for some time."

. . . .

The firm of Grubman and Indursky, with its long-standing ties to Sony and other labels, must be especially careful about conflict of interest, Fields said. "The firm has a policy of disclosing any potential conflict to clients. In a real conflict, they bring in another lawyer. I know. Allen (Grubman) had asked me to replace him in major deals when there was a conflict."

Another legal superpower in the music industry is John Branca and his firm of Ziffrin, Brittenham and Branca, who have brokered many of the recent megadeals for artists like Prince, the Rolling Stones and Aerosmith, and who shared in the Michael Jackson deal.

Branca said his firm was meticulous about informing clients of potential conflict and obtaining waivers. "We are very sensitive and aware in this area, and follow the letter and spirit of the law. We have specific guidelines."

But are waivers enough? Some attorneys don't think so, especially in the case of young bands who are hungry for a deal.

"I don't know if it's totally waivable," Cooper said. "If you have a waiver is the attorney home free? I don't know." He added, in a note that could chill the attorneys whose income relies on the waiver, "Soon, the waiver will be challenged."

"Can you ever really get informed consent?" Sloane asked. "We'll soon find out."

NOTES

When the Billy Joel suit was first filed, Fields, Grubman's lawyer, was quoted in the Hollywood *Reporter* as saying "I don't think there is a conflict of interest involved here. I haven't investigated it yet, but if they disclosed it to his manager, that was disclosing it to Joel. And then it's no impropriety." Does this explanation hold up? Or should Joel, the client, himself be entitled to notice? Fields' remarks were particularly unusual in light of the fact that part of Joel's complaint alleged the malfeasance of his manager and the collusion of the manager and attorney Grubman.

A year after the Joel lawsuit was filed, the parties announced a settlement, although the terms were kept highly confidential. Some speculated that Grubman paid Joel nothing in settlement, while others estimated a settlement figure as high as $10 million. The questions about conflict of interest remained. Among them were these: Is a lawyer ever justified in not disclosing potential conflicts of interest? Is Grubman's nondisclosure justified where he can demonstrate his presence works to the benefit of both clients? Or does this beg the question?

The justification offered by entertainment lawyers like Grubman — that everyone benefits from having the lawyers' hands on all sides of a deal — harkens back to early in the last century, when future Supreme Court Justice Louis D. Brandeis espoused the view of being a "lawyer for the situation" — that is, a lawyer acting to resolve the issues among all parties to achieve common goals.[7] Some lawyers may see their role as similar when they represent a divorcing couple, or a family in estate planning situations. One noted scholar with a Christian legal perspective has suggested that the family unit effectively creates a situation that the lawyer can properly "represent."[8]

But can one truly consider a situation, or even a family, to be a "client"? Or must attorneys recognize that they represent *clients*, whether singly or multiply? Most observers believe that calling oneself a lawyer for the situation begs the question — and allows the lawyer to avoid the ordinary conflict analysis required of others. After all, to echo the question asked at the end of the Billy Joel article, how effectively can a lawyer represent the "situation" when one relatively weak client — like a "young band hungry for a deal" — is negotiating with another client who is much stronger?

A few more questions about multiple related representations: What happens when a law firm like Grubman, Indursky represents not only Billy Joel but Madonna, Bruce Springsteen, and other artists whose deals, and the money for them, depend in part on what similar musicians earn? Or when a sports lawyer represents a dozen pro quarterbacks, all of whom are compared to each other in salary negotiations? Or, as it might concern more ordinary people, when a law firm specializing in private adoptions provides the birth parents with the pictures and files of only one, or two, of the firm's eighty prospective adoptive couples? See *In re Petrie*, 154 Ariz. 295, 742 P.2d 796 (1987), which disciplined an attorney for choosing one adoption client couple over another.

6. Prospective Waivers. What happens when a lawyer represents fifteen homeowners who receive a lump sum settlement for defective construction from the subdivision developer? ABA Model Rule 1.8(g) says that the clients must consent to an aggregate settlement. Assuming that the clients, fully informed, consented to a carefully drafted waiver of conflicts back in the beginning of the case, how does the attorney now divide up the pot? Is the

---

[7] Prof. Geoffrey C. Hazard, Jr. has taken a particular interest in this concept. *See* his ETHICS IN THE PRACTICE OF LAW 64-65 (1978) and HAZARD & W. WILLIAM HODES, THE LAW OF LAWYERING § 2.2:102 (1999 ed.).

[8] *See* THOMAS SHAFFER, AMERICAN LEGAL ETHICS 302 (1985); Shaffer, *The Legal Ethics of Radical Individualism*, 65 TEX. L. REV. 963 (1987).

original prospective conflicts waiver enough? What about the fact that by the end of the case, after discovery and investigation has been conducted, the relative values of each homeowner's claim are materially different than when the waiver was executed?

Advance or prospective waivers have been approved in a number of ethics opinions and a smattering of court cases. But the approval has usually been either guarded or limited, and sometimes, as in the case of ABA Formal Opinion 93-372, both. First, Opinion 93-372 concludes that any potential conflict of interest would have to be described "with sufficient clarity" for the client's consent to be considered fully informed. Second, even if all clients were so informed and consented, the waiver would have to be reevaluated later if circumstances changed, to see whether a further waiver was necessary, or indeed whether the representation could continue at all. Clearly, prospective waivers of conflicts that are unknown, can't be sufficiently described, or — as we saw above — can't be adequately disclosed, would not pass muster under this ABA opinion. However, in 2005, ABA Formal Opinion 05-436 (May 11, 2005) withdrew a large portion of the older opinion and liberalized prospective waivers substantially, particularly where the client is a sophisticated business.

Case law is still developing. A California case accepting prospective waivers,[9] held that when a law firm got the agreement of co-defendant clients that if they wound up in a dispute with each other, the firm could withdraw as to one "notwithstanding any adversity that may develop," and remain as counsel to the other, its longtime client. A dispute soon occurred, and the law firm actually filed a cross-complaint on behalf of its ongoing client against its former client. Nevertheless, since the waiver anticipated precisely the situation that occurred, the court upheld its validity and allowed the firm to continue its representation. While the court didn't expressly rely on this, it is of no small consequence that the dropped former client had expressly asked to be taken in by the firm, which was already representing its ongoing client and which made it clear it did not want to jeopardize that longstanding relationship.

Other courts are at least arguably more restrictive. In *Worldspan v. Sabre Group Holdings, Inc.* 5 F. Supp. 2d 1356 (N.D. Ga. 1998), a six-year-old advance waiver was not considered effective prospective consent to allow the law firm to represent otherwise conflicted clients.

7. Conflicts and Criminal Defense. What happens when a lawyer's ethical obligations are viewed in the context of a criminal defendant's Sixth Amendment right to the effective assistance of counsel? Read the following excerpt of a case decided by the United States Supreme Court.

CUYLER v. SULLIVAN
446 U.S. 335, 100 S. Ct. 1708 (1980)

Mr. Justice Powell delivered the opinion of the Court. . . .

Respondent John Sullivan was indicted with Gregory Carchidi and Anthony DiPasquale for the first-degree murders of John Gorey and Rita Janda. The

---

[9] *Zador Corp. v. Kwan*, 31 Cal. App. 4th 1285, 37 Cal. Rptr. 2d 754 (1995).

victims, a labor official and his companion, were shot to death in Gorey's second-story office at the Philadelphia headquarters of Teamsters' Local 107. Francis McGrath, a janitor, saw the three defendants in the building just before the shooting. They appeared to be awaiting someone, and they encouraged McGrath to do his work on another day. McGrath ignored their suggestions. Shortly afterward, Gorey arrived and went to his office. McGrath then heard what sounded like firecrackers exploding in rapid succession. Carchidi, who was in the room where McGrath was working, abruptly directed McGrath to leave the building and to say nothing. McGrath hastily complied. . . . The victims' bodies were discovered the next morning.

Two privately retained lawyers, G. Fred DiBona and A. Charles Peruto, represented all three defendants throughout the state proceedings that followed the indictment. Sullivan had different counsel at the medical examiner's inquest, but he thereafter accepted representation from the two lawyers retained by his codefendants because he could not afford to pay his own lawyer.[10] At no time did Sullivan or his lawyers object to the multiple representation. Sullivan was the first defendant to come to trial. The evidence against him was entirely circumstantial, consisting primarily of McGrath's testimony. At the close of the Commonwealth's case, the defense rested without presenting any evidence. The jury found Sullivan guilty and fixed his penalty at life imprisonment.

. . . .

DiBona and Peruto had different recollections of their roles. . . . Peruto recalled that he had been chief counsel for Carchidi and DePasquale, but that he merely had assisted DiBona in Sullivan's trial. . . . DiBona said he had encouraged Sullivan to testify even though the Commonwealth had presented a very weak case. Peruto remembered that he had not "want[ed] the defense to go on because I thought we would only be exposing the [defense] witnesses for the other two trials that were coming up." . . . Carchidi claimed he would have appeared at Sullivan's trial to rebut McGrath's testimony about Carchidi's statement at the time of the murders.

. . . .

The Pennsylvania Supreme Court affirmed both Sullivan's original conviction and the denial of collateral relief. The court saw no basis for Sullivan's claim that he had been denied effective assistance of counsel at trial. It found that Peruto merely assisted DiBona in the Sullivan trial and that DiBona merely assisted Peruto in the trials of the other two defendants. Thus, the court concluded, there was "no dual representation in the true sense of the term." . . .

The Court of Appeals . . . held that the participation by DiBona and Peruto in the trials of Sullivan and his codefendants established, as a matter of law, that both lawyers had represented all three defendants. The court recognized that multiple representation " 'is not tantamount to the denial of effective

---

10 [1] DiBona and Peruto were paid in part with funds raised by friends of the three defendants. The record does not disclose the source of the balance of their fee, but no part of the money came from either Sullivan or his family. *See United States ex rel. Sullivan v. Cuyler*, 593 F.2d 512, 518, and n. 7 (3d Cir. 1979).

assistance of counsel. . . .'" But it held that a criminal defendant is entitled to reversal of his conviction whenever he makes "'some showing of a possible conflict of interest or prejudice, however remote. . . .'" The court found support for its conclusion in Peruto's admission that concern for Sullivan's codefendants had affected his judgment that Sullivan should not present a defense.

. . . .

Sullivan's claim that he was denied the effective assistance of counsel guaranteed by the Sixth Amendment because his lawyers had a conflict of interest . . . raises two issues expressly reserved in *Holloway v. Arkansas,* 435 U.S., at 483-484. The first is whether a state trial judge must inquire into the propriety of multiple representation even though no party lodges an objection. The second is whether the mere possibility of a conflict of interest warrants the conclusion that the defendant was deprived of his right to counsel.

In *Holloway,* a single public defender represented three defendants at the same trial. The trial court refused to consider the appointment of separate counsel despite the defense lawyer's timely and repeated assertions that the interests of his clients conflicted. This Court recognized that a lawyer forced to represent codefendants whose interests conflict cannot provide the adequate legal assistance required by the Sixth Amendment. . . .

Holloway requires state trial courts to investigate timely objections to multiple representation. But nothing in our precedents suggests that the Sixth Amendment requires state courts themselves to initiate inquiries into the propriety of multiple representation in every case. Defense counsel have an ethical obligation to avoid conflicting representations and to advise the court promptly when a conflict of interest arises during the course of trial. Absent special circumstances, therefore, trial courts may assume either that multiple representation entails no conflict or that the lawyer and his clients knowingly accept such risk of conflict as may exist. Indeed, as the Court noted in *Holloway,* trial courts necessarily rely in large measure upon the good faith and good judgment of defense counsel.

. . . .

Holloway reaffirmed that multiple representation does not violate the Sixth Amendment unless it gives rise to a conflict of interest. [A] possible conflict inheres in almost every instance of multiple representation. . . . But . . . a reviewing court cannot presume that the possibility for conflict has resulted in ineffective assistance of counsel.

. . . .

The Court of Appeals granted Sullivan relief because he had shown that the multiple representation in this case involved a possible conflict of interest. We hold that the possibility of conflict is insufficient to impugn a criminal conviction. In order to demonstrate a violation of his Sixth Amendment rights, a defendant must establish that an actual conflict of interest adversely affected his lawyer's performance. Sullivan believes he should prevail even under this standard. He emphasizes Peruto's admission that the decision to rest Sullivan's defense reflected a reluctance to expose witnesses who later might have testified for the other defendants. The petitioner on the other hand, points to DiBona's contrary testimony and to evidence that Sullivan himself wished to avoid taking the stand. [J]udgment is vacated and the case is remanded for further proceedings consistent with this opinion.

MR. JUSTICE MARSHALL, concurring in part and dissenting in part. . . .

[T]he potential for conflict of interest in representing multiple defendants is "so grave," see ABA Project on Standards for Criminal Justice, Defense Function, Standard 4-3.5 (b) (App. Draft, 2d ed. 1979), that whenever two or more defendants are represented by the same attorney the trial judge must make a preliminary determination that the joint representation is the product of the defendant's informed choice. . . . If the Court's holding would require a defendant to demonstrate that his attorney's trial performance differed from what it would have been if the defendant had been the attorney's only client, I believe it is inconsistent with our previous cases. Such a test is not only unduly harsh, but incurably speculative as well. The appropriate question under the Sixth Amendment is whether an actual, relevant conflict of interests existed during the proceedings. If it did, the conviction must be reversed. . . . An actual conflict of interests negates the unimpaired loyalty a defendant is constitutionally entitled to expect and receive from his attorney. . . .

NOTES

The Supreme Court's opinion in *Cuyler* was hardly the last word on the issue. For defendant Sullivan, his case returned to the court of appeals, where his claim that he was denied effective assistance of counsel was upheld. Meanwhile, Federal Rule of Criminal Procedure 44(c), pending at the time of *Cuyler*, soon became law. It provides that:

> The court shall promptly inquire with respect to such joint representation and shall personally advise each defendant of his right to the effective assistance of counsel, including separate representation. Unless it appears that there is good cause to believe no conflict of interest is likely to arise, the court shall take such measures as may be appropriate to protect each defendant's right to counsel.

Wheat v. United States, 486 U.S. 153 (1988), presented the inverse circumstance to *Cuyler*. Justice Rehnquist's 5-4 opinion upheld the conviction of a criminal defendant who *sought* to have the same counsel as two codefendants, and was expressly willing to waive any conflicts of interest. The district court, in the words of Rule 44(c), "inquire[d] with respect to joint representation," and found what was, in its view, an irreconcilable conflict. The lower court then took "measures as may be appropriate to protect [the] right to counsel," and denied the defendant counsel of choice based on the conflict.

Interestingly, while Rule 44(c) serves on its face to protect criminal defendants, it has come to be used in conjunction with *Wheat* as a tactic to disqualify a defendant's attorney of choice, such as where counsel has represented potential adverse witnesses. See *United States v. Moscony*, 927 F.2d 742 (3d Cir. 1991), *cert. denied,* 501 U.S. 1211, 111 S. Ct. 2812, in which the court disqualified counsel who had represented four targets of a federal investigation, one of whom was indicted while the others became probable witnesses.

A similar tactic was used by the prosecutors in the John Gotti case to disqualify Gotti's attorney of choice, Bruce Cutler, even after the pair had been through two "hung juries" together.[11] And in August, 1994, another New York court disqualified famed attorney William Kunstler from representing any of the World Trade Center bombing defendants, because he had originally spoken to three different defendants, causing the judge to conclude that he could not represent any of them without harming the others. *The New York Times*[12] said that the court's decision meant that "the lawyers who have been most in demand by various defendants, and have been the most visible public advocates of those accused, have now been entirely squeezed out of the case in what has to be seen as a major victory for the Government."

The basis for such disqualifications largely comes down to the same issue we discussed earlier — whether the client's waiver of a conflict of interest must be objectively reasonable in order to be effective. The difference in the criminal setting, of course, is that *courts,* rather than the clients and their attorneys, are now making these determinations.

8. Criminal Defense Conflicts, Waivers, and Effective Assistance of Counsel. Where have the Supreme Court cases left the issue of jointly representing criminal defendants? Courts have looked at this issue in both *Cuyler* and *Wheat* contexts, that is, direct or collateral attacks on conviction itself, and pre-trial prosecutorial claims of "unwaivable" joint representations. Meanwhile, some observers and ethics experts continue to see an inherent underlying conflict of interest between any two criminal defendants, and claim that joint representation should never be undertaken, at least during trial or plea negotiations.[13]

In trial, the inherent problems seem clear: Joint representation affords no opportunity for any inconsistencies in the defense of the respective clients. In *Griffin v. McVicar*, 84 F.3d 880 (7th Cir. 1996), the court reversed a conviction where one lawyer represented both co-defendants in the same trial. The lawyer, Goldenhersh, had presented a joint defense of an alibi and faulty eyewitness identification. But in pre-trial motions, Goldenhersh had essentially admitted that conflicts of interest existed between his two clients: He moved to sever the two trials both because Griffin had made admissions that could prejudice co-defendant Smith, and because Smith's serious prior record could prejudice Griffin. Fifteen years after trial, on habeas corpus, the appellate court agreed that prejudice had indeed occurred.[14]

---

[11] *United States v. Locascio*, 6 F.3d 924 (2d Cir. 1993). Here, the alleged conflict dealt with tapes of conversations between Cutler and Gotti that could be interpreted as involving planning illegal acts. The prosecution asserted the tapes could make Cutler a witness and at the least would put the lawyer in the position of defending his own conduct as well as Gotti's as he dealt with the tapes.

[12] (Aug. 26, 1994) at 1.

[13] *See* Peter R. Jarvis & Bradley F. Tellam, *Conflicts About Conflicts*, [ABA] Professional Lawyer (May 1996) at 22-23, in which sophisticated ethics experts were informally surveyed and agreed overwhelmingly that such circumstances "should" amount to an unwaivable conflict.

[14] It is worth noting that before trial, the prosecution challenged whether Goldenhersh could represent both co-defendants because their defenses could become "antagonistic to each other." This argument, made in 1981, several years before *Wheat*, went nowhere.

In *U.S. v. Newell*, 315 F.2d 510 (5th Cir. 2002), an attorney for two defendants wound up with a defense for one that pointed the finger at the other. The existence of a conflict waiver didn't prevent reversal of a conviction because the conflict that occurred was not foreseeable by that defendant. And in a far more defendant-protective case, *U.S. v. Schwarz*, 283 F.3d 76 (2d Cir. 2002), one of the police assault cases stemming from the highly publicized attack on Abner Louima in New York, the defendant officer's waiver of conflict of interest was held ineffective as to the defense lawyer, who was under contract to the police union, or working for the PBA handicapped the lawyer in blaming one of the other involved officers for the assault. The policeman's conviction was reversed.

However, that same year, the U.S. Supreme Court spoke again and in another closely divided opinion held in *Mickens v. Taylor*, 535 U.S. 162 (2002), that defense counsel's conflict of interest, because he had represented the murder victim on other charges at the time of the homicide, was *not* enough for a new trial under *Cuyler* unless there was a demonstrable effect on the representation.

In plea bargaining, prosecutors are often inclined either to offer "package deals" to resolve the entire case, or agreements that require one defendant to testify against others. This would seem necessarily to set off one defendant against another. Thus, in *Thomas v. Foltz*, 818 F.2d 476 (6th Cir. 1987), one attorney represented all three co-defendants in a murder case. The DA offered a package deal to reduce charges if, and only if, all three pled guilty. Thomas was reluctant to do so, but eventually did based at least partly on the knowledge that he had to plead guilty for any of the co-defendants to get the plea bargain. The court found a conflict of interest existed. The co-defendants had competing interests which the attorney could not protect due to the "all or nothing" group offer. In contrast, in *Hanna v. Indiana*, 714 N.E.2d 1162 (Ind. App. 1999), prosecutors attempted to disqualify two law firms jointly representing six co-defendants, police officers charged with abuse of their office. The DA argued that joint representation would interfere with the state's ability to negotiate with individual defendants to cooperate in return for leniency. The court, after analyzing *Wheat*, held that the lawyers should not be disqualified. Not only had defense counsel explained the waivers of conflict to the defendants, but so had both a magistrate and independent outside counsel.

How do the standards applied to pre-trial *Wheat* disqualifications compare to the showing required to reverse a conviction? Take two similar cases in which a lawyer represented one criminal defendant in a first trial, then the co-defendant in a subsequent case. In one case, the Ninth Circuit upheld the pre-trial disqualification of Defendant #2's counsel because the lawyer had represented Defendant #1. During her representation of the first defendant, the attorney had disparaged and even pointed the finger at Defendant #2. But Defendant #2 wanted the lawyer because she knew the case and had successfully gotten a reduced sentence for the first defendant. Besides, none of her arguments, most of which took place at sentencing, could have been admitted against Defendant #2.[15] In the other case, the Eleventh Circuit refused to

---

[15] *United States v. Stites*, 56 F.3d 1020 (9th Cir. 1996). Note the implication this case has for so-called "positional conflicts," which we discuss in Problem 9.

reverse the murder conviction of Defendant #2 after the same law firm had represented Defendant #1.[16] The majority of the court, sitting *en banc*, noted that the defendant claimed an insanity defense, and interpreted *Cuyler* as requiring direct and specific "inconsistent interests" before reversal was required.

9. Practice-Specific Conflicts Issues. This Problem and its readings have touched on several practice areas in which conflicts can and often do arise. But these examples are by no means exhaustive. Several specific practice areas and practice situations provide difficult and recurring issues of conflicting loyalties. We will discuss several in the other problems in this chapter, particularly Problem 8 and Problem 11. But even that review will not be nearly exhaustive.

Take, for example, the situation facing estate planning attorneys who would like to represent the entire family, or at least husband and wife, in coordinating an estate plan that makes sense for everyone. This common-sense approach is handicapped by numerous questions of impaired loyalty. May the lawyer know husband's and wife's ultimate bequest desires without careful conflict waivers? How are "mirror wills" done without shared confidences? What if one partner wants to make a change and not tell the other? And what about working with children, particularly adult children with their own families, who may not only have their own estate planning issues — ones that may be dependent at least in part on their parents' plans — but who also may be prospective executors and trustees, and, of course, beneficiaries?

Some of the other issues raised in this problem also apply in this area, including whether conflict waivers must include a waiver of confidences, whether prospective waivers are possible and renewed waivers necessary, and even whether waivers are available at all in certain instances.

While full treatment of all loyalty issues for every practice area is not possible in this volume, it *is* possible for us all to recognize that such issues are systemic and may exist in different forms in many, many venues.

SUPPLEMENTAL READINGS

1. May a lawyer represent both sides in a divorce case? In *Klemm v. Superior Court*, 75 Cal. App. 3d 893, 142 Cal. Rptr. 509 (1977), an attorney friend represented both the husband and wife in an uncontested divorce. The parties were in agreement on all issues. Both signed written consents to the joint representation. The court found that "with full disclosure to and informed consent of both clients," the attorney could represent both. But the court sounded a "note of warning," reminding lawyers that they "owe the highest duty to each [client] to make a full disclosure of all facts and circumstances which are necessary to enable the parties to make a fully informed decision. . . . Failing such disclosure, the attorney is civilly liable [and] lays himself open to charges, whether well founded or not, of unethical and unprofessional conduct."

---

[16] *Freund v. Butterworth*, 165 F.3d 839 (11th Cir. 1999) This case is discussed further in the Supplemental Readings.

2. Several jurisdictions have both malpractice and disciplinary cases in which lawyers representing both sides in a real estate deal — even the simple purchase of a home — face a conflict of interest. In those situations where consent is not clear and unambiguous, courts tend to find against the attorneys. See *Colorado v. Bollinger*, 681 P.2d 950 (Colo. 1984), and *In re Lanza*, 65 N.J. 347, 322 A.2d 445 (1974), both involving sales of single family homes. This trend has continued through more recent case law.

3. Thomas D. Morgan, *Suing a Current Client*, 9 Geo. J. Legal Ethics 1157 (1996). This noted ethics professor argues the interesting and rather unusual proposition that law firms should not be prevented from suing their own clients on entirely unrelated matters. Analyzing the history of conflicts rules, concluding that the current rule "snuck up on the bar," and reducing the importance of loyalty by using a test of "whether a reasonable client in the circumstances of the case would perceive a breach of loyalty," Morgan favors a rule that would allow an adverse lawsuit unless it would have a "'material' adverse effect on representation" of one of the firm's clients.

4. Georgetown student Alice Brown has written a helpful Note, *Advance Waivers of Conflicts of Interest: Are the ABA Formal Ethics Opinions Advanced Enough Themselves*, 19 Geo. J. Legal Ethics 567 (2006). Brown evaluates both the 1993 and 2005 ABA opinions and the current state of Model Rule 1.7, and suggests and describes additional standards that she believes are warranted.

5. Peter R. Jarvis & Bradley F. Tellam, *When Waiver Should Not Be Good Enough: An Analysis of Current Client Conflicts Law*, 33 Willamette L. Rev. 145 (1997). This is a valuable review of when current conflicts should be nonwaivable. The authors focus on the conflicts rules of Oregon and the District of Columbia to compare, contrast, and conclude.

6. For further analysis of lawyers representing family members in divorces or estate planning, see Russell Pearce, *Family Values and Legal Ethics: Competing Approaches to Conflicts in Representing Spouses*, 62 Fordham L. Rev. 1253 (1994), and Teresa S. Collett, *Disclosure, Discretion, or Deception: The Estate Planner's Ethical Dilemma from a Unilateral Confidence*, 28 Real. Prop. Prob. & Trust J. 683 (1994). Prof. Pearce argues that ethical guidelines should allow lawyers to represent families as a group to mediate among the members. We will look at this concept more closely in Problem 21. Prof. Collett criticizes the fundamental unfairness of one spouse in a joint representation being able to maintain unilateral confidences in a manner that hurts the other spouse.

7. *Freund v. Butterworth*, 165 F.3d 839 (11th Cir. 1999), was decided *en banc* after its initial panel opinion (117 F.3d 1543 (1997)). In both decisions, the court refused to overturn Freund's murder conviction, even though the same law firm had earlier represented his co-defendant. While the majorities reasoned that the test of *Cuyler v. Sullivan* had not been met, particularly because Freund sought an insanity plea, Judge Tjoflat, writing in dissent, called the case "a classic example of how a conflict of interest can prevent a law firm from adequately representing a criminal defendant." Tjoflat (and other dissenters *en banc*) noted that by undertaking the exceptionally difficult course of seeking a finding of not guilty by reason of insanity, the law firm essentially admitted that Freund had actually committed the homicide. The firm's disinclination to attempt to shift the blame to the co-defendant, or attempt to plea bargain for leniency in return for testimony against the co-defendant, demonstrated to the dissenters a direct conflict of interest requiring reversal.

8. *Castillo v. Estelle*, 504 F.2d 1243 (5th Cir. 1974), concerns a lawyer appointed to represent a criminal defendant while also representing one of the principal prosecution witnesses, the owner of the company that had been the victim of a theft. Though the lawyer's representation of the witness was unrelated to the criminal charges, the court reversed the conviction, noting that the lawyer had not disclosed the situation to the defendant, and that the lawyer "is likely to be restrained in the handling of that client/witness," making the situation "so inherently conducive to divided loyalties as to amount to a denial of the right to effective representation."

9. Catherine Houston Richardson, *A "Rest in Peace" Guide of Estate Planning Ethics*, 28 J. Legal Prof. 217 (2003-04), explores potential conflicts of interest for attorneys in estate planning such as representing spouses and multiple family members; being named as beneficiary for a will the attorney is drafting; and being named as the fiduciary of the probate estate. The author, an Alabama estate planning lawyer, suggests that the ABA Model Rules do not adequately address the problems faced by estate planners, and highlights guidelines created by ACTEC, an organization of trust and estate lawyers, to illustrate steps such lawyers can take to avoid conflicts of interest.

10. Simone A. Rose & Debra R. Jessup, *Whose Rules Rule? Resolving Ethical Conflicts During Simultaneous Representation of Clients in Patent Prosecution*, 44 IDEA 283 (2004), discusses the specific conflicts faced by patent attorneys, particularly the inconsistencies between the ABA Model Rules and the United States Patent and Trademark Office Code of Professional Responsibility. The authors argue that the duty of confidentiality must "dominate the practice of all law, including patent law," and assert that when an attorney simultaneously represents two clients and discovers information from one relating to the other that would be required to be disclosed under the PTO duty of candor, the duty of confidentiality supersedes the PTO duty of candor and disclosure should not be required.

PROBLEM 8

In the last problem, we examined several typical conflicts of interest. Before specific conflicts are evaluated, however, a threshold issue must be answered: Who is the client? "Isn't that obvious?" you might ask. "Isn't the client the person who walked into my office asking for help?" Often it is, especially when the client is a single individual. But when the client is an organization, it gets complicated. Again, try to think of it in terms of "divided loyalty": "Do I know to whom I owe my duty as a lawyer? Is it clear and unambiguous?" If the answer to each question is not a clear and unequivocal "yes," there may be a question about the identity of your client. Consider the situation facing attorney Esperanza Dejos.

Who Is My Client?

Esperanza Dejos represents HiFly Realty. HiFly was started by Gary Lavin, a real estate broker and developer with whom Dejos had worked on previous projects. Lavin organized HiFly as a limited partnership. Lavin and his two codevelopers became the three general partners. Lavin then brought in seven airline pilots as investors and limited partners. Lavin was installed as managing general partner and began receiving a monthly salary for managing the business. HiFly purchased commercial real estate in a new industrial park at the edge of town and leased out the space. The partnership has recently been looking at acquiring another similar property.

Dejos has handled several matters for HiFly, including leases and lease-backs, a few eviction matters, and a property damages lawsuit. She's also been asked by Lavin to help renegotiate HiFly's bank loan to fund the new acquisition. Dejos finds Lavin always to be cooperative, and HiFly pays its bills promptly. Though she is not on retainer, Dejos considers herself the partnership's counsel, and considers HiFly to be one of her best clients.

One day, Dejos gets a call from Andy Arthursen, the accountant who is examining the books to put HiFly's financial papers in order for the new bank loan. "Esperanza, something's come up and I'm worried," he tells Dejos. "I've got to see you right away."

At a meeting that afternoon, Andy tells Esperanza that "I think someone's been cooking the books. Not only can't we show this to the bank, but it looks like the partnership has failed to make distributions to the pilots. It's like Gary's set up his own slush fund."

"Andy, are you saying Gary is stealing from the pilots?" asks Dejos.

"Not exactly, Esperanza. Technically, the partnership is, since the money is still in partnership accounts. But Gary's the one who controls the money, and it looks to me like it's being concealed from the investors."

"How sure are you about this, Andy?" asks Dejos.

"Well . . ." Andy says, then pauses. "I guess I'm pretty darn sure."

QUESTIONS

1. What are Esperanza's obligations? What advice should she give, and to whom? What disclosures should she make, and to whom? For example, should

she advise the limited partners, even though she has never even met most of them?

2. Suppose Eddie O'Neill calls Esperanza, introduces himself as one of the investors, and says, "Gary's been talking about a new acquisition, and I want to know what you think. I've been looking at buying a new Cessna with Red Farber, one of the other limited partners, and I've only got so much to invest. Is buying another property a good idea?" How does Esperanza answer O'Neill? What, if anything, does she say about what the accountant has learned? Are her obligations to O'Neill different than under Question 1? Are her obligations to O'Neill different than to the other limited partners?

3. Would it make a difference if Esperanza actually helped Lavin put the original deal together and drafted the partnership agreement?

4. Finally, assume that it is the president and treasurer of a local union chapter who are "cooking the books," and that Dejos represents the local. Since a union is generally defined as an association of its members, would Dejos have an obligation to disclose the problem to every rank and file member? If not, what should she do?

READINGS

1. Whom Do You Represent? The question "Who is my client?" would be relatively straightforward if it could simply be answered by saying, "It's the entity or organization." But saying that the client is the entity is the beginning, not the end, of the inquiry. The lawyer for the entity must also ask several other questions: We'll start with these: Who within the entity speaks for it? With whom does the attorney have confidential and privileged communications? Is the attorney sure whom he or she does *not* represent?

Let's focus for a moment on this last issue. Representing an entity is usually complicated by the fact that a lawyer may have close relationships with many of the organization's management and directors. Particularly in a closely-held organization like HiFly, those individuals, in turn, may seek to consult the attorney about personal issues, including their own potential personal liability, and they may have expectations that communications with "their lawyer" are confidential. What should the lawyer tell these individuals? What confidentiality may the lawyer maintain with them?

In 1992, William Aramony, the former president of United Way of America, was indicted for stealing hundreds of thousands of dollars by diverting United Way funds for his own personal use. Aramony eventually was sentenced to seven years in prison. His appeal was denied by the United States Supreme Court in June 1999. Before that happened, though, his criminal defense lawyers accused his former civil attorneys — or were they only counsel for the entity United Way? — of violating their duty of confidentiality. Here is the report from *Legal Times*, Washington D.C.'s weekly legal newspaper.

EVA M. RODRIGUEZ, INDICTED EX-UNITED WAY CHIEF
SAYS LAWYERS RATTED ON HIM
Legal Times (January 16, 1995)[1]

WASHINGTON—"Three of William Aramony's former counsel have betrayed him."

So begins a motion submitted by the current legal team for the indicted former president of United Way of America. Using quasi-biblical terms, Aramony's attorneys allege that their client was stabbed in the back by the three lawyers at Washington's Verner, Liipfert, Bernhard, McPherson and Hand who Aramony once believed looked after his legal interests. . . .

Aramony says his former lawyers breached a "sacred" attorney-client relationship when they disseminated highly personal — and perhaps damning — information about him. The Verner, Liipfert partners vigorously dispute Aramony's conflict-of-interest charge and say their loyalties were with their client — United Way, which Aramony headed until he was fired in 1992.

Unfortunately for Aramony, U.S. District Judge Claude Hilton ruled Jan. 6 that he couldn't have been betrayed because the Verner, Liipfert partners — Lisle Carter Jr., Berl Bernhard and James Hibey — were never his counsel: They were hired and paid by United Way. And although Aramony was president of the organization and dealt frequently with the Verner, Liipfert team, the lawyers' legal obligations were to the organization, not to him.

[Aramony's] allegation could be interpreted as a last-ditch tactic to try to derail the prosecution. But, association lawyers say, it also offers a cautionary tale for association executives never to confuse their own interests with those of the organization they serve.

"There's a potential difficulty at a human level because the real relationships are with a person, not with an abstraction called an entity," says Robert Boisture, a partner at Washington's Caplin & Drysdale and outside counsel to Independent Sector, the country's largest coalition of charities and nonprofit organizations.

"So, you may feel a sense of loyalty to the individual," he continues. "But you're paid and hired by the organization and it seems to me that [the organization] is invariably where your obligations lie." . . .

But according to Aramony's current attorneys, William Moffit and John Cline, the situation for their client was anything but clear. . . . Moffitt and Cline filed a motion asking Judge Hilton to suppress any evidence that the government may have gleaned from interviewing the Verner, Liipfert lawyers — evidence that Aramony considers confidential.

Moffitt and Cline lay out examples of how Aramony could have believed that he had an attorney-client relationship — or at the very least, an implied attorney-client relationship — with Verner, Liipfert.

For starters, Carter had represented Aramony personally in 1984 or 1985 for about one month when Aramony was engaged in contract negotiations with

---

[1] Copyright © 1995 by Legal Times. Reprinted by permission of Legal Times.

United Way. According to Moffitt and Cline, Carter or other Verner, Liipfert lawyers also represented Aramony in personal matters on other occasions.

Aramony hired Carter as general counsel for United Way in 1988. When Carter retired in 1991, Kathryn Baerwald took over as general counsel to United Way and recommended to Aramony that the organization hire outside counsel. Aramony, in turn, recommended to Baerwald that she hire Verner, Liipfert, which she did in January 1992.

Moffitt and Cline claim that Aramony saw the Verner, Liipfert lawyers as his confidants and believed that they were acting as his attorneys. . . .

The lawyers also claim in their 32-page motion that both Bernhard and Hibey told Aramony that if his interests diverged from those of the organization, they would represent him and drop United Way as a client.

In separate affidavits, Verner, Liipfert's Hibey and Carter insist that their "sole and exclusive" client was United Way, even though they had handled some personal matters for Aramony in the past.

Bernhard, in an affidavit and in an interview, also strongly denies that he ever told Aramony that he considered himself the executive's lawyer or that he would represent Aramony should he and the organization's interests conflict.

Bernhard calls the allegations made by Moffitt and Cline "offensive, appalling, and inaccurate."

"In a desperate attempt to save their client from trial, [Aramony's current lawyers] have made personal and scurrilous attacks on three reputable attorneys, even to the point of baldly accusing [Bernhard and Hibey], two of the most honorable and respected attorneys in the District of Columbia, of selling out their client for money," wrote [prosecutor Randy] Bellows. . . .

Moffitt and Cline's arguments were of no avail. On Jan. 6, Judge Hilton, one of the judges that has carved out a reputation for speediness on Alexandria's so-called Rocket Docket, dismissed Aramony's motion out of hand. "I find from the submissions and the affidavits presented, that there is not a sufficient issue presented to require an evidentiary hearing," Hilton said.

Aramony's lawyers have appealed Hilton's decision, and have asked the Fourth Circuit U.S. Court of Appeals to force Hilton to hold a hearing on the matter.

In the meantime, . . . association executives should take heed of this most recent tangle over attorney-client relationships. They should take a close look at the retainer agreement between the organization and the firm.

NOTES

As we move on, think about the other two questions we asked: Who within the entity speaks for it? And with whom does the attorney have confidential and privileged communications? It is very difficult — perhaps impossible — for a lawyer to evaluate the role as attorney for the entity without answering these two questions. It's clear, however, that lawyers generally cannot communicate to the entire entity at once; they must do so through its appropriate representatives. Similarly, attorney-client confidentiality must have some limits, or it would extend to every employee of the organization, and make the job of corporate counsel impossible. Keep these issues in mind as you look at the rest of the readings for this problem.

2. Whom Do You Tell in the Organization? When you represent an organization against an outside entity, traditionally there is no question to whom you owe your professional responsibilities; you will protect the organization's interests as against the outsider.[2] We will also examine further what happens when there is internal conflict. Like Hi-Fly, any organization is merely a structural entity that can only act through its constituents. But for our purposes here, we begin by focusing on who the client is and who the clients speak through. That requires recognizing that sometimes, individual members, officers, or employees can take unauthorized actions that are adverse to the organization. What do you do in that instance? Who do you go talk with then? And how do you determine what is adverse to the organization?

What should be the lawyer's relationship to the CEO, or to the governing board as an entity? When an action has been taken that is adverse to the entity, to whom does the lawyer go, and when, if at all, is there an obligation to "blow the whistle"?

A generation before Enron, the Securities and Exchange Commission had already entered this debate by suspending well-known Wall Street lawyers William Carter and Charles Johnson from practice before the SEC for failing to force its client the National Telephone Co. to disclose its true financial condition or reveal the truth themselves: That was near bankruptcy in 1974 and 1975, while it was attempting to find new capital. Carter and Johnson were not parties to the obfuscation; indeed, after they found out about it, they advised the company's CEO to fully disclose the company's true finances to the SEC, but he refused. Eventually, the board of directors, sensing something in the air, asked the lawyers what was going on, and the lawyers responded with the full story.

But were the lawyers wrong to wait for the Board to ask "the right question"? An administrative law judge at the SEC thought so and suspended them. On appeal the reviewing commission called it "a close judgment," but reinstated the lawyers by finding the evidence "insufficient to establish that either respondent acted with sufficient knowledge and awareness or recklessness. . . ."

Even back in 1981, this was hardly a ringing endorsement. Now, as we'll see later in this volume, the duties of lawyers have changed materially and Carter and Johnson likely would have had a different result to their appeal.

3. The _Garner_ Case. The following Fifth Circuit case, _Garner v. Wolfinbarger,_ provides a historic background for understanding the genesis of ABA Model Rule 1.13. _Garner_ was often cited and relied on during the debate over that rule. Note the absolutist positions advanced by the shareholders, the

---

[2] With Enron and other scandals and the Sarbanes-Oxley regulations, this simplistic view is changing rapidly. We will study the post-Enron era at length later in this volume, and evaluate the sometimes difficult issue of when lawyers _can't_ shut the door on outside regulators.

corporation, and, notably, the American Bar Association as amicus on behalf of the corporation. Note also the court's reliance on *Wigmore on Evidence*. Of what significance is it that the issue of corporate attorney-client confidentiality has been joined here not in the context of the lawyer's ethical obligations, but on the issue of evidentiary privilege in a litigation matter?

What do you think of the *Garner* court's conclusion? Does the case-by-case balancing test employed by the court offer a reasonable solution between the extreme positions of the litigants? Or is the court splitting the baby in half in order to avoid setting forth a more concrete standard of conduct for corporate counsel?

GARNER v. WOLFINBARGER
430 F.2d 1093 (5th Cir. 1970)

This case presents the important question of the availability to a corporation of the privilege against disclosure of communications between it and its attorney, when access to the communications is sought by stockholders of the corporation in litigation brought by them against the corporation charging the corporation and its officers with acts injurious to their interests as stockholders. . . .

Stockholders of First American Life Insurance Company of Alabama (FAL) brought, in the Northern District of Alabama, a class action alleging [securities violations], seeking to recover the purchase price which they and others similarly situated paid for their stock in FAL. The defendants are FAL and various of its directors, officers and controlling persons. The plaintiffs also claim that FAL was itself damaged by alleged fraud in the purchase and sale of securities, and they assert against various individual defendants a derivative action on behalf of the corporation.

FAL filed a cross-claim against all other defendants, asserting in its own behalf the rights the plaintiff shareholders had claimed in the derivative aspect of their complaint.

R. Richard Schweitzer served as attorney for the corporation in connection with the issuance of the FAL stock here involved. After the transactions sued upon were complete he became its president. On deposition Schweitzer was asked numerous questions concerning advice given by him to the corporation about various aspects of the issuance and sale of the stock and related matters. Other questions went into the content of discussions at meetings attended by him and company officials and information furnished to him by the corporation. All questions related to times at which Schweitzer acted solely as attorney, before he became an officer of the company and before the filing of suit. Objections were made by counsel for the corporation and by Schweitzer himself that the attorney-client privilege barred his revealing both communications to him by the corporation and the advice which he gave to the corporation. . . .

The District Judge held that the privilege is not available to the corporation as against these plaintiff stockholders.

. . . .

Background and Choice of Law

Turning to the merits, [plaintiffs'] argument is that the privilege is not available to FAL in the circumstances of this case against the demands of the corporate stockholders for access to the communications. The corporation says that its right to assert the privilege is absolute and of special importance where disclosure is sought in a suit brought by the shareholders against the corporation. The American Bar Association appears as amicus curiae and supports the view of an absolute privilege.

The privilege does not arise from the position of the corporation as a party but its status as a client. However, in this instance plaintiffs deny the availability to the corporation of the otherwise existent privilege because of the role of the corporation as a party defending against claims of its stockholders.

We do not consider the privilege to be so inflexibly absolute as contended by the corporation, nor to be so totally unavailable against the stockholders as thought by the District Court. We conclude that the correct rule is between these two extreme positions.

. . . .

There is no comprehensive federal body of law surrounding the attorney-client privilege, and no opinion of the circuit courts of appeals discussing the precise issue at hand. . . .

The competing interests in disclosure on the one hand and confidentiality on the other, neither of which lies exclusively within the state or federal realm, are the subject of the next part of our discussion.

The Availability of the Privilege

The privilege must be placed in perspective. The beginning point is the fundamental principle that the public has the right to every man's evidence, and the exemptions from the general duty to give testimony that one is capable of giving are distinctly exceptional. 8 Wigmore, Evidence, § 2102 at 70. An exception is justified if — and only if — policy requires it be recognized when measured against the fundamental responsibility of every person to give testimony. Id., § 2285 at 527. Professor Wigmore describes four conditions, the existence of all of which is prerequisite to the establishment of a privilege of any kind against the disclosure of communications.

. . . .

The problem before us concerns Wigmore's fourth condition, a balancing of interests between injury resulting from disclosure and the benefit gained in the correct disposal of litigation. We consider it in a particularized context: Where the client asserting the privilege is an entity which in the performance of its functions acts wholly or partly in the interests of others, and those others, or some of them, seek access to the subject matter of the communications.

It is urged that disclosure is injurious to both the corporation and the attorney. Corporate management must manage. It has the duty to do so and requires the tools to do so. Part of the managerial task is to seek legal counsel when desirable, and, obviously, management prefers that it confer with counsel without the risk of having the communications revealed at the instance of one or more dissatisfied stockholders. The managerial preference is a rational one, because it is difficult to envision the management of any sizeable corporation pleasing all of its stockholders all of the time, and management desires protection from those who might second-guess or even harass in matters purely of judgment.

But in assessing management assertions of injury to the corporation it must be borne in mind that management does not manage for itself and the beneficiaries of its action are the stockholders. . . . For example, it is difficult to rationally defend the assertion of the privilege if all, or substantially all, stockholders desire to inquire into the attorney's communications with corporate representatives who have only nominal ownership interests, or even none at all. . . . [W]hen all is said and done management is not managing for itself.

. . . .

The ABA urges that the privilege is most necessary where the corporation has sought advice about a prospective transaction, where counsel in good faith has stated his opinion that it is not lawful, but the corporation has proceeded in total or partial disregard of counsel's advice. The ABA urges that the cause of justice requires that counsel be free to state his opinion as fully and forthrightly as possible without fear of later disclosure to persons who might attack the transaction. . . .

[W]e reject the idea that the prospective decision of the client on whether to abide by advice or disregard it, or the guarantee of a veil of secrecy, either establishes or narrows the attorney's obligation in the giving of advice. And to grant to corporate management plenary assurance of secrecy for opinions received is to encourage it to disregard with impunity the advice sought.

Two traditional exceptions are also persuasive in negativing any absolute privilege in a corporation in the circumstances of this case. These are the exceptions for communications in contemplation of a crime or fraud, and for communications to a joint attorney.

Communications made by a client to his attorney during or before the commission of a crime or fraud for the purpose of being guided or assisted in its commission are not privileged.

. . . .

A second exception is also instructive. In many situations in which the same attorney acts for two or more parties having a common interest, neither party may exercise the privilege in a subsequent controversy with the other. This is true even where the attorney acts jointly for two or more persons having no formalized business arrangement between them. This exception applies to partners, makers of mutual wills, and joint trustors . . . and many others.

. . . .

In summary, we say this. The attorney-client privilege still has viability for the corporate client. The corporation is not barred from asserting it merely because those demanding information enjoy the status of stockholders. But where the corporation is in suit against its stockholders on charges of acting inimically to stockholder interests, protection of those interests as well as those of the corporation and of the public require that the availability of the privilege be subject to the right of the stockholders to show cause why it should not be invoked in the particular instance.

Good Cause

There are many indicia that may contribute to a decision of presence or absence of good cause, among them the number of shareholders and the percentage of stock they represent; the bona fides of the shareholders; the nature of the shareholders' claim and whether it is obviously colorable; the apparent necessity or desirability of the shareholders having the information and the availability of it from other sources; whether, if the shareholders' claim is of wrongful action by the corporation, it is of action criminal, or illegal but not criminal, or of doubtful legality; whether the communication related to past or to prospective actions; whether the communication is of advice concerning the litigation itself; the extent to which the communication is identified versus the extent to which the shareholders are blindly fishing; the risk of revelation of trade secrets or other information in whose confidentiality the corporation has an interest for independent reasons. The court can freely use *in camera* inspection or oral examination and freely avail itself of protective orders, a familiar device to preserve confidentiality in trade secret and other cases where the impact of revelation may be as great as in revealing a communication with counsel.

The order relating to availability of the attorney-client privilege is Vacated. The cause is Remanded for further proceedings not inconsistent with this opinion.

NOTES

Although *Garner* was decided over 30 years ago, it is a case that has often been discussed by other courts and used by ethics authorities. Some courts have formally adopted the *Garner* reasoning, while others have criticized the "good cause" test as vague and overbroad, or have limited corporate privilege only through the crime fraud exception. Most often, though, courts have accepted the *Garner* concepts in principle that the best interests of the corporation are not congruent with the best interests of management, and that the fiduciary duties owed to those such as shareholders mean there is no absolute privilege. How do the new ethics rules, especially MR 1.13, deal with these same issues? Would the outcome of *Garner* be different today?

After the *Upjohn* case (our next reading) was decided, some predicted the demise of the *Garner* doctrine. The contrary has proved to be the case, as courts have sought to carve out public policy exceptions for corporate privilege. Interestingly, *Upjohn* was the first Supreme Court case to directly affirm that a corporate attorney-client privilege even *existed*.[3] As recently as 1962, only

---

[3] In 1906, the high court had held that corporations did not have a privilege against self-incrimination. *Hale v. HenkelI*, 201 U.S. 43 (1906).

eight years before *Garner*, an Illinois federal judge had held that the privilege was "historically and fundamentally personal in nature," something that could only "be claimed by natural individuals." In his opinion the judge wondered who, among all the corporate employees, would be able to claim the privilege, and noted that with corporations, "with their large number of agents, masses of documents and frequent dealings with lawyers, the zone of silence grows large." The Court of Appeal reversed the trial court, noting that "certainly, the privilege would never be available to allow a corporation to funnel its papers and documents into the hands of its lawyers for custodial purposes and thereby avoid disclosure.[4]

4. Upjohn. *Upjohn Co. v. United States* remains a key case in defining the scope of the corporate attorney-client privilege. The United States government was investigating possible illegal payments by Upjohn Company, a pharmaceutical manufacturer, to foreign governments. Upjohn instructed its general counsel, Gerard Thomas, to conduct an internal investigation, which produced interviews with and answers to questionnaires from Upjohn employees throughout the world. The government subpoenaed the files "relative to the investigation conducted under the supervision of Gerard Thomas." The lower court held that communications between counsel and the company's "control group" were privileged, but communications with lower level Upjohn employees were not. The Supreme Court reversed, with Justice Rehnquist writing an opinion that the privilege applies to more than just a "control group." The following is an excerpt from that opinion.

UPJOHN CO. v. UNITED STATES
449 U.S. 383, 101 S. Ct. 677 (1981)

In the case of the individual client the provider of information and the person who acts on the lawyer's advice are one and the same. In the corporate context, however, it will frequently be employees beyond the control group as defined by the court below — "officer and agents . . . responsible for directing [the company's] actions in response to legal advice" — who will possess the information needed by the corporation's lawyers. Middle-level — and indeed lower-level — employees can, by actions within the scope of their employment, embroil the corporation in serious legal difficulties, and it is only natural that these employees would have the relevant information needed by corporate counsel if he is adequately to advise the client with respect to such actual or potential difficulties. . . .

The control group test adopted by the court below thus frustrates the very purpose of the privilege by discouraging the communication of relevant information by employees of the client to attorneys seeking to render legal advice to the client corporation. The attorney's advice will also frequently be more significant to noncontrol group members than to those who officially sanction the advice, and the control group test makes it more difficult to convey full and frank legal advice to the employees who will put into effect the client corporation's policy.

---

4 *Radiant Burners, Inc. v. American Gas Association*, 207 F. Supp. 771 (N.D. Ill. 1962), *rev'd*, 320 F.2d 314 (7th Cir. 1963). Interestingly, at the time of the appeals court opinion, this kind of concealment had already been in place in the tobacco industry, although the revelations did not occur until the 1990s. We will tell something of this story in Problem 17.

The narrow scope given the attorney-client privilege by the court below not only makes it difficult for corporate attorneys to formulate sound advice when their client is faced with a specific legal problem but also threatens to limit the valuable efforts of corporate counsel to ensure their client's compliance with the law. In light of the vast and complicated array of regulatory legislation confronting the modern corporation, corporations, unlike most individuals, "constantly go to lawyers to find out how to obey the law," particularly since compliance with the law in this area is hardly an instinctive matter. . . . The test adopted by the court below is difficult to apply in practice . . . . An uncertain privilege, or one which purports to be certain but results in widely varying applications by the courts, is little better than no privilege at all. . . .

The communications at issue were made by Upjohn employees to counsel for Upjohn acting as such, at the direction of corporate superiors in order to secure legal advice from counsel. As the Magistrate found, "Mr. Thomas consulted with the Chairman of the Board and outside counsel and thereafter conducted a factual investigation to determine the nature and extent of the questionable payments *and to be in a position to give legal advice to the company with respect to the payments.*" Information, not available from upper-echelon management, was needed to supply a basis for legal advice concerning compliance with securities and tax laws, foreign laws, currency regulations, duties to shareholders, and potential litigation in each of these areas. The communications concerned matters within the scope of the employees' corporate duties, and the employees themselves were sufficiently aware that they were being questioned in order that the corporation could obtain legal advice. The questionnaire identified Thomas as "the company's General Counsel" and referred in its opening sentence to the possible illegality of payments such as the ones on which information was sought. . . . Pursuant to explicit instructions from the Chairman of the Board, the communications were considered "highly confidential" when made, and have been kept confidential by the company. Consistent with the underlying attorney-client privilege, these communications must be protected against compelled disclosure.

The Court of Appeals declined to extend the attorney-client privilege beyond the limits of the control group test for fear that doing so would entail severe burdens on discovery and create a broad "zone of silence" over corporate affairs. Application of the attorney-client privilege to communications such as those involved here, however, puts the adversary in no worse position than if the communications had never taken place. The privilege only protects disclosure of communications; it does not protect disclosure of the underlying facts by those who communicated with the attorney. . . . Here the Government was free to question the employees who communicated with Thomas and outside counsel. Upjohn has provided the IRS with a list of such employees, and the IRS has already interviewed some 25 of them. While it would probably be more convenient for the Government to secure the results of petitioner's internal investigation by simply subpoenaing the questionnaires and notes taken by petitioner's attorneys, such considerations of convenience do not overcome the policies served by the attorney-client privilege. As Justice Jackson noted in his concurring opinion in *Hickman v. Taylor*, 329 U.S., at 516:

"Discovery was hardly intended to enable a learned profession to perform its functions . . . on wits borrowed from the adversary." . . .

NOTES

Upjohn concerns the evidentiary privilege of Rule 501 of the Federal Rules of Evidence. Other courts have adhered to the control group test. See, e.g., *Consolidation Coal Co. v. Bucyrus-Erie Co.*, 89 Ill. 2d 103, 432 N.E.2d 250 (1982) (rejecting *Upjohn*'s approach because it has the "potential to insulate so much material from the truth-seeking process"). Is it so clear that the *Upjohn* questionnaires were "confidential communications" protected by the attorney-client privilege? Would there have been a different result if someone other than counsel sent out the questionnaires? After *Upjohn*, the Supreme Court decided *United States v. Arthur Young & Co.*, 465 U.S. 805 (1984), in which it held that a certified public accountant firm, as the independent auditor responsible for reviewing the corporation's financial statements under federal securities laws, was required to release its tax work papers in response to an IRS summons.

5. Whither the Privilege After *Upjohn*? Does *Upjohn* mean a corporation may keep internal investigations private simply by asking its legal department to handle them? Or that any documents prepared with litigation in mind will be covered by the attorney work product privilege? Is the breadth of corporate attorney-related privileges getting broader or narrower? Like the answer to many questions, it depends on whom you ask. In 1970, the same year as *Garner* and a decade before *Upjohn*, the federal court in the District of Columbia held that the minutes of a hospital's meetings investigating the death of a patient could remain confidential so that the hospital would feel free to conduct a candid inquiry.[5] This so-called "self-critical analysis" privilege was later approved by several other courts, while rejected by others. Still other courts have debated about whether there should be an attorney "work product" privilege not merely for documents prepared "primarily or exclusively for litigation," but those which are simply prepared with the expectation they *may* be used in litigation.[6] The New Jersey Supreme Court tackled these issues in a 1997 opinion excerpted below, in a case dealing with the plaintiffs' efforts to discover the employer-defendant's internal investigation of sexual harassment charges.

PAYTON v. NEW JERSEY TURNPIKE AUTHORITY
691 A.2d 321 (N.J. 1997)

The privilege of self-critical analysis exempts from disclosure deliberative and evaluative components of an organization's confidential materials. According to one court, "[t]he primary justification for this privilege is the encouragement of candor and frankness toward the ends of discovering the reasons for

---

[5] *Bredice v. Doctor's Hospital, Inc.*, 50 F.R.D. 249 (D.D.C. 1970), *aff'd*, 479 F.2d 920 (D.C. Cir. 1973).

[6] See, e.g., *United States v. Adlman*, 134 F.3d 1194 (2d Cir. 1998), broadening this privilege in a 2-1 decision.

past problems and preventing future problems." Although some courts have rejected the privilege, others have adopted it.

Several lower courts in this State have adopted the privilege and granted seemingly absolute protection to evaluative and deliberative portions of organizations' files. Others have accommodated the confidentiality concerns arising from potential disclosure of deliberative and evaluative processes by employing a balancing test instead of a more rigid privilege.

We decline to adopt the privilege of self-critical analysis as a full privilege, either qualified or absolute, and disavow the statements in those lower court decisions that have accorded materials covered by the supposed privilege near-absolute protection from disclosure. Instead, we perceive concerns arising from the disclosure of evaluative and deliberative materials to be amply accommodated by the "exquisite weighing process."

. . . . Although trial courts should accord significant weight to self-critical analysis and although confidentiality concerns about such information at times may outweigh competing interests in disclosure (especially if the information is obtainable through other sources), certain interests in disclosure are strong enough, in their reflection of important public policies, to outweigh such confidentiality concerns under most, if not all, circumstances.

We recognized one such public policy in *Dixon*, where we stressed the paramount public interest in the eradication of discrimination, an interest that outweighed the interest in confidential communications in the tenure process. [W]e believe that the balance, assuming a valid claim and relevance, is normally best struck in favor of disclosure. As we described in *Dixon,* however, acknowledging the need to order disclosure does not end the inquiry. Instead, [a court can use] "a protective order that limits access to persons directly involved in the case." Consequently, we reject the privilege of self-critical analysis in favor of a case-by-case balancing approach.

Defendant maintains that the attorney-client privilege protects the entire investigatory process because attorneys employed by defendant participated in the investigation. We disagree with that blanket contention. . . .

While an organization or corporation like defendant can be a "client" for purposes of the privilege [citing, *inter alia, Upjohn*], a fine line exists between an attorney who provides legal services or advice to an organization and one who performs essentially nonlegal duties. An attorney who is not performing legal services or providing legal advice in some form does not qualify as a "lawyer" for purposes of the privilege. Thus, when an attorney conducts an investigation not for the purpose of preparing the litigation or providing legal advice, but rather for some other purpose, the privilege is inapplicable.

NOTES

Payton contains a thorough analysis of the law in many jurisdictions. The case is also part of what may be a growing trend to focus on public policy as an important enough goal to curtail certain aspects of corporate attorney-client protections. But *Payton* also concerns a defendant that is a public agency. Do the public policy arguments apply with equal force to private corporations? What *should* the trend be regarding institutional confidentiality or privilege? There are valid arguments on both sides.

6. Subsidiaries. What constitutes a corporation? Is a wholly-owned subsidiary the same as the parent corporation for purposes of conflicts of interest? This has long been the subject of ethics opinions, scholarly articles, and, increasingly, case law, particularly since ABA Ethics Opinion 95-390 (January 25, 1995). In one of its most factionalized opinions, the committee's majority concluded that lawyers were not "necessarily barred" from undertaking representation adverse to corporate affiliates of their current clients. Only if the affiliate is an actual client, or if the new representation "will materially limit" the lawyer's duties to the original client, will conflict of interest rules prevent representation. The majority opinion contains good advice about what "prudence and good practice" may dictate, but leaves it at that: Advice. As for a holding, the opinion states that any effect on the original client is "indirect rather than direct, since its immediate impact is on the affiliate and only derivatively upon the client."

It is rare when an ABA opinion has written dissents or even concurrences. This opinion had three. Lawrence J. Fox, a partner in a prestigious "white shoe" Philadelphia law firm and a longtime advocate of stringent conflicts rules, wrote one dissent. After commending the opinion's "laudable practical advice," Fox wrote that the "advice" would have become "ethically mandated as well if the majority had not strained the meaning of Model Rule 1.7 to permit what everyone on this Committee agrees is ill-advised: suits against corporate affiliates of corporate clients."

Fox's complaints include the fact that the original client does not even have to be informed of the new matter by the law firm. In his view, the notion of loyalty *is* directly impacted. A Northwestern University law student laid out his concerns about whether effects were truly "indirect" in two succinct scenarios.

MICHAEL SACKSTEDER, NOTE: FORMAL OPINION 95-390 OF THE ABA'S ETHICS COMMITTEE: CORPORATE CLIENTS, CONFLICTS OF INTEREST, AND KEEPING THE LID ON PANDORA'S BOX
91 Northwestern University Law Review 741 (1997)[7]

Consider these two seemingly dissimilar hypothetical scenarios.

Scenario One: Your law firm represents Clip-Rite Corporation from time to time in prosecution and protection of trademarks for "Clip-Rite" brand nail clippers. Clip-Rite Corporation is a wholly owned subsidiary of Humongous Corporation, a multinational conglomeration of enterprises ranging from bituminous coal mining to baby food production. One day, your largest client, Big Cat Pistons, asks you to bring a comparatively insignificant lawsuit against another wholly owned subsidiary of Humongous Corp., Thunder Diesel Engines. Humongous Corp. has recently acquired Thunder Diesel without your knowledge. Although you have done no work for either Thunder Diesel

---

[7] Copyright © 1997 by Northwestern University School of Law, Northwestern University Law Review. Reprinted by permission.

or directly for Humongous Corp., you wonder whether your representation of Clip-Rite presents a conflict of interest that prohibits you from undertaking a representation adverse to Clip-Rite's sibling company Thunder Diesel. Your firm's ethics guru consults Formal Opinion 95-390 and determines, quite reasonably, that such a remotely adverse representation is ethically permissible.

Scenario Two: Your law firm represents a small welding company called Mom-N-Pop, Incorporated, in most of its legal matters. Several years earlier, Mom-N-Pop had purchased an acetylene supply company called Ace Acetylene. Your firm did not participate in the acquisition and has performed no legal work for the subsidiary, which kept its existing officers and board of directors following the buyout. Since the acquisition, Ace has flourished, generating almost all the profits in Mom-N-Pop's (very limited) corporate empire. But once again, Big Cat Pistons has entered the picture. This time, Big Cat wants you to institute a multimillion dollar breach of contract suit against Ace. Although you know that an adverse judgment in the suit could cripple Ace and do serious economic harm to Mom-N-Pop, your ethics guru again tells you that the representation is ethically permissible under Formal Opinion 95-390.

In each of these scenarios, adherence to Formal Opinion 95-390 permits the lawyer to disregard the economic impact of the representation on the original client, even when that impact is potentially devastating, as it is in the second scenario.

NOTES

Is this law note too facile, or do Sacksteder's illustrations make a valid point? What should the standard be? Look at Comment 34 to Model Rule 1.7. Does that help?

7. Who in the Corporation Gets a Confidential Relationship? In light of *Upjohn* and other extensive case law — and in light of the obvious, that you can't take a "corporation" to lunch but only its individuals — who in the corporation is entitled to a confidential relationship with the corporate lawyers so that those confidences are never revealed? Who is bestowed with "client-hood," and under what circumstances? Here are two takes, the first a piece by practicing lawyers evaluating employees' confidentiality and privilege in light of an important 2005 case, the second a more tongue-in-cheek but no less compelling effort by a lawyer-writer discussing what to do about confidentiality with corporate higher ups.

IVONNE MENA KING & NICHOLAS A. FROMHERZ, GETTING THE *UPJOHN* WARNING RIGHT IN INTERNAL INVESTIGATIONS
17 Practical Litigator 59 (2006)[8]

What is an *Upjohn* warning, and what purpose does it serve? In essence, an *Upjohn* warning is a disclaimer issued by an attorney for a company to an employee of the company, wherein the employee is advised that that the attorney does not represent the employee, but rather the company as legal entity.

When the third-party employee knows that she is not the client, the privilege clearly belongs to the company alone.

From the company's perspective, a finding that an employee also holds the attorney-client privilege with respect to certain communications can pose a serious dilemma. Any holder of the attorney-client privilege can block disclosure of privileged communications by another holder. Thus, potential conflicts can arise when the company-holder wishes to disclose, and the employee-holder does not. The gravity of this problem is magnified by the fact that companies now have a very strong incentive to disclose the findings of internal investigations, because disclosure of such discoveries is one of the main ways that companies can avert more serious government action. On the other hand, employees who have communicated wrongdoings will often have a strong disincentive to disclose if it is their personal action that lies at the heart of the wrongdoing. Naturally, the wrongdoing employee, who may face serious criminal and civil charges, has no interest in being the proverbial sacrificial lamb that saves the company from harm at his own expense. . . .

[M]any of these pitfalls can be avoided by a properly given *Upjohn* warning, which ensures that the attorney-client privilege belongs only to the company, enabling it to waive or hold the privilege at will.

In re Grand Jury Subpoena: Under Seal

The importance of a properly-given *Upjohn* warning was recently affirmed by the Fourth Circuit case of *In re Grand Jury Subpoena: Under Seal*, [415 F.3d 33 (4th Cir. 2005)]. Although the court ultimately held that the *Upjohn* warning issued was adequate to preclude the relevant employees from asserting the attorney-client privilege, . . . this opinion offers a stern warning to those attorneys who would not take seriously the exact protocol of delivering these warnings.

The pertinent facts: . . . AOL Time Warner began an internal investigation into its relationship with another firm. [AOL] hired outside counsel to assist in the investigation, and over the next several months, outside and in-house counsel interviewed three Company employees (hereinafter the "Employees"). . . . [W]hen the company agreed to waive the attorney-client privilege and disclose the contents of these interviews pursuant to a grand jury subpoena,. . . . [p]resumably to serve their own (diametrically opposed) interests, the Employees moved to quash the interview disclosures on the grounds that they, too, held the attorney-client privilege with respect to the interviews. The issue before the *In re Grand Jury Subpoena* court thus centered around the nature of the *Upjohn* warnings given by the attorneys conducting the interviews. . . .

Counsel's *Upjohn* warning stated:

> We represent the company. These conversations are privileged, but the privilege belongs to the company and the company decides whether to waive it. If there is a conflict, the attorney-client privilege belongs to the company. . . . You are free to consult with your own lawyer at any time.

When conducting the interviews, however, outside counsel told the Employees that it "could" represent them "as long as no conflict appear(ed)." Other similar statements were made to the Employees as well, such as "(w)e can represent (you) until such time as there appears to be a conflict of interest," and "we represent AOL, and can represent (you) too if there is not a conflict." These latter statements were the basis of the Employees' argument that they reasonably believed, at the time of the interviews, that the investigating attorneys represented both them and the Company.

Nevertheless, considering these facts, the court explained that all of the "essential touchstones for the formation of an attorney-client relationship between the investigating attorneys and the (Employees) were missing at the time of the interviews," so that the attorney-client privilege as to these communications was solely possessed by the Company. In particular, the court noted that:

> There is no evidence of an objectively reasonable, mutual understanding that the (Employees) were seeking legal advice from the investigating attorneys or that the investigating attorneys were rendering personal legal advice. . . .

The Trouble With Watered-Down Warnings

However, notwithstanding the Company's success in the case, the court offered a strong critique of the *Upjohn* warning practice used by the investigating attorneys. Indeed, explaining that its opinion should not be construed as an affirmation of "watered-down" *Upjohn* warnings, the court stated that the attorneys' practice represented a "potential legal and ethical mine field." In the court's view, the stakes were high:

> Had the investigating attorneys, in fact, entered into an attorney-client relationship with (the Employees), as their statements . . . professed they could, they would not have been free to waive the (Employees') privilege when a conflict arose. It should have seemed obvious that they could not have jettisoned one client in favor of another. Rather, they would have had to withdraw from all representation and to maintain all confidences.

This would have surely complicated the Company's ability to cooperate with the government.

[A]s the *In re Grand Jury Subpoena* case demonstrates, many dangers accompany a careless *Upjohn* warning practice. For the corporation's sake, counsel should make it abundantly clear that the corporation is the client, not the employee. To do otherwise may be tantamount to giving up valuable government leniency and exposing the company to unnecessary harm.

NOTES

And now to continue in a slightly lighter vein, although in view of Enron and other corporate scandals that have occurred since this article, the issue of "Miranda warnings" for those who consider corporate counsel *their own* lawyers has become only too real.

JOEL COHEN, WARNING YOUR CLIENT THAT YOU'RE NOT HIS LAWYER
New York Law Journal (November 5, 1993)[9]

PICTURE THIS: Armed with a search warrant, a team of FBI agents raid company headquarters of Graftco, Inc. (Graftco) to establish proof of payoffs made to gain subcontracting work on military contracts. They seize boxes of records and interview several senior executives, including the chief executive officer — Jim Upcreek. At the opening volley, some of the executives make incriminating statements. Others lie. Still others, panicked by the unfolding events, implicate the company and top management, including Upcreek. A few add that two members of the board of directors should also be investigated.

When the dust begins to settle, Upcreek, a lawyer by training who has never practiced law, telephones Graftco's outside counsel whom he had actually retained for Graftco years before. With criminal law expert in tow, outside counsel arrives shortly after the FBI has left. After sizing up the warrant and talking to Upcreek and other executives, they get a better fix on what occurred and quickly try to define the parameters of the FBI's investigation.

Upcreek's longstanding relationship with outside counsel, coupled with a mounting case of nerves, leads Upcreek to blurt out, "the FBI asked pointed questions about me." After that comment, the lawyers decide that it is imperative to debrief Upcreek as fully as they can. After everyone else is gone, they quiz him thoroughly, emptying out every possible bit of information, incriminating to him or not.

The lawyers don't want to frighten Upcreek by telling him that, in truth, they represent Graftco, not him. Indeed, to warn Upcreek now that anything he says may someday be divulged to the government (if outside counsel's true client, Graftco, later decides that it suits its purpose to do so) would devastate him. In what might be called Machiavellian altruism, they decide not to advise him who their real client is.

Thus, this law-trained Upcreek, drawing on the widely held belief that any communications between an individual and the attorney he perceives to be

---

representing him are privileged, tells all. He begins by saying that he lied to the FBI to limit his own criminal exposure, which, it turns out, is substantial. Significantly, though, from everything Upcreek tells the lawyers, the conduct under investigation does not implicate the board of directors.

. . . .

The belief, largely held by the public, that any conversation with a lawyer is sacrosanct — that it cannot be repeated, or re-uttered in testimony by the lawyer — is incorrect. The mere fact that a corporate employee, however high a position he or she occupies, was interviewed by the company's counsel will not automatically spread the protective umbrella of the attorney-client privilege. . . . The determination . . . will depend on the employee's "reasonable" belief that he or she, in addition to the corporation, was actually a client.

. . . . [M]uch depends on the words exchanged between the participants before the employee's interview substantively begins. So, if the lawyer tells the employee the following, there is little risk that the employee will mistakenly conclude that the conversation is safeguarded.

- "I do not represent you. I represent the company;

- "If you tell me that you have done something wrong, I must report it to my client and perhaps recommend to my client that action be taken against you;

- "If you feel more comfortable in talking to your lawyer before talking to me, I would encourage you to do so;

- "In fact, just so you understand, there may come a time when the company may want me to repeat to a prosecutor what you tell me today. That statement could conceivably be used against you.

- "All right? Having heard all of that, are you willing to talk to me now?"

. . . .

8. Side-Switching and Changing Loyalties. What happens when control of the organization changes, particularly when the take-over is hostile? And what about organizations other than corporations? To whom do attorneys representing unions, trade consortiums, or partnerships owe their duty of loyalty? With whom may they speak confidentially? First, read this interesting New York Court of Appeals case, in which Chief Judge Kaye walks an interesting tightrope between competing interests.

TEKNI-PLEX v. MEYNER AND LANDIS
89 N.Y.2d 123, 674 N.E. 2d 663, 651 N.Y.S.2d 954 (1996)

KAYE, CHIEF JUDGE.

Central to this appeal, involving a dispute over a corporate acquisition, are two questions. First, can long-time counsel for the seller company and its sole shareholder continue to represent the shareholder in the dispute with the buyer? And second, who controls the attorney-client privilege as to pre-merger communications? We conclude that counsel should step aside, and that the buyer controls the privilege as to some, but not all, of the pre-merger communications.

Facts

Tekni-Plex, Inc., incorporated under the laws of Delaware in 1967, manufactured and packaged products for the pharmaceutical and other industries. In 1986, Tang became the sole shareholder of Tekni-Plex. From that time until the corporation's sale in 1994, Tang was also the president, chief executive officer and sole director of Tekni-Plex.

Appellant Meyner and Landis (M&L), a New Jersey law firm, was first retained as Tekni-Plex counsel in 1971. During the ensuing 23 years, M&L represented Tekni-Plex on various legal matters, including environmental compliance. . . . Additionally, during this period M&L represented Tang individually on several personal matters.

In March 1994, Tang and Tekni-Plex entered into an Agreement and Plan of Merger (the Merger Agreement) with TP Acquisition Company (Acquisition), whereby Tang sold the company to Acquisition for $43 million. M&L represented both Tekni-Plex and Tang personally. The two instant lawsuits grow out of that transaction.

Acquisition was a shell corporation created by the purchasers solely for the acquisition of Tekni-Plex. Under the Merger Agreement, Tekni-Plex merged into Acquisition, with Acquisition the surviving corporation, and Tekni-Plex ceased its separate existence. Tekni-Plex conveyed to Acquisition all of its tangible and intangible assets, rights and liabilities. Acquisition in return paid Tang the purchase price "in complete liquidation of Tekni-Plex," and all of Tang's shares in Tekni-Plex — the only shares outstanding — were canceled.

The Merger Agreement contained representations and warranties by Tang concerning environmental matters, including that Tekni-Plex was in full compliance with all applicable environmental laws and possessed all requisite environmental permits. It further provided for indemnification of Acquisition by Tang for any losses incurred by Acquisition as the result of misrepresentation or breach of warranty by either Tang or Tekni-Plex. Acquisition, in turn, agreed to indemnify Tang and Tekni-Plex for any similar losses suffered by them.

Following the transaction, Acquisition changed its name to "Tekni-Plex, Inc." (new Tekni-Plex). In June 1994, new Tekni-Plex commenced an arbitration against Tang, alleging breach of representations and warranties contained in the Merger Agreement regarding the former Tekni-Plex's (old Tekni-Plex) compliance with environmental laws. . . .

Tang retained M&L to represent him in the arbitration. New Tekni-Plex moved [in court for an] order against M&L (1) enjoining the law firm from representing Tang in any action against new Tekni-Plex, (2) enjoining M&L from disclosing to Tang any information obtained from old Tekni-Plex, and (3) ordering M&L to return to new Tekni-Plex all of the files in the law firm's possession concerning its prior legal representation of old Tekni-Plex. . . . [The trial court ruled for new Tekni-Plex.]

We agree with the courts below that, in the circumstances presented, M&L should be disqualified from representing Tang in the arbitration. As for confidential communications between old Tekni-Plex and M&L generated during the law firm's prior representation of the corporation on environmental compliance matters, authority to assert the attorney-client privilege passed to the corporation's successor management. Moreover, because the record fails to establish that M&L also represented Tang individually on these matters, the exception to the privilege for co-clients who subsequently became adversaries in litigation is inapplicable. . . .

New Tekni-Plex, however, does not control the attorney-client privilege with regard to discrete communications made by either old Tekni-Plex or Tang individually to M&L concerning the acquisition — a time when old Tekni-Plex and Tang were joined in an adversarial relationship to Acquisition. Consequently, new Tekni-Plex cannot assert the privilege in order to prevent M&L from disclosing the contents of such communications to Tang. Nor is new Tekni-Plex entitled to the law firm's confidential communications concerning its representation of old Tekni-Plex with regard to the acquisition.

Disqualification of Counsel

Is New Tekni-Plex a "Former Client" of M&L? It is undisputed that M&L represented old Tekni-Plex for over 20 years on a variety of legal matters. As counsel to the corporation, the law firm's duties of confidentiality and loyalty ran to old Tekni-Plex on these matters. Concomitantly, the attorney-client privilege attached to any confidential communications that took place between M&L and Tekni-Plex corporate actors in the course of this representation. The power to assert or waive the privilege, moreover, belonged to the management of old Tekni-Plex, to be exercised by its officers and directors.

[Tang and M&L] argue that the purchase of old Tekni-Plex by Acquisition did not transfer the corporation's attorney-client relationship to the newly formed entity. According to appellants, the transaction effected nothing more than a transfer of assets, with old Tekni-Plex expiring upon the merger, there being no "former client" still in existence. . . .

When ownership of a corporation changes hands, whether the attorney-client relationship transfers as well to the new owners turns on the practical consequences rather than the formalities of the particular transaction. In *Commodity Futures Trading Commn. V. Weintraub*, 471 U.S. 343, 348 (1985), the Supreme Court held:

> "when control of a corporation passes to new management, the authority to assert and waive the corporation's attorney-client privilege passes as well. New managers . . . may waive the attorney-client privilege with respect to communications made by former officers and directors."

Weintraub establishes that, where efforts are made to run the pre-existing business entity and manage its affairs, successor management stands in the shoes of prior management and controls the attorney-client privilege. . . .

Here, appellants emphasize that old Tekni-Plex merged into Acquisition and ceased to exist as a separate legal entity. That Acquisition, rather than old Tekni-Plex, was designated the surviving corporation, however, is not dispositive. Acquisition was merely a shell corporation, created solely for the purpose of acquiring old Tekni-Plex. Following the merger, the business of old Tekni-Plex remained unchanged. . . .

As a practical matter, then, old Tekni-Plex did not die. To the contrary, the business operations of old Tekni-Plex continued under the new managers. Consequently, control of the attorney-client privilege with respect to any confidential communications between M&L and corporate actors of old Tekni-Plex concerning these operations passed to the management of new Tekni-Plex. An attorney-client relationship between M&L and new Tekni-Plex necessarily exists.

Indeed, M&L's earlier representation of old Tekni-Plex provided the firm with access to confidential information conveyed by old Tekni-Plex concerning the very environmental compliance matters at issue in the arbitration. M&L's duty of confidentiality with respect to these communications passed to new Tekni-Plex; yet its current representation of Tang creates the potential for the law firm to use these confidences against new Tekni-Plex in the arbitration. . . .

Confidential Communications

As a final matter, we must determine whether M&L was properly enjoined from revealing to Tang any confidential communications obtained from old Tekni-Plex and whether new Tekni-Plex owns the confidences created during the law firm's prior representation of old Tekni-Plex. For analytical purposes, the attorney-client communications must be separated into two categories: general business communications and those relating to the merger negotiations. . . .

[T]o grant new Tekni-Plex control over the attorney-client privilege as to communications concerning the merger transaction would thwart, rather than promote, the purposes underlying the privilege. . . . Where the parties to a corporate acquisition agree that in any subsequent dispute arising out of the transaction the interests of the buyer will be pitted against the interests of the sold corporation, corporate actors should not have to worry that their privileged communications with counsel concerning the negotiations might be available to the buyer for use against the sold corporation in any ensuing litigation. Such concern would significantly chill attorney-client communication during the transaction.

NOTES

Do you agree with Judge Kaye's analysis? Or do you believe that somehow, the original client of this closely-held corporation wound up with the short straw? Is this a decision too dependent on formulaic technicalities or one necessitated by the realities of business transfers in today's fluid economic climate?

9. The United Mine Workers Litigation. *Yablonski v. United Mine Workers of America*, 448 F.2d 1175 (D.C. Cir. 1971), was one of several cases that came out of the struggle to control the UMW between Tony Boyle and

Joseph Yablonski. Yablonski, a reformer, brought suit under the Labor-Management Reporting and Disclosure Act, more commonly known as the Landrum-Griffith Act or the LMRDA. The Yablonski forces had strong evidence that the leadership of UMW President Boyle was corrupt, and that it had stolen both union funds and union elections. They believed that honest elections would have installed Yablonski as union President. The LMRDA action was brought to examine Boyle's conduct in running the union, and to demand an accounting of union and pension funds.

LMRDA actions are brought by union members against the union as well as its individual leaders. The UMW was represented in the Yablonski matter by the same law firm which represented Boyle on other matters. Yablonski objected, arguing that *he*, not Boyle, actually represented the best interests of the union, and that the union's law firm, one clearly loyal to Boyle personally, should be replaced. The court agreed, likening Yablonski's suit to a shareholder derivative action. The court evaluated the proper role of union counsel in this way:

> We are not required to accept at this point the charge of the appellants that the "true interest" of the union is aligned with those of the individual appellants here; this may or may not turn out to be the fact. But in the exploration and the determination of the truth or falsity of the charges brought by these individual appellants against the incumbent officers of the union and the union itself as a defendant, the UMWA needs the most objective counsel obtainable. After Boyle's private law firm was disqualified, the union's in-house general counsel, also beholden to Boyle, took over the Yablonski case on behalf of the union. Again the Yablonski group objected, and again the Court of Appeals agreed. [10]

The matter ended favorably for the Yablonski side, but tragically for Yablonski himself. In 1969, during the pendency of the litigation, Yablonski and his wife and child were murdered during a break-in at their home. Eventually, "Tough Tony" Boyle was convicted of conspiracy to murder Joe Yablonski, and sent to prison. During the pendency of the ongoing Yablonski litigation, the Yablonski forces gained control of the union, and the union petitioned to switch sides. Interestingly, the Boyle defendants then made the same claim about new union counsel that Yablonski had previously made, but this time, the Court of Appeals — making perhaps a largely political decision that the best interests of the union were now being served — denied Boyle's motion. [11]

10. Lawyers for Partnerships. Last but not least — and vital to Esperanza Dejos — what about partnerships? Despite the widespread existence of partnerships, and the common use of limited partnerships which, like HiFly, are created for the ownership and development of real estate, there is not a great deal of authority — and even less agreement — defining whom the lawyers for those partnerships represent, and with whom they may share confidential information.

---

[10] *Yablonski v. United Mine Workers*, 454 F.2d 1036 (D.C. Cir. 1971).

[11] *Weaver v. United Mine Workers*, 492 F.2d 580 (D.C. Cir. 1973).

ABA Formal Opinion 91-361 (July 12, 1991) addresses these issues. It concludes that Model Rule 1.13 applies to partnerships, and that a lawyer for the partnership represents the entire entity. "There is no logical reason to distinguish partnerships from corporations or other legal entities in determining the client." The opinion recognizes that individual partners — unlike corporate officers, for example — continue to have individual rights and to carry personal liability for partnership acts. Nevertheless, the ABA concludes that a lawyer does not necessarily have an attorney-client relationship with any of the individual partners. Whether this relationship exists will depend on "the specific facts" of the situation.

What about confidences? Generally, says Opinion 91-361, they are gained by the lawyer on behalf of the partnership, and thus shared among all partners. On this point too, however, the ABA hedges in a footnote excepting from this general rule situations in which the lawyer is representing the partnership in a dispute against one of its partners. But how is "dispute" defined? Do Gary Lavin's actions create a dispute between him and the partnership, at least once Esperanza Dejos is aware of the situation?

To support both its proposition that the entity is the client, and its view that the individual partners are not necessarily clients, ABA Opinion 91-361 cites *Margulies v. Upchurch*, 696 P.2d 1195 (Utah 1985). But *Margulies* also holds that the reasonable beliefs of partners that the lawyer represented them individually must be considered in determining whether an attorney-client relationship existed.[12] Moreover, the ABA opinion specifically notes that for a limited partnership, application of Model Rule 1.13 might be different. Since limited partnerships are quite common, more complex structurally, and at least as likely to wind up in litigation as general partnerships, one wonders why the ABA chose to consider limited partnerships the exception to the rule. Perhaps it was recognition of the difficulty in developing clear guidelines for limited partnerships.

Does justification for the dichotomy in ABA Opinion 91-361, between whom the attorney represents and who may share confidences, depend on why the representation is being scrutinized? For example, some California courts have held that a partnership lawyer does not necessarily represent the individual partners. See, for example, *Responsible Citizens v. Superior Court*, 16 Cal. App. 4th 1717, 20 Cal. Rptr. 2d 756 (1993), which is described further in the Supplemental Readings. Other cases hold that confidences imparted by one partner to the attorney must be shared with all partners, even limited partners, according to *McCain v. Phoenix Resources, Inc.*, 185 Cal. App. 3d 575, 230 Cal. Rptr. 25 (1986), a case cited by Opinion 91-361. Still another case claims that whether or not the limited partners are considered clients "is of no great moment," since the lawyer for the general partner necessarily

---

[12] Consideration of the putative client's reasonable belief in personal representation is not unique to *Margulies*. For example, see *Rosman v. Shapiro*, 653 F. Supp. 1441 (S.D.N.Y. 1987), using this standard for a closely-held corporation. And in *Westinghouse Elec. Corp. v. Kerr-McGee Corp.*, 580 F.2d 1311 (7th Cir. 1978), a law firm represented a trade association. The court considered the "reasonable belief" of the association's members that they had confidential relationships with the law firm and held that the law firm had a professional obligation to maintain those confidences.

owes "a fiduciary duty to the partnership to look out for all the partners' interests."[13]

The imprecision and lack of uniform authority about entity representation does not mean that the issue has been poorly treated either by courts or by ethics commentators. Rather, it emphasizes the difficulty of grappling with this issue. We can't say how much comfort this might be to Esperanza Dejos as she tries to resolve her dilemma, but we are confident she is not alone.

SUPPLEMENTAL READINGS

1. *Fassihi v. Sommers, Schwartz, Silver, Schwartz & Tyler, P.C.*, 107 Mich. App. 509, 309 N.W.2d 645 (1981). Defendant attorneys represented a closely-held corporation with two officers and shareholders, both radiologists and employees of the corporation, each with 50% ownership. When one physician, the corporation's president, ousted the other, the ousted doctor sued, and the attorney claimed attorney-client privilege and confidentiality. The court held that the attorney for the corporation had a fiduciary relationship with both shareholders and a duty to advise the ousted shareholder of his individual representation of the president, and that no privilege could be asserted against the ousted shareholder because, as a member of the corporate board, he was part of the entity's "control group." The court also cited the *Garner* case for the proposition that disclosure is warranted where a corporation seeks to defraud one of its shareholders.

2. *Responsible Citizens v. Superior Court*, 16 Cal. App. 4th 1717, 20 Cal. Rptr. 2d 756 (1993), cited four factors in determining whether the lawyer for a partnership represented the individual partners: the type and size of the partnership; the nature and scope of the lawyer's representation; the amount of contact between the lawyer and the partner in question; and the lawyer's access to information relating to the specific partner's interests.

3. Two New York City ethics opinions take the position that lawyers for limited partnerships not only may, but *must* disclose a general partner's malfeasance to the limited partners. Ass'n Bar City of N.Y. Opinion 1986-2 allows disclosure, while Opinion 1994-10 requires it; even though the limited partners are not clients, disclosure is required to protect the interests of the partnership.

4. Darian M. Ibrahim, *Solving the Everyday Problem of Client Identity in the Context of Closely Held Businesses*, 56 Ala. L. Rev. 181 (2004), proposes a new model rule for closely held corporations that would allow an attorney to represent the entity on external matters and one of the shareholders on internal matters. An interesting discussion of what would be a substantial departure from the existing norm.

5. Ellen A. Pansky, *Between an Ethical Rock and a Hard Place: Balancing Duties to the Organizational Client and Its Constituents*, 37 So. Tex. L. Rev. 1165 (1996), is a good, brief, and readable survey of the problems faced by organizational attorneys.

---

[13] *Johnson v. Superior Court*, 38 Cal. App. 4th 463, 477, 45 Cal. Rptr. 2d 312, 321-22 (1995).

6. Sherman L. Cohn, *The Organization Client: Attorney-Client Privilege and the No-Contact Rule*, 10 Geo. J. Leg. Ethics 739 (1997), is an interesting and frank critique of the common policy of organizational lawyers advising organizational employees in a way that may be in the best interests of the organization but stretches the bounds of the relationship between those employees and the attorney.

7. Ronald D. Rotunda, *Conflicts Problems When Representing Members of Corporate Families*, 72 Notre Dame L. Rev. 655 (1997), and Lara E. Romansic, *Note: Stand by Your Client?: Opinion 95-390 and Conflicts of Interest in Corporate Families*, 11 Geo. J. Leg. Ethics 307 (1998) are two valuable articles on this controversial subject.

8. Richard W. Painter, *Ethics in the Age of Un-incorporation: A Return to Ambiguity of Pre-Incorporation or an Opportunity to Contract for Clarity?*, 2005 U. Ill. L. Rev. 49 (2005). One of the primary authors of Sarbanes-Oxley related regulations suggests that relationships between lawyers and unincorporated entities, including scope of representation, should be determined by contract between them, rather than reliance on rules and case law that often do not apply to the unique circumstances involved.

9. An excellent analysis of the duties of union counsel is contained in Russell G. Pearce, *The Union Lawyer's Obligations to Bargaining Unit Members: A Case Study of the Interdependence of Legal Ethics and Substantive Law*, 37 So. Tex. L. Rev. 1095 (1996). An earlier article, James Gray Pope, *Two Faces, Two Ethics: Labor Union Lawyers and the Emerging Doctrine of Entity Ethics*, 68 Ore. L. Rev. 1 (1989), examines whether the corporate model ought to apply to unions, and evaluates the alternatives.

10. *United States v. International Brotherhood of Teamsters*, 119 F.3d 210 (2d Cir. 1997), was decided in the aftermath of a hotly contested — and government-supervised — election for Teamsters' president between Ron Carey and James Hoffa, Jr., son of the notorious former Teamster boss. When Carey won, Hoffa objected to the union's court-appointed Election Officer. Although Carey cooperated with the Election Officer's investigation and waived any attorney-client confidentiality between him and his campaign's lawyers, Carey's campaign manager, Jere Nash, refused to do so. When Nash did not accede to the Election Officer's demands, the government took the issue to court. Both the district court and the Second Circuit Court of Appeal agreed that Nash had no independent rights of privilege and confidentiality. (Though Carey cooperated, his election was eventually invalidated, and Hoffa wound up winning a new election from which Carey was barred from being a candidate.)

PROBLEM 9

An attorney's loyalty to a client and independence of professional judgment may be compromised whenever the lawyer's own interests are affected by the representation. Most apparent among these interests are financial gain. Charging clients a fee comes with the territory, but lawyers must make sure their own financial interests don't interfere with their clients' cases. There are myriad other interests that may affect a lawyer's actions on behalf of a client — everything from the attorney's personal relationships, to the desire to withdraw from a case that's lost its luster, to the desire for an intimate relationship with the client. This problem addresses conflicts that can arise from lawyer-client fee arrangements, and examines whether a lawyer's desire to withdraw from a case, and a number of other extrinsic interests of the lawyer, can also create a conflict of interest.

What Happens When Your Personal Interests Get in the Way?

I. Melanie Cameron is a sole practitioner. Consider these two scenarios:

1. Cameron represents William Simons. He is accused of stealing a car. Cameron has agreed to represent Simons for $3,500 if the case resolves before trial, and $10,000 (an additional $6,500) if the case goes to trial.

The DA has offered a plea bargain that both Melanie and Will think is far too stiff. Cameron advises him that he might want to take his chances at trial. He says, "I'd like to, you know, but I'm worried about the extra bucks for you. You deserve it, but my folks are just barely making it as it is, and I work at McDingle's for five bucks an hour. I guess it's just too expensive for us to go to trial. So I better plead guilty."

What should Cameron do?

2. Cameron also represents Lola Lipp in a contingency-fee case concerning injuries Lipp received in an auto accident. Cameron has taken her case on the understanding that Lipp will pay all costs incurred along the way, including deposition fees, investigation, and experts. Cameron's written agreement reflects this, and Melanie also has written Lipp a letter outlining these costs and advising that "while I think that beyond a few depositions, these costs will be modest, I cannot of course guarantee this. It is possible, though unlikely, that significant investigation or expert advice will be necessary."

Unfortunately, discovery has revealed that there are potential eyewitnesses, necessitating extensive investigation, and questions about liability for which an accident reconstruction specialist is needed. Costs will be substantially greater than anticipated. But when Cameron approaches Lipp about this, the client seems taken aback, and says she doesn't have the money. What should Cameron do? Specifically:

(a) If Cameron wants to continue to represent Lipp, must she provide the funds for these unexpected expenses?

(b) Suppose on the other hand that Cameron determines that it is impossible for her to fund the extra expenses and also that the new issues about liability make the case far less attractive by substantially reducing the settlement value. May Cameron withdraw from the case?

(c) What if Lipp, frustrated by Cameron's refusal to pay for the additional costs, fires her and hires another lawyer? What rights (if any) does Cameron have?

II. Arnie Berkowitz is a sole practitioner. Arnie has a stock portfolio which he manages himself. He owns 500 shares of stock in Globetrotting Airways, Inc., which represents about 9% of his portfolio. He is asked by the Airline Pilots Association to head the negotiating team for their new contract with "Globie." Money, of course, is a big concern, but the pilots are also concerned with the safety of the airline's fleet of BX-15s. While the pilots' association has so far said nothing about these aircraft, they have unreleased documentation which they believe shows the planes are unsafe. They don't want to reveal the information, but have threatened privately to do so if their demands for a full BX-15 repair and recall program are not met in the new collective bargaining agreement.

QUESTIONS

1. May Arnie undertake this representation? Should he? What, if anything, must he do beforehand? Does the size of his holdings in Globetrotting make a difference? Why (or why not)?

2. Suppose Arnie did not own stock in Globie at all, but was a golfing partner of the company's chief financial officer. Is this the kind of relationship which creates a conflict? Could Arnie represent the pilots in this circumstance?

3. What if Arnie's wife worked for Globie in a non-managerial capacity? Could Arnie represent the pilots? What if the Globie employee were his brother-in-law?

III. Sam Shade has been in sole practice for twenty-five years. One day, Bernard Bentley comes in with a personal injury case. Shade agrees to take the case for one-third of the gross recovery if the case does not go to trial and 40% if the case is tried. Shade looks at jury verdicts in comparable cases and determines that the estimated value of this case at trial is $70,000. He also estimates that if the case goes to trial, it will require 250 hours of his time.

Instead of filing a complaint, Shade telephones the defendant's insurance carrier. After the medical information is verified, the carrier's adjuster offers Shade $18,000 to settle the case now. Since Bentley does not have any residual injury, Shade decides to recommend settlement now. This way, he reasons, he can get a $6,000 fee for ten hours of work, rather than the larger fee he would hope to get, but may not get, if the case goes to trial. "After all," he advises his client, "jury awards are unpredictable." Is this proper?

READINGS

1. When Lawyers Have Something to Gain. What happens when a lawyer develops a close relationship with a client, even becoming like a surrogate relative, particularly when the client has no other family? American Bar Association guidelines specifically prohibit lawyers who practice estate planning from preparing trusts or wills in which they are beneficiaries, and those guidelines have been adopted by a majority of states. Moreover, many question the propriety of an attorney serving as a trustee managing trust assets. Read what one enterprising lawyer did.

JACK EWING, LAWYER'S ROLE IN ESTATE CHALLENGED; ELDERLY WOMAN LEFT EVERYTHING TO "DEAREST FRIEND"

The Hartford Courant (November 16, 1991)[1]

Irene Burkhardstmayer used to greet lawyer Richard Lafferty warmly when he visited her at the convalescent home where she lived. After all, the mildly senile 85-year-old Hartford woman had no children, no living brothers or sisters. Lafferty, appointed by a judge to oversee Burkhardstmayer's affairs, was one of her only visitors.

But it appears that Lafferty was getting more out of the arrangement than just the satisfaction of helping a lonely old woman.

Over a 32-year period, he collected legal fees that totaled more than $150,000, according to documents on file at Hartford Probate Court. He set up a trust to handle her financial affairs, according to the documents, and put her money — several hundred thousand dollars apparently accumulated through years of saving — into high-risk investments, including a Hollywood movie that flopped.

And last year, Lafferty arranged to have Burkhardstmayer's will rewritten. Signed by Burkhardstmayer in a trembling hand, it said that she wished to acknowledge all the "kindness, attention, support and love" provided by "my dearest friend."

The will stipulated that, unless some other lawful heirs were discovered, the dear friend would collect all the money in the estate.

A separate document signed at the same time stipulated that this friend, in consultation with a doctor, would be the one to decide whether to keep Burkhardstmayer on life support "if my condition is deemed terminal."

The dear friend's name? Richard Lafferty.

Lafferty, who works out of an office in Rocky Hill, denies through his lawyer doing anything improper in the handling of the affairs of Burkhardstmayer, a former employee of Underwood Olivetti Typewriter Co. She died in September.

Lafferty's attorney, William F. Gallagher of New Haven, said Lafferty drew up the will only after Burkhardstmayer asked him to. Lafferty spent an "enormous amount of time" looking after Burkhardstmayer and her sister, Anna Burkhardstmayer, who died in 1989, Gallagher said. "He became the only person to take an interest in the care of these ladies," Gallagher said.

But in April, after court officials became concerned about Lafferty's handling of the case, another lawyer was appointed to scrutinize the estate. She soon began raising questions about the way the will was drawn up, about the

---

[1] Reprinted by permission.

investments Lafferty made, and about the multiple roles he took on in Burkhardstmayer's life — roles that gave him almost total control over her finances and legal affairs.

She and others also have questioned how hard Lafferty worked to find relatives of Burkhardstmayer who might be entitled to her money. In documents filed with Hartford Probate Court, Lafferty said she had no known heirs. Later, however, lawyers assigned to sort out the estate had little trouble finding four first cousins living in Willington, Coventry and Tolland. Under law, cousins are considered legitimate potential heirs.

"He had no idea they existed. He would have contacted them," Gallagher said of Lafferty.

Lafferty gave up his financial role in the estate in July under pressure from Hartford Probate Judge Robert K. Killian Jr. Burkhardstmayers' cousins are challenging Lafferty's claim on the assets. A series of hearings has been scheduled for December.

However, this week lawyers involved in the case said they were close to a settlement in which Lafferty would give up any claim to Burkhardstmayer's estate — by some estimates worth $500,000 — and buy back some questionable investments, including a $100,000 loan to Howard Baldwin, former managing general partner of the Hartford Whalers. The loan, used to finance a film that was a financial failure, is in default, according to documents on file at the probate court.

The settlement would allow Lafferty to keep the more than $150,000 in fees he collected, including time charged for visiting Burkhardstmayer at the nursing home.

According to Gallagher, Lafferty collected about $35 an hour — a low rate for an attorney — for his work on the estate, including hours he visited Burkhardstmayer.

At that rate, Lafferty would have spent more than 4,000 hours on the Burkhardstmayer estate, about two years of steady 40-hour weeks. "My assessment is that Richard Lafferty works very long hours," Gallagher said when asked about the hours.

Nothing in the settlement suggests that action be taken against Lafferty's license to practice law.

. . . .

No one has alleged that Lafferty in any way hastened Burkhardstmayer's death after she suffered heart failure. She died Sept. 6 at Hartford Hospital after more than a month in intensive care. A report prepared by a convalescent home nurse 10 months after the last will was signed said Burkhardstmayer was able to dress, wash and go to the bathroom on her own, but had a poor short-term memory, suffered from mild senile dementia, and required 24-hour supervision. The report noted: "Attorney Lafferty visits client often for socialization as well as for financial reasons and they seem to have a strong friendship."

2. Can We Expect Lawyers to Act "Better"? No, says Professor Leonard E. Gross, an "economic behavioralist" who did empirical research to determine if the existing conflicts rules square with what economic behaviorists would predict about how lawyers and clients will behave.

LEONARD E. GROSS, ARE DIFFERENCES AMONG THE ATTORNEY CONFLICT OF INTEREST RULES CONSISTENT WITH PRINCIPLES OF BEHAVIORAL ECONOMICS?
9 Georgetown Journal of Legal Ethics 111 (2006)[2]

Lawyers' Behavior in Assessing Conflict of Interest Situations will be Largely Self-Motivated

Do lawyers behave like other people when it comes to determining whether to conform their behavior to ethical norms?

. . . .

To test whether lawyers actually behave the way behavioral economics would predict, I have conducted a survey of lawyers. I have also reviewed statistics on lawyer discipline and compared the results to statistics on discipline for other professionals committing similar types of misconduct. This data confirms the hypothesis that lawyers will be inclined to behave in ways that are consistent with their self-interest, and that clients will generally defer to their attorney's suggestion to waive conflicts of interest. . . .

Empirical Results

A survey concerning behavior in conflict of interest situations was sent to 439 graduates of Southern Illinois University School of Law (all the alumni for which we have e-mail addresses), and 157 people responded. The demographics of the attorneys who responded to the survey were similar to those in Illinois as a whole. Illinois is reasonably representative of the country, though it has more large firms than does the nation as a whole. The results of the survey reveal some interesting information about how lawyers and clients behave (or at least how lawyers say they behave). The results were inconclusive with respect to how frequently lawyers discussed conflicts of interest with their clients. [Substantial numbers of responses ranged from] one to two times per month or more [to] less frequently than once a year.

When lawyers do identify conflicts and inform their clients about them, they overwhelmingly indicate that they believe the conflicts are waivable. . . . A follow-up question asked how often attorneys told their clients that they could do a good job notwithstanding the conflict. Here, the results were more mixed. Twenty-seven percent of attorneys told their clients virtually all the time that they could do a good job, [but] another 34% of attorneys told clients this less than half the time. Both small firms and medium sized ones were much less likely to tell clients that they could do a good job notwithstanding the conflict than were large firms.

The seeming contradiction between the overwhelming majority of attorneys telling their clients that conflicts were waivable almost all of the time and

---

[2] Reprinted with permission of the publisher, Georgetown Journal of Legal Ethics © 2006.

attorneys being more evenly divided on how frequently they told their clients they could do a good job notwithstanding the conflict may be explained in a number of ways. One possibility is that many lawyers and firms may make calculated business decisions that they will gain more clients than they will lose by adopting self-interested definitions of conflicts and obtaining broad consents to future conflicts while revealing as little as possible to clients.

Clearly, it is easier to hide the ball from the client when the client lacks sophistication. Survey results reveal that clients almost invariably consent to waiving conflicts. . . . Furthermore, clients very rarely raise conflicts sua sponte. Seventy-two percent of lawyers reported that clients never raised possible conflicts that the lawyer had not first raised with them. . . .

One possible explanation for the relative absence of discussion between lawyers and clients about conflicts of interest is that lawyers rarely have conflicts of interest; and they virtually never have conflicts of interest that they do not raise with clients. Another perhaps more plausible explanation is that because of self-interest, lawyers do not reveal many conflicts to their clients. One possible explanation for clients' failure to raise conflicts sua sponte is that there are few such conflicts that are not disclosed to them by their attorney. More plausibly, clients do not raise conflicts with their lawyers because they do not recognize the conflict, or because they have already put their trust in the lawyer and are disinclined to look for potential problems in the relationship. . . .

An outstanding case study by Susan P. Shapiro based on interviews with lawyers in Illinois supports the notion that lawyers, when faced with conflicts of interest, act in self-interested ways. . . . Shapiro observes that only a small number of the firms she surveyed stuck their head in the sand when it came to conflict of interest between multiple clients. Instead, most firms performed some type of conflict check, though the degree of sophistication with which the check was performed differed widely from firm to firm. When confronted with conflicts, lawyers reacted in a number of ways. A few would decline to represent a client for fear that a conflict of interest would preclude them from subsequently accepting a more lucrative client. Shapiro observed, however, that for every respondent who indicated that his firm declined to take a case because of a potential conflict, several others described identical situations in which they would take the case, explaining that they would deal with the conflict later if and when it arose. . . .

Principles of Behavioral Economics do not Support Disparate Treatment of Certain Kinds of Conflicts of Interest

The ethics rules permit clients to waive some attorney conflicts of interest but not others. . . . Rule 1.8(j) now absolutely precludes a lawyer from having sexual relations with a client unless a consensual sexual relationship existed between them when the lawyer-client relationship commenced. This apparent anomaly, which precludes lawyers from having sexual relations with existing clients but permits business relations with existing clients, may be predicated on the assumption that lawyers will be more likely to take advantage of clients sexually than they will financially. However, none of the principles of behavioral economics would suggest that lawyers are more inclined to put their interests ahead of their clients' in the personal realm rather than the financial area.

. . . .

[W]e must address why Rule 1.8(a) permits lawyers to have business dealings with clients (subject to disclosure and waiver and provided that the transaction is "fair") and why Rule 1.8(c) permits lawyers to draft documents on behalf of clients who are relatives, thereby leaving themselves substantial bequests. One cannot plausibly argue that there is little danger of the lawyer taking advantage of the client in those situations. The cases are legion in which attorneys have exerted undue influence over relatives while drafting wills or inter vivos bequests which leave them or other relatives substantial amounts of money. Likewise there are many cases in which attorneys who engaged in business dealings with their clients put their own interests ahead of those of their clients.

Rule 1.5 permits lawyers to charge contingency fees in a wide variety of cases, though not in criminal matters or in domestic relations matters. The rule has been interpreted by the ABA as even permitting lawyers to charge contingent fees when liability is clear and the only uncertainty is the amount in question. . . . One way of [diminishing contingency fee conflicts] is to have the lawyer's percentage recovery be less for settlement than for trial. However, if the percentage were not calibrated carefully, one could create an inappropriate inducement causing the lawyer to take a case to trial when settlement was in the client's best interest. It is perhaps for this reason that many states have statutorily limited the amounts that attorneys can recover in medical malpractice cases.

. . . .

[P]ermitting contingent fee agreements is somewhat inconsistent with Rule 1.8(e), which forbids lawyers from advancing financial assistance to a client in connection with pending or contemplated litigation except for court costs and expenses of litigation if either (a) repayment is contingent on the outcome of the case or (b) the client is indigent. In both situations, there is a conflict of interest, where an attorney would be tempted to put his own financial interests above the interests of the client. . . .

One might argue that contingent fees are needed to enable clients to hire lawyers in situations in which they could not otherwise afford them or in which they were unwilling to assume the risk of the litigation. However, the same argument could be made with respect to advancement of medical costs and living expenses. Clients may fall victim to low ball offers from insurance companies if they are unable to obtain money to pay their medical bills and living expenses. Although one might argue that clients will be less inclined to fire lawyers in whom they have lost confidence if they would still owe them money from the advancement of living expenses or medical bills, the same issue arises when clients consider firing lawyers whom they have retained on a contingent fee basis. In many jurisdictions, they still owe the lawyer a reasonable fee for his services on a quantum meruit basis, regardless of whether the contingency ultimately occurs. Thus, we are still left struggling for an explanation for the disparate treatment between permitting contingent fees generally but not permitting the advancement of living expenses and medical bills.

. . . .

Although one could argue that permitting a greater degree of latitude in contingent fee situations is a necessary tradeoff for encouraging lawyers to handle cases, this justification of the rule is incomplete. It does not explain the failure to adequately inform clients of the conflict, which would be necessary if the rule is truly designed to benefit clients in obtaining representation. It also does not explain why lawyers are not required to offer hourly fees when clients desire representation on that basis. Therefore, unless the rule permitting contingent fees is designed to benefit lawyers at client expense (certainly a possibility), it would seem to be partially the product of unwarranted assumptions about lawyer and client behavior.

NOTES

Do Professor Gross' conclusions sound too harsh? Or is there a reasonable likelihood that lawyers are that self-interested? Even in the face of their so-called "fiduciary duty" to always put the client's interest ahead of themselves? What part of Gross' conclusions resonate with you? Do you agree, for example, that sex with a client is no more problematic, in terms of "behavioral economics," than a lawyer-client business deal?

3. Fee Arrangements and Conflicts of Interest. What about more subtle financial conflicts than the self-interested overreaching of attorney Lafferty in section 1? The following article argues that almost *any* fee arrangement can create a conflict between the interests of the lawyer and those of the client. Is this true? If it is, what can the attorney do to avoid such a conflict? Are such conflicts inherent in the practice of law, or are there ways of charging fees which would avoid or at least minimize the problem?

RICHARD ZITRIN, WHEN FEES ARE UNETHICAL
California Lawyer (November 1989)[3]

Abby Perkins, a young lawyer who's been passed over for partner, decides to go out on her own. She struggles financially; she's behind in her rent and hasn't paid her secretary in two weeks. When the defense offers to settle a contingency fee case, she's tempted to take the first offer.

Abby asks her friend Stuart Markowitz, a partner at her former firm, to help evaluate the case. Markowitz tells her she's settling for too little, but she recommends the offer to her client anyway. Only after her client refuses to settle and fires her does Abby realize she's acted unethically. She's allowed her own financial problems to interfere with the interests of her client.

If this story sounds familiar, it's because you saw it on last season's *L.A. Law.* But real lawyers know that, as the California Supreme Court put it in *Maxwell v. Superior Court* (1982) 30 C3d 606, "Almost any fee arrangement between attorney and client may give rise to a 'conflict.'" This doesn't mean

---

attorneys should stop getting paid. It simply means lawyers must always consider the effect their fees have on their clients.

. . . .

[M]any potential conflicts have been subject to very little comment. The court in *Maxwell* mentioned three:

● Either the attorney or the client in a contingency fee arrangement "needs a quick settlement while the other . . . would be better served by pressing on."

● A lawyer receiving a flat fee may have an incentive "to dispose of the case as quickly as possible, to the client's disadvantage."

● An attorney paid by the hour might be tempted to "drag the case on" without real benefit to the client.

Contingency fees aren't just necessary, they're desirable. They increase access to the courts for those who can't otherwise afford it.

Theoretically an identity of interest exists between attorney and client in a contingency fee case: The higher the recovery, the larger the fee. But most plaintiffs attorneys know that a lawyer can make far more money per hour by turning cases over quickly than by doing the preparation necessary to maximize recovery for each client. "The vagaries of a contingency fee practice don't always lend themselves to even cash flow," says Oakland plaintiffs litigator David W. Rudy.

Early disposition may be best for some clients, such as an accident victim with relatively minor injuries. But in more complex contingency fee cases, the responsible plaintiffs attorney will usually need to conduct discovery before fully evaluating the case.

How a specific case should be litigated always involves judgment calls and matters of strategy difficult to second-guess. But the client must come first. "You simply make your judgments based on the client's best interests. That's just part of the job," says Rudy.

Sometimes it is in the client's interest to settle. A San Francisco sole practitioner recalls winning a multimillion-dollar verdict, then being ready to litigate the appeal against the defendant's offer to settle for about 50 percent of the verdict. "I was sure we were going to prevail, and I couldn't help thinking I could retire on the fee I'd receive," says the lawyer.

Then he realized that his client, who was destitute, would do very well with the amount offered in settlement and would remain impoverished during the years of appeal. "I was looking at the appeal from my economic perspective, not my client's. When I put myself in my client's shoes, I had to resolve the case."

On the other side is the defense lawyer, who generally bills at an hourly rate. The longer the case goes on, and the more work done, the larger the fee.

"I try to make our work as efficient as possible," says Peter E. Romo, a partner in the San Francisco office of Adams, Duque & Hazeltine. That means ongoing communications with clients and a balancing of the need for discovery against the opportunity for quick case resolution. . . .

Principles can get in the way of a settlement that makes economic sense, as when a defendant refuses to settle because it would seem an admission of wrongdoing. It's then, notes Romo, the ethical defense lawyer takes the size of his fee into consideration by advising the client of the likely costs.

Sometimes the lawyer should ask if it's ethical to represent the client at all when the vast majority of the recovery will be spent on hourly fees even if the client wins. "I think it's important to be right up front with my client," says Ronald S. Smith of Beverly Hills. "I ask, 'Do you want to give Ron Smith $7,500 to pursue a $10,000 claim?'"

Similarly, the cost of hiring a lawyer may not always be justified in criminal cases. Smith, who was a deputy district attorney for five years, questions whether it is fair to charge a drunk driving defendant $1,500 just to walk him through a standard guilty plea.

He prefers to review the police report first, for little or no fee, to determine if the client has a defense. "Then I tell them what the practical consequences are and suggest they can go to court on their own."

Most criminal law practitioners in California's major metropolitan areas charge flat fees for representing criminal defendants. However, because it's often impossible to determine how much work a case will require — in particular, whether it will actually go to trial — this fee structure gives the lawyer three uncomfortable choices: Assume the case will go to trial and charge a larger sum, to the detriment of the client; assume it will not, to the lawyer's potential financial detriment; or split the difference, which may average out over time but doesn't serve the needs of either the client or the lawyer in any particular case.

James Larson, of the San Francisco criminal defense firm of Larson & Weinberg, no longer sets his fees this way. He says it is fairer to charge one fee for preparation until trial — work that almost always must be done — and a second fee for the trial itself. Larson's clients don't pay for trials that never take place, and Larson has eliminated the conflict that might tempt him to encourage a questionable guilty plea.

Unfortunately, other problems may arise with this type of fee structure. Criminal clients often don't have the funds to pay the entire fee in advance and may be unable on the eve of trial to pay the trial fee. Larson says courts themselves sometimes look favorably on his request to be appointed and paid by the court if an incarcerated client is indigent. Otherwise, he says, "My job is to try the case anyway, with or without the rest of the fee."

Surprisingly, nowhere do the California Rules of Professional Conduct say that legal fees can cause a conflict of interest. Rule 3-300 says a lawyer "shall not . . . knowingly acquire an ownership, possessory, security, or other pecuniary interest adverse to a client." But the "discussion" appended to this rule explains that it was not intended to apply to most fee agreements.

California Business and Professions Code sections 6147 and 6148 now require that most fee agreements between attorneys and noncorporate clients be in writing, and that they include the basic provisions regarding rates and the nature of legal services. But these provisions may lead to the erroneous conclusion that the mere written recitation of a fee agreement resolves all potential conflicts of interest regarding those fees.

The clearest words yet may be those of U.S. Supreme Court in *Evans v. Jeff D.* [,475 U.S. 717 (1986)]. The court permitted a settlement in a civil rights action that required the plaintiff's attorney to waive his fee. While this result is harsh, Justice John Paul Stevens's description of a lawyer's ethical obligation sounds like hornbook law: The lawyer "must not allow his own interests, financial or otherwise, to influence his professional advice." Thus a lawyer should "evaluate a settlement offer on the basis of his client's interests, without considering his own interest in obtaining a fee."

Charging a fee is an intrinsic and necessary part of the practice of law. When care is taken to avoid any adverse consequences to the client, a lawyer can provide the best possible representation without worrying about compensation.

4. The Problem of Determining the Attorney's Fee Independently of the Client's Recovery. What happens when opposing counsel, or even the judge, drives a wedge between a client's recovery and a lawyer's fee? What is the proper balance between lawyers protecting the interests of their client and protecting their own fees? Read the excerpt from this most appropriately titled case.

IN RE FEE
182 Ariz. 597, 898 P.2d 976 (1995)

Respondents' client gave birth to a severely brain-damaged boy. In 1987, after unsuccessfully seeking representation from three other attorneys, she retained respondents [Attorneys Fee and Montijo] on a 40% contingent fee. They filed a medical malpractice suit against the State of Arizona and Pima County. . . .

The medical negligence claim was admittedly weak. Respondents' success in developing a colorable racketeering theory, however, prompted negotiations. After an unproductive initial settlement conference, a second was scheduled for January 21, 1991, the day before trial. On Friday the 18th, the defense offered a structured settlement consisting of a cash lump sum followed by periodic payments. This proposal designated a separate amount for attorneys' fees. After consulting an annuities expert, respondents and their client decided that her needs would likely be greater than those contemplated by the offer.

The following Monday at 3:30 P.M., the parties, attorneys, and annuities experts met with the settlement judge. In a private conference with respondents' group, the judge brought up the latest proposal. This prompted a discussion about the "common defense tactic" of making separate offers of attorneys' fees. Respondents and the judge agreed that such a move frequently had the effect of "driving a wedge" between a plaintiff's lawyer and his or her client by causing fees to become a source of discomfort, disagreement, and potential conflict.[4] Despite his recognition of this strategy, however, and

---

4 [2] Indeed, the defense here has since acknowledged that this was its purpose in making a separate offer of fees.

respondents' argument that the reasonableness of their fee was an issue for the trial court at the conclusion of the case, the settlement judge indicated that, in his opinion, the contingent fee being charged here was excessive. Testimony before the disciplinary hearing committee shows that the relationship between the court and respondents deteriorated from that point and became progressively antagonistic over this year. . . .

Respondents asserted at the disciplinary hearing that during these negotiations they spoke with their client about the insufficiency of the attorneys' fees being offered by the defense. They claimed that she authorized them to demand more money for the care of her son, thereby possibly securing an increase in fees as well. Although he was not technically a party to these proceedings, the record shows that the son's interests were important to all participants, particularly the court. Consequently, following respondents' pleas, the judge agreed to seek more money from the defendants.

Late in the day, the settlement judge called both sides into the courtroom to discuss a new offer, consisting of $175,000 in cash, annuities for both mother and son, $400,000 in attorneys' fees, and $55,000 in costs. According to the judge, this offer was higher than the previous one because of respondents' representations that the client needed, among other things, better housing and "specially equipped transportation" for her son, as well as additional funds for his possible future surgeries.

After conferring briefly, respondents met privately with the client and proposed that she pay them an additional $85,000 in attorneys' fees from her share of the cash proceeds. During this discussion, the judge approached the trio and asked if they needed his help. Respondent Fee testified that he felt pressed by the judge's presence and told him, "I don't want you here." Fee also told the client that she should not allow herself to feel coerced by her attorneys or the judge and that she could refuse the offer or take additional time to consider it.

After repeatedly advising the client of her right to seek independent advice and obtaining numerous assurances from her that she was satisfied with the arrangement, Fee prepared a handwritten agreement concerning the additional fees.

The three then returned to the courtroom where respondents informed their annuities expert about the new agreement. They asked the expert to review the proposed settlement with the client one final time to ensure that the available funds would be sufficient to meet her needs and that the overall agreement was fair. . . .

Respondent Fee announced that they agreed "in principle" to the settlement. However, when the judge repeated the terms previously discussed, nobody disclosed the existence of the newly-enacted fee agreement. Both the [disciplinary] committee and the commission found that respondents, not wanting to upset the settlement and believing it was not this judge's role to determine reasonableness of fees, planned to reveal the separate agreement to the trial judge in connection with the formal approval of attorneys' fees . . . .

Ten days after the conference, the client telephoned the settlement judge, informed him of the separate agreement and asked whether she was required to comply with it. The judge obtained a copy of the agreement, held a hearing during which he removed respondents from the case, appointed pro bono counsel to complete the settlement, and provided for the proceeds to be relayed through the clerk of the court for "proper" distribution. He then initiated these disciplinary proceedings.

A majority of the disciplinary commission recommended 60-day suspensions.[5]

We agree that respondents breached ER 3.3(a)(1), which states: "A lawyer shall not knowingly . . . make a false statement of material fact or law to a tribunal." . . . Respondents knowingly failed to disclose the separate agreement to the settlement judge in violation of this rule. At the same time, they engaged in "conduct involving dishonesty, fraud, deceit or misrepresentation" in violation of ER 8.4(c).

There are remarkably few cases applying the rules of professional conduct in a settlement contest and none that we can find directly on point.

. . . .

Respondents did not want to lose a favorable settlement for their client. At the same time, they neither wished to permit the defense to dictate the amount of their fees, nor felt comfortable with pressure from the judge to reduce them. Moreover, respondents clearly attempted to ensure that their client fully understood and concurred in the separate agreement. Both the committee and commission specifically found the modification was fair and that the client understood it. The uncontradicted evidence also suggests that respondents thought they were not obligated to disclose the arrangement to the settlement judge.

Nevertheless, we cannot condone their conduct. In our judgment, respondents should have either disclosed the complete arrangement or politely declined any discussion of fees. Fear that this might have jeopardized the settlement, while understandable, does not excuse their lack of candor with the tribunal. The system cannot function as intended if attorneys, sworn officers of the court, can lie to or mislead judges in the guise of serving their clients. "Zealous advocacy" has limits. It clearly does not justify ethical breaches.

Although we adopt the factual findings of both the committee and the commission, we are compelled to agree with the dissenting commissioners that the recommended sanction "exceeds the misconduct."[6] Nothing in the record suggests that respondents pose any threat to the public. Moreover, they already have suffered a considerable penalty by virtue of the extensive negative publicity surrounding this case.

We wish to discourage the previously-described tactic of "driving a wedge" between lawyer and client in negotiations. . . .

CORCORAN, JUSTICE, dissenting:

I respectfully dissent.

---

[5] [7] Two commissioners dissented, finding the recommended penalty overly harsh for what they considered a technical violation.

[6] [10] . . . Under these specific facts, we disagree that suspension is required.

I view the facts in this case differently from the majority. The respondents Fee and Montijo lied to the settlement judge so that they would get more money and their client would get less money. It is especially egregious for a lawyer to lie to a judge for the purpose of increasing his own fees at the direct expense of his client. I cannot agree with the committee, the commission, and the majority that respondents lacked dishonest or selfish motives. *Res ipsa loquitur.* Such conduct warrants at least a suspension and not a mere censure.

. . . .

For lawyers dealing with judges, whether they be trial or settlement judges, the guiding rule is never lie to or mislead a judge. Respondents claim they were lying in order to secure the best settlement agreement for their client. Nonetheless, it is often the case that lawyers who lie for the client will also lie to the client.

NOTES

In contrast to the *Fee* court's majority, in December 1997 California's State Bar Court unanimously suspended attorney Stephen Yagman for one year for pocketing not only the $378,000 in attorneys' fees awarded by the court, but also insisting on his percentage of his clients' jury award of about $44,000.[7] His insistence on this additional fee, just under $20,000, was enough for the court to conclude Yagman acted with "moral turpitude" towards his clients. The decision on Yagman, a well-known Los Angeles gadfly who will reappear later in this volume, may have been influenced, pro and con, by his reputation for both his willingness to take on tough police misconduct cases and his abrasive demeanor that many consider uncivil and some find offensive.

5. Contingency Fees in Criminal Cases? All American jurisdictions forbid contingency fees in criminal cases. The reasons most often advanced are first, that there is no economic recovery from which to take a fee (an argument also heard with regard to contingency fees in divorce cases); and second, that paying lawyers a premium for acquittal would cause them to encourage their clients to turn down "favorable" plea bargains and go to trial. But the current practice of many criminal defense lawyers is to charge their clients "flat fees," receiving the same amount whether the case goes to trial or not. Doesn't this practice cause lawyers to encourage their clients *not* to go to trial and to accept possibly *unfavorable* plea bargains?

William Simons doesn't have what is traditionally thought of as a contingency fee. Yet, since he must pay $6,500 in the event the case goes to trial, couldn't it be argued that this is a kind of contingent payment? Is William Simons' fee any less contingent than paying a premium for "winning"? Is it fair to argue that in each of these three situations, the contingent premium for winning, the flat fee, and the bifurcated fee for William Simons, the lawyer's interests are potentially placed at odds with the client's interests? There is a dearth of reported appellate cases on this issue, though the second and third types of fee arrangements are rather common in many jurisdictions.

---

[7] *In re Yagman*, 98 Cal. Daily Op. Service 166, 98 D.A.R. 195, *review denied*, 1998 Cal. LEXIS 6210 (Cal. Sup. 1998).

There are anecdotal reports, however, of the issue being raised by appellate lawyers trying to overturn a conviction. For example, in 1997, a Georgia lawyer was accused of ineffective assistance of counsel by the convicted defendant's appellate attorneys because he accepted a $25,000 fee but promised — in a handwritten note on the bottom of the fee contract — to refund $15,000 "should all charges against [defendant] be dismissed and another perpetrator either arrested or identified." This arrangement appears to show little more than the lawyer's willingness to receive less should it be discovered before trial that the authorities were prosecuting the wrong man. But the defendant's expert witness, a member of the state bar's board of governors, testified that "the fact that the ultimate fee is contingent on something makes it a contingency contract." The expert also testified that this contingency created an "incentive" for the lawyer to take the case through trial rather than "work[ing] towards early termination."[8] This seemingly ignores the requirement that another perpetrator be found before the fee is refunded, a circumstance that no lawyer (except perhaps Perry Mason in novels and on television) is likely to accomplish. It also underscores the point that almost any fee can be interpreted as creating a lawyer-client conflict.

6. Failure to Pay Fees and Withdrawal. If a client doesn't make agreed-upon payments, may the lawyer then withdraw from representation? Virtually every jurisdiction has a rule of professional conduct that would allow a lawyer to seek withdrawal if the client fails to meet agreed-upon financial obligations. But seeking withdrawal and obtaining it can be two different things. ABA Model Rule 1.16 specifies several grounds that would permit a lawyer to withdraw so long as the client's interests are not adversely affected. But that withdrawal is *permissive*, not mandatory. Subsection (c) of the rule notes that when a court orders the lawyer to remain on the case, "a lawyer shall continue representation notwithstanding good cause. . . ."

While it is perhaps not the most common occurrence, judges, vested with great discretion to permit or deny withdrawal for reasons relating to fees, do deny those requests. The more acute the problem and the closer to trial, the greater the possibility withdrawal will be denied. In one well-publicized New York case some years ago, one outspoken jurist refused to let a lawyer withdraw from a difficult "matrimonial" matter. Here is a brief excerpt of what he said from the bench, as reprinted in the New York legal press.

SAMUEL G. FREDMAN, A WORD TO THE WISE . . . FROM THE BENCH
New York Law Journal (May 8, 1991)[9]

. . . .

As I myself stated from the bench, there is no involuntary servitude in America, and I have no right to make any attorneys work without payment, but in this case they made their own agreement and a balancing of the equities involved at this time, as I see the picture, makes it necessary that they carry

---

[8] *See* Lolita Browning, *Assault Case Deal Labeled Contingency Fee*, Fulton County (Ga.) DAILY REPORT, April 14, 1997.

[9] Reprinted with the permission of The New York Law Journal. Copyright © 1991 by The New York Law Publishing Company.

out their responsibilities to this plaintiff, however cumbersome that is going to be for them.

. . . .

I was myself an active practitioner for just shy of 40 years before I moved to this other side of the bench. I have a great appreciation for lawyers and their problems, all of which I have myself suffered during that period of time. . . .

. . . .

[But] the facts of the case cry out for good legal support for both parties. There is, primarily, the welfare of a 13-year-old child involved, who presents the kind of custodial and visitation problems to a court which challenges [sic] the entire process of what we judges who work in this field are charged with doing. The independent psychiatrist has not been paid and refuses, at the moment, to present her report. The plaintiff claims to be a battered woman and was living in a shelter for housing such people in Danbury, Conn., at the time this motion came before me. With no proof of any reason to remove either party from the family home, the parties are presently under one roof, each making claims against the other, some of them of an extraordinary nature which makes the trier of facts want to scream at the parties to effectuate their own settlement, because no court is able to do so at this time.

. . . .

At the risk of offending my old colleagues at the matrimonial bar . . . I feel that lawyers who enter into a retainer agreement with clients which include [sic] payment of a minimum retainer fee (here $3,500 . . .), calling for billing on an hourly basis (whatever the specifics of that part of the fee arrangement), which agreements are either silent or unclear as to what will happen if the case turns out to be more difficult than it was expected to be when the retainer was signed, or when there is an application to the court for fees which is turned down or referred to the trial court, ought not to be allowed to withdraw from the case on the ground alone that they have run up thousands of dollars of additional time and there is no one to pay them that amount at that time. . . .

We have all been taught and we know that law is a profession as well as a business. . . . I do not question the right of lawyers to assign a value to their services. If the client accepts the responsibility of paying that price, then so long as the client wishes the relationship to continue, the lawyer has no right to withdraw from his or her part of the bargain merely because the client is deferring the method of payment . . . . [T]here is no excuse for clients in a matrimonial, who may have borrowed or scrimped or saved to have enough money to pay a retainer, being forced into either seeking new counsel, often at the most difficult stages of a litigation, and often without any source to pay a new retainer, or having to choose to represent themselves at such serious times.

NOTES

Do you think most courts would agree with the judge and require the lawyer to continue to represent the client? Does it matter that it was a custody case?

Or that fees in domestic cases may come from the other spouse as part of the findings in the case? What kind of service do you think the client got after the lawyer was prohibited from withdrawing? What would you have done in this situation? And, finally, do you think the judge's decision was appropriate?

Some jurisdictions have held that attorneys should be able to get attorneys' fees when they file collections cases against their clients for failure to pay, and allow for interest on unpaid attorneys' fees so long as the retainer agreement makes clear to the client that such interest will accrue.[10] Other jurisdictions disagree with such provisions, arguing that their existence creates an unnecessary and burdensome conflict of interest between the lawyer and the client. Given that practicing law is a business, do you think it is nœive to prohibit lawyers from having such provisions in their retainers? Or is the practice of law, as Judge Fredman claimed, at least in part still a profession? If so, does that make a difference here?

7. "Don't Slam the Door Behind You." There are many grounds for withdrawal that are considered appropriate in most states as well as under ABA Model Rule 1.16. Despite Judge Fredman's admonitions, the failure of the client to fulfill a fee agreement is one such ground. So is the lawyer's desire to withdraw when the client insists on doing something the lawyer sees as "repugnant or imprudent," or where the client has made the lawyer's continued representation "unreasonably difficult." Indeed, a lawyer may withdraw for *any* reason at all if it "can be accomplished without material adverse effect" on the client. All these grounds are permissive only — not mandatory, as in the case of an emerging and direct conflict of interest — but leave lawyers with relatively wide latitude to withdraw, subject to the approval of the tribunal hearing the matter.

Some states' rules are more strict. For instance, a member of the State Bar of California may not withdraw at all, even *with* legitimate grounds, "until the member has taken reasonable steps to avoid reasonably foreseeable prejudice to the rights of the client. . . ."[11]

How can a lawyer successfully get out of a case without endangering the client's position? What does it mean to "avoid reasonably foreseeable prejudice" to the client? Obviously, courts will insist on a lawyer demonstrating adequate grounds for withdrawal. But even under the more flexible ABA rule, may an attorney file a declaration in support of a motion to withdraw that lays out, chapter and verse, exactly how the client has been "unreasonably difficult" or insists on a "repugnant or imprudent course"? Read the different approaches and views expressed in the following article.

---

[10] *See, e.g.,* D.C. Ethics Opinion No. 310 (2002).

[11] Cal. R. Prof'l Conduct 3-700(A)(2).

ABDON M. PALLASCH, BREAKING OFF THE ATTORNEY-CLIENT RELATIONSHIP
Chicago Lawyer (June 1996)[12]

Edward M. Genson of Genson, Steinbeck, Gillespie & Martin stood before Cook County Circuit Judge Fred G. Suria Jr.

"Why do you want to drop your client?" the judge asked.

" 'Ethical, moral' reasons," Genson replied.

Would he elaborate? No, Genson would not. Then I'm not letting you off the case, said Suria, unless your client agrees. The client didn't.

And with that, Genson went right back to zealously defending U.S. Rep. Mel Reynolds, D-Dolton. Reynolds is under indictment for allegedly sleeping with underage girls and offering them money to lie to the government.

Dropping a client can be a gut-wrenching decision for the attorney who can't stomach his client for any of a number of reasons. Convincing a judge the withdrawal is warranted can be equally trying. Professional model codes and court rules may conflict. Case law and a lawyer's own personal code make the process even more complex. Nevertheless, decisions to withdraw — and questions about how to do it — are becoming more and more common.

. . . .

Requests for withdrawal affect more than high-profile cases.

"It's one of the biggest issues for the '90s — the heart of a lot of ethics classes," said James J. Grogan, Chief Counsel of the Attorney Registration and Disciplinary Committee. "I get so many phone calls on a weekly basis on this topic."

Examples? My client owes me money — can I withdraw? . . . My client might be planning to do something terrible here, but I don't want to broadcast it. What can I do?

. . . .

When judges deny leave to withdraw, it's generally because the attorney waited too long. "It was never a tough choice if it came on the eve of trial — it was denied," said Cook County Circuit Court Judge Earl E. Strayhorn, who sat in Criminal Courts before taking over the First Municipal District.

But every now and again comes a situation that forces an attorney to make a tough call on whether to seek leave to withdraw — and leaves a judge with a difficult choice of whether to grant it. Ethics rules, case law and opinion all clash over whether an attorney's first duty is to his client's confidentiality, the integrity of the court, or the attorney's conscience.

The bind Genson finds himself in with Reynolds — according to prosecutors — is that while Genson was defending Reynolds against the initial indictments, Reynolds allegedly tampered with witnesses and fabricated documents that he gave to Genson to use in his defense. Those charges against Reynolds were included in the second round of indictments, handed down the day Genson asked to withdraw.

---

[12] Copyright © 1996 by Law Bulletin Publishing Company. Reprinted by permission.

But were Genson's two words — "ethical, moral" — uttered in open court too much? At least one expert says Genson violated his client's confidence by saying as much as he did. . . . Prof. Monroe Freedman argues that attorney-client privilege is paramount and should never be compromised, even if the attorney suspects his client may commit perjury. "The lawyer has no business revealing that kind of information to the judge in the first place; and once that has happened, there certainly cannot be an appropriate lawyer-client relationship," Freedman said.

Defense attorney E. Michael Kelly of Hinshaw & Culbertson agreed with Freedman that the attorney-client privilege is paramount but said Genson did not reveal too much.

"Genson was quite prudent and moderate in his approach," Kelly said. "You have to say something to make the claim for withdrawal meritorious and Genson has done it the right way. God only knows what the ethical, moral problem is — and that's the way it should be. Genson's a pro."

. . . .

Freedman said Genson could have at least appeared with a substitute counsel and said, " 'Your Honor, for personal reasons I'm moving to withdraw; but here is so and so, who I have made sure is fully up to speed, and he's prepared to take over.' " When he does it that way, it's very hard for the judge to deny the substitution."

[T]he other can of worms that opens is whether the attorney who withdraws has a responsibility to disclose the client's planned perjury to his replacement counsel. Freedman argues no, but George Rutherglen, in his 1992 American Journal of Criminal Law article on client perjury, says the attorney should. "The threat of withdrawal won't convince the client to tell the truth if the client is free to obtain another attorney who will then remain ignorant of the planned perjury," Rutherglen wrote.

. . . .

The closeness to trial is often a deal-breaker, judges said, no matter how meritorious the request for withdrawal.

Jack J. Carriglio of Fran & Schultz remembers one case in which a trial-eve request for leave to withdraw was shot down. "It was a multi-defendant case, and another lawyer in the case came into the court the day before the trial, he had a conference with his clients, and they told him they would not be paying fees," Carriglio said. "We were working at a three-month trial. He said, 'I'm a sole practitioner, and I can't be here three months without being paid.' He said the court should consider getting substitute counsel and suggested the court delay the trial to allow them to do so.

"The judge said if he left the courtroom, the marshals would be sent to send him back. Once he filed papers in the case, it was not the court's concern that he was having fee problems. That lawyer stayed and represented the client and did a pretty good job. He was never paid."

NOTES

Whether one agrees with Prof. Freedman that even using the words "ethical" and "moral" is stating too much or with those who feel that this vague, generalized approach is appropriate, it is clear that most lawyers see the need for considerable circumspection. This can put a lawyer between a rock and a hard place — being clear enough to convince the court to grant withdrawal, while not being so clear as to slam the door on the client's case while leaving the courtroom.

In *United States v. Bruce*, 89 F.3d 886 (D.C. Cir. 1996), the court evaluated the conduct of Bruce's court-appointed lawyer, Rudasill, after Bruce was convicted on bank fraud charges. Bruce and Rudasill were at odds, with Bruce eventually insisting that Rudasill lie to the court about his inability to represent the defendant in hopes Bruce would be given another lawyer. Instead, Rudasill went to the judge in the middle of trial and revealed, ex parte, that Bruce had insisted that Rudasill lie to the court. The trial continued, and the appeals court upheld Bruce's conviction, though it was critical of the lawyer:

> Bruce's persistence created a dilemma for Rudasill, but not one which required him to request an ex parte hearing. The wiser course of action, we think, would have been for Rudasill to tell the judge, as he did, that he and his client had reached an impasse and that he would like to be removed from the case. In describing the "impasse," however, the lawyer should have avoided any mention of the fact that his client had asked him to lie to the court.

Id. at 895.

While this course might have been more pure, the trial court had just made it clear to Bruce that the case would not be postponed no matter what. The strategy suggested by the appeals court would likely have either left Rudasill in the case as counsel, or forced the defendant to represent himself. Neither choice is appealing, which emphasizes the problem faced by counsel who is at once expected to be circumspect and to provide competent, effective representation.

In Problem 10, we will briefly return to the issue of withdrawal in the context of lawyers changing law firms.

8. Who "Owns" the Case File? Suppose a lawyer successfully withdraws from a case, and in a way that does no harm to the client. Who "owns" the case file, client or lawyer? Almost all jurisdictions agree that if the client has paid the lawyer's bills, the file belongs to the client. But that is only the beginning of the story. Two of the issues that arise most frequently are what happens when the client has *not* paid the legal fees, and to what extent a lawyer's work product should be included in the definition of "the file."

The ABA rules provide surprisingly little guidance on these issues. State ethics opinions and a few court cases have been more illuminating. Calif. Formal Opinion 1994-134 takes a strong pro-client view, making it clear that the file belongs to the client, and that clients are "entitled to constant access" to the file during the case. It concludes that even where the client discharges the attorney and demands the file before a formal substitution of counsel, "the attorney may not withhold the file from the client or successor counsel merely to await the technicality of formal withdrawal." The lawyer may "retain possession and control of the file only to the extent necessary to represent the client competently" until formally relieved. Finally, this opinion concludes that "a discharged attorney who wants to keep a copy of the file normally must bear the copying expense."

Most other states don't go quite this far, though in the past 25 years, many states have held that where fees are still owed the lawyer, the attorney may not hold the file hostage, even if the fee agreement has a provision for a "retaining lien." A retaining lien is, simply, a contractual provision in which the client agrees the lawyer can retain the file until the fees are paid. Such liens are considered to be void as against public policy in many states, including California[13] while other states, including New York, continue to permit them. Other jurisdictions, such as the District of Columbia, fall somewhere in between. D.C. Rule 1.8(i) leaves the narrowest of retaining liens: only attorney work product, and only when withholding the work product poses no "significant risk to the client of irreparable harm."

What about the general obligation of lawyers to produce their attorney work product? While the law is still far from clear in many jurisdictions, courts and ethics counsel are more and more frequently requiring law firms to turn over this work product as part of the "file." Perhaps the leading case, further profiled in the Supplemental Readings, is *In re Sage Realty Corp. v. Proskauer Rose Goetz & Mendelsohn, LLP*, 91 N.Y.2d 30, 689 N.E.2d 879 (1997), in which the New York Court of Appeals required the Proskauer firm to turn over all work product except material created only for internal law firm use.

9. What Relationships Are Too Close? It now seems settled that spouses working on opposite sides of a case will be disqualified as counsel. It is less clear to what extent courts may allow the spouses' firms to continue in the case with the informed consent of all clients, though ABA Model Rule 1.8(i) allows for such consent. Still less clear are the rules that control other relationships. MR 1.8(i) specifically mentions "parent, child, sibling or spouse." In this day of other intimate personal relationships, should disclosure and consent be required for other situations? The answer is "yes" under Calif. Rule of Prof'l Conduct 3-320, although the rule fails to define the phrase "intimate personal relationship." The California rule also refers to people who live together, while other states have used the term "cohabiting."

Even the ABA's Ethics 2000 Commission, perhaps mindful of the increasing openness of gay and lesbian relationships as well as other non-marital relationships, toyed with broadening its "relationship" definition. One suggestion was a "cohabiting relationship closely approximating marriage." But later Commission drafts returned to the original Model Rule definition.

Does defining which relationships must be disclosed and consented to in such formulaic terms make sense to you? Or should the real test include a subjective component? That subjective element could be defined as any

---

[13] *See, e.g., Academy of Calif. Optometrists v. Superior Court*, 51 Cal. App. 3d 999, 124 Cal. Rptr. 668 (1975).

relationship that the lawyer feels may have an effect on the representation, or even any relationship that the client reasonably believes *could* have such an effect. What is your view?

10. Sex With Clients. One relationship obviously fraught with problems is a sexual relationship with a client. This will almost always create a professional conflict of interest to one degree or another. Many jurisdictions have laws that ban medical practitioners and psychotherapists from having sex with their patients. Should there be a *per se* rule prohibiting all lawyer-client sex? Should such rules be limited to certain types of representations, such as divorce? Or are existing ethical rules adequate to address any problems that could arise from such relationships? When we asked these same questions in 1995 for the first edition of this book, we noted that only two jurisdictions — California and Oregon — had explicit rules on the subject. This has changed. As we enter the new millenneum, fully half the states have passed prohibitions against sex with clients, as has the ABA.

The theories behind these rules focus on one or more of three concepts: the existence of a conflict of interest; questions about the ability of a sexually-involved attorney to perform legal services competently; and the potential for a lawyer's position of power over and responsiblity for the client — in short, the attorney's fiduciary duty — being used to unduly influence the client into having the relationship. Most of these rules prohibit using the attorney-client relationship as a launching pad for a sexual liaison, but don't prohibit representing clients where the relationship is pre-existing.

A word or several about civil liability: Using one's position as attorney to engage in sex with a client may now be a *per se* violation of the ethical rules of many states, but that behavior is not necessarily tantamount to malpractice. In *Vallinoto v. DiSandro*, 688 A.2d 830 (R.I. 1997), for example, Rhode Island's highest court reversed a jury verdict against a lawyer who had a sexual relationship with his client during a divorce case. The *Vallinoto* court held that the client had not proven she had been damaged in the case by the lawyer's action, and that alone required reversal and a new trial. But the court went further, concluding that in order for the client to show that the lawyer's services departed from the standard of care, she would have to show more than the sexual relationship. Indeed, the court also concluded that the sexual conduct did not consitute a breach of the lawyer's fiduciary duty. *Id.* at 835.

In *Suppressed v. Suppressed*, 206 Ill. App. 3d 918, 565 N.E.2d 101 (1990), the court concluded that even if the sex was coerced by fear the lawyer would not otherwise do his job, legal malpractice and even breach of fiduciary duty claims did not lie where there was "no specific harm other than [the client's] own emotional distress."[14] Although the issue is civil liability rather than discipline, one must wonder whether this last case would be decided the same way just a decade later.

11. Lawyers' Personal and Political Agendas. Some lawyers believe that a no-sex-with-clients rule is not needed because of the breadth of rules such as ABA Model Rule 1.7(b), which says that a lawyer may not represent

---

[14] But see *Tante v. Herring*, 264 Ga. 694, 453 S.E.2d 686 (1994), further described in the Supplemental Readings, for a somewhat different perspective.

a client if the lawyer's representation is "materially limited . . . by the lawyer's own interests." Nothing in the language of this rule, or its comments, would limit it to financial, as opposed to personal, interests.

Most observers do agree, however, that a "lawyer's own interests" can be very broad, relating to anything which could affect the attorney's ability to provide the client independent professional judgment. Are these personal interests broader than financial, sexual, or romantic? Can they relate to professional or political agendas which are personal to the attorneys?

In the aftermath of the Tawana Brawley case, when it appeared that Ms. Brawley, an African-American teenager, had manufactured a story about being sexually assaulted by a group of white racists, many lawyers raised questions about Brawley's attorneys' personal agendas. Suspicions were raised that Brawley's attorneys helped perpetuate a hoax in order to focus media attention on racial issues, and, possibly, enhance their own reputations. "What if the lawyers didn't care about Miss Brawley's interest and were simply using her plight to advance their own ulterior aims?" asked Professor Stephen Gillers, a leading ethics expert, in a 1988 *New York Times* piece. "The legal profession's code of ethics forbids such disloyalty." Presumably, Prof. Gillers was referring to the language of Model Rule 1.7(b).

Here is another example in a different context. In 1995, noted Chicago personal injury lawyer Philip H. Corboy, Jr. withdrew from representing Illinois state senator Robert Raica on a medical malpractice claim because Raica had voted for "tort reform" that would limit damages of the kind the politician was seeking with Corboy's help. Corboy acknowledged to *Chicago Lawyer* that he had first lobbied his client for his vote, a fact which Raica likened to "a surgeon [who] had me on the operating table [and] said, 'Well, Senator, how are you going to vote on tort reform?' " After Raica's vote, Corboy withdrew because Raica "took away the rights of people but retained them for himself. . . . Having devoted 40 years of my life to protecting the rights of victims, I did not feel I could represent him." In short, when his personal beliefs got in the way of his representation, Corboy got out of the case. But was his lobbying effort proper?

12. A Word About "Positional Conflicts." Are lawyers permitted to take a legal position in one case and advocate an opposite legal theory in another? There is little law on this issue. Yet most authorities see no grounds on which to prevent this unless taking position #1 will have a direct and significant adverse effect on the client advocating position #2. Comment 24 to ABA Model Rule 1.7 states this standard: A lawyer may take inconsistent legal positions in different courts at different times. But if taking position #1 creates "a significant risk" that client #2 will be seriously compromised, such as "when a decision favoring one client will create a precedent likely to seriously weaken the position taken on behalf of the other," a conflict exists. These relatively broad standards leave a lot of questions unanswered by either ethics opinions or case law. May a lawyer take opposite positions in the same court if at significantly different times? Or in different courts at proximate times? Does the lawyer owe any duty to the court to make consistent legal arguments, at least where those arguments are in front of the same court? The nuances of the issue of "positional conflicts" have yet to be clearly resolved.

SUPPLEMENTAL READINGS

1. *Maxwell v. Superior Ct.*, 30 Cal. 3d 606, 180 Cal. Rptr. 177 (1982). An attorney agreed to represent a defendant facing robbery charges in exchange for the right to exploit the defendant's life story. The trial court ruled that an inherent conflict was created which demands the disqualification of the attorney. The California Supreme Court reversed, stating that the defendant's consent after extensive discussions with his attorney constituted an adequate waiver which precludes counsel's removal.

2. Douglas E. Rosenthal, *Lawyer and Client: Who's In Charge?* (1974). This book retains vitality more than a generation after its publication. The author takes a strong view about lawyers and how they receive their fees, including blunt views about quick recovery contingency fee cases that pay off for the lawyer but not the client.

3. *United States v. Hurt*, 543 F.2d 162 (D.C. Cir. 1976), presented an interesting issue that has come up periodically in several jurisdictions. The defendant's appellate attorney argued that the trial attorney did not provide effective assistance of counsel. The defendant's trial attorney in turn sued the appellate attorney for defamation. The appellate attorney then sought to be excused as the defendant's appellate counsel on the grounds that the defamation suit created a conflict of interest between himself and the defendant. The court agreed, finding a conflict between the client's interest in the appellate attorney pursuing the theory of trial counsel's ineffective assistance of counsel and the appellate attorney's interest in not worsening his position in the defamation suit.

4. *People v. Barboza*, 29 Cal. 3d 375, 173 Cal. Rptr. 458 (1981). The county's contract with the public defender specified that $15,000 is deposited in an account to pay for defense counsel who are appointed when the public defender is disqualified from representing a defendant. The public defender was to pay for any deficiencies in the account, but at the end of the year any remaining balance was returned to the public defender's office. The court ruled that this contract created a conflict of interest between the county and the public defender, because it gives the public defender a disincentive to declare himself disqualified for a case.

5. *In re Sage Realty Corp. v. Proskauer Rose Goetz & Mendelsohn, LLP*, 91 N.Y.2d 30, 689 N.E.2d 879 (1997). Sage Realty hired the Proskauer firm in a complex real estate restructuring for which Proskauer billed — and Sage paid — about $1 million in fees. After a falling out, Sage fired Proskauer and hired another firm. Proskauer resisted giving Sage a large number of documents including internal memos, drafts of instruments, research, and lawyers' notes written on contracts, transactions and charts. The New York Court of Appeal held that this information, even though work product, must be turned over to Sage, except internal law office memos intended solely "for lawyers to be able to set down their thoughts." Sage's payment of its legal fees seems critical to the decision, the court noting that Sage had paid for the creation of the documents it sought. Also, the court determined that copying the material, which amounted to fourteen volumes containing over 500 documents, was properly chargeable to the client.

6. Stephen W. Simpson, *From Lawyer-Spouse to Lawyer-Partner: Conflicts of Interest in the 21st Century*, 19 Geo. J. Legal Ethics 405 (2006), discusses the history of family law conflict of interest rules and examines the impact of same sex marriage laws on those rules. He then proposes an alternative scheme of rules that would avoid the issues created by same sex marriage laws.

7. In *In re Lewis*, 262 Ga. 37, 415 S.E.2d 173 (1992), the Georgia Supreme Court suspended a lawyer from practice for three years even though his sexual relationship with his divorce client was uncoerced, did not adversely affect his representation, and predated the representation. The court held that the lawyer's professional judgment could or might reasonably have been affected by the relationship: "Every lawyer must know that an extramarital relationship can jeopardize every aspect of a client's matrimonial case — extending to forfeiture of alimony, loss of custody, and denial of attorney fees." Two years later, the same court, in *Tante v. Herring*, 264 Ga. 694, 453 S.E.2d 686 (1994), decided that the lawyer's adulterous relationship with his client may have been a violation of legal ethics, but "a satisfactory result . . . by necessity precludes a claim for legal malpractice." However, the court sustained the client's claim for breach of fiduciary duty, since this claim included the allegation the lawyer had misused confidences about the client's medical and emotional condition to persuade her to engage in a sexual relationship. The court noted it might have taken a stronger pro-client stance had the matter been a divorce case.

8. *In re Maternowski*, 674 N.E.3d 1287 (Ind. Sup. 1996), presents an interesting twist on the potential conflict caused by a lawyer's personal principles. Two criminal defense lawyers had long taken the position, as a policy matter, not to represent clients who cooperate with the government. They nevertheless continued to represent a client who was indecisive about whether he wanted to cooperate with the authorities. This continued representation, in the face of their stated beliefs, coupled with the fact that their fees were being paid by third parties who were alleged accomplices of the defendant, resulted in the two lawyers being suspended from practice for thirty days for having a personal conflict of interest with their client that could interfere with their ability to exercise independent professional judgment.

9. Note, *The Plaintiff as Person: Cause Lawyering, Human Subject Research, and the Secret Agent Problem*, 119 Harv. L. Rev. 1510 (2006), describes the "cause lawyer's" conflicts of interest between advocating for the client in the traditional sense and advocating for the principled cause. The author presents a middle ground approach where the lawyer advocates primarily for the client, discloses any potential conflicts of interest arising from the cause for which the lawyer is advocating, and allows the client to make an informed decision mindful of the risks and benefits of representation by a lawyer who focuses on a cause.

PROBLEM 10

The conflicts of interest we have already discussed in this chapter concern a single lawyer representing more than one client. But life in the legal fast lane is rarely that simple. Many lawyers work as part of a law firm. And, as we saw in our examination of organizational clients, relationships between lawyers and clients can be far more complex than a simple one-on-one.

During the last quarter century the old patterns of law practice have changed dramatically. The legal market place has a fluidity that didn't exist a generation ago. Law firms expand and diversify by merging, or acquiring whole practice sections of other firms. "Lateral transfers" move from one firm to another. These partners or senior associates bring "books of business" — that is, their own stable of clients. Meanwhile mergers and acquisitions of large corporations have created numerous conflict of interest problems even for attorneys who just stay put.

These recent developments create increasingly complex issues for both lawyers and the courts. Nowhere is this more clearly manifested than in the exponential increase in the number of litigated motions to disqualify law firms and recent attempts to limit such motions. There has been an enormous amount of case law devoted to disqualification and related issues.[1] This problem explores the modern realities of law firm conflicts of interest from a variety of perspectives.

Conflicts of Interest and the Business of Being a Profession

I. Meeker, Reynolds and Stearns began as an intellectual property law "boutique" that catered to high tech and other start-up companies. But the downturn in dot.coms led to the loss of some of Meeker, Reynolds' biggest clients and a slowdown in new business. The partners eventually decided to expand into other areas, including real estate litigation. They have had some serious discussions about merging with ten to twelve lawyers from the litigation department of Burton & Barrows across town.

Talks between Meeker, Reynolds and Burton & Barrows litigators heat up. Before their firm's monthly partnership meeting, Leonard Meeker and Elizabeth Reynolds meet to discuss presenting their expansion proposal to the firm.

"Beth," says Meeker, "I just learned that B&B has sued Royster Homes on behalf of Hoosier Trust over that joint venture agreement with Royster a few years ago. Their guy Pete Markovich is taking the case with him when he comes over here. Didn't we represent Royster on its initial public offering just before it entered into that joint venture?"

"Yeah, we did, Len," says Reynolds. "In fact, we had to learn about Royster's assets, its earning potential, its board of directors, everything. We had to pass muster with the SEC, and we had to arrange with Arbenz Accounting to get their books in order. It was quite a job, and we earned quite a fee. Does that give us a conflict with the B&B litigators?

---

[1] Much of this case law stems from the Second and Seventh Circuits and the state of California, which are thus heavily represented in the cases cited here.

"I don't know, Beth," replies Meeker. "Not everyone who worked on the case would be joining our firm. Besides, we only represented Royster in its IPO. Isn't that OK? I mean, putting together an IPO has nothing to do with a lawsuit over a joint venture agreement. Right?"

"Maybe so, Len," concludes Reynolds, "but we'd better check it out before we pitch our partners on this deal."

QUESTIONS

1. If Meeker, Reynolds absorbs the Burton & Barrows litigators, will any conflict exist if their new partners continue to represent Hoosier in its lawsuit against Royster? Does Meeker, Reynolds have confidential information about Royster Homes that would be of use to Hoosier in its lawsuit against Royster? Does that make a difference?

2. Does it matter whether Meeker, Reynolds is continuing to represent Royster on other intellectual property and securities matters unrelated to the lawsuit? Why or why not?

II. At the partnership meeting Meeker and Reynolds inform the other members of the firm about the merger details and their would-be new partners' potentially troublesome representation of Hoosier in the lawsuit against Royster. Ed Stearns suggests that the firm simply set up an ethical wall around the litigators in the Hoosier/Royster lawsuit. " 'Screening' is done all the time when lawyers leave government work. I don't see why we can't do it here."

QUESTIONS

1. Can the new lateral transfers to Meeker, Reynolds continue to represent Hoosier if Royster moves to disqualify them?

2. If Meeker, Reynolds establishes an ethical screen, what would it look like?

3. Assume that Royster moves to disqualify the former Burton & Barrows attorneys from representing Royster. Can Royster also disqualify the entire Meeker, Reynolds firm wall around the former B&B attorneys?

4. May a law firm drop a client to avoid a conflict? Under what circumstances?

READINGS

1. Conflicts and Motions to Disqualify Counsel. When a lawyer has a conflict, how does that conflict affect that attorney's law firm? And what happens when lawyers move from firm to firm, or when two firms merge? A few ethics rules address the conduct of lawyers as members of firms. ABA Model Rules 1.7, 1.9, and 1.10 are perhaps the most significant examples. But rules of professional conduct are designed to discipline individual lawyers, not law firms.[2] So it would be very unusual to have a law firm's conflict of interest

---

[2] In 1993, the Committee on Professional Responsibility of the Association of the Bar of the City of New York published a report recommending that New York State's disciplinary rules be revised to permit disciplining law firms. This controversial report has not spawned a vast

addressed directly through disciplinary rules. The law firm's conflict can be addressed in an after-the-fact malpractice lawsuit, but in actual practice, the issue is most often joined in a motion to disqualify counsel. We begin with a conflict between current clients of a law firm and then look at an example of what can happen when law firms merge and thereby create conflicts — either with current clients or between current and former clients which, as we will see, is a considerably more complicated issue.

SUSAN ORENSTEIN, "TECHNICAL" CONFLICT, MAJOR CONSEQUENCE
The Recorder (San Francisco) (December 9, 1992)[3]

Pettit & Martin beat out six other firms in a beauty contest last spring to take on a large construction case for Orange County. The county was being sued for more than $35 million and was making multimillion-dollar counterclaims over problems with the construction of John Wayne International Airport.

Today, Pettit is off the case because of a conflict — the victim, it says, of an innocent, minor slipup that was seized upon by the other side to gain an edge in the litigation.

Pettit's appeals of the disqualification, for all practical purposes, were exhausted last week, and Orange County is debating how much the firm should be paid for the 2,000 hours it worked on the case. Worse still, the dispute has pitted the firm against a major insurance client Pettit specifically had tried to accommodate.

"It's a big case. It's a serious disappointment for me and the firm to be disqualified, particularly in the circumstances of this case, where No. 1, you think the order was mistaken, and No. 2, where you think it was filed as a litigation tactic," said John Clark, the Pettit partner who had been lead counsel for the county.

Even if Clark's interpretation of events is correct, however, Pettit's disqualification is more than just an example of being burned on a technicality. Its dismissal not only points out the potentially high stakes involved in dealing with seemingly minor conflicts, it shows how a simple oversight can come back to haunt a firm, how clients' concerns can never be taken for granted and how even lawyers need to remember to get everything in writing.

Pettit was retained by the county in June as trial counsel for separate cases involving delays in building the airport terminal and an elevated roadway and parking structure. The cases involve multiple parties, including . . . two subsidiaries of American International Group — American Home Assurance Co. and National Union Fire Insurance Co. of Pittsburgh.

The latter is a client worth millions to Pettit over the years, largely because of litigation work involving the mid-80s collapse of Technical Equities Corp., a San Francisco investment firm that National Union insured.

---

movement. While there are Sarbanes-Oxley and other newer regulations open more avenues for such discipline, ethical sanctions are rare. Thus our focus on the most common sanction — disqualification.

[3] Susan Orenstein was a reporter for *The Recorder* in San Francisco. Copyright © 1992 by The Recorder.

Clark had asked the partner who was primarily responsible for National Union work, D. Wayne Jeffries, to contact the company about any possible problems with Pettit representing the county. The call was a courtesy, Clark says. National Union was being sued by subcontractors in one of the airport cases, not by the county. Clark says he saw no possible conflict, but he wanted to be upfront with National Union. . . .

A Conflict The Firm Didn't See

Based on Jeffries' interpretation of the call to [his client's general counsel], Pettit took the county's case without submitting a request for a written waiver. . . .

But what Jeffries and Clark were apparently unaware of was that the firm clearly did need a written waiver. American Home Assurance, it turned out, was also a Pettit client, and was being sued by the county in the roadway case. That put Pettit in the position of representing an adverse interest of a client — a violation of state ethics rules unless the client has signed a waiver.

Pettit's initial conflicts check did not turn up American Home as a client, Clark says. . . . Had he known of the American Home work, Clark adds, he would have delayed taking on the roadway case until he had a written waiver or until Pettit's American Home cases were completely settled in August, shortly after an associate brought the conflict to Clark's attention.

"There was, for a brief time, a technical conflict with American Home," Clark says. "Obviously, the mistake was made, but in terms of fault, I don't see that."

Clark insists, however, that the firm's representation of American Home was merely a vehicle for opposing counsel's disqualification motion, not a substantive conflict. Pettit was representing American Home in three disputes at the request of the Kuman Corp. . . . American Home, the firm says, never paid a bill.

Moreover, says Clark, "If I knew everything there was to know about American Home, it would have no bearing on this case at all. . . ."

In a September letter to the lawyer for National Union and American Home, Clark angrily implied that it was the contractor, Taylor Woodrow, whose interests were really being served.

. . . . "Behind your escalating demands is a calculated effort by Taylor Woodrow to derail this case, by disrupting the current ambitious discovery program, delaying the trial and denying to the county the right to employ the counsel of its choice. . . ."

R. Donald McIntyre, the attorney for National Union and American Home, dismisses Clark's conspiracy theory as irrelevant, saying a surety and its principal would almost always have the same interests.

. . . .

Clark says he doubts American Home cared if Pettit represented the county. But the fact that there was an actual conflict, he says, "became very convenient because it added to their arguments."

Meanwhile, the county is trying to decide who it will name as trial counsel. . . . The county also is "reviewing all its options in regard to payment to Pettit & Martin.

. . . .

"Although we're unhappy at being disqualified," Clark says, "it's not so much that it takes away business as it's frustrating. Conflicts present a difficult problem for lawyers, as I've learned the hard way."

NOTES

Motions to disqualify have become so common that many argue they are not really ethical matters, but legal and tactical ones. Indeed, an enormous body of case law has developed setting standards and tests for disqualification. Pettit & Martin's cry of "litigation tactic" is one that is echoed throughout the country as these motions become more widespread. Still, no matter how much a law firm might want to avoid it, at the heart of the matter is the basic issue of conflicts of interest. In the following pages, we will examine how the individual lawyer's conflicts of interest are "imputed" to, or adopted by, that attorney's law firm, and what standards are used in determining whether law firms may or may not engage in representation. Whether it is a legal or ethical issue, or some of both, no problem discussed in this book is more complex.

SHANNON P. DUFFY, CONFLICT MEANS DUANE MORRIS MUST DROP CLIENT: FIRM DIDN'T ERECT ETHICS SCREEN FAST ENOUGH FOLLOWING MERGER
Legal Intelligencer (March 3, 1999)[4]

[A] federal judge has disqualified Duane Morris & Heckscher from representing a woman in an age discrimination suit because the firm merged with another firm that previously represented the company she is suing.

In his 13-page opinion in James v. Teleflex Inc., U.S. District Judge Lowell A. Reed Jr. found that when Duane Morris merged with Miller Dunham & Doering, the entire firm incurred a conflict of interest because attorney Jane Dalton was already representing JoAnne Skowronski James in a suit against Teleflex, an existing client of incoming attorney Edward Dunham. . . . And the conflict was not cured when Dunham withdrew from representing Teleflex in a trade secrets case and stopped working on the company's Year 2000 problems, Reed said.

"The fact that Dunham withdrew, or at least told Teleflex that he was withdrawing, as counsel for Teleflex in [its suit against Aeroutfitters Inc.] and other matters when the conflict of interest was brought to his attention indicates behavior that violates an attorney's duty of loyalty to his client," Reed wrote. . . . Reed found that "an attorney may not drop one client like a 'hot potato' in order to avoid a conflict with another, more remunerative client."

---

[4] Copyright © 1999 by ALM Properties, Inc. Reprinted by permission.

According to court papers, Dunham was the lead counsel at Miller Dunham on all Teleflex matters, and as of May 30, 1998, he was the attorney of record for Teleflex in the lawsuit against Aeroutfitters.

On May 28, 1998, Dunham wrote a letter to Steven K. Chance, the vice president and general counsel of Teleflex, informing him that Miller Dunham would be merging with Duane Morris effective the following Monday, June 1, 1998, and requesting authority to transfer Teleflex's matters to Duane Morris. The next day, Chance called Dunham and informed him that Duane Morris was handling James' lawsuit against Teleflex. Dunham told Chance he would look into the problem and contact him with a solution.

Several days later, Dunham informed Chance that Duane Morris was "very embarrassed about missing the conflict" and requested more time to resolve the issue, to which Chance agreed.

Dunham joined Duane Morris on June 1 and on June 19, he contacted Chance's office while Chance was on vacation to inform his secretary that Duane Morris had decided to continue its representation of James and that Dunham would withdraw as counsel for Teleflex in the Aeroutfitters case.

In its motion demanding that Duane Morris be disqualified from any further handling of James' case, Teleflex argued that it had never consented to Duane Morris' continued representation of James.

As a result, it argued, Duane Morris is ethically precluded from continuing to represent James under three of Pennsylvania's Rules of Professional Conduct.

Under Rule 1.7(a), it argued, the firm's representation of James is in direct conflict with its representation of Teleflex in another lawsuit currently pending. Under Rule 1.9, it said, their representation is in direct conflict with Dunham's past representation of Teleflex in a substantially related matter which is at issue in James' lawsuit. And under Rule 1.10, the conflicts have not been waived by Teleflex, are imputed to the entire Duane Morris law firm, and cannot be remedied short of Duane Morris' disqualification in James' case.

Dalton explained that Duane Morris did not initially detect the potential conflict with Dunham's representation of Teleflex because the name "Teleflex" was inadvertently omitted from the list of Dunham's clients entered into the firm's computer to check for potential conflicts.

She also said that an ethics screen or "firewall" had been established so that Dunham and others associated with the Miller Dunham firm would have had no contact with the attorneys, paralegals or staff working on James' lawsuit. . . . As a result, Dalton argued, there was no reasonable risk that confidences of Teleflex would or could be used to the detriment of Teleflex.

. . . .

Reed found that "the prior representation of Teleflex by Dunham is substantially related to this lawsuit. . . ."

As a result, Reed said, Duane Morris "has the burden of establishing that Dunham was screened from participation in the pending lawsuit before becoming associated with Duane Morris and that written notice was given to Teleflex promptly. . . ."

Reed found that Duane Morris failed to carry its burden or proving that the ethics screen was effective.

"While the features of the screen implemented by Duane Morris appear facially sufficient, other factors weigh against the sufficiency of the screen under Rule 1.10," Reed wrote.

"There was no lapse of time between the representation of Teleflex by Dunham and the representation of James by Duane Morris; in fact, it appears that both clients were being concurrently represented for at least a period of time after the merger of the two law firms." And the relationship between Dunham and Teleflex "was substantial," Reed added. . . .

After concluding that the entire firm did, in fact, suffer from a conflict of interest, Reed said that his final task was to conduct a balancing test — weighing the interest in enforcing the Rules of Professional Conduct against the hardship that disqualification would impose on James to retain new counsel, especially since the case "is on the brink of trial."

Factors to be included in such a balancing test, he said, included Teleflex's interest in attorney loyalty; James' interest in retaining her chosen counsel; and the risk of prejudice to James.

But in the end, Reed found that disqualification was required to further the court's own interest in "protecting the integrity of the proceedings and maintaining public confidence in the judicial system."

NOTES

The Duane Morris disqualification raises several issues we'll return to in the following readings: law firm imputation, the "substantial relationship" test, the "hot potato" rule and law firm screening. After you read these sections ask yourself whether this well-intentioned judge analyzed the conflicts issue correctly. Our thoughts appear at the end of our "hot potato" section. The first issue we return to is law firm imputation.

2. Law Firm Imputation. Here's the issue: What happens when one member of a law firm represents X in a lawsuit against Y, while another member of that same firm *currently* represents Y in another venue in an entirely unrelated matter? Will courts disqualify the entire firm even if, as Pettit & Martin claimed, the conflict is only "technical"? Or must there be some relationship between the two matters? When the conflict is *concurrent*, courts have generally disqualified law firms, regardless of the relationship between the two matters. The rationale is threefold. First, because confidences and access to information are shared within law firms, with cases discussed and worked on in teams, and financial interests also shared by firm members, that firm is considered like a single entity for purposes of conflict of interest. Thus, when a lawyer represents a client, that representation is "imputed" to the entire firm. Accordingly, ABA Model Rule 1.10(a) states that no lawyers associated in a firm "shall knowingly represent a client when any one of them practicing alone would be prohibited from doing so" by Model Rule 1.7 or 1.9, the rules against conflicts of interest.

Second, then, the question of whether a law firm may represent X and Y becomes almost identical to whether an individual attorney may do it. Every American jurisdiction prohibits a lawyer from representing one client in a matter directly adverse to another current client without both clients' consents, regardless of whether there is a relationship between the two matters. The third part of the analysis is whether the clients — usually the issue is with Y, the client in the collateral matter who is also adverse in *X v. Y* — are willing to consent. Where consent is given, the representation may continue. Where it is not, the next step is often withdrawal or a motion to disqualify.

Where current adverse representations are involved, even most of those who favor the use of ethical screens (see sections 5 and 6, below) agree that such screens are inadequate to resolve the conflict.

Suppose a large law firm with several offices is involved, the representations of the clients have nothing at all to do with each other, and the two lawyers themselves have nothing to do with each other. Why shouldn't the representation be allowed? The Second Circuit Court of Appeals, the court which has led the way in addressing conflicts of interest disqualification issues, answered that question in *Cinema 5, Ltd. v. Cinerama, Inc.*, excerpted here. In *Cinema 5*, a New York City law firm was disqualified from representing Cinema 5 against Cinerama because one of its partners, Fleischmann, was also a partner in a separate Buffalo firm which was already representing Cinerama in another matter. Even though two law firms were involved, the only common thread being attorney Fleischmann, the court upheld the disqualification of the New York firm. The reason was not the relationship between the two cases, but the right of each client to the undivided loyalty of its attorney.

CINEMA 5, LTD. v. CINERAMA, INC.
528 F.2d 1384 (2d Cir. 1976)

Cinerama . . . was entitled to feel that at least until that litigation was at an end, it had [Fleischmann's] undivided loyalty as its advocate and champion . . . and could rely upon his "undivided allegiance and faithful, devoted service. . . ." Needless to say, when Mr. Fleischmann and his New York City partners undertook to represent Cinema 5, Ltd., they owed it the same fiduciary duty of undivided loyalty and allegiance. . . . [T]he professional judgment of a lawyer must be exercised solely for the benefit of his client, free of compromising influences and loyalties, and this precludes his acceptance of employment that will adversely affect his judgment or dilute his loyalty. . . .

[T]he lawyer who would sue his own client, asserting in justification the lack of "substantial relationship" between the litigation and the work he has undertaken to perform for that client, is leaning on a slender reed indeed. Putting it as mildly as we can, we think it would be questionable conduct for an attorney to participate in any lawsuit against his own client. . . .

Where the relationship is a continuing one, adverse representation is prima facie improper, and the attorney must be prepared to show, at the very least, that there will be no actual or *apparent* conflict in loyalties or diminution in the vigor of his representation. . . . [S]o long as Mr. Fleischmann and his

Buffalo partners continue to represent Cinerama, he and his New York City partners should not represent Cinema 5, Ltd. in this litigation.

NOTES

Cinema 5 is a case which has often been cited by other courts and commentators. Since the conflict in *Cinema 5* is attenuated, the case stands in strong opposition to bending the rule prohibiting law firm conflicts. Thus, a conflict can't be cured by screening off the offending lawyer, creating a "wall" or "cone of silence"[5] around that attorney so that no confidences or secrets are revealed or received. This is because the law firm's *current* loyalties would still be divided. According to *Westinghouse v. Kerr-McGee Corp.*, 580 F.2d 1311 (7th Cir. 1978), this is true even where a national law firm had offices in different cities, and representation was indirect through a trade association.

Some authority does exist for a narrow exception to the rule forbidding concurrent representation of adverse clients. *Hughes v. Paine, Webber, Jackson & Curtis, Inc.*, 565 F. Supp. 663 (N.D. Ill. 1983), argues somewhat anomalously that where an attorney-client confidential relationship has formed through a consultation but the lawyer does not ultimately represent the client, although the individual lawyer may have had an attorney-client relationship with the client, the law firm did not.

3. The "Hot Potato" Doctrine. What if the law firm avoided the direct conflict of interest problem by withdrawing from representing the less interesting (or less lucrative) client? Suppose X wants the law firm to sue Y, and Y is a minor client in an unrelated case. May the firm withdraw its representation of Y in order to take X's case? According to several courts, the answer in these so-called "hot potato" cases is "no."[6]

Such legal finesses may occur because of the pressure on large firms, given the mobility of today's modern lawyer. How can law firms risk merger, or even taking on additional "lateral hires," if they are confronted with insoluble conflict of interest problems?

Picker Int'l, Inc. v. Varian Assocs., 869 F.2d 578 (Fed. Cir. 1989), addressed some of these issues. The firms of Jones, Day, Reavis & Pogue and McDougall, Hersh & Scott merged. At the time of the merger, Jones, Day was representing long-time client Picker in a suit against Varian. Varian was a client of the McDougall firm in unrelated matters. McDougall asked Varian for consent to have Jones, Day continue to represent Picker after the merger, but Varian refused. At that point, McDougall purported to withdraw as Varian's counsel just before the merger. The court rejected this withdrawal, and instead required Jones, Day to withdraw as Picker's counsel, reaffirming the idea that a law firm cannot drop a client like a "hot potato," even where a major merger is at stake.

---

[5] We prefer to avoid the now appropriately discredited term "Chinese wall."

[6] *See, e.g., Unified Sewerage Agency v. Jelco, Inc.*, 646 F.2d 1339 (9th Cir. 1981); *Stratagem Dev. Corp. v. Heron Int'l NV*, 756 F. Supp. 789 (S.D.N.Y. 1991); *Truck Ins. Exch. v. Fireman's Fund Ins.*, 6 Cal. App. 4th 1050, 8 Cal. Rptr. 2d 228 (1992).

And in the Duane Morris disqualification discussed in section 1 above, Judge Reed cited the hot potato concept as an inappropriate way to avoid a conflict. In light of this clear circumstance — and that *concurrent* representation was taking place before the withdrawals — it is a bit puzzling to us why the judge seemed to base his decision on conflicts involving a "former" client and use of the "substantial relationship" test, which is generally necessary only in *former* client conflict situations. We now look more closely at that test.

4. The "Substantial Relationship" Test. What happens where a law firm wants to take on representation which is adverse not to a current client, but a *former* one? The standards used in both ethics rules and case law are significantly different than the almost blanket prohibitions involving current clients. The threshold test is commonly called the "substantial relationship" test: that is, is there a substantial relationship between the subject matter of the current representation ($X v. Y$) and the former engagement (involving ex-client Y)? In most jurisdictions, if the answer is yes, it is presumed that the law firm received confidential information *from* the former client which is material to the current case *against* that former client.[7]

The purposes of the test are to assure attorney loyalty and protect confidentiality, while still allowing clients counsel of choice when possible. As Judge Weinfeld wrote in the *T.C. Theatre*[8] case, "a lawyer's duty of absolute loyalty to his client's interests does not end with his retainer." Moreover, the lawyer has the continuing obligation to preserve the client's confidences and secrets *after* the representation. The presumption that the lawyer received material confidences avoids making the former client state its case for disqualification by revealing the very confidence it told its former lawyer and doesn't want used.

While the substantial relationship test may sound simple on the surface, in its application it is anything but. Among the questions raised about this test are these:

- *What constitutes a former client?* Is an actual case necessary? Is it sufficient that the client consulted the lawyer even if counsel was never retained?

- *What does "matter" mean?* Is it required that the "matter" be in litigation? May a lawyer be disqualified for representing one client against a former client in a business negotiation? What about an attorney who provides ongoing business advice to a company that is a competitor of the former client?

- *What constitutes "adversity"?* Is "adversity" limited to direct representation of one client against the former client, or can the "adverse" relationship be more subtle or indirect? Courts have disagreed broadly on this question. Some cases have interpreted the term literally, while others have held that "adverse" can mean "differing" or even "not exactly aligned."[9]

---

[7] The test was first articulated in *T.C. Theatre Corp. v. Warner Bros. Pictures, Inc.*, 113 F. Supp. 265, 268-69 (S.D.N.Y. 1953), and has been used, essentially unchanged, in countless cases since. The substantial relationship test is now embodied in ABA Model Rule 1.9, and interpreted at length in the Comment to that rule.

[8] *See* Footnote 7.

[9] *See In re Blinder, Robinson & Co.*, 123 B.R. 900 (Bankr. Colo. 1991).

● *What constitutes a "substantial relationship" between the current and former representations?* This is the very core of the test. It is subject to the most analysis and scrutiny by the courts, but at the same time remains the most difficult concept to define. Some courts look to the facts of each representation. Others examine the common legal issues. Others seem to invert the presumption about confidences by arguing that a substantial relationship turns on whether the lawyer has obtained confidential information which can be used against the former client.

A number of cases decided under California law illustrate some of the more nuanced issues. In *Trone v. Smith*, 621 F.2d 994 (9th Cir. 1980), the first review of the test applying California law, the federal appeals court concluded that among the determining factors in finding a substantial relationship was the knowledge the lawyer had gained of the "policies, practices and procedures" of the former client. To many this seemed to make sense. After all, shouldn't a court's inquiry focus on whether the attorney has learned *anything* which could be used against the former client? What could be more useful than "inside" knowledge about how the former client thinks — how litigation decisions are made, or settlement postures are taken?

However a decade later, *H.F. Ahmanson & Co. v. Salomon Bros., Inc.*, 229 Cal. App. 3d. 1445, 280 Cal. Rptr. 614 (1991), developed an oft-cited and somewhat more limited three-part test relating more directly to the underlying facts of the two cases: (1) whether the cases are similar factually; (2) whether they are similar legally; and (3) the extent of the lawyer's involvement.

But more recent California cases seem to have broadened *Ahmanson*'s test for disqualification. In *Jessen v. Hartford Casualty Insurance Co.*, 111 Cal. App. 4th 698, 3 Cal. Rptr. 3d 877 (2003), the court held that if the former representation "placed the attorney with respect to the prior client" in a "direct and personal" relationship, the third *Ahmanson* factor was determined as a matter of law, and "the only remaining question is whether there is a connection between the two successive representations. . . ." Then, in *Farris v. Fireman's Fund Insurance Co.*, 119 Cal. App. 4th 671, 14 Cal. Rptr. 3d 618 (2004), an insurance company sought disqualification of a law firm prosecuting a bad faith case against it because former coverage counsel for the insurer now worked for the plaintiff's firm. *Farris* discussed *Jessen* and *Ahmanson* at length, cited *Trone v. Smith* with approval, and disqualified the lawyer despite acknowledging that "the services [in the two cases] are distinct." *Farris* concluded that there remained a substantial risk that the work the lawyer had performed in the former case could be used in the current adverse representation.

● *"Playbooks" and "poker tells."* Some commentators criticized *Jesson* and *Farris* as they had *Trone* — for advocating the generally disfavored "playbook" approach to former client relationships. As ABA Formal Opinion 99-415 put it, a lawyer's general knowledge of the strategies, policies, or personnel of the former employer, without more, is not enough to establish a substantial relationship. The Restatement Third of the Law Governing Lawyers, § 132, also avoids the so-called "playbook" approach. But the *Farris* court argued strongly that *Jessen* was not a "playbook" case, because it "mandates that the information acquired during the first representation be . . . directly at issue in, or have some critical importance to, the second representation." *Farris* cites favorably the portion of Restatement § 132 that states that if a lawyer performed work and "there is a substantial risk that [the present representation] will involve the use of information acquired" while doing that first work, a substantial relationship exists.

What about "poker tells"? All good lawyers know that the more personal the knowledge -how to "push the client's buttons," or the personal idiosyncrasies of the client, such as what it means when the client scowls, or giggles, in deposition, or even more significant, how the client rubs her nose when she's telling less than the whole truth -the more valuable that knowledge is. If the idea behind the substantial relationship test is truly to avoid harm to the former client, these factors are crucial ones. Do they amount to the kinds of information that is barred by the case law discussed above, or by the Restatement? At this juncture, despite the substantial body of law on this issue, the answer is less than clear.

• *Were material confidences imparted?* This question actually relates to the *presumption* about confidences. First, is it presumed that the attorney received confidences from the former client? Second, may this presumption be rebutted?[10] Jurisdictions generally agree that there is a presumption, but disagree as to whether it may be rebutted. For example, in *Silver Chrysler Plymouth, Inc. v. Chrysler Motors Corp.*, 518 F.2d 751 (2d Cir. 1975), the court said that a lawyer who performed only minimal tasks and who never shared in any of the former client's confidences would not be presumed to have acquired those confidences:

> [T]here is reason to differentiate for disqualification purposes between lawyers who become heavily involved in the facts of a particular matter and those who enter briefly on the periphery for a limited and specific purpose relating solely to legal questions. . . . Under the latter circumstances the attorney's role cannot be considered "representation" within the meaning of *T.C. Theatre Corp.* . . .

The idea that somehow, not all members of a law firm "represent" its clients was clearly a minority view when *Silver Chrysler* was decided. But passage of ABA Model Rule 1.9 lends support to this position. Rule 1.9(b) prevents a lawyer from representing a client in a substantially related matter against the ex-client of the lawyer's old firm if *the lawyer* (as opposed to the lawyer's former firm) received material confidential information. Extensive comments to Model Rule 1.9 discuss this liberalized rule and the competing interests involved when lawyers migrate from one firm to another, including the business realities of modern law firm migration.

---

[10] An interesting case is *Casco Northern Bank v. JBI Associates, Ltd.*, 667 A.2d 856 (Maine 1995), which holds that actual transmission of confidential information is not required to disqualify a firm once a substantial relationship between past and present representations has been established. The Maine Supreme Court disqualified an attorney for a limited partnership in litigation against a general partner whom the attorney had previously represented in setting up the partnership. The court held that even if the former client had no reasonable expectation that the information the lawyer received was confidential, the client still had a reasonable expectation of *loyalty*.

But what about the former client's perspective? How does that client know that the lawyer changing firms has not received material confidential information? Why should the former client have to trust the former lawyer's claims, when the lawyer now works for a firm on the other side, and where the economic consequences to the lawyer's new firm can be substantial? The District of Columbia bar has twice taken the former client's point of view. First, in Opinion 212 (1990), it held that a law firm must be disqualified unless *all* lawyers who worked on the former client's matter have left the firm, and no remaining lawyer has ever received confidences about the matter. Then, the D.C. bar amended its version of Model Rule 1.10(b) to require imputed law firm disqualification when there is *either* (rather than both) a substantially related matter *or* any remaining lawyer who had material confidential information.

The Nebraska Supreme Court has adopted a "bright line" rule of disqualification: If the lawyer's prior firm represented the former client in a way in which confidential information was transmitted to that firm, then those confidences are imputed to all other lawyers of that firm, no matter how peripheral their participation in the former representation. *Creighton Univ. v. Hickman*, 245 Neb. 247, 512 N.W.2d 374 (1994). Indeed, here the disqualification related to a paralegal and her new law firm.

The issue of whether a lawyer is presumed to have received confidences of a client of the lawyer's former firm is particularly significant when it comes to law firm imputation, discussed next.

● *How shall the lawyer's former involvement be imputed to the lawyer's new law firm?* It is this question which faces Meeker, Reynolds and which we evaluate further here.

Once it has been determined that the migrating lawyer has (or is presumed to have) received confidential information from the former client of the old law firm, the next question is whether this information is now imputed to the lawyer's new firm. Remember that the imputation of shared confidences from the former client is based on whether there is a "substantial relationship" between the old representation and the new one. Where the representations are the same case, there is no question about this.

Where the representations concern different matters the same analysis applicable to the imputation of knowledge at the old firm also applies to the imputation of knowledge with the new firm. Thus, an attorney who worked on the "periphery" of a case at the old firm may argue that such work did not amount to an actual "representation," and thus would not preclude that lawyer from working on the new firm's matter adverse to the interests of the old firm's client. Certain jurisdictions, such as the Second Circuit, have adopted this approach.

However, the Seventh Circuit in *Novo Terapeutisk Laboratorium A/S v. Baxter Travenol Laboratories*, 607 F.2d 186 (7th Cir. 1979), held that the length of the former representation, while a factor, should not be given great weight, as confidences can be transmitted even in a short period of time. The *Novo* court held that whether there was a substantial relationship between the two representations rested on "the possibility, or appearance thereof, that confidential information *might* have been given to the attorney in relation to the subsequent matter in which disqualification is sought." (Emphasis added.) The court concluded that it would be inappropriate for a trial court to inquire into whether actual confidences were disclosed, because this would require the client claiming a breach of its confidences to reveal them in order to prove that they were communicated, thus defeating the very purpose of the motion. In order for the trial court to find that there was *not* a substantial relationship, it must be "clearly discernable" that the issues involved in the current case did not relate to the former representation.

Thus, in analyzing whether there is a substantial relationship between two representations, the court must first determine the scope of the original representation; second, determine whether it is reasonable to infer that the migrating lawyer received confidential information regarding the original representation; and third, decide whether that information is relevant to the new representation against the former client. The *Novo* court did not require that the third step be the new firm's actual receipt of the confidential information.

It is generally the case that the analysis used to determine whether confidential information is to be imputed to an attorney for the work at the old firm for the old client is similar to the determination that if the migrating attorney is said to have obtained such information, it will be imputed to the new firm as well. The new firm will be disqualified unless it can rebut the presumption that it received the confidences. This almost always involves the assertion that an ethical wall at the new firm shielded the attorneys working on the case from receiving any information from the migrating attorney that could possibly assist them.

Not surprisingly, a great debate rages over whether such ethical walls or screens should be permitted to rebut the presumption of imputed confidences.

5. Screening: A Brief History. We come now to the issue of whether the "tainted" lawyer can successfully be "screened." If a court rules that the former client's confidences *are* imputed to the lawyer who leaves the firm, is creating a wall around the lawyer to prevent any involvement in the new case sufficient to protect the former client's interests? A growing number of jurisdictions, while still in the minority, have begun to approve some form of screening mechanism beyond those that historically have been afforded former government employees. The minority has grown, gaining support from new language in the ABA Ethics 2000 Commission's drafts and the American Law Institute's proposed final language in its Restatement. As screening gains a larger foothold, the opposition to ethical screens, far from receding, has also strengthened its voice.

Under the old ABA Model Code, DR 5-105 supported the position now taken by the Nebraska "bright line" rule: No attorney can "switch sides" against a client, even if the lawyer switching sides personally had little or nothing to do with that client.

The first exception to this prohibition against screens was ABA Formal Opinion 342 (1975), which applied to former government attorneys. DR 9-101(B) provided that "a lawyer shall not accept private employment in a manner in which he had substantial responsibility while he was a public employee." The committee interpreted this rule liberally, stating that there were weighty policy reasons why it should not be applied to broadly limit a lawyer's new employment after government service. The imposition of harsh restraints on future private practice would impair the government's ability to recruit attorneys.

Subsequently, most jurisdictions that prohibited screening for private attorneys eventually accepted the government lawyer exception. The ABA Model Rules even have a distinct rule on the subject, MR 1.11. We will address the work of government lawyers, including the conflicts of interest they confront, in a later chapter.

It was not long after ABA Formal Opinion 342 was issued that various commentators and private firms began pushing for ethical screens for private attorneys who had changed firms. For example, the Seventh Circuit, which took a broad stand on the substantial relationship test, also fashioned a relatively liberal screening test. In *Schiessle v. Stephens*, 717 F.2d 417 (7th Cir. 1983), the court, after determining if there is a "substantial relationship" between the present and former matters, would next examine "whether the presumption of shared confidences . . . has been rebutted with respect to the prior representation. . . ." The *Schiessle* court then developed this test:

> In other words . . . the presumption of shared confidences could be rebutted by demonstrating that "specific institutional mechanisms" . . . had been implemented to effectively insulate against any flow of confidential information from the "infected" attorney to any other member of his present firm. Such a determination can be based on objective and verifiable evidence presented to the trial court and must be made on a case-by-case basis. Factors appropriate for consideration by the trial court might include, but are not limited to, the size and structural divisions of the law firm involved, the likelihood of contact between the "infected" attorney and the specific attorneys responsible for the present representation, the existence of rules which prevent the "infected" attorney from access to relevant files or other information pertaining to the present litigation or which prevent him from sharing in the fees derived from such litigation.

In the years since *Schiessle*, cases — and rules makers — have continued to answer the screening question in a variety of ways. It appears to be the case that jurisdictions that take a narrow, limited circumstances view of disqualifying conflicts tend not to make screening available, while if the jurisdiction has broader conflicts disqualifications, like the Seventh Circuit, courts seem to feel that equity may require the availability of screening. (California is a notable exception here.) Does this make sense to you? What should the court consider if creating that balance?

6. The Screening Debate. The deep division in the legal profession and among courts and rule-makers over whether the imputation of confidential information to the new firm should be rebuttable and whether ethical screens are desirable is illustrated by comparing the following excerpted articles. The views of these commentators are almost diametrically opposed. We highlight several specific issues, moving back and forth between the commentators.

ANDREW P. ROMSHEK, THE NEBRASKA "BRIGHT LINE" RULE: THE AUTOMATIC DISQUALIFICATION OF A LAW FIRM DUE TO A NEW LAWYER'S PRIOR AFFILIATIONS . . . SENSIBLE SOLUTION OR SERIOUS SETBACK?
28 Creighton Law Review 213 (1994)[11]

NEIL W. HAMILTON & KEVIN R. COAN, ARE WE A PROFESSION OR MERELY A BUSINESS?: THE EROSION OF THE CONFLICTS RULES THROUGH THE INCREASED USE OF ETHICAL WALLS
27 Hofstra Law Review 57 (Fall 1998)[12]

On Client Choice:

Romshek: [D]isqualifying law firms restricts the client's right to employ and keep a qualified lawyer. Potentially, a client could lose the benefit of longtime counsel who has specialized knowledge of the client's situation. . . .

For example, in *FirsTier Bank, N.A., Omaha* [*v. Buckley*, 244 Neb. 36, 503 N.W.2d 838 (1993)], through the use of the bright line rule, the court could have disqualified at least thirty-four law firms from representing the defendants because of prior associations with FirsTier Bank.

Hamilton & Coan: Lurking in the shadows of every policy discussion citing the right of client choice is the fact that the client's dilemma in this type of conflict is caused exclusively by the fact that a lawyer has moved in the first place. . . . [C]ourts have exhibited an increased willingness to decide against disqualification based on the quality of client choice. The client choice rationale is necessarily a function of the policy of accommodating lawyer mobility. [T]he client choice rationale is thus implicitly a policy of giving more weight to lawyers' financial interests and the concept of the profession as a business.

On Client Hardships:

Romshek: A client whose attorney is disqualified may encounter hardships. Before disqualification is complete, the attorney may be motivated to settle early. After the attorney's disqualification, the client's chance of losing the case might increase, or the client might be forced to settle. In the end, the client loses time and possibly the work product.

Hamilton & Coan: Courts allowing ethical walls may encourage litigants to choose firms that possess confidential information of adversaries. . . . There is no compensatory benefit to the former client. . . . The existing client whose firm is disqualified because the firm recruited a migrating lawyer who created a former client conflict has a malpractice claim to compensate for damages. . . . The former client whose confidences are compromised has almost no chance either to discover the wrong or to prove damages.

On Lawyer Mobility:

Romshek: As a practice, large law firms tend to hire more young attorneys than are actually expected to attain partnership status. . . . [Y]oung attorneys may seriously jeopardize their careers by working for a large firm for a short period of time. A law firm would be reluctant to hire an attorney who previously worked at a large firm if the imputation doctrine would automatically disqualify the firm from all cases in which a client is represented by the former firm.

Hamilton & Coan: [The] dramatic increase in the mobility of law firm partners . . . is occurring because a substantial source of larger law firms' growth during the last fifteen years has been the recruitment of laterals, including partners, who have lucrative books of business. These lawyers move for more attractive financial packages.

. . . [T]he growing perception of the practice of law as solely a business, and that lawyer mobility . . . must be accommodated . . . is a fundamental shift away from the conception that the practice of law is also a profession shaped principally by its commitment to a transcendental purpose, justice.

On Public Criticism of the Bar:

Romshek: [(Quoting *Lemaire v. Texaco, Inc.*, 496 F. Supp. 1308, 1308-1309 (E.D. Texas 1980)]: "[T]he more frequently a litigant is delayed or otherwise disadvantaged by the unnecessary disqualification of his lawyer under the appearance of impropriety doctrine, the greater the likelihood of public suspicion of both the bar and judiciary."

Hamilton & Coan: Lawyers assure clients of absolute confidentiality. However, the former client's inability to ensure that confidences are protected, combined with the firm's interests both as advocate for the current client and in its own financial gain, are factors that undermine the former client's trust, and in turn the public's trust, in a legal system that would permit such a situation to exist without the former client's consent.

NOTES

Other commentators argue about whether lawyers may be trusted to maintain an ethical screen effectively. Screen proponents focus on the rights of the clients of the new firm and of the migrating lawyers; opponents focus on the rights of the former client. Sometimes it appears that the two sides are talking past each other. Those arguing for a screen claim no one has produced evidence screens have ever been breached; those arguing against screens claim there is no way for the former client to know if such breaches ever occurred since the attorneys benefitting by such a breach would never voluntarily disclose it, and because the pressure to win is so great that "peep holes" in the wall may result without a conscious decision to make it happen. The former client is in the position of having to trust the *new* firm of the tainted lawyer, the firm now zealously representing the other side.

Nothing better demonstrates this schism than the examples Romshek and Hamilton and Coan used to buttress their arguments:

Romshek: "Lawyer A joins Lawyer B as an associate, handling litigation matters. While Lawyer A is still an associate, Lawyer B drafts a will for Client X, Lawyer A having no knowledge or participation in the representation. Lawyer A leaves to open his own law office. Ten years later, Lawyer B retires from practice. Thereafter, Lawyer A is asked to represent the heir of Client X in a suit against the executor of the estate of Client X. Lawyer A would be disqualified."

Hamilton & Coan: "Imagine . . . that you are a construction subcontractor who has had the same lawyer from a large firm for a number of years. . . . [T]he lawyer has represented your interests in disputes against several general contractors. Your lawyer has become very familiar with your methods of operation, your financial position, and the contracts you use . . . . Recently, your lawyer has been drafting documents and giving advice concerning your dispute with . . . Contractor A. Now imagine that your lawyer switches firms . . . because of a more lucrative offer . . . , but you decide to stay with the same large firm. Later, you find out that your former lawyer has joined the firm representing Contractor A. . . . She [tells you] that the new firm has set up an ethical wall to . . . safeguard your confidential information. Is this ethical wall enough to ensure your absolute confidence that what you shared with your attorney will not be used against you?"

It seems that the only area of agreement between the two sides is that screening exists to promote the business of practicing law. Whether this is desirable is the source of much of the disagreement. A comment to ABA Model Rule 1.9 emphasizes that the duty of loyalty, absent the consideration of confidentiality, is insufficient to require the disqualification of the new firm, seemingly supporting the idea of law as a business over law as a profession. The Ethics 2000 Commission proposed adding subsection (c) to Model Rule 1.10 to permit "timely" screening of migrating lawyers who did not have a "substantial role" adverse to the new firm's client, but the House of Delegates did not approve it. But Section 204 of the Restatement goes even further, approving ethical screens to segregate migrating lawyers who have obtained confidential information from former clients who now oppose clients of the new firm.

But if maximizing business opportunities for lawyers is more important than the principles of loyalty and client confidentiality, one must ask what possible interest the new firm has in protecting the tainted lawyer's former client, now known as "the opposing party." Even if such a firm acted in complete good faith, is it fair to ask the former client to accept the word of opposing counsel? Is screening an idea whose genesis is in the reality of law as a business rather than a profession? Can ethical precepts and client obligations come first if screening is allowed?

Perhaps because of these questions, as late as mid-2006, despite all the discussion about the implementation of ethical screens, and despite the reality of law as a big business, the number of jurisdictions allowing screening (except for government lawyers) has increased only modestly in recent years. According to ALAS,[13] only eleven states allow for screening of lateral hires with

---

[13] The Attorneys' Liability Assurance Society, Inc., which describes itself as a "risk retention group" and which compiles statistics on a number of significant ethics issues jurisdiction by jurisdiction. These figures are based on the 2006 edition of ALAS's Loss Prevention Manual.

various caveats regarding notice to the client and limitations on receipt of fees for the screened lawyer. Seven other states allow for more limited screening, but in some of those states, case law makes those limits quite narrow.

For example, in *Lennartson v. Anoka-Hennepin Independent School District No. 11*, 662 N.W.2d 125 (Minn. 2003), the Minnesota Supreme Court narrowly interpreted that state's screening rule: "We are properly reluctant to interpret the rule as contradictory to its plain meaning, especially when the plain meaning is consistent with the purpose behind the rule — to instill confidence in the legal profession. Therefore, we conclude . . . that the subparts of the rule be read conjunctively." Thus, the court held, where the lawyer who moved to the law firm on side A received confidential information from side B, the firm "is unable to meet the first subpart of our rule and any screening measures it enacted are irrelevant," and disqualification is required.

Since the promulgation of the 2002 ABA Model Rules, 26 states have revised their rules, but only four that had not previously adopted screening mechanisms have added them to their rules.

7. Corporate Subsidiaries, Client Interests, and Disqualification. What happens in the world of corporate conglomerates, where a parent may own several subsidiaries, some of which are far-flung and have little connection to the parent? May a firm represent a client against the parent (or subsidiary) of a former corporate client? This is another emerging issue, and the courts that have considered it have not agreed on how to analyze the situation. One question is whether courts will look beyond corporate organizational charts to the practical effect on the client.

In *Teradyne, Inc. v. Hewlett-Packard Co.*, 20 U.S.P.Q.2d 1143 (N.D. Cal. 1991), Teradyne sued Hewlett-Packard for patent infringement. One law firm representing Teradyne in the litigation also represented H-P's wholly owned subsidiary, Apollo Computer, in related trademark matters. The court found that there was an "identity of interests" between H-P and Apollo, and that the firm had a conflict of interest by simultaneously representing Apollo while representing Teradyne against H-P. The court disqualified the firm from representing Teradyne.

Two other courts reached different results based on the same facts in lawsuits brought in New York and California: *Brooklyn Navy Yard Cogeneration Partners LP v. PMNC* (N.Y. Super. Ct. 1997)[14] and *Brooklyn Navy Yard Cogeneration Partners LP v. Superior Court*, 60 Cal. App. 4th 248, 70 Cal. Rptr. 2d 419 (1997). The far-reaching opinion below discusses the California version of *Brooklyn Navy Yard*, bucks the law-as-a-business trend, and provides a thoughtful analysis of both corporate subsidiary conflicts and the need to focus on the *interests* of a party, rather than just the party's status as "client."

---

[14] See a report in *ABA/BNA Manual on Professional Conduct*, p. 319 (1997) for a discussion of the opinion.

MORRISON KNUDSEN CORP. v. HANCOCK, ROTHERT & BUNSHOFT

69 Cal. App. 4th 223, 81 Cal. Rptr. 2d 425 (1999)

HANLON, P. J.

This is an appeal from a preliminary injunction preventing the law firm of Hancock, Rothert & Bunshoft (Hancock) from representing the Contra Costa Water District (District) in any dispute with Morrison Knudsen Corporation (Morrison), or Morrison's wholly owned subsidiary, Centennial Engineering, Inc. (Centennial) concerning the Vasco Road or Los Vaqueros construction projects in Livermore. . . .

Hancock seeks to represent the District in proceedings on a cross-complaint against Centennial [the Unimin sand dispute], and the alleged conflict stems primarily from Hancock's ongoing representation of Morrison's insurance underwriters in matters involving Morrison, rather than from representation of Morrison itself or of Centennial. We conclude: (1) that the court could consider the information Hancock received as underwriter's counsel in determining whether there was a conflict; (2) that this information could be deemed to create a conflict if it was "substantially related" to the District's dispute with Centennial; (3) the court could reasonably find that the information was substantially related to the Centennial dispute; (4) the court could reasonably find that there was a sufficient "unity of interest" between the Centennial and Morrison to treat them as one entity for purposes of the alleged conflict; and (5) the determination that Hancock should be disqualified was not an abuse of discretion under all of the circumstances. . . .

. . . .

Hancock had never represented Centennial, but Centennial's parent, Morrison, had retained Hancock on various matters until about 1990. Beginning in the 1980s, and continuing up to the time of the District's dispute with Centennial herein, Hancock was retained by the underwriters of Morrison's primary comprehensive insurance policy to monitor the defense attorneys Morrison retained on errors and omissions claims. In its capacity as "monitoring counsel," Hancock received detailed confidential communications from Morrison's defense counsel concerning the progress of cases and Morrison's potential liability.

. . . .

This case is "a square peg which does not fit into the round holes of the rules most commonly applied in attorney disqualification cases." . . . An attorney is forbidden from undertaking a representation adverse to a former client if there is a "substantial relationship" between the current and former matters. This prohibition stems from the attorney's duty to maintain client confidences. . . .

The [trial] court wrote, with italics added, that "[Hancock's] prior direct representation of Morrison, *coupled with its current status as monitoring counsel for [Morrison's] underwriters*, supports the conclusion that [Hancock] has acquired substantial knowledge of the policies, attitudes and practices of [Morrison's] top management with respect to litigation of this type."

Thus, this case does not fit neatly into the former representation rule. Two issues not generally presented in former representation cases are raised here. First, could the court properly consider the information Hancock obtained as counsel for Morrison's underwriters in determining whether Hancock should be disqualified herein? Second, if the answer to the first question is "yes," was the information Hancock gained from its prior representation of Morrison and its present representation of Morrison's underwriters sufficiently relevant to the Unimin sand dispute to create a conflict of interest?

. . . .

[A]n attorney's receipt of confidential information *from a nonclient* may lead to the attorney's disqualification. In this case, Morrison's declarations testified to an understanding that its communications with Hancock in Hancock's capacity as "monitoring counsel" for Morrison's underwriters would be kept confidential, even if Morrison was not Hancock's "client" in those matters. This was a reasonable expectation. Hancock's own declarations acknowledged that it treated information received from Morrison "confidentially, given the Underwriters' good faith obligations to their insured." Accordingly, we conclude that the court could properly take into account the confidential information Hancock received as "monitoring counsel" . . . . While Morrison had a reasonable expectation that this information would be kept confidential, it could not expect "fidelity" from Hancock as if Hancock were an attorney sitting on its board of directors. Hancock's loyalty ran to its client, the underwriters, not to Morrison, and Morrison could expect that the information might be used against it to further the underwriters' interests. . . . Like a case of successive representation, the primary consideration for the (non)client in this instance is one of confidentiality rather than loyalty. . . .

We therefore conclude that the proper standard for assessing whether the information Hancock received as the underwriters' counsel disqualified it from representing the District is . . . the "substantial relationship" test ordinarily applied in successive representation cases.

. . . .

Application of the Substantial Relationship Test

As for the nature and extent of Hancock's involvement in Morrison's cases, the evidence established that the involvement was substantial, even in Hancock's capacity as monitoring counsel for the underwriters. The declarations averred that in those matters, attorneys at Hancock discussed litigation strategy with Morrison's officers and defense counsel, conducted defense research, and participated in settlement discussions and mediations. Morrison personnel declared that from 1990 to 1996, they had received advice from Hancock on the "value" of cases [and], "the upside and downside of settlement alternatives. . . ."

[T]here was substantial evidence that as monitoring counsel Hancock had considerable exposure to Morrison's litigation policies and strategies.

. . . .

A final factor militating in favor of a "substantial relationship" finding, and one not present in the usual successive representation case [is that], Hancock was privy by virtue of this continuing role to information about Morrison's financial condition which could be useful to a Morrison adversary. As counsel put it to the court, a monitoring attorney at Hancock could potentially report to a Hancock attorney for the District that "[Morrison] is going to have to pay out a lot of money [on a monitored claim]. This is a great time for the [D]istrict to come in, make a reasonable demand on [Morrison]. They're going to settle quickly because we've already exhausted certain amounts within their policy. . . ."

The Unity of Interests Test

It is undisputed that Hancock had never represented Centennial, or monitored any claim against Centennial on behalf of the underwriters. Since any conflict of interest arose solely from Hancock's dealings with Morrison, the remaining question is whether Morrison and Centennial are to be treated as separate entities for purposes of the alleged conflict.

The court disqualified Hancock based on the "close relationship" it found between Morrison and Centennial. In support of this finding, the court cited among other things the District's tender of PG&E's $ 12.4 million Unimin sand claim to Morrison as well as Centennial. . . . The court also cited . . . evidence confirm[ing] that as counsel for Morrison's underwriters, Hancock had ongoing communications about litigation matters with Richard Edmister and Edwin Appel, the in-house attorneys at Morrison who would be managing Centennial's defense.

. . . .

[California State Bar Ethics Opinion 1989-113] opined, in the context of its hypothetical involving a suit against a client's subsidiary, that "if the attorney has obtained confidential information directly from the nonclient subsidiary under circumstances where the subsidiary could reasonably expect that the attorney had a duty to keep such information confidential, the attorney might be precluded from acting adversely to the subsidiary in matters related to the subject on which the attorney had obtained such confidential information."

. . . .

The *Brooklyn Navy Yard* court referred extensively to the State Bar Opinion, and conceded it stated that corporations could be treated as one entity for conflict purposes if they were either alter egos or had a unity of interests. However, the court thought that the "unity of interests" standard was too uncertain to provide any useful guidance. . . . *Brooklyn Navy Yard*'s analysis conflicts with formal ethics opinion No. 95-390 of the American Bar Association's Committee on Professional Ethics.

The ABA Committee addressed "whether a lawyer who represents a corporate client may undertake a representation that is adverse to a corporate affiliate of the client in an unrelated matter, without obtaining the client's consent." The ABA Opinion concluded that while corporate affiliation alone did not necessarily create an attorney-client relationship, there were "particular circumstances" in which an affiliate could be considered an additional client. "This would clearly be true," the ABA Committee thought, "where one corporation is the alter ego of the other. It is not necessary, however, for one corporation to be the alter ego of the other as a matter of law in order for both to be considered clients."

. . . .

The weight of the foregoing authorities supports Hancock's disqualification in this case. A number of considerations apply. First, as previously discussed, in the course of the firm's work involving the parent corporation, it received confidential information. . . .

[Second,] the parent in this instance controls the legal affairs of the subsidiary. . . .

A third set of considerations stems from the evidence of Morrison's participation in the construction project at issue. Here the record shows that Morrison personnel administered Centennial's contract, that Centennial had no contractual authority independent of Morrison, and that the District was aware of Morrison's controlling role.

. . . .

In light of all of the foregoing considerations, the trial court could reasonably find that Morrison and Centennial were, in the court's word, "closely" enough related to be treated as one entity for purposes of the conflict herein. . . .

Centennial and Morrison do not claim to be alter egos, and the question is whether the absence of such a relationship is dispositive. We conclude that it is not.

. . . .

The "unity of interests" test will continue to develop on a case-by-case basis, and take more definite and useful shape in the process. . . . [H]ere, the principal focus should be the practical consequences of the attorney's relationship with the corporate family. If that relationship may give the attorney a significant practical advantage in a case against an affiliate, then the attorney can be disqualified from taking the case. There is substantial evidence of such a potential advantage in this instance, and that is as close as we can come to defining a "bottom line."

NOTES

Does this opinion make good solid common sense, or is the decision simply unfair to the District, which lost a lawyer that had never represented the other side?

8. Shared Space and Non-Lawyer Migration. As if lawyer migration and imputed law firm disqualification were not complicated enough, several other "twists" on these issues exist. Two bear brief mention here. Many lawyers who keep separate law firms and separate books share office space, receptionists, phone systems, and libraries. These shared space situations present difficult issues of imputed conflicts of interest.

When lawyers conduct themselves as a firm or even hold themselves out to the public or to a client in a way that suggests that they are a firm, they will be treated as one law firm for conflicts purposes. This is also often true when it comes to disqualification, responsibility to work on a case, and, ultimately, malpractice liability. The comment to Model Rule 1.10 recognizes shared space arrangements and emphasizes the issue of whether confidences are shared as well. But what about those situations where it appears reasonably possible that information will be shared unintentionally? Many state ethics opinions, as well as a few cases, address these issues. The majority seem to turn on how much a lawyer protects against inadvertent disclosure of confidences, the easier the access other attorneys have to the confidential information, and the greater the likelihood that the lawyer will be considered to be breaching the confidentiality. When attorneys in the same suite keep their separate files sacrosanct, use a separate telephone and fax machine, have different support staff, and make it clear they are in separate practices, they are far more likely to be permitted to represent adverse interests than if these protections are not in place. Even then, however, when there is close proximity of lawyers within a suite of offices, representing adverse interests is dangerous under any circumstances at least from the point of view of potential liability in the form of a "shotgun" malpractice claim.

We have discussed lawyers who change firms, but what about non-lawyer personnel? These personnel serve under the lawyer's "umbrella," and the lawyers who supervise them must ensure that they respect attorney-client confidences just as the attorney does.[15] But does a change of employment lead to the same disqualification standard that confronts law firms who take on migrating attorneys? Despite the *Casco* case footnoted above, most recent cases hold that such migrating personnel will not lead to the disqualification of the law firm as long as the personnel are screened.

Perhaps the first case to deal with this issue is *In re Complex Asbestos Litigation*, 232 Cal. App. 3d 572, 283 Cal. Rptr. 732 (1991). A paralegal moved from a firm which handled asbestos defense work to a plaintiff's asbestos firm, reviewing many of his former firm's files before he left. Although the court found that the paralegal's new firm was tainted by his knowledge, it nevertheless set up a future test less stringent than the substantial relationship test in one respect, and much like the *Schiessle* test in another. First, the court held that since a paralegal, and not a lawyer, was involved, the usual presumption of confidences didn't apply; rather, the burden was on the former client to show that the employee had obtained material confidences. Second, the receipt of confidences could be rebutted by showing that the paralegal did not disclose them to the new law firm due to screening measures, or what the court termed a "cone of silence" employed by the new firm. But cases since have generally not made this distinction between lawyer and paralegal.

For example, *In re American Home Products*, 985 S.W.2d 68 (Tex. 1998), concerned a legal assistant who had formerly worked for a defense firm representing one of the Norplant defendants. She spent significant time interviewing potential witnesses and investigating plaintiffs, meeting with counsel, and preparing memoranda about the evidence. Thereafter she went

---

[15] Non-lawyers, of course, are not subject to discipline under rules of professional conduct. But they can, for example, be contractually bound to maintain confidences as a condition of employment.

to work for a plaintiffs' lawyer who failed to screen her. The lawyer was disqualified.

In *Ciaffone v. Eighth Judicial District Court*, 945 P.2d 950 (Nev. 1997), a plaintiff's firm hired a secretary who had worked for two months for the opposing law firm in a case the plaintiff's firm was handling. Although she was not assigned to a lawyer working on the case, the firm did not screen her. The court applied the confidentiality rule to nonlawyer employees and disqualified the plaintiff's firm. And in a series of cases in Florida in 2000, 2001 and 2002, lawyers hiring paralegals who had worked for the other side were uniformly disqualified.[16]

Does it make sense to have a different standard for support staff than for lawyers? What might justify such different treatment? Are support staff any more mobile than lawyers? And, finally, how might this issue apply to *you* as a law student working for one law firm one summer and another the next?

9. Withdrawing From a Case. In disqualifications, lawyers are forcefully ejected from a case. There are also various reasons that lawyers voluntarily withdraw from a representation. Some of these are mandatory, required by the circumstances. Others are permissive, justified at the lawyer's request, assuming permission is sought and granted by the relevant tribunal. And then, of course, there are those occasions where the attorneys' services are "no longer required" by the client. We discuss all three situations here.

Mandatory Withdrawal. Lawyers are *required* to withdraw from representation for a variety of reasons, among them issues relating to their health or ability to continue on a case, or to avoid complicity with a client who is about to commit a crime.

While disqualification motions provide the bulk of the case law on conflicts withdrawals, many prudent firms examine their potential conflicts after their own mergers and acquisitions of new attorneys, and evaluate their chances of being forcibly removed. These firms may then decide themselves to withdraw voluntarily. Increasingly, disgruntled clients, unhappy about being surprised by a motion to withdraw and, ultimately, losing their law firm, have looked to their own lawyers to see whether their firm should have anticipated the problem. Legal malpractice suits have arisen where the firm "played ostrich," or simply failed to advise the client of the possible dangers of disqualification.[17]

Permissive Withdrawal. A client's insistence in pursuing a course of conduct or a strategy that is either fraudulent or criminal, or that involves the submission of false evidence, gives an attorney good cause to withdraw from a representation. A client's failure to pay fees may also constitute good cause for permissive withdrawal, but not always. For example, in *Kriegsman v. Kriegsman*, 375 A.2d 1253 (N.J. Super. Ct. App. Div. 1977) the court refused to allow a firm to withdraw from representing an indigent woman in a divorce

---

[16] In a December 31, 2002 article in the Miami Daily Business Review, *Costly Lesson: Miami Lawyer Ordered Off Big Negligence Case Because He Hired a Paralegal Who Had Worked for the Opposing Law Firm*, reporter Laurie Cunningham reviews several of these Florida cases.

[17] *See, e.g.*, Richard A. Zitrin, *Knowing When to Disqualify Yourself From a Case*, CAL. BAR J., Feb. 1994.

action when she paid $2,000 in fees but her husband made the representation so difficult the attorneys actually billed $7,500. The court was not sympathetic to the lawyers' pleas, reasoning that "obligations [to the client] do not evaporate because the case becomes more complicated or the work more arduous or the retainer not as profitable as first contemplated. . . ."

Other reasons justifying a lawyer's permissive withdrawal are more subjective. As Model Rule 1.16(b) suggests, no matter how "repugnant or imprudent" a client, or how "unreasonably difficult," withdrawal is not automatic, and an attorney who seeks to withdraw must do so in a way that reasonably protects the client's interests. Protecting a client's interests means, among other things, not withdrawing at a critical point in a case, or spilling the beans in an all-too-candid declaration in support of a withdrawal motion, or refusing to cooperate with successor counsel. Even if withdrawal is granted in such cases, a malpractice suit may lurk right around the corner.

There are relatively few authorities that discuss whether an attorney may *threaten* withdrawal in order to pressure a client to act in a certain way, such as to accept a settlement offer. If a lawyer says "Accept this offer or I'll withdraw," can the client's subsequent acceptance be truly voluntary? Clearly, an attorney may threaten withdrawal to get a client to cease doing something that is criminal or fraudulent, but the issue is much more dicey once the lawyer uses the threat of withdrawal to limit or curtail the client's rights. Such threats create great danger; they also may be seen by a jury in a malpractice case as tantamount to client abandonment. While there is always a problem proving malpractice damages, particularly where a case settles, such a conclusion could put the law firm on the hook for any lost opportunity suffered by the client as a result of the lawyer's ultimatum.

At a minimum, in every case of permissive withdrawal an attorney who threatens to withdraw should also explain how the withdrawal may be carried out. Thus, in a case where the court's permission is needed for the attorney to withdraw, the attorney should advise the client that a motion is required and the client will have an opportunity to oppose it. All factors that will help the client determine whether to risk the attorney's withdrawal should be explained to the client so that the client can make an informed decision.

What happens with representations that do not involve litigation? How may a lawyer withdraw, for example, from a contract negotiation or the preparation of legal documents? The rules are unclear. If a lawyer simply writes a letter and returns the file and any unearned fees, is that sufficient to protect the client's interests? What if the negotiations are in a particularly delicate stage, and a serious strategic dispute arises between the client and the lawyer? Is this sufficient ground for the lawyer to withdraw? While the rules governing permissive withdrawal apply to transactional situations, how can a client enforce such rules, if there is no court to oversee the process and to conduct a hearing, or evaluate the client's perspective?

An attorney who withdraws from representation must return the client's files and other property to the client as soon as practicable. Because it is now the rule in almost every jurisdiction that the file is the client's and not the attorney's, the attorney may not hold the file hostage until the client has paid all fees and costs then owing.[18] What happens to the file if the withdrawing attorney was representing two clients? In an insurance situation, where the attorney is hired by the insurer to represent the insured, it seems clear that the insured should get the file, since the insured is a party to the action and not the insurance company, an issue we'll examine in greater detail in the next problem. But what if the lawyer represented two partners in a commercial venture? If there is no "primary" client and the clients cannot agree, there are no set procedures for resolving such a dispute. In major cases or major disagreements, the law firm could seek the guidance of the court in the form of declaratory relief. To do so could jeopardize confidentiality, but might also encourage a resolution among the affected clients.

Client Discharge. It is an implied term of attorney-client fee agreements that a client may fire an attorney at any time, with or without cause. Generally, most jurisdictions hold that a discharged attorney is entitled to reasonable compensation for the work done, or quantum meruit. The rules about file retention are even more important here. A law firm that has been fired and does not respond quickly to requests for the file risks a lawsuit for breach of fiduciary duty. This can be frustrating for lawyers who have not been paid, but it is far more prudent to accept the course of events, turn over the file, and battle about fees later.

SUPPLEMENTAL READINGS

1. Committee on Professional Responsibility, "Discipline of Law Firms," *Record of the Association of the Bar of the City of New York*, June 1993, Vol. 45, No. 5. This controversial report advocates extending disciplinary rules to govern the conduct of law firms. Noting that certain disciplinary rules already apply to law firms, such as advertising regulations, the committee advocates applying conflict of interest rules to law firms as a whole, to require their participation in avoiding conflicts, rather than keeping the disciplinary focus solely on individual attorneys.

2. *IBM v. Levin*, 579 F.2d 271 (3d Cir. 1978), involved a law firm which had represented IBM over the years on various labor matters. The firm filed an antitrust suit against IBM, and IBM sought disqualification. The law firm was disqualified even though it was not on retainer to IBM and had no specific open file at the time the antitrust action was filed. The court held that "the pattern of repeated retainers, both before and after the filing of the complaint, supports the finding of a continuous relationship."

3. *Hartford Acc. & Indem. Co. v. RJR Nabisco, Inc.*, 721 F. Supp. 534 (S.D.N.Y. 1989). This case is a twist on the "hot potato" scenario described in the readings. Here, instead of "firing" its client, the law firm fired the "tainted" lawyer. A law firm sued RJR Nabisco on behalf of the Hartford. The law firm then fired its lawyer, who represented RJR. That lawyer took RJR with him. Even though the conflict arose during concurrent representation, the court allowed the law firm to remain as counsel for Hartford, reasoning that RJR had only been with the firm because of the departed lawyer.

---

[18] A few states, including New York, still have some exceptions to this rule.

4. James M. Altman, "A Young Lawyer's Nightmare,"*N.Y. Law Journal* (February 16, 2001), describes the sad story of a young would-be associate who lost his job because of a previous representation, and discusses how transient lawyers have become and the difficulties of navigating conflicts rules.

5. Joanne Pelton Pitula, "Clearing Up Before Moving On: Conflicts of Interest Increase Complications When Switching Firms," 82 *ABA Journal* 91 (April 1996) discusses ABA Formal Opinion 96-400. The issue there was whether lawyers may explore employment possibilities with a firm representing a party adverse to the lawyer's current client, without running afoul of Model Rules 1.7(b), 1.9, and 1.10.

6. *Chrysler Corp. v. Carey*, 5 F. Supp. 2d 1023 (E.D. Mo. 1998), approves the chilling prospect that lawyers who switch sides in a case may not only be subject to disqualification, but may be sued for malpractice as well. The case holds that either a breach of the duty of confidentiality *or* the duty of loyalty would support a finding of professional negligence.

7. Joshua Horn, Abraham C. Reich & Scott L. Vernick, *Screening Mechanisms: A Broader Application? Balancing Economic Realities and Ethical Obligations*, 72 Temp. L. Rev. 1023 (1999), examines the interrelationship of multi-disciplinary practice and screening rules. The authors discuss how conflicts and, especially, screening would be handled if lawyers were allowed to set up a one stop professional shop for clients that included accountants, social workers, financial planners, realtors, and other professionals.

8. *Hitachi, Ltd. v. Tatung Co.*, 419 F. Supp. 2d 1158 (N.D. Cal. 2006), contains a thorough review of the California case law that both implies, in one state Supreme Court case, that screening might be appropriate in certain circumstances and, in other cases, holds that it is not permitted.

9. California State Bar Formal Opinion 1997-150 lays out the parameters for shared space arrangements among lawyers to avoid problems among their clients. Although the opinion focuses mostly on the confidentiality of communications and not on conflicts of interest, it acknowledges that such conflicts may arise particularly from shared staff, advertising, or the inadvertent or careless sharing of confidences.

10. For an expanded description of what an ethical screen should look like and how it should work, see Lee A. Pizzimenti, *Screen Veritt: Do Rules About Ethcial Screens Reflect the Truth About Real-Life Law Firm Practice?*, 52 U. Miami L. Rev. 305 (Oct. 1997).

PROBLEM 11

We have seen in the several problems in this chapter first how conflicts of interest affect a single lawyer's representation of single clients, and then, in Problem 10, how law firms are affected. But the ethical rules describing both conflicts of interest and the duty of loyalty were designed for a traditional paradigm of legal representation: one lawyer and one client. While the rules and case law have been extensively broadened to address multiple lawyers taking on multiple clients, there are two situations, insurance defense representation and class action cases, where the rules lag farther behind the reality of actual practice. Either the existing rules don't seem to apply in the same way they do to other situations, or other considerations, including public policy ones, excuse what would otherwise be unacceptable behavior. As will be seen, there is no agreement on how either insurance or class action situations should be handled, with sometimes troubling results.

A Day in the Life of Lynch, Dahl & Wong

Lynch, Dahl & Wong is a 25-lawyer litigation firm which primarily does insurance work, but is also developing a plaintiffs' class action practice. Firm founder Leonard Lynch and managing partner Danielle Dahl have worked hard to cultivate their insurance carrier clients, and have formed close working relationships with their best clients' senior executives. The firm's bread and butter practice is its insurance defense work, where it is hired by an insurance carrier client to represent one of its insureds. Recently, New States Insurance Company, one of the firm's largest clients, announced a new policy: All defense lawyers' fees and costs will be subject to billing guidelines and audits. Part of this new program requires firms to obtain advance approval for the hiring of any expert where the anticipated cost would exceed $400.

I. Dahl has been defending 18-year-old Midge Trasky in an auto intersection accident case for Secured Home and Life Insurance, another of the firm's best clients. The complaint claims Midge struck a pedestrian in a crosswalk with her father's car, causing the pedestrian to suffer a compound fracture of the leg.

Lynch, Dahl provides periodic reports on each Secured Home file, including the lawyer's summary of the facts, information on the latest discovery, and an estimate of case value. To provide current information, and because Midge's deposition is to be taken in a few weeks, Dahl has just interviewed Midge for the first time since the beginning of the case. During the interview, Midge hesitated and then asked Dahl if there would be a problem if someone else had been driving the car, someone who shouldn't be driving. Danielle was immediately concerned that Midge was on the verge of admitting that someone else had been driving at the time of the accident, a fact which, if known by the insurance company, could cause it to potentially drop the defense. Nevertheless, Danielle reassured Midge that telling her the truth was the best course. Midge then admitted that she was not driving after all, because shortly before the accident, she had allowed her 15-year-old cousin, Madge, to get behind the wheel. Madge is unlicensed and uninsured.

QUESTIONS

1. Dahl knows that Midge's admission means that Secured Home very likely would have no responsibility to pay for the accident. What should Danielle advise Secured? May she remain in the case?

2. Did Dahl have a duty to give Midge advice about the ramifications to her coverage if someone else was driving before Midge divulged that Madge was driving? Could Danielle give Midge such advice in view of her relationship with the insurance company?

3. What should Dahl do if Midge repeats at deposition what she told Danielle privately? Must she tell Secured? *May* she? May she stay in the case?

II. At a partner's meeting to discuss what to do about New States' new policy, senior partners Dahl and Lynch seemed resigned, albeit uncomfortable, about having an insurance company dictate what they could do to work up a case. But Malcolm Wong, the youngest and most outspoken of the three, was outraged: "Come on! This amounts to practicing law without a license, or at the least a direct interference with our ability to represent our client. How can they make the decision on what's necessary for a case and what isn't? We'd be violating our ethical duties to agree to this!"

QUESTIONS

1. Do Wong's concerns make sense or is he out of line? If New States thought that a particular expert was unnecessary to defend an insured, but the insured wanted the company to hire one and Lynch, Dahl agreed, whose preferences should control?

2. Is Wong right that the firm's lawyers might be violating ethical duties by agreeing to New States' billing and auditing requirements? What rules of professional conduct could be involved?

III. New partner Jocelyn Nyala came to the firm with a background in class action cases. One day over dinner, Joella Winston, a friend of Nyala's, complained that she had purchased a computer from Great Guys/Great Buys, a regional electronics store, expecting to get a free printer. The store had advertised that anyone buying a new computer and monitor would get the printer free-of-charge. "I knew the printer was a bottom-of-the-line model," said Joella, "but it had to be better than what I had. I ended up buying two computers, one for the office, and one for my daughter, but I never did get a printer."

Nyala investigated and discovered that when GG/GB ran out of stock of the giveaway printers, they simply told customers that they would have to call back later. Since the printers were a discontinued model, the store was never able to restock them. Those customers who called back were eventually told that the offer had expired.

Nyala smelled a good class action suit, based on GG/GB's deceptive advertising. Since the store had advertised the printer as "a $189 value," a class action could be quite remunerative. But Nyala's friend Joella made it clear she wanted no part of being a class representative. So Nyala found herself in need of some GG/GB customers to become her "named plaintiffs," or class representatives.

QUESTIONS

1. What can Nyala do to solicit the store's customers to become her clients? May she contact friends she knows shop at the store, even if they have never been her clients? May she have someone hand out flyers in front of the store's branches?

2. What if after filing the case Nyala discovers that three computer purchasers from one of GG/GB's suburban stores are suing one of Malcolm Wong's clients in a serious auto accident? Does Nyala have a conflict of interest unless these claimants "opt out" of the class action? Or may she continue to represent the class as a whole and the named class representatives?

3. After filing, Nyala conducted discovery and learned that during the ad campaign, Great Guys/Great Buys sold 14,000 computers but gave away only 3,200 printers. Nyala receives a settlement offer from GG/GB's attorneys: For customers of GG/GB's four city and five suburban locations, the store will give each customer who has proof of purchase $10.00 and a coupon for a $90.00 store credit. However, the customers of GG/GB's four "remote," or more rural, locations — about 2,000 in all — will receive only the $10.00 check. The store's attorneys claim that these stores, run by independent franchisees, simply couldn't afford the store credit. Still, with an arguable "settlement value" of $1,220,000 ($100 for 12,000 customers and $10 for 2,000 customers), the defense lawyers are offering Nyala a fee of $244,000, representing 25% of the total "recovery," a most generous sum given the amount of legal work done.

May Nyala accept the offer? What about those who are getting only $10.00? Is this settlement fair to them? Does it matter? Does it matter whether any of Nyala's "class reps" shopped at a rural store?

READINGS

1. Loyalty and the Insurance Defense Lawyer. Insurance is one of the few industries which is in the business of litigating cases. Not surprisingly, then, insurance carriers can be highly desirable clients. An insurance practice includes coverage work, in which the law firm determines whether an event involving a particular insured is covered under the policy, and subrogation cases, after-the-fact claims among insurance companies to resolve the relative liabilities of their insureds. But the bread and butter of most insurance practices is the litigation of liability claims, or insurance defense work, in which the insurer hires an attorney to represent the insured under its policy.

To whom does the lawyer owe a duty of loyalty in an insurance defense case? Read the following excerpt from a case decided by the Arizona Supreme Court.

PARSONS v. CONTINENTAL NATIONAL AMERICAN GROUP
113 Ariz. 223, 550 P.2d 94 (1976)

We accepted this petition for review because of the importance of the question presented. We are asked to determine whether an insurance carrier in a garnishment action is estopped from denying coverage under its policy when its defense in that action is based upon confidential information obtained by the carrier's attorney from an insured as a result of representing him in the original tort action.

. . . .

[T]he Parsons filed a complaint alleging that Michael Smithey [age 14] assaulted the Parsons and that Michael's parents were negligent in their failure to restrain Michael and obtain the necessary medical and psychological attention for him. . . .

[Insurance carrier] CNA's retained counsel undertook the Smitheys' defense and also continued to communicate with CNA and advised. . . .

"The above referred-to confidential file shows that the boy is fully aware of his acts and that he knew what he was doing was wrong. It follows, therefore, that the assault he committed on claimants can only be a deliberate act on his part."

After CNA had been so advised they sent a reservation of rights letter to the Smitheys stating that the insurance company, as a courtesy to the insureds, would investigate and defend the Parsons' claim, but would do so without waiving any of the rights under the policy. The letter further stated that it was possible the act involved might be found to be an intentional act, and that the policy specifically excludes liability for bodily injury caused by an intentional act. This letter was addressed only to the parents and not to Michael.

. . . .

Appellants contend that CNA should be estopped to deny coverage and have waived the intentional act exclusion because the company took advantage of the fiduciary relationship between its agent (the attorney) and Michael Smithey. We agree.

. . . .

The attorney in the instant case should have notified CNA that he could no longer represent them when he obtained any information (as a result of his attorney-client relationship with Michael) that could possibly be detrimental to Michael's interests under the coverage of the policy.

The attorney representing Michael Smithey in the personal injury suit instituted by the Parsons had to be sure at all times that the fact he was compensated by the insurance company did not "adversely affect his judgment on behalf of or dilute his loyalty to [his] client, [Michael Smithey]." Ethical Consideration 5-14. Where an attorney is representing the insured in a personal injury suit, and, at the same time advising the insurer on the question of liability under the policy it is difficult to see how that attorney could give individual loyalty to the insured-client. "The standards of the legal profession require undeviating fidelity of the lawyer to his client. No exceptions can be tolerated."

. . . .

The attorney in the present case continued to act as Michael's attorney while he was actively working against Michael's interests. When an attorney who is an insurance company's agent uses the confidential relationship between an attorney and a client to gather information so as to deny the insured coverage under the policy in the garnishment proceeding we hold that such conduct constitutes a waiver of any policy defense, and is so contrary to public policy that the insurance company is estopped as a matter of law from disclaiming liability under an exclusionary clause in the policy.

2. Who Is the Insurance Lawyer's Client? Who is the client in an insurance defense case — the insured or the insurance carrier? The insured is the subject of the litigation and the one who indirectly pays for representation as part of the insurance policy. But the carrier retains the attorney and is responsible for direct payment. It is the carrier whose claims personnel form personal relationships with the lawyers, and which determines how many cases to send to the law firm. Finally, it is usually the carrier which decides on a settlement value after receiving reports from the attorney.

Many cases and commentators describe insurance defense as a "dual representation." The issue almost always comes up in the context of a lawyer who failed to protect the interests of the *insured* as against the insurance carrier. In *Parsons*, for instance, the court addresses this dual representation in passing, noting that "[t]he attorney in the instant case should have notified CNA that he could no longer represent them. . . ." The excerpted analysis in the following case, upholding the insured's malpractice liability claim against the insurance defense lawyer, describes that dual representation.

BETTS v. ALLSTATE INSURANCE CO.
154 Cal. App. 3d 688, 201 Cal. Rptr. 528 (1984)

In accepting employment to render legal services, an attorney impliedly agrees to use such skill, prudence and diligence as lawyers of ordinary skill and capacity commonly possess, and he is subject to liability for damage resulting from failure so to perform. Furthermore, it is an attorney's duty to "protect his client in every possible way," and it is a violation of that duty for the attorney to "assume a position adverse or antagonistic to his client without the latter's free and intelligent consent given after full knowledge of all the facts and circumstances." The attorney is "precluded from assuming any relation which would prevent him from devoting his entire energies to his client's interest." [Citations omitted.]

These traditional obligations of an attorney are in no way abridged by the fact that an insurer employs him to represent an insured. Typically, in such a situation, the attorney in effect has two clients, to each of whom is owed a "high duty of care." To the insured, the attorney owes "the same obligations of good faith and fidelity as if he had retained the attorney personally." (*Lysick v. Walcom* (1968) 258 Cal. App. 2d 136, 146 [65 Cal. Rptr. 406].)

Provided there is full disclosure and consent, an attorney may undertake to represent dual interests. However, whether in the insurer-insured context or otherwise, the attorney who undertakes to represent parties with divergent interests owes the "highest duty" to each to make a "full disclosure of all facts and circumstances which are necessary to enable the parties to make a fully informed decision regarding the subject matter of litigation, including the areas of potential conflict and the possibility and desirability of seeking independent legal advice."

The loyalty owed to one client by an attorney "cannot consume that owed to the other." Thus a lawyer who, while purporting to continue to represent an insured and who devotes himself to the interests of the insurer without notification or disclosure to the insured breaches his obligations to the insured and is guilty of negligence. (*Lysick v. Walcom, supra.* . . .)

NOTES

Recently, some authorities have recognized that the special problems of this "tripartite" relationship have to be addressed in special ways, including section 134 of the Restatement Third of the Law Governing Lawyers, which reaffirms the *Parsons* holding on confidentiality and the duty of a lawyer to exercise independent professional judgment. More recently, a few states now require more. In 2002, the Florida Supreme Court approved a "Statement of Insured Client's Rights," codified as Florida Rule 4-1.8(j): "Conflicts of Interest; Prohibited and Other Transactions." Read the following story about that rule.

ROBERT A. CLIFFORD, SUNSHINE STATE ENLIGHTENS CLIENTS' RIGHTS
Chicago Lawyer 13 (January 2003)[1]

Lawyers hired by insurance companies to defend policyholders in Florida must give them a Statement of Insured Client's Rights under a new mandatory disclosure rule adopted last year by the Florida Supreme Court. It is believed to be the first of its kind in the country, and I believe it should be more widespread.

The Statement informs the client of possible conflicts of interest faced by his or her lawyer. The document spells out the policyholder's rights and, in the case of an insurance contract, explains the three-way relationship between the lawyer, the policyholder and the insurance carrier that often can lead to competing loyalties.

Initially, it had been reported that the insurance industry resisted these new rules; but, after increasing support from other factions, insurance representatives participated in the drafting of the document. The effort to adopt these rules was instigated by lawyers who formed a special committee in 1999 to examine a number of insurance defense ethics issues including these questions:

● When an insurance company hires a lawyer to defend a policyholder, can the company's claims adjuster tell the lawyer how to conduct the defense?

● Can the company require the lawyer to sacrifice independent professional judgment in favor of cost-cutting guidelines imposed by the company?

● Can the law firm hired by the insurance company send an itemized bill containing confidential client information to the insurer's outside auditor?

● What happens when the insurance company agrees to pay for the policyholder's lawyer but reserves the right not to pay any judgment if it decides that the claim wasn't covered?

• Does a policyholder have any greater say in his legal defense when he faces a judgment that exceeds his policy limits?

Following a year of study and hearings, the committee found it was unable to definitively answer these and other questions.

There's no bright line. What the insurance industry calls "controlling the litigation," many attorneys call "treading on the attorney's professional conduct," the committee said. . . .

The Statement is a breakthrough in professional conduct involving representation in insurance coverage disputes in that it contains 10 paragraphs of information to the client about the lawyer-client relationship, fees, confidentiality, conflicts of interest and risks. It also addresses who has the right to direct the lawyer, the right to hire independent counsel and the right to report disciplinary violations to the bar. . . .

Frankly, I think the Statement doesn't go far enough. Defense lawyers often don't advise their clients of the inherent conflicts in insurance matters; and this Statement is a step toward informing a client, which is paramount in any representation.

. . . .

Although many defense lawyers recognize that the client is their priority, too often lawyers are conflicted because of the dueling loyalties to those who are signing their paychecks. Privately, many will admit to this ethical dilemma.

It is difficult to make these conflicts disappear, but it is wise to disclose as much as possible to the client so that s/he is well-informed and can make decisions based upon accurate and full information.

And, it is heartening to see, as in Florida, that the insurance industry finally is embracing this effort.

NOTES

Anomalously, New York approved a "written letter of engagement" rule a month before the Florida rule was approved. Here, however, greater confusion may have resulted when a comment was added that stated, "For purposes of this rule, where an entity (such as an insurance carrier) engages an attorney to represent a third party, the term 'client' shall mean the entity that engages the attorney."

3. Is Dual Representation Realistic? Is a "Unique" Relationship Workable? Recall our discussion in Problem 7 about the effectiveness of certain consents, particularly where the parties do not have equal power. Can the insured's consent truly be "free and intelligent" in the insurance situation, when a refusal of consent might be tantamount to refusing legal counsel? When an insured signs an insurance contract, does that include a consent to joint representation? Even with Florida-style rules, does the insured have any real choice other than to consent? Some argue that most of the time, consenting to dual representation is not a problem, since conflicts between insurer and insured occur only rarely. Here's how one court put it: "[T]he attorney has two clients whose primary, overlapping and common interest is the speedy and successful resolution of the claim and litigation."[2] But is this really true? Does "successful resolution" mean the same to the insurer and the insured? The insurer's primary goal is usually to resolve the case as inexpensively as possible, minimizing both the costs of defense and the cost of settlement. The insured's goal may be very different: to have minimal intrusion on the insured's time, or minimal disruption of his or her life, or to avoid the traumatic experiences of being deposed or sitting through trial as the named defendant.

The ostensibly common interests of insurer and insured may suddenly diverge at the moment of settlement. Most insurance policies require the consent of the insured in order to settle. On the other hand, sometimes the lawyer may need to advise the insurer to settle. Several courts have followed the language from this early leading New York case: "The attorney may not seek to reduce the company's loss by attempting to save a portion of the total indemnity in negotiations for the settlement of a negligence action, if by so doing he needlessly subjects the assured to judgment in excess of the policy limit."[3] And several cases have held that where a client refuses to settle, the lawyer hired by the carrier may not be able to settle the case, *even if* the insurance policy does not require the insured's consent. For example, in *Rogers v. Robson, Masters, Ryan, Brumund & Belom*, 81 Ill. 2d 201, 407 N.E.2d 47, 49 (1980), the Illinois Supreme Court held that a physician could maintain an action against the lawyers who represented him in a malpractice case and settled without his consent:

> Although defendants were employed by the insurer, plaintiff, as well as the insurer, was their client . . . and was entitled to a full disclosure of the intent to settle the litigation without his consent and contrary to his express instructions. . . . Defendants' duty to make such disclosure stemmed from their attorney-client relationship with plaintiff and was not affected by the extent of the insurer's authority [under the insurance policy] to settle.

Some commentators, like Denver law professor Stephen L. Pepper, have argued for a "single client model" in which lawyers have only one client, the insured. Pepper postulates that the single client model is necessary to act "as a substantial counterbalance to the lawyer's self-interest," since lawyers face "the bias created by the economic power of the insurance companies which pay them on the one hand, and the arguable ethical obligation to assist the insured *against* the company, on the other."[4] Others, like Texas law professor Charles Silver, believe that the opposite is true: The insurance defense lawyer

---

[2] *American Mut. Liab. Ins. Co. v. Superior Ct.*, 38 Cal. App. 3d 579, 592, 113 Cal. Rptr. 561, 571 (1974).

[3] *American Employers Ins. Co. v. Goble Aircraft Specialties, Inc.*, 205 Misc. 1066, 131 N.Y.S.2d 393 (1954).

[4] Stephen L. Pepper, *Applying the Fundamentals of Lawyers' Ethics to Insurance Defense Practice*, 4 CONN. INS. L.J. 27 (1997-1998).

can have two *equal* clients at all times, as envisioned by the insurance contract.[5]

It is interesting to note that *Rogers*, like most other authorities, refers to dual representation. As we have learned, joint representation means that the highest duty of care is owed to both clients. It also means that the confidences of both must be either shared or carefully guarded. It means that the lawyer must maintain the balancing act of protecting one client's confidences and zealously representing the other. Is this balancing act feasible for the insurance defense lawyer?

Courts have understandably been reluctant to declare insurance carriers mere third party payors who do not enjoy the status of clients. This might cost them rights and remedies to which they feel entitled, without which the insurance system as we know it might not exist. Nevertheless, if insurance carriers are clients, the weight of authority suggests their rights may be secondary to the rights of insureds. Can there be such a thing as a "second class" client?

In *Atlanta International Insurance Co. v. Bell*, 438 Mich. 512, 475 N.W.2d 294 (1991), the Michigan Supreme Court, noting that "the defense counsel-insurer relationship is unique," upheld the right of an insurance carrier to maintain a malpractice action against the defense attorney. To avoid the clienthood trap, that court came up with this inventive solution: "To hold that an attorney-client relationship exists between insurer and defense counsel could indeed work mischief, yet to hold that a mere commercial relationship exists would work obfuscation and injustice. The gap is best bridged by resort to the doctrine of equitable subrogation to allow recovery by the insurer."

Does the Michigan court's emphasis on a practical approach reconcile with the ethical rules on conflicts of interest? Or is this practical solution, complete with what some would call a "legal fiction," justified by the social reality of the usefulness of insurance, even if the ordinary rules of conduct are bent to fit that reality?

4. Limiting Defense Costs vs. Insureds' Confidentiality. In recent years insurance companies have undertaken two measures to limit their own defense costs, and have earned themselves scorn and enmity from many, including some of the "panel" attorneys the companies have traditionally hired to defend their insureds. One measure involves instituting billing guidelines and audits; the other involves using in-house or "captive" counsel to defend their cases.

---

[5] See especially, and most pungently, Charles Silver & Kent Syverud, *The Professional Responsibilities of Insurance Defense Lawyers*, 45 DUKE L.J. 255 (1995), and Charles Silver & Michael Sean Quinn, *Are Liability Carriers Second-Class Clients? No, But They May Soon Be: A Call to Arms Against the Restatement (Third) of the Law Governing Lawyers*, 6 COVERAGE (March/April 1996).

SYLVIA HSIEH, BILLING GUIDELINES AND FEE AUDITS OF DEFENSE LAWYERS STRUCK DOWN
2000 Lawyers Weekly USA 435 (May 15, 2000)[6]

Where insurance defense lawyers have to comply with insurance companies' billing guidelines and submit to third-party audits, this violates the Rules of Professional Conduct unless the insured consents, says the first state supreme court to address this issue. . . .

"This is very hot news," says Lloyd Milliken, Jr. of Indianapolis, president of the Defense Research institute (DRI). "This is going to change the way the defense business is being run," says Gary M. Zadick of Great Falls, Mont., one of the lawyers who brought the case.

The guidelines have become a standard feature in defense work and typically require pre-approval before a lawyer can take a deposition, hire an expert or spend money on other litigation costs. In addition, lawyers are often required to submit detailed billing statements to third-party auditors who oversee the expenses.

But the Montana Supreme Court unanimously held that a defense lawyer's sole client is the policyholder, not the insurance company. Therefore, the pre-approval process interferes with lawyers' independent judgment and the use of outside auditors violates client confidentiality, the court said.

Thirty-two state ethics committees have already reached the same conclusion. However, the insurance industry has largely ignored them as non-binding, says Great Falls, Mont. attorney Robert James, a co-petitioner in the case who says he has received calls from lawyers in every state about it. . . .

[D]efense lawyers and insurance companies will be trying to fashion agreements to avoid similar litigation in other states, including ways to seek the insured's "informed consent" to the billing guidelines, says Michael Aylward, a Boston defense attorney and vice chair of DRI's insurance committee.

Milliken says third-party auditing is already "on its way out," judging from recent meetings between DRI and insurance industry representatives, many of whom said they are dropping their outside auditors. . . .

The insurance companies argued that the lawyers represent two clients — the insured and the insurance company that foots the bill. Courts in other jurisdictions have held this way in other contexts. But the Montana court said that none of those decisions addresses whether they are clients for purposes of the Rules of Professional Conduct.

"[T]he stark reality [is] that the relationship between an insurer and insured is permeated with potential conflicts . . . . In cases where an insured's exposure exceeds his insurance coverage, where the insurer provides a defense subject to a reservation of rights, and where an insurer's obligation to indemnify its insured may be excused because of a policy defense, there are potential conflicts of interest," the court said.

The insurance companies argued that the pre-approval process is necessary to control litigation costs.

But the court said that "the requirement of prior approval fundamentally interferes with defense counsel's exercise of their independent judgment."

I. . . .

The court next addressed a requirement in the insurer-imposed guidelines that defense lawyers submit detailed descriptions of their work to independent auditors hired by the insurance companies. The defense lawyers argued that this practice violated a professional conduct rule that bars a lawyer from revealing information to third parties unless the client consents.

The insurance companies argued that auditors fell within the "magic circle" of people with whom information can be shared, such as secretaries, interpreters and computer technicians.

But the court disagreed, finding that the auditors don't have a common interest with the insured.

"Their mission . . . is to find fault with legal charges, not to further the representation of insureds. Further, unlike secretaries and computer technicians who are engaged to assist defense counsel, third-party auditors are not employed by defense counsel and . . . they are potential adversaries of defense counsel. . . ."

One question is whether the insured can consent by signing a provision in the policy agreeing to the billing guidelines and third-party auditing.

Defense lawyers say this won't fly. "Putting it in a policy where there's no negotiation would not be 'fully informed consent.' It would be a contract of adhesion," says Zadick.

NOTES

In this instance, not only did Montana lead the nation, but the nation reacted swiftly. By 2001, the ABA had joined the Montana court and the dozens of state ethics committees cited in the article in condemning the auditing practice as violative of the insured's confidential relationship with the assigned attorney.

5. Insurance Company Employee and Defense Counsel: Another Dual Role? Can an insurance company employee serve as counsel for the insured, or is the conflict of interest so direct that it simply is not permissible? What about other issues, such as the insurer's unauthorized practice of law? Cases and ethics opinions go both ways. Here is one view.

AMERICAN INSURANCE ASS'N v. KENTUCKY BAR ASS'N
917 S.W.2d 568 (Ky. 1996)

In this consolidated action, Complainants [all insurance companies] timely filed a motion seeking review by this Court of Advisory Ethics Opinion E-368 which was issued by the Board of Governors of respondent, Kentucky Bar Association. . . . In addition, State Farm requests that this Court review that portion of Unauthorized Practice of Law Opinion U-36 which proscribes the use, by insurance companies, of salaried attorneys to provide defense services under the insurers' policies of insurance. . . .

[W]e hereby approve and adopt E-368 as written, and choose not to disturb U-36. At issue is the following question presented in E-368: (1) May a lawyer enter into a contract with a liability insurer in which the lawyer or his firm agrees to do all of the insurer's defense work for a set fee?

The Board of Governors answered "no" to this question. . . . The Board, indicating that the lawyer's duty to the insured client was a function of the attorney-client relationship and not governed by or limited by the terms of the insurance contract, expressed concern that this set fee arrangement would result in the loss of control of the insured client vis-a-vis actions taken by counsel. . . . The Board characterized [this] as but the latest issue to arise from attempts by insurers to cut costs. One such cost-cutting measure . . . involved the practice of insurers to provide defense services directly through salaried attorney employees, a practice, the Board concluded, that "is not permitted in Kentucky, for in addition to the obvious conflicts of interest . . . the practice would violate the law governing unauthorized practice."

The opinion relied upon . . . long-standing Kentucky case law which proscribes a corporation from being licensed to practice a learned profession, such as law. Ethical rules and legal precedent were merged in the opinion to reach the conclusion that in the typical action on an insurance contract, the insured, and not the insurer, was the party-defendant, and that, therefore, "the insurance company must hire members of the private bar to undertake representation of their insured."

Notwithstanding the trends of other jurisdictions, [t]he age-old adage of "if it ain't broke, don't fix it" seems appropriate in disposing of Complainants' argument herein. . . .

In fact, no situation is more illustrative of the inherent pitfalls and conflicts therein than that in which house counsel defends the insured while remaining on the payroll of the insurer. "No man can serve two masters," regardless here of either any perceived "community of interest," or Complainants' Pollyanna postulate that house counsel will continue to provide undivided loyalty to the insured.

. . . .

[W]e do not wear the blinders that Complainants apparently have in place, for we view the situation surrounding the set fee agreement as ripe with potential conflicts. Respondent was able to cite to nineteen such conflicts, including representation of the insured which becomes more complex than anticipated, resulting in financial hardship for the attorney; policy and/or coverage defenses asserted by the insurer against the insured; and disagreement between the insured and the insurer with regard to settlement negotiations. . . . Inherent in all of these potential conflicts is the fear that the entity paying the attorney, the insurer, and not the one to whom the attorney is obligated to defend, the insured, is controlling the legal representation.

NOTES

The sometimes salty Kentucky court opinion adopts a position quite similar to that espoused by Prof. Pepper. But it is by no means reflects a unanimous view, as the court itself recognizes. For example, in *Cincinnati Ins. Co. v. Wills*, 717 N.E.2d 151 (Ind. 1999), the Indiana Supreme Court cited the Kentucky opinion but came to a different conclusion. The Indiana case began somewhat differently, with *plaintiffs* moving to disqualify defense counsel who were "captive" insurance company employees, arguing that the insurers were engaged in the unauthorized practice of law. The trial court agreed, but the Indiana Supreme Court reversed, holding that the companies may represent insureds so long as counsel were mindful of their ethical duties to their insureds/clients. The court did ban the lawyers from using a law firm name, since it misled the public by not clearly acknowledging their captive status.

In Formal Opinion 03-430 (July 9, 2003), however, the ABA ethics committee not only supported the concept of insurance company staff lawyers representing insureds, but favored the use of law firm style names instead of requiring that the "firm" state that "XYZ Insurance" was defending. And while the opinion stated that the insured client would have to be advised of the lawyers' employee status, the plaintiffs and their counsel would be left not knowing.

6. Who Is the Lawyer's Client in a Class Action? Representing a class may present the most complicated, and the most multifaceted, issues of loyalty a lawyer is likely to face. Many of the issues addressed in this chapter are ones class counsel must answer, including: identifying the client; representation of multiple clients; conflicts of interest among clients; and conflicts between the attorney's own interests, including fees, and those of the clients. When it comes to class action ethics issues, that's just for starters.

Class actions are lawsuits in which lawyers represent a "class" of similarly-situated people whose interests are protected by one or more "class representatives," whose duties include protecting the passive members of the class — many of whom may not even know they are class members. After they are given notice, class members generally are given the opportunity to "opt out" of the class should they wish to pursue their claims individually. Historically, though, few chose to do this since the damages for such things as defective toasters or bank overcharges were too small for people to pursue individually. Indeed, the very point behind class actions was to provide a remedy for these "little" wrongs by banding people together in a "class."

Class actions increased dramatically in popularity in the 1960s, when a change in the Federal Rules of Civil Procedure allowed individual members of a class to collect money damages. With increasing popularity came increasing difficulty in applying ethical rules designed with individual clients in mind. The use of class actions to litigate mass tort and employment claims raised the stakes substantially, changing the traditional class action into a major, "big ticket" item, multi-jurisdictional litigation.

As we have seen, even in multiple-plaintiff cases, each individual remains a separate client, entitled to the lawyer's loyalty to his or her particular case. Class actions don't — indeed, *can't* — work that way. The sheer number of potential class members means that if each were considered an individual client, with the full right to settle only upon individual approval, it would be impossible to ever pursue, much less resolve a case. Running a conflicts check — or obtaining a conflicts waiver — would be impossible, as often, the *number* of individual class members is not known, much less the name of each class participant.

Lawyers often begin a class action themselves, creating the class, defining its scope and objectives, and finding representative class members. Class action lawyers thus have far more power than attorneys in traditional litigation. In many jurisdictions, they have the power to settle the case themselves. But who is, or are, the clients, and what power (if any) do they have? The individual named plaintiffs, or class representatives, are generally considered to be clients of the lawyer. In the reading below, we will see that even class representatives may not be accorded the usual privileges of being a client.

KAREN DONOVAN, HUH? *I'M* THE LEAD PLAINTIFF?
The National Law Journal (May 24, 1999)[7]

His question was simple enough.

"I would specifically like to know if I am your 'client' according to your records," Charles D. Chalmers asked in a May 28, 1998, e-mail to Barrack, Rodos & Bacine, a Philadelphia law firm that specializes in filing securities fraud class actions.

He didn't get a yes or no answer. But meanwhile, Barrack Rodos was busy putting him forth as a "lead plaintiff" in a class action that settled without his knowledge, input or consent.

At the time, Mr. Chalmers, a San Francisco lawyer, also had no idea what it meant to be a "lead plaintiff." But he did some research on it. . . .

Mr. Chalmers' strange relationship with Barrack Rodos stems from his investment in Digital Lightwave Inc., a Clearwater, Fla., maker of test products for high-speed telecommunications networks. On Jan. 22, 1998, the company announced that it would restate revenues sharply downward, citing the "discovery of certain errors in the timing of revenue recognition and a review of accounting policies and procedures."

The next day, the first of 23 class actions alleging securities fraud was filed in federal district court in Tampa. Mr. Chalmers monitors his investments on the Internet. . . . After Digital Lightwave dropped its bombshell announcement, Mr. Chalmers noticed a slew of press releases from law firms notifying investors of class actions. A Jan. 26, 1998, release from Barrack Rodos was among the first.

"I wanted to follow it," recalls Mr. Chalmers, who lost about $39,360 on his investment. He e-mailed Barrack Rodos on Sunday, March 1, 1998, inquiring how he could "monitor" the suits. Several hours later, he got an e-mail response, a form letter from Maxine S. Goldman, "shareholder relations manager" at the law firm. "Please be advised that we would be delighted to have you join our action," it began, urging him to send back information on how much stock he had purchased "as soon as possible."

---

[7] Reprinted with permission from the May 24, 1999 edition of The National Law Journal © 1999 by NLP IP Company. All rights reserved. Further duplication without permission is prohibited.

From his brief experience with securities class actions in the 1970s, Mr. Chalmers recalled these cases as a race to the courthouse that put the first law firm to file its complaint in charge of the suit. While he didn't realize it, the flurry of press releases he had seen on the Internet were evidence of a different sort of race by the plaintiffs' bar, triggered by the 1995 law.

When Congress passed the Securities Litigation Reform Act, the debate centered on "lawyer-driven" class actions, which often had nominal plaintiffs. Lobbyists pushing to pass the law invariably cited a quote from William S. Lerach, the most successful class action lawyer and the prime target. He said, according to Forbes magazine, "I have the greatest practice in the world. I have no clients."

The law's "lead plaintiff" provision was supposed to take control away from the law firms and put it in the hands of the investor with the largest financial stake, which would then select counsel. It provides for a 60-day notice period, after which anyone can move to be a lead plaintiff. In practice, it has led to a 60-day scramble by law firms to solicit investors like Mr. Chalmers.

E-mailing Maxine

By March 16, [Maxine Goldman] forwarded a letter with papers to sign. "Our intention is to join you in the litigation," she wrote. The letter asked him to sign and return an enclosed "Sworn Certification" the next day. The certification, another requirement of the 1995 law, states that Mr. Chalmers will not accept payment for being a "representative party."

When he signed the form, Mr. Chalmers says, he thought that being a representative party meant that he had agreed to be deposed and to show his investment record to assist the case. Of lead plaintiffs, he admits, "I didn't know from bupkis."

When Mr. Chalmers asked Ms. Goldman if he was, indeed, the law firm's client, she responded, "An agreed order has been submitted which would appoint our group of plaintiffs the lead plaintiff and us as lead counsel."

Mr. Chalmers e-mailed Ms. Goldman on July 22 with a list of nine questions, asking her to identify the named plaintiffs in the case and whether discovery had begun. She replied that the firm had sent out the "Digital Lightwave newsletter" earlier that month, and she asked whether he had received his copy.

Mr. Chalmers sent back a curt e-mail on July 23, telling her that the newsletter contained "very little 'news.'"

Mr. Chalmers got no response from Ms. Goldman. . . .

"We are having a strange correspondence," Mr. Chalmers wrote back, reminding her that he was a lawyer. . . .

That's when Mr. Chalmers had his first contact with a lawyer from Barrack Rodos. Ms. Goldman referred him to M. Richard Komins. Mr. Chalmers claims that he also got the run-around from Mr. Komins, who finally forwarded a copy of the settlement stipulation in early December, after U.S. District Judge Susan C. Bucklew said from the bench that she was inclined to approve the deal. When Mr. Chalmers got the document on Dec. 12, he says, he was stunned to see his name referenced as a "lead plaintiff" in the case. "They wanted to be sure that I didn't find out who I was until after they had obtained her preliminary approval," he surmises.

Mr. Chalmers sprang into action once he discovered what the 1995 law had to say about lead plaintiffs, demanding to contact the other nine investors listed as lead plaintiffs. He got little satisfaction.

In February he addressed his concerns with Judge Bucklew in a lengthy letter. By then, he had tracked down two other "lead plaintiffs," who said they had never been told that they were being proposed for such a role and that settlement had never been discussed with them. One of them was Bob McMurtry, of Depew, Okla., who says that he first learned of the proposed settlement when Mr. Chalmers called.

Judge Bucklew took up Mr. Chalmers' objections at a day-long hearing on March 12. When Mr. Chalmers related his first conversation with Mr. Komins, when the Barrack Rodos lawyer told him that he could not look at the evidence in the case because it was subject to a protective order, the judge became alarmed. She had never issued a protective order. . . .

[I]t was clear that Barrack Rodos never consulted with Mr. Chalmers before cutting a deal with Digital Lightwave. . . .

Lawyers on both sides suggested that increased participation by plaintiffs in these settlements would amount to an annoyance. Glen DeValerio, of Boston's Berman, DeValerio & Pease, concedes that the 1995 law demands increased participation by investors in these suits. But, he says, "the language is one thing, and the practicalities are another."

Digital Lightwave's defense counsel, Michael D. Torpey, says that the 1995 law envisioned one lead plaintiff. "Glen's right, we do a better job of settling without them." Judge Bucklew said "there was a very poor job of communication" with Mr. Chalmers, but she approved the settlement.

NOTES

Comment 1 to ABA Model Rule 1.4 states: "The client should have sufficient information to participate intelligently in decisions concerning the objectives of the representation and the means by which they are to be pursued, to the extent the client is willing and able to do so." Is there a justification for suspending this rule in class actions? Is it true that having actual plaintiffs participate in settlement negotiations will only interfere with the negotiating process? If so, do the plaintiffs' lawyers have a real client?

The flip side of having an unsuspecting "client" as lead plaintiff may be having a professional lead plaintiff. In 2006, a federal grand jury in Los Angeles indicted the well-known plaintiffs' securities class action firm Milberg Weiss Bershad & Schulman and two named partners, David Bershad and Steven G. Schulman, for allegedly participating in a conspiracy to pay secret kickbacks to individuals who repeatedly appeared as Milberg's lead plaintiffs in different cases. News stories reported that the U.S. attorney had targeted powerhouse San Diego class action counsel William Lerach, who is quoted in the above article. Some said he may not have been indicted because he and most of his West Coast colleagues had split from the New York-based Milberg not long before. Indictments are not convictions, of course, and only time will tell whether the charges had merit or were, as some argued, a political effort to stifle shareholder class action suits.

7. Are Passive Class Members Clients? What about the absent members of the class, those who may qualify as class members but do not even know yet that the class exists? Fed. R. Civ. P. 23(a)(4) says that those who represent the class must "fairly and adequately protect the interests of the class." Most commentators, and most cases that have addressed the issue, agree this means that even if only the named plaintiffs are accorded the full-service status of "clients," the class lawyer nevertheless undertakes certain fiduciary duties to all class members. It also means that class counsel generally may not settle a case on behalf of the named plaintiffs alone while leaving the class out while class certification is pending.[8] But is there a meaningful distinction between a "client" and a passive class member to whom fiduciary duties are owed but who may not be anointed with full client status?

Surprisingly, several courts have held that even passive class members have an attorney-client relationship with class counsel, at least when it comes to whether opposing counsel is communicating with a represented party when contacting *any* member of a certified class. In *Kleiner v. First National Bank of Atlanta*, 751 F.2d 1193, 1207, n. 28 (11th Cir. 1985), the court said that "at a minimum, class counsel represents all class members as soon as a class is certified." *Resnik v. American Dental Association*, 95 F.R.D. 372, 376 (N.D. Ill. 1982) states: "Without question the unnamed class members, once the class has been certified, are 'represented by' the class counsel. Class counsel have the fiduciary responsibility and all the other hallmarks of a lawyer representing a client." *Fulco v. Continental Cablevision*, 789 F. Supp. 45, 47 (D. Mass. 1992), states it bluntly and broadly: " 'Once the court enters an order certifying a class, an attorney-client relationship arises between all members of the class and class counsel.' "

One issue that case law has barely touched on is this: If a million member class means a law firm has a million "clients" upon certification, how does the firm run a conflicts check to ensure, for example, that the firm is not adverse to any of the million clients in any firm cases? The answer, of course, is that it cannot. Does this mean that courts that call the passive class members "clients" are naïve or unsophisticated? Or that different rules about client conflicts must be applied?

When it comes to settlement authority, courts generally take a different position on clienthood. For example, in *Kincade v. General Tire and Rubber Company*, 635 F.2d 501 (5th Cir. 1981), the court refused to interfere with class counsel's authority to settle, despite an appeal brought by several named representatives as well as passive class members: Appellants' argument that the settlement cannot be applied to them because they did not authorize their attorneys to settle the case or otherwise consent to the settlement is also easily

---

[8] *See, e.g., Roper v. Consurve, Inc.*, 578 F.2d 1106 (5th Cir. 1978).

disposed of. Because the "client" in a class action consists of numerous unnamed class members as well as the class representatives, and because "[t]he class often speaks with several voices . . ., it may be impossible for the class attorney to do more than act in what he believes to be the best interest of the class as a whole . . . ." [Citation] Because of the unique nature of the attorney-client relationship in a class action, the cases cited by appellants holding that an attorney cannot settle his individual client's case without the authorization of the client are simply inapplicable.

8. Other Class Action Conflicts Issues. Not only do class actions have more than one named plaintiff, but conflicts can also arise between these plaintiffs and the absent class members. For example, what happens if a lawyer finds potential class representatives and decides to pursue claims that fit their situations, while ignoring others? Has the attorney failed to act on behalf of the whole class? Some classes are so large that it is impossible for all class members to have the same interests in settlement. Can a class attorney adequately represent all the members of the class when the interests of the class members are diverse and potentially adverse to each other? The Supreme Court addressed this in *Amchem Products, Inc. v. Windsor*, 521 U.S. 591 (1997), excerpted below.

Increasingly, conflicts exist among segments of a class, some members getting a smaller measure of recovery than others or, as in *Amchem*, potentially no recovery at all. As class actions become more common in mass tort cases, ethical issues become more dicey and difficult. How much attention must plaintiffs' class action attorneys pay to each segment, or sub-class? May they settle for the greater good rather than get something for everyone?

What if a favorable settlement is offered to the class as a whole which excludes the named plaintiffs? While the lawyer works with the class representatives and not individual class members, the named plaintiff's obligation to the class under Rule 23(a)(4) still applies. And courts have consistently held that class representatives cannot act in a way which holds the absent members of the class hostage against their best interests.

Unfortunately, the Ethics 2000 Commission chose not to deal with these and other uniquely class action-related issues in a special rule. That means that class action lawyers remain governed — and guided — only by the ordinary rules regarding conflicts of interest, and a body of case law that lacks uniformity.

Sometimes, of course, the existing rules *can* be helpful. For example, in some cases settlement can turn a class action into a mass series of individual cases. Take, for example, an employment discrimination claim where the settlement involves individual hearings to see whether particular class members would have received specific jobs or promotions had discrimination not taken place. In these situations, it would appear that the class character of the individual members is gone; they are no longer absent, no longer anonymous, and no longer all similarly situated. Rather, they have developed what are, in effect, individual claims. At this point, the law firm representing the class may find itself engaged in the individual representation of several (or several hundred) plaintiffs, each of whom is a client, and each of whom is entitled to the lawyers' undivided loyalty. At that point, the ordinary rules about conflicts of interest may be required.

Finally, although conflicts can occur over the scope and objectives of the representation, or the actual certification of a class, the largest area of conflict is, of course, fees. Class actions are expensive to litigate and prepare. In mass torts, they often involve committees of lawyers who each pledge to "front" specific sums of money to help fund the litigation. As a result, when settlement is at hand, lawyers feel that they have earned their sometimes very substantial fees. But no less true than in simpler fee situations is the concept with which we have addressed at length before — there is often a conflict between the client and the lawyer who wishes to receive fees. We examine that issue in section 9, below.

AMCHEM PRODUCTS, INC. v. WINDSOR
521 U.S. 591, 117 S. Ct. 2231 (1997)

JUSTICE GINSBURG delivered the opinion of the Court.

This case concerns the legitimacy under Rule 23 of the Federal Rules of Civil Procedure of a class-action certification sought to achieve global settlement of current and future asbestos-related claims. The class proposed for certification potentially encompasses hundreds of thousands, perhaps millions, of individuals tied together by this commonality: each was, or some day may be, adversely affected by past exposure to asbestos products manufactured by one or more of 20 companies. Those companies, defendants in the lower courts, are petitioners here.

The United States District Court for the Eastern District of Pennsylvania certified the class for settlement only, finding that the proposed settlement was fair and that representation and notice had been adequate. That court enjoined class members from separately pursuing asbestos-related personal-injury suits in any court, federal or state, pending the issuance of a final order. The Court of Appeals for the Third Circuit vacated the District Court's orders, holding that the class certification failed to satisfy Rule 23's requirements in several critical respects. We affirm.

. . . .

The class action thus instituted was not intended to be litigated. Rather, within the space of a single day, January 15, 1993, the settling parties — CCR defendants [defendant asbestos companies joining forces under the name Center for Claims Resolution] and the representatives of the plaintiff class described below — presented to the District Court a complaint, an answer, a proposed settlement agreement, and a joint motion for conditional class certification.

. . . .

More than half of the named plaintiffs alleged that they or their family members had already suffered various physical injuries as a result of the exposure. The others alleged that they had not yet manifested any asbestos-related condition. The complaint delineated no subclasses; all named plaintiffs were designated as representatives of the class as a whole. . . .

A stipulation of settlement accompanied the pleadings; it proposed to settle, and to preclude nearly all class members from litigating against CCR companies, all claims not filed before January 15, 1993, involving compensation for present and future asbestos-related personal injury or death. An exhaustive document exceeding 100 pages, the stipulation presents in detail an administrative mechanism and a schedule of payments to compensate class members who meet defined asbestos-exposure and medical requirements. . . .

Class members, in the main, are bound by the settlement in perpetuity, while CCR defendants may choose to withdraw from the settlement after ten years. A small number of class members — only a few per year — may reject the settlement and pursue their claims in court. Those permitted to exercise this option, however, may not assert any punitive damages claim or any claim for increased risk of cancer.

. . . .

Objectors raised numerous challenges to the settlement. They urged that the settlement unfairly disadvantaged those without currently compensable conditions in that it failed to adjust for inflation or to account for changes, over time, in medical understanding. They maintained that compensation levels were intolerably low in comparison to awards available in tort litigation. . . . And they objected to the absence of any compensation for certain claims, for example, medical monitoring, compensable under the tort law of several States.

. . . .

Objectors maintained that class counsel and class representatives had disqualifying conflicts of interests. In particular, objectors urged, claimants whose injuries had become manifest and claimants without manifest injuries should not have common counsel and should not be aggregated in a single class.

. . . .

Rule 23(a) states four threshold requirements applicable to all class actions: (1) numerosity (a class [so large] that joinder of all members is impracticable"); (2) commonality ("questions of law or fact common to the class"); (3) typicality (named parties' claims or defenses "are typical . . . of the class"); and (4) adequacy of representation (representatives "will fairly and adequately protect the interests of the class").

. . . .

In setting out these factors, the Advisory Committee for the 1966 reform anticipated that in each case, courts would "consider the interests of individual members of the class in controlling their own litigations and carrying them on as they see fit."

. . . .

As the Third Circuit observed in the instant case: "Each plaintiff [in an action involving claims for personal injury and death] has a significant interest in individually controlling the prosecution of [his case]"; each "has a substantial stake in making individual decisions on whether and when to settle."

While the text of Rule 23(b)(3) does not exclude from certification cases in which individual damages run high, the Advisory Committee had dominantly in mind vindication of "the rights of groups of people who individually would be without effective strength to bring their opponents into court at all."

. . . .

Among current applications of Rule 23(b)(3), the "settlement only" class has become a stock device. . . . Although all Federal Circuits recognize the utility of Rule 23(b)(3) settlement classes, courts have divided on the extent to which a proffered settlement affects court surveillance under Rule 23's certification criteria.

. . . .

We granted review to decide the role settlement may play, under existing Rule 23, in determining the propriety of class certification. We agree with petitioners to this limited extent: settlement is relevant to a class certification. The Third Circuit's opinion bears modification in that respect. But the Court of Appeals in fact did not ignore the settlement; instead, that court homed in on settlement terms in explaining why it found the absentees' interests inadequately represented. . . .

Confronted with a request for settlement-only class certification, a district court need not inquire whether the case, if tried, would present intractable management problems, for the proposal is that there be no trial. But other specifications of the rule — those designed to protect absentees by blocking unwarranted or overbroad class definitions — demand undiluted, even heightened, attention in the settlement context. Such attention is of vital importance, for a court asked to certify a settlement class will lack the opportunity, present when a case is litigated, to adjust the class, informed by the proceedings as they unfold.

. . . .

The Third Circuit highlighted the disparate questions undermining class cohesion in this case:

> Class members were exposed to different asbestos-containing products, for different amounts of time, in different ways, and over different periods. Some class members suffer no physical injury or have only asymptomatic pleural changes, while others suffer from lung cancer, disabling asbestosis, or from mesothelioma. . . . Each has a different history of cigarette smoking, a factor that complicates the causation inquiry. "The [exposure-only] plaintiffs especially share little in common, either with each other or with the presently injured class members. It is unclear whether they will contract asbestos-related disease and, if so, what disease each will suffer. They will also incur different medical expenses because their monitoring and treatment will depend on singular circumstances and individual medical histories."

Differences in state law, the Court of Appeals observed, compound these disparities.

. . . .

Nor can the class approved by the District Court satisfy Rule 23(a)(4)'s requirement that the named parties "will fairly and adequately protect the interests of the class." . . .

As the Third Circuit pointed out, named parties with diverse medical conditions sought to act on behalf of a single giant class rather than on behalf of discrete subclasses. In significant respects, the interests of those within the single class are not aligned. . . .

The settling parties, in sum, achieved a global compromise with no structural assurance of fair and adequate representation for the diverse groups and individuals affected. Although the named parties alleged a range of complaints, each served generally as representative for the whole, not for a separate constituency. . . .

The Third Circuit found no assurance here — either in the terms of the settlement or in the structure of the negotiations — that the named plaintiffs operated under a proper understanding of their representational responsibilities. That assessment, we conclude, is on the mark.

Impediments to the provision of adequate notice, the Third Circuit emphasized, rendered highly problematic any endeavor to tie to a settlement class persons with no perceptible asbestos-related disease at the time of the settlement. Many persons in the exposure-only category, the Court of Appeals stressed, may not even know of their exposure, or realize the extent of the harm they may incur. Even if they fully appreciate the significance of class notice, those without current afflictions may not have the information or foresight needed to decide, intelligently, whether to stay in or opt out.

Family members of asbestos-exposed individuals may themselves fall prey to disease or may ultimately have ripe claims for loss of consortium. Yet large numbers of people in this category — future spouses and children of asbestos victims — could not be alerted to their class membership.

Affirmed.

NOTES

The Supreme Court followed its decision in *Amchem* with another asbestos case, *Ortiz v. Fibreboard Corp.*, 527 U.S. 815, 119 S. Ct. 2295 (1999). In *Ortiz* the Court rejected a proposed global settlement, holding that there were significant disparate interests within the class that called for the establishment of subclasses with their own representatives. This settlement was especially vulnerable because it included a "no-opt-out" provision, which would have prevented asymptomatic "exposure-only" class members from preserving their own individual claims. Given the Supreme Court's two pronouncements, is there any room for plaintiffs' class action attorneys to ethically represent an entire class in large mass tort cases? Is it possible for attorneys to settle such wide-ranging cases without bringing in other counsel to ensure representation of each subdivision of the class? Finally, while the Supreme Court did not answer the question, remember that the class action in *Amchem* was filed, answered, and settled in one day. What is the future of classes created for settlement purposes only? Is there any scenario in which such extraordinary timing would *not* at least imply collusion?

9. Collusion, Attorneys' Fees, and Settlements of Dubious Value. In 1994, an Alabama state court judge approved a settlement in a class action against the Bank of Boston. The case charged the bank with holding escrow account interest that belonged to its borrowers, rather than paying it to them as it was earned. The 715,000 class members each had had mortgages issued through the bank at one time or another. Plaintiffs' and defense counsel told the judge that their settlement was worth over $40 million. But according to The New York *Times*, the maximum individual recovery was only $8.76.[9] Besides, there was no dispute that the money belonged to the class members; the only question was *when* it would be paid. The court also approved $8.5 million in class counsel's fees, despite the fact, according to Illinois federal judge Milton I. Shadur, that the bank had offered essentially the same settlement two years earlier, *except* that the plaintiffs' lawyers fees were then only $500,000. To make matters worse, under the first offer, the bank would pay the fees, but under the final settlement, the fees were to be paid out of the *class'* recovery. Since class members who no longer had mortgages had no funds left in the bank, the entire attorneys' fees bill had to be paid by those who still had their mortgages.

This gave the case the unique feature of charging some class members far more in fees than they "won" in back interest. One Maine couple "recovered" $2.19 from the class action, but had to pay out $91.33 in attorneys' fees. Many claimed they never even knew they were members of a class until they had "miscellaneous deductions" used to pay the lawyers charged to their escrow accounts. Eventually, some of these class members filed their own class action against the plaintiffs' attorneys and the bank for fraud. This case, however, was dismissed, barred by the statute of limitations.

The Bank of Boston settlement aroused the ire of many, including Judge Shadur, who bluntly called the case the "Willie Horton of the class action." The Attorney General of Florida, where the bank's principal mortgage company was located, undertook an investigation. But lawyers for both the plaintiffs and the bank pointed out that the bank did change its accounting practices as part of the agreement. "Nothing fraudulent or improper took place," one of the chief plaintiffs' counsel, Chicago's Daniel Edelman, told the *New York Times*.[10]

While not quite as onerous, fees being paid by defendants also create conflicts of interest. In 2003, Joseph Rice, a leading class-action lawyer from South Carolina, accepted a $20 million fee from an asbestos class defendant's parent company as well as from the class settlement. At the same time, he was being criticized for creating a settlement trust that worked to the disadvantage of more seriously ill plaintiffs. Despite criticism from Professor

---

[9] *See* Barry Meier, *Math of a Class Action Suit: Winning $2.19 Costs $91.33*, N.Y. TIMES, Nov. 21, 1995.

[10] Barry Meier, *Math of a Class Action Suit: Winning $2.19 Costs $91.33*, N.Y. TIMES, Nov. 21, 1995; *see also* Hon. Milton Shadur, *The Unclassy Class Action*, 23 LITIGATION; Kimberly Blanton, *Class-action Suit Winners Sue Lawyers*, BOSTON GLOBE, Nov. 22, 1995.

Susan P. Koniak (see below) among others, his fees were accepted.[11] And a 2004 Missouri case held that plaintiffs' class counsel could not be retained by one group of potential broker defendants to file a class action against another group of brokers.[12] Particularly significant was the lawyer's disclaimer that certain underwriter brokers would be off limits in the class action he intended to pursue.

Consider the testimony before Congress of two individuals with very different perspectives: Phoenix attorney John Frank, long a class action skeptic, and the always-outspoken Susan P. Koniak, a Boston University ethics professor and long a critic of class action abuses. It is more than a little interesting that they share a strong concern over collusive settlements.

HEARING OF THE COURTS AND INTELLECTUAL PROPERTY SUBCOMMITTEE OF THE HOUSE JUDICIARY COMMITTEE
Federal News Service (March 5, 1998)

MR. FRANK: What I wish to call to your attention is what I think is a serious problem here, that the class action rule wholly, without regard to its original purpose, has become something of a device for social administration, which should never have been the product of the rules at all. These are matters which should be handled by the Congress and by the administrative agencies, and not by attempted effort to govern various parts of the economy by lawsuits which give more to the counsel — in any case the lawyers' relief act is what the rule has become — than they do to those who should benefit from them. . . .

I completely subscribe to the view . . . that class actions in state court, where the industry involves interstate commerce, should be removable to the federal courts. . . . As a major recommendation, particularly in cases where potential recovery to individuals is very small, the class should exist only on an opt-in basis, permitting res judicata to follow only for those who opt in, and we should eliminate the system of opt out. . . .

[T]he decision of the Supreme Court [in *Amchem*], which permits settlement and fees to be decided in the same case at the same time, was a reversal of the position of the Third Circuit. . . . Allowing settlement and fees to be settled together, to put it bluntly, permits the defendant to bribe plaintiff's counsel by giving him a large settlement figure for fees, without paying any attention to what the [class'] recovery is.

MS. KONIAK: Abuse in class actions is rampant. The world of class action practice is a world in which plaintiffs' lawyers get rich by selling out their clients. It's a world in which corporate defendants dispose of serious liability at bargain-basement rates, paying pennies on the dollar for serious injuries they cause and the frauds that they perpetrate.

It's a world in which judges — and I include in this category federal judges — are more interested in clearing their dockets and keeping lawyers happy than protecting the absent class, which is supposed to be the job of a judge in a class action.

---

[11] Alex Berenson, *Lawyer Cashes in on Both Sides*, INT'L HERALD TRIBUNE, March 13, 2003.

[12] *State ex rel. Union Planters Bank, N.A. v. Kendrick*, 142 S.W.3d 729 (Mo. 2004).

It's a world in which class members end up with worthless coupons . . . for injuries that may cause their death or serious illness. . . .

This world of corruption flourishes because there is too little law regulating what can and cannot be done in connection with a class action. There are almost no rules in this world. The same judge who orchestrates and all but writes a settlement may sit in judgment on that settlement to decide whether it's fair. Defendants may offer class counsel all kinds of inducements, including side settlements, to get them to accept a settlement that is bad for their own clients, the class.

NOTES

While it is impossible to undertake here an exhaustive study of all the nuances of unfair and arguably unethical class action practices, coupons, mentioned by Prof. Koniak, are a particularly sensitive issue. When coupons or discounts become the class' compensation, the actual money paid is both indirect and uncertain, making an accurate determination of the value of the settlement problematic at best. For example, a class action suit against major airlines involved over 4,000,000 people and attorneys' fees of $14 million. While these fees totaled less than four percent of the claimed recovery, none of the settlement was "paid" in cash but in coupons good for $10 or $25 off future fares. Restrictions on these coupons limited their use; most significantly, the coupons couldn't be "stacked," or all used at one time for one flight. Since they were usable only in small increments ($10 maximum on any fare under $250, and $25 on any fare under $500), most customers found the coupons not worth the trouble.

10. Frivolous Filings. Conflicts of interest and collusive settlements are not the only ethical issues facing class action attorneys. The defense bar has its own perspective about frivolous filings, as well as sharing skepticism about plaintiffs' lawyers' fees. Read the following.

DEBORAH ROSENTHAL, ABUSE OF POWER
Daily Journal Verdicts and Settlements 10 (December 1, 2000)[13]

Many attorneys believe that class-action abuse is widespread and severe. John Sullivan, president of the Civil Justice Association of California, says that abuses have increased in recent years as plaintiffs' lawyers, motivated by "greed and desperation for legitimate business," file more and more meritless lawsuits. "The role models of the current crop of personal injury lawyers are lawyers who hit the . . . class-action jackpot," Sullivan says.

Luanne Sacks, a business litigator in the San Francisco office of Crosby, Heafey, Roach & May, agrees. "Cases that would be deemed clearly lacking in merit if they were brought on behalf of an individual or handful of individuals gain a toehold [through the class-action procedure] simply because of the numbers," Sacks says.

But errors at the outset of class actions make up only half of the problem. Sullivan says that unfair settlements and lawsuits pursued primarily for attorney fees present "a bad situation that is approaching being out of control."

---

[13] Copyright © 2000 by Daily Journal Corporation. All rights reserved.

But the efficacy of legislative reform is hotly disputed by plaintiffs' attorneys and plaintiffs' bar organizations.

Consumer attorneys and the Department of Justice lambaste the Class Action Fairness Act of 1999. According to Elizabeth Strawn, legislative fellow for the consumer rights organization Public Citizen, the bill proposes an unconstitutional expansion of federal power which would effectively enable companies to "evade the justice of state courts" by rendering virtually every class action removable to federal court.

Furthermore, Arthur H. Bryant, executive director of the Trial Lawyers for Public Justice, states that, because the federal court docket "is already massively overloaded," legislation which allows defendants to remove more cases from state to federal court will cause "massive delay and far less opportunity to obtain justice for class members."

Nor is there any evidence that the proposed legislation will curb abuses, Bryant says, because the alleged abuses occur in federal and state courts. In fact, "the two largest and most notorious instances of class-action abuse took place in federal court and were approved by federal district court judges," Bryant says [referring to *Amchem* and *Ortiz*.]

However, the *Amchem* and *Ortiz* decisions addressed most of the abuses which were occurring, and, as a result, "those kinds of abuses are now relatively isolated, especially compared to the number of class actions that do good," Bryant says.

. . . .

Most attorneys agree that genuinely unreasonable fee awards could be eliminated if the fees were based on the actual benefit which the plaintiffs derived from the settlement, as opposed to a theoretical value ascribed to the settlement at the front end. . . . Class counsel then would have incentive to encourage coupon redemption so the award to the class would have real-world value. . . .

. . . .

[T]he legal community may soon engage in a collaborative effort which combines suggested reforms. A comprehensive study of "class-action dilemmas" published earlier this year by the RAND Institute for Civil Justice offers a detailed recipe for reform. The study concludes that attorneys and legislators must work to educate judges, increase public expenditures for the courts, invite greater participation by class members and intervenors, call for additional information and/or neutral testimony with regard to settlement amounts and disbursement plans before allowing judges to approve settlements and publicize class-action practice and outcomes.

11. Notice to the Class and Freedom of Speech. Generally an attorney or firm may send written notices of intended or existing class actions as long as the notices comport with the general limitations on lawyer advertising. Model Rule 7.3, subsection (c) requires the words "Advertising Material" on any written communication sent to non-clients "known" to the attorney to be in need of legal services. Are potential class members "known" to an attorney to be in need of legal services?

Most notices are protected by commercial free speech under the First Amendment, an issue we discuss more fully in Problem 30. In *Coles v. Marsh*, 560 F.2d 186, 189 (3d Cir. 1977), the court held that "the district court lacked power to impose any restraint on communication for the purpose of preventing the recruitment of additional parties plaintiff or of the solicitation of financial or other support to maintain the action."

In *Gulf Oil Co. v. Bernard*, 452 U.S. 89, 101 S. Ct. 2193 (1981), the United States Supreme Court cited *Coles* with approval. Plaintiffs in *Gulf* had claimed racial and sex discrimination in a claim before the EEOC, and Gulf entered into an agreement with the government to cease its discriminatory practices and to implement affirmative action programs to rectify its prior conduct. It also agreed to offer back pay to alleged victims of the discrimination, and sent out notices to these claimants offering that back pay if the claimants would agree to waive all their claims against Gulf. When plaintiffs' attorneys proposed sending a letter to these claimants suggesting that they decline the proffered settlements, Gulf requested and obtained an order from the court prohibiting such communications between plaintiffs' attorneys and the potential class members.

The Supreme Court held that the order unnecessarily interfered with the claimants' ability to obtain information about whether they should accept Gulf's offer, and it interfered with the attorneys' attempts to gather facts about the case. The Court also found that any order truncating communications between the attorneys and potential class members should be as limited as possible. . . . However, in a footnote, the Court also noted "heightened susceptibilities of non-party class members to solicitation amounting to barratry as well as the increased opportunities of the parties or counsel to 'drum up' participation. . . ."

SUPPLEMENTAL READINGS

1. *San Diego Navy Fed. Credit Union v. Cumis Insurance Society*, 162 Cal. App. 3d 358, 208 Cal. Rptr. 494 (1984). The plaintiff's insurer, Cumis, provided counsel to defend its insured San Diego Federal Credit Union in an action for general and punitive damages for tortious wrongful discharge. Cumis nonetheless sent notice to the credit union reserving its right to assert at a later date that the credit union was not covered for certain damages. The credit union retained independent counsel to protect its interests. The court found that under these circumstances there is a conflict of interest between the insurer and the insured, and the insured thus has a right to independent counsel paid for by the insurer.

2. The first number of Volume 4 of the *Connecticut Insurance Law Journal* (1997-1998) contains not only the article by Prof. Stephen Pepper mentioned above on the single client model of insurance defense, but articles by professors Charles Silver, Nancy J. Moore, Thomas Morgan, and others.

3. Eugene R. Schiman & Michelle J. Benycar, "Tripartite Relationship: Who Protects the Rights of the Insured?" *N.Y. Law Journal*, April 30, 2003, deals with New York's version of a written engagement letter, referred to in the notes at the end of section 2 of the Readings. The New York letter, unlike the Florida letter described above, does *not* ensure the primacy of the insured. The authors criticize the New York rule, explain why they feel it is inappropriate, and suggest what can be done.

4. The insurer's desire to save costs is exemplified by the efforts of Allstate Insurance Company, which was accused of penalizing claimants who hired their own attorneys to pursue claims on their policies. For example, if an uninsured motorist caused an accident injuring someone insured by Allstate, Allstate would send their own insured a notice suggesting that it was not in their interest to hire an attorney to try to obtain the fullest possible coverage under the Allstate policy. A Washington trial court found that these practices amounted to the unauthorized *and negligent* practice of law by Allstate, which was also found to have breached its fiduciary duties to its insureds. Similar claims were made against Allstate in California, Illinois, Indiana, West Virginia and Florida. Reporter Mark Ballard has been following the Allstate story for some time. Two of his reports can be found in *The National Law Journal*: "Allstate's Master Plan?" (November 9, 1998) and "Allstate Tactics Under Fire" (January 31, 2000). See also Deborah Lohse, "Insurer's Anti-Counsel Stance Gains Enemies," *Daily Journal* (July 29, 1998), describing the West Virginia Bar's unathorized practice decision.

5. Gail Diane Cox, "Captive Firms of Insurers Get Stung in Court," *National Law Journal* (May 15, 2000), reports that Kentucky is no longer alone in condemning the practice of having insurance company in-house or employee attorneys represent the companies' insureds. Montana strictly forbids such a practice, and the Florida State Bar Board of Governors gave preliminary approval to a measure acknowledging the potential for conflict between insurers and their insureds when the insurers use employee attorneys.

6. Martha Matthews, *Ten Thousand Tiny Clients: The Ethical Duty of Representation in Children's Class Action Cases*, 64 Fordham L. Rev. 1435 (1996), is a thorough explication of the problems and suggested solutions faced by those representing children in class actions. Matthews believes that children in class actions are rarely, if ever, consulted and their feelings are usually ignored by generally well-meaning but paternalistic lawyers. Matthews favors consultation with the children, their parents or guardians and others who are claiming to speak for them before determining the goals of a class action.

7. *The Future of Class Action in Mass Tort Cases: A Roundtable Discussion*, 66 Fordham L. Rev. 1657 (1998), provides a good explanation of the claimed abuses of class actions and discusses the effects of *Amchem*. Participants include plaintiffs' and defense counsel and judges.

8. Jack B. Weinstein, *Ethical Dilemmas in Mass Tort Litigation*, 88 Nw. U. L. Rev. 469 (1994). The federal judge who pioneered mass tort class actions writes about his belief that lawyers must act in the public interest in such cases. "It is my impression," he writes, "that few of the groups of plaintiffs I have dealt with in Agent Orange, asbestos, or DES were helped systematically or sympathetically as communities by lawyers handling their cases. Most lawyers were focused on getting cash for the individual client, obtaining a large fee, and closing the file." An interesting article by an outspoken, activist judge.

9. Perhaps the most controversial coupon case involved General Motors pickup trucks with side-mounted gas tanks. In July 1993, a federal district court in Philadelphia approved a class settlement covering roughly 5.7 million owners of these trucks. The owners would get coupons good for $1,000 off their next light duty truck; the coupons, however, were neither "stackable" nor transferable other than to family members. The plaintiffs' lawyers fees were set at $9.5 million. In *In re: General Motors Corp. Pick-Up Truck Fuel Tank Products Liability Litigation*, 55 F.3d 768 (3d Cir. 1995), the court reversed the settlement, which Judge Edward R. Becker called "a GM sales promotion device." The court found that the settlement "provided absolutely nothing to those unwilling or unable to purchase another GM truck." A similar class action later settled in Louisiana. This settlement allowed fully transferrable and "stackable" coupons, creating a "secondary market" that gave the coupons an actual street value, and also allocated $5 million to fire safety research, including $1 million of the attorneys' fees.

10. David J. Kahne, *Curbing the Abuser, Not the Abuse: A call for Greater Professional Accountability and Stricter Ethical Guidelines for Class Action Lawyers*, 19 Geo. J. Legal Ethics 741 (2006), states that Fed. R. Civ. P. 23 is not an adequate "procedural safeguard for class claimants," and that the Model Rules are "inapplicable in the eyes of the courts" and have "stalled any effort to introduce meaningful alternative ethical guidelines." The author argues that "clear ethical boundaries for the professional behavior of lawyers" involved in mass tort litigation are sorely needed.

11. The Rand Institute for Civil Justice has produced a substantial work on class actions and the attendant ethical issues. Its report, *Class Action Dilemmas: Pursuing Private Goals for Public Gain* (2000), is available from the Rand Institute. An extensive "Executive Summary" is available on Rand's website at http://www.rand.org/publications/MR/MR969.1.pdf.

Chapter 5

WHO CONTROLS THE CASE? HOW SHOULD LAWYERS AND CLIENTS SHARE DECISIONMAKING?

PROBLEM 12

What should a lawyer do when the client doesn't want to follow the lawyer's advice? What if the client insists on a course of conduct that the lawyer is convinced is not in the client's best interests? The answers to these questions are even more difficult when the client is not a mature, reasonably objective adult, when the client is mentally impaired, or when the client is under extraordinary pressure, such as facing a potential death sentence. In many respects, we see these issues as the most difficult lawyers have to face. And almost no lawyer is immune from being put in these difficult circumstances. In the following problem the lawyer is confronted with difficult choices while representing a juvenile offender with a mind of his own.

Is the Lawyer the Client's Savior or Mouthpiece?

I. You are a sole practitioner with considerable juvenile court experience. One day, Joseph Umberto, age fourteen, and his parents come in to see you. Joseph has been charged in juvenile court with robbery and assault with a deadly weapon, charges stemming from an incident in which a young woman was shot in the leg and her purse was taken. Joe says he was so shaken by the incident he can't remember anything other than his and two friends' presence at the scene. You agree to take the case and reach an agreement for fees with Joe's parents, first explaining that even though they will pay you, your responsibility is to Joe, not to them. They agree, saying, "We only want what's best for Joe."

In talking to Joe and checking school records, you learn that while he has no previous record, he has a history of learning difficulties and of some psychological abnormalities which have only, to this point, been vaguely diagnosed. You find Joe pleasant enough, though decidedly withdrawn. Joe agrees to a psychiatric examination done by a doctor you trust. This doctor reports that Joe is in need of intensive psychiatric counseling to avoid more serious problems. He believes that without this intensive program, the boy's withdrawal is likely to become more pronounced and potentially irreversible.

You and Joe contest the charges, but at the hearing the juvenile court referee finds that Joe is guilty. The DA now intends to argue for placement either at the Youth Authority ("YA") or at the new Juvenile Hall "secure facility," where there is little in the way of psychiatric counseling. You believe that with the help of the doctor and a sympathetic probation officer, you could still persuade the referee to grant probation, with placement at home and therapy under the doctor's direction.

You discuss these alternatives with Joe. Although you question him closely about how much he knows about YA or the local lock-up, he expresses a clear preference for those alternatives: "I don't like talking to these guys about what's going on inside my head, anyway." You know how tough the Hall can be, much less YA, and you are concerned that what Joe may now consider an adventure he could eventually strongly regret.

How should you advise Joe? Specifically:

1. How hard should you push Joe to adopt your view? Gentle persuasion, (figurative) arm-twisting, or somewhere in between?

2. To what extent should the views of Joe's parents be taken into account?

3. If you can't persuade Joe to your point of view, should you override his wishes and make the decision for him?

4. Does Joe's age or maturity matter? How much?

Ultimately, who decides "what's best for Joe" — you, the parents, or Joe?

II. Consider the death penalty cases discussed in the readings. What is your duty to a client who tells you to abandon all efforts to mitigate a possible sentence of death, or even argue *in favor* of a death sentence?

READINGS

1. Paternalism and "Instrumentalism." Who makes the decisions, the lawyer or the client? Are there some issues that are solely for the attorney to decide? Are there issues that the client must decide? How is decisionmaking authority established in the attorney-client relationship? One commentator divides lawyer-client decisionmaking patterns into two extreme models and offers some observations about each. Read this brief excerpt defining these models.

JUDITH L. MAUTE, ALLOCATION OF DECISIONMAKING AUTHORITY UNDER THE MODEL RULES OF PROFESSIONAL CONDUCT

17 University of California at Davis Law Review 4, 1049, 1050 (1984)[1]

The traditional decisionmaking patterns between lawyers and their clients can be described by two theoretical models: The paternalist and the instrumentalist. Both models allocate decisionmaking authority based on status as lawyer or client. [There is] the paternalist lawyer who presumes to know what the client wants and pursues those ends without regard for what the client may actually desire. The paternalist assumes moral responsibility for the representation. Conversely, the instrumentalist lawyer will do the client's bidding, with little regard for the consequences, so long as her actions are not clearly prohibited by law.

---

[1] Copyright © 1984 by Judith L. Maute. Reprinted by permission.

. . . .

[L]awyers disserve their clients when they pursue ends that they have imputed to their clients through means that they have not discussed with them. At the other extreme, lawyers diminish the legitimacy of the legal system and profession when they act purely as technicians, awarding their clients too much authority and abdicating responsibility for the consequences of their actions. Social scientists, legal philosophers, and others have expressed concern that the paternalist model subverts client autonomy. On the other hand, the instrumentalist model gives short shrift to legitimate societal interests.

NOTES

Professor Maute implies that lawyers must strike a balance between the paternalist and instrumentalist views. Is this the correct approach? Should a lawyer always strive to balance these two extremes, or are there circumstances in which one extreme is the correct choice? Can you posit circumstances in which clients force lawyers to adopt one or the other extreme?

2. Balancing Decisionmaking. Balancing the decisionmaking between lawyer and client is often a delicate task. It is generally accepted that lawyers have control over purely "tactical" considerations, while clients control the "ultimate issues." But what constitutes tactics in one case may be an ultimate issue in another. Ethical rules have generally resorted to rather ambiguous standards. EC 7-7 of the ABA Model Code allocates authority as follows:

> In certain areas of legal representation not affecting the merits of the cause or substantially prejudicing the rights of a client, a lawyer is entitled to make decisions on his own. But otherwise the authority to make decisions is exclusively that of the client and, if made within the framework of the law, such decisions are binding on the lawyer.

Model Rule 1.2 describes settlement and the "objectives of representation" as matters for the client to decide, while the attorney decides other matters. But what does this language mean? Does "affecting the merits of the cause" arguably limit the lawyer's role to ministerial duties only? How do lawyer and client determine what actions will "substantially prejudice the rights of clients"? How does one evaluate what are and are not the "objectives of representation"?

For example, in most litigation matters, lawyers ordinarily decide what discovery should be conducted. The client does not consent to each and every set of interrogatories or document requests. But is this always the case? What if the client has clearly made cost a factor? What about where granting opposing counsel an extension of time, ordinarily appropriate, would result in a calendaring consequence that may be important to the client? Ordinarily, the lawyer decides most questions of trial strategy, but this may be subject to a client's power to preempt those decisions.

Some commentators have suggested that a form of the informed consent doctrine, of the type used in medicine, be applied to the legal profession.[2] What information is an attorney obligated to provide the client? Is an attorney in a position to manipulate the client's decision by selecting the information which is given the client?

If the client seeks an end that the lawyer considers imprudent, to what extent must the attorney follow the client's stated choices? Under what circumstances should, or may, the attorney override the client?

3. Client Circumstances and the Temptations of Paternalism. A lawyer may have additional responsibilities depending upon the maturity, intelligence, experience, mental condition, or age of a client. But does the attorney always know better than the client what is in the client's "best interests"? When does "helping" become controlling or masterminding people's lives? Consider what you would do in the following hypothetical situations:

a. You represent a pregnant teenager who doesn't want to live at home anymore. She wants you to petition the court for an order emancipating her from her parents. If the petition is granted, the teenager, who has no financial resources of her own, will be living in a tenement in the worst part of town, or, even worse, might wind up homeless.

b. You represent a client who has Down's Syndrome. The client lives off income from a trust fund left by his deceased parents. You believe that the client's brother, who manages the fund, is making highly imprudent investments and wasting assets. Your client adores his brother and will hear nothing of your concerns.

c. Your client is a ninety-one-year-old widow. She recently has been befriended by her gardener. She calls you and tells you she wants to change her will, leaving all of her substantial financial assets to the gardener. You know that her current will leaves everything to her two children.

4. Life or Death for David Mason. In many cases, most lawyers would consider the filing of motions and the creation of other pleadings "tactical" or "technical" issues where decisionmaking rests with the attorney. But in the case of David Mason and his two competing attorneys, filing a motion or appeal took on a life-or-death significance, addressing the ultimate point of the representation itself. While reading the following article, consider the difficult choices that the attorneys for this death row inmate faced.

RICHARD BARBIERI, A FIGHT TO THE DEATH
The Recorder (San Francisco) (April 17, 1993)[3]

For the last nine years, Charles Marson has been trying to get David Edwin Mason out from under a death sentence. In January, Marson filed a 106-page *habeas corpus* petition in federal court seeking a new trial.

---

[2] *See, e.g.*, Susan R. Martyn, *Informed Consent in the Practice of Law*, 48 GEO. WASH. L. REV. 307 (1980); Mark Spiegel, *Lawyering and Client Decisionmaking: Informed Consent and the Legal Profession*, 128 U. PA. L. REV. 41 (1979).

[3] Richard Barbieri was an associate editor for *The Recorder* in San Francisco. This article is reprinted from the April 17, 1993 issue. Copyright © 1993 by The Recorder.

Meanwhile, his client was trying to get him fired. The condemned prisoner no longer wishes to fight his execution and believes he has found the right lawyer to smooth the way to his own demise — Sacramento's Michael K. Brady.

Mason and the 41-year-old trial lawyer, who says he handles mostly death penalty trials and drunken-driving cases, seem well suited to each other in one significant way: They both believe that executions are appropriate in certain cases.

"Dave has asked me to perform a particular task — that is to help him waive his appellate rights," Brady said in an interview last week.

Mason is seeking a judge's permission to fire Marson, a Remcho, Johansen & Purcell partner who was appointed to represent him in 1984. Marson is not following his wishes, Mason charges, because the former American Civil Liberties Union attorney is personally opposed to capital punishment.

By agreeing to help Mason in his unusual pursuit, Brady finds himself in a high-stakes dispute with Marson, who by his actions remains as committed to saving Mason's life as Brady is to helping end it.

Marson informed Brady in a March 16 letter he would no longer send him copies of any court papers he files on Mason's behalf. "I hope you have reconsidered your involvement in the effort to rush Mr. Mason into the gas chamber," Marson added.

Brady responded March 30: "I am not trying to rush David Mason into the gas chamber. That decision was already made. . . . He is going to die. The only question is when."

Mason was sentenced to death in 1984 for murdering four elderly Oakland residents over eight months in 1980, and then fatally strangling a fellow inmate in jail two years later. The California Supreme Court has already unanimously affirmed Mason's sentence and denied two state *habeas* petitions.

Marson filed a new *habeas* in San Jose federal court Jan. 7. It claims Mason should be granted a retrial because of new evidence he has turned up. But the *habeas* petition has become a sidelight in the case.

U.S. District Judge Ronald Whyte has scheduled a May 13 hearing to consider Mason's competence. And while he's not formally appointed Mason's lawyer, Brady is waiting in the wings.

If Mason is deemed mentally fit, he'll immediately fire Marson and stop all appeals, Brady said. And there's little in the law to stop him.

The U.S. Supreme Court has held that condemned prisoners judged sane enough to make an intelligent decision about their fates can forgo their appeals.

. . . .

"I become his lawyer, and we withdraw the *habeas* petition and [Mason] goes to the top of the list," Brady said.

"He's A Smart Guy"

Although Mason's psychiatric records are sealed, Brady said he's confident that Mason is competent. It's an opinion shared by Mason's prosecutor, Deputy Attorney General Catherine Rivlin, conceding that "this case makes for strange bedfellows."

"Mason's a real smart guy," she said. "He's a stone-cold killer, but he's a smart guy."

For his part, Mason, 36, says he knows what he's doing. "I'm sure it has crossed your mind that anyone who wants to die has to be a fool," Mason wrote to Brady on Jan. 26. "I disagree with that thought, I'm no fool. I am pro-death penalty, always have been, more since my years here. So now that I'm caught up in it, I can't exclude myself."

Although most condemned prisoners fight to the end, Mason's position is not unique. The states have carried out nearly 200 executions nationwide since 1973, with 21 involving so-called volunteers — prisoners who seek out their own executions by waiving their appeals.

Brady is not threatening to take such extreme measures on Mason's behalf. But his role in the case, which had not been widely known until it surfaced in press reports last week, is likely to draw increasing attention from other lawyers.

"A lawyer's job is to represent his client effectively, and you don't represent your client effectively by seeking his execution," said James Thomson, a Sacramento criminal defense lawyer and former death penalty committee chairman of the California Attorneys for Criminal Justice. "There's already a prosecutor in the picture," he said.

Boalt Hall professor Franklin Zimring added: "He's going to become the Jack Kevorkian of San Quentin's death row."

But Brady defends himself, saying he's just carrying out his client's wishes.

"The way I look at it is, if he doesn't deny the action and thinks he got a fair trial, and society thinks it's OK to put people to death, then he should be put to death," he said.

He said he doesn't plan to make a practice of taking cases like Mason's. Indeed he's not yet been paid for this case and doesn't intend to ask for fees even if he is appointed.

. . . .

In a letter dated Feb. 23, Mason charges that Marson is "not counsel for petitioner, he is counsel and lobbyist for the anti-death penalty movement. . . . I would ask you to appoint [Brady] as counsel for petitioner, allowing Mr. Marson to pursue his objective without censoring my own."

. . . .

Marson, 50, who was legal director of the ACLU Northern California chapter between 1972 and 1977, is well known among capital defenders. "He's a real good lawyer and highly respected by everybody in the defense bar," one lawyer said.

Brady says he views his task as a defense lawyer as giving clients "fair and vigorous representation." "That doesn't mean that when some of my clients are convicted I'm sorry to see them go to jail. They deserve it, in some cases."

In an interview on Friday, Brady said he had just spoken to Mason, who informed Brady that he had chosen the method of execution he prefers — gas chamber. Brady said he had told Mason that lethal injection was a less painful way to die.

"He said, 'My mind is made up.' He doesn't want to die lying on his back and wants to take his punishment like a man."

NOTES

In the Spring of 1993, David Mason finally fired Charles Marson and hired Michael Brady, but that did not end the controversy. While Brady filed papers requesting the abandonment of appeals and habeas petitions on Mason's behalf, other attorneys continued to file numerous pleadings trying to save the life of David Mason. Most prominent among these was Charles Marson, who, though he had been fired, "filed one appeal after another to try to save the condemned inmate's life — until the final hours," according to the San Francisco *Chronicle* of August 24, 1993.

Marson and others argued to the last that because of Mason's history of childhood abuse, mental illness and attempted suicide, Mason was not competent to decide for himself whether he should live or die. Ultimately, Judge Whyte disagreed, lifting all stays, and Mason died just after midnight on the morning of August 24, 1993. That morning's San Francisco *Chronicle* said this about attorney Michael Brady:

> With the execution only moments away, Brady stood waiting for a signal from Mason to stop the execution and refile a federal appeal the inmate had chosen to withdraw in January. Prison officials and state prosecutors said they would honor any decision by Mason to pursue that appeal, even if he changed his mind while sitting in the gas chamber.
>
> But the signal never came.[4]

Who was right, Michael Brady or Charles Marson? Was Brady "the Kevorkian of death row," or merely doing his client's bidding? Was Marson a hero trying to save a man's life, or presumptuously inserting his own set of beliefs for those of his client? From Brady's perspective, Mason was a clearheaded individual who had the right to decide his own fate. From Marson's perspective, Mason was a severely mentally disabled person, and part of the proof of that disability was his "volunteering" to die.

This question has hardly abated in the years since Mason's execution. Current statistics of the Death Penalty Information Center in Washington, D.C. show that over ten percent of the people executed nationwide since the death penalty was restored in 1977 are so-called "volunteers." This means that

---

[4] *Mason Put to Death*, CHRONICLE (San Francisco), Aug. 24, 1993, at 1.

an increasing number of lawyers face this same difficult and perhaps insoluble dilemma.

5. Is It Possible for a Lawyer to Act Objectively About the Client's Desires? How difficult is it for a lawyer whose client is facing a death sentence to evaluate the client's needs objectively? How much is the lawyer's perception of the client's ability to make decisions slanted by the counsel's strong disagreement with the client's stated desires? Or by the lawyer's concern that the client, faced with the ultimate penalty, may be less capable than the typical client to make decisions on his or her own behalf? In the following case, a lawyer struggles to make the most objective determination possible, ultimately arriving at a different approach than Charles Marson.

PEOPLE v. DEERE
53 Cal. 3d 705, 280 Cal. Rptr. 424 (1991)

Defendant Ronald Lee Deere was convicted of one count of first degree murder and two counts of second degree murder . . . . The penalty was fixed at death. The penalty judgment was subsequently reversed by this court in *People v. Deere* (1985) 41 Cal. 3d 353, 222 Cal. Rptr. 13, 710 P.2d 925 (*Deere I*).[5] Following a remand for retrial of the penalty phase, the sentence was again fixed at death. This appeal is automatic.

I. *Factual and Procedural Background*

Because defendant does not deny responsibility for the three killings, we need not dwell unduly on the evidence linking him to the crimes. Apparently despondent over the termination of his relationship with Cindy Gleason, defendant shot and killed the husband and two young children of Ms. Gleason's sister, Kathy Davis. Defendant had previously threatened to kill "everyone" in Ms. Gleason's family if she stopped seeing him. . . .

Defendant initially pleaded not guilty but later moved to withdraw his plea. The trial court appointed a psychiatrist, Dr. Tommy Bolger, to examine him. Following the examination and a report confirming defendant's competence, the court found defendant competent to plead guilty, waive jury trial and cooperate with counsel in the event his plea was withdrawn. The court then permitted defendant to withdraw his plea of not guilty, waive his rights, and plead guilty to each count and admit the special circumstance allegation. His counsel concurred in the change of plea. Based on the transcript of the preliminary hearing, the court then found defendant guilty of one count of first degree murder in the killing of Don Davis, and two counts of second degree murder in the killings of Michelle and Melissa Davis. The court also found true the multiple-murder special circumstance allegation.

Thereafter, defendant also waived jury on the penalty issue. Pursuant to stipulation, the court considered the testimony at the preliminary hearing and an earlier hearing to suppress evidence. While defendant offered no mitigating evidence, he made a brief statement voicing remorse for his crimes and announcing that he deserved to die. Counsel argued that the aggravating

---

[5] [All further citations to *"Deere I"* have been omitted. Eds.]

circumstances did not outweigh those in mitigation and therefore that the penalty should not be death.

Counsel also explained to the court the reasons which impelled him to agree to the guilty plea, the waiver of jury trial and the failure to offer mitigating evidence. According to counsel, he argued with defendant over each of these decisions, but ultimately grew to appreciate and concur in his client's point of view. Defendant, counsel explained, believed that to call mitigating witnesses would "'cheapen' his relationship with his family and remove 'the last vestige of dignity he has.'" The decision not to offer evidence, counsel stated, was "'made . . . in close consultation with [defendant]. It has been based on his desires and my conclusion that I have no right whatsoever to infringe upon his decisions about his own life.'"

In his first appeal, defendant claimed, inter alia, that counsel had been deficient in failing to offer any evidence in mitigation during the penalty phase apart from defendant's testimony at the preliminary hearing. A majority of this court agreed, holding that a defense counsel's failure to present any mitigating evidence in the penalty phase of a capital trial deprives the defendant of effective assistance of counsel. The judgment was, accordingly, reversed as to penalty, but affirmed in all other respects.

At the penalty retrial (to be discussed more fully below) defendant again waived jury trial. The prosecution offered no evidence in aggravation beyond that already presented at the first trial. Defense counsel, at defendant's insistence, failed to present any mitigating evidence apart from certain testimony at the preliminary hearing. The trial court, in response, held counsel in contempt for refusing to obey its order to present any available mitigating evidence, in conformity with this court's decision in *Deere I* . . . .

II. *Discussion*

A. *Ineffective Assistance of Counsel*

. . . .

[D]efendant contends that counsel rendered ineffective assistance in failing to present evidence in mitigation. The claim is totally without merit, if not specious.

As noted earlier, we held in *Deere I, supra* that defendant was denied adequate representation at the penalty phase as a result of counsel's failure to present evidence in mitigation, notwithstanding defendant's unequivocal desire that no such evidence be presented. Defendant was represented at the penalty retrial by the same deputy public defender who had appeared on his behalf at the first trial. Defendant's views with respect to the presentation of mitigating evidence also remained unchanged; defendant was adamant, in counsel's words, that "[h]e does not want any evidence presented on his behalf because in his heart that is his private life and to bring that evidence into court would violate his relationships with everybody he holds dear and respects in this world. And to him, those relationships are more important than anything else, including his life."

Thus, counsel was confronted with the unenviable and wrenching choice of obeying the law as defined by this court in *Deere I,* or honoring his client's deeply held convictions. To make the dilemma even more acute, the trial court ordered counsel to present whatever mitigating evidence was available in accordance with our decision, or be held in contempt.

Forced to choose between the Scylla of his duty to his client and the Charybdis of his obligation to the law, counsel chose his client. As he explained: ". . . I think I am obligated to argue for [defendant] in this situation. If the Court — if I were to follow the Court's order and present mitigating evidence, assuming for the purpose of argument it is available, [defendant] would object to the very depth of his soul. He's told me that. I know he would do that." Counsel explained that his client's clear and unequivocal wishes simply left him no choice: "I feel under the unique circumstances of this case I must make this decision. . . . [Defendant] has never once altered his position. . . . His position today is the same as it was the first day I met him. And although we argued vigorously on many occasions concerning what we should do in this case, . . . slowly but surely he convinced me his position is the correct one. He's made his decisions consciously, temperately, and not in the heat of passion, but based on his true and sincere and honest beliefs about what is right for him. I stand with him 100 percent. And to accede to the Court's order to either offer mitigating evidence or state for the record that there is none available would be the most gross conflict of interest I can imagine for an attorney in a case like this. So I cannot do it. I hope the Court doesn't feel that denial is contemptuous, but if the Court sees it that way, so be it."

Thus, under severe legal constraints, and at personal risk, counsel courageously performed the duty owed to his client. The trial court, as it had warned, thereupon held counsel in contempt for willful failure to comply with its order. The court then weighed the evidence before it, found that the aggravating outweighed the mitigating circumstances, and sentenced defendant to death. Subsequently, however, the court stayed the sentence for the purpose of obtaining additional mitigating evidence. . . .

At the continued hearing, the prosecution presented no additional evidence. Defense counsel reiterated that it was defendant's desire not to present any mitigating evidence. Thereafter, defendant, through [newly appointed] Attorney Landau, presented six witnesses in mitigation. . . . [and] an example of defendant's art work, which he had obtained from defense counsel pursuant to a subpoena duces tecum. In argument, Landau stressed defendant's artistic talent and the work he could accomplish in prison if his life were spared. Defense counsel also argued in favor of life, stressing the absence — in his view — of aggravating circumstances, and the psychological stress defendant was under at the time of the offenses.

In light of the foregoing, we find defendant's assertion that he was denied effective assistance of counsel to be totally without merit. [Death penalty affirmed.]

. . . .

Mosk, J., concurring:

To permit a defendant convicted of a potentially capital crime to bar his counsel from introducing mitigating evidence at the penalty phase . . . would . . . prevent this court from discharging its constitutional and statutory duty.

. . . .

"To allow a capital defendant to prevent the introduction of mitigating evidence on his behalf withholds from the trier of fact potentially crucial information bearing on the penalty decision no less than if the defendant was himself prevented from introducing such evidence by statute or judicial ruling. In either case the state's interest in a reliable penalty determination is defeated." (*People v. Deere, supra,* 41 Cal. 3d at pp. 363-364, citations omitted.)

. . . .

I turn now to the case at bar. In my view, no *Deere* error occurred or, if it did, it was effectively cured. To be sure, at defendant's request counsel again declined to present available evidence in mitigation. By so doing, he violated his obligation to the court and the adversarial process. But this time, the court . . . appointed special counsel. . . .

NOTES

Defendant Deere's deputy public defender made impassioned speeches "on behalf" of his client at the penalty phase of both trials. When he spoke at the second trial of arguing "for" his client, and "stand[ing] with him 100%," Deere's attorney really meant arguing *against* the introduction of mitigating evidence and in favor of his client's expressed desires. What do you think of this lawyer's actions under what he himself called these "unique circumstances"? Did he perform his client a service by being the one person in the "system" to express his client's deeply held wishes, or did he abrogate his role as counsel to become merely a "mouthpiece"?

Although the propriety of defense counsel's conduct was not directly before the court, the *Deere* justices themselves disagreed on the issue. While the court's majority lauded the lawyer's ethics for "courageously" performing his duty to his client "at personal risk," the concurrence saw this same behavior as a clear ethical breach — the failure of an attorney to perform his duty to the court.

In a 1998 Arizona case, the trial lawyers for Douglas Alan Smith went even further than the public defender in *Deere*. At their client's request, they affirmatively argued for a death sentence, even though the prosecution sought only imprisonment. Unlike Michael Brady, Jamie McAlister, Smith's lawyer, was an avowed death penalty opponent. Arguing for a death sentence was "difficult," McAlister told the *ABA Journal*, "but when my client makes a careful, rational, legal decision, I have an obligation to be a vigorous advocate on his behalf." McAlister's advocacy failed to get Smith what he wanted; he received a sentence of 62 years in prison. But the lawyer left the case "at peace with myself," confident she had made the right call. "what would bother me more would be to see somebody stripped of his right to make his own decisions about the course of his life."[6]

What would you have done if you were the defendant's lawyer in *Deere*? Would you be "at peace" with yourself if you had argued in favor of a death sentence for your own client? Tennessee Ethics Opinion 84-F-73 (1984) states: "Counsel is not ethically required to accept the moral and legal choices of the client and has no ethical obligation in this instance to advocate [for death] on behalf of the client." But that language still leaves it up to the lawyer to decide how to argue. Can any trial lawyer, who often must make ethical judgment calls in the heat of battle, ever be sure what the right decision is?

Finally, when considering what to do in such extraordinarily difficult circumstances, recent U.S. Supreme Court decisions have weighed in on both sides of the issue. In *Florida v. Nixon*, 543 U.S. 175, 125 S. Ct. 551 (2004), defense counsel conceded guilt at trial without express client consent. The defendant's lawyers felt that the only chance to avoid the death penalty was to make this concession and argue sentence, but the defendant was unresponsive each time the strategy was explained. The Florida court found the lawyers' acts were "the functional equivalent of a guilty plea," and reversed. The Supreme Court disagreed, called the decision strategic, and reinstated the death penalty.

On the other hand, in *Rompilla v. Beard*, 545 U.S. 374, 125 S. Ct. 2456 (2005), a 5-4 majority held that defense counsel had a duty to investigate what turned out to be the horrific childhood of the defendant, rather than merely rely on the defendant's understated representations. This defendant there, however, did not refuse mitigation testimony.

6. When a Client's Ability Is "Impaired." ABA Model Rule 1.14(a) provides that when a client's ability "to make adequately considered decisions" is impaired (whether because of minority, mental disability, or for some other reason) "the lawyer shall, as far as possible, maintain a normal client-lawyer relationship with the client." What does this rule mean in practice? Who decides whether the client has the ability to make an "adequately considered decision"? Is a lawyer competent to make that determination?

What does Model Rule 1.14(a) mean by "as far as possible"? Or decisions which are "adequately considered"? Is a client who chooses to fight a death sentence necessarily more "competent" than one who chooses to accept it? Is this issue analogous to "right to die" cases, where a terminally ill patient wants to cease life-prolonging measures?

Consider Theodore Kaczynski, the man convicted as the Unabomber, and his two lawyers.

---

[6] *See* Mark Hansen, *Death's Advocate*, ABA J., Dec. 1998, at 22.

RICHARD A. ZITRIN, THE KACZYNSKI DILEMMA, A DEFENSE LAWYER'S ETHICAL DUTY TO A SELF-DESTRUCTIVE AND MENTALLY ILL CLIENT
Legal Times (Washington, D.C.) (February 2, 1998)[7]

The Kaczynski case is over, ended with a guilty plea that seemed to satisfy most participants and observers, and even many of the victims. But this resolution was achieved only after Theodore Kaczynski had been denied the ability to decide the course of his own defense.

Kaczynski's counsel, Quin Denvir and Judy Clarke, faced what might be the toughest ethical dilemma any lawyer can have: How to represent your client when the strategy you firmly believe is in your client's best interests is totally unacceptable to the client. Making this situation worse was their belief that Kaczynski was seriously mentally ill, if not legally insane. Were this not enough, they had to determine their defense strategy under the watchful eyes of media representatives in numbers rivaling the Oklahoma City trials.

First, a somewhat oversimplified summary: Kaczynski wanted nothing to do with any defense that suggested he was mentally ill. Whatever consideration Denvir and Clarke gave to actually presenting an insanity defense was effectively stymied by the client's refusal to submit to a psychiatric evaluation. The lawyers continued to insist, over Kaczynski's objections, that they would present a "mental defect" defense, although it remained unclear exactly how.

Judge Garland Burrell Jr. agreed to allow the defense team to raise the issue of Kaczynski's mental state, but the government filed an unusual document objecting to the use of Kaczynski's mental illness as a defense, and demanding a hearing on the issue. Judge Burrell then ordered a competency evaluation. After Kaczynski was found competent, Burrell denied Kaczynski's request to conduct his own defense, and the plea of guilty and sentence of life imprisonment soon followed.

On the surface, the plea arrangement seems to have gotten most people what they wanted. Kaczynski's brother, David, and his mother were grateful that Ted's life had been spared. Prosecutors avoided the growing criticism over their insistence on the death penalty for one so obviously mentally ill. And Judge Burrell got off the horns of several legal dilemmas: Had he correctly ruled that Denvir and Clarke could use Kaczynski's mental condition in court? Should he have allowed Kaczynski to hire San Francisco defense lawyer Tony Serra to come in and put on a political defense, a move that would have delayed the trial for several months and created a possible circus? Was he justified in denying Kaczynski, now found competent, the right to represent himself?

Who Decides Best Interests?

It's likely that no one was more relieved by the guilty plea than Kaczynski's dedicated attorneys. Their care for their client and concern for his welfare were manifest, and helped them avoid a complete breakdown in their relationship, even when they were completely at odds with him. This undoubtedly contributed to the successful plea negotiations. But did Ted Kaczynski get what *he* wanted from this plea bargain? And ultimately, did his attorneys act in his best interests, not as they saw those interests, but as *he* saw them?

We will never know, and even the participants may never know, what would have happened had Denvir and Clarke acted as Kaczynski's "mouthpieces" by representing his views in court as strongly as they could. Perhaps they would have gone to trial and their client would have received the death penalty, although this seems unlikely. Perhaps Judge Burrell's refusal to allow Kaczynski to represent himself would have led to conviction but would have been reversed on appeal. Or perhaps Serra would have been allowed to represent Kaczynski, or advise him in his self-representation, presenting a political defense. Perhaps the very nature of that defense would have convinced a jury that Kaczynski was indeed crazy and did not deserve to die.

All this, of course, is rank speculation. But it's based on what could have happened had Kaczynski's lawyers chosen to do his bidding — acting in what *he* thought were his best interests, rather than what they thought. By never presenting their client's view of his case, they may have put Kaczynski in the position of accepting a plea he really didn't want — an offer he couldn't refuse.

How much of a mouthpiece must a lawyer be, particularly where the client is mentally impaired?

. . . .

It's difficult to be critical of Kaczynski's lawyers in making this hard, almost impossible, decision — especially under such trying circumstances. But I must disagree with their choice. Who in the courtroom spoke for what Ted Kaczynski wanted, crazy as that may have sounded to us? The answer is no one. It's obvious that no defense lawyer would have voluntarily presented the case Kaczynski's way or advocated his "strategy." But ultimately, it was Kaczynski's life at stake, and his call to make. As members of the criminal law community often say, "We don't do the time."

. . . .

Several lessons can be drawn from the Kaczynski case. First, a defendant's competency should be evaluated as early as possible in the case, not as a virtual afterthought.

Second, before indictment, the prosecutors ought seriously to consider, if not actually resolve, how they will deal with plea negotiations where their case is based on information provided by an immediate family member, or where the defendant obviously is materially impaired. There was no need for the Kaczynski play to drag on through so many acts.

Third, the predicament of defense counsel representing a mentally impaired defendant is ultimately everyone's problem, judge and prosecution included. Everyone should focus on assuring the defendant that his voice will indeed be heard, not by what Kaczynski felt forced to resort to — tossing a pencil across a table or making a speech during jury selection — but from the very beginning of the case.

NOTES

After his conviction, Kaczynski continued to maintain that he was sane and to try to set aside his guilty plea because it was based on his own lawyers' threats to use a "mental defect" defense. Indeed, while he ultimately lost in the Ninth Circuit Court of Appeals, he got a vote for reversal on this ground from the homonymous Judge Alex Kozinski. But sometimes, when clients of questionable competence *are* given the right to decide the course of their defense, it doesn't turn out at all the way the client intended, as in the case of Daniel Colwell.

TRISHA RENAUD, KILLER'S DEMAND TO DIE CHANGES TO PLEA FOR LIFE
Fulton County Daily Report (July 14, 1999)[8]

From the beginning, Daniel Morris Colwell said he wanted to die.

When he appeared at the Americus police station in 1996 to confess gunning down two strangers only minutes before, he told police he had killed because he wanted to die in the electric chair.

And, at his 1998 sentencing trial, he said the same thing repeatedly to his lawyers who tried to save his life by arguing that his death wish was a manifestation of mental illness. He said the same thing to the judge who told his lawyers they should accede to his wishes that they argue for death. The Sumter County Superior Court jury obliged him by sentencing him to die.

To celebrate the verdict, Colwell asked his lawyers to bring him a steak dinner.

Now, however, Colwell wants to live.

His lawyer says Colwell changed his mind because, for the first time in years, he is receiving the medication and dosage needed to treat his mental illness. . . .

Colwell, diagnosed by the state's doctors as a schizophrenic and manic depressive . . . "now realizes what happened to him," [his lawyer Michael] Mears says.

He says the judicial and mental health systems failed a mentally ill man, adding, "a very sick individual was allowed to try to commit suicide."

Colwell, says Mears, wants to withdraw his guilty plea and plead not guilty by reason of insanity. His client, he adds, now has "tremendous remorse for what he did."

Mears filed a motion for a new trial . . . Colwell "realizes that the decision which he made before and during his trial were decisions which were not the acts of a sane and rational human being," the motion says, adding that the sentencing trial "was a proceeding fundamentally tainted by Mr. Colwell's mental illness" and should be set aside.

Attached to the motion is a June 28th letter Mears received from Colwell. Colwell wrote his lawyer to say "Mears, I very much want to go to a state mental hospital to get help to save my life. I am very sorry for killing those people."

Those were very different words from those Colwell used at his trial.

In a booming voice, he told jurors that "God is ordering you jurors to give Daniel Colwell the death penalty." He also gave them a warning. "How do you know I won't escape and torture your loved ones?" he said. "Jurors, why take the risk?"

NOTES

The Colwell case is thoroughly laced with irony. Colwell's lawyers strongly resisted his efforts to control his own defense; his guilty plea was entered over their objection. Eventually the trial judge ordered the lawyers to follow Colwell's demands. But Colwell ultimately decided to allow his lawyers to present a defense because he feared that their failure to do so might result in a reversal of his conviction and a delay of his death sentence.

7. How Impaired Must a Client Be? A lawyer's personal belief of what is in the client's "best interests" might interfere with more than the lawyer's zealous representation and desire to make decisions for the client. It may also have a substantial effect on counsel's determination whether the client has the capacity to make his or her own decisions in the first place. May or should an attorney try to establish a client's incompetence where the client wants to be found competent? Should the lawyer hire an independent expert to examine that competence? May or should counsel reveal information communicated in confidence in order to establish the client's incompetence?

In contrast to the narrow language of ABA Rule 1.14(a), Rule 1.14(b) says an attorney may seek a guardian or "other protective action" where the lawyer "reasonably believes" the client is not able to act in his or her own interest. But the seeking of a guardianship — or the assistance of an expert to determine the necessity of a guardianship — may intrinsically involve the disclosure of information which the lawyer is usually not entitled to reveal. ABA Informal Opinion 89-1530 (1989) implies that such disclosures are implicitly authorized. Is this a persuasive argument?

ABA Formal Opinion 96-404 acknowledges that there are times when maintaining an ordinary lawyer-client relationship may be difficult, even impossible. But the opinion cautions that the lawyer's independent intervention is not authorized when *the lawyer believes* the client's actions are "ill-considered" or against the client's best interest. Rather, the lawyer can only act when *the client cannot* "act in his own interest." Even then, the lawyer must take the "least restrictive action under the circumstances." Thus, appointing a guardian, a "serious deprivation of the client's rights," ought to occur only when no "other less drastic, solutions" are available.

Several states, in ethics opinions and court decisions, have addressed the question of what a lawyer should do because of the client's perceived mental incompetence. For the most part, they have been in accord with a "least restrictive" approach. For example, Michigan Informal Opinion CI-882 (1983) holds both that a lawyer must resolve all doubt in favor of the client's competence before seeking a guardianship and that, even if that doubt is resolved, the attorney must still avoid the use of any confidential information. Alaska Ethics Opinion 94-3 (1994) requires that even where a guardian exists, "it is the lawyer's duty to make his client's wishes known to the court. The disabled client has no one but his attorney to speak for him." And in *Matter of M.R.*, 135 N.J. 155, 638 A.2d 1274 (1994), described further in the Supplemental Readings, the court admonished an attorney to "advocate the decision that the client makes" unless it is "patently absurd" or "pose[s] an undue risk of harm."

What if the client is severely delusional and cannot possibly assist the lawyer in the preparation of a defense, including an insanity defense? This is the situation that confronted the lawyer in the following case.

PEOPLE v. BOLDEN
99 Cal. App. 3d 375, 160 Cal. Rptr. 268 (1979)

Samuel Othello Bolden, Jr., appeals the order finding him mentally incompetent to stand trial based upon a jury verdict of incompetence. Bolden contends he was denied due process by Penal Code section 1368 which requires his attorney to give an opinion of his client's competence, and was denied effective assistance of counsel when his counsel offered evidence of his incompetence although Bolden desired to be found competent.

Bolden was charged with robbery, two counts of assault with intent to murder, and two counts of assault with a deadly weapon. Criminal proceedings were suspended to determine if Bolden was competent to stand trial. . . . Two psychiatrists testifying for the People said Bolden was not competent to stand trial, as he was suffering delusions. He believed the people he was charged with assaulting, his father and brother, were actually aliens from outer space who were inhabiting the bodies of his father and brother.

Out of the jury's presence Bolden's counsel explained to the court his client wanted to testify in his own behalf and wanted to be found competent to stand trial. While counsel felt he had a duty to pursue his client's desires, he also felt he had a duty to represent his client's best interests. He had been told by professional people a not-guilty-by-reason-of-insanity defense was available for his client. He felt he needed his client's cooperation to pursue this defense. Bolden's current mental state interfered with such cooperation. Counsel's solution to this dilemma was to place Bolden on the witness stand to testify to his competence, and then to offer his own psychiatric witness who testified Bolden was not competent to stand trial.

After 10 minutes of deliberation, the jury returned a verdict of not competent to stand trial. Bolden was committed to Patton State Hospital for treatment.

Penal Code section 1368 requires a judge who doubts the mental competence of the defendant to "inquire of the attorney for the defendant whether, in the opinion of the attorney, the defendant is mentally competent." Bolden contends this section violates the attorney-client privilege by requiring the attorney to reveal knowledge gained in the course of his relationship with his client.

This statute does not, however, require the disclosure of a confidential communication. "What the attorney observes of or hears from his client is not always privileged. It is apparent that some ingredient of disclosure or revelation is essential to the element of communication." Although an attorney's opinion of his client's competence may be principally drawn from confidential communications he has had with that client, merely giving the opinion does not reveal any protected information.

. . . .

No complaint is made about the skill of his attorney or the attorney's dedication to his client. Bolden's contention is the attorney was acting in what he felt was the best interest of his client rather than as an *advocate* of his client's position. By his attorney "siding" with the People in offering evidence of incompetence, Bolden contends, his desire to be found competent went unrepresented.

Diligent advocacy does not require an attorney to blindly follow every desire of his client. An attorney can ordinarily make binding waivers of many of his client's rights as to matters of trial tactics. When the attorney doubts the present sanity of his client, he may assume his client cannot act in his own best interests and may act even contrary to the express desires of his client. To do otherwise may cause prejudicial error.

Bolden's attorney provided effective assistance to his client.

NOTES

Is Bolden's lawyer's acting parentally — following his view of his client's best interests — more justified here by the clear disability of his client than it was in the *Deere* or *Kaczinski* cases? Is disability a matter of degree, as ABA Model Rule 1.14 suggests, or a matter of ascertainable fact, such as an in-court determination of competence?

What do you make of the lawyer's decision in *Bolden* to let his client testify in support of a claim of competence, while the expert testified against this finding? Was this "splitting the baby in half," or was it no more than a gesture from a lawyer who was taking a position at odds with his client's wishes? Finally, are you persuaded by the *Bolden* court's reasoning that Bolden's lawyer's disclosures — including his opinion on competence — did not reveal any confidential communications?

8. Representing Children. A lawyer's responsibility to a child presents an issue of particular difficulty. Read the following article. Some children's advocates take the position that a lawyer is always obligated to advocate for the child's point of view, no matter what the lawyer thinks is in the child's best interest. Do you agree? If not, where would you draw the line? When are children old enough to have the capacity to make their own "adequately considered decisions"?

JAN HOFFMAN, WHEN A CHILD-CLIENT DISAGREES WITH THE LAWYER
The New York Times (August 28, 1992) [9]

When a client gives marching orders to a lawyer about the course the client wants to pursue, the lawyer generally has to obey or risk getting dismissed. But if that client is a child, and the marching orders strike the lawyer as dangerous, does the lawyer still have to obey the client?

Just such a question has been posed in a Chicago juvenile court. It goes to the heart of a lawyer's responsibility to a client who is a child, and it would probably stump King Solomon. The case involves a 13-year-old girl in foster care who is eager to return home and who is being fought over by two lawyers who want to represent her.

The lawyer that the girl wants to drop is her court-appointed guardian, who is obligated to argue for what he determines to be in the girl's best interest. But his plan collides with what she wants. So another lawyer has stepped forward. This lawyer would be willing to be a traditional advocate for her, representing her marching orders in court. Hearings on which lawyer will be able to speak for her are set for Sept. 4.

The girl wants to resume overnight visits with her mother and stepfather, but the stepfather recently completed four years in prison after being convicted of sexually assaulting her. The guardian insists that the visits take place during the day and that they be supervised, and that the stepfather undergo therapy for sex abuse before the family can be reunited.

"This fight is not about the child's right to have her wishes granted; that's up to the judge," said Barry A. Miller, the lawyer the girl wants to retain. "It's about the right to have her voice heard in the legal process. The question is whether a child can be considered adequately represented by a court-appointed attorney who refuses to advocate for what she wants."

The clash over the lawyers' role is emblematic of the internal conflict faced by many lawyers and lay volunteers who represent children: Should they perform in the traditional role of a lawyer, arguing for their client's point of view, or be more of a third parent, presenting to a judge what they think would be best for the child?

. . . . Children were rarely seen and almost never heard in the courts until 1967, when the Supreme Court gave the right to counsel to juveniles charged with crimes. In the 70s, children's advocates, like Hillary Clinton, argued that children should be heard in cases that significantly affected their well-being.

Certainly children's voices have been growing louder in a number of legal arenas. Twenty-seven states now permit lawyers or guardians, who may or may not be lawyers, to be assigned to children in custody disputes. If the Mia Farrow-Woody Allen custody fight had been filed in Connecticut, for example, the children would have been entitled to counsel; because it was filed in New York, which has no such requirement, they are not so entitled.

And in July, a Florida juvenile court judge ruled for the first time that Gregory K, a 12-year-old boy in foster care, could sue to terminate the parental rights of his natural mother so that he can be adopted by his foster parents.

---

[9] Copyright © 1992 by The New York Times Company. Reprinted by permission.

The Chicago girl is fighting for exactly the tool that Gregory K. had: A lawyer to represent her position.

Lawyers in Conflicting Roles

In Chicago, virtually all children in neglect and abuse proceedings are represented by the Cook County Office of the Public Guardian, a brigade of 71 lawyers who work with 25,000 children. The office is supervised by Patrick T. Murphy, a high-profile figure among children's rights advocates. The public Guardian's office has a two-pronged role: As a guardian ad litem who argues for what the guardian thinks is in the best interests of a child, and the child's lawyer, who represents the child's point of view in legal matters.

The Chicago office is one of the few that combine these roles. The roles are at odds in this case because of the objection raised by the girl, so Mr. Miller and Barbara S. Shulman of Miller, Shakman, Hamilton & Kurtzon argue that they should now step in on her behalf, a move Mr. Murphy opposes.

"Usually you're advocating something the parents don't want, so let the parents' lawyers represent the other point of view," Mr. Murphy said.

In 1987, the girl's stepfather was convicted of having sexually assaulted the girl since she was 3 years old, and he was imprisoned. Since then the girl has been living with her maternal grandmother and permitted frequent visits with her mother, who was declared unfit by the state's Department of Children and Family Services because she refused to acknowledge that her husband had abused her daughter. The stepfather was released from prison last year and has rejoined his wife. Now the girl wants overnight visits and to rejoin her family eventually.

Warning Signals Raised

Mr. Murphy said his office initially allowed the girl to have overnight visits with the couple. But last March, he said, he learned that the stepfather, supported by the mother, had recanted his confession, proclaimed his innocence and, although he was in counseling, said he had not sought specific therapy for sex abusers. Mr. Murphy complained to the juvenile court judge, who ordered that visits to the home be stopped.

At a recent court hearing, the girl's therapists said the girl had grown despondent about not seeing her family, so the therapist suggested the girl get a new lawyer. The Legal Assistance Foundation of Chicago, which handles suits on behalf of children, contacted Ms. Shulman and Mr. Miller.

Associate Judge Stephen V. Brodhay of Cook County Circuit Court, Juvenile Division, who has been presiding at hearings in this case, will decide whether the girl was manipulated into substituting lawyers. "Just because a young incest victim decides she wants to go home, does that mean her attorney has to go along with that decision?" asked Miriam Soloveichik, an assistant public guardian who is active in the case. "Can she make a reasoned, adult decision? The answer has to be no."

At the bar convention a few weeks ago, a number of positions on the role of children's lawyers was staked out by a panel. While legal experts agree that representing very young children poses its own set of difficulties, children who are about 7 to 14 years old offer baffling ethical and practical obstacles. They are old enough to talk about whether they want to go back to a neglectful home or why they want to live with mom or dad, but their reasons may seem immature and ill-advised to the lawyer.

"Where does your job end?" said Sara D. Eldrich, a New Haven lawyer who is chairwoman-elect of the family law section of the Connecticut Bar Association, which is trying to write its own guidelines. If a lawyer asks a psychologist for an opinion in a custody case, she said, and the psychologist's recommendation is at odds with what the child wants, "have you breached your responsibility?"

These questions have reached a boiling point, in part because more courts are allowing children to have some sort of advocate speak on their behalf. But a 1990 study sponsored by the United States Department of Health and Human Services concluded that among the states requiring guardian ad litems for abused and neglected children, there was little consistency over who could serve as a child's representative, what the responsibilities entailed, and how ethical conflicts should be handled.

. . . .

Consensus about who should do what for children eluded [an] A.B.A. panel, whose members include scholars, lawyers and lay advocates. "Maybe what we have to do as a committee is just figure out when and if you can take off your lawyer's hat and do something else for your client," said Katherine Hunt Federle, co-chairwoman of the bar's panel and a professor at Tulane Law School.

In the Chicago case, as lawyers wrangle and the court deliberates over how the girl will be best represented, Ms. Soloveichik of the Public Guardian's office said: "the sad part is that the kid is lost in the middle. All the progress in the case has been held up just because a bunch of grownup attorneys are fighting with each other over her."

NOTES

Many states now have child abuse reporting statutes that require a wide variety of professionals, sometimes lawyers, to disclose suspected instances of child abuse. But these reporting statutes may directly conflict with the ordinary requirements of a confidential lawyer-client relationship. The result of this conflict can be a difficult balancing test. Formal Opinion 1997-2 of the Association of the Bar of the City of New York holds that even if a social services lawyer has a confidential relationship with an abused child, the lawyer's physical observation of abuse may be revealed.

9. May a Lawyer Manipulate a Client's Competence? Andrew Goldstein came perilously close to losing his insanity defense at his first trial. For the retrial, his new lawyers decided to take more desperate measures.

DAVID ROHDE, FOR RETRIAL, SUBWAY DEFENDANT STOPS TAKING HIS MEDICATION
The New York Times (February 23, 2000) [10]

As a jury selection began yesterday in the second murder trial of a schizophrenic man who pushed a young woman in front of a subway train, attention focused on a rare tactic by his new lawyers: the defendant, Andrew Goldstein, stopped taking his anti-psychotic medication two weeks ago.

Mr. Goldstein, 30, sat calmly and attentively yesterday between his new court-appointed lawyers, who advised him to go off his drugs in an effort to demonstrate to the jury the debilitating effects of his mental illness. But some experts described the move as desperate and unethical.

No one knows whether the lack of medication will have an incremental or sudden effect on Mr. Goldstein's state of mind over the course of the trial, which is expected to last more than a month.

Mr. Goldstein, who has pleaded not guilty by reason of insanity, is "very comfortable" with the new tactic, according to his lawyers, who said he was eager to testify.

"We've talked about it," said Kelvin Canfield, one of the defense lawyers. "He wants to testify; he does. Whether or not he'll change his mind, I don't know."

The move adds another twist to a high-profile case that has exposed the inadequacies of the state's mental health system. Mr. Goldstein, who has cycled in and out of mental institutions for more than a decade, has admitted that he pushed Kendra Webdale to her death on Jan. 3, 1999, but has said he was not responsible because of his schizophrenia. His first trial, in November, ended with the jury deadlocked 10 to 2 in favor of conviction.

Taking a mentally ill defendant off anti-psychotic medication during a trial is an unusual legal tactic that divides lawyers and psychiatrists. Doctors currently treating Mr. Goldstein at Bellevue Hospital Center strongly oppose taking him off his medication, his defense lawyers said.

Others were also skeptical. "It seems irresponsible to take a man off medication to produce some kind of dramatic effect before a jury," said Richard Uviller, a Columbia University law professor. "A lawyer's first duty is to preserve his client's health."

But other experts said it was an ugly but necessary step. Dr. E. Fuller Torrey, an expert on schizophrenia who heads the Stanley Research Foundation in Bethesda, MD., said he had intentionally given homeless mentally ill patients less medication than they needed before court competency hearings to keep them from being put back on the street.

"If I were his lawyer, I would argue for the same thing," he said. "If I were Andrew Goldstein, I would want the jury to see how psychotic I could be."

Dr. Torrey said it was not clear whether allowing a mentally ill person to suffer a breakdown causes long-term damage, but he said a breakdown would surely be harrowing for Mr. Goldstein. "I've never seen anyone with schizophrenia who enjoyed being in a psychotic state," he said.

The tactic, like the insanity defense itself, is extremely rare, according to legal experts. Lawyers for Russell E. Weston Jr., a mentally ill man accused of killing two guards in a shooting rampage at the United States Capitol in July 1998, refused to put him on anti-psychotic medication. Subsequently, a judge ruled him incompetent to stand trial for murder and committed him to a mental institution. But in other cases, judges have forced defendants to take their medications.

In the Goldstein case, Justice Carol Berkman of State Supreme Court in Manhattan has said she would allow Mr. Goldstein to stop taking his medication for as long as he appears competent to stand trial. If he appears not to understand his surroundings, she ruled, he will be forcibly given his medication.

. . . .

Odd behavior by Mr. Goldstein in front of the jury should not technically affect his case, legal experts say. . . . [But] juries in insanity defense cases are known to go with their inner sense of whether or not a defendant is unsound or just faking it. Several jurors in Mr. Goldstein's first trial said they noted his demeanor in the courtroom, which they said appeared normal.

If neither side presents new evidence in the second trial, an appearance by Mr. Goldstein on the witness stand could be pivotal. . . . But the defense may gamble that the image of a frightened and disoriented mentally ill defendant is their best hope.

NOTES

Ironically, Goldstein's long and thoroughly-documented psychiatric history included over a dozen efforts to voluntarily hospitalize himself and obtain the medications he ultimately declined to take for his retrial. An overcrowded hospital system repeatedly discharged him, even though there was clear evidence he was dangerous. "The tragedy," wrote Jonathan Gregg in *Time*, "is that in repeatedly seeking help, Andrew Goldstein behaved more responsibly than the state that is now prosecuting him."

There are significant differences between Goldstein's case and the decision by the lawyers for accused U.S. Capitol shooter Russell Weston to refuse to give him anti-psychotic medication. Goldstein, competent at the time, consented to his lawyers' strategy. Weston, incompetent at the time, had no ability to consent. Does that make a difference in how a lawyer should act? After all, if Goldstein's tactic succeeded, he could have suffered a severe psychotic break. Within a week of the start of his trial, Goldstein had indeed begun to show signs of psychotic behavior, twice assaulting the social worker who accompanied him to court. The judge ordered that Goldstein's medication be offered to him twice a day in case he changed his mind. Eventually he did, unable to handle the increasing mental illness that lack of medication brought on. Weston, on the other hand, had even less ability to control his own fate than Samuel Bolden.

As these cases show, the advances made in recent years in administering powerful psychotropic drugs have materially complicated the already difficult ethical issues that lawyers face. The Supreme Court has ruled that no death sentence can be carried out unless the defendant is competent. *Ford v. Wainwright*, 477 U.S. 399 (1986). But the issue of whether courts are empowered to force a defendant to take medication is less well-settled. *Riggins v. Nevada*, 504 U.S. 127 (1992), has language that both supports the due process rights of those who wish to refuse psychotropic drugs, and acknowledges the state's interest in requiring medication if medically justified and if it were impossible to "obtain an adjudication of guilt or innocence by using less intrusive means." Lower courts are split.

All this leaves the lawyer (as well as doctors ordered to medicate) with this near-impossible situation: Allow a client to become or remain incompetent in order to avoid a life-or-death trial or, worse, to prevent a sentence of death from being carried out. Or permit medication, restored mental health, and, potentially, execution.

SUPPLEMENTAL READINGS

1. David Luban, *Paternalism and the Legal Profession*, 1981 Wisc. L. Rev. 454. This article is an excellent academic and philosophical discussion of the paternalistic model of decisionmaking. Professor Luban begins his article with seven hypotheticals which set forth circumstances similar to those confronting the attorney for Joe Umberto.

2. Paul Tremblay, *On Persuasion and Paternalism: Lawyer Decisionmaking and the Questionably Competent Client*, 1987 Utah L. Rev. 515. This article discusses six alternative strategies for the lawyer who deals with a client of questionable competence. These alternatives range from acceding to the client's wishes regardless of the consequences, to using persuasion, to seeking a guardian, acting as a de facto guardian, or allowing a family member to do so.

3. Philip Heymann & Lance Liebman, "Rita's Case," *The Social Responsibilities of Lawyers* 2-21 (1988). This is a compelling account of an attorney working on a child custody case in a public interest setting who must balance the duty to represent the client's best interest and her stated desires. This account also provides a glimpse into the world of public interest law and how the legal and social service needs of the clientele often intertwine.

4. Rebekah Denn, "Dispute Embroils Killer's Request to Die," *Seattle Post-Intelligencer* (July 7, 2001) tells the sad and compelling story of James Elledge, another "volunteer" for death who insisted his appeals be abandoned. Elledge suffered from mental illness, committed his crimes while under the influence of alcohol, and had a horrific home life as a child. While in prison he educated himself, risked his life to save a prison guard in a racially motivated riot, and informed prison officials about a planned breakout. Yet he insisted on dying: "I don't look at this as an execution, I look at it as a separation. There's a dirty part of my soul, and I want it destroyed."

5. Adam Liptak, assisted by other staff reporters, wrote a compelling series of articles in the *New York Times* in October 2005 called "No Way Out" on the plight of both adults and juveniles who were sentenced to "LWOP," or "life without possibility of parole." Given the hopelessness of their situations and the dismantling of prison rehabilitation programs, many defendants were ready to choose the death penalty over life in prison without parole. Among the articles are: Adam Liptak, "No Way Out: The Changing Rules to More Inmates, Life Term Means Dying Behind Bars," *New York Times* (October 2, 2005), Adam Liptak, "No Way Out: The Youngest Lifers Locked Away Forever After Crimes as Teenagers," *New York Times* (October 3, 2005), and Adam Liptak, "No Way Out: Dashed Hopes, Serving Life, With No Chance of Redemption," *New York Times* (October 5, 2005).

6. *Matter of M.R.*, 135 N.J. 155, 638 A.2d 1274 (1994), involved a young adult with Down's Syndrome whose parents were divorced and who had expressed the desire to move from her mother's home to her father's. The trial court appointed a lawyer to represent the woman. The New Jersey Supreme Court engages in an excellent discussion about the attorney's role as advocate even where "incompetency is uncontested." The court concludes, *inter alia*, that "with proper advice and assistance," generally incompetent people are capable of making their own decisions on certain matters, and that the role of the attorney is to "protect [the client's] right to make decisions," and "to advocate the decision that the client makes."

7. *In re K.M.B.*, 462 N.E.2d 1271 (Ill. 1984). In contrast, in this case, a delinquent juvenile violated probation. Prior to the disposition hearing, K.M.B. informed her court-appointed attorney that she wanted to be placed in her mother's home. Upon recommendation of her counsel, the court placed K.M.B. in a children's home. K.M.B. appealed, alleging that she was denied the right to counsel because counsel did not follow her wishes at the hearing. The court affirmed, finding that unlike other court-appointed counsel, juvenile court-appointed counsel must not only protect the juvenile's legal rights but must also act in his or her best interests, even when the juvenile does not agree.

8. Marvin R. Ventrell, *Rights & Duties: An Overview of the Attorney-Child Client Relationship,* 26 Loy. U. Chi. L.J. 259 (Winter 1995), contains a historical review of the legal rights of children and a worthwhile review of the duties of attorneys for children, including a valuable section on how to deal with circumstances when the child's objectives differ from the lawyer's.

9. A series of articles at 64 Fordham L. Rev. 1379 *et seq.* (1996), grew out of a symposium on conflict of interest issues relating to the representation of children. One of the principal conflicts discussed is the tension between a lawyer acting as advocate for what a child wants vs. advocating what the attorney believes is in the child's best interests. Of particular interest are articles by Christopher N. Wu, the managing partner of a public interest law firm that represents children, on representing children in dependency cases (at pages 1857 *et seq.*) and Professor Nancy J. Moore's article at page 1819, especially her analysis at 1844 *et seq.* of the effect of parents as "interested third persons."

PROBLEM 13

Sometimes "differences" make a difference and sometimes they do not. Regardless of who you are or where you use your legal skills, you will be working with people with whom you share some common traits and with others who you percieve as very different because of culture, class, race, gender, sexual orientation, family background and a myriad of other reasons. A lawyer's learning and decisionmaking preferences may affect the ability to communicate the information that a client needs and that lawyer's effectiveness at aiding the client in making a decision. Not surprisingly, then, several states now require lawyers to learn about "multi-culturalism" as part of the Continuing Legal Education requirements because of a recognition that these differences can impact a lawyer's ability to deliver services. When do "differences" become a professional or ethical issue? And how can lawyers deal with these differences to provide competent and diligent representation to all their clients?

The demographics of our clients are changing. Whether lawyers work domestically or globally, they and their clients will inevitably be addressing cross-cultural issues. As one article sums it up: "US demographers predict that women, people of color and ethnic minorities will represent over 50 percent of all new entrants to the US workforce by 2008. . . . The next and future generations will reflect a very different world. This changing demographic landscape is demonstrated in the dramatic increase in the number of same-sex households, an increase in the number of Americans identifying themselves as multi-racial, and the fact that Latinos now surpass African Americans as the largest minority segment."[1]

One thing we can guarantee: All this *will* have an effect on the way you practice law.

Practicing Law in a Multi-Cultural World

I. JoAnne Bronson represents a battered woman, a relatively recent immigrant, who is now separated from her husband. She refuses to prosecute her husband or seek a restraining order because the husband has threatened her with bodily harm. She also tells you that she will not seek custody of her two children, including an infant, because of fears of retribution against her and her family in the "old country." You know that the circumstances of her case make it very likely that your client would be awarded custody, and there are available legal remedies that would serve to protect her, but those remedies are not, of course, infallible.

QUESTIONS

What would you do? Would it make a difference if your client's husband is abusive to the children as well as his wife? What other things would make a difference?

---

[1] *See, e.g.*, Velma E. McCuiston, Barbara Ross Wooldridge & Chris K. Pierce, *Leading the Diverse Workforce: Profit, Prospectus and Progress*, LEADERSHIP & ORG. DEV. J., Sept. 30, 2004, at 173.

II. Kayla Hotchkiss works for a large firm whose main office is in a major metropolitan area in the United States but has offices all over the world. She grew up in the city in which she practices, knows people from a wide range of ethnic and cultural backgrounds, has traveled widely, and sees herself as a "global" citizen. She is meeting with a client who has asked her to finalize negotiations on an import contract with a small Japanese firm that produces unique silks. The client explains that he is frustrated because the person with whom he has been negotiating does not seem to be able to make independent decisions and does not seem to understand that time is of the essence in coming to closure on the transaction.

QUESTIONS

What, if any, role should Kayla take in helping her client understand differences in culture? What should Kayla do to prepare herself to engage in the negotiations with the Japanese firm? Whose cultural norms should be followed?

READINGS

1. Open-Minded and Intelligent Decisionmaking in a "Global Village." How should lawyers approach their decisionmaking tasks? How do your own pre-law school experiences and background help you understand the law? How about your own sense of morality? What kind of analysis do you primarily rely on for problem solving? Or for legal decisionmaking?

Increasingly in the cultural "global village" of our nation, it is easy to find oneself in a situation where communications are breaking down because the other person is using different analytical tools. Where that other person is a client, resorting to multiple kinds of "intelligences," as Professor Angela Olivia Burton terms them, can assist the lawyer in bridging the gap.

ANGELA OLIVIA BURTON, CULTIVATING ETHICAL, SOCIALLY RESPONSIBLE LAWYER JUDGMENT: INTRODUCING THE MULTIPLE LAWYERING INTELLIGENCES PARADIGM INTO THE CLINICAL SETTING
11 Clinical Law Review 15 (2004)[2]

. . . .

The ethical rules guiding lawyer-client relationships mandate that lawyers exercise "independent professional judgment" in representing clients. In accordance with the dominant view of the lawyer's role, the profession's ethical norms specify that lawyers provide clients "with an informed understanding of the client's legal rights and obligations" and explain the practical implications of those rights and obligations. Along with this deeply embedded and preeminent emphasis on legal rights in the ethical rules governing lawyer conduct, there is also a recognition (albeit a sort of off-handed one) of the law's inseparability from practical, moral, and ethical concerns inherent in the realities of human conflict situations. Authorizing the lawyer to refer to concerns such as "moral, economic, social and political factors" when advising a client, the Comment to Rule 2.1 notes that because such concerns "may decisively influence how the law is applied," advice premised entirely upon a technical interpretation of legal rules "may be of little value to a client."

. . . [I]t seems unlikely that a lawyer fulfills her duty to provide a client with adequately informed assessments of the strengths and weaknesses of alternatives, and to provide reasoned opinions about the relative propriety of various options if she has not factored both legal rules and relevant contextual considerations into her deliberative calculus. Given the prevalence of influences other than rights, powers, and obligations derived from formal legal rules, the notion that lawyer's judgment can be either truly "independent" or "professional" without reference to the potential impact of social, cultural, and structural factors operating within the situation appears untenable.

. . . . The lawyer therefore acts more consistently with her professional role when she brings to the client's attention the potential impact of the client's decision on other people, and when she engages in dialogue with a client around issues of "the right thing to do" than when she fails to do so. . . .

In addition [e]ach lawyer is a "representative of clients, an officer of the legal system, and a public citizen having special responsibility for the quality of justice." In accordance with this caretaking obligation, the expectation of the profession is that lawyers will act "in conformance with justice, fairness, and morality" by counseling clients to take non-doctrinal considerations into account "when the client makes decisions or engages in conduct that may have an adverse effect on other individuals or on society," as well as when functioning as an agent for clients. When lawyers do not account for social, cultural, and structural influences in their decision-making processes, cumulatively, and over time, decisions made and actions taken in contemplation of lawyers' judgments can and do result in a variety of negative consequences to clients, to non-clients, and to the quality of justice.

. . . . The often competing responsibilities of lawyers to clients, third parties, and the public demand . . . that the lawyer appreciate and integrate a broad range of influences, concerns, and interests into her deliberative process as she prepares to counsel and advise her clients. Noticeably, the rules of professional responsibility do not provide specific guidance to assist lawyers in this complex undertaking. As a result, some have argued, lawyers do not sufficiently consider or counsel clients with respect to non-doctrinal issues and the interests of third parties, with the result that "[e]veryday, lawyers and clients make decisions that do violence to others and create harshness and suffering, through the assertion of positions sanctioned by law."

. . . .

The lawyering intelligences model is a product of the collaborative efforts of Workways, a group of law professors, social scientists, and education specialists devoted to the study of the varieties of work necessary to effective and socially responsible lawyering. Primarily the brainchild of Workways' founder Peggy Cooper Davis, the model comprises logical-mathematical, linguistic, narrative, interpersonal, intrapersonal, categorizing, and strategic intelligences, a set of distinct yet interconnected intellectual capacities that animate every kind of legal work. The conceptual framework . . . defines "intelligence" in terms of specific intellectual frames — for example, linguistic, logical, interpersonal or intrapersonal — through which information is processed "in a cultural setting to solve problems or create products that are of value to a culture." [E]ffective problem solving or intelligent behavior [thus arises] from the interaction among numerous forms of intelligence, rather than from the operation of a single unitary faculty. . . .

To exercise critical judgment lawyers need to . . . gather, analyze, and synthesize information from a variety of sources and disciplines, while understanding that each source has its own perspective. They need to recognize and deal with ambiguity. They need to communicate effectively, orally and in writing with people as different from each other and themselves as clients, government officials, judges, jurors and experts in various fields. In today's multi-cultural "global village" lawyers will need to engage in difficult discussions about complex and contentious issues such as the law's relationship to matters of race, culture, and gender. Further, because so much of being an effective lawyer is learned through experience and reflection, they need to apply the same critical skills that they apply to a problem brought to them by a client in order to examine their work as lawyers.

NOTES

Professor Burton reprises the concept of "moral lawyering" but takes it a step or two further. Do you agree with her that using a multi-intelligence approach is a necessary part of lawyering? Is it an ethical issue? And does sensitivity to and understanding of cultural differences rise to the level of an ethical issue in your mind?

2. Client-Centered Lawyering in Abuse Cases. In the following piece, the authors, a clinical law professor and his student assistant, passionately argue that the lawyer's job is to empower the client to make decisions and then defer to the client's choices. Do you agree that the lawyer should defer to the client in the domestic abuse problem described above? The authors assume paternalism on the part of the lawyer is a always a bad thing, but are there circumstances in which the lawyer should substitute his or her own judgment? Think also about the lawyer's advisor function. What obligation does the lawyer have to directly explain these client-vs. lawyer-centered dynamics to the client? Would it depend on the client's level of sophistication and ability to comprehend?

In Problem II, should Kayla insist her American client comply with the Japanese norm or visa versa? What distinguishes Problem I from Problem II in terms of the lawyer's role in deferring or controlling the client's decisionmaking?

V. PUALANI ENOS & LOIS H. KANTER, WHO'S LISTENING? INTRODUCING STUDENTS TO CLIENT-CENTERED, CLIENT-EMPOWERING, AND MULTIDISCIPLINARY PROBLEM-SOLVING IN A CLINICAL SETTING
9 Clinical Law Review 83 (2002)[3]

The client-centered advocate works to understand the client's perspectives regarding the substance and context of the client's problem(s). This approach also involves addressing the client as a whole person, recognizing her place within the community and her relationships with family, friends and others. It necessitates seeing the abuse in the context of the client's life, rather than defining the client in terms of the abuse.

A client-centered approach involves addressing the multitude of issues facing each client and recognizing that legal relief such as restraining orders, criminal prosecution, custody and visitation orders, or immigration benefits typically address only a few of the client's needs. Additionally, legal relief may further the client's legal goals but have a negative impact on the client's emotional recovery from abuse or her economic, educational, employment or health care goals. While the services and resources available to her are important issues to discuss, her alternatives do not always turn on using services. A client-centered approach focuses on the client's articulated desires, even when system solutions are not apparent.

Empowering a client involves an effort by her advocate, reaffirmed in every stage of the relationship between them, to ensure that the client has the information, capacity and opportunity to articulate her needs, determines what course of action will best meet those needs, and obtains from others the resources and cooperation necessary to keep herself and her children safe. Client empowerment, therefore, begins with a client-centered analysis of the problem presented, so that the advocate — whether a lawyer or other provider — sees the problem through the client's eyes and is therefore in a position to assist the client in addressing her problem the way she deems best. Once the problem is defined from the client's perspective, the advocate's role can best be viewed as partnering with a client to exchange information, assisting the client in prioritizing her needs and desires, and strategizing with her to devise alternatives that best address the client's priorities. The advocate can then support the client in analyzing alternatives by weighing the benefits and risks of each alternative carefully and honestly, including the potential time and resources to be expended by the client and the impact of any action taken on the client's long term goals. To maintain a true partnership throughout this process, the advocate must accept and respect the client's right to make and execute decisions, no matter whether, or how slowly, she is prepared to act.

This model of client-centered and client-empowering advocacy shifts the power dynamic inherent in traditional lawyer/client roles with the intent of equalizing power and status between an attorney and client and tapping into the strengths and knowledge of the client as well as the attorney. It emphasizes information sharing and joint problem-solving, as opposed to limiting

---

[3] Copyright © 2002 by Clinical Law Review, Inc. Reprinted by permission.

the client's understanding and directing the client toward service-based solutions. Using this approach, the empowering advocate works to provide the client with the opportunity to form her own relationships with other helping professionals, and supports her in maintaining these relationships, rather than representing the client in all of her dealings with others. Moreover, limiting the preeminence of the attorney in speaking on behalf of the battered client can increase her safety. . . . Co-opting the client's power, even if intended to further the best interests of the client, is dangerous because it mirrors the power and control dynamic central to abusive relationships. Repeating this pattern, even if it feels familiar and appealing to the client, can only be harmful. We have found that attorneys who have been trained through traditional legal methods find this approach particularly challenging, even when they are obviously committed to assisting victims of violence. However, we have personally experienced the increased client satisfaction that accompanies this shift from a hierarchical power relationship to an empowering partnership, and believe that client satisfaction can provide even the most skeptical lawyer with the incentive to achieve competency in this method. . . .

Most importantly, however, this approach avoids the most dangerous and unhelpful thing an advocate can do, which is to give a victim of domestic violence advice and instructions about how best to ensure her safety and that of her children. Advocates do not have enough time to learn all the facts and do not have enough control over enough factors to predict with reliability the results of any particular action or course of conduct. While the client herself may not have all the facts, and certainly cannot control all of the factors vital to her continued safety, she has greater access to the facts and control over her environment than does her advocate. Also, in the end, it will be the client who must live with the consequences of all decisions.

NOTES

In an abuse situation, the authors' argument for client-centered lawyering, as they term it, seems to make a lot of sense. After all, paternalistic lawyering may repeat some elements of the abusive situation. But do you agree that client-centered lawyering is always the right approach? The authors say that a more traditional approach "can only be harmful." Do you agree, or do you think some clients would prefer that the lawyer be more directive and assertive, perhaps to the point of making the decisions for the client? Might this depend on both the client and the circumstances? Or the cultural background of the client, as Part I of the Problem suggests? Might it even depend on the relationship between the particular lawyer and the particular client?

3. White Lawyers and Culturally Diverse Clients. In the next article, Fordham ethics Professor Russell Pearce, long a leading thinker on the relationship of race and culture, acknowledges the difficulties all white lawyers have dealing with — and getting over — being part of the predominating group in this country. After the Pearce piece we'll look at a famous example of white paternalistic lawyering done with the best intentions that nevertheless did not work out too well.

RUSSELL G. PEARCE, WHITE LAWYERING: RETHINKING RACE, LAWYER IDENTITY, AND RULE OF LAW
73 Fordham Law Review 2081 (2005)[4]

This Essay will explore what it means to be a white person in the legal profession and how recognition of whiteness as racial identity requires a dramatic rethinking of professional norms.[5] As white people, we too often view racial issues as belonging to people of color. We tend to do that in one of two ways. Some whites believe that race generally does not matter except in the rare case of an intentional racist. Other whites view whites generally as racists and look to people of color to tell them how to understand issues of race. This Essay rejects both of these approaches. The Essay argues that for white lawyers, as well as lawyers of color, increased "competence [in] dealing with racial matters" and "speak[ing] openly, frankly, and professionally about relations" is necessary both to competent client representation and equal justice under law.

. . . [W]hether they view themselves as color-blind or racist, white lawyers understandably have a tendency to treat whiteness as a neutral norm or baseline, and not a racial identity, and tend to view racial issues as belonging primarily to people of color, whether lawyers or clients. This approach is consistent with, and reinforces, the prevailing professional norm that lawyers should "bleach out" their racial, as well as their other personal, identities.

As this Essay explains, this unfortunate symbiosis of whiteness and professionalism undermines the work of lawyers both in their representation of clients and in their systemic efforts to promote the rule of law. The latest research in the field of organizational behavior suggests that the assumption of lawyer neutrality so central to lawyer professionalism is not only wrong descriptively, but that it also undermines the very goals it seeks to promote. In particular the pathbreaking research of Robin Ely and David Thomas demonstrates that in a diverse society and legal profession an integration-and-learning perspective that openly acknowledges and manages racial identity would far better promote excellent client representation and equal justice under law than the currently dominant commitment to color blindness. . . .[6]

. . . .

As a general descriptive matter, white people are the dominant racial group in legal organizations. They represent 83.2% of judges, 89.2% of lawyers, and 79.5% of law students, percentages which exceed the 75.1% of the American population that is white. In elite legal jobs, the white domination is even greater. Whites represent almost 98% of partners in the 100 top law firms.

---

[4] Copyright © 2005 by Russell G. Pearce. Reprinted by permission.

[5] [FN3] This Essay focuses on whiteness; it makes no claims — and indeed rejects the notions — that race is the only significant identity in lawyering or that racial identity does not intersect and interact with other identities. A number of scholars have discussed how nonracial identities influence lawyering. [Here, Professor Pearce sets forth an extensive bibliography of related articles. Eds.]

[6] [FN10] Robin J. Ely & David A. Thomas, Cultural Diversity at Work: The Effects of Diversity Perspectives on Work Group Processes and Outcomes, 46 Admin. Sci. Q. 229, 260-65 (2001) [hereinafter, Ely & Thomas, Cultural Diversity]; Robin J. Ely & David A. Thomas, Team Learning and the Racial Diversity-Performance Link 23-35 (2004) (Harvard Business School Working Paper No. 05-026) [hereinafter Ely & Thomas, Team Learning].

As the dominant racial group, whites can view ourselves as having no particular racial identity. An African-American friend recently described his impression that newspaper stories describing lawyers usually identified the race of lawyers of color but mentioned no race for white lawyers. As a member of the dominant group in the legal profession, the white lawyer is the norm. With regard at least to our race, we start by looking around the room and feeling like we belong, as is so often the experience of white students, particularly the men, in my seminar who do not see race as a useful way to discuss their experience. . . .

The experience of law students and lawyers of color is quite different. As a minority group in the legal profession, they have "no choice except to learn about white culture if they are to survive." When people of color look around the room, they know they are not the dominant culture and do not necessarily assume the same fit and the same authority. Enhancing this effect is the congruence of white dominance in the legal profession with white dominance in a society where whites have a greater share of wealth and power. When white lawyers, judges, and court personnel assume my students of color are tenants and not legal representatives, or assume a summer associate of color is a member of the support staff, they are applying generalizations about race relations congruent with the relative distribution of racial power found in society in general. The incongruence of the authority position of being a lawyer, or of having a position of authority within the legal profession, complicates the organizational tasks of lawyers of color.

While race makes a significant difference in our experiences as lawyers, intergroup theory reminds us that it is not determinative. These experiences, like those relevant to organizational groups and other identity groups to which we belong, provide us with data. How we manage that data — whether we acknowledge it consciously and how we respond to it — is a matter of choice on both an individual and group level. One way I choose to manage my white identity is to acknowledge and discuss issues of race with my students and colleagues and, indeed, to write this Essay as a way of communicating with a broader group of legal academics, lawyers, and law students. Although this Essay represents a preliminary account of the white experience in the legal profession, this part offers at least two conclusions: White racial identity exists and whites tend to avoid acknowledging their identity.

NOTES

Professor Pearce's postulate is proposed not to engender sympathy but to underscore the difficulty in bridging the cultural gap that whites — especially straight white males — have never had to deal with in much of their practice of law. He gives all of this vast majority quite a challenge, though he's a little short on solutions. Before we look at solutions, read the next section about a white lawyer dealing with a group of Cuban refugees who not only brought different cultural and linguistic barriers to their representation but an enormous political/cultural issue — their loyalty, above all else, to their bosses at the CIA.

4. The Watergate "Foot Soldiers" Plead Guilty. If there was one seminal event that focused the attention of America on legal ethics, that event was the Watergate break-in in 1972. The debacle of Watergate included the infamous "Saturday night massacre," in which one lawyer, President Richard M. Nixon, ordered another lawyer, then-Attorney General Elliot Richardson, to fire a third, Watergate Special Prosecutor Archibald Cox. When Richardson refused, he too was fired, and Nixon moved down the Department of Justice chain of command until he found someone willing to carry out his orders. The fall of lawyers, from the President, who resigned in disgrace in August 1974, to a United States Attorney General (John Mitchell), to the White House counsel (John Dean), to the creator of the campaign of "dirty tricks" against political opponents (Donald Segretti), focused our country on the ethics of lawyers as never before.

One lawyer who did not fall, but who played a small though fascinating and important role in the Watergate case, was Washington, D.C. criminal defense attorney Henry Rothblatt, Jr.

Most lawyers would agree that whether a criminal defendant pleads guilty or not guilty is a decision ultimately controlled by the client. Yet, under the unusual circumstances in which he found himself in early 1973, Rothblatt refused to accede to the guilty pleas of his four clients, and instead withdrew from the case. Rothblatt represented Messrs. Barker, Martinez, Sturgis, and Gonzalez, four of the seven defendants in the original Watergate break-in case.[7]

These four, the "Watergate foot soldiers," were all Cuban refugees from Castro and veterans of the abortive "Bay of Pigs" invasion, in which the CIA attempted to invade Cuba to eliminate Castro in 1961. They all were intelligence operatives for the CIA willing to do almost anything to bring the Castro government down. They were charged along with their three Anglo superiors, E. Howard Hunt, G. Gordon Liddy, and James McCord, with the burglary of Democratic National Committee headquarters at the Watergate apartments in June 1972, during Nixon's reelection campaign.

The "foot soldiers" had all worked for Hunt, one of the chief CIA agents involved in the "Bay of Pigs" invasion, and were extraordinarily loyalty to him and "the Agency." After their arrest, the four "foot soldiers" maintained that they engaged in the Watergate operation at the behest of Hunt, carrying out the break-in in the belief that Hunt was operating under authority of the CIA.

The trial of the seven Watergate defendants began in Washington in January 1973, before United States District Court Judge John J. Sirica. In his opening statement, Rothblatt outlined his clients' defense as that of four soldiers with no criminal intent following the orders of superiors. Immediately after opening statements, however, E. Howard Hunt changed his plea to guilty. This, the four "foot soldiers" would later argue, was a signal from their superior that they too were to plead guilty. As Barker later put it in an affidavit:

---

[7] We do not here address the propriety of Rothblatt representing multiple defendants. See our discussion in Problem 7.

After we came to Washington for our trial . . . I was told by Mr. Hunt that he had decided to plead guilty and that we did not have any defense. This represented to me a final decision that there would be no disclosure at the trial as to the true nature of the operation we had engaged in and that the plan which was to be followed was for us to plead guilty. . . .

Right after Hunt's guilty plea, the four soldiers wrote a letter to Rothblatt insisting that they be allowed to change their pleas to guilty. But Rothblatt believed his clients had legitimate defenses and were being duped into not using them. He believed that the CIA had had *no* authority to conduct the break-in, and that the "foot soldiers" were being used as pawns in a yet-unknown and dangerous high-stakes political game. Having failed in his attempts to convince his clients, Rothblatt then refused to participate in their guilty pleas. He gave the letter to Judge Sirica, and told the court he "couldn't in good conscience, as a member of the bar, knowing my professional responsibilities," participate in his clients' efforts to plead guilty.

After ascertaining that each of the four defendants still wished to plead guilty, the judge replaced Rothblatt with another attorney. Within a few days, and with the concurrence of new counsel and after extensive *voir dire* by the court, the four guilty pleas were accepted. In September, 1973, however, before their final sentences were imposed, Barker, Martinez, Sturgis, and Gonzales had come around to Rothblatt's perspective — that they had been duped and never should have pled guilty. They moved to withdraw their guilty pleas. In November, 1973, however, Judge Sirica denied the motions to withdraw the pleas. The circuit court of appeals, sitting *en banc*, in a highly factionalized decision, affirmed that ruling, the majority noting that the defendants had knowingly overruled Rothblatt's advice and pled guilty with the competent assistance of successor counsel.[8]

As for Rothblatt, who had taken the highly unusual step of refusing to accede to what is clearly a client decision, his paternalism was proved correct — at least on this particular occasion. Were his actions justified? Perhaps the answer lies in part in the fact that the ultimate decision in the case was not determined by him, but by the clients themselves after his withdrawal. Not much is known about the manner in which Rothblatt approached his clients, so it is difficult to speculate what he did to bridge the gap between his experiential and cultural view of the world and clients who were not only culturally different but must have seemed mentally "impaired," or even delusional in their slavish adherence to a master who, as it turned out, was selling them out.

5. Multi-Cultural Lawyering. We have learned much about multi-cultural lawyering in the 30-plus years since Watergate, but we are still in the embryonic stages. In the following article, a clinical professor attempts to come up with some answers for how lawyers can bridge experiential, cultural, and perceptual gaps today.

---

[8] *United States v. Barker*, 514 F.2d 208 (D.C. Cir. 1975).

CARINA WENG, MULTICULTURAL LAWYERING: TEACHING PSYCHOLOGY TO DEVELOP CULTURAL SELF-AWARENESS
11 Clinical Law Review 369 (2005)[9]

Crafting a good solution to a client's problem could require familiarity with more than just the relevant legal facts; indeed, familiarity with more facts about the client's situation could determine whether the lawyer even is thinking about the right legal claim. . . . [C]lient-centered models of lawyering have [now] developed. The first model, promulgated by Binder and Price,[10] (hereinafter the Binder-Price model) recognizes that the client has superior knowledge about her values, goals and situation, which will enable her to better choose a satisfactory resolution. . . .

However, the original formulation of client-centered lawyering was often inapt, at least as applied to clients many students encounter in clinical and legal services practice. Critics noted that the Binder-Price model conceptualized the client as a copy of the lawyer, minus the legal know-how. This copy shared the lawyer's socioeconomic status, perspective, organizational modes, etc. — for example, related his situation in clear, chronological order — and thus was ready, willing, and able to participate in the lawyering model promulgated by Binder and Price. Other clients, who might ramble, evince reluctance to discuss certain topics or to commence an interview, lie, or display anger or hostility were, in the Binder-Price parlance, "difficult" and "atypical."

The early Binder-Price model does offer some explanation as to why clients might be 'difficult,' but the reasons do not take into account culture, whether based on race, socioeconomic status, or other factors, except age. The model thus ignores the fact that culture and other power and privilege differences also affect the client's participation in the lawyering relationship . . . .

In *Constructions of the Client within Legal Education*, Ann Shalleck points out that this undifferentiated model of client-centered lawyering in fact maintains the lawyer as the dominant player. She notes that the model favors a chronological narrative over other forms of storytelling, depends on the lawyer to determine the importance of both legal and nonlegal concerns, assumes a standardized client, and ignores power imbalances. . . .[11]

Concerns about a "one-size-fits-all" training model arose among mental health professionals before they arose among law clinicians. Derald and David Sue warned that an 'ethnocentric' model of counseling teaches students to practice in a way that can harm their clients. The model views the experiences of clients of color "from the 'White, European-American perspective'. . . . [and] the focus tends to be on their pathological lifestyles and/or a maintenance of false stereotypes." For example, a counselor might view a patient's reluctance to self-disclose as paranoia, when in fact that reluctance might be "a healthy reaction to racism" from the counselor. . . .

---

[9] Copyright © 2005 by Clinical Law Review, Inc. Reprinted by permission.

[10] [FN27] David A. Binder & Susan C. Price, *Legal Interviewing and Counseling: A Client-Centered Approach* (1977).

[11] [FN35] Ann Shalleck, "Constructions of the Client within Legal Education," 45 Stan. L. Rev. 1731, 1742-48 (1993).

Small wonder, then, that Michelle Jacobs should find the Binder-Price client-centered model troubling when applied to the primary consumer at her clinic, namely poor, black clients. Jacobs reminds us that clients labeled difficult by textbooks espousing client-centered lawyering might be resisting the lawyer's invitation to participate in the lawyering process. Rather than dismiss the client as difficult, lawyers need to ask ourselves why the client might be resisting our invitation. Might the client's response be a reaction to behavior by the lawyer who fails to recognize "the real client in her full context — culturally, politically and economically?" Or based on the client's perception of a lawyer who is culturally different from her?

. . . . Jacobs' and Shalleck's critiques raise questions about how well the standard model of client-centered lawyering works with clients who are disenfranchised and often economically and racially/ethnically diverse from their lawyers. Even though client-centered lawyering focuses on respecting and empowering the client, it does not address the dynamics of power and subordination (historical, actual, or perceived) in the attorney-client interaction. Thus, suggestions to improve client-centered lawyering also draw on the theory of rebellious lawyering. . . . With rebellious lawyering, the emphasis is on the client: How the client's life — including her membership in an outsider group and her group's history of subordination — defines the legal problem, generates the solutions, and determines the course of action. With this emphasis, the client might more effectively participate as an equal in the decision-making process.

. . . .

Building this bridge is not an easy task. Empathy and active listening may elicit more details from the client, and questioning the premises of the American legal system may help the lawyer consciously to avoid its biases. But the lawyer's cultural lens will operate automatically to filter this information and to create expectations about the lawyer-client interaction. So, unless the lawyer understands her own culture and the ways it affects her interactions with others, she risks perpetuating the status quo of discrimination.

. . . .

Training in multicultural lawyering brings together [many] approaches. . . . As a starting point, multiculturalists focus on a broad understanding of culture as "unstated assumptions, shared values, and characteristic ways of perceiving the world that are normally taken for granted by its members." Multicultural lawyering training teaches the student to be aware of the cultural basis for his own behavior and champions using "a 'cultural lens' as a central focus of professional behavior . . . recogniz[ing] that all individuals including themselves are influenced by different contexts, including the historical, ecological, sociopolitical, and disciplinary." Thus, the student develops a "personal-cultural orientation" toward lawyering in which she considers how her and others' behavior is guided by culturally learned expectations and values. With such knowledge and regular practice, the student is better equipped to develop more accurate decision making that is less biased by the cultural backgrounds of either the lawyer or the client or by the complexity of the problem presented. . . .

For practical guidance to develop cultural self-awareness, student "lawyers" can turn to the five habits for cross-cultural lawyering that Bryant and Jean Koh Peters have devised. . . . For example, Habit 1, Degrees of Separation and Connection, . . . asks students to identify similarities and differences between the student and the client and to consider how these aspects affect information gathering/processing and professional distance/judgment. By deliberately identifying similarities and differences, the lawyer can challenge assumptions about himself and the client, probe for facts, and lawyer based on fact. Habit 5, The Camel's Back, encourages cultural self-awareness, specifically with regard to bias and stereotype. First, the student identifies factors like stress, lack of control, and burn out that disrupt the lawyer-client interaction and make bias and stereotype more likely to intrude. That identification permits proactive efforts to minimize future interference. Second, and in conjunction with Habit 1, the student identifies client traits and personal traits that cause the lawyer to treat the client with insensitivity. . . .

The Psychological Underpinnings of Multicultural Lawyering Training

Why is some understanding of cognitive and social psychology necessary? Because, currently in our society, we typically do not discriminate intentionally against people who differ from ourselves. So, lawyers treat clients in culturally insensitive ways due to "unconscious or aversive racism," which can stem from categorization errors that characterize cognitive functioning and from unconscious tendencies to favor members of social groups similar to themselves over members of other groups. Learning more about these psychological processes provides a basis for understanding how lawyers behave in ways that cause discrimination and, therefore, how to assess their own beliefs and lawyering practices.

A lawyer who understands that he has subconscious cognitive categories — called schemas — and that the way he automatically employs them can cause subordinating treatment might be less defensive about acknowledging that his behavior is discriminatory. In addition, awareness of how a schema is created might enable a dominant-culture lawyer to understand how that culture influences the contents of his schemas and to make conscious efforts to diversify his interactions and to question the contents of his schemas in an effort to act with more accuracy regarding members of different cultures. Such a change could more easily allow the client's life, including her membership in an outsider group and that group's history of subordination, to define the legal problem, generate the solutions, and determine the course of action.

NOTES

The adjectives "difficult" and "atypical," as much as anything else, bring home the point of the last article that client-centered lawyering is not nearly enough to succeed in providing lawyering that is both client-sensitive and culturally sensitive and sophisticated. We provide our own personal example.

Some years ago, one of us, hired as an ethics and malpractice avoidance speaker on behalf of an insurance company, was touring California giving presentations with a colleague about the need to get conflict of interest waivers and fee agreements in writing. All went well until we got to a town in California's central valley, where, ten minutes into our presentation, one lawyer stood up and asked this question: "That's all well and good if you're dealing with Western culture. But we have many Hmong clients and it simply doesn't work this way in their culture. How do we make our ethical requirements conform to their cultural needs?" This thoughtful and caring question took over the entirety of our three-hour program, and while we can't say that we answered it, the attempt to address client needs on the client's own home ground made better lawyers of us all.

6. Lawyer-Client Dialogues Across Cultural Lines. In this interesting role-playing piece, a group of clinical law professors attempt to show by two dialogues how difficult bridging cultural gaps can be — and why it is of paramount importance not to make assumptions, since superficial similarities can easily turn out to be differences. Read the two scenarios described below and the professors' comments. See if they help you gain a better understanding for how the two lawyers in our problems might approach their clients.

ROBERT DINERSTEIN, STEPHEN ELLMANN, ISABELLE GUNNING, & ANN SHALLECK, CONNECTION, CAPACITY AND MORALITY IN LAWYER-CLIENT RELATIONSHIPS: DIALOGUES AND COMMENTARY
10 Clinical Law Review 755 (2004)[12]

In the following dialogue, Allen Anderson, an employment discrimination attorney, is a white male in his 40's who, due to a shooting, cannot walk and uses a wheel chair. His client, Anthony Braxton, is also a white male and in a wheel chair, but in his late 20's. The encounter between Anderson and Braxton reflects that there can be even more challenging divisions for lawyers searching for ways to connect with their clients — despite profound similarities that lawyer and client may also share:

L1: Hello, Mr. Braxton. Come in. Ah! I see I don't have to offer you a chair since you like me have brought your own. Get comfortable here.

C1: Mr Anderson, I hadn't realized when I called to make an appointment that you were in a wheelchair too. Call me Tony.

L2: Tony it is and I am Al. And yes, I was the victim of a shooting in my teens. Wrong place at the wrong time. But I didn't let that stop me from finishing college and going on to law school.

C2: I respect that a lot. I was in a car accident. I would have been a pro football player but for it. I had been picked in the draft and everything. But with a lot of prayer and help from friends and family and God, I got through and have recreated my life as a stock broker. I work for a large company . . . where I have had my troubles.

L3: My staff told me that this was an employment discrimination case. Does your boss know nothing of the Americans with Disabilities Act?

---

[12] Copyright © 2004 by Clinical Law Review, Inc. Reprinted by permission.

C3: It's not that, Al. At least I don't think so. The head of our firm is a born-again Christian. He is a member of Pat Robertson's church, and he hates gays and lesbians. He thought I was great, wheelchair and all, when I was hired because he saw me as a church-going former football player. Which of course is exactly what I am. But I am also gay and when he found that out . . . well, everything changed and my work life became hell.

L4: Uh, well . . . Mr. Braxton. I think it only fair to tell you that I too am a member of Reverend Robertson's church. My religious views on homosexuality are separate from my job in helping you make sure that your boss follows the law.

Here Al Anderson starts out assuming that he and his client, Tony Braxton, could identify very closely as physically challenged men who, through faith, have overcome difficulties to create successful careers, only to discover that other differences — their different sexual orientations and different moral and religious views on this — may cause them to be quite distant. These differences alone may make Anderson feel that Braxton is in the "we have nothing in common" category, although clearly as a factual matter that is not true. Anderson will have to think carefully and honestly about whether his religious beliefs will allow him to zealously represent his client. . . .

This aspect of the Anderson-Braxton relationship highlights the reality that while lawyers can and should work to bridge differences with their clients, they must also be prepared for the possibility that some differences are unbridgeable. Just as Braxton may be unable to trust Anderson, so Anderson may be unable to fully commit himself to representing Braxton. Again, self-awareness and honesty are key.

Here, Anderson has not revealed the details of his religiously based moral code other than to implicitly confirm that it views homosexuality in some kind of negative light. Whether Anderson should politely refuse to represent Braxton is highly contextualized — as the specifics of any attorney-client relationship are. The key issue for the lawyer is not what outside observers might conclude about the fundamental tenets of his church, but how Anderson understands whatever those tenets are. While there may be some church doctrine that reflects a disapproval of gay and lesbian people or homosexual behavior, there probably are also tenets on the connection between all people in the eyes of God and the primacy of love as a moving force in one's life. How Anderson understands and balances these two broad moral approaches will be decisive for his ability to represent Braxton. If Anderson's disapproval of homosexual behavior means that he, personally, dislikes anyone he discovers is gay or lesbian and feels a discomfort with and disrespect for them, then he needs to let Braxton find an attorney who can represent him with zeal. On the other hand, Anderson, who is a civil rights attorney, may find that his religious views are more focused on the aspects of brotherly love. He could decide that their shared physical challenges and the ways in which both men have relied on God and faith to succeed constitute a much greater connecting force than their differences around their sexual orientations. . . .

You are, of course, always "getting to know the client" as an interview progresses, and part of what you may get to know is about difference, as in the following conversation, which takes place in the office of attorney Bryan

Culbert in Seattle, Washington, sometime in late November or early December of 1999:

L1: (After greetings and small talk) Ms. Yamashita, how can I help you?

C1: Well, Mr. Culbert, I was arrested. It is an absolute outrage! And frankly I may want to sue the Seattle police.

L2: I see. You have been arrested and feel that this was unjust. Do you have a lawyer for the criminal matter? And by the way, what were you arrested for?

C2: Destruction of property, assault, resisting arrest. I was arrested near the World Bank meetings during the demonstrations downtown. And the cops just went wild! I don't have a lawyer for the arrest; that's why I came to you but I want to sue as well. I mean what happened to the First Amendment?

L3: Okay. Well, let's start with the criminal matter first since that will move faster than any civil matter we might choose to bring and, frankly, the outcome of the criminal case may well affect our civil case.

C3: What?! You mean I can't sue the cops for beating me because they made up these charges?

L4: No. But if we don't "beat" the criminal charges, so to speak, while you can sue, a judge or jury may, I stress may, feel that whatever injuries you suffered were within the officer's line of duty because you assaulted him or her or were destroying property. So we can sue, but our case is harder. Remember there was a good deal of publicity around the demonstrations opposing the World Bank and International Monetary Fund economic policies in third world countries. Some people already believe that the Seattle cops lost it with the protestors. And that will help us. But others think that the protestors got out of line, but even here we can focus in on you and your behavior and your right to protest peacefully and be treated with respect and dignity regardless of how others were behaving. But let's get back to the criminal situation — you were arrested demonstrating against the World Bank and the cops roughed you up. Tell me exactly what you were doing in the demonstration when the cops approached you and what they said and did.

C4: And here is my problem again! I was not demonstrating! I'm a reporter for . . . .

[Here,] Culbert is confronted with a client who is quite upset about her criminal case and the circumstances of her arrest. Culbert immediately starts using active listening (L2); he mirrors his client's statement of fact by restating the substance ("you were arrested") and he identifies the feelings she expressed ("and you feel that this was unjust"). His client, Yamashita, is so angry that she is focused on a civil case rather than the more pressing criminal matter. Culbert, in his attempt both to calm her down and to redirect her attention to the criminal case, makes some logical assumptions about what happened. If she was arrested during the demonstrations against the World Bank and IMF policies, it's likely that she was participating in the demonstrations. But in fact this didn't have to be the case. The effects of demonstrations, and police action directed at them, can involve local residents and bystanders as well as demonstrators (and this was true in Seattle in 1999).

In this case, the logical but incorrect assumption has managed to offend the client because, unbeknownst to the lawyer, the client feels that the crux of her case rests on inappropriate stereotyping and racial assumptions. You could imagine, too, that if Yamashita had not had a legitimate reason for being out past curfew — if she was neither lawfully working nor engaged in civil disobedience — the lawyer could have missed an opportunity to explore what she in fact was doing out on the streets. What if Yamashita were a drug dealer and was working, but not lawfully so? Culbert's defense might still focus in on all the confusion of the Seattle demonstrations but if he had not asked his client about her activities in an open and nonjudgmental manner, he would not be prepared for any "surprises" about his client's history. He would generally be better off if he explored carefully whether or not his client really was on the street for the demonstrations rather than making even plausible, but premature, assumptions. Having made this mistake, however, he now must try to recover from it:

L5: Ms. Yamashita, I am sorry. I shouldn't have assumed. You said First Amendment and I heard right to protest when you were talking about freedom of the press. Both important rights. Again I'm sorry. Let's back up. What were you doing that night exactly?

C5: I was downtown at about 8 PM. It was after curfew but it was clear there were protestors out and I wanted to . . . well, do my job. Observe what actions they were engaged in. Maybe interview people. Some were obviously our own homegrown petty criminals out looting, but some people were mad and were able to tell me about their issues.

L6: And that means you were doing what . . . walking or in a car? On the streets or inside stores or what?

C6: I was walking. I had left my car so that I could really see what people were doing. I did not go into any stores because they were all closed. I just talked to people I saw on the street.

L7: What happened right before the police approached you?

C7: I was talking with some people who were real protestors when some other people came and broke a store window. I was trying to call to my photographer who was with me but way down the street. And then I started to shout to the people going in. Saying things like, "What are you doing? Is this part of your protest? How does breaking into a store help your cause?" And then the police came.

L8: Did you say who you were as soon as you saw them?

C8: Why? I'm black so I have to identify myself as legitimate?

L9: No, but you were out past curfew and as you said, you were near people who had broken into a store. The cops could make an honest mistake given the heat of the moment.

C9: Yeah, well. . . . I didn't see them right away. I was trying to stop the looters from going in and the cops came from behind and grabbed me and threw me to the ground. And that is when I said "Hey! I'm a reporter! I'm not with them!"

L10: Did they hear you?

C10: Of course they heard me! I was screaming as one would if your arms were twisted and you had been thrown down. They didn't care!

L11: Okay, I'm sorry. I'm just trying to get a sense of what it was like out there. And these are questions — how easily able the cops were to hear you — that will come up and we have to be ready for them. What did they say to you when you said that you were a reporter?

C11: Well there were two on me. One guy, the older one, was saying "Shut up, bitch!" And the other guy was trying to cuff me. The one who said shut up, hit me too. And I screamed again that I was a reporter and the younger guy pulled out my press badge which was on a chain around my neck and started to say something like "It does say she's a reporter" and the older cop said "what!" and looked at the badge for . . . less than a second and said "Yamashita! Her! She stole that to sneak through. Take her and let's get her friends." And then they took me to the police van.

L12: Did either of these officers hit you again or say anything to you as they took you to the van?

From the conversations, we can tell that Yamashita is mixed race, African American and Asian American, and we can infer that she "looks" black. Culbert's race is unknown, but it is apparent that he is not black. That is clear from Yamashita's reaction to his question about identifying herself to the police (C8), a reaction whose heat suggests that she does not feel she is talking to someone who can identify with the problem of being presumptively perceived to be "up to no good" rather than an "upright citizen." Had Culbert been African American, he might have been able to ask the same question about identifying herself without getting quite the same reaction of anger and resentment. Then Yamashita might have assumed that he knows law enforcement shouldn't be that way but that he himself has had to endure such questions just to ensure his own safety when stopped by the police. Context matters. But it is important to note that non-black Culbert uses other skills in the face of his client's misunderstanding of his intent. He freely apologizes for his initial mistaken assumption about her involvement in the demonstration (L5), and apologizes again for another question that annoys her, even though he thinks he had a good reason for the question (L11). And in each case he also provides the legitimate explanation for his questions without resentment. These kinds of reactions can go a long way in encouraging a client, over time, to trust you even if your initial interactions have been less than ideal.

7. The Arrival of Global Law. As attorney Kayla Hotchkiss struggles with how to get a frame of reference to assist her in helping her client, she will not be alone. Professor Laurel S. Terry, our foremost expert on ethics and globalization, has looked at the history of American legal ethics and sees a strong movement towards international comparative analysis because of the growing number of lawyers working globally. Read the brief excerpt below.

LAUREL S. TERRY, U.S. LEGAL ETHICS: THE COMING OF AGE OF GLOBAL AND COMPARATIVE PERSPECTIVES
4 Washington University Global Studies Law Review 463 (2005)[13]

In order to understand why there may have been a sea change in the nature of the U.S. legal ethics dialogue, it is useful to examine the current practice context for lawyers. Recent U.S. trade statistics help explain the importance of global and comparative legal ethics discussions because they reveal a significant amount of both inbound and outbound international trade by clients. . . . International trade has increased significantly over the past few decades, with a forty-three-fold increase in exports between 1960 and 2004 and a seventy-seven-fold increase in imports during this period. . . .

Another important development that affects the practice context in which lawyers work is the dramatic increase in the foreign-born U.S. population. . . . Since the last census . . . a 57% increase . . . This increase has affected large states and small states, states on the coasts and states such as Missouri, that are in the middle of the country. . . .

Logic and the data . . . suggest that individual clients, as well as business clients, are increasingly likely to need the services of both U.S. and foreign lawyers. Some of these foreign born individuals may need to handle family matters in their home country at some point in their lives, such as inheritance or custody matters. In a business context, foreign born residents may be more likely to set up joint ventures, distributorship relationships, or other business relationships, with individuals in their home countries. When they do so, U.S. lawyers may find themselves working with lawyers from other countries.

Given the dramatic increase in international trade of goods and services and the movement of individuals across borders, it should come as no surprise that there also has been a dramatic increase in the amount of international trade in legal services. For example, U.S. statistics show $3.37 billion in outbound U.S. legal services trade in 2003 and $879 million in inbound U.S. legal services trade. . . .

Moreover, the increase in international legal services trade has not been limited to the United States. . . . Trade in legal services has also been significantly growing in other countries [including, significantly] Hong Kong, China . . . and Australia. . . . Because of the dramatic increase in legal services trade, it should come as no surprise to learn that foreign offices of law firms have grown dramatically, even within the past five years. For example, Carole Silver recently reported that for a group of forty-seven U.S. law firms with foreign branch offices in London, the average firm size in 1999 was twenty lawyers; five years later, in 2004, it was forty-four lawyers.In the two years between 1998 and 2000, U.S. law firms opened forty-one new foreign offices.

What is even more striking is the degree to which law firms are truly global. Of the ten largest law firms in the world, all had offices in ten or more countries. Strikingly, six of the world's ten highest-grossing law firms had more than 50% of their lawyers working in countries outside of the firm's home country.

---

[13] Copyright © 2005 by Washington University. Reprinted by permission.

8. The Impact of U.S. Foreign Policy. Not only does young attorney Hotchkiss need to be mindful of cultural differences, developing new communication skills, especially the listening ones, culturally-biased thought processes on both sides, culturally diverse business practices, and long-distance communication in the global marketplace (among many other issues), she may also need to be sensitive to American and Japanese treaty and trade regulations and — like it or not — American foreign policy itself. The following cites but one example of the problem.

CLAYTON COLLINS, NOW, BEING A YANKEE ISN'T DANDY
Christian Science Monitor (June 28, 2004)[14]

After 14 years of regular travel to Brazil, Andrew Odell was thunderstruck by what he found there on a trip last month. "I have never run into such a consensus view on US politics," says the contract negotiator and partner at Bryan Cave, a New York law firm. "People condemn the US (for its Middle East policy), and are frightened by the US."

In subtle and not-so-subtle ways, America's troubled world standing is beginning to color its business relationships abroad. So far, the practical impact seems minimal. Many executives, including Mr. Odell, see their foreign counterparts distinguishing politics from business — especially when a cheap dollar makes American goods and services attractive overseas.

On the other hand, perceptions count. In what many view as an era of bold political unilateralism by the United States, negotiators working cross-border deals for US firms in Latin America, Europe, and Asia now find themselves facing a precipitous shift in their homeland's image abroad. And they're struggling with whether and how to adjust to it.

"I would say it creates a backlash for everybody in an interdependent world," says Bruce Patton, deputy director of the Harvard Negotiation Project in Cambridge, Mass. "If you're a really big kid and you don't lean over backward not to be coercive, people think you're a bully. . . . If you get what you want just because you can, they hate you for it."

That's what appears to be happening with America's image abroad. For example, only 15 percent of Indonesians felt somewhat favorable or very favorable toward the US, down from 61 percent a year earlier. The Roper survey of 30,000 people in 30 countries also found declines in non-Muslim countries: Russia, down 25 percentage points; France, down 20 points; Italy, down 10.

"Overseas, they perceive Americans as being aggressive and uncompromising," says Sheida Hodge, managing director of the cross-cultural division for Berlitz International in Princeton, N.J. Ms. Hodge spent the last half of 2003 on the road. "Everywhere I went I heard the same thing: 'Americans want to have their way.' The Japanese tell you; the Chinese tell you; the French tell you."

. . . .

---

[14] Copyright © 2004 Christian Science Monitor. All rights reserved. Reprinted with permission.

Some observers say overseas companies are simply pessimistic about whether the US can sustain its recovery, with crude-oil prices at historic highs, and don't see the US as a place to invest serious money. Others attribute it to a less hospitable US stance toward foreign business since 9/11.

But a Harvard Business School study released early this year suggested only minimal effects from overseas anger at the US. In 12 countries, only 12 percent of consumers preferred a local brand to a global (often US) brand. One reason the backlash is minimal, experts suggest, is that many US multinationals, such as Eastman Kodak, have worked hard to establish a local identity in the countries where they operate.

The question is whether consumer antipathy will grow — and how American business should react.

Instead of a softer stance, one emerging school of negotiating calls for tougher tactics. According to this view, the US is losing business because its win-win approach fails overseas.

"So often, especially where culture is used as a barrier, the excuse is that 'Well, it's our culture, so you have to give us something. It's our culture, so in order for you to do business here, you're going to have to compromise,' " says Jim Camp, a negotiating coach in Vero Beach, Fla., and author of the contrarian new book "Start with No."

Mr. Camp, who has worked with nearly 200 public-and private-sector clients, cites a major American supplier to the photographic-instruments industry. "That American supplier has not had one year of profitability in the past nine years," he says. "They've had a win-win mind-set, and they've compromised away their margins of profit. . . . They'll cut their price trying to get someone to like them."

But other dealmakers aren't panicked. Experts say that it's still about individual relationships built on mutual respect and trust. And anecdotes suggest that America may still have some goodwill to draw upon.

. . . .

"People can separate what they feel about the current administration's politics from their desire to do a deal," says [another American lawyer].

NOTES

Do you think that if America is unpopular in the eyes of most of the world that unpopularity can materially hurt international negotiations, or is it still, as one commentator put it, a matter of personal relationships? While a negotiating attitude of "Start With No" would seem to perpetuate the "bully" image of Americans and be antithetical to bridging cross-cultural gaps, is it possible that Americans *do* start by giving away too much? Is it possible that this is a viable principle for American lawyers? Or would we be better off sticking with increased cross-cultural understanding and better communication skills?

SUPPLEMENTAL READINGS

1. Kimberley Crenshaw, *Mapping the Margins: Intersectionality, Identity Politics, and Violence Against Women of Color*, 43 Stan. L. Rev. 1241 (1991), and Leslie Espinoza Garvey, *The Race Card: Dealing with Domestic Violence in the Courts*, 11 Am. U. J. Gender Soc. Pol'y & L. 287 (2003), are two extremely valuable pieces that help think through the issues of cross-cultural lawyering in domestic violence cases. Crenshaw's article, now 15 years old, was an important groundbreaking work and is still valuable.

2. Blanca M. Ramos, *Acculturation and Depression Among Puerto Ricans in the Mainland*, 6/1/05 Soc. Work Research 95 (2005), describes the distinctive manner in which depression manifests itself for Puerto Ricans who have moved to the mainland. Although it is written for social workers, it discusses the challenges all professional service providers face in understanding how their clients are experiencing their services.

3. Susan Bryant, *The Five Habits: Building Cross-Cultural Competence in Lawyers*, 8 Clin. L. Rev. 33 (2001). This groundbreaking article, referenced above in the Readings, contains a full explanation of the five principal cross-cultural habits. The article is the product of years of teaching cross-cultural lawyering and has become the cornerstone for those interested in a successful methodology for doing that.

4. On the issues of race and gender and differences in communication, see, among other good pieces in the field, Leslie Espinoza & Angela P. Harris, *Afterword: Embracing the Tar-Baby — LatCrit Theory and the Sticky Mess of Race,* 10 La Raza L. J. 499 (1998), 85 Cal. L. Rev. 1585 (1997), and Bryna Bogoch, *Gendered Lawyering: Difference and Dominance in Lawyer-Client Interaction*, 31 Law & Soc'y Rev. 677, 681 (1997).

5. Robert E. Lutz, Philip T. von Mehren, Laurel S. Terry, Peter Ehrenhaft, Carole Silver, Clifford J. Hendel, Jonathan Goldsmith & Masahiro Shimojo, have written an ambitious and comprehensive work, *Transnational Legal Practice Developments*, 39 Int'l Law. 619 (2005), that attempts to provide an up to date review of international and domestic regulatory schemes that affect lawyers engaged in international multijurisdictional practice. This report, written for the American Bar Association, explains the history and development of WTO negotiations designed to liberalize "trade in services," or the work lawyers do across international lines. The United States is not included in these various agreements because our individual states insist on regulating the practice of law within their jurisdictions. The article points out that while the ABA supports the federalistic regulation of legal services in the United States, it also urges all states to adopt rules permitting foreign lawyers to open offices to practice as "foreign legal consultants" (FLCs) without taking a U.S. qualification examination. By the beginning of 2005, 24 jurisdictions (23 states and the District of Columbia) had FLC rules in place — states that have in the ABA's estimate 80 percent of the U.S. "market for legal services" overseas, including New York, California, Illinois, and Texas.

PART TWO
BALANCING THE DUTY OF ADVOCACY WITH THE DUTY TO THE LEGAL SYSTEM

"The most difficult ethical dilemmas result from the frequent conflicts between the obligation to one's client and those to the legal system and to society. It is in this area that legal education has its greatest responsibility, and can have its greatest effects."

—Jack B. Weinstein, 1975

Chapter 6

WHAT PRICE TRUTH? WHAT PRICE JUSTICE? WHAT PRICE ADVOCACY?

PROBLEM 14

May a lawyer represent a client he or she firmly believes to be guilty? Or knows in fact is guilty? How far should or must the lawyer go in representing such a client? What if the lawyer finds the client to be personally distasteful, even repugnant? In the following hypothetical, a lawyer who represents such a criminal client must decide how far to go in presenting a defense in which the lawyer does not believe, in cross-examining a truthful witness, and in arguing the case. As you reflect on this situation, consider how much you would or should do for such a client. If you provide vigorous representation to a client who is "bad" or "guilty," are you then aligned with that client? Do you abdicate your role as a seeker of justice? Or should the client's conduct and personality not make any difference, because of the job you have to do?

How Far Should Richie Go to Get His Client Off?

It is the question perhaps most frequently asked of lawyers: "How can you justify representing someone you're convinced is guilty?" Richie Richewski has heard it hundreds of times, at friends' cocktail parties, his kids' soccer games, wherever he goes in his life away from the courthouse. To Richie, the answers are clear, but many lawyers are themselves uncomfortable with these questions, and would never do what Richie Richewski does for a living.

Simeon "Richie" Richewski is one of the most respected criminal defense lawyers in River City. Although he is a private lawyer, not a public defender, he accepts more than his share of "assigned cases" where he's appointed by the court. These cases don't pay very well, but Richie likes the work more than defending wealthy clients accused of drunk driving, or white collar embezzlement cases. Richie often says that assigned cases are "what doing criminal defense work is all about."

Not all of Richie's cases are a walk in the park, however, and Kirk Hopman is a case in point. Richie has been appointed by the court to represent Hopman on three counts of child abuse with great bodily injury. The indictment charges that on several occasions, Hopman struck his girlfriend Rowena Soo's three-year-old child, and once threw the child against the walls of their apartment, causing brain damage. Soo is also accused and faces the same charges, though the deputy D.A. assigned to the case has made it clear that she considers Hopman the perpetrator and Soo only an aider and abettor.

In a jail conference room, Hopman denies he did anything wrong, but tells a story that includes several factual inconsistencies. Richie is almost certain that Hopman is guilty, but can't be absolutely sure, since Hopman denies everything. Richie finds the allegations repugnant. Besides, though he likes most of his clients, Richie finds Hopman manipulative and demanding. Nevertheless, Richie knows that there are "winning chances" if the case goes to trial, because the witnesses against his client — especially the one witness who claims to have seen Hopman actually "tossing that kid around" — are "flaky," not exactly model citizens, the type of witnesses Richie knows he has an excellent chance of impeaching successfully.

1. At the pretrial conference, should Richie convince Hopman to accept a guilty plea? May he go to trial with a client whom he is convinced is guilty? Or whom he finds personally repugnant?

2. Assume that at the pretrial conference, Hopman insists on going to trial, but Soo pleads guilty and agrees to testify against Hopman. Since the district attorney has a policy of only accepting "packaged deals," allowing a plea bargain only if both defendants agree to it, she refuses to negotiate with Soo. The judge, however, tells Soo that she will consider probation after the trial if Soo pleads guilty. Given no alternative other than trial, Soo "pleads to the sheet" — that is, she pleads guilty to all of the charges, including that Soo personally committed great bodily injury on her own child, even though she has steadfastly denied this, and even though the DA herself believes the perpetrator was Hopman.

Richie realizes that although Soo will testify against Hopman, her guilty plea could help create a reasonable doubt defense that Soo, not Hopman, committed the injuries. After all, reasons Richie, he can use Soo's plea to the sheet as an admission that she herself caused her son's injuries. May Richie use this defense? Should he? *Must* he? Should he come out "with both guns blazing" in cross-examination of Soo even if he believes Hopman, not Soo, caused the injuries? How vigorously can he argue to the jury that Hopman is not guilty?

3. Assume that on the eve of trial, Hopman admits to Richie that he took Soo's child in a fit of rage and threw him against the wall, and that he had "hit the child a few other times pretty hard" in the past. Does this change how Richie deals with the plea bargain? If Richie and Hopman decide that Hopman will not testify at trial, may Richie still try the case? Or vigorously cross-examine the independent witnesses? What about the cross-examination of Soo and the argument that Soo committed the acts? Is there a difference in how vigorously Richie may argue to the jury that Hopman is not guilty?

READINGS

1. The "Adversary Theorem" Revisited. We began Part II of this book by reprising the quote from New York federal judge Jack B. Weinstein that we first encountered in one of the *Belge* opinions in Problem 4. Judge Weinstein's remark was as accurate today as when it was written a quarter century ago. In Chapter One, we called balancing advocacy for our client on one hand and our duty to society and the legal system on the other "the central ethical question." Weinstein takes this one step further, describing this "dilemma," in essence, as the most important issue in legal education.

The traditional adversary role of lawyers — and the traditional concept that lawyers best act in the public interest when they diligently and zealously serve the needs of their clients — has been seriously challenged continually since the attacks in the early 1970s by such people as Ralph Nader and "Nader Raider" and legal commentator Mark Green, who twenty years later became Ombudsman for the City of New York. It was the era of Watergate, a time when lawyers in the Nixon administration were being accused of highly unethical conduct. But the most telling criticisms of the profession have come not from journalists, commentators, or consumer spokespersons, but from the public itself — the average legal consumer who either uses the services of lawyers or falls victim to them. Not surprisingly, to the average member of the public, the O.J. Simpson trial and others like it define the American justice system.

The negative image of the legal profession has grown steadily in the last three decades, as the average layperson began asking questions about why lawyers do what they do. Many of these questions are the ones we address in this critical part of this volume: Are lawyers ever justified in helping their clients lie? Can they justify hiding the truth? Do they ever have a duty to reveal the truth? How much trickery can they use and then justify in the name of "strategy" or "tactics"? How nasty or "hardball" can they be in representing their clients, even if it means hurting innocent people? Is the analysis the same or different when comparing the lawyer who represents a corporation that is stealing money from its shareholders or worse, promoting cigarettes to minors, as opposed to the lawyer who represents the factually guilty criminal defendant? And, of course, how can lawyers zealously and aggressively represent criminal defendants whom they know to be guilty?

2. Is Advocacy a Search for Truth? In his 1975 book *The Other Government*, Mark Green launched an overt attack on the adversarial system. He argued that when influential Washington law firms lobbied against the public interest on behalf of powerful clients such as the Tobacco Institute or major car manufacturers, the lawyers did so as "a matter of personal choice, not professional compulsion." Green argued that these lawyers should be held morally responsible for assisting such clients. He wanted these lawyers to "make a judgment about the likely impact on the public" of their representation, and to withdraw their representation if the client wanted to act in a way which would create a "demonstrable though avoidable public harm." Among the lawyers he criticized was Lloyd Cutler, who lobbied on behalf of General Motors to postpone automobile safety regulations, and whose offices were picketed, spawning the debate between Monroe Freedman and Michael Tigar that is referred to in Problem 2. Two decades later, as one of Washington's most highly respected lawyers, Cutler agreed to become President Clinton's chief White House counsel to help increase White House credibility during the Whitewater controversy.

Among the lawyers responding to attacks like Green's was Simon Rifkind, a highly respected attorney, political advisor, and observer of the legal scene, and the guiding force of one of New York's most powerful law firms. He articulated a cogent and thought-provoking counterattack, a portion of which is reproduced below.

SIMON H. RIFKIND, THE LAWYER'S ROLE AND RESPONSIBILITY IN MODERN SOCIETY

30 The Record of the Association of the Bar of the City of New York 534 (1975)[1]

"How could you represent so-and-so?" is a question frequently put to me. . . . The tone of voice which accompanies the question sufficiently discloses that the questioner has consigned the client to some subhuman category of untouchables.

As you know, there are fashions in untouchability. One season it is a sharecropper in Mississippi, the next season it is a multi-million share corporation in Detroit. From the viewpoint of the adversary system, the applicable principle is the same.

. . . .

Recently, a group of law students picketed a prominent Washington lawyer [Cutler] in order to give expression to their disapproval of his representation of a large corporation. Had they mastered the meaning of the adversary system they would have known that their conduct was subversive of the central tenet of the profession they were about to enter.

. . . .

Experience tells me that the adversary system has been good for liberty, good for peaceful progress and good enough to have the public accept that system's capacity to resolve controversies and, generally, to acquiesce in the results.

Those who have voiced [contrary] views have not taken account of the operation of the adversary process. The utility of that process is that it relieves the lawyer of the need, or indeed the right, to be his client's judge and thereby frees him to be the more effective advocate and champion. Since the same is true of his adversary, it should follow that the judge who will decide will be aided by greater illumination than otherwise would be available.

Lord MacMillan in his famous address on the ethics of advocacy delivered in 1916 quotes this exchange:

> *Boswell:* "But what do you think of supporting a cause which you know to be bad?"

> *Johnson:* "Sir, you do not know it to be good or bad till the judge determines it. You are to state facts clearly; so that your *thinking*, or what you call *knowing*, a cause to be bad must be from reasoning, must be from supposing your arguments to be weak and inconclusive. But, sir, that is not enough. An argument which does not convince yourself may convince the judge to whom you urge it; and if it does convince him, why then, sir, you are wrong and he is right. It is his business to judge; and you are not to be confident in your opinion that a cause is bad, but to say all you can for your client, and then hear the judge's opinion."

---

[1] Copyright © 1975 by The Association of the Bar of the City of New York. Reprinted by permission.

. . . .

This change in the professional wind has caused to bloom a body of lawyers who call themselves public interest lawyers. Instead of advancing the cause of a client who has selected the lawyer as his advocate, the public interest lawyer selects the client and advances his own cause. He pretends to serve an invisible client, the public interest. . . . Inevitably the lawyer is driven to identify his predilections with the public interest. That is unctuous.

. . . . [T]he most baffling problem of substance is how to locate the public interest. It simply will not do to accept a set of simplistic labels and to decide, a priori, that in a contest between an employer and an employee the public interest demands that the employee shall always prevail; or that in a landlord-tenant controversy, the latter is always to be preferred. . . . Oh, if only life were that simple!

The traditional relationship of lawyer to client does not contemplate that the lawyer will be a hired hand or a hired gun. He is a professional counsel and not a menial servant. He takes instructions only in those areas in which it is appropriate for the client to give them. In other respects the lawyer is in command. To the client he owes loyalty, undivided and undiluted, zeal and devotion. . . . His object is to achieve for his client the best which is available within the law by means compatible with the canons of ethics.

. . . .

In general terms, truth commands a very high respect in our society. No one can be heard to challenge judges when they pay homage to truth.

With some trepidation I should like to tender the suggestion that in actual practice the ascertainment of the truth is not necessarily the target of the trial, that values other than truth frequently take precedence, and that, indeed, courtroom truth is a unique species of the genus truth, and that it is not necessarily congruent with objective or absolute truth, whatever that may be.

When I once casually expressed this notion to a group of laymen, they expressed shock and dismay as if I were a monk uttering some unutterable heresy to a Tenth Century congregation of bishops. But that reaction has not deterred me. . . . [T]he object of a trial is not the ascertainment of truth but the resolution of a controversy by the principled application of the rules of the game. In a civilized society these rules should be designed to favor the just resolution of controversy; and in a progressive society they should change as the perception of justice evolves in response to greater ethical sophistication.

NOTES

In one sweeping statement, Rifkind not only defended the traditional advocacy system which to this day dominates our conduct as lawyers, but took a strong swipe at Mark Green's concept that lawyers have an obligation to serve consistent with a clearly defined public interest. By quoting Samuel Johnson, he also made the telling point that the job of an advocate is not to judge the client, but to advocate the client's cause. Nevertheless, in the quarter century since, largely because of public opinion, the underlying controversy has deepened rather than gone away. More and more "traditional" lawyers have come to argue a moral imperative in legal representation.

3. "Cause Lawyers": The Opposite of the "Neutral" Advocate? In the following article, a longtime public defender, now a law professor, argues in in favor of "cause lawyering" and suggests that the major ethical problem for criminal defense attorneys is the conflict between the interests of one client and another, not between the individual client and the lawyer's interest in a cause.

MARGARETH ETIENNE, THE ETHICS OF CAUSE LAWYERING: AN EMPIRICAL EXAMINATION OF CRIMINAL DEFENSE LAWYERS AS CAUSE LAWYERS
95 Journal of Criminal Law & Criminology 1195 (2005)[2]

In 1990, Jose Orlando Lopez retained a prominent criminal defense attorney, Barry Tarlow, to represent him on serious narcotics charges. Mr. Tarlow's understanding with his client was that Tarlow would "vigorously defend and try" the case but that he would not negotiate on Lopez's behalf if Lopez decided to turn over State's evidence and become an informant in exchange for a reduced sentence. For moral and ethical reasons, it was Tarlow's general policy "not to represent clients in negotiations with the government concerning cooperation.". . . According to Tarlow, such cooperation negotiations were "personally, morally and ethically offensive" and he would no sooner represent a snitch than he would represent "Nazis or an Argentine general said to be responsible for 10,000 'disappearances.'"

Whatever one thinks of Tarlow's policy, this case highlights an important truth. For Barry Tarlow and many other defense attorneys, the practice of criminal defense is about much more than helping individual clients achieve their individual goals. Criminal defense attorneys are often motivated by an intricate set of moral and ideological principles that belie their reputations as amoral (if not immoral) "hired guns" who, for the right price, would do anything to get their guilty clients off. Some of the collateral causes advanced by these attorneys are laudable while others are not. But almost all of them raise ethical concerns that the rules . . . are not well-equipped to resolve. . . .

The cause-motivated approach to lawyering contradicts the traditional view of those in the legal profession as rights-enforcers or as neutral advocates of their clients' interests. Weighing the virtue of neutrality in an advocate versus that of activism, the ethics and professional responsibility literature seems to embrace the former as the more appropriate of the two. Lawyers are strongly advised to be zealous but neutral advocates of their clients' interests. They also have a duty of loyalty to clients that may prohibit them from representing clients in cases where the attorney feels the pull of professional, personal, or political interests distinct from those of the client.

These conflicts raise significant ethical concerns for cause lawyers — activist lawyers who use the law as a means of creating social change in

---

[2] Reprinted by special permission of Northwestern University School of Law, The Journal of Criminal Law and Criminology.

addition to a means of helping individual clients. These lawyers are known by many names in the legal and sociological literature, including . . . public interest lawyers. . . . The worry for the cause lawyer is that the pursuit of her "cause" may at times conflict with the client's interest. A lawyer's professionalism is measured in part by her ability to keep her personal and political agendas apart from (and secondary to) her clients' agendas. . . . Tarlow's particular policy of not representing snitches is open to criticism on this ground, but is merely one example of an overall approach to criminal defense lawyering in which the attorney's moral and political values play centrally in her advocacy decisions.

In this Article — the first to seriously evaluate whether criminal defense lawyers are cause lawyers — I consider several examples of cause lawyering as described by defense lawyers during the course of forty interviews. Through their discussions, I explore the types of values or commitments that animate defense lawyers' approaches to the practice of law and the impact of such "cause lawyering" on the criminal defendant. I consider whether the cause lawyering approach in the criminal context is compatible with ethical and professional rules, and argue that it should be. Sometimes criminal defendants are better represented by defense attorneys who are "cause lawyers" passionately seeking to advance their political and moral visions through the representation of their clients than by attorneys who have no overriding "cause" other than the representation of the individual client. Ethical and professional norms should be more adaptive to these instances.

My conclusion provides no quarrel with the notion that the defendant's goals should take priority over the attorney's personal or political goals. Rather, [t]his paper challenges the well-established view that neutrality (or at least client-centrality) is the only ethical approach to lawyering. I provide empirical evidence supporting the contention that in many instances the cause lawyer's approach is not only defensible but preferable.

NOTES

Do you find it interesting that the term Rifkind uses so disparagingly — "public interest lawyer" — is one Etienne refers to so favorably? Is this just a semantic disconnect or do these two perspectives really embody irreconcilable differences about what it is to be a good lawyer?

4. Representing the Guilty Client. One of the most difficult issues for the public understanding of the legal profession is how the criminal defense lawyer justifies representing the guilty client. Almost all of us have been brought up with one generation or another of Perry Mason, a lawyer who uses all the tricks in the book, but only for his seemingly limitless stable of innocent clients. Going back almost a hundred years, the West Coast's first great criminal defense attorney, Earl Rogers, claimed that he only represented people he believed innocent, at least according to his biographer and daughter, the noted journalist Adela Rogers St. Johns.[3]

---

[3] ADELA ROGERS ST. JOHNS, FINAL VERDICT (1962).

TV shows and movies make heroes of lawyers who, like Atticus Finch in *To Kill a Mockingbird*, do their level best to get justice for their falsely accused clients.

But often, the reality of the criminal defense lawyer at trial (as opposed to the frequent pretrial job of negotiating the best possible plea for a client) is the use of skill and persuasion to convince the jury to acquit a *guilty* client. The public may be asking, "How can you try to get that guilty person off?" But to most experienced criminal defense lawyers, that question is old news, as old as the Courvoisier case we discussed in the first chapter.

We have a long history of such representation, including the legal career of Clarence Darrow, whose impassioned defense of the guilty Leopold and Loeb, among others, was the stuff of legend. But we also have the explicit requirements of the Fifth Amendment, to due process of law, and of the Sixth Amendment, that criminal defendants be afforded "the *effective* assistance of counsel." And, as innumerable cases from *Powell v. Alabama*[4] on have held, "effective" means far more than sitting around waiting for something to happen. So when we turn on the television of the new millennium, we see not Perry Mason, but the lawyers on "The Practice" using the strategy they call "Plan B": pointing the finger at someone else — anyone else — so that their client, innocent or guilty, might avoid conviction.

Let's return for a moment to the idea espoused by Dr. Samuel Johnson — that the lawyer must avoid judging the client. Wouldn't it be impossible for criminal defense lawyers to perform their functions if they sat in judgment of their clients as well as defended them? Representing criminal defendants is not everyone's cup of tea; many lawyers choose not to do it. But those who do undertake a serious and often difficult responsibility.

5. True Evidence, False Defense. Effective assistance of counsel is one thing, even if it means doing your best for a client in whom you do not believe. But how far does a lawyer have to go in that representation? May an attorney, knowing the client is guilty, put on evidence which, though truthful in itself, misleads the jury into thinking that the client did not commit the crime? *Must* a lawyer put on such evidence? The State Bar of Michigan addressed these questions in a 1987 opinion.

MICHIGAN OPINION CI-1164
(1987)

Client is charged with armed robbery. He proposes to call some friends as witnesses at trial, who will give truthful testimony that he was with them at the time of the crime. At the preliminary examination the victim had testified that the robbery occurred at the same hour and time to which the friends will testify. Client has confided to attorney that he robbed the victim; his theory on the time mix-up is that he stole the victim's watch and rendered him unconscious so that the victim's sense of time was incorrect when relating the circumstances of the robbery to the investigating detectives. Months later, at the preliminary examination, the victim relied on the detectives' notes to help him recall the time. Client and attorney have decided that client will

---

[4] 287 U.S. 45 (1932).

not testify at trial. Would it be ethical for attorney to subpoena the friends to trial to testify that client was with them at the alleged time of the crime?

DR 7-101 requires counsel to represent the client zealously. A defense attorney can present any evidence that is truthful; if the ethical rule were otherwise it would mean that a defendant who confessed guilt to his counsel would never be able to have an active defense at trial.

The danger of an opposite approach is that sometimes innocent defendants "confess guilt" to their counsel or put forth a perceived "truthful" set of facts that do not pass independent scrutiny. Many crimes have degrees of guilt, as in homicide, where the "true facts" go to the accused's intent; something a jailed defendant may not be in a reflective mood to assess. Criminal defense counsel are not sent to the jail's interview room to be their client's one person jury and they certainly are not dispatched to court to be their client's hangman. Our society has made the decision to permit a person charged with crime to make full disclosure to his counsel without fear that, absent the threat of some future conduct (such as a threat to kill a witness), the lawyer will not disclose the information so provided.

The role of criminal defense counsel is to zealously defend the client within the boundaries of all legal and ethical rules. Therefore, if the information confidentially disclosed by the client were to prevent counsel from marshaling an otherwise proper defense, the client would, in effect, be penalized for making the disclosure. Such a policy, over a longer run, would tend to cause future defendants to fail to disclose everything to their lawyer; the result would be that they would receive an inadequate defense. Such an approach would be fundamentally inconsistent with the implicit representation made to defendants as a part of procedural due process that they may disclose everything to their lawyer without fear of adverse consequence.

It is the prosecution's responsibility to marshal relevant and accurate testimony of criminal conduct. It is not the obligation of defense counsel to correct inaccurate evidence introduced by the prosecution or to ignore truthful evidence that could exculpate his client. Although the tenor of this opinion may appear to risk an unfortunate result to society in the particular situation posed, such an attitude by defense counsel will serve in the long run to preserve the system of criminal justice envisioned by our constitution.

DR 7-102(4) prohibits counsel from using perjured testimony or "false evidence," but it is perfectly proper to call to the witness stand those witnesses on behalf of the client who will present truthful testimony. The testimony of the friends will not spread any perjured testimony upon the record. The client indeed was with the witnesses at the hour to which they will testify. The victim's mistake concerning the precise time of the crime results in this windfall defense to the client. . . .

6. Criminal Defense Justifications. One can readily understand that to the public, the use of the "true testimony — false alibi" suggested by the Michigan opinion is not justice served but justice denied. Yet for those who do this work, techniques like this are not only accepted, they are taught, practiced, polished, and even applauded. Defense lawyers learn how to "try someone, anyone, other than the defendant," or to point the finger at a person or persons unknown (sometimes called the "dude done it" defense.)

Since in a criminal trial the state must be put to its proof and proof must be beyond a reasonable doubt, criminal defense lawyers reason, cogently, that their job — their sworn duty — is to do anything within the bounds of ethical rules to raise such a doubt in the minds of the jurors. Put another way, truth must be measured not by whether the accused is guilty, but by whether the state has met its constitutional burden. That, these lawyers argue, is truly justice served, since justice, to paraphrase legendary federal appeals court judge Learned Hand, should be measured by how well we treat the worst members of our society, not the best. Thus, for lawyers to do less than *their* best would truly be justice denied.

Do you agree? Or is this kind of defense beyond the appropriate role of a lawyer, even in a criminal case? Consider where you fit on this spectrum as you review the rest of the readings for this problem.

Are there other reasons which criminal defense lawyers use to justify their defense of guilty clients? We've read Margareth Etienne's views above. Briefly excerpted here are several justifications suggested some years ago by a Stanford law professor and former public defender.

BARBARA BABCOCK, DEFENDING THE GUILTY
32 Cleveland State Law Review 175 (1983)[5]

The Garbage Collector's Reason. It is dirty work but someone must do it. We cannot have a functioning adversary system without a partisan for both sides. . . . The civil libertarian tells us that . . . [i]n protecting the constitutional rights of criminal defendants, we are only protecting ourselves.

The Legalistic or Positivist's Reason. Truth cannot be known. Facts are indeterminate, contingent, and in criminal cases, often evanescent. . . . [T]here is a difference between legal and moral guilt; the defense lawyer should not let his apprehension of moral guilt interfere with his analysis of legal guilt. The example usually given is that of a person accused of murder who can respond successfully with a claim of self-defense. The accused may feel morally guilty but not be legally culpable. . . .

The Political Activist's Reason. Most people who commit crimes are themselves the victims of horrible injustice. This statement is true generally because most of those accused of rape, robbery and murder are oppressed minorities. . . . Moreover, the conditions of imprisonment may impose violence far worse than that inflicted on the victim. . . .

The Social Worker's Reason. Those accused of crime, as the most visible representatives of the disadvantaged underclass in America, will actually be helped by having a defender, notwithstanding the outcome of their cases. Being treated as a real person in our society and accorded the full panoply of rights and the measure of concern afforded by a lawyer can promote rehabilitation. . . .

The Egotist's Reason. Defending criminal cases is more interesting than the routine and repetitive work done by most lawyers, even those engaged in what passes for litigation in civil practice. . . . Actual court appearances, even jury trials, come earlier and more often in one's career than could be expected in any other area of law. And winning . . . has great significance because the cards are stacked for the prosecutor. . . .

NOTES

Are the reasons offered by Babcock valid ones? Which are more persuasive than others? Which appear to you to be more ethical? More moral? How do these reasons compare to Etienne's, or with the other reasons articulated in these Readings? How do they compare to those given in the following article by a young public defender in San Diego?

TAMARA RICE LAVE, EQUAL BEFORE THE LAW
Newsweek (July 13, 1998)[6]

"How can you represent *those* people? How can you be a public defender?" Jane (not her real name), a former nurse, asked me both questions. The daughter of a California police officer, she is young, pretty and white. Jane was charged with, and pleaded guilty to, stealing from a disabled patient. Taken aback, I stared at her: "But I am representing you!"

This "us/them" philosophy lies at the heart of such questions. There are some defendants, white and middle class, who do not see themselves as criminals. They believe it is "them" — the poor and minorities — who violate the law. . . .

When I first started my job, I thought like a social worker. I justified representing those who were guilty because I believed I could help them . . . . After two years, my conscience no longer requires such justification. It doesn't matter to me whether my client really committed a crime. My job is to advocate, and [m]y goal is to expose reasonable doubt. When I succeed, jurors sometimes say "we thought he probably did it, but we just had too many questions to convict."

This end result makes many people uncomfortable. They expect something more from a trial; they want truth. Their vision of justice is fostered by a Perry Mason sense that what happened will become glaringly clear. Trials are rarely like this. It's not until someone sits on a jury that they really understand the phrase "has been proved guilty beyond a reasonable doubt." [W]hatever I think, as the voice of my client, I must ensure that the prosecution proves its case.

In effect, I've accepted the presumption of innocence . . . .

Sometimes the work can be unpleasant. The days are long and stressful. I spend a good deal of time in jail, which reeks of stale food and body odor. My clients often think that because I'm court-appointed, I must be incompetent. In jailhouse parlance, I am just a "dump truck," a person who wants nothing more than to plead them guilty.

Most trying is dealing with prosecutors who aren't sympathetic to the tribulations of lives unlike their own. In one memorable case, a city attorney

---

[6] Copyright © 1998 by Newsweek. Reprinted by permission.

argued that a homeless client should get 60 days behind bars for illegal posses-sion of a shopping cart because he had prior convictions for the same offense and didn't seem to be "learning his lesson."

Despite the frustrations, I've never regretted becoming a public defender. If I had gone to a law firm or become a prosecutor, I would have been surrounded by people like me. This would have given me little opportunity — and indeed, in the case of the prosecutor, little reason — to challenge my own prejudices. As a public defender, I must bridge the divide between us and them, myself and my client, proving that everyone is equal before the law. Doing so requires empathy and patience, two characteristics that everyone, particularly the Janes of society, could use.

7. How Far Can a Lawyer Stretch the Truth? The Oklahoma City bombing trial had an effect on the entire nation. The following brief excerpt describes how Timothy McVeigh's attorney Stephen Jones reacted to press reports that his client had admitted his guilt.

RICHARD ZITRIN & CAROL M. LANGFORD
The Moral Compass of the American Lawyer 178-180 (1999) [7]

In March 1997, just before jury selection began in the Timothy McVeigh trial, the Dallas *Morning News* reported that McVeigh's lawyers had a written confession from their client admitting he had driven the truck filled with explosives that killed 168 people in Oklahoma City. There was no question that the confession, if it existed, was inadmissible in court: it was made only to the defense team, and the *Morning News* acknowledged it had obtained its documentation from a member of that team; this made the statements a confidential attorney-client communication. But the story was still damning to McVeigh both in the court of public opinion and in the minds of prospective jurors. Chief defense counsel Stephen Jones, about to select a supposedly "unbiased" jury in a case involving the worst act of terrorism in our country's history, needed instant damage control.

At first, Jones said the confession was a hoax — it didn't exist. Within a day, Jones changed his story, claiming that the "confession" had been con-cocted by the defense to persuade a reluctant witness to talk. The witness would only talk if he was not suspected; the "confession," Jones said, was created to lull the witness into speaking with the defense. The press, especially the legal trade press, immediately focused its attention on whether Jones was justified in lying. . . .

The press figured Jones was a liar either way: he had lied by creating the "concocted" confession and fooling a witness, or the confession was actually the truth, in which case Jones had lied to the press. Legal ethics experts lined up on both sides of the issue. Many cited the American Bar Association's ethics rule which prohibits making false statements not just to the court or opposing counsel, but to any "third person." Either the witness, if the confession was a fake, or the press, if the confession was true, would qualify as a "third person." Talk circulated about whether Jones should be referred for discipline

---

to the State Bars of Oklahoma, his home state, and Colorado, where the trial was held.

No one knows whether this "confession" was true or concocted. Assuming for the moment that his client's confession was true, Jones was in a tough situation. Already confronted by a horrible case with a wealth of evidence against him, he found himself faced with three choices: admit its truth, effectively damning his client to the public and the potential jurors; remain silent, knowing that this would have the same effect as an admission; or come up with a plausible denial. . . .

Concocting a confession to persuade a witness to talk raises a more difficult issue. Many ethics experts who approved of this said it amounted to a lawyer simply doing his job. "Lawyers are not truth-seeking, unless the truth happens to help clients," said Prof. Stephen Gillers. Others pointed out that the prosecution often does worse things. Even the local District Attorney justified Jones's fake confession ploy as a matter of strategy, and said that if he had a witness who wouldn't talk as long as his mother was alive, he would "send someone from the funeral home out and say his mother was just killed." But to argue that Jones was justified because prosecutors lie even more is to invoke "the Doctrine of Relative Filth" — I can do it because *they* are doing something worse.

8. Taking Advantage on Cross-Examination. We now spend some time with two cross-examination scenarios — the elderly witness or victim whose ability to recall is questioned, and the rape victim who is known by the lawyer to be telling the truth. First, consider the elderly woman in the next article. Is the described cross-examination justified? Does the witness' age make any difference? Does it matter that the witness is also the victim? Or what further damage or humiliation is inflicted on her? Does the nature of the crime make a difference? What about the potential penalty to the client? Or should zealous representation of the client be the lawyer's only concern in all cases, no matter what?

E.R. SHIPP, FEAR AND CONFUSION IN COURT PLAGUE ELDERLY CRIME VICTIMS
The New York Times (March 13, 1983)[8]

An 89-year-old woman sat in a wheelchair next to the witness stand in State Supreme Court in Manhattan and, during questioning over two days, pleaded with the judge and the defense attorney to let her go home.

"I was never in a mix-up like this in my life," she said. "I feel as though I am just sitting here being persecuted for nothing, absolutely nothing."

Thousands of New York City's elderly citizens are the victims of crime each year. For the woman on the witness stand, Eleanor Cosgrove, the attempt to describe her case — in which a lawyer was charged with stealing from her — was made difficult by poor health, a faltering memory and fear. "I am scared to death," she repeatedly said.

The police and prosecutors say they are increasingly concerned about the physical or psychological barriers that prevent elderly victims from becoming

---

witnesses and that make it difficult to prosecute those who prey upon them. . . .

Both the police and the District Attorneys' offices say they are spending more time working with the elderly, teaching them how to prevent crime and encouraging them to come forward to report it.

But in preparing cases for trial, they say, three main hurdles must be overcome: the victim's fear, deliberate delay by the defense and, if the case progresses that far, rigorous cross-examination during trial.

"They're afraid," said Acting Justice Francis N. Pecora of State Supreme Court in Manhattan. "They're intimidated, and they are then more or less browbeaten by the defense attorney. It's like being assaulted a second time."

. . . .

Linda A. Fairstein, chief of the Sex Crimes Bureau of the Manhattan District Attorney's office, estimated that 10 percent to 20 percent of the victims of sexual crimes prosecuted by her office were 65 or older.

Sherry Roman, the chief of the Major Offense Bureau of the Bronx District Attorney's office, said, "A very significant portion of our cases involves the elderly as victims."

But because of such physical disabilities as failing eyesight, these elderly victims "generally make poor witnesses," said Sgt. Michael W. Gerhold, who heads one of Manhattan's two senior robbery units.

. . . .

"A major problem is stalling tactics by defense lawyers to delay the trial," said Judge Irving Lang of the city's Criminal Court. "Everybody's memory fades with time, but older people have particular problems in that regard."

Finally comes the trial and the sometimes grueling cross-examination by the suspect's attorney.

Many defense attorneys, Miss Fairstein said, try to show that the elderly witness does not really know what went on.

"They do that," Miss Fairstein said, "by asking so many detailed questions that will have to result in an 'I don't know' or 'I don't remember' answer, trying to shake the foundation of the case and give the impression of faulty memory, obtuseness and senility. They prey on mistakes."

A defense lawyer, Donald O. Weinberger, gave another view: "There's a responsibility you take on when you become a defense attorney. You've got to cross-examine that witness and make sure that witness is correct about what he's saying. That's not so easy, whether or not it's an old person."

At the age of 89, Mrs. Cosgrove was one of the oldest witnesses to appear in recent cases, and the defense tried to show that, because of her advanced age and uncertainty about so many details, the jury should not believe any of her testimony.

The defendant, Erich Reisch, had been her attorney and was charged with stealing $129,000 from her and using the money for such things as a 1981 Cadillac, certificates of deposit listed in his and his wife's names, and real-estate investments, also in his wife's name.

Mr. Reisch maintained that he was not guilty. He contended that Mrs. Cosgrove had wanted "a greater yield" than she was receiving on her savings accounts and thus he had made investments for her, even though some were in other names. He further said that Mrs. Cosgrove had lent him money for the car and other items, and that he had given her promissory notes but that he had neglected to keep copies for himself. Mrs. Cosgrove did not recall such notes.

On cross-examination, Mr. Reisch's attorney, Bruce H. Goldstone, immediately began to raise doubts about her memory. He asked, "Have you found that as you get older your memory perhaps is not as good as it was years ago?" She answered: "I wouldn't say so. I'm pretty keen."

That led to a dispute about her birthdate. After Mrs. Cosgrove said that she was born on April 22, 1893, Mr. Gladstone read from the transcript of a February 1982 hearing — one of three previous proceedings at which Mrs. Cosgrove had been required to give testimony — showing her saying: "I was born in 1903."

"Oh, no, I never said that," Mrs. Cosgrove replied. "I never said 1903. I was in school then. So I had no occasion to use 1903."

The longer the questioning proceeded, the more confused Mrs. Cosgrove appeared to become.

The assistant district attorney in the case, Seth Rosenberg, urged the jury to focus upon what Mrs. Cosgrove did clearly recall — that she had not authorized Mr. Reisch to use her money for investments or his personal affairs.

. . . .

After deliberating several days, the jury deadlocked 11 to 1 in favor of conviction, leading Justice Clifford A. Scott to declare a mistrial. A new trial, at which Mrs. Cosgrove will again have to testify, is set to begin April 5.

9. How Far Should One Go With a Guilty Client? Several years ago, for the first volume of a new journal on legal ethics, a noted criminal law professor, Harry I. Subin, analyzed a case he had encountered as the director of a law school clinic. The client, charged with rape, had at first denied his guilt. While Subin doubted this story of innocence, he also recognized "some strength to [his client's] arguments, and that there were questionable aspects to the complainant's story." Eventually, though, the client confessed to Subin that his alibi was false and he in fact was guilty. Years later, and with ethical hindsight, Subin analyzed how he had behaved upon learning of his client's guilt. Troubled by his actions, he proposed a far less adversarial role for the criminal defense lawyer that would have avoided presenting a "false defense" for a client known to be guilty.

HARRY I. SUBIN, THE CRIMINAL DEFENSE LAWYER'S "DIFFERENT MISSION": REFLECTIONS ON THE "RIGHT" TO PRESENT A FALSE CASE

1 Georgetown Journal of Legal Ethics 125 (1987)[9]

II. *Truth Subversion in Action: The Problem Illustrated*

[When my client finally admitted guilt] I did not pause very long to ponder the problem, however, because I concluded that knowing the truth in fact did not make a difference to my defense strategy, other than to put me on notice as to when I might be suborning perjury. Because the mission of the defense attorney was to defeat the prosecution's case, what I knew actually happened was not important otherwise. What did matter was whether a version of the "facts" could be presented that would make the jury doubt the client's guilt.

Viewed in this way, my problem was not that my client's story was false, but that it was not credible. . . . To win, we would therefore have to come up with a better theory than the alibi, avoiding perjury in the process. Thus, the defense would have to be made out without the client testifying. . . .

There were two possible defenses that could be fabricated. The first was mistaken identity. . . . [But] it seemed doubtful that the mistaken identification ploy would be successful. The second alternative, consent, was clearly preferable. . . . To prevail, all we would have to do would be to raise a reasonable doubt as to whether he had compelled the woman to have sex with him. The doubt would be based on the scenario that the woman and the defendant had met before, and she voluntarily returned to his apartment. . . .

The consent defense could be made out entirely through cross-examination of the complainant, coupled with argument to the jury about her lack of credibility on the issue of force. I could emphasize the parts of her story that sounded the most curious. . . . [An] allegedly stolen watch was never found, there was no sign of physical violence, and no one heard screaming or any other signs of a struggle.

. . . .

How all of this would have played out at trial cannot be known. Predictably, the case dragged on so long that the prosecutor was forced to offer the unrefusable plea of possession of a gun. As I look back, however, I wonder how I could justify doing what I was planning to do had the case been tried. I was prepared to stand before the jury posing as an officer of the court in search of the truth, while trying to fool the jurors into believing a wholly fabricated story: that the woman had consented, when in fact she had been forced at gunpoint to have sex with the defendant. I was also prepared to demand an acquittal because the state had not met its burden of proof when, if it had not, it would have been because I made the truth look like a lie. If there is any redeeming social value in permitting an attorney to do such things, I frankly cannot discern it.

---

9 Reprinted with the permission of the publisher. Copyright © 1987 by The Georgetown Journal of Legal Ethics and Georgetown University.

. . . .

III. *Can Lawyers "Know" the Truth?*

. . . .

The argument that the attorney cannot know the truth until a court decides it fails. Either it is sophistry, designed to simplify the moral life of the attorney, or it rests on a confusion between "factual truth" and "legal truth." The former relates to historical fact. The latter relates to the principle that a fact cannot be acted upon by the legal system until it is proven in accordance with legal rules. . . .

Given that the attorney is not the trier of fact in the case but the representative of the defendant, it seems appropriate that the lawyer be directed to apply a burden of proof in favor of the client. Because there is a strong societal interest in providing the defendant the opportunity to state a case, the presumption should be strong. It would seem, therefore, that the attorney should be permitted to offer a defense unless he or she "knew" beyond a reasonable doubt that the defense was false.

Applying this standard to the case under discussion, I would conclude that I "knew" beyond a reasonable doubt that the proposed consent defense was false. . . .

IV. *Does the Truth Matter? Appraising the Different Mission*

[One cannot sensibly] defend the utterly arbitrary line we have drawn between deliberately offering perjured testimony and deliberately attempting to create false "proof" by offering truthful but misleading evidence, or by impeaching a truthful witness. Instead [one should] recognize that the right to put forward a defense is limited, not absolute. . . .

V. *Accomplishing the Defense Attorney's Different Mission —*
Morally

I propose a system in which the defense attorney would operate not with the right to assert defenses known to be untrue, but under the following rule:

> It shall be improper for an attorney who knows beyond a reasonable doubt the truth of a fact established in the state's case to attempt to refute that fact through the introduction of evidence, impeachment of evidence, or argument.

In the face of this rule, the attorney who knew there were no facts to contest would be limited to the "monitoring" role. Assuming that a defendant in my client's situation wanted to assert his right to contest the evidence against him, the attorney would work to assure that all of the elements of the crime were proven beyond a reasonable doubt, on the basis of competent and admissible evidence. This would include enforcing the defendant's right to have privileged or illegally obtained evidence excluded: The goal sought here is not the elimination of all rules that result in the suppression of truth, but only those not supported by sound policy. It would also be appropriate for the attorney to argue to the jury that the available evidence is not sufficient to sustain the burden of proof. It would not, however, be proper for the attorney to use any of the presently available devices to refute testimony known to be truthful. I wish to make clear, however, that this rule would not prevent the attorney from challenging *inaccurate* testimony, even though the attorney knew that the defendant was guilty. . . .

Applying these principles to my rape case, I would engage fully in the process of testing the admissibility of the state's evidence, moving to suppress testimony concerning the suggestive "show-up" identification at the precinct, and the gun found in the defendant's apartment after a warrantless search, should the state attempt to offer either piece of evidence. At the trial, I would be present to assure that the complainant testified in accordance with the rules of evidence.

Assuming that she testified at trial as she had at the preliminary hearing, however, I would not cross-examine her, because I would have no good faith basis for impeaching either her testimony or her character, since I "knew" that she was providing an accurate account of what had occurred. Nor would I put on a defense case. I would limit my representation at that stage to putting forth the strongest argument I could that the facts presented by the state did not sustain its burden. . . .

NOTES

Noting that evidence rarely falls into neatly wrapped packages labeled "true" and "false," attorney and law professor John B. Mitchell, writing in the same Georgetown Law School ethics journal that had published Subin's article, tested the practical difficulty of Subin's proposal by trying to present a closing argument that both provided a defense to the accused and avoided resting on falsehoods.

Mitchell hypothesized that he was defending a young woman accused of shoplifting a Christmas tree star. The store manager stopped the defendant when she walked straight through the store and out the door with the star in her hand. When stopped, the woman burst into tears. Just as the manager was about to take her to the store's security office, a small fire broke out in the camera section, and he rushed off to help put it out. When he returned five minutes later, the woman was still sitting where he had left her. Back in the security room, the manager asked her to empty her pockets. He found that the woman had nothing else belonging to the store, but did have a ten-dollar bill. The star cost $1.79.

Mitchell's fictitious client admitted her guilt to him: "[The star] was so pretty. . . . I would have bought it, but I also wanted to make a special Christmas dinner for Mama and didn't have enough money to do both. . . . But that star . . . I could just see the look in Mama's eyes if she saw that lovely thing on our tree."

First, Mitchell describes how he would defend the case. Then we read a final excerpt: Subin's response to Mitchell's proposed defense.

JOHN B. MITCHELL, REASONABLE DOUBTS ARE WHERE YOU FIND THEM: A RESPONSE TO PROFESSOR SUBIN'S POSITION ON THE CRIMINAL LAWYER'S "DIFFERENT MISSION"

1 Georgetown Journal of Legal Ethics 343 (1987)[10]

My defense is not that the defendant accidentally walked out, but rather that the prosecution cannot prove the element of intent to permanently deprive beyond a reasonable doubt. Through this theory, I am raising "doubt" in the prosecution's case. . . . In my effort to carry out this legal theory, I will *not assert* that facts known by me to be true are false or those known to be false are true. As a defense attorney, I do not have to prove what *in fact* happened. That is an advantage in the process I would not willingly give up. . . . Thus, in this case I will not claim that my client walked out of the store with innocent intent (a fact which I know is false); rather, I will argue:

> The prosecution claims my client stole an ornament for a Christmas tree. The prosecution further claims that when my client walked out of that store she intended to keep it without paying. Now, maybe she did. None of us were there. On the other hand, she had $10.00 in her pocket, which was plenty of money with which to pay for the ornament without the risk of getting caught stealing. Also, she didn't try to conceal what she was doing. She walked right out of the store holding it in her hand. Most of us have come close to innocently doing the same thing. So, maybe she didn't. But then she cried the minute she was stopped. She might have been feeling guilty. So, maybe she did. On the other hand, she might just have been scared when she realized what had happened. After all, she didn't run away when she was left alone even though she knew the manager was going to be occupied with a fire inside. So, maybe she didn't. The point is that, looking at all the evidence, you're left with "maybe she intended to steal, maybe she didn't." But, you knew that before the first witness was even sworn. The prosecution has the burden, and he simply can't carry any burden let alone "beyond a reasonable doubt" with a maybe she did, maybe she didn't case. . . .

Is this a "false defense" for Professor Subin? Admittedly, I am trying to raise a doubt by persuading the jury to appreciate "possibilities" other than my client's guilt. Perhaps Professor Subin would say it is "false" because I know the possibilities are untrue. But if that is so, Professor Subin will have taken a leap from defining "false defense" as the assertion that true things are false and false things are true, for I am doing neither of those things here. . . .

Another perspective from which to look at the function of a defense attorney involves understanding that function in the context of the nature of evidence at trial. Professor Subin speaks of facts and the impropriety of trying to make "true facts" look false and "false facts" look true. But in a trial there are no such things as facts. There is only information, lack of information, and chains of inferences therefrom. . . .

---

[10] Reprinted with the permission of the publisher. Copyright © 1988 by The Georgetown Journal of Legal Ethics and Georgetown University.

In our shoplifting example, the prosecution will elicit that the defendant burst into tears when stopped by the manager. From this information will run a chain of inferences: defendant burst into tears; people without a guilty conscience would explain their innocence, not cry; defendant has a guilty conscience; her guilty conscience is likely motivated by having committed a theft. Conversely, if the defense brings out that the manager was shaking a lead pipe in his hand when he stopped the defendant, defense counsel is *not asserting* that defendant did not have a guilty conscience when stopped. Counsel is merely *weakening* the persuasiveness of the prosecution's inference by raising the "possibility" that she was crying not from guilt, but from fear. By raising such "possibilities," the defense is making arguments against the ability of the prosecution's inferences to meet their burden of "beyond a reasonable doubt." . . . In a system where factual guilt is not at issue, Professor Subin's "falsehoods" are, in fact, "reasonable doubts."

HARRY I. SUBIN, IS THIS LIE NECESSARY? FURTHER REFLECTIONS ON THE RIGHT TO PRESENT A FALSE DEFENSE
1 Georgetown Journal of Legal Ethics 689, 691-692 (1988)[11]

John B. Mitchell has written a thought-provoking response to my argument. While there is much in his presentation with which I disagree, I think that he has stated as well as anyone can the case for what I have called the "false" defense. He has not persuaded me. But he has demonstrated a flaw in my formulation, which I would like to correct here. In essence, Mitchell has convinced me that precluding the defense attorney from attacking a truthful case against the defendant may be incompatible with the defense attorney's responsibility to assure that the prosecution meets its high burden of proof at trial. I shall therefore offer this modification of my original proposal: when the defense attorney knows that the prosecution's evidence is true, he or she may nonetheless suggest to the jury alternative explanations of the facts, for the purpose of assisting the jury to measure the weight of the evidence. The jury must, however, be instructed as to the limited purpose for which these alternative explanations, made without a good faith basis, are being offered.

I applaud [Mitchell's] apparent concession that presenting a false defense might be ethically wrong. (Why else would Mitchell go to the trouble of making the argument?) I believe, moreover, that if defense attorneys were required to give this kind of closing argument in "reasonable doubt" cases, it would help to reconcile the goals of assuring a truthful verdict and putting the state to its proof. Mitchell's presentation is, however, flawed in two respects. In the first place, the closing argument which he offers, with its intimations that the defense theory is not dependent upon the facts, is much more forthright than those which most attorneys would give. What they would actually say would be more cryptic with respect to what the jury should conclude about the truth, something like:

> The prosecution claims that my client walked out of the store intending not to pay. I ask you, members of the jury, why would this young

[11] Reprinted with the permission of the publisher. Copyright © 1988 by The Georgetown Journal of Legal Ethics and Georgetown University.

lady, with $10.00 in her pocket, steal a $1.79 Christmas tree ornament? Isn't it more likely that in the hustle and bustle of Christmas shopping she saw the ornament, focused for a second on the beautiful Christmas tree she was decorating, picked it up and then forgot she had it when she left the store? At the very least, don't you believe that possibility creates a reasonable doubt about whether she intended to steal the ornament?

Moreover, even if Mitchell's sanitized closing was given, it is still designed to persuade the jury of the existence of facts he knows to be not true: here, that the woman in fact left the store accidentally (i.e., "maybe she did (leave accidentally). None of us was there."). That is not a lie, but it certainly creates a false impression, which amounts to the same thing.

10. The Supreme Court Speaks. Who is right, Subin or Mitchell? Does Subin's final point — that Mitchell's "sanitized closing" is unrealistic — mean that Mitchell's argument is the same as overtly arguing falsehoods? Or could it be that *neither* has gotten it right, at least in the eyes of defense lawyers? As unpleasant as this may sound to most of the public, is it the job of criminal defense lawyers to argue what they know to be false, so long as it's in the arena of testing the prosecution's case? Read what Subin cites in his first article as the standard he wants to abandon, from the pen of Justice Byron White.

UNITED STATES v. WADE
388 U.S. 218, 256-57, 87 S. Ct. 1926, 1947-48 (1967)

[D]efense counsel has no . . . obligation to ascertain or present the truth. Our system assigns him a different mission. He must be and is interested in preventing the conviction of the innocent, but . . . we also insist that he defend his client whether he is innocent or guilty. . . . If he can confuse a witness, even a truthful one, or make him appear at a disadvantage, unsure or indecisive, that will be his normal course. Our interest in not convicting the innocent permits counsel to put the State to its proof, to put the State's case in the worst possible light, regardless of what he thinks or knows to be the truth. . . . In this respect, as part of our modified adversary system and as part of the duty imposed on the most honorable defense counsel, we countenance or require conduct which in many instances has little, if any, relation to the search for truth.

11. Cross-Examining the Truthful Witness. Professor Monroe Freedman has long been one of the most controversial but articulate and enlightening commentators on the adversary system. Beginning with a 1966 law review article[12] and continuing through numerous other articles and two books,[13] Freedman has evaluated the role of lawyer — especially the criminal defense lawyer — as advocate, and the limits that law and ethics place on that role. Like Subin, Freedman questions how the rules of ethics can justify prohibiting perjured testimony on the one hand while permitting — even requiring —

---

[12] *Professional Responsibility of the Criminal Defense Lawyer: The Three Hardest Questions*, 64 MICH. L. REV. 1469 (1966).

[13] LAWYERS' ETHICS IN AN ADVERSARY SYSTEM (1975); UNDERSTANDING LAWYERS' ETHICS (1990).

cross-examination of a known truthful witness on the other. But Freedman comes to a very different conclusion than Subin, as we shall see when we examine his opinions about client perjury in Problem 14.

Interestingly, though, despite the language in *Wade*, Freedman has long held that cross-examining a truthful and accurate witness in order to make the witness appear mistaken or lying is more difficult to accept even than presenting known perjury. To make his points, Freedman uses as a factual vehicle a rape case not unlike Professor Subin's, a scenario which was originally used in a 1966 Washington, D.C. symposium on legal ethics which included former Chief Justice (then appeals court judge) Warren Burger. Professor Freedman has discussed this scenario in different contexts and various forums, and his 1990 book is a significant modernization of his thoughts. We use here his analysis from his seminal 1975 book, which has been called both the most controversial and the most important volume on the ethics of legal advocacy.

MONROE FREEDMAN, CROSS-EXAMINATION: DESTROYING THE TRUTHFUL WITNESS
Lawyers' Ethics in an Adversary System ch. 4 (1975)[14]

Should the defense lawyer use the information supplied by [a rejected suitor of the victim, even though this information was suspect and related to her prior sexual conduct in a jurisdiction which then allowed such evidence]?

One of the panelists who spoke to that question was Chief Justice (then Judge) Warren Burger. The Chief Justice first discussed the question in terms of "basic and fundamental rules." One of those rules, which he characterized as "clear-cut and unambiguous," is that "a lawyer may never, under any circumstances, knowingly . . . participate in a fraud on the court." That rule, he said, "can never admit of any exception, under any circumstances," and no other consideration "can ever justify a knowing and conscious departure" from it. Moreover, only the "naive and inexperienced" would take a contrary position, which is a "perversion and prostitution of an honorable profession." Indeed, the Chief Justice held any other view to be "so utterly absurd that one wonders why the subject need even be discussed among persons trained in the law."[15]

After that powerful rhetoric, Chief Justice Burger's response to the question [of cross-examining the truthful witness] is a matter of some astonishment. The function of an advocate, and "particularly the defense advocate in the adversary system," is to use "all legitimate tools available to test the truth of the prosecution's case." . . .

That, of course, is sanction for nothing less than a deliberate attempt to perpetrate a fraud upon the finder of fact. The lawyer knows that the client is guilty and that the [victim] is truthful. In cross-examining her, the lawyer

---

[14] Copyright © 1975 by Monroe H. Freedman. Reprinted by permission. Professor Freedman has updated and expanded his analysis in UNDERSTANDING LAWYERS' ETHICS (1990) and along with co-author Abbe Smith published a third volume in 2004.

[15] [1] Burger, *Standards of Conduct for Prosecution and Defense Personnel: A Judge's Viewpoint*, 5 AM. CRIM. L.Q. 11-15 (1966).

has one purpose only: to make it appear, contrary to fact, that [she] is lying in testifying that she was raped.

There is only one difference in practical effect between presenting the defendant's perjured alibi — which the Chief Justice considers to be clearly improper — and impeaching the truthful [victim]. In both cases the lawyer participates in an attempt to free a guilty defendant. In both cases, the lawyer participates in misleading the finder of fact. In the case of the perjured witness, however, the attorney asks only nonleading questions, while in the case of impeachment, the lawyer takes an active, aggressive role, using his professional training and skills, in a one-on-one attack upon the client's victim. The lawyer thereby personally and directly adds to the suffering of the [victim]. In short, under the euphemism of "testing the truth of the prosecution's case," the lawyer communicates, to the jury and to the community, the most vicious of lies.

That case takes us to the heart of my disagreement with the traditional approach to dealing with difficult questions of professional responsibility. That approach has two characteristics. First, in a rhetorical flourish, the profession is committed in general terms to all that is good and true. Then specific questions are answered by uncritical reliance upon legalistic norms, regardless of the context in which the lawyer may be acting, and regardless of the motive and the consequences of the act. Perjury is wrong and therefore no lawyer, in any circumstance, should knowingly present perjury. Cross-examination, however, is good, and therefore any lawyer under any circumstances and regardless of the consequences, can properly impeach a witness through cross-examination. The system of professional responsibility that I have been advancing, on the other hand, is one that attempts to deal with ethical problems in context — that is, as part of a functional sociopolitical system concerned with the administration of justice in a free society — and giving due regard both to motive and to consequences. In that respect, the debate returns us to some fundamental philosophical questions that have not been adequately developed in the literature of professional responsibility.

The classic exposition of a legalistic, anti-utilitarian ethical system is that of Immanuel Kant. In assessing moral worth, Kant rejects any concern with motive or purpose, but relies exclusively upon fulfillment of duty as expressed in a maxim of conduct. . . .

Kant's only test of the validity of a maxim is whether one is prepared to will the maxim to be a universal law. Referring specifically to lying, Kant suggests that it is improper to reason: "I should not lie, because then no one would thereafter believe me." The error in that, Kant says, is that one would then be telling the truth "from apprehension of injurious consequences," rather than from duty to principle. Assume, for example, that one is in a difficult situation that can be avoided only by telling a lie. One might say that everyone may tell a lie in order to escape a difficulty that otherwise cannot be avoided. However: "I presently become aware that while I can will the lie, I can by no means will that lying should be a universal law." From there Kant reasons that telling the truth is a universal law, and that it cannot be violated under any circumstances. Thus, if a victim is fleeing from a murderer, one must answer the murderer truthfully when asked where the victim is hiding. Lying — violation of principle — cannot be justified by mere expediency.

In response to that proposition, it would seem to be adequate to observe that there is something wrong with a system of morality that places a higher value upon one's moral rectitude with respect to lying, than upon the preservation of an innocent person's life. The legalistic mind, however, does not recognize such conflicts of principle; for example, what if one had already promised the victim to give him protection, and could only be truthful to the murderer by breaking one's word to the victim? That difficulty, of course, precisely parallels the problems faced by the criminal defense lawyer who has entered into an obligation of trust with the client. . . . One can agree with Chief Justice Burger that lying is wrong, and still not know the answer to the question of whether it is worse to lie to the client or to lie to the court.

There is an extremely important aspect of Kant's rejection of utilitarianism, however, which is frequently overlooked. That is, holding that one must obey a maxim without regard to consequences, Kant is speaking at the level of personal morality. When he leaves the level of personal morality, and addresses himself to morality in systemic terms, Kant is entirely pragmatic. Thus, the fundamental question of whether a maxim is valid in the first instance (as distinguished from whether a valid maxim should be obeyed) is determined by the utilitarian concern with whether that maxim can be universalized, that is, with whether that maxim can be embodied into a viable system. . . .

One of the major flaws in the traditional approach to legal ethics is that it seeks to answer the difficult questions in a legalistic fashion at the personal level, but begs completely the critical questions raised at the systemic level. . . .

Let us return, then, to the case involving the street robbery at 16th and P Streets, in which the defendant has been wrongly identified as the criminal, but has been correctly identified by [another witness,] the nervous, elderly woman who wears eyeglasses, as having been only a block away five minutes before the crime took place. If the woman is not cross-examined effectively and her testimony shaken, it will serve to corroborate the erroneous evidence of guilt. On the other hand, the lawyer could take the position that since the woman is testifying truthfully and accurately, she should not be made to appear to be mistaken or lying.

But if a similar course were to be adopted by every lawyer who learned the truth through confidential disclosures from the client, such disclosures would cease to be made. The result, for practical purposes, would be identical with the practice, disapproved in the ABA Standards, of "selective ignorance. . . ." Of course, if that is the result we want, it would be far better that lawyers take a direct and honest approach with their clients, telling them to be less than candid, rather than lying to their clients by impressing upon them a bond of trust that the lawyers do not intend to maintain. Thus, when we examine the problem in a systemic context, we reach the conclusion that Chief Justice Burger was correct, although for the wrong reason, in supporting cross-examination of the [victim] in the rape case.

Obviously, the rape case is a much harder one, because the injury done to the [victim] is far more severe than the more limited humiliation of the public-spirited and truthful witness in the case of the street robbery. Nevertheless,

I come to the same conclusion in the case of cross-examining the rape victim. Unlike the Chief Justice, however, I find it a far more difficult and painful choice than that of client perjury.

SUPPLEMENTAL READINGS

1. Randy Bellows, "Notes of a Public Defender," in Phillip B. Heymann & Lance Liebman, *The Social Responsibilities of Lawyers* (1988), in which then-public defender Bellows grapples compellingly with his obligation to represent his clients to the best of his ability, while finding himself increasingly uncomfortable, even appalled, by his role as their advocate.

2. In 1911, the infamous Triangle Shirtwaist fire killed over 100 sweatshop workers, mostly immigrant women, and created an atmosphere which helped revolutionize the rights of workers and conditions of the workplace. In the aftermath of the fire, famed criminal defense lawyer Max D. Steuer defended the factory owners on criminal charges, successfully getting them acquitted by cross-examining a young survivor of the fire who spoke little English, and proving her direct testimony had been rehearsed and memorized word for word. Steuer's efforts have been extolled as the best example of zealous advocacy and pilloried as the worst example of an advocacy system run amok. Steuer and the Triangle trial have been the subject of many treatments over the years. A few of those are: Aaron Steuer, *Max D. Steuer, Trial Lawyer* (1950); Leon Stein, *The Triangle Fire* (1962) and, more recently, on the 75th anniversary of the fire, Daniel J. Kornstein, "A Tragic Fire — A Great Cross-Examination," *New York Law Journal*, March 28, 1986. Most of these treatments have justified Steuer's actions.

3. Thomas L. Shaffer, *Serving the Guilty*, 26 Loy. L. Rev. 71 (1980). This article explores, from a moral and religious perspective, whether a lawyer may represent a guilty client.

4. *Johnson v. U.S.*, 360 F.2d 844 (D.C. Cir. 1966). There, in a concurrence, Warren Burger further articulates his views about the role of the criminal lawyer as a "highly important but nonetheless limited function" of "put[ting] the prosecution to its proof, to test the case against the accused."

5. Nothing served to galvanize the American public on the behavior of criminal defense lawyers as much as the O.J. Simpson trial. For two worthwhile books on the subject from very different perspectives, we suggest Gerald F. Uelmen, *Lessons From the Trial* (1996), and *Birth of a Nation 'hood* (Toni Morrison, ed., 1997). Prof. Uelmen was part of the Simpson "dream team" and is a former dean of Santa Clara Law School and a frequent commentator on the ethics of criminal defense lawyers. The Morrison volume focuses on sociology and race, not law, from a variety of interesting individual perspectives and includes a valuable piece by the late Federal Court of Appeals Judge A. Leon Higgenbotham.

6. The Washington University Journal of Law and Policy contains a debate regarding the role of lawyers as zealous advocates, as opposed to adopting more of the traits of social workers. One might term it a modernized version of the famous Subin-Mitchell debate in the readings. The three pieces of particular note are: Jane Aiken & Stephen Wizner, *Law as Social Work*, 11

Wash. U. J.L. & Policy 63 (2003), Abbe Smith, *The Difference in Criminal Defense and the Difference It Makes*, 11 Wash. U. J.L. & Policy 83 (2003), and Katherine R. Kruse's response, *Lawyers Should be Lawyers, but What Does that Mean? A Response to Aiken & Wizner and Smith*, 14 Wash. U. J.L. & Policy 49 (2004).

PROBLEM 15

This problem concerns one of the most difficult ethical problems that arises in practice — what to do when your client lies, or you suspect your client is going to lie? Should you remain silent and do nothing? Urge your client to correct the lie? Withdraw from the representation? Tell the court? The perjurious client pits two important ethical obligations directly against each other: the duty to the client to preserve confidences and provide loyal, even zealous, representation versus the lawyer's obligation to society and the system of justice to avoid untruthfulness. There are no easy answers, as you will find when you consider the following problem and the accompanying readings.

When the Client Insists on Lying

I. Review Professor Monroe Freedman's scenario about the 16th and P Streets robbery case, on page 406.

QUESTIONS

1. What would you do if your client insisted on testifying falsely in the manner described by Freedman?

2. Of the suggested solutions to the "perjury trilemma," which would you adopt, and why?

3. Does it make a difference in how you would handle the situation that you know, as Professor Freedman tells you, that your client is actually not guilty?

II. Review the dialogue of the movie *Anatomy of a Murder* on page 421 and Professor Freedman's description of the book.

QUESTIONS

1. Does the defense lawyer in *Anatomy of a Murder* suborn perjury by the way in which he advises the defendant, or is this the legitimate tactic of a hard-nosed trial lawyer who is informing his client of the law?

2. Compare the *Anatomy of a Murder* scenario to Professor Freedman's description of the defendant who is asked how often he carries a penknife, at page 422 below. Would you make a distinction between the two scenarios? Is there a distinction in the propriety of the advice given in each scenario? Why, or why not?

READINGS

1. Henry Drake, and "Pop" Campbell's Two Lawyers. What should a lawyer do when he or she believes a client is going to commit perjury? Does the lawyer have any obligations to the legal system in addition to those owed the client? Or are lawyers required to keep their clients' secrets, even at the cost of a client's dishonesty, and pursue every means on behalf of their clients, leaving it to the adversary process to produce a just result?

Read the following article about the case of Henry Drake, who was wrongly convicted of murder and sent to death row on the basis of his friend "Pop" Campbell's perjurious testimony. Campbell's lawyers knew that Drake was innocent, but kept quiet. One of Campbell's lawyers advised him to keep quiet even after he expressed a desire to recant. Was their conduct within ethical bounds? If within the literal bounds of ethical rules, was it the "right thing" to do? Or should morality even be an issue?

DAVID A. KAPLAN, DEATH ROW DILEMMA
The National Law Journal (January 25, 1988)[1]

Four men knew Henry Drake didn't belong on Georgia's death row.

One was Henry Drake. Another was his co-defendant, William "Pop" Campbell, a sociopath and a liar whose perjurious testimony sent Mr. Drake away. The other two were Mr. Campbell's lawyers, and they said not a word.

They knew Mr. Drake was innocent because their client told them. But, because of their duty as lawyers, they felt bound to silence.

So was posed the Ultimate Ethical Dilemma, the stuff of law school exams and theoretical symposia: What does a lawyer do when fidelity to keeping a client's confidence may cost someone's life? For Floyd Keeble and Patrick Beall, two attorneys from the piney woods of northeast Georgia, the classic hypothetical of the law became a reality.

Mr. Drake is out of prison now. The state parole board freed him two days before Christmas, believing he spent eight years on death row for a crime he did not commit. Mr. Campbell is dead, of natural causes. The two lawyers, captives in a conundrum they did not create, continue to practice law in the Georgia countryside.

The story of Henry Drake, told through interviews and court records, is a tale of many things. . . . But perhaps most of all, it is a story about the unkind inexactitudes of ethics and inevitable shadows in any system of rules.

Late one December afternoon, 13 years ago, someone walked into Charlie Estee Eberhart's little barbershop in Colbert, Ga., and crushed the skull of the 74-year-old proprietor with a claw hammer. Mr. Eberhart also was stabbed in the chest with a pocket knife and robbed of about $400.

. . . .

Henry Drake and Pop Campbell both were charged with the murder. The two had become friends in 1974 — at Reidsville State Prison. . . . When Mr. Drake got out of jail, he returned home to his parents in Colbert. He soon took up with his girlfriend, Mary Carruth, in nearby Madison, just across the county border. Mr. Campbell followed a short time later; his prison buddy had told him to stop by if he needed a place to stay upon his release from Reidsville. The three were not the most popular of citizens. The two men were white, Ms. Carruth was black, and the living arrangement, by all accounts, was the big scandal in town.

---

[1] Reprinted with the permission of The National Law Journal. Copyright © 1988 by The New York Law Publishing Company.

On Dec. 5, 1975, Mr. Drake, accompanied by his girlfriend, set out to visit his mother in Colbert. Mr. Campbell wanted to come along to get a haircut in town. At his trial, Mr. Drake testified that he and Ms. Carruth dropped Mr. Campbell off at the Eberhart barbershop, and arranged to pick him up later on the way back to Madison.

"Campbell was waiting at the Laundromat when we got there," is how Mr. Drake tells it. "After we got about halfway home, in Athens, he told me he and the barber had been in a fight because 'the old man messed my hair up.' "

Mr. Drake asked how badly hurt the barber was. "Pretty bad," was the answer. He said he did not learn how bad until word got around the next day.

Pop Campbell offered a very different version of events. At his own trial in August 1976, he testified that, as he was getting a haircut, Mr. Drake walked in, brandishing a hammer. He attacked, before the barber even saw him. The jury didn't buy it, convicting Mr. Campbell and sentencing him to the electric chair.

A year later at Mr. Drake's trial, a different jury believed Mr. Campbell's story, despite changes in it. This time, Mr. Campbell said Mr. Drake entered the shop disguised in Ms. Carruth's black wig. After Mr. Drake struck the barber on the head, the two struggled. The wig fell off, Mr. Eberhart recognized Mr. Drake — a regular customer — and exclaimed, "I wouldn't believe you could do something like this." Mr. Drake continued the attack.

The testimony constituted the main part of the state's case against Mr. Drake. Twelve jurors sentenced him to join his former friend on death row.

. . . .

But while Mr. Drake told a story or two, Mr. Campbell had dozens. Floyd W. Keeble Jr., his 36-year-old court-appointed lawyer at trial, recalls that Mr. Campbell "would say something different almost every time I talked to him." However, the one thing on which his client did not waver was Mr. Drake's innocence.

"Before Campbell even went to trial, I was convinced in my own mind Drake was not involved," Mr. Keeble says. "But what was I supposed to do? I couldn't reveal it. I was bound by the rules of confidentiality. And I certainly couldn't prevent Campbell from exercising his right to testify."

. . . .

In November 1978, Mr. Campbell's case was taken over by Patrick T. Beall, a 31-year-old staff lawyer with the University of Georgia School of Law's prisoner counseling project, which had an office conveniently located near death row. He immediately found out about Mr. Campbell's secret.

"I first learned of Drake's innocence in my very first interview with Campbell," Mr. Beall wrote in an August 1987 court document. "Campbell informed me he had 'killed the old man.' He explained he had lied . . . because he thought Drake had turned him in to the law." Mr. Campbell "kept on lying through Drake's trial," Mr. Beall continued, "because Drake and his family were 'ugly' to him after he blamed Drake and because Drake told him he was glad Campbell 'got the chair.' "

The lawyer sternly advised his client "to keep his mouth shut about it and tell no one else."

. . . .

"I was on the horns of a dilemma here," he [Mr. Beall] says. "On the one hand, I had a client who was guilty of murder, and who lied and caused his co-defendant to be convicted and sentenced to death; and on the other, I had a client who was under sentence of death whom I had to protect from that fate."

Without revealing his or his client's identity, Mr. Beall sought guidance from the ethics committee of the State Bar of Georgia. Over the telephone, a committee staffer advised him his "sole focus" should be Mr. Campbell.

"I would let Drake's attorneys worry about Drake," Mr. Beall says, adding that he also decided, if the situation arose, he would "never put Campbell on the stand to testify to what happened on that night in December 1975." This would prevent Mr. Beall from any complicity in Mr. Campbell again perjuring himself. . . .

. . . .

[A]s Ms. Davis recalls, [Campbell] was "beside himself with guilt over the fact that Henry was still on death row because of his lie." Mr. Beall continued to direct his client to keep quiet, advising him that recantation would "virtually destroy my ongoing attempts to obtain sympathetic treatment for him, undermine my legal arguments to have his death sentence set aside, [and] subject him to a potential perjury prosecution."

Despite his efforts to keep Mr. Campbell "from proclaiming the truth to the severe detriment of his own appeals," [as Beall put it] . . . Mr. Campbell set it all out, concluding, "I want to get this off my conscience and try to be forgiven by Henry and God Almighty."

Pat Beall knew nothing of the affidavit. "When he found out," [said Drake's Appellate lawyer, Mary J. Wilkes], "he was irate, thinking I was operating behind his back. He learned I didn't prompt it, and [he] tried to talk Pop out of the statement — to recant his recantation." Pop Campbell did not yield, and the affidavit . . . was used by Ms. Wilkes in a motion for a new trial. Mr. Campbell even testified at a hearing, but to no avail. The motion was denied.

. . . .

In March 1983, Pop Campbell died in prison from his various respiratory ailments. Henry Drake remained there for two more years until the full 11th U.S. Circuit Court of Appeals threw out his conviction and death sentence on technical grounds: flawed instructions to the jury by the trial judge. The court did not discuss the recantation issue.

NOTES

Henry Drake's troubles did not end with the reversal of his conviction. He was tried twice more for the murder of Charlie Eberhart. The jury in the first retrial hung 10-2 for acquittal, while the second jury, despite evidence of "Pop" Campbell's recantation, convicted him, this time with a sentence of life imprisonment. He spent eight more months in prison before the Georgia Board of Pardons and Paroles, while denying a pardon, granted Drake early parole.

But what of Campbell's lawyers, Floyd Keeble and Pat Beall? According to the *National Law Journal* article, both look back at their actions and feel they did the right thing. "Under the state bar code, I had no choice," Beall told his interviewer. "It's unfortunate a lawyer has to have such a myopic view, but I couldn't sell my client down the river." Yet both lawyers admit that if Henry Drake had exhausted his appeals and was actually facing imminent death, they might well have revealed that "Pop" Campbell perjured himself in order to save Drake's life.[2]

Was the refusal to reveal Campbell's perjured testimony the same for Keeble, Campbell's trial lawyer, as it was for Beall, the appellate attorney who learned of the perjury only after the fact? Did Keeble have an obligation to reveal the perjury before or as it happened at trial to avoid assisting his client in its commission? What about Beall? Was the justification for his silence similar to that of the New York attorneys who refused to reveal the location of their client's victims' bodies (see Problem 4)? Here, of course, the innocent party was still alive. And if Beall's silence was justified, was it equally justified to affirmatively try to prevent Campbell from recanting? Consider your answers to these questions in light of the comments and readings that follow.

2. A Brief Rules History. No debate on ethical issues arouses more emotion or causes more controversy than what a lawyer — especially a criminal defense lawyer — should do about a client's perjured testimony. The modern history of this debate can be dated from a series of law review articles by Professor Monroe Freedman in the mid-1960s. Before we turn to the writings of Professor Freedman, and his scenarios which form the basis of Problem 15, it is useful to review briefly the history of the prevailing ABA rules in the last quarter century.

By 1969, the ABA had passed the Model Code. But to some, the Code seemed to add fuel to the debate rather than resolve it. DR 4-101(C) sets forth an exception to the rule of confidentiality: a lawyer *may* reveal a client's intention to commit a crime. DR 7-102(A)(4) says a lawyer *shall not* knowingly *use* perjured testimony. When first passed, DR 7-102(B) said that a lawyer who learns that a client has "perpetrated a fraud" on a tribunal must call on the client to rectify the fraud and if the client does not, *shall* reveal the fraud to the tribunal.

Many felt that these disciplinary rules were inherently inconsistent and that none fully addressed the issue at hand. How, for example, does one reconcile the mandatory language of DR 7-102 with the permissive language of DR 4-101? Is perjury a crime within the meaning of 4-101, or — since the perjury relates directly to the underlying case for which the lawyer is giving representation — should the client's intent to lie at trial *not* be considered

---

[2] Recall Abbe Smith's article in Problem 5 and how she comes down on this issue — or *says* she would come down.

as part of the "future crime exception" to the rule of confidentiality? What is meant by "knowingly using" perjury?[3] In 1975, DR 7-102(B) was amended to provide an exception to revealing the fraud "when the information is protected as a privileged communication." But many felt this exception swallowed the rule.

In the early 1970s, the ABA developed a set of standards for prosecutors and criminal defense lawyers. Standard 7.7 called upon lawyers faced with a perjurious client to allow the testimony to occur, but only in the narrative, as opposed to the usual question and answer format. Then, the lawyer was to refrain from arguing this testimony to the jury. This method found some favor with institutionalized criminal defense organizations, such as public defenders' offices, which were searching for a way to take a position which walked the tightrope between "snitching off" one's client and permitting outright perjury. It also found favor with courts, several of which upheld trial court orders that a defense lawyer act in accordance with this standard.

The problem with the narrative method, however, is that it fools absolutely no one, especially the jury. Many feel it is tantamount to hanging a sign around the defendant's neck that says "LIAR." When it revised the criminal law standards, the ABA first reaffirmed but then abandoned Standard 7.7, preferring to rely on Model Rule 3.3.

Model Rule 3.3 was amended substantially in 2002. Under Rule 3.3(a)(3) a lawyer *shall not knowingly* offer evidence "that the lawyer *knows* to be false," (our emphasis), while the "lawyer *may* refuse to offer evidence, other than the testimony of a defendant in a criminal matter, that the attorney *reasonably believes* is false." No longer is this prohibition limited to a "material" falsehood. Comments 7 and 9 of the new Rules attempt to clarify both this change and the ABA's position on this oft-debated issue. Comment 7 exempts testifying in the narrative in those jurisdictions that favor it, even if the lawyer knows it's perjury. And Comment 9 reinforces that the permissive portion of MR 3.3(a)(3) does *not* apply to testimony by a criminal defendant.[4] In a moment, we will examine how the United States Supreme Court dealt with this rule, in *Nix v. Whiteside*, 475 U.S. 157, 106 S. Ct. 988 (1986).

3. The Perjury "Trilemma." Professor Monroe Freedman's views about what he calls "the perjury trilemma" were sufficiently controversial that the District of Columbia Bar sought (unsuccessfully) to take disciplinary action against him. We met Professor Freedman in the last problem. Now, we excerpt at some length his ideas about "the perjury trilemma," and explore his best known and most controversial thesis — that if necessary, a lawyer in a criminal case must present the client's perjurious testimony before the court, even when the lawyer knows it is perjury. We begin with a brief expostulation of the "trilemma" from Professor Freedman's 1990 volume,[5] and continue with a longer excerpt from his 1975 book, which we use as the foundation for Problem 15.

---

[3] Prof. Freedman has written cogently on the difficulty of using these Code provisions. See especially UNDERSTANDING LAWYERS' ETHICS 125-29 (1990).

[4] Note that in *civil* cases, the anomaly between these two phrases of Rule 3.3(a)(3) is more pronounced.

[5] Since updated with the assistance of co-author Abbe Smith in 2004.

MONROE H. FREEDMAN, UNDERSTANDING LAWYERS' ETHICS
109-11 (1990)[6]

Is it ever proper for a criminal defense lawyer to present testimony that she knows is perjurious? Our answer is yes.[7]

. . . .

Underlying proposed solutions to the problem of client perjury are two sharply different models of the lawyer-client relationship. The traditional model . . . is one of trust and confidence between lawyer and client. The client is urged to confide in the lawyer and is encouraged to do so by a pledge of confidentiality.

The other model is one referred to in the literature as selective ignorance (or, sometimes, intentional ignorance). That is, the lawyer puts the client on notice that the lawyer would prefer not to know certain kinds of facts, and/or that the lawyer can be expected to pass on to the judge or the other party information that the client would prefer to keep confidential. The burden is then on the uncounseled client to speculate about whether to entrust potentially harmful facts to the lawyer — to decide, that is, what is relevant and what is irrelevant, what is incriminating and what is exculpatory. . . .

The problem for the client is illustrated by a case related by a lawyer who practiced selective ignorance. The client was accused of stabbing her husband to death with a kitchen knife. In conferences with her lawyer, she consistently denied committing the crime. The facts, however, were damning. The killing had taken place in the couple's kitchen; only her fingerprints were on the knife; she was in the apartment at the time; and she had no other suspect to offer. An investigator informed the lawyer, however, of reports from neighbors that the husband had had a habit of getting drunk and brutalizing the wife. Confronted with that information by her lawyer, the defendant broke down and "confessed." Her husband had been drunk and was about to attack her again. As she backed away, her hand fell upon the knife and, in her terror, she stabbed him.

Why, expostulated the lawyer, had she not volunteered the information to him in the first place? Because, explained his client — who was unsophisticated about the law of self-defense — "it proved I did it."

Apart from the practical problems of requiring clients to do their own lawyering, we might question whether selective ignorance is a moral resolution of the lawyer's ethical problem. Certainly, lawyers who practice selective ignorance have the comfort of saying that they have never knowingly presented a client's perjury. On the other hand, by remaining ignorant, these same

---

[6] Copyright © 1990 by Matthew Bender & Co., Inc. Reprinted with permission. All rights reserved. Professor Freedman and Georgetown Professor Abbe Smith published the third edition of this volume in 2004.

[7] [1] An overwhelming proportion of trial lawyers agree. *See, e.g.*, Steven Allen Friedman, *Professional Responsibility in D.C.: A Survey*, 1972 RES IPSA LOQUITUR 60. The conclusion is also confirmed by extensive discussions I have had at innumerable professional meetings around the country over the course of a quarter of a century. Law professors, however, generally disagree with my answer. I think it is significant that law professors have made a career choice that removes them from service to clients. . . .

lawyers have disabled themselves from being in a position to dissuade their clients from committing the perjury. Lawyers can remain aloof from client perjury, but that does not prevent it from happening. . . .

The American Bar Association has taken a strong stand against selective ignorance, using unusually strong rhetoric in doing so. To advise the client at the outset not to admit anything that might "handicap the lawyer's freedom in calling witnesses or in otherwise making a defense" is "most egregious" and is advocated only by "unscrupulous" lawyers. Nevertheless, as we will see, the ABA appears to have adopted the solution of selective ignorance in its [Model Rules of Professional Conduct.]

The Trilemma

The lawyer's ethical difficulty has been called a trilemma, because it derives from three obligations. First, in order to give clients the effective assistance of counsel to which they are entitled, lawyers are required to seek out all relevant facts. Second, in order that clients will feel free to give lawyers the information necessary to effective representation, the lawyer is under a duty of confidentiality with regard to information obtained in the professional relationship. In addition, the lawyer is expected to be candid with the court.

A moment's reflection makes it clear, however, that one cannot do all three of those things — know everything, keep it in confidence, and reveal it to the court over the client's objections. To resolve this trilemma, therefore, one of the three duties must give way.

If we sacrifice the first duty, that of seeking all relevant information, we would be adopting the model of selective ignorance. If the second duty is abrogated, that of confidentiality, clients would quickly learn that their lawyers could not be trusted and would withhold damaging information; again, the result is selective ignorance. Only by limiting the third duty — by allowing lawyers to be less than candid with the court when that is necessary to protect clients' confidences — can we maintain the traditional lawyer-client model.

4. The Perjury Described. From Monroe Freedman's seminal first book, a description of facts that results in perjury. Please read this story.

MONROE H. FREEDMAN, LAWYERS' EITHICS IN AN ADVERSARY SYSTEM
30-41 (1975)[8]

Your client has been falsely accused of a robbery committed at 16th and P Streets at 11:00 p.m. He tells you at first that at no time on the evening of the crime was he within six blocks of that location. You are able to persuade him that he must tell you the truth and that doing so will in no way prejudice him. He then reveals to you that he was at 15th and P Streets [one block away from the scene of the crime] at 10:55 that evening, but that he was going east, away from the scene of the crime, and by 11:00 p.m., he was six blocks away.

---

[8] Copyright © 1975 by Monroe H. Freedman. Reprinted by permission. Professor Freedman has updated and expanded his analysis in UNDERSTANDING LAWYERS' ETHICS. *See* footnote 6.

At the trial, there are two prosecution witnesses. The first mistakenly, but with some degree of persuasiveness, identifies your client as the criminal. . . . The second prosecution witness is an elderly woman who is somewhat nervous and who wears glasses. She testifies truthfully and accurately that she saw your client at 15th and P Streets at 10:55 p.m. She has corroborated the erroneous testimony of the first witness and made conviction extremely likely. However, on cross-examination her reliability is thrown into doubt through demonstration that she is easily confused and has poor eyesight. . . .

The client then insists upon taking the stand in his own defense, not only to deny the erroneous evidence identifying him as the criminal, but also to deny the truthful, but highly damaging, testimony of the corroborating witness who placed him one block away from the intersection five minutes prior to the crime. Of course, if he tells the truth and thus verifies the corroborating witness, the jury will be more inclined to accept the inaccurate testimony of the principal witness, who specifically identified him as the criminal.

In my opinion, the attorney's obligation in such a situation would be to advise the client that the proposed testimony is unlawful, but to proceed in the normal fashion in presenting the testimony and arguing the case to the jury if the client makes the decision to go forward. Any other course would be a betrayal of the assurances of confidentiality given by the attorney in order to induce the client to reveal everything, however damaging it might appear.

A frequent objection to the position that the attorney must go along with the client's decision to commit perjury is that the lawyer would be guilty of subornation of perjury. Subornation, however, consists of willfully procuring perjury, which is not the case when the attorney indicates to the client that the client's proposed course of conduct would be unlawful, but then accepts the client's decision. Beyond that, there is a point of view, which has been expressed to me by a number of experienced attorneys, that the criminal defendant has a "right to tell his story." What that suggests is that it is simply too much to expect of a human being, caught up in the criminal process and facing loss of liberty and the horrors of imprisonment, not to attempt to lie to avoid that penalty. For that reason, criminal defendants in most European countries do not testify under oath, but simply "tell their stories." It is also noteworthy that subsequent perjury prosecutions against criminal defendants in this country are extremely rare. However, the judge may well take into account at sentencing the fact that the defendant has apparently committed perjury in the course of the defense. That is certainly a factor that the attorney is obligated to advise the client about whenever there is any indication that the client is contemplating perjury.

. . . .

The most obvious way to avoid the ethical difficulty is for the lawyer to withdraw from the case, at least if there is sufficient time before trial for the client to retain another attorney. The client will then go to the nearest law office, realizing that the obligation of confidentiality is not what it has been represented to be, and withhold incriminating information or the fact of guilt from the new attorney. In terms of professional ethics, the practice of withdrawing from a case under such circumstances is difficult to defend, since the identical perjured testimony will ultimately be presented. Moreover, the new attorney will be ignorant of the perjury and therefore will be in no position to attempt to discourage the client from presenting it. Only the original attorney, who knows the truth, has that opportunity, but loses it in the very act of evading the ethical problem.

The difficulty is all the more severe when the client is indigent. In that event, the client cannot retain other counsel, and in many jurisdictions it is impossible for appointed counsel or a public defender to withdraw from a case except for extraordinary reasons. Thus, the attorney can successfully withdraw only by revealing to the judge that the attorney has received knowledge of the client's guilt,[9] or by giving the judge a false or misleading reason for moving for leave to withdraw. . . .

. . . .

Another solution that has been suggested is that the attorney move for leave to withdraw and that, when the request is denied, the attorney then proceed with the case, eliciting the defendant's testimony and arguing the case to the jury in the ordinary fashion. Since that proposal proceeds on the assumption that the motion will be denied, it seems to me to be disingenuous. If the attorney avoids the ethical problem, it is only by passing it on to the judge. Moreover, the client in such a case would then have grounds for appeal on the basis of deprivation of due process and denial of the right to counsel, since the defendant would have been tried before, and sentenced by a judge who had been informed by the defendant's own lawyer that the defendant is guilty both of the crime charged and of perjury. . . .

Another unsuccessful effort to deal with the problem appears in the ABA Standards Relating to the Defense Function. . . . [T]he Standards present a most extraordinary solution. If the lawyer knows that the client is going to commit perjury, Section 7.7 of the Standards requires that the lawyer "must confine his examination to identifying the witness as the defendant and permitting him to make his statement." That is, the lawyer "may not engage in direct examination of the defendant . . . in the conventional manner." Thus, the client's story will become part of the record, although without the attorney's assistance through direct examination. The general rule, of course, is that in closing argument to the jury "the lawyer may argue all reasonable inferences from the evidence in the record." Section 7.7 also provides, however, that the defense lawyer is forbidden to make any reference in closing argument to the client's testimony. . . . There is, of course, only one inference that can be drawn if the defendant's own attorney turns his or her back on the defendant at the most critical point in the trial, and then, in closing argument, sums up the case with no reference to the fact that the defendant has given exculpatory testimony. . . .

Ironically, the Standards reject any solution that would involve informing the judge, but then propose a solution that, as a practical matter, succeeds in informing not only the judge but the jury as well.

---

9 [*]The typical formula is for the attorney to advise the judge of "an ethical problem." The judge understands that [generally] to mean that the client is insisting upon a perjured alibi over the lawyer's objections. . . .

. . . .

I continue to stand with those lawyers who hold that "the lawyer's obligation of confidentiality does not permit him to disclose the facts he has learned from his client which form the basis for his conclusion that the client intends to perjure himself." What that means — necessarily, it seems to me — is that the criminal defense attorney, however unwillingly in terms of personal morality, has a professional responsibility as an advocate in an adversary system to examine the perjurious client in the ordinary way and to argue to the jury, as evidence in the case, the testimony presented by the defendant.

NOTES

Note Freedman's antipathy towards withdrawal, on the grounds that it will foster lack of candor from the client in discussions with the second lawyer, thus resulting in that lawyer's ignorance. Freedman is hardly the only commentator who has criticized the withdrawal solution. Dean Norman Lefstein has said that "withdrawal from a defendant's case should never be viewed as a solution to the perjury dilemma."[10]

Freedman's conclusion that putting on perjured testimony should be distinguished from "subornation" has received less support. Do you agree with him, or does he take an overly narrow view of subornation in order to justify his conclusions?

5. Practicality and Morality. Almost all lawyers recognize the potentially conflicting duties to client and court which make up two-thirds of Professor Freedman's "trilemma." Freedman tries to solve this conflict by the way he treats the third trilemma component — full and complete knowledge of the relevant facts. A lawyer should "make continuing, good faith efforts to dissuade the client" from perjurious testimony. According to Freedman, this will work only if the client entrusts his or her story to the attorney, meaning that the lawyer must avoid "selective ignorance of the facts." If the client is successfully dissuaded from perjury, both the client's and society's needs are served.

But what if the lawyer fails to dissuade the client from perjury? Ultimately, Freedman would present the perjured testimony, because he believes that the duty to the client is paramount over the duty to the justice system. It is this choice which puts him at odds with the majority of other commentators. Indeed, one of the most oft-cited examples of this majority view is the concurrence of Freedman's frequent adversary, then Appellate Judge Warren Burger, in *Johnson v. U.S.*, 360 F.2d 844 (D.C. Cir. 1966), which we cited in the Supplemental Readings to the last problem. Here's how another court put it:

In our system the courts are almost wholly dependent on members of the bar to marshal and present the true facts. . . . When an attorney adds or allows false testimony . . . he makes impure the product and makes it impossible for the scales [of justice] to balance.[11]

---

[10] *Client Perjury in Criminal Cases: Still in Search of an Answer*, 1 Geo. J. Legal Ethics 521 (1988).

[11] *Dodd v. Florida Bar*, 118 So. 2d 17, 19 (Fla. 1960).

Yet Freedman would argue that, based on surveys of actual practitioners, *his* view, not most courts', is truly the majority view. As a practical matter, criminal defense lawyers would find their jobs far more difficult if they had to place their duties to the court above their "loyalties" to their clients, who frequently start out mistrustful, are scared throughout, and in the end are often sent to prison with only their lawyers to take their side.

As the last paragraph of the previous reading notes, Professor Freedman felt in 1975 that the criminal defense attorney must present and advocate false testimony no matter how morally uncomfortable it made the lawyer. In his 1990 volume, Freedman is still less than fully comfortable with presenting perjured testimony. But he is more comfortable with the morality of his choice: "I find deep moral significance in the dignity of the individual and in the way that dignity is respected in the American constitutional adversary system." Thus, with the exception of a situation involving an even higher moral value — such as acting to save the life of Henry Drake, an innocent person on death row — he could not, "consistent with my own sense of morality," break his pledge to his client, even if the client insists on testifying falsely.

6. Nix v. Whiteside. In 1986, the United States Supreme Court decided the case of *Nix v. Whiteside*, 475 U.S. 157, 106 S. Ct. 988 (1986). Whiteside was facing murder charges, and claimed he acted in self-defense. He told his lawyer, Robinson, that he believed the deceased was coming at him with a gun. About a week before trial, Whiteside told Robinson for the first time that he had actually seen something metallic in the deceased's hand. Robinson questioned Whiteside closely, and when pressed, Whiteside admitted that "[i]f I don't say I saw a gun, I'm dead." Robinson then took very strong steps to dissuade Whiteside from testifying to having seen a metallic object. He threatened to tell the court of the presumed perjury, and to impeach the testimony himself, and also threatened to withdraw.

Ultimately, the dissuasion was successful. Whiteside testified, but only that he believed the deceased had a gun, not that he had seen it. He was convicted, and brought a habeas corpus action alleging ineffective assistance of counsel due to Robinson's admonitions. The Court decided 9-0 against Whiteside, but split 5-4 in its discussion of Robinson's conduct. In dicta in his majority opinion, Chief Justice Burger went well beyond whether Robinson's efforts at dissuasion were appropriate to broadly evaluate the ethical obligations of attorneys confronted with perjurious clients.

NIX v. WHITESIDE
475 U.S. 157, 106 S. Ct. 988 (1986)

. . . . We must determine whether, in this setting, Robinson's conduct fell within the wide range of professional responses to threatened client perjury acceptable under the Sixth Amendment.

. . . .

Although counsel must take all reasonable lawful means to attain the objectives of the client, counsel is precluded from taking steps or in any way assisting the client in presenting false evidence or otherwise violating the law. This principle has consistently been recognized in most unequivocal terms by expositors of the norms of professional conduct since the first Canons of Professional Ethics were adopted by the American Bar Association in 1908.

. . . .

Indeed, both the Model Code and the Model Rules do not merely *authorize* disclosure by counsel of client perjury; they *require* such disclosure. See Rule 3.3(a)(4) [now 3.3(a)(3)]; DR 7-102(B)(1); *Committee on Professional Ethics and Conduct of Iowa State Bar Association v. Crary*, 245 N.W.2d 298 (Iowa 1976).

These standards confirm that the legal profession has accepted that an attorney's ethical duty to advance the interests of his client is limited by an equally solemn duty to comply with the law and standards of professional conduct; it specifically ensures that the client may not use false evidence. . . .

Whether Robinson's conduct is seen as a successful attempt to dissuade his client from committing the crime of perjury, or whether seen as a "threat" to withdraw from representation and disclose the illegal scheme, Robinson's representation of Whiteside falls well within acceptable standards of professional conduct. . . .

. . . .

Robinson's action, at most, deprived Whiteside of his contemplated perjury. Nothing counsel did in any way undermined Whiteside's claim that he believed the victim was reaching for a gun. . . . On this record, the accused enjoyed continued representation within the bounds of reasonable professional conduct and did in fact exercise his right to testify; at most he was denied the right to have the assistance of counsel in the presentation of false testimony. . . .

The rule adopted by the Court of Appeals, which seemingly would require an attorney to remain silent while his client committed perjury, is wholly incompatible with the established standards of ethical conduct. . . .

NOTES

In concurrences, Justices Brennan, Blackmun, and Stevens became the first of many to criticize the Chief Justice's conclusions about a lawyer's ethical mandates. Said Brennan:

> [I]t is not surprising that the Court emphasizes that it "must be careful not to narrow the wide range of professional conduct acceptable under the Sixth Amendment so restrictively as to constitutionalize particular standards of professional conduct and thereby intrude into the State's proper authority. . . ." Unfortunately, the Court seems unable to resist the temptation of sharing with the legal community its vision of ethical conduct. But let there be no mistake: the Court's essay regarding what constitutes the correct response to a criminal client's suggestion that he will perjure himself is pure discourse without force of law. . . . Lawyers, judges, bar associations, students and others should understand that the problem has not now been "decided."

Justice Stevens said the following:

> [T]he post-trial review of a lawyer's pre-trial threat to expose perjury that had not yet been committed — and, indeed, may have been prevented by the threat — is by no means the same as review of the way in which such a threat may actually have been carried out. Thus, one can be convinced — as I am — that this lawyer's actions were a proper way to provide his client with effective representation without confronting the much more difficult questions of what a lawyer must, should, or may do after his client has given testimony that the lawyer does not believe.

Professor Freedman was also quick to criticize his old adversary the Chief Justice.[12] But this time, he was joined by a loud chorus of others who criticized both Burger's use of Supreme Court dicta to set attorneys' ethical standards and his conclusion that lawyers *must* disclose client perjury. Many pointed to Burger's use of the *Crary* case, which deals with civil perjury at deposition, a decidedly different issue with no Fifth or Sixth Amendment implications.

7. The ABA Speaks. In Opinion 87-353 (1987), however, the ABA ethics committee agreed with the *Whiteside* majority's analysis of a lawyer's ethical duties. There, the committee reconsidered its previous Opinion 287 in light of Model Rule 3.3. Opinion 287 dealt with how a criminal defense lawyer should respond when the judge inquires about a client's prior criminal record.

It held that even if the lawyer knows the client has a record, he or she should not reveal it to the court in any of three situations: when the records custodian erroneously informs the court that the defendant has no record; when the lawyer is asked directly by the judge (in which case the lawyer should remain silent); and where the client falsely replies in the negative when asked by the court. The new opinion concluded that under Rule 3.3, this last situation "imposes a duty on the lawyer, when the lawyer cannot persuade the client to rectify the perjury, to disclose the client's false statement to the tribunal. . . ."

Opinion 87-353 then discussed the *Whiteside* case, noting that Rule 3.3 was written to apply to both civil and criminal cases except as the Fifth and Sixth Amendment rights of an accused might limit that application. *Whiteside*, concludes the opinion, stands for the proposition that these rights do not interfere with applying Rule 3.3.

Citing Freedman, Opinion 87-353 then discusses whether its holding interferes with an effective attorney-client relationship. It answers this question with a resounding "no," pointing out that "neither the adversary system nor the ethical rules permit the lawyer to participate in the corruption of the judicial process by assisting the client in the introduction of [false] evidence. . . ." The duty to avoid perjury and to refuse to have it play a part in the court proceedings "is not inconsistent with the lawyer's duty to preserve the client's confidences. . . . Implicit in the promise of confidentiality is its nonapplicability where the client seeks the unlawful end [of giving] false evidence."

---

[12] *The Aftermath of* Nix v. Whiteside: *Slamming the Lid on Pandora's Box*, 23 CRIM. L. BULL. 25 (1987).

Clearly, however, the duty of confidentiality and the duty to prevent the presentation of false evidence to the court *are* inconsistent in those rare instances of client perjury. The Opinion chooses to beg this question, in two ways. First, it claims that the lawyer's professional relationship to the client remains unchanged. But imagine yourself in the client's place; how would you feel about the relationship with your lawyer if he or she went to the court and told it you had lied?

Second, the Opinion closes with the admonition that it is strictly limited to a situation "where the lawyer *knows* that the client has committed perjury." This conclusion brings us right back to the third prong of Freedman's trilemma — knowing the facts of the case — and the danger of what he calls "selective ignorance."

8. When Do You "Know" It's Perjury? The current version of ABA Rule 3.3 makes critical the determination of whether the lawyer "knows" the evidence is false. By their very narrow definitions of "knowing," both *Whiteside* and ABA Opinion 87-353 in effect provide a de facto "solution" to the perjury trilemma. Opinion 87-353 explicitly says that knowledge will ordinarily be based on a client's own admissions, and that "[t]he lawyer's suspicions are not enough." Both the ABA opinion and Justice Blackmun's *Whiteside* concurrence cite *United States ex rel. Wilcox v. Johnson*, 555 F.2d 115 (3d Cir. 1977), for the proposition we have seen espoused by Dr. Samuel Johnson — that lawyers should not assume "the role of the judge or jury to determine the facts."

This narrow view is bolstered by the language of Model Rule 3.3(a)(3) itself, which requires disclosure only where the lawyer "knowingly . . . offer[s] evidence that the lawyer knows to be false." With its double use of the verb "to know," Rule 3.3(a)(3) stands in strong contrast to the later section of the rule, that *permits* the lawyer to refuse to offer what the attorney *reasonably believes* is false evidence.

Courts since *Whiteside* have largely agreed with this narrow vision of knowledge. Thus, in *United States v. Long*, 857 F.2d 436, 444 (8th Cir. 1988), a lawyer "concerned" about the testimony of his client did not put the client on the stand. The court reversed the conviction, stating that a lawyer cannot act against the client's interests unless the client gives "a clear expression of intent to commit perjury." More recently, in *United States v. Midgett*, 342 F.3d 321 (4th Cir. 2003), a lawyer believed that his client was going to testify falsely about a third person in a vehicle who could have committed the robbery. The lawyer had no corroborating evidence, and advised the court, which gave the defendant the choice of having his lawyer withdraw, representing himself and being permitted to testify, or agreeing not to testify. The defendant didn't testify. The Fourth Circuit Court of Appeals reversed the conviction, and distinguished *Whiteside* by noting that unlike that case, this defendant "never told his lawyer or otherwise indicated to him that his intended testimony was perjurious." Another 2003 case, this time in Wisconsin, went even further: requiring an affirmative admission by the client in order for a lawyer to know his client will commit perjury. [13]

---

[13] *State v. McDowell*, 669 N.W.2d 204, 266 Wis. 2d 599 (Wis. App. 2003).

Others, including some ethics professors, have been critical of this narrow definition of knowing. Samuel Dash, former chief of staff to the Senate Watergate Committee and a long-time ethics professor, argued that the Wisconsin rule directly undermined Rule 3.3. In a 2003 article, South Carolina ethics professor Nathan Crystal argued for a "factual inconsistency test." Perjury, for Crystal, would be known "if the defendant's testimony will be inconsistent with facts that defendant has admitted (the factual admission test) or with facts known to the lawyer through independent investigation (the factual inconsistency test)."[14] But what if the lawyer's investigation is incomplete?

Crystal claims that his test is consistent with the "firm factual basis" test adopted by the Restatement of the Law Governing Lawyers. The Restatement states that a "firm factual basis" only exists "when facts known to the lawyer or the client's own statements indicate to the lawyer that the testimony or other evidence is false," but "facts known" may prove to be significantly narrower language.

Brent R. Appel, who argued *Whiteside* before the Supreme Court for the State of Iowa, also adopts the narrow view of "knowing." In a 1988 law review article, *The Limited Impact of* Nix v. Whiteside *on Attorney-Client Relations*, 136 U. Pa. L. Rev. 1913 (1988), he argues that *Whiteside* will rarely have a direct impact on actual cases. The duty to take affirmative action to prevent perjury arises "only when an attorney 'knows' that the client intends to testify falsely. Only rarely will a lawyer know both that proposed testimony is false and that the client is determined to offer the false testimony at trial."

This narrow definition of "knowing" wouldn't make Professor Harry Subin happy.[15] Nor, of course, does it please Professor Freedman. It works well, however, for many criminal defense lawyers, one of whom expressed his methodology to us as follows:

> I try not to ask my clients to tell me what they did. Instead, at the first interview, I ask "what do *they say* you did?" Let's face it; clients are changing their stories all the time. Sometimes, the "facts" just get in the way. Anyway, how do I know what version is the truth and what's not? I once had a client who was a notorious liar. One time, when I asked him to tell me what occurred, he looked me right in the eye and said, "do you want the truth, or do you want the *whole* truth? Or do you really want to know what happened?" Look, my job is to defend my client; I have to know enough about the case to be able to put together the best possible defense. But it's not my job to give my clients lectures about trusting me with the truth, or to give them the third degree every time they tell me a story.

Freedman decries the "tell me what they said you did" method as a victory of tactics over ethics, calling it "sophistry . . . produced by unrealistic rules." Indeed, he clearly believes that presenting perjured testimony is preferable to avoiding the truth. Given the high "knowledge" threshhold, selective

---

[14] Nathan Crystal, *False Testimony by Criminal Defendants: Still Unanswered Ethical and Constitutional Questions*, 2003 U. Ill. L. Rev. 1529.

[15] See Subin's discussion of "knowledge" in the Problem 14 readings.

ignorance will almost inevitably allow the lawyer to duck the trilemma issue, by turning it into a dilemma that, practically speaking, will almost never occur.

One thing that Professor Crystal writes that would garner widespread agreement is the very title of his law review article: *False Testimony by Criminal Defendants: Still Unanswered Ethical and Constitutional Questions.*[16] The meaning of "knowing" continues to be unknown.

9. Is There a Solution to the "Trilemma"? No commentator has yet offered an entirely satisfactory solution to the perjury trilemma. When David A. Kaplan of the *National Law Journal* sought the reactions of ethics experts to the Henry Drake case, Yale Law School Dean Guido Calabresi told him that there are no rules capable of governing all situations. "Any system breaks down in the extreme case," he said, "and one never knows what one will do."[17]

Interestingly, although it was twice expressly rejected by the ABA, the idea of allowing the defendant to testify in the narrative continues to have vitality. District of Columbia Rule 3.3 actually lays out a procedure for narrative testimony, and decisions in Pennsylvania and California endorse the procedure.[18] In *People v. Johnson*, 62 Cal. App. 4th 608, 72 Cal. Rptr. 2d 805 (1998), the court engaged in an extensive discussion of the right of a criminal defendant to testify, and then evaluated six possible solutions to the perjury problem, everything from Prof. Freedman's position to refusing the defendant the opportunity to take the stand. The court concluded that the narrative approach was "the best accommodation of the competing interests" involved. Almost all commentators would agree that the narative solution is only a compromise. Some compromises provide the lowest common denominator, but not this one. To us, it provides the worst of both worlds — the presentation of the false story *and* the breach of client confidentiality.

Perhaps the best solution is suggested by the lawyer, above, who describes his client as "telling a story." Indeed, Freedman notes that in most European countries, criminal defendants are not sworn at all, but merely tell their stories. Some commentators have suggested that juries should be advised that some lawyers might present perjurious testimony. Apart from enormous constitutional problems, such instructions are probably not necessary. Juries are not easily fooled, and experienced prosecutors know that full well. When they argue the motives of witnesses to lie, number one on the hit parade is the defendant. It is partly for this reason that many defense lawyers are reluctant to have their clients testify, regardless of the perjury issue. Indeed, the vast majority of criminal defendants are convicted at trial. Given these circumstances, it is reasonable to conclude that the jury already views the testimony of the defendant as "telling a story," rather than as the truth told under oath.

---

[16] 2003 U. Ill. L. Rev. 1529.

[17] David A. Kaplan, *What Would Ethics Experts Do?*, Natl L.J., Jan. 25, 1988. So difficult is this issue that at least one state ethics opinion failed to resolve it, pointing not only to a conflict in the ethics rules but between those rules and decisional law. *See* Maine Professional Ethics Commission Opinion 140 (1994).

[18] *Pennsylvania v. Jermyn*, 652 A.2d 821 (Pa. 1995); *People v. Guzman*, 45 Cal. 3d 915, 248 Cal. Rptr. 467 (1988); *People v. Jennings*, 70 Cal. App. 4th 899, 83 Cal. Rptr. 2d 33 (1999); *People v. Gadson*, 19 Cal. App. 4th 1700, 24 Cal. Rptr. 2d 219 (1993).

10. Perjury in Civil Cases. Most of the debate on client perjury — as with the issues we raised in Problem 14 — has occurred in the context of criminal cases, with all of the constitutional components those cases bring. But what about perjury in the context of a civil case? First, unlike perjury in criminal cases, civil perjury is most likely to occur before trial, in responses to discovery, either by written interrogatories or at deposition. Because of this, there is both more time to rectify the perjury and more time to allow the lawyer to withdraw if the client refuses to rectify.

There are relatively few cases directly addressing civil perjury. In *Doe v. Federal Grievance Comm.*, 847 F.2d 57 (2d Cir. 1988), the court reversed a suspension by following *Whiteside*'s narrow definition of knowledge: perjury is "clearly established when the client acknowledges [the fraud] to the attorney."[19] The most oft-cited case — the one cited by Chief Justice Burger in *Whiteside* — has a relatively unusual set of facts. In *Committee on Prof. Ethics v. Crary*, 245 N.W.2d 298 (Iowa 1976), Crary, a lawyer who was his client's lover, did not attempt to prevent or correct her false testimony that she was in Chicago for a period of time when she was actually with Crary. Crary was disbarred. Similarly, the court in *In re Attorney Discipline Matter*, 98 F.3d 1082 (8th Cir. 1996), had little difficulty upholding a lawyer's disbarment where an in-court tape machine, inadvertently left running, recorded the lawyer actively suggesting that the client lie.

But what are the practical realities of civil perjury, where the lawyer is not an active participant but, at least in the beginning, an innocent bystander? Here is how one Chicago trial lawyer deals with client perjury in his civil litigation practice.

WILLIAM R. McERLEAN, WHAT DO YOU DO WHEN YOUR CLIENT LIES?
Litigation (Winter 1989)[20]

[U]sually you can believe your client. Sure, he may see things only his way. His enthusiasm for the suit may color his recollection, but the trust you develop with a client is normally the benchmark against which the rest of the case can be evaluated.

What if your client lies? It can be more than upsetting to suspect client dishonesty: Your whole case will seem built on a foundation of sand. The positions you have stoutly defended will instantly appear baseless. The arguments you have ridiculed will suddenly have substance.

Faced with such suspicion, what do you do next? Implore your lying client to tell the truth or confess he is a perjurer? Tell the court? Pull out of the case? Rely on attorney-client privilege, stay silent and hope for the best?

. . . .

In civil litigation — the focus here — . . . [a] lying client's constitutional rights usually do not complicate counsel's dilemma. Given the scope of civil

---

[19] *Doe* involved an underlying civil case but concerned an *adverse witness*, not the lawyer's own client. Nevertheless the narrow definition of knowledge is significant.

[20] Copyright © 1989 by William M. McErlean. Reprinted by permission.

discovery and extended trial preparation time, lawyers rarely should be surprised by client perjury at trial or by a client's proposal, on the eve of trial, to lie in court.

In fact, the civil ground rules are easily stated: A lawyer must try to dissuade his client from committing perjury. If perjury has already occurred, the lawyer must try to get the client to correct it. Counsel cannot permit a client to commit perjury or allow perjury to remain in the record. If the client cannot be persuaded to refrain from or correct perjury, the lawyer must withdraw.

Beyond these basics, things get muddier. The problem is that disclosure of perjury to the court can conflict with other ethical obligations.

. . . .

How, in actual practice, do you deal with possible dishonesty?

Obvious liars do not often walk into lawyers' offices. More often, an apparently credible potential client asks you to represent him. Parts of his story are confusing, inconsistent, or illogical. You do not know whether your doubts are well founded. Is it a matter of faulty recollection or lying? Experience teaches that nearly everyone has flawed recall. . . . What do you do?

In the most diplomatic way, point out the inconsistency or illogic. If that does not clear things up, explain how inconsistencies can foul up prosecution of the suit. If that fails to help, explain your own ethical duties and your obligation under Rule 11 to investigate the facts. Point out the consequences, to both attorney and client, of a violation of those duties.

. . . .

Paradoxically, the most dangerous situation is the client interview where nothing seems wrong. You have no doubts about the client's recollection or veracity. You take the case. Then, in discovery, you learn that the client's story is riddled with inconsistencies and possible falsehoods.

. . . .

[A] client's lie in civil litigation, if not revealed earlier, is most likely to surface just before, or at, his deposition.

A good way to ensure a truthful deposition is to keep your client informed of the results of discovery. Without loading on too much extraneous information, send him the opponent's answers to interrogatories and key documents. Insist that he review selected deposition transcripts with you. Schedule regular meetings to go over the case and keep his recollection fresh. If inconsistencies arise, point them out. Require clear explanations, and insist that he try to recall as much as he can.

Client communication at regular intervals over the course of discovery is essential when you suspect the client may be lying. Rather than forcing an explosive confrontation the day before a deposition, repeated examination of the client's inconsistencies gives him time to sort out his recollection, if recollection is the problem. If it is a lie, constant exposure to the consequences of the lie gives the client an opportunity to save face and retreat gracefully from the untruth.

. . . .

If you learn before your client's deposition that he is lying and that the lie has surfaced in a court paper, act immediately. You can no longer try diplomatically to prevent the deception. . . . In all jurisdictions, continuing to litigate after you discover a falsehood will be considered in assessing sanctions. *Orange Prod. Credit Ass'n v. Frontline Ventures, Ltd.*, 792 F.2d 797 (9th Cir. 1986).

Suppose your client's deposition is only days away, and you still believe he is lying or intends to. . . . This is your last chance to prevent big trouble. You must confront the client with your belief. Now is the time to use unsubtle, high-powered tactics. Tell him about the penalties for perjury. Outline your ethical obligation not to present perjured testimony and to withdraw if he insists on proceeding with a lie. You also can tell him that if perjury is committed, you are ethically obliged to tell the court and that the attorney-client privilege cannot stop you from doing so. . . .

After a few salvos like that, you may no longer have a client. But suppose, despite such heavy artillery, you cannot budge your client from his intended perjury and, improbably, he admits the lie but says he will stick to it at his deposition. Then your course is clear. Move to withdraw, cancel the deposition, and, if called upon by ethical rules in your jurisdiction, explain to the court why you are withdrawing.

. . . .

If a lie slips out while the lawyer sips coffee, lights his cigar, or dozes off, he can still act. I have seen attorneys who, when they realized perjury has occurred, react as if poked with a cattle prod, rise up, and demand a break. After some time, they come back with the client, who sheepishly says that he didn't really understand the question or was confused. There is no limit to the variety of possible excuses. After this, the witness "corrects" the false testimony.

The correction dodge is not always contemporaneous with the false testimony. I have seen lawyers wait for days after the deposition to change the offending testimony. But there is one thing I have never experienced: Never have I heard counsel come in after a break and say this: "My client wants to correct testimony he gave this morning because he lied." Always, the correction is said to be based on mistake or confusion.

Correcting false deposition testimony by saying it is a "mistake" is ethically suspect. Still, the fact that the lie has been corrected is probably enough for an attorney to escape disciplinary proceedings. The longer a lawyer waits to correct his client's perjury, however, the greater the risk he runs that the delay will be seen as an unethical strategic decision to wait and see if the other side will be able to prove perjury.

. . . .

A final note: The message of this article is not that a litigator must always view his clients with suspicion, holding them at arm's length and doubting their every word. Instead, the advice here is mostly for lawyers who have developed doubts and misgivings on their own. But everyone should pay attention.

NOTES

New Hampshire attorney Steven E. Feld could have benefitted from McErlean's advice. In *Feld's Case*, 737 A.2d 656 (N.H. 1999), when Feld learned the full extent of a client's false deposition testimony over the lunch recess, he failed to advise his client to correct the falsehood and did nothing to clarify it himself. While Feld did not help create the perjury, he compounded his conduct by later allowing the client to respond inaccurately to interrogatories on a similar subject. The New Hampshire Supreme Court punished Feld, but despite his double violation, only by public censure, nowhere close to the disbarment sought by the state's disciplinary committee.

11. Knowledge, Rectification, and *Jones v. Clinton*. Undoubtedly the best-known example of possible perjury in a civil discovery context is the January 17, 1998 deposition given by President Clinton in the lawsuit brought against him by Paula Jones. The deposition came ten days after Monica Lewinsky's affidavit, which she later admitted was partly false, that denied sexual involvement with the President. At his deposition, Clinton denied having sex with Lewinsky and testified that he had never been alone with her. Most damning may have been his answer to his own lawyer Robert Bennett's question referring to Lewinsky's affidavit: "In paragraph eight of her affidavit, she says this, 'I have never had a sexual relationship with the President, he did not propose that we have a sexual relationship. . . .' Is this a true and accurate statement as far as you know it?" Clinton's answer: "That is absolutely true."

Given that Bennett himself asked this question, it's reasonable to conclude that the President's lawyer did not know the truth of the situation until later, perhaps not until shortly before the August 17, 1998 grand jury testimony of his own client. Indeed, after learning from special prosecutor Kenneth Starr's report that Lewinsky had disavowed parts of her own affidavit, Bennett wrote Judge Susan Webber Wright, who presided over the *Jones* case, that "portions of her affidavit were misleading and not true. Therefore, pursuant to our professional responsibilty, we wanted to advise you that the court should not rely on Ms. Lewinsky's affidavit." Interestingly, Bennett did *not* advise the judge not to rely on the President's testimony, including Clinton's answer regarding the very part of Lewinsky's affidavit she had disavowed.

Was Bennett's failure to rectify the President's deposition testimony disingenuous? Self-serving? Was it arguably unethical? One argument made in opposition to Clinton's impeachment — that the President's deposition statements about Lewinsky were not "perjury" because they were not material to the *Jones* suit — might support Bennett. But how would Bennett explain attempting to rectify the status of Lewinsky's affidavit while remaining silent on his own client's deposition? Interestingly, Judge Wright had no trouble seeing the fallacy in this distinction. In her ruling holding the President in contempt for "giving false, misleading and evasive answers," she cited Bennett's letter in concluding that Clinton's answer about Lewinsky's affidavit had been just as "misleading and not true" as Lewinsky's affidavit itself.[21]

---

[21] *Jones v. Clinton*, 36 F. Supp. 2d 1118, 1130, n.15 (E.D. Ark. 1999).

There is no unanimity of authority on a civil lawyer's duty to rectify false statements. For example, the *Feld* court, while noting in passing that "[o]f course, a lawyer always has a duty to correct errors created by his client when the attorney learns of them," based its decision more on the attorney's failure to stop his client's falsehoods. Numerous state ethics opinions have addressed what a lawyer must do upon learning that the client has given a false response in a civil matter. Most, but not all (see the Supplemental Readings), require that the lawyer at least advise the client to rectify the false statements and, if that is not done, then withdraw.[22] Other states go further, requiring that the lawyer actually reveal the perjury if the client refuses to correct it.[23]

On the surface, ABA Formal Opinion 93-376 (August 6, 1993) seems to agree with the latter view. But the language of the opinion equivocates, further clouding the issue: "If all else fails, direct disclosure to the court *may* prove to be the only effective remedial measure. . . ." (Emphasis added.) Formal Opinion 98-412 (September 9, 1998) continues the ABA's tightrope walk by noting that rectification is necessary only where the court or opposing party may rely on the false statement. How are these opinions affected by the amendments to Rule 3.3? Is it possible that Robert Bennett could justify his silence about President Clinton's statements at deposition because by August, no one was likely to rely on them?

12. Witness Preparation and Its Limits: "The Most Difficult Question." The one area of almost universal agreement among commentators is that a lawyer should do all things possible to dissuade a client from testifying falsely. In "real world" terms, this dissuasion solves the perjury problem far more often than it fails.

But what about witness preparation? In "going to the woodshed," or coaching, to prepare a client's testimony, how does the lawyer draw the line between giving valid legal advice and information which suggests false testimony? Judge John D. Voelker, who served on the Michigan Supreme Court in the 1950s, provided one of the most famous examples of the fine line between advising a client and assisting in a fraud. It comes not from one of Voelker's opinions, but from his novel *Anatomy of a Murder*, which he wrote under a pseudonym, and which became both a best-seller and a blockbuster movie. In the novel, the defense attorney narrator describes "the Lecture" he gives his clients:

> [C]oaching clients, like robbing them, is not only frowned upon, it is downright unethical and bad, very bad. Hence the Lecture, an artful device as old as the law itself, and one used constantly by some of the nicest and most ethical lawyers in the land. "Who, me? I didn't tell him what to say," the lawyer can later comfort himself. "I merely explained the law, see."[24]

Here is the crucial dialogue from the award-winning movie. An army lieutenant, played by Ben Gazzara, is accused of murdering a man named Barney

---

[22] *See, e.g.,* Alabama Opinions 83-61 (April 7, 1983) and 84-54 (April 5, 1984), Calif. Formal Opinion 1983-74 (1983), North Carolina Opinion 203 (1995).

[23] *See, e.g.,* Maryland Opinion 85-67 (Feb. 11, 1985), Michigan Opinion CI-1103 (Aug. 4, 1985), New Jersey Opinion 520 (Oct. 6, 1983), Virginia Opinion 1451 (1992).

[24] Robert Traver, (John D. Voelker), ANATOMY OF A MURDER (1958).

Quill, shortly after Quill raped Gazzara's wife. Jimmy Stewart, representing Gazzara, tells his client that of all the defenses to murder, only one — that Gazzara had a "legal excuse" — might apply. Stewart tells Gazzara that he is just explaining the "letter of the law," but Gazzara thinks Stewart has something more in mind:

> Ben Gazzara: Go on.
>
> Jimmy Stewart: Go on with what?
>
> Ben: With whatever it is you're getting at.
>
> Jimmy (smiling): You're bright, Lieutenant. Now let's see how really bright you can be.
>
> Ben: Well, I'm working at it.
>
> Jimmy: Now because your wife was raped, the sympathy will be with you. What you need is a legal peg so the jury can hang up their sympathy on your behalf, you follow me? (Pause while Gazzara thinks hard.) What's your legal excuse, Lieutenant? What's your legal excuse for killing Barney Quill?
>
> Ben (thinking): Excuse. Just excuse. (Stands up and walks to window, back to Stewart.) Well, what excuses are there?
>
> Jimmy: How should I know? You're the one who plugged Quill.
>
> Ben (staring out window, thinking): I must have been mad.
>
> Jimmy: No, bad temper's no excuse.
>
> Ben (walking back towards Stewart): Well, I mean I must have been crazy. (Pause.) Am I getting warmer? (Jimmy walks to door, starts to open it.)
>
> Ben (insistently): Am I getting warmer?
>
> Jimmy: I'll tell you that after I talk to your wife. In the meantime, see if you can remember just how crazy you were.[25]

Eventually, Gazzara comes up with the legal "excuse" of killing under an "irresistible impulse," a kind of temporary insanity defense discovered by Stewart's law associate in the dark recesses of an old Michigan case.

To evaluate "the Lecture" and other coaching, we return to the writing of Monroe Freedman.

MONROE H. FREEDMAN, LAWYERS' ETHICS IN AN ADVERSARY SYSTEM
59-75 (1975)[26]

When I first attempted to analyze problems of professional responsibility several years ago, I suggested that the question of interviewing and counseling the client prior to trial is probably the most difficult of all. As I have thought

---

[25] ANATOMY OF A MURDER (Columbia Pictures 1959, renewed 1987, 8 Otto Preminger Films, Ltd.). All rights reserved. Courtesy of Columbia Pictures.

[26] Copyright © 1975 by Monroe H. Freedman. Reprinted by permission. Professor Freedman has updated and expanded his analysis in UNDERSTANDING LAWYERS' ETHICS. See footnote 6.

about issues of legal ethics and discussed them with others over the ensuing years, I have become more and more persuaded that it is indeed the most difficult question. . . .

If people do respond to suggestion, and if the lawyer helps the client to "fill in the gaps" and to avoid being "tripped," by developing "new ideas" in the course of repeated rehearsals, it is reasonably clear that the testimony that ultimately is presented in court will have been significantly affected by the lawyer's prompting and by the client's self-interest. Whether the end product is "well within the truth, the whole truth and nothing but the truth" is therefore subject to considerable doubt

. . . .

[I] might seem to suggest that the conscientious lawyer should avoid giving a client or other witness an understanding of what is relevant and important and should rely only upon narrative statements unassisted by questions that seek to elicit critical facts. However, anyone who has conducted interviews will immediately recognize that such a procedure would be highly impractical. An untrained and perhaps inarticulate person cannot be expected to relate all that is relevant without a substantial amount of direction. That is why one of the most important functions of the lawyer is to provide an awareness of what is legally relevant. . . . What prompting can do is to trigger recognition, which is a less complex process than remembering. . . . That is, if we rely only upon unprompted narrative, many important facts will be omitted, facts which can be accurately reported if memory is prompted by recognition, such as through leading questions. Obviously, therefore, we are faced with another dilemma. On the one hand, we know that by telling the client that a particular fact is important, and why it is important, we may induce the client to "remember" the fact even if it did not occur. On the other hand, important facts can truly be lost if we fail to provide the client with every possible aid to memory. Furthermore, since the client's memory is inevitably going to be affected by reconstruction consistent with self-interest, a client who has a misunderstanding of his or her own legal interest could be psychologically inclined to remember in a way that is not only inconsistent with the client's case, but also inaccurate.

. . . .

Particularly effective in illustrating the difficulty is the so-called *Anatomy of a Murder* situation. . . . Before attempting to deal directly with the *Anatomy of a Murder* situation, in which the facts are unambiguous and the lawyer is suggesting a defense based upon radically different facts from those related by the client, let us deal with some situations in which there is necessarily a degree of ambiguity.

. . . .

[I]ssues of judgment or degree [may] be colored by the client's understanding (whether correct or incorrect) of his or her own interest. For example, assume that your client, on trial for his life in a first-degree murder case, has killed another man with a penknife but insists that the killing was in self-defense. You ask him: "Do you regularly carry the penknife in your pocket, do you carry it frequently or infrequently, or did you take it with you only on that particular occasion?" He replies: "Why do you ask me a question like that?" It is entirely appropriate to inform him that his carrying the knife only on that occasion, or infrequently, might support an inference of premeditation, while if he carried the knife invariably, or frequently, the inference of premeditation would be negated. Thus, your client's life may depend upon his recollection as to whether he carried the knife frequently or infrequently. Despite the possibility that the client or a third party might infer that the lawyer was prompting the client to lie, the lawyer must apprise the defendant of the significance of his answer. There is no conceivable ethical requirement that the lawyer trap the client into a hasty and ill-considered answer before telling him the significance of the question. As observed by Professor John Noonan of Boalt Hall (in an article otherwise generally critical of my position): "A lawyer should not be paternalistic toward his client, and cannot assume that his client will perjure himself." Professor Noonan continued: "Furthermore, a lawyer has an obligation to furnish his client with all the legal information relevant to his case; in fulfilling this duty to inform his client, a lawyer would normally not violate ethical standards."

Up to this point, the analysis presented in this chapter parallels that in my earliest article. . . . I now believe, however, that I erred in going on to conclude that the *Anatomy of a Murder* situation is "essentially no different from that just discussed" . . . I concluded that it should not be unethical for the lawyer to give the advice. Although I did not articulate it at the time, I also had in mind the "I am a law book" rationale, that is, that the attorney would be doing no more than informing the client of what is in the applicable statutes and court decisions. After considerable reflection, I now consider that decision to have been wrong . . . (It is the same as if, in the penknife case, the defendant had in fact bought the knife the very day of the killing, and the lawyer had advised him to say instead that he had been carrying it daily for several months.)

. . . .

Referring specifically to the *Anatomy of a Murder* case, I suggested . . . [that t]o withhold the advice would not only penalize the less well-educated defendant, but would also prejudice the client because of his initial truthfulness in telling his story in confidence to the attorney.

The fallacy in that argument is that the lawyer is giving the client more than just "information about the law," but is actively participating in — indeed, initiating — a factual defense that is obviously perjurious. To suggest that the less well-educated defendant is entitled to that extent of participation by the attorney in manufacturing perjury carries the "equalizer" concept of the lawyer's role too far. Moreover, even though the client has initially been truthful in telling his story to the attorney in confidence, it does not follow that there is any breach of confidentiality if the lawyer simply declines to create a false story for the client.[27]

---

27 [*] That is a very different matter from accepting a client's decision to commit perjury, and presenting that perjury to the court, recognizing that to do otherwise would undermine the confidential relationship.

NOTES

This isn't just the stuff of movies. In 1997, a well-known Dallas plaintiffs' asbestos firm, Baron & Budd, accidentally turned over to the defense a memo entitled "Preparing for Your Deposition" that read to many observers like a primer in how to stretch the truth in litigation. The memo advises clients to "STOP TALKING IMMEDIATELY" if their lawyer interrupts, because "your attorney is trying to fix something you said wrong. . . ." It instructs clients to listen closely to any "suggestion" made in their lawyer's questions, and offers examples that sound like much more than hints: "You meant that insulating cement was used on steampipes, didn't you?" or "You didn't see the product before the 1960s, right?" Trial judges in both Texas and Ohio were sufficiently upset to order the document disclosed in discovery and to sanction the firm's conduct. We will look at the results of the Ohio case upholding sanctions in Problem 17. Baron & Budd fared better in Texas, where a divided appeals court held that the memorandum was privileged. One Texas trial judge referred the matter to the grand jury, but no action was ever taken. Named partner Fred Baron remains one of the highest-profile plaintiffs' asbestos lawyers in the nation.

SUPPLEMENTAL READINGS

1. There are an enormous number of articles on client perjury. Among the commentators, Charles W. Wolfram is among the most prolific and significant. He has written several articles on the issue. *Client Perjury*, 50 S. Cal. L. Rev. 809 (1977), is one of the few treatises which focuses on perjury in civil cases. *Client Perjury: The Kutak Commission and the Association of Trial Lawyers on Lawyers, Lying Clients, and the Adversary System*, 921 Amer. Bar Found. Res. J. 964 (1980), addresses the varieties of client perjury and various proposals under consideration for dealing with client perjury at the time the Model Rules were being considered.

2. Norman Lefstein has also written frequently and cogently on perjury. In addition to the 1988 article mentioned in the readings, see *The Criminal Defendant Who Proposes Perjury: Rethinking the Defense Lawyer's Dilemma*, 6 Hofstra L. Rev. 665 (1978), in which Dean Lefstein responds to Professor Freedman's writings with his own approaches for handling client perjury; and "Reflections on the Client Perjury Dilemma and *Nix v. Whiteside*," Crim. Justice Summer 1986, in which he took a stand strongly critical of the majority opinion analysis in *Whiteside*.

3. A symposium issue of the Loyola (Los Angeles) Law Review on "Executing the Wrong Person" contains an *Introduction*, at 29 Loy. L.A. L. Rev. 1547 (1996), by W. William Hodes that focuses on the issues raised by the Henry Drake/"Pop" Campbell case. Hodes also compellingly tells the story of the famous 1913 Leo Frank murder and rape case, and the behavior of a well-respected lawyer who knew Frank to be innocent but said nothing. Frank, a Jewish factory manager in Atlanta, was wrongfully convicted and ultimately hanged by an anti-Semitic mob.

4. Among the early criticisms of Justice Burger's mandatory disclosure requirement in *Nix v. Whiteside* is Carl A. Auerbach, *What Are Law Clerks For?*:

Comments on Nix v. Whiteside, 23 San Diego L. Rev. 979 (1986), which strongly criticizes the opinion for its errors of law and analysis.

5. A few ethics opinions on perjury in civil cases come to surprising outcomes. N.Y. County Opinion 712 (1996) holds that an attorney who cannot persuade the client to recant false testimony not only may conceal the perjury but *may not* disclose it. Moreover, the lawyer need not withdraw "if the attorney reasonably believes that he can argue or settle the case without using the false testimony." Philadelphia Ethics Opinion 95-3 (1995) holds that an attorney who knows a client testified falsely at deposition need not reveal it if the testimony is not material, and may continue as counsel, so long as the lawyer doesn't offer the deposition in court, which would trigger the prohibition against presenting false evidence.

6. Arnold Rosenfeld and Nancy Kaufman, "Client Fraud: A Critique of Three MBA Opinions," 20 *Mass. Law Weekly* 2107, June 22, 1992. The authors of this article criticize three opinions issued by the Massachusetts Bar Association that mandate disclosure of past perjury when the lawyer knows that the client intends to repeat the perjury or rely upon it in the future.

7. Erin K. Jaskot & Christopher J. Mulligan, *Witness Testimony and the Knowledge Requirement: An Atypical Approach to Defining Knowledge and its Effect on the Lawyer as an Officer of the Court*, 17 Geo. J. Legal Ethics 845 (2004). This student note provides a good summary of the current case law in which courts have attempted to create a knowledge standard under Rule 3.3.

8. Among the many articles on the Baron & Budd memorandum are Bob Van Voris, "Client Memo Embarrasses Dallas Firm," *National Law Journal*, October 13, 1997, which first gave the memo national attention, and Michael Higgins, "Fine Line," 84 *A.B.A. Journal* 52 (May 1998), which analyzes the line between preparing a witness and suborning perjury in light of the Baron & Budd memo and the *Jones v. Clinton* case.

9. Peter J. Henning, *Lawyers, Truth, and Honesty in Representing Clients*, 20 Notre Dame J.L. Ethics & Pub. Pol'y 209 (2006), is part of a Symposium on Law and Politics as Vocation. In this piece, Professor Henning suggests that the lawyers should strive to be "honest" and that the focus in the ethics literature on "truth" is misplaced. He contends that requiring lawyers to ensure that the truth is revealed undermines their duty of zealous advocacy. A focus on honesty is a better approach because it strikes a balance between the lawyers competing duty to the court and his or her client.

PROBLEM 16

This problem explores the tension between the duties of candor to the court on the one hand, and diligent and dedicated — what some might call "zealous"— representation of the client's cause on the other. As you contemplate the quandaries faced by lawyers Gabrielle Yetzi and Annette Friel, below, ask yourself whether disclosure of the complete "truth" is the ultimate goal of litigation. Also consider these questions, and where you might draw the line: How much knowledge of the truth is necessary in order to pursue a case? Should an affirmative duty be imposed on all lawyers to investigate the facts *before* taking a position? What if the purpose of filing a complaint is merely to delay or harass? May the complaint still be filed so long as there is a legitimate legal justification? Does the amount of candor depend on whether the lawyer is grappling with disclosure of the law of the case, as opposed to the probative facts? Does it make sense to have different standards for disclosing the law as opposed to the facts?

Pushing the Envelope and Coming Clean to the Court

I. Attorney Gabrielle Yetzi is an environmental lawyer. She represents Save Our Land ("SOL"), an environmental group dedicated to preserving open space. A developer is planning to build a large shopping mall on the only remaining undeveloped land within the city. The massive project will require, among other things, the cutting of 1,000 mature oak trees. SOL wants the site to be converted to public park land, but the site is zoned commercial/retail and the local planning commission has already approved the project since it conforms to the city's general plan.

SOL wants Yetzi to file a lawsuit on its behalf to stop the project. SOL knows that the developer is in a precarious financial condition, and that if development doesn't proceed quickly, the project may die. SOL President Ernest Green tells Yetzi "we don't really care if we win or not, but our lawsuit could tie up this project. You don't have to be aggressive. You don't have to get the case on the active trial list. Just buy us some time. Maybe we can find a public funding source to acquire the land. And maybe in the meantime the developer goes bankrupt."

QUESTIONS

1. Would it be proper for Yetzi to file the suit requested by SOL? Is it sufficient if the sole justification for filing is that the land would be permanently altered once development begins?

2. Suppose Yetzi finds a city ordinance requiring a hearing before the Parks Commission before any tree 100 years old or more may be cut down. She asks Green whether there were any such hearings. Green checks with his staff and reports back to Yetzi that no one at SOL could recall. Are there sufficient grounds for Gabrielle to file the lawsuit? Even if SOL's primary goal remains simply to delay development?

3. Suppose, instead, the most Yetzi can find is the possibility that there was not a quorum at one of the many City Council and Planning Committee

meetings where pieces of the development plan were on the agenda. Would this alone be a sufficient basis for filing the complaint?

4. Assume Yetzi files the lawsuit. Must she follow her client's instructions about using various delay tactics? Are there times when *inaction* could amount to inappropriate delay or harassment under Rule 11 of the Federal Rules of Civil Procedure or other relevant standards?

II. Annette Friel is a plaintiff's personal injury attorney. On behalf of client Daniel Hathaway, she is defending against a summary judgment motion in state court in a products liability case that turns on the definition of what constitutes a "defective product design." Friel's research showed that, while it is a close question, the law supports her client's position, and she has filed a strong brief. She feels that oral argument went very well, and that the judge is inclined to deny the defendant's motion. At the conclusion of the hearing, the judge stated that she would take the matter under submission and render a decision within one week.

The next day, Friel spends some time reviewing the stack of recent opinions which has been accumulating on her desk. She sees a case in these "advance sheets" which is directly against her client's position. Neither she nor opposing counsel cited this case.

QUESTIONS

1. Does Friel have a duty to disclose the new case's holding to the judge before a decision is rendered? Would doing so cause her to violate any duty to her client?

2. Suppose that upon rereading the case carefully, Friel concludes that harmful language redefining the meaning of "design defect" is not absolutely necessary to the case's holding. May she now avoid raising the issue with the court because the bad language is merely dicta?

3. What if Friel learns of the new case only after the court clerk has posted a "tentative ruling" in her favor, which under the local court rules will become final unless her opposing counsel gives notice that he intends to argue the matter further?

III. In another state court case, Friel also represents Mary Cooper, who has been injured in a car accident. Cooper claims that the defendant drove through a stop sign at a four-way stop, hitting her and causing her injury. There are no independent witnesses. Although the police were called and their report tends to corroborate Mary, Friel knows that the report only represents one officer's opinion based largely on the client's statement. So the week before trial, Friel sends her investigator back to the scene to canvass the neighborhood for eyewitnesses one last time. To her surprise, the investigator turns up an eyewitness who had been out of the country for some months after the accident. Unfortunately, the witness, who appears entirely credible, clearly recalls that it was Mary, not the defendant, who ran the stop sign.

QUESTIONS

1. Assume that the discovery deadline has passed and (as is the law in many states) there is no order for the exchange of "ongoing discovery." Must Friel disclose this information to the court or opposing counsel? May she?

2. May she argue at trial that there is no evidence other than the driver's testimony to refute her client's story? In closing argument, may she say the following: "Unfortunately, no one witnessed the accident except the parties, so we have to rely on Mary's recollection and the defendant's, and the statements of the police officer, to piece together what happened."

READINGS

1. Rule 11. While the rules of ethics speak to the issues raised here, of equal and perhaps greater practical importance are the effects of a variety of court-imposed sanctions, and the dangers of liability for malpractice or malicious prosecution. Most lawyers who are accused of abusing the court system by the use of a frivolous pleading will not face disciplinary charges, but a court's threatened imposition of sanctions. Federal courts employ several methods to control litigation by imposing sanctions against errant lawyers and their clients. The most important has been Fed. R. Civ. Proc. 11. Many states have similar provisions. *See, e.g.*, Calif. Code of Civ. Proc. § 128.5. Here is an article giving a brief history of Rule 11, and offering some thoughts about the relationship of Rule 11 and discipline under the ethics rules.

PETER A. JOY, HAPPY (?) BIRTHDAY RULE 11
37 Loyola of Los Angeles Law Review 765 (2004)[1]

Rule 11's Role in Controlling Lawyers' Litigation Conduct

Rule 11 was a little used federal rule until it was amended in 1983 to provide for a more meaningful system of sanctions for frivolous filings. Under the pre-1983 Rule 11, a lawyer's signature on a pleading certified that there was good cause for the pleading and that it was not brought for the purpose of delay. This earlier version of Rule 11, in effect from 1938 until the 1983 amendments, was criticized "on the grounds that 'good cause' was poorly defined and that other abuses, such as litigation intended to harass or to force the opposing party to incur unnecessary expenses, were not prohibited."

In response to these concerns, as well as growing complaints among lawyers, judges, and the public over frivolous litigation, the [federal courts'] Advisory Committee amended Rule 11 in 1983. The 1983 version of Rule 11 expanded the significance of the lawyer's signature to require an affirmative duty upon the lawyer to conduct a "reasonable [prefiling] inquiry" demonstrating that the filing "is well grounded in fact and is warranted by existing law or a good faith argument for the extension, modification, or reversal of existing law." In addition, the signature certified that the filing "is not interposed for any improper purpose, such as to harass or to cause unnecessary delay or needless increase in the cost of litigation."

The changes to Rule 11 proved to be significant. First, a "reasonable inquiry" or objective standard replaced the "good faith" or subjective standard of the old version of Rule 11. Second, the amended version of Rule 11 expanded the

---

improper purposes for filing to include "any improper purpose" and not just delay. Third, the 1983 version of Rule 11 required the judge to sanction the offending lawyer for violating Rule 11 rather than leaving discretion with the judge. . . . These changes combined to expand the scope of Rule 11 violations to make them easier to prove, and to require a sanction for every violation. . . .

As Professor Georgene Vairo has pointed out, at least one thing is certain about the 1983 version of Rule 11 — every empirical study showed that the amended version caused lawyers to "stop and think" and engage in "significantly more prefiling research than they had before Rule 11 was amended." The 1983 version of Rule 11 also began to take up a significant portion of lawyers' energies and court deliberations. One multi-circuit study found that in a one-year period nearly 25% of lawyers who practiced in federal court had been involved in cases in which Rule 11 motions or show cause orders had been filed but did not lead to sanctions, and nearly 8% had been involved in cases where judges imposed sanctions. In addition, this study found that during the same one-year period over 30% of lawyers had received out-of-court threats of sanctions and nearly 25% had received in-court threats of sanctions in cases where no formal Rule 11 sanctions requests or procedures were initiated.

Understandably, the threats and sanctions took a toll on lawyer relations. A Federal Judicial Center study in 1991 demonstrated that over 50% of the 483 federal judges responding to the survey believed that Rule 11 motions "exacerbate unnecessarily contentious behavior of counsel toward one another." Similarly, a 1992 study by the American Judicature Society (AJS) found that 64% of the lawyers surveyed thought that Rule 11 had caused a decline in lawyer civility.

Responding to these and other studies and complaints about Rule 11, the Advisory Committee . . . concluded that in many ways the 1983 version was counterproductive to promoting efficient and ethical litigation conduct, and it proposed amendments designed to correct some of the problems and inefficiencies.

Among its changes, the 1993 version of Rule 11 provided that the purpose of Rule 11 sanctions is solely the deterrence of objectionable filings, made the imposition of sanctions discretionary, provided a "safe harbor" against sanctions for filings that are withdrawn, permitted the filing of factual allegations without evidentiary support at the time of filing provided they were likely to have evidentiary support after discovery, and removed discovery activity from the scope of the rule. The Advisory Committee's note emphasized that a "court has available a variety of possible sanctions to impose for violations, such as striking the offending paper; issuing an admonition, reprimand, or censure; requiring participation in seminars or other educational programs; ordering a fine payable to the court; [and] referring the matter to disciplinary authorities."

A few years after the 1993 amendments to Rule 11, the Federal Judicial Center surveyed judges and lawyers for their views on the effects of the amendments. Among the issues surveyed, the questionnaires asked whether Rule 11 should be modified to better deter groundless filings, and whether sanctions should be mandatory rather than discretionary. Of those respond-ing, the largest percentages — 52% of judges, 41% of plaintiffs' attorneys, 37% of defendants' attorneys, and 40% of other attorneys — stated that Rule 11 "is just right as it now stands."

. . . .

The Use of Rule 11 and Subsequent Professional Discipline

Several challenges exist to investigating the use of Rule 11 sanctions. There are no reporting requirements for the federal courts to track and report the use of Rule 11, so researchers must use surveys of lawyers and judges, research actual court dockets, or rely on electronic database searches to understand the uses of Rule 11. [Here, Professor Joy disusses at length the methods he used for his empirical research to correlate Rule 11 cases and disciplinary cases under ethics rules.]

Despite the difficulties of using electronic databases for researching issues concerning the use of Rule 11 sanctions, the data from those searches do tell a story that is useful in understanding the interplay between Rule 11 sanctions and lawyers' discipline for the same conduct. . . .

Of the 1473 district court cases citing to Rule 11 [during 1993-2003], trial judges imposed sanctions on lawyers or lawyers and parties in only 274 cases and imposed sanctions solely on parties in ninety-two additional cases. Further analysis of the cases reveals that the circuit courts affirmed sanctions against lawyers in 170 cases and against parties in fifty-eight cases. . . .

The foregoing analyses of reported Rule 11 cases involving lawyer sanctions tell a partial story. The data illustrate the frequency of Rule 11 sanctions against lawyers, but they do not provide us with information about disciplin-ary referrals under Rule 11, nor professional discipline against lawyers for the conduct underlying their Rule 11 sanctions. . . .

[T]he data reveal a very low number — only four cases — of disciplinary referrals in [Rule 11] cases reported to computer databases. After discipline was referred in these cases, disciplinary authorities could either decide not to take action, to issue private discipline, or to issue public discipline. Because only the public discipline cases appear as reported cases, correlating Rule 11 sanctions that include referrals to disciplinary authorities with resulting discipline captures only the public discipline cases, which comprise slightly less than sixty percent of all lawyer discipline cases.

. . . .

As a final step to uncover the relationship between reported Rule 11 sanc-tions against lawyers and discipline against these lawyers for that same conduct, I reviewed published discipline cases against the lawyers after the date of their Rule 11 sanctions. I read each discipline case to see if the basis for the discipline explicitly referred to the Rule 11 sanction.

As discussed previously, trial judges imposed Rule 11 sanctions against lawyers in 274 district court cases, and circuit courts affirmed sanctions against lawyers in 170 cases. In searching subsequent discipline cases involving the lawyers from the combined total of 444 district and circuit cases,

. . . only three of the lawyers were disciplined in whole or in part for the same conduct that triggered their Rule 11 sanctions.

. . . .

The foregoing analysis of reported cases demonstrates very little correlation between reported state discipline cases based upon the same conduct triggering Rule 11 sanctions since the 1993 amendments. This data is consistent with a survey of lawyer disciplinary authorities in 1992 and 1993 revealing that "few, if any, Rule 11 violations had been reported" under the 1983 version of Rule 11. Although this investigation demonstrates little empirical evidence of a relationship between Rule 11 sanctions and subsequent lawyer discipline, it begs the question, advanced by some commentators, of whether there should be such a relationship.

2. Should the Rule 11 Pendulum Swing Again? As Professor Joy notes, the Rule 11 pendulum has swung back and forth from mild (1938-1983), to stringent (1983-1993) to more moderate (1993 onward). There is a move afoot to amend Rule 11 yet again to eliminate the safe harbor provision under which otherwise sanctionable pleadings may be withdrawn. The following article reviews and argues in favor of pending federal legislation that would again make Rule 11 more strict. Do you agree that this would be a reform? Or is this legislation little more than client (or defendant) protectionism?

SANDRA DAVIDSON, FRCP 11: A WOUNDED REMEDY FOR UNETHICAL BEHAVIOR
62 Journal of Missouri Bar 16 (2006)[2]

The argument for eliminating the 21-day grace period is not only an ethical one concerning the current law's failure to deter, but also an economic one. Forcing the wrongfully sued defendant to have to challenge the frivolous charges or misrepresentations, but then denying any financial recovery to that defendant, deprives him or her of funds. Thus, the defendant suffers an irretrievable loss. This loss constitutes an injury that the federal rule on sanctions should not permit. (Of course, it may also be that a plaintiff must attack a frivolous defense or misrepresentation, so this problem of loss is not just an issue for defendants. This article will, however, for convenience only, argue in terms of defendants having to challenge frivolous claims or misrepresentations made by plaintiffs.)

The Lawsuit Abuse Reduction Act of 2004, H.R. 4571, targeted Rule 11 for change. Introduced by Rep. Lamar Smith (R-Tex.), the bill supported both mandatory sanctions for frivolous suits and elimination of nationwide forum shopping. Under that proposed legislation, Rule 11 sanctions would become mandatory instead of discretionary, and the 21-day "safe harbor" period would be eliminated. The bill passed the House on a 229 to 174 vote, but the legislation was not introduced in the Senate.

[Now, current proposed legislation] is garnering both support and opposition. Among supporters is a newly formed coalition called the Lawsuit Abuse Reform Coalition (LARC)[, c]omprised of more than 70 member organizations

---

from the business world. . . . Another supporter of the legislation is the American Tort Reform Association.

The Judicial Conference of the United States opposes the Lawsuit Abuse Reduction Act. Also opposing that law is the American Judicature Society. In part, their opposition seems to be a classic battle over the separation of powers. Judges may well be opposed philosophically to legislators trying to become too intimately involved in courtroom procedure.

According to the 2005 survey of federal district judges released by the Federal Judicial Center, more than 80% of the 278 district judges indicated that "Rule 11 is needed and is just right as it now stands." In evaluating the alternatives, 87% of the respondents preferred the current Rule 11, 5% preferred the version in effect between 1983 and 1993, and 4% preferred the version proposed in H.R. 4571. . . .

Also, the American Association of Trial Lawyers' web site has harsh words about the Lawsuit Abuse Reduction Act. But this article, "Proposal Unfairly Targets Civil Rights Plaintiffs and Chills Meritorious Claims," which appears under the hearing of "Factsheets & Resources," says that "[i]n 1993, the U.S. Congress amended Rule 11 . . . in large part because it was being abused by defendants in civil rights cases. . . ." That language is perhaps misleading. . . .

The battle over Rule 11 will continue. Of course, whatever one thinks about the current Rule 11 may well be colored by personal experiences. Fairly recently, I received payment of my attorney fees as a result of Rule 11 sanctions. But I held my breath during the 21-day waiting period. Had the other side simply withdrawn its complaint, either my client would have paid my bill or I would have written the time and effort off as a pro bono contribution to a conscientious client who should never have been put through the ordeal of a federal lawsuit. Not surprisingly, my view is that the safe harbor of Rule 11 can have a dual effect of tolerating arguably unethical behavior by attorneys and depriving wronged defendants from the ability to recover their economic loss caused by such behavior.

Perhaps more important than making up our own minds about Rule 11 is that we attorneys be aware that this debate is ongoing. The future of Rule 11 may, in effect, be controlled by legislators, not judges. And even we who do not particularly like Rule 11 can have qualms about that potential turn of events.

NOTES

Despite the 1993 amendments, the current Rule 11 is hardly toothless, as one might suspect from the wide judicial support the current rule enjoys from the bench. No one, even "tort reformers," consider the liberalized amendments to be a return to the pre-1983 days of a largely symbolic rule. Take the case of *U.S. Bank National Ass'n, N.D. v. Sullivan-Moore*, 406 F.3d 465 (7th Cir. 2005.). There, a federal trial court sanctioned an entire law firm, Fisher and Fisher, P.C., a "high volume operation" dealing in real estate closings, foreclosures, and other similar matters, for mishandling of a foreclosure action against an elderly woman named Mattie Sullivan-Moore, who, as the court noted, "never received proper notice of the proceedings." Fisher and Fisher eventually discovered the address was wrong, but aside from moving to correct "a scrivener's error," did nothing to stop the eviction from proceeding.

"Instead of exploring at that point whether Sullivan-Moore had received adequate process," noted the appeals court, "Fisher and Fisher pressed forward. . . . [A]lthough she had never received the requisite notice of the proceedings, Sullivan-Moore was evicted." The trial court identified numerous Rule 11 violations, including failing to reasonably review the complaint and repeatedly exacerbating or failing to correct the error. The trial court concluded that the initial mistake as to Sullivan-Moore's address "was an honest one" for which Fisher and Fisher should not be faulted. But, it nevertheless sanctioned the entire firm by requiring all the lawyers to attend a 16-hour course on civil procedure. Neither the finding of Rule 11 violation nor the nature of the sanctions was erroneous, concluded the court of appeals: "Neither the firm's caseload nor its practice of shuffling cases from one attorney to another within the firm excuses the type of negligent action that caused Sullivan-Moore to be evicted."

3. Adequate Investigation and Relying on the Client. In addition to the "safe harbor" provision discussed above, another significant softening of Rule 11 in the 1993 amendments is the language in subsection (3) affording lawyers the opportunity to identify certain contentions for which they may not yet have discovered evidentiary support, and in subsection (4) allowing denials based on "lack of information and belief." Since a lawyer's advocacy is continuing, this language buys the lawyer time to investigate, but not the option to hide behind a shield of ignorance forever.

Again, courts have split over whether to use a subjective or objective test. In *Garr v. U.S. Healthcare,* 22 F.3d 1274 (3d Cir. 1994), a divided appeals court upheld sanctions where the pleadings turned out to be meritorious, but the majority described the lawyer's pleading as a "shot in the dark [that] somehow hits the mark." *In re Keegan Mangagement Co. Securities Litigation,* 78 F.3d 431 (9th Cir. 1996), came out the opposite way in another 2-1 vote: Even if the lawyer hadn't adequately investigated, sanctions were reversed where it turned out the claim was not objectively frivolous. The key difference between these cases may be that *Garr* was based on Rule 11 before the 1993 amendments, while *Keegan* was based on the more liberal post-1993 rule.

An objective test can cut both ways. It can get a shot-in-the-dark lawyer off the hook, but it can also result in sanctions despite counsel's personal good faith in filing or continuing an action. In the words of an Oklahoma appeals court that acknowledged the lawyer's subjective good faith under its state version of Rule 11, "if at any point in this inquiry we find either that [counsel] had no reasonable basis in fact or law to initially file the claim, or that after filing the claim he could not produce evidence which would reasonably support the continuation of the claim, we will not hesitate to affirm the trial court's imposition of proper sanctions."[3]

The following case, focusing on the extent to which a lawyer may rely on the representations of a client rather than conducting an independent

---

[3] *Warner v. Hillcrest Medical Center,* 944 P.2d 1060 (Okla. App. 1996).

investigation, was also decided under the post-1993 changes. Would the censure of famed New York lawyer William Kunstler have come out differently if the case had been based on the 1983 version of the rule?

HADGES v. YONKERS RACING CORP.
48 F.3d 1320 (2d Cir. 1995)

Background

This appeal concerns the most recent dispute arising out of the efforts of plaintiff-appellant Hadges to compel various racetracks and state agencies to permit him to pursue his career as a harness racehorse driver, trainer and owner. We set forth below the factual background . . . .

Hadges was first licensed by the New York State Racing and Wagering Board (Racing Board) in 1972. His license was suspended and revoked in 1974 because he failed to disclose the full extent of his criminal arrest record in his initial license application. Hadges was relicensed in 1976.

In early 1989, the Racing Board again suspended Hadges's license for six months after determining that Hadges had illegally passed wagering information to a member of the betting public at Roosevelt Raceway in 1986. According to the Racing Board, as Hadges approached the starting gate, he trailed behind the other horses and shouted, "Get the '7'," to someone in the stands. The number seven horse did in fact win, and Hadges's horse, number two, drove erratically and interfered with the other horses.

In September 1989, although the Racing Board had reissued Hadges's license, YRC denied Hadges the right to work at its racetrack, Yonkers Raceway. In response, Hadges [who throughout was represented by attorney William M. Kunstler] filed an action against YRC in the district court under 42 U.S.C. § 1983, which resulted in the decision in Hadges I. Hadges alleged that YRC had violated his Fourteenth Amendment right to due process in banning him. In the course of the Hadges I litigation, YRC submitted an affidavit of its General Manager, Robert Galterio, who stated that the YRC ban did not prevent Hadges from pursuing his profession because he could still work at other regional tracks, including the Meadowlands in New Jersey.

In March 1990, the district court granted YRC's motion for summary judgment, finding that YRC's practices were not state action and thus could not give rise to liability under § 1983. In two footnotes, the district court indicated its apparent understanding that Hadges was not barred from racing at other facilities but "that proof that other tracks in the state followed YRC's decision could establish state action."

. . . .

In 1993, Hadges brought another § 1983 action, this time against the Meadowlands Raceway. . . . In the course of that action, Meadowlands General Manager Bruce Garland submitted an affidavit stating that Meadowlands had banned Hadges based on the YRC ban. . . .

After successfully settling the Meadowlands suit . . . Hadges brought the instant Rule 60(b) action in the Southern District of New York. He sought to vacate the court's decision in Hadges I on the ground that YRC had perpetrated a fraud on the court in that action by submitting the Galterio affidavit stating that Hadges could continue to work at other tracks despite the YRC ban. [T]he district court ruled against Hadges and granted YRC's motion for summary judgment. In response to a request by YRC, the court also imposed sanctions under Fed.R.Civ.P. 11 on both Hadges and Kunstler.

Facts Underlying Rule 11 Sanctions

In support of his claim for relief in the Rule 60(b) action, Hadges submitted a sworn statement that 1993 was his "fifth year . . . out of work, with the boycott by Yonkers still in effect." Plaintiff's memorandum of law, signed by Kunstler, also asserted that Hadges "has not worked for more than four years." Hadges claimed that he had applied to race at other tracks in New York State, but that these tracks refused to act upon the applications, thereby barring him from racing. He also asserted that upon the advice of a former attorney, Joseph A. Faraldo, he had written to the general managers of these tracks to apply for driving privileges in mid-1990 but received no reply. Hadges presented the court with an affidavit of Faraldo stating that Faraldo had so advised Hadges.

In response, YRC produced documents revealing that Hadges had in fact raced at Monticello Raceway five times in 1991 and seven times in 1993. The most recent race took place less than one month before Hadges submitted his affidavit stating that he had been banned from racing by all tracks in New York State for more than four years. YRC also submitted letters of current and former Racing Secretaries from race tracks in Saratoga, Batavia Downs, Fairmount Park, Vernon Downs and Buffalo who asserted that Hadges had not applied (or they had no recollection of his having applied) for racing privileges at their respective tracks in the relevant time period.

. . . .

After YRC requested sanctions, Hadges submitted an affidavit dated December 28, 1993, admitting that he had raced in Monticello in 1991 and 1993, but explaining that he considered the races insignificant because he had earned less than $ 100 in the two years combined. That affidavit also described a so-called "scratching incident" that Hadges claimed had taken place at Yonkers Raceway on October 31, 1989. He stated that although his state racing license had been restored in 1989, New York State Racing Board judges "scratched" him from that race, in which he was to have ridden the horse "Me Gotta Bret." After this scratching incident, YRC informed him of its independent ban. Hadges argued to the district court that this sequence of events supported his theory that YRC was acting as a state agent in banning him and thus could be held liable in a § 1983 action. Hadges submitted to the court a "scratch sheet," purporting to document his version of the event.

YRC then submitted what the district court later described as "overwhelming proof" that the scratch sheet did not refer to an October 1989 race, but rather to a November 1987 race.

[T]he district court . . . was "quite concerned" that Hadges and Kunstler had attempted "to indicate that [Hadges] had not raced in four years when, in fact, he had privileges at Monticello in both 1991 and 1993." The court stated that Hadges had "made matters worse by attempting to strengthen his claim of state involvement alleging that he was scratched from driving Me Gotta Bret on October 31, 1989 by the judges of the racing board." The court further found that submission of the undated scratch sheet was a "flagrant misrepresentation . . . suggesting the need for sanctions, certainly against the plaintiff and possibly against his counsel." The judge invited Hadges and Kunstler to submit papers opposing the imposition of sanctions.

Thereafter, Hadges submitted an affidavit admitting that he had made a misstatement about the scratching incident but expressing his objection to sanctions. He stated that this error was the result of a simple memory loss, and that the scratch sheet involved was bona fide proof of his having been scratched in 1987 rather than in 1989. He went on to describe yet another 1989 incident in which he had been scratched from racing the horse "Dazzling GT" at YRC.

Hadges also submitted an affidavit of his then-assistant Erik Schulman, which also described the 1989 Dazzling GT scratching incident. Further, Hadges repeated that he had written to the General Managers (not the Racing Secretaries relied upon by YRC) of the various tracks to request driving privileges but had received no reply. He attached copies of the letters along with copies of postal receipts.

Kunstler also submitted a sworn response, which stated that he "had no idea" that the scratch sheet was from 1987 rather than 1989, and set forth the facts of the Dazzling GT incident. Kunstler maintained that the error regarding the date of the scratch sheet was unintentional but would not have affected the outcome of the case in any event. Regardless of its date, he argued, the scratch sheet was evidence that YRC was acting as an agent of the state Racing Board and could therefore be held liable in a § 1983 action. Thus, he maintained that submission of the document was not sanctionable. Kunstler's affidavit did not describe the efforts he had undertaken to verify his client's factual claims. YRC then submitted further affidavits stating that it had no records concerning the alleged Dazzling GT incident.

[T]he judge imposed a Rule 11 sanction of $2,000 on Hadges [and] also censured Kunstler under Rule 11 for failing to make adequate inquiry as to the truth of Hadges's affidavits. . . . In the course of his opinion, the judge stated:

> Mr. Kunstler is apparently one of those attorneys who believes that his sole obligation is to his client and that he has no obligations to the court or to the processes of justice. Unfortunately, he is not alone in this approach to the practice of law, which may be one reason why the legal profession is held in such low esteem by the public at this time.

Rule 11 Sanctions

[A]n amended version of Fed.R.Civ.P. 11 came into effect on December 1, 1993, five days before Hadges filed his complaint. . . . The 1993 amendment to Rule 11 is "intended to remedy problems that had arisen" under the 1983 version of the Rule and is expected to "reduce the number of motions for sanctions presented to the court." Advisory committee note on 1993 amendment. The new Rule liberalizes the standard for compliance and provides procedural safeguards to enable parties to avoid sanctions. Of particular relevance here, the 1993 amendment establishes a "safe harbor" of 21 days during which factual or legal contentions may be withdrawn or appropriately corrected in order to avoid sanction.

If Hadges had received the benefit of the safe-harbor period, the record indicates that he would have "withdrawn or appropriately corrected" his misstatements, thus avoiding sanctions altogether. Hadges did in fact correct one of his misstatements by admitting in an affidavit, sworn to on December 28, 1993, just 12 days after YRC asked for sanctions, that he had raced at Monticello in 1991 and 1993. Thus, this misstatement is not sanctionable.

Hadges also explained and corrected his misstatement about the 1989 date of the first scratching incident and described another scratching incident in 1989 involving another horse (Dazzling GT). This correction was supported by his own affidavit sworn to on March 17, 1994, and the affidavit of Erik Schulman, sworn to on March 16, 1994. Both were filed with the district court on March 21, 1994, just one week after the court issued its order stating that it was considering imposition of sanctions. . . . We note that Kunstler also filed an affidavit making similar retractions.

Kunstler did not receive the benefit of the safe-harbor period. The district court imposed sanctions on Kunstler for failing to adequately investigate the truth of Hadges's representations prior to submitting them to the court . . . .

[We have held] that "an attorney is entitled to rely on his or her client's statements as to factual claims when those statements are objectively reasonable." Calloway v. Marvel Entertainment Group, 854 F.2d 1452, 1470 (2d Cir. 1988), rev'd in part on other grounds sub nom. Pavelic & LeFlore v. Marvel Entertainment Group, 493 U.S. 120, 107 L. Ed. 2d 438, 110 S. Ct. 456 (1989). This interpretation is in keeping with the advisory committee notes on former Rule 11, which indicates that the reasonableness of an inquiry depends upon the surrounding circumstances, including

> such factors as how much time for investigation was available to the signer; whether he had to rely on a client for information as to the facts underlying the pleading . . . ; or whether he depended on forwarding counsel or another member of the bar. Advisory committee note on 1983 amendment to Fed.R.Civ.P. 11.

In Calloway, at least one of the plaintiff's claims "was never supported by any evidence at any stage of the proceeding," and we affirmed the district court's imposition of sanctions. Calloway, 854 F.2d at 1470 & 1473. However, we went on to set forth a procedure for district courts to follow in analyzing whether an attorney has conducted a reasonable inquiry into the facts underlying a party's position.

> In considering sanctions regarding a factual claim, the initial focus of the district court should be on whether an objectively reasonable evidentiary basis for the claim was demonstrated in pretrial proceedings or at trial. Where such a basis was shown, no inquiry into the

adequacy of the attorney's pre-filing investigation is necessary. Id. at 1470.

The new version of Rule 11 makes it even clearer that an attorney is entitled to rely on the objectively reasonable representations of the client. No longer are attorneys required to certify that their representations are "well grounded in fact." Fed.R.Civ.P. 11 (1983) amended 1993. The current version of the Rule requires only that an attorney conduct "an inquiry reasonable under the circumstances" into whether "factual contentions have evidentiary support." Fed.R.Civ.P. 11(b) & (b)(3). Thus, the new version of Rule 11 is in keeping with the emphasis in Calloway on looking to the record before imposing sanctions.

In its first sanction decision in April 1994, the district court here stated:

> There is nothing to indicate that, on the serious factual misrepresentations made in plaintiff's papers, Mr. Kunstler had independent knowledge of their falsity. However, it is equally clear that he made no attempt to verify the truth of the plaintiff's representations prior to submitting them to the court.

Apparently, the district court did not focus, as Rule 11 now requires, on whether the pretrial proceedings provided "evidentiary support" for the factual misrepresentations with which the court was concerned. It is clear that the record before the district court contained evidentiary support for Kunstler's incorrect statements. . . . We reverse the Rule 11 sanction of Hadges and the censure of Kunstler.

NOTES

The *Hadges* court combined the post-1993 "safe harbor" provision and liberalized standard for alleging facts with the Second Circuit's rule that an attorney may rely on "objectively reasonable" evidence. While liberalization of Rule 11 was seen by many as necessary to allow reasonable access to the courthouse, particularly in such matters as civil rights cases, does *Hadges* swing the pendulum too far back, allowing lawyers too much leeway? Or did it work fairly for Kunstler, who claimed he knew of no falsehoods, moved quickly to correct them, and had supporting evidence of his client's claims? The jury is still out about "the new Rule 11," and it's too early to tell to what extent the duty to investigate may be diminished by the 1993 amendments.

4. Tort Claims for Frivolous Lawsuits. In addition to sanctions under Rule 11 and ethical rules that can result in discipline, parties and their lawyers who pursue frivolous claims may also be liable to the opposing party for the common-law tort of malicious prosecution. That tort requires substantially more than a favorable finding on the original case. In most states, there must be both malicious intent and a lack of probable cause to file or continue the action. Probable cause in a civil context has generally been defined as an honest belief after a reasonable investigation that the client has a tenable claim, and that a reasonable attorney after a reasonable investigation would have thought it tenable. It does not mean, however, that the client must prevail, because an attorney does not and cannot ensure victory.

Liability for malicious prosecution and sanctions for Rule 11 under the 1993 amendments have some distinct similarities. Some courts will continue to invoke Rule 11 for meritorious actions taken for an "improper purpose" — not unlike the malicious intent standard required for malicious prosecution. Also, courts in both Rule 11 and malicious prosecution cases continue to examine what weight should be given to the lawyer's adequacy of investigation and reliance on the statements of a client, and the question of whether subjective or objective standards — or both — should apply.

For example, *Tool Research & Engineering Corp. v. Henigson*, 46 Cal. App. 3d 675, 120 Cal. Rptr. 291 (1975), holds that where the lawyer erroneously relied on the client, "the attorney's reasonable and honest belief that his client has a tenable claim" is sufficient to defeat the malicious prosecution cause of action, at least "after a reasonable investigation and industrious search of legal authority" by counsel. The Michigan Supreme Court studied *Henigson* in a malicious prosecution and abuse of process action arising out of an underlying medical malpractice claim, and concluded that the investigation bar set by *Henigson* was too high: "[T]he lawyer risks being penalized for undertaking to present the client's claim to a court unless satisfied, after a potentially substantial investment in investigation and research, that the claim is tenable. . . . Time will not always permit 'a reasonable investigation and industrious search of legal authority' before the lawyer must file a complaint to preserve the client's claim."[4] But the California Supreme Court, in *Sheldon Appel Co. v. Albert & Oliker*, 47 Cal. 3d 863, 765 P.2d 498 (1989), pushed the *Henigson* test in a different direction, allowing a subjective evaluation of malice only in those cases where the prior action was not tenable "as an objective matter":

> [I]f the court finds that the prior action was in fact tenable, probable cause is established — and the malicious prosecution action fails — without regard to the adequacy or inadequacy of the attorney's legal research efforts.

What happens in the opposite situation? Suppose that a lawyer *refuses* to undertake an action desired by a client — for example, by joining a particular party in a lawsuit — because counsel personally believes it to be unwarranted under Rule 11 standards. Should an objective test be used in this situation when the lawyer's client sues for professional negligence? The answer appears to be "no," at least according to *Mills v. Cooter*, 647 A.2d 1118 (D.C. App. 1994). Here, the attorney's subjective belief that a filing is unwarranted will control — at least where it occurs well before the statute of limitations runs and the client is informed: "[T]he second-guessing after the fact of Cooter's professional judgment was not a sufficient foundation for a legal malpractice claim. . . . An attorney is under no obligation to maintain a position which the attorney does not believe that he can honorably defend."

To what extent are law suits against attorneys an abusive tactic designed to create a conflict? In *Creating Conflicts of Interest: Litigation as Interference with the Attorney-Client Relationship*, 43 Am. Bus. L.J. 173 (2006), T. Leigh Anenson discusses this practice and argues that it can violate Rule 11 and

---

[4] *Friedman v. Dozorc*, 412 Mich. 1, 312 N.W.2d 585 (1981).

create a cause of action for tortious interference with attorney client relationship. Does this mean that lawyers could spiral into an endless cycle of suits against each other?

5. Other Rules, Statutes, and Methods of Sanctions. Rule 11 and its state equivalents do not form the only bases for sanctions for a lawyer's improper use of a judicial forum. Several other mechanisms exist in federal law, and in most states. Fed. R. Civ. Proc. 26, also amended in 1993, has become perhaps the most important of these rules. Rule 26(a)(1) now *requires* each party to affirmatively disclose information to the other side "without waiting for a discovery request." Moreover, Rule 26(g) mandates that these disclosures be both signed and certified by the lawyer in the same manner as Rule 11 certification, while Rule 37 specifically authorizes sanctions. 1993 changes to several other federal discovery rules have served to require both a more open exchange of discovery and increased scrutiny of attorneys who make frivolous or over-extensive discovery demands. 28 U.S.C. § 1927 provides authority for monetary sanctions against lawyers who act unreasonably or vexatiously. Various federal rules of appellate procedure have been invoked to discipline lawyers, as the *Hendrix* case, which we excerpt in a few pages, demonstrates.

Another method of deterrence, still in its formative stages, is anti-SLAPP legislation. The following article explains how it works.

JUDITH MILLER, STATES HAVE MOVED TO KEEP PLAINTIFFS FROM USING COURTS TO MUZZLE CRITICS
The New York Times (June 11, 1996)[5]

A university that offers a doctorate in sensuality, including courses in "nice and meanness," "teasing" and "mutual pleasurable stimulation of the human nervous system," was an irresistible story to The San Francisco Chronicle.

So in 1992, the newspaper published the curriculum offered by More University, calling the school "an academy of carnal knowledge" in one of several articles detailing More's many problems. That June, the school sued for libel, citing this description and The Chronicle's account of its other activities.

Though the suit might seem frivolous — a court held that on its face More's complaint was without merit — lawyers say it is one of thousands that have been filed mainly to retaliate against critics or to intimidate them into silence.

Few of the suits, called strategic lawsuits against public participation or Slapps, are successful. But with defendants sometimes spending years and hundreds of thousands of dollars just to get one of these suits dismissed, many are too scared ever again to speak out on a public issue.

For The Chronicle, the price of justice was not too onerous. In August 1994, a California court dismissed More's lawsuit and later ordered it to pay The Chronicle's $60,000 in legal expenses. A state appellate court upheld the dismissal earlier this year, though further appeal on the legal fees is possible. The Chronicle has yet to recover any of the money it spent defending itself.

But the dispute would have lasted far longer and cost even more if not for the fact that in 1992, California adopted a law to prohibit Slapps.

As the number of such suits grew since becoming common in the 1970s, so did the outcry against them. Since 1989, anti-Slapp laws have been passed in eight states besides California — Delaware, Massachusetts, Minnesota, Nebraska, Nevada, New York, Rhode Island and Washington. Anti-Slapp bills have been considered in Florida, Georgia, New Jersey, Pennsylvania, Tennessee and Texas.

Mark Goldowitz, the director of the California Anti-SLAPP Project, which monitors the law's implementation, said such legislation was vital.

"It encourages people to get involved in current affairs without fear of getting dragged down into a litigation morass," Mr. Goldowitz said.

These suits have arisen from many types of citizen involvement:

In Michigan, animal rights advocates were sued for demanding that local agencies stop dealing with a kennel that sold animals for medical experiments. The kennel owners, who claimed business interference and defamation, reportedly received more than $800,000 in settlements.

In Connecticut, a Greenwich man has sued neighbors who complained to town officials after he cut down 95 trees, some on town property.

And in Oklahoma last year, lawyers filed a class-action suit against a group supporting tort reform, saying they had libeled trial lawyers.

The most extensive study of the lawsuits found that most involved development issues but that one-fifth were filed by government agencies or officials against taxpayers.

Because uninhibited public debate is considered a vital part of American government, laws to prevent such suits provide special rules for those who are sued for speaking out.

They outline which cases will be covered — generally libel, defamation and restraint of business suits in which the defendant was speaking out in a public forum or seeking or criticizing a government action. They allow for a speedy hearing by a judge and a quick dismissal. They also allow a defendant to sue the plaintiff for legal fees or even punitive damages.

It is not clear how many such suits are filed because the definition of a Slapp can be subjective, especially in states without anti-Slapp laws. But interviews with defense lawyers, policy makers and advocates suggest that the laws are working.

"I deal with citizens and citizen groups an awful lot," said John E. Grzybek, a St. Paul lawyer, who wrote Minnesota's law, "and they say that knowing the law exists gives them a kind of courage to continue."

California's law is "one of the most important weapons in our First Amendment arsenal," said James M. Wagstaffe, a lawyer who has successfully fought such suits.

George Pring, a law professor at the University of Denver who, with Penelope Canan, a sociology professor at the university, has written the leading work on such lawsuits, "Slapps: Getting Sued for Speaking Out,"

(Temple University Press, 1994), said the scope and effectiveness of the laws varied widely.

New York State's statute, which was passed in 1992, protects only people who "speak their minds about permit applications, zoning changes, leases and licenses," Professor Pring said. As such, he said, it applies to about half of the retaliatory lawsuits that are typically filed . . . .

Minnesota has the broadest law, Professor Pring said. It states that it protects "lawful conduct or speech" aimed at getting "favorable government action." Like most of the strong laws, it puts the burden on the plaintiff to prove that the defendant should not be protected.

Some plaintiffs have claimed that the laws infringe on their constitutional right to jury trial on their claims of injury. Other critics have said that the laws could be used to dismiss valid libel and defamation suits involving matters having nothing to do with government.

Striking a balance between protecting the First Amendment right to "petition the government for redress of grievances" and assuring citizens ready access to the courts is often difficult, lawyers agree. For that reason, some of the new state laws are deliberately vague or narrowly drawn, to withstand judicial review.

California's law, which has had one of the more extensive records of appeals, has been frequently upheld. "We now have published appellate decisions in 10 cases under the California anti-Slapp law," Mr. Goldowitz said. "So far, every decision on the merits has ruled for the defendant who was 'Slapped.'"

. . . .

NOTES

Many states have passed anti-SLAPP legislation. In addition to the First Amendment issues, some observers fear that strong anti-SLAPP laws create a danger that Goliaths as well as Davids will cry "SLAPP," turning what was supposed to be a shield into a sword.

Beyond specific statute and rule authority, some courts have relied on their "inherent powers" to sanction unwarranted attorney conduct. The U.S. Supreme Court has acknowledged this "inherent power." In *Alyeska Pipeline Co. v. Wilderness Society*, 411 U.S. 917 (1973), the Court said that assessing attorneys' fees was justified when a party "has acted in bad faith, vexatiously, wantonly, or for oppressive reasons." And in *Chambers v. NASCO, Inc.*, 501 U.S. 1269, 112 S. Ct. 12 (1991), the Court held that federal courts have the inherent power to sanction bad faith conduct and award attorneys' fees whether or not the conduct is subject to a specific federal sanctioning provision.

Do federal and state practice rules regulating attorney conduct constitute supplementary ethical requirements over and above the rules of professional conduct? What about judicial decisions based on the "inherent power" of courts? Are these efforts on the part of our courts attempts to legislate morality without changing the rules of ethics themselves? The answers to these questions are not simple. Lawyers in all jurisdictions are bound by applicable rules of professional conduct. But it would be overly simplistic to claim that ethical codes, and *only* those codes, govern attorney conduct.

6. Disclosure of Adverse Authority. The following article, written by one of the ethics counsel at the ABA's Center for Professional Responsibility, describes the perils of failing to cite adverse authority. But while the court may appreciate full disclosure of adverse authority, a client may be quite unhappy with a lawyer who is completely honest with the court, perceiving that lawyer as less than a zealous advocate. Is it possible to be a diligent and effective advocate and fully disclose adverse authority to the extent advocated in this article?

JOANNE PITULLA, PLAYING OSTRICH
ABA Journal (August 1993)[6]

Fundamental to a lawyer's role as an officer of the court is the duty to disclose adverse authority — or to describe that duty more precisely, the "legal authority in the controlling jurisdiction known to the lawyer to be directly adverse to the position of the client and not disclosed by opposing counsel." (See Model Rule 3.3(a)(3) [now 3.3(a)(2)] and DR 7-106 (B)(1) of the predecessor Model Code of Professional Responsibility.)

. . . .

Many lawyers say, "Why should I do research and supply argument for the other side? That's their job. My duty is to my client!" But courts must rely on lawyers to supply the law that governs a particular case. As the Comment to Rule 3.3 says, "A lawyer is not required to make a disinterested exposition of the law, but must recognize the existence of pertinent legal authorities." The lawyer can then distinguish the authority or argue for a new precedent.

. . . .

While the federal circuits are divided on whether a failure to acknowledge a binding adverse precedent is in violation of Fed. R. Civ. P. 11, several federal district courts have adopted the Rules of Professional Conduct of the states where they are located. In *U.S. v. Collins*, 920 F.2d 619 (10th Cir. 1990), the court ruled that a lawyer violated Western District of Oklahoma Rule of Professional Conduct 3.3 by directing the court's attention to legal authority with constructive knowledge that such authority had been superseded. This constituted a "brazen subversion of legal argument."

Extent Of Duty

The duty to reveal adverse authority continues to the end of the case and must be met whenever the lawyer becomes aware of the precedent's existence. (See Model Rule 3.3(b) [now 3.3(c)].) The Standing Committee on Ethics and Professional Responsibility concluded in Informal Opinion 84-1505 (1984) that even when an issue is not presently under consideration but may be revisited, the lawyer who learns of a controlling court decision that may be interpreted as adverse to the client's position must promptly advise the court.

---

[6] Copyright © 1993 by American Bar Association. Reprinted by permission.

. . . .

Note that the standard is defined in terms of authority in the "controlling jurisdiction" and may vary according to the nature of the legal question involved. It is not necessary that the adverse authority itself be "controlling. . . ."

A bright line standard for determining when authority is "directly adverse" is found in ABA Formal Opinion 280 (1949): "We would not confine the Opinion [requiring lawyers to disclose adverse legal authority] to controlling authorities — i.e., those decisive of the pending case — but . . . would apply it to a decision directly adverse to any proposition of law on which the lawyer expressly relies, which would reasonably be considered important by the judge sitting on the case. . . . The test in every case should be: . . . Might the judge consider himself misled?"

Professors Hazard and Hodes in "The Law of Lawyering," 3.3:206 (2d ed. 1990), provide even more succinct guidance: "[T]he more unhappy a lawyer is that he found an adverse precedent, the clearer it is that he must reveal it." Playing ostrich can result in sanctions for the lawyer and the loss of the client's case.

NOTES

Are you persuaded by the author's reasoning, which implies that the standard of when to reveal adverse authority is relatively simple and straight-forward? For example, Pitulla cites a 1949 ethics opinion as containing a "bright line standard" to define what authority is "directly adverse." Did you find that standard clear?

Pitulla also points out that under what is now Rule 3.3(c) there are continuing duties to reveal adverse information. As a practical matter, will attorneys like Annette Friel be willing to make such revelations on their own after the issue has been resolved — albeit without prejudice? This rule may be difficult to enforce if nothing is before the court when the lawyer learns of the adverse authority. After all, how would the court ever know if the lawyer fails to provide the appropriate law?

7. Failure to Disclose and Sanctions. How does the failure to reveal controlling authority get applied in practice? Read this brief excerpt from a Seventh Circuit court which took a very dim view of the failure to cite the controlling case, and a very broad view of the possible consequences.

IN RE HENDRIX
986 F.2d 195 (7th Cir. 1993)

This appeal concerns the effect of a discharge in bankruptcy on litigation against the debtor's liability insurer outside of bankruptcy. *In re Shondel*, 950 F.2d 1301 (7th Cir. 1991), decided well before the appeal briefs were filed yet cited by neither party, dooms the appeal, but we shall not stop with that observation, as there are a few new wrinkles in this case.

. . . .

We [address] the parties' failure to cite *Shondel*. Although the cases are not identical, this appeal could not succeed unless we overruled *Shondel*. Needless to say, the appellant failed to make any argument for overruling *Shondel,* for it failed even to cite the case. This omission by the Atlanta Casualty Company (the real appellant) disturbs us because insurance companies are sophisticated enterprises in legal matters, *Shondel* was an insurance case, and the law firm that handled this appeal for Atlanta is located in this circuit. The Pages' lawyer, a solo practitioner in a nonmetropolitan area, is less seriously at fault for having failed to discover *Shondel* — and anyway his failure could not have been a case of concealing adverse authority, because *Shondel* supported his position. At all events, by appealing in the face of dispositive contrary authority without making arguments for overruling it, Atlanta Casualty filed a frivolous appeal.

. . . .

There is a further point. Although as we noted in *Thompson v. Duke*, 940 F.2d 192, 196 n.2 (7th Cir. 1991), the circuits are divided (and we have not taken sides) on whether a failure to acknowledge binding adverse precedent violates Fed. R. Civ. P. 11, if Atlanta Casualty's counsel knowingly concealed dispositive adverse authority it engaged in professional misconduct. ABA Model Rules of Professional Conduct Rule 3.3(a)(3) [now 3.3(a)(2)] (1983). The inference would arise that it had filed the appeal for purposes of delay, which would be an abuse of process and thus provide an additional basis for imposition of sanctions under Fed. R. App. P. 38 ("damages for delay"). A frivolous suit or appeal corresponds, at least approximately, to the tort of malicious prosecution, that is, groundless litigation; a suit or appeal that is not necessarily groundless but was filed for an improper purpose, such as delay, corresponds to — indeed is an instance of — abuse of process.

We are not quite done. Rule 46(c) of the appellate rules authorizes us to discipline lawyers who practice before us. In deciding whether a lawyer has engaged in conduct sanctionable under that rule, we have looked not only to the rules of professional conduct but also to Rule 11 of the civil rules, which makes it sanctionable misconduct for a lawyer to sign a pleading or other paper, including a brief, if he has failed to make a reasonable inquiry into whether his position "is well grounded in fact and is warranted by existing law or a good faith argument for the extension, modification, or reversal of existing law." Reasonable inquiry would have turned up *Shondel*. The lawyer who signed Atlanta Casualty's briefs in this court is therefore directed to submit a statement within 14 days as to why he should not be sanctioned under Rule 46(c).

Affirmed, with order on sanctions.

8. Arguing for "Extension of Existing Law." If the rule about citing adverse authority is to be strictly applied, what may a lawyer do in making "a good faith argument for an extension, modification or reversal of existing law," as expressly permitted by both Model Rule 3.1 and Model Code DR 7-102? (With the exception of substituting the word "nonfrivolous" for "good faith," Rule 11 uses the identical language.) In *Golden Eagle Distrib. Corp. v. Burroughs Corp.*, 801 F.2d 1531 (9th Cir. 1986), a three-judge appellate panel examined this question. The district court judge had sanctioned the law firm of Kirkland & Ellis under Fed. Rule Civ. Proc. 11 for failure to cite three adverse cases. Even though California does not have either Model Rule 3.3 or DR 7-102, the court found that Rule 3.3 was a "necessary corollary" to interpreting Rule 11.

The appeals court reversed the sanctions order. On appeal, the law firm claimed, among other things, that its brief was a good faith argument for an extension or reversal of existing law. The appeals panel held that it was not necessary for the law firm to "identify" its argument in that manner:

> It is not always easy to decide whether an argument is based on established law or is an argument for the extension of existing law. . . . In even a close case, we think it extremely unlikely that a judge, who has already decided that the law is not as a lawyer argued it, will also decide that the loser's position was warranted by existing law.

Then, in excusing the failure to cite adverse authority, the court said the following:

> Were the scope of the rule to be expanded as the district court suggests, mandatory sanctions would ride on close decisions concerning whether or not one case is or is not the same as another. . . . The burdens of research and briefing by a diligent lawyer anxious to avoid any possible rebuke would be great. And the burdens would not be merely on the lawyer. If the mandatory provisions of the Rule are to be interpreted literally, the court would have a duty to research authority beyond that provided by the parties to make sure that they have not omitted something.

> . . . .

> [N]either Rule 11 nor any other rule imposes a requirement that the lawyer, in addition to advocating the cause of his client, step first into the shoes of opposing counsel to find all potentially contrary authority, and finally into the robes of the judge to decide whether the authority is indeed contrary or whether it is distinguishable. It is not in the nature of our adversary system to require lawyers to demonstrate to the court that they have exhausted every theory, both for and against their client. Nor does that requirement further the interests of the court. It blurs the role of judge and advocate. . . .

A substantial minority of the Ninth Circuit court was unhappy with these views and requested *sua sponte* to rehear the case *en banc*. That request was denied (*Golden Eagle Distrib. Corp. v. Burroughs Corp.*, 809 F.2d 584 (9th Cir. 1987)). Five judges joined in a strongly worded dissent, which contained the following paragraph:

> How can a brief be warranted by existing law if its argument goes in the face of directly contrary authority from the highest court of the jurisdiction whose law is being argued? How can a brief be warranted to be a good faith argument for the extension, modification, or reversal of existing law when there is not the slightest indication that the brief is arguing for extension, modification or reversal?

Just as the Ninth Circuit court split on this issue, so too have other circuits, with the Seventh and Eleventh Circuit siding with the dissenters in *Golden Eagle*. For example, in *DiSisto College, Inc. v. Line*, 888 F.2d 755 (11th Cir. 1989), counsel was sanctioned for failing adequately to research the relevant law, which would have prevented unnecessary litigation, and for citing law in another circuit. The court concluded that a lawyer arguing for modification of existing law must first articulate what that existing law is.

9. Disclosing Facts. Failing to disclose adverse authority is an issue which has been widely litigated and thoroughly analyzed. As we have seen, client perjury is another issue which has been subject to great analysis and debate. But what of Annette Friel's factual dilemma? What ethical obligations does a lawyer have to disclose a witness not subject to ordinary discovery? Model Rule 3.3 is clear about a lawyer's duty to take remedial measures, including disclosure to the tribunal, when the lawyer knows that the person is engaging in criminal or fraudulent conduct. It is far less clear when it comes to witnesses and information that adversely affect a client's case. Rule 3.3(a)(1) states that the lawyer shall not knowingly "make a false statement of fact or law to a tribunal or fail to correct a false statement of material fact or law" to the court." Does arguing to the judge or jury in the manner suggested in the problem violate this rule? What about Model Rule 3.3(a)(3), which permits (but does not require) a lawyer to refuse to offer evidence she believes to be false? While it might be a major leap to call it perjury, does Mary Cooper's testimony now fall into this "false evidence" category? Note the difference between the "believes to be" standard here, and the "knows" standard we discussed with respect to client perjury.

What if Mary Cooper had been drinking on the day of the accident? Paragraph 9 of the Comment to Rule 3.3 states that a lawyer may refuse to offer testimony that the lawyer "reasonably believes is false." The reason given is that "[o]ffering such proof may reflect adversely on the lawyer's ability to discriminate in the quality of evidence and thus impair the lawyer's effectiveness as an advocate." But is this reasoning likely to be persuasive to Annette Friel? Or is it more likely that her *failure* to present Mary Cooper's testimony as effectively as possible will call into question her role as an advocate?

A lawyer in Friel's position may also consider the possible malpractice consequences of revealing factually strong information that is not subject to discovery and that hurts the client's case. It may be quite difficult for a lawyer to justify revealing adverse facts. Contrast that with the attorney who, in *Mills*, above, refused to file claims he honorably believed were not reasonable. Realistically, when it comes to facts, isn't there a greater danger that the aggrieved client, if the case is lost, will see counsel as disloyal and sue for malpractice and breach of fiduciary duty?

A brief note about disclosure of facts by prosecutors, a subject we will address more fully elsewhere. In *Brady v. Maryland*, 373 U.S. 83, 83 S. Ct. 1194 (1963), the Supreme Court held that as a matter of constitutional right, a prosecutor is required to disclose evidence favorable to a criminal defendant, an issue we discuss more fully in Problem 220. Anomalously, in *People v. Jones*, 44 N.Y.2d 76, 404 N.Y.S.2d 85, 375 N.E.2d 41 (1978), there was no denial of due process when the prosecutor failed to disclose during plea negotiations that the complaining witness had died. We will look more closely at this case in Problem 18.

SUPPLEMENTAL READINGS

1. Phillip B. Heymann and Lance Liebman, "When to Give Up a Law Suit," in *The Social Responsibilities of Lawyers* 336-54 (1988). This is an excellent case study of a close call, on the border between frivolous filing and dedicated and loyal advocacy.

2. For a liberal extreme on the lawyer's duty to investigate in light of a client's assertions, see *Driskill v. Babai*, Summit Co. Appellate Dist. No. 17914, 1997 Ohio App. LEXIS 1162 (Ohio App. 1997). *Driskill* was a wrongful death medical malpractice action in which plaintiff's lawyer filed a complaint relying solely on "plaintiff's description of the medical care [the decedent] received," and then voluntarily dismissed the case before trial. The defendants sought sanctions under Ohio's Rule 11, but the appellate court upheld the trial court's denial: While "it might be preferable practice for attorneys to acquire the injured party's medical records and have an expert review them before filing, . . . [a]ttorneys do not act in bad faith or engage in 'frivolous conduct' if they reasonably rely on the representations of the injured party and/or his or her family. . . ."

3. David H. Taylor, *Filing With Your Fingers Crossed: Should a Party Be Sanctioned for Filing a Claim to Which There Is a Dispositive, Yet Waivable, Affirmative Defense?*, 47 Syracuse L. Rev. 1037 (1997). This is an important and dicey issue that arises frequently. Prof. Taylor covers the territory well, evaluating the difficult balance between meeting the procedural burden to assert defenses while still avoiding frivolous filings.

4. Lauren A. Weeman, *Bending the (Ethical) Rules in Arizona: Ethics Opinion 05-06's Approval of Undisclosed Ghostwriting May be a Sign of Things to Come,* 19 Geo. J. Legal Ethics 1041 (2006). Should lawyers be able to avoid Rule 11 Sanctions by "ghostwriting" a brief for a pro se litigant? This student note examines a recent Arizona opinion approving the practice.

5. Daisy Hurst Floyd, *Candor Versus Advocacy: Courts' Use of Sanctions to Enforce the Duty of Candor to the Tribunal*, 29 Ga. L. Rev. 1035 (1995). This article contains a good review of post-1993 standards on what constitutes reasonable inquiry, and good faith arguments for modification or extension of existing law.

6. Several United States Supreme Court cases have addressed the issue of what happens when appointed criminal appellate counsel concludes that there are no nonfrivolous issues that can be addressed on appeal. *Anders v. California*, 386 U.S. 738, 87 S. Ct. 1396 (1967), required that even if counsel felt there were no nonfrivolous issues, counsel could not withdraw without setting forth in a brief to the court "anything in the record that might arguably support the appeal." More recent cases have narrowed *Anders*. In *Jones v. Barnes*, 463 U.S. 745, 103 S. Ct. 3308 (1983), Barnes' appellate attorney raised some issues on appeal that his client insisted on, but rejected others. Chief Justice Burger's majority opinion held that "counsel's professional evaluation" of the merits of various claims was sufficient. In *McCoy v. Court of Appeals,*

486 U.S. 429, 108 S. Ct. 1895 (1988), the Court upheld Wisconsin's rule requiring that the appellate attorney's "*Anders* brief" discuss the principal facts and law that led the attorney to believe that an issue was meritless, in effect forcing the lawyer to argue against the client. Finally, in *Smith v. Robbins*, 528 U.S. 259, 120 S. Ct. 746 (2000), the Court, in a 5-4 vote, approved the California Supreme Court's own modification of the *Anders* procedure: A lawyer need not file an *Anders* brief or a *McCoy* discussion, merely a brief reciting the case's "procedural and factual history," and then ask the appellate court to review the record to see if it found any issues worth briefing, while remaining available to brief those issues should the court request. The *Robbins* dissenters argued that this abrogated counsel's role as an advocate. The majority maintained that they were not overruling *Anders*, and that those states that chose to require an *Anders* brief could still do so.

7. Barbara Arco, *Comment: When Rights Collide: Reconciling the First Amendment Rights of Opposing Parties in Civil Litigation*, 52 U. Miami L. Rev. 587 (1998). This Comment offers a good analysis of the important competing First Amendment issues that arise in SLAPPs and anti-SLAPP legislation.

8. Christopher W. Deering, *Candor Toward the Tribunal: Should an Attorney Sacrifice Truth and Integrity for the Sake of the Client?*, 31 Suffolk U. L. Rev. 59 (1997). This Comment offers a first-rate history on the development of the duty to disclose adverse authority.

9. *Commonwealth v. Pavao*, 423 Mass. 798, 672 N.E.2d 531 (1996), suggests that the duty to disclose law adverse to the client is at least more ambiguous when it comes to constitutional rights in criminal cases. In *Pavao*, a judge failed to conduct a personal colloquy with the defendant before accepting a waiver of the right to a jury. Defense counsel knew that the failure was grounds for automatic reversal, yet he said nothing to correct this error of law as it occurred. The appellate court said that this deliberate omission "exceeded the bounds of acceptably zealous representation," and refused to reverse the conviction. The Massachusetts Supreme Court disagreed as to the conviction, since the defendant should not be saddled with counsel's strategy where the point of the waiver was that it must come personally from the accused. The higher court also stopped short of calling the lawyer's conduct unethical: "We express no opinion on the propriety of defense counsel's inaction but do suggest to the [disciplinary powers] that they consider whether such conduct should be subject to an explicit disciplinary rule."

10. Chenise S. Kanemoto, *Bushido in the Courtroom: A Case for Virtue-Oriented Lawyering*, 57 S.C. L. Rev. 357 (2005). In this piece, a practicing attorney recommends that lawyers adopt the virtues of the Samauri including politeness, honor, humility, integrity, and courage. The author argues that adherence to these principles would greatly enhance law practice. It is possible that they might, if followed, eliminate the need for such sanctions as Rule 11.

Chapter 7

TACTICS, FREE SPEECH, AND PLAYING BY THE RULES

PROBLEM 17

The place where most of the modern "advocacy game" is played is not the courtroom, but the discovery arena. In recent years, much of the analysis of lawyer overzealousness has focused on abuses in the discovery process. Attorney Clancy Garrett's methods can and should be analyzed in light of the black letter rules; one's conclusions would be fairly subjective, with reasonable lawyers differing significantly in opinion. But also think about Clancy Garrett's actions in the larger sense — whether certain tactics, assuming they're technically "ethical," might nevertheless not be moral. We ask again whether there should be a difference between morals and ethics. Can or should a technical definition of what is "ethical" be used as a sword?

Is Discovery Survival of the Fittest?

Clancy Garrett is a senior litigation partner with Williams, Ruth, Foxx, Mantle & Henderson, a 250-lawyer firm in the southern part of the state. He is in charge of training first through fourth year associates in litigation techniques. Here are some of the views he espouses.

• "We *do not* give away discovery. We do not give them *anything.* If you can argue with a straight face that you don't understand *exactly* what they mean, then object on grounds of ambiguity. If you can think of a claim to make, then make it. Your job is to get in their way, not to give them information."

•"If you are ordered to turn everything over, try to back up the truck and bury the important stuff. Even when we have to give discovery, we don't have to provide a road map."

• "We will ask for every conceivable piece of information, and go to the mat on it. We want personal stuff, voluminous stuff, the stuff that will wear the other side down. Let them have second thoughts about whether they want to stay the course."

• "So in employment termination cases, insist on every scrap of paper to every prospective employer to make them prove what they've done to mitigate damages. And concentrate on getting medical records if they so much as whisper the words 'emotional distress.'"

• "We must hold our settlements to the eleventh hour. Our job is to protect our clients, not to dole out money to lightweights who can't stay the course. Litigation is a war of attrition. We have the resources here, and our clients have the resources to back us up."

•"If we litigate every case to the nth degree, giving no quarter and offering nothing, we will see our opponents fold nine out of ten times. The tenth time, they may roll the dice and go to trial, but even then, their chances are no better than even. And there's always an appeal. So give no quarter."

Clancy also tells the associates how he manipulates opposing counsel in the discovery process. For instance, although he is known by his male friends to be very supportive of gender equality issues, he purposely calls female attorneys "honey" during deposition and has been heard to make such remarks as, "You know, you're beautiful when you're angry!" when they object to his questions. "This way," he explains, "I get the upper hand even before trial!"

Consider these views. Which practices do you think are ethical and which are not? Why? When do tactics that are merely "hardball" become unethical?

READINGS

1. Discovery "Hardball": Bogle & Gates and the "Dear Doctor" Letters. How far can a law firm go in stonewalling discovery? And how far must young firm associates play along silently or put their jobs in jeopardy? The pressures on law firm associates can, of course, be considerable, and each firm's "culture" is important in determining how its lawyers are "supposed" to act. Take the case of Bogle & Gates, described at length in the Stuart Taylor article *Sleazy in Seattle*, cited in the Supplemental Readings, and reported in part in *Washington State Physicians Ins. Exch. & Assoc. v. Fisons Corp.*, 858 P.2d 1054 (Wash. 1993).[1]

In 1986, Bogle & Gates began representing the drug company Fisons in a case filed by the parents of a three-year-old girl named Jennifer, who was permanently brain damaged from a dose of theophylline, the active ingredient in Fisons's Somophyllin Oral Liquid. The parents also sued the girl's pediatrician for prescribing the drug. Theophylline can be toxic when given to children like Jennifer who are also suffering from a viral infection. Though Fisons knew of this problem, the pediatrician did not, because the company had never warned him. The doctor filed a counter-claim against Fisons, saying he never would have prescribed the drug had he been told.

During discovery, Jennifer's lawyers requested "all documents pertaining to any warning letters including 'Dear Doctor' letters or warning correspondence to the medical profession regarding the use of the drug Somophyllin Oral Liquid." The pediatrician's lawyers asked Fisons for "any letters sent by your company to physicians concerning theophylline toxicity in children." The law firm knew of at least two documents fitting these descriptions: a 1981 letter addressed "Dear Doctor" on the subject of "Theophylline and Viral Infections" sent to 2,000 physicians, but not Jennifer's doctor; and a 1985 memo warning of an " 'epidemic' of theophylline toxicity." However, Bogle & Gates advised Fisons not to produce either document.

Eventually, with no proof that Fisons had misled him, the doctor settled with Jennifer's parents. The parents' lawsuit against Fisons continued until, in March 1990, the pediatrician's lawyer received in the mail from an anonymous source a copy of the 1981 "Dear Doctor" letter. A month later, with

---

[1] In the below account, we have drawn on our treatment of this case in THE MORAL COMPASS OF THE AMERICAN LAWYER 62-65 (1999).

this document now the cornerstone of Jennifer's case, Fisons settled for $6.9 million. The pediatrician, wanting to clear his name, kept alive his lawsuit against Fisons, and also complained of discovery abuse. At trial, the pediatrician won a million dollar verdict against Fisons, and another $450,000 in attorneys' fees.

The doctor was less successful on his plea for sanctions for discovery abuse. Rather than conceding it had erred, Bogle & Gates defended its position, arguing, as to the "Dear Doctor" letter, that the firm had interpreted this request as being limited to the "term of art referring to a warning letter mailed at the FDA's request to all physicians," and not merely to *any* letter addressed "Dear Doctor." As for the 1985 memo, they argued that they had simply limited their response to information about Fisons's Somophyllin *brand name*, even though the request referred to theophylline. Bogle produced the sworn declarations of 14 experts, including eminent ethics authorities and two past presidents of the Washington State Bar. Typical of the declarations was one that said, in part: " 'Practitioners' see discovery as a part of, not an exception to, the adversary system. . . . Tendentious, narrow, and literal positions with regard to discovery are, in my opinion, both typical and expected. . . ."

Faced with this array, the trial judge refused to sanction Bogle for discovery abuse, finding that Bogle's conduct was "consistent with the customary and accepted litigation practices in the bar of this community and this state."

On appeal, the Washington Supreme Court unanimously reversed the trial court. "It appears clear," wrote Chief Justice James Anderson, "that no conceivable discovery request could have been made by the doctor that would have uncovered the relevant documents." The higher court remanded the case with instructions to punish Bogle in an amount "severe enough to deter these attorneys and others" from engaging in such conduct again.

Bogle agreed to pay $325,000, made a public admission of its mistake, and said it had "taken steps to ensure that all attorneys at Bogle & Gates understand that the rules . . . must be complied with in letter and spirit." Yet less than two years after the *Fisons* opinion, in the view of federal Judge Robert Bryan, litigators from Bogle & Gates obfuscated, stonewalled, and "gave answers that were just plain wrong" while defending Subaru of America on charges that the driver's seatbacks in Subaru's Justy could collapse in a rear-end accident. In one request, plaintiffs had asked for National Highway Traffic Safety Administration records that showed the collapse of driver's seats from a rear-impact "force" of 30 miles per hour. Bogle's response was that the request was "vague, confusing and unintelligible. . . . Specifically, 30 miles per hour is a velocity, not a force, and due to this confusion of technical terms, no meaningful response can be given." Judge Bryan called this "lawyer hokum," and forced Bogle to pay the other side's attorneys' fees.

Was this a repeat performance or a legitimate objection? In any event, it's impossible to know for certain why Bogle would risk more judicial wrath. It is possible that Bogle's sanction, even at $325,000, was seen merely as the cost of doing business. Perhaps a stronger signal than the *Fisons* court opinion was the signal sent by the firm when the two lawyers primarily responsible for the Fisons discovery remained with Bogle in good standing, with one promoted to partner.

Was Bogle & Gates, a firm that ceased to exist in the late 1990s, an isolated case? It seems unlikely. One more brief example: Atlanta's powerful Alston & Bird and its client, chemical giant Du Pont. They were accused by judges in Florida, Hawaii, and Georgia of concealing test results that would have helped plaintiff growers prove that their crops were damaged by herbicide after they used Du Pont's product, Benlate. Georgia federal judge J. Robert Elliott called the misrepresentations in the case he tried the worst instance of discovery abuse he had ever seen. He sanctioned Du Pont and Alston & Bird *jointly* for $114 million, saying he would forgive $100 million if Du Pont publicly admitted wrongdoing. Du Pont appealed and won, ironically, on the basis of an appeals court finding that a full due process hearing was required because "Du Pont and its counsel may very well have engaged in criminal acts."[2] After remand, Alston & Bird ultimately settled the sanctions issue by agreeing to pay $250,000 to the Georgia Supreme Court's Commission on Professionalism. Alston attorneys remained adamant in justifying their actions, and it seemed unlikely that the Benlate controversy would dissuade the firm from similar behavior in the future.

Consider what you would do if you were a young associate in a firm and were asked to engage in a discovery tactic that you believed was wrong. Should you, or may you, refuse a partner's instructions if the practice is technically "ethical," i.e., within the four corners of the ethics rules? How can you at least educate yourself about such conduct and its potential consequences? When you become a partner, will you be able to avoid the same practices?

2. Sources of Discovery Abuse. Is abusive discovery inevitable? A quarter of a century ago, a study conducted by the American Bar Foundation and published in 1981 evaluated the civil discovery system and found it replete with abuses and problems, and a marked lack of judicial decisiveness. As you read this report, written by a longtime federal magistrate judge, think about whether these problems sound familiar today. More recent studies, including two in the late 1990s — by the Rand Institute for Civil Justice on the effects of the federal Civil Justice Reform Act of 1990, and the ABA Litigation Section's Special Task Force on Ethics: Beyond the Rules — reached similar conclusions. See the Supplemental Readings for further reference to these studies. The early study also found that there is greater discovery abuse in large litigation than smaller cases, another conclusion that is consistent with later studies.

In the years since Magistrate Judge Brazil's article, our legal system has undergone several reforms in addition to the 1990 Act, including changes in the Federal Rules of Civil Procedure in both 1993 and 2000. Yet to some, little seems to have changed. Can the failings of the discovery system be rectified? Consider who is more responsible for the problems of the discovery system — lawyers or judges. How can lawyers monitor themselves or their clients to avoid discovery abuses, or is discovery so embedded at the core of litigation that only closer judicial activism will help?

---

2 *Bush Ranch, Inc. v. E.I. Du Pont de Nemours & Co.*, 918 F. Supp. 1524 (M.D. Ga. 1995), *rev'd, In re E.I. DuPont De Nemours & Co. (Benlate Litigation)*, 99 F.3d 363 (11th Cir. 1996).

WAYNE D. BRAZIL, CIVIL DISCOVERY: HOW BAD ARE THE PROBLEMS?
67 ABA Journal 450 (1981)[3]

During the last few years many practicing lawyers, judges, and legal scholars have criticized the way pretrial discovery is working in civil litigation. . . . In 1979 the American Bar Foundation began sponsoring a study whose purpose was to meet this need.

We . . . [interviewed] 180 lawyers who practice in the Chicago area. Because we interviewed lawyers from a wide range of civil practices, we were able to compare the experiences and complaints of groups of quite differently situated attorneys.

. . . . The data show that there are great differences between the character of discovery in large cases and in smaller cases and that in larger lawsuits the system is plagued with severe problems that prevent it from effectively serving the purposes for which it was designed. The interviews also produced a dramatically intense and consistent chorus of criticism of the role the courts play in the discovery arena. An overwhelming majority of the lawyers we interviewed blame the judiciary for many of the discovery system's most severe problems. Four of every five respondents believe the courts should impose sanctions more frequently. And litigators who primarily handle large matters call in loud and remarkably united voices for more help from the courts in controlling what appears to be a runaway system.

. . . .

. . . [B]ig case lawyers portrayed a system whose most salient characteristic is gross inefficiency. Among the sources of that inefficiency, none plays a more pervasive, troublesome role than evasion. Evasive responses to discovery requests have become a ubiquitous feature of the system in sizeable lawsuits. . . . Providing evasive or only partly responsive answers to discovery requests is not the only form of "foxholing" that plagues larger lawsuits. Another widely used avoidance technique is delay. . . . Doctrinal shields of information — the attorney-client privilege, the work product doctrine, and rules protecting trade secrets — also are significant sources of friction and inefficiency in the discovery stage of major lawsuits.

. . . .

These deficiencies or limitations, however, by no means are always self-imposed. The big case litigators we interviewed made it quite clear that they spend considerable time and creative energy trying to increase the odds that opposing counsel will fail to discover damaging information from their clients. As one declared, "Most attorneys still see discovery as a game and play it to the hilt to avoid disclosure."

. . . .

Several lawyers admitted that only a small percentage of the information their own discovery efforts produce is really useful. Many also reported that to uncover key information they had to develop elaborate systems of discovery probes, employing different kinds of discovery devices in carefully orchestrated

---

sequences, and that they had to commit substantial resources not only to sifting through immense amounts of material produced by their opponents but also to framing careful follow-up inquiries.

. . . .

Some of this inefficiency is attributable, of course, to the complex legal theories on which some large cases turn and to the large data bases the theories sometimes require. The lawyers we interviewed, however, left us with no doubt that whatever inefficiency is inherent in the development of big cases is substantially aggravated by adversarial maneuvering that intensifies through cycles of mutual mistrust. The kind of attitude that both reflects and generates mistrust was succinctly articulated by one interviewed litigator. "In the adversarial system it's one group's job to get information and the other's not to give it to them."

The inefficiency of the discovery process in larger cases might be tolerable if it regularly accomplished the goal of distributing all the important information about a case among all the parties. Unfortunately, the system as it operates in larger cases has no such redeeming feature. . . . [I]n half of the larger, more complex lawsuits that are closed by settlement, at least one of the attorneys believes he knows something of significance about the case that counsel for other parties have not discovered. [Moreover,] in half of the cases they settle they believe that another party still has [undiscovered] relevant information. . . .

. . . .

As a group, lawyers who primarily handle smaller cases [$25,000 or less in dispute] are measurably less dissatisfied with how the discovery system works than are their larger case counterparts. . . . In smaller matters there is less money available to support elaborate tactical plans, there tends to be less data to process, and the existence and sources of relevant evidence tend to be more predictable. . . .

. . . .

The lawyers interviewed readily acknowledged that lawyers and ways of lawyering are responsible for many of the defects of the discovery system. Despite these concessions, however, many lawyers feel that the principal culprits in the discovery system's failings are judges. The only partly articulated theory supporting this belief seems to be that irresistible economic and adversarial pressures will compel attorneys to adopt evasive and sometimes abusive tactics unless the courts impose a system of predictably tight and telling restraints.

. . . .

. . . [T]here is one aspect of judicial behavior that provoked far more complaints than any other. Eighty per cent of *all* the interviewed lawyers believe that the courts should more frequently sanction discovery abuse. . . . Many litigators are intensely angry about what they perceive as the courts' failure to provide the discipline the system requires.

. . . .

We should report one additional result of our study that has important implications for reform efforts. Contrary to some assumptions, there is no broad support for the notion that the scope of discovery should be narrowed. While among all the lawyers we interviewed 30 per cent favored cutting back the scope of discovery, twice as many (60 per cent) favored leaving the scope as it is and 10 per cent favored broadening it. . . .

At least according to the lawyers in our sample, it would be a mistake to focus efforts to reform discovery on the formal descriptions of its proper scope. Instead, litigators believe the real need is to devise a system of restraints and rewards that will combat the pervasive problem of evasion and curb misuse of the system's tools.

NOTES

Before we move on, consider a few additional questions. Does how discovery is conducted in a particular case depend on the tone that's set in that case? If so, who sets that tone? Some academics have argued that plaintiffs typically are the seekers of discovery, while defendants are the resisters. If this is so, is it defense counsel who generally sets the discovery tone? Many plaintiffs' lawyers feel this way, and claim to be ready for an open and friendly exchange until a Clancy Garrett type appears in opposition. Others argue that the tone is really set by plaintiff's counsel, who determines how broadly the case is pled and thus how much resistance is necessary.

3. Choosing Sides? The following article has a clear point of view — not surprising from a lawyer who works at a think tank largely funded by ATLA, primarily a plaintiffs' lawyers' group. Nevertheless, he is not the only one with this perspective. Is his point of view justified?

JAMES E. ROOKS, JR., WILL E-DISCOVERY GET SQUEEZED?
40 Trial 18 (2004)[4]

For at least the past 15 years, the ability of requesting parties — which, in products liability cases, usually means the plaintiffs — to use the broad discovery rights originally envisioned in the Federal Rules of Civil Procedure, and the notice-pleading regime they complement, has been steadily curtailed. Similar developments have been seen in state courts, owing to the trickle-down effect of the federal rules on their state counterparts.

In major part, discovery rights have been truncated through neither the intransigence of opposing parties nor the rulings of judges — but through amendments to the rules themselves by the federal courts' own official rule-makers, urged on by the lobbying of tort "reform" advocates. During that period, federal court litigants have lost at least the following:

• the right to obtain information through lawyer-managed discovery, not through mandatory, limited disclosure requirements;

---

[4] Copyright © November 2004 by the Association of Trial Lawyers of America. Reprinted by permission.

- the right to determine how many interrogatories and depositions are necessary to develop adequate proof;

- the right to depose a witness for as long as it takes to get answers to relevant questions;

- the right to get all relevant information, not merely what the opposing party decides is supportive of claims and defenses;

- the right to complete discovery without repeated hearings before judges or discovery masters, with the attendant cost in time and money.

Throughout this period, for every de jure right lost, an opposite de facto right has been created for defendants. Most of this occurred in the rule amendment cycles of 1993 and 2000.

The 1993 discovery amendments. The 1993 amendments established the federal courts' current system of initial disclosure, which relieved federal judges of some of their discovery workload. The amendments also established presumptive limits of 25 interrogatories and 10 depositions per side in each case. Escape from the presumptive limits requires at least one motion by a requesting party and a decision by a judge, magistrate judge, or discovery referee. The net effect has been increased time and money spent on discovery — a change that has benefited defendants more than plaintiffs.

The 2000 discovery amendments. These changes included proposals long advocated by both the American Bar Association's Section of Litigation and the American College of Trial Lawyers — organizations that, while nominally neutral, are populated largely by corporate and insurance defense counsel.

The rule-makers made initial disclosure mandatory for nearly all cases, in all courts; limited the required disclosure to information supporting the disclosing party's claim rather than requiring disclosure of all information relevant to the case; established a presumptive limit of "one day of seven hours" for depositions; and — most critically — narrowed the scope of discovery defined in Rule 26(b)(1) from "the subject matter involved in the action" to "the claim or defense of any party."

What — or who — drives this curtailment of discovery rights? The public comments on the 2000 amendments show clearly the interests that promote this kind of rule-making: A number of the proposals that led to the 2000 amendments were supported by officers of, or advocates for, business and defense bar organizations. Among them were the Chemical Manufacturers Association, the Defense Research Institute, Dow Chemical Co., the Federation of Insurance and Corporate Counsel, Ford Motor Co., the International Association of Defense Counsel, Lawyers for Civil Justice, the National Association of Manufacturers, the Product Liability Advisory Council, Roche Pharmaceuticals, Shell Oil Co., and various defense bar organizations.

Several proposals were opposed by consumer, public interest, and trial lawyer organizations, and by academics. Among the groups were the Lawyers' Committee for Civil Rights Under Law, the NAACP Legal Defense Fund, the National Association of Consumer Advocates, the New York State Bar Association's Commercial and Federal Litigation Section, and ATLA. And both the scope-of-discovery amendment and a cost-shifting proposal (which the Judicial Conference later rejected) were opposed by the U.S. Department of Justice.

NOTES

The most dramatic changes in the federal discovery rules were to Federal Rule of Civil Procedure 26. Rule 34 was also significantly impacted. A further revision to Rule 26 affecting electronic discovery (we discuss this in section 7, below) was pending Supreme Court approval as we go to press.

4. Are Depositions Incubators for Abuse? The deposition room has long been the place where young lawyers cut their teeth. Some observers feel it has too often become the place where lawyers cut up each other. Some of the worst examples follow.

Some years ago, the young Dallas firm of Bickel & Brewer made itself a national reputation when the firm's witness preparation and deposition methods became an issue in a Texas case resulting in a $15,000 sanction. As reported by *Texas Lawyer* and later by the *New York Times*, part of the testimonial exchange between an Akin Gump associate and a Bickel & Brewer client went like this:

> Attorney: When did you review those documents?
>
> Witness: What do you mean by "when"?
>
> Attorney: The documents that were reviewed, where were they located?
>
> Witness: They were located . . . what do you mean by "where"?

Partner William Brewer was quoted in the *New York Times* saying he encourages witnesses to challenge deposition questions by telling them "to interrogate the interrogator . . . . The question 'Did you review the document?' could mean anything from acknowledging the existence of the document to memorizing it."

Another broadly reported example: Famed Texas lawyer Joe Jamail defending a witness in the Delaware case of *Paramount Communications, Inc. v. QVC Network, Inc.*,[5] as follows:

> [Opposing Counsel] JOHNSTON: No, Joe —
>
> MR. JAMAIL: He's not going to answer that. Certify it. I'm going to shut it down if you don't go to your next question.
>
> MR. JOHNSTON: No. Joe, Joe —
>
> MR. JAMAIL: Don't "Joe" me, asshole. You can ask some questions, but get off of that. I'm tired of you. You could gag a maggot off a meat wagon.

While the Delaware Supreme Court criticized Jamail, who was not a member of the Delaware bar, it did not attempt to discipline him.

In *Principe v. Assay Partners*, 154 Misc. 2d 702, 586 N.Y.S. 2d 182 (N.Y. Sup. Ct. 1992), a young associate from a New York law firm had to put up with these comments from a less-than-politic male attorney: "I don't have to talk to you, little lady"; "Tell that little mouse over there to pipe down"; "Be quiet, little girl"; and "Go away, little girl." The court reviewing this behavior

---

[5] 637 A.2d 34 (Del. 1994).

called the offending lawyer's conduct unprofessional and "offensive," "a paradigm of rudeness, [to] condescend, disparage, and degrade a colleague upon the basis that she is female." The court then ordered a fine of $1,000; whether this was enough to serve as disincentive or small enough to act as an invitation is open to question.[6]

Finally, the following brief excerpt from a book about the Dalkon Shield litigation demonstrates how abusive deposition discovery can be. The Dalkon Shield was an intrauterine birth control device made by A.H. Robins & Co. It caused many different injuries to both women and their babies, including pelvic inflammatory disease, the "PID" described in the excerpt. Its use resulted in tens of thousands of lawsuits and the payment of hundreds of millions of dollars.

MORTON MINTZ, AT ANY COST: CORPORATE GREED, WOMEN AND THE DALKON SHIELD
(1985)[7]

No one disputes that certain sexual activities or unhygienic habits can enhance the environment for pelvic inflammatory disease, even if they do not *cause* PID. This is why A.H. Robins had a right to make inquiries into highly private aspects of the lives of women who filed lawsuits blaming the Dalkon Shield for PID-related injuries. But it did not have a right to make *unreasonable* and *irrelevant* inquiries.

The record shows that Robins attorneys took depositions from Shield victims in which they asked not only intimate, but also demeaning and even intimidating questions. Although certain judges required defense counsel to show a connection between the questions and women's injuries, others did not do so and allowed Robins to ask at public trials what plaintiffs' lawyers call "dirty questions."

[In] the Shield suit of an Iowa mother of two children who had suffered PID and the consequent loss of her ovaries and womb Robins's counsel took depositions from her and her husband, each in the presence of the other. To her, the company attorney put queries about her sexual relations before their marriage in 1963, *ten years before she was fitted with a Shield, and fifteen years before she was stricken with PID.* Her lawyer, Kenneth W. Green of Minneapolis, objected, calling such questions "disgusting as well as irrelevant."

. . . .

Pantyhose can't cause PID; not even defense experts suggested they could. But in a case involving another Shield litigant, a Robins attorney made pantyhose an issue. Among his questions was whether she wore them and what fabric was used in the crotch. To the latter query she replied, "I'll answer that, but this sounds more like an obscene phone call than anything else."

During a deposition in Minnesota in May 1982, lawyers for a Boston woman directed her not to answer questions by Robins counsel about which way she

---

[6] See a reference to this case in the *Wunsch* case in Problem 20.

[7] Copyright © 1985 by Morton Mintz. Reprinted by permission of Pantheon Books, a division of Random House, Inc.

wiped, and whether, and how often she engaged in oral and anal intercourse and used so-called marital aids. Five months later, however, a judge compelled her to return to Twin Cities to answer the questions.

NOTES

In the Dalkon Shield case, the judge spoke out strongly. From the appendix to Mintz's book come these words of Judge Miles W. Lord, who presided over the Dalkon Shield litigation, addressed to A.H. Robins's CEO, chief of research and development, and general counsel in his Minneapolis courtroom in 1984:

> [W]hen the time came for these women to make their claims against your company, you attacked their characters. You inquired into their sexual practices and into the identity of their sex partners. You exposed these women — and ruined families and reputations and careers — in order to intimidate those who would raise their voices against you. You introduced issues that had no relationship whatsoever to the fact that you planted in the bodies of these women instruments of death. . . .

Consider these questions: What will be expected of new associates at a law firm when it comes to dealing with depositions and other discovery behavior? Is there hope for a view that honorable lawyers can act in good faith, or are obfuscation, game-playing, and stonewalling more likely to be part of the task demanded of the new associate?

Finally, do the rules apply in the same way for men and women? Do our images and expectations about women and how they act vary from our images and expectations of men? Despite all efforts to create a "level playing field," do most of us still expect men to take a more "macho" approach while women are expected to be "kinder and gentler"?

5. One Solution: "Issue" Sanctions and Dismissal. If discovery sanctions such as the $325,000 fine Bogle & Gates received in the *Fisons* case or Alston & Bird's quarter million dollar "contribution" are viewed by law firms as part of the cost of doing business, abusive discovery behavior is unlikely to be cured by limiting the penalties imposed on these firms to "mere" money. "Stonewalling" may be seen as cost-effective.

But courts have a powerful alternative to monetary fines: the ability to use "issue sanctions," which can be tailored to respond to the particular discovery abuse found by the court. Issue sanctions raise the stakes significantly for law firms caught stonewalling in discovery, since they materially limit the law firm's *client* from presenting or defending its case. In the extreme situation, a case can be dismissed, a course of action ratified by the United States Supreme Court in *National Hockey League v. Metropolitan Hockey Club, Inc.*, 427 U.S. 639, 96 S. Ct. 2778 (1976). There, the plaintiffs in an antitrust suit failed to respond fully and timely to hundreds of interrogatories over a period of seventeen months. The trial court finally sanctioned the plaintiffs by dismissing their case. After the court of appeals had modified the trial court's order, the high court reaffirmed the dismissal.

The Court noted the "natural tendency . . . to be heavily influenced by the severity of outright dismissal as a sanction for failure to comply with a discovery order." Nevertheless, to "deter those who might be tempted" to abuse the discovery process, the district court's dismissal was upheld. The Court concluded "that the extreme sanction of dismissal was appropriate in this case by reason of respondents' 'flagrant bad faith' and their counsel's 'callous disregard' of their responsibilities."

National Hockey League raised questions as well as answering them: Is it fair to punish discovery violators for the sake of example? How much discretion should a judge have to impose a "death penalty" sanction? Of what import is the judge's perception of the merits of the case? The stage of the litigation? How much is at stake? Should the judge's discretion be limited by strict guidelines? And what if the fault lies only with the lawyers — what remedy does their client have?

In the years since *National Hockey League*, there were few discovery-induced dismissals and no more than a trickle of significant "issue sanctions" — at least until the 1990s. In recent years, courts have seemed to be more willing to consider issue sanctions, perhaps increasingly frustrated with the nonresponsiveness of law firms not only to the discovery requests of opposing counsel, but to the courts' own orders.

In the late 1990s, General Motors and its counsel ran afoul of more than one court in cases relating to gas tank fires in various GM vehicles. The following article describes how one Georgia judge dealt with discovery abuse by imposing a series of issue sanctions that seriously interfered with GM's ability to defend the case.

BILL RANKIN, DID GM AND ITS LAWYERS SUBORN PERJURY IN GEORGIA CASE?
The National Law Journal (October 26, 1998) [8]

ATLANTA—Recently sanctioned by a Georgia Judge, General Motors Corp. and its legal team from Chicago's Kirkland & Ellis and Atlanta's King & Spalding must now defend themselves at an upcoming hearing against allegations that GM suborned perjury and obstructed justice in court cases across the country.

On October 27 here, GM and its attorneys are expected to refute accusations that a key GM witness gave false pretrial testimony on numerous occasions and that knowing GM lawyers sat mute during the depositions and allowed it to happen.

The allegations were filed by Jim Butler, of Columbus, Ga.'s Butler, Wooten, Overby, Pearson & Daughtery. In March, Mr. Butler filed a wrongful-death lawsuit against GM on behalf of a woman whose husband died from burn-related injuries after a May 21, 1997 auto accident. His 1985 Chevrolet Chevette was clipped in the rear by a Volvo, causing the Chevette's fuel tank to leak gasoline and the car to burst into flames, the lawsuit contends.

---

[8] Copyright © 1998 by The National Law Journal. Reprinted by permission.

"Better Boxes"

Repeated discovery violations by GM and its attorneys in the case led to a scathing Oct. 8 order by Fulton County State Judge Gino Brogdon.

In it, Judge Brogdon said the last straw involved 81 boxes of documents he had ordered GM to produce for Mr. Butler by June 19. Instead GM's lawyers sent 71 boxes, explaining that they had consolidated the documents in "better boxes."

But during an Oct. 5 hearing, King & Spalding's Philip Holladay admitted that GM lawyers had removed, without the judge's permission, 2,300 documents from the boxes because they were, he said, "nonresponsive" to Mr. Butler's discovery requests. Mr. Holladay also told the judge that there were four more documents in the boxes — a sealed court transcript and three documents he claimed were protected by attorney work-product — that GM did not want to provide.

"Despite heartfelt admonishment from the court as to questionable discovery tactics and plain misconduct, GM has engaged in perhaps the most bold and flagrant discovery abuse and defiance of its kind," Judge Brogdon wrote.

Judge Brogdon struck GM's defenses and skipped over jury questions by finding that GM's Chevrolet Chevette had a defectively designed fuel system which caused it to become engulfed in flames; that the fuel tank was susceptible to puncture in foreseeable collisions; and that the car was made in a way that created an "unreasonable risk" of fuel leakage and post-collision fuel-fed fires. All a jury must do now is determine whether the Chevette, already found to be defective, caused the driver's injuries and death and the amount of damages needed to compensate them.

The severe sanctions were necessary, the judge said, to prevent the abuse from continuing. "A Swahili proverb provides 'When two elephants struggle, it is the grass that suffers,'" he wrote. "Similarly, where litigants and their lawyers engage in this type of reprehensible misconduct, the integrity of the judicial process suffers." General Motors said that it believed Judge Brogdon's ruling was "in error."

NOTES

The war over this General Motors case escalated for the next year. In March 1999, Judge Brogdon held a crime fraud hearing on the issue of perjury by the witness described in the article, former GM engineer Edward Ivey. Ivey had done a cost-benefit analysis of how much GM would have to spend to prevent post-collision fuel fires. Ivey claimed that he had done this analysis on his own, rather than under the direction of his GM superiors, and had so testified in many depositions. Plaintiffs claimed to have proof he did the cost-benefit analysis under GM directive.

Judge Brogdon did not conclude that GM's in-house or outside lawyers overtly suborned Ivey's perjury, but he found that there was "a shameful scheme by GM to defraud and mislead several courts, to thwart and obstruct justice and to enjoy the ill-gotten gains of likely perjury," including the GM lawyers' refusal to provide Ivey-related documents in a series of cases. In September 1999, the judge ordered further issue sanctions — the loss of GM's attorney-client and work-product privileges for documents relating to the Ivey report and testimony. Three weeks later, rather than produce the documents now required by Judge Brogdon's order, GM settled the case.[9]

Although the evidence is largely anecdotal, courts have seemed to pick up the pace of issue sanctions. In 1996, for example, when federal district court judge Gladys Kessler found that Union Oil of California (Unocal) had hidden its own highly damaging test results from plaintiffs, she ruled that Unocal was forbidden to claim that its product contained lower levels of dangerous benzene. Initially, the judge also ordered that the plaintiff could present evidence that Unocal altered and suppressed the tests, but later withdrew this sanction in fear it might "divert the jury from its main task."[10]

A few years earlier, Suzuki Motors was fighting numerous lawsuits claiming that their Samurai sports utility vehicle was prone to roll over. In 1991, when Suzuki was asked in a written interrogatory whether General Motors had turned down an offer to market the Samurai in the United States because GM had safety concerns, Suzuki's lawyer, Atlanta's Joe Freeman, Jr., claimed Suzuki was "unaware of any decision by General Motors not to market the Samurai." When plaintiffs' attorneys proved this false by subpoenaing GM's own records, including correspondence between GM and Suzuki showing that GM had specifically mentioned safety problems in backing away from marketing the Samurai, federal judge B. Avent Edenfield described the lawyers' actions as a "cover-up" having "the same result as an outright lie." In addition to fining the lawyers, Edenfeld also entered a judgment against Suzuki on liability, leaving the company to fight only about damages.[11]

Finally, recall the Baron & Budd witness preparation memorandum we examined in Problem 15. Word of that memo spread from Texas, where it was first uncovered, to other states where Baron & Budd was engaged in litigation, including Ohio. There, after the memo was brought to the attention of state trial court judge George Elliott, he ordered Baron & Budd to disclose witness preparation documents in the case before him, stating that any claim of work product or attorney-client privilege should be submitted to the judge for his *in camera* review. The Ohio Supreme Court, in its opinion upholding the issue sanctions eventually levied by Judge Elliott, picks up the story from there.

STATE EX REL. ABNER v. ELLIOTT, JUDGE
85 Ohio 3d 11, 706 N.E.2d 765 (1999)

Despite Judge Elliott's September and October 1997 orders, appellants did not provide the defendants in the asbestos cases with any witness preparation documents and, although claiming that all of these materials were protected from disclosure by the attorney work product and attorney-client privileges, appellants did not submit the materials to Judge Elliott for an *in camera*

---

[9] *Bampoe-Parry v. General Motors Corp.*, Fulton Co. (Ga.) No. 98VS138297.

[10] *Richardson v. Union Oil Company of California*, 167 F.R.D. 1 (D.D.C. 1996), modified at 170 F.R.D. 333 (D.D.C. 1996).

[11] *Malautea v. Suzuki Motor Corp.*, 148 F.R.D. 362 (S.D. Ga. 1991), *aff'd*, 987 F.2d 1536 (11th Cir. 1993).

inspection. In addition, at a November 1997 deposition, after Judge Elliott overruled appellants' objections, appellants' counsel instructed the deponent not to answer questions concerning witness preparation based on work-product and attorney-client privileges.

As a result of the foregoing actions by appellants, defendant North American Refractories Company filed a motion for sanctions. In December 1997, after a hearing, Judge Elliott issued an order in which he found that the Texas deposition preparation document constituted evidence of improper coaching of prospective deponents, that it was reasonable to infer that similar deposition materials had been used to coach clients and witnesses in asbestos litigation in Butler County that had been filed by the same law firm that prepared the Texas document, that the court thereby issued its September and October 1997 discovery orders, and that appellants had not complied with those orders. Judge Elliott consequently ordered the following:

"Therefore, at the trial of this case, upon request of defense counsel, the jury will be instructed to accept and consider the following as being conclusively proved facts established by the greater weight of the evidence, viz.:

"1. Prior to trial plaintiff and his co-workers met with plaintiff's attorneys and paralegals to prepare for this lawsuit.

"2. At least one such meeting occurred before (a) the preparation of plaintiff's answers to written interrogatories, (b) the deposition of plaintiff by defendants' counsel, and (c) the deposition of each co-worker.

"3. During each of those meetings, plaintiffs' attorneys or paralegals either gave to or showed plaintiff and the co-workers certain lists, photographs, or other items which disclosed the product name, manufacturer name, product type, product description, packaging description, location of use, time of use, and typical trade or job of the Armco workers who used numerous products manufactured by defendants.

"4. Before, during, or immediately after the disclosure of that information to plaintiff and, or, the co-workers, plaintiff's attorneys informed plaintiff and, or, the co-workers that it would be to their advantage for them to name as many of the defendants' products as possible during their depositions.

"The foregoing instruction shall also be given to the jury in any other asbestos-related personal injury action in this county wherein court-ordered discovery of improper witness coaching techniques either has been or will be prevented by the objections of plaintiffs' counsel."

. . . .

NOTES

Dismissal and/or judgment are the most extreme sanctions possible. Under Rule 37 of the Federal Rules of Civil Procedure, a "willful" abuse is required before such sanctions can be imposed. But what does "willful" mean? What is the necessary degree of culpability required for dismissal or judgment? Should the same standards apply to a finding of liability? And who is responsible for sanctions? What conflicts of interest may arise between lawyers and clients over who should pay for monetary sanctions? Could a client successfully argue a law firm's malpractice liability for issue sanctions by claiming that it refused to produce important documents only because it relied on the firm's advice?

6. The Extremes of Discovery Abuse: Two Examples. When lawyers feel that they are beyond the power of courts to sanction their conduct, they can all too easily be sucked into the vortex of injurious advocacy — protecting the client regardless of cost, the rules, or ordinary morality. The following article describes how lawyers for the tobacco industry advocated document destruction, suppression of research reports, and "junk science" to avoid disclosing the risks of tobacco.

MILO GEYELIN & ANN DAVIS, BIG TOBACCO'S COUNSEL ACCUSED OF CONSPIRACY
The Wall Street Journal (April 23, 1998) [12]

Tobacco lawyers are in the hot seat.

Thus far, the conduct of the $45 billion tobacco industry has been the focus of both civil lawsuits and the government's criminal inquiries. But now anti-tobacco forces are mobilizing on a new front: war with the industry's hired guns.

In recent years, thousands of damaging internal industry documents have surfaced, including the bitterly contested trove of 39,000 that was released Tuesday. With each new round, a starker picture has emerged of the extensive role played by lawyers in directing sensitive research about smoking and health — and hiding the findings from the public.

The documents released Tuesday for example include a 1985 report prepared by outside lawyers for R.J. Reynolds Tobacco Co. that suggests that they were aware of the company's efforts to suppress and destroy research that could have hurt their client in lawsuits.

Already, law firms have been named as codefendants with the industry in two of the three dozen state suits seeking to recover public health-care costs linked to smoking. The allegation? The firms participated in a conspiracy to deceive the public. Now anti-tobacco lawyer Cliff Douglas says he plans to file complaints against tobacco lawyers with state bar disciplinary authorities and to urge the American Bar Association and Congress to look into the lawyers' conduct.

In Minnesota, where a trial is under way in the state's case, attorney General Hubert "Skip" Humphrey strongly condemned the attorneys Tuesday and provided the media with a summary prepared by his office of the 1985 law firm report.

Humphrey contends that the 104-page report describes a history of document destruction at Reynolds dating to 1953. It was prepared by Cleveland's Jones, Day, Reavis & Pogue. But Jones Day litigation department head John Strauch challenged the attorney general's summary, saying that the report it was based on referred to possible document destruction only twice and that

---

in both instances the documents were saved on microfilm and turned over to plaintiffs in Minnesota.

The law firms involved in tobacco cases include some of the best-known names in the legal world. Chadbourne & Parke and King & Spaulding both represent Brown & Williamson Tobacco Co. and Arnold & Porter represents Philip Morris Cos.

The lawyers maintain that they were merely doing what all good lawyers are supposed to do: advise clients how to avoid liability and vigorously defend the clients when they are sued.

"The role is the same as the roles of lawyers representing any client faced with litigation and that is provide the best legal and factual defense that can be mustered," said Tom Bezanson of Chadbourne Tuesday. Reynolds also defended its lawyers Tuesday, saying they "were doing what lawyers are supposed to do preparing the company to defend itself in litigation and regulatory challenges."

But many say it isn't so simple. At least when litigation is involved, the rules of civil procedure require lawyers to hand over any documents that plaintiffs lawyers have a legitimate reason for requesting. Failing to do so could lead to either court sanctions or, in extraordinary cases, criminal charges or professional disciplinary action.

"If you are under court order to turn over documents or hang on to them and you destroy documents, that's obstruction of justice and you can go to jail for that," said Charles Wolfram, a Cornell University legal ethics professor.

Ethics experts say it isn't always a crime or a violation of disciplinary rules for lawyers to destroy documents if they haven't been sought in a lawsuit. If lawyers suppressed research decades ago, before anyone knew a study was being conducted, it might be morally wrong to hide the results but hard to use as the basis of a disciplinary case. "I don't think lawyers like to let the world know this, but the rule is you can advise a client to do anything that is barely legal to do," Professor Wolfram said.

. . . .

If bar officials were to go after tobacco lawyers for furthering a criminal conspiracy, there would be few precedents that involve major law firms and allegations of this magnitude, Professor Wolfram said. Still, the anti-tobacco camp is energized. "I find it extremely offensive that the companies and their lawyers say this is what lawyers do," said Richard Daynard, a Northeastern University law professor. "It's not what lawyers do. It's not the normal work of corporate counsel to help their clients defraud their customers." He adds that he is encouraging plaintiffs to name law firms as defendants in civil suits.

"The lawyers are likely to continue fighting the release of documents by invoking the privilege shielding communications between lawyers and clients from disclosure. That privilege can be breached only after a judicial finding that there is evidence of a crime or fraud."

While such a finding by a Minnesota judge ultimately led to the release of the latest trove of documents, which the state has been using in its trial, fights over the attorney-client privilege are long and arduous. The tobacco companies, in fact, fought all the way to the U.S. Supreme Court to keep the latest documents secret.

Depositions of lawyers aren't likely to go smoothly either. When lawyers for Oklahoma, which has named Shook, Hardy & Bacon as a defendant, tried to take the deposition of former Shook partner William Shinn last year, he refused to answer any questions. He did so on the advice of his lawyers at the high-powered criminal defense firm Williams & Connelly.

Still, there is growing evidence that since the first public health alarms linking cigarettes to lung cancer were sounded in the early 1950s, lawyers have cautioned the industry against conducting internal research to get to the bottom of the public health debate to avoid negative results that could hurt in court.

The 1985 Jones Day report released Tuesday depicts widespread involvement by Reynolds's outside lawyers in editing and, in some cases, suppressing scientific research reports. The report noted "very strong interaction" between scientists and the law department saying that lawyer involvement went beyond mere "word-smithing" of research reports to "efforts to prevent the distribution or production of certain reports."

After the Surgeon General's report linking smoking to cancer in 1964, lawyers' "influence" over "research objectives" at Reynolds increased, the document said. The lawyers, it explains, "did not want anyone performing research that would appear to acknowledge that cigarettes or cigarette smoke contained harmful constituents or posed a health problem."

The law firm with the deepest ties to the tobacco industry — and the one that has come under the most scrutiny — is Shook Hardy in Kansas City, Mo. Since successfully representing Philip Morris in a smoker's suit in 1954, it has represented four of the six major tobacco companies. In the process, it has emerged as the industry's top trouble shooter.

More than a half-dozen judges have found that industry documents the firm claimed were shielded by the attorney-client privilege could be turned over to plaintiffs because they contained evidence of a crime or fraud. Plaintiffs have accused the firm of working behind the scenes to generate junk science for the tobacco industry's independent research arm, the Council for Tobacco Research, and of abusing the attorney client privilege to keep negative research results from reaching the public. . . . And at a meeting with Brown & Williamson in 1981, Shook lawyer Richard Northrip recommended doing testing of tobacco additives in house, rather than contracting with outsiders, so the company could terminate any research that yielded negative results, remove the additive and "destroy the data," according to a document describing the meeting. Brown & Williamson maintains it ignored the advice.

Shook declined to comment.

NOTES

The disclosure of 39,000 documents referred to in the article came when the House Commerce Committee opened its files after the Supreme Court refused to overturn Judge Kenneth J. Fitzpatrick's broad December 1997 disclosure order in the Minnesota case. That case was eventually settled while in trial for $6.6 billion. As for the attorney-client privilege, it was relied on by tobacco lawyers for far more than refusing to answer deposition questions. It was the primary reason for the creation of the so-called "special projects" unit of the Council for Tobacco Research referred to in the article. According to documents uncovered in 1992 during litigation in a case in New Jersey federal court, the "special projects" unit was supervised by lawyers rather than scientists, and lawyers had decision-making authority over both the hiring and firing of scientific employees and the selection of research projects.

Hon. H. Lee Sarokin, the judge who presided in that case, quoted a CTR participant as saying, "When we started CTR Special Projects, the idea was that the scientific director of CTR would review a project. If he liked it, it was a CTR special project. If he did not like it, then it became a lawyers' special project. . . . We wanted to protect it under the lawyers. We did not want it out in the open." "No evidence," wrote Sarokin in his opinion overruling all claims of privilege, "could be more damning. . . . [E]ven more disturbing is defendants' announced practice of using the 'special projects' division in order to shield damaging research results from the public and the FTC."[13]

On a somewhat lighter note, read this next brief excerpt in which the exasperated judge resorted to a game of rock, paper, scissors when the lawyers could not even agree on something as simple as the location of a deposition.

ADAM LIPTAK, LAWYERS WON'T END SQUABBLE, SO JUDGE TURNS TO CHILD'S PLAY
The New York Times (June 9, 2006)[14]

Fed up with the inability of two lawyers to agree on a trivial issue in an insurance lawsuit, a federal judge in Florida this week ordered them to "convene at a neutral site" and "engage in one (1) game of 'rock, paper, scissors'" to settle the matter.

Childish lawyers are commonplace, but the use of children's games to resolve litigation disputes is apparently a new development. The judge, Gregory A. Presnell of Federal District Court in Orlando, wrote that his innovation was "a new form of alternative dispute resolution."

The proximate cause of Judge Presnell's ruling, issued Tuesday, was a motion saying the two lawyers in the case could not agree about where to conduct the deposition of a witness. The choices were the building where they both work, four floors apart, or a court reporter's office down the street.

Judge Presnell's order indicated that deciding such things was not part of the job of a federal judge. Still, wary that the lawyers would start a new battle over where to conduct the rock-paper-scissors showdown, Judge Presnell gave them a default site: the front steps of the federal courthouse in Tampa.

That will not be necessary, said David J. Pettinato, a lawyer for the plaintiff. He and his adversary have agreed to meet on June 30, Mr. Pettinato said, at "an undisclosed location."

---

[13] *Haines v. Liggett Group, Inc.*, 140 F.R.D. 681 (D.N.J. 1992), *rev'd*, 975 F.2d 81 (3d Cir. 1992). For more on this fascinating case, see the reference in the Supplemental Readings, below.

[14] Copyright © 2006 by the New York Times Company. Reprinted by permission.

Mr. Pettinato added that he had been wasting no time since the order came down and had been training with his daughters, who are 5 and 9. They have advised him to open with rock. Mr. Pettinato said he was inclined to agree "because my case is solid as a rock." . . .

The second lawyer in the case, D. Lee Craig, declined through a spokesman to preview his strategy. Judging from the spokesman's tone, Mr. Craig did not find the matter especially amusing.

That would be in keeping with the compliment Mr. Craig paid to Mr. Pettinato in a letter last week.

"Apparently you think it is in your client's interest to create as much misery and bad feeling as you are able," Mr. Craig wrote. "In those endeavors, you are most able."

7. The Next Frontier: Electronic Discovery. The following piece is not about discovery abuse, but electronic discovery in the modern age. It is not unheard of for first and second-year associates at some firms to spend the vast majority of their time doing document review. They accordingly are often the gatekeepers for the kinds of discovery described below. As you read this article, think about how law firms might use technology to avoid providing appropriate discovery — and what protections could be developed to prevent this from happening.

MARK E. BORZYCH, AVOIDING ELECTRONIC DISCOVERY DISPUTES: PRACTICE QUESTIONS ANSWERED
41 Arizona Attorney 36 (January 2005) [15]

In a partnership dispute, plaintiff's attorney requested from opposing counsel electronic files of accounting records, contracts, e-mail and other correspondence for a specific period of time. This information was copied onto a CD and turned over to her.

Unfortunately, her discovery request did not demand imaging of the computer hard drives on which those files had originally resided. Subsequently, those computers were forensically examined, and when the contents of the hard drive were compared to the material on the CD, it became apparent that the production was incomplete, in part because important electronic evidence was missing.

When most attorneys think of "documents" as they prepare or respond to discovery requests, they probably think of paper — hard-copy — documents. Unfortunately, an attorney who applies such a limited scope to the discovery process risks either overlooking important information or not producing crucial evidence. "Moreover," said one court in stating the common view, "it is a well accepted proposition that deleted computer files, whether they be e-mails or otherwise, are discoverable." A requesting party also may miss an important opportunity to obtain possibly relevant information in the form of metadata, residual or "inaccessible" data, and other operating system artifacts.

---

[15] Originally published in Arizona Attorney magazine, State Bar of Arizona, January 2005. Reprinted by permission.

"Document" Definition in Flux

Some file formats contain embedded metadata, which is "descriptive and historical information about an electronic file, such as the date it was created, modified or deleted, its location on the hard drive," and the name of the person who created it. In fact, "programs such as Microsoft Word or Adobe Acrobat can store a myriad of information" about a file, including the names of several of its authors, the amount of time spent editing it, editing comments, the name of the person who made the edits, the last time it was printed, and, in some cases, even previous versions. . . .

. . . .

One court recently explained that computerized data and "other electronically-recorded information" includes, but is not limited to, the following:

Voice mail messages and files, back-up voice mail files, e-mail messages and files, backup e-mail files, deleted e-mails, data files, program files, backup and archival tapes, temporary files, system history files, web site information stored in textual, graphical or audio format, web site log files, cache files, cookies, and other electronically-recorded information.[16]

Unlike paper documents, however, electronic documents or data may be compromised, destroyed or lost as new files or data are created, saved to or deleted from a hard drive. This is the case because new information continuously overwrites old data. Simply turning on a typical Windows-based computer can alter hundreds of files and potentially destroy relevant electronic evidence.

Preservation Letters and the Duty To Preserve

Due to the volatile nature of electronic data, the timing of a preservation request may be critical. In Arizona, "Litigants have a duty to preserve evidence which they know, or reasonably should know, 'is relevant in the action, is reasonably calculated to lead to the discovery of admissible evidence, is reasonably likely to be requested during discovery and/or is the subject of a pending discovery request.'" . . .

To protect the integrity of electronic evidence, the preservation letter should also include a request for the computer to be taken out of service until a forensically accurate mirror image of the hard drive can be created. That last step may require more specialized knowledge.

Neutral Third Parties

Courts recognize the value of forensically accurate hard drive "mirror images" to preserve electronic evidence and to analyze the computer data properly. A forensic mirror image is a "byte-for-byte copy of everything on the hard drive," including deleted files and unused disk space. In contrast, a "functional copy" only duplicates disk structures and active files..

---

[16] [4] *Super Film of America, Inc. v. UCB Films, Inc.*, 219 F.R.D. 649, 657 (D. Kan. 2004) (quoting *Kleiner v. Burns*, No. 00-2160-JWL, 2000 WL 1909470 (D. Kan. Dec. 15, 2000)).

When forensically imaging a hard drive, a computer forensic specialist's objective is to establish that the image is identical to the original. The accuracy of the image is determined by calculating the "hash value" of the contents of the hard drive using an "algorithm known as MD5 (Message Digest 5). This algorithm computes a unique hexadecimal alphanumeric identifier for the data on the hard drive." Once the hash value of the data in the image is determined, it is compared to the hash value of the data on original media. The image is considered forensically accurate if the two hash values are the same.

. . . .

Spoliation and Sanctions

To avoid sanctions, a party should preserve potentially relevant electronic evidence once litigation is reasonably foreseeable. Although Arizona has not recognized a separate tort for spoliation of evidence, a court may still sanction a "litigant who is on notice that documents and information in its possession are relevant to litigation, or potential litigation, or are reasonably calculated to lead to the discovery of admissible evidence, and destroys such documents and information."

. . . .

As technology continues to advance, lawyers must be prepared to confront and address electronic discovery issues. Not long ago, there was virtually no case law addressing these issues. Now, case law in this area is evolving rapidly. With that evolution, the learning curve for lawyers is starting to diminish as more published opinions emerge, and judges' expectations continue to rise regarding electronic discovery matters.

8. Issues Sanctions and E-Discovery. We now come to the intersection of two cutting edge concepts: issues sanctions and electronic discovery. In June 2005, financier and corporate raider Ronald Perelman won a $1.45 billion fraud verdict in Florida against the Wall Street brokerage Morgan Stanley. The verdict was given a large assist by Judge Elizabeth Maass' pre-trial ruling that Morgan Stanley's repeated failure to produce electronic discovery mandated a partial default judgment against the firm on the issue of fraud. This opinion piece explains the basis of Judge Maass' decision.

GRETCHEN MORGENSON, ALL THAT MISSING E-MAIL . . . IT'S BAAACK,
The New York Times (May 8, 2005)[17]

Ronald O. Perelman, the financier who is also chairman of Revlon, is not usually considered a friend to individual investors. But to anyone who has lost money as a client of Morgan Stanley in recent years, Mr. Perelman may turn out to be a true pal.

Why? Because . . . Morgan Stanley's document production in the Perelman case was so woeful and obstructionist that the judge in the case criticized it. After that, the firm decided to conduct a new search for any materials it might

---

[17] Copyright © 2005 by the New York Times Company. Reprinted by permission.

have overlooked. The documents it unearthed may or may not have a bearing on arbitrations won by the firm, but if any do, decisions that supported the firm could be reversed.

In recent weeks, Morgan Stanley sent a letter to lawyers who represented clients in cases against the firm, alerting them to the e-mail trove. "Morgan Stanley DW Inc. has recently come to appreciate that there are additional sources that might contain additional responsive e-mail," the letter said. "Although there may or may not be material responsive in this matter, MSDW will make reasonable accommodations as appropriate."

Morgan Stanley had long argued that many of its documents were lost in the destruction of the World Trade Center, where it had offices. But the documents relevant to the Perelman case turned up in Brooklyn . . . .

All Wall Street firms play hardball when clients bring arbitration cases. But Morgan Stanley is famous for its scorched-earth tactics. The firm often stonewalls routine requests for documents and stalls even when arbitration panelists order that materials be produced. During an October 2003 arbitration, for example, Morgan Stanley was penalized $10,000 a day until it complied with an order that documents be produced. "Enough is enough," the arbitration panel wrote . . . .

Elizabeth T. Maass, the circuit court judge overseeing the Perelman suit in West Palm Beach, Fla., wrote a blistering opinion about Morgan Stanley's tactics. "The conclusion is inescapable that MS & Co. sought to thwart discovery in this specific case," she noted.

. . . .

Last week, [Florida attorney Darren C. Blum] filed a class-action suit against Morgan Stanley on behalf of the Quintanas and others who brought cases against the firm from January 1999 to April 2005. The suit contends that lapses in document production meant that arbitrations lost by Morgan Stanley clients may have been decided unfairly. "It is clear that they violated discovery rules and there is a price to pay," Mr. Blum said.

. . . .

Lewis D. Lowenfels, an expert in securities law at Tolins & Lowenfels, said: "Our present era combines highly sophisticated electronic tools used to retain and produce corporate records with a deep judicial suspicion of the integrity of corporate management. Therefore firms that fail to respond to reasonable discovery requests may expose themselves to draconian penalties."

9. Winning — And Making Money. Is it possible to "win" without using the kind of tactics described in many of the readings to this problem? The author of the following article thinks so, though he contends, like most litigators, that "winning" is the only thing that matters. Is *how* a lawyer wins as important as whether the lawyer wins? Or is this attorney merely trying to sugar-coat a "kinder, gentler" system by claiming that "winning is everything" could still apply? As you read this article, consider whether you can win for your clients while remaining ethical.

MARK A. DOMBROFF, WINNING IS EVERYTHING!
The National Law Journal (September 25, 1989) [18]

With increasing regularity, lawyers confront a wide range of articles in legal periodicals and seminars put on by bar associations on such topics as "Dealing With The S.O.B. Litigator" or "Combating Hardball Litigation Tactics." What all of these offerings share in common is that they almost universally condemn the hardball approach to litigation and the trial lawyers who use hardball tactics . . . .

The fact of the matter is, however, that like it or not, for better or worse, to a litigator winning is everything. Justice is done when your client wins and being right isn't enough. It may give you a warm feeling inside to know you're right and that your opponent isn't, but it doesn't win cases. What wins cases in the courtroom is, plain and simple, persuading the jury you're right. Like it or not, in our system, whoever has the better lawyer will frequently prevail. . . .

The real question to be focused on is what does "winning" mean. Well, in any given case it may mean a good settlement, a dismissal on motion or perhaps a jury trial. Winning doesn't necessarily always have to mean a verdict in your client's favor. Winning is a state of mind. It's whatever your client thinks it is in a particular case.

Accepting for the sake of argument that, as Vince Lombardi said, "Winning isn't everything. It's the only thing," we then move to the next level . . . .

The following are just a few of the things that should be considered . . . .

● How you win is as important as if you win. Don't be an "obnoxious" winner.

Remember, the adversary you vanquished today will frequently be your opponent again tomorrow.

● Discuss with your client at the outset of the case and regularly thereafter what winning means in the context of the case. Frequently, a "win" is a settlement with which your client is happy.

● "Scorched earth" is not the same as winning. In fact, the scorched earth school of litigation gives all litigators a bad name.

. . . .

So then what's wrong with hardball tactics and aggressive litigators? . . . Whomever the critics, the articles and the programs may be directed at, I prefer to believe that they are not focused upon those of us who believe that winning for our clients is the only thing that matters so long as we do it within the ground rules established by our profession and our society. After all, isn't that the kind of lawyer you want representing you if you get sued?

NOTES

Many observers of modern American litigation see another important motive for discovery wars besides winning — money. The increased

-----

importance at many law firms of litigation *support* — that is, the machinery of the discovery process — serves as proof to some that discovery is regarded by these firms as a major profit center. Is money driving the discovery engine? At a 1995 legal administrators' conference, one consultant estimated legal services as a $98 billion industry, with litigation making up $70 billion of that figure, and discovery $45 billion.[19] It is hard to estimate the accuracy of this figure. But it is equally hard to discredit this story, told by Charles R. Morgan, former vice president, general counsel, and secretary of Chiquita Brands International Inc., and senior corporate counsel of Kraft Foods: "When I was thinking about going back to private practice, I interviewed some very big firms. I was talking to the head of the litigation department at a very large firm and explained that I had an interest in helping companies settle or resolve cases early on. He told me that it was a terrible idea. I asked, 'Why?' And he said, " 'Because we make all of our money at this law firm in discovery practice.' "[20]

As you enter the practice of law and encounter the Clancy Garretts of your firm, how should you evaluate the possibility that extensive, exhaustive, and contentious discovery may be one of the principal ways in which that firm makes money? Is it possible to determine whether this kind of discovery is taking place only with the informed consent of the firm's clients? How should this affect your behavior during discovery?

SUPPLEMENTAL READINGS

1. James S. Kakalik, et al., *Discovery Management: Further Analysis of the Civil Justice Reform Act Evaluation Data*, reprinted in 39 B.C. L. Rev. 613 (1998), and also available as Rand Institute Abstract No. MR-941-ICJ (1998), is the analysis by the Rand Institute for Civil Justice on discovery and the federal Civil Justice Reform Act of 1990.

2. A summary and analysis of the results of the surveys undertaken by the ABA Litigation Section's Special Task Force on Ethics: Beyond the Rules has been written by Professor Robert W. Gordon, published through the American Bar Association, and reprinted at 67 Fordham L. Rev. 709 (November 1998), as *The Ethical Worlds of Large-Firm Litigators: Preliminary Observations*.

3. In two interesting law review articles, Professor Linda S. Mullenix has debunked what she considers the "myth" of discovery abuse, and the link between our society's supposed litigiousness and such abuse. She suggests that the reforms of the past decade were likely unnecessary. *Discovery in Disarray: The Pervasive Myth of Pervasive Discovery Abuse and the Conse-quences for Unfounded Rulemaking*, 46 Stan. L. Rev. 1393 (1994), and *The Pervasive Myth of Pervasive Discovery Abuse: The Sequel*, 39 B.C. L. Rev. 683 (1998).

4. In *Cincinnati Bar Ass'n v. Statzer*, 800 N.E.2d 1117 (Ohio 2003), a lawyer was disciplined for intentionally misleading a witness in deposition by placing a series of audio cassettes before the witness, each labeled to make it appear they contained conversations between the witness and the lawyer. The tapes

---

[19] Rebecca Morrow, *Bottom Line Changes*, LEGAL ASSISTANT TODAY (May-June 1995).

[20] CORPORATE LEGAL TIMES, June 1997, at 1.

were all blank. The lawyer contended the subterfuge was necessary to draw out truthful testimony, but the court disagreed: When the lawyer resorts to "subterfuge that intimidates a witness," the deception is no more likely to induce the truth than a lie based on the threat.

5. In *Rambo Depositions: Controlling an Ethical Cancer in Civil Litigation*, 25 Hofstra L. Rev. 561 (1996), Jean M. Cary discusses the problem of attorneys who use rude, profane, and intimidating behavior, which she calls "Rambo tactics," to seize control of a deposition. Cary examines and then disputes the claim that these lawyers are simply zealously representing their clients and are behaving no differently than other attorneys. She highlights three court rulings finding this behavior unacceptable and resulting in various sanctions including case dismissal.

6. A symposium issue at 26 U.S.F. L. Rev. (Winter 1992) contains interesting articles on reform of the discovery process. *See* Earl C. Dudley, Jr., *Discovery Abuse Revisited: Some Specific Proposals to Amend the Federal Rules of Civil Procedure*, 26 U.S.F. L. Rev. 189 (Winter 1992); Edwin W. Green & Douglas S. Brown, *Back to the Future: Proposals for Restructuring Civil Discovery*, 26 U.S.F. L. Rev. 225 (Winter 1992).

7. Stuart Taylor, Jr., "Sleazy in Seattle," *American Lawyer,* April 1994, describes the Bogle & Gates/Fisons affair in detail and with considerable style. An excellent "read" about an amazing discovery story.

8. Bradley F. Wendell wrote *Rediscovering Discovery Ethics*, 79 Marq. L. Rev. 895 (1996), while an associate at Bogle & Gates. Wendell provided an interesting and often provocative analysis of discovery in an adversary system, sanctions as the means of policing abuses, and whether it is possible to infuse lawyers with sufficient morality so they can begin to "take their public responsibilities seriously."

9. *Haines v. Liggett Group, Inc.*, 140 F.R.D. 681 (D.N.J. 1992), *rev'd*, 975 F.2d 81 (3d Cir. 1992). The trial court opinion in *Haines* makes for fascinating reading. It is the first such opinion that in effect accuses tobacco company lawyers of collusion by intentionally assisting in hiding cigarette dangers and using the attorney-client privilege to do so. Judge H. Lee Sarokin overruled his own magistrate in voiding all privileges, finding that the hearings before a special master had disclosed numerous instances of improper behavior by both the tobacco industry and its lawyers. Despite what appears in hindsight to be a clear case for disclosure, Sarokin's order was reversed by the Third Circuit Court of Appeals, and Sarokin was removed from the case, tainted, said the appeals court, by his presiding over an earlier cigarette case, *Cipollone v. Liggett*, 683 F. Supp. 1487, 1490-93 (D.N.J. 1988), which he had referred to in his *Haines* opinion. However, Sarokin's detailed published opinion, including some specifics of the information uncovered before the special master, remained available to be used by others attacking the tobacco industry's discovery shield.

10. Christine Hatfield, *The Privlege Doctrines — Are They Just Another Discovery Tool Utilized by the Tobacco Industry to Conceal Damaging Information?*, 16 Pace L. Rev. 525 (1996), is a thorough discussion of the tobacco company disclosures in the *Haines* case and elsewhere, from a pro-disclosure, anti-privilege perspective.

PROBLEM 18

Whether they do transactional work or litigation, or handle civil, criminal, or administrative matters, most lawyers find that they negotiate as a daily part of their professional lives. Negotiation by its very definition involves providing something less than "the truth, the whole truth, and nothing but the truth." But is there a difference between a direct misstatement and one which is less direct but ultimately no less misleading? When does a misrepresentation become a lie, and when is it merely a legitimate negotiation tactic — "puffing," or "playing poker"? And is there ever a time when an attorney is obligated to share with the other side the hidden weaknesses of his or her position? Read how negotiator Ross Davids deals with these issues, and, after reading a selection of other viewpoints, decide where you stand.

The Fine Line Between Posturing and Lying in Negotiation

I. Ross Davids is a lawyer with a statewide reputation for artful negotiating techniques. In a recent seminar he gave on negotiation, Ross described a few of his methods.

"I want to protect my client. One of my favorite ways is by answering a question with another question. When opposing counsel in a small business purchase asked how solvent my client was, I just replied, 'Do you really think he'd be doing this deal if he wasn't?' Later, when my client's finances came up again, I pretended to get angry, and objected to all those 'personal' questions. In actuality, my client's balance sheet was not as clean as we'd like it, but it was a pretty small deal, and the other lawyer never did check it out.

"I never want to lie, but stretching the truth is not lying. Let me tell you what I mean. We just did a mediation in a construction defect case. I told them that we had architectural, framing and soils experts all lined up. Actually, we'd put the architect to work already, and I'd talked to the soils expert, but I didn't want to be wasting thousands on him or a framer if the mediation was successful. So I just took what the architect and I *thought* they'd say, and told the mediator that's what we'd be able to prove at trial. I figure it's no harm, no foul, since we almost definitely would get that testimony anyway.

"In that same case, we told them we had a corroborating witness who heard our client twice ask the general contractor about earth movement and get told that it was 'no problem.' Actually, we do have the name of this person, but we've had some problems tracking her down. We believe she's a Mexican citizen who's back in Mexico. But sometimes, your strongest case is the one you can present at a mediation or settlement conference, since that's the time you can 'tell a little white lie,' or 'play poker' and run a bluff.

"I always want to use my client as a shield to deflect committing to a deal when I may be able to get a better one. Sometimes, when I have my client's authority, I'll pretend to conspire with the other lawyer. I'll say something like, 'Tell you what, if you and I can agree that X dollars is fair, I'll sell it to my client if you do the same to yours.' That gets me off the hook of being the one to blink.

"Or say an insurance company client evaluates a case at $50,000. That doesn't mean I can't say to a weak opponent that the company won't pay more than twenty. In negotiating a deal, it's the same idea. Say my client gives me authority to purchase at $500,000. I'll try to close the deal for a lot less. If opposing counsel is foolish enough to come down to five hundred right away, I'll say something like, 'I'll tell my client, but frankly, he or she simply won't go for anything this high.' I know my client would pay five hundred, but why shouldn't I find out how good a deal I can get? If I'm selling, I'll do the same thing. Lawyers have to be put to the test to find out just how good they think their position really is."

Evaluate each of Ross Davids' tactics.

II. Take two of the examples in the negotiation ethics roundtable article in section 3, below, and evaluate how you would behave, and why.

III. Assume a deputy district attorney is going to trial with an eyewitness who is a drug addict and has several "failures to appear" on his record, when the addict failed to make his scheduled court appearance. Must the DA share this information with the defense during a plea negotiation session in the DA's office? What if the plea bargaining takes place in chambers in the presence of the judge? What if the deputy DA knows that the witness "temporarily" cannot be found?

READINGS

1. Squaring Negotiation With Candor. It all seems so simple: ABA Model Rule 4.1, titled "Truthfulness in Statements to Others," says that a lawyer may not "make a false statement of material fact" to a third party. And yet, even the strongest proponents of full and candid disclosure acknowledge that negotiation, by its very nature, involves misleading the opponent, concealing one's true position, and — to use the poker parlance often adopted to describe the process — running a bluff. In short, negotiation is not, and will never be, a matter of "putting all our cards on the table."

Indeed, paragraph 2 of the Comment to Rule 4.1 acknowledges that "puffing" in negotiation is a fact of life: "Whether a particular statement should be regarded as one of fact can depend on the circumstances. Under generally accepted conventions in negotiation, certain types of statements ordinarily are not taken as statements of material fact [such as] estimates of price or value . . . and a party's intentions as to an acceptable settlement of a claim . . . ."

The requirement of being truthful to the tribunal is a long-established ethical precept. But lawyers — litigators and transactional attorneys alike — have long had difficulty squaring principles of fairness and candor with the give and take of negotiation. Perhaps it is not surprising that negotiation is governed by relatively vague and equivocal rules of professional conduct, since it generally occurs behind closed doors, under conditions which would make it difficult in any event to enforce a bright line disciplinary standard. Thus, in discussing negotiation ethics, we will also revisit an increasingly familiar issue — whether conduct which may be technically "ethical," in the sense that one can "get away with it," is nevertheless "wrong," in the sense that one should not do it.

Iowa law professor Gerald B. Wetlaufer is a proponent of this last view. In a 1990 article[1] he submits that lawyers should both own up to the fact that they lie, and do so under his broad definition: any effort "to create in some audience a belief at variance with one's own." Citing the Random House Dictionary, which goes beyond direct falsehoods to define "lie" as "something intended or serving to convey a false impression," Wetlaufer argues that concealments and omissions are also lies. He catalogues the ways in which lawyers lie — and fool themselves into believing either that they don't, or that the lies don't "count." Many sound familiar. We summarize:

- *"I didn't lie,"* which includes "My statement was literally true" (though misleading), "I was speaking on a subject about which there is no Truth," and "I was merely putting matters in the best light."

- *"I lied, if you insist on calling it that, but it was . . ."*: "ethically permissible" (and thus OK); "legal" (and thus OK); "just an omission"; or ineffectual, because it was just a white lie, or was simply not believed.

- *"I lied but it was justified by the very nature of things."* This includes situations where lying is considered part of the rules of the game, such as negotiations, where most lawyers feel that candor defeats the very purpose of the exercise.

- *"I lied but it was justified by the special ethics of lawyering,"* especially the duties owed clients: loyalty, confidentiality, and, of course, zealous representation.

- *"The lie belongs to someone else,"* usually the client, so that the lawyer is "just the messenger."

- *"I lied because my opponent acted badly."* This includes "self-defense," or "having to lie" before the opponent does, and lying to teach the opponent a lesson, or because bad behavior means the opponent has forfeited any right to candor.

- *"I lied but it was justified by good consequences,"* that is, justice triumphed.[2]

As we examine lying vs. negotiating and misleading vs. posturing, consider Wetlaufer's perspective. Does he ask too much of lawyers to avoid these excuses, or is he asking for just enough?

2. Candor, Judge Rubin's Views, and the "Prisoner's Dilemma." Although there are various versions of what has been described as the "prisoner's dilemma," the basic scenario is the same: Two defendants are accused of committing a serious crime. The prosecutor, looking to strengthen the state's case, promises each prisoner that informing on the co-defendant will result in probation for the informant, while the other defendant will receive a very heavy sentence, perhaps life. Each prisoner, thinking alone, will be tempted to inform. But they can cooperate with each other if they choose to. They know that if they *both* inform, the prosecutor's case is made and both will be sentenced heavily to, say, 20 years, while if *neither* informs,

---

[1] Gerald B. Wetlaufer, *The Ethics of Lying in Negotiations*, 75 Iowa L. Rev. 1219 (1990).

[2] We have adopted this summary from Zitrin & Langford, The Moral Compass of the American Lawyer 163-64 (1999).

the prosecutor's case will remain weak and they will be convicted of lesser crimes and serve only a year or two. For any individual, the best obtainable result is immediate freedom, but this result requires betrayal by one, and trust by the other. The best result for the prisoners in the long run would be to cooperate with each other. But this cooperation requires trust, and therein lies the dilemma. Can either trust the other to follow through and not inform, knowing that the other could inform and gain freedom?[3]

There are many similarities between the prisoners' dilemma and litigation. Litigation, played out to its conclusion through trial — and then appeals — will result in a winner, a loser, and the enormous expenditure of resources, both money and the time and labor of lawyers (who are often the *only* ones who win in extensive litigation). When one party believes it can win while the other side will lose, it will either not negotiate, or negotiate in bad faith. However, if both sides trust each other to cooperate, including the candid revelation of the strengths, and even the weaknesses, of their positions, they can engage in a successful negotiation.

Judge Alvin Rubin would certainly agree with this last sentence. In the past 25 years, numerous commentators have written about the ethics of negotiation. Perhaps the first significant modern commentary is that of Judge Rubin, then a federal district judge in Louisiana, and later a member of the court of appeals for the Fifth Circuit. Concerned about the lack of guidance provided by the ABA Code, then the prevailing standard, Judge Rubin raised many questions about how lawyers should negotiate, and developed two principles for lawyers to live by. His thoughts, excerpted here, stimulated a great deal of critical thinking on the subject.

ALVIN B. RUBIN, A CAUSERIE ON LAWYERS' ETHICS IN NEGOTIATION
35 *Louisiana Law Review* 577 (1975)[4]

[T]here are few lawyers who do not negotiate regularly, indeed daily, in their practice. . . . Neither the Code of Professional Responsibility nor most of the writings about lawyers' ethics specifically mention any precepts that apply to this aspect of the profession. The few references to the lawyer's conduct in settlement negotiations relate to obtaining client approval and disclosing potentially conflicting interests. . . . It is scant comfort to observe here, as apologists for the profession usually do, that lawyers are as honest as other men. . . . If it is an inevitable professional duty that they negotiate, then as professionals they can be expected to observe something more than the morality of the market place. . . .

There are a few rules designed to apply to other relationships that touch peripherally the area we are discussing. A lawyer shall not:

---

[3] Game theorists have written extensively about the prisoners' dilemma. (We've moved the apostrophe for grammatical reasons.) See for an early example, Robert D. Luce & Howard Raiffa, GAMES AND DECISIONS 94-102 (1957). There are literally hundreds of Internet sites focused on studying this dilemma. Or watch a DVD of the first season of the television show *Survivor,* in which alliances and trust played a central theme in Richard Hatch's winning strategy.

[4] Copyright © 1975 by Louisiana Law Review. Reprinted by permission.

- knowingly make a false statement of law or fact.
- participate in the creation or preservation of [false] evidence. . . .
- counsel or assist his client in conduct that [is] illegal or fraudulent, or
- knowingly engage in *other illegal conduct*.

. . . .

But nowhere is it ordained that the lawyer owes any general duty of candor or fairness to members of the bar or to laymen with whom he may deal as a negotiator, or of honesty or of good faith. . . .

Is the lawyer-negotiator entitled, like Metternich, to depend on "cunning, precise calculation, and a willingness to employ whatever means justify the end of policy"? Few are so bold as to say so. Yet some whose personal integrity and reputation are scrupulous have instructed students in negotiating tactics that appear tacitly to countenance that kind of conduct. In fairness it must be added that they say they do not "endorse the *propriety*" of this kind of conduct and indeed even indicate "grave reservations" about such behavior; however, this sort of generalized disclaimer of sponsorship hardly appears forceful enough when the tactics suggested include:

- Use two negotiators who play different roles. (Illustrated by the "Mutt and Jeff" police technique: "Two lawyers for the same side feign an internal dispute . . . .")
- Be tough — especially against a patsy.
- Appear irrational when it seems helpful.
- Raise some of your demand as the negotiations progress.
- *Claim* that you do not have authority to compromise.
- After the agreement has been reached, have your client reject it and raise his demands.

. . . .

The professional literature contains many instances indicating that, in the general opinion of the bar, there is no requirement that the lawyer disclose unfavorable evidence in the usual litigious situation. The *recants* of lawyers and judges with their peers are full of tales of how the other side failed to ask the one key question that would have revealed the truth and changed the result, or how one side cleverly avoided producing the critical document or the key witness whom the adversary had not discovered. The feeling that, in an adversary encounter, each side should develop its own case helps to insulate counsel from considering it a duty to disclose information unknown to the other side. Judge Marvin Frankel, an experienced and perceptive observer of the profession, comments, "Within these unconfining limits [of the Code] advocates freely employ time-honored tricks and stratagems to block or distort the truth."

. . . .

Interesting answers are obtained if lawyers are asked whether it is proper to make false statements that concern negotiating strategy rather than the facts in litigation. Counsel for a plaintiff appears quite comfortable in stating, when representing a plaintiff, "My client won't take a penny less than $25,000," when in fact he knows that the client will happily settle for less; counsel for the defendant appears to have no qualms in representing that he has no authority to settle, or that a given figure exceeds his authority, when these are untrue statements. . . . [E]stimable members of the bar support the thesis that a lawyer may not misrepresent a fact in controversy but may misrepresent matters that pertain to his authority or negotiating strategy because this is expected by the adversary.

To most practitioners it appears that anything sanctioned by the rules of the game is appropriate. From this point of view, negotiations are merely, as the social scientists have viewed it, a form of game; observance of the expected rules, not professional ethics, is the guiding precept. But gamesmanship is not ethics.

. . . .

The lawyer must act honestly and in good faith. Another lawyer, or a layman, who deals with a lawyer should not need to exercise the same degree of caution that he would if trading for reputedly antique copper jugs in an oriental bazaar. . . . Good conduct exacts more than mere convenience.

. . . .

While some difficulty in line-drawing is inevitable when such a distinction is sought to be made, there must be a point at which the lawyer cannot ethically accept an arrangement that is completely unfair to the other side, be that opponent a patsy or a tax collector. So I posit a second precept: *The lawyer may not accept a result that is unconscionably unfair to the other party.*

. . . .

The unconscionable result in these circumstances is in part created by the relative power, knowledge and skill of the principals and their negotiators. . . . The imposition of a duty to tell the truth and to bargain in good faith would reduce their relative inequality, and tend to produce negotiation results that are within relatively tolerable bounds.

But part of the test must be in result alone: whether the lesion is so unbearable that it represents a sacrifice of value that an ethical person cannot in conscience impose upon another. The civil law has long had a principle that a sale of land would be set aside if made for less than half its value, regardless of circumstance. This doctrine, called lesion beyond moiety, looks purely to result. . . . [T]here certainly comes a time when a deal is too good to be true, where what has been accomplished passes the line of simply-a-good-deal and becomes a cheat. . . . This duty of fairness is one owed to the profession and to society; it must supersede any duty owed to the client.

. . . [J]udges hear not only of the low repute the public has for the bench but also of the even lower regard it has for the bar. . . . We will not change the attitude by Law Days alone. . . . Surely if its practitioners are principled, a profession that dominates the legal process in our law-oriented society would not expect too much if it required its members to adhere to two simple principles when they negotiate as professionals: Negotiate honestly and in good faith; and do not take unfair advantage of another — regardless of his relative expertise or sophistication. This is inherent in the oath the ABA recommends be taken by all who are admitted to the bar: "I will employ for the purpose of maintaining the causes confided to me such means only as are consistent with truth and honor."

NOTES

Was Judge Rubin's view that of a bench-bound Polyanna, or a realistic visionary? Whatever view you might have, his reasoning, and some of his aphorisms — "gamesmanship is not ethics"; "an adversary system . . . is means, not end"; "good conduct exacts more than mere convenience" — struck a chord with attorneys, law professors, and his colleagues on the bench, who cited his article as authority in several opinions. There is no question that the increased scrutiny of the lawyer as negotiator, and the existence of Model Rule 4.1, owe more than a little to Rubin's strong and articulate stand.

3. A Roundtable on Negotiation Ethics. In the years since Rubin framed the issue, commentators have continued to be interested in the ethics of negotiation, perhaps because of the anomaly of how to tell the truth in a process which inherently involves deception, and perhaps because there is so little clear authority which governs a lawyer's conduct. In 1988, one writer gathered most of the major academic commentators, seasoned the mix with a number of practicing attorneys, sprinkled in a couple of judicial officers, including Judge Rubin, and surveyed the 15-member group on four hypothetical negotiation problems. The results show a wide variety of opinions even among those who have devoted much thought to the issue.

LARRY LEMPERT, IN SETTLEMENT TALKS, DOES TELLING THE TRUTH HAVE ITS LIMITS?
Inside Litigation (March 1988)[5]

Law professor Charles Craver, who teaches courses and workshops on legal negotiation and settlement, likes to begin by saying, "I've never been involved in legal negotiations where both sides didn't lie." It tends to get some "shocked responses," he admits.

Craver, a former litigator and labor law practitioner, does not stop there. He goes on to defend some lies in the course of settlement talks as perfectly proper.

To U.S. Magistrate Wayne Brazil, on the other hand, lying is anathema, and nothing about the settlement setting excuses it. "My opinion is, no lying," he says, adding, somewhat wryly, "Strike one blow for naiveté."

Whether naive or not, Brazil does seem to be in a minority. Not all lawyers are as unapologetic as Craver, but interviews with experts who have focused on negotiation and ethics, plus several litigators and judicial officers, indicate that most believe lying in settlement talks is not always prohibited (and that volunteering the truth is not always required).

---

[5] Reprinted from Inside Litigation, March 1988, Volume 2, Number 5, with the permission of Prentice Hall Law & Business.

In the 15 interviews, *Inside Litigation* asked what a lawyer ought to do in each of four hypothetical settlement situations. The hypotheticals were elaborations on suggestions made by Craver, who teaches at George Washington University's National Law Center.

Participants included nine law professors who have written on ethics, negotiation, or both; five experienced litigators; a federal circuit court judge; and a U.S. magistrate. . . . Most specified what they believed prevailing ethics rules would allow. A few answered in terms of what they would do but did not venture opinions on the formal ethics rules. In several instances, some noted that ethics rules might permit lying but that, personally, they would not do it. The lawyers also volunteered suggestions on tactics.

. . . .

[Model Rule 4.1 implies] the lawyer would not be lying because according to well-established custom, he or she would be speaking in a context where puffing is part of the game. Of course, says Craver, "It's easy to characterize your own statement as puffing, and the other's as mendacity."

Situation No. 1: Lying About Authorized Limits

Your clients, the defendants, have told you that you are authorized to pay $750,000 to settle the case. In settlement negotiations, after your offer of $650,000, the plaintiffs' attorney asks, "Are you authorized to settle for $750,000?" Can you say, "No, I'm not"?

(Two of the litigators well-known for representing plaintiffs were asked essentially the same question with the roles reversed, so that the plaintiffs' attorney is asked whether he or she is authorized to settle for a specific amount.)

Of those willing to give a straight yes or no answer, six say no, you cannot say that. Seven say yes, you can — but all but one of these add that as a matter either of personal ethics or strategy, they would not give such an answer.

"Outright lying always is out of bounds," according to David Luban of the University of Maryland. It's not that one can never be misleading in the admittedly adversarial game of negotiation, he explains. But the way the process works, when one side makes an evasive statement, the other side can ask a question to clarify that position. A flat, declarative statement sends no signal that clarification is needed. "People have to be able to rely on flat-out declarations," Luban says, or the process breaks down or, at best, becomes "incredibly time-consuming."

Geoffrey Hazard Jr., the author of the ABA Model Rules, agrees that "you're allowed to make an evasive statement." He too says that an outright lie in Situation No. 1 would violate Rule 4.1.

Statements of Material Fact?

Litigator Jacob Stein, however, argues that this is one of those statements, referred to in the comment to Rule 4.1, that "ordinarily are not taken as statements of material fact." If the opponent says he or she is not authorized to pay more, "I don't rely on that," says Stein. "In the realm of negotiation, the issue is whether there's reliance."

Several participants contend that the ethics rules would permit the lie but their personal standards would not. Stein is in this camp. So is James White of the University of Michigan: "A flat denial of that sort" — although permissible — "makes me uncomfortable. It's questionable morally," White says.

Craver, on the other hand, not only believes that lying is permissible in Situation No. 1 but says "I don't have any hesitancy in lying about my authorized limits"; he has done it before and would do it again, he says. Lying is an acceptable response to the inquiry, in his view, because "the other side has no right to that information."

Avoiding the Problem

Most of those interviewed point out that a negotiator who is asked about authorized settlement limits can dodge the question or deflect it in a variety of ways. "The way to avoid [the problem] is to think ahead and have answers ready," says White. He recalls, for example, negotiators who would simply laugh and say, "You don't think I'm going to tell you answers to questions like that."

. . . .

A no-lying rule, Craver complains, means that the negotiator would always have to swear off the "limited authority" technique — a Mutt and Jeff kind of approach that casts the negotiator as a nice guy whose flexibility is limited by a tough-minded client. The negotiator could never say, "I'm sorry, I'm just not authorized . . . ," even when the statement is true, because he or she would be forced to tell the truth — and cut off a possible better deal for the client — when the opponent probes further and hits on the actual authorized figure. Yet, "limited authority" is a "very, very common technique," Craver says. And saying, "No, I'm not authorized," he notes, is much more forceful than saying, "You know you can't ask me that."

Some experienced practitioners, however, eschew that technique anyway. For one thing, they say, it would imply a lack of influence with the client that the opponent would not find credible. Says plaintiffs' lawyer Leonard Ring, "I don't use the word authorize. . . . I have a lot of persuasion with my client."

Situation No. 2: Lying About an Injury

You represent a plaintiff who claims to have suffered a serious knee injury. In settlement negotiations, can you say your client is "disabled" when you know she is out skiing?

The score: no, 14; yes, one. This question was the only one of the four that yielded a solid consensus. Actually all 15 participants agree that a negotiator cannot lie about the client's injury — he or she cannot say a leg has been broken when an X-ray shows the contrary. The only disagreement is over the possible interpretation of "disabled." (Told that this one question produces a nearly unanimous response, Hazard chuckles. "Thank heaven for small blessings," he says.)

The principle, adhered to by all, is that negotiators cannot misrepresent specific, verifiable facts. Not only is it wrong, but many of the lawyers add that it is, to use Ring's characterization, "dumb."

. . . .

Situation No. 3: Exaggerating an Injury

You are trying to negotiate a settlement on behalf of a couple who charge that the bank pulled their loan, ruining their business. Your clients are quite upbeat and deny suffering particularly severe emotional distress. Can you tell your opponent, nonetheless, that they did?

The score: no, eight; yes, five (with two not answering directly).

. . . .

[S]everal lawyers who find the assertion of disability in No. 2 to be unethical do not object to the assertion of emotional distress in No. 3. Obviously, some distress has occurred — "if they didn't care at all, there wouldn't be a legal matter," says Craver. "I'm embellishing the concern." White agrees that exaggeration of the degree of pain experienced by a client is "well within the range of puffing . . . ."

Explaining further, White draws an analogy to sales law, which distinguishes between puffing and making a warranty by asking whether reliance on the statement would be reasonable. In this analogy, lawyers are sophisticated buyers and sellers; the defense lawyer is a buyer, the plaintiff's lawyer, a seller. "Because they're sophisticated, a fair amount of puffing is permitted without it being a warranty," White says. "It's like two car dealers' negotiating the sale and purchase of a car." (Independently, [Professor Ronald] Rotunda arrives at a similar analogy but draws a different conclusion. Contending that the exaggeration in Situation No. 3 is improper, Rotunda observes, "If lawyers want to be like used car salesmen, this is a good place to start.")

. . . .

Several who say the lawyer in No. 3 cannot make an outright assertion about emotional distress do acknowledge that the issue can be raised in a more oblique way. Hazard, for example, would let the negotiator say that cutting off a loan is the kind of act that can produce serious distress. . . . Or you can ask a rhetorical question, says Luban: "Wouldn't *you* feel as though the world has caved in on you?"

. . . .

Situation No. 4: A Mistaken Impression

In settlement talks over the couple's lender liability case, your opponent's comments make it clear that he thinks the plaintiffs have gone out of business, although you didn't say that. In fact, the business is continuing, and several important contracts are in the offing. You are on the verge of settlement; can you go ahead and settle without correcting your opponent's misimpression?

The score: no, four; yes, nine (with two not answering directly).

The participants agree that you cannot say anything to further or ratify the misimpression. But beyond that point, disagreement sets in.

Hazard says no on the ground that the ethics rules incorporate the law of fraud — "and the law of fraud," adds Hazard, "is more exacting than most lawyers think." The opponent's belief that the client is out of business is "a manifest misapprehension that goes to the bargain itself," Hazard says. . . .

Interestingly, Craver, outspoken in his support for lying in Situation No. 1, finds No. 4 so difficult a situation that he cannot give a definite answer. If he thought that correcting the misimpression would not hurt the client, he says, he would do it. But if it looked like the settlement would fall apart on that issue alone, he's not so sure. By contrast, Luban — who flatly says no to the outright lie in No. 1 — generally approves keeping quiet in No. 4.

The difference for Luban lies in his rule that flat-out declarations have to be true — No. 4, obviously, involves no such declaration. "It's not my job to do their job for them," Luban says of the opponent in No. 4, "as long as my word isn't on the line."

. . . .

Luban cites a Minnesota Supreme Court case from 1962 to show what he means about consequences. In *Spaulding v. Zimmerman* (116 N.W.2d 704), a car crash had led to a personal injury suit. The defense doctor examined the plaintiff and discovered a potentially fatal medical problem that neither the plaintiff, the plaintiff's lawyer, nor the plaintiff's doctor knew about. The defense doctor revealed his finding to the defendant's lawyer, who settled the case without mentioning that the plaintiff could drop dead any second (presumably, that fact would have affected the settlement value adversely from the defense point of view). The defendant's lawyer was not responsible for the plaintiff's misimpression about the value of the case. "But it's perfectly clear that any lawyer with a grain of conscience would tell the plaintiff he had to see a doctor. You don't let somebody drop dead to save your client some money," Luban says.

. . . .

In *Spaulding v. Zimmerman,* the Minnesota court did not say the defendant's lawyer had acted unethically, but it did void the settlement, as the plaintiff had asked it to do. As a practical matter, that points to a problem with keeping quiet in Situation No. 4, as several interviewees emphasize — if an attack on the settlement ensues once the opponent learns the facts, your client might not have the peace he thought he was buying. "That's one practical reason for taking the ethical high road," says Brazil.

But Stein, who says that correction of the misimpression is not required, believes that a well-crafted release would probably foreclose an attack on the settlement.

Not surprisingly, given the range of reactions to the hypotheticals, experts approach the issue of truth in the settlement process from a variety of perspectives.

"I don't see why the law should allow attorneys to tell a bald-faced lie," says Rotunda. As he sees it, the comments to Rule 4.1, which forgive certain lies because of "generally accepted conventions in negotiation," are an attempt to "slice the baloney [too] thin."

. . . .

At the same time, countervailing forces exist — and not just moral or religious ones — in favor of candor. One such force is reputation. Legal practice would be cumbersome indeed if other lawyers were never willing to take you at your word, Craver notes. "There has to be a level of candor if one is going to practice law," he says. Moreover, he observes, candor can be a good tactic. In this regard, he says a possible approach to Situation No. 4 would be to correct the misimpression and build on the boost in credibility with the opponent that such a step would bring.

[Michigan attorney Thomas] McNamara has another reason to tell the truth — he knows he would not be a good liar. "I can't be my most convincing when I'm lying," he says.

NOTES

How do these different views square with your own? How did you feel about Professor White's equating negotiations between lawyers with negotiations between car salesmen? Is this an apt analogy, or do you agree with Professor Rotunda that this is exactly the comparison lawyers should attempt to avoid? And what about responses like rhetorical questions, or saying "you know I can't answer that"? Are these likely to be seen by opposing counsel as weak responses? Do they give the opposition too clear an indication of the truth?

4. The Practicing Lawyer's Perspective. Although the preceding article appeared in a litigation periodical, the negotiation principles discussed there are equally applicable to transactional settings, such as the purchase and sale of a business. In the following articles, two corporate lawyers, both partners in large law firms, discuss the dangers of lying in such negotiations.

JAMES C. FREUND, LYING IN NEGOTIATION PROCESS CAN BE PERILOUS
Legal Times (June 3, 1985) [6]

Recently, I was representing a public company that was in the process of being acquired — not entirely of its own volition. Negotiations over price and other key subjects were hot and heavy, but on price the purchaser wasn't giving an inch. At a crucial point, the purchaser's investment banker asked me pointblank whether we had another corporate buyer for the company.

In fact, though there had been nibbles, we had no other corporate buyer. To reply that one existed would have been a lie. I couldn't do it — even though the purchaser might well have upped his price with an active corporate rival in the field.

---

[6] Reprinted with permission of Legal Times. Copyright © 1985.

On the other hand, to reply in the negative would provide important information — information that would undoubtedly strengthen his stand on price. So I bobbed and weaved as best I could, mumbling something like, "We're not without options, I can assure you, but I'm not at liberty to disclose what they are. . . ."

Whatever it was, my response had little effect; the other side didn't budge. And since nothing else materialized, my client ultimately had to take what was offered.

Misplaced Scruples?

Reflecting on the incident that night, I couldn't help but wonder whether my scruples were misplaced. The fact is, a great deal of lying goes on daily at negotiating tables across the land — and not just by non-lawyers. People may use euphemisms to describe their conduct, but what it really comes down to is one side attempting to mislead the other in order to gain an advantage.

. . . .

In addition [to established principles of contract and tort law], lawyers are subject to certain ethical rules concerning negotiation. While courts have been reluctant to use ethical rules as a basis for imposing civil liability on lawyers for the benefit of third parties, attorneys have been disciplined in a number of cases for making factual misrepresentations to third parties.

. . . .

The Classic Paradox

You see, the real problem here is the classic paradox facing all negotiators, which one of the commentators summed up in these candid terms:

On the one hand the negotiator must be fair and truthful; on the other hand he must mislead his opponent. Like the poker player, a negotiator hopes that his opponent will overestimate the value of his hand. Like the poker player, in a variety of ways he must facilitate his opponent's inaccurate assessment . . . . To conceal one's true position, to mislead an opponent about one's true settling point, is the essence of negotiation.

So, where should the line be drawn? . . . [D]istortion concerning the value of one's case (or other subject matter of the negotiation) — puffery if you will — is part of the game. . . .

. . . .

Lying about [a client's intention] may be reprehensible, but I would have doubted that a contract or tort action could be based on it.

"Perla" Wisdom

That is, until my attention was directed to *Chase Manhattan Bank, N.A. v. Perla* (65 A.D. 2nd 207, 411 N.Y.S.2d 66 (1978)), in which a New York court ruled that an injured lender could sue the debtor's lawyer for fraud on the basis of a statement concerning what the debtor would do in the future.

According to the court, if the lawyer has knowledge that the future action will not be carried out, the statement as to the client's intention is a fraudulent misrepresentation of fact. . . .

[Freund then contrasts one statement, "My client does not *want* to accept less than $10 million at prime plus two percent interest" with another: "My client *will not* agree" to those terms, knowing the client *will* accept the $10 million if nothing better is offered. Freund argues that the first statement is ethical even though designed to mislead, while the second is a close call ethically because it is plainly untruthful.]

Blocking Techniques

So, what should you do . . . ? Here, according to one authority (Harbaugh and Britzke, "Primer on Negotiation," P.L.I., 1984), are some of the so-called blocking techniques that can be used (and that I'll apply to [the sale of a house where the seller wants to sell quickly because of a commitment to buy another property, and does not have another firm offer to purchase]):

• Answer incompletely. Respond with the least harmful data. Answer general questions specifically, specific questions generally. ("Obviously, I will have to live somewhere; I'm not about to take to the streets.")

• Answer another question. Give information on a related non-sensitive query. ("Funny you should ask. The broker was just saying the other day that this would be a perfect house for a doctor who has his office at home . . . .")

• Overanswer the question. Give all possible answers without making a commitment to any one response. ("I may have other buyers; I may have one buyer; I may have a prospective buyer . . . .")

• Answer a question with a question. ("Are you bidding on any other houses?")

• Rule the question out of bounds. ("I think my financial needs are an inappropriate, irrelevant area of inquiry.")

• Ignore the question. This can be done either by silence or by changing the topic. ("How do you like the icemaker on the refrigerator?")

These kinds of techniques often require advance planning; spur-of-the-moment responses may inadvertently communicate information one wants to protect.

But remember, if you use these techniques too often — if you're too evasive — your adversary may feel he's located a "soft spot" that he'll then proceed to exploit.

My own preference is to take a somewhat more aggressive tack. On the "other buyer" issue, I might say:

I don't want to get into that. Make up your mind on the merits of the house itself. I'm telling you, it will take $200,000 to buy this house. Or: I don't have a firm offer at this time. But I do have a potential purchaser (assuming there is one) who, if he decides to buy, is clearly capable of paying $200,000. Are you willing to take the risk that I'll pass up your lowball bid for the greater expectancy?

On the "other house" and resultant need for speed, I might try this:

I love this house. It was a wrench for me to decide to sell it. Now that I've decided, I want it to happen quickly. You're well-advised to get me signed, sealed, and delivered before I change my mind and take it off the market.

STUART K. FLEISCHMANN, CONTRACT NEGOTIATING: HOW MUCH TRUTHFULNESS IS REQUIRED
The Professional Lawyer 123 (1999 ABA Symposium)[7]

The point of this outline is to raise consciousness about the limits on corporate lawyering or negotiating. Many articles have raised the issue of whether there are or should be ethical limits on corporate lawyering, questioning whether it is permissible to lie in negotiations or engage in less than truthful behavior. While there may be no formalized set of ethics in the business that underlies corporate law negotiations, lawyers are bound by certain standards and rules of professional conduct. The standards in this are unclear; what is clearer are the various types of behavior in which corporate negotiators often engage.

Are There Limits on Negotiating?

The "art" of negotiating is what some call it. The practice of lying — or tolerating inadequate disclosures or omissions — is what others call it.

. . . . The lawyer is under several distinct duties to Client, including the duty of loyalty, the duty of confidentiality, the duty of obedience and the duty to exercise sufficient skill and care to best attempt to achieve Client's objectives. Obviously, Lawyer is not permitted to engage in illegal conduct in attempting to achieve Client's objectives. . . . Ethical considerations also affect the limits of negotiations. . . .

Reading and taking to heart the Model Rule prohibitions, one would assume that it is *never* permissible to lie or condone outright lying in negotiations. Yet, as the literature and case law make clear, it all depends on what you mean by "lying."

Some Difficult Situations

It probably goes without saying that most lawyers would not knowingly tolerate fraud on the part of their clients and would seek to resign from the relationship if the client insists on perpetrating a fraud. This is the easy case. But there are a number of circumstances that arise in virtually all contract negotiations that raise questions about a client's behavior and the lawyer's response thereto that are much harder to deal with. Consider the following:

● *The Risk Allocation Situation* — Many Clients believe that since representations and warranties are in essence a risk sharing mechanism, truthfulness isn't necessarily required. Assume that Other Side requests a representation or warranty on a specific situation (*i.e.*, the non-existence of ERISA or environmental liabilities). Client is not aware of any problems, but feels it

---

[7] Reprinted by permission.

will be too expensive and one never knows what an internal investigation could uncover. Client decides instead to make a "flat" representation that no liabilities exist and to give an indemnity to Other Side for breach of this warranty. Other Side agrees to go ahead based on the flat representation. . . . Since Other Side thinks the indemnity is "belt and suspender" protection, it does not concern itself with whether the Client will financially be able to honor its indemnity or whether the possible existence of liabilities alone would cause it to cancel the deal. In this circumstance, is it acceptable for Lawyer to allow Client to give a false representation and agree to bear the consequences without so informing Other Side and letting Other Side decide if it is willing to bear the risk?

• *The Promissory Fraud Situation* — Clients are typically asked to agree to undertake certain activities in contracts and agreements (reporting obligations, information sharing, covenants not to compete, financial tests, etc.). . . . What does the Lawyer do if the Client tells you that it so badly needs the funds now that it doesn't care whether it can honor the covenants, preferring instead to renegotiate the covenants later on once its problems become known?

• *The "No Meeting of Minds" Situation* — Sometimes in legal and business negotiations there is a disconnect between what parties believe to be the "business understanding" and the particular legal language used in the final agreement to represent this "understanding." For example, some Clients may agree to make certain payments, yet it is often unclear whether the payments are to be made on a "before" or "after" tax basis. If the two sides actually discuss a provision that Lawyer has drafted and Lawyer feels Other Side is confused, does Lawyer have a duty to correct the misunderstanding? If Lawyer knows or believes that the provision is susceptible to different interpretation by Other Side, does Lawyer have a duty to raise the matter in a specific discussion and correct the possible misunderstanding? Is there any difference if . . . the Other Side (or its counsel) drafted the provision?

• *The Greater Expertise Situation* — If Lawyer believes that an independent accountant or other non-legal professional has made a mistake that will be relied on by Other Side, is Lawyer under any duty to raise the issue for Other Side? Can Lawyer and Client assume that Other Side is "on its own"? Does any of this change if, instead of accountants, Lawyer believes that the Other Side or its counsel is inexperienced or worse?

• *The Materiality Situation* — Any transaction will have its "material" points that both sides would agree go to the heart of the business arrangement or rationale for entering into a transaction. Just as obviously, there are innumerable details that, while interesting, are relatively unimportant to either side. . . . [I]s it up to the Lawyer to decide whether something is material and, if not, must a Lawyer correct all misstatements or omissions? Is there a duty to correct Other Side's misunderstanding?

• *The False Demands Situation* — In many negotiations, a Lawyer or Client may put forth a series of demands several of which may in fact be irrelevant to the Client and which, in fact, are nothing more than "bargaining chips." They are included nonetheless to give the impression that Client has a number of important points that must be addressed. In fact the real purpose is to afford the Client points that can be bargained away in hopes of getting the Client the deal it really wants. Is putting forth so-called "false demands" and claiming their importance under these circumstances appropriate behavior?

• *The Duty of Confidentiality Situation* — In all negotiations, there are issues that are sensitive to Client and may not be able to be disclosed due to confidentiality concerns and, therefore, an issue arises as to whether truthfulness is always required. For example, in attempting to settle a case or agree to a payment amount, Other Side may inquire about Client's ability to take an action or the amount of its insurance coverage. . . . In such cases, being truthful and responding fully to an inquiry or volunteering information could breach the Lawyer's duty of confidentiality and disclosure could be adverse to Client. Is Lawyer free to disclose information in these circumstances?

• *Lying vs. Misleading Situation* — In negotiations, there is often a distinction between lying and providing misleading information. It would seem to be inappropriate for Lawyer to say "I don't know" to a request for specific information when he in fact does have the information. But what about the Lawyer who responds (in a misleading way?) to a question about whether the Client has a long-term supply contract by saying "yes" when he knows the contract party has recently indicated an intention not to renew the arrangement at the end of the contract period.

Conclusions

It has been said that when one deals with the Lawyer in a contract negotiation, the Other Side should not have to approach the situation as if it were bargaining for copper pots in a sidewalk bazaar. The involvement of Lawyer in the process, a trained and licensed professional, is meant [to] and should convey that the negotiations are tempered by a code of reasonable conduct. In the absence of a judge, arbitrator or other independent party to monitor behavior, it must be up to lawyers individually and the profession itself to encourage full and fair dealing in corporate negotiations.

NOTES

What do you think of Freund's approach? How do you think he would act in the situations posited by Fleischmann? For instance, take Fleischmann's risk allocation situation. Freund's position seems to indicate that he would stand silent if the other side had a mistaken belief in his client's ability to meet its guarantee. Is silence in the face of such an important misconception ethical? How do you react to Freund's claim that saying a client "does not want" a particular loan interest does not create an ethical problem, but stating that the client "will not agree" to that interest crosses the line? Is this semantic difference enough to justify the ethical distinction he makes?

Recall our discussion of Monroe Freedman's *Anatomy of a Murder* and penknife scenarios in Problem 15, and the semantics the lawyer uses to inform the client of how the law and facts interrelate. Is the semantic distinction proposed by Freund similar? Does it differ only in that it is being set forth to a third party, rather than one's own client? Or does Freund simply beg the question?

How would you resolve Fleischmann's hypotheticals? He has obviously read Judge Rubin's article closely. Is it equally apparent that he suffers from a rose-colored glasses view? Or is his suggestion of a higher moral standard of lawyering both laudable and workable? Finally, does Fleischmann's suggestion that lawyers' negotiation tactics be restricted by "a code of reasonable conduct" give any greater guidance than the existing rules of professional conduct?

5. Civil Liability and Malpractice Concerns. Freund was not only concerned with potential ethical violations in negotiations. He also posited that there were significant liability risks involved in making misrepresentations in negotiations. For example, if the lawyer/negotiator affirmatively misrepresents a material fact that induces the other party to rely on it, and if that reliance is justified, then the injured party may void the contract. The lawyer who made the misrepresentations may be liable in tort to the injured party, unless the client has lied to the lawyer.

Additionally, a lawyer whose misrepresentations or other unethical conduct in negotiations lead to a void contract or damages assessed against the client may be subject to a malpractice action by the lawyer's own client. Lawyers who conceal their misconduct during negotiations have also been held to be liable to clients in malpractice lawsuits.[8] Moreover, a large number of courts have held that a client may establish a malpractice claim against an attorney arising out of negotiations when, for example, the lawyer fails to adequately investigate the other side's assets;[9] or when the lawyer fails to adequately prepare for trial, forcing the client to accept a low settlement or to pay more than the client otherwise would have had to pay, had the attorney been prepared.[10]

6. Can an Omission be a Lie? Read this excerpt from a more recent article by a New York practitioner who believes that there should be a "safe harbor" for lawyers who *omit* telling the truth. Note the interesting reference to Prof. Wetlaufer. How would Freund or Fleischmann address the "out of business" hypothetical?

BARRY R. TEMKIN, MISREPRESENTATION BY OMISSION IN SETTLEMENT NEGOTIATIONS: SHOULD THERE BE A SILENT SAFE HARBOR?
18 Georgetown Journal of Legal Ethics 179 (2004)[11]

The commentary to Model Rule 4.1, as noted above, provides that a lawyer "generally has no affirmative duty to inform an opposing party of relevant

---

[8] *See Muhammed v. Strassburger, McKenna, Messer, Shilobod & Gutnick*, 526 Pa. 541, 587 A.2d 1346 (1991). Note that *Muhammed* also held that short of fraud or misrepresentations, attorneys could not be sued for negligence when their clients agreed to settle the underlying case. This is by no means a universally held position. For a further discussion of this issue, see the Epstein article described in the Supplemental Readings.

[9] *See, e.g., Patrick v. Ronald Williams P.A.*, 102 N.C. App. 355, 402 S.E.2d 452 (1991).

[10] *See Fishman v. Brooks*, 396 Mass. 643, 487 N.E.2d 1377 (1986).

[11] Copyright © 2004 by Georgetown Journal of Legal Ethics. Reprinted by permission.

facts." Yet the same comment also states that an impermissible misrepresentation "can also occur by partially true but misleading statements or omissions that are the equivalent of affirmative false statements."

Under the silent safe harbor proposal, as under comment 1 to Model Rule 4.1, a lawyer who does not introduce into settlement negotiations the topic of a client's ability to pay a judgment is under no obligation to disclose information that would be advantageous to the adversary, such as the existence of an insurance policy, assuming that there is no requirement of substantive or procedural law for that disclosure. However, once the lawyer departs from the safe harbor and elects to speak, what is said should not consciously and materially mislead. A lawyer who affirmatively introduces the concept of a client's ability to pay a judgment should also disclose the existence of the liability insurance. A lawyer who pleads poverty in settlement negotiations in order to place on the table the client's ability to pay a judgment should disclose the existence of the insurance policy.

The following hypotheticals illustrate possible scenarios in which the defendant's ability to satisfy a judgment comes into play:

Hypothetical 1: Defense counsel states "My client is going out of business." Defense counsel does not disclose the existence of a substantial liability policy which is available and sufficient to pay any resulting judgment.

The permissibility of this statement in settlement negotiations may depend on its context, whether elicited by the claimant or volunteered by the defense, and whether adduced to create the impression of the collectibility of a future judgment. For example, the following variations on this hypothetical illustrate a continuum of misdirection, ranging from simple avoidance to outright deception.

Hypothetical 1A:

Claimant's attorney: "Tell me a little about your client."

Defense counsel: "I don't want to talk about my client. Let's talk about how you think you are going to prove your case without a credible witness."

Hypothetical 1B:

Claimant's attorney: "Tell me a little about your client."

Defense counsel: "Well it's going out of business."

Hypothetical 1C:

Defense counsel: "I am offering you ten cents on the dollar. Take it or leave it, because my client is going out of business."

Hypothetical 1D:

Claimant's attorney: "I am a little concerned about whether a judgment would be collectible against your client."

Defense counsel: "My client is going out of business."

Hypothetical 1E:

Defense counsel: "I am offering you ten cents on the dollar on this case. You'd better take it because my client is going out of business and you will not be able to collect on your judgment."

In each of the five hypothetical examples, defense counsel omits the existence of insurance coverage, and in the last four, counsel tells the claimant that the defendant corporation is going out of business. On one end of the spectrum of responses, Hypothetical 1A is beyond reproach, as defense counsel desists from making any factual representations about the client's financial status. The defense attorney in that example remains in the safe harbor. Hypothetical 1B is ethically acceptable, as it is not clear from the context that defense counsel is attempting to create a false impression that the firm is without assets with which to pay a judgment. The plaintiff's attorney asked an open-ended question asking for general background information, and the defense attorney replied in kind. On the other end, Hypothetical 1E is manifestly false under the terms of the hypothetical, which postulate the availability of insurance coverage, and should subject the attorney to discipline for falsely stating that a judgment would be uncollectible.

Hypotheticals 1C and 1D are more interesting, as the attorney is implying without expressly stating that a judgment would be uncollectible, thereby creating a false impression without deliberately misstating the facts. In Hypothetical 1C, the defense attorney suggests that the offer may not be available in the future due to the defendant's plan to go out of business.

. . . .

While it has long been apparent that an attorney may not make affirmative factual misrepresentations in settlement negotiations, a growing body of authorities and commentators has posited that an attorney is ethically obligated to correct misimpressions caused by half-truths or omissions which are relied upon by adversaries to their detriment.

. . . .

An explicit and fundamental premise of the safe harbor proposal is, as Professor Wetlaufer has pithily observed, that lying is endemic in the legal profession and in settlement negotiations in particular. The range of lying runs the full gamut, from Wetlaufer's curious definition of disingenuous arguments, or "a belief at variance with one's own," through misdirection, omissions, and half-truths right up through good old-fashioned, Mark Twain-style whoppers. The adversary system assumes and requires the zealous and vigorous advocacy of attorneys on behalf of their clients. The more aggressive negotiators, including the most ethically aggressive, often obtain optimal results for their clients and develop successful practices. The best bluffers frequently clean up at the poker table . . . .

Accordingly, the safe harbor proposal posits that absent court rule, principle of substantive law, or prior factual representation, an attorney should have no duty to make any affirmative factual representations in the course of settlement negotiations, subject only to the crime/fraud exception. Once an attorney speaks, what is said should be truthful.

Reconciling the duty of zealous advocacy with the highest standards of honesty and fair dealing is one of the most difficult tasks facing attorneys. It is hoped that by critical analysis of existing ethical principles, the debate on reconciling these perennially conflicting values will be advanced.

7. The Gulf Between Theory and Practice. It is clear from the "roundtable" results that many commentators see the issue of truth in negotiation as framed by one standard under a technical reading of the rules ("would it be ethical?" equates with "can I get away with it?"), and another standard based of "doing the right thing." But the average practicing lawyer likely has given little thought to this distinction. Rather, this practitioner is "in the field" day in and day out, closing deals, negotiating settlements, and, most likely, telling opposing counsel what he or she thinks the other side should hear in order to obtain the desired result.

We talked with several lawyer-mediators of our acquaintance to find out their thoughts about what lawyers tell them in mediation caucus rooms. The majority felt they were not told the truth, even when the lawyers said that they were at the limit of their client's authority, or that their client "would not accept a dime less than (X)." "It would be ridiculous for me to expect that a lawyer is going to tell me, much less opposing counsel, the real bottom line, or the real limit of authority," says one highly skilled and successful lawyer-mediator. "I expect them to hold back, to run a bluff, to exaggerate. I have to be realistic; that's how the negotiation process works, and — for better or worse — most mediations work the same way."

What does this say about our justice system's methods of negotiation and dispute resolution? Perhaps it means that those few who have thought and written on the subject are more sophisticated in their thinking than the average practitioner in the trenches. Perhaps it also means the formal rules of ethics have not yet addressed these issues with sufficient specificity and clarity to tell those practicing lawyers not only what kind of behavior is *preferred* for them, but what kind of behavior is *required*.

8. The Duty of the Prosecutor. What about the prosecutor's behavior in plea negotiations? Are the rules which apply to prosecutors the same ones which apply to other advocates? Are they more stringent? When we discussed the necessity of disclosing material facts in Problem 14, we had occasion to cite to *Brady v. Maryland*, 373 U.S. 83, 83 S. Ct. 1194 (1963), which held that as a matter of constitutional right, a prosecutor *must* disclose material evidence favorable to a criminal defendant. In our present problem, do the eyewitness' drug addiction and history of failures to appear constitute material evidence favorable to the defense? What about the possible unavailability of the witness?

In the following case, the New York Court of Appeals held that a prosecutor's silence during plea negotiations about the death of the complaining witness/victim did not violate either the defendant's due process rights or the prosecutor's ethical obligations.

PEOPLE v. JONES
44 N.Y.2d 76, 404 N.Y.S.2d 85,
375 N.E.2d 41 (1978)

Plea negotiations had been conducted before the complaining witness had been located, were continued after the case had been marked ready, and culminated on April 26, 1976 when defendant withdrew his prior plea of not guilty and pleaded guilty to robbery. . . .

When defendant appeared for sentencing, defense counsel moved to withdraw the plea of guilty on the ground that it had come to his attention the previous day that the District Attorney's office had been informed of the death of Rodriguez, the victim, on April 22, 1976, four days prior to the acceptance of the plea.

In support of the motion to withdraw the plea, counsel for defendant contended that "in the spirit of *Brady v. Maryland*" the prosecution was obliged to disclose the fact of Rodriguez' death to the defense and averred that had counsel . . . "been informed of that fact I would not have allowed, at least I would have advised my client not to make the plea . . . ." At no time did defendant assert, nor does he now, that he was innocent of having committed the criminal acts charged.

It advances analysis to focus on the precise nature of the matter which was not disclosed by the prosecutor during the plea negotiations — information with respect to the death of the complaining witness. The circumstance that the testimony of the complaining witness was no longer available to the prosecution was not evidence at all. Further to the extent that proof of the fact of the death of this witness might have been admissible on trial, it would not have constituted exculpatory evidence — i.e., evidence favorable to an accused where the evidence is material either to guilt or to punishment. Accordingly, it does not fall within the doctrine enunciated by the Supreme Court of the United States in *Brady v. Maryland*. . . .

The question remains as to the extent of the prosecution's obligation to disclose information in its possession which, as here, is highly material to the practical, tactical considerations which attend a determination to plead guilty, but not to the legal issue of guilt itself . . . [that] is whether the pretrial conduct of the prosecutor in the course of plea negotiation was such as to constitute a denial of due process.

. . . .

Counsel cite no reported case, nor has our independent research disclosed any, in which judicial attention has been focused on the failure of a prosecutor before trial or during plea negotiations to disclose nonevidentiary information pertinent to the tactical aspects of a defendant's determination not to proceed to trial. No particularized rule can or need be laid down; some comments may usefully be assayed, however. At the threshold we assume that, notwithstanding that the responsibilities of a prosecutor for fairness and open-dealing are of a higher magnitude than those of a private litigant, no prosecutor is obliged to share his appraisal of the weaknesses of his own case (as opposed to specific exculpatory evidence) with defense counsel. . . . All the reported instances of deceitful persuasion appear to have involved positive misstatement or misrepresentations; none has considered the effect to be accorded silence only. Consistent with legal principles recognized elsewhere in our jurisdiction, it would seem that silence should give rise to legal consequences only if it may be concluded that the one who was silent was under an affirmative duty to speak. . . .

NOTES

The ABA Standards Relating to the Administration of Criminal Justice, Standard 3-4.1(c), says: "A prosecutor should not knowingly make false statements or representations as to fact or law in the course of plea discussions with defense counsel or the accused." The *Jones* court found that this provision did not require the prosecutor to make an affirmative disclosure of a nonevidentiary fact. But didn't this prosecutor's silence clearly mislead defendant Jones, by leaving him with an erroneous understanding of the strength of the case against him? And didn't Jones clearly rely on this erroneous understanding when pleading guilty? Standard 3-3.11 relates to the prosecutor's duty to make *Brady* disclosures. But it also requires disclosure of information which "would tend to reduce the punishment of the accused." Does this standard apply, in that if Jones had known of the death of the victim, he likely would have gotten a much better "deal," thus "reducing his punishment"?

It is impossible to say how *People v. Jones* would be decided today, after the intense discussions about negotiating tactics that have taken place in the years since. But to date, the *Jones* holding has not been disputed in other reported decisions, either in New York or elsewhere. What do you think our commentators on negotiation ethics would say about the prosecutor's actions in *Jones*? One thing is almost certain: there would be no unanimity of opinion. Think about how the individual commentators might view *Jones,* as well as how you, yourself, see it.

SUPPLEMENTAL READINGS

1. Roger Fisher & William Ury, *Getting to YES* (1981). This seminal bestselling book on the keys to successful negotiation is not primarily about ethics, but it is referred to by many who specialize in mediation and negotiation techniques, and those who deal with the ethics of negotiation. It is must reading for anyone with a particular interest in the negotiation process.

2. James J. White, *Machiavelli and the Bar: Ethical Limitations on Lying in Negotiation*, 1980 Am. B. Found. Res. J. 921. Professor White, quoted at some length by Lempert, wrote an interesting and valuable article. Among its important points is that negotiation has an "almost galactic scope," used not just in the legal system, but in business, labor disputes, family situations, even war and terrorism. White also points to significant community, ethnic, and other cultural variables which affect how different people negotiate. He provides an interesting example of a negotiation between two of his better students, one African-American, one Jewish, who — although from the same city — had assimilated very different negotiation patterns, which resulted in very different approaches and reactions in their negotiation.

3. *Virzi v. Grand Trunk Warehouse & Cold Storage Co.*, 571 F. Supp. 507 (E.D. Mich. 1983). This case sets aside a settlement that was based on a negotiation consummated after the death of the plaintiff, because the plaintiff's attorney did not inform defense counsel of the death. ABA Formal Opinion 95-397 (September 18, 1995) addressed the same issue and also concluded that the attorney had to disclose the client's death. Upon that death the attorney is without a client, and the failure to disclose this fact is "tantamount to making a 'false statement of material fact' " to the opponent. *Virzi* and Formal Opinion 95-397 provide a contrast both to *People v. Jones*, above, and to Virginia State Bar Opinion 952 (1987). Virginia Opinion 952 holds that where a lawyer was preauthorized by both his deceased client and the client's estate to accept a settlement offer, the lawyer had no affirmative duty to advise the opposing insurance defense counsel of the client's death unless opposing counsel specifically inquired as to the health of the client.

4. Charles Craver, *Effective Legal Negotiation and Settlement* (1986). This book, written by one of the "hardliners" of Lempert's negotiation roundtable (and the man who created the hypotheticals), is a complete study of the "art" of negotiation, with a specific chapter devoted to negotiation ethics.

5. Geoffrey Hazard Jr., *The Lawyer's Obligation to Be Trustworthy When Dealing with Opposing Parties*, 33 S.C. L. Rev. 181 (1981). This article is written from Professor Hazard's perspective as reporter for the Kutak Commission, which was then drafting the ABA Model Rules. Hazard points to the Commission's efforts to strengthen substantially the truth-telling requirements of the Model Rules, and the resistance it encountered. By the time this article was written, the Commission's reforms had already been significantly diluted. They were to become more diluted by the time the Rules were passed by the ABA.

6. Sissela Bok, a philosopher and an acute observer of the legal system, wrote an oft-referenced book, *Lying: Moral Choices in Public and Private Life* (1978), in which she states that "what the liar perceives as harmless or even beneficial may not be so." Bok examines lying in the context of our whole society, in which "the veneer of social trust is often thin." Lying, she argues, can damage or even destroy this trust. When trust is damaged, she argues, the whole community is damaged; when trust is destroyed, "societies falter and collapse."

7. Gary T. Lowenthal, *The Bar's Failure to Require Truthful Bargaining by Lawyers*, 2 Geo. J. Legal Ethics 411 (1988). This article examines the ABA's treatment of potentially dishonest behavior in negotiation. The author argues that while much exaggeration may be tactical posturing, the temptation to misrepresent or conceal information during negotiations is too great and requires stronger regulation. He concludes that unless the ABA seriously hopes to provide more than a guide on how to avoid civil liability, it should drop the pretense that it regulates bargaining behavior at all.

8. Lynn A. Epstein, *Post-Settlement Malpractice: Undoing the Done Deal*, 46 Catholic U. L. Rev. 453 (1997). This article criticizes the willingness of courts to permit clients to sue their attorneys after they have settled a case. Professor Epstein bases her argument in part on the "type of gamesmanship" in negotiations supported by the Model Rules. The author acknowledges that the *Muhammed* case, which immunized lawyers from malpractice claims (other than fraud) after their clients had accepted settlements, has been soundly criticized by most other jurisdictions.

9. Steven Lubet, *Lawyer's Poker* (2006). There are so many references in this Problem to poker that it would be imprudent to leave out this Northwestern ethics professor's recent book, subtitled "52 Lessons that Lawyers can

Learn from Card Players." While not just about negotiation, the book does say, at page 7, that "just like litigation, poker is all about winning."

PROBLEM 19

The line dividing legitimate trial tactics from trickery and sharp practices can be a very thin one indeed. Although there are prohibitions against material misrepresentations (see, e.g., MR 3.6 and 3.7) and a requirement of candor to the tribunal (see, e.g., MR 3.3), the Model Rules — and the Model Code before it — provide little in the way of concrete guidance about the tactical tricks of a lawyer's trade. Read about the tactics used by "Honest Abe" Dennison and his law partner. On which side of the line do they fall, and why?

"Honest Abe's" Trial Tactics

Abe Dennison is one of the most successful trial lawyers in Port City. He and his law partner, Arthur McCabe, provide general litigation services for some of the greater Bay Area's wealthiest families, especially among the social elite. Dennison is president of the Marina Yacht Club, where he engages in lunchtime and "happy hour" rainmaking, and is quite often seen playing $100 "Nassaus" on the city's most exclusive golf course.

Although Dennison is smoother than silk out of the courtroom, in court he takes on a bumbling, "aw shucks" persona. This, he explains to clients and friends, gives jurors the impression he's just a "hick from the sticks," thus creating juror sympathy. He carries this persona right through the trial. He rarely objects without hesitating, starting over, and making a little speech, which he privately calls "my Jimmy Stewart Method." Instead of "objection, irrelevant," Dennison is inclined to say "I'm sorry, Your Honor, but I don't under . . . I can't put my finger on why . . . I just can't figure out why that question has anything to do with this case." Dennison's persona has earned him from his courthouse colleagues the sarcastic sobriquet "Honest Abe."

Dennison also tries to mask the sophistication of his clients, insisting they "dress down" in court by wearing off-the-rack discount store clothes rather than the stylish outfits they favor. He has even bought bus or subway passes for clients, and then placed them conspicuously in his clients' pockets or handbags.

Dennison justifies these practices as "trial tactics" necessary to ensure winning verdicts. One time in a personal injury case, he hired his secretary's sister for the sole purpose of sitting in the first row behind Dennison's table and acting as if she was the girlfriend of his client. The case was tried in a county where Dennison feared the presence of his client's gay lover would bias the jury against his client.

In a rare criminal case, Dennison was hired by a wealthy yacht club friend to represent his son, who had been accused of rape. Dennison knew that the jury would be acutely aware of the cross-racial nature of the alleged assault — Dennison's client being white, the alleged victim first generation Chinese-American. In order to diffuse this, Dennison recruited an attractive Chinese-American woman from his Trial Practice class at the law school to act as his law clerk during the trial. He emphasized to her the importance of being friendly to the defendant during the course of the trial, "complete," as he put it, "with touching."

Arthur McCabe considers himself a mentor to the young associates at the firm. He advises them that they must manipulate the jury and use all available tricks of the trade to defend against large jury verdicts. McCabe tells the associates that "selecting a jury is the most important part of trial. In fact, a well selected jury will win your case." McCabe then recounts a case where he defended two wealthy immigrants from Mexico City in a breach of contract action brought by a real estate sales company. McCabe confides that it was very important to pack the jury with working class individuals and persons of Hispanic descent. "Having dressed my clients to look like immigrants who had scraped their life savings together to buy this property, it was important to get people on the jury who would readily accept the idea that these poor souls were struggling against a rich, white brokerage firm. Although we never mentioned the words 'race' or 'prejudice,' we made it very clear in other ways that this was an out-and-out case of racial and ethnic discrimination."

I. Evaluate these trial tactics. Are they ethical? Would you use them? Can tactics be devious and still be ethical?

II. Examine the tactics of attorneys Darrow and Dodd, and, especially, evaluate the tactics of Max Wildman, described below.

READINGS

1. Courtroom Tactics and "Parlor Tricks." A story is attributed to Clarence Darrow. Back in the early part of this century, when everyone smoked and people smoked freely in the courtroom, Darrow was sitting at counsel table listening to the prosecutor's closing argument. He lit a big Havana cigar and started smoking it. As the DA's argument progressed, the cigar ash grew longer and longer. Darrow had placed a straight wire down the center of the cigar, which kept the ash attached. As time went by, the jury paid less and less attention to the prosecutor and more and more to the cigar. The defendant was ultimately acquitted.

It is said that famed Chicago insurance defense lawyer Max Wildman once hired an attractive young woman to sit behind the plaintiff in a case concerning the wrongful death of the plaintiff's wife. The woman's job was to make friendly small talk with the plaintiff during court recesses; the idea was that the jury would observe the plaintiff's "new relationship" and lose sympathy for his loss.

Often, the tricks and devices used in the "trade" are told in "war stories" and set out like trophies to be admired. Take the following article, in which a practicing lawyer gleefully describes some of the devices he has used to persuade the jury. Written for the self-described "TV generation," it is equally relevant in the Internet era.

ROGER J. DODD, INNOVATIVE TECHNIQUES: PARLOR TRICKS FOR THE COURTROOM
Trial (April 1990) [1]

What happens in the courtroom is necessarily serious. That work requires and deserves respect. I mean no disrespect by referring to demonstrative evidence and other demonstrative techniques as parlor tricks. But I want to emphasize how important it is to stimulate, impress, and sometimes entertain during the trial of a case. This is the TV generation, and mere words from the witness may no longer be enough to persuade or convince.

Creative Approach

. . . . No matter how uncreative we think we are, each of us can bring a case alive for a jury by following a simple thought process.

• To begin the thought process, the trial lawyer must target the dominant emotion of the case — the emotion that the jury must feel in order to acquit.

• The lawyer must develop a theme that targets that emotion, and organize and present the case around that theme. A good theme will be a simple slogan, a few vivid words that will stick in the jurors' minds. . . .

• The trial lawyer must think through the emotion and theme to be targeted using the five senses: smelling, seeing, hearing, touching, and tasting. . . .

• If at all possible, the trial lawyer should be part of the demonstration. We lawyers have a public relations problem. We come across as holier-than-thou in attitude — particularly in our native habitat, the courtroom. By becoming a part of the demonstration, we lose that attitude and become human beings. Jurors relate to us . . . .

Sweet Smell of Success

Demonstrative evidence in one court-martial resulted directly in a verdict of acquittal of possessing and distributing cocaine and LSD. . . .

The "drunk" witness testified before the trial that he had consumed about a quart of Jack Daniels whiskey but that he still remembered the defendant possessing and distributing marijuana, cocaine, and LSD. We began thinking about how to convince the jurors that this witness was too drunk to see, to remember, or to be cognizant of what was going on around him.

Mental buzzers went off, lights flashed, and we decided that we would introduce into evidence a quart of Jack Daniels. We obtained the quart, placed an exhibit sticker on it, and leaned back to admire the brilliance of our work. Then we decided that we could easily buy another quart for an exhibit and we should sample this one. It was only when we opened the bottle and poured some into a glass that this fair idea became a much better one.

As soon as the bottle was opened, we realized that what stimulates most people about liquor is its smell, not just its taste. It is not the sight of the bottle. If you have a question about that, think back to your college days when

---

you would enter a room where there had been a party the night before and smell the stale alcohol. Remember that impact?

We decided that we must open the bottle in the courtroom so the jury could actually smell the alcohol. Again, reverting back to the thought process, we decided that the most acceptable reason for opening the bottle was to pour it into cups to show how many cups of alcohol are in a quart.

Now we were targeting sight as well as smell. Of course we would have people testify; that would target hearing. We decided against going so far as to suggest that the jury should exercise their sense of taste.

. . . .

Once the alcohol was poured, the smell of Jack Daniels permeated the courtroom. The bourbon sat on the jury rail throughout the closing argument. We are confident of the effectiveness of this demonstration because after the verdict was announced the jury foreman told us, "That sure was one hell of a lot of bourbon."

. . . .

Putting It All Together

A murder case is a difficult test of trial lawyers. One murder case, premised on the fact that my client, Ms. D.S. (5 feet 9 inches, 162 lbs.), sank a knife into the chest of Mr. R.G. (5 feet 4 inches, 143 lbs.) with enough force to bend the steak knife over at the handle on a 45-degree angle, brought on visions of early retirement.

The knife had pierced R.G.'s heart, slicing the aorta and killing him in about 45 seconds. Unfortunately, during those 45 seconds, my client had managed to push him down to the floor of the bar in front of some 30 or more people. They all agreed that my client said to the victim, "Say it again, _____!"

For the longest time we struggled to understand why someone would do such a stupid thing. In the process of asking ourselves why, a staff member suggested that under the right circumstances, anyone might have done it. After the snickers died down, we started to talk about the circumstances.

The entrance to the bar was dark. The only light at that entrance was a flashing Michelob sign. The temperature was in the high 90s. The humidity in south Georgia in August is always close to 100 percent. The temperature and humidity had been at these levels for some two weeks before this stabbing.

Using the thought process, we determined that the only sound that the patrons heard before my client's farewell statement to the deceased was a certain popular rap song with a driving bass. The only smell was that of stale beer.

During the trial we managed to get in all these facts. When we tendered into evidence the neon Michelob sign (having subpoenaed it), the prosecutor's reaction was neutral. When we tendered into evidence a tape recording of the song that was playing at the time of the alleged crime, the prosecutor obviously wanted to object but could think of no better objection than relevancy. It was overruled.

No one objected to our establishing the time that the acts occurred, the darkness of the hour, the heat, the humidity, and the duration of that August's heat wave and humidity.

When we offered into evidence an open beer can that obviously smelled stale (we left it open for about a week before we tried the case), the prosecutor knew something was afoot. But she could not determine what it was and, again, could only object on relevancy grounds. The judge pointed out that she had not objected to our line of questioning when we were establishing that the smell in the bar and at the entrance was of stale beer. Therefore, the actual smell should be permitted.

All these items lay on the clerk's bench without effect until closing argument. Just before closing, we asked the court to recess and turn the air conditioner off to permit the courtroom temperature to rise to the 90s and let the humidity rise as high as possible. After the court denied this request, we asked the court to turn the lights out for my closing argument, on the theory that it was dark when all of this happened. This, too, was denied.

The closing argument began this way:

If we had it within our power to put you jurors into the circumstances that existed at the time Ms. D.S. admittedly stabbed Mr. R.G., we would do so. We do not deny that she stabbed him, but you must understand the circumstances to understand why.

It is beyond our control to raise the temperature in this room to the temperature she had felt for two weeks. It is beyond our control to raise the humidity and have you feel the humidity she felt for two weeks. It is even beyond our control to darken the room so that you could better understand what happened that night.

The best we can do is to provide the music that was pounding in the background. [We turned the music on low enough so we could talk over it and let it play throughout the closing argument. We had looped the tape so it continuously played the song over and over again.] We can show you the only light. [I picked up the Michelob light and held it.] We can recreate the smell. [I put the stale beer in the can on the jury rail.]

It is up to you in your collective wisdom to think about and imagine how these other conditions affected what we recreate.

If you would close your eyes perhaps you will better understand how dark it was. [Two jurors did close their eyes.]

The remaining closing argument was given. Our client was acquitted.

The sign cost nothing. It was subpoenaed. The tape cost $1. The beer cost 75 cents.

Finale

Perhaps the best way to conclude this article is to relate what the judge told us after the acquittal in that murder case. He said that until our closing argument, when we pulled together those trivial pieces of evidence that he should not have permitted into the trial, no one would have bet that our client would have been found not guilty. Our closing was a direct appeal to the jury's emotions. We were admonished to be ashamed of ourselves.

2. Contempt and Client Identification. One of the ways in which unethical conduct can be directly regulated by the court is by the court's use of its power to hold a lawyer in contempt. The following case concerns the appeal of a federal district judge's finding of criminal contempt against an attorney who appeared before him. The opinion attempts to draw the line between zealous advocacy and obstructing the administration of justice. Is it possible to establish a "bright line" test?

UNITED STATES v. THOREEN
653 F.2d 1332 (9th Cir. 1981)

I. *Introduction*

The issue before us is whether an attorney may be found in criminal contempt for pursuing a course of aggressive advocacy while representing his client in a criminal proceeding such that, without the court's permission or knowledge, he substitutes someone for his client at counsel table with the intent to cause a misidentification, resulting in the misleading of the court, counsel, and witnesses; a delay while the government reopened its case to identify the defendant; and violation of a court order and custom.

We affirm the district court's finding of criminal contempt.

II. *Facts*

By February 1980, Thoreen, an attorney, had practiced law for almost five years. He was a member of the bars of the State of Washington and of the Western District of Washington. He had made numerous court appearances and participated in one trial and several pretrial appearances before Judge Jack E. Tanner of the Western District of Washington.

In February 1980, he represented Sibbett, a commercial fisher, during Sibbett's non-jury trial before Judge Tanner for criminal contempt for three violations of a preliminary injunction against salmon fishing. In preparing for trial, Thoreen hoped that the government agent who had cited Sibbett could not identify him. He decided to test the witness identification.

He placed next to him at counsel table Clark Mason, who resembled Sibbett, and had Mason dressed in outdoor clothing denims, heavy shoes, a plaid shirt and a jacket-vest.

Sibbett wore a business suit, large round glasses, and sat behind the rail in a row normally reserved for the press.

Thoreen neither asked the court's permission for, nor notified it or government counsel of, the substitution.

On Thoreen's motion at the start of the trial, the court ordered all witnesses excluded from the courtroom. Mason remained at counsel table.

Throughout the trial, Thoreen made and allowed to go uncorrected numerous misrepresentations. He gestured to Mason as though he was his client and gave Mason a yellow legal pad on which to take notes. The two conferred. Thoreen did not correct the court when it expressly referred to Mason as the defendant and caused the record to show identification of Mason as Sibbett.

Because of the conduct, two government witnesses misidentified Mason as Sibbett. Following the government's case, Thoreen called Mason as a witness and disclosed the substitution. The court then called a recess.

When the trial resumed, the government reopened and recalled the government agent who had cited Sibbett for two of the violations. He identified Sibbett, who was convicted of all three violations.

On February 20, 1980, Thoreen was ordered to appear on February 27 and show cause why he should not be held in criminal contempt. At the hearing, Judge Tanner found him in criminal contempt.

. . . .

B. Contempt

Judge Tanner found Thoreen in criminal contempt for the substitution because it was imposed on the court and counsel without permission or prior knowledge; the claimed identification issue did not exist; it disrupted the trial; it deceived the court and frustrated its responsibility to administer justice; and it violated a court custom. He found Mason's presence in the courtroom after giving the order excluding witnesses another ground for contempt because Thoreen planned that Mason would testify when the misidentification occurred. . . .

Thoreen's principal defense is that his conduct was a good faith tactic in aid of cross-examination and falls within the protected realm of zealous advocacy. He argues that as defense counsel he has no obligation to ascertain or present the truth and may seek to confuse witnesses with misleading questions, gestures, or appearances.

He argues also that (1) in the absence of a court rule controlling who may sit at counsel table, his failure to give notice of the substitution is not misbehavior within 18 U.S.C. § 401(1) (1976); (2) he did not intend to deceive; and (3) the exclusion order was not directed at Mason.

1. Zealous Advocacy

While we agree that defense counsel should represent his client vigorously, regardless of counsel's view of guilt or innocence, we conclude that Thoreen's conduct falls outside this protected behavior. . . . When we review this conduct and find that the line between vigorous advocacy and actual obstruction is close, our doubts should be resolved in favor of the former. [But t]he latitude allowed an attorney is not unlimited. He must represent his client within the bounds of the law. As an officer of the court, he must "preserve and promote the efficient operation of our system of justice."

Thoreen's view of appropriate cross-examination, which encompasses his substitution, crossed over the line from zealous advocacy to actual obstruction because as we discuss later, it impeded the court's search for truth, resulted in delays, and violated a court custom and rule. Moreover, this conduct harms rather than enhances an attorney's effectiveness as an advocate.

. . . .

2. *Criminal Contempt*

18 U.S.C. § 401 (1976) provides

> A court of the United States shall have power to punish by fine or imprisonment, at its discretion, such contempt of its authority . . . as
>
> (1) Misbehavior of any person in its presence or so near thereto as to obstruct the administration of justice;
>
> . . . .
>
> (3) Disobedience or resistance to its lawful . . . command.

. . . .

Making misrepresentations to the court is also inappropriate and unprofessional behavior under ethical standards that guide attorneys' conduct. These guidelines, in effect in Washington and elsewhere, decree explicitly that an attorney's participation in the presentation or preservation of false evidence is unprofessional and subjects him to discipline.

Substituting a person for the defendant in a criminal case without a court's knowledge has been noted as an example of unethical behavior by the ABA Committee on Professional Ethics. See Informal Opinion No. 914, 2/24/66.

. . . .

Making misrepresentations to the fact finder is inherently obstructive because it frustrates the rational search for truth. It may also delay the proceedings. In *In re Dellinger*, 502 F.2d 813, 816 (7th Cir.1974), *cert. denied*, 420 U.S. 990, 95 S. Ct. 1425, 43 L. Ed. 2d 671 (1975), for example, the Seventh Circuit held that an attorney obstructed justice by putting inadmissible evidence before the jury, hampering its ability to decide the case according to the legal principles provided them.

. . . .

To be held in criminal contempt, the contemnor must have the requisite intent.

"An attorney possesses the requisite intent only if he knows or reasonably should be aware in view of all the circumstances, especially the heat of the controversy, that he is exceeding the outermost limits of his proper role and hindering rather than facilitating the search for truth." Proof of an evil motive or of an actual intent to obstruct justice is unnecessary.

Good faith is a defense to a finding of intent, but it does not immunize all conduct undertaken by an attorney on behalf of a client [citing *United States v. Seale*, 461 F.2d 345 (7th Cir. 1972)]. It requires only that a court allow an attorney great latitude in his pursuit of vigorous advocacy.

Thoreen admits he planned and intended the substitution, but defends by asserting that (1) it was a good faith effort to prove misidentification and attack the credibility of the government witnesses; (2) he never intended to misrepresent any facts to the court or to obstruct justice; and (3) he believed the court knew Sibbett's identity from the pretrial hearing.

. . . .

His alleged lack of intent to deceive the court or to obstruct justice is irrelevant. Section 401(1) does not require specific intent. It suffices that he should have been aware that his conduct exceeded reasonable limits and hindered the search for truth.

Conclusion

Thoreen's error in judgment was unfortunate. The court's ire and this criminal contempt conviction could have been avoided easily and the admirable goal of representing his client zealously preserved if only he had given the court and opposing counsel prior notice and sought the court's consent.

Nonetheless, viewing the evidence in the light most favorable to the government, we find that there is sufficient evidence to find beyond a reasonable doubt that Thoreen violated 18 U.S.C. § 401(1) and (3). The district court's findings were not clearly erroneous. We AFFIRM the contempt conviction. . . .

NOTES

Interestingly, two Seventh Circuit cases cited by the *Thoreen* court in supporting contempt charges, *In re Dellinger* and *U.S. v. Seale*, related to the explosive Chicago 7 trial, whose defendants were antiwar and civil rights activists on trial for organizing disruptions at the 1968 Chicago Democratic convention, at the height of the Vietnam War and shortly after the assassinations of Dr. Martin Luther King, Jr. and Senator Robert F. Kennedy. No trial in modern American history was more politicized or provided more of a circus atmosphere than this one. Defendants and lawyers alike disrupted the proceedings, and contempt citations flew. Eventually, the judge too was censured for his conduct, and the defendants' convictions were reversed.

The opinion in *Thoreen*, while upholding the contempt citation as "not clearly erroneous," seemed to have some substantial sympathy for the attorney. A decade later, in another case involving a defendant/stand-in switch, Illinois attorney David Sotomayor had his state court criminal contempt upheld by a 4-3 Illinois Supreme Court decision, although this court also sounded sympathetic to the attorney. The dissenting justices noted that Sotomayor had a legitimate reason to show the unreliability of the witness' identification. By sanctioning the lawyer for providing an objective identification test, "[t]he case points out how arguably meaningless in-court I.D.'s are," Fordham ethics professor Bruce A. Green told the *New York Times*.

Unlike Thoreen, Sotomayor acted spontaneously on a single day, never misrepresented that the person sitting next to him at counsel table was the defendant, and didn't dress up the defendant or dress down the stand-in (both wore similar modest attire). Moreover, identification was not an irrelevant issue; indeed, the judge who made the contempt finding also dismissed all charges against Sotomayor's client.[2] The big problem may have been Sotomayor's failure to inform the judge in advance of what he said was a lunchtime inspiration. But no rule existed requiring the defendant to be at counsel table, just in the courtroom.

The *Thoreen* court says that in a close case, doubts should be resolved in favor of vigorous advocacy. Why, then, did Sotomayor suffer the same fate as Thoreen? "We ought to give the guy a medal," the incoming president of the National Association of Criminal Defense Lawyers told the *New York Times*.

3. Racial Issues in Court. In the last few years many of the most highly publicized trials in the nation have had a large racial component: among others, trials concerning Howard Beach, Bernhard Goetz, the beatings of both Rodney King and Reginald Denny, Marion Barry's drug trial, and especially the O.J. Simpson murder case, with its allegations of a racially bigoted police investigator. After Simpson was acquitted, one of his own defense attorneys, Robert Shapiro, criticized lead counsel Johnnie Cochran on national television for "playing the race card" and "dealing it from the bottom of the deck." Many others in the mainstream media accused Cochran of achieving what to them seemed to be an unjust result by injecting the issue of race into the trial.

But was it the defense who placed race at issue in the Simpson case? Read the following article by a highly regarded federal appeals judge and his law clerks.

A. LEON HIGGINBOTHAM, JR., ADERSON BELLEGARDE FRANCOIS & LINDA Y. YUEH, THE O.J. SIMPSON TRIAL: WHO WAS IMPROPERLY "PLAYING THE RACE CARD"?
Toni Morrison and Claudia Brodsky Lacour, editors, in Birth of a Nation'hood: Gaze, Script and Spectacle in the O.J. Simpson Case *(1997)*[3]

[The authors first describe the evidentiary rules on bias and credibility.]

The foregoing cases, statutes, and jury instructions represent a formal modern enactment of the ancient maxim *falsus in uno, falsus in omnibus* — originally construed as "he who speaks falsely on one point will speak falsely upon all" — and serve as means to enforce the Supreme Court's admonishment that "the exposure of a witness's motivation in testifying is a proper and important function of the constitutionally protected right of cross-examination." This plethora of unequivocal state and federal jurisprudential precedents sanctioned the defense team's efforts to inquire about the racial bias of detective Mark Fuhrman.

Was Mark Fuhrman Biased?

The Simpson trial presented the case of an African-American man accused of killing his white ex-wife and her white male friend. Mark Fuhrman, the

---

[2] See the report on this case in Jan Hoffman's article, *At the Bar*, N.Y. TIMES, July 29, 1994. This case is reported in *People v. Simac*, 641 N.E.2d 416 (Ill. 1994).

[3] Copyright © 1997 by Pantheon Books, a division of Random House. Used by permission. All rights reserved.

prosecution's main police witness, whom Mr. Cochran referred to as a "lying genocidal racist," once admitted that "when he sees a nigger driving with a white woman, he pulls them over" for no reason other than the fact that the man is African American and the woman is white. So strong was Mr. Fuhrman's bias toward African Americans that he wished "nothing more than to see all niggers gathered together and killed." So deep were Mr. Fuhrman's prejudices that he allowed himself to be taped using the word "nigger" at least forty-two times. Yet, when questioned on the stand about whether he harbored a bias toward African Americans, Mr. Fuhrman denied that he did so. Indeed, Mr. Fuhrman went on to emphatically deny having used the word "nigger" at all in the past ten years.

The jury, therefore, had at least four reasons to consider Mr. Fuhrman a less than credible witness against Mr. Simpson. First, the fact that Mr. Fuhrman lied about using the word "nigger" (*falsus in uno*) meant that he could have been lying about other aspects of his testimony (*falsus in omnibus*). Second, the jury had cause to disbelieve Mr. Fuhrman's testimony because Mr. Fuhrman perjured himself on the witness stand. . . . Third, the jury could have reasonably determined that Mr. Fuhrman was biased against Mr. Simpson for having been married to a white woman because Mr. Fuhrman held and acted upon a strong bias against interracial couples made up of African-American men and white women. Fourth, the jury could have reasonably found that Mr. Fuhrman's investigation and testimony against Mr. Simpson was tainted because it was Mr. Fuhrman's fervent wish to have "all niggers gathered together and killed." Thus, the Simpson defense team had a legal and professional obligation to introduce to the jury this very substantial and damning evidence of Mr. Fuhrman's lack of credibility.

This may seem to be an obvious point. However, during and after the trial, it appeared as if most Americans considered it morally wrong, socially irresponsible, and generally "unfair" for Mr. Cochran and his co-counsel to have "interjected" race into the trial.

Why was it unfair?

If Different Biases Had Been Involved, Would the Commentators Have Been as Critical of a Defense Counsel's Strategy to Raise the Issue of Race, or Gender, or Religion?

Any critical evaluation of the fairness of the commentary on the O.J. Simpson case should start with the assessment that there were several factors present during the trial that affected the public reaction to the verdict and that may have led commentators to claim that the defense improperly "played the race card": the race of the defendant, his fame and wealth, the race and gender of the victims, the race of the main police witnesses, the particular racial bias held by these witnesses, the race of lead counsel for the defense, and even the race of the judge. Since the interplay of these factors undoubtedly contributed to the incorrect perception that the defense had improperly played the race card, it then follows that changing one or more of these factors might also conceivably alter the perception that the defense improperly interjected race into the trial.

For example, if the main police witnesses had been African Americans with a history of hatred of and hostility toward whites, and if O.J. Simpson had been white, would the commentators have been as critical of any defense counsel who raised the "bias issue" as to the black police officers' prior conduct? Or, if Mr. Simpson's wife had been black, would these same commentators have been just as vehement in condemning the verdict as an outrage?

Underlying all these scenarios described below is the basic question of whether, assuming that the violence and the commission of the crime were precisely the same, the intensity of the criticism would have been the same, less or more, if the variables as to race, gender, or religious were different than those involved in the O.J. Simpson case.

If the defendant had been Jewish and the prosecution's main police witness had a history of calling Jewish individuals "kikes" and then lying about in on the witness stand, automatically stopping any motorist wearing a yarmulke, and wishing that "all kikes should be gathered together and killed," would the critics claim that it was unfair for the defense to introduce evidence that the witness was a lying, anti-Semitic neo-Nazi? Probably not.

If the defendant had been a woman, and the prosecution's main police witness had a history of calling women "bitches" and then lying about it on the witness stand, sexually harassing women at work, and wishing that "all bitches should be gathered together and killed," would the critics claim that it was unfair for the defense to introduce evidence that the witness was a lying, misogynistic harasser? Probably not.

If the defendant had been gay, and the prosecution's main police witness had a history of calling gays "faggots" and then lying about it on the witness stand, arresting any men seen holding hands, and wishing that "all faggots should be gathered together and killed," would the critics claim that it was unfair to introduce evidence that the witness was a lying, genocidal homophobe? Probably not.

Would it be unfair for the defense to argue that any witness — particularly a law enforcement officer charged with protecting all citizens — who harbors and acts upon sexist, anti-Semitic or homophobic tendencies should be disbelieved when the defendant against whom the witness is testifying represents the very object of the witness's hate? Probably not.

Under any of the above scenarios, would the defense be accused of unfairly playing the gender card, or the religion card, or the ethnicity card, or the sexual-orientation card? Probably not.

The Tensions Between the Rhetoric of Seeking a Color-Blind Society and the Reality of Living in a Race-Conscious Nation

Perhaps it is both inevitable and understandable that the Simpson case would be used as a metaphor for the seemingly intractable problem of race in America. In the larger scheme, the case did not really involve any major public policy issues. However, the public paid so much attention to the trial that by the time the verdict was finally announced, there seemed to be a need to infuse the case with a measure of deeper social importance in order to justify all of the time and money spent on it. Unfortunately, the lessons that most Americans took from the trial were wrong.

. . . . [T]he public recrimination over the verdict only served to rake over and over again the dirt from the freshly covered graves of the victims, revealing in the churned-up mud corpses only half buried and souls only half put to rest. Perhaps it is only in that way that the trial and the verdict may — carefully, very carefully — be used as a metaphor for race in America. The victims' graves were not the only ones that were disturbed by the public recrimination over the verdict. In the process, we also stirred up the shallow grave where is stored the vestiges of centuries of slavery, segregation, racial oppression, biases, and prejudices, also revealing in that ancient muddy racial pit corpses only half buried and souls only half put to rest. The trial was merely the shovel we used to dig up that grave.

The Simpson trial *did not create* the racial tensions that American society experiences and desperately attempts to conceal. To pretend to be shocked at the differences in racial attitudes in the reactions to the verdict is, therefore, more than a little disingenuous. The "racial divide" in public opinion over the verdict is not a phenomenon newly created by the Simpson trial; it has existed all along, and it took the tragic double murder of two innocent people to expose the hypocrisy of our collective consciousness. It is this same self-deception that Americans engage in when politicians and even the courts declare that race-conscious remedies in public policies are evils that keep us from reaching the promised land of a color-blind society.

NOTES

In a postscript to the article, Higginbotham noted ironically that the press paid little attention to officer Mark Fuhrman's plea of no contest and resulting conviction for perjury, or to the fact that, although he apologized to the police department, his family, and the general public, he never expressed any remorse for his diatribes against African Americans over the years.

"Playing the race card" is merely a catch phrase unless it is placed in context. Some cases necessarily involve issues of race, sex, or ethnicity. Racially and ethnically motivated incidents occur, as do sexual harassment and discrimination, and criminal sexual behavior. In these cases, no one seriously argues with lawyers who emphasize issues of race, ethnicity, or sex.

But what about playing the race card, as Abe Dennison did with his law clerk? Does the race card have a place in the courtroom, even when race itself is not *directly* an issue? After all, most racism in the United States is *indirect*. Experienced lawyers don't decide to raise race in a vacuum; they know that to make it an effective tool they must tie it to something in the case — what the police did, what a witness saw or said, what opposing counsel has charged. Does this justify Dennison's actions? Excuse them? And what about Johnnie Cochran's strategy in the Simpson case?

What about when race comes into play in how a lawyer selects a jury? Read what famed (or is it infamous?) trial lawyer Melvin Belli was quoted as telling the Association of Trial Lawyers of America in 1982: "The g__d__ Chinese won't give you a short noodle on a verdict. You've got to bounce them out of there. In the last case that I tried, I used all my challenges getting rid of those sons of the Celestial Empire."[4] These remarks caused an uproar in Belli's hometown of San Francisco, where Asian-American civil rights groups were quick to demand an apology. But aside from the overt offensiveness of the remarks, is the *strategy* which underlies them justified? And how does this strategy compare to Arthur McCabe's in selecting a jury for his Mexican-American clients?

4. Courtroom Attire. Issues of race may arise in relation to counsel's attire. How would you feel if opposing counsel, an African-American, presented his opening argument to a predominantly black jury wearing a kente cloth scarf? Kente cloth has become a symbol of ethnic pride for many African-Americans. Does wearing it give opposing counsel an unfair advantage? And should that advantage be the test for whether the attorney's garb is suitable or his trial behavior unethical?

PATRICE GAINES-CARTER, D.C. LAWYER TOLD TO REMOVE AFRICAN KENTE CLOTH FOR JURY TRIAL
The Washington Post (May 23, 1992)[5]

Could a piece of cloth associated with black pride cause a black jury to be prejudiced in favor of a defendant and his attorney?

D.C. Superior Court Judge Robert M. Scott told a defense attorney yesterday that he could not keep the kente cloth he wears around his suit collar if he wants a jury trial for his client.

Defense attorney John T. Harvey III was given the options of removing the kente cloth, removing himself as a lawyer in the case or entering a plea of guilty for his client.

Scott, who is white, has said that he is not personally influenced either way by the brightly colored cloth traditionally worn by West African royalty. Thus, Harvey may wear the cloth if he chooses to try his case in front of the judge.

But Harvey refused all options. He did not enter a plea and said he would stay on as a lawyer in the case and continue wearing the kente cloth. . . .

Scott could have held Harvey in contempt of court. But he skirted the issue — for now — and set an arraignment for Harvey's client for June 11. The judge left the impression that he will remove Harvey from the case if the trial goes to a jury.

Harvey was accompanied in the courtroom by about 20 supporters dressed in kente cloth ties, stoles and hats and by the president of the District chapter of the NAACP. The lawyer has said he wears his kente scarf for religious and cultural reasons and has compared it to a yarmulke worn by Jews.

The cloth with a distinctive pattern has become a powerful symbol of ethnic pride for many black Americans. Former D.C. mayor Marion Barry wore a kente cloth scarf during his trial and at most of his recent public appearances. Harvey said that his church, Faith United Church of Christ in the District,

---

[4] As quoted in THE NATIONAL LAW JOURNAL, (Aug. 2, 1982).

[5] Copyright © 1992 by The Washington Post. Reprinted by permission.

requires officers to wear kente cloths and that he has worn one for the last seven months, appearing before other judges, none of whom objected.

"You are in conflict with all your other colleagues," Harvey, 32, told the judge yesterday.

"I run my court. I do whatever I think is proper," Scott, 70, retorted.

Area lawyers said that what is at issue is interpretation of constitutional law and First Amendment rights, and that cases such as this one are rare. . . .

One lawyer who did not want to be identified said it is generally accepted that judges determine the decorum in their courtrooms, what "apparel is considered duly disruptive or distracting to jurors."

But Harvey and his supporters interpret Scott's objections as a personal questioning of their cultural and religious beliefs.

"Kente literally means 'Whatever happens to it, it will not tear,' which really is the epitome of the struggle of us as African Americans . . . that whatever attempt to divide us must not happen," said the Rev. Joseph E. Taylor, Harvey's pastor. . . .

At Scott's request, Harvey submitted a memo last month saying that the cloth is "historically significant" and that he had no "intent to send any message to the jury."

The judge had no comment. Some months ago in court, when the fight began, Scott referred Harvey to a New York case in which a lawyer who also was a priest was prohibited from wearing his priest's collar. In that decision, it was determined that the jury process was ineffective in ferreting out people who might be biased in favor of the priest.

Harvey had asked that the judge remove himself from the case, but Scott denied the request yesterday.

Outside the court, Harvey called the judge's action "discriminatory" and said, "I ask the community to help and put pressure on the Superior Court system so that it will be more inclusive." The lawyer said he is considering asking Chief Judge Fred B. Ugast to intervene in the dispute.

NOTES

What about garb worn for religious reasons? We presume the case referred to in the above article is *LaRocca v. Lane*, 37 N.Y.2d 575, 376 N.Y.S.2d 93, 338 N.E.2d 606 (1975), in which the New York Court of Appeals required a criminal defense lawyer priest to abandon his clerical collar because it might unduly prejudice the jury. But the same lawyer won the right to use the collar four years later in another reported case, where the court found no prejudice that could not be dealt with in voir dire.[6] In *Jensen v. Superior Court*, 154 Cal. App. 3d 533, 201 Cal. Rptr. 275 (1984), a lawyer was allowed to wear his turban *and* to decline to explain the religious beliefs behind the attire; the court held that there was no showing of disruption or interference with

---

[6] *People v. Rodriguez*, 424 N.Y.S.2d 600 (1979).

the administration of justice. Finally, in *Ryslik v. Krass*, 279 N.J. Sup. 293, 652 A.2d 767 (1995), the court found that a priest defendant in a vehicle accident case who testified in clerical garb did not unduly prejudice the jury. The court found that any potential bias for the priest (who was *not* found liable) was cured when the court addressed the problem during jury selection. Are there different standards for attorneys acting as lawyers, witnesses and parties? If so, why? Would curative jury instructions work with attorneys as well as non-attorneys?

Prejudice and disruption or interference also appear to be the test for non-religious attire. Thus, in a Florida case, a lawyer who had gone to jail for contempt when he refused to wear a tie then took to wearing string ties. His case went to the Florida Supreme Court, which, in *Sandstrom v. State*, 336 So. 2d 572 (Fla. 1976), decided against him, but not without a strongly worded dissent that argued there had been no showing of disruption, interference with "the search for truth," or peril to the judicial system. A more egregious case occurred in *Florida Bar v. Burns*, 392 So. 2d 1325 (Fla. 1981), in which an attorney was disciplined for appearing in court on a stretcher, dressed in bedclothes, ostensibly because he had been advised by his doctors to have complete bed rest due to an illness. It did not help that the attorney walked to and from his doctor's appointment the previous day.

Women have suffered far more significant limitations on their attire than the kind of ties they may wear. For example, one superior court judge in Seattle (a woman) is reported to have insisted that women lawyers appearing before her wear skirts, not pants.[7] Gradually, the absence of disruption, distraction, and disrespect have been cited to justify a variety of women's attire, from slacks and a sweater[8] to miniskirts.[9]

Is attire, then, an ethical issue? Arguably yes, at least to the extent that it is designed to prejudice either the jury or the court. Thus, a lawyer was not permitted to appear in court wearing a World War II German officer's uniform, complete with Nazi insignia, because it was prejudicial to the administration of justice.[10]

5. Ethics, Trial Tactics, and Modern Techniques of Jury Selection. This is not only the TV generation, as trial lawyer Roger Dodd put it, but the generation of technology. Trial tactics may not have travelled quite as far down the information superhighway as other technologies, but the last generation has seen an explosion of new techniques. Videotaped depositions, laser-assisted demonstrative evidence and computer modelled incident reconstruction have all become more common. Other techniques focus on understanding the jury. Jury focus groups help lawyers determine in advance the kind of jury they want, and "shadow juries" are hired by the lawyers to follow the case moment by moment, available for debriefing every evening. It is a rare trial on Court TV that takes place without the services of an in-court jury consultant to help select the chosen few who will hear the case.

---

[7] Birkland, *No Skirting the Issue in This Courtroom*, SEATTLE TIMES, Sep. 30, 1999, at B1.

[8] *See In re DeCarlo*, 357 A.2d 273 (N.Y. 1976).

[9] *See Peck v. Stone*, 304 N.Y.S.2d 881 (1969).

[10] *In re Price*, 709 P.2d 986 (Kan. 1985).

More subtle but perhaps no less manipulative of the fact-finding process are the books, articles, and seminars which teach the science — for it has become a science as much as an art — of storytelling. Psychologists and social scientists can develop the perfect storytelling profile for the average jury — extroverted, relaxed delivery, slightly rapid conversational mode of speech, and plenty of eye contact, hand gestures, and facial expression. They evaluate the different physical demeanors of witnesses — upright or relaxed on the stand, legs straight or crossed, and so on. They analyze racial, ethnic, and socioeconomic class distinctions between witnesses and jurors, to decide how best to bridge the gaps. And, of course, they make a scientific study of selecting the right jury to hear the particular story in question. Read the following excerpt.

FRANKLIN STRIER & DONNA SHESTOWSKY, PROFILING THE PROFILERS: A STUDY OF THE TRIAL CONSULTING PROFESSION, ITS IMPACT ON TRIAL JUSTICE AND WHAT, IF ANYTHING, TO DO ABOUT IT
1999 Wisconsin Law Review 441[11]

A considerable part of the impetus for ethical standards crystallizes around pretrial investigations of prospective jurors by trial consultants. Many investigational procedures skirt the outer limitations of acceptable practices. Some investigations may even constitute jury tampering, obstruction of justice or invasion of privacy or constitute ethical violations by the attorney. MRPC Rules forbid attorneys from communicating with or seeking to influence jurors or prospective jurors and extend vicarious liability for the actions of those working under them or retained by them for conduct that would be a violation of the rules if engaged in by the attorney.

[Some commentators] offer the following illustration of how an ostensibly innocuous pretrial investigation procedure can run afoul of the law. In developing a community network model, trial consultants usually rely on friends of the defendant or other non-professionals untrained in the skills necessary for this type of information gathering. There is a high probability some of these nonprofessionals will act or appear "suspicious." If a person so contacted by such a person in the network informs a prospective juror that persons of questionable character or motive are conducting an investigation into his or her personal affairs, the prospective juror may well feel threatened or intimidated. This type of practice may constitute obstruction of justice. The federal statute, for example, defines obstruction of justice as "whoever corruptly . . . endeavors to influence, intimidate, or impede any grand or petit juror . . . in the discharge of his duty." Importantly, this section has been held to apply to prospective jurors as well as sworn jurors.

Prospective jurors may experience another invasion of their privacy in court, during *voir dire*. The questioning of prospective jurors can sometimes delve protractedly into intensely private and intimate details of the questioned individual's life. Responsibility often lies with the trial consultant as well as with the interrogating attorney. All trial attorneys want to make the most informed

---

[11] Copyright © 1999 by University of Wisconsin Law Review, University of Wisconsin. Reprinted by permission.

and effective use of their peremptory challenges. To this end, they employ trial consultants who may suggest *voir dire* interrogations that might violate privacy. This affront to the sensibilities of the panelists might nonetheless be justifiable, on balance, if there were clearly demonstrable countervailing benefits. That assessment, however, has not been universal. Contrasting our system with that of England, where both peremptory challenges and pretrial investigations have been virtually eliminated, one scholar observed: "In the United States, where *voir dire* allows for vast intrusions into individuals' lives, the result has not been greater impartiality, but a proliferation of methods by which skilled litigators and expensive consultants tailor juries to their clients' needs."

NOTES

The authors discuss several remedies to address the potential abuses that can arise from the use of jury consultants, but they only recommend licensing such consultants and improving self-imposed industry standards. They point out that as the use of trial consultants increases, so does the likelihood that attorneys who fail to use such experts may expose themselves to claims of malpractice if they lose.

Are these commentators right that jury selection has gotten too personal? Or as many trial lawyers would argue, do the parties' rights to a fair trial trump such privacy concerns in the interests of getting a fair and impartial jury?

In addition to professionals who help attorneys investigate jurors, develop evidence, or prepare for trial, some actors and directors are also offering their services to trial lawyers. As with other consultants, theater consultants help lawyers map out their strategy, advise witnesses on effective presentation of testimony, help lawyers improve their own courtroom effectiveness, and help create visual aids. According to one source, the "tricks" they teach lawyers include bending at the waist to show informality, and moving from the jury's right to its left when discussing a weak point of a case — opposite to the usual left-to-right reading direction by which people generally take in information.[12]

Many of these methods are both cost-and labor-intensive, making them difficult for the average small firm lawyer to access. Except for videotaped depositions, whose "production values" have been regulated by many of the courts that have passed on their admissibility, the ethical issues of using these techniques have not yet been directly addressed. Perhaps it is sufficient to say that to many lawyers, these techniques are becoming part of the duties of competence and zealous advocacy. But it is important to be aware that technological advances, when taken to the extreme, could affect the fact-finding process far more than just suggestion, persuasion and manipulation. The more sophisticated the computer modelling, the more difficult it may be to detect its fraudulent application. The more widespread and detailed the jury investigation, the more difficult it may be to discover an invasion of the privacy of

---

[12] Sands, *For Argument's Sake, Lawyers Engage in Trial to Stage Courtroom Victories,* Washington Times, Feb. 5, 1996, at A16.

members of the jury panel. Modern techniques are here to stay, several of which we would use ourselves. We merely suggest that, as with any other developments in the profession, understanding their use should be coupled with an understanding of their potential abuse.

6. Jury Selection and Race. Read this article by a Georgia law professor tying ethics and constitutional law together in instances of racially discriminatory jury selection.

LONNIE T. BROWN, JR., RACIAL DISCRIMINATION IN JURY SELECTION: PROFESSIONAL MISCONDUCT, NOT LEGITIMATE ADVOCACY
22 Review of Litigation 209 (2003)[13]

Although many regard the duty and privilege of participating in our judicial process through jury service with about as much warmth and respect as they view telemarketing calls at suppertime, it is nevertheless an opportunity that must be afforded to all citizens, regardless of race, ethnicity, or gender. Furthermore, Supreme Court jurisprudence over the years has established that the mere "opportunity" to serve on a jury through inclusion on jury lists or venires is not enough. The Constitution also requires that potential jurors not be excluded from actual juries as a result of intentional racial or gender-oriented discrimination. The Supreme Court embarked on the development of this constitutional principle in Swain v. Alabama, in which it held that prosecutors' use of their discretionary strikes of prospective jurors, commonly referred to as "peremptory challenges," to systematically exclude Blacks from petit juries in "case after case" might be deemed unconstitutional. Later, in Batson v. Kentucky, the Court narrowed and strengthened this concept by holding that it was unconstitutional for a prosecutor to exercise his or her peremptory challenges in a fashion that intentionally discriminated against Blacks on the basis of race, even within the context of a single case.

The Court's prohibition against the discriminatory use of peremptory challenges was originally founded on the concept of safeguarding the equal protection rights of criminal defendants alone, but later shifted to a focus on the protection of these rights with regard to prospective jurors. In addition, the Supreme Court gradually expanded Batson's initial reach beyond addressing discriminatory conduct by prosecutors only. The dictates of Batson now apply equally to criminal defense counsel as well as civil trial attorneys.

Hence, attorneys' striking of jurors in an intentionally discriminatory fashion has unequivocally and in all respects been deemed improper and indeed unconstitutional . . . .

[But] the Supreme Court has actually eased the burden of avoiding a charge of discrimination in jury selection by requiring only a race-neutral explanation for a peremptory strike that has been properly challenged, rather than one that is both race-neutral and rational. As a result, some commentators have posited, and evidence suggests, that judges have become more willing to accept proffered race-neutral explanations for alleged discriminatory use of peremptory challenges, no matter how suspect. Furthermore, even if a violation of

---

[13] Copyright © 2003 by Review of Litigation. Reprinted by permission.

Batson's dictates is found by a court, the modest penalties imposed on offending lawyers provide little incentive to refrain from such behavior in the future . . . .

Equally troubling is the apparent insulation now provided by the ethics rules to attorneys who engage in the discriminatory use of peremptory challenges, notwithstanding alleged efforts by bar authorities to the contrary. Specifically, Rule 8.4(d) of the American Bar Association's (ABA) Model Rules of Professional Conduct prohibits lawyers from engaging in conduct that is "prejudicial to the administration of justice," but provides in the Rule's explanatory comments as follows:

A lawyer who, in the course of representing a client, knowingly manifests by words or conduct, bias or prejudice based upon race, sex, religion, national origin, disability, age, sexual orientation or socioeconomic status, violates paragraph (d) when such actions are prejudicial to the administration of justice. Legitimate advocacy respecting the foregoing factors does not violate paragraph (d). A trial judge's finding that peremptory challenges were exercised on a discriminatory basis does not alone establish a violation of this rule.

. . . . Even if a lawyer is found to have committed a Batson violation by a trial court, according to the Comment, that finding "alone" would not subject the lawyer to discipline. There is no indication, however, as to how much weight, if any, should be given to such trial-level determinations. As a result, this sentence seems to undermine the importance of these findings and give the impression that something more than intentional discrimination must be established before an attorney can be subject to discipline under Rule 8.4(d). One cannot overlook, however, the fact that this type of intentional misconduct constitutes a violation of the Constitution, and therefore is supremely worthy of the attention of lawyers, as well as those who regulate them. Unfortunately, this has not been the reality of the situation.

. . . .

[T]he ABA and every state should enact an ethical rule expressly articulating that a Batson-type violation is a disciplinable offense and, therefore, one that lawyers and judges have a clear obligation to report to the appropriate disciplinary authorities. Under this proposed rule, any lawyer found to have violated Batson should automatically be reported to the proper disciplinary body . . . .

The increased accountability created by the proposed procedural innovations will cause counsel to give greater consideration to their exercise of peremptories ex ante and will thereby serve as a deterrent for those predisposed to strike jurors for racial reasons. Furthermore, in instances in which prophylactic measures are unsuccessful and Batson violations occur, the recommended disciplinary modifications more appropriately treat and denominate such behavior as what it truly is — professional misconduct.

SUPPLEMENTAL READINGS

1. Robert E. Keeton, *Trial Tactics and Methods* (1973). This seminal volume on the art of trying cases keeps a careful eye on the ethics of trial work.

2. *Hawk v. Superior Court*, 42 Cal. App. 3d 108, 116 Cal. Rptr. 713 (1974), is a textbook case of all the trial tactics *not* to engage in. While defending Juan Corona on twenty-five counts of murder in a highly publicized trial, attorney Hawk amassed fourteen counts of contempt, $3,000 in fines, and a 54-day jail sentence. Hawk's conduct ran the gamut from the most severe, such as advising his client to disobey an order of the court and making comments during jury voir dire that improperly attempted to influence jurors, to the seemingly innocuous — calling his client by his given name. All but two of the judgments of contempt were sustained.

3. W. Lance Bennett & Martha S. Feldman, *Reconstructing Reality in the Courtroom: Justice and Judgment in American Culture* (1981). This book is an in-depth analysis of how best to tell a story in the courtroom that will be found believable by the jury. It discusses many of the psychological techniques and devices mentioned above.

4. D. A. Clay, *Race and Perception in the Courtroom: Nonverbal Behaviors and Attribution in the Criminal Justice System*, 67 Tul. L. Rev. 2335 (1993). This interesting law review note discusses racial attitudes of jurors as they affect jury verdicts, and how racial bias can and cannot be controlled. It also provides a good summary of the literature in the field.

5. Stuart Taylor, Jr., "Selecting Juries: Dumb and Dumber," *Legal Times*, April 14, 1997. Taylor reports on election campaign revelations by Philadelphia District Attorney Lynn Taylor that her Republican opponent, who was also a senior prosecutor, urged colleagues to exclude whole categories of African-Americans (among other groups) from juries. The prosecutor, Jack McMahon, also argued for keeping highly educated and well-informed people off juries because "they take those words, 'reasonable doubt,' and actually try to think about them."

6. How race can properly be used in jury selection, including by the *defense*, has been a rather hotly debated issue. Notable among articles on the subject are these:

● Abbe Smith, *Nice Work if You Can Get It: "Ethical" Jury Selection in Criminal Defense*, 67 Fordham L. Rev. 523, 531 (1998). Smith argues that an attorney's obligation to fight cultural stereotypes or to serve the interests of the broader community cannot conflict with the duty to the client. She states it is unethical for a criminal defense attorney to ignore the impact of race and sex on juror attitudes and that *Batson*'s prohibition against race-based peremptory challenges directly conflicts with an attorney's obligation to zealously advocate for his or her client.

● Anthony V. Alfieri, *Race Prosecutors, Race Defenders*, 89 Geo. L.J. 2227 (2001). Contrary to Smith, Alfieri claims that criminal defense lawyers should use a socially-conscious approach which does not exploit stereotypes, and that claiming that the use of stereotypes is zealous advocacy is unfounded and an inapt.

● David C. Baldus et al., *The Use of Peremptory Challenges in Capital Murder Trials: A Legal and Empirical Analysis*, 3 U. Pa. J. Const. L. 3 (2001). The author presents an overview of the literature on peremptory challenges and an empirical study performed in the 1980s and 1990s in Philadelphia revealing that discrimination in the use of peremptory challenges on the basis of race and gender continues to be widespread despite Supreme Court decisions banning these practices. The study also found that prosecutors are more successful than defense attorneys at controlling the composition of the jury.

PROBLEM 20

This problem concerns two important facets of litigation: lawyers' relations with each other and the tension between free speech rights and protecting the goal of a fair trial. The lawyers in the problems use various "tricks of the trade" to gain advantage. Consider whether these attorneys' actions are the effective strategies of smart and zealous but ethical advocates, or the sneaky tricks of unethical lawyers. Consider whether the behavior described here is prohibited by the letter of the rules, and whether attorneys have free speech rights like every other citizen. Note also that more than purely "ethical" issues are involved: the notion of "civility," the court's contempt powers, and constitutional law.

Civility, Contempt of Court, Free Speech, and Publicity

I. Attorney E.Z. Boyette, a local sole practitioner who's been practicing in Suburban County for 30 years, and Samantha Courbasier, a partner in a mid-sized firm in Urban City across the river, represent opposing parties in Suburban Superior Court. The trial date is 60 days off.

1. Boyette needs an order that would shorten the normal time for hearing a motion to compel production of documents sufficiently in advance of trial to avoid close of discovery. The local court rules state that such orders "shall, with appropriate accompanying declaration, be presented to the Presiding Judge, and if that judge is not reasonably available, then to any Superior Court Judge."

The current P.J. is a notorious stickler on procedure, and Boyette is concerned his excuse in support of the motion for shortened time may not be sufficient. So he decides to present his motion between 9:00 and 9:15, the one time in the day when the P.J. is unavailable since he sits as Master Trial Judge during that time. Sure enough, Boyette finds the P.J. unavailable, but does find Judge Braithwaite still in chambers. Braithwaite, never known for promptness or exacting procedure, signs the order shortening time.

Boyette, having gotten his order signed, now goes to the clerk's office to calendar the motion. The clerk tells him that all motions filed this date are being set for hearing on the following Tuesday. Recalling that motions Judge Hickenlooper takes a very narrow view of discovery, and further that Hickenlooper will be at a judges' weekend retreat through Monday, Boyette tells the deputy clerk who calendars the motion, "If you can set this on Monday, it'll make my life a whole lot easier. It's gonna be real tough on me if I gotta be here on any other day." The clerk, who is on friendly terms with Boyette due to occasional shared coffee breaks and miscellaneous other pleasantries over the years, assumes that Boyette has genuine scheduling difficulties and agrees to calendar the hearing for Monday. Braithwaite will now hear the motion.

2. The court grants Boyette's motion. He then serves Courbasier with a request for production of documents, while readying to leave town for a week on a long-planned backpacking trip. He informs Courbasier of his plans, and gives her an additional week to produce the documents. Courbasier, however, decides to seek a protective order allowing her to redact, or "black out," a portion of the documents, on grounds of privilege. She knows this is a "long

shot," but decides to give it a try, especially since she's now angry with Boyette.

Courbasier now needs an order shortening time for a hearing on her motion for a protective order, but she knows that Boyette would oppose an OST. She realizes that, with Boyette's opposition, the court might not grant her request, since her motion is more tactical than substantive. So she waits two days until the first day of Boyette's vacation, when she calls Boyette's office, as required by the court's local rules, and leaves the following message with Boyette's secretary: "Will make ex parte request for OST tomorrow, Department 12 at 9:00 A.M."

Courbasier's request for an OST is heard and, not surprisingly, is unopposed because Boyette is out-of-town. The hearing on the motion for the protective order is set for the day after Boyette returns from vacation.

QUESTIONS

1. Evaluate the conduct of attorneys Boyette and Courbasier. Which conduct of these lawyers do you feel is unethical? Do some of these lawyers' actions, while they may not strictly violate ethical rules, nevertheless fail to meet a reasonable standard of conduct for an attorney? Which actions, and why?

2. Consider the two scenarios on page 536. Are these two examples ethical? Sleazy? Might they be considered both ethical and sleazy?

II. Miles Bethea is one of the best-known products liability lawyers in the state. He and his opposing counsel, the equally celebrated Michael Epstein, have been litigating the case of *McVie v. Reliable Motors* for the past two years. Plaintiff Doreen McVie claims the brakes on her new Reliable failed, causing her to crash into a light pole. She sustained a severe spinal injury and as a result is paralyzed below the waist. During the two months that she owned the car, she returned it to her dealer three times, complaining that the brakes felt "soft." The dealer's service mechanics checked the car each time and found nothing wrong.

The case is now in trial. Bethea believes that one of his most important pieces of evidence is that as of the date McVie bought her car, Reliable's zone service offices had received at least 13 complaints from car owners about braking problems and "soft" brakes. Although only three of the complaints involved accidents, Bethea believes that these reports show that even before McVie bought her car, Reliable was on notice that cars like hers may have had brake problems.

Unfortunately for Bethea, he and McVie have drawn Judge Marcia MacAboo, a jurist with a restrictive view of evidence in products liability and punitive damages cases. Bethea supports his offer to admit the complaints with several cases in which similar evidence had been received in courts in his state. On the second day of trial, when the admissibility of the complaints is argued, the following discussion takes place on the record:

BETHEA: We ask now that these documents be admitted into evidence as plaintiff's Exhibit numbers 4(a) through (m).

EPSTEIN: Objection, Your Honor, these reports. . . .

THE COURT: Sustained, counsel, the objection is sustained. These documents are completely irrelevant; no foundation.

BETHEA: Would the Court be more specific? I . . . .

THE COURT: I don't have to explain my ruling to your satisfaction. There will be no more said about this.

BETHEA: But refusing to admit these complaints will perpetuate a false impression about auto safety. It's absurd to have dangerous . . . .

THE COURT: Counsel!

BETHEA: It makes no sense at all to . . . .

THE COURT: That's enough, and that's contempt! Two days in jail at the close of this case.

Is this contempt or proper zealous advocacy? Would this finding of contempt be affected by whether the jury was present at the time of this colloquy?

III. Mike Epstein's investigators have learned that McVie was in and out of three alcohol rehabilitation clinics over a five-year period ending a year before the accident. Records at the state's Motor Vehicles Bureau show that McVie has two convictions for driving under the influence, one eight years ago, and the other 15 months before the accident. The last conviction resulted in a year's suspension of McVie's license, which ended just 10 weeks before the accident.

McVie's case against Reliable Motors is both newsworthy and emotionally charged. Reliable is known for its "safe" yet economical cars. Local TV stations and newspapers have been following the progress of the case since McVie filed suit two years ago.

On the fourth trial day, McVie testifies before the jury and Epstein grills her on cross-examination. At the end of the day, Epstein is bombarded by news people on the courthouse steps. "Look," he tells reporters, "in this case, *I* represent the good guys. A reasonable jury can't possibly find McVie credible," he continues. "There's nothing wrong with these cars. McVie caused her own injuries. She's a lush and shouldn't have been on the road. She took her life into her own hands and now she's looking for a deep pocket to pay her."

QUESTIONS

1. Did Epstein act within the bounds of propriety in making these statements to the press? How important is determining whether the statements are likely to prejudice the case or interfere with the plaintiff's ability to get a fair trial? What if Epstein had made these comments before trial?

2. Suppose Bethea, frustrated by Judge MacAboo's adverse rulings, lashed out at her his in after-court press conference: "If she knew how to apply rules of evidence, we wouldn't be trying this case with one hand tied behind our backs and one foot stuck in cement." Is this comment proper?

READINGS

1. Is There an Ethical Duty of Civility and Fair Dealing? Besides their duties to clients, the courts, and the public, should lawyers have professional obligations to each other? Some years ago, the author of the following article, a Second Circuit Court of Appeals judge, set the bar of civility and "fair dealing."

But can the rules of ethics define lawyers' obligations to each other? Is the duty of zealous representation incompatible with maintaining professional courtesy? Is there a "hierarchy" of professional duties? If a lawyer's overriding duty is to the client, does this obligation supersede any obligations that lawyers may owe each other?

ROGER J. MINER, LAWYERS OWE ONE ANOTHER
National Law Journal (December 19, 1988)[1]

The ethics of the profession command members of the bar to act honestly in their relations with each other. . . .

. . . .

Closely related to the duty of honesty is the duty of fair dealing. . . . Fairness also requires that lawyers keep their word in their dealings with one another. The erroneous notion that responsibility to clients supersedes all other professional responsibilities seems to be gaining popularity among the members of the bar. This notion has led an increasing number of lawyers to ignore agreements they have made with opposing counsel in order to advance the perceived interests of their clients. It also has led to a general decline in fair dealing between counsel.

. . . .

Uncivil conduct in lawyer-to-lawyer relations demonstrates a lack of respect for the legal system and for those who serve it. It tends to diminish public confidence in the system and in the legal profession, and is prejudicial to the administration of justice. It should be condemned strongly as a most serious violation of the ethical standards of the profession. . . .

Few lawyers condone coarse and uncivilized behavior or physical assault. All too many, however, condone and utilize tactics [that] variously are described as "hardball," "scorched earth," "take no prisoners," and "giving go quarter." They are practiced by lawyers who are pleased to compare themselves to Rambo and Attila the Hun. I call them legal terrorists and barbarians of the bar. . . .

The good news, of course, is that lawyers are beginning to talk about drawing a line between zealous advocacy and unacceptable conduct. Finding that valuable judicial and attorney time is consumed in resolving unnecessary contention and sharp practices between lawyers, the judges of the U.S. District Court for the Northern District of Texas recently adopted standards of conduct for attorneys practicing before their court. The Cleveland Bar Association has adopted "A Lawyer's Creed of Professionalism" to deal with "uncivil, counter-productive and unprofessional conduct."

2. Can Courtesy and Civility Be Regulated? Judge Miner refers to the idea of "fair dealing," certainly a laudable concept. But do the rules of ethics

---

[1] Reprinted with the permission of the author and The National Law Journal. Copyright © 1988 by Roger J. Miner and The New York Law Publishing Company.

actually adopt this term or its equivalent? Miner cites to two of the old ABA Code's ethical considerations to support his conclusion that the existing rules are sufficient to deal with issues of civility, comity, and fair play. But ethical considerations by definition are aspirational precepts only, meaning that lawyers are generally not subject to discipline for violating them. Miner also quotes from the comment to ABA Model Rule 1.3, but that merely vests the attorney with "professional discretion."

How, then, is such conduct to be regulated? Or should it be the subject of disciplinary rules at all? When the ABA's Commission on Professionalism published its report, it understandably emphasized public service as the goal of the legal professional. But what about courtesy, civility, and fair play? In 1988, two years after the professionalism report, the ABA adopted a Creed of Professionalism which included the lawyer's responsibilities to the courts, the justice system, and opposing counsel and parties. But the Creed was intended to be aspirational; indeed, a disclaimer explicitly states that it is not intended to supersede or modify any disciplinary rule.

Nevertheless, such "creeds" can serve a valuable purpose, by creating a community standard that encourages a "kinder, gentler" way of thinking and, perhaps, some amount of peer pressure to conform to what have been defined as reasonable behavioral norms. One of the earliest of such modern "civility creeds" is "the Texas Lawyers' Creed," formally adopted by the Texas Supreme Court in 1989. We quote briefly from it below. In reading this excerpt, ask yourself whether these aspirational guidelines are effective or mere homilies.

TEXAS RULES OF COURT, TEXAS LAWYER'S CREED — A MANDATE FOR PROFESSIONALISM
(November 7, 1989)

The conduct of a lawyer should be characterized at all times by honesty, candor, and fairness. In fulfilling his or her primary duty to a client, a lawyer must be ever mindful of the profession's broader duty to the legal system.

. . . [A]busive tactics range from lack of civility to outright hostility and obstructionism. Such behavior does not serve justice but tends to delay and often deny justice. The lawyers who use abusive tactics instead of being part of the solution have become part of the problem.

. . . .

I know that professionalism requires more than merely avoiding the violation of laws and rules. I am committed to this creed for no other reason than it is right.

I. *Our Legal System*

A lawyer owes to the administration of justice personal dignity, integrity, and independence.

I am passionately proud of my profession. Therefore, "My word is my bond."

. . . .

II. *Lawyer to Client*

I will advise my client that civility and courtesy are expected and are not a sign of weakness. . . .

I will advise my client that we will not pursue conduct which is intended primarily to harass or drain the financial resources of the opposing party.

I will advise my client that we will not pursue tactics which are intended primarily for delay.

. . . .

I reserve the right to determine whether to grant accommodations to opposing counsel in all matters that do not adversely affect my client's lawful objectives. A client has no right to instruct me to refuse reasonable requests made by other counsel.

III. *Lawyer to Lawyer*

A lawyer owes to opposing counsel, in the conduct of legal transactions and the pursuit of litigation, courtesy, candor, cooperation, and scrupulous observance of all agreements and mutual understandings.

. . . .

I can disagree without being disagreeable. I recognize that effective representation does not require antagonistic or obnoxious behavior. . . .

I will not, without good cause, attribute bad motives or unethical conduct to opposing counsel nor bring the profession into disrepute by unfounded accusations of impropriety.

NOTES

The Texas Creed is informal and, on its face, aspirational only: It is explicitly "not a set of rules that lawyers can use and abuse to incite ancillary litigation." Obeying the Creed "depends primarily upon understanding and voluntary compliance, secondarily upon re-enforcement by peer pressure and public opinion," and only lastly on the courts' inherent powers. It is clear that certain standards of behavior are expected by Texas' highest court. But what happens if the standards aren't met?

To date, rules of courtesy and fair play have not been included in disciplinary rules themselves. In *Aspen Services, Inc. v. IT Corporation*, 583 N.W. 2d 849 (Wis. App. 1998), the court found that although civility rules may not be enforceable in a disciplinary court setting, they can be used to support a sanctions award in litigation. The most likely way such aspirational principles can become required modes of behavior is through their incorporation into local rules of court that govern the practice of individual jurisdictions.

Thus far, however, even the few jurisdictions which have formally incorporated rules of civility and courtesy use primarily aspirational language.

3. Is Regulating Civility an Oxymoron? Rules of court stating general prohibitions can only go so far in suspending a lawyer from practice. In *In* *re Snyder*, 472 U.S. 634, 105 S. Ct. 2874 (1985), the United States Supreme Court ruled unanimously that a North Dakota lawyer who wrote a mean-spirited, even nasty, note to the district court's secretary on the subject of the inadequacy of a court-appointed fee could not be suspended under federal practice rules prohibiting "conduct unbecoming a member of the bar" despite the strong, even offensive language of his letter. Said Chief Justice Burger, "even assuming that the letter exhibited an unlawyer-like rudeness, a single incident of rudeness or lack of professional courtesy — in this context — does not support . . . a finding that a lawyer is 'not presently fit to practice. . . .'"

Is it possible to enforce civility by ethical rule? Perhaps, but this is no easy task. Read the following case and its discussion of § 6068(f) of the California Business & Professions Code, which reads in relevant part: "It is the duty of an attorney . . . to abstain from all offensive personality."

UNITED STATES v. WUNSCH
84 F.3d 1110 (9th Cir. 1996)

This matter arose during the course of a criminal tax prosecution brought by the United States against three defendants, William and Beverly Wunsch and their daughter, Teri Sowers. Shortly after Sowers' arrest by federal agents on March 18, 1993, Frank Swan telephoned Assistant United States Attorney Elana Artson, counsel for the United States. Swan identified himself as Sowers' lawyer and asked about the charges pending against his client including the conditions for her release. Swan also told Artson that he would be unable to attend Sowers' bail hearing that afternoon, but would send another attorney, Gerald Wilson, in his stead.

On March 24, 1993, Artson moved to disqualify Swan and Wilson from representing Sowers, arguing that their representation of both Sowers and her parents, who at that time were the targets of a grand jury investigation, amounted to a conflict of interest. . . . On April 28, 1993, the district court granted the motion to disqualify them from representing the Wunsches, and denied Sowers' motion to reconsider.

On May 6, 1993, Artson received a letter from Swan. Appended to the letter was a single sheet of paper with the following photocopied words, all enlarged and in capital letters:

MALE LAWYERS PLAY BY THE RULES, DISCOVER TRUTH AND RESTORE ORDER. FEMALE LAWYERS ARE OUTSIDE THE LAW, CLOUD TRUTH AND DESTROY ORDER.

The district court cited as authority for its disciplinary action Local Rules 2.2.6, 2.5.1, and 2.5.2; section 6068(f) of California's Business and Professions Code; "and the Court's inherent power[.]" With respect to the court's inherent power, we note that an attorney admitted to a particular bar may be disciplined for conduct that violates the bar's local rules of professional conduct. This power to discipline is not limited to conduct that occurs within the course of litigation.

We begin by noting that, "Once a lawyer is admitted to the bar, although he does not surrender his freedom of expression, he must temper his criticisms in accordance with professional standards of conduct." No reference to any court or judge appears or is even hinted at in the letter of attachment. Moreover, Swan's criticism "cannot be equated with an attack on the motivation or the integrity or the competence of the judge."

Interference with the Administration of Justice

The district court cited to two published decisions in support of its conclusion that Swan's sexist communication constituted an interference with the administration of justice under Local Rule 2.5.2. See *Matter of Swan*, 833 F. Supp. at 798 (citing *In re Plaza Hotel Corp.*, 111 Bankr. 882 (Bankr. E.D. Cal.); *Principe v. Assay Partners*, 154 Misc. 2d 702, 586 N.Y.S. 2d 182 (N.Y. Sup. Ct. 1992)). Neither of these decisions supports the district court's conclusion.

[I]n *Principe*, the court sanctioned an attorney for unprofessional conduct in the litigation process, based on a series of demeaning remarks directed against a female attorney at deposition. The remarks, which included references to the female lawyer as "little lady," "little mouse," "young girl," and "little girl," were accompanied by rude hand gestures and had been made in front of other counsel, the witness, and a court reporter. . . .

In both cases the courts imposed sanctions based on facts showing that each attorney's sexist behavior was not only deplorable, but clearly interfered with the administration of justice. In the instant case, however, we have a single incident involving an isolated expression of a privately communicated bias. . . . While we decline to hold that a single egregious act of bigotry could never subject an officer of the court to disciplinary sanctions, . . . [e]qually clearly, however, the courts cannot punish every expression of gender bias by attorneys without running afoul of the First Amendment.

. . . . Our review of the California case law dealing with "offensive personality" in the context of the administration of justice fails to reveal a single controlling decision — much less a clear line of authority — that either specifically discusses the scope of section 6068(f) or explicitly limits its applicability to, e.g., courtroom interactions.

To be sure, there are a few reported decisions which give some hint of the limits of section 6068(f). . . . Nevertheless, we are unable to discern from these cases any clearly delineated bounds to the reach of Cal. Bus. & Prof. Code § 6068(f).

. . . .

Clearly, "offensive personality" is an unconstitutionally vague term in the context of this statute. See, e.g., *Cohen v. California*, 403 U.S. 15, 25, 29 L. Ed. 2d 284, 91 S. Ct. 1780 (1971) ("disturbing the peace . . . by . . . offensive conduct" fails to give sufficient notice of what was prohibited). As "offensive personality" could refer to any number of behaviors that many attorneys regularly engage in during the course of their zealous representation of their clients' interests, it would be impossible to know when such behavior would be offensive enough to invoke the statute. For the same reason, the statute is "so imprecise that discriminatory enforcement is a real possibility[,]" *Gentile v. State Bar of Nevada*, 501 U.S. at 1051 (1991) (Kennedy, J., minority opinion), and is likely to have the effect of chilling some speech that is constitutionally protected, for fear of violating the statute.

. . . .

The question before us is not whether Swan displayed a deplorable lack of sensitivity, but whether the district court's decision to impose sanctions on Swan . . . can be upheld as a matter of law based on the authorities cited. For the reasons set forth above, we conclude that it cannot.

Reversed.

NOTES

Other courts *have*, albeit rarely, sanctioned lawyers for uncivil conduct. In *Matter of Golden*, 496 S.E.2d 619 (S.C. 1998), a lawyer narrowly escaped suspension from practice but was publicly reprimanded for making gratuitously insulting, threatening, and demeaning comments in the course of two depositions. Golden asked a deponent if he was "cheap," and a "janitor." He then told the deponent he was "not smart enough to argue with" and referred to him as an "inmate" of a hospital. Finally, he called a female opposing party "a mean-spirited, vicious witch and I don't like your face and I don't like your voice. What I'd like, is to be locked in a room with you naked with a sharp knife."

Reversal of discipline or sanctions for even the nastiest possible lawyer behavior is more common. *Saldana v. Kmart Corp.*, 84 F. Supp. 2d 629 (D. V.I. 1999), disciplined a lawyer for repeated bad behavior including the ongoing use of the word "f—k" in deposition colloquy and conversations with opposing counsel. That ruling was later overturned by the appellate court, which reasoned that although it could not condone use of such language, no discipline was warranted since the attorney did not use the language in court or in her pleadings.[2]

Revson v. Cinque & Cinque, 70 F. Supp. 2d 415 (S.D.N.Y. 1999), involved a dispute between a client, Revson, and her former lawyers. Burstein, Revson's new lawyer, was sanctioned $50,000 by the trial court for numerous acts of bad behavior, among other things writing a letter to attorney Cinque threatening to "tarnish" his reputation with the "legal equivalent of a proctology exam"; making a sham offer to settle by setting an unreasonable deadline and then immediately filing suit even though Cinque met that deadline; publicly accusing Cinque of fraud without any evidence; threatening to interfere with the lawyers' other clients, and contacting former clients to ask about "experiences, good or bad," about their billing practices. But the appellate court reversed the sanctions award based on its conclusion that the substance of the claims brought was not "so completely without merit as to require the conclusion that they must have been undertaken for some improper purpose."[3]

---

[2] *Saldana v. Kmart Corp.*, 260 F.3d 228 (V.I. 2001).

[3] *Revson v. Cinque & Cinque, P.C.*, 221 F.3d 71 (2d Cir. 2000).

4. *Should* Civility Be Regulated? To give one view on this subject we turn once again to the words of Professor Monroe Freedman.

MONROE FREEDMAN, MASKING THE TRUTH TO RESOLVE COMPETING DUTIES
Legal Times (September 11, 1995)[4]

. . . [T]hose who proclaim a lack of civility disagree wildly as to what they are talking about. For an increasing number of judges, civility means that lawyers should sacrifice their clients' interests in order to protect "brother lawyers" from real practice claims — for example, not raising a statute of limitations counsel has missed. Most lawyers would agree that that kind of "civility" is inconsistent with the bar's traditional ethic of zealous representation of our clients' interests.

Nevertheless, when a survey was conducted in the 7th Circuit by a committee chaired by Judge Marvin Aspen, a majority of lawyers and judges agreed that there is a civility problem. But what type of conduct did those lawyers and judges agree was a problem? Were they talking about good manners, which might include such things as promptly returning telephone calls or being accommodating about scheduling? If that's what the fuss is about, it's hard to justify the enormous investment of time and effort that has been lavished on the issue. Or were they talking about more serious matters, like discovery abuse or willful misrepresentations in pleadings? If so, that kind of conduct is already outlawed by statutes, rules of procedure, and ethical rules.

The answer is that the Aspen committee respondents were talking about all of the above and a lot more. In defining civility, the Aspen committee's survey said that it means "professional conduct in litigating proceeding." It would be hard to get much broader or vaguer than that, but the committee contrived to do so; it went on to say that "civility" includes "good manners or social grace." I know that's hard to believe, but you can look it up.

. . . .

In view of the committee's all-inclusive definition of civility, it's hardly surprising that a majority of those surveyed answered yes when the committee asked: "As so defined, do you believe there is a problem of 'civility?'" Under the "social grace" definition, the respondents could have been referring to anything from slurping coffee to wearing large pinkie rings, mismatched socks, or garish lipstick. Others, of course, might have been referring to matters that go beyond the dictionary definition of civility, like suppressing documents in discovery.

In addition to meaningless (or overinclusive) definitions, there's a serious problem of perception when lawyers are asked about incivility. Consider a common enough situation. The plaintiff's lawyer attempts to ask a long series of questions, some of which are embarrassing to the defendant. The plaintiff's lawyer has a theory, and the questions might lead to relevant evidence to support her theory. The defendant's lawyer doesn't see the theory or doesn't consider it meritorious, views the questions as harassment, and advises her

---

client not to answer. Both lawyers have acted in good faith to advance or protect their clients' interests. And both lawyers are likely to leave the deposition complaining that the other has engaged in discovery abuse, one by asking improper questions, the other by obstructing legitimate discovery. The result is that two of two lawyers concur that there's a problem of civility, each one referring to her adversary's conduct, and each one mistaken in her perception.

Competing Values

But there's a deeper problem with the perception of incivility in discovery. Our civil discovery rules have created an unresolved tension between competing values — on the one hand, disclosure requirements, and on the other hand, lawyer-client confidentiality and work product. A similar point was made by Justice Antonin Scalia, dissenting from the Supreme Court's approval of the 1993 amendments to the Federal Rules of Civil Procedure. Joined by Justices David Souter and Clarence Thomas, Scalia warned that the new requirement of Rule 25(a), to give one's adversary information that is "relevant" to "disputed facts," is "potentially disastrous" to America's traditional adversary system. This new requirement, he explained, puts an "intolerable strain upon lawyers' ethical duty to represent their clients and not to assist the opposing side." Making a judgment about what is relevant, Scalia noted, "plainly requires [the lawyer] to use his professional skills in the service of the adversary."

. . . .

[T]here is an obvious tension between those policies that has not been resolved. The result is that lawyers have developed the practice of reading discovery requests extremely strictly (read disingenuously) and the courts have condoned that practice. . . .

Making Hard Choices

There is a way to deal effectively with this kind of unresolved tension, to deal with what Justice Scalia called the "intolerable strain" that is placed upon lawyers who are told by the discovery rules to serve their clients' adversaries. The way to do that is to make the hard choices. One choice is to favor discovery over confidentiality. That would require creating a bench and bar that will take discovery rules at face value and abandon the American lawyer's traditional ethic of client loyalty. I seriously doubt that can be done, short of mass purges like those Stalin employed to get rid of landowners who couldn't adjust to communism. Another hard choice is to favor client loyalty and confidentiality over discovery. That would mean abandoning or restricting discovery, which has not fulfilled its initial promise of streamlining litigation and reducing costs by encouraging prompt settlements. But those who write the rules of procedure, including a majority of the Supreme Court, are going in the opposite direction.

The way not to resolve these kinds of tensions, however, is by dithering on about "civility" and calling upon lawyers to make the hard choices that the established bar and the bench are unwilling to make. That way, we are sure to continue to pay the price of widespread disingenuousness and dishonesty.

NOTES

Do you agree with Freedman's analysis? Does the focus on civility and professionalism detract from a focus on *ethics*? Or is civility an integral component of the ethical attorney?

Carla Messikomer, a non-lawyer writing in the Fordham Law Review,[5] studied lawyers' comfort levels with certain terms. She was struck by the way in which words like "rules" and "norms" were within attorneys' comfort zones, but terms like "ethics" and "misconduct" made them "uneasy." She noted the "soft, polite, rather amorphous" acceptance of terms like "incivility," a word she also called "euphemistic."

Finally, consider this thought: Whatever protections are afforded by creeds and rules on civility, they do not regulate the cajoling and schmoozing that takes place between lawyers and court personnel, particularly by those lawyers who know their way around the local courthouse. Consider there two examples:

1. The court clerk's office closes at 5:00. Lawyer shows up at the clerk's office at 5:03 and begs to be let in to file a motion with today's date, absolutely the last date on which the motion may be filed. Using all of the force of her friendly personality, she tries to convince the clerk to let her file the motion. The last thing the clerks do before leaving is to change the "FILED" date stamp to tomorrow's date. They haven't changed the stamp yet, and Lawyer begs to be allowed to file with today's date on her pleading.

2. Attorney is in trial, and during cross-examination he obtains testimony that he would really like transcribed for his closing argument the next day. He goes to the court reporter after court and pleads with her to type up "just an itty bitty piece of the transcript" for him overnight. He flirts, smiles, and cajoles, and the reporter, who's known him for years as a friendly acquaintance, agrees to help, though she's under no obligation to do so.

Are such activities acceptable? Should they be regulated? Is it even possible to do so?

5. Speech as Contempt. Judges have wide latitude to deal with what they perceive as contempt. Contempt is vaguely defined as a disrespectful obstruction of justice. This definition applies equally to attorneys, clients, and trial spectators. Should a lawyer, however, be allowed more latitude than a party or a spectator? After all, mustn't the lawyer make sure that the trial court record is complete? Or is it true that in acquiring the privilege to practice law, an attorney waives some free speech privileges in return?

In *In re Kunstler*, 168 A.D.2d 146, 571 N.Y.S.2d 930 (1991), famed defense attorney William M. Kunstler was held in contempt for the following colloquy with the trial court in what had become known as the Central Park Jogger Rape Case. The occasion was Kunstler's motion for a new trial.

---

[5] *Ambivalence, Contradiction and Ambiguity: The Everyday Ethics of Defense Litigators*, 67 FORDHAM L. REV. 739 (1998).

MR. KUNSTLER: It is outrageous. You will not have an evidentiary hearing despite all the law that calls for it?

THE COURT: I will not hear oral argument. Call the next case.

MR. KUNSTLER: You have exhibited what your partisanship is. You shouldn't be sitting in court. You are a disgrace to the bench.

THE COURT: Sir, I hold you in contempt of court.

MR. KUNSTLER: You can hold me in anything you wish. I am outraged.

THE COURT: I am giving you an opportunity to be heard right now.

MR. KUNSTLER: I am saying this, judge. Every case in the world says you should hold a hearing in order to determine whether outside influences affected a juror. Every case there is. I submitted them to you. Even when a juror falls asleep, the Second Department has held there should be a hearing. And for you to deny it without a hearing, I think it is outrageous. You are violating every standard of fair play.

THE COURT: I am holding you in contempt of court. You are fined $250 or 30 days in jail.

Contempt resulting from the words used by counsel is generally summary in nature — the order of contempt immediately follows the words, without hearing or due process. Kunstler was held in contempt because the judge found his words insulting and offensive. Should decorum be the standard which determines contempt? Or is this standard as vague as "offensive personality"? Should more be required, such as an obstruction of justice? In *Kunstler*, one appellate department jurist, Judge Wallach, wrote in dissent that offending a judge's sensibilities is insufficient: The test for summary contempt should be either that the lawyer disrupted the hearing or that his statements interfered with the court's calendar. "On this record," he concluded, "it would appear that the good ship Justice sailed serenely on, without a one-degree compass point deviation from its appointed course."

It appears that the United States Supreme Court is in substantial agreement with that dissent. Here's what the Court said in *In re McConnell*, 370 U.S. 230, 236, 82 S. Ct. 1288 (1962): "The arguments of a lawyer in presenting his client's case strenuously and persistently cannot amount to a contempt of court so long as the lawyer does not in some way create an obstruction which blocks the judge in the performance of his judicial duty." In an earlier case[6] the Court said that a trial judge should give "due allowance for the heat of controversy," even if the claim seems "far fetched and untenable," before summarily holding an attorney in contempt. Yet Kunstler's contempt was upheld.

Standards for what constitutes contempt based on the words spoken by counsel continue to vary by jurisdiction, court, and circumstance. One significant factor appears to be whether counsel is engaged in the good-faith albeit persistent efforts to make a clear record so that an appellate court can rule later on the disputed issue. But the manner and means of presentation to the court — respect or the lack of it, insult, or sarcasm — will undoubtedly have an effect on the trial court's decision to pull the contempt trigger. Compare

---

[6] *Sacher v. U.S.*, 343 U.S. 1, 78 S. Ct. 842 (1952).

·ases cited in the Supplemental Readings, one in which a lawyer was not ˌust held in contempt but suspended from practice for calling the trial a farce,[7] and one in which a contempt citation for calling the trial a joke was reversed because the lawyer couched his comments in otherwise respectful terms.[8] A more recent case[9] reversed a contempt citation though counsel asserted that the government's use of an informant was "prostituting this Court's integrity." The appeals court concluded: "While judges as individuals may question the use of the particular word chosen [i.e., "prostituting"], as a court we cannot objectively conclude that the language used was calculated to be contemptuous of the court process."

6. Disruption of the Administration of Justice. If disruption of the administration of justice is the standard for contempt, this recent Hawaii case is one Miles Bethea might well consider.

OFFICE OF DISCIPLINARY COUNSEL v. BREINER
89 Haw. 167, 969 P. 2d 1285 (1999)

The trial judge first cited Breiner for contempt of court after Breiner refused to desist from arguing during his opening statement. The record reflects that Breiner was stubborn, argumentative, sarcastic, and disrespectful; as illustrated by the following exchange:

THE COURT: Mr. Breiner, this is opening statement, not argument.

BREINER: I'm not arguing, I'm stating the facts. . . .

THE COURT: Do not enter into argument. I've warned you, this is the last warning.

BREINER: To what extent are you going to help the prosecution with this case?

THE COURT: No intention of helping either party. Proceed.

BREINER: Seem to be helping, prosecution openly argued her case, you didn't admonish her.

THE COURT: You're afraid to object?

BREINER: Afraid? That's beautiful.

Breiner then resumed his opening statement to the jury.

> Shortly, ladies and gentlemen, we will prove that in order to find Raita Fukusaku guilty you have to assume he did everything possible to make himself the suspect short of calling up Keith Kaneshiro [the Prosecutor] and saying I did it.

The deputy prosecuting attorney (DPA) objected and argued that Breiner was being argumentative again. The trial court agreed and, out of the presence of the jury, cited Breiner for criminal contempt.

. . . .

---

[7] *In re Friedland*, 376 N.E.2d 1126 (Ind. 1978).

[8] *In re Carrow*, 40 Cal. App. 3d 924, 115 Cal. Rptr. 601 (1974).

[9] *Murrell v. State*, 595 So. 2d 1049 (Fla. App. 1992).

The fourth incident occurred when the trial court called for a bench conference during the DPA's direct examination of yet another witness, Julie Ann Cooper. While en route to the bench, Breiner muttered, in a tone loud enough for the jury to overhead, "I'm tired of this crap." The trial court cited Breiner for criminal contempt of court.

Although the Disciplinary Board's report and recommendation only address the incidents described above, the record that was before us in *Fukusaku*, of which we take judicial notice, reflects, inter alia, that Breiner also characterized the proceedings as a "kangaroo court" and then, pursuing the metaphor in a testy exchange with the trial court, explained that he was not a "marsupial."

. . . .

The sole issue presented by this disciplinary case is whether the recommended suspension in the present case is sufficient to protect the public, the integrity of the legal profession, and the dignity of the courts.

Discussion

We begin our analysis with the understanding that vigorous and zealous advocacy is a necessary component of our judicial system. Likewise, "respect for and confidence in the judicial office [is] essential to the maintenance of any orderly system of justice."

Under our judicial system "it is the lawyer's duty to make his objections and other points in his client's behalf, [and] it must follow that he is entitled to a timely opportunity to make them. From this it necessarily follows that the judge is without power to foreclose that opportunity by any order or admonition to sit down or to be quiet or not to address the court. The power to silence an attorney does not begin until a reasonable opportunity for appropriate objection or other indicated advocacy has been afforded."

Nevertheless, we have made it clear that when an attorney's in-court conduct and statements are deliberately and flagrantly contemptuous of the court, the trial judge has the discretion to proceed summarily and find the attorney guilty of criminal contempt of court, as a petty misdemeanor, if such a course is necessary to ensure the orderly administration of justice.

. . . .

The prohibition of our Disciplinary Rules against "undignified or discourteous conduct degrading to a tribunal" . . . is not for the sake of the presiding judge but for the sake of the office he or she holds. Respect for and confidence in the judicial office are essential to the maintenance of any orderly system of justice. This is not to suggest that a lawyer should be other than vigorous, even persistent in the presentation of a case, nor is it to overlook the reciprocal responsibility of courtesy and respect that the judge owes to the lawyer.

When a lawyer is pitted against an abusive judge, who is also harming the lawyer's client with his rulings, the lawyer faces a dilemma. If he responds in an obstreperous manner, the controversy may escalate, and the proceedings will indeed be interrupted. That the judge committed the first infraction would not excuse the lawyer's conduct, although it might later mitigate the sanction.

On the other hand, a lawyer should not be so concerned with pleasing a judge as to leave his client's rights unprotected. The lawyer must have the courage to stand respectfully firm long enough to insist that a record be made for appellate scrutiny.

Even if the judge's order is clearly improper, the lawyer should obey it and then seek review. . . . Temporary disobedience might be justified in a rare case where the judge attempts to prohibit even the making of a record, or in which even temporary compliance would result in irreparable harm to a client. In such a case it could be said that the lawyer has not "intended" to disrupt the tribunal at all, but has attempted to insure that the overall course of the litigation will proceed more smoothly, not less. Such a lawyer would not be liable for a disciplinary infraction, but would probably be found in contempt of court, and could then pursue his remedies through a "test-case" appeal.

Breiner apparently believed that he was the object of abuse at the hands of the trial court. Such a belief, however, would not and could not serve as a justification for his abusive and obstreperous conduct. . . . We have no doubt that Breiner's behavior during the Fukusaku trial interfered with the proceedings. Breiner could simply have preserved issues regarding the conduct of the trial by voicing his objections on the record and moving on. . . .

Breiner's contemptuous behavior undoubtedly denigrated the legal profession and the dignity of the courts. A suspension of less than six months would be insufficient to express the extent of our concern that the public, the legal profession, and the courts be protected from such unprofessional conduct.

NOTES

It is interesting that the court saw fit to increase Breiner's punishment. Do you think this was because Breiner's transgression directly involved "degrading" the trial court?

7. Publicity and the *Gentile* Case. ABA Model Rule 3.6 was designed to limit a lawyer's free speech outside the courtroom to ensure a fair trial. Subsection (a) limited a lawyer's speech when the lawyer should know that it "will have a substantial likelihood of materially prejudicing" a proceeding. Subsection (c) of the rule offered several exceptions, including a so-called "safe harbor" allowing a lawyer to state "without elaboration . . . the general nature of the claim or defense."

In 1991, the United States Supreme Court decided *Gentile v. State Bar of Nevada*, 501 U.S. 1030, 111 S. Ct. 2720 (1991). Dominic Gentile was a well-known and well-regarded criminal defense lawyer in Southern Nevada. Within hours of his client, Sanders, being indicted on criminal charges, Gentile held a televised press conference. Below is a portion of his prepared remarks at that press conference, reproduced from Appendix A of the Supreme Court opinion.

[T]his indictment is a significant event in the history of the evolution of sophistication of the City of Las Vegas, because things of this nature, of exactly this nature have happened in New York with the French connection case and in Miami with cases — at least two cases there — have happened in Chicago as well, but all three of those cities have been honest enough to indict the people who did it; the police department, crooked cops.

When this case goes to trial, and as it develops, you're going to see that the evidence will prove not only that Grady Sanders is an innocent person and had nothing to do with any of the charges that are being leveled against him, but that the person that was in the most direct position to have stolen the drugs and money, the American Express travelers' checks, is Detective Steve Scholl.

There is far more evidence that will establish that Detective Scholl took these drugs and took these American Express Travelers' checks than any other living human being.

And I have to say that I feel that Grady Sanders is being used as a scapegoat to try to cover up for what has to be obvious to people at Las Vegas Metropolitan Police Department and at the District Attorney's office.

Now, with respect to the . . . so-called other victims, . . . four of them are known drug dealers and convicted money launderers; three of whom didn't say a word about anything until after they were approached by Metro and after they were already in trouble and are trying to work themselves out of something.

Gentile went to trial on Sanders' case, and his client was acquitted. But the Nevada State Bar disciplined Gentile for his remarks, giving him a private reproval, the lightest form of punishment. Because of the importance of the issue, Gentile allowed his confidential discipline file to become public, and took his case first to the Nevada and then the United States Supreme Court.

Gentile's discipline was eventually overturned, though in the unusual circumstance of a divided court with two separate majority opinions, one by Chief Justice Rehnquist, the other by Justice Kennedy. The Rehnquist majority opinion held, 5-4, that the standard used in the disciplinary rule, the "substantial likelihood" of material prejudice, did not violate the First Amendment and was constitutionally justifiable. Kennedy's opinion dissented on this issue, arguing that the rule ought to require the higher standard of prejudice. But Kennedy's opinion was in the majority, 5-4, in holding that the safe harbor provision was void as unconstitutionally vague. Justice O'Connor, the swing vote, was a member of both majorities. We briefly excerpt first Kennedy's and then Rehnquist's opinion.

GENTILE v. STATE BAR OF NEVADA
501 U.S. 1030, 111 S. Ct. 2720 (1991)

JUSTICE KENNEDY [Majority opinion as to Part III and Judgment]: Nevada Supreme Court Rule 177 is a rule governing pretrial publicity almost identical to ABA Model Rule of Professional Conduct 3.6. . . .

Nevada's application of Rule 177 in this case violates the First Amendment. Petitioner spoke at a time and in a manner that neither in law nor in fact created any threat of real prejudice to his client's right to a fair trial or to the State's interest in the enforcement of its criminal laws. Furthermore, the

Rule's safe harbor provision, Rule 177(3), appears to permit the speech in question, and Nevada's decision to discipline petitioner in spite of that provision raises concerns of vagueness and selective enforcement.

I

Model Rule 3.6's requirement of substantial likelihood of material prejudice is not necessarily flawed. Interpreted in a proper and narrow manner, for instance, to prevent an attorney of record from releasing information of grave prejudice on the eve of jury selection, the phrase substantial likelihood of material prejudice might punish only speech that creates a danger of imminent and substantial harm. A rule governing speech, even speech entitled to full constitutional protection, need not use the words "clear and present danger" in order to pass constitutional muster.

. . . .

Under those principles, nothing inherent in Nevada's formulation fails First Amendment review; but as this case demonstrates, Rule 177 has not been interpreted in conformance with those principles by the Nevada Supreme Court.

II

Even if one were to accept respondent's argument that lawyers participating in judicial proceedings may be subjected, consistent with the First Amendment, to speech restrictions that could not be imposed on the press or general public, the judgment should not be upheld. The record does not support the conclusion that petitioner knew or reasonably should have known his remarks created a substantial likelihood of material prejudice, if the Rule's terms are given any meaningful content.

. . . .

As petitioner explained to the disciplinary board, his primary motivation was the concern that, unless some of the weaknesses in the State's case were made public, a potential jury venire would be poisoned by repetition in the press of information being released by the police and prosecutors, in particular the repeated press reports about polygraph tests and the fact that the two police officers were no longer suspects. . . . Far from an admission that he sought to "materially prejudice an adjudicative proceeding," petitioner sought only to stop a wave of publicity he perceived as prejudicing potential jurors against his client and injuring his client's reputation in the community.

Petitioner gave a second reason for holding the press conference, which demonstrates the additional value of his speech. Petitioner acted in part because the investigation had taken a serious toll on his client. Sanders was "not a man in good health," having suffered multiple open-heart surgeries prior to these events. . . .

An attorney's duties do not begin inside the courtroom door. He or she cannot ignore the practical implications of a legal proceeding for the client. Just as an attorney may recommend a plea bargain or civil settlement to avoid the adverse consequences of a possible loss after trial, so too an attorney may take reasonable steps to defend a client's reputation and reduce the adverse consequences of indictment, especially in the face of a prosecution deemed unjust or commenced with improper motives. A defense attorney may pursue lawful strategies to obtain dismissal of an indictment or reduction of charges, including an attempt to demonstrate in the court of public opinion that the client does not deserve to be tried.

. . . .

Petitioner's judgment that no likelihood of material prejudice would result from his comments was vindicated by events at trial. While it is true that Rule 177's standard for controlling pretrial publicity must be judged at the time a statement is made, ex post evidence can have probative value in some cases. . . .

The trial took place on schedule in August, 1988, with no request by either party for a venue change or continuance. The jury was empaneled with no apparent difficulty. The trial judge questioned the jury venire about publicity. Although many had vague recollections [about the case,] not a single juror indicated any recollection of petitioner or his press conference.

At trial, all material information disseminated during petitioner's press conference was admitted in evidence before the jury, including information questioning the motives and credibility of supposed victims who testified against Sanders, and Detective Scholl's ingestion of drugs in the course of undercover operations (in order, he testified, to gain the confidence of suspects). The jury acquitted petitioner's client. . . .

III

As interpreted by the Nevada Supreme Court, the Rule is void for vagueness, in any event, for its safe harbor provision, Rule 177(3), misled petitioner into thinking that he could give his press conference without fear of discipline. Rule 177(3)(a) provides that a lawyer "may state without elaboration . . . the general nature of the . . . defense." Statements under this provision are protected "[n]otwithstanding," subsection 1 and 2(a-f). By necessary operation of the word "notwithstanding," the Rule contemplates that a lawyer describing the "general nature of the . . . defense" "without elaboration" need fear no discipline, even if he comments on "[t]he character, credibility, reputation or criminal record of a . . . witness," and even if he "knows or reasonably should know that [the statement] will have a substantial likelihood of materially prejudicing an adjudicative proceeding."

Given this grammatical structure, and absent any clarifying interpretation by the state court, the Rule fails to provide "fair notice to those to whom [it] is directed." A lawyer seeking to avail himself of Rule 177(3)'s protection must guess at its contours. The right to explain the "general" nature of the defense without "elaboration" provides insufficient guidance because "general" and "elaboration" are both classic terms of degree. . . .

Petitioner testified he thought his statements were protected by Rule 177(3). A review of the press conference supports that claim. He gave only a brief opening statement, and on numerous occasions declined to answer reporters' questions seeking more detailed comments. One illustrative exchange shows petitioner's attempt to obey the rule:

> QUESTION FROM THE FLOOR: Dominick, you mention you question the credibility of some of the witnesses, some of the people named as victims in the government indictment.
>
> Can we go through it and *elaborate* on their backgrounds, interests —
>
> MR. GENTILE: *I can't because ethics prohibit me from doing so.*
>
> Last night before I decided I was going to make a statement, I took a close look at the rules of professional responsibility. There are things that I can say and there are things that I can't. Okay?

. . . .

The judgment of the Supreme Court of Nevada is reversed.

CHIEF JUSTICE REHNQUIST [Majority opinion as to Parts I and II, dissent as to Part III and Judgment]: We conclude that the "substantial likelihood of material prejudice" standard applied by Nevada and most other states satisfies the First Amendment.

. . . .

The Southern Nevada Disciplinary Board found that petitioner knew the detective he accused of perpetrating the crime and abusing drugs would be a witness for the prosecution. It also found that petitioner believed others whom he characterized as money launderers and drug dealers would be called as prosecution witnesses. Petitioner's admitted purpose for calling the press conference was to counter public opinion which he perceived as adverse to his client, to fight back against the perceived efforts of the prosecution to poison the prospective juror pool, and to publicly present his client's side of the case. The Board found that in light of the statements, their timing, and petitioner's purpose, petitioner knew or should have known that there was a substantial likelihood that the statements would materially prejudice the Sanders trial.

. . . .

It is unquestionable that in the courtroom itself, during a judicial proceeding, whatever right to "free speech" an attorney has is extremely circumscribed. An attorney may not, by speech or other conduct, resist a ruling of the trial court beyond the point necessary to preserve a claim for appeal. Even outside the courtroom a majority of the Court in two separate opinions in the case of *In re Sawyer*, 360 U.S. 622, 79 S. Ct. 1376, 3 L. Ed. 2d 1473 (1959), observed that lawyers in pending cases were subject to ethical restrictions on speech to which an ordinary citizen would not be.

. . . .

Because lawyers have special access to information through discovery and client communications, their extrajudicial statements pose a threat to the fairness of a pending proceeding since lawyers' statements are likely to be received as especially authoritative. . . . We agree with the majority of the States that the "substantial likelihood of material prejudice" standard constitutes a constitutionally permissible balance between the First Amendment rights of attorneys in pending cases and the state's interest in fair trials.

NOTES

There are few post-*Gentile* cases delineating the permissible scope of attorney speech under the First Amendment. In *U.S. v. Cutler*, 58 F.2d 825 (1995), the Second Circuit found that a showing of actual prejudice was not important, but that a showing of intent to counter prejudicial publicity is a crucial factor in deciding whether there is a reasonable likelihood that attorney speech interferes with a fair trial.

8. The Revised ABA Rule and Other Alternatives. In 1994, the ABA substantially modified Rule 3.6, significantly narrowing it and expanding its exceptions. Taking a page from Justice Kennedy's opinion in *Gentile*, Rule 3.6(c) allows a lawyer to make a statement that is reasonably required "to protect a client from the substantial undue prejudicial effect of recent publicity. . . ." It appears that this provision is not limited to counteracting prejudice to the jury, but could also be used to defend a client, to use Kennedy's words, "in the court of public opinion." And to solve the unconstitutionally vague provision allowing a public description of the "general nature" of a claim or defense, the ABA eliminated the offending phrases "without elaboration" and "general nature"; now, an attorney may simply describe the client's defense. Retaining this exception is understandable, since without it, a prosecutor could refer to available court documents, such as indictments and search warrants, while a defense lawyer could not respond with a client's defense unless and until some document about it was filed with the court. Clearly under this new rule, Dominic Gentile's press conference would not have subjected him to discipline.

Several states — and commentators — continue to question why a lower First Amendment standard should be used only for lawyers. The leading case decided under the Model Code, *Chicago Council of Lawyers v. Bauer*,[10] held that DR 7-107 was unconstitutionally vague and overbroad, and that only comments that pose a "serious and imminent threat" of interference with the fair administration of justice may be prohibited.[11] The "serious and imminent threat" language appears much closer to the "clear and present danger" standard used in other First Amendment prior restraint cases. Several states and the District of Columbia use the "serious and imminent" standard in their own rule.

With California's joining the parade following the massive publicity in the O.J. Simpson case, every jurisdiction in the country now has a rule that limits lawyers' free speech in cases of prejudicial publicity. In most jurisdictions, however, remaining First Amendment protections and the realities of disciplinary agencies' enforcement priorities mean that such rules will likely only

---

[10] 522 F.2d 242 (7th Cir. 1975). See a further discussion of this case in the Supplemental Readings.

[11] Other circuits have disagreed. For instance, the Fourth Circuit, in *Hirschkop v. Snead*, 594 F.2d 356 (4th Cir. 1979), upheld one state's version of DR 7-107 in criminal trials, although it invalidated it for other litigation.

rarely be the source of attorney discipline. Many enforcement agencies simply find it too difficult to sustain a violation, and so rarely try. And the exceptions to MR 3.6 may effectively swallow the rule.

Moreover, since a violation turns on the likely prejudicial effect on the judge or jury, and a disciplinary hearing usually occurs after the fact of a trial, it is difficult to show any *actual* prejudice. Although Rehnquist's opinion makes it clear that no actual prejudice is necessary for the "substantial likelihood" standard to be violated, one must question why such a rule is necessary if careful jury voir dire successfully eliminates or cures the prejudice anyway. As the *Gentile* case and many studies[12] have shown, potential jurors rarely remember the details of pretrial publicity by the time trial rolls around, and even if they do, they view what they read in the press and see on television with healthy skepticism. Perhaps the emphasis on prejudicial *pretrial* publicity has been misplaced. Thus, the District of Columbia rule is limited to cases currently in trial, when curing the prejudice can be far more difficult.

9. Criticizing the Judge. Does lawyers' free speech narrow when it comes to criticizing a judge? The ABA has a specific rule covering the issue: Model Rule 8.2 prevents a lawyer from making a statement critical of a judge, either when the lawyer knows the statement is false, or when the lawyer recklessly disregards whether it is true or false.

Former Congresswoman Elizabeth Holtzman ran afoul of a similar New York rule. Holtzman was elected Kings County (Brooklyn) District Attorney, where she continued a highly visible political career that included a run for the United States Senate. When she read in a deputy DA's memo that a judge had asked a rape victim to get down on the floor in chambers and show the position she was in at the time of the assault, Holtzman was outraged, and fired off a letter to the judge who chaired the state's Task Force on Women in the Courts. Then, she released her letter to the press in the form of a "news alert."

This press release resulted in a disciplinary investigation of Holtzman. Despite Holtzman fighting the matter to the United States Supreme Court, the private letter of admonition she received was upheld by the New York Court of Appeals,[13] which was unpersuaded by the fact that Holtzman thought the allegations were true. The sanction was warranted, said the court, because Holtzman did nothing to investigate the charges, not even talking to her staff attorney. The court rejected her argument that actual malice, such as that required for defamation of public figures, was required in order to sustain a disciplinary violation: "Accepting [Holtzman's] argument would immunize all accusations, however reckless or irresponsible, from censure as long as the attorney uttering them did not actually entertain serious doubts as to their truth."

What about lawyers who express opinions about a judge, rather than alleging particular "facts"? In *In re Westfall*, 808 S.W.2d 829 (Mo. 1991), a

---

[12] *See, e.g.*, Martin F. Kaplan, *Cognitive Processes in the Individual Juror, in* THE PSYCHOLOGY OF THE COURTROOM (N. L. Kerr and R. M. Bray eds., 1982). Kaplan's chapter cites numerous other studies.

[13] *In re Holtzman*, 78 N.Y.2d 184, 573 N.Y.S.2d 39, 577 N.E.2d 30 (1991).

Missouri prosecutor went on television to criticize the opinion of an appeals judge who rejected a criminal prosecution. Westfall said the judge's opinion "distorted the statute . . . and convoluted logic to arrive at a decision that he personally likes." He characterized the judge as "a little bit less than honest." Westfall defended his statement by arguing first, that he was merely expressing his personal opinion about the judge, not stating facts, and second, that he was criticizing the judge's opinion, not the judge. In light of the words used, this last defense simply doesn't hold up. But Westfall's first argument also failed to impress both the majority of the Missouri Supreme Court (though the Chief Justice wrote a strong dissenting opinion), and the U.S. Supreme Court, which denied certiorari on the same day it was denied for Holtzman[14]

More recently, in *Office of Disciplinary Counsel v. Gardner*, 793 N.E.2d 425 (Ohio 2003), the Ohio Supreme Court upheld a six month suspension of attorney Gardner for making accusations of judicial impropriety against a panel of appellate judges. Among other things, Gardner declared that the panel had issued an opinion so "result driven" that "any fair-minded judge" would have been "ashamed to attach his/her name" to it. The court found that this was not protected speech even though no malice was found, and adopted "an objective standard" based on whether a reasonable attorney, "considered in light of all his professional functions," would so act, and "whether the attorney had a reasonable factual basis for making the statements."

Other courts have been more lenient in allowing lawyers to express their opinions, blunt though they may be, about judges. Thus, where a Texas attorney called a judge "a midget among giants," a court refused to discipline the lawyer because he was merely expressing his own personal beliefs. *State Bar v. Semaan*, 508 S.W.2d 429 (Tex. 1974). In 1959, the Supreme Court decided *In re Sawyer*, 360 U.S. 622, 79 S. Ct. 1376 (1959). Some commentators believe that *Gentile* effectively overruled much of this case. But others believe that part of the *Sawyer* holding still controls: that opinions about judges should be protected unless the lawyer's speech obstructs justice, even in a pending case. But what constitutes obstruction of justice? Interestingly, the *Holtzman* court itself agreed that "obstruction of justice" was the appropriate standard, claiming that Holtzman's criticism did more than merely attack one judge's reputation. Was Holtzman's press release a broad attack on the administration of justice? Essentially, the court's finding was "yes."

Read the opinion of another court, in which noted jurist Alex Kozinski, widely considered both a conservative and an intellectual, carefully analyzed the over-the-top behavior of a well-known Los Angeles legal gadfly and came to an interesting result.

STANDING COMMITTEE ON DISCIPLINE, UNITED STATES DISTRICT COURT FOR THE CENTRAL DISTRICT OF CALIFORNIA v. YAGMAN
55 F.3d 1430 (9th Cir. 1995)

Never far from the center of controversy, outspoken civil rights lawyer Stephen Yagman was suspended from practice before the United State District

---

[14] 502 U.S. 1009 (1991).

Court for the Central District of California for impugning the integrity of the court and interfering with the random selection of judges by making disparaging remarks about a judge of that court. We confront several new issues in reviewing this suspension order.

The convoluted history of his case begins in 1991 when Yagman filed a lawsuit *pro se* against several insurance companies. The case was assigned to Judge Manuel Real, then Chief Judge of the Central District. Yagman promptly sought to disqualify Judge Real on grounds of bias. The disqualification motion was randomly assigned to Judge William Keller, who denied it. *Yagman v. Republic Ins.*, 136 F.R.D. 652, 657-58 (C.D. Cal. 1991), and sanctioned Yagman for pursuing the matter in an "improper and frivolous manner."

A few days after Judge Keller's sanctions order, Yagman was quoted [in the L.A. *Daily Journal* legal newspaper] as saying that Judge Keller "has a penchant for sanctioning Jewish lawyers: me, David Kenner and Hugh Manes. I find this to be evidence of anti-semitism." The district court found that Yagman also told the *Daily Journal* reporter that Judge Keller was "drunk on the bench." . . .

Around this time, Yagman received a request from Prentice Hall, publisher of the much-fretted-about Almanac of the Federal Judiciary, for comments in connection with a profile of Judge Keller. Yagman's response was less than complimentary.[15]

Soon after these events, Yagman ran into Robert Steinberg, another attorney who practices in the Central District. According to Steinberg, Yagman told him that, by leveling public criticism at Judge Keller, Yagman hoped to get the judge to recuse himself in future cases. Believing that Yagman was committing misconduct, Steinberg described his conversation with Yagman in a letter to the Standing Committee on Discipline. A few weeks later, the Standing Committee received a letter from Judge Keller [stating] "there is clear evidence that Mr. Yagman's attacks upon me are motivated by his desire to create a basis for recusing me in any future proceeding."

1. We begin with the portion of Local Rule 2.5.2 prohibiting any conduct that "impugns the integrity of the Court." As the district court recognized, this provision is overbroad because it purports to punish a great deal of constitutionally protected speech, including all true statements reflecting adversely on the reputation or character of federal judges.

To save the "impugn the integrity" portion of Rule 2.5.2, the district court read into it an "objective" version of the malice standard enunciated in *New York Times Co. v. Sullivan*, 376 U.S. 254 (1964) . . . to prohibit only false statements made with either knowledge of their falsity or with reckless disregard as to their truth or falsity, judged from the standpoint of a "reasonable attorney."

---

15 [4] The portion of the letter relevant here reads as follows:

. . . . It is an understatement to characterize the Judge as "the worst judge in the central district." It would be fairer to say that he is ignorant, dishonest, ill-tempered, and a bully, and probably is one of the worst judges in the United States. . . .

. . . .

Though attorneys can play an important role in exposing problems with the judicial system, false statements impugning the integrity of a judge erode public confidence without serving to publicize problems that justifiably deserve attention. . . .

Attorneys who make statements impugning the integrity of a judge are, however, entitled to other First Amendment protections applicable in the defamation context. To begin with, attorneys may be sanctioned for impugning the integrity of a judge or the court only if their statements are false; truth is an absolute defense. . . .

It follows that statements impugning the integrity of a judge may not be punished unless they are capable of being proved true or false; statements of opinion are protected by the First Amendment unless they "imply a false assertion of fact."

With these principles in mind, we examine the statements for which Yagman was disciplined.

2. We first consider Yagman's statement in the *Daily Journal* that Judge Keller "has a penchant for sanctioning Jewish lawyers: me, David Kenner and Hugh Manes. I find this to be evidence of anti-semitism." Though the district court viewed this entirely as an assertion of fact, we conclude that the statement contains both an assertion of fact and an expression of opinion.

Yagman's claim that he, Kenner and Manes are all Jewish and were sanctioned by Judge Keller is clearly a factual assertion: The words have specific, well-defined meanings and describe objectively verifiable matters. Nothing about the context in which the words appear suggests the use of loose, figurative language or "rhetorical hyperbole." Thus, had the Standing Committee proved that Yagman, Kenner or Manes were not sanctioned by Judge Keller, or were not Jewish, this assertion might have formed the basis for discipline. The committee, however, didn't claim that Yagman's factual assertion was false, and the district court made no finding to that effect. We proceed, therefore, on the assumption that this portion of Yagman's statement is true.

The remaining portion of Yagman's *Daily Journal* statement is best characterized as opinion; it conveys Yagman's personal belief that Judge Keller is anti-Semitic. As such, it may be the basis of sanctions only if it could reasonably be understood as declaring or implying actual facts capable of being proved true or false.

. . . .

3. The district court also disciplined Yagman for alleging that Judge Keller was "dishonest." This remark appears in the letter Yagman sent to Prentice Hall in connection with the profile of Judge Keller in the Almanac of the Federal Judiciary. The court concluded that this allegation was sanctionable because it "plainly implies past improprieties." Had Yagman accused Judge Keller of taking bribes, we would agree with the district court. Statements that "could reasonably be understood as imputing specific criminal or other wrongful acts" are not entitled to constitutional protection merely because they are phrased in the form of an opinion.

When considered in context, however, Yagman's statement cannot reasonably be interpreted as accusing Judge Keller of criminal misconduct. The term "dishonest" was one in a string of colorful adjectives Yagman used to convey the low esteem in which he held Judge Keller. The other terms he used — "ignorant," "ill-tempered," "buffoon," "sub-standard human," "right-wing fanatic," "a bully," "one of the worst judges in the United States" — all speak to competence and temperament rather than corruption; together they convey nothing more substantive than Yagman's contempt for Judge Keller. Viewed in context of these "lusty and imaginative expressions," the word "dishonest" cannot reasonably be construed as suggesting that Judge Keller had committed specific illegal acts . . . .

Were we to find any substantive content in Yagman's use of the term "dishonest," we would, at most, construe it to mean "intellectually dishonest" — an accusation that Judge Keller's rulings were overly result-oriented. Intellectual dishonesty is a label lawyers frequently attach to decisions with which they disagree. . . . Because Yagman's allegation of "dishonesty" does not imply facts capable of objective verification, it is constitutionally immune from sanctions.

4. Finally, the district court found sanctionable Yagman's allegation that Judge Keller was "drunk on the bench." Yagman contends that, like many of the terms he used in his letter to Prentice Hall, this phrase should be viewed as mere "rhetorical hyperbole." The statement wasn't a part of the string of invective in the Prentice Hall letter, however; it was a remark Yagman allegedly made to a newspaper reporter. Yagman identifies nothing relating to the context in which this statement was made that tends to negate the literal meaning of the words he used. We therefore conclude that Yagman's "drunk on the bench" statement could reasonably be interpreted as suggesting that Judge Keller had actually, on at least one occasion, taken the bench while intoxicated. Unlike Yagman's remarks in his letter to Prentice Hall, this statement implies actual facts that are capable of objective verification. For this reason, the statement isn't protected.

For Yagman's "drunk on the bench" allegation to serve as the basis for sanctions, however, the Standing Committee had to prove that the statement was false. This it failed to do; indeed, the committee introduced no evidence at all on the point. . . .

As an alternative basis for sanctioning Yagman, the district court concluded that Yagman's statements violated Local Rule 2.5.2's prohibition against engaging in conduct that "interferes with the administration of justice." The court found that Yagman made the statements discussed above in an attempt to "judge-shop" — i.e., to cause Judge Keller to recuse himself in cases where Yagman appeared as counsel.

The Supreme Court has held that speech otherwise entitled to full constitutional protection may nonetheless be sanctioned if it obstructs or prejudices the administration of justice. Given the significant burden this rule places on otherwise protected speech, however, the Court has held that prejudice to the administration of justice must be highly likely before speech may be punished.

In a trio of cases involving contempt sanctions imposed against newspapers, the Court articulated the constitutional standard to be applied in this context.

Press statements relating to judicial matters may not be restricted, the Court held, unless they pose a "clear and present danger" to the administration of justice. The standard announced in these cases is a demanding one: Statements may be punished only if they "constitute an imminent, not merely a likely, threat to the administration of justice. The danger must not be remote or even probable: it must immediately imperil." . . .

Yagman's criticism of Judge Keller was harsh and intemperate, and in no way to be condoned. It has long been established, however, that a party cannot force a judge to recuse himself by engaging in personal attacks on the judge.

. . . .

The question remains whether the possibility of voluntary recusal is so great as to amount to a clear and present danger. We believe it is not. . . . Judge Real, for example, despite receiving harsh criticism from Yagman, did not recuse himself in *Yagman v. Republic Ins.*, where Yagman was not merely the lawyer but also a party to the proceedings. . . .

We can't improve on the words of Justice Black in *Bridges* [*v. California*, 314 U.S. 252, 62 S. Ct. 190 (1941)] at 270-71 (footnote omitted):

> The assumption that respect for the judiciary can be won by shielding judges from published criticism wrongly appraises the character of American public opinion. For it is a prized American privilege to speak one's mind, although not always with perfect good taste, on all public institutions. And an enforced silence, however limited, solely in the name of preserving the dignity of the bench, would probably engender resentment, suspicion and contempt much more than it would enhance respect.

Reversed.

SUPPLEMENTAL READINGS

1. Susan E. Davis, "Uncivil Behavior: The Tactics Lawyers Resort to When They're Not Restrained," *California Lawyer* (July 1999). This article is a pungent, to-the-point view of the lack of civil behavior in the profession, complete with a list of root causes, including: "because it works," "testosterone poisoning," and "it's contagious." Davis also offers some valuable proposed solutions.

2. Brenda Smith, *Civility Codes: The Newest Weapons in the "Civil" War Over Proper Attorney Conduct Regulations Miss Their Mark*, 24 Dayton L. Rev. 151 (1998). This article questions whether civility codes are really the best solution for improving the legal profession.

3. Terry Carter, "A Search for Civility: 'Inns of Court' Movement Taming 'Rambo' Lawyers," *National Law Journal*, June 5, 1989, focuses on the Inns of Court movement as a way of promoting civility and collegiality.

4. Christopher J. Piazzola, *Ethical Versus Procedural Approaches to Civility: Why Ethics 2000 Should Have Adopted a Civility Rule*, 74 U. Colo. L. Rev. 1197 (2003), focuses on how rules commissions have yet to adopt ethical rules requiring civility or professionalism by attorneys. It cites the case of Lee

Rohm, the lawyer in the *Saldana* case cited in section 3, among other interesting examples.

5. Two older cases that reached opposite results in explosive circumstances remain of interest. *In re Carrow*, 40 Cal. App. 3d 924, 115 Cal. Rptr. 601 (1974). Attorney Carrow won reversal of an order of contempt in a highly politicized trial that the appeals court acknowledged had been difficult on both the judge and the lawyers. Carrow's comment about the trial becoming a "joke" was made in response to a witness' runaway narrative and couched in otherwise respectful terms. ("I submit, Your Honor, that this trial has become a joke.") In *In re Friedland*, 376 N.E.2d 1126 (Ind. 1978), by contrast, discipline was sustained against a lawyer who called the trial a farce. This was held to be "conduct prejudicial to the administration of justice," and a false accusation against the judicial officer. Here, however, the attorney was otherwise disrespectful.

6. Kevin Cole & Fred C. Zacharias, People v. Simpson: *Perspectives on the Implications for the Criminal Justice System: The Agony of Victory and the Ethics of Lawyer Speech*, 69 So. Calf. L. Rev. 1627 (May 1996). A thorough analysis of extrajudicial statements made in the O.J. Simpson case.

7. Two valuable law review articles on lawyers' free speech are cited here. In *Free Speech for Lawyers*, 28 Hastings Const. L.Q. 305 (2001), Cornell Professor W. Bradley Wendel analyzes and criticizes the disparate treatment of free speech in cases that don't deal with lawyers as opposed to those that do. Katrina M. Kelly, *Comment: The "Impartial" Jury and Media Overload: Rethinking Attorney Speech Regulations in the 1990s*, 16 N. Ill. U. L. Rev. 483 (Spring 1996) examines the rationale behind attorney speech regulations and analyzes the ineffectiveness of the standard that the majority of states apply.

8. Lonnie T. Brown, Jr., *"May It Please the Camera, I Mean the Court"* — *An Intrajudicial Solution to an Extrajudicial Problem*, 39 Ga. L. Rev. 83 (2004), re-examines pre-trial publicity after *Gentile* and suggests that in the modern era of high-visibility trials like Scott Peterson's and Michael Jackson's and the post-9/11 politicization of cases like that of the so-called "American Taliban," John Walker Lindh, we need rules that "equate the court of public opinion with courts of law for purposes of professional regulation."

9. *Chicago Council of Lawyers v. Bauer*, 522 F.2d 242 (7th Cir. 1975). An association of local lawyers sought declaratory relief and an injunction against the enforcement of a local criminal "no-comment" rule of court and disciplinary rule. The "no-comment" rule, in the criminal context, prohibited the extrajudicial comments by lawyers in connection with pending cases if there was a reasonable likelihood that the release of such information would interfere with a fair trial. The plaintiffs argued that the "no-comment" rules deprived lawyers of their freedom of speech under the First Amendment. The court agreed, holding that the "no-comment" rule in the criminal context may bar only those comments which pose a serious and imminent threat of interference with the fair administration of justice. The court also criticized rules which purported to sanction lawyers for criticizing judges, as violative of "pure" free speech.

PROBLEM 21

This problem explores ethical issues relating to mediation, an increasingly common and important method of resolving disputes. Many of these issues have been touched on elsewhere in this volume: confidentiality, conflicts of interest, and negotiation tactics among them. But mediation brings a new spin to these issues, particularly because of its lack of black letter rules. We also address how both advocates and mediators engage in balancing acts, between the parties and, on occasion, between the client and the public welfare, when a settlement is offered only on the condition of secrecy. When a mediator sees a disparity in power between the parties or a litigator sees a danger in "secretizing" a settlement about an issue that endangers the public, they must ask whether and how to reconcile personal morality and the practice of their profession.

Advocates' and Mediators' Ethical Dilemmas in Mediation

I. Peter van Lund of Cooper, van Lund & Winters LLP, represents Benedict, Inc., a corporation with diverse pharmaceutical holdings. One of Benedict's most lucrative subsidiaries is Kimoprimo, a company that manufactures *Annihilator*, a chemotherapy that drug trials have shown is particularly effective for treating ovarian cancer.

Marla Justice is a partner at Fisler & Nichols, a small firm that represents plaintiffs in injury cases. She has developed a niche doing products liability work. Justice represents Jacob Stephens, whose wife, Joy, had unsuccessfully undergone *Annihilator* chemotherapy and died at age 38. Justice and her experts believe that the chemotherapy used on Joy was tainted, resulting in her death.

Justice and van Lund have engaged in constant discovery battles, so she is surprised when, shortly before the hearing on her latest discovery motion, van Lund suggests mediating the case. Though aware of Cooper, van Lund's adage, "Litigate and never blink!" she readily agrees. She suggests the names of a few lawyers whom she knows are skilled "neutrals" knowledgeable in products liability matters. Van Lund, however, demands Jimmy Springer, a recently-retired judge who has rejoined Emile & Springer, van Lund's former firm. Van Lund insists that "only Springer can get this done."

QUESTIONS

1. Does Justice have an ethical duty to suggest mediation to her client in the first place? What if Justice is opposed to mediation because she believes that individual plaintiffs are at a disadvantage when facing powerful mega-companies? What about here, where van Lund has made the offer but will only mediate with Springer?

2. Does van Lund's previous employment with Springer's firm pose ethical concerns? How should they be resolved? Does van Lund's hand-picking Springer raise any ethical issues?

3. What duties, if any, does Springer or van Lund have to disclose their relationship? What if van Lund has used Springer as a mediator on 10 prior

occasions? What if van Lund and Springer had a close, personal relationship instead of a professional one? *Who*, if anyone, should disclose?

II. At the mediation, after several difficult hours with little progress toward settlement, Springer calls Justice into the coffee room for a "private chat." Van Lund, he says, has just made a surprising one-time offer: Settle the case today for $3,000,000 or get ready to go to trial. Justice is shocked, especially since the offer is substantially higher than her own private evaluation. She asks Springer what's going on. Springer tells her he will only speak if she promises silence, even with her client. He then tells her that her latest discovery motion will likely result in "smoking gun" documents revealing "adverse incidents" that show tainted *Annihilator* was directly responsible for the deaths of several women and the near-death poisoning of others.

Springer then meets with just the lawyers. Van Lund places two conditions on his offer: first, that the parties enter into a settlement agreement in which neither the amount nor the information about other adverse incidents may be revealed; and second that Justice may tell Stephens only of the existence of a problem without mentioning any specifics.

QUESTIONS

1. Was it ethical for Justice to meet Springer or van Lund without Stephens?

2. May Justice ethically recommend settlement while keeping the specifics about adverse incidents from her client? Would a totally "confidential" settlement be ethical if she *could* tell Stephens what she knows? In considering the offer, would it be appropriate for Justice to tell Stephens her concerns about future harm to the public if secrecy shrouds the discovery?

3. What, if anything, may Springer say about the mediation? May he write about it in his bi-monthly newsletter if he changes all the names? If this were court-ordered mediation and he were ordered to do so, could he write a report to the court detailing how he thought the case should be resolved?

III. Virginia Westport is a successful full-time lawyer-mediator. She is mediating a case with Lester Granot, who represents Al Pottman, a self-employed 48-year-old landscaper who was hit and injured by a Quick Cab taxi, and John Quincy, an experienced defense lawyer representing Quick Cab and its driver.

During an early "caucus" with Westport, Granot, who strikes her as having little litigation experience, confides that Pottman's medical bills are only $10,000 and that while Pottman is in great pain and can no longer handle the physical rigors demanded of his livelihood, he has only soft-tissue injuries, though his improvement is unlikely. Granot tells Westport that his demand is $50,000.

During a later caucus with Quincy, he notes the weakness of opposing counsel and makes it clear that he considers the case to be worth little. He offers to pay only a $15,000 "nuisance value." He pressures Westport to resolve matters "so we can all get back to more important things."

As Westport leaves that caucus she runs into Pottman, who had gone for a cup of coffee. He tells Westport that he is worried about his case, his attorney, and his future. He had been a landscaper for 20 years and is concerned about providing for his family. He found Granot through a friend of a friend, and feels stuck because Granot's contingency fee contract, which calls for the lawyer to get 40% of the recovery, contains a lien against any recovery should Pottman fire him. Pottman makes it clear he feels intimidated by the whole mediation process and does not know who to trust. He pleads for Westport's help.

QUESTIONS

1. What should Westport do? May she reply to Pottman at all? Suppose that given her experience, she believes that the true value of his case is $150,000 to $250,000. Should she tell either Granot or Pottman? Would your answer change if Quincy had told her "I'd offer $100,000 or more, but *not* against that lightweight lawyer"?

2. What if Westport believes that Granot is incompetent or that his fee is unethically high? May she tell Pottman to get a different attorney? Should she? May she simply stop the mediation?

READINGS

1. What Is Mediation? As the world of litigation evolves, so does the way in which people respond to conflict. ADR[1] has become "part and parcel of the practice of law and constitutes a tool of equal rank with litigation to achieve, in the proper case, prompt and cost-effective dispute resolution."[2] There are many types of ADR, including mediation, arbitration (where the "neutral" is a private decisionmaker, acting as trier of both fact and law), judicial reference to a special master, early neutral evaluation, "med/arb" (unsuccessful mediation turns into binding arbitration), and "arb/med" (arbitrator attempts to get the parties to resolve the case consensually before arbitration). The use of ADR is likely to increase dramatically as more courts promote "fast track" timetables that discourage delay. Today, less than 5% of civil filings end up going to trial. That leaves 95% that resolve another way. Ninety percent of cases that go to mediation settle at the mediation or shortly after. Why do you think this is so?

According to Black's Law Dictionary[3] mediation is defined as "the act of a third person who interferes between two contending parties with a view to reconcile them or persuade them to adjust or settle their dispute." Mediation has been described as a facilitated negotiation among the parties to a dispute, or "shuttle diplomacy" by a neutral third party. The parties and their attorney meet with the mediator and the opposing side in a "joint session" and privately with the mediator in a "caucus."

Artful mediators, either in joint session or private caucuses, do more than merely convey information between disputants. They listen carefully to both advocates and parties to be able to frame the case's issues and highlight

---

[1] An acronym for Alternative Dispute Resolution. Former U.S. Attorney General Janet Reno has used the term "Appropriate Dispute Resolution" in her speech to the Society of Professionals in Dispute Resolution, October 19, 1996, San Diego, CA.

[2] New Jersey Joint Ethics and Advertising Opinion 676/18 (April 4, 1994).

[3] Sixth edition (1990).

particular strengths and weaknesses of each side. There are many techniques that mediators use to move parties from polarization to resolution. How they do this may raise ethical concerns for both mediator and advocate.

The beauty of mediation is that it allows litigants and their lawyers control over the outcome of their disputes. No third party, whether judge, jury, or arbitrator, makes rulings or issues awards. The process generally saves both time and money. More importantly, it provides some measure of satisfaction to all, while allowing for more creative solutions than traditional litigation. Moreover, parties can resolve disputes without destroying ongoing relationships. And because mediation is generally a voluntary process, there is no risk. If the matter doesn't settle, the parties can just walk away and resume litigating. In their writings and discussions, mediators often refer to "the process," and to "letting the process work." Some state that preserving the process is their main goal, not settlement.

Some have criticized mediation as little more than a forum for a fishing exhibition, allowing free discovery without the hammer of the court. But for a case to resolve, there must be an adequate exchange of information. What information is provided and how it is ultimately used is largely dependent on the attorneys. Should a lawyer refuse to reveal information in an attempt to save the "smoking gun" for trial? Or is a client best served by a more open, candid approach? These issues are even more apparent when the mediation is court-ordered, with the parties and counsel required to make a "good faith" effort at settlement. Mandated good faith for an essentially voluntary process is difficult at best. It requires litigators to walk an ethical tightrope, particularly in those situations where they consider resolution unlikely or untimely.

Once parties decide to mediate, their selection of the mediator is voluntary, a decision usually based on the mediator's style, reputation, and experience with certain types of cases. There are times when some lawyers may insist on a specific mediator. This often occurs when a "repeat customer — say an insurance carrier — has learned to trust a particular individual's style, approach, and — most important — word. Mediators have no actual power in forcing parties to settle, but they often have enormous informal influence over the disputants. Many are retired judges or attorneys with formidable reputations in the legal community.

Mediator selection criteria, whether based on real or perceived data, can raise ethical concerns. For instance, what if an attorney bases selection on the perception that the particular mediator has a reputation for extracting large settlements from insurance carriers? Or that the mediator is known to be close to one party or another? Or particularly tough-minded and tough-talking, even intimidating? Market forces may afford the best protection against mediator bias. After all, mediators would not stay in business long if their neutrality were frequently questioned.

2. Ethical Rules for Mediators. Historically, ADR was used by stipulation of the parties. As a result, formal rules governing the process have been slow to develop. Today, rules for arbitration and mediation are becoming more formalized. Arbitration has two foundational statutes: the federal Arbitration Act of 1954 requires courts to recognize and enforce arbitration awards that are fundamentally fair, while the Uniform Arbitration Act, adopted in 49 states, outlines a series of arbitration requirements that, if met, make overturning an arbitration award nearly impossible.[4] While it is generally accepted that the mediator should be a neutral third party with no vested interest in the outcome of a dispute,[5] mediation has been subject to even less codification.

There are a number of ethics codes for ADR neutrals that have been promulgated by national ADR professional organizations, state-wide regulatory or judicial bodies, individual courts, community ADR programs, and individual ADR provider organizations.[6] Surprisingly, some of these codes apply to both arbitrators and mediators, despite the fact that arbitrators act more like judges.

Some basic principles are common to most sets of rules, but no codified rules formally result in disciplinary action for failure to comply, except within private organizations for conduct that might cause removal from a panel of neutrals. Some mediators talk about the primacy of neutrality and "symmetry," a concept that is more than equality — a balance of fair dealing and equal treatment for all sides. But it remains the case that it is not formal rules but the free market system — and reputation — that are the ultimate arbiters of a mediator's ethics.

The 2002 changes to the ABA Model Rules eliminated a rule addressing the lawyer as "intermediary" and added Rule 2.4, titled Lawyer Serving as Third-Party Neutral. What are the underlying assumptions about representation in Rule 2.4? Some things to think about in light of the current state of the ABA rules include how this rule and its comments are to be applied, whether the rule is sufficiently specific, and whether the rule is sufficiently prescriptive.

There has been criticism that the relatively modest change created by Ethics 2000 in revising the rules was not adequate to address the ethical concerns that ADR lawyer-neutrals face. Proposed ethics rules that take into account issues such as confidentiality, conflicts of interest, fees, court obligations, and competency standards are areas likely to be addressed as the rules develop. Also of note is the lack of distinction in Rule 2.4 between mediators and arbitrators, despite the vast differences in these neutrals' roles, most significantly that the former are decisionmakers while the latter are not. It is thus open to substantial question whether Rule 2.4 will be sufficient to serve as the basis for a uniform, systematic approach to ethics for lawyer-mediators.

3. Confidentiality. The expectation that mediation is a confidential process is the touchstone of its desirability and success. Confidentiality encourages an open forum, enhancing the likelihood of resolution. The Federal Rules of Evidence provide a limited privilege for settlement discussions, while state laws offer widely varying degrees of protection. Some jurisdictions, such as California,[7] hold that all communications related to the mediation are

---

[4] *See generally* William C. Smith, *Much to Do About ADR*, ABA J., June 2000, at 62.

[5] Many mediators say this lack of investment should extend even to the issue of whether the case settles — the only goal being to protect the neutrality of the mediation process itself.

[6] *See* the CPR-Georgetown Commission on Ethics and Standards of Practice in ADR monograph, *Principles for ADR Provider Organization*, June 2000, at 18.

[7] *See* Calif. Evidence Code § 1119; *see also NLRB v. Maculuso*, 618 F.2d 51 (9th Cir. 1980) (held that "complete exclusion of mediator testimony is necessary" for effective mediation).

confidential and can never be disclosed. The drafters of the Uniform Mediation Act (UMA), which combines the efforts of an ABA group and the National Conference of Commissioners on Uniform State Law, counted some 2,500 statutes around the country that deal in some way with confidentiality in mediation, but there is nothing close to uniformity. The confusing array of inconsistent confidentiality guarantees points to a need for more uniformity.

The UMA itself takes a middle road on confidentiality.[8] Under that proposal, the default position is that "mediation communications are not subject to discovery or admissible in evidence in a civil proceeding. . . ." Exceptions to this broad exclusion include mediations that by law are open to the public and threats of future criminal acts or violence, a significant parallel to Model Rule 1.6 as defined in many states. However, a court may also choose to override the privilege for information related to claims of fraud, duress, incapacity, or malpractice actions, or where there are "mediation communications that evidence a significant threat to public health or safety."

The UMA also has language that allows a mediator to be subpoenaed to testify against a disputant if there is later disagreement as to a settlement.[9] Another view, as articulated in Calif. Evidence Code section 703.5, is that "no mediator shall be competent to testify, in any subsequent civil proceeding, as to any statement, conduct, decision or ruling occurring at or in conjunction with the prior proceeding, except as to [one] that could constitute a crime . . . or give rise to disqualification . . . ."

In order to facilitate settlement, it is almost invariably necessary that parties share with the mediator information that would ordinarily be client confidences, with the clear expectation that such discussions will be absolutely protected. Where this confidentiality protection is not statutorily mandated as in California, it is often well-established convention that the mediator's ethical duty is to keep the information confidential when instructed. Even though the mediator cannot disclose such information to the other side, the mediator can and often does *use* the information without revealing it in suggesting solutions to the parties.

However, even jurisdictions with a seemingly ironclad rule of mediation confidentiality have exceptions. In California, where mediation is better established and more widespread than most other states, there also has been more developed case law. Three key California cases raised questions about the extent of mediation confidentiality. *Rinaker v. Superior Court*, 62 Cal. App. 4th 155, 74 Cal. Rptr. 2d 464 (1998), held that a mediator's testimony could be compelled if it would protect a party's constitutional rights by preventing perjury. In *Olam v. Congress Mortage Co.*, 68 F. Supp. 2d 1110 (N.D. Cal. 1999), the plaintiff claimed to have signed a settlement agreement in distress. Later *all* the parties wanted the mediator to testify. The court ordered the testimony to determine the plaintiff's capacity to contract. The settlement agreement was ultimately enforced.

In *Foxgate Homeowners' Association v. Bramalea California Inc.*, 78 Cal. App. 4th 653, 92 Cal. Rptr. 2d 916 (2000), an appointed hybrid mediator/discovery master required the parties to appear with their experts for five days

---

[8] *See* Uniform Mediation Act, Interim Draft, February 20, 2001.

[9] *See* UMA § 2(c)(8).

of hearing. Defense counsel refused to bring his experts, saying he didn't want to respond to the plaintiff's frivolous claim. The mediator prepared a report to the court, a procedure the parties had agreed to, and based on that report's conclusion that counsel had delayed and obstructed the mediation process, the trial court sanctioned defense counsel. The appeals court wrote that "[w]hile confidentiality is essential to make mediation work, so too is the meaningful, good faith participation of the parties and their lawyers." Concluding that no privilege should be read so broadly as to immunize parties and their lawyers from sanctions for disobeying court orders, the court held the mediation privilege to be waived notwithstanding the clear statutory language:

Muzzling the parties and the mediator in such circumstances would not only effectively preclude a party from seeking and obtaining sanctions. Because the court would have no way of learning that its orders had been disobeyed or that some serious misconduct occurred which warrants judicial oversight, the court would be stripped of its inherent power to police and control its own processes.

Fortunately for those concerned about maintaining mediation confidentiality, this opinion was short-lived, overruled by the California Supreme Court in July 2001.[10] That court held that confidentiality is essential to effective mediation, and concluded that the statute "unqualifiedly bars disclosure of communications" — even those that could be used to demonstrate that a party approached a session in bad faith.

But what about a lawyer's duty to report misconduct by another attorney? Should the lawyer-mediator wear a "neutral" hat or a hat that says "member of the Bar"? The lawyer-mediator's duty to report attorney misconduct during mediation can create an ethical dilemma when it conflicts with mediation confidentiality.

In *In re Waller*, 573 A.2d 780 (D.C. 1990), a mediator was concerned about the unethical behavior of attorney Waller, who represented plaintiff in a medical malpractice case, sued the hospital and a tissue bank that supplied tissue for a bone implant, but didn't sue the surgeon. When the mediator asked during a court-ordered mediation why the surgeon had not been named, Waller acknowledged that he was the surgeon's lawyer. The mediator reported the conflict of interest to the court.

D.C. had no confidentiality statute, but the court's mediation order included a provision that "no statement of any party or any counsel shall be disclosed to the court or be admissible for evidence for any purpose at the trial of this case." Nevertheless, the mediator reasoned that disclosure was appropriate because it concerned a matter *unrelated* to the subject of the mediation. Though it is hard to separate the allegation of wrongful conduct from the subject matter of the case, both the District of Columbia's disciplinary board and the D.C. appeals court agreed, and upheld Waller's 60-day suspension from practice.

4. Must a Lawyer Offer Mediation? Does a lawyer have an ethical obligation to offer mediation to the client? Could a failure to advise about ADR

---

[10] *See* 26 Cal. 4th 1, 108 Cal. Rptr 2d 642 (2001).

ever fall below the standard of care and result in malpractice? Clearly, litigation is not always the best choice for every client's case. If a lawyer has a duty to effectively serve the client, does it follow that discussing mediations as a potential resolution should be mandated?

The ethical duty to inform clients of alternatives to litigation is referred to in several sections of the ABA Model Rules. Model Rule 2.1 Comment 5 has the simple sentence that "when a matter is likely to involve litigation, it may be necessary under rule 1.4 to inform the client of forms of dispute resolution that might constitute reasonable alternatives to litigation." Is such a requirement reasonable? Or should it be made even more clear by requiring or at least suggesting that a lawyer not wait until an issue is already in litigation before it is referred to an alternative means of resolution?

Some states have amended the model rules to specifically address lawyers suggesting ADR. Colorado's rules imply an ethical duty, while Georgia's rule mandates a non-discretionary duty. Other states have imposed the requirement through other means. The Texas Lawyer's Creed states, "I will advise my client regarding the availability of mediation, arbitration, and other alternative methods of resolving and settling disputes." Federal district court rules in Massachusetts require attorneys to discuss ADR with their clients.[11]

The failure to advise clients about ADR methods may ultimately be determined to be malpractice, though to date no cases have been reported with that specific finding. But the possibility of this result in the future is real, for several reasons. First, legal malpractice, like medical malpractice, often turns on informed consent, while litigation may be viewed as the legal equivalent to surgery: not always the most desirable means to resolution, and one for which the client should make the ultimate choice. The client, after all, bears most of the risk. Second, since lawyers have the inherent conflict that comes with receiving any fee, offering ADR — almost always more cost-effective and fee-reducing — may come to be seen as part of an attorney's fiduciary duty. Third, as mediation becomes more common, even routine, considering its use in appropriate cases may come to be part of the basic standard of care which the competent practice of law requires.

Law firms' financial realities, however, do not always provide the best environment in which to emphasize the benefits of mediation, as the following excerpted article describes.

JOHN G. BICKERMAN, LEAVING THE FIRM, CONFLICTS, FIRM ECONOMICS AND ISSUES OF CULTURE CAN STIFLE ADR PRACTICE
Dispute Resolution Magazine (Winter 1998)[12]

At first, I believed my former firm would embrace a meaningful dispute resolution practice. It seemed logical that such a practice could complement and enhance the firm's litigation department. After several years of generating

---

[11] *See* Monica L. Warmbrod, *Comment: Could an Attorney Face Disciplinary Actions or Even Legal Malpractice for Failure to Inform Clients of Alternative Dispute Resolution?*, 27 CUMBERLAND L. REV. 791 (1997).

[12] Copyright © 1998 by Dispute Resolution Magazine. All rights reserved.

hundreds of thousands of dollars in fees for the firm, I drafted a detailed business plan showing how the firm could develop a profitable dispute resolution practice area. The firm's response to the proposal was lukewarm. Over the next three years, I slowly realized that my vision of a full-time mediation practice could not be realized within a large national firm.

. . . .

Conflicts presented a daily concern for me. . . . Several attorneys in Florida approached me about mediating the litigation brought by the state's Attorney General against the major tobacco manufacturers. . . . [This case] could have generated considerable income for the firm if I had been selected. The response from several partners was swift and negative. Mediating this case would have foreclosed the firm representing any of the tobacco company participants in the pending litigation. Although no one at the firm was engaged in such representation, the possibility . . . posed a sufficient threat to potential business opportunity that I was discouraged from expressing further interest in this assignment. . . .

[Conflicts of interest are complicated, for example by such matters as what are called] "settlement facts" and how these facts are used after the mediation ends. Information learned during a mediation that may not go directly to the merits of the dispute may still be of strategic importance to the party. For example, a mediator may learn that a party is contemplating a merger or that a party is teetering on bankruptcy.

Now fast forward several months and consider the dilemma whereby the firm and perhaps an attorney in the firm are engaged in a business transaction adverse to this mediation participant but that is not substantially related to the subject of the mediation. The knowledge of these settlement facts poses a very practical problem. Arguably, the attorney in possession of this information has an ethical obligation to share it with the firm's present client. Yet, sharing this information would breach the confidentiality of the mediation process.

. . . .

The driving force that predicts behavior in most firms is money or, less charitably, self-interest. . . . Litigators in my former firm saw themselves as dispute resolvers [but] because many lawyers had only a partial understanding of how mediation works, they underestimated its utility to clients, or, more cynically, worried that using effective dispute resolution processes might cut short a lucrative litigation.

More troubling, they viewed mediation as contrary to the business of litigation. Seeing themselves as true warriors who go to battle to vindicate the rights of their clients, they feared signaling to either clients or adversaries that they would prefer to settle instead of going to war. They had little interest or incentive to tinker with a business that had elevated them to the senior ranks of the firm.

Mediation cannot provide the leverage, and thus the profit margin per case, that large-scale litigation generates. Profits for most firms rest squarely on the pyramid of leverage. Litigation and most business transactions frequently require many layers of lawyers. The very efficiency that mediation seeks to achieve, eliminating the time and expense of litigation, strikes at the heart of a law firm profit model.

***

NOTES

This is not the first time we have seen lawyers' self-interest, particularly in generating income, conflicting with the best interests of clients. Is there anything different about the mediation setting that makes this a more difficult conflict to deal with? Less difficult? How can this problem be solved so lawyers initiate mediation in those cases where it is truly in the client's best interests?

5. The Lawyer as Advocate in Mediation. The question of whether the lawyer must advise their client about the availability of mediation is only one piece of the puzzle. When the client opts for mediation and the lawyer serves as the advocate, is this the same or different than participating in a negotiation? How? In 2006, the ABA issued Formal Opinion 06-439 which addresses part of this question. What do you think are the similarities and distinctions between mediation and negotiation? Do they warrant disparate treatment?

AMERICAN BAR ASSOCIATION, FORMAL OPINION 06-439 LAWYER'S OBLIGATION OF TRUTHFULNESS WHEN REPRESENTING A CLIENT IN NEGOTIATION: APPLICATION TO CAUCUSED MEDIATION
(April 12, 2006)

Under Model Rule 4.1, in the context of a negotiation, including a caucused mediation, a lawyer representing a client may not make a false statement of material fact to a third person. However, statements regarding a party's negotiating goals or its willingness to compromise, as well as statements that can fairly be characterized as negotiation "puffing," ordinarily are not considered "false statements of material fact" within the meaning of the Model Rules.

In this opinion, we discuss the obligation of a lawyer to be truthful when making statements on behalf of clients in negotiations, including the specialized form of negotiation known as caucused mediation.

It is not unusual in a negotiation for a party, directly or through counsel, to make a statement in the course of communicating its position that is less than entirely forthcoming. For example, parties to a settlement negotiation often understate their willingness to make concessions to resolve the dispute. A plaintiff might insist that it will not agree to resolve a dispute for less than $200, when, in reality, it is willing to accept as little as $150 to put an end to the matter. Similarly, a defendant manufacturer in patent infringement litigation might repeatedly reject the plaintiff's demand that a license be part of any settlement agreement, when in reality, the manufacturer has no genuine interest in the patented product and, once a new patent is issued, intends to introduce a new product that will render the old one obsolete. In the criminal law context, a prosecutor might not reveal an ultimate willingness to grant immunity as part of a cooperation agreement in order to retain influence over the witness.

. . . .

Having delineated the requisite standard of truthfulness for a lawyer engaged in the negotiation process, we proceed to consider whether a different standard should apply to a lawyer representing a client in a caucused mediation . . . .

It has been argued that lawyers involved in caucused mediation should be held to a more exacting standard of truthfulness because a neutral is involved. The theory underlying this position is that, as in a game of "telephone," the accuracy of communication deteriorates on successive transmissions between individuals, and those distortions tend to become magnified on continued retransmission. Mediators, in turn, may from time to time reframe information as part of their efforts to achieve a resolution of the dispute. To address this phenomenon, which has been called "deception synergy," proponents of this view suggest that greater accuracy is required in statements made by the parties and their counsel in a caucused mediation than is required in face-to-face negotiations.

It has also been asserted that, to the contrary, less attention need be paid to the accuracy of information being communicated in a mediation — particularly in a caucused mediation — precisely because consensual deception is intrinsic to the process. Information is imparted in confidence to the mediator, who controls the flow of information between the parties in terms of the content of the communications as well as how and when in the process it is conveyed. Supporters of this view argue that this dynamic creates a constant and agreed upon environment of imperfect information that ultimately helps the mediator assist the parties in resolving their disputes.

Whatever the validity may be of these competing viewpoints, the ethical principles governing lawyer truthfulness do not permit a distinction to be drawn between the caucused mediation context and other negotiation settings. The Model Rules do not require a higher standard of truthfulness in any particular negotiation contexts. Except for Rule 3.3, which is applicable only to statements before a "tribunal," the ethical prohibitions against lawyer misrepresentations apply equally in all environments. Nor is a lower standard of truthfulness warranted because of the consensual nature of mediation.

6. Dealing with Mediator Conflicts of Interest. How a mediator deals with conflicts issues in mediation is a matter of considerable debate with no clear consensus. One of the biggest differences between a mediator's and an advocate's role is that the mediator has no duty of loyalty to the parties (or perhaps more accurately an equal duty of loyalty to all parties). A mediator also has no duty of independent judgment, or to communicate with one side without regard to the other side's point of view. Indeed, the very nature of the process is one in which the mediator selectively offers each side's view to the other in an effort to move towards settlement. And, of course, a major hallmark of mediation is that each side can communicate with the mediator *ex parte* in confidence.

Clearly this process gives the mediator much discretion in determining what information should, or should not, be conveyed to the other side. Part of a mediator's strategy is in determining what to convey, to whom to convey it, and when, if at all, to do so.

Conflicts of interest for mediators have not been clearly or uniformly regulated. In part this is due to the voluntary nature of mediation — the free choice to use this method to resolve a dispute. Unlike a judge or arbitrator, the mediator has no actual power to force parties to resolve anything. The mediator's power lies in the ability first to gain trust and then to persuade. As a result, there has not been a uniformly perceived need for a tightly-controlled system of conflicts checks, disclosure, and consent. In fact, what may be perceived as "problem" conflicts of interest, such as past relationships or prior business dealings between the mediator and a party or attorney, may actually be beneficial in the mediation context. Who better than someone known and trusted to tell them the truth about the strengths and weaknesses of their case?

Moreover, mediators often do not know the identity of all the actual parties in interest. They may never be actually aware of this until some time during the mediation session itself. For example, the only "named" parties may be the plaintiff and defendant; while the existence of an insurance carrier may be expected, there may be an "excess carrier," or another entity which has partially indemnified the defendant as the result of an assignment, an anticipated buy-out, or a merger. The party's desire for confidentiality may have led to this information being concealed from the opposing party and the mediator prior to the mediation. Since mediation is a party-driven process, the parties are the ones who determine what information they want to convey, and when.

Some lawyer-mediators believe that these factors, and their roles as facilitators, mean that conflict checking is not necessary to the extent it is for arbitrators — or lawyers and law firms. On the other hand, there is much to be said for the mediator making the fullest possible disclosure to the parties. It is hard to argue that *too much* disclosure is likely to be harmful to those participating in the mediation. And since one of the primary goals of the mediator is to build trust, disclosure of any prior relationship with the parties or counsel — often not a disabling factor in using that mediator — can serve as a trust-builder. Moreover, when a mediator has an ongoing relationship with one side, such as an insurer who brings a particular neutral a good deal of repeat business, it would seem the other parties have a right to know this. Do the new Model Rules help you resolve this? Whatever the lawyer-mediator decides to disclose, there are few rules and little hard and fast law to use for guidance.

7. Power: An Ethical Issue? One of the best and most interesting features of mediation is that no one comes to the process with *de jure* power. But while mediators may make no decision nor force the parties to agree to anything, they usually have substantial *de facto* power. They control both the process and the flow of information between the parties. Even orchestrating the seating arrangement at the joint session may have significant repercussions, as can deciding how and when to break up into caucuses. And clearly, determining when to reveal information to each side, and how much to reveal, can have a large impact.

Perhaps the most important ethical issue related to a mediator's use of power is how he or she deals with power imbalances among the parties and their representatives. The parties are the ultimate decisionmakers, but they come to the table from inherently unequal bargaining positions. Such imbalances are heightened when parties are unrepresented. Concerns also exist where one lawyer is more knowledgeable or experienced or has more resources than the others. Issues relating to unequal power are particularly prevalent in domestic law mediation. However, race, gender, and economic disparities between the parties also can create power issues.

On the one hand, mediators must guard against taking the easy path of siding with the more powerful party, or allowing that party's will to control the result. On the other hand, mediators must avoid the temptation to balance out power by "putting a thumb on the scales," or presenting facts, law, or negotiating positions slanted in favor of the weaker party. Such efforts undermine neutrality and create the danger that the *mediator's* version of fairness will supplant that of the parties. Most mediators agree that good settlements are not only based on probable court results but also on people's own sense of fairness and justice.

Selecting a mediator for a particular case may also relate in part to power. Mediators are often chosen because of their expertise in a particular subject: employment law, intellectual property, or construction defects, for example. Parties and their attorneys frequently want and even expect mediators to be more than passive facilitators, and to offer advice and input based on their expertise in an area of law. Sometimes, mediators are chosen precisely because the parties and lawyers *want* them to exert power. While it is controversial among mediators, some adopt a style in which throwing their weight around is part of the ordinary course of business. Indeed, a lawyer may select a mediator to serve as a "reality check" for a client who needs to hear about the weaknesses of a case from a neutral third party, or who wants the mediator to give a personal opinion of the value of the case.

Where should the ethical lines be drawn? Is it acceptable for a mediator to "throw weight around" or express a personal belief in the "right" amount for settlement? Should a mediator attempt to neutralize power discrepancies between the parties? Is this necessary to ensure fairness, or does it fly in the face of the true meaning of the word "neutral"? And, finally, is there an inconsistency between any effort to balance power and the duty of confidentiality? What happens when, as in the *Waller* case above, a lawyer acts unethically? Does that change the neutral's appropriate course of action? Should it?

8. The Fine Line Between "Lawyer" and "Mediator." In addition to disclosing unethical lawyer conduct, at least two other issues arise as to what role a lawyer-mediator adopts: How does the lawyer/mediator deal with conflicts of interest between parties in mediation and the lawyer's own firm, and to what extent, if any, is the mediator engaged in the practice of law? We look briefly at the first issue in the following piece.

D. ALAN RUDLIN, GREER D. SAUNDERS & BARBARA L. HULBURT, ATTORNEY-MEDIATORS FACE IMPORTANT ETHICAL ISSUES

The National Law Journal (November 18, 1996) [13]

In addition to participating in the [mediation] process as advocates, lawyers are increasingly interested in working as neutrals. The current codes of professional responsibility for lawyers . . . have not evolved to keep pace with the growth of lawyer participation in ADR. At the same time, statutes and rules governing ADR are being developed around the country.

As a result, attorneys interested in incorporating ADR into their practice may find that there are inconsistencies between the Model Rules and specific ADR rules that exist in certain states. Those mediating in a state without such rules may find that there is simply no guidance.

. . . .

[An] issue for the attorney-mediator is whether it is appropriate for an attorney to act as an advocate for parties who have previously participated in mediation sessions conducted by that attorney acting as a mediator. Two cases, *Poly Software Int'l Inc. v. Su* [880 F. Supp. 1487 (D. Utah 1995)] and *Cho v. Superior Court* [45 Cal. Rptr. 2d 863 (Cal. App. 1995)], call for disqualification of both the former attorney-mediator and the attorney-mediator's firm from representing parties who previously participated in mediations or settlement conferences.

In *Poly Software*, the court held that an attorney who serves as a mediator cannot subsequently represent anyone in a "substantially factually related" matter without the consent of the original parties when the mediator has received confidential information in the course of a mediation session. In *Cho v. Superior Court*, the court . . . disqualified a law firm as trial counsel when a former judge who had joined the firm had presided over settlement negotiations in the same case.

The *Poly Software* and *Cho* decisions also may have an effect on the use of mediation. Firms may limit their mediation practice for fear that it will decrease the pool of potential clients for their more lucrative and traditional adversarial practice. Firms that establish separate ADR sections within the firm may not go far enough to prevent conflict-based disqualification motions. Whether the firm's establishment of an ADR "subsidiary" would cure the problem remains an open issue.

. . . . The benefits to attorneys of incorporating ADR into their practices, both as advocates and as neutrals, outweigh the difficulties, but these questions must be addressed to ensure that attorneys will not unwittingly run afoul of the rules governing the ethical exercise of their profession.

---

[13] Reprinted with permission from the November 18, 1996 issue of The National Law Journal © 1996 by NLP IP Company. All rights reserved. Further duplication without permission is prohibited.

NOTES

What about the question of whether mediators practice law? Most claim firmly that they do not. And yet, we have remarked on the desire of some parties and lawyers in mediation to actively seek the substantive advice and knowledge of lawyer-mediators with expertise in a particular area of law. If the mediator gives this advice, doesn't that constitute the practice of law? Taking it a step farther, what happens when the parties are not represented by counsel? Can a lawyer-mediator's statement that "nothing shall be construed as my practicing law or giving you legal advice" override the reality that the neutral does just that? Finally, how is malpractice insurance affected by whether or not the lawyer is "merely" mediating or is also giving legal advice?

There are (you may not be surprised by this point to learn) no clear answers to these questions in this still-developing area. But something a leading mediator — an attorney with over 25 years' experience mediating family law cases, many without counsel — told us years ago still makes sense. This particular mediator routinely both advised litigants of the likely court outcome, and memorialized marriage settlements himself, knowing that leaving these matters to the parties alone might result in guesswork or errors neither intended. As for whether he was practicing law, he saw the distinction between a "yes" or "no" answer as little more than semantic, a matter of form over substance.

9. Secret Settlements: Justice for Whom? A lawyer's foremost loyalty is to the client. But what about when public safety is also at risk? Should advancing the client's interests always outweigh the rights of the public as a whole?

It is not uncommon that as part of a settlement agreement, key information remains "secret" to all but the parties to the initial dispute. By contract, parties can agree to prevent discovered evidence from ever being made public. This perhaps most frequently occurs in products liability cases or those involving high-profile or highly scrutinized individuals such as ministers, doctors, or teachers. When individual cases settle secretly, the public remains at risk.

Perhaps the most widely-publicized example of secret litigation in the last decade concerned defective Firestone tires that shredded during normal use.[14] Some other examples of secrecy agreements involving products include: defective heart valves and other medical prostheses; prescription medicines with fatally adverse side effects; exploding automobile fuel tanks; toxic oil spills and chemically contaminated water; and dangerous cribs and playground equipment.[15] The fatally defective Dalkon Shield intrauterine device, which

---

[14] Estimates of the number of people killed in crashes before the Firestone story was made public range from 88, see Bob Van Voris, *Lawyers Caught Between Clients and Public Safety in Tire Cases*, AMERICAN LAWYER MEDIA (Sept. 22, 2000) and NATIONAL LAW JOURNAL (Sept. 25, 2000), to almost 200, see Keith Bradsher, *S.U.V. Tire Defects Were Known in 1996 But Not Reported*, N.Y. TIMES, June 24, 2001 at 1.

[15] In a 1992 article for the *Connecticut Law Tribune*, well-known plaintiff's lawyer Richard

we discussed in Problem 17, was the subject of many secret settlements, to the point where some lawyers were asked to promise never to take another Dalkon Shield case.

Outside the products liability arena, private agreements have been made by a home for the mentally ill whose administrator had sexually abused a Down syndrome patient; the Catholic Church in resolving child molestation cases; and law firms settling severe AIDS discrimination in exchange for silence.

"Secret settlements" actually injure individuals twice; though "compensated" for their injury, the aggrieved cannot share their stories with the world, forcing them to live with the knowledge that many others are placed at great risk. It is obvious that the ethical and moral implications for lawyers on both sides are substantial.

10. What Is a "Secret Settlement"? Secret settlements can come in several forms:

Protective orders are intended to legitimately restrict the use of discovery, such as where trade secrets are involved in litigation. These orders, especially when they are stipulated to by both sides and approved by a judge without close scrutiny, have sometimes been used to protect defendants from having to reveal a potentially dangerous situation to the public. Federal Judge H. Lee Sarokin, who handled several New Jersey tobacco cases in the early 1990s and who first revealed previously secret information that exposed "Big Tobacco" wrongdoing,[16] described how he routinely granted protective orders until the first litigated tobacco case, *Cipollone v. Liggett Group, Inc.*, 106 F.R.D. 573 (D.N.J. 1985): "I must confess that for a considerable period of time, as a routine matter I signed consent orders on the theory that since the parties agreed and the lawyers agreed, there was no reason for us to examine the agreement. But I slowly came to the realization that there were other interests involved."[17] Those interests, of course, belonged to the public.

Stand-alone secrecy agreements come in the form of either "private protective orders" or agreements to return discovery at the close of the case. Often the settlement offer seems "too good" for plaintiff to turn down, though some later regret accepting it when they realize the likely harm to others.[18]

Sealing court files and/or changing the names of the parties on court documents. These extreme measures, which seem to directly subvert the court

---

Silver stated: "In every medical malpractice case I've had in the last five years, they've required secrecy. It hurts because terrible things are happening." Silver discussed the "Safety Rail," a crib extender with which babies could wedge their necks between the device's bars, resulting in death. Silver says he found that another child had died in the same manner a year before his case. "It has always been my belief that had the media publicized the first death, the product would have been taken off the market as it eventually was after the second child's death." Joseph Calve, *Restricting Settlement Secrecy*, CONN. L. TRIB. March 16, 1992.

16 See our further discussion of this in Problem 25.

17 Quoted in Jaffe, *Public Good vs. Sealed Evidence*, STAR-LEDGER (Newark), Sept. 2, 1990.

18 See, e.g., *60 Minutes II* of October 10, 2000, depicting a lawyer who felt it necessary to enter a secrecy agreement on behalf of the mother of a man who died in a Firestone case, while the mother, knowing others had died, expressed regret at having ever agreed to secrecy, and felt that *she* was responsible.

processes, serve to deny the public access to ordinarily-public information in court records. They generally can be accomplished only by stipulation and court approval.

Stipulated reversals and depublication are two ways litigants who reach a settlement after trial can effectively change the decision of the trier of fact. Depublication, somewhat less onerous, avoids adverse precedent by permitting an opinion to stand as "unpublished," without affecting the case's actual result. Stipulated reversals involve agreements to wipe the trial court's judgment off the books by stipulating to reverse that judgment on appeal in return for immediate payment. For example, if a doctor lost a medical malpractice case in court, the physician might offer to settle now for 100 cents on the dollar in exchange for erasing a judgment that might affect the doctor's future insurability. [19]

In this gold-from-dross procedure, the loser of the case becomes the *de jure* winner, and can trumpet that "victory."

11. Is Secrecy an Ethical Issue? One view, to which we acknowledge our adherence, says that it is. Lawyers — those on *both* sides — are indispensable participants in secrecy agreements. After all, they not only engage in secret settlements in the name of "zealous advocacy," they create the documentation. But given the stakes involved, the issue is whether zeal and loyalty to the client's interests outweigh the public's right to know of significant dangers to health or safety.

We have seen in our examination of confidentiality, how the rules, especially Model Rule 1.6, balance lawyers' abilities to protect their client's confidences with their duties to protect society. The fulcrum of that balance has moved somewhat in many states as a result of the 2002 and 2003 rules revisions. But "secretizing" information in settlements *does not* interfere with confidentiality at all, as it pertains only to matters subject to discovery during litigation.

One problem with the current lack of ethical standards relating to secrecy is that attorneys who believe it to be in their client's economic interests to enter into such agreements will do so; their perceived duty of advocacy will trump any possibility of disclosing, even if a lawyer believes disclosure is permitted under MR 1.6. So long as such agreements are "ethical," they will be entered into regardless of any danger to the public, on the theory that the client's interests (usually considered by lawyers to be financial ones) come first. A fair share of the blame lies with current ethics rules that, in the view of most lawyers, *require* their participation.

We know many plaintiffs' lawyers who would prefer not to feel compelled to accept secret deals. We know that many defense lawyers and in-house counsel would like nothing better than to say, "I can't help you hide the truth about a danger." But lawyers are doing exactly what they've been taught to do: Put the client first. The Sarbanes-Oxley rules discussed elsewhere in this volume have given some lawyers pause about how far this "client first"

---

[19] See *Neary v. Regents of the Univ. of Calif.*, 3 Cal. 4th 273, 10 Cal. Rptr. 859 (1992), which authorized stipulated reversals absent "extraordinary circumstances." Note that *U.S. Bancorp Mortgage Co. v. Bonner Mall Partnership*, 513 U.S. 18, 115 S. Ct. 386 (1994), disapproved of this practice.

attitude may go. But a sea change on the issue of secrecy is likely to occur only when lawyers are widely prohibited from contracting away their ability to disclose known, discovered dangers to the public so that their sole client may benefit.

Read the following excerpt, which explores some of the issues of ethics and responsibility that flow from secret settlements.

ALAN F. BLAKLEY, TO SQUEAL OR NOT TO SQUEAL: ETHICAL OBLIGATIONS OF OFFICERS OF THE COURT IN POSSESSION OF INFORMATION OF PUBLIC INTEREST
34 Cumberland Law Review 65 (2003-2004) [20]

One Clergy Sex Abuse Set

In October 1998, Paul J. Marcoux settled a claim against Archbishop Rembert Weakland and the Archdiocese of Milwaukee. The claim arose from Marcoux's allegations that he and the archbishop had an illicit sexual affair that began with Marcoux's being sexually abused by the archbishop. Marcoux claimed that at one time the archbishop had written him a "love letter," which Marcoux still possessed. The parties executed a settlement agreement prior to the initiation of any litigation. Among other things, the settlement agreement required Marcoux to return all originals and copies of any correspondence (including presumably the "love letter") or documents that he had received at any time from anyone concerning the Archdiocese of Milwaukee including, but not limited to, Archbishop Weakland. In return for Marcoux's compliance and agreement to refrain from further action, the archdiocese paid him $450,000.00. . . .

The sexual relationship between Archbishop Weakland and Marcoux began in 1979. During the time between 1979 and May of 2002, many people found some of Archbishop Weakland's views on a variety of sexual subjects inexplicably odd. For instance, it has been reported that in 1988, Archbishop Weakland wrote a column in which he said that, "[S]ome adolescent sex abuse victims were 'not so innocent' and were sexually active, street wise, and aggressive." . . . However, prior to the disclosure of the settlement did anyone have reason to suspect that Archbishop Weakland's . . . policies and practices concerning priests in his archdiocese accused of sexual abuse influenced primarily by his own past, or by his honest desire to protect the privacy of victims and victimizers alike?

In 1990, prior to the Marcoux-Weakland settlement, but during the Marcoux-Weakland relationship, John Ramstack settled a lawsuit against the Reverend David Hanser of the Archdiocese of Milwaukee. . . . Ramstack claimed that Reverend Hanser had sexually abused John and three of his brothers. The resulting settlement for $65,000.00 included a confidentiality provision . . . .

Had the Hanser-Ramstack settlement received public notice, would someone have uncovered the Marcoux-Weakland affair in 1990? Would the Archdiocese

---

of Milwaukee or the Catholic Church of the United States have developed a sexual abuse policy a decade earlier than it did? Would the revelations about a well-known archbishop have been sufficient to cause widespread change and saved countless victims? . . .

The example of the Archdiocese of Milwaukee typifies the ethical questions involved in settlements concerning underlying allegations of private matters having public interest. A plethora of additional questions arise. In 1990, how should the attorney representing John Ramstack have approached the competing interests of his client and the interests of the public at large? Should attorneys ever have any obligation to consider those questions? How should the attorney for Reverend Hanser in 1990 have balanced his duty to the archdiocese to keep additional claims from awakening, his duty to help prevent additional abuse, and his duty to insure that Reverend Hanser received treatment and was prevented from being in contact with additional potential victims? What duty did the district attorney have to investigate Archbishop Weakland's statement to him about the sexual affair? What should he have done? Similar questions arose at the time of the Marcoux-Weakland settlement. Finally, . . . [i]f the archdiocese had used the Ramstack-Hanser litigation as a catalyst of change and implemented a socially responsible policy for addressing sexually abusive priests, would the undisclosed settlement, protecting the parties' privacy, have been completely justified?

Products Liability Cases

Since 2000, Ford Motor Co., Bridgestone Tire Co., and Firestone Inc. have been involved in products liability litigation concerning the failure of tires installed on Ford sport utility vehicles that resulted in roll-over accidents. However, as early as 1991 lawsuits began, thus indicating that even then Firestone knew of the problems and was involved in settlements that included confidentiality provisions. In current litigation, many documents are kept in a "reading room," accessible only to the attorneys working on the case. Presumably, the court and the parties still wish their records to remain private.

On December 5, 2000, Bloomberg, LP and Dow Jones and Co., Inc. filed a motion to intervene for the purpose of having information in the Bridgestone/Firestone case removed from the confidential "reading room." Even though the court noted that 6.5 million tires were recalled on August 9, 2000, and that congressional hearings had been held concerning the tires, the court refused to allow public access to the documents. The court drew a distinction between documents filed with the court and documents that had simply been produced in discovery. While it held that a court has a special obligation to the public, it held that when the parties stipulate to secrecy, the intervening press should be allowed to argue for disclosure only if one of the parties seeks to have discovery information disclosed or seeks the intervention of the court.

Is this an abdication of responsibility by the court? What is the role of the court in a case of a defective or dangerous product when litigants have no incentive to disclose the information? Do the parties have any incentive to seek disclosure? . . . Who advocates for the public when the news media is not even aware of an issue? With increasingly busy court dockets, is this an additional task heaped on the courts that will further slow the judicial process? Should courts second-guess attorneys and litigants who know more about their disputes? . . . Didn't the companies have the right to try to fix the problems they discovered through these claims without being hounded by the press? Did the attorneys for the companies have an obligation to notice a trend . . . ? If so, when did that obligation arise? After the tenth claim? The hundredth claim? Should the plaintiffs' attorneys, in an effort to recognize the public interest of the litigation, advise their clients not to accept a settlement because it has a confidentiality provision?

NOTES

Could a rule of professional responsibility solve these ethical quandaries? One of the authors of this volume thinks so, and has proposed a modification to the ABA Model Rules.[21]

On the other hand, shouldn't litigants have a reasonable expectation of privacy, particularly when they opt *voluntarily* to resolve a matter in mediation, without the assistance of the court system? One of the strongest benefits of alternative dispute resolution is that it assists parties in the resolution of their disputes while also affording them strict confidentiality of *all* proceedings. This provides a safe harbor for parties to take risks without fear of public exposure. Parties contractually bind themselves to arbitration to assure the highest degree of confidentiality, as well as more control over the triers of fact and the forum in which the case will be heard. Others voluntarily opt for mediation largely because of these same confidentiality considerations.

Many criticize the idea of forcing litigants to reveal information that they have stipulated be kept secret; they argue this will discourage early settlement of their disputes. How does involving the court system change this? Should parties' stipulations ever trump the public's right of access to court documents? How attenuated can health and safety issues be as a factor in making these determinations? The following excerpt explains the argument in favor of the private resolution of disputes.

ARTHUR R. MILLER, CONFIDENTIALITY, PROTECTIVE ORDERS AND PUBLIC ACCESS TO THE COURTS
105 Harvard Law Review 427 (1991)[22]

Litigants do not give up their privacy rights simply because they have walked, voluntarily or involuntarily, through the courthouse door. Yet precisely such a surrender of privacy can often result from litigation. The mere payment of a filing fee entitles a plaintiff to compel production of intensely personal and confidential information, such as medical records, marital information, religious documents, financial records, and even trade secrets or intellectual property. The defendant, of course, can respond in kind. The loss

---

[21] The rule has been published in several articles. *See, e.g.*, Richard A. Zitrin, *The Case Against Secret Settlements (Or What You Don't Know Can Hurt You)*, 2 J. INST. FOR STUDY OF LEGAL ETHICS 115 (1999).

[22] Copyright © 1991 by Harvard Law Review. All rights reserved.

of privacy through litigation is compounded when the information is disclosed to the media, competitors, political adversaries, and even curious members of the public.

The rulemakers who crafted our broad discovery regime to promote the disposition of civil disputes on their merits never intended that rights of privacy or confidentiality be destroyed in the process. The broad discovery procedures in the Federal Rules were designed solely to improve the dispute resolution system. The drafters had no intention of using these procedures to undermine privacy; nor were they expanding discovery in the name of promoting public access to information.

Courts exist to serve private parties bringing a private dispute. Courts are designed to resolve disputes, not to be information ombudsmen.

NOTES

Professor Miller suggests that the need for greater public access has been exaggerated. He opposes reforms that allow greater public access, and argues that heightening this access would wreak havoc on the efficient functioning of the litigation process and jeopardize personal and commercial interests. Is this true? Or might there be efficiency *and* public access? Miller suggests that if the judge's discretion to issue protective orders becomes undercut, the only way to maintain parties' privacy might be to deny discovery altogether. Is this a valid conclusion?

A few states have responded to secrecy by enacting "sunshine in litigation" laws: legislation or court rules that recognize the importance of public access.

Florida, Texas, and Washington have the strongest laws, but only Washington's makes an attorney's failure to comply a disciplinary violation. Perhaps the strongest "sunshine in litigation" law is Texas Rule of Civil Procedure 76(a), which affects filed and *unfiled* court documents, including documents produced pursuant to discovery requests that never go to court. Passed in 1990 by a 4-3 vote of the Texas Supreme Court with the staunch support of then-associate justice Lloyd Doggett, the rule has been seen by some as a model for other jurisdictions interested in open court records.

"That judicial records should be open to public inspection is not a novel idea," wrote Justice Doggett in 1991.[23] "As expressed by Justice Tom Clark, 'The principle that justice cannot survive behind walls of silence has long been reflected in the Anglo-American distrust for secret trials.'" Doggett noted that "greater access to civil justice records promotes health and safety for the public," and argued that "by presuming open access by the public, the rule strengthens democracy." Concluded Doggett: "To close a court to public scrutiny of the proceedings is to shut off the light of the law."

What do you think about these widely divergent opinions?

---

[23] Lloyd Doggett & Michael J. Mucchetti, *Public Access to Public Courts*, 69 Tex. L. Rev. 643 (1991).

SUPPLEMENTAL READINGS

1. Barbara Ashley Phillips, *Mediation: Did We Get It Wrong?*, 33 Willamette L. Rev. 649 (1997), discusses whether courts and lawyers will remain at the center of civil dispute resolution, and how much of the stage they will have to share with those from other disciplines.

2. For an overview of proposed standards of conduct for mediators see John D. Feerick, *Toward Uniform Standards of Conduct for Mediators*, 38 S. Tex. L. Rev. 455 (May 1997).

3. Pamela A. Kentra, *Hear No Evil, See No Evil, Speak No Evil: The Intolerable Conflict for Attorney-Mediators Between the Duty to Maintain Mediation Confidentiality and the Duty to Report Fellow Attorney Misconduct*, 1997 B.Y.U. L. Rev. 715 (1997), and Monica L. Warmbrod, *Comment: Could an Attorney Face Disciplinary Actions or Even Legal Malpractice for Failure to Inform Clients of Alternative Dispute Resolution?*, 27 Cumb. L. Rev. 791 (1997), are two excellent pieces analyzing this increasingly-discussed issue involving mediators who wear two different hats.

4. Of the many articles on power disparities in mediation, perhaps the most important are those by Tina Grillo. Two of Grillo's pieces are *The Mediation Alternative: Process Dangers for Women*, 100 Yale L.J. 1545 (1991), and "Respecting the Struggle: Following the Parties' Lead," 13 *Mediation Q.* 279 (1996). These articles evaluate the mediation process as it affects relatively unempowered women, especially in domestic cases.

5. Diversity awareness and recognition that cultural differences can profoundly affect a mediation's outcome are also important factors to consider. Two articles in the Summer 1999 *Mediation Quarterly* address this issue: Howard H. Irving, Michael Benjamin, and Jose San-Pedro, "Family Mediation and Cultural Diversity: Mediating with Latino Families," Vol. 16, at 325 and Cherise D. Hariston, "African Americans in Mediation Literature: A Neglected Population," Vol. 16, at 357.

6. Opposite sides of the secrecy coin are represented by Richard J. Vangelisti, *Proposed Amendment to Federal Rule of Civil Procedure 26(c) Concerning Protective Orders: A Critical Analysis of What It Means and How It Operates*, 48 Baylor L. Rev. 163 (1996), discussing the debate about the availability and scope of protective orders, and Wayne Brazil, *Protecting the Confidentiality of Settlement Negotiations*, 39 Hastings L.J. 955 (July 1988), which makes the case for why settlement negotiations should be protected as confidential. Two of the authors of this volume have written a chapter on secret settlements for their book *The Moral Compass of the American Lawyer* (1999), and modified part of that chapter in two articles, one of which focused on an explosive case involving secrecy and Prozac. Richard Zitrin & Carol M. Langford, The Moral Compass: Hide & Secrets II — The Louisville Prozac Trial, *Law News Network* (on-line magazine) and American Lawyer Media, April 1999. The proposed rule of professional conduct prohibiting secret settlements, discussed in Section 11 is discussed in Richard A. Zitrin, *Why the Laudable South Carolina Rules Must Be Broadened*, 55 S. C. L. Rev. 883 (2004), and *The Case Against Secret Settlements (Or What You Don't Know Can Hurt You)*, 2 J. Inst. for Study of Legal Ethics 115 (1999), among other places.

7. An excellent objective review of the status of secrecy agreements in the courts is contained in Laurie Kratky Doré, *Secrecy by Consent: The Use and Limits of Confidentiality in the Pursuit of Settlement*, 74 Notre Dame L. Rev. 283 (1999). For an excellent bibliography of the literature in the area and a catalogue of state regulations, see The Roscoe Pound Institute monograph "Materials on Secrecy Practices in the Courts" (July 2000).

Chapter 8

THE SPECIAL PROBLEMS OF THE GOVERNMENT LAWYER

PROBLEM 22

The job of the prosecutor comes with special responsibilities. Prosecutors have what many consider a quasi-judicial function, in that they are the ones who decide what to investigate, whom to charge and what to charge. They also must balance their advocacy with their other role — a seeker of justice. In most states, there are special rules which specifically address their conduct. All prosecutors, after all, whether deputy district attorneys or state or federal justice department employees, are lawyers licensed to practice in their particular jurisdictions. But in recent years some have questioned whether prosecutors' conduct is subject to the same scrutiny as that of their colleagues in the private sector. These issues raise questions about the seemingly ever-increasing power that prosecutors wield.

Must a Prosecutor Play by Different Rules?

I. Heather Hunt is the district attorney of the City and County of Metropolis. When Hunt won election, she did it with a pledge to concentrate on violent crimes. Part of her "priorities pledge" was a promise not to prosecute anyone on "simple loitering" charges, so long as the individual was not otherwise disturbing the peace. In the three years since Hunt's election, despite the increasing presence of the homeless in several areas of Metropolis, the district attorney's office has not prosecuted loitering cases. Police have done no more than occasionally moving or breaking up larger gatherings of homeless.

Is Hunt's refusal to prosecute loitering cases proper? Why, or why not?

II. The Mission District is a pleasant middle class residential neighborhood. Recently, the Mission District Safe Neighborhood Coalition met with Hunt to complain about an influx of homeless in Mission Park and the nearby Town Square shopping mall. The coalition complained that the park is no longer comfortable for the families and kids who live in the neighborhood. The Town Square representatives showed how their businesses are losing money. Hunt orders her charging deputies to send out the word to police that her office will enforce the loitering statute in Town Square and Mission Park but will continue its prior policy in all other areas of the city.

QUESTIONS

1. Is this an appropriate exercise of prosecutorial discretion or an improper selective enforcement of the laws?

2. What if the state's highest court had recently upheld the loitering statute in a case involving the homeless?

3. What if the loitering statute was in disuse not because Heather chose not to enforce it, but because it had not been enforced by anyone in the state for 50 years?

4. Suppose again that the loitering statute has been in disuse for the last 50 years. Suppose, too, that Hunt receives a report that reputed drug lord Leonard Sheldon is in Metropolis to organize and take over much of the city's drug trade. May Hunt tell the police chief that her office would prosecute Sheldon for anything, including loitering? Is this use of the loitering statute proper?

III. Michael Stone is a trial deputy in the district attorney's Serious Crime Unit. Metropolis police Inspector Ronald Rico of the robbery detail approaches Mike and asks him to charge Benjamin Sisk for the robbery of Whit Moore. Last week, Moore was robbed by a young black male after he withdrew money from an automatic teller machine. Three days later, Moore was having a drink in a local bar across town, The Lucky 7, when Sisk walked in. Moore, sure that Sisk was the man who robbed him, called the police, and Sisk was arrested.

Rico puts Sisk in a lineup, at which Moore makes a positive identification. Moore is a 57-year-old white male with poor eyesight, though he was wearing his glasses at the time of the robbery. He admits to having had two drinks in the bar before Sisk walked in. After the robbery, Moore had described the robber as a black male in his early twenties, muscular, short black hair, moustache, between 6'1" and 6'3" tall. This description fits Sisk, except that he is 5'11."

Stone knows he has enough to charge Sisk, but harbors some doubts. First, he checks Sisk out, and finds that he is a longtime resident of the city, he has had one adult arrest, three years ago at age 19, for disturbing the peace, and no convictions. Sisk has held the same job for the past 18 months, as a supermarket checker. Second, Stone wonders about the size discrepancy in the description, which, though not enormous, could be significant. Third, although Metropolis has a large black population, Moore, who two years before moved from a small town in the Midwest, has apparently had little close exposure to African-Americans and has no black friends. Stone is concerned that Moore's "i.d." may possibly have been unintentionally motivated by the coincidence of seeing a black man of similar looks and attire to the robber in the bar just a few days later.

QUESTIONS

1. Should Stone file robbery charges against Sisk? Which of Stone's musings, above, is appropriate for him to consider?

2. Suppose Stone decides to talk directly to Moore, and Moore seems certain of his identification. How should this affect Mike's decision?

3. Suppose Rico had previously arrested Sisk's brother on similar robbery charges two years ago. Should Stone consider this fact in deciding whether to charge Sisk?

4. Assume that Rico unlawfully searches Sisk's apartment in violation of state and federal search and seizure laws, and finds Moore's driver's license

inside the apartment. Should Stone take this evidence into account in deciding whether to charge Sisk, even though he knows the evidence will be excluded at trial?

5. Suppose deputy DA Peter Sling is assigned the case for trial. After reviewing the file, Sling harbors significant doubts about Sisk's guilt. In light of this, would it be appropriate for Peter to dismiss the case? What about offering Sisk a better plea bargain? If Sisk turns down the deal, proclaiming his innocence, may Peter argue at trial the absolute accuracy of Moore's "i.d.," even if he himself is not convinced?

READINGS

1. Are a Prosecutor's Ethical Standards Different? Prosecutors, we are often reminded, are not merely advocates but objective administrators of the criminal justice system. As such, they should be held to a different — indeed, a *higher* — ethical standard than the average advocate, since their duty is "to seek justice, not merely to convict."[1]

This dual function manifests itself in some important respects. District attorneys and U.S. attorneys have enormous discretion in deciding whether a case should be filed; under which criminal statutes it should be filed; whom it should be filed against (and what other individuals should be given immunity); and how certain criminal statutes should be applied. They also have discretion to determine when a case is appropriate for prosecution, and whether it warrants a plea negotiation. Eventually, at trial, they turn into advocates, whose ego drive and desire to win are every bit as strong as any other advocate's — and, generally, whose belief in the correctness of their position is honestly and deeply held.

With this dual role come some special responsibilities, both of constitutional[2] and ethical dimension, such as Model Rule 3.8, which enumerates a series of special requirements for prosecutors. Some of those special responsibilities have been defined by the ABA's specific standards for prosecutors, selected portions of which are set forth below.[3]

---

[1] ABA Standards Relating to the Administration of Criminal Justice, 3-1.2(c), adopting language from *Berger v. United States*, 295 U.S. 78, 55 S. Ct. 629 (1935).

[2] See *Brady v. Maryland*, 373 U.S. 83, 83 S. Ct. 1194 (1963), and *United States v. Bagley*, 473 U.S. 667, 105 S. Ct. 3375 (1985), on the requirement to turn over exculpatory evidence.

[3] The ABA has developed standards for lawyers on both sides of the criminal law fence. We looked at the criminal defense standard on perjury in Problem 15.

AMERICAN BAR ASSOCIATION STANDARDS FOR CRIMINAL JUSTICE
(3d ed. 1992)[4]

Standard 3-1.2 The Function of the Prosecutor

(a) The office of prosecutor is charged with responsibility for prosecutions in its jurisdiction.

(b) The prosecutor is an administrator of justice, an advocate, and an officer of the court; the prosecutor must exercise sound discretion in the performance of his or her functions.

(c) The duty of the prosecutor is to seek justice, not merely to convict.

(d) It is an important function of the prosecutor to seek to reform and improve the administration of criminal justice. When inadequacies or injustices in the substantive or procedural law come to the prosecutor's attention, he or she should stimulate efforts for remedial action.

Standard 3-2.8 Relations With the Courts and Bar

(e) A prosecutor should strive to develop good working relationships with defense counsel in order to facilitate the resolution of ethical problems. In particular, a prosecutor should assure defense counsel that if counsel finds it necessary to deliver physical items which may be relevant to a pending case or investigation to the prosecutor, the prosecutor will not offer the fact of such delivery by defense counsel as evidence before a jury for purposes of establishing defense counsel's client's culpability. . . .

Standard 3-3.1 Investigative Function of Prosecutor

(d) A prosecutor should not discourage or obstruct communication between prospective witnesses and defense counsel. A prosecutor should not advise any person or cause any person to be advised to decline to give to the defense information which such person has the right to give.

(e) A prosecutor should not secure the attendance of persons for interviews by use of any communication which has the appearance or color of a subpoena or similar judicial process unless the prosecutor is authorized by law to do so.

Standard 3-3.4 Decision to Charge

(c) The prosecutor should establish standards and procedures for evaluating complaints to determine whether criminal proceedings should be instituted.

Standard 3-3.6 Quality and Scope of Evidence Before Grand Jury

(a) A prosecutor should only make statements or arguments to the grand jury and only present evidence to the grand jury which the prosecutor believes is appropriate or authorized under law for presentation to the grand jury. . . .

(b) No prosecutor should knowingly fail to disclose to the grand jury evidence which tends to negate guilt or mitigate the offense.

(c) A prosecutor should recommend that the grand jury not indict if he or she believes the evidence presented does not warrant an indictment under governing law.

Standard 3-3.9 Discretion in the Charging Decision

(a) A prosecutor should not institute, or cause to be instituted, or permit the continued pendency of criminal charges when the prosecutor knows that the charges are not supported by probable cause. A prosecutor should not institute, cause to be instituted, or permit the continued pendency of criminal charges in the absence of sufficient admissible evidence to support a conviction.

(b) The prosecutor is not obliged to present all charges which the evidence might support. The prosecutor may in some circumstances and for good cause consistent with the public interest decline to prosecute, notwithstanding that sufficient evidence may exist which would support a conviction. Illustrative of the factors which the prosecutor may properly consider in exercising his or her discretion are:

   (i)   the prosecutor's reasonable doubt that the accused is in fact guilty;

   (ii)   the extent of the harm caused by the offense;

   (iii) the disproportion of the authorized punishment in relation to the particular offense or the offender;

   (iv)   possible improper motives of a complainant;

   (v)   reluctance of the victim to testify;

   (vi)   cooperation of the accused in the apprehension or conviction of others; and

   (vii) availability and likelihood of prosecution by another jurisdiction.

(c) A prosecutor should not be compelled by his or her supervisor to prosecute a case in which he or she has a reasonable doubt about the guilt of the accused.

(d) In making the decision to prosecute, the prosecutor should give no weight to the personal or political advantages or disadvantages which might be involved or to a desire to enhance his or her record of convictions.

(e) In cases which involve a serious threat to the community, the prosecutor should not be deterred from prosecution by the fact that in the jurisdiction juries have tended to acquit persons accused of the particular kind of criminal act in question.

(f) The prosecutor should not bring or seek charges greater in number or degree than can reasonably be supported with evidence at trial or than are necessary to fairly reflect the gravity of the offense.

Standard 3-3.11 Disclosure of Evidence by the Prosecutor

(a) A prosecutor should not intentionally fail to make timely disclosure to the defense, at the earliest feasible opportunity, of the existence of all evidence or information which tends to negate the guilt of the accused or mitigate the offense charged or which would tend to reduce the punishment of the accused.

Standard 3-4.1 Availability for Plea Discussions

(a) The prosecutor should have and make known a general policy or willingness to consult with defense counsel concerning disposition of charges by plea.

(c) A prosecutor should not knowingly make false statements or representation as to fact or law in the course of plea discussions with defense counsel or the accused.

Standard 3-4.2 Fulfillment of Plea Discussions

(a) A prosecutor should not make any promise or commitment assuring a defendant or defense counsel that a court will impose a specific sentence or a suspension of sentence; a prosecutor may properly advise the defense what position will be taken concerning disposition.

(b) A prosecutor should not imply a greater power to influence the disposition of a case than is actually possessed.

Standard 3-5.7 Examination of Witnesses

(a) The interrogation of all witnesses should be conducted fairly, objectively, and with due regard for the dignity and legitimate privacy of the witness . . . and without seeking to intimidate or humiliate the witness unnecessarily.

(b) The prosecutor's belief that the witness is telling the truth does not preclude cross-examination, but may affect the method and scope of cross-examination. A prosecutor should not use the power of cross-examination to discredit or undermine a witness if the prosecutor knows the witness is testifying truthfully.

Standard 3-6.1 Role in Sentencing

(a) The prosecutor should not make the severity of sentences the index of his or her effectiveness. To the extent that the prosecutor becomes involved in the sentencing process, he or she should seek to assure that a fair and informed judgment is made on the sentence and avoid unfair sentence disparities.

NOTES

These ABA standards pay more than lip service to the notion that the prosecutor's role is special. Note that some of these rules set different standards for prosecutors than would be applied to other advocates. For example, Standard 3-2.8(b) talks about the *appearance* of a proper relationship, echoing the old "appearance of impropriety" standard that the Model Rules have generally abandoned. Another example is Standard 3-5.7(b), which admonishes prosecutors that they should not use cross-examination to impeach a witness known to be telling the truth. This is in direct contrast to the ethical rules — and the vast weight of authority — that pertain to criminal defense counsel, as we saw in Problem 14.

Some would suggest that the existing standards for prosecutors have failed to diminish prosecutor misconduct. Richard Rosen's research found that disciplinary charges have been "brought infrequently under the applicable rules and that the meaningful sanctions have been applied only rarely."[5] Professor Bennett L. Gershman, a former deputy district attorney who served on the front lines and as special assistant to New York State's attorney general and has written frequently about prosecutors, reported that he reviewed "[l]iterally hundreds of truly egregious instances of prosecutorial misconduct," none of which resulted in punishment of the prosecutor by either his superiors or the bar.[6]

Despite the specifics of prosecution standards, they have not been fully codified in most jurisdictions, making their proscriptions and requirements largely advisory. Note that the standards themselves have not been amended at all in the last decade, leaving one to wonder about the extent of their continued vitality. Without these standards having the "force of law," how well is the conduct of prosecutors actually regulated?

It has been suggested that often, the criminal justice system relies on the personal integrity of the district attorney. This is, of course, most irrevocably true in death penalty cases. In May 2000, the *New York Times* published a detailed evaluation of executions of Texas death row prisoners. A sidebar article focused on five specific cases in which criminal defendants of questionable culpability were executed, and concluded that overzealous prosecutors were largely to blame.[7] Article 2.0.1 of the Texas Code of Criminal Procedure codifies ABA Standard 3-1.2(c): "It shall be the primary duty of all prosecuting attorneys, including any special prosecutors, not to convict, but to see that justice is done." Nevertheless, at least in Texas, as one parole board member who voted against an execution told the *Times*, "if the prosecutor doesn't have integrity, there won't be justice."

2. The District Attorney in Trial. Before we look at how some prosecutors conduct themselves in trial, it is important to recognize that saying a prosecutor must be both advocate and seeker of justice is a lot easier than doing it. Famed death penalty defense attorney (and former prosecutor) Anthony Amsterdam put it this way: Two adversaries in trial are like two prize-fighters; "Consider how very difficult it is for any human being to stand in the ring getting pummeled by left jabs and right hooks from an adversary whose avowed, legitimate and obvious purpose is to knock the hell out of you . . . and in that atmosphere to remember that your goal is not to strike back

---

[5] Richard A. Rosen, *Disciplinary Sanctions Against Prosecutors for Brady Violations: A Paper Tiger,* 65 N.C. L. Rev. 693 (1987).

[6] Bennett L. Gershman, Prosecutorial Misconduct 13-2 n.4 (6th ed. 1991).

[7] Raymond Bonner & Sara Rimer, *On the Record: Capital Punishment in Texas* and *A Closer Look at Five Cases That Resulted in Executions of Texas Inmates,* N.Y. Times, May 14, 2000.

. . . but rather to do justice. . . ." One's instinct, says Amsterdam, is "to hit back first and worry about doing justice later."[8]

While this may help us understand the difficult task prosecutors face, many observers believe that prosecutors' behavior in trial is directly due to the fact that their conduct is largely unencumbered by either court scrutiny or external ethical checks. Read the following article about a top-notch Chicago prosecutor, one of the few to be criticized by the appellate courts.

KEN ARMSTRONG & MAURICE POSSLEY, REVERSAL OF FORTUNE, TRIAL & ERROR: HOW PROSECUTORS SACRIFICE JUSTICE TO WIN
Chicago Tribune (January 13, 1999)[9]

On a weekday afternoon one year ago, in a conference room 39 floors above LaSalle Street, two men sat at opposite ends of a long oval table ringed by a dozen lawyers and a court reporter.

At one end was Dennis Williams, a man who had spent much of his life in prison, awaiting execution. At the other was Scott Arthur, the prosecutor who put him there.

It was a moment 20 years in the making. Williams, now exonerated, was seeking financial retribution for a life lost to Death Row. And Arthur, now in private practice, was under oath, forced to answer the sort of hardball questions he usually relished firing at others. Do you have a criminal record? Were you ever suspended? Did you cut secret deals with witnesses?

The confrontation arose from a lawsuit filed by Williams and three other men, now known as the Ford Heights 4, alleging that sheriff's deputies framed them for a gang rape and a double murder in 1978. Although he is not a defendant, prosecutors are immune from such lawsuits, Arthur has been the one constant at the prosecution table in three trials over nine years. In many ways, he personified the miscarriage of justice that imprisoned the Ford Heights 4.

But on this afternoon, questioned as a witness in the still pending lawsuit, Arthur offered no apologies, second thoughts or self-doubts about the prosecution he helped lead.

"Sitting here today, Mr. Arthur, do you believe that any of the Ford Heights 4, Willie Rainge, Kenny Adams, Verneal Jimerson and Dennis Williams, had any involvement in the murders of Larry Lionberg and Carol Schmal?" asked one of Jimerson's attorneys.

"Yes," Arthur said. "I think they did."

Arthur clings to his belief even though other men have confessed; even though DNA tests implicated one of those who confessed and eliminated

---

[8] Amsterdam, now a New York University law professor, made these remarks at a December 1986 retreat of the Association of the Bar of the City of New York. The remarks were reported by ethics professor Stephen Gillers in *The Prosecution and Defense Functions: Do They Promote Justice?*, 42 THE RECORD OF THE ASS'N OF THE BAR OF THE CITY OF N.Y. 626, reprinted by Professor Gillers in his book REGULATION OF LAWYERS: PROBLEMS OF LAW AND ETHICS, now in its fifth edition.

[9] Copyright © 1999 by Chicago Tribune. Used by permission. All rights reserved.

Williams and his friends as suspects; even though prosecution witnesses have either recanted or been discredited, and the scientific evidence at the trial exposed as bunk; even though Williams and his friends have received pardons from the governor and apologies from the state's attorney's office.

When Arthur looked down that long oval table at Williams, he still saw a murderer. When Williams stared back, he saw the man who wanted him executed for a crime he did not commit.

Since 1963, at least 381 people in the United States have had a homicide conviction reversed because prosecutors engaged in the worst kind of deception — withholding evidence favorable to a defendant or allowing witnesses to lie. Jimerson is one of those defendants. His conviction was reversed because Scott Arthur allowed his star witness to lie, according to an Illinois Supreme Court ruling.

. . . . As a prosecutor — the lawyer for the people — Arthur was, in many ways, a lawyer the people could be proud of . . . . Many of the defendants Arthur put away were monstrous criminals who generated little sympathy and whose guilt few doubted. In 1982, Arthur prosecuted Edgar Hope Jr. on a charge of murdering a police officer. After winning a conviction, Arthur asked jurors to sentence Hope to death. Pacing around the courtroom, Arthur pointed to all the Chicago police officers packed into the gallery, then grabbed the murder weapon and waved it at the jurors.

"This gun is talking to you. What it says is worth more than 10,000 words. It killed a man who wears this badge," Arthur said, picking up the victim's police star.

The jury returned a sentence of death, and the courtroom erupted in cheers and shouts of congratulation.

But 10 years later, that moment lost its luster. The Illinois Supreme Court granted Hope a new trial, ruling that Arthur and his trial partner had improperly excluded African-Americans from the jury. Hope had to be retried, reopening emotional wounds and taxing public resources. [Eventually the Illinois Supreme Court vacated Hope's death sentence.]

Other courtroom victories of Arthur's also evaporated on appeal because he and his trial partners broke the rules of a fair trial, allowing a key witness to lie, making improper arguments, or engaging in abusive behavior toward defense attorneys and witnesses. . . .

Indeed, Arthur's conduct in [one] case was so egregious that it became a touchstone used by appellate courts in evaluating other prosecutors' behavior. The case has been cited more than 100 times in published appellate rulings, although they do not name Arthur. In the protective atmosphere of the legal world, lawyers who behave badly usually remain anonymous.

NOTES

Note that even in the cases involving Scott Arthur's egregious conduct, the courts not only did not discipline him but assiduously *avoided using his name* — an unfortunate practice but an all-too-common occurrence when courts address prosecutorial abuse.[10] "Prosecutors today wield greater power, engage in more egregious misconduct, and are less subject to judicial or bar association oversight than ever before," wrote Professor Gershman in 1992.[11] Gershman details how prosecutors use a series of trial tricks that he considers ethically suspect, but notes that the offending behavior is rarely disciplined.

These tricks include character assassination and insinuation of the defendant, intentionally presenting improper evidence, arguing to the jury's prejudices, and violating the defendant's rights against self-incrimination. If a prosecutor's status lends more credibility to the attorney than the average litigator gets, do these trial tricks have more serious consequences than, for example, Honest Abe's?

One example of discipline is *In re Zawada*, 92 P.3d 862 (Ariz. 2004). There, the Arizona Supreme Court suspended a prosecutor who had a history of misconduct for his actions in a trial involving an insanity defense. Without any basis in fact, Zawada attacked the testimony of six psychiatrists who testified on insanity, including the state's witnesses. Among other things, he accused the defense of fabricating testimony by paying off the experts. The defendant's conviction was reversed. The court described Zawada as "single-handedly responsible for much of the law in Arizona on . . . extreme prosecutorial misconduct." Zawada's actual suspension was for six months. This prosecutor was both named and disciplined, in contrast to some circumstances described in this Problem. But given the extraordinarily egregious nature of the misconduct and the prosecutor's history, do you think the six months suspension was adequate? What should courts do in such extreme situations?

3. Prosecutorial Discretion and Selective Prosecution. Prosecutorial discretion is necessary. It is impossible to prosecute every individual for every crime committed. And a certain amount of selective prosecution is appropriate as well — choosing to file charges against Smith while declining them against Jones, for articulable and judicious reasons.

But when does prosecutorial discretion become an abuse of power, and selective prosecution become discriminatory enforcement? In the late 1960s and into the 1970s, as the ABA made its first efforts to codify ethical rules for prosecutors, there was a wide-ranging debate about the appropriate level of discretion. Standard 3-3.9, which articulates the criteria for prosecutorial discretion in charging a crime, gives considerable leeway to the prosecutor's subjective evaluation of circumstances. This rule has remained the standard since its formation.

Should the standard have added language to regulate prosecutors' conduct in selectively charging and prosecuting? Professor Monroe Freedman has long argued that the decision to prosecute should not be based on personal vendetta or personal bias. To bolster his argument, Freedman cited Justice Robert Jackson, a former United States Attorney General, who spoke often on the duties of the moral prosecutor: "Picking the man and then searching the law books or putting investigators to work, to pin some offense on him" is wrong,

---

[10] See generally the discussion of this practice *ad passim* in EDWARD HUMES, MEAN JUSTICE (1999).

[11] *Tricks Prosecutors Play*, TRIAL, April 1992.

because it allows the prosecutor to decide whom to investigate based on personal biases. Freedman cited *Yick Wo v. Hopkins*, 118 U.S. 356, 6 S. Ct. 1064 (1886), the constitutional law case read by practically every law student, which holds that it was discriminatory to deny permits for laundries in wooden buildings only to Chinese, and then prosecute them for violating the ordinance. He quotes *Yick Wo* about a law "fair on its face" but applied "by public authority with an evil eye and an unequal hand."

Then, stretching it one step further, Freedman argued that Robert Kennedy's effort to prosecute and convict Jimmy Hoffa — complete, he points out, with a team Kennedy called the "Get-Hoffa squad" — was wrong because it was motivated by Hoffa's personal insults. The young Attorney General's efforts, claimed Freedman, meant that "satisfying [Kennedy's] grudge became the public policy of the United States."[12]

On the other hand, Prof. Richard Uviller, writing in 1973 at about the time the standard was proposed,[13] and current commentators evaluating the leeway needed by special prosecutors such as Kenneth Starr in the Whitewater controversy, have argued that prosecutors *should* be able to consider the particular individual being scrutinized. Uviller noted that all prosecutors would consider an individual's personal character and prior record in determining a plea bargain. Why not then, he argued, in deciding whom to investigate? Many who defended the lengths to which Starr went to investigate and seek prosecution of President Bill Clinton for the Monica Lewinsky affair make a similar argument: The fact that Clinton was the president made it especially important to the public interest that he be held accountable. Others, of course, saw Starr's actions as nothing but vendetta — a more extreme version of Freedman's take on Robert Kennedy.

We will return to examine Starr's role as independent counsel more closely. For the moment, we remain focused on the "real world" problems of prosecutorial discretion and selective enforcement that occur every day in district attorneys' offices throughout the country. Below are four specific examples, the first involving broad policy questions and large numbers of people, the second involving selecting one particular person to investigate, the third involving selecting one particular person *not* to charge, and the final example being the compelling story of a 12-year-old murder defendant and the prosecutor who wanted both a conviction on the maximum charge and lenient sentence for a penalty.

San Francisco's Homeless. First, we turn to San Francisco, which like many cities across the country, has faced an increasingly difficult problem of how to deal with the homeless. A subsection of California's trespassing statute prohibits lodging "in any building, structure, vehicle, or place, whether public or private, without the permission of the owner . . . ." In early 1991, San Francisco's police commission decided on new guidelines to enforce this subsection, including permitting the arrest of anyone "settling in a public place for more than a momentary or brief stop. . . ."

---

[12] LAWYERS' ETHICS IN AN ADVERSARY SYSTEM 81-83 (1975).

[13] *The Virtuous Prosecutor in Quest of an Ethical Standard: Guidance from the ABA*, 71 U. MICH. L. REV. 1145 (1973).

Some of San Francisco's homeless had been congregating for some time in the park across from City Hall, which then served as the city's main courthouse. Under the new guidelines, police could evenhandedly apply the law to arrest a homeless person sitting on a park bench and a court clerk eating a lunchtime sandwich by the park's fountain. But arresting both was clearly not the result desired. The alternative was to distinguish between the homeless person and the court clerk, resulting in a pattern of selective enforcement. The district attorney eventually concluded that this particular code section was not the best way to address the homeless problem.

Celebrity Justice? Marion Barry, Martha Stewart, and George Ryan. Second, we examine whether celebrity can result in selective prosecution. In 1990, Washington, D.C. Mayor Marion Barry found himself the focus of federal agents who mounted a sting operation against him. The government went to substantial lengths to set its trap, including the use of a false "friend" who overtly encouraged him to use drugs. Barry was videotaped using "crack" cocaine, and then arrested. Many felt that had Barry been anyone other than the mayor, and a rather controversial one, the sting operation never would have occurred, or at least never would have gone to such lengths to encourage his criminal behavior. Some argued that the sting had more to do with the federal prosecutors' political dislike of Barry than his actual drug use. But federal authorities argued that any lengths within the bounds of the law were appropriate when the alleged drug user is none other than the mayor of the nation's capital.

Barry eventually pled guilty to reduced charges.[14] By 1994, declaring himself rehabilitated, Barry, made a stunning political comeback, winning reelection as mayor. But was it fair to single him out for prosecution in the first place?

Then we have the case of Martha Stewart, sent to prison for crimes many felt would not have been prosecuted had she not been a celebrity. Did prosecutors use her as a "poster child" to warn off others? If so, did her name recognition justify making Stewart an example of what can happen when insider trading takes place, or was it selective and thus unfair?

Former Illinois Governor George Ryan commuted the sentences of all Illinois death row inmates in 2003 as he was leaving the Governor's office. In 2006, he was convicted of racketeering, fraud, lying, and obstruction for acts done between 1991 and 2003. Some argued he was the epitome of the corrupt Illinois politician while others have suggested he did nothing out of the ordinary and that his prosecution was related to his death penalty commutations.

"Butch" Hallinan and the Singleton *Case.* Should selective *avoidance* of enforcement be permitted as legitimate prosecutorial discretion? May a prosecutor let a criminal defendant free, or offer a sweet plea arrangement or sentence reduction in exchange for testimony? Clearly, this happens all the time. Supposedly, the deal is offered to someone whom the prosecutor sees as being less of a threat to society. But can this discretion also be abused?

---

[14] This plea itself caused some controversy, in that it was conditioned on Barry's resignation as mayor.

Take the widely-reported case of Patrick "Butch" Hallinan, a well-known San Francisco lawyer whose brother served as the city's district attorney.[15] The U.S. Attorney in Reno, Nevada indicted Hallinan in 1993 for allegedly conspiring with his drug-lord client, Ciro Mancuso, to assist in Mancuso's criminal enterprise. The chief prosecution witness? Mancuso himself, who, facing a sentence of up to 60 years, gave his expertise and testimony to the government in return for a promise of leniency. The case against Hallinan collapsed embarrassingly at trial, but Mancuso was sentenced to only nine years in prison, a vastly reduced sentence. Had Hallinan been convicted, many observers speculated Mancuso would have received little if any further time in custody.[16] Was it legitimate to argue that Mancuso posed less of a threat to society than did his lawyer?

For a brief moment in 1998, at least one court had concluded that inducing a prospective criminal defendant to become a witness by offering leniency or immunity was a violation of the federal bribery statute. "If justice is perverted when a criminal defendant seeks to buy testimony from a witness, it is no less perverted when the government does so," wrote the appeals court panel in *United States v. Singleton*, 144 F.3d 1343 (10th Cir. 1998). Within weeks, however, the Kansas prosecutors who made the leniency/immunity offers in a drug-trafficking case had successfully sought a stay. They soon got an *en banc* decision that decisively reversed the three-judge panel.[17]

The *en banc* court held that the anti-bribery statute refers to an individual offering the bribe and that an assistant U.S. attorney offering leniency is acting on behalf of the government itself. The court also implied that applying the anti-bribery statute could restrict the sovereign prosecutorial powers of the executive branch. Not everyone agreed. Georgetown law professor Paul Rothstein, who closely followed the case, told the *ABA Journal* that the original three-judge panel had correctly interpreted the bribery statute's plain meaning: "The majority opinion appears to give the words an illogical reading in order to preserve a practice it feels is necessary and desirable for law enforcement purposes."

Post 9/11 Scrutiny of Muslims and Arabs. Many have raised the issue of whether since September 11, 2001, individuals with Arab and Muslim backgrounds have been singled out for investigation, scrutiny, detention, and prosecution.

In a widely-reported case in 2004, Brandon Mayfield, a Portland attorney and convert to Islam, was arrested and detained for two weeks in connection with the 2004 terrorist bombings in Madrid. The FBI said his fingerprints had been found on a bag connected to the bombing, but the Spanish investigators disagreed and quickly ruled him out. Spain informed the FBI through official diplomatic channels that their police had linked the fingerprint to an

---

[15] See, *inter alia*, the extensive series of articles by Howard Mintz in the RECORDER (San Francisco) and by several reporters, especially Rob Haeseler of the SAN FRANCISCO CHRONICLE, from August 1993 through mid-1997.

[16] In fact, Mancuso complained in his appeal to the Ninth Circuit that he should have received a shorter sentence in light of his good efforts as an informant. See Mr. Mintz's RECORDER article of July 23, 1996, *Hallinan Witness Says He Got Less Than He Bargained For.*

[17] *United States v. Singleton*, 165 F.3d 1297 (10th Cir. 1999).

Algerian man and that Mayfield was innocent. But despite the clear evidence, the U.S. government did nothing to release Mayfield for several days.

These issues relate not only to actual allegations of terrorist activities, but to other endeavors facially irrelevant to terrorism. For example, *U.S. v. Alameh,* 341 F.3d 167 (2d Cir. 2003), involved a person of Arab ethnicity who claimed he was being selectively prosecuted for unlawful procurement of naturalization — marrying a citizen to get a green card. His lawyers argued that prior to 9/11, 85% of those prosecuted for this activity had non-Arab non-Muslim names, but after 9/11, the percentages were inverted — 85% of those prosecuted did have Arab or Muslim names. However, the court held that Alameh had failed to meet his burden of presenting sufficient evidence to warrant discovery on a selective prosecution claim.

Lionel Tate and His Prosecutor. Finally, we come to the sad irony of Lionel Tate. Lionel's case raises the issue of whether a prosecutor may file a charge for which he thinks the penalty is too severe. The case, which got a great deal of publicity due to the youth of the defendant, also raises a collateral question: What happens when a prosecutor changes opinions about the initial charges midstream?

In March 2001 in Broward County Florida, Lionel Tate, then 14, was sentenced to life without possibility of parole for the murder of a six-year-old committed when Lionel was 12. At sentencing, the prosecutors requested leniency for Lionel, and even talked afterwards about joining the defense's appeal to the governor for leniency. But the judge, Joel T. Lazarus, who imposed the full adult sentence, took that opportunity to criticize the prosecution, saying that if the state did not believe the boy deserved a life sentence, prosecutors should have tried Lionel only on lesser charges: "To talk about travel to the governor to seek a reduction in charge or sentence, if accurate, is of tremendous concern to this court. It not only casts the prosecutor in a light totally inconsistent with his role in the criminal justice system, but it makes the whole court process seem like a game. . . ."[18]

The prosecutor defended his handling of the case by saying that the severity of the crime justified trying Lionel as an adult but should have included leeway in sentencing. He also noted that the defense had summarily dismissed a generous plea bargain.[19] But should the prosecutor be allowed to seek a *conviction* resulting in the severest possible penalty and then turn around at *sentencing* to request leniency? Or was Judge Lazarus right that the prosecution should not speak out of both sides of its mouth, but go to trial only on a charge whose consequences it could accept at sentencing? Or, put another way, did the prosecution abuse its discretion by overcharging the case?

4. Abuse of Power? Inside the Beltway. There has undoubtedly been more written about the investigation and possible prosecution of President

---

[18] *See, e.g.,* Dana Canedy, *A Sentence of Life Without Parole for Boy, 14, in Murder of Girl, 6,* N.Y. TIMES, March 10, 2001, at 1.

[19] Interestingly, particularly in light of our discussion in Problem 12, Lionel's mother, a Florida state trooper, seemed to have had decisionmaking power over Lionel's plea. She rejected several offers by the prosecutors to have her son plead guilty to second-degree murder and accept a sentence of three years in a juvenile detention center and 10 years of probation.

Clinton by special prosecutor Kenneth Starr — and Clinton's subsequent impeachment and acquittal — than any other event in American legal history. We do not intend here to add to the verbiage. We do feel it is important, however, to pause briefly and examine an issue that tens of millions of Americans debated daily: Did prosecutor Starr abuse his power by the manner in which he investigated the President concerning his relationship with White House intern Monica Lewinsky?

With one exception, we don't evaluate Starr's office's conduct from the perspective of his role as independent counsel; largely as a result of Whitewater, that office no longer exists, and is unlikely to reappear any time soon. Rather, we briefly review some of Starr's office's conduct in light of the dichotomy we suggest above: Does prosecutorial discretion permit the targeting of an individual when that individual — here, a sitting President — is so vital to the public interest that higher scrutiny or broader discretionary leeway is justified? Or did the zeal applied amount to an attempt at selective prosecution — an abuse of prosecutorial discretion, under Justice Jackson's theory (as interpreted by Professor Freedman) that it is simply wrong to be "picking the man and then searching the law books, or putting investigators to work, to pin some offense on him"?[20]

The first point to consider, and the one in which Starr's role as special prosecutor *is* relevant, is that Starr was appointed for the very purpose of focusing on President Clinton and his wife Hillary Rodham Clinton. This clearly vitiates the issue of singling out an individual. On the other hand, many observers argued that Starr focused on a collateral matter (Clinton's relationship to Lewinsky) and an offense for which few, if any, ordinary citizens would be prosecuted (alleged perjury by denying a sexual relationship in a deposition in a civil matter otherwise unrelated to the prosecutorial investigation). In this respect, Starr's office may well have violated Justice Jackson's admonition not to search to "pin an offense on him."

Other than the very existence of an investigation on the collateral subject of the Lewinsky matter, Starr's office was perhaps most heavily criticized in three areas: the manner in which the investigation of Lewinsky was conducted, including her initial detention; the manner in which witnesses subpoenaed before the grand jury were treated; and the manner of Starr's testimony before Congress in the impeachment inquiry. This last issue — accusations that Starr's testimony before Congress, rather than being a neutral recitation of facts, was accusatory and prosecutorial in nature — while seemingly a reasonable interpretation, relates directly to Starr's brief as independent counsel and his and his staff's interpretation of that brief. We accordingly leave it there.

The other two issues, the treatment of Lewinsky and the treatment of witnesses (whether considered unfriendly or neutral), both relate, again, to the question of whether Starr's zealous investigative practices, given the importance of his target, justified an abrupt and sometimes peremptory prosecutorial style. St. John's University law professor John Q. Barrett, a former member of special prosecutor Lawrence Walsh's staff, has often pointed

---

[20] This is not unlike Marion Barry's case, albeit on a much grander scale.

out that every prosecutor's office allocates resources, and every prosecutor's office will be more zealous in pursuing a key witness in an alleged crime lord's case than in a routine bank robbery. Barrett's point is not only well-taken, it is accurate and even necessary.

Assume for a moment a justifiable increased scrutiny in light of the importance of Starr's investigation. It is nevertheless difficult to see how the peremptory subpoenaing of a privately-owned bookstore, Kramerbooks, for records of Lewinsky's purchases, forcing that bookstore to defend its customer's rights of privacy at its own expense, is consistent with a proper understanding of the meaning of ABA Standard 3-1.2 that the "duty of the prosecutor is to seek justice, not merely to convict."[21]

More recently, the memorandum written in substantial part by Justice Department lawyer Jay S. Bybee justifying certain acts of torture by United States personnel, came under tremendous scrutiny. We will discuss the "torture memo" in substantially greater length in Problem 25. Here we ask whether as a government prosecutor Bybee had a duty of objectivity and candor in advising the president, or whether his duties allowed him to slant the opinion letter in favor of the president's authorization of torture.

5. Abuse of Power? Outside the Beltway and Over in Colorado. Whatever one concludes about special prosecutor Starr and his staff in their handling of the Lewinsky matter, there can be little question that they had an extraordinary amount of power. This is true of most prosecutors; indeed, we will focus most of our remaining discussion on why this is so. In Starr's case, it made him, for a time, arguably the most powerful person in America. In the case of a Colorado prosecutor, the power was more fleeting but no less overwhelming.

In April 2001, a veteran prosecutor in Jefferson County, Colorado was disciplined for posing as a public defender to persuade a suspected ax murderer, who soon confessed, to surrender. The prosecutor, Chief Deputy District Attorney Mark Pautler, was unrepentant after being put on 12 months' probation but not actually suspended from practice, and appealed the disciplinary committee's 2-1 vote against him to the state Supreme Court, which unanimously upheld the discipline.[22]

"Members of our profession must adhere to the highest moral and ethical standards," said Justice Rebecca Kourlis, writing for the court.

"Those standards apply regardless of motive. Purposeful deception by an attorney licensed in our state is intolerable, even when it is undertaken as a part of attempting to secure the surrender of a murder suspect."

In July 1998, Pautler had posed as public defender "Mark Palmer" after William "Cody" Neal, suspected in a triple murder earlier the same day as

---

[21] The Kramerbooks subpoena was also widely reported. It is our understanding both from news accounts and our own unpublished sources that the bookstore was offered and accepted financial help from the American Booksellers Association, the primary association of independent booksellers, in fighting the subpoena, and that legal fees had reached several hundred thousand dollars when Lewinsky reached an immunity agreement with the special prosecutor and then consented to the bookstore's revealing a list of her purchases.

[22] *See In re* Pautler, 47 P.3d 12175 (Colo. 2002).

well as several other crimes, had been on a cell phone with investigators and insisted on speaking with a public defender. Pautler told the disciplinary panel that he didn't trust the public defenders, and that providing one was out of the question because the defense lawyer would have had to advise Neal to say nothing more.

Instead, Pautler decided that he would pose as a public defender, reasoning that only a real attorney could pull off the deception. According to Denver's *Rocky Mountain News*, "When Neal asked Pautler what his rights were, the prosecutor-turned-defense attorney dodged the question."[23] Pautler told the disciplinary panel that he had checked with his boss before acting.

Although it is certainly understandable why law enforcement officers would not want to leave a dangerous fugitive at large — Neal surrendered peacefully and many have written that Pautler deserved a medal — one wonders why the lawyers didn't let competent police officers do their job. One must also ask on what basis Pautler believed he had the authority or power to participate in such an overt lie. Indeed, the court made it clear that "noble motives" don't allow prosecutors to ignore the Rules of Professional Conduct. "[W]e are adamant that when presented with choices, at least one of which conforms to the rules, an attorney must not select an option that involves deceit or misrepresentation," wrote Justice Kourlis.

Nevertheless, Pautler remained unrepentant even after the Supreme Court ruling. "Lawyers are told not to do the right thing but to do the expedient thing to keep their license," Pautler was quoted as saying by the *Denver Post*. "I think it is more important to save lives. I think this slavish adherence to the code even though human lives are going to be lost doesn't make sense. Neal indicated he had killed literally hundreds of people, was armed and would kill again . . . . I don't know how you can minimize somebody who just killed three women."[24]

Phil Cherner, a lawyer speaking on behalf of the Colorado criminal defense bar saw it differently, telling the *Post* the ruling was an "emphatic statement that we are held to the highest responsibility and . . . [that] the rules apply to everybody, including prosecutors. I'm glad she (Kourlis) put a stop to this nonsense."

It must be noted, however, that the state's high court, while critical of Pautler's conduct, placed him on probation without requiring actual suspension.

Best-selling author and former prosecutor Scott Turow put it this way in describing Los Angeles prosecutors in the aftermath of the Rampart District scandal: "Police officers [who lie] usually just want to convict the guilty, . . . 'tightening up the case.' Thus it falls to the courts and lawyers to insist on strict adherence to all those rules that the police often regard as a pesky hindrance." Sometimes, Turow suggests, prosecutors — seen as the cops'

---

[23] Sarah Huntley, *Prosecutor Admits He Lied,* ROCKY MOUNTAIN NEWS (Denver), March 8, 2001. *See also* Marlys Duran, *Attorney Pautler appeals to state high court; He says he was right to lie to fugitive killer,* ROCKY MOUNTAIN NEWS (Denver), April 24, 2001.

[24] Howard Pankratz, *Deception By Lawyers Ruled Out Decision Stems From Attempt To Get Murder Suspect's Surrender,* DENVER POST, May 14, 2002.

lawyers — will allow the falsehoods to take place.[25] For some, it is a relatively small step from allowing lies to go forward to telling one's own lie.

Most prosecutors, to be sure, play it by the book. But why does it seem that those who take ethical risks feel that they are unlikely to be punished by the courts or disciplinary authorities? The rest of our discussion will explore that question, first by looking at whether prosecutors have to play by the same ethical rules as all other lawyers, and then by examining how, if at all, prosecutors are held accountable for their actions.

6. Must Prosecutors Play by the Same Rules? It has long been a rule of professional conduct that a lawyer may not communicate with a party represented by counsel. Every state has a rule embodying this principle, most based either on Model Rule 4.2 or old DR 7-104(A). In 1989, however, then-Attorney General Richard Thornburgh authored what became known as the Thornburgh Memorandum. This memorandum claimed that because MR 4.2 or DR 7-104(A) might interfere with legitimate law enforcement interests, federal prosecutors were not bound to follow these rules. The Thornburgh Memorandum argued that under the Supremacy Clause, states had no power to discipline federal prosecutors.

It was generally thought that the Thornburgh Memorandum was issued as a response to *United States v. Hammad*, 858 F.2d 834 (2d Cir. 1988). In *Hammad*, the court sanctioned a prosecutor for communicating with a represented individual who was being investigated for Medicaid fraud. Although the appeals court held that the prosecutor violated the rule, the court's ruling was narrow. It noted that the "authorized by law" exception found in both DR 7-104(A) and MR 4.2 would allow wide latitude to a prosecutor investigating a crime, to prevent "career criminals with permanent 'house counsel'" from forever immunizing themselves from informants.

Nevertheless, the Thornburgh Memorandum soon followed. When new Attorney General Janet Reno took over in 1993, many felt she would at least significantly qualify the Thornburgh Memorandum. She did not, and in mid-1993 published a virtually identical memorandum. Little Thornburgh memos began cropping up in various states, where prosecutors couldn't resort to the Supremacy Clause, but could still argue, persuasively, their need to engage in ongoing investigations.

One of the focuses of controversy in the Reno Memorandum was the distinction it drew between "represented parties," the words of MR 4.2 at the time, and "represented persons," the term used in the memorandum. The difference can be substantial. There are allegations, though disputed, that Kenneth Starr's staff had occasion to use this distinction in avoiding Monica Lewinsky's entreaties to speak with her lawyer during her day-long detention. The ABA, angered by prosecutors saying they were not required to abide by state ethical rules largely based on the Model Rules, first drafted a formal opinion stating that "parties" really referred to all represented persons,[26] and then actually amended Rule 4.2 to state it applied to represented "persons" rather than "parties." The battle was on.

---

[25] Scott Turow, *Lying to Get the Bad Guys,* N.Y. Times, Feb. 20, 2000.

[26] Formal Opinion 95-396, July 28, 1995.

The fight ultimately played itself out in the congressional arena. First, in 1995 Senate Judiciary Chairman Orrin Hatch co-sponsored legislation that would have exempted federal prosecutors from state ethics rules. The legislation failed. Partly in response, The Citizen Protection Act (also known as the McDade-Murtha Amendment) was drafted, passed, and went into effect in 1999.[27] This act confirmed that federal prosecutors — indeed, all government lawyers — are subject to the same professional conduct rules as all other lawyers.

The Thornburgh and Reno memoranda came in for a great deal of criticism from many quarters — state appellate courts, the American Corporate Counsel Association (ACCA), and ethics experts from all areas of the spectrum. But much of the criticism focused on points of constitutional law, concerning separation of powers, the Supremacy Clause, and the balance of power between the federal government and the states. What about the issue from a purely ethical context?

First, the extent to which prosecutors may participate directly in pre-filing prosecutorial investigations — an issue recognized by the *Hammad* court just before the controversy enflamed — is still an open question. There is no consensus as to where to draw the line between proper prosecutorial investigation and violation of ethical rules. In the last generation, federal courts have, generally speaking, expanded the power of the Justice Department and other prosecutors. Now, the states will once again decide what restrictions apply.

Finally, the Reno Memorandum insisted that a prosecutor may talk to a represented *and charged* party where there is a perceived conflict of interest. This is directed at situations where organized crime third parties are paying the fees of the accused. But the determination whether such a conflict is genuine and unwaivable rests entirely with the government. This is hardly an objective forum. Nevertheless, this is another issue that may be decided differently by different states. Only time will tell what leeway is allowed prosecutors in the investigatory stage of a case — and in which jurisdictions.

7. Prosecutorial Accountability. Almost all commentators, including prosecutors, agree that prosecutors must live up to a higher ethical standard than other lawyers. Ironically, most also agree that prosecutors are less likely to be subject to discipline than the average attorney, and less likely to be disciplined than a generation ago. At the same time, the tools prosecutors have at their disposal in this modern era of law enforcement are increasingly broad. In 1974, Congress authorized federal undercover sting operations. In the mid-1980s, the strengthening of 18 U.S.C.§ 1963 (commonly called the "RICO" Act), and 21 U.S.C. § 848 *et seq.* (the Continuing Criminal Enterprise Statute) gave prosecutors forfeiture tools that they did not previously have. These forfeitures enable prosecutors to seize or freeze a defendant's property, to file

---

[27] It is interesting to note that the sponsorship of Joseph McDade, a Pennsylvania Republican, was undoubtedly colored by his seven-week trial in 1996 in which he was acquitted of charges that he had accepted $100,000 in bribes from defense firms in exchange for supporting millions of dollars' worth of government contracts. Several jurors later described themselves as "incredulous" at the weakness of the government's case. McDade had been in line to become chairman of the House Appropriations Committee when Republicans won control of the House in 1994, but was passed over for Louisiana's Bob Livingston, who was later nominated as Speaker of the House, before he himself resigned from Congress under a cloud.

suit in civil courts to seize property if it can be linked to a crime, and to affirmatively question the source of a defense attorney's fees. Supreme Court rulings in the 1980s loosened the standard for search warrants; prosecutors use subpoena and search warrant powers far more aggressively against defense counsel than ever before, in an attempt to gain possession of records detailing defense counsel's clientele.[28]

Why is it that in this era of enormous prosecution power, the accountability of prosecutors under ethical rules has significantly diminished? One reason, of course, is that the effect of the Thornburgh and Reno memoranda are unquestionably still being felt. But this is hardly the only answer. Bennett Gershman has written an excellent law review article[29] which posits some other possibilities for why the behavior of prosecutors is not more frequently sanctioned. First, he argues, ethical rules were designed on a private attorney-client model, in which the prosecutor increasingly does not fit; second, the prosecutor is an increasingly powerful figure, one with considerable public support, whose prosecutorial zeal is politically and practically difficult to sanction; third, prosecutorial abuse, being a more subjective matter than disciplining private attorneys for "garden variety" violations, is simply too difficult for many disciplinary agencies to tackle.[30]

We suggest some other reasons (hardly original to us — we paraphrase here the comments of many) why prosecutors are not more often sanctioned for improper conduct. First, there is simply an absence of ordinary accountability. That is, most advocates have easily identifiable clients, to whom the lawyer must report, and whose interests the lawyer must protect. While many prosecutors feel that they indeed have a client, be it the United States government or the citizenry of the particular jurisdiction, this is not a client in the ordinary sense, the kind that makes decisions on each case. Thus, the prosecutor, not the amorphous client "the People," decides policy and what is in "the client's" best interests. Too often, this lack of accountability leads to an insular climate, where a deputy DA can sign off on his or her decisions — or, as with Colorado DA Pautler, needs only his boss' pro forma approval before acting as he chooses.

This lack of client accountability is coupled with full access to all the investigative powers that modern law enforcement can provide. Since prosecutors have these vast powers at their disposal, and are vested with enormous discretionary powers of their own, their acts take on a quasi-judicial aura. Moreover, enforcing abusive conduct is made more difficult by separation of powers problems — that is, the difficulty of officers of the judiciary branch disciplining lawyers working for the executive branch. The result is that if prosecutors decline to police themselves, they may not be policed at all.

---

[28] Model Rule 3.8(e) specifically limits the appropriate use of the subpoena power against defense counsel.

[29] *Symposium*: *The New Prosecutors*, 53 U. PITT. L. REV. 393 (1992). We refer further to this article in the Supplemental Readings below.

[30] Gershman suggests that prosecutorial discipline be taken out of the ordinary discipline system, placed not in the hands of the Attorney General but in special "prosecutor misconduct commissions" which would be similar to the commissions which govern judicial conduct. This is appropriate, he submits, because prosecutors have, after all, quasi-judicial functions. Gershman's idea is an interesting one, though how effectively it would discipline prosecutorial abuses is open to serious question, particularly in light of the frequent criticism of judicial conduct commissions for *their* failures to effectively discipline members of the bench.

Moreover, even where prosecutors are cited for misconduct, they may not be disciplined and, as significantly, their misconduct does not lead to reversal of the criminal conviction unless the appellate court determines the result was reasonably likely to be different. For example, for a *Brady* suppression of evidence to result in a new trial, the Supreme Court has held that it must be found that the defendant was deprived of a fair trial: "[N]o purpose would be served by requiring a new trial simply because an inept prosecutor incorrectly believed he was suppressing a fact that would be vital to the defense."[31] Even in cases of admitted *Brady* error, the defendant must show a " 'reasonable probability' of a different result" on retrial.[32] Moreover, *Arizona v. Youngblood*, 488 U.S. 51, 109 S. Ct. 885 (1988), held that when evidence that could have exonerated a defendant was destroyed (there, clothing worn by a rape victim containing semen stains), a conviction will not be reversed "unless a criminal defendant can show bad faith" on the part of the police. It is far too easy to have *Brady* information fall through a *Youngblood* crack, particularly where evidence of guilt appears overwhelming.

What happens when a prosecutor risks not moving forward with a prosecution in an effort to do "the right thing"? Will there be repercussions in the political arena? Can there be retaliation from within the prosecutor's own office? Consider the recent closely divided United States Supreme Court case below involving a supervising deputy district attorney in Los Angeles.[33]

GARCETTI V. CEBALLOS
__ U.S. __, 126 S. Ct. 1951 (2006)

JUSTICE KENNEDY delivered the opinion of the Court.

. . . .

In February 2000, a defense attorney contacted Ceballos about a pending criminal case. The defense attorney said there were inaccuracies in an affidavit used to obtain a critical search warrant. The attorney informed Ceballos that he had filed a motion to traverse, or challenge, the warrant, but he also wanted Ceballos to review the case . . . . After examining the affidavit and visiting the location it described, Ceballos determined the affidavit contained serious misrepresentations . . . . He relayed his findings to his supervisors, petitioners Carol Najera and Frank Sundstedt, and followed up by preparing a disposition memorandum. The memo explained Ceballos' concerns and recommended dismissal of the case. On March 2, 2000, Ceballos submitted the memo to Sundstedt for his review . . . .

Despite Ceballos' concerns, Sundstedt decided to proceed with the prosecution, pending disposition of the defense motion to traverse. The trial court held a hearing on the motion. Ceballos was called by the defense and recounted his observations about the affidavit, but the trial court rejected the challenge to the warrant.

---

[31] *United States v. Agurs*, 427 U.S. 97, 110, 96 S. Ct. 2392, 2401 (1976).

[32] *Kyles v. Whitley*, 514 U.S. 419, 115 S. Ct. 1555 (1995).

[33] The case was argued twice, once before and once after the appointment of Justice Alito; with eight members of the court, it appeared that the vote would be 4-4, thus upholding the circuit court.

Ceballos claims that in the aftermath of these events he was subjected to a series of retaliatory employment actions . . . . Ceballos sued in the United States District Court for the Central District of California, asserting, as relevant here, a claim under Rev. Stat. § 1979, 42 U. S. C. § 1983. He alleged petitioners violated the First and Fourteenth Amendments by retaliating against him based on his memo of March 2.

Petitioners responded that . . . Ceballos' memo was not protected speech under the First Amendment. Petitioners moved for summary judgment, and the District Court granted their motion. Noting that Ceballos wrote his memo pursuant to his employment duties, the court concluded he was not entitled to First Amendment protection for the memo's contents . . . .

The Court of Appeals for the Ninth Circuit reversed, holding that "Ceballos's allegations of wrongdoing in the memorandum constitute protected speech under the First Amendment." 361 F. 3d 1168, 1173 (2004). In reaching its conclusion the court looked to the First Amendment analysis set forth in *Pickering* v. *Board of Ed. of Township High School Dist. 205, Will Cty.,* 391 U. S. 563 (1968) . . . .

We granted certiorari, 543 U. S. 1186 (2005), and we now reverse.

. . . .

The question becomes whether the relevant government entity had an adequate justification for treating the employee differently from any other member of the general public. See *Pickering*, 391 U. S., at 568. This consideration reflects the importance of the relationship between the speaker's expressions and employment. A government entity has broader discretion to restrict speech when it acts in its role as employer, but the restrictions it imposes must be directed at speech that has some potential to affect the entity's operations.

. . . .

The Court's decisions, then, have sought both to promote the individual and societal interests that are served when employees speak as citizens on matters of public concern and to respect the needs of government employers attempting to perform their important public functions.

. . . .

The controlling factor in Ceballos' case is that his expressions were made pursuant to his duties as a calendar deputy . . . . That consideration — the fact that Ceballos spoke as a prosecutor fulfilling a responsibility to advise his supervisor about how best to proceed with a pending case — distinguishes Ceballos' case from those in which the First Amendment provides protection against discipline. We hold that when public employees make statements pursuant to their official duties, the employees are not speaking as citizens for First Amendment purposes, and the Constitution does not insulate their communications from employer discipline.

. . . .

Ceballos did not act as a citizen when he went about conducting his daily professional activities, such as supervising attorneys, investigating charges, and preparing filings. In the same way he did not speak as a citizen by writing a memo that addressed the proper disposition of a pending criminal case. When he went to work and performed the tasks he was paid to perform, Ceballos acted as a government employee. The fact that his duties sometimes required him to speak or write does not mean his supervisors were prohibited from evaluating his performance . . . .

. . . . Supervisors must ensure that their employees' official communications are accurate, demonstrate sound judgment, and promote the employer's mission. Ceballos' memo is illustrative. It demanded the attention of his supervisors and led to a heated meeting with employees from the sheriff's department. If Ceballos' superiors thought his memo was inflammatory or misguided, they had the authority to take proper corrective action.

JUSTICE BREYER, dissenting.

Like the majority, I understand the need to "affor[d] government employers sufficient discretion to manage their operations." *Ante*, at 11. And I agree that the Constitution does not seek to "displac[e] . . . managerial discretion by judicial supervision." *Ibid.* Nonetheless, there may well be circumstances with special demand for constitutional protection of the speech at issue, where governmental justifications may be limited, and where administrable standards seem readily available — to the point where the majority's fears of department management by lawsuit are misplaced. In such an instance, I believe that courts should apply the *Pickering* standard, even though the government employee speaks upon matters of public concern in the course of his ordinary duties.

This is such a case. The respondent, a government lawyer, complained of retaliation, in part, on the basis of speech contained in his disposition memorandum that he says fell within the scope of his obligations under *Brady* v. *Maryland*, 373 U. S. 83 (1963). The facts present two special circumstances that together justify First Amendment review.

First, the speech at issue is professional speech — the speech of a lawyer. Such speech is subject to independent regulation by canons of the profession. Those canons provide an obligation to speak in certain instances. And where that is so, the government's own interest in forbidding that speech is diminished . . . .

Second, the Constitution itself here imposes speech obligations upon the government's professional employee. A prosecutor has a constitutional obligation to learn of, to preserve, and to communicate with the defense about exculpatory and impeachment evidence in the government's possession. *Kyles* v. *Whitley,* 514 U. S. 419, 437 (1995); *Brady, supra* . . . .

Where professional and special constitutional obligations are both present, the need to protect the employee's speech is augmented, the need for broad government authority to control that speech is likely diminished, and administrable standards are quite likely available. Hence, I would find that the Constitution mandates special protection of employee speech in such circumstances. Thus I would apply the *Pickering* balancing test here.

NOTES

Does it make sense to treat a government lawyer — indeed, a prosecutor — the same as any government employee for free speech purposes? Or does Justice Breyer's reliance on not only the position of "lawyer" but of "prosecutor," and his multiple references to the *Brady* case, make more sense? If a prosecutor is not afforded the free speech Breyer suggests, would s/he be able to fulfill all the duties articulated in section 1 above? See particularly Standard 3-3.9. Would it affect the actions of the DAs in the problem?

8. The Case of the Anonymous Prosecutor. Finally, the problem of refusing to name the names of offending prosecutors continues to plague our courts. To illustrate this problem, we close with an irony — a brief excerpt of an opinion of Judge Alex Kozinski excoriating the conduct of Assistant United States Attorney Jeffrey S. Sinek and reversing the defendant's conviction because of Sinek's repeated failures to tell the truth about a plea agreement with an informant, Nourian.

UNITED STATES v. KOJAYAN
8 F.3d 1315 (9th Cir. 1993)

[T]he defense attorneys — experienced criminal lawyers — had a strong hunch Nourian must have cut a deal pursuant to which he promised to testify if the government called him. At trial, they decided to make hay out of the government's failure to do so: They argued that, because the prosecution (and only the prosecution) could have called Nourian to the stand but didn't, the jurors should infer that his testimony would have undercut the government's case. . . .

Unfortunately for the defendants, they had no proof that Nourian was actually available to the government. Thwarted in their attempt to obtain this information under *Brady*, defense counsel were in the unenviable position of having to raise the point without any support in the record. Though they urged the jury to infer the existence of a deal from the circumstances, without any direct evidence of an agreement, their claims naturally seemed weak.

As the prosecutor, Assistant United States Attorney Jeffrey S. Sinek, forcefully argued to the jury, the defense's contentions appeared to be a classic example of asking the jury to speculate. Sinek, however, was not telling the truth. Defense counsel had guessed right — Nourian had entered into a cooperation agreement with the government.

. . . .

In determining the proper remedy, we must consider the government's willfulness in committing the misconduct and its willingness to own up to it. [The court then detailed that willfulness at length, then quoted Justice William O. Douglas:]

As Justice Douglas once warned, "the function of the prosecutor under the Federal Constitution is not to tack as many skins of victims as possible to the wall. His function is to vindicate the right of people as expressed in the laws and give those accused of crime a fair trial."

. . . .

Evidence matters; closing argument matters; statements from the prosecutor matter a great deal. Sinek deprived the defendants of an opportunity to put on what could have been a powerful defense.

NOTES

The irony? When the opinion was first published on August 4, 1993, it prominently featured Sinek's name.[34] After a petition by the U.S. Attorney to remove Sinek's name from the opinion, however, the court, with the generally-outspoken Kozinski still the opinion's author, agreed to do it. The November 1, 1993 version of the opinion refers only to "the prosecutor" or "the AUSA."[35] This despite Kozinski's statement in the *Kojayan* opinion that "[m]uch of what the United States Attorney's office does isn't open to public scrutiny or judicial review." The *Kojayan* case, unfortunately, seems to have become another example of lack of judicial scrutiny, at least for one prosecutor who, through the court's ultimately anonymous handslap, at best learned a mixed lesson.[36]

SUPPLEMENTAL READINGS

1. *Donnelly v. DeChristoforo*, 416 U.S. 637, 94 S. Ct. 1868 (1974), is perhaps typical of cases in which the United States Supreme Court found the prosecutor's behavior in error, but refused to reverse the conviction. During summation, the prosecutor stated, "I quite frankly think that they [defendant and his attorney] hope you find him guilty of something a little less than First Degree murder." The jury convicted the defendant of first degree. Such comments, held the Court, did not meet the previously outlined standard required for reversal: "consistent and repeated misrepresentation." It was in this case, in dissent, that Justice Douglas made the remarks quoted decades later by Judge Kozinski in *Kojayan*, above.

2. *United States v. Ofshe*, 817 F.2d 1508 (11th Cir. 1987). This case represents perhaps the most extreme example of a prosecutor communicating with a defendant: using an informant who is also the defendant's lawyer. Ofshe, facing drug charges, hired attorney Glass. When Glass himself became the target of an investigation, Assistant United States Attorney Scott Turow (yes, the famous author) wired Glass for a meeting with Ofshe. When Ofshe discovered this, his other attorney moved to set aside the indictment, a motion which was denied. The court held this remedy was not necessary because Glass was instructed not to violate the attorney-client privilege (though how

-----

[34] 1993 U.S. App. LEXIS 19873.

[35] 1993 U.S. App. LEXIS 28301.

[36] Avoiding using the prosecutor's name is not invariable or inevitable. In addition to disciplinary matters, occasional mention of names does occur. *See, e.g., People v. Hill*, 17 Cal. 4th 800, 72 Cal. Rptr. 2d 656 (1998), in which the offending prosecutor, Rosalie Morton, was repeatedly named by the California high court, which reversed defendant Hill's conviction. "The most disturbing aspect of this case was the outrageous and pervasive misconduct on the part of the state's representative at trial: the public prosecutor," said the opinion. The court called Morton's misconduct "continual" and "constant". Though excoriated in a unanimous high court opinion, Morton received no public discipline for her behavior.

this could be avoided is not made clear), and because no useful information was developed.

3. Bennett L. Gershman, *Symposium: The New Prosecutors*, 53 U. Pitt. L. Rev. 393 (1992). This article, referred to above, is a thoughtful and provocative study. Among other things, Gershman details the cases of four murder defendants who he argues were wrongly convicted because of prosecutorial misconduct, and cites evidence of widespread patterns of prosecutorial abuse.

4. *United States v. Goodwin*, 457 U.S. 368, 102 S. Ct. 2485 (1982), involved a prosecutor who originally filed misdemeanor charges against the defendant, but when the defendant demanded a jury trial, returned to the grand jury to get an indictment on a felony charge. The Supreme Court found that this action did not abuse prosecutorial discretion or interfere with a defendant's constitutional right to demand a jury: "[A] prosecutor may file additional charges if an initial expectation that a defendant would plead guilty to lesser charges proves unfounded."

5. Two *N.Y. Times* articles by Jonathan D. Glater exploring issues of "celebrity justice" are "Stewart's Celebrity Created Magnet for Scrutiny," *N.Y. Times*, Mar. 7, 2004, and Glater and Nick Madigan, "Weighing Celebrity Justice: Blind or Biased," *N.Y. Times*, Jun. 15, 2005. The articles address the role celebrity plays in criminal justice system, and refer to other "celebrity" prosecutions, among them Mike Tyson's, and the child molesting charges against Michael Jackson.

6. Are prosecutors abusing their power in their prosecution of corporations and their higher-ups? In "Convictions Drive Home the Point Again," *Washington Post*, May 26, 2006, Steven Pearlstein contends that the convictions of former Enron executives Ken Lay and Jeff Skilling were selective prosecutions, and that lawyers have escaped responsibility and may have profited from the prosecution of others by hiding behind the attorney-client privilege. In "Over Before It Started," *N.Y. Times*, Jan. 14, 2005, Joseph A. Grundfest claims that Arthur Andersen was destroyed not at trial, but when it was indicted. He argues that prosecutors have the power to destroy corporations simply by indicting them on serious charges and that this prosecutorial power should be subject to review to ensure that is not abused.

7. There is increasingly overwhelming evidence that sentencing disparity exists among those of different races who stand convicted of crimes. How or even whether this is caused by the manner in which prosecutorial discretion is exercised remains an open albeit hotly debated question. Many articles in the last several years have addressed the issue. Two of many valuable articles worth reading are Marc Mauer, "Disparate Justice Imperils a Community," *New Jersey Law Journal*, Oct. 30, 1995, and Andrew Blum, "Jail Time by the Book," *ABA Journal*, p. 18, May 1999.

8. After September 11, 2001, the U.S. implemented a federal registration and fingerprinting system in order to track people with temporary visas. Several articles have been critical of that program as resulting in the arrests or detentions of hundreds of innocent Middle Eastern men and teenagers who voluntarily complied with the program. See, e.g., these two early pieces: Karen Brandon, "INS Detentions Spark Protests; Debate Grows Over Targeting of

Middle Easterners in the U.S.," *Chicago Tribune*, Dec. 20, 2002, and Peter Skerry, "Muslims Never Had to Unite — Until Now," *Washington Post*, Jan. 5, 2003.

9. Kathleen Clark & Julie Mertus, "Torturing the Law: The Justice Department's Legal Contortions on Interrogation," *Washington Post*, June 20, 2004, argues that Jay S. Bybee distorted the law in the famous "torture memo" by saying that the president could authorize torture even though the country's laws and treaties prohibit it. They contend that Bybee was obligated by his role as an advisor to be frank rather than slanted when advising the executive branch about the law.

10. *People v. Eubanks*, 14 Cal. 4th 580, 59 Cal. Rptr. 2d 200 (1996), raises an interesting issue of prosecutorial conflict of interest. In a close case before a divided court, the California Supreme Court evaluated when a prosecutor could be disqualified for receiving financial assistance in investigating possible white collar crimes. One high tech firm offered about $13,000 in financial assistance to a district attorney investigating other high tech companies' use of trade secrets. While the *Eubanks* court was careful not to set clear precedent or hard and fast guidelines, it reversed the intermediary appeals court and upheld a trial court's ruling disqualifying the DA's office.

11. In *Banks v. Dretke,* 540 U.S. 668, 124 S. Ct. 1256 (2004), the Supreme Court gave some hope to defendants seeking post-conviction redress for *Brady* error. In *Banks,* the prosecutor failed to disclose that the key witness was a paid informant and allowed the witness to testify falsely that he had never spoken to the police, then relied on the false evidence in closing argument. The Supreme Court held that Banks was entitled to seek post-conviction remedy because his failure to investigate the informant and develop impeachment information was the direct result of the prosecutor's ongoing misrepresentations concerning the informant.

12. In *The Professional Discipline of Prosecutors*, 79 N.C. L. Rev. 721 (2001), Fred Zacharias evaluates the prospect of future discipline against prosecutors in the post-McDade Act era. Zacharias notes the long-standing Supreme Court rule under *Imbler v. Pachtman*, 424 U.S. 409, 96 S. Ct. 984 (1976), that prosecutors are immune from civil suit because other adequate remedies exist to discipline their misconduct. Recognizing the checkered history of discipline by state agencies, Zacharias evaluates whether, where, and how the new authority of the states over prosecutorial behavior is likely to result in discipline, and the extent to which it is likely to make a real difference.

PROBLEM 23

One of the least understood and least studied ethical conundrums facing lawyers concerns the role of the civil government attorney. Frankly, this is an area which has received far too little attention from ethicists, though it causes great concern for practicing government lawyers. There are several important questions about this role. First, whom does the government attorney represent, the larger governmental entity (e.g., the state or municipality), or the particular governmental agency to whom the lawyer directly answers? Second, who speaks for the client and from whom must the governmental attorney take direction? Third, does attorney-client confidentiality and the attorney-client privilege exist in the ordinary sense, and if so, with whom? Finally, how does the government attorney reconcile representing a governmental entity and the individuals employed by that entity?

As we shall see, there are often no clear answers to these questions. We have seen the difficulty that counsel for a corporation or partnership has in determining these issues. These problems are compounded when the lawyer is counsel to a government or a governmental agency. Examine the situation faced by Joe Hannah.

What's a City Attorney to Do?

I. Joe Hannah is a deputy city attorney for the City of Big Boondock. The city attorney's office is responsible for representing the city as well as its agencies and its employees while acting within the scope of their employment.

Joe is currently assigned the city's property assessment division. This division assesses the value of all properties within the city limits for tax purposes. The higher the assessed value of the property, the more taxes collected by the city.

Part of Joe's job is to represent the Office of Assessor in appeals before the assessment appeals board. The appeals board is an administrative board set up by the city to resolve disputes between the assessor's office and property owners regarding the assessed value of their land. In addition to representing the assessor's office in those appeals, Joe is also responsible for advising the appeals board on evidentiary questions that arise.

Roger Sturges is a property owner whose land was recently assessed at $350,000. Sturges felt that this assessment was far too high and appealed to the assessment appeals board. Before the appeals hearing, Joe reviews papers that Sturges' counsel has filed urging a lower assessment based on comparable property in the area. Joe realizes that Sturges' argument is strong, but may turn on the admissibility of the information forming the basis of the "comp" analysis. When Joe shares this information with Chief Assessor Martine Ferrara, Ferrara tells Joe: "Let's stand by our assessment. There's no reason for the city to lose all of that tax revenue unless it's absolutely necessary. And who knows whether Sturges has information that's admissible."

QUESTIONS

1. May Joe represent the Assessor's Office in Sturges' appeal to the Board while at the same time advising the Board regarding evidentiary questions that arise during that appeal?

2. What if the evidentiary issues *did not* have a direct impact on the ultimate assessment determination?

3. Should Joe be able to advise the Board on whether Sturges' evidence is admissible or supports a lower assessment even though doing so would hurt the city's position? What if he does and the Board chooses to ignore that information?

4. Should or must Joe inform a "higher" authority within city government? If so, whom?

5. What if the Board were advised by another attorney in Joe's office? Does that solve all these problems?

II. Joe has been hearing rumors that individual assessors have been extorting money from property owners in exchange for lower assessment valuations. When Joe confronts Arnold Shostrand, one of the assessors, about these rumors, Shostrand acknowledges that it is not uncommon for other assessors to suggest to property owners that they are willing to "deal." Shostrand insists, however, that he found this practice "disgusting," and only participated in the scam on two isolated occasions.

QUESTIONS

Should Joe report the assessors' practice? If so, to whom? Would doing so violate a duty of confidentiality to Shostrand?

III. The Boondock *Daily Grind* gets wind of the assessors' practice of extorting money in exchange for lower property valuations and publishes an exposé. Citizens throughout Big Boondock are outraged. Within two weeks, three lawsuits are filed by property owners against the city. Joe is assigned to represent the city.

Later in that week, Joe receives a call from the mayor, who says that the suits are an embarrassment to the current administration. The mayor urges Joe to settle the suits quickly so that it is all old news by the time of the next election.

QUESTIONS

Can Joe represent both the city and the individual assessors? What if Joe believes that the city could argue that the assessors were acting outside the course and scope of their employment? What if there are punitive damages claims against the assessors individually which are not available against the city as an entity? If he represents the city and the assessors, how does he deal with maintaining confidential communications?

May Joe take into account the mayor's request in reaching a decision on whether to settle or go to trial? *Must* he consider the mayor's views? What if, instead of the mayor, it is the City Council applying the pressure to settle?

READINGS

1. Conflicting Advice in Los Angeles. To give a flavor of the kinds of conflicts of interest that can confront a city attorney, we turn again to the aftermath of the Rodney King case, and in particular the question of discharging Los Angeles Police Chief Darryl Gates. Los Angeles has more people and a larger economy than many states. Intra-administrative conflicts are bound to exist in such a complex jurisdiction; the Gates matter can hardly have been the first. But in the Gates case the whole country was watching. How should a city attorney deal with answering to more than one "client"?

RICH CONNELL, CITY ATTY. ROLE RAISES CONFLICT OF INTEREST ISSUE
Los Angeles Times (April 9, 1991)[1]

A potential conflict of interest by the Los Angeles city attorney's office — which has given legal advice to opposing factions in the Darryl F. Gates controversy — was raised as a central legal issue Monday in the court battle over the police chief's reinstatement.

City Atty. James K. Hahn's office told the Police Commission that it had the legal authority to place Gates on leave and, within days, advised the City Council on a legal maneuver to reverse the action, documents and interviews show.

"There appears to exist ample legal authority, in both law and practice, to support the imposition of an involuntary administrative leave on the chief of police," Hahn's office advised the Police Commission in a confidential March 27 legal opinion, a copy of which was obtained by The Times.

Commissioners said they relied on the city attorney's advice last Thursday when they ordered Gates to take a 60-day paid leave, pending completion of an investigation of the Rodney G. King beating.

In a closed session the next day, the council asked Hahn and several of his office's lawyers for advice on legal steps it was considering taking to reinstate Gates. One of the council's tactics — settling a lawsuit that Gates was expected to file — was approved by the council Friday. . . .

As part of their argument against the settlement, attorneys for the commissioners and civil rights groups alleged that Hahn had a conflict of interest that should invalidate the settlement.

Hahn has a "gross, unlawful three-cornered conflict of interest, which precludes his serving either the legitimate interests of the city or the public interests," said Pete L. Haviland, an attorney for several civil rights groups trying to block the settlement. The judge postponed a ruling on the issue.

Hahn's office denied there was a conflict in its advice to the Police Commission and City Council because both panels are part of the same legal entity — the city of Los Angeles. . . .

Erwin Chemerinsky, USC law professor and an expert on legal ethics, said Hahn's office appeared to have a conflict of interest.

"A lawyer can't represent adverse interests in a single matter," he said, adding that "the question of how to deal with Daryl Gates at this time is a single question."

---

[1] Copyright © 1991 by Los Angeles Times. Reprinted by permission.

"Once (Hahn) advised the commission, he was the lawyer for the commission," Chemerinsky said. "He shouldn't be then helping the council undo what the commission did on the basis of his legal advice."

James Ham, former chairman of the Los Angeles County Bar Assn.'s ethics committee, said . . . "[t]hey have a conflict issue that is legitimate."

Ham and Chemerinsky said it would have been preferable for Hahn to disqualify his office from giving advice to both the commission and council.

. . . .

Mike Qualls, Hahn's spokesman, said the city attorney has only one client — the city of Los Angeles — and the power to settle lawsuits rests with the City Council. . . .

Council President John Ferraro said the city attorney's staff answered questions and assured council members that what they were doing was legal. "They helped draw up the motion," he said.

Qualls said the city attorney has remained neutral in the dispute between the commission and the council and there was nothing contradictory in the legal advice provided to the two panels. He said the only potential conflict of interest would have been representing the city in an adversarial case against Gates, whose department it also represents in numerous lawsuits.

NOTES

Should the city attorney have advised just the police commission, or just the city council? Should the council have paid for independent outside counsel, a method used in several states? What about the council members' rights to have their lawyer, Hahn, advise them? The answers to these questions turn at least in part on the question of who is the client.

2. Who Is the Client? Three weeks after the above article appeared, former Los Angeles City Attorney Burt Pines wrote an editorial page opinion for the *Los Angeles Times* which defended Hahn's advising both the police commission and the city council. He cited a memorandum he himself had written, saying that the city attorney had only one client — the city itself.

"This precept is fundamental to understanding why the city attorney does not have a conflict of interest in advising various city departments that may sharply disagree with one another at any particular time," opined Pines. "These departments are not separate legal entities but simply administrative arms of the city, a municipal corporation. Only that corporation is the city attorney's client. Only that municipal corporation is a legal entity, able to sue or be sued."[2]

Pines cited numerous instances where both he and his successor, Ira Reiner, resolved conflicts among the city's thirty-some departments and commissions. He argued that the very reason a city attorney can resolve such "squabbles" is that the client remains the municipality. Moreover, to give separate counsel to all 30 departments and 18 elected city officials would involve astronomical

---

2 Los Angeles Times, April 30, 1991.

cost and potential advocacy of one department's interests as against another, instead of finding the best objective solution for the city as a whole.

Who is right, Pines or the ethics experts found by the *L.A. Times*? Pines' prose sounds persuasive, but does it hold up in the face of what appears to be clearly contradictory advice given by Hahn's office in the Gates case? After all, if the city attorney is one big law firm, how can it justify giving conflicting opinions in the same matter? Is determining what entity can be sued the best criterion for determining who is the client? Must we change the meaning of conflicts of interest in the government context to conform to the reality of what governments today actually do and can afford?

Before we analyze the loyalties and duties owed by the government attorney, let us explore identifying the client a little further. Neither the ABA nor most states have specific rules defining the roles and responsibilities of the government attorney. Model Rules 1.7 and 1.13 both make reference to the government lawyer, but provide virtually no black-letter guidance. Comment 9 to MR 1.13 acknowledges that "defining precisely" who is the client in a government setting may be more difficult than in other organizational settings and acknowledges that it is beyond the scope of the Rules. This is not encouraging, given the difficulties lawyers have even in non-governmental organizational settings. The comment goes on to state, equivocally and unhelpfully, that "[a]lthough in some circumstances the client may be a specific agency, it may also be a branch of governement, such as the executive branch, or the government as a whole." Finally, Comment 9 acknowledges that statutory and regulatory schemes defining the duties of government lawyers are not limited to the ethics rules. The ABA rules thus will be of little aid and comfort to either James Hahn or Joe Hannah.

One commentator, R.P. Lawry, has written two interesting law review articles which dispute the need to specifically identify the client in the government context.[3] Identifying the client is not really possible in the traditional sense, Lawry argues. It is more important for the government attorney to determine from whom to take direction on matters for which the lawyer is responsible. We saw an important and similar issue in the representation dilemma facing Esperanza Dejos in Problem 8.

3. How Limited Is the Governmental Attorney-Client Privilege?
Whatever else it was, the "Whitewater" scandal during the Clinton administration gave legal scholars a veritable bouquet of issues concerning the proper behavior of lawyers. We already examined, in Problem 5, whether deputy White House counsel Vincent Foster's attorney-client privilege survived his death. In the last problem, we examined issues relating to whether Independent Counsel Kenneth Starr had abused his power as special prosecutor. Here, we focus on attorney-client privilege and confidentiality in the government context.

Three cases stemming from the Whitewater investigation illuminate the status of the government attorney-client privilege. First in time was *In re Grand Jury Subpoena Duces Tecum*, 112 F.3d 910 (8th Cir. 1997), *cert. denied,*

---

[3] *Who Is the Client of the Federal Government Lawyer? An Analysis of the Wrong Question,* 37 FED. B.J. 61 (1978); *Confidences and the Government Lawyer,* 57 N.C. L. REV. 625 (1979).

117 S. Ct. 2482 (1997), in which Starr sought notes taken by White House lawyers about conversations with then-first lady Hillary Rodham Clinton concerning Mrs. Clinton's testimony before a federal grand jury and her activities following the death of Foster. In a 2-1 decision that the Eighth Circuit termed a case of first impression, Mrs. Clinton's lawyers were compelled to turn their notes over to the Independent Counsel. The court wrote that even assuming the existence of an attorney-client privilege, there is a "strong public interest in honest government and in exposing wrongdoing by public officials" that is inconsistent with asserting an attorney-client privilege in the face of a criminal investigation. The majority relied on *United States v. Nixon*, 418 U.S. 683 (1974), in which then-president Nixon was forced to turn over audiotapes relating to the Watergate affair. Though Nixon's claim was one of "executive privilege," the Supreme Court's *Nixon* holding affirmed, in the Eighth Circuit's view, "the general principle that the government's need for confidentiality may be subordinated to the needs of the government's own criminal justice processes."

A year later, it was President Clinton and his lawyers on the spot, and time for the D.C. Circuit's own case of first impression.

IN RE LINDSEY

148 F.3d 1100 (D.C. Cir. 1998), reported with previously-sealed portions at 158 F.3d 1263 (D.C. Cir. 1998)

PER CURIAM:

In these expedited appeals, the principal question is whether an attorney in the Office of the President, having been called before a federal grand jury, may refuse, on the basis of a government attorney-client privilege, to answer questions about possible criminal conduct by government officials and others. To state the question is to suggest the answer, for the Office of the President is a part of the federal government, consisting of government employees doing government business, and neither legal authority nor policy nor experience suggests that a federal government entity can maintain the ordinary common law attorney-client privilege to withhold information relating to a federal criminal offense. . . . See *United States v. Nixon*, 418 U.S. 683, 707-12 (1974); *In re Sealed Case (Espy)*, 121 F.3d 729, 736-38 (D.C. Cir. 1997). In the context of federal criminal investigations and trials, there is no basis for treating legal advice differently from any other advice the Office of the President receives in performing its constitutional functions. The public interest in honest government and in exposing wrongdoing by government officials, as well as the tradition and practice, acknowledged by the Office of the President and by former White House Counsel, of government lawyers reporting evidence of federal criminal offenses whenever such evidence comes to them, lead to the conclusion that a government attorney may not invoke the attorney-client privilege in response to grand jury questions seeking information relating to the possible commission of a federal crime.

. . . .

On January 30, 1998, the grand jury issued a subpoena to Bruce R. Lindsey, Deputy White House Counsel and Assistant to the President. On February 18, February 19, and March 12, 1998, Lindsey appeared before the grand jury and declined to answer certain questions . . . . On March 6, 1998, the Independent Counsel moved to compel Lindsey's testimony. The district court granted that motion on May 4, 1998.

. . . .

The attorney-client privilege protects confidential communications made between clients and their attorneys when the communications are for the purpose of securing legal advice or services. It "is one of the oldest recognized privileges for confidential communications." *Swidler & Berlin v. United States*, 118 S. Ct. 2081 (1998).

The Office of the President contends that Lindsey's communications with the President and others in the White House should fall within this privilege both because the President, like any private person, needs to communicate fully and frankly with his legal advisors, and because the current grand jury investigation may lead to impeachment proceedings, which would require a defense of the President's official position as head of the executive branch of government, presumably with the assistance of White House Counsel. The Independent Counsel contends that an absolute government attorney-client privilege would be inconsistent with the proper role of the government lawyer and that the President should rely only on his private lawyers for fully confidential counsel.

. . . .

Courts, commentators, and government lawyers have long recognized a government attorney-client privilege in several contexts. Much of the law on this subject has developed in litigation about exemption five of the Freedom of Information Act ("FOIA") . . . . "In the governmental context, the 'client' may be the agency and the attorney may be an agency lawyer." In Lindsey's case, his client — to the extent he provided legal services — would be the Office of the President.

. . . .

Recognizing that a government attorney-client privilege exists is one thing. Finding that the Office of the President is entitled to assert it here is quite another.

. . . .

The grand jury, a constitutional body established in the Bill of Rights, "belongs to no branch of the institutional Government, serving as a kind of buffer or referee between the Government and the people," while the Independent Counsel is by statute an officer of the executive branch representing the United States. For matters within his jurisdiction, the Independent Counsel acts in the role of the Attorney General as the country's chief law enforcement officer. Thus, although the traditional privilege between attorneys and clients shields private relationships from inquiry in either civil litigation or criminal prosecution, competing values arise when the Office of the President resists demands for information from a federal grand jury and the nation's chief law enforcement officer. . . .

The question whether a government attorney-client privilege applies in the federal grand jury context is one of first impression in this circuit. . . . In

Swidler & Berlin, the Supreme Court, [a]fter finding that the Independent Counsel was asking the Court "not simply to 'construe' the privilege, but to narrow it, contrary to the weight of the existing body of caselaw," . . . concluded that the Independent Counsel had not made a sufficient showing . . . .

In the instant case, by contrast, there is no such existing body of caselaw upon which to rely and no clear principle that the government attorney-client privilege has as broad a scope as its personal counterpart. Because the "attorney-client privilege must be 'strictly confined within the narrowest possible limits consistent with the logic of its principle,'" and because the government attorney-client privilege is not recognized in the same way as the personal attorney-client privilege addressed in *Swidler & Berlin*, . . . pursuant to our authority and duty under Rule 501 of the Federal Rules of Evidence to interpret privileges "in light of reason and experience," we view our exercise as one in defining the particular contours of the government attorney-client privilege.

When an executive branch attorney is called before a federal grand jury to give evidence about alleged crimes within the executive branch, reason and experience, duty, and tradition dictate that the attorney shall provide that evidence. With respect to investigations of federal criminal offenses, and especially offenses committed by those in government, government attorneys stand in a far different position from members of the private bar. Their duty is not to defend clients against criminal charges and it is not to protect wrongdoers from public exposure. The constitutional responsibility of the President, and all members of the Executive Branch, is to "take Care that the Laws be faithfully executed." U.S. Const. art. II, § 3. Investigation and prosecution of federal crimes is one of the most important and essential functions within that constitutional responsibility. . . . Unlike a private practitioner, the loyalties of a government lawyer therefore cannot and must not lie solely with his or her client agency.

. . . . As Judge [Jack B.] Weinstein put it, "if there is wrongdoing in government, it must be exposed . . . . A [government lawyer's] duty to the people, the law, and his own conscience requires disclosure . . . ." Furthermore, "to allow any part of the federal government to use its in-house attorneys as a shield against the production of information relevant to a federal criminal investigation would represent a gross misuse of public assets." *In re Grand Jury Subpoena Duces Tecum*, 112 F.3d 910, 921 (8th Cir.), cert. denied, 117 S. Ct. 2482 (1997).

. . . .

Lloyd Cutler, who served as White House Counsel in the Carter and Clinton Administrations, discussed the "rule of making it your duty, if you're a Government official as we as lawyers are, a statutory duty to report to the Attorney General any evidence you run into of a possible violation of a criminal statute." . . . Similarly, during the Nixon administration, Solicitor General Robert H. Bork [according to an interview Bork gave in 1997] told an administration official who invited him to join the President's legal defense team: "A government attorney is sworn to uphold the Constitution. If I come across evidence that is bad for the President, I'll have to turn it over. I won't be able to sit on it like a private defense attorney."

. . . .

In sum, it would be contrary to tradition, common understanding, and our governmental system for the attorney-client privilege to attach to White House Counsel in the same manner as private counsel. When government attorneys learn, through communications with their clients, of information related to criminal misconduct, they may not rely on the government attorney-client privilege to shield such information from disclosure to a grand jury.

TATEL, CIRCUIT JUDGE, dissenting from Part II and concurring in part and dissenting in part from Part III.

The attorney-client privilege protects confidential communication between clients and their lawyers, whether those lawyers work for the private sector or for government. Although I have no doubt that government lawyers working in executive departments and agencies enjoy a reduced privilege in the face of grand jury subpoenas, I remain unconvinced that either "reason" or "experience" (the tools of Rule 501) justifies this court's abrogation of the attorney-client privilege for lawyers serving the Presidency. . . .

My colleagues and I have no disagreement . . . about political advice given to the President by advisers who happen to be lawyers. Such advice is protected, if at all, by the executive privilege alone. Our disagreement centers solely on whether a grand jury can pierce the attorney-client privilege with respect to official legal advice that the Office of White House Counsel gives a sitting President.

. . . .

This court now holds that for all government attorneys, including those advising a President, the attorney-client privilege dissolves in the face of a grand jury subpoena. . . . Clients, in this case Presidents of the United States, will avoid confiding in their lawyers because they can never know whether the information they share, no matter how innocent, might some day become "pertinent to possible criminal violations." Rarely will White House counsel possess cold, hard facts about presidential wrongdoing that would create a strong public interest in disclosure, yet the very possibility that the confidence will be breached will chill communications. As a result, Presidents may well shift their trust on all but the most routine legal matters from White House counsel, who undertake to serve the Presidency, to private counsel who represent its occupant.

. . . .

I think the court seriously underestimates the independent role and value of the attorney-client privilege. Unlike the executive privilege — a broad, constitutionally derived privilege that protects frank debate between President and advisers — the narrower attorney-client privilege flows not from the Constitution, but from the common law. The attorney-client privilege does not protect general policy or political advice — even when given by lawyers — but only communications with lawyers "for the purpose of obtaining legal assistance." . . . In other words, the unique protection the law affords a President's communications with White House counsel rests not, as my colleagues put it, on some "conceit" that "lawyers are more important to the operations of government than all other officials," but rather on the special nature of legal advice, and its special need for confidentiality, as recognized by centuries of common law. . . .

. . . .

Preserving the official presidential attorney-client privilege would not place the President above the law, as the Independent Counsel implies. To begin with, by enabling clients — including Presidents — to be candid with their lawyers and lawyers to advise clients confidentially, the attorney-client privilege promotes compliance with the law. Independent Counsels, moreover, have powerful weapons to combat abuses of the attorney-client privilege. If evidence suggested that a President used White House counsel to further a crime, the crime-fraud exception would abrogate the privilege.

. . . .

Accordingly, before abrogating the official attorney-client privilege for all future Presidents, this court should have remanded to the district court to allow the Independent Counsel to recall Lindsey to the grand jury to determine whether, with respect to each question that he declines to answer, he can demonstrate the elements of the attorney-client privilege, namely that each communication was made between privileged persons in confidence "for the purpose of obtaining or providing legal assistance for the client." If Lindsey failed to meet this burden, that would end the matter. . . . On the other hand, if Lindsey demonstrated that his communications involved official legal advice, the district court could use the remand to enrich the record. . . . This would create an infinitely more useful record for us, or eventually the Supreme Court . . . .

NOTES

Lindsey expanded considerably on the Hillary Clinton case by, among other things, clearly reaffirming the existence of a governmental attorney-client privilege. (Interestingly, without stopping to analyze the issue anew, the opinion adheres to — and almost assumes — the proposition that the "client" of a government lawyer is the agency, in Lindsey's case the Office of the President.) But how narrow is the *Lindsey* holding? On its facts, it deals only with a situation in which two parts of the federal executive branch are at odds with each other, and there is an active federal criminal grand jury investigation.[4]

But it is also reasonable to interpret the *Lindsey* opinion far more broadly. Judge Tatel, early in his dissent, concludes that the majority's opinion applies to "all government attorneys," wherever they may be. Moreover, *Lindsey* uses broad language supporting "public interest in honest government and in exposing [governmental] wrongdoing," and relies on a "tradition and practice" of federal lawyers reporting evidence of a crime "whenever such evidence comes to them." This language, and *Lindsey*'s reference to the statements of

---

[4] Narrowing the facts still further, the case deals only with the Office of President itself, although in *Espy*, the third Whitewater privilege case and cited in *Lindsey*, the court similarly limited the attorney-client privilege of a cabinet member, then-Secretary of Agriculture Mike Espy.

three well-known commentators from across the political spectrum, Jack B. Weinstein, Lloyd Cutler, and Robert Bork, while not necessary to the court's holding, seem to imply an *affirmative* duty to reveal criminal conduct whenever it occurs in a government context — or at least a federal government context — with or without subpoena.

However, the *Lindsey* view is by no means unanimously adopted. Circuits have split when attorneys for state officers assert attorney-client privilege in the course of criminal investigations. In 2002, the Seventh Circuit followed a 1997 Eighth Circuit decision, and held that chief legal counsel for a state's Secretary of State could not assert the privilege before a federal grand jury.[5] But in 2005, the Second Circuit held that that the chief legal counsel for the Governor could assert attorney-client privilege before a federal grand jury that was investigating state corruption.[6]

Other apparent conflicting determinations have occurred in the elevation of our two newest Supreme Court justices. During Senate confirmation hearings for Chief Justice John Roberts, the Bush Administration raised attorney-client privilege as a rationale to refuse to release many documents from the period when Roberts acted as Principal Deputy Solicitor. Neither the Senate nor the public were allowed to see the documents. Shortly thereafter, now Justice Samuel Alito was nominated but during his confirmation hearings, his writings as a government attorney in the Department of Justice were released to the Senate and the public. Is a confirmation closer to a civil matter and thus arguably subject to privilege, or is the judicial confirmation process one that should require disclosure?

Do you think both privilege positions can be supported by the current version of Comment 9 to Rule 1.13? Or could these differing results be part of the fallout from an overly vague rule? Reconsider the policy rationales for having the attorney/client privilege in a government setting. Should it matter if the government lawyer worked for the Chief Executive (the President or Governor) or reported to a head of a governmental agency?

4. Limits on Confidentiality? Cindy Ossias Blows the Whistle. *Lindsey* leaves many questions unanswered, including these: If the attorney-client privilege is abrogated by an active investigation into criminal activity, what about *confidentiality*, a concept that we have seen is far broader than the evidentiary privilege? Is a governmental attorney permitted affirmatively to blow the whistle in the face of wrongdoing when there is no ongoing investigation? Might whistleblowing even be *required*, as some of those quoted in *Lindsey* suggest?

The *Lindsey* dicta is not alone in raising these issues. Indeed, Comment 9 to MR 1.13 states, in part, "Thus, when the client is a governmental organization, a different balance may be appropriate between maintaining confidentiality and assuring that the wrongful act is prevented or rectified, for public business is involved." Lawry's articles discussed in section 2 argue that when "whistleblowing" is involved, the government lawyer, in the public interest, can rely on a broad definition of "client." In order to protect the abilities of

---

[5] *In re: A Witness Before the Special Grand Jury 2000-2 (Witness)*, 288 F.3d 289 (7th Cir. 2002).

[6] *In re: Grand Jury Investigation (John Doe)*, 399 F.3d 527 (2d Cir. 2005).

government employees to disclose government wrongdoing to public scrutiny, the federal government passed two reform acts to protect such conduct, in 1978 and 1989. Several states have also passed such "whistleblowing" statutes.

These employees may include lawyers, with the ordinary rules of confidentiality suspended. However, how far a lawyer can go in abrogating confidences is only beginning to be tested. In California, the first test came from the actions of California Department of Insurance lawyer Cindy Ossias.

Ossias was a staff attorney for the California Department of Insurance (DOI) when she began reviewing insurance companies' good-faith compliance with claims resulting from the 1994 Northridge earthquake. Eventually, she and a team of DOI staffers reported that four insurance companies had violated their duties to settle earthquake claims in good faith. Her group recommended substantial financial penalties, restitution, and remedial action. But after giving the recommendations to Insurance Commissioner Chuck Quackenbush, Ossias and her colleagues were suddenly excluded from the process of negotiating with the insurers.

Ossias soon learned that Quackenbush had cut deals with the insurers to pay nominal sums totaling $12 million — a small fraction of nine-figure totals she had recommended — as contributions to foundations established by Quackenbush. She was shocked to learn that certain of the DOI/insurer settlement agreements found the insurer had not acted in bad faith, or were used as platforms for self-serving statements by the insurers themselves. Her team's original unfavorable reports had been buried.

Early in 2000, suspicion began to focus on Quackenbush's actions, both in the state legislature, and in the Los Angeles *Times*, where a reporter was investigating whether Quackenbush was using the newly-created foundations as a resource for his own personal public relations benefit. When Ossias was asked by an acquaintance from the state Assembly's insurance committee what was going on, she provided the Assembly committee copies of the four original recommendations and supporting documentation. The story — both the insurers' sweetheart deal and Quackenbush's foundation boondoggle — hit the front pages across California, and remained there for months. In June 2000, Ossias, now subpoenaed by the Assembly to testify, described what she believed to be Quackenbush's malfeasance. Within a week, Quackenbush had resigned in disgrace.

As for Ossias, after her disclosure the Office of Trial Counsel of the State Bar of California opened an investigation into her conduct. One conclusion trial counsel could have reached is that the state, rather than the office of insurance commissioner, was her true client, especially when the chief of her agency acted as he did. But trial counsel did not take this arguably easier way out. Instead, the bar prosecutors bit the bullet and exonerated Ossias on whistleblowing *and* public policy grounds. The text of the letter from trial counsel to Ossias' counsel Richard Zitrin appears below in its entirety save for citations.

CALIFORNIA STATE BAR TRIAL COUNSEL, LETTER TO COUNSEL FOR CINDY OSSIAS
State Bar Case No. 00-O-12989 (October 11, 2000)[7]

The State Bar of California

Office of the Trial Counsel-Enforcement

October 11, 2000

Dear Mr. Zitrin:

We are sending this letter to you based on our understanding that you represent Ms. Ossias in this matter. Please let us know immediately if this understanding is incorrect.

We are writing to advise you that we have decided to close our investigation relating to whether Ms. Ossias violated the Rules of Professional Conduct or the State Bar Act when she disclosed materials from the Department of Insurance to legislative staff members. We have concluded that Ms. Ossias did not engage in conduct which warrants disciplinary prosecution.

In reviewing this matter, we found that the facts were not in serious dispute. Ms. Ossias, while employed as an attorney with the Department of Insurance, provided legislative committees with materials pertaining to the department's settlement of claims against insurance companies arising out of the Northridge Earthquake. We have carefully reviewed the question of whether Ms. Ossias violated client confidences, whether Ms. Ossias complied with the obligations of attorneys representing an organization, and whether Ms. Ossias' conduct was permissible under the California Whistleblower Protection Act.

We have not found it necessary to decide whether the Department of Insurance could have asserted that the documents in question were confidential as to legislative committees. Rather, we have determined that Ms. Ossias' conduct should not result in discipline because: (1) It was consistent with the spirit of the Whistleblower Protection Act; (2) it advanced important public policy considerations bearing on the responsibilities of the office of insurance commissioner; and (3) it is not otherwise subject to prosecution under the guidelines set forth in this office's Statement of Disciplinary Priorities.

We note that the acting insurance commissioner, based on reports from the California Highway Patrol and the California attorney general's office, commended Ms. Ossias for her actions and reinstated her to active employment with the department.

We appreciate the cooperation that we have received from you and your client in this matter. Please feel free to contact us if you have any questions or concerns.

Sincerely,

Donald Steedman

Deputy Trial Counsel

---

[7] This letter is reprinted here, as it has been elsewhere, with the consent of Cindy Ossias. As the subject attorney, Ossias has the right to keep such a letter confidential. She has chosen, however, to allow its widespread publication.

NOTES

What does this letter mean? Los Angeles *Times* reporter Virginia Ellis, who first broke the Quackenbush story, wrote that the statements in the State Bar's letter could represent "an important breakthrough," possibly "the first decision of its kind in the nation." But it is a *letter*, without clear precedential value. Nevertheless, the letter appears to have obvious public policy significance, although the State Bar's general counsel claimed, after the fact, that no policy position should be inferred from the document, merely an exercise of "prosecutorial discretion." The letter, written by senior staff counsel who had been told it would be made public, seems to accept Ossias' affirmative actions in a manner consistent with the *dicta* in *Lindsey*.[8]

Ultimately, the Ossias letter, like the *Lindsey* opinion, speaks for itself. Read it again and make up your own mind. The letter opens the door to many questions: Why did trial counsel avoid the easy way out by stating that "we have not found it necessary" to determine whether the Department of Insurance (as opposed to the state or a legislative committee) had a confidential relationship with Ms. Ossias? Did the bar prosecutors want to address the case's public importance head on? Was their reference to the state's Whistleblower Protection Act an effort to create a safe harbor for public lawyers? Since the whistleblower statute cited applied specifically to state employees, was the reference to Ossias' conduct having "advanced important public policy considerations" an indication that these considerations might apply to lawyers other than government attorneys, such as in-house counsel? Finally, was any precedent established, or was this simply a case of "prosecutorial discretion," as the Bar claimed?

5. Representing Different Governmental Agencies. Have courts and ethics opinions supported governmental lawyers who represent different agencies at the same time? The answer is "it depends." And sometimes even within states there are clearly contradictory holdings. For example, in *In re Opinion 415*, 81 N.J. 318, 407 A.2d 1197 (1979), the New Jersey Supreme Court used a strict "appearance of impropriety" standard to disallow joint representation of two different governments, a municipality and the surrounding county. But in another case, the court held that a single government lawyer may represent several different boards which are part of the same township, when there is little likelihood of a conflict arising. *DeLuca v. Kahr Bros.*, 171 N.J. Sup. 100, 407 A.2d 1285 (1979), required the boards to consent to being defended by the same counsel, but permitted the joint representation as being in the public interest. Nevertheless, the state ethics advisory committee, in New Jersey Opinion 560 (1985), applied the narrow "appearance of impropriety" standard to a lawyer's representation of different agencies within the same governmental entity, warning against this even where there is no apparent conflict.

Connecticut has an intriguing ethics opinion, Opinion 85-13 (1985). This opinion characterizes each of the individual members of a local board as

---

[8] Note, however, that the *Lindsey dicta* implies not merely that a lawyer in Ossias' position may blow the whistle, but that she *must*.

"clients," though it acknowledges that if these individuals act antithetically to the board, counsel would have a duty to inform the board.

What guidance exists in California for Messrs. Hahn and Pines? Perhaps not surprisingly, there are somewhat conflicting messages in the case law. *Civil Service Comm'n of San Diego Cty. v. Superior Court*, 163 Cal. App. 3d 70, 209 Cal. Rptr. 159 (1984) concerned an underlying labor dispute. County counsel had advised both the county department of social services and the civil service commission, which eventually found against the department. But county counsel, concluding the commission was in error in deciding for the employees against the county, then filed an action on the county's behalf to overturn the commission's decision. The court disqualified county counsel, holding that given the necessary independence of a civil service commission, it was too simplistic to conclude that "the county" was the only client. Yet the court notes its holding is narrow.

CIVIL SERVICE COMM'N OF SAN DIEGO COUNTY v. SUPERIOR COURT
163 Cal. App. 3d 70, 209 Cal. Rptr. 159 (1984)

While we have determined that county counsel must be disqualified from representing the County in this case, we wish to indicate the limits of our holding. First, it should again be emphasized that a conflict of this nature only arises in the case of and to the extent that a county agency is independent of the County such that litigation between them may ensue. Second, disqualification of county counsel is not necessarily mandated in future cases involving quasi-independent agencies. We have noted that a fundamental conflict arises whenever county counsel is asked to represent both the Commission and the County. Moreover, it is clear from the course of this case that county counsel, with good reason, views his primary responsibility as being to the board of supervisors. If the Commission is afforded access to independent legal advice, however, there is no reason county counsel may not continue to vigorously represent the County even when such representation results in litigation against the Commission. We need not and do not decide whether the Commission, appropriately informed and advised in a given case, could validly waive the conflict at the advisory stage. At most, we deal here with a manifestation of the system's general insensitivity to conflict of interest questions as they affect the government attorney. By our comments we do not mean to suggest that government attorneys must necessarily be treated identically with attorneys in private practice. But neither are they immune from conflict problems similar to those which confront the private bar. Our decision is but one small step in what should be a continuing process to develop standards of conduct which accurately reflect the realities of practice in the private and public sectors.

NOTES

Both Messrs. Hahn and Pines and the ethics experts who dispute them can take some comfort from this case. On the one hand, the court prevented representation in litigation after counsel gave advice to two different government agencies. On the other, the giving of the advice, in and of itself, was not criticized by the court. In 1992, another California appeals court affirmed that advising two agencies of the same municipality may be permissible. In *Howitt v. Superior Court*, 3 Cal. App. 4th 1575, 5 Cal. Rptr. 2d 196 (1992), county counsel was allowed to represent one government agency (here, a sheriff's department) in an employee hearing before an appeals board, while also giving advice to that appeals board. The court permitted the dual representation so long as appropriate screening procedures protected the independence of the separate deputy county counsel.

6. Representing the Government and Its Individual Employees. The most frequent forum for employer/employee conflicts is the lawsuit against a municipality and its police officers. Consider *Dunton v. County of Suffolk*, 729 F.2d 903 (2d Cir. 1984). There, plaintiff sued Suffolk County (N.Y.) and two of its police officers for malicious prosecution and battery. On appeal, the court found that the defendant police officers had been deprived of a fair trial, as the county and the cops had all been represented by the same counsel. The lawyer argued, successfully, that the county was not liable because the officers were acting outside the scope of employment. The court held that where there was a "likely conflict of interest," the trial court should carefully scrutinize the arrangement before the county attorney may represent all parties.

In response to this case, Suffolk County proposed to set up a panel of three lawyers, and have the officers choose their attorneys from among the three. In *Suffolk Cty. Patrolmen's Benevolent Ass'n v. County of Suffolk*, 751 F.2d 550 (2d Cir. 1985), the union representing the two officers sued the county to seek the appointment of independent counsel chosen by the defendants themselves. The court refused to extend *Dunton*. While the defendants were entitled to independent counsel, it was up to the county to select the attorneys; otherwise the county would have no way of controlling costs.

Connecticut has a statutory requirement of indemnification for its police officers. General Statute 7-101-a requires a municipality to "protect and save harmless any municipal officer from financial loss or expense . . . arising out of any claim. . . ." This is certainly a pure solution, albeit not economical, and thus not likely to achieve widespread adoption. Even with indemnification, however, the U.S. District Court in Connecticut has required the fully informed consent of individual employees to the joint representation. *Manganella v. Keyes*, 613 F. Supp. 795 (D. Conn. 1985).

Cases in other jurisdictions have both extended and limited *Dunton*. In a Texas police brutality case, *Shadid v. Jackson*, 521 F. Supp. 87 (E.D. Tex. 1981), the court held that when a city and its police officer employees were to be represented by the same counsel, in "circumstances present[ing] . . . an obvious potential for conflict," the conflict is unwaivable, and separate representation is required. But in *Rodick v. City of Schenectady*, 1 F.3d 1341 (2d Cir. 1993), the court found that, because a trial had already occurred, and the police officers accused of undue force and misconduct had not shown any actual prejudice to their case because of joint representation by Schenectady's counsel, no *Dunton* review was needed. Would the outcome have been different had the appellants moved for disqualification of the city's attorney before trial?

The *Barkley* case below contains a thorough ethical analysis of conflicts in the governmental attorney sphere. Compare it with the cases cited above.

BARKLEY v. CITY OF DETROIT
204 Mich. App. 194, 514 N.W.2d 242 (1994)

This is an action for declaratory judgment concerning the duty of defendant, the City of Detroit, to provide legal counsel to police officers being sued for injuries allegedly inflicted by the officers during the performance of their official duties. Plaintiffs, who are all police officers and members of the Detroit Police Officers Association (DPOA), and the City of Detroit were named as defendants in nine separate civil suits that alleged various acts of police misconduct. At issue is whether ethical considerations prevent attorneys from the city's law department from fulfilling the city's obligation to provide counsel for plaintiffs in those civil actions. . . .

The Detroit Charter, § 6-403 provides that, "upon request, the corporation counsel may represent any officer or employee of the city in any act or proceeding involving official duties." [Also, the] Detroit Code states that, "where there is willful misconduct or lack of good faith in the doing of such acts, the same shall not constitute the performance of the official duties . . . ."

Detroit Code, art. XI, § 13-11-5 provides that the corporation counsel shall represent an employee in an underlying suit until the city council determines otherwise . . . . However, the collective bargaining agreement . . . provid[es] that the city council's determination is subject to final and binding arbitration and that representation will be provided in the underlying suit until the conclusion of arbitral proceedings.

Plaintiffs argue that as soon as the city's corporation counsel (acting through the city's law department) decides to recommend to the city council that no representation be provided, a conflict of interest arises. This conflict, they argue, requires that the corporation counsel withdraw from representing them in the underlying suit. Thus, in order to meet its obligation under the city code and the collective bargaining agreement, the city must pay for plaintiffs to be represented by attorneys of their own choosing.

. . . .

The trial court held that there is indeed a conflict of interest that arises when the city council refuses to provide representation and an employee seeks to overturn that decision through arbitration. That conflict arises because the corporation counsel would be representing the employee in the underlying suit while at the same time representing the city in the arbitration proceeding, in effect, arguing for the employee in one forum and against the employee in another. The parties do not challenge this determination, which we agree is a correct holding.

The trial court also held that, once a conflict arises, the city should pay for the employee to be represented in the underlying suit by independent counsel. . . . The court further found that no conflict of interest existed before an adverse determination by the city council. . . . Plaintiffs argue that a conflict arises when the corporation counsel represents both the city and an employee in an underlying suit while at the same time arguing to the city counsel that no representation should be provided. We agree.

. . . .

The [Michigan State Bar] Ethics Committee has [stated]:

Where a City Attorney rendered advice on a matter to members of City Council who later sued the City over the same matter, the City Attorney may defend the City in the case only if he did not gain and did not appear to gain confidential information from the council members involved and his contact with them would not affect or appear to affect his independent professional judgment on behalf of the City. [Informal Opinion CI-335 (January 16, 1978).]

. . . .

The ethical issue presented is whether the representation of these individual plaintiffs by an attorney from the city's law department "may be materially limited by the lawyer's responsibilities" to the city, given that these plaintiffs obviously do not wish to consent to such dual representation. In such a situation, the parties seem to agree that an actual conflict is unlikely because access to the party perceived to have the deeper pockets would be obtained by showing that the employee acted within the scope of employment, thereby imposing liability on the city. However, there is a danger that the evidence will show otherwise and liability will rest solely on the individual plaintiff. . . . Therefore, such dual representation should not be undertaken.

We now return to the issue whether the city's law department should be treated in the same manner as a private law firm, so that the disqualification of one attorney should be imputed to others. *See* MRPC 1.10. We find that it should. . . .

It might be argued that a so-called "Chinese wall" might be erected such that a disqualified attorney would have neither any role in the case nor any contact with the attorneys actually involved. . . . The present case, however, does not involve a particular attorney with a particular disqualification. Rather, because all attorneys in the department represent the city and owe it the duties discussed above, none of them are free to also represent an individual employee once a conflict arises. For this purpose, we find that the department should be considered a law firm.

We, therefore, hold that assuming that the city law department is representing the city in the underlying suit, no attorney from the city law department may also represent plaintiffs in the same suit.[9] This, however, does not mean that plaintiffs should be allowed to choose who will represent them at city expense. . . . [T]he city may select plaintiffs' counsel in the underlying cases as long as it selects an independent and unbiased counsel with none of the ethical problems discussed above. . . .

---

[9] [7] We do not decide whether different departments of, for example, the Attorney General's office, may represent parties on both sides of a dispute. Although some references were made in this regard, that is not an issue before us.

NOTES

When two different but related parties are sued, one party's theory of the case can create problems for the other. Where a police director who sought advice of counsel when acting in his official capacity was later sued in his individual capacity, he raised advice of counsel as the basis of his qualified immunity defense. The city was also sued, and claimed attorney-client privilege to protect the communications between the police director and the city attorney. The Sixth Circuit had to resolve whether the *director* invoking advice of counsel impliedly waived the *city's* attorney-client privilege held by the city. The Court said no: "Having concluded that a municipality can assert the attorney-client privilege in civil proceedings, we now hold that a municipal official's assertion of the advice of counsel defense does not require the City to relinquish the privilege it holds." *Ross v. City of Memphis*, 423 F.3d 596, 603 (6th Cir. 2005).

7. Screening Revisited. Note the reference in the *Howitt* case (see Section 5 above) to screening as a justification for allowing two different departments of the county counsel to represent two different agencies of the same government. Screening, you may recall from Problem 10, is the evolving but still generally disfavored tactic resorted to by law firms in an effort to prevent their total disqualification. In *Barkley,* the court correctly points out that in that particular case, the systemic nature of the conflict — with the party being the municipality itself, not merely different agencies within the city government — means that screening of separate attorneys would not solve the conflict of interest. But the language of the court's opinion certainly allows for the possibility that setting up a screen would be permitted in an appropriate case.

Indeed, it appears that, whether stated or not, principles of screening are frequently behind those court decisions that permit representation of two or more different governmental agencies by the same government "law firm," a circumstance that simply would not be allowed for a private firm in most states, at least if the agency is considered the client. Anyone who is considered a "client" is going to have significant expectations about confidentiality of communications. Several cases make reference to the fact that one office of government lawyers has little or no interaction with another office, thus allowing confidences to be preserved and justifying dual representation. This is particularly true in the case of the federal government.

Sometimes, the courts have acknowledged de facto screening. *In re Lee G.,* 1 Cal. App. 4th 17, 1 Cal. Rptr. 2d 375 (1991), concerned the dependency of a minor. Two separate and distinct offices of county counsel were permitted to represent both the department of social services, seeking to place the child away from the mother, and the conservator for the mother. The court pointed to the lack of connection between the two offices in denying the mother's motion for independent counsel.

As we discussed in Problem 10, screening of government lawyers has special status after the fact as well. That is, screening is far more liberally allowed when the lawyer in question is a former government attorney. Model Rule 1.11 directs itself specifically and extensively to this question.

But before we move on, what if the boss has a conflict? The California Supreme Court decided that vicarious disqualification of an entire government law firm was required when the elected San Francisco City Attorney had, in private practice, represented a client that was being sued by the city in a matter substantially related to the chief attorney's prior representation.[10] The California Supreme Court found that as the chief attorney of his office, the City Attorney could neither successfully delegate the representation nor create a valid ethical screen.

8. The Part-Time Government Lawyer. What happens when a lawyer works part-time as a government attorney and part-time in a private practice? Several states have used a broad "appearance of impropriety" standard which excludes any conflicting employment. And when the constitutional rights of the criminally accused are at stake, the restrictions are even more pronounced. In *Utah v. Brown*, 201 Utah Adv. Rep. 4, 853 P.2d 851 (1992), the court appointed a part-time municipal prosecutor as a criminal defendant's trial counsel. The court held that "as a matter of public policy and pursuant to our inherent supervisory power over the courts, as well as our express power to govern the practice of law, counsel with concurrent prosecutorial obligations may not be appointed to defend indigent persons." The defendant's conviction was reversed and a new trial ordered.

Compare *Brown* to a more recent 1997 Utah Supreme Court case. In *V-1 Oil Company, aka V-1 Propane v. Dept of Environmental Quality*, 317 Utah Adv. Rep. 11, 939 P.2d 1192 (1997), the court held that an administrative governmental agency, the Solid and Hazardous Waste Control Board, could appoint one of its own employees to preside at a formal hearing on a respondent's alleged hazardous waste violation. The agency employee was a part-time staff attorney in the same division charged with investigating and prosecuting violations. The lawyer's duties did not involve investigating the kind of violation at hand (underground storage leaks). Still, the state court of appeals disqualified the appointee. The Supreme Court reversed, denying the assumption that the lawyer-appointee would automatically act in the interest of his employer, the Board: "His duty of loyalty toward his employer required him to function as an impartial adjudicator. [F]ailure to do so would constitute a serious breach of loyalty. We do not accept the proposition that the employing agency is a client or that the appointee owes the same duty of loyalty to that agency that he would owe a client." Do you agree?

Is *V-1* easily reconciled with *Brown*? Is there a legitimate distinction because *Brown* involved a criminal case while *V-1* only involved civil administrative penalties? What about when the penalties have a quasi-criminal effect?

9. The Government Lawyer as Employee. It is significant that government attorneys are not only the legal advisors to their entities, but also the employees of those entities. One emerging issue, which can affect corporate house counsel as well as government lawyers, is what happens when an attorney is terminated or otherwise leaves employment unwillingly. Can the lawyer sue for discrimination, wrongful discharge, and so on? Would such a suit involve revealing attorney-client confidences and secrets? For example, what

---

[10] *City & County of San Francisco v. Cobra Solutions, Inc.*, 38 Cal. 4th 839, 135 P.3d 20, 43 Cal. Rptr. 3d 771 (2006).

if the lawyer is privy to information demonstrating the agency's lack of good faith in its open hiring policy? May the lawyer use this information later in an employment suit? If a lawyer may do this, it may have a chilling effect on how much confidential information is disclosed to such attorneys in the first place.

May government attorneys be disciplined for their attempts to bring matters to the attention of their superiors where they feel the government's interests would be best served? Recall *Garcetti v. Ceballos*, __ U.S. __, 126 S. Ct. 1951 (2006), in the last problem. A sharply divided United States Supreme Court has now answered this question "yes," at least as to First Amendment grounds.

Another issue, more likely to affect governmental attorneys than their brothers and sisters in the private sector, is organized labor efforts. Issues of confidentiality and its breach arise when all deputy city counsel, for instance, unionize or threaten a strike unless they receive an acceptable collective bargaining agreement. These issues have not yet thoroughly been addressed by the courts of most states, a situation we expect will change in the near future.

At least one state, California, has permitted public attorneys to unionize and even to sue their own employers through their employee associations, and actually sue their employers. In *Santa Clara County Counsel Attorneys Assn. v. Woodside*, 7 Cal. 4th 525, 869 P.2d 1142, 28 Cal. Rptr. 2d 617 (1994), the court upheld a California statute that permitted government lawyers to form collective bargaining units and sue if they believed, as happened in this case, that the employer had failed to negotiate in good faith. The court stopped short of "approv[ing] the general proposition that an attorney suit against a present client is ethically permissible." "[W]e are not unmindful," wrote the court, "of the fact that attorneys suing their clients, in any circumstance, put a strain on the attorney/client relationship, and may tend to diminish the client's confidence in their attorneys' loyalty." But, emphasizing that the legislature had specifically given public attorneys a limited statutory employment right, the court allowed the lawsuit to proceed.

10. Who Is the Client, Revisited. The following article demonstrates how difficult it can be to define who a government attorney's client really is. Especially in the context of the federal government lawyer, can it ever be defined with precision?

L.J. PENDLEBURY, BAR, AGENCIES HAGGLE OVER DEFINING "CLIENT": FOR WHOM DOES THE GOVERNMENT LAWYER TOIL?
Legal Times (November 14, 1988)[11]

Who is a lawyer's client? For private attorneys, that question is usually a simple one. But take a Customs Service lawyer: Is this lawyer's client the Customs Service, the Treasury Department, or the whole U.S. government?

This may sound like only a matter of semantics, but it is much more. A debate being waged in government circles and at the D.C. Bar is bringing to

---

[11] Reprinted with permission of Legal Times. Copyright © 1988.

the surface strong differences over the definition of *client* for government lawyers, and the issue's ultimate resolution could significantly affect how these lawyers function. . . .

. . . .

At the monthly meeting of the bar's board of governors last Tuesday, President-elect Charles Ruff of Covington & Burling, a former U.S. attorney for the District, focused the issue sharply.

Ruff objected vigorously to a special bar committee's proposal to ask the appeals court to define the government lawyer's *client* as the agency, department, or individual whose interests the attorney is directly representing.

Under this definition, the hypothetical Customs Service attorney would represent only the service or any individual he or she is assigned to represent. The lawyer's duty would run only to those clients.

Moreover, if this lawyer shared confidential information with any other office, including another agency within the Treasury Department like the Internal Revenue Service, he could face a bar disciplinary proceeding for violating the confidentiality of his client, the Customs Service.

The court's version doesn't distinguish between private and government lawyers for the purpose of the ethics rules.

Ruff strenuously contended that in view of the complexities of the issue, the bar ought to define the client in every possible instance or, if that is impossible, just stay away from the issue and leave it up to the agencies themselves.

"I wonder whether we're serving any real purpose here by serving up an all-purpose definition of who the client is," said Ruff. "It is not our role to solve the problems of the world regarding the inner workings of government lawyers."

Just a "Rule of Thumb"

Joe Sims, partner in the D.C. office of Cleveland's Jones, Day, Reavis & Pogue, who chaired the special bar committee, pointed out that the report calls its conclusion merely a "rule of thumb, a benchmark from which deviations can be made as appropriate."

Sims later conceded, however, that "it is optimistic in the extreme to think you can serve up an ethics rule that can spell out exactly who the government client is in all cases."

Despite Sims' concession, the measure passed overwhelmingly, with Ruff the only dissenter. The bar committee will now submit to the court suggested revisions of the ethics rules that attempt to define the client in a narrow manner.

. . . .

[The D.C. bar received a series of comments on its proposals from high-ranking government lawyers.]

Russell Bruemmer, general counsel of the Central Intelligence Agency, for example, described interagency meetings at which "lawyers from within the executive branch communicate with each other and discuss legal issues in a manner that goes beyond the interests of a particular agency."

Bruemmer suggested that, in such a meeting, the client of the lawyers present might be the United States or, at least, the executive branch.

William Parler, general counsel of the Nuclear Regulatory Commission, asked whether a federal attorney might run afoul of confidentiality rules if he responds to a White House or congressional oversight committee request for information.

Parler also wondered how a government attorney should respond if the Office of Government Ethics requests a meeting regarding the activities of officials in the attorney's agency. Would a breach of attorney-client privilege occur?

The Federal Bar Association proposed going even farther than the Sims committee in limiting the definition of the client. In a letter submitted by association president Bonnie Gay, a Justice Department lawyer, the voluntary bar group urged that the client agency be clearly described as "the lowest common denominator, . . . a bureau or office and not the entire department or other bureaus or offices with which the attorney does not have a close working relationship."

SUPPLEMENTAL READINGS

1. *Ward v. Superior Court*, 70 Cal. App. 3d 23, 138 Cal. Rptr. 532 (1977), is an older case similar to the facts in our problem. It involved a volatile dispute between the Los Angeles County assessor and the county board of supervisors that ended in litigation. The assessor, one Philip Watson, ultimately sued the board in his individual capacity "and as a taxpayer and resident of the County" for violations of the Civil Rights Act (42 U.S.C. § 1983). When county counsel represented the board, Watson moved to disqualify that office, since it represented him as well, as assessor. The trial court granted the motion, but the appeals court reversed. It held that the assessor's office is "merely an arm of county government" supervised by the board, and that communications between county counsel and the assessor, "an agent of the county," could not "be considered secret confidential communication so as to bar the county, acting through the board of supervisors, from obtaining that information." This harsh language on confidentiality may have been motivated by the personal nature of Watson's lawsuit against the county.

2. Michael Stokes Paulsen, *Who "Owns" the Government's Attorney Client Privilege?*, 83 Minn. L. Rev. 473 (1998). This is a good overview evaluating the attorney-client privilege in the context of an Independent Counsel investigating executive branch officials.

3. Two significant articles addressing whistleblowing by governmental attorneys are Roger C. Cramton, *The Lawyer as Whistleblower: Confidentiality and the Government Lawyer*, 5 Geo. J. Leg. Ethics 291 (1991), and Richard C. Solomon, *Wearing Many Hats: Confidentiality and Conflicts of Interest Issues for the California Public Lawyer*, 25 Sw. U. L. Rev. 265 (1996). Cramton's piece is a valuable study charting the interrelationship between the ethical rules on whistleblowing and confidentiality and the recent development of whistleblowing statutes. Solomon begins by stating that "California has rejected the concept of lawyer as whistleblower," and then discusses how and when an attorney would be warranted in going to the highest authority when wrongdoing antithetical to the public interest occurs.

4. Jesselyn Radack, a federal whistleblower in the case of "American Taliban" John Walker Lindh, has written two articles worthy of note. In *The Government Attorney-Whistleblower and the Rule of Confidentiality: Compatible at Last,* 17 Geo. J. Legal Ethics 125 (2003), she discusses the new, broader MR 1.6 exceptions and whistleblower protection laws, as they combine to provide the beginnings of a solution for government attorney-whistleblowers. In *Tortured Legal Ethics: The Role of the Government Advisor in the War on Terrorism,* 77 U. Colo. L. Rev. 1 (2006), she explores both an agency and public interest approach to the ethical duties of government lawyers. She argues for the primacy of a public interest approach when government lawyers give advice "on morally perilous questions."

5. The New Jersey Supreme Court has written several opinions dealing with the ethical requirements of the governmental attorney. In *In re Opinion 552,* 102 N.J. 194, 507 A.2d 233 (1986), the court overturned its own advisory committee on professional ethics, ruling that a municipal attorney may represent the city and its employees in a federal discrimination action where the defendants have potential diverging interests, provided there is a substantial identity of interests between them. In *In re Opinion 452,* 87 N.J. 45, 432 A.2d 829 (1981), the court affirmed the opinion of its ethics panel that it was a conflict of interest for two partners in the same law firm to work for the same city as municipal prosecutors and attorneys for the planning board. In *In re Opinion 653*, 132 N.J. 124, 623 A.2d 241 (1993), the court ruled no inherent conflict existed when two partners in the same law firm served in positions for the same county, one as county counsel and the other as counsel to the county vocational school board.

6. Heather E. Kimmel, Note, *Solutions to the City Attorney's Charter-Imposed Conflict of Interest Problem*, 66 Ohio St. L.J. 1075 (2005), is a law review note discussing conflict of interest problems that may arise when city attorneys are required by charter to represent both the mayor and the city council, and other difficulties dealing with the who is the client dilemma.

7. *United States v. Reynoso,* 6 F. Supp. 2d 269 (S.D.N.Y. 1998), involves a liberalized screening standard for quasi-governmental lawyers, such as those contracted to do defense work through New York's Legal Aid Society. In *Reynoso*, the prosecution requested to disqualify a federal Legal Aid Society lawyer because another legal aid lawyer had represented a witness in the current case four years before on another matter. The defendant wanted to keep his lawyer. The court denied the motion, which had been joined by the former client/witness.

8. James R. Harvey III, *Note: Loyalty in Government Litigation: Department of Justice Representation of Agency Clients*, 37 Wm. & Mary L. Rev. 1569 (1996), examines the issue of whom the Department of Justice represents, and what happens in situations in which an agency such as DOJ is asked to litigate a matter it does not consider to be in the government's best interest. Harvey examines the ethical standards that define the duty of both the individual lawyer and the agency itself.

9. Pam Smith, "Court Bangs Head on 'Ethical Wall,'" *The Recorder* (San Francisco), March 9, 2006, has a good discussion of the ethical issues raised by *City & County of San Francisco v. Cobra Solutions, Inc.*, cited in section 7 of the Readings.

10. Steven K. Berenson, *The Duty Defined: Specific Obligations that Follow from Civil Government Lawyers' General Duty to Serve the Public Interest*, 42 Brandeis L.J. 13 (2003) discusses the differences between a civil government lawyer's ethical duties in serving the public interest and those of a private practitioner.

Chapter 9

THE LAWYER ACTING AS ADVISER

PROBLEM 24

This problem raises several issues for the lawyer who is asked for advice. First, how should an attorney approach the task of giving the advice? Second, when does a lawyer know a client is using advice for a fraudulent purpose? This issue of knowledge is similar to others we have encountered before (for example, see Problems 14 and 15). Third, what should the lawyer do when the client wants more than advice — active assistance in what may be fraudulent conduct? We will look at several scandals involving lawyers, including Enron, in examining the line between advice and active assistance.

What's Most Important — What You Say, How You Say It . . . or Whether You Should Say It at All?

Lonnie Pomeranian is a lawyer specializing in immigration matters. One day she is visited by an old client, Solomon Tovarich, whose family Pomeranian has helped over the years. The following conversation takes place:

> "Lonnie," says Solomon, "my best friend Mischa's family is visiting from Ukraine. His brother and sister-in-law and their beautiful daughter Elena. And they say things are no better there. Sure, it's better for some than the old days, but for Jews it's even worse. Mischa's brother says it's too late for them, but Elena is twenty and wants to emigrate. But with the quotas filled, it's impossible. I was thinking, I'm a widower, my kids are grown, I got a good job, maybe I could marry Elena. She's a beautiful young lady, intelligent. She could stay here, go to college."

> "You know, Sol, marrying a foreigner to avoid immigration quotas is a serious crime."

> "I'm aware of that," replies Tovarich. "Why do you think I came to you?"

Consider the following alternative responses that Pomeranian could make to Tovarich. For purposes of this problem, assume the legal accuracy of the advice given.

Scenario #1: "If this is what you really want, my advice to you is to court Elena every minute while she's here on her visitor's visa. Spend holidays with her, your birthday, and hers. Look for a new apartment together, and furnish it. Even write her love letters. And she should do the same. She'll have to be convincing about why a young woman like her is falling in love with an old goat like you."

"Is all that necessary?"

"Only if you want immigration to believe that this is a marriage made of love, not quotas."

Scenario #2: "Well, Sol, I'll go through it piece by piece. The key issue is whether your marriage to Elena is one of convenience. That is, are you marrying her for real, or to get her a legal 'status adjustment' that would let her stay in the States? Marrying her so she can live here would be defrauding the Immigration Service."

"So what will Immigration do?" asks Tovarich.

"Well," says Pomeranian, "immigration applications are now investigated by the USCIS, which is part of Homeland Security. They can't investigate every marriage, and you're not in the groups they scrutinize most closely, but they do check out a sizable random sample. They investigate a much higher sample of people who fit their sham marriage 'profile.' I guarantee that with your age difference and the full immigration quota, you fit right into that profile."

"Of course, whether your marriage is real or a sham is a question of fact. The USCIS can only look at how the two of you act and what you say to determine the legitimacy of your marriage. For example, if you can prove you spent months in each other's company before you got married, or exchanged long letters of devotion and affection, or were always together on important occasions, that would all tend to show that your marriage is for real."

"I'll guarantee you something else: If they do investigate, you'll each be interviewed separately, and they'll ask you where you were on various dates you might be expected to remember — July 4, Thanksgiving, your birthday, hers. They'll ask you where you've been in the week just before the interview. They'll ask what kind of toothpaste and soap she uses. If your answers don't match, they'll use it against you and probably see it as fraud. But if it's clear by your answers that you've really spent the time together, it will be very strong evidentiary support for a marriage made in heaven."

"Lonnie, that's very helpful. Every day I'm more in love."

QUESTIONS

1. Is the first scenario unethical? Ethically, does it differ from the second?

2. Recall Professor Freedman's penknife and *Anatomy of a Murder* scenarios discussed in Problem 15. Compare those scenarios to these. What are the differences? The similarities?

3. Suppose Tovarich decides to go forward with his plan to marry Elena, and asks Pomeranian for her help in filling out the necessary documents for Elena's legal status. May Lonnie help him and Elena? What else, if anything, should Pomeranian consider before giving herself to this effort?

4. Suppose the USCIS challenges Tovarich's marriage and the issue turns on his state of mind as to the reason for the marriage. Could Lonnie represent Solomon before the USCIS? Does it matter whether she prepared the papers originally? Finally, which do you find easier, preparing the documents or defending the couple afterwards? Why?

READINGS

1. How Should Lawyers Advise Their Clients? To what extent does the lawyer owe a duty of full disclosure? What about where the lawyer believes the client may put the advice to improper use? Or where the lawyer thinks the advice may encourage the client to "get away with" something because of the small likelihood of getting caught? Should these issues affect how the lawyer gives advice? Here is a view from a professor who teaches both ethics and tax about one of the most complex of all areas of legal counseling — tax advice.

JOEL S. NEWMAN, THE AUDIT LOTTERY: DON'T ASK, DON'T TELL?
Tax Notes 1438 (March 6, 2000)[1]

In Book II of Plato's *Republic,* Socrates tells of the shepherd Gyges, who discovered a ring that would make him invisible whenever he wished. With a twist of the ring, he could do anything he pleased, and never get caught. For centuries, philosophers have argued over whether Gyges should have lived a moral life anyway.

The tax version of Gyges's ring is the audit rate, which has rarely exceeded 2 percent of all returns filed. Of course, 98 percent invisibility does not quite reach the 100 percent invisibility that Gyges achieved, but it is close enough for tax work. Many taxpayers have twisted the ring, and played the audit lottery. They have taken questionable or worse positions on tax returns, betting that they would not be audited. . . .

Whether Gyges the taxpayer should twist the ring and play the audit lottery is one thing. Whether his lawyer should tell an unknowing Gyges what the ring can do is quite another. I propose to discuss the latter question. May a lawyer discuss the audit lottery with her client? Must she?

. . . .

[T]he national audit rate for the average, individual taxpayer is very low. If we know that our client is indeed average, with none of the peculiarities that might raise an IRS eyebrow, then the audit probability is indeed 1 percent. Why can't we tell them that?

The problem arises if we know that our client intends to take a questionable or worse position on a tax return. Arguably, advising such a client that, with a low audit rate, he is unlikely to get caught is tantamount to helping the client break the law. However, if we don't tell the client, then we are failing in an essential lawyering function. Some people already know about the low audit rate. Shouldn't everyone know? Shouldn't all taxpayers start with the same information in their dealings with their government?

Model Rules of Professional Conduct

The Model Rules of Professional Conduct do not provide many helpful answers, but they do ask the right questions. That is more than the specific

---

tax authorities do. The relevant portion of Model Rule 1.2(d) is set forth below. Its two clauses have been separated, so that its possible contradictions will be more apparent:

> A lawyer shall not counsel a client to engage, or assist a client, in conduct that the lawyer knows is criminal or fraudulent,

> but a lawyer may discuss the legal consequences of any proposed course of conduct with a client. . . .

For the remainder of this discussion, then, consider a client who wishes to take a position on a tax return that in your view is neither criminal, fraudulent, nor even frivolous. However, you do not believe that the position satisfies the realistic possibility standard of section 6694.[2] The client has no plans to disclose the position adequately. . . . May you tell that client about the low audit rate?

As discussed above, the first clause of Model Rule 1.2(d) should not apply at all, since the proposed conduct is neither criminal nor fraudulent. However, parsing Model Rule 1.2(d) might still be helpful in raising the legal and ethical issues that are involved. The uses of "counsel," "assist," and "legal consequences" are especially intriguing.

"Counsel" and "Assist"

Here is the argument for a broad interpretation of "counsel" and "assist." Advising a client on a proposed course of action usually means helping her to weigh its costs and benefits. Anything that lowers the costs in the client's eyes will make the course of action more probable. Telling her that she probably won't get caught is one way of lowering those projected costs. Therefore, discussing the low audit rate is counseling and assisting the client to engage in the conduct.

The interpretation sketched out above is too broad. Assume that the client proposes criminal or fraudulent conduct. Pursuant to the broad interpretation, any time a lawyer discusses a legal consequence of that conduct that is even remotely positive, the lawyer is counseling or assisting that conduct. Therefore, the first clause of Rule 1.2(d) ["counsel" or "assist"] would contradict the second ["discuss legal consequences"]. Surely, such contradictions were not intended.

Mere advice, without more, should never be construed as a violation of Model Rule l.2(d). If it were, then it would be very difficult for lawyers to give any advice at all. Advice is, after all, the most worthwhile thing we have to give.

"Legal Consequences"

The notion of what constitutes law, and hence, what constitutes "legal consequences" has been greatly expanded, thanks to the Legal Realism

---

2 [21] Section 6694 levies a fine on the income tax return preparer if: (1) any part of the understatement of liability with respect to any return is due to a position for which there was not a realistic possibility of being sustained on its merits. . . .

movement. No longer a sterile discussion of statutes and cases, an analysis of "legal consequences" now must include consideration of the way in which government actually works. Surely, such an analysis properly includes a consideration of governmental enforcement patterns. However, one must be careful not to take this notion too far. Without proper limits, encouraging lawyers to discuss enforcement patterns leads to the notion that what is lawful is whatever one can get away with. At that point, Legal Realism loses its coherence and moral force.

Yet, within limits, it is not only appropriate, but necessary to consider patterns of government enforcement when advising clients about legal consequences. Two relevant parameters concern the difference between "never enforced" and "rarely enforced," and the difference between intentional and unintentional underenforcement.

Never Enforced and Rarely Enforced

Imagine that there is a statute on the books in your state that criminalizes the playing of bingo, even if no money changes hands, even if the game is played among friends in their private homes. Imagine further that this statute has not been enforced for 50 years, and that the local prosecutors have no intention of ever enforcing it again. Your client proposes to play bingo, at home with his friends, for no money.

If you tell your client that playing bingo is a crime, and say no more, then you are doing your client a major disservice. Your statement would not be an accurate description of the legal consequences of playing bingo. There is general agreement that if a law is never enforced, it is appropriate, and necessary, to say so.

When one goes from "never enforced" to "rarely enforced," certainty and consensus break down. However, [w]ho among us has not had the experience of driving at 62 in a 55-mile-per-hour zone, only to be passed by almost everyone else on the road, including a few state troopers? Clearly, the enforcers know that the law is being broken. Yet, they rarely choose to enforce it. . . . As to the question of what the law is, the speed limit is not really 55. As to the question of consequences, the legal consequences of driving 62 in a 55-miles-per-hour zone are usually zero. . . .

Intentional vs. Unintentional Underenforcement

Tax law enforcement, however, is not the same as traffic enforcement. There is no tax law counterpart to going just a little bit over the speed limit. If your tax return is incorrect, even just a little bit, and the IRS finds out about it, you will be required to correct it, and to pay whatever taxes, interest, and penalties that might result.

It is the IRS problem with detection, however, that is the rub. In a sense, our traffic laws are not fully enforced because the government won't enforce them; our tax laws are not fully enforced because the government can't enforce them. Arguably, instances of "the government won't" can properly be discussed with clients; instances of "the government can't" cannot. . . .

However, even if the underlying distinction between "can't" and "won't" is accepted, it is not clear which side tax law enforcement is on. Note that it would not be impossible for the IRS to audit every return. The low audit rate is caused primarily by a refusal of Congress to staff and fund the IRS at the requisite levels. Congressional funding levels of IRS have been pretty consistent since 1913; the IRS has never had the personnel to audit more than a tiny fraction of submitted returns. Hasn't this been going on long enough so that we can call it a policy? . . . [S]urely the taxpaying public at least has a right to know of the conscious underfunding of IRS, and of its consequences in policy and practical terms.

The Moral Dimension: Crime and Fraud Redux

[Denver ethics professor] Stephen Pepper argues that the propriety of discussing legal consequences and enforcement policy with respect to a proposed course of conduct should depend on how bad the proposed course of conduct would be. He distinguishes *malum prohibitum* — something that is prohibited only because the law says so — from *malum in se* — something that is wrong by its very nature. A lawyer should feel perfectly free to discuss any and all legal consequences of a breach of a contract, but a lawyer should be much more circumspect in discussing the legal consequences of murder. On his continuum, Pepper locates taking an aggressive position on a tax return as somewhere in the middle.

. . . .

Bear in mind that the lawyer is merely communicating information. It is up to the client whether or not to use that information, and how. We should be loath to assume either that our morals are better than our clients', or that we should be making decisions that are properly theirs to make. . . .

Lawyers should give their clients all relevant information. They may then, if they wish, give their clients their opinion on the moral dimensions of the client's decision. They may even enter into a moral dialogue with the client, and try to persuade the client to do the right thing, in their view. Having done all of those things, however, the lawyer must then let the client decide.

Conclusion

Had he asked me, I would have told Gyges exactly what the ring could do. Of course, I would have insisted on being paid in cash for my advice up front, before he disappeared on me.

NOTES

Professor Newman raises many issues in his lucid statement of the problem. Are you fully persuaded by his arguments? Do you accept Newman's reasoning for negating the distinction between a government that "can't" rather than "won't" enforce? Or is it too facile, like his statement that "the speed limit is not really 55" because it's rarely enforced at that level? Do you accept the argument that lawyers who advise their clients even in ways that could be put to fraudulent purpose are "merely communicating information"? Is there, as the Model Rule comment claims, really a "critical distinction" between analyzing legal issues and recommending fraud? What about when your client's fraudulent intent is clear? Finally, does Professor Pepper's distinction between *malum prohibitum* and *malum in se* make sense?

2. Advising on Torture. In the days after September 11, 2001, Americans captured a severely wounded Abu Zubaydah, an important Osama bin Laden lieutenant. By the Spring of 2002, Zubaydah, still gravely wounded, was taken to a safe house in Thailand by a CIA security team. There, after he was sufficiently recovered, Zubaydah was at first interrogated by FBI agents using standard interviewing techniques. The FBI tried to convince him they knew the details of his participation in terror by showing him a box of blank audiotapes that they said, falsely, contained recordings of his phone calls.

While Zubaydah soon began providing information, the CIA agents present believed that he was withholding far more than he told, and took over the interrogation. With the CIA in charge, Zubaydah, still weak, was subjected to coercive interrogation techniques including being stripped, held in an icy-cold room without bed or blankets, sometimes until he turned blue, and blasted with the earsplitting sounds of the Red Hot Chili Peppers (and other loud rockers).[3]

It has since been reported that the FBI and CIA strongly disagreed about Zubaydah's treatment — both its utility and its legality. The *New York Times* reported that three former CIA officials said that their "techniques had been drawn up on the basis of legal guidance from the Justice Department, but were not yet [then] supported by a formal legal opinion."

Accordingly, then CIA Director George Tenet requested a legal memo to protect the interrogators and their superiors from any future prosecution under the 1994 anti-torture act and to ensure — or at least claim — compliance with the United Nations' Convention Against Torture.

The Justice Department's Office of Legal Counsel (OLC) was assigned the task of writing the memo. The head of OLC, Jay Bybee, now a federal appeals judge, eventually signed the August 1, 2002 "torture memo," but the memo was a group effort. OLC staff, particularly John Yoo, now a University of California law professor, drafted the memo, while then White House Counsel Alberto Gonzales, his staff, then Attorney General John Ashcroft's staff, and even Vice President Dick Cheney's legal counsel gave input on drafts. Among other things, the memo stated that treatment of prisoners such as Zubaydah was not torture unless it was "equivalent in intensity to the pain accompanying serious physical injury, such as organ failure, impairment of bodily function, or even death."

Although the Bush administration disavowed the Bybee memo in mid-2004, as late as September 9, 2006, President Bush maintained that the Zubaydah

---

[3] These facts are taken from various news reports, most recently David Johnston, *At a Secret Interrogation, Dispute Flared over Tactics*, N.Y. TIMES, Sept. 10, 2006. Other information in this section has been variously reported by David Johnston, Neil A. Lewis and others for *The New York Times*, Mike Allen, Dana Priest, Professor Kathleen Clark (whose piece on the torture memo appears in Problem 26), for *The Washington Post*, and Stuart Taylor for the *National Review* and the *National Law Journal*.

interrogation was legal: "These procedures were designed to be safe, to comply with our laws, our Constitution and our treaty obligations," Mr. Bush said. Moreover, "the Department of Justice reviewed the authorized methods extensively and determined them to be lawful."

Was the Bybee torture memo a matter of lawyers giving the clients — here, the CIA and, indeed, the President — the answers they wanted to hear, to the denigration of reasonable interpretations of law? Or were the memos honest advice within the bounds of colorable claims of law? Read the following article, which quotes from several former high-ranking government lawyers.

ADAM LIPTAK, HOW FAR CAN A GOVERNMENT LAWYER GO?
The New York Times (June 27, 2004)[4]

A client asks his lawyer a question: During an interrogation of a suspected terrorist, how much pain can I legally inflict?

The lawyer should:

a) Explore every legal avenue available for his client, including all possible defenses should criminal charges be filed.

b) Give legal guidance but add advice on the wisdom and morality of what the client is considering.

c) Tell the client to take a walk.

The lawyers at the Justice Department who prepared the memos concerning torture seemed to have decided on Option A.

These memos raise profound questions about the ethical and moral limits of what lawyers can and should do in advising their clients. It is hardly unusual, of course, for lawyers in private practice to give narrow and comprehensive advice on how to comply with, say, the tax laws to maximum advantage. But lawyers serving private clients rarely confront questions as morally perilous as torture.

[The August 2002 Bybee memo] concluded that only physical pain as intense as that accompanying organ failure or death qualified as torture . . . . John Yoo, a former deputy in the Legal Counsel's office, has said that the exploration of the question of what constitutes torture is important and legitimate. A good analogy, he said, was the legal advice police officers receive on the use of force . . . .

Geoffrey C. Hazard Jr., who teaches legal ethics at the University of Pennsylvania, said "It was very appropriate for lawyers" in the government "to think in concrete terms about what is meant by torture."

Other lawyers stressed that a lawyer's proper task is a narrow one.

"When a government is faced with a situation and is faced with options," said Charles Fried, a law professor at Harvard and a former solicitor general in the Reagan administration, "surely one of the questions it asks — but only one of them — is, what does the law require? Another question is, is it

---

effective? Another is, is it moral? Those are not the same questions." The lawyer's role, he said, is to answer the first question.

Still, government lawyers have more complicated obligations than those in private practice do. The government lawyer's ultimate client, after all, is the public, and government lawyers have not infrequently told their bosses things they did not want to hear.

Attorney General Francis Biddle, for instance, opposed the internment of American citizens of Japanese ancestry during World War II. His boss, President Franklin Roosevelt, overruled him.

Douglas W. Kmiec, who led the Office of Legal Counsel in the Reagan administration, recalled delivering bad news himself. "One of the least happy days in my life," he said, "was telling President Reagan that he could not exercise an inherent line-item veto," because it wasn't implicit in the Constitution, "even though he dearly wanted it."

Walter Dellinger, who ran the office in the Clinton administration, said the torture memos represent a departure from the disinterested advice the office has historically given to presidents in both parties.

The development is particularly unfortunate because it indicates that the no-holds-barred advocacy common in the private sphere has started to infect the work of government lawyers, argued Philip Lacovara, who served in the Nixon administration and as a Watergate prosecutor. "If you set loose very smart and very energetic lawyers and tell them their task is to justify the unjustifiable, they will do it," he said.

Which, according to critics, is just what happened, giving potential abusers a road map for how to avoid prosecution. "It reminded me," Mr. Lacovara said, "of the first time I heard one of the Nixon tapes, when Nixon was giving a little primer on how to escape prosecution for perjury . . . ."

NOTES

Obviously, the torture memos raise a host of important questions. How similar is the advice in Professor Newman's tax scenario and the advice government lawyers gave in the torture memo? Is the "only" distinction the extent of the harm involved — and the explosive political consequences? Do all lawyers have an obligation to advise clients about the moral implications of a legal course of action? Must *government* lawyers take into account, as Liptak's article suggests, that on some level they represent the public? Recall our discussion in the last problem. Should they take into account — as Alberto Gonzales and John Yoo have argued — issues of national security and that they are fighting a war on terrorism? Or should they provide the "disinterested" advice that Walter Dellinger suggests?

3. Knowledge and the Story of O.P.M.'s Lawyers. Lawyers who compromise their ethics by the way they advise their clients are hardly a new story. Each recent decade seems to have had its own top-rated scandal. In recent years, it's been Enron. In the 1990s, it was the Lincoln Savings & Loan debacle, about which more later. In the 1980s, it was the extraordinary story of O.P.M. Leasing. There is much to be learned from each of these stories. We begin with O.P.M. (the acronym stood for "other people's money") and its attorneys, the New York firm of Singer, Hutner, Levine & Seeman.[5]

Beginning in the early 1970s, Singer Hutner began representing O.P.M. Leasing, Inc. O.P.M. was founded in 1970, the brainchild of two partners, childhood friends, and brothers-in-law, Myron Goodman and Mordecai Weissman. O.P.M.'s business involved purchasing computers — the old-fashioned main-frame kind — from IBM, and then leasing them to companies like Rockwell International, AT&T, and Polaroid. The more O.P.M. leased, the more banks were willing to lend money for more computers, using the leases with the megacompanies as collateral. By the late '70s, O.P.M. was one of the country's five largest computer-leasing companies, all of it done with O.P.M., "other people's money."

This apparent success masked the reality that the entire business was a fraud, a pyramid scheme. Not only were most of the leases fake, most of the computers never existed. The same computer would be used again and again for different leases and different loans. O.P.M.'s biggest "client," Rockwell, was less an actual client than a name used on forged leases, created by Goodman crouching under a glass-top table to shine a flashlight through signature pages that Weissman traced onto fake documents. In all, according to investigative reporter Stewart Taylor, Jr., between 1978 and 1981 alone, O.P.M. obtained almost $200 million in loans from 19 lenders secured by forged Rockwell leases.

Not long after it opened its doors, O.P.M. became Singer Hutner's largest client. The lawyers had no indication of anything amiss until June 1980 when Goodman, knowing his accountant had discovered the Rockwell fraud and was threatening to tell all, first swore his attorneys to secrecy, and then told them he had done something wrong, something he couldn't fix because it would take millions of dollars he didn't have. According to Taylor, Goodman refused to be specific about his wrongdoing, in light of senior partner Joseph L. Hutner's statement that he couldn't promise to keep the details confidential, because O.P.M. itself was the firm's client.

While Goodman kept his story vague, the accountant hired his own lawyer, William J. Davis, to meet with O.P.M.'s counsel. Davis later described his meetings with Joseph Hutner as "a macabre dance." He says he offered Hutner a letter from the accountant outlining the fraud, but Hutner "didn't want it [and] didn't want to know what was in it." Hutner behaved, said Davis, as if he were about to "clamp his hands over his ears and run out of the office." Meanwhile, Goodman, while admitting to past mistakes, swore to his lawyers that his days of dishonesty were behind him.

But the lawyers knew it wasn't that simple. The accountant's message had gotten through: A Singer Hutner memorandum drafted during this period

---

[5] In developing this narrative, we are indebted to Stuart Taylor, Jr., whose fascinating and comprehensive article, *Ethics and the Law: A Case History*, N.Y. Times, Jan. 9, 1983 (Magazine), describes the case in detail, and to Heidi Li Feldman, *Can Good Lawyers Be Good Ethical Deliberators?*, 69 So. Cal. L. Rev. 885 (March 1996). The narrative itself is adapted from our treatment in Zitrin & Langford, The Moral Compass of the American Lawyer (1999), for which we owe thanks to Ballantine Books and Random House.

referred to evidence of multimillion-dollar frauds. To get that money, O.P.M. had used the law firm's own opinion letters about the worthiness of the loans, which in turn were based on fake documents. Even worse, the firm knew that in the accountant's opinion, O.P.M., "in order to survive, would probably have to continue the same type of wrongful activity."

Given all this, Singer Hutner considered stopping all its work for O.P.M. But no firm wants to lose its largest client; if Goodman's assurances could be taken at face value, all his "mistakes" were in the past. The lawyers decided to seek the advice of an outside expert in legal ethics. They chose Henry Putzel 3d, who had taught ethics at Fordham University and came recommended by the law school's dean. Putzel gave Singer Hutner the answers the firm wanted to hear.

First, Putzel concluded that despite the accountant's opinion, Singer Hutner knew of "no fact which in any way indicated the commission of an ongoing fraud." Therefore, said Putzel, the firm had no duty to say anything about what had happened in the past, including telling the banks that existing, *ongoing* loans were based on false information. Second, relying on Goodman's new assurances, the firm could even continue to close new loans for O.P.M. Third, it was not necessary for Singer Hutner to check to be sure each new O.P.M. deal was legitimate so long as Goodman swore in writing that it was, which of course he was only too happy to do by simply adding to his litany of lies.

So during the summer of 1980, Singer Hutner continued to assist O.P.M. in obtaining new loans. They claimed later that they didn't "know" Goodman was continuing his fraudulent ways, though Davis, the accountant's lawyer, had written a memorandum after his June meeting with Hutner that remarked on his firm's "apparent willingness to stick his head in the sand and ignore these problems." But the lawyers couldn't keep their heads in the sand forever. In September 1980, Goodman admitted more details about his past frauds and acknowledged that they totaled over $80 million. At that point, with the evidence overwhelming and, according to Stewart Taylor, some partners concerned about their fees and O.P.M.'s possible bankruptcy, the law firm finally decided to resign as counsel.

But with Putzel's approval, Singer Hutner did not resign at once. Rather, they set up a staged withdrawal between September and December to ensure that the client was not abandoned without a lawyer, which the firm feared would immediately put the company under. The lawyers justified staying on despite Goodman's admissions since, after all, he had sworn yet again that all fraud had finally stopped.

O.P.M. found new lawyers to represent them: Peter Fishbein and his firm of Kaye, Scholer, Fierman, Hays & Handler. In October, Fishbein called his old friend Hutner to ask whether there were any problems with O.P.M. that caused Singer Hutner to give up its largest client. But Putzel instructed Hutner he couldn't tell Fishbein anything about fraud without violating O.P.M.'s confidentiality. The end result was that Kaye, Scholer, knowing nothing of O.P.M.'s past history, assisted O.P.M. in obtaining another $15 million in bogus loans before the fraud was exposed. Putzel even advised

Singer Hutner that it could not tell O.P.M.'s own in-house lawyer about the frauds.

When O.P.M.'s house of cards collapsed and the tangled web of litigation began, everyone got a lawyer, including the lawyers, Singer Hutner, and the lawyers' lawyer, Putzel. O.P.M. went into bankruptcy and Goodman and Weissman were sent to prison. Lawsuits flew, and Singer Hutner wound up paying $10 million. The firm collapsed, but the principals went on practicing law, none sanctioned by the bar, and all claiming they did the right thing.

Perhaps the most sanctimonious was Putzel, whose legal brief defended his seemingly indefensible advice: Under the adversary system, "a lawyer's primary obligation . . . must be to his client, rich or poor, likeable or despicable, honest or crooked." There are times, Putzel's lawyers argued, when lawyers are "duty-bound to stand up for and protect liars and thieves." But here, by advising Singer Hutner essentially to turn a blind eye toward the truth, had Putzel encouraged the lawyers to stand up and *assist* liars and thieves?

NOTES

The O.P.M. case raised many questions back in the 1980s about the extent to which lawyers could suspend disbelief and ignore obvious reality. Here is what Stuart Taylor wrote in the conclusion of his *New York Times Magazine* article:

> Whether or not Singer Hutner violated the ethical code, a basic question remains: Is there not something wrong with a code that can plausibly be used to justify the extreme lengths to which Singer Hutner went to protect its criminal client? Indeed, there is growing concern both inside and outside the legal profession that the current rules make it too easy for lawyers to condone or even actively assist their clients' ongoing crimes, frauds and cover-up conspiracies.

Could such disingenuous behavior happen again in today's far more sophisticated legal environment? Some argue that it has, in the Enron case and elsewhere, and that little has changed.

4. Knowledge and the Duty to Investigate. What should a law firm affirmatively be required to do to verify the legitimacy of the client's statements and position? Should an investigation be required, such as one might do before filing a complaint to avoid Rule 11 attack, before advice is given or an opinion rendered? Or should the lawyer be able to take what the client says at face value? Look at ABA Model Rule 1.1 and the Comments to 1.2 and see if they provide any insight. What is the difference between the standard of "knowing" and one of "should have known"?

The ABA has addressed this issue on several occasions over the years. In Formal Opinion 335 (1974), the ABA discussed an attorney's duty of inquiry in the context of giving an opinion about whether the sales of securities have to be registered under the Securities Act of 1933: "It is, of course, important that the lawyer competently and carefully consider what facts are relevant to the giving of the requested opinion and make a reasonable inquiry to obtain such of those facts as are not within his personal knowledge." Where the lawyer does not have "sufficient confidence as to all the relevant facts," or fails to make further inquiries, the attorney should not provide the client with an opinion. When the lawyer has no reason to believe the facts are "incomplete," "suspect," "inconsistent," or "on the basis of known facts open to question," the lawyer may assume they are accurate without doing more. But when one of these factors is present, the lawyer must either decline the opinion or do further verification.

In ABA Revised Formal Opinion 346 (1982), the ABA analyzed the role of a lawyer in rendering an opinion as to the propriety of a tax shelter. Opinion 346 reiterated the requirements of Opinion 335 to investigate and inquire, and stated:

> The lawyer who accepts as true the facts which the promoter tells him, when the lawyer should know that a future inquiry would disclose that these facts are untrue, also gives a false opinion. It has been said that lawyers cannot "escape criminal liability on a plea of ignorance when they have shut their eyes to what was plainly to be seen."

In both these ABA opinions, the work of the lawyer becomes more than simple advice. The lawyer is being asked to actively convert that advice into an opinion on which the client will rely and, in the case of the tax shelter opinion, on which the public may rely, since the lawyer's opinion may be referred to in the offering or promotional literature. What about the lawyer who is simply asked for advice, not a formal opinion? Are the same standards required before such advice is given?

5. Enron: Legal Advice As Cover-Up, or Just Client Protection? We are all familiar with the story of Enron — the rise, the fall, the scams, and the criminal convictions of CFO Andrew Fastow and CEO Ken Lay. The roles of Enron's many lawyers, especially Vincent & Elkins, have also been closely analyzed. Did the lawyers advise and then appropriately act as advocates, defending Enron as they are sworn to do? Or did their advice and assent to frauds make them co-conspirators in Enron executives' crimes? Read the following.

ROBERT W. GORDON, A NEW ROLE FOR LAWYERS?: THE CORPORATE COUNSELOR AFTER ENRON
35 Connecticut Law Review 1185 (2003)[6]

Lawyers seem to have played a relatively minor part in the theater of deception and self-dealing that has led to the collapse of Enron and other corporate titans of the 1990s. The spotlight has been on the grasping managers at the heart of the drama, debased accounting standards and practices, corrupt politicians pressing to abolish or weaken regulations and cripple enforcement, opportunistic investment bankers, conflicted stock analysts, and a credulous business press. But lawyers — both in-house lawyers and outside law firms — were participants in many of the central transactions that ultimately brought about the companies' ruin.

---

[6] Copyright © 2003 by Connecticut Law Review. Reprinted by permission.

I. *Some Problems with What Lawyers Did*

Non-Disclosure by (Technical) Disclosure

Securities laws require accurate and transparent financial statements, so that investors can know the financial condition of the company. Enron arranged to borrow money from banks through transactions disguised as sales of real assets. No real assets ever changed hands, nor were they going to; Enron was going to repay the money with interest and cancel the sales. The purpose was to show the debt on the company's books as earnings . . . . Lawyers wrote opinions certifying the disguised loans as "true sales." Enron moved other debt off of its own books by creating sham transactions with limited-partner-entities. By law, these must be "independent" — i.e., conform to the (incredibly lax) requirement that a minimum of investors (three percent) must be from "outside" the parent firm. In some cases, even the outside investors were creatures of Andrew Fastow, Enron's CFO. Lawyers — both inside the company and outside counsel — approved all of these transactions. More generally, lawyers repeatedly facilitated Enron's strategy of structuring dubious transactions so that nobody could understand them, by using language to describe them in proxy and financial statements that, although literally and technically correct, was in practice completely opaque . . . .

Facilitating Self-Dealing

Special Purpose Entities ("SPEs") paid enormous sums to managers (again, Enron officers — Fastow's subordinates and designates) for managing them. Fastow personally received over $30 million in management fees from one set of SPEs . . . . SEC rules require that disclosure is required "where practicable" of the amount of compensation being paid to interested parties. Fastow had a "strong desire" to avoid disclosure of his compensation, and apparently was accustomed to treating the lawyers as his own personal vassals. The lawyers — in this case, Vinson & Elkins ("V&E") — obliged, by reasoning that since it was uncertain how much Fastow would eventually earn from all the transactions, Enron did not have to disclose even what he had already earned. In their SEC filings, the lawyers also asserted, as required by law, that these "related-party" transactions were negotiated at "arm's-length" and on "comparable terms" to deals with non-related parties, but apparently did not look for any factual support for these assertions, although the deals seemed questionable on their face.

The Investigation that Wasn't

Sherron Watkins, a vice president for corporate development at Enron, warned company chairman Kenneth Lay that the company was about to "implode in a wave of accounting scandals" because of dubious accounting by Enron's auditors, Arthur Andersen, for the many limited-partnership investment deals it had used to keep debt off the parent company's books and inflate Enron's earnings. Watkins said that many senior executives had complained loudly about these practices, that the company was "crooked," and that the side deals either had to be undone (if not too late to escape detection) or disclosed. She advised the chairman to ask an independent outside law firm to investigate, noting that Enron's regular law firm of V&E should be disqualified because it had signed off (given "true sale" opinions) on some of the deals and had a conflict of interest. Contrary to her advice, Lay did ask V&E to review the transactions, but to stop short of looking into Andersen's treatment of them. V&E, overlooking its own conflict and the patent contradiction in Lay's instructions to avoid looking at the very source the whistleblower had identified as the cause of the problem, duly reported back that the transactions seemed fine — because Andersen had, after all, approved them. The lawyers interviewed only eight senior executives, who all denied knowledge of any problems, and failed to interview any of the lower-level employees who had been identified as people who might provide helpful information. The lawyers then warned that "the bad cosmetics" of the partnerships could result in "a serious risk of adverse publicity and litigation," but concluded with the advice that no further investigation was necessary.

Was there anything illegal or unethical about what these lawyers did? Scholars who have studied these transactions in detail have argued that there was, that the lawyers' conduct subjects them to potential liability for criminal fraud, civil fraud, and violation of the securities laws. In addition, they could face discipline under state ethical codes for facilitating fraud, or malpractice liability for failing to competently represent their actual clients, the corporate entities. Of course, the lawyers themselves vigorously deny any wrongdoing or ethical lapses, some even going so far as to say they would do it all over again.

. . . .

II. *Some Excuses for What the Lawyers Did*

It is clear that the advice both in-house lawyers and outside law firms gave to the managers of Enron and other companies like it was instrumental in enabling those managers to cream off huge profits for themselves while bringing economic ruin to investors, employees, and the taxpaying public. Although the lawyers were not principally responsible for these acts [s]uch fraud could not have been carried out without the lawyers' active approval, passive acquiescence, or failure to inquire and investigate. Nonetheless, not only the lawyers involved but large numbers of practitioners and bar committees . . . vigorously justify the conduct as consistent with the highest conceptions of legal, ethical, and professional propriety . . . . This attitude is not universal . . . but it is pervasive.

How are we to understand why the lawyers acted as they did, and why they are justifying their actions now? Observers from outside the profession, and even some from within the profession, are tempted to say that the lawyers were simply weak and corrupt, or, for those who prefer to talk this way, that the lawyers were rational economic actors. They want the client's business, in an intensely competitive market, and so they will wish to approve anything senior management of the client firm asks, averting their eyes from signs of trouble and their noses from the smell of fish. Asking too many questions and (horrors) refusing to bless a transaction risks losing the client to another firm across town. Demonstrating ingenuity in giving the managers the results they want despite apparent legal obstacles wins praise and repeat business. Sailing close to or even over the line of illegal conduct is not unduly risky, because lawyers who advise on complex transactions for corporate clients almost never face sanctions.

But this is the amoral rational calculator's perspective, and professionals in high-status jobs at respectable blue-chip institutions do not like to think of themselves as amoral maximizers.

. . . .

Law as Neutral Constraint: The Lawyer as Risk-Manager

In this view, law is simply a source of "risk" to the business firm; it is the lawyers' task to assess and, to the extent possible, reduce it. These lawyers do not feel a moral imperative, as libertarians do, to defy or undercut the law; but neither do they feel one to comply . . . .

This restates what Holmes called the "bad man's" view of legal rules as prices discounted by sanctions — or, to reduce it still further, by the probability of enforcement of sanctions . . . . The lawyer objectively assesses the risks, then games the rules to work around the constraints and lower the tariffs as much as possible. If some constraints are unavoidable he "not only may but should" advise breaking the rules and paying the penalty if the client can still make a profit.

[This story-line was] not available in the case of Enron, for the obvious reasons that managers were looting the companies for their own benefit while concealing debts and losses from workers and investors. When the lawyers and accountants outwitted the pesky regulators — who, had they known what was happening, might have put a stop to it — they were not helping heroic outlaws add value to the economy and society by defying timid convention, but enabling, if not abetting, frauds and thieves. Nor were the professionals objectively, if amorally, assessing risks and weighing benefits against costs of efficient breach. It seems not to have occurred to them that outsiders might find out that the many-sided transactions with special entities were not actually earning any real returns, but merely concealing debts and losses, and that when that happened, Enron's stock price would tumble, and with it, all the houses of cards secured by that stock. The company they advised is now facing at least seventy-seven lawsuits as a result of its conduct. At best, the lawyers were closing their eyes to the risk of disaster; at worst, they were helping to bring it on.

"We Din' Know Nothin'": The Lawyer as Myopic or Limited- Function Bureaucrat

These are claims that the lawyers were not at fault because their role was limited: We didn't know, we weren't informed; the accountants said the numbers were okay; management made the decisions; our representation was restricted to problems on the face of the documents or to information submitted to us.

Many of these claims of innocent ignorance now look pretty dubious. Some of the outside law firms, such as V&E and Andrews & Kurth, in fact worked closely with Andersen accountants in structuring many of the transactions. Sometimes lawyers made notes that they needed further information or managers' or the board's approval to certify a deal, but signed opinions and proxy statements even if they never got it. Sometimes they expressed doubts about the deals. An in-house lawyer, Jordan Mintz, once even hired an outside law firm to look more closely into some of Fastow's deals. Ronald Astin of V&E repeatedly objected to some of Fastow's deals, saying they posed conflicts or weren't in Enron's best interests; but when Fastow persisted, Astin expressed unease to in-house attorneys or executives but not to the board. Moreover, in V&E's report on the whistleblower Watkins' allegations, Astin minimized suspected problems. In the end, the doubting lawyers never pressed the issues.

Some of their claims of limited knowledge are plausible, however, because Enron never trusted any one set of lawyers with extensive information about its operations — it spread legal work out to over 100 law firms. If one firm balked at approving a deal, as V&E occasionally did, Enron managers would go across town to another, more compliant firm such as Andrews & Kurth. Even Enron's General Counsel, James Derrick, had no means of controlling or supervising all of the legal advice the company was receiving, because the different divisions all had their own lawyers and outside firms. It is this layering of authority, fragmentation of responsibility, and decentralization that has made it possible for the chairman, CEO and board of directors of Enron, as well as the lawyers, to claim that they did not know much . . . .

The Lawyer as Advocate

The classic defense of the corporate lawyer's role, both most often advanced and held in reserve if other defenses fail, is of course that we are advocates, whose duty is zealous representation of clients. We are not like auditors, who have duties to the public; our duties are only to our clients. Our job is to help them pursue their interests and put the best construction on their conduct that the law and facts will support without intolerable strain, so as to enable them to pursue any arguably-legal ends by any arguably-legal means . . . .

For the advocate . . . [u]ltimate responsibility for determining the facts and interpreting the law rests with other actors and institutions — the authoritative decision-makers, especially the courts. The lawyer does not look for truth or justice, although of course to play his role he needs to know what courts are likely to say, and how far he can get them to see the facts and bend the rules his client's way . . . .

Unlike the . . . neutral risk-assessor, the advocate is not hostile or indifferent to law . . . . [T]he advocate is loyal to the law seen as the outer boundaries of the arguably-legal, the point beyond which facts and law can no longer be stretched. He will push up to the boundaries, and even to creative plausible extensions of the boundaries, but not beyond . . . .

What is less clear and more debated about the corporate lawyer-as-advocate is whether he has any obligation to try to induce his clients to comply with the law. It is clear that the lawyer may not actively help clients engage in what he knows to be a crime or a fraud. It is not at all clear what steps lawyers should take to prevent this from happening, to encourage the client to walk in the paths of legality, or to respond if the client strays off the paths. Most state ethics codes . . . say that lawyers who become aware of fraud, especially if it has been accomplished through lawyers' efforts, must try to get clients to correct the wrong, and that if the client does not comply, the lawyer may or must withdraw and disaffirm any documents he has helped to prepare; and if serious harm is likely to result, may or must disclose to relevant parties or authorities.

In the post-Enron debates — as in the wake of past corporate scandals — the view of the lawyer-as-advocate has most often been invoked to resist rule-changes that would give corporate lawyers positive obligations as monitors or gatekeepers of the legality of corporate conduct, especially by requiring them to report, if all else fails, managers' violations of law to authorities. Law firms and bar associations almost always take the position that such reporting requirements would turn lawyers into "cops," "snitches," or "informers," and thus pervert their function as confidential advisors and advocates. If clients do not trust their lawyers, they will not be candid and forthcoming with the information that the lawyers need to do their job.

But what is their job? One view . . . is that the lawyer needs his client's trust so that he can learn about possibly illegal plans and take steps to stop them. The argument for confidentiality here recognizes that one of the lawyer's functions is to monitor compliance and head off wrongdoing — not just to put the best face on things if the client goes ahead and breaks the law.

6. Lincoln Savings, Its Lawyers, *Their* Lawyer, and "Litigation Counsel." During the 1980s, several hundred savings and loan associations failed, many of which were engaged in improprieties on a grand scale. The savings and loan scandals rocked the financial world and the country. Perhaps the most highly publicized was that involving Lincoln Savings & Loan and its chief, Charles Keating, Jr. Keating and Lincoln engaged in massive frauds which would cost taxpayers billions. The federal Office of Thrift Supervision (OTS), charged with cleaning up the S&L mess, was not satisfied with going after Keating.

On March 2, 1992, the OTS set out after Lincoln's attorneys, the New York firm of Kaye Scholer, Fierman, Hays & Handler and its managing partner Peter Fishbein — the same lawyer and law firm that took over OPM a decade before. The OTS, accusing Kaye, Scholer of conspiring with its client Lincoln to provide false information to the Federal Home Loan Bank Board, and assisting Lincoln's fraudulent conduct, froze the law firm's assets. Within a matter of days, Kaye Scholer — its assets frozen, its lines of credit being called in by its banks — settled its dispute with OTS for $41 million. Two partners, including Fishbein, the firm's driving force, agreed to never again represent federally insured deposit institutions. Kaye Scholer and Fishbein maintained their innocence throughout, and placed the blame for the settlement on the high-handed tactics of OTS, including the freezing of the law firm's assets. Indeed, many felt that the OTS's tactics *were* extreme and overreaching, and may have unfairly invaded the attorney-client relationship — a claim not unlike those made by lawyers objecting to today's Sarbanes-Oxley and SEC reporting regulations that we will discuss in the next problem. The validity of these claims of overreaching notwithstanding, many believed that Kaye Scholer's focus on the "big brother" tactics of OTS was being used to deflect scrutiny from the law firm's own conduct.

That conduct, according to the OTS accusations, involved Kaye Scholer interposing itself between regulators and Lincoln during two federal examinations, and then providing banking regulators with incomplete and incorrect statements, while withholing material facts about questionable transactions, Lincoln's net worth, and the compromising circumstances under which the accounting firm of Arthur Andersen — the same Arthur Andersen that was involved in the Enron affair — resigned.

Some felt Kaye Scholer's conduct was far worse than the bare-bones OTS accusations. *American Lawyer* reporters Susan Beck and Michael Orey wrote a lengthy article in May 1992 entitled *They Got What They Deserved*, which chronicled Kaye Scholer's behavior, including this language, taken from the law firm's public 1987 submission to the Bank Board on behalf of Lincoln, as evidence of Kaye Scholer's complicity:

- "Lincoln unquestionably is not in unsafe and unsound condition. To the contrary, as set forth below, Lincoln's new management has created an extraordinarily successful, financially healthy institution."

- "Lincoln prudently manages and thus minimizes the risks associated with real estate lending."

- "In making real estate loans, Lincoln has always undertaken very careful and thorough procedures to analyze the collateral of the borrower. What is unusual about Lincoln's underwriting is its particular emphasis on, and the thoroughness of its understanding of, the collateral."

- "The ultimate proof of the pudding of Lincoln's comparative advantage, its sound investment selection, and its prudent underwriting is the unqualified success of Lincoln's program."

The *American Lawyer* exposé also documented the law firm's knowledge of backdated documents that were authored after a key deadline but dated the month before to grandfather in the investments in question. It described Kaye Scholer as "intimately familiar" with Lincoln employees' efforts to take files that were "empty or inadequate" and create documents "intended to look like they were part of the file at the time the investment or loan was made." The exposé also accused Kaye Scholer of knowing that files were "sanitized" by removing negative information about borrowers or risky investments, and numerous other instances of complicity with Lincoln. Indeed, a reading of Kaye Scholer's publicly-submitted documents raises many of these same issues.

Like Singer, Hutner before it, Kaye Scholer hired outside ethics counsel — in this case, one of the deans of the profession, Professor Geoffrey Hazard, then at Yale.

Kaye Scholer, with Hazard's support, claimed that its conduct was appropriate because it was acting as Lincoln's "litigation counsel' — much as Enron's lawyers have claimed their behavior was justified in their roles as "advocates."

Although no litigation was then pending between federal regulators and Lincoln, Kaye Scholer claimed that it undertook Lincoln's representation only after an adversary relationship had already developed between Lincoln and the bank board. This, claimed the law firm, meant that its submissions to the bank regulators, including a lengthy June 1987 submission that responded to the 1986 examination, were the responses of litigation counsel "advancing arguments on its client's behalf which it believed were supported by the facts and law, without going further and disclosing weaknesses in its client's position." For his part, Prof. Hazard, according to the law firm's press release, gave the opinion that had the firm complied with the OTS, it "would have violated the standards of ethical conduct . . . applicable to Kaye Scholer in its role as litigation counsel."

Could Kaye Scholer, by declaring the situation to be adversarial, change from advisor to "litigation counsel" by fiat? Years later, could Enron's lawyers justify their conduct in signing off on phantom deals as "advocates" under the same theory? One month after the short but sharp Kaye, Scholer affair, Professor Hazard set forth his view of litigation counsel's responsibilities, in his *National Law Journal* column, reprinted here.

GEOFFREY C. HAZARD, ETHICS
The National Law Journal (April 27, 1992) [7]

The Kaye Scholer case has now come and gone, having been settled on terms that most observers consider very onerous for the law firm. However, the major issue in the case has not been resolved for other cases in the future. This issue is a lawyer's duty concerning disclosure of facts adverse to a client, and to what third parties that duty runs. Continuing uncertainty about this question subjects lawyers to jeopardy of the kind to which Kaye Scholer was exposed.

The Office of Thrift Supervision's principal accusation against Kaye Scholer was its alleged failure to disclose to the bank regulatory authority facts that might have revealed serious financial weakness in Lincoln Savings and Loan Association. The law firm's position was that all its statements to the agency were true. The agency's position was that other facts were known to the firm that should have been disclosed and which would have given a different picture of the S&L's condition. Whether there were such other facts was itself in dispute.

The Kaye Scholer case has been mooted by the settlement. But the question remains open as to what standard of disclosure was applicable.

The bottom line is that there is no single standard for disclosure of facts adverse to a client. Many litigators seem to think there is a single standard: A lawyer may never disclose any facts adverse to a client. But this is erroneous. . . .

Under modern discovery rules . . . lawyers for all parties generally have several duties to make adverse disclosures. These include identifying

---

[7] Reprinted with the permission of The National Law Journal. Copyright © 1992 by The New York Law Publishing Company.

witnesses who may be adverse and producing documents that may be "smoking guns."

The civil litigation lawyer's duty of disclosure nevertheless is conditional and indirect. It is conditional because disclosure is required only upon a discovery demand by an opposing party. It is indirect because the discovery rules directly address the client rather than the lawyer. However . . . the lawyer necessarily assumes at least minimal responsibility for the client's compliance with the demand. In practical effect, therefore, the civil litigator has to make disclosures that are adverse to the client.

. . . .

However, the litigation lawyer's disclosure duty remains tightly circumscribed. Clearly it does not require an inquisitorial search of the client's mind. Except in ex parte presentations it does not require search of the client's files to produce everything that the opposing party should have demanded if it had similar access. These limitations are the whole point of the lawyer's work product privilege, created by the Supreme Court in *Hickman v. Taylor*, 329 U.S. 495 (1947).

More fundamental, a lawyer for a client in litigation is not a grand inquisitor against the client. If such were the duty, a client would be better off dealing directly with grand inquisitors, who at least are identifiable as the adversary. A litigation lawyer, on the other hand, is supposed to be the client's friend.

In any event, three propositions hold. First, even a litigation lawyer has some duty to disclose facts adverse to the client. Second, even the maximum disclosure rules do not require revealing confidential conversations with the client about how the litigation should be conducted. Third, the scope of the duty of disclosure is defined by legal rules applicable in specific context.

7. Kaye Scholer, Enron, Factual Assertions, and Three Bar Opinions. Some questioned how strongly Professor Hazard had really supported Kaye Scholer's position. *American Lawyer*'s Beck and Orey reported that Kaye Scholer actually prepared the text of Hazard's opinion statement, that it was prepared before the full OTS charges and documentation had been filed, and that it contained assumptions of fact that took up 14 of the opinion's 22 pages.

Nevertheless, as his article shows, Hazard's central point on the issue of "litigation counsel" transcends the specific facts. Most observers did not buy his justification, as most today have not accepted Vincent and Elkins' claim of acting as advocates. Those who deconstructed Hazard's opinion after-the-fact (and with, of course, the easy clarity of hindsight) were widely critical of the litigation counsel claim, pointing out that a Bank Board report did not come close to reaching such an adversarial level that the law firm could justify being in litigation mode. Similarly, there intuitively seems little reason to excuse Enron's lawyers' behavior as "advocacy" when their work product was used to create and approve sham transactions.

William H. Simon, Columbia law professor and prolific writer on issues of lawyers' morality and personal responsibility, wrote an extensive review of the Kaye Scholer case in 1998 that applies with equal force to Enron.[8] The

---

[8] *The Kaye Scholer Affair: The Lawyer's Duty of Candor and the Bar's Temptations of Evasion and Apology*, 23 LAW & SOC. INQUIRY 243 (1998).

problem, said Simon, was not so much the use of the term "litigation counsel" but "the distinction between factual assertion and argument." Kaye Scholer, he claimed, violated its ethical duties by claiming to make factual assertions while actually engaging in argument. Vincent & Elkins and other Enron lawyers, one might argue, did the same.

A footnote: Three interesting ethics opinions emerged from the Kaye Scholer affair. First, in New York, a disciplinary investigation was opened but eventually closed with no action taken. Second, the ABA issued Formal Opinion 93-375 (August 6, 1993), which concluded that "in representing a client in a bank examination, a lawyer may not under any circumstances lie to or mislead agency officials, either by affirmative misstatement or by omitting a material fact . . . ." "However," continued the opinion, mirroring the words of Kaye Scholer's defense, "she is under no duty to disclose weaknesses in her client's case or otherwise to reveal confidential information that would be protected under Rule 1.6."

Third, however, California, Formal Opinion 1996-146, also seemingly written with an eye on Kaye Scholer, and perhaps anticipating Enron, asked the following question: May a lawyer for a subdivision developer, knowing that substandard plumbing material has been used by a sub-contractor, write a letter to homeowners saying "The warranty in your contract means that [developer] has promised that all materials, including plumbing lines, meet plans and specifications, including all code requirements. The warranty speaks for itself"? While strictly true, and while the lawyer does not represent the original malfeasant, the letter clearly seems to mislead. The opinion concludes that the lawyer *may not* write such a letter: "A lawyer acts unethically where she assists in the commission of a fraud by implying facts and circumstances that are not true in a context likely to be misleading."

8. Putting the Advice Into Action. Beyond lawyers who advise on the law or on arguably improper courses of action are those who may be involved in actually implementing strategies of questionable legality. Read the following article about asset protection trusts.

DEBRA BAKER, ISLAND CASTAWAY
84 ABA Journal 54 (October 1998)[9]

David Westrate claims his only reason for setting up a family trust in 1994 was to preserve his family's fortune for the benefit of himself, his wife and his four children.

As the owner and operator of National Business Institute, a multi-million-dollar company that sponsored legal education seminars for lawyers, Westrate says he wanted to guard against the threat of frivolous lawsuits and claims by unforeseen creditors.

But Barbara Westrate, his wife of 11 years, says she had no idea her husband had shipped 90 percent of their assets — an estimated $11 million — to the Cook Islands, located 1,900 miles off the coast of New Zealand.

And, she says, he never mentioned that the trust did not specifically name her as a beneficiary, referring instead to "spouse of the settlor."

---

[9] Copyright © by American Bar Association, 1998. Reprinted by permission.

. . . .

Estate Planning or Money Hiding?

Over the last decade, the off-shore trust industry has emerged as a popular estate-planning mechanism for wealthy entrepreneurs, executives, doctors and lawyers seeking to safeguard their funds.

But as the Westrate case suggests, there are growing concerns that these trusts are being used to hide money from spouses and other legitimate creditors. Significant questions also are being asked about the role lawyers play in designing trusts for use by clients with fraudulent intentions.

David Westrate's lawyers came under scrutiny in June when a central Florida judge found a prima facie case existed to apply the crime-fraud exception to the attorney-client privilege between him and his lawyers.

. . . .

Barry S. Engel, who co-authored the trust laws in the Cook Islands in 1989 and set up the trust in the Westrate case, says these trusts help wealthy individuals who believe the legal system can't protect them. "What we're doing is a response. We're leveling the playing field," says Engel. . . .

Moving money to locales such as the Cook, Channel and Cayman islands provides a layer of insulation for the settlor of the trust because creditors or others who win a judgment from a U.S. court must then go to the foreign jurisdiction where the trust sits if they want to collect.

The laws of these debtor-friendly jurisdictions make it difficult and costly to prevail. A well-drafted offshore trust provides other benefits, as well. For example . . . an offshore trust, unlike a U.S. trust, may allow settlors to maintain significant control over their assets.

. . . .

Christopher J. Redmond, a Kansas City, Mo., lawyer who specializes in tracking down funds that have been fraudulently transferred outside the country, says each case ends up being considered on its own facts.

"The real issue is intent," says Redmond, who is the chair of the International Bankruptcy Committee of the ABA Business Law Section. "No one is going to say, 'I did this because of a divorce or because of creditors.' The only way you can establish it is from the totality of evidence."

. . . . The matter of attorney liability is equally vague. Legal and ethics rules, as well as interpretations of those rules, vary by state. Many suggest, however, that lawyers may expose themselves to discipline, disbarment or even jail time for assisting in conduct that violates rules prohibiting fraud, deceit or misrepresentation.

But some attorneys say they are not violating ethical rules, no matter what the intent of their clients. They argue that because fraudulent transfer laws are merely remedial statutes, lawyers who assist clients in making such transfers are doing nothing illegal.

The Right to Move Money

Denis Kleinfeld, an asset protection attorney in Miami, says the legal nuances relating to client intent are not relevant because the attorney's only involvement is in making the transfer, which is a legal transaction. If the client has a fraudulent intent, the creditor has a means, through the statute, to go after the money, he says.

Attorneys have a right, even a duty, to set up a workable estate plan for clients regardless of intent, Kleinfeld says. And clients have a right to do what they wish with freely alienable property, he says.

"The question is: Do you have a lawful right to draft a will and a trust? Of course you do. There is no law that says you can't. If property is freely alienable, [you] can move it anywhere in the world."

Kleinfeld says that representing trust clients with suspect motives is no different from a criminal defense attorney representing child molesters or murderers.

But [Arnold D.] Levine, the lawyer for Barbara Westrate, sees a clear distinction. "There is a difference between a client who says, 'I committed a crime; represent me,' and one who says, 'Help me commit a crime,'" he says. "If an attorney had knowledge of marital discord and set up a trust, unquestionably he is involved in the perpetration of fraud." Even among staunch advocates of asset protection trusts, few are willing to read the law as broadly as Kleinfeld.

. . . .

Attorneys should not be able to close their eyes to a client's true intent merely because he or she says the trust is for a legitimate purpose, [Levine] adds.

"When someone hides behind the fact that their client did not specifically ask them to perpetrate a fraud, I say that's bull," Levine says. "It at least runs up to the line, and I'm satisfied an ethical practitioner would say it is going over the line. It's certainly sleazy."

. . . .

A Lawyer Protection Device

For his part in the Westrate case, Engel says he was merely a special counsel retained by another Westrate attorney and not by David Westrate himself. As a result, he is one step removed from Westrate.

Because 90 percent of Engel's work is in creating the structures for clients of other lawyers, he is able to shift the burden to those lawyers to ensure their clients are not harboring fraudulent intent.

For his own clients, Engel insists they fully disclose to him all relevant information, and he has them sign a written statement to that effect.

. . . .

[Barbara] Westrate says she is fortunate. She ended up with $ 4.3 million, including the trust assets, from her husband. She also secured $ 2.5 million from National Business Institute, which the foreign trustee had sold, allegedly for less than fair market value.

. . . .

With cases such as the Westrates' often ending in settlement, it likely will be some time before the boundaries for using offshore asset-protection trusts will be more clearly defined.

NOTES

Recall the "critical distinction" made in comment 6 to Model Rule 1.2. Have lawyers like Engel and Kleinfeld crossed the threshold between "presenting an analysis of legal aspects of questionable conduct and recommending the means by which a crime or fraud might be committed with impunity"? Have they even gone a step farther, by creating the trust themselves? Or do they have the right to assume their clients' innocence? After all, even the trust-busting lawyers admit intent is always an issue. Finally, what about attorney Engel's stance that since he is hired by the client's lawyers, he is "one step removed" from the client and his or her fraudulent intent?

The propriety of lawyers creating offshore asset protection trusts remains very much of an open issue. While Westrate's attorney-client privilege was voided by the trial court, the case eventually settled without a written appellate opinion. Other courts, including federal bankruptcy court and at least two federal courts of appeal,[10] have examined the propriety of asset protection trusts, but none to date has directly addressed the behavior of the lawyers involved.

SUPPLEMENTAL READINGS

1. Stewart Taylor, Jr.'s excellent classic article about O.P.M., "Ethics and the Law: A Case History," from *The New York Times Magazine* of January 9, 1983, gives the complete story of O.P.M. in the words of one of our most astute observers of the legal profession. The article is worth reading for anyone wanting to learn the whole case study, including details of the O.P.M. story such as Myron Goodman, told at last by his lawyers that they will no longer assist in his frauds, standing "at the head of the law firm's staircase, shaking with anger," and shouting, "If you . . . bring down the company, I will bring down this firm."

2. For an excellent recitation of the O.P.M. case, together with some thoughtful questions about its implications, see Phillip B. Heymann & Lance Liebman, *The Social Responsibilities of Lawyers* (1988).

3. Stephen Gillers & Roy D. Simon, Jr., "The Kaye Scholer File," in *Regulation of Lawyers: Statutes and Standards* (1993 ed.), provides an interesting and thorough treatment of the Kaye Scholer case, largely because of the inclusion of a comprehensive excerpt of the OTS charging document.

4. Jim Schachter, "Oft-Snubbed Lawyers May Finally Get Some Respect," *Los Angeles Times*, May 4, 1987, is an article about the Immigration and

---

[10] The Second and Ninth circuits; see the Supplemental Readings.

Naturalization Service's efforts to crack down on immigration attorneys who "know" that their clients are lying in order to gain residency, and the immigration bar's efforts to fight back.

5. Susan P. Koniak, *When Courts Refuse to Frame the Law and Others Frame It to Their Will*, 66 So. Cal. L. Rev. 1075 (1993). Professor Koniak reviews the Kaye Scholer case in the context of powerful law firms and powerful governmental regulatory agencies acting with little oversight from the judicial system.

6. *Federal Deposit Ins. Corp. v. O'Melveny & Meyers*, 969 F.2d 744 (9th Cir. 1992), is a difficult case to negotiate, but an important one. It holds that a law firm could have a duty to a corporation's investors to reveal fraud on the part of insiders. The case was overruled on other grounds dealing with choice of law, at 512 U.S. 79, 114 S. Ct. 2048 (1994).

7. There have been at least three federal appeals court cases addressing the propriety of offshore asset protection trusts. A Second Circuit case, *S.E.C. v. Brennan*, 230 F.3d 65 (2d Cir. 2000), refused to exempt the SEC from the stay provisions of the Bankruptcy Code in its effort to repatriate assets, even though the SEC had already won a judgment against defendants, who created the offshore asset protection trust during trial and then declared bankruptcy right after trial. The Ninth Circuit has taken a more negative view, most recently by enjoining a tax consulting firm (albeit not one involving lawyers) from rendering tax-shelter advice, though the reason for the injunction was false advertising, not fraud. *United States v. Estate Preservation Services*, 202 F.3d 1093 (9th Cir. 2000). Perhaps more significantly in terms of long-term distrust of such trusts, *FTC v. Affordable Media, LLC*, 179 F.3d 1228 (9th Cir. 1999), upheld a trial court's order demanding the defendants repatriate monies held offshore, despite defendants' claim of "inability to comply with a judicial decree." "It is readily apparent," said the court, "that [trutstors] the Andersons' inability to comply . . . is the intended result of their own conduct — their inability to comply and the foreign trustee's refusal to comply appears to be the precise goal of the Andersons' trust."

8. *Brouwer v. Raffensperger, Hughes & Co.*, 199 F.3d 961 (7th Cir. 2000), expanded the interpretation of the civil RICO statute by reinstating causes of action against a defendant law firm. The Seventh Circuit held that personal participation in the operation or management of an enterprise is not necessary in order to violate the racketeering statute. It is enough to allege that a law firm knowingly agreed to facilitate the operation of an enterprise.

9. William H. Simon, *Wrongs of Ignorance and Ambiguity: Lawyer Responsibility for Collective Misconduct*, 22 Yale J. on Reg. 1 (2005). Professor Simon's latest focuses on "deliberate ignorance and calculated ambiguity" as "key recurring themes in modern scandals from Watergate to Enron." Simon discusses lawyers' efforts to avoid responsibility, the "trend in recent legal doctrine, exemplified by the Sarbanes-Oxley Act, to strengthen duties of inquiry," and the established legal bar's resistance to the regulation.

PROBLEM 25

What should in-house counsel do when confronted with a corporation's mistakes? Is there an obligation to tell the company to "do the right thing"? Is there ever an obligation to "blow the whistle" and reveal the error? When? When the corporation has clearly made a mistake that poses a serious physical threat to the public? What about mistakes, or frauds, that involve no physical harm? And what is the effect of new rules — both from the ABA and the federal government — that address a client's fraudulent conduct?

Advising the Corporate Client That's Made a Mistake

Ernesto Valencia is chief assistant general counsel to Giant Automobile, Inc., one of the nation's "Big Four" automotive companies.

I. Giant's electronics division produces its own stereo radio and CD systems for all Giant cars except the top-of-the-line Luxurios. Giant's electronics laboratory tests have disclosed that the standard automobile CD player has a defective gear mechanism that causes an estimated 34% failure rate after 2,000 hours of use and a 49% failure rate after 3,000 hours. Failures generally occur when the CD starts "skipping" due to the worn gear. CDs may also become pitted and thus unplayable. Because the defect is wear-related, the failure rate is only about 2% to 3% for the first 1,000 hours, which represents the warranty period. The gear has now been changed, but 2,400,000 of the CD players have already been installed.

The complete electronic package — stereo, AM-FM radio, CD player, and speaker hook-up — costs Giant about $82 each to produce. The package is sold as part of a $980 "upgrade package" in the economy compact Midget, and is standard equipment on all other models.

Despite the fact that almost all the gear failures occur outside the warranty period, Giant has received a large number of complaints asking for a replacement CD player. Some have also asked for between $10 and $250 for CDs that no longer play.

QUESTIONS

1. May Valencia advise Giant to replace the CD players and pay the claims for those who have complained? Should he? Even if he believes that most car owners will not follow up on their claims either by filing suit or taking other action?

2. What about customers who bought these models but who have not complained? Since there is an admitted defect, should Ernie advise that *all* the CD players be recalled and replaced?

3. May or should Ernie advise Giant to defend against any small claims suits, rather than paying immediately, on the theory that many customers will not see their claims through? May he advise Giant to settle for 50 cents on the dollar?

4. May Ernie say anything about the defect to anyone outside Giant? What if he discovers evidence of a fraudulent financial arrangement between Giant and the subcontractors producing the defective gear mechanisms?

II. Giant has discovered in controlled proving grounds tests that its most popular model, the Venezia sedan, has defective brake fluid distribution that under certain changes in climatic conditions can cause complete brake failure. There are two million Venezias on the road.

Company climate experts and statisticians have written a report noting that the likelihood of complete brake failure is slight, and estimating that complete brake failure is likely to cause no more than one accident per every 100,000 vehicles per year. It is not known precisely how many of these accidents would result in a fatality, but based on reports "in the field," the company's internal auditors have been able to identify a small number of "serious accidents" — between 12 and 15 per year — as being caused by the brake failure.

Finally, repair of the Venezias is complicated. The cost to repair these vehicles is estimated at $135 per car. That would cost the company $270,000,000 for a complete recall.

QUESTIONS

1. May Valencia advise the company to litigate all claims as they occur, on grounds of proximate cause, contributory negligence, etc.?

2. When these facts are presented to him, must or should Ernie advise Giant to recall all affected cars? What should he do if Giant refuses? What *may* he do? Would the analysis be different if Valencia were outside counsel?

3. Does it matter that the estimated number of accidents each year is 15 or 20? What if it were 50? Or 200? Or 3?

4. Does it matter that the cost of a recall is $270,000,000? What if it were only $27,000,000? What if it were $2,700,000,000, and would put Giant in bankruptcy? May Ernie consider the potentially ruinous consequences both financially and emotionally of the car company going broke on Giant workers and their families?

5. Does it matter what version of the ABA Model Rules apply in Ernie's state? Or is it the case that regardless of the rules, Ernie will have to make a decision balancing ethics rules, personal morality, and the economic reality of facing the possible loss of his job? How should he balance these considerations?

READINGS

1. Should Counsel Ever "Blow the Whistle"? At what point should general counsel "blow the whistle" on his or her own client — the company that employs the lawyer? "Bean counters," or actuarial analysts, can determine the risk of harm to the public of all kinds of products which have an inherent level of danger stemming from their use. Are these mere actuarial statistics, or is there a point at which such danger, including death, must be prevented by the company? Or by the lawyer acting if the company refuses to act? Professor David Luban uses one of modern corporate America's most dramatic examples of death caused by a product of a generation ago — the Ford Pinto cases — to posit an ethical requirement of whistleblowing. As you read about the Pinto case, consider whether the revised ABA Model Rules result in a different course of action or change the responsibilities for lawyers in the 21st century.

DAVID LUBAN, LAWYERS AND JUSTICE: AN ETHICAL STUDY
ch. 10 (1988)[1]

The Pinto Case

The shockers came on three successive days, October 13, 14 and 15, 1979, in three successive front-page *Chicago Tribune* headlines:

> October 13 FORD IGNORED PINTO FIRE PERIL, SECRET MEMOS SHOW

> October 14 HOW FORD PUT A PRICE TAG ON AUTOS' SAFETY

> October 15 U.S. OFFICIAL SEES COVER-UP IN FORD SAFETY TEST POLICY

Of course, everyone knew about the celebrated exploding Pinto long before that time. In February 1978, a California jury had awarded $125 million — later reduced to $6.6 million by a judge — to a teenager who had suffered horrendous burns in a Pinto accident. . . . [T]he *Tribune*'s research was initiated because a grand jury in Indiana had indicted Ford for reckless homicide in the burning deaths of three teenage women whose 1973 Pinto had exploded after being struck from behind by a van on August 10, 1978.

The secret internal Ford memos revealed in the first two *Tribune* articles made it all the worse. They seemed to show a level of foreknowledge and coldblooded calculatedness on Ford's part that appalled many readers.

The first day's memos showed that Ford engineers knew that Pinto gastanks would be pierced by bolts when struck from behind at speeds as low as 21 m.p.h. This would allow gasoline to leak out, so that any spark, caused, for example, by metal scraping over pavement, would explode the fuel supply. Other memos discussed several modifications in the Pinto design that would make it safer. These were rejected on the grounds that they cost too much money (various figures were cited, ranging from $5.08 to $11 per car), and because some would decrease trunk space.

According to the first *Tribune* article, a Ford memo of November 10, 1970 commented that government-proposed fuel tank safety standards "are too strict and come too soon. Ford executives list lesser standards that the Department of Transportation 'can be expected to buy' as alternatives." A "confidential" memo dated April 22, 1971 recommended that one of the safety devices not be installed until 1976, to save Ford $20.9 million. Another "confidential" memo of October 26, 1971 stated that no additional "fuel system integrity" changes would be made until "required by law." As a result of lobbying by the auto industry, the more stringent legal requirements did not

---

go into effect until 1977; the 1977 Pinto was designed to meet the new requirements.

These memos, in short, indicated that Ford engineers and executives were aware of Pinto's design problem, and that instead of repairing it, they acted deliberately to avoid regulatory and financial consequences to the company. The next day's revelations were summarized by Lee Strobel of the *Tribune* as follows:

> Saving 180 people from burning to death and another 180 from suffering serious burns in car fires each year would not be worth the cost of adding $11 per car for safety improvements, Ford Motor Co. officials concluded in a financial study obtained by the *Tribune* from court files.
>
> After preparing a cost analysis that amounted to putting a price tag on human lives and suffering, the automaker concluded that the $11 increased cost on 12.5 million cars and light trucks would be almost three times greater than the estimated costs stemming from persons killed and injured in vehicles lacking the safety measures, according to the document.
>
> The document does not state whether or not Ford viewed the costs as being related to potential legal liability payments.

. . . .

Ford was acquitted of reckless homicide in the Indiana trial. . . . [T]he key to the defense lay in the facts of the Indiana case. The young women's car was struck by a van moving fifty m.p.h., enough to rupture the fuel tank on any comparable car. . . . According to the *Tribune*, Ford engineers had known since 1968 that fuel tanks in the position of the Pinto's were liable to rupture "at very low speed," and discussions of how to deal with the problem in Pintos had been going on since at least 1970. Yet until the lawsuits began, the public had no inkling of the matter. . . . During 1976 and 1977 alone "thirteen Pintos — more than double the number that might be expected in proportion to their numbers — were involved in fiery rear-end crashes, resulting in deaths" while the VW Rabbit and Toyota Corolla suffered none. Some might say that it is a mistake to dwell on the particulars; it makes our reactions too emotional. On the contrary, I think that in problems such as this we cannot afford to forget the three teenagers who perished in a one-thousand-degree fire. And, if the *Tribune* stories are accurate, Ford knew precisely what it was doing. Shouldn't someone at Ford have made the information public in an act of preventive whistleblowing?

The obvious people to do so would have been Ford engineers or executives. I wish to consider a different problem, however, and that is whether attorneys in Ford's legal department (its "general counsel") who reviewed the cost-benefit and crash-test documents should have disclosed the terrible menace posed by the Pinto fuel tank. According to former Ford executive Harley Copp, the lawyers "definitely knew" what was in those documents.

It is perhaps obvious that, before calling Jack Anderson or the Department of Transportation, a Ford attorney should have gone through internal company procedures to get the Pinto recalled or to reverse the decision to build unsafe Pintos. Reminding the client of the common good (in the fashion of Brandeis) is after all the fundamental requirement of morally activist legal practice. Let us suppose, as would perhaps have been the case, that this proved fruitless. Then, unless some special argument to the contrary can be found, the attorney should have alerted the public to the menace of the Pinto. . . . Ask not with whom the buck stops, it stops with thee. Life is unfair. . . .

What's Wrong With Trading Lives for Cash?

. . . [A]ssuming that the facts of the case are as the newspapers stated them, did Ford do anything immoral?

This question sounds absurd. If allowing innocent people to be immolated for no other reason than cold, cold cash isn't immoral, what is? . . .

Despite this understandable reaction, there is another way to look at the matter. What was it that Ford did? It traded off cost for safety. But that is what car manufacturers must also do. Safety costs money, and people may not be willing to pay the price. Hence, the cheaper, in both senses, car. . . . Government regulations set minimum safety standards, but after these are met, the marketplace sets the level of safety.

. . . .

To a sophisticated reader, Ford's cost-benefit study is nothing to get excited about. First of all, that number of deaths is simply an actuarial statistic and does not by any means show a callous attitude toward human life, any more than does a similar study by your insurance company or by the manufacturer of the safest car money can buy. . . . One hundred and eighty deaths out of 12.5 million vehicles translates into the statistic that the gastank Ford was using increased your chance of death by one in seventy thousand over the safer alternative. . . . (Many people would bet their lives against eleven dollars at seventy thousand to one odds; you take a worse bet by far every time you ride without a seatbelt.)

. . . .

So, at any rate, goes the argument.

We should reject this argument for several reasons. The most important and obvious one is that the Pinto did not represent a safety-versus-price trade-off. It represented a blunder. Ford could have built Pintos with safer over-the-axle rather than puncturable behind-the-axle gastank mountings, but it did not, because it had tooled up too quickly. Its cost-benefit analyses did not, as a consequence, address the question of safety-versus-price; rather, they addressed the question of recall-versus-price, given the prior mistake.

. . . .

What the Rules Say

To begin our analysis of the corporate lawyer's problem, let us review the requirements of the ethical codes. First of all, it is important to realize that in their official formulations the rules of confidentiality may not cover the

Pinto case. That is because the Pinto problem concerns preventive whistle-blowing, and even in its most stringent formulations, confidentiality is absolute only regarding past events. Thus, the ABA . . . Model Rules allow a lawyer to reveal information relating to. the representation of a client "to prevent the client from committing a criminal act that the lawyer believes is likely to result in imminent death or substantial bodily harm . . . ."

One might wonder whether the purely statistical risk to Ford owners would allow preventive whistleblowing under these last rules. The answer, I believe, is "yes."

None of these rules, I believe, is perfect.

NOTES

Since Prof. Luban wrote his book, the rules have changed more than once. As we shall shortly see, they have moved closer to Luban's morality-based position, though they are not yet there. Note Luban's reference to Ford's efforts to postpone new car safety regulations. In Problem 2, we saw references to Lloyd Cutler's efforts to postpone other car safety regulations. Clearly, the timing of safety requirements has a material and substantial economic effect on automakers.

Luban clearly believes that lawyers should be held morally accountable. That is particularly relevant here, as Ernesto Valencia struggles to determine his appropriate course of conduct. Is the moral imperative sufficient to cause Valencia to act? Do you agree with Luban that there is also an *ethical* imperative, at least in the case of the Pinto's flaming gas tanks? Or is his claim that whistle-blowing is *ethically* required colored by his belief that it is *morally* required?

Professor Luban himself acknowledges that evaluating the "price range" for life is not an evil thing so much as it is routine, something that governmental agencies do on an almost daily basis. How does the "price of life" evaluation affect a lawyer's decision on whether to blow the whistle? Luban says that it is not the price of lives lost in the Pinto case that created the ethical mandate to disclose, but the fact that the lives were being lost because of Ford's "blunder." Do you agree that this trumps the value of life analysis?

Finally, if you agree there is an ethical imperative, when does that imperative operate? Is it enough to be reasonably certain about ensuing death or great bodily injury? Or must there be no doubt? And how imminent must the harm be? Where does the Venezia fit?

2. Roger Tuttle's *Mea Culpa.* In his 1985 book about A. H. Robins and their lawyers,[2] which we excerpted briefly in Problem 17, Morton Mintz describes the trials of Roger Tuttle. In the 1970s Tuttle served as a Robins in-house lawyer; by 1984 he was a law professor in Oklahoma when he testified in deposition about the role of Robins' general counsel's office a decade earlier. In his testimony, Tuttle admitted that early in 1975, as lawsuits over Robins' defective Dalkon Shield mounted and government scrutiny increased,

---

[2] AT ANY COST: CORPORATE GREED, WOMEN AND THE DALKON SHIELD (Pantheon 1985).

he was told by his boss, General Counsel and corporate vice president William A. Forrest, to oversee the destruction of "troublesome" Shield documents — those that pointed to the dangers of the Dalkon Shield and to Robins' early knowledge of those dangers.

At the time, Tuttle not only said nothing, but had the destruction carried out. As a "sop to my conscience," he ordered his subordinates to do the job, using the same forced-air furnace Robins used to burn contaminated drugs to destroy hundreds of documents.[3]

Had these documents become public, tens of thousands of women with Shields still implanted would have learned of their danger and been able to remove them before further damage was done. And, of course, sue Robins. A decade later at his deposition, Tuttle was asked by the plaintiffs' lawyers about these women, and what if anything was done to warn them. Nothing, he admitted, nor was anything disclosed to the FDA.

Tuttle clearly recognized the gravity of his failure to speak out. He testified that he was well aware of the implications of the documents as evidence, and acknowledged that destroying them was both legally and morally wrong.

Tuttle also admitted that he "personally lacked the courage to throw down the gauntlet," knowing that his job was at stake. "[W]ith a wife and two young children, I'll have to confess to you that I lacked the courage to do then what I know today was the right thing."

Tuttle didn't forsake his morals entirely. Instead of destroying everything he was asked to, he selected the "most damaging of the documents" and saved copies, hiding them in the basement of his home. He turned these over at the time of his deposition. A few months later, all of the Minnesota Dalkon Shield cases were settled, in no small measure due to the information he provided.

3. Sea Change, Part One — Sarbanes-Oxley and the SEC. The rules affecting Ernesto Valencia and his fellow in-house counsel — and, in many respects, outside counsel as well — changed substantially in the first half of the century's first decade. First was the passage of the Sarbanes-Oxley Act, then the passage of SEC ethics rules, then the completion of the two-step modification to ABA Model Rules 1.6 and 1.13. We will look at each in turn, starting with an article about another financial implosion — Global Crossing — and the passage of Sarbanes-Oxley, followed by our Note describing the SEC rules.

MICHELLE COTTLE, WHY NO ONE BLAMES THE LAWYERS
New Republic (October 14, 2002)[4]

By late last summer Roy Olofson, then the vice president of finance for Global Crossing, was convinced something was rotten with the company's books. Hit hard by the deflating telecom bubble, Global Crossing, Olofson suspected, had begun using a range of accounting tricks to artificially inflate its revenue statements. So on August 6, 2001, he sent a five-page letter to

---

[3] Forrest and those acting under Tuttle's direction all denied Tuttle's charges.

[4] Reprinted by permission of The New Republic. Copyright © 2002 by The New Republic, LLC.

the corporation's general counsel, James Gorton, outlining his concern that company shareholders and bankers, as well as the Securities and Exchange Commission (SEC), had been intentionally misled about the organization's financial health.

Faced with Olofson's accusations, Gorton asked Global Crossing's outside counsel, the New York law firm of Simpson Thacher & Bartlett, to launch an independent inquiry. After conducting a round of interviews and reviewing company documents, the firm reported its findings back to Gorton. On February 4, 2002, Global Crossing issued an official statement asserting that after "consultation with outside counsel," management was confident that the company's accounting methods had been appropriate and that it had made adequate disclosure both to the public and to the SEC. The "allegations made by Mr. Olofson were without merit."

Today, of course, it seems clear that the folks at Simpson Thacher missed a few details. Global Crossing is under investigation by both the SEC and the U.S. Attorney's office in Los Angeles for possible accounting and disclosure improprieties. The New York attorney general is scrutinizing the company's relationships . . . while the Labor Department examines its employee stock policies. Some four dozen class-action suits alleging violations of securities law have been filed . . . . This week both Gorton, who left the firm early this year, and Chairman Gary Winnick appeared before a House Energy and Commerce subcommittee to discuss — among other things — the contents of Olofson's letter. Meanwhile [Global] filed for the fourth-largest bankruptcy in history. . . .

What about all that "consultation with outside counsel"? Apparently, Simpson Thacher's review followed the see-no-evil model that Vinson & Elkins made famous in its review of Enron . . . . The Simpson Thacher team not only failed to contact Global Crossing's board of directors and its outside auditor, the now-defunct Arthur Andersen, it didn't even interview Olofson. Rather, attorneys relied largely on information provided by a handful of company executives, many of whom may have been involved in — or knowingly benefited from — the schemes in question. . . .

But as subpoenas are issued, briefs filed, and Global Crossing self-destructs in spectacular Enron style, it's business as usual at Simpson Thacher. The firm faces no threat of legal action from the government or the public. . . . This, despite the fact that . . . the cozy relationship between Global Crossing and Simpson Thacher may well have inclined the law firm to conduct a less-than-strenuous inquiry. In addition to the millions in legal fees . . . each year, a number of Simpson Thacher attorneys owned stock in the telecom company. . . .

For its part, Simpson Thacher maintains that the firm had no legal obligation to conduct a more thorough inquiry into Olofson's accusations. Since no charges had been leveled directly at Gorton or Winnick, the review team had no reason to contact company board members, asserted the chairman of Simpson Thacher's executive committee, Richard Beattie, to the Los Angeles Times in February. Insisted Beattie, "I don't believe we did anything wrong."

But Simpson Thacher shouldn't get off that easily — nor should the legal profession as a whole. When accused of professional misconduct, lawyers often argue that their code of ethics — with its emphasis on protecting the client — actually requires them to dispense cutting-edge (read: questionable) legal advice and to overlook a client's suspicious behavior . . . . Many legal ethicists, however, say such arguments intentionally misinterpret certain aspects of the rules governing lawyers. And in other instances the rules themselves need to be changed . . . .

Members of the bar have periodically tried to increase lawyers' public accountability by loosening these attorney-client privilege rules. But a vocal opposition has successfully countered with ominous scenarios about what would result: Clients will no longer be honest with their attorneys, attorneys will be afraid to launch zealous defenses of their clients, and our entire legal system will come tumbling down . . . .

Reform-minded lawyers, however, point to a number of flaws in these apocalyptic claims. For starters, says Jonathan Macey, a professor at Cornell University Law School, one of the most pervasive problems in corporate law is that lawyers forget who "the client" is. "The lawyer's true ethical responsibility is to the corporation, not the individual officer who hires him," says Macey . . . . This is precisely the sort of thinking that helped fuel the savings-and-loan crisis, says University of Illinois law professor Richard Painter. Painter served on the ethics committee of the New York bar back in the early '90s when federal banking regulators were fighting to hold lawyers accountable for their part in the meltdown. "One issue was lawyers' failure to inform the full board when client firms were obviously in violation of federal law," he recalls . . . .

The new wave of corporate scandals has again spotlighted the need for change. In March, Painter drafted a letter to SEC Commissioner Harvey Pitt — signed by 40 reform-minded law professors — recommending that the commission enforce tougher ethics standards for lawyers. Three weeks later Painter received a polite rebuff from SEC general counsel David Becker, suggesting that the professor take the matter up with Congress. So Painter did just that, sending his recommendations to Senator John Edwards, who used them as the basis for an amendment to the Sarbanes-Oxley corporate-accountability act, which President Bush signed on July 30. The amendment directs the SEC to establish rules of conduct for all lawyers doing business with the commission. These rules must, among other things, require lawyers to report "evidence of material violation of securities law or breach of fiduciary duty" to a client company's general counsel or CEO. If the CEO or counsel fails to respond adequately, the lawyer must proceed up the chain of command to the audit committee or even the full board of directors.

Reformers say Sarbanes-Oxley should be uncontroversial since it allows lawyers to keep even the dirtiest of client secrets in the family. "It's really rather tame," says Stephen Gillers, vice dean and professor of legal ethics at New York University. "It does not mandate reporting outside, and so in no way compromises confidentiality or privilege." Nonetheless, the American Bar Association (ABA), which has repeatedly beaten back efforts at external oversight, lobbied hard against the amendment.

. . . .

Sarbanes-Oxley may not be enough. An even hotter topic under debate is a lawyer's right (and responsibility) to report a client's misdeeds to outside parties such as the SEC. Currently, the ABA's Model Rules . . . allow lawyers to breach confidentiality only when failure to do so is likely to result in imminent death or substantial bodily harm. Not long ago the ABA's Ethics 2000 committee recommended expanding this exemption to include preventing a client from "using the lawyer's services to commit a crime or fraud." The change was rejected . . . .

Stunned by the passage of Sarbanes-Oxley and desperate to head off further government meddling, the ABA has pledged to revisit the confidentiality issue at its February [2003] meeting.

. . . .

Some observers believe that by refusing to seriously address ethics reform until this latest series of scandals forced Congress to get involved, the legal profession has outsmarted itself. For years lawyers, like accountants, have done as they please, assuming they would always remain totally self-regulating, says [Columbia law professor John] Coffee. "Both professions have behaved much like French aristocrats one year before the revolution. . . . And now it's gonna cost both of them."

NOTES

Section 307 of the Sarbanes-Oxley Act, passed in July 2002, mandated that the Securities & Exchange Commission promulgate "minimum standards of professional conduct for attorneys appearing and practicing before the Commission in . . . the representation of public companies."

On January 29, 2003, the SEC complied, adopting much of § 307 of the statute's language. The SEC required that an attorney representing a client (or "issuer") must report up the ladder to the chief legal officer or chief executive officer of the company when the lawyer "becomes aware" of "evidence of a material violation of securities law or breach of fiduciary duty or similar violation" by the company or any of its agents. If the general counsel or CEO does not respond "appropriately" to the evidence, the attorney must report it to an independent audit committee or to the company's full board of directors.

The new SEC rules also require the general counsel or chief legal officer to conduct a reasonable inquiry once the matter has been reported to that individual. The general counsel must then notify the reporting attorney of the results of the inquiry, and, unless s/he believes that no material violation is involved, take reasonable steps to ensure that the client takes appropriate remedial measures and makes appropriate disclosures. (The SEC rules also clarified — as if there were any doubt — that lawyers represent the entity rather than the officers or other corporate constituents, and that attorneys must therefore act in the best interests of the entity.)

Disclosures under this rule, of course, would involve the company "going public," but the SEC rules currently do not independently require that either the reporting lawyer or the GC do more than performing their duties to make and take all reasonable reporting steps within the company. But when the SEC promulgated its rules in early 2003, it also drafted a proposed rule that would require that if internal reporting was insufficient, the lawyers would have to withdraw and notify the SEC. It is here that the next battle may be fought.

What about Global Crossing? The company went bankrupt, but went more quietly than its Houston neighbor, Enron, without indictments or much fanfare.[5]

4. Sea Change, Part Two — The ABA Model Rules. As the last article discusses, the ABA House of Delegates had a pitched battle over the exceptions to confidentiality relating to financial fraud. In 2002, as those changes failed, the ABA modified and simplified the "death or substantial bodily harm" exception to Model Rule 1.6 with relatively little controversy. Instead of allowing an exception to confidentiality only "to prevent the client from committing a criminal act that the lawyer believes is likely to result in imminent death or substantial bodily harm," the ABA followed what was by then the majority of states and eliminated both the phrase "criminal act" and the requirement that the harm be "imminent." These changes focused the issue on *harm* rather than behavior. Thus, if "slow-harm" dangers like toxic pollutants in the groundwater table are as dangerous as deadly car defects or even ex-spouses armed for revenge they are as disclosable. And the new rule no longer requires that the client be the actor at all, much less that the act be criminal, only that the harm be "reasonably certain." The American Law Institute approved similar changes in its Restatement of the Law Governing Lawyers.

As for the financial fraud changes, the battle was renewed in the summer of 2003, as this article describes.

PATRICIA MANSON, LAWYER-ETHICS CODE UNDERGOES SEA CHANGE
Chicago Daily Law Bulletin (August 12, 2003)[6]

Reversing course, American Bar Association delegates have approved an ethics rule allowing lawyers to blow the whistle on a client who has made the lawyer an unwitting pawn in a financial scheme.

The policy-making House of Delegates had rejected an identical proposal to amend Rule 1.6 of the Model Rules of Professional Conduct at the ABA's 2001 annual meeting.

But citing the accounting scandals and corporate meltdowns that have occurred since then, proponents pushed the measure at the current annual meeting — and on Monday they won.

And on Tuesday, proponents also successfully urged delegates to amend Rule 1.13 to allow attorneys — either in-house counsel or outside lawyers —

---

[5] For those wanting to read about Global's demise and an argument about why Global didn't suffer the same fate as Enron, read Timothy L. O'Brien, *A New Legal Chapter for a 90s Flameout*, N.Y. TIMES, Aug. 15, 2004.

[6] Copyright © 2003 by Law Bulletin Publishing Company. Reprinted by permission.

to reveal confidential information in some circumstances if a corporate client refuses to address a violation of law . . . .

Peter F. Langrock of Middlebury, Vt., said a lawyer should not be forced to stand by and do nothing when an erring client manipulates the lawyer to inflict harm on others. "I didn't go to law school, I didn't spend 43 years practicing law, to have a client make use of my services to perpetrate a fraud on a widow who's trying to save money toward her daughter's education," Langrock said.

But opponents took a different view of the proposed changes to Rule 1.6. Former ABA president William G. Paul of Oklahoma City argued that the rule "asks us to barter away a piece of our professional soul" by breaching the obligation to maintain the confidentiality of communications with clients.

. . . .

In a 218-201 vote, delegates amended Rule 1.6 to allow lawyers to reveal confidences in order to block a client from using the lawyer's services in a financial fraud or crime.

Delegates also amended Rule 1.6 to permit lawyers to disclose confidences in a bid to repair any substantial harm that the client's wrongful acts have inflicted on the financial interests of another . . . .

Tuesday, delegates came back to amend Rule 1.13 to require attorneys who represent corporations or other organizations to report to authorities within the client the unlawful conduct of an officer or employee.

Delegates also modified Rule 1.13 to allow an attorney to go outside the organization with confidential information if the organization's authorities fail to act in the face of a violation of the law.

Attorneys may reveal such information only if they reasonably believe that the move is necessary to prevent substantial harm to the client.

Delegates approved the amended rule after deleting a provision that would have required lawyers to report conduct that a reasonable lawyer should have known was criminal or fraudulent.

. . . .

In a vote on another resolution, delegates endorsed a series of corporate governance practices that included requiring boards of directors to "engage in active, independent and informed oversight of the corporation's business and affairs, including its senior management."

NOTES

Of course, only individual states will determine what the disciplinary rules will be. How many of the ABA reforms to either Rule 1.6 or Rule 1.13 will be adopted by the states is still unclear as of this writing, though several states had acted before the ABA, and many others have since. States continue to have wide differences about permissive vs. mandatory disclosure. Thus, the broad exceptions to confidentiality in New Jersey, for example, have only passing resemblance to the narrow exceptions in California.

The "up-the-ladder" requirements of Sarbanes-Oxley and the SEC, the possibility — discussed by many "SOX" commentators — that the application of those requirements may be broadened to include a much wider range of entities than publicly-traded corporations, and the possibility of going outside the corporation raised by both federal law and the 2003 version of Model Rule 1.13, are areas in-house counsel must research carefully before deciding what to do. Regardless of the results of research, of course, lawyers will always be confronted by the moral issues Prof. Luban raises.

5. Can Corporate Criminal Guidelines Foster Ethical Conduct? Before the SOX-SEC transformation and the new Ethics 2000 ABA Rules, there were the corporate criminal sentencing guidelines. These guidelines, in place since the early '90s, offer a series of challenges to in-house and outside counsel, and continue to be important today, as we will see in Section 8 below.

JOSEPH J. FLEISCHMAN, WILLIAM J. HELLER & MITCHELL A. SCHLEY, THE ORGANIZATIONAL SENTENCING GUIDELINE AND THE EMPLOYMENT AT-WILL RULE AS APPLIED TO IN-HOUSE COUNSEL
Business Lawyer (February 1993)[7]

The Organizational Sentencing Guidelines (Guidelines) place new and serious professional obligations on in-house counsel. Both in-house and outside counsel may face professional disciplinary proceedings, and, in extreme circumstances, civil and criminal liability, if they do not withdraw from the lawyer-client relationship and report continuing corporate wrong-doing to prosecuting authorities, even if the report may involve information protected by the attorney-client privilege. These external pressures often conflict with the lawyer's paramount duties of loyalty and confidentiality to the client.

. . . .

The Guidelines determine an organization's penalty for violating federal-criminal law. Under the Guidelines, the sentencing judge performs an eight-step analysis to determine the amount of the mandatory fine. Each organization begins with a "base" fine which can range from $5,000 to $72.5 million, and a culpability score of five points, which can be increased or decreased depending on several factors. This culpability score is applied as a multiplier against the base fine, and it can have a significant impact upon the amount of the ultimate penalty levied against the corporation. The culpability score is a function of aggravating factors, which increase the score, and mitigating factors, which decrease the score.

Points are added — and penalties are increased under the Guidelines — for:

1. willful ignorance or condoning behavior by "high level" personnel or pervasive intolerance by "substantial authority" personnel;

2. prior criminal or civil adjudications based on similar conduct;

3. violations of an injunction or judicial order; and

---

[7] Copyright © 1993 by American Bar Association. Reprinted by permission.

4. willful obstruction or knowing failure to prevent the crime.

Points are subtracted — and penalties are mitigated under the Guidelines — for:

1. the existence of an "effective" compliance program to prevent and detect violations of law;

2. self-reporting promptly after becoming aware of the violation and prior to government investigation;

3. organizational cooperation; and

4. acceptance of responsibility. . . .

The Guidelines offer significant reductions in fines when the organization implements an effective compliance program . . . .

Frequently, and understandably, the burden of implementing a compliance program falls to counsel, especially in-house counsel. They also have responsibilities under the rules of professional conduct, such as the duty to maintain a client's confidences. Indeed, they may jeopardize their licenses to practice law for failure to comply with these ethical rules, which may conflict with the Guidelines' disclosure and other requirements.

. . . .

With the advent of the Guidelines, in-house counsel, to whom most corporations turn for legal compliance, now have a reinforced duty to detect wrongdoing and to disclose it to the entity, and possibly to prosecuting authorities. Yet, the very act of enforcing compliance or disclosing wrongdoing may lead to a sharp conflict between in-house lawyers and their supervisors.

6. Roger Balla's Stand. As the title of the last article indicates, the authors include a rather lengthy discussion of the availability of employment law remedies to in-house counsel who feel compelled to blow the whistle on their employers. Corporations have defended against retaliatory discharge and similar allegations brought by whisteblowing lawyers by arguing that such claims, necessarily based on communications between counsel and client, are barred by the attorney-client privilege and the confidential relationship. Read what happened to one in-house counsel who, under the affirmative reporting language of Illinois' version of MR 1.6 had a duty, rather than a mere option, to report his client's wrongdoing.

BALLA v. GAMBRO, INC.
145 Ill. 2d 492, 584 N.E.2d 104 (1991)

The issue in this case is whether in-house counsel should be allowed the remedy of an action for retaliatory discharge. . . .

Gambro is a distributor of kidney dialysis equipment manufactured by Gambro Germany. Among the products distributed by Gambro are dialyzers which filter excess fluid and toxic substances from the blood of patients with no or impaired kidney function. The manufacture and sale of dialyzers is regulated by the United States Food and Drug Administration (FDA). . . .

Appellee, Roger J. Balla, is and was at all times throughout this controversy an attorney licensed to practice law in the State of Illinois. On March 17, 1980, appellee executed an employment agreement with Gambro which contained the terms of the appellee's employment. . . . [A]ppellee's specific responsibilities included, inter alia . . . compliance with applicable laws and regulations. . . .

In July 1985, Gambro Germany informed Gambro in a letter that certain dialyzers it had manufactured, the clearances of which varied from the package insert, were about to be shipped to Gambro. . . . Appellee told the president of Gambro to reject the shipment because the dialyzers did not comply with FDC regulations. The president notified Gambro Germany of its decision to reject the shipment on July 12, 1985.

However, one week later the president informed Gambro Germany that Gambro would accept the dialyzers and "sell [them] to a unit that is not currently our customer but who buys only on price." Appellee contends that he was not informed by the president of the decision to accept the dialyzers but became aware of it through other Gambro employees. Appellee maintains that he spoke with the president in August regarding the company's decision to accept the dialyzers and told the president that he would do whatever was necessary to stop the sale of the dialyzers.

On September 4, 1985, appellee was discharged from Gambro's employment by its president. The following day, appellee reported the shipment of the dialyzers to the FDA. The FDA seized the shipment and determined the product to be "adulterated . . . ."

On March 19, 1986, appellee filed a four-count complaint in tort for retaliatory discharge seeking $22 million in damages.

. . . .

We agree with the trial court that appellee does not have a cause of action against Gambro for retaliatory discharge. . . . In this case it appears that Gambro discharged appellee, an employee of Gambro, in retaliation for his activities, and this discharge was in contravention of a clearly mandated public policy . . . . In appellee's eyes, the use of these dialyzers could cause death or serious bodily harm to patients. As we have stated before, "[t]here is no public policy more important or more fundamental than the one favoring the effective protection of the lives and property of citizens." However, in this case, appellee was not just an employee of Gambro, but also general counsel for Gambro.

In his brief to this court, appellee argues that not extending the tort of retaliatory discharge to in-house counsel would present attorneys with a "Hobson's choice." According to appellee, in-house counsel would face two alternatives: either comply with the client/employer's wishes and risk both the loss of a professional license and exposure to criminal sanctions, or decline to comply with the client/employer's wishes and risk the loss of a full-time job and the attendant benefits. We disagree. . . . In-house counsel do not have a choice of whether to follow their ethical obligations as attorneys licensed to practice law, or follow the illegal and unethical demands of their clients. In-house counsel must abide by the Rules of Professional Conduct. Appellee had no choice but to report to the FDA.

. . . .

If extending the tort of retaliatory discharge might have a chilling effect on the communications between the employer/client and the in-house counsel, we believe that it is more wise to refrain from doing so.

Our decision not to extend the tort of retaliatory discharge to in-house counsel also is based on other ethical considerations. Under the Rules of Professional Conduct, appellee was required to withdraw from representing Gambro if continued representation would result in the violation of the Rules of Professional Conduct. . . . [A]ccording to appellee's claims herein, his continued representation of Gambro would have resulted in a violation of the Rules of Professional Conduct. Appellee argues that such a choice of withdrawal is "simplistic and uncompassionate, and is completely at odds with contemporary realities facing in-house attorneys." These contemporary realities apparently are the economic ramifications of losing his position as in-house counsel. However difficult, economically and perhaps emotionally, it is for in-house counsel to discontinue representing an employer/client, we refuse to allow in-house counsel to sue their employer/client for damages because they obeyed their ethical obligations.

JUSTICE FREEMAN, dissenting:

I respectfully dissent from the decision of my colleagues. In concluding that the plaintiff attorney, serving as corporate in-house counsel, should not be allowed a claim for retaliatory discharge, the majority first reasons that the public policy implicated in this case, i.e., protecting the lives and property of Illinois citizens, is adequately safeguarded by the lawyer's ethical obligation to reveal information about a client as necessary to prevent acts that would result in death or serious bodily harm. I find this reasoning fatally flawed.

The majority so reasons because, as a matter of law, an attorney cannot even contemplate ignoring his ethical obligations in favor of continuing in his employment. I agree with this conclusion "as a matter of law." However, to say that the categorical nature of ethical obligations is sufficient to ensure that the ethical obligations will be satisfied simply ignores reality. Specifically, it ignores that, as unfortunate for society as it may be, attorneys are no less human than nonattorneys and, thus, no less given to the temptation to either ignore or rationalize away their ethical obligations when complying therewith may render them unable to feed and support their families.

I would like to believe, as my colleagues apparently conclude, that attorneys will always "do the right thing" because the law says that they must. However, my knowledge of human nature, [is] more than sufficient to dispel such a belief.

. . . .

. . . [T]his court must take whatever steps it can, within the bounds of the law, to give lawyers incentives to abide by their ethical obligations, beyond the satisfaction inherent in their doing so. We cannot continue to delude ourselves and the people of the State of Illinois that attorneys' ethical duties, alone, are always sufficient to guarantee that lawyers will "do the right thing." In the context of this case, where doing "the right thing" will often result in termination by an employer bent on doing the "wrong thing," I believe that the incentive needed is recognition of a cause of action for retaliatory discharge.

NOTES

Who do you think is right in *Balla* about the "contemporary realities" of how general counsel will behave, the majority or the dissent? Recall that even "good" lawyers like Roger Tuttle don't always act ethically with their jobs on the line.

Note that Illinois' affirmative duty to report, rather than working in Roger Balla's favor, seemed to hurt his case. Do you think the court would have upheld his ability to sue if Illinois only had a permissive disclosure rule? It is interesting that *Balla* does not bar Balla's claim because it would necessarily violate the attorney-client privilege. To the contrary, it seems to *require* the lawyer to disclose.

7. Whither Protection for In-House Whistleblowers? The idea of in-house counsel suing an employer for retaliatory discharge is relatively new. As the case law develops, the effect of Sarbanes-Oxley and the SEC rules may be felt in future court decisions, though they have yet to have significant impact. We review that case law here.

Balla was one of the first reported cases, although, interestingly, not the first Illinois case. *Herbster v. North Am. Col. For Life & Health Insurance*, 150 Ill. App. 3d 21, 501 N.E.2d 343 (1986), cited with approval in *Balla*, barred a suit by in-house counsel who refused to do what Roger Tuttle did — destroy documents that showed his company's fraud. *Balla*'s approval of *Herbster* is odd in light of *Herbster*'s different approach towards a lawyer's duties. Citing *Upjohn*, *Herbster* emphasized that "confidential communications related by a client remain inviolate by the attorney both during the attorney-client relationship and after it has been terminated." *Herbster*'s somewhat oblique holding criticized both sides for "focus[ing] on the privilege aspect of the relationship only. We find that all aspects are so necessary to our system of jurisprudence that extending this tort to the attorney-client relationship here is not justified." And what are these aspects? "The mutual trust, exchanges of confidence, reliance on judgment, and personal nature of the attorney-client relationship [that] demonstrate the unique position attorneys occupy in our society."

In another 1991 case the court in *Mourad v. Automobile Club Insurance Ass'n*, 186 Mich. App. 715, 465 N.W.2d 395 (1991), concluded that in-house counsel who had refused to let his non-attorney employees supervise lawyers had a contract cause of action for wrongful discharge, based on an implied understanding that the lawyer was bound by ethical rules, and could not be terminated without just cause if expected to act outside those rules.

While *Mourad* was limited to contract claims, in the years since courts have begun to recognize causes of action for retaliatory discharge. Most significantly, in 1994, the California Supreme Court in *General Dynamics Corp. v. Superior Court*, 7 Cal. 4th 1164, 32 Cal. Rptr. 2d 1 (1994), both agreed that a "just cause" contract action applied and upheld a retaliatory discharge tort claim based on in-house counsel Andrew Rose's assertion that he was discharged because of the advice he had given to his corporate employer about the company's required course of conduct. Soon after, a Massachusetts court, in *GTE Products Corp. v. Stewart*, 653 N.E.2d 161 (Mass. 1995), cited *General Dynamics*, and also recognized a retaliatory discharge tort.

But these retaliatory discharge cases give only modest comfort to in-house counsel who feel an ethical compulsion to speak out. While *General Dynamics* overcame the issue of whether attorney-client duties limited corporate counsel's remedies against a former employer, it permitted a tort cause of action only where "it can be established without breaching the attorney-client privilege or unduly endangering the values lying at the heart of the professional relationship." Where did this leave matters? California then had a strict confidentiality rule, ostensibly with no exceptions, so establishing a case without violating confidences could be a daunting task. But the court's opinion completely dodged this question, focusing instead on the narrower privilege: "[M]any of the cases in which house counsel is faced with an ethical dilemma will lie outside the scope of the statutory privilege," such as the crime fraud exception, or where "disclosure is necessary to prevent the commission of a criminal act likely to result in death or substantial bodily harm . . . ."

In *Stewart*, plaintiff house counsel fared less well. First, the *Stewart* court required that "the claim can be proved without any violation of the attorney's obligation to respect client confidences and secrets," a broader prohibition than abrogating only the privilege. Indeed, *Stewart* noted that exceptions to confidentiality "are extremely limited." Then, stating that Stewart did not show "that remaining in his position would have required him to violate his ethical obligations as an attorney," or that, despite a poor performance review soon after he urged the company to comply with federal hazardous waste requirements, he had established that his new working conditions were so difficult that he was compelled to resign, the court granted summary judgment against him. Similarly, in *Willy v. Coastal States Management Co.*, 939 S.W.2d 193 (Tex. App. 1996), a case that had bounced around the Texas courts for so long that a 1986 version had been cited in *Balla*, the court allowed a retaliatory discharge tort at least in theory, then created the same Catch-22 for former in-house counsel Willy, saying he could not prove his claim without resorting to forbidden client confidences.

To date, the most permissive interpretation of wrongful discharge suits (and in this particular case a sex discrimination claim) may be *Kachmar v. Sungard Data Systems, Inc.*, 109 F.3d 173 (3d Cir. 1997), in which a Sungard subsidiary's allegedly discriminatory policies towards women were challenged by in-house counsel Lillian Kachmar, who was eventually fired. Not only did the court allow her causes of action to go forward, but the court wrote: "We do not suggest that concerns about the disclosure of client confidences in suits by in-house counsel are unfounded, but these concerns alone would not warrant dismissing a plaintiff's case, especially where there are other means to prevent unwarranted disclosure of confidential information." The court then cited *General Dynamics'* suggestions of protective orders, limited admissibility of evidence, and in camera hearings. *Kachmar* is particularly interesting because the nature of the company's violation did *not* involve potential harm to the public at all, nor did Kachmar directly refuse to act in an unethical manner.

But the Fifth Circuit came to a very different conclusion in *Douglas v. DynMcDermott Petroleum Operations Co.*, 144 F.3d 364 (5th Cir. 1998), where corporate in-house counsel complained first in-house and then to the EEOC about job discrimination, was fired, and won a substantial trial court judgment for sex and race discrimination. The opinion overturned that award and called Douglas' revelation of attorney-client confidences a violation of her ethical obligations.

What about recourse for in-house counsel under the whistleblower protection statutes that exist in most states? So far, these have generally not been applied to lawyers, at least those in private employment.[8] One notable exception is New Jersey, which has long had a narrower view of attorney-client confidentiality than most venues. In *Parker v. M & T Chemicals, Inc.*, 566 A.2d 215 (N.J. App. 1989), in-house attorney Sheldon Parker was demoted when he refused to participate in receiving deposition transcripts from a competitor's case that were subject to a protective order.

Pointing out that "the commission of a crime or fraud is excepted from the attorney-client privilege," the court had little difficulty in refusing the defendant's entreaties to follow *Herbster*, and held the whistleblower statute applicable to lawyers: "[I]t reinforces the Court's constitutional mission to encourage and insure the ethical practice of law. We see no constitutional incompatibility and will not read in-house attorneys out of the Act's protection." As for confidentiality (as opposed to the privilege), the court said: "The employer-client is still free to file an ethics complaint against the former employee-attorney . . . . The attorney is still subject to the same discipline as before the adoption of the [Whistleblower] Act."

Despite the fact that *Parker* was one of the first cases decided on this issue, other courts have not specifically evaluated the question of whether whistleblower act protection should be afforded in-house lawyers.

One final thought: It is of more than passing interest that of all these cases, only *Balla* and *Douglas* actually involved an in-house lawyer who went *outside* the company to blow the whistle. And in *Balla*, that occurred only after Balla had been fired. Thus, in almost every reported case, termination came about not as a result of public disclosure of the company's practice, but rather, *private*, *internal* pressure on the part of in-house counsel to get the company to do the right thing.

8. Whither (Wither?) the Corporate Attorney-Client Privilege? Part One — Prosecutorial Pressure. Note the "modern" use of the corporate sentencing guidelines to extract privilege waivers, as discussed in this next article.

---

[8] Recall our discussion of public attorneys' whistleblowing in Problem 23.

DAVID B. FEIN & ROBERT S. HUIE, ATTACKS ON CLIENT PRIVILEGE INCREASING: GOVERNMENT INSISTENCE ON WAIVER JEOPARDIZES VALUES OF CORPORATE PRIVILEGE

Connecticut Law Tribune (June 23, 2003)[9]

In a recent public talk, Mary Jo White, former U.S. Attorney for the Southern District of New York, lamented that waiver of corporate privilege has become a litmus test for whether a company is cooperating with an investigation. Her lament is apt.

Federal prosecutors increasingly demand waiver of attorney-client privilege and work product protection at the inception of investigations. As described by Deputy Attorney General Larry Thompson in his January 2003 memorandum, entitled "Principles of Federal Prosecution of Business Organizations," waiver is not "an absolute requirement," but prosecutors should consider willingness to waive "as one factor in evaluating the corporation's cooperation." Thompson's memorandum revised 1999 guidelines and increased the "emphasis on and scrutiny of the authenticity of . . . cooperation." Pursuant to the 2003 revisions, prosecutors use willingness to cooperate as one of eight factors to determine whether to bring charges against a business organization.

Although prosecutors demand waiver more frequently, corporate privilege continues to serve an essential purpose. Attorney-client privilege and work product privilege protect communications between attorneys and their corporate clients. As the U.S. Supreme Court recognized 20 years ago in *Upjohn Co. v. United States*, corporate privilege is essential because it facilitates "communication of relevant information" between attorneys and clients. Such uninhibited dialogue enables companies to comply with applicable laws, because compliance with "the vast and complicated array of regulatory legislation confronting the modern corporation" is "hardly an instinctive matter." Without legal advice unfettered by the risk of disclosure, corporations may be less able to make informed decisions in accordance with the law. . . . Without assurances that communications will remain confidential, organizations may not only be hindered in their efforts to determine what laws apply and how to follow them, but may turn a blind eye to existing wrongdoing.

Federal prosecutors who aggressively pursue waiver show little regard for the importance of privilege. Prosecutors . . . not only decide whether to seek criminal charges, but they also determine what charges and sentences to seek. Since principles of corporate criminal liability are extremely broad, almost all acts of all employees may be imputed to the organization. . . . Given that authority, [p]rosecutors requesting waiver present corporations a difficult choice between seeking leniency and safeguarding privilege.

Tough Choices

. . . . Government requests for corporate waiver often arise at the outset of an investigation, and almost certainly prior to any resolution of possible

---

enforcement actions. On occasion, companies must decide whether to waive without even knowing what information they are ceding. In all these events, it is unlikely the company will know what benefits, if any, it will receive by virtue of its waiver.

In some situations, waiver may result in prosecution rather than leniency. Perhaps the most chilling example of this first problem is the 2002 indictment of Arthur Andersen. According to public reports, Andersen agreed to waive attorney-client privilege during the government investigation in an effort to cooperate and was rewarded with an indictment . . . . At Andersen's criminal trial, . . . once-privileged communications between Andersen employees and Andersen in-house counsel . . . formed the basis for the jury's conviction. . . .

Although the government's decision to charge Andersen led many experienced white-collar practitioners to question the value of a company waiving privilege, the pressure to waive still exists. Credit Suisse First Boston ("CSFB") recently decided to waive its attorney-client privilege, possibly out of fear of corporate prosecution . . . after [prosecutors] learn[ed] of a December 2000 e-mail message by CSFB star banker Frank Quattrone, regarding "time to clean up those files." . . . At the prosecutors' request, CSFB waived its attorney-client privilege with respect to some e-mail communications between Quattrone and CSFB's attorneys. A chain of e-mail messages between Quattrone and CSFB's then-general counsel surfaced, showing that, at the time Quattrone urged others to destroy documents, he had already been told of the government investigations of CSFB. Quattrone was subsequently indicted on obstruction of justice and witness tampering charges . . . .

Private Plaintiffs

The law is unsettled, but some court decisions suggest that waiver in a government investigation also may act as waiver in concurrent or subsequent private actions . . . .

In January [2003], a district court judge ordered McKesson Corp., the medical supply and information company, to produce the results of an internal investigation [of] two former executives who had been indicted for securities, mail and wire fraud. In 1999, McKesson had announced accounting irregularities . . . and conducted an internal investigation. McKesson turned the final report of that investigation over to the SEC and DOJ pursuant to a confidentiality agreement, and the DOJ used the report to indict two former executives. . . . In finding waiver despite the confidentiality agreement — which by its terms authorized the DOJ to disclose the report as it saw fit — the district court declined to follow decisions that allowed a party to waive privilege "selectively" to government agencies . . . .

Waiver essentially turns a corporation's lawyers into an investigative arm of the government. Some commentators have pointed out that this arrangement allows prosecutors to evade the Fifth Amendment: whereas employees might invoke their right against self-incrimination when questioned by the government, they are unable to assert it against their employer without the very real possibility of losing their jobs. As a result, employees who know that privilege has been or will be waived are understandably skittish about talking with the corporation's lawyers. . . . As the Supreme Court in *Upjohn* recognized, ". . . [a]n uncertain privilege . . . is little better than no privilege at all."

Better Solutions?

. . . . Ultimately, a policy change is called for to resolve the present dilemma. One solution is for the DOJ to reconsider, on a department-wide basis, the appropriateness of its requests for waiver of attorney-client privilege by organizations. Given Thompson's recent memorandum and the current climate of financial scandals, this result is extremely unlikely.

A recent report by the SEC suggests a more feasible, albeit partial, solution. The Sarbanes-Oxley Act . . . directed the SEC to report findings to Congress, including recommended regulations or legislation, which the SEC did in January. The report recommends amending the Securities Exchange Act of 1934 "to allow parties who choose to produce privileged or protected material to do so without fear that their production to the Commission will be deemed to waive privilege or protection as to anyone else." The report concludes that this change "would enhance the Commission's access to significant, otherwise unobtainable, information."

. . . . Whether Congress will act on this recommendation remains to be seen.

NOTES

It is of more than passing interest that both Arthur Andersen the entity and Frank Quattrone the individual had their convictions set aside by appeals courts. These events, especially the Andersen reversal, in light of the reality of Andersen's demise, have made prosecutors a bit more guarded about pressing too hard for privilege waivers lest they force other entities out of business without ultimately getting a conviction.

On the other hand, this article begins with the traditional apologia for why the corporate attorney-client privilege is essential. Do you agree? Before deciding, first read the following section. (One other note: The authors' reference to the Fifth Amendment in the above article is interesting given that corporations themselves have never had a Fifth Amendment — as opposed to attorney-client — privilege.)

9. Whither (Wither?) the Corporate Attorney-Client Privilege? Part Two — Corporate Self-Destructive Behavior. Only 25 years after the Supreme Court in *Upjohn* formally affirmed the corporate attorney-client privilege, many commentators, some of them in-house counsel, see serious signs that this privilege may be eroding. The use by prosecutors of pressured waivers, as in the Salomon Brothers case, is one reason for this concern, as is the increasing prevalence — and the possible trend — of decisions that allow causes of action for in-house counsel who refuse to act unethically. On another front, Loyola (Los Angeles) law professor Robert Benson has moved to revoke the corporate charter of Union Oil of California (Unocal), charging that it is a "repeat offender" in environmental and labor matters. If such petitions gain any currency, they would also undermine the corporate privilege.

The most significant challenge, however, comes from courts' increasing use of the crime-fraud exception to the privilege. In that arena, no one has caused corporate officers and boards more concern than the tobacco companies, for it has been in tobacco cases that the crime-fraud exception has been most widely applied.

By the 1950s, tobacco companies had set up a system of reporting unfavorable information directly to lawyers in an effort to protect as much as possible under the umbrella of the attorney-client privilege. One memo from in-house counsel advised that "direct lawyer involvement is needed in all [company] activities pertaining to smoking and health, from conception through every step of the activity," while another, from outside counsel, advised that a survey on the dangers of smoking be directly commissioned by lawyers, so that "[s]hould the results prove unfavorable, there will be nothing in the [survey takers'] records to subpoena. . . ."[10]

The Council on Tobacco Research (CTR), created in the 1950s by a consortium of tobacco companies, had a "special projects" unit supervised by lawyers, not scientists. The lawyers even had decision-making authority over hiring and firing of scientific employees and the selection of research projects. But this was not known until the trial court's rulings on discovery in *Haines v. Liggett Group, Inc.,* 140 F.R.D. 681 (D.N.J. 1992). There, judge H. Lee Sarokin reviewed his magistrate's discovery findings and then voided the attorney-client privilege on crime-fraud grounds. Among other things, discovery in *Haines* uncovered a memo acknowledging that CTR had been set up as "an industry 'shield' . . . a front," [Seligman, 1978 memo, cited in Haines, see Nader & S.] and a CTR participant as saying, "When we started CTR Special Projects, the idea was that the scientific director of CTR would review a project. If he liked it, it was a CTR special project. If he did not like it, then it became a lawyers' special project. . . . We wanted to protect it under the lawyers. We did not want it out in the open."

Sarokin was reversed by the Third Circuit in *Haines v. Liggett Group, Inc.,* 975 F.2d 81 (3d Cir. 1992), and disqualified from the case. But his opinion, already published, served as a road map for those trying to crack open "Big Tobacco's" shield of secrecy by exposing the industry's abuse of the attorney-client privilege. In 1997, a Florida court voided the tobacco companies' privilege on crime-fraud grounds, ultimately resulting in a $144 billion verdict in favor of the state to reimburse health care costs.[11] Finally, the floodgates opened when, in March 1998, Minnesota Judge Kenneth J. Fitzpatrick ordered the public release of 865 tobacco company documents. Fitzpatrick accused the

---

[10] See Christine Hatfield, *The Privilege Doctrines — Are They Just Another Discovery Tool Utilized by the Tobacco Industry to Conceal Damaging Information?,* 16 PACE L. REV. 525 (1996), quoting a 1984 memo from Brown & Williamson in-house counsel J. Kendrick Wells, and Mike France, *Inside Big Tobacco's Secret War Room,* BUSINESS WEEK, June 15, 1998, quoting a 1968 Arnold & Porter memo.

[11] *American Tobacco Company v. Florida,* 697 So. 2d 1249 (Fla. App. 1997). For the verdict, see newspapers of July 15, 2000, e.g., Rick Bragg, *Jurors in Florida Give Record Award in Tobacco Case,* N.Y. TIMES at 1.

industry of claiming privilege for many documents "clearly and inarguably not entitled to protections." This "intentional and repeated misuse" of the privilege "is intolerable in a court of law . . . ."[12] By the end of April 1998, when the Supreme Court denied the tobacco companies' requests for a stay, a congressional committee ordered the public release of 39,000 tobacco documents. It was the beginning of the end of the tobacco companies' long-standing "hardball" defense of cigarettes.

The tobacco companies are not alone, however, when it comes to lawyers' involvement in possible fraud and the use of the crime-fraud exception. We saw in Problem 17 how in 1999 one Georgia court found General Motors and its lawyers complicit in concealing information about a key witness, voiding the attorney-client and work product privileges, and forcing GM into an expensive settlement. It appears that courts are more willing to investigate the propriety of questionable corporate attorney-client privilege claims than ever before.

Finally, in New York, a federal district court voided a company's attorney-client privilege after finding that its in-house lawyer's act of negotiating the environmental details of a contract was a business matter, not the practice of law.[13] The case, never appealed, raised eyebrows because the judge did not consider *any* of the lawyer's work to be privileged. "It is my view that courts have steadily been narrowing [corporate] attorney-client privilege," Nikko general counsel C. Evan Stewart, a frequent commentator on corporate privilege issues, wrote soon afterwards. Several others, including Frederick J. Krebs, president of the American Corporate Counsel Association, saw a double standard in which in-house counsel was accorded less respect than other lawyers when it came to the privilege. Perhaps summing it up best, Sun Co. general counsel Jack Foltz told *The National Law Journal* that the corporate attorney-client privilege "is a fragile privilege. If you don't treat it right and take care of it, it will evaporate."[14]

SUPPLEMENTAL READINGS

1. Marianne Lavelle, "Placing a Price on Human Life," *The National Law Journal*, October 10, 1988, is a valuable review of how various entities, including governments, put a value on human life. This unpleasant but nevertheless real issue will almost inevitably be considered in evaluating facts such as those posited in this Problem. The range Lavelle found was from $70,000 to $132 million, with the average jury verdict for a male in his 30's right in the middle at $950,000.

2. Shelley Stucky Watson, *Keeping Secrets That Harm Others: Medical Standards Illuminate Lawyer's Dilemma*, 71 Neb. L. Rev. 1123 (1992), discusses whether lawyers should follow a medical model in the case of a serious threat of harm, at least where there are "identifiable" potential victims.

---

[12] *State by Humphrey v. Philip Morris, Inc.*, 1998 Minn. App. LEXIS 431 (1998).

[13] Georgia-Pacific Corp. v. GAF Roofing Mfg. Corp., 1996 U.S. Dist. Lexis 671 (S.D.N.Y. 1996).

[14] Claudia MacLachlan, *Corporate Counsel Defend Attorney-Client Privilege*, NATIONAL L.J., July 29, 1996.

3. Brian M. Smith, *Note: Be Careful How You Use It or You May Lose It: A Modern Look at Corporate Attorney-Client Privilege and the Ease of Waiver in Various Circuits*, 75 U. Det. Mercy L. Rev. 389 (1998), provides a valuable pre-SOX update on the ease with which the attorney-client privilege may be breached by the courts in various venues.

4. Several relatively recent law review articles have examined the role of in-house counsel as attorney/employee, as repository of confidences, and as potential litigant against a former employer. Among the most valuable: Sally R. Weaver, *Client Confidences in Disputes Between In-House Attorneys and Their Employer-Clients: Much Ado About Nothing — Or Something?*, 30 U. C. Davis L. Rev. 483 (1997), and Nancy J. Moore, *Conflicts of Interest for In-House Counsel: Issues Emerging from the Expanding Role of the Attorney-Employee*, 39 So. Texas L. Rev. 497 (1998).

5. Elizabeth Chambliss, *Empirical Studies of the Legal Profession: What Do We Know about Lawyers' Lives? The Professionalization of Law Firm In-House Counsel*, 84 N.C. L. Rev. 1515 (2006), is an article by a law professor who also holds a Ph.D. in Sociology. She used focus groups, interviews, and participant observervation to gather information on the evolution of the professionalization of in-house counsel.

6. It seems that innumerable Sarbanes-Oxley articles exist. Here is one of many. Jeffrey I. Snyder, *Regulation of Lawyer Conduct Under Sarbanes-Oxley: Minimizing Law-Firm Liability By Encouraging Adoption of Qualified Legal Compliance Committees*, 24 Rev. Litig. 223 (2005), is an article that, according to its summary, "will briefly discuss the period prior to passage of the Sarbanes-Oxley Act and what, if anything, the legal profession might have done differently to prevent the sweeping nature of the regulation under the Act." Then Snyder discusses the ramifications of the SEC rules, the possibility of compulsory "noisy withdrawal," and the reason why corporations should adopt the compliance committee structure created by the SEC.

7. Two more good SOX articles are: Andrew Longstreth, "In the New Era of Internal Investigations, Defense Lawyers have Become Deputy Prosecutors," *American Lawyer* (February 2005), explains how lawyers must now help in investigations of corporate wrongdoing lest they themselves be subjected to sanctions. A good, well-written piece, Meredith M. Brown, "Reporting By Lawyers of Evidence of Material Violations," 1462 PLI/CORP 535 (2005) provides a thorough and cogent explanation of the reporting requirements of Sarbannes-Oxley.

8. Thomas Morgan, *The Client(s) of a Corporate Lawyer*, 33 Capitol U. L. Rev. 17 (2004), is an article by one of the nation's most respected ethics theorists, a professor at George Washington, who argues that "a lawyer's role is clean and simple . . . . [T]he lawyer exists to implement that which the client wants to do and could do itself if the client had the lawyer's training and experience. The lawyer's duty is not to think; it is to accept the directions given by those people who are authorized to direct . . . ." Morgan acknowledges recent modifications to the ethics rules, but encourages lawyers not to act like "Lone Rangers."

9. H. Lowell Brown, *The Crime-Fraud Exception to the Attorney-Client Privilege in the Context of Corporate Counseling*, 87 Ky. L. J. 1191 (1999), is an article that reviews the status of this increasingly fragile privilege and how corporate counsel should behave in order to maximize privilege protection for their clients.

10. We usually think of reporting as the responsibility of in-house counsel, but what are the responsibilities of the plaintiff's bar? According to the *New York Times'* "S.U.V. Tire Defects Were Known In '96 But Not Reported," by Keith Bradsher, (June 24, 2001), in 1996 personal injury lawyers and traffic safety consultants identified a pattern of tire failures from the Firestone ATX tires, but they did not report those defects to government regulators because they did not want to jeopardize their own cases on behalf of plaintiffs.

11. Christine Hatfield, *The Privilege Doctrines — Are They Just Another Discovery Tool Utilized by the Tobacco Industry to Conceal Damaging Information?*, 16 Pace L. Rev. 525 (1996), is a thorough account of the tobacco companies' use and abuse of corporate attorney-client privilege.

12. Arthur Miller, *All My Sons* (1949). This play, by the Pulitzer Prize-winning playwright, revolves around the consequences of one man's interpretation of his corporate responsibility. Although it does not deal with the legal profession, the story is a compelling and clear tale centered on business ethics.

PART THREE
THE PRESSURES, ECONOMICS, AND DIVERSITY OF MODERN PRACTICE

"My fantasy of getting up from my desk, walking out my office, going to the head of my department and quitting to be a bartender is sounding extremely appealing. HELP!"

—a young lawyer posting on a "Greedy Associates" on-line board, 1999

Chapter 10

THE LAWYER AS PART OF THE LAW FIRM STRUCTURE

PROBLEM 26

Clients ask lawyers for their opinions all the time. Sometimes, they want these opinions in the formal setting of an opinion letter, a document on which the client can rely in determining how to act. How far may a lawyer stretch his or her own beliefs in drafting an opinion letter? Is it acceptable to draft a letter that does not comport with one's objective opinion but may be justifiable under the facts? If the opinion "stretches" the law, must the lawyer tell *that* to the client?

The problem of writing such an opinion letter is a difficult enough issue. But it is even more difficult where a law firm associate is being asked, or perhaps *told*, to write an opinion in which he or she does not believe. Should a law firm have rules that permit associates to refuse to perform an assignment if they consider it improper? What if the associate is not sure whether performing the work is unethical? What about the duty of the law firm to the client, and the duty of the associate to the partner *and* the client? Consider the difficult dilemma of Steven Green.

The Senior Associate's Serious Dilemma

Steven Green is a senior associate at Swenson & DeLuca, a mid-sized firm that specializes in litigation and real estate law. Steven has been at Swenson for only 18 months, but he first spent almost six years in the regional counsel's office of the Environmental Protection Agency. He has become his firm's resident expert on hazardous substances and toxic torts. Sheila Dern, one of the firm's real estate partners, asks Steven to meet with one of her best clients, George Reynolds. Reynolds owns a building which had been leased for the last 10 years to a company whose business used extensive quantities of a chemical called Thorzac. The company recently went bankrupt, and now Reynolds is looking to sell the building.

At the meeting, Reynolds tells Steven and Sheila that he has been approached by Doggy-Days, a company that boards and trains dogs, about purchasing Reynolds' building. But Reynolds knows that the prior lessee intentionally placed Thorzac in a man-made cement pond because it seemed to help the growth of the pond's lily pads. Steven and Sheila tell Reynolds that not disclosing hazardous waste to the buyer could make him liable for civil and criminal penalties.

"I know that," says Reynolds, "but what about the Thorzac? Is it hazardous or not? Look, I don't know anything about the disposal of hazardous waste. If this stuff is considered hazardous, my once-valuable piece of property may not be worth spit. And I need to move quick; this dog guy is ready to buy and wants an answer yesterday."

Sheila asks Steven to research Thorzac and get back to her within a week.

Steven reviews the federal law and the laws of his state, and concludes that a waste is deemed hazardous if it is specifically identified as such by the EPA, or if it is any of the following: (1) toxic, (2) corrosive, (3) an irritant, (4) a strong sensitizer, (5) flammable, or (6) generates pressure through decomposition. Steven's research discloses that Thorzac has not been specifically identified by the EPA as a hazardous waste. Therefore, Steven knows he must determine whether it has any of the proscribed characteristics.

Although there is no evidence that Thorzac fits the last four definitions for hazardous waste, Steven is concerned that it might be considered either corrosive or toxic. He believes a regulatory agency would use the following definition of a toxic substance: "having the capacity to produce personal injury or illness to humans through ingestion, inhalation, or absorption through the body surface."

Steven researches Thorzac, a substance that only came into common usage in the last several years. He finds four studies. The earliest study and one conducted under a grant from the chemical's manufacturer concluded that the toxicity of Thorzac could not be established. Two other studies, one at a Midwestern university, the other a recent study by a public interest research group called SafeChem, show preliminary results that indicate toxicity. Both these studies concluded that prolonged exposure to Thorzac causes birth defects in rats, though the effect on humans was not definitively established. Moreover, the SafeChem study also concluded that Thorzac has corrosive properties, and that it is capable of penetrating building materials so that the fumes may be present long after the chemical itself has been removed.

Steven meets with Sheila. He suggests they hire an expert, but Sheila reminds him that time is too short, and that Reynolds wants to move on the sale right away. They then discuss the results of Steven's research.

"What does all that mean, Steven?" says Sheila when Steven is finished. "Look, I just talked to George this morning, and he made it real clear that what he needs is an opinion letter from us saying Thorzac is not a hazardous substance, as that term is now defined. He's sitting on a 4.5 million dollar property that he may not be able to sell to anyone."

"I understand that, Sheila," says Steven, "but I think Thorzac fits the definition of a hazardous substance. I don't see how I can write an opinion letter saying it's not."

"Nonsense," Sheila replies. "We can't base our opinion on a study by SafeChem. They don't know what they're doing. Besides, the results of those two studies are just preliminary, and other studies disagree. If that's all you've been able to find, I don't have any problem with an opinion letter which says that Thorzac is not a hazardous substance. And by the way, I want *you* to write this, not me. You're the toxic expert around here and you're the guy who worked for the EPA. George is going to need *your* opinion, not mine."

QUESTIONS

1. Should Steven write the opinion letter? *May* he?

2. If Steven is considering refusing to write the letter, how sure would he have to be that he is right? What if he thinks that although he *believes* Thorzac is hazardous, he cannot be certain the government would reach the same conclusion, at least based on current evidence? Is this enough to warrant his refusal to write the letter?

3. In the end, what alternatives, if any, does Steven have to writing the letter?

4. Would Steven be in a different position if Swenson & DeLuca had been hired to defend Reynolds in a lawsuit filed by Doggy-Days for Reynolds' failure to disclose the Thorzac?

5. Suppose that, on Sheila's advice, Reynolds does not disclose the presence of Thorzac to Doggy-Days. Should Steven tell Doggy-Days about the Thorzac and the dangers he believes it presents? Should he tell Doggy-Days to keep the dogs out of the pond?

READINGS

1. Peter Kelly Takes a Stand. The following article describes the trials and tribulations of a young lawyer who felt he had to take a stand in reporting the unethical behavior of one of his firm's partners. One of the questions any associate in Peter Kelly's — or Steven Green's — position will have to answer is whether it is "worth it" to make the ethical but sometimes very difficult choice. Kelly, if asked, maintains that it was, although his decision cost him dearly, as the article describes. Ask yourself how you would go about making this choice if you were in his position.

JAMES M. ALTMAN, ASSOCIATE WHISTLE BLOWING
New York Law Journal (September 10, 1999)[1]

Discovering that a partner at your law firm has engaged in a significant violation of New York's Code of Professional Responsibility is not merely disillusioning. The Code's imperative to report the ethical misconduct of your fellow lawyers also places you in a potential conflict with your firm and puts you at personal risk. Just how complicated and serious such a situation can become is illustrated by the case of Peter Kelly, the former Hunton & Williams associate who allegedly was discharged for blowing the whistle on the fraudulent billing of partner Scott Wolas, now a fugitive from justice. Ultimately, Mr. Kelly sued Hunton and won a settlement on the eve of trial, but not before joblessness and presumably a lot of angst along the way. Mr. Kelly's case is a cautionary tale that raises many questions about how to act ethically without jeopardizing your employment when you suspect that one of your "superiors" has engaged in unethical conduct.

The factual recitation of Judge John Gleeson's decision in *Kelly v. Hunton & Williams*[2] denying the firm's summary judgment motion reads like a John

---

[1] Copyright © 1999 by The New York Law Publishing Company.

[2] 1999 U.S. Dist. Lexis 9139, 1999 WL 408416.

Grisham novel. Mr. Kelly joins Hunton's New York office in 1990 as a first-year litigation associate. The office's tightly knit litigation department has fewer than 10 partners and associates. Mr. Kelly works primarily for Mr. Wolas and Franklin Stone, another partner, and with Christopher Mason, then an associate. His first-year reviews are highly complimentary and he earns the maximum pay raise for his class. But during that first year, apparently because he was involved in preparing attorneys' fee applications, Mr. Kelly begins to suspect Mr. Wolas of billing for time not worked. He shares his suspicions with Joseph Saltarelli, another litigation associate, whose own experiences confirm Mr. Kelly's concern.

During his second year, Mr. Kelly tells Mr. Mason, now a partner, that he believes Mr. Wolas is engaged in billing fraud. Unbeknownst to Mr. Kelly, Mr. Mason, along with partner Mr. Stone, has been investing heavily with Mr. Wolas in what, it later turns out, is a multi-million dollar Ponzi scheme. "Mason respond[s] curtly, telling [Kelly] that things are not always what they seem, and that Mr. Wolas's billing is not [his] concern."[3] Shortly thereafter, Mr. Kelly starts to get negative feedback about his work.

Mr. Saltarelli expresses his concerns about Mr. Wolas's billing to the managing partner of the New York office. The managing partner refuses to approach Mr. Wolas for an explanation of his billing, suggesting instead that Mr. Saltarelli raise it with Mr. Wolas "in a non-accusatory manner, under the guise of asking his help in explaining billing records. . . ."

Having been advised that they might have an ethical obligation to disclose Mr. Wolas's billing irregularities to disciplinary authorities, Messrs. Kelly and Saltarelli and another litigation associate meet a few months later with James Jones, the former managing partner of the New York office, about Mr. Wolas's billing. Eventually, he informs them that the former managing partner of Hunton's flagship office in Richmond will investigate.

Mr. Mason and another partner, aware of the investigation, meet with Mr. Kelly the day before he is to be interviewed about Mr. Wolas's billing. They give Mr. Kelly a Hobson's choice: either be fired immediately, without severance pay and a favorable job reference, or announce his resignation, stay with the firm for several months, and get a favorable reference. Mr. Kelly chooses the coerced resignation.

Hunton then concludes billing fraud was not clearly established and informs Mr. Kelly he has no duty to file a disciplinary complaint with authorities.

Four years later, Mr. Kelly sues Hunton for breach of contract under *Wieder v. Skala*, the 1992 New York Court of Appeals decision holding that a law firm cannot discharge an associate for insisting that the firm report to disciplinary authorities the professional misconduct of one of its lawyers. By that time, Mr. Wolas has vanished, leaving Hunton as a co-defendant in multi-million dollar lawsuits brought by investors in Mr. Wolas's Ponzi scheme. Mr. Kelly seeks more than $250,000 in compensatory damages, plus punitive

---

[3] [2] Just as every novel distorts reality, Judge Gleeson is aware that his decision denying Hunton's summary judgment motion also may distort reality because it sets forth "the central facts viewed in the light most favorable to plaintiff . . . ." Except where expressly indicated, the statements in this column about Mr. Kelly and Hunton are based upon that decision.

damages of more than $ 2.5 million. A month after Judge Gleeson denies Hunton summary judgment, the parties settle for an undisclosed sum.

In Mr. Kelly's case, the firm is the obvious loser. It rallied behind one of its popular and powerful rainmaking partners before determining whether loyalty was warranted. Because the firm failed to respond to legitimate ethical concerns of its associates, it never discovered Mr. Wolas's billing fraud, nor the Ponzi scheme covered up by Mr. Wolas's billing for time not worked. . . .

Professional Duty

Hunton's alleged conduct shows just how a law firm should *not* respond when one or more associates questions whether a firm lawyer is acting unethically. Law firms have a professional duty to create an atmosphere supportive of ethical practice. That certainly includes refraining from taking action against an associate who raises an ethical issue. But for some firms, that duty is sometimes trumped by economics or firm politics. . . .

Even if the firm was the loser, Mr. Kelly surely did not achieve anything close to a complete triumph. He was plagued by his discharge and an unfavorable reference from his only legal employer. Unable to secure suitable legal employment in New York, the lawyer moved to Texas, but the circumstances of his discharge traveled with him. After a year's unemployment, he obtained a lawyering job, but his legal career had been derailed. No settlement could fully compensate for that or for the painful anxieties and emotional distress that he must have suffered as an inexperienced lawyer fearing unemployability.

Yet Mr. Kelly did the right thing. Indeed, he did the only thing an ethical associate could do. . . . [O]nce Mr. Kelly's suspicions ripened to "knowledge," [New York] DR 1-103(A) required him to report Mr. Wolas's fraudulent billing, lest he himself commit an ethical violation.

In Mr. Kelly's case, DR 1-103(A) was harsh and unforgiving. It was DR 1-103(A)'s duty to blow the whistle on a fellow attorney — whether friend, colleague, or in Mr. Kelly's case, a powerful partner — that created the collision with a stonewalling law firm. Could he have acted ethically but still averted that destructive collision?

Mr. Kelly's career was derailed because he had not lined up another job by the time Hunton clearly showed it was unreceptive to his ethical concerns. Mr. Mason's "butt out" response to Mr. Kelly's comment about Mr. Wolas's billing was the initial tip-off that the Hunton partners in New York would rally behind Mr. Wolas. At that time, more than a year and a half after he joined the firm, Mr. Kelly was still well regarded. He probably could have left for employment with another firm without any problem. . . . If by then he felt he had "knowledge" of Mr. Wolas's fraud, Mr. Kelly could have satisfied his ethical obligation by filing a disciplinary charge shortly after securing a new job.

. . . .

It is often difficult for an associate to assess the likely reaction of law firm partners to concerns about possible ethical improprieties. There are numerous factors to consider: How committed is the firm to professional standards? Has the firm established a mechanism — such as an ethics committee or an outside ethical adviser — for dealing with such situations? Does the alleged impropriety reflect carelessness or intentional misconduct? What is the magnitude of the transgression? Can the impropriety be rectified and, if so, how easily? How powerful within the firm, both economically and politically, is the offending lawyer? Can the offending lawyer save face vis-a-vis the firm?

[If] your firm is unlikely to shoulder its own responsibility to create an ethical environment. . . . then it is probably prudent to start evaluating your job prospects before raising the issue with the firm. If you miscalculate and raise the issue to an unreceptive firm, then it becomes more urgent to think seriously about leaving before the situation deteriorates.

As the *Kelly* case demonstrates . . . [t]he stakes can be enormous.

NOTES

At least Peter Kelly had Howard Wieder's precedent on his side. In 1987 Wieder insisted that the partners at his 12-lawyer firm report for discipline a fellow associate who was engaged in a pattern of lying to and deceiving clients. The law firm did so three months later — begrudgingly, says Wieder — and shortly thereafter fired Wieder.

Wieder maintained he was fired for insisting on reporting his colleague. "All I did was what I am ethically bound to do," Wieder told *Manhattan Lawyer*. He sued for retaliatory discharge, but saw his case thrown out by both the trial court and first-level appeals court, both of which held Wieder had no cause of action under New York's at-will employment law. The Court of Appeals finally gave Wieder satisfaction, reversing the lower courts and reinstating his dismissed causes of action against the firm. Here is a brief excerpt from the high court's opinion:

> We agree with plaintiff that in any hiring of an attorney as an associate to practice law with a firm there is implied an understanding so fundamental to the relationship and essential to its purpose as to require no expression: that both the associate and the firm in conducting the practice will do so in accordance with the ethical standards of the profession.[4]

Note that unlike the retaliatory discharge cases we examined in Problem 25, the law firm is only an employer, not a *client*. This avoids one of the principal obstacles to maintaining a cause of action for retaliatory discharge: client confidentiality. Despite this and despite the fact that most states, like New York, *require* lawyers to report ethical violations, neither the law nor the courts have always been sympathetic to the Peter Kellys of the legal world. Before leaving this subject, we should report the good news: Kelly has become a highly successful trial lawyer in Houston.

We will return to the issue of the ethical obligations of law firm associates, and partners, but first a word or two from one of the deans of legal ethics, Professor Geoffrey Hazard.

---

[4] *Wieder v. Skala*, 80 N.Y. 2d 628, 593 N.Y.S. 2d 752, 609 N.E. 2d 105 (1992).

2. Advice From Professor Hazard. How should a young lawyer deal with being asked to do something which he or she is convinced is unethical? Read this advice from Prof. Hazard's *National Law Journal* column.

GEOFFREY C. HAZARD, ETHICS
The National Law Journal (January 17, 1994)[5]

On several occasions, I have had telephone calls from former students asking how they should respond to demands by supervising lawyers that they do something seriously unethical. Should they go along, thus violating the rules of ethics and perhaps other laws as well; or should they risk losing their jobs? . . . The problem attracts great attention at continuing legal education programs when the audience includes young lawyers in law firms or law departments. . . .

The problem arises when both a junior and senior are working on a legal task involving a judgment call that has significant ethical consequences.

One example is . . . whether a corporate matter involving possible illegal activity — for example, illegal payments — should be referred upward in the corporate chain of command. In litigation, the problem may be whether certain files containing potentially damaging information are within the scope of the opposing party's discovery demand . . . .

When clear-cut illegality is involved, the ethical question is not difficult to answer — or should not be. A junior lawyer who assists in illegal conduct is equally as responsible as a senior lawyer, whether in the context of disciplinary charges, civil liability or criminal responsibility. Thus it would be no defense to digging into trust account funds to say that everyone in the firm was doing the same thing. If the ethical question is plausibly arguable, however, then the junior lawyer may look to the senior lawyer to determine the question and, at least in the disciplinary context, may invoke that determination by way of exculpation. Rule 5.2 of the Model Rules of Professional Conduct provides:

> A subordinate lawyer does not violate the Rules of Professional Conduct if that lawyer acts in accordance with a supervisory lawyer's resolution of an arguable question of professional duty.

As a practical matter, however, the situation confronting the junior may be very perilous. Put bluntly, the senior may engineer the assignment so the junior is directly responsible while the senior leaves no fingerprints. For example, the junior may be invited or instructed to sign the disclosure opinion or the pleading to which Rule 11 applies. Or the senior may absent himself conveniently when the crucial decision has to be made. Afterward, it can be foretold, the senior and the junior may have very different recollections of their roles in the transaction.

When a junior lawyer calls me for advice in such a situation, my initial inquiry — after getting the facts — is this: Is there a lawyer in your shop (law firm or law department) who has real clout in the organization, and whom

---

you really trust? Having "real clout" means being able to carry the day with the senior partners or a management committee. . . .

The junior needs a person who could deal with the matter on such a basis without thinking badly of the junior. The junior has to be reasonably confident that seeking "back channel" consultation will be protected.

Unfortunately, there may not be anyone trustworthy in the firm who has clout. In that event, the question to the junior will be to the effect of: How many children do you have and how big is your mortgage? That is, can you afford to quit your job? If quitting is a realistic possibility, then the junior's career plan should be redirected along that line. A shop that demands juniors be the fall guys in ethics matters is no place to work, if one can help it.

The possibility of legal redress is only a last resort, notwithstanding decisions such as *Wieder v. Skala*. The chances of winning or getting a good settlement may be less than even.

The firm will have drawn the wagons around, for its professional reputation is also at stake. If redress is realized, it will come later, after wracking controversy, great expense and damage to the junior's professional reputation and employability. Waiting a long time, and bearing great expense and damage to reputation, is not easy for anyone. It is especially burdensome for a young lawyer in the formative years of professional development.

No one can say how often these situations arise, and doing a survey of the subject would be ludicrous. I believe the problem is pervasive with respect to relatively minor infractions, however, and more than occasional in terms of serious ones. The incidence certainly is far greater than would appear from grievance proceedings and malpractice litigation.

NOTES

Clearly, Hazard's suggestion to find a trustworthy superior with clout in the law firm is good advice. But as he himself recognizes, this may be almost impossible for many if not most associates.

Professor Hazard's question — "How many children do you have and how big is your mortgage?" — can hardly be comforting to Steven Green. More comforting may be Hazard's recourse to MR 5.2. How sure must Steven be in order to refuse the orders of his superior, Sheila Dern? Or does this rule beg the question, since Steven, not Sheila, is the acknowledged expert?

Hazard focuses on partners who set up the associate so that the partner "leaves no fingerprints." Just as common may be the law firm whose day-to-day operations involve questionable ethics that are ingrained in that firm's "culture." These questionable practices may relate to several of the issues raised in this volume, such as discovery practices, trial tactics, or billing irregularities. They may include an attitude that fosters the writing of opinion letters of questionable propriety. When the firm's culture is involved, it means that "just saying no" becomes even more difficult, and the likelihood of finding a sympathetic partner with clout even more remote, since the partners with clout are the ones who set the tone for the firm.

In light of this, how can Steven avoid writing such an opinion letter and survive in his law firm environment? Can you think of a successful way out?

3. To Report or Not to Report? Let us return to the duty to report unethical conduct. Is Prof. Hazard correct that MR 5.2 provides a shield? Joanne Pitula, long one of the American Bar Association's ethics counsel, sees it a little differently. In a 1995 article,[6] she pointed out that both Model Rules 8.3 and 8.4 require lawyers to report professional misconduct. "In effect," she writes, "professional conduct rules create an attorney-client relationship between every lawyer in a firm and each of the firm's clients. Model Rules 5.1 and 5.2 articulate this concept. . . . Simply put, playing dumb about the misconduct of other lawyers in your firm is wrong." Pitula cites a 1989 Connecticut ethics opinion[7] that concluded a lawyer was directly responsible to a client under Rule 5.1 when the lawyer's partner missed the statute of limitations in filing a lawsuit: "The . . . lawyer was required to report his former partner to the disciplinary authorities, even though in so doing he 'may also be reporting himself.'"

The strongest statement of the duty to report violations comes from *In re Himmel*, 112 Ill. 2d 531, 533 N.E.2d 790 (1988), which held that lawyers have an "absolute duty" to report unethical behavior. Apparently, *Himmel* has had an effect. The number of lawyer-reported ethical violations dramatically increased in Illinois since *Himmel*. Michael Oths, then president of the National Organization of Bar Counsels, told the *National Law Journal* in 1999 that the Illinois reporting rate was much higher than in any other state.[8]

Needless to say, as Messrs. Kelly and Wieder learned, it's not always as simple as reporting ethics violations when they occur and then going about one's business. Kelly, as the article notes, would have been far better off strategically to leave the firm for another job, and then, from a safe distance, report the unethical conduct directly to the disciplinary authorities.

But most people don't operate that way; they want to work things out "within the family," if possible, as both Kelly and Wieder tried to do. Indeed, *Himmel* itself is conspicuously silent on the degree of evidence a lawyer must have before the duty to report to a disciplinary agency is triggered.

When partner Colette Bohatch tried to report what she believed were billing improprieties to her managing partner at a Texas law firm, the managing partner exonerated the accused partner and "encouraged" Bohatch herself to leave. Bohatch sued for constructive discharge and for the firm's retaliatory conduct, including denying her access to clients, reducing her partnership compensation, and breaching the fiduciary duties owed by partners to one another. On appeal, the court allowed Bohatch's claim for breach of the partnership compensation agreement, but reversed the remainder of her award, including $4 million in punitive damages.[9] A dissent argued that the failure to allow a breach of fiduciary duty claim allowed the law firm to punish a partner for trying to get the firm to comply with its ethical duties.

---

[6] *Firm Commitments: Lawyers Cannot Ignore Duty to Report Ethics Violations by Colleagues*, ABA J., April 1995.

[7] Informal Opinion 89-21 (1989).

[8] *See* Darryl Van Duch, *Partner Accused, Career Damaged*, NATIONAL L.J. March 8, 1999.

[9] *Bohatch v. Butler & Binion*, 977 S.W.2d 543 (Tex. App. 1998).

But other courts have been similarly unsympathetic. A District of Columbia court denied an attorney a retaliatory discharge remedy after she was dismissed for reporting ethical violations to her superiors, though they allowed her to pursue a defamation claim for falsehoods in her work evaluations.[10] And in Illinois, home of *Himmel*, a 1998 case refused to allow an associate to sue a law firm after he was fired for objecting to superiors on three occasions about a partner's repeated violations of the Fair Debt Collection Agency Act.[11] The court pointed out that after all, the associate should have gone directly to the disciplinary board, as required in *Himmel*. A vigorous dissent emphasized the effect of the majority's opinion: harsh economic and practical disincentives for speaking out.[12]

4. The Torture Memorandum — May a Lawyer Give Less Than an "Honest" Opinion? — A Case Study. Steven Green has been asked to write an "opinion letter" in which he does not personally believe. May he do this? To help examine this question, we take a look at perhaps the most explosive opinion letter in recent years — the Justice Department's "torture memorandum." While there are obvious differences between the torture memorandum and Steven's pending Thorzac memorandum, the analysis of the ethics of writing the torture memorandum, here by Washington (St. Louis) law professor Kathleen Clark, who has developed a sub-specialty in "security law," is both interesting and illuminating.

KATHLEEN CLARK, ETHICAL ISSUES RAISED BY THE OLC TORTURE MEMORANDUM
1 Journal of National Security Law & Policy 455 (2005)[13]

In the fall of 2001, the Bush Administration was looking for a place to imprison and interrogate alleged al Qaeda members away from the prying eyes of other countries and away from the supervision of US courts. The Defense Department believed that the Naval Base at Guantanamo, Cuba might work, and so commissioned the Justice Department's Office of Legal Counsel (OLC) for legal advice on whether federal courts would consider habeas petitions filed by prisoners at Guantanamo, or whether they would dismiss such petitions as beyond their jurisdiction. On December 28, 2001, OLC responded with a thorough and balanced analysis of whether federal courts would assert habeas jurisdiction. It explained the arguments against such jurisdiction, but also explored weaknesses in that argument and possible strengths in the opposing position. The memo opined that federal courts would not exercise jurisdiction, but explained the risk of a contrary ruling. Acting in reliance on this memo, the government started imprisoning and interrogating alleged al Qaeda members at Guantanamo the following month cognizant of the risk that a federal court might find habeas jurisdiction.

In 2004, the Supreme Court considered habeas corpus claims by prisoners at Guantanamo, and reached a result contrary to that predicted by the Justice

---

[10] *Wallace v. Skadden, Arps, Slate, Meagher & Flom*, 715 A.2d 873 (D.C. 1998).

[11] *Jacobson v. Knepper & Moga, P.C.*, 706 N.E.2d 491 (Ill. 1998).

[12] Recall that Illinois was also the state that denied the claims of Roger Balla, discussed in Problem 25.

[13] Copyright © 2005 by the Journal of National Security Law & Policy. Reprinted by permission.

Department memorandum, ruling that the district court did have jurisdiction. The fact that the Court came to a different conclusion than that advanced by OLC does not, however, mean that the OLC attorneys failed to fulfill their professional obligations to their client. The authors appropriately explained the risk of an adverse decision, and they provided enough information for the client to understand that risk and make decisions accordingly.

Whenever a lawyer offers a legal opinion, there is a possibility that other legal actors will take a contrary view. If the lawyer apprises the client of that risk and explains the magnitude of that risk, the lawyer has adequately advised and informed the client. The authors of the habeas jurisdiction memo certainly met this standard.

During the summer of 2002, CIA officials grew frustrated with the interrogation of al Qaeda member Abu Zubaydah, who had stopped cooperating with his interrogators. The CIA wanted to use harsher interrogation techniques against Zubaydah, but sought the imprimatur of the Justice Department for those techniques. In particular, they were concerned that certain harsh techniques might violate the international Convention Against Torture and implementing federal legislation, which makes it a crime to engage in torture under color of law outside the United States. White House Counsel Alberto Gonzales commissioned OLC for legal advice about the scope of the torture statute . . . . Deputy Assistant Attorney General John Yoo drafted a memorandum that was signed in August 2002 by Assistant Attorney General Jay Bybee, . . . the "Bybee Memorandum." . . . The government apparently acted in reliance on this memorandum in setting interrogation policies for alleged al Qaeda members.

The Bybee Memorandum purported to provide objective legal advice to government decision makers. Nevertheless, its assertions about the state of the law are so inaccurate that they seem to be arguments about what the authors (or the intended recipients) wanted the law to be rather than assessments of what the law actually is . . . .

I. *The Substantive Inaccuracies in the Bybee Memorandum*

The Bybee Memorandum consists of 50 pages of text supporting three assertions: (1) the federal criminal statute prohibiting torture is very narrow in scope, applying only where an interrogator specifically intends to cause the kind of extreme pain that would be associated with organ failure or death; (2) an interrogator who is prosecuted for violating the torture statute may be able to use an affirmative defense to gain an acquittal; and (3) the torture statute would be unconstitutional if it interfered with the President's war-making powers, including the power to detain and interrogate enemy combatants as he sees fit. The memorandum's claims about the state of the law in each of these areas are grossly inaccurate.

The first major inaccuracy is in the memorandum's assertion that the federal criminal statute prohibiting torture applies only where a government official specifically intends to and actually causes pain so severe that it "rise[s] to . . . the level that would ordinarily be associated with . . . death, organ failure, or serious impairment of body functions." This claimed standard is bizarre for a number of reasons. . . . [T]his legal standard is lifted from a statute wholly unrelated to torture. It comes from a Medicare statute setting out the conditions under which hospitals must provide emergency medical care. That statute . . . define[s] "emergency medical condition" as one in which failure to provide medical care could result in "serious jeopardy" to an individual's health, "serious impairment to bodily functions," or "serious dysfunction of any bodily organ or part." The Bybee Memorandum twists this legal standard, and . . . purports to give interrogators wide latitude to cause any kind of pain short of that associated with "death, organ failure, or serious impairment of body functions."

A second major inaccuracy is the memorandum's discussion of [the] defenses available . . . — necessity and self-defense. . . . The memorandum's analysis of the self-defense option is somewhat measured. It . . . asserts that a government official charged with violating the torture statute could make a self-defense (or defense of another) argument, but it does not assert that such an affirmative defense would necessarily succeed. The memorandum also asserts that an interrogator charged with torture might well be able to gain an acquittal using the necessity defense. Yet as David Luban has noted, the memorandum never mentions the fact that the Convention Against Torture itself seems to proscribe such a defense when it declares that " '[n]o exceptional circumstances whatsoever, whether a state of war or . . . any other public emergency, may be invoked as a justification of torture.' " . . .

A third major inaccuracy is found in the memorandum's discussion of presidential authority. The Bybee Memorandum asserts that the President can, at least under some circumstances, authorize torture despite the federal statute prohibiting it. This position is based on a expansive view of inherent executive power, but the memorandum does not even mention — let alone address — *Youngstown Sheet & Tube Co. v. Sawyer*, the leading Supreme Court cae on this aspect of separation of powers. *Youngstown*, colloquially known as the *Steel Seizure Case* because it invalidated President Truman's seizure of the nations's steel mills during the Korean War, seriously undermines any claim of unilateral executive power. The Bybee Memorandum does not even acknowledge that the constitution explicitly grants to *Congress* the power to define "Offences against the Law Of Nations . . ." which suggest[s] that Congress was well within its constitutional authority in banning torture.

On each of these three points . . . the Bybee Memorandum presents highly questionable legal claims as settled law. It does not present either the counter arguments to these claims or an assessment of the risk that other legal actors — including courts — would reject them. Despite these obvious weaknesses, the memorandum apparently became the basis for the CIA's use of extreme interrogation methods. . . . In fact, much of the memorandum was used verbatim in . . . the [written] basis for Defense Department policy.

The legal analysis in the Bybee Memorandum was so indefensible that it could not — and did not — withstand public scrutiny. Press reports about and excerpts from the memorandum began to surface in early June, 2004, and there was a wave of criticism. The Justice Department resisted congressional pressure to turn over the memorandum, insisting that the president had a right to confidential legal advice. When *The Washington Post* posted the complete text of the memorandum on its Web site, the wave of criticism turned into a flood. Eight days later, the Bush administration disavowed the memorandum. Six months later, in December 2004, OLC issued a new torture memorandum that offered legal analysis that was more accurate, repudiating the Bybee Memorandum's analysis of "specific intent" and "severe pain," adopting a broader definition of torture, and omitting the troublesome sections claiming inherent presidential power . . . .

II. *The Substantive Inaccuracies in the Bybee Memorandum*

The substantive inaccuracies in the Bybee Memorandum are so serious that they implicate the legal ethics obligations of its authors. In analyzing the legal ethics implications, it is important to make three preliminary observations. First, lawyers who work for the federal government are subject to state ethics rules . . . . Both Jay Bybee and John Yoo were subject to the D.C. Rules of Professional Conduct . . . .

Second, these OLC lawyers had as their client an organization — the executive branch of the United States government — rather than any individual officeholder. Although White House Counsel Alberto Gonzales requested the Bybee Memorandum, he was not the client. Instead, he was simply a constituent of the organizational client. Ordinarily, lawyers must accept the decisions made by such constituents when those constituents are authorized to act on behalf of the organization. But where a lawyer knows that a constituent is acting illegally and that conduct could be imputed to the organization, the lawyer must take action to prevent or mitigate that harm . . . .

Third, in analyzing the performance of the lawyers who wrote the Bybee Memorandum, it is important to analyze whether they were acting as legal advisors or as legal advocates.

When a lawyer gives legal advice, she has a professional obligation of candor toward her client. In advising a client, the lawyer's role is not simply to spin out creative legal arguments. It is to offer her assessment of the law as objectively as possible. The lawyer must not simply tell the client what the client wants to hear, but instead must tell the client her best assessment of what the law requires or allows.[14]

David Luban has described this obligation of candor in the following way: [Where] there is not absolute agreement among lawyers about the state of the law . . ., knowledgeable lawyers' opinions usually fall somewhere in a range similar to the familiar bell curve. If a lawyer advised a client that the law is at an extreme end of that bell curve (rather than that . . . where most knowledgeable lawyers would view it), then the obligation to give candid legal

---

[14] [51] Comment 1 to D.C. Rule 2.1 states that "a lawyer should not be deterred from giving candid advice by the prospect that the advice will be unpalatable to the client.". . . Model Rule 2.1 is identical . . . . A leading treatise on legal ethics explains:

[A] client may consult a lawyer to have her own preconceptions confirmed rather than to seek genuine advice. A Lwyer may be tempted to play sycophant to such a client, to ensure continued employment. Rule 2.1 prohibits such an approach, however, first by requiring that a lawyer's advice be candid; and second, by requiring the lawyer to exercise judgment that is both independent and professional. 1 Geoffrey C. Hazard & W. William Hodes, *The Law of Lawering*, 3rd edition (2001), §23.2 . . . .

advice requires the lawyer to inform the client that the lawyer's interpretation is at the extreme end . . . .

In giving legal advice, a lawyer may provide advice that is contrary to the weight of authority, spinning out imaginative, even "forward-leaning" legal theories for the client to use. When doing so, however, the candor obligation requires the lawyer to inform the client that the weight of authority is contrary to that advice.

. . . .

The harm to the client from failing to advise about the illegal character of proposed conduct may be even greater when the clients is an entity rather than an individual. Indeed, a lawyer working for an entity client has an enhanced obligation to guard the interests of the entity against wrongdoing by the entity's constituents.

The Bybee Memorandum purports to offer legal advice. Its authors, Jay Bybee and John Yoo, had an obligation to be candid with their client, the executive branch. The constituent who requested the Bybee Memorandum, Gonzales, may have wanted a particular answer to his questions about the torture statute. But the OLC lawyers had a professional obligation to give accurate legal advice to their client, whether or not the client's constituents wanted to hear it. Based on the available facts, it appears that Bybee and Yoo failed to give candid legal advice, violating D.C. Rule 2.1, and that they failed to inform their client about the state of the law of torture, violating D.C. Rule 1.4 . . . .

If bar disciplinary authorities investigate Yoo and Bybee, these two attorneys . . . might assert that the ethincal obligations of candor and adequately informing their client did not apply because the Bybee Memorandum was never intended as legal advice in the traditional sense. In fact, David Luban and other scholars have speculated that this Bybee Memorandum was not intended as legal advice at all, but instead as an immunizing document, to ensure that CIA officials who engage in torture would not be prosecuted for that conduct . . . .

But if the authors of the Bybee Memorandum intended to immunize torturers in this way, they might have violated a different ethical rule which prohibits an attorney from assisting a client's criminal conduct . . . .

Bybee and Yoo are not the only government lawyers for whom the Bybee Memorandum may raise ethical concerns. News reports indicate that several White House lawyers reviewed drafts of the Bybee Memorandum. Did the White House lawyers object to the flawed analysis in the memorandum, or did they instead actually insist that the memorandum include such analysis? . . .

Not all government lawyers accepted the patently inaccurate claims of the Bybee Memorandum. Career military lawyers who were involved in developing Defense Department interrogation policy objected to the Bybee Memorandum, and they went up the chain of command to register their objections. The contrast between the career military lawyers . . . and most of the politically appointed lawyers, who championed it, is quite striking.

NOTES

Obviously, the torture memoranda have become politically charged. But it would be unfortunate if scholars avoided evaluating these documents on that basis. Harold Koh, Dean of Yale Law School, recently offered this evaluation:

> To me, the saddest part of this entire episode is not how the President's lawyers failed, but how they failed to understand how they had failed. . . . [W]e see hard cases all the time, where lawyers are forced to choose between law and morality . . . . But here, sadly, morality and law pointed in the same direction. Nor was this just government lawyers doing their job . . . . You are under no obligation as a government lawyer to tell your boss how to violate the law, particularly since a government lawyer's prime obligation is not to his or her boss, but rather, to uphold and protect the Constitution and laws of the United States of America.[15]

5. Duties to Third Parties? Opinion letters, of course, are not just used by clients, but by third parties with whom the client is attempting to do business. Clearly, Mr. Reynolds intends to use Steven Green's letter in his efforts to sell his property. Clients often give their lawyers' opinion letters to others to further their goals. Paralleling the "noisy withdrawal" opinion is a series of court cases about lawyers' *liability* to third parties when their opinion letters have been used for improper purposes. There are many ways that lawyers can be swept up into their clients' wrongdoing. Here are a few — and how some courts saw the responsibilities of the lawyers involved.

In *Petrillo v. Bachenberg*, 623 A.2d 272 (N.J. Super. 1993), aff'd, 655 A.2d 1354 (N.J. 1995), a seller of land had performed soil testing that revealed the land was unsuitable for a septic system. The seller's lawyer, knowing the problem, nevertheless provided the buyer with a misleading single report that gave the buyer a false sense of security about the transaction. When the buyer sued, the court found that when the lawyer handed over the test results, he assumed a duty to the buyer to render reliable information, even though the document was not created by the lawyer.[16]

In *Rubin & Cohen v. Schottenstein, Zox & Dunn,* 143 F.3d 263 (6th Cir. 1998), the court en banc reversed a three-judge panel and held the lawyers for a company liable where the attorneys, knowing that the company had advised potential investors to contact them, confirmed, inaccurately, the financial soundness of the company. The court emphasized that the lawyers knew exactly why their input was being sought, and that the investors had a right to rely on the lawyers' candor. Similarly, in *Vega v. Jones, Day, Reavis & Pogue*, 121 Cal. App. 4th 282, 17 Cal. Rptr. 3d 26 (2004), the court allowed a fraud claim where the law firm for a company that was purchasing another had written a disclosure schedule that was not candid about how the client was financing the purchase. The "half-truth" told in the schedule was tantamount to "active concealment."

---

[15] Harold Hongiu Koh, *Can the Predient Be Torturer In Chief?*, 81 IND. L.J. 1145, 1165, 1166 (2006).

[16] Note the similarities between this case and California Formal Opinion 1996-146, discussed in Problem 24.

A 1995 Colorado case[17] held that where a lawyer's opinion letter to *the client* about the merits of a lawsuit is used by the client to entice third-party purchasers, and the lawyers knew that the letter was being used, the lawyers could be liable to the *third parties* for misrepresentation (though not ordinary professional negligence).[18]

Ackerman v. Schwartz, 947 F. 2d 841 (7th Cir. 1991), goes half a step further. There, investors in a fraudulent tax shelter brought an action for securities fraud against an attorney who wrote the client an opinion letter that incorrectly stated that investors would be entitled to tax credits. The court decided that the lawyer had no affirmative duty to blow the whistle on his clients or to correct the letter. The lawyer did not agree to have his letter circulated to investors. But he did not object when his clients included his letter in an offering. The court concluded that this was enough to hold the attorney liable as a principal in the fraud.

Now read about the *Klein* case in New Jersey — a case that went yet another step further in finding potential lawyer liability to third parties.

LAWRENCE M. ROLNICK & EDWARD T. DARTLEY, "KLEIN v. BOYD" RATIONALE MAY STILL BE ARGUED IN OTHER CASES
New York Law Journal (February 8, 1999)[19]

In February 1998 the Third Circuit Court of Appeals shocked the legal community when it ruled, in *Klein v. Boyd*,[20] that a claim under § 10(b) of the Securities and Exchange Act of 1934 could be maintained against a law firm that participated in the drafting of a client's securities disclosure documents. The panel held that liability could be imposed even though the law firm did not sign or endorse the documents, and its role was unknown to plaintiffs-investors.

The decision was followed by a flurry of articles by practitioners and academics criticizing the decision as reintroducing a form of secondary liability that most people believed had been eliminated by the U.S. Supreme Court's 1994 decision in *Central Bank of Denver v. First Interstate Bank of Denver*.[21] Shortly thereafter, the Third Circuit granted rehearing en banc and vacated the *Klein* panel's decision.[22]

Then, last fall, before the Third Circuit had the opportunity to hear the case, the parties quietly settled their dispute and withdrew the appeal. As a result, securities lawyers face substantial uncertainty as to what courts in the Third Circuit will do when presented with the issue in the future.

---

[17] *Mehaffy, Rider, Windholz & Wilson v. Central Bank Denver N.A.*, 892 P.2d 230 (Colo. 1995).

[18] *See also McCamish, Martin, Brown & Loeffler v. F. E. Appling Interests*, 42 Tex. Sup. J. 597, 991 S.W.2d 787 (1999).

[19] Reprinted with the permission of The New York Law Journal. Copyright © 1999 by The New York Law Publishing Company.

[20] [1] Nos. 97-1142 and 97-1261, 1998 U.S. App. Lexis 2004, unpublished.

[21] [2] 511 U.S. 164 (1994).

[22] [3] 1998 U.S. App. Lexis 4121.

The "Klein" Decision

In *Klein*, a law firm prepared a disclosure package for a limited partnership investment, but allegedly failed to include information concerning a long history of regulatory problems of one of the principals, disciplinary actions against another principal, and restrictions imposed on the general partner. . . .

The Third Circuit, of course, concluded that lawyers and other secondary actors could be primarily liable under § 10(b) if they "significantly participate[d] in the creation of their client's misrepresentations, to such a degree that they may fairly be deemed authors or co-authors of those misrepresentations."

. . . .

As a practical matter, the *Klein* decision created uncertainty for securities lawyers about what level of participation in an offering would expose them to liability under the federal securities laws. It also raised concern that the panel's ruling would effectively create a duty to "blow the whistle" on their clients.

. . . .

Unfortunately, the parties' decision to settle has deprived the Third Circuit of the opportunity to give the sort of definitive relief hoped for by the legal community. . . . [S]ecurities lawyers are left to speculate about whether they may be held primarily liable . . . for misstatements in documents which they helped to prepare, even if their names do not appear on the document and they are otherwise invisible to investors. . . .

Use of "Klein" Rationale

It should come as no surprise that future plaintiffs in the Third Circuit may try to use the *Klein* court's reasoning to distinguish the *Central Bank* decision. Klein did in fact recognize *Central Bank* and acknowledged that secondary actors cannot be held liable for aiding and abetting a violation of § 10(b).

However, the court ruled that a lawyer in certain circumstances may not be a "secondary actor" but could instead "fairly be characterized as an author or a co-author of a client's fraudulent document [and thus] may be held primarily liable to a third-party investor under the federal securities laws." . . .

As a result, proponents of *Klein* undoubtedly will argue that the analysis employed by the Third Circuit does not depart from *Central Bank*'s holding. . . . Instead, . . . under the *Klein* analysis, [a] lawyer's failure to sign the document containing the misstatement or otherwise identify himself or herself to investors should not, on its own, insulate the lawyer from liability. . . .

Securities practitioners should not discount the potential appeal of such an argument. . . . [L]awyers in the Third Circuit and elsewhere have been subject to primary liability under § 10(b) where they participated in the creation of the alleged misstatements and had some direct contact with the investors.

In such circumstances, a securities lawyer may not have an independent duty under § 10(b) or Rule 10b-5 to disclose information about the client, but must provide complete and non-misleading information when he or she elects to speak. The only difference between the facts in those cases and those which gave rise to the decision in *Klein* is the investors' lack of knowledge about the defendant lawyers' role.

NOTES

It is interesting that the authors focus on the fact that the third parties did not know of the lawyers' involvement in the false documents, and that the lawyers, while involved, did not themselves sign anything. Should this be the test of lawyer liability? Should lawyers be immune so long as the third parties don't know the lawyers are involved? Or should the *results* of the lawyers' actions be the key to determining liability — the lawyers' participation in the inaccurate disclosure, whether named or not?

The trial judge in the Enron litigation in Texas[23] seemed less concerned with who signed documents and more with participation. The court found that Vinson & Elkins did more than remain silent about high management's fraudulent deals, and that the law firm was a de facto "co-author" of the disclosure statements regardless of whether V&E was so identified. V&E thus could be held liable because it participated in issuing the statements knowing third parties would rely on them. Of course, unlike in *Klein*, V&E's involvement in Enron's frauds was hardly unknown.

6. Discipline for Law Firms? ABA opinions about the requirements for "noisy withdrawal" and the like are all well and good, but do they solve Steven Green's dilemma? They certainly don't address Prof. Hazard's question about losing a job, paying the mortgage, and feeding the kids. Would a system that disciplines law firms as well as lawyers help such associates? Would it tend to improve a law firms's "culture"? University of Arizona law professor. Ted Schneyer wrote this next article some years ago as a cutting-edge statement of the case in favor.

TED SCHNEYER, PROFESSIONAL DISCIPLINE FOR LAW FIRMS?
77 Cornell Law Review 1 (November 1992)[24]

1. In 1989 a partner at Baker & McKenzie made improper racist and sexist remarks while interviewing a University of Chicago Law School student for a job with the firm. Shortly after the incident was reported to the firm, the interviewer opted for early retirement. But matters did not end there. Instead of treating the incident as the isolated wrongdoing of a "bad apple," the school insisted that the firm submit a written description of the measures it was taking to prevent similar incidents before the school would allow the firm to recruit on campus again. The firm complied with this demand. . . .

---

[23] *In re Enron Corp. Securities, Derivative & ERISA Litigation*, 235 F. Supp. 2d 549 (S.D. Tex. 2002).

[24] Copyright © 1992 by Cornell University. All rights reserved.

2. A company represented by Fried, Frank, Harris, Shriver & Jacobson sued the federal government to obtain documents under the Freedom of Information Act. The company's name was to be kept confidential under a protective order. In 1989, Fried, Frank inadvertently filed in court an unredacted document that divulged the client's name. . . .

3. During the pretrial phase of a major antitrust suit against Kodak, the company's lawyer, a senior partner at Donovan, Leisure, Newton & Irvine, lied to opposing counsel and the judge when he told them that documents sought in discovery no longer existed. Though an associate who worked closely with the partner allegedly reminded him that the documents were still at the firm, the partner did not correct his previous statement. The associate kept the partner's lie to himself, but it later came disastrously to light . . . .

4. A federal judge determined that Lord, Bissell & Brook aided in a violation of the antifraud provisions of the securities laws by failing to notify the shareholders of its client company when the firm learned that the earnings of an intended merger target had been grossly inflated in merger documents. A partner working on the case held stock in the target company and was interested in the deal's success. The judge, however, refused to grant the SEC an injunction that would have required Lord, Bissell & Brook to change its internal procedures to discourage such incidents in the future. The court noted the professional duty of the firm's lawyers to "conform their conduct to the dictates of the law" and expressed confidence that the firm would voluntarily take "appropriate steps." But the firm failed to take those steps and was later sued for securities violations in a similar matter, which resulted in a 24 million dollar settlement.

. . . .

Law practice in the United States is regulated in many ways, but most comprehensively through a specialized system that metes out professional discipline to those who violate the rules of legal ethics. . . . Disciplinary agencies have always taken individual lawyers as their targets. They have never proceeded against law firms either directly, for breaching ethics rules addressed to them, or vicariously, for the wrongdoing of firm lawyers in the course of their work. The traditional focus on individuals has probably resulted from the system's jurisdictional tie to licensing, which the state requires only for individuals, and from the system's development at a time when solo practice was the norm.

Legal practice, however, has changed. While as late as 1951, sixty percent of the bar practiced alone, two-thirds now work in law firms and other organizations . . . . Law firms themselves have also changed. As a result of internal growth and mergers, the top 100 law firms now account for nearly twenty percent of all legal fees. While only thirty-eight American law firms had more than fifty lawyers in the late 1950s, by 1986 over 500 firms did so and over 250 had more than 100 lawyers. As of 1984, 95 of the 100 largest firms had at least one branch office. Branching has made intrafirm coordination both more difficult and more important. Firms have also become highly leveraged — that is, the ratio of relatively inexperienced associates to partners has risen as high as four-to-one. The proportionally larger number of inexperienced lawyers within firms has heightened the need for supervision. . . .

As law firms grow, the potential harm they can inflict on clients, third parties, and the legal process grows as well. At the same time, the law firm, at least the larger firm, is ripening into an institution that presents new opportunities for bureaucratically controlling the technical and ethical quality of law practice. . . .

So far, however, those who make disciplinary policy have taken little notice of these developments. True, the . . . Model Rules of Professional Conduct, note that "the ethical atmosphere of a firm can influence the conduct of its members." The Model Rules also make clear for the first time that supervisory lawyers are responsible for monitoring their subordinates, an obligation with particular significance in the hierarchical setting of a large firm. But the ABA, the state supreme courts that adopt the ABA codes, and the agencies that assist the courts in disciplinary enforcement have yet to confront the infrequency of disciplinary proceedings against lawyers in firms.

Proceedings against lawyers in large or even medium-sized firms are very rare. In 1981-82, for example, more than eighty percent of the lawyers disciplined in California, Illinois, and the District of Columbia were sole practitioners, and none practiced in a firm with over seven lawyers. Yet, judging from the frequency with which larger firms and their lawyers are the targets of civil suits, motions to disqualify, and sanctions under the rules of civil procedure disciplinable offenses occur with some regularity in those firms. . . .

These factors may help to explain the infrequency of disciplinary proceedings against large-firm lawyers, but additional explanations, so far neglected, have important implications for disciplinary policy. These explanations stem from the nature of group practice. First, even when a firm has clearly committed wrongdoing, courts may have difficulty, as an evidentiary matter, in assigning blame to particular lawyers, each of whom has an incentive to shift responsibility for an ethical breach onto others in the firm. Many, perhaps most, of the tasks performed in large firms are assigned to teams. Teaming not only encourages lawyers to take ethical risks they would not take individually, but also obscures responsibility. . . .

Second, even when courts and disciplinary agencies can link professional misconduct to one or more lawyers in a firm as an evidentiary matter, they may be reluctant to sanction those lawyers for fear of making them scapegoats for others. . . .

Third and most important, a law firm's organization, policies, and operating procedures constitute an "ethical infrastructure" that cuts across particular lawyers and tasks. . . . Even a firm with a well-defined management structure does not delegate the duty to make firm policy and maintain an appropriate infrastructure solely to management. To varying degrees this remains every partner's business — and sometimes, as a result, no one's. In no aspect of law firm work is teaming, and thus collective responsibility, more important than in the development of firm structure, policy, and procedures.

[A] disciplinary regime that targets only individual lawyers in an era of large law firms is no longer sufficient. Sanctions against firms are needed as well.

. . . .

A disciplinary system for law firms may not be immediately attractive to the lawyers who practice in firms. It could, after all, encourage their firms to monitor their work and limit their individual discretion more sharply — phenomena to which many lawyers are hostile. Yet a system of law firm discipline may actually benefit these lawyers. It could promote firm practices that reduce the risk not only of discipline but also of civil liability, disqualification, and other nondisciplinary sanctions. It could encourage disciplinary authorities not to proceed against firm lawyers individually when proof problems, fairness, or deterrence considerations point to the firm itself as the more appropriate target. It could give firms a new and attractive basis on which to compete for clients by helping them develop firmwide ethical track records over time. . . .

The Emerging Status of Law Firms as Appropriate Disciplinary Targets

While law firm discipline would depart from the traditional disciplinary focus on the individual, the idea is not as radical as it may seem. Close administrative analogies exist. The stock exchanges and the Securities and Exchange Commission maintain disciplinary systems for brokerage houses, and not just for the individuals who work in those firms. . . . And of course law firms as such are already subject to civil liability, fee denials, and disqualification; these sanctions complement lawyer discipline as a regulatory technique. Moreover, four developments in modern ethics rules and disciplinary techniques suggest that the legal profession is already edging toward the use of law firm discipline.

A. Prophylactic Ethics Rules

Modern ethics rules already require lawyers to take certain prophylactic measures to prevent misconduct. For example, . . . lawyers must take reasonable steps to prevent breaches of confidentiality by their employees and associates. . . .

The Model Rules also make it clear that when one lawyer in a firm is barred from handling a case on conflict grounds, other lawyers in the firm are generally barred as well. This rule seeks to avoid the risk that a lawyer who possesses confidential information about a client will be tempted or pressed to communicate that information to others in the firm.

When one views ethics rules in this modern light, as a tool to minimize lawyers' opportunities to commit fundamental wrongs, disciplining law firms for failing to take preventive, institutional measures hardly seems a radical step.

B. Firm-Directed Ethical Norms

A second and more curious point about modern ethics rules is that occasionally they directly address law firms. . . . Moreover, bar association ethics opinions sometimes construe ethics rules that do not explicitly address law firms as if they did. For example, one ABA opinion holds that when a lawyer who is handling a client's matter leaves her firm, the withdrawal [rules], though addressed only to individual lawyers, require the firm to continue representation. . . .

Since only licensed individuals are now subject to professional discipline, these rules and interpretations seem odd. . . . Yet the rules may not be mere slips of the professional tongue. They have a common theme: each rule deals with matters that in law firms require collective action. . . .

C. Ethics Rules on Matters of Law Firm Governance

. . . [E]thics rules have also begun to regulate matters of law firm governance that bear on ethical compliance. These rules, themselves prophylactic in nature, so far are addressed only to individual lawyers. Model Rule (MR) 5.1(b) . . . exposes a supervising lawyer to discipline for failure to make reasonable efforts to monitor a direct subordinate. MR 5.1(c) prohibits knowing acquiescence in the wrongdoing of other lawyers in one's firm. . . .

Of special interest here is MR 5.1(a), which recognizes that the duty to prevent ethical breaches within a law firm is a matter of indirect as well as direct supervision. The rule requires lawyers who have "supervisory authority over the professional work of a firm" to "make reasonable efforts to ensure that the firm has in effect measures giving reasonable assurance that all lawyers in the firm conform to the rules of professional conduct.". . . Clearly, MR 5.1(a) is concerned with matters of ethical infrastructure. . . .

Although the importance of an ethical infrastructure would seem to vary directly with firm size, the prospects for using MR 5.1(a) . . . are best where small firms are involved. . . . As one moves up the scale toward firms of intermediate size, the prospects for enforcing MR 5.1(a) dim. . . . The spectacle of disciplining all the partners in the firm remains a possibility of course, but not a very realistic one in a mid-sized firm.

With still larger firms, MR 5.1(a) has so far been a disciplinary dead letter. So long as the rule's up-to-date recognition of the importance of firm infrastructure is tied to the horse-and-buggy of individual discipline, the rule seems likely to remain so. . . . Disciplinary authorities may have difficulty pinning this structural defect on particular partners (even on a managing partner), and they may be reluctant to try, for fear of scapegoating some lawyers for sins shared by others . . . . Accordingly, . . . if we are to pursue the regulatory aims of MR 5.1(a) in the very firms where such programs are most important, then we may have to give disciplinary authorities the options of fining or censuring the firm or putting it on probation.

D. The Growing Use of Firm-Appropriate Disciplinary Sanctions

Before 1970, many states used disbarment or suspension from practice as their chief disciplinary sanction. A system of law firm discipline could never rely heavily on analogous sanctions.

. . . .

The post-1970 development of probation as a sanction illustrates the shift toward a disciplinary philosophy compatible with firmwide discipline. . . . Probation is used "to help lawyers who have violated the disciplinary rules, but whose conduct likely can be corrected so that they can continue to serve the public." . . . When probationers work in a firm, their partners are used as supervisors and are required to ensure that the probationers use proper office practices.

Conclusion

A number of questions remain concerning the implementation of a system of law firm discipline which this Article has not fully addressed — how to fund the system, how disciplinary bodies will gain jurisdiction over law firms, whether they should also take jurisdiction over other entities in which lawyers practice, and who should have jurisdiction over a firm with branches in several states. These matters are secondary. For now, debate should focus on the merits of the general proposal.

NOTES

Note Prof. Schneyer's discussion of the development of "ethical infrastructures" for law firms. Since this article was written, many more firms have developed such infrastructures, perhaps out of necessity given the increase in the various forms of non-disciplinary regulation that Prof. Schneyer cites. In addition, of course, the growth of big firms has exploded exponentially.

Recall the Bowen McCoy article in Chapter One about the inability of several mountain trekkers to develop a group ethic that could have helped a holy man to safety while individuals acting alone could not. Do you see a parallel between McCoy's lesson on corporate ethics and Schneyer's arguments about ethical infrastructures? Interestingly, Schneyer uses corporate models for his proposals on developing law firm ethical cultures and firm-wide discipline.

A last question: Is Schneyer being "fair" to large firms by saying it is in those firms where the biggest problem lies?

In the years since Schneyer's ambitious article, only two states, New York and New Jersey, have instituted law firm discipline. In New York, the basic rule of general application, DR 1-102 (no one may violate disciplinary rules, interfere with the administration of justice, etc.), was amended to apply to law firms. Other rules were amended to require that law firms "ensure that all lawyers in the firm conform" to the ethics rules, and that firms must "supervise, as appropriate," the work of associates, partners, and nonlawyers alike. New York now also requires that law firms keep records sufficient to run adequate firm-wide conflicts checks.[25] Given the history of discipline as an individual lawyer-by-lawyer matter, these changes are substantial, though they have not — at least not yet — produced a pattern of firm-wide discipline. Meanwhile, several other states, including California, have begun to consider adding a component of law firm discipline to their ethical rules.

---

[25] DR 5-105(E).

7. Modern Law Firm Culture and "Greedy Associates."[26] With the continued consolidation and mergers of big firms and the increasing view that law is a business first and a profession second, mentoring for young associates has become more problematic.

Any law firm's culture is a combination of its personality, its traditions, and its core values. These core values include many issues we have discussed in these pages, such as policies about the kinds of clients the firm takes, or how the firm acts towards its opponents. These values also include how much the firm focuses on making more money as opposed to "quality of life" issues — everything from part-time partnerships to parental leave policies.

Firms also define their cultures by the way they treat their associates. Some firms see their younger lawyers as profitable engines to be run at full tilt, and make little effort to convince them to stay the course to partner, while others are far more nurturing.

But firms with strong mentoring programs are increasingly rare. Many law firms give little or no feedback to their new attorneys. Annual reviews often last a mere 30 minutes. Associates come to know that they will get little insight into the quality of their work, and a lot of talk about billing.

Law firms do make efforts of varying kinds to inculcate their young lawyers with the firm's core values. But the activities for "summer associates" — the law student interns who form the recruitment pool for permanent jobs — are too often opportunities to wine and dine while the firm delivers its best PR pitch. Law firms promote retreats and annual meetings as a chance for all employees to "bond." Instead, at many firms these events are expensive weekends where drinking or playing golf form the social schedule, and the business meeting focuses on the firm's financial health. Many firms offer little opportunity at these retreats to consider or create new directions or philosophies.

Some firms provide training for young associates from more senior lawyers or outside consultants, while others have senior partners who serve as real role models and mentors.[27] But increasingly, it is a world of lawyer mobility, lateral transfers — experienced lawyers from other firms who arrive with "books of business" — and diminishing loyalty to The Firm.

When law firms become revolving doors and values and traditions give way to free market economics and the question "What have you done for me lately?" the associate, at the bottom of the food chain, usually feels the pressure the most. Increasingly, these young associates have turned to their peers for what we might term "self-mentoring." Among the most popular outlets for peer talk therapy and general venting have been the Greedy Associates boards, or chat

---

[26] We are again indebted to the Ballantine Books division of Random House for "borrowing" in this section from pages 87-91 of RICHARD ZITRIN & CAROL M. LANGFORD, THE MORAL COMPASS OF THE AMERICAN LAWYER (1999).

[27] One interesting example is Washington's Howrey Simon Arnold & White, which in the summer of 2000 decided to stop the typical summer associates' country club and replace it with a "boot camp," where law students could learn what joining the firm would really be like. Prospective hirees were expected to work hard each day, participate in a mock trial, and travel to work in one of Howrey's satellite offices. *See* David Leonhardt, *Law Firm Plans Radical Revision of Summer Program for Students*, N.Y. TIMES, Aug. 1, 2000.

groups, that have sprung up on the Internet in the past decade. The following excerpted article is our own take on this phenomenon.

RICHARD ZITRIN & CAROL M. LANGFORD, THE MORAL COMPASS: ASSOCIATED STRESS
American Law Media and Law News Network (September 1999)[28]

Greedy associates care. They care about pay, perks, and prestige, and whether their firm is as hot as the competition. On line, they post the latest in salaries, bonuses, mergers, and layoffs, with Internet links to news stories announcing major law firm changes.

Greedy associates kvetch. They complain when they have to spend Labor Day in the office while their partners enjoy the weekend. And they complain when the partners *are* in the office: "Which is worse: knowing the partner for whom you are working is enjoying his Labor Day with his family, or having him hovering to make sure you are working diligently on his project?"

Greedy associates are comedians. "Newbies" who don't know the lingo had better be quick studies. And sometimes, "GAs" will even joke about themselves, their lives — even their sex lives, or the lack thereof — and their lot in life.

And they do it all publicly, on line, in a series of "Greedy Associates" clubs, or "boards". . . . Originally the boards served to exchange information about the perks offered by large firms (called "BIGLAW" on line). They still do, but they've expanded well beyond this limited scope. There are regional GA boards, specialized boards, boards for summer associates. . . . The most popular and interesting is "RealGAs," [which] has posts about salaries, bonuses, and raises. But there are also wide-ranging discussions about almost everything, from the pros and cons of punitive damages, to moral philosophy, to where to vacation in Greece. . . .

It's impossible to profile the average Greedy Associate with accuracy, since people don't identify themselves by their real names. To do so would make it impossible for a candid discussion of what's troubling them. . . . Still, it's possible to make some generalizations, particularly about those who post rather than just lurk.

Greedy associates are egotistical, sharp-tongued, prideful, competitive, and bright. Mostly bright. And young — young enough to be egotistical, sharp-tongued, prideful, and competitive about how bright they are — and to constantly compare their intelligence to others. Typical is their intentional misspelling of the word "REdiculous," their creation of "sock puppet" alter egos who are free to express themselves sarcastically, even scatalogically, in ways their usual identities would not, and their on-line identities themselves: Lady Greediva, postassociatestressdisorder and the like.

Greedy associates are also disillusioned. They grouse about doing work paralegals could easily handle, far from the action and even farther from the courtroom, on cases they don't choose for clients they don't know or, even worse, don't like. The irony is that these highly intelligent young lawyers — many, if one can believe their claims, from the top of their class at the best law schools — feel they're being wasted on tasks better suited for "lesser" beings. But though many would deny it on line, beneath the hard shell of cynicism and sarcasm — the side they tend to show on the GA boards — lurk some sensitive souls.

Greedy associates worry. They worry about the meaning of their lives, why they've chosen a profession that forces them to give up so much for, well, so *much*, at least economically. But their unhappiness is palpable.

They are expected to perform quickly, at a high level of competence, and with a billable hours quota that makes the forty-hour work week look like chump change. . . . One RealGAs associate put it this way: It's like the high school competition she used to hate — swim under water for as long as possible, and see who can hold her breath and stay under water the longest. . . .

The Greedy Associates boards do more than provide an outlet for the frustrations of the law business. They also allow participants to create their own group culture. Even though people's true identities remain anonymous, many on-line comments and most of the messages we've received "off-list" show that GAs are fiercely loyal to and protective of each other. To many, the culture of the Board, and their loyalty to its participants, is more real than what they find in their own firms.

But for some, it's not enough. Wrote one Greedy Associate in a moment of despair:

> "Does anyone else on this board feel like being a lawyer in BIGLAW is slowly but surely deadening them inside? It is such mind-numbing work that I feel like I'm losing my sense of humor and find it very difficult to appreciate anything, either inside or outside work. Pure ambivalence. I've gotta get out before I go completely postal. FYI — I'm stuck here working with a partner to turn a document that does not need to be turned. It's in an area of law for which I have no experience that I got roped into because I'm a new lateral and haven't learned the politics yet. When does this end? I'm sick of being an adult and having most of my waking life dictated by people I don't like or respect, doing work for which there is no passion. My fantasy of getting up from my desk, walking out my office, going to the head of my department and quitting to be a bartender is sounding extremely appealing.
>
> "HELP!"

We must find a way to give those who swim under water a chance to come up for air.

SUPPLEMENTAL READINGS

1. The incredible story of law student/whistleblower Richard G. Poff, Jr. sounds like a tale from a Grisham novel. Michael D. Goldhaber has written an excellent *National Law Journal* article, "Crazy in Alabama," December 20, 1999, describing how Poff blew the whistle on well-known Alabama lawyer

Robert "Coach" Hayes and his partners, only to find himself sued by Hayes for slander (despite Hayes's criminal conviction and bar suspension), thrown in jail by one judge, and ordered to undergo a psychiatric evaluation by another. Also worth reading is the Alabama Supreme Court opinion in *Poff v. Hayes*, 763 So. 2d 234 (Ala. Sup. 2000) reversing the seven-figure default judgment entered in favor of Hayes after a judge improperly denied both Poff's pre-trial motions and his right to jury trial.

2. Two relatively recent articles from the Georgetown Journal of Legal Ethics on the duty to report misconduct that so damaged Peter Kelly are Arthur F. Greenbaum, *The Attorney's Duty to Report Professional Misconduct: A Roadmap for Reform*, 16 Geo. J. Legal Ethics 259 (2003), and Nikki A. Ott and Heather F. Newton, *A Current Look at Model Rule 8.3: How Is It Used and What Are Courts Doing About It?*, 16 Geo. J. Legal Ethics 747 (2003).

3. Irma S. Russell, *Cries & Whispers, Environmental Hazards, Model Rule 1.6, and the Attorney's Conflicting Duties to Clients and Others*, 72 Wash. L. Rev. 409 (1997), tests the ethical prohibition against disclosure in the extreme circumstance of widespread environmental harm.

4. Morgan Shipman, *The Liabilities of Lawyers in Corporate and Securities Work*, 62 U. Cin. L. Rev. 513 (1993), focuses on third party liability, particularly in securities work, and is also useful in exploring and understanding the ethics of writing a securities opinion letter.

5. *Kline v. First W. Sec., Inc.*, 24 F.3d 480 (3d Cir. 1994), contains a thorough treatment of third party reliance on securities opinion letters, in which a divided court held that an opinion letter's misrepresentations, even the omissions, may allow a third party plaintiff to maintain a cause of action against the law firm which wrote the letter.

6. *R.T.C. v. Latham & Watkins*, 909 F. Supp. 923 (S.D.N.Y. 1995), is one of the relatively rare recent cases to find no liability owed by a law firm. Here, however, the firm issued an opinion letter valid under one state's laws but reviewed by buyers in other states. The court attributed a certain level of sophistication to the buyers of the securities involved.

7. Leonard Gross, *Ethical Problems of Law Firm Associates*, 26 Wm. & Mary L. Rev. 259 (1985), is a "pre-modern" survey of several ethical problems facing law firm associates. It provides guidance for how these problems may best be resolved. Patrick J. Schiltz's more modern view, *On Being a Happy, Healthy, and Ethical Member of an Unhappy, Unhealthy, and Unethical Profession*, 52 Vand. L. Rev. 871 (1999), will have a second excerpt in the next problem.

8. Lawrence J. Fox, *Legal Tender*, American Bar Association Section of Litigation (1995). The former chair of the ABA's ethics committee and a staunch defender of clients' rights has written a book about the trials and travails of a large American law firm that looks suspiciously like his own Drinker Biddle & Reath.

9. Two worthwhile colloquial articles about law firm culture and the pressures on associates are Susan Hightower & Brenda Sapino, "Cultural Evolution: It Takes More Than Money to Succeed Over the Long Haul in the Law Business," *Texas Lawyer*, January 22, 1996, and Carol A. Leonard &

Kelly A. Fox, "Sometimes, the Enemy Comes From Within," *New York Law Journal*, July 9, 1996.

PROBLEM 27

As clients become more concerned about the costs of legal services, and the legal marketplace, saturated with lawyers, becomes more competitive, billing practices of lawyers have come under much closer scrutiny. The traditional practice of sending an unannotated bill and expecting it to be paid is a thing of the past. But questionable billing practices continue, in large firms and small law offices alike. And pressures increase on young lawyers with every extra hour they are required to bill.

Billing Practices at Prager & Dahms

I. Carrie Waters was excited to accept an offer at Prager & Dahms, a large Southland City law firm. Carrie was told that as a new associate, she would receive a basic salary of $125,000 per year, plus a year-end $10,000 bonus if she billed over the requisite 1,850 hours, and another $10,000 if she could get her billings up to 2,000 hours.

Seven months have passed. Carrie is frustrated because she barely makes her billing quota and thinks she will never reach the year-end bonus goal. Moreover, she is concerned that if she doesn't reach bonus status, Prager & Dahms might give her a bad year-end review for not pulling her weight. She tells her concerns to her friend Billy Shears, a fifth-year Prager & Dahms associate. Shears tells Carrie that billing is an art and that there are certain "tricks of the trade" that will help her make her billing goals.

QUESTIONS

1. First, Shears advises Carrie that he bills for any and all time that he spends on a case. He tells her that he bills even when he thinks about a case while showering in the morning. He calls it "strategizing client's case" or "evaluating tactics for trial."

2. Second, Shears informs Carrie that since she often flies to Capital City for depositions, she should bill one client for traveling to and from the deposition and simultaneously bill another client for reviewing that client's file on the same flight. "I do it each time I travel," he says.

3. Shears suggests billing clients in minimum quarter-hour increments instead of tenths of an hour (six minutes). "That way," Shears tells Carrie, "if I call opposing counsel and he or she is not in, I leave a voice mail message and bill a quarter-hour. When I call again that afternoon and get voice mail again, it's another quarter-hour. Two one-minute phone calls, a half-hour billed!"

4. Shears tells Carrie that he recently worked on a complex antitrust research issue. He devoted over 30 hours to the project: 20 hours researching and 10 drafting a winning brief. One month later, Shears was assigned another case with the same issues. Shears simply modified the brief he had already prepared and changed the parties' names. He spent two hours revising the brief, but charged the client 20 hours for the same research and writing he had billed on the previous project. "I had the special expertise," he said. "The second client got a 10 hour discount and has nothing to complain about."

Evaluate Shears' tactics and advice.

II. Thurston Prager, founding partner of Prager & Dahms, has been practicing law for over 35 years. He is a very experienced and well-respected attorney. He charges $450 per hour for his time, and still runs the firm through its management committee.

QUESTIONS

1. When new clients are brought to the firm, Prager prefers to negotiate a fixed billing agreement with his clients. His fee agreement says he will charge a minimum of two hours for any court appearance, even if it takes less time. Last week, Prager scheduled three consecutive court appearances starting at 9:00 a.m. Prager was finished by 10:15. He billed six hours of work and then went out to the golf course. Is this proper?

2. Prager has suggested to the firm's compensation committee that the bonus system for associates should change. Instead of paying a flat bonus like Carrie Waters' $10,000 increments, he presents the idea of basing the bonus on the total income brought in by that associate. This, he reasons, will reduce the amount of time of first and second year associates that their reviewing partners "write down" as being wasted or part of the associates' learning curve and thus unbillable to the client. Prager also believes that this bonus system will encourage associates to work harder on cases where they are billed out at the highest rates, which in turn will generate more profit for the firm. Is this proper?

READINGS

1. The Development of "Billable Hours." It hasn't been that long since hourly billing was considered the wave of the future. Fifty or sixty years ago, the amount of the typical lawyer's bill was determined by what the attorney considered appropriate. This method of billing involved a largely subjective assessment of the value of legal services, and resulted in a fee that was somewhere in between today's "flat fee" and what we today would call "value billing," a term we will look at briefly later in these readings.

One major difference between the "good old days" and modern practice is that in years past, the bill was rarely based on a formal fee agreement or even an engagement letter. Many lawyers of an earlier era felt it was unprofessional or at least undignified to have written fee agreements with clients. As recently as a generation ago, a written fee agreement was unusual except in contingency cases, where the lawyer's fee was based on a percentage of the recovery. The American Bar Association rules have only required a client's informed consent to a written contingency fee contract since the Ethics 2000 changes were implemented in 2002, and still do not require written fee contracts in non-contingency cases, though many individual states, including California, do have such a requirement.

Many localities had standard rates for certain kinds of services, such as real estate closings, simple wills, and probates. In some places, some of these rates, such as probate fee schedules, became codified. Other rates were institutionalized in the rules of local practice and in ethics rules. Thus, both the Model

Code and the Model Rules still use as one of the factors to be considered in determining the propriety of a fee "the fee customarily charged in the locality for similar legal services." Formalized fee schedules, including schedules setting minimum fees, were widely used 40 years ago, and their use continued until the United States Supreme Court held, in *Goldfarb v. Virginia State Bar*, 421 U.S. 773, 95 S. Ct. 2004 (1975), that these fee schedules violated antitrust laws.

The modernization of law practices and centralization of lawyers in larger firms are circumstances which called for more uniform billing practices. And the consumers of legal fees began to think that they should be paying on the same time-for-money basis that much of America used to earn its wages. Indeed, the 1950s saw an enormous increase in hourly billing not only for lawyers, but for other service people, from auto mechanics and plumbers to accountants. Only physicians and dentists seemed to escape this trend.

Hourly billing had numerous advantages over the traditional discretionary billing methods it replaced. The "time sheet" became a way to quantify a lawyer's work, allowing the consumer to be sure that "you get what you pay for." But hourly billing presented its own host of problems. The currency of the new law firm became hours, and the measurement of the worth of law firm associates — and of many partners as well — became "billable hours."

As the starting salaries in large law firms escalated dramatically in the 1980s, so, too, did the billing requirements, which climbed beyond 1,800 billable hours a year to 2,000, 2,200 and more for associates in some firms. Below, we will examine at length the effect of these billable hours requirements on the associates who must meet them. For the moment, though, put aside the issue of whether lawyers can render ethical, competent representation at that exhausting level. There is little question among commentators and ample empirical evidence that we practice law today in an environment ripe for billing abuses. Many factors are at work in addition to the escalation of billable hours requirements themselves: the profession's increasing bottom-line obsession during the last generation; the recession in the law "industry" by the end of the 1980s, resulting in what has come to be called an "eat-what-you-kill" mentality, or every-lawyer-for-oneself; the resurgence of law firm profitability, at unprecedented levels, at the end of the 1990s; and the steep, sudden, and dramatic rise in salaries, even for first-year associates, as the law profession (perhaps now more accurately called the "law business") reached the millennium.

2. No Free Lunch? Clients Fight Back About Overbilling. Unfortunately for the consumer of legal services, then, the development of hourly billing was hardly a panacea, and seems to have created new problems. After a period of acceptance, clients, especially large "institutional" clients, who used to pay their lawyers' periodic invoices automatically, began not only to question, but to fight back. In turn, lawyers themselves have objected to clients bringing in outside auditors to examine their bills, especially in the area of insurance defense. Read the following article about legal bill auditors and the tension it has created between lawyers and their own clients, a tension that continues to this day.

DAVID MARGOLICK, AT THE BAR: KEEPING TABS ON LEGAL FEES MEANS GOING AFTER THE PEOPLE WHO ARE HIRED TO GO AFTER PEOPLE
The New York Times (March 20, 1992)[1]

"If a client does not complain about a bill, it isn't high enough." This aphorism was part of the lawyerly wit and wisdom John J. McCloy, the former diplomat and New York lawyer, gave each year to the tenderfoots in his firm.

But such an attitude was by no means limited to Milbank, Tweed, Hadley & McCloy. Reluctant to dirty themselves on such unseemly matters, lawyers long set their fees arbitrarily, often erring on the side of extravagance. Conversely, clients, either intimidated by counsel or unduly deferential to them, rarely kept close tabs.

In the past few years, though, as the economy has slumped, belts have tightened, and sentimental traditions have yielded to hard-headed pragmatism, all this has begun to change. For a fee, a number of companies will now monitor legal bills. The oldest and busiest, it seems, is Legalgard Inc. of Philadelphia.

In its promotional literature, the company describes its mission euphemistically. "Legalgard conducts an objective and detailed review of in-force attorney billing and utilization practices to determine a baseline for billing and case management problems and to identify opportunities for savings," it states. Translated into English, that means investigating ripoffs.

The growth of Legalgard, which primarily serves insurance companies and corporations, reflects the fertility of the territory. Begun only five years ago, it has expanded 300 percent annually ever since. It has opened branch offices in Woodland Hills, Tampa, Fla., and Chicago and now employs 80 people. Most are lawyers-turned-investigators, presumably familiar with all the fine points of padding.

"Lawyers were the last of the sacred cows, the last people on the face of the earth to be held accountable to anyone," said Legalgard's chairman, John J. Marquess. He recalled how, only a few years ago, a potential client of his balked at second-guessing his lawyer.

"He told me, 'If you can't trust your lawyer, it's like not being able to trust your wife,'" Marquess said. "I told him, 'Based on what your legal costs have looked like for the last five years, maybe you should go home and check what your wife is doing.'"

Marquess, who practiced law for 15 years himself, said his investigators found irregularities on four of every five legal bills, ranging between 10 percent and 30 percent of the total. With legal fees in the United States totaling $100 billion a year, he said, "the target market is gigantic."

Since 1987, Marquess' minions have found all manner of machinations, including these:

● A lawyer in Century City who, on three occasions, billed a client for 50-hour workdays. "I don't care what you say, nobody has an excuse for billing more than 24 hours a day," Marquess indignantly declared.

- A Los Angeles lawyer who charged a client in 135 separate cases for the same piece of legal research: the meaning of a "collapsed" condominium.

- A San Francisco firm that passed on to clients the $17,000 cost of its program for summer law clerks — all under the guise of "legal research." "It was really devious," Marquess said.

- Boston lawyers who either billed their clients for the cost of heating and air-conditioning their offices, or commuting between their homes and offices.

- A lawyer in Cleveland who charged his client for the suit, shirts and underwear he purchased in the midst of a long trial.

- A prominent New York firm that charged $375 an hour for the time one of its partners spent making photocopies.

- A Chicago firm that put 79 of its 82 lawyers, along with all of its paralegals, on a single products liability case, racking up a $6 million tab for work that, Marquess estimates, should have cost no more than $200,000. Another Chicago lawyer, he said, charged $25,000 for "ground transportation" during an assignment in San Francisco. "Either the attorney was renting a limousine on top of a rental car, or was renting an escort," Marquess said.

- A firm in New Orleans that routinely billed four hours of work for letters that were one sentence long.

Since he signs confidentiality agreements with his clients, Marquess would not identify any of the malefactors. But he offered some clues.

Abuses, he said, tended initially to be more novel on the West Coast. But the worst offenders, he said, were the largest and ostensibly the most prestigious law firms — a fact he attributed to a combination of bureaucracy and arrogance.

"The big firms on Wall Street are having it both ways: They're billing $400 an hour and massaging the billings on top of that," he said.

NOTES

Now firms are billing far more than the $400 per hour suggested at the end of the last article. And the worst billing practices have not improved. Horror stories are legion, and while it is not a primary purpose of this volume to tell lawyers' "war stories," a few examples on this particular issue are worth noting:

- Gary and Maureen Fairchild, husband and wife, worked individually at their separate Chicago law firms creating not just fraudulent bills but fraudulent clients, and padded those bills with personal expenses, extra hours, and more. Both were caught, disbarred, and charged with felonies. Professor Lisa Lerman of Catholic University, perhaps the most prolific writer on the subject of inappropriate billing practices, profiled this particular couple in *The Slippery Slope from Ambition to Greed to Dishonesty*, 30 Hofstra L. Rev. (2002).

- Bobby Glenn Adkins Jr. of Marietta, Georgia billed his clients in three matters for "legal services" that was actually time spent prosecuting lawsuits and perfecting liens against these same clients, and defending himself on disciplinary charges. He was disbarred in 2004.

• Raleigh, North Carolina bankruptcy attorney Mark Kirby was indicted on 16 counts of billing fraud. Among his offenses were: "double billing" clients enough to manage 90 hours in one day; and billing a total of *13,000 hours* in a 13-month period, even though that period, calculated at 24 hours a day seven days a week, was only 9,500 hours long. Kirby somehow managed to get a hung jury in federal court before a plea negotiation resolved his case.

Of course, it is not the extreme and outrageous story that is our main focus here, but the issue of day-to-day overbilling or at the least, pressures to over-bill. We will examine this a bit further in the next two articles.

3. Overbilling at the Top. According to the Legalgard official in the Margolick article above, the worst billing offenders seemed to be prestigious law firms charging "Wall Street" rates. Can this be? And if it is so, then why? Is it simply the "bureaucracy and arrogance" cited by Mr. Marquess? Is it arrogance? The Fairchilds were both successful lawyers at large Chicago firms. Or are there other explanations for the "blue chip" overbillers described in the following article?

MICHAEL D. GOLDHABER, OVERBILLING IS A BIG-FIRM PROBLEM TOO
The National Law Journal (October 1999) [2]

Every few months, an elite firm partner is caught in a billing or expense fraud. Predictably, the rogue's partners dismiss him as "just one rotten apple." Then the issue of overbilling is ignored until the next scoundrel comes along.

A new study in the *Georgetown Journal of Legal Ethics*, "Blue-Chip Billing," takes a longer view and tallies the rotten apples. Lisa Lerman of Catholic University . . . counts exactly 16 elite firm partners during the past 10 years who allegedly stole at least $100,000 in a billing or expense scam. Seven were managing partners. "I wanted to make a point about rot at the top," Professor Lerman says.

She sees her 16 cases as "the tip of an iceberg."

Prof. Lerman would bring the iceberg into view, if only she could. She uses her study as an occasion both to look back on the outrageous cases we know about and to speculate about the outrageous cases we don't know about. She partly blames the bar for failing to catch overbillers.

"There's a complete disconnect between the occurrence of misconduct and the rate of discipline," she says in an interview. In her article, she writes, "The lawyer regulatory system has focused most of its attention on lawyers whose practices are far more modest than the sixteen lawyers on this list."

"Blue-Chip Billing" trots out a host of silk-stocking rascals, among them: Scott Wolas, the fugitive who allegedly padded bills to mask the time he spent on a Ponzi scheme to resell Scotch whiskey in Asia; Webster Hubbell, the former associate U.S. attorney general and chair of the Arkansas bar ethics committee who used Rose Law Firm funds to pay off 10 personal credit cards; and Harvey Myerson, who spent his $2.5 million in fraudulent billings on dog

---

[2] Reprinted with the permission of The National Law Journal. Copyright © 1999 by The New York Law Publishing Company.

food, toupees and helicopter rides. Mr. Myerson moved to a villa in Key West, Fla., after getting out of prison.

How Common?

"They are terrible cases, no question," says Robert O'Malley, of the American Legal Assurance Society, which insures firms against legal malpractice claims, "but she's got 16 cases out of millions of client representations. I don't think what she describes is widespread."

Cornell Law School ethics professor Roger Cramton counters, "These big cases are clearly outliers, but systematic bill padding is pretty widespread."

Most attorneys draw a sharp line between padding and fraud. "Inefficient or excessive billing is not remotely in the same category as falsifying bills," says Steven Krane, of Proskauer Rose L.L.P.

Yet Prof. Lerman believes that there's plenty of outright fraud, and the more subtle cases of overbilling are often blameworthy. "It's a significant deception when you put down four hours and you've only worked one," she says. Other academics agree.

William G. Ross, author of the book "The Honest Hour: The Ethics of Time-Based Billing by Attorneys" (1996) conducted surveys in the early '90s. About half the lawyers surveyed confessed to at least some double-billing . . . . "This is a problem that most definitely goes beyond 16 people," Prof. Ross said in an interview.

. . . .

One reason for big-firm fraud, says billing auditor James Schratz, of Glen Ellen, Calif., is that partners are driven to overbill by financier envy. "They say to themselves, 'If [ex-junk-bond dealer Michael] Milken could make 500 million in one year, I'm worth at least a couple of million' . . . . "

Prof. Lerman suggests that big firms get away with more because they "send huge bills to large institutional clients every month." She also argues that abuses flow from arrogance, and that "law firms are magnets for people with convention-center-size egos."

Finally, Prof. Lerman attributes the crisis to the billable hour. "By setting annual billable targets for lawyers," she writes, "law firms may invite — perhaps almost require — dishonest recordation of time."

Prof. Ross found that even in the early 90s, half of all associates recorded billing more than 2,000 hours. Taking into account routine slack time, 2,000 honestly recorded billables translates into 3,000 hours worked — more than eight hours, seven days a week — by Prof. Ross's reckoning. . . .

But if big-firm lawyers are routinely padding, they're not getting caught. A 1981-82 study cited by Prof. Lerman showed that 80% of those disciplined that year in California, Illinois and Washington, D.C., were sole practitioners — and none practiced in firms of more than seven lawyers. An updat[ed] survey by *The National Law Journal* shows that . . . solos and small firms dominate the time of bar discipline offices.

. . . .

The obvious radical alternative is to abolish the billable hour. Auditor John Toothman, of the Arlington, Va., firm The Devil's Advocate, calls for simpler changes in law firm culture.

Mr. Toothman tells firms not to rent expensive space or depend on a few clients because high overhead and sudden drops in business rachet up the pressure to overbill. He also tells lawyers to lower their expectations: If they want to get rich, they should switch fields. . . .

Prof. Ross . . . and Prof. Cramton, of Cornell, say that a firm with a pervasive culture of overbilling could be punished through "firmwide discipline." Rules allowing a whole firm to be disciplined have been on the books for two years in New York and New Jersey. So far, however, they've been used sparingly, to the dismay of some experts.

"Firmwide discipline hasn't been used in elite theft cases," reports David E. Johnson Jr., director of New Jersey's office of attorney ethics. "It tends to be used when there's no individual who can be held responsible."

. . . James J. Grogan, chief counsel to the Illinois disciplinary commission, reports that indeed, "Illinois' big billing cases have come to us by virtue of *Himmel* reporting."[3] Illinois, out of proportion to its size, accounted for three of the 16 cases on Prof. Lerman's all-time baddie list, and all three were brought to the bar by their partners, through *Himmel* reports.

None of the 16 cases came from Texas, where last year the high court held that Houston's Butler & Binion was permitted to expel a partner after she had reported suspected overbilling by another partner. . . .

Prof. Lerman herself offers no prescriptions, but her avowed ambition, in calling attention to what she perceives as the crisis of big-firm overbilling, is characteristically sweeping. "My aspiration," she says, "is to make it unsafe."

NOTES

Professor Lerman, as we've noted, and Professor Ross have focused much of their work on billing issues, from slightly different perspectives, as this article indicates. Lerman, often using real-life examples to illustrate her points, has also closely examined the issue of lawyers as liars. Ross has used surveys and statistics both to crunch billing numbers and to demonstrate lawyer dissatisfaction. Some of their work product is further described in the Supplemental Readings. Two other individuals mentioned in the last article are worthy of further note: James P. Schratz was an auditor for an insurance company who blew the whistle on a San Francisco law firm, destroying the firm almost single-handed and subjecting the partners to disciplinary proceedings. And Patrick Schiltz's *Happy, Healthy, Ethical* law review piece, destined to be a classic and quoted briefly above, will be excerpted for the second time in this volume in just a few pages.

Before we get there, we take one more recent view of what the author calls "the inflation temptation," based on an annual survey of big-firm associates done by the magazine *American Lawyer*.

---

[3] See our discussion in Problem 26.

HELEN COSTER, THE INFLATION TEMPTATION:
WHAT HAVE YOU DONE FOR YOUR CLIENT
IN THE PAST SIX MINUTES?
New Jersey Law Journal (October 4, 2004)[4]

Like surfing the Internet during a conference call, bill padding is the sort of activity that many lawyers do, but few will admit to.

However, The American Lawyer's annual Midlevel Associates Survey shows 160 associates from 79 law firms — or about 4 percent of respondents — reporting that inflating their hours on time sheets is an accepted practice at their firms.

The associates come from various firms, practice groups, and cities, although New York seems to have a concentration of firms with bill inflators.

Thirty-nine percent of this group practices in New York . . . .

[The survey question] "Does the firm train you in how you should track and record your time?" [got a response of] Yes: 63.8 percent, No: 36.2 percent.

. . . .

Many agree that the tendency to inflate hours is an unavoidable, albeit unfortunate, byproduct of the bill-or-burn culture of big-firm life. They blame hefty billing requirements, a downturn in business, inadequate training, and the difficulty of accurately recording six-minute intervals of work.

"I know people who sit down at the end of the day and say, 'What's a defensible amount of time that I could say I've been here?' " says an associate at a New York-based firm. "They think of what number they can rationally allocate to each task. The way that you write your time can be an art, and people can get quite creative."

Managing partners dispute this message. "I am surprised, shocked, and disagree a thousand percent," says Cesar Alvarez, chief executive of Greenberg Traurig, one of six firms who had five or more associates reply yes to the question, "Is inflating hour reports on time sheets an accepted practice at your firm?" (The others were Baker & McKenzie; King & Spalding; O'Melveny & Myers; Paul, Hastings, Janofsky & Walker; and Skadden, Arps, Slate, Meagher & Flom.) "We train our people and tell them on a regular basis that this behavior is not acceptable. These are lawyers, and they know the ethics."

Some associates are selective about whose bills they pad. "If a client is a jerk, I might take a walk around the hall and bill him for my time," says a fourth-year associate at a Milwaukee firm. Others are more likely to pad the bills of clients with deep pockets, or those who have agreed to an estimate. "If we've been given an estimate from a client, then the firm wants us to come up with enough hours," says an associate at a Houston firm. "I've had [partners] say, 'We gave this client an estimate of $10,000, and you only billed $8,000. That's $2,000 we could have made and you didn't bill for.' Later, I went into accounting and saw that they had added some additional document review to the bill."

---

[4] Copyright © 2004 by ALM Properties, Inc. Reprinted by permission.

But inflating hour reports doesn't always mean creating work out of nowhere. "It's so absurd to think that anyone can be completely accurate when they have ten different things going on," says a third-year associate in Washington, D.C. "I have a certain amount of paranoia because I find being completely accurate so difficult, and it's both a legal and ethical necessity to get it right."

Some associates say that the billable hour system itself is part of the problem. "Things that I could dictate to my secretary, I type out because it could take a little longer," says the Milwaukee-based fourth-year. "I've had partners say in my review, 'Work less efficiently.'"

NOTES

Note that the question asked of these associates was not "Do you personally overbill" but whether their firm allows such a practice. Do the protestations of managing partner Alvarez regarding the training his firm's associates receive ring true? Or are his statements unlikely in light of the number of associates who reported that overbilling is accepted? What role in overbilling does the firm play? Is it the dominant one, the creation of a firm culture where this behavior is expected? Or is pointing the finger at their law firm just an excuse for unethical associates?

4. The ABA Speaks Out on Billing Practices. Some agree with ALAS's Robert O'Malley that Prof. Lerman's examples and Prof. Ross' statistics are not indicative of widespread billing fraud. But what about relatively common practices that law firms have traditionally used? Where should the line be drawn? In 1993, the ABA's ethics committee spoke out strongly on the propriety of a wide range of billing practices, a view that remains the ABA's — and many states' — current thinking. We excerpt that opinion here.

AMERICAN BAR ASSOCIATION FORMAL OPINION 93-379, BILLING FOR PROFESSIONAL FEES, DISBURSEMENTS, AND OTHER EXPENSES
(December 6, 1993)[5]

The legal profession has dedicated a substantial amount of time and energy to developing elaborate sets of ethical guidelines for the benefit of its clients. Similarly, the profession has spent extraordinary resources on interpreting, teaching and enforcing these ethics rules. Yet, ironically, lawyers are not generally regarded by the public as particularly ethical. One major contributing factor to the discouraging public opinion of the legal profession appears to be the billing practices of some of its members.

It is a common perception that pressure on lawyers to bill a minimum number of hours and on law firms to maintain or improve profits may have led some lawyers to engage in problematic billing practices. These include

---

[5] Copyright © 1993 American Bar Association. Reprinted by permission. Copies of this publication are available from Service Center, American Bar Association, 750 North Lake Shore Drive, Chicago, IL 60611.

charges to more than one client for the same work or the same hours, sur-charges on services contracted with outside vendors, and charges beyond reasonable costs for in-house services like photocopying and computer searches. Moreover, the bases on which these charges are to be assessed often are not disclosed in advance or are disguised in cryptic invoices so that the client does not fully understand exactly what costs are being charged to him.

The Model Rules of Professional Conduct provide important principles applicable to the billing of clients, principles which, if followed, would ameliorate many of the problems noted above. The Committee has decided to address several practices that are the subject of frequent inquiry . . . .

The first set of practices involves billing more than one client for the same hours spent. In one illustrative situation, a lawyer finds it possible to schedule court appearances for three clients on the same day. He spends a total of four hours at the courthouse, the amount of time he would have spent on behalf of each client had it not been for the fortuitous circumstance that all three cases were scheduled on the same day. May he bill each of the three clients, who otherwise understand that they will be billed on the basis of time spent, for the four hours he spent on them collectively? In another scenario, a lawyer is flying cross-country to attend a deposition on behalf of one client, expending travel time she would ordinarily bill to that client. If she decides not to watch the movie or read her novel, but to work instead on drafting a motion for another client, may she charge both clients, each of whom agreed to hourly billing, for the time during which she was traveling on behalf of one and drafting a document on behalf of the other? A third situation involves research on a particular topic for one client that later turns out to be relevant to an inquiry from a second client. May the firm bill the second client, who agreed to be charged on the basis of time spent on his case, the same amount for the recycled work product that it charged the first client?

The second set of practices involve billing for expenses and disburse-ments. . . .

Disclosure of the Bases of the Amounts to be Charged

At the outset of the representation the lawyer should make disclosure of the basis for the fee and any other charges to the client. This is a two-fold duty, including not only . . . the basis on which fees and other charges will be billed, but also a sufficient explanation in the statement so that the client may reasonably be expected to understand.

. . . .

A corollary of the obligation to disclose the basis for future billing is a duty to render statements to the client that adequately apprise the client as to how that basis for billing has been applied. [For hourly fees,] a billing setting out no more than a total dollar figure for unidentified professional services will often be insufficient. . . . [B]illing other charges without breaking the charges down by type would not provide the client with the information the client needs to understand the basis for the charges.

Professional Obligations Regarding the Reasonableness of Fees

Implicit in the Model Rules and their antecedents is the notion that the attorney-client relationship is not necessarily one of equals, that it is built on trust, and that the client is encouraged to be dependent on the lawyer, who is dealing with matters of great moment to the client.

. . . .

An unreasonable limitation on the hours a lawyer may spend on a client should be avoided as a threat to the lawyer's ability to fulfill her obligation under Model Rule 1.1 to "provide competent representation to a client." . . .

On the other hand, the lawyer who has agreed to bill on the basis of hours expended does not fulfill her ethical duty if she bills the client for more time than she actually spent on the client's behalf. In addressing the hypotheticals regarding (a) simultaneous appearance on behalf of three clients, (b) the airplane flight on behalf of one client while working on another client's matters and (c) recycled work product, it is helpful to consider these questions, not from the perspective of what the client could be forced to pay, but rather from the perspective of what the lawyer actually earned. A lawyer who spends four hours of time on behalf of three clients has not earned twelve billable hours. A lawyer who flies for six hours for one client, while working for five hours on behalf of another, has not earned eleven billable hours. A lawyer who is able to reuse old work product has not re-earned the hours previously billed and compensated when the work product was first generated. Rather than looking to profit . . . the lawyer who has agreed to bill solely on the basis of time spent is obliged to pass the benefits of these economies on to the client. The practice of billing several clients for the same time or work product . . . is contrary to the mandate of . . . Model Rule 1.5.

Moreover, continuous toil on or over-staffing a project for the purpose of churning out hours is also not properly considered "earning" one's fees. One job of a lawyer is to expedite the legal process . . . .

If . . . the lawyer is particularly efficient in accomplishing a given result, it nonetheless will not be permissible to charge the client for more hours. . . . [T]he economies associated with the result must inure to the benefit of the client, not give rise to an opportunity to bill a client phantom hours . . . .

Charges Other Than Professional Fees

. . . . The Rules provide no specific guidance on the issue of how much a lawyer may charge a client for costs incurred over and above her own fee. However, we believe that the reasonableness standard explicitly applicable to fees under Rule 1.5(a) should be applicable to these charges as well.

. . . . In the absence of disclosure to the client in advance of the engagement to the contrary, the client should reasonably expect that the lawyer's cost in maintaining a library, securing malpractice insurance, renting of office space, purchasing utilities and the like would be subsumed within the charges the lawyer is making for professional services.

At the beginning of the engagement lawyers typically tell their clients that they will be charged for disbursements. When that term is used clients justifiably should expect that the lawyer will be passing on to the client those actual payments of funds made by the lawyer on the client's behalf. . . .

[I]n the absence of disclosure to the contrary, it would be improper if the lawyer assessed a surcharge on these disbursements over and above the amount actually incurred. . . .

Perhaps the most difficult issue is the handling of charges to clients for the provision of in-house services. In this connection the Committee has in view charges for photocopying, computer research, on-site meals, deliveries and other similar items. Like professional fees, it seems clear that lawyers may pass on reasonable charges for these services. Thus, in the view of the Committee, the lawyer and the client may agree in advance that, for example, photocopying will be charged at $.15 per page, or messenger services will be provided at $5.00 per mile. However, the question arises what may be charged to the client, in the absence of a specific agreement to the contrary. . . . [U]nder those circumstances the lawyer is obliged to charge the client no more than the direct cost associated with the service (i.e., the actual cost of making a copy on the photocopy machine) plus a reasonable allocation of overhead expenses directly associated with the provision of the service (e.g., the salary of a photocopy machine operator).

NOTES

The billing practices described in this opinion are hardly the most outrageous we have seen in these readings. No one is billing 135 clients for the same opinion, or 785 hours in one month. Indeed, many law firms have engaged in some of these practices for years, and many lawyers consider them perfectly appropriate. Take the cross-country plane ride. Do you agree that a lawyer, already committed to a paid trip on behalf of Client A, cannot work on Client B's file and bill it? The lawyer would still be paid for the plane ride while reading John Grisham's latest novel instead. And why shouldn't a law firm be able to "value bill" by charging for work done for another client? What if this work is the product of the firm's expertise, rather than just the lucky coincidence the ABA opinion implies? Perhaps the ABA committee's point relates more to notice and consent than to per se unreasonableness. Its analysis, after all, begins with a discussion on disclosure about billing practices, rather than unfairness. Would such notice and consent have resolved the examples posited by the ABA?

Note the ABA's concern over the public image of lawyers. Will abiding by Opinion 93-379 improve the image of lawyers? How easy will it be to comply, given the pressure to produce billable hours? Might the answer lie in law firms being more modest in their billable hours requirements, or in restructuring salaries? What other alternatives might work?

Finally, the ABA created a Commission on Billable Hours that has issued periodic reports on the continued use of this now-questioned billing practice. The latest reports can be found on the web at *http://abanet.org/ careercounsel/billable/toolkit/bhcomplete.pdf.*

5. Happy, Healthy, and Ethical — And Still Billing? We now return to Professor Patrick Schiltz, who has written eloquently and straightforwardly (and, admittedly, with both a perspective and an attitude) about the dangers to associates inherent in the cultures of large firms. In our earlier excerpt,[6] Schiltz discussed generally how a young lawyer could remain ethical. In this excerpt, Schiltz's position is blunt, unlikely to achieve uniform agreement from his readers. But he is clear-eyed and direct. Here he focuses on money: law firms' bottom-line mentality, playing the money "game," and what he sees as the associate's inevitable path toward billing abuse.

PATRICK J. SCHILTZ, ON BEING A HAPPY, HEALTHY, AND ETHICAL MEMBER OF AN UNHAPPY, UNHEALTHY, AND UNETHICAL PROFESSION
52 Vanderbilt Law Review 871 (1999)[7]

Thirty years ago, most partners billed between 1200 and 1400 hours per year and most associates between 1400 and 1600 hours. As late as the mid-1980s, even associates in large New York firms were often not expected to bill more than 1800 hours annually. Today, many firms would consider these ranges acceptable only for partners or associates who had died midway through the year.

[Schiltz cites studies by Professor William Ross, the ABA, Michigan Law School, and Altman Weil Pensa, a legal consulting firm, all showing that a high percentage of associates bill over 2000 hours a year, many as much as 2150 to 2400 hours per year.] Workloads, like the job dissatisfaction to which they so closely relate, are not distributed equally throughout the profession. Generally speaking, lawyers in private practice work longer hours than those who work for corporations or for the government. . . . Within private practice, the general rule of thumb is the bigger the firm, the longer the hours. . . .

The long hours that big firm lawyers must work is a particular source of dissatisfaction for them. While roughly half of all attorneys in private practice complain about not having enough time for themselves and their families, in big firms, the proportion of similarly disaffected lawyers is about three quarters. . . . [Y]oung attorneys in large firms who are interested in finding a new job are more likely than similarly situated associates in small firms to be motivated by "a desire for more personal time."

The unhappiness of lawyers may puzzle you. At first blush, these billable hour requirements may not seem particularly daunting. You may think, "Geez, to bill 2000 hours, I need to bill only forty hours per week for fifty weeks. If I take an hour for lunch, that's 8:00 a.m. to 5:00 p.m., five days per week. No sweat." Your reaction is common among law students — particularly among law students who are in the process of talking themselves into accepting jobs at big firms. Your reaction is also naive.

There is a big difference — a painfully big difference — between the hours that you will *bill* and the hours that you will *spend at work*. If you're honest, you will be able to bill only the time that you spend working directly on matters for clients. Obviously, you will not be able to bill the time that you

---

[6] *See* Problem 2.

[7] Copyright © 1999 by Vanderbilt Law Review, Vanderbilt University School of Law. Reprinted by permission.

spend on vacation, or in bed with the flu, or at home waiting for the plumber. But you will also not be able to bill for much of what you will do at the office or during the workday — going to lunch, . . . visiting your favorite websites, going down the hall to get a cup of coffee, reading your mail, . . . attending the weekly meeting of your practice group, filling out your time sheet, . . . sending e-mail to friends, preparing a "pitch" for a prospective client, . . . interviewing a recruit, doing pro bono work, reading advance sheets, . . . attending CLE seminars, writing a letter about a mistake in your credit card bill, going to the dentist, . . . and so on.

Because none of this is billable — and because the average lawyer does a lot of this every day — you will end up billing only about two hours for every three hours that you spend at "work." And thus, to bill 2000 hours per year, you will have to spend about sixty hours per week at the office, and take no more than two weeks of vacation/sick time/personal leave. If it takes you, say forty-five minutes to get to work, and another forty-five minutes to get home, billing 2000 hours per year will mean leaving home at 7:45 a.m., working at the office from 8:30 a.m. until 6:30 p.m., and then arriving home at 7:10 p.m. — and doing this *six days per week*, every week. That makes for long days, and for long weeks. And you will have to work these hours not just for a month or two, but year after year after year. That makes for a long life.

Now do you understand why so many attorneys are unhappy? And why, generally speaking, the more lawyers work, the less happy they are? What makes people happy is the *nature* of the work they do and the quantity and quality of their lives outside of work. Long hours at the office have no relationship to the former and take away from the latter. . . . There's no mystery about why lawyers are so unhappy: They work too much.

The Money

Why do lawyers work too much? At this point, I'm afraid that we have to leave the realm of fact and enter the realm of opinion. No one knows for certain. . . . Admittedly, my opinion is just an opinion, but it is based on a lot of experience. I practiced law for eight years in a big firm — six as an associate, two as a partner — and spent much of that time working with and against other big firm lawyers. . . .

In one sense, the answer to the question of why so many lawyers work so much is easy: It's the money, stupid. It begins with law students, who, like most Americans, seem to be more materialistic than they were twenty-five or thirty years ago. . . . The vast majority of law students — at least the vast majority of those attending the more prestigious schools (or getting good grades at the less prestigious schools) — want to work in big firms. And the reason they want to work in big firms is that big firms pay the most.

Of course, students deny this. Students — many of whom came to law school intending to do public interest work — don't like to admit that they've "sold out," so they . . . insist that the *real* reason they want to go to a big firm is the training, or the interesting and challenging work, or the chance to work with exceptionally talented colleagues, or the desire to "keep my doors open." . . . Or they reluctantly admit that, yes, they really are after the money, but they have no choice: Because of student loan debt, they *must* take a job that pays $80,000 per year. $60,000 per year just won't cut it.

Most of this is hogwash. As I will explain below, almost all of the purported non-monetary advantages of big firms either do not exist or are vastly overstated. Moreover, there are few lawyers who could not live comfortably on what most corporations or government agencies pay, whatever their student loan debt . . . . The hiring partner of any major firm will tell you that if his firm offers first year associates a salary of $69,000, and a competitor down the street offers them $72,000, those who have the choice will flock to the competitor — even if the competitor will require them to bill 200 hours more each year. I realize that I am not exactly flattering law students. But if this were not true, would big firms get into bidding wars for the services of the best law school graduates? Of course not. But big firms do get into bidding wars — all the time — and, as a result, the salaries of first year associates get pushed to extraordinary levels. . . . [I]n 1997, some New York firms broke the magic $100,000 barrier and began paying six figure salaries to first year associates — many of whom, of course, had not yet even passed the bar exam.

As the salaries of first year associates go up, the salaries of senior associates must rise to keep pace. After all, no sixth year associate wants to be paid less than a first year associate. And as the salaries of senior associates go up, the salaries of junior partners must rise to keep pace. After all, no junior partner wants to be paid less than a senior associate. And, of course, as the salaries of junior partners go up, so must the salaries of senior partners.

How do firms pay for this ever-spiraling increase in salaries? . . . The market for lawyers' services has become intensely competitive. . . . Clients insist on getting good work at low hourly rates. . . . If clients do not get what they want, they will move their business to one of the thousands of other lawyers who are chomping at the bit to get it. Raising billing rates to pay for spiraling salaries is simply not much of an option for most firms. As a result, firms get the extra money to pay for the spiraling salaries in the only way they can: They bill more hours. . . .

I am leaving out one wrinkle — an important wrinkle that you should know about [that] big firm partners euphemistically refer to as "leverage." I like to call it "the skim." Richard Abel calls it "exploitation." The person being exploited is you.

It is common for the top partners in the biggest firms to earn upwards of $2 million per year. . . . Not one of these highly paid partners could personally generate the billings necessary to produce such an income. . . .

Basically, what happens is that big firms "buy associates' time 'wholesale and sell it retail.'" Here is how it works: As a new associate in a large firm, you will be paid about one-third of what you bring into the firm. . . . Another third will go toward paying the expenses of the firm. And the final third will go into the pockets of the firm's partners. Firms make money off associates. That is why it's in the interests of big firms to hire lots of associates and to make very few of them partners.

. . . .

This, then, is life in the big firm: It is in the interests of clients that senior partners work inhuman hours, year after year, and constantly be anxious about retaining their business. And it is in the interests of senior partners that junior partners work inhuman hours, year after year, and constantly be anxious about retaining old clients and attracting new clients. And it is in the interests of junior partners that senior associates work inhuman hours, year after year, and constantly be anxious about retaining old clients and attracting new clients and making partner. And most of all, it is in everyone's interests that the newest members of the profession — the junior associates — be willing to work inhuman hours, year after year, and constantly be anxious about *everything* — [including] their billable hours. The result? Long hours, large salaries, and one of the unhealthiest and unhappiest professions on earth.

The "Game"

. . . . Almost every one of these problems would be eliminated or at least substantially reduced if lawyers were simply willing to make less money. . . . The notion that lawyers could get by with less money is not exactly absurd. In 1994, the median income for American men employed full-time during the entire year was $31,612; for women, the comparable figure was $23,265. In 1995, the median income for partners in firms of all sizes was $168,751. . . . Even in the smallest firms (firms of eight or fewer lawyers), the median income for partners was $134,294. . . . It's not as if lawyers are just scraping by.

. . . . Lawyers could enjoy a lot more life outside of work if they were willing to accept relatively modest reductions in their incomes. Take, for example, a partner who is billing 2000 hours and being paid $200,000. If we assume that a 20% reduction in billable hours will translate into a 20% reduction in pay (an assumption that is unlikely to be exactly true, but that is close enough for our purposes), this lawyer could trade $40,000 in income for 600 more hours of life outside work (assuming that three hours at work translates into two hours billed).

Our hypothetical partner has a choice, then: He can make $200,000 per year and work many nights and most weekends — routinely getting up early, before his children are awake, driving to the office, eating lunch at his desk, leaving the office late, picking up dinner at the Taco Bell drive-through window, and then arriving home to kiss the cheeks of his sleeping children. Or he can make $160,000 per year and work few nights and weekends. He can spend time with his spouse, be a parent to his children, enjoy the company of his friends, pursue a hobby, do volunteer work, exercise regularly, and generally lead a well balanced life — *while still making $160,000 per year*. If all such lawyers making $160,000 per year sat down and asked themselves, "What will make me a happier and healthier person: another $40,000 in income (which, after taxes, will mean another $25,000 or so in the bank) or 600 hours to do whatever I enjoy most?," it is hard to believe that many of them would take the money.

But many of them do take the money. Thousands of lawyers choose to give up a healthy, happy, well-balanced life for a less healthy, less happy life dominated by work. And they do so merely to be able to make seven or eight times the national median income instead of five or six times the national median income. Why? Are lawyers just greedy?

Well, some are, but it is more complicated than that. For one thing, lawyers . . . don't sit down and think logically about why they are leading the lives they are leading any more than buffalo sit down and think logically about why they are stampeding. That is the primary reason I am writing this Article: I hope that you *will* sit down and think about the life that you want to lead before you get caught up in the stampede.

More importantly, though, the flaw in my analysis is that it assumes that the reason lawyers push themselves to make so much money is the money itself. . . . What you need to understand, though, is that [t]hey are doing it for a different reason.

Big firm lawyers are, on the whole, a remarkably insecure and competitive group of people. Many of them have spent almost their entire lives competing to win games that other people have set up for them. First they competed to get into a prestigious college. Then they competed for college grades. Then they competed for LSAT scores. Then they competed to get into a prestigious law school. Then they competed for law school grades. Then they competed to make the law review. Then they competed for clerkships. Then they competed to get hired by a big law firm.

Now that they're in a big law firm, what's going to happen? Are they going to stop competing? Are they going to stop comparing themselves to others? Of course not. . . . They're playing a game. And money is how the score is kept in that game.

Why do you suppose sixty year old lawyers with millions of dollars in the bank still bill 2200 hours per year? Why do you suppose lawyers whose children have everything money can buy but who need the time and attention of their parents continue to spend most nights and weekends at the office — while continuing to write out checks to the best child psychologists in town? Why do you suppose one big firm partner I know flew into a rage after learning that his year-end bonus would be only — only — $400,000, while the bonus of one of his rivals in the firm would be $425,000? . . .

What's driving these lawyers is the desire to *win the game*. . . . If a lawyer's life is dominated by the game — and if his success in the game is measured by money — then his *life* is dominated by money. For many, many lawyers, it's that simple.

. . . .

Becoming Unethical

Unethical lawyers do not start out being unethical; they start out just like you — as perfectly decent young men or women who have every intention of practicing law ethically. They do not become unethical overnight; they become unethical just as you will (if you become unethical) — a little bit at a time. And they do not become unethical by shredding incriminating documents or bribing jurors; they become unethical just as you are likely to — by cutting a corner here, by stretching the truth a bit there.

Let me tell you how you will start acting unethically: It will start with your time sheets. One day, not too long after you start practicing law, you will sit down at the end of a long, tiring day, and you just won't have much to show for your efforts in terms of billable hours. It will be near the end of the month. You will know that all of the partners will be looking at your monthly time report in a few days, so what you'll do is pad your time sheet just a bit. Maybe you will bill a client for ninety minutes for a task that really took you only sixty minutes to perform. However, you will promise yourself that you will repay the client at the first opportunity by doing thirty minutes of work for the client for "free." In this way, you will be "borrowing," not "stealing."

And then what will happen is that it will become easier and easier to take these little loans against future work. And then, after a while, you will stop paying back these little loans. You will convince yourself that, although you billed for ninety minutes and spent only sixty minutes on the project, you did such good work that your client should pay a bit more for it. After all, your billing rate is awfully low, and your client is awfully rich.

And then you will pad more and more — every two minute telephone conversation will go down on the sheet as ten minutes, every three hour research project will go down with an extra quarter hour or so. You will continue to rationalize your dishonesty to yourself in various ways until one day you stop doing even that. And, before long — it won't take you much more than three or four years — you will be stealing from your clients almost every day, and you won't even notice it.

You know what? You will also likely become a liar. A deadline will come up one day, and, for reasons that are entirely your fault, you will not be able to meet it. So you will call your senior partner or your client and make up a white lie for why you missed the deadline . . . . And then, in preparing a client for a deposition, you will help the client to formulate an answer to a difficult question that will likely be asked — an answer that will be "legally accurate" but that will mislead your opponent. And then you will be reading through a big box of your client's documents — a box that has not been opened in twenty years — and you will find a document that would hurt your client's case, but that no one except you knows exists, and you will simply "forget" to produce it in response to your opponent's discovery requests.

Do you see what will happen? After a couple years of this, you won't even notice that you are lying and cheating and stealing every day that you practice law. None of these things will seem like a big deal in itself . . . . But, after a while, your entire frame of reference will change. You will still be making dozens of quick, instinctive decisions every day, but those decisions, instead of reflecting the notions of right and wrong by which you conduct your personal life, will instead reflect the set of values by which you will conduct your professional life — a set of values that embodies not what is right or wrong, but what is profitable, and what you can get away with. The system will have succeeded in replacing your values with the system's values, and the system will be profiting as a result.

Does this happen to every big firm lawyer? Of course not. It's all a matter of degree. The culture in some big firms is better than in others . . . . The big firm at which I practiced was as decent and humane as a big firm can be. Similarly, some big firm lawyers have better values than others. I owe a lot to a partner who sacrificed hundreds of hours of his time and tens of thousands of dollars of income to act as a mentor to me and to many other young lawyers like me.

. . . .

"Big Picture" Advice

My "big picture" advice is simple: Don't get sucked into the game. Don't let money become the most important thing in your life. Don't fall into the trap of measuring your worth as an attorney — or as a human being — by how much money you make.

If you let your law firm or clients define success for you, they will define it in a way that is in their interest, not yours. It is important for them that your primary motivation be making money. . . . If you end up as an unhappy or unethical attorney, money will most likely be at the root of your problem.

You cannot win the game. If you fall into the trap of measuring your worth by money, you will always feel inadequate. There will always be a firm paying more to its associates than yours. . . . There will always be a lawyer at your firm making more money than you. . . . You will run faster and faster and faster, but there will always be a runner ahead of you, and the finish line will never quite come into view . . . .

Most likely, when you were a child, your parents or grandparents told you money does not buy happiness. They were right.

NOTES

Remember that Prof. Schiltz comes to a much more upbeat conclusion in the segment we excerpted in Problem 2. Please feel free to return to that excerpt to reread his advice about how to be happy, healthy, *and* ethical.

6. Inflated Salaries, Inflated Expectations? In the brief time between Schiltz's article and our drafting of this text, associates' salaries have risen dramatically. A few days before the turn of the millennium, and less than a year after Schiltz's article, a relatively modest-sized Silicon Valley firm, Gunderson, Dettmer, Stough, Villeneuve, Franklin & Hachigian, jumped first-year associates' salaries to $150,000 a year — $125,000 plus guaranteed bonuses of $25,000. This was not the small, incremental leap-frogging increase that marked the salary wars of the '80s and '90s. It was a "statement" by the new kids on the block, clearly fueled by the boomtown-like dot.com economy. It was, founding partner Scott Dettmer told *California Lawyer*, a "benchmark . . . to attract high-powered laterals from out of town . . . and to hold on to associates who were otherwise tempted to move to start-ups."[8]

In the first months of 2000, the salary war focus quickly shifted from Wall Street to Silicon Valley. By mid-January, Silicon Valley giants Cooley Godward, Wilson Sonsini, and Gray Cary had matched Gunderson, Dettmer.

---

[8] CALIFORNIA LAWYER, July 2000. *See* Supplemental Reading 3.

Other San Francisco giants soon followed suit, including Morrison Forester, Heller Ehrman, and Brobeck, Phleger, and Harrison, which had become the richest and largest Northern California-based firm. Those that were slow to act found themselves attacked by the habitues of on-line "greedy associates" boards, who monitored and reported every move in detail.

Was this only about lawyers making more money? Not exactly. There were increased expectations as well. Brobeck, for example, claimed to raise its salaries above the Gunderson benchmark. But in order to earn the extra money, the 1,950 annual billable hours previously required of Brobeck associates would no longer be enough. To earn incremental bonuses to get them to Gunderson levels, associates would need to raise their "billables" to 2,100, 2,250, and — for the big payoff — 2,400 hours a year. Brobeck chairman Tower Snow, Jr. announced, somewhat anomalously, "We don't want our people working these excessive hours, but if they do, we want to acknowledge them." More than a few found this statement disingenuous.

The Silicon Valley salary escalation seemed to affirm Prof. Schiltz's analysis — that young lawyers would play "the game" and work many more hours for just a few more dollars than the competitor paid, and that many law firms saw associates as commodities to be bought wholesale and sold retail.

With lawyers leaving — or threatening to leave — for in-house dot.com jobs, complete with stock options, dozens of firms raised their salaries by extraordinary percentages between December 1999, when Gunderson moved, and the beginning of the NASDAQ's downturn in March 2000. A year later, with the NASDAQ at less than half its previous level and "start-up" closings already an old story, most associates' salary structures remained the same. But the business environment that surrounded the law firms had changed materially for the worse. Many a newly-minted dot.com house counsel was not just out of stock options but out of work. A few law firms had found it necessary to lay off associates — the fungible commodities Schiltz described. Gunderson, which started it all, cancelled its guaranteed bonuses, effectively dropping its salaries by $20,000.[9] And by 2003, Brobeck had collapsed into bankruptcy.

One final thought: The enormous salary increases for young attorneys have increased the disparity between their pay and that of experienced legal support staff. This doesn't sit terribly well with some staff members, who in some areas of the country have voiced complaints, demanded salary increases, and even thought about unionization.[10]

7. Modern Alternatives to Hourly Billing. In light of the problems that hourly billing has caused, many law firms and clients have looked for different ways to charge for legal services. Here are a few of those ways:

Flat or fixed fees have long been used by criminal defense lawyers and estate planners to set the value of their services. Now larger firms and their clients are looking at flat fees, particularly where the task involved is familiar and relatively quantifiable. Often, they call this "value billing" or "task-based"

---

[9] See series in THE RECORDER (San Francisco) by Renee Deger, including *Gunderson's Guaranteed Bonus a Goner*, June 13, 2001.

[10] *See, e.g., Salary Slight?* THE RECORDER (San Francisco), California Legal Pro Supplement, Spring 2000.

billing. A modification of the flat fee arrangement is one where the attorney charges hourly up to a maximum cap for a particular case. The advantage to the client of such arrangements is clear: knowing from the outset what the fee will be. The advantage to the lawyer is that, so long as the services are well performed, the client will be happy even if the lawyer finds ways to save time and costs. The disadvantage to the lawyer, however, is that very careful time estimates are required, and will not always prove accurate. The law firm may find itself committed to a case which is taking far more time than the flat fee covers. This can be a disadvantage to the client as well, since a law firm in such circumstances might be disinclined to spend all the time necessary for the client's case.

One more caveat about flat or fixed fee arrangements: Some courts have criticized, even invalidated, flat fees deemed "non-refundable."[11] But if law firms protect their financial interests when performing a set task, would they ever enter such a fee arrangement? Many other courts have found that flat-fee or non-refundable fee contracts are not necessarily improper, for instance where the law firm does the work,[12] makes itself available on an as-needed basis,[13] or is fired for refusing to engage in requested action that it believes might be unethical.[14]

Hybrid hourly and contingency fees allow lawyers who are not sufficiently confident about a matter to take it entirely on contingency to represent clients who can't or don't want to pay the full hourly freight. These situations might include business, real estate, or insurance litigation, where monetary damages are at stake but where the liability issues are more complicated than those of the typical personal injury contingency case. Hybrid fees mean the lawyer gets a substantially discounted hourly fee, and then a discounted contingency fee in the event the case is successful.

Incentive bonuses are similar to these hybrid fees. Here, the attorney might receive a reduced hourly rate plus a percentage bonus for any recovery over a specified sum of $X, or any savings to the client of more than $Y. Both hybrid fees and incentive bonuses have the advantages to the lawyer of rewarding both the time spent and results obtained, while helping the client by reducing the expenditures substantially if the case is not successful.

Discounts and "blended" rates, where the law firm charges a single median rate for the work of both partner and associate, are becoming more common, particularly where the law firm and client have known each other for a long time. Discounts to the firm's best clients may be a way of keeping those clients happy. But by creating a compensation "hierarchy," they may also encourage lawyers to spend their available time on matters compensated at higher rates. Moreover, many observers believe that the most frequent abuses for "churning files" (overworking them) and "writing up" (or inflating) hours occur in the

---

[11] *See, e.g., Matter of Cooperman*, 83 N.Y.2d 465, 633 N.E.2d 1069 (1994); *In re Hirschfeld*, 960 P.2d 640 (Ariz. 1998).

[12] *In re Gastineau*, 317 Or. 545, 857 P.2d 136 (1993).

[13] *Kelly v. MD Buyline, Inc.*, 2 F. Supp. 2d 420 (S.D.N.Y. 1998) (limiting the scope of *Cooperman*).

[14] *Ryan v. Butera, Beausang, Cohen & Brennan*, 193 F.3d 210 (3d Cir. 1999).

field of insurance defense, a highly competitive area in which substantial hourly discounts are often given.

No fee arrangement is perfect. But as clients become more sensitized to the need for control over fees, they and their lawyers will work more closely to come up with acceptable solutions.

SUPPLEMENTAL READINGS

1. Volume 50, No. 4 of the Rutgers Law Review contained four valuable articles about unethical billing practices, all based on Lisa Lerman's narrative of the true story of a lawyer named, for purposes of publication, "Nicholas Farber." Her *Scenes From a Law Firm*, 50 Rutgers L. Rev. 2153 (1998), is accompanied by articles by William Ross, James P. Schratz, and Lawrence J. Fox, formerly both an ABA ethics committee chair and a big-firm managing partner.

2. Patrick Schlitz's article, reprinted above, was part of a symposium issue of the Vanderbilt Law Review, Volume 52, number 4, with the title "Attorney Well-Being in Large Firms: Choices Facing Young Lawyers." Other articles provided perspectives on Schiltz's "feature" piece, and Schiltz closed with a response to those other commentators. These other articles provide varied and valuable viewpoints on Schiltz's theme.

3. In a slightly different vein, the July 2000 issue of *California Lawyer* contains an excellent series of articles on life, salary escalation, and the expectations of both law firms and associates. The enlightening profiles and interviews with associates and partners include one with the woman who is believed to have been Gunderson's first beneficiary of Silicon Valley generosity.

4. Among others, Lisa Lerman's contributions to this subject include *Blue-Chip Bilking: Regulation of Billing and Expense Fraud by Lawyers*, 12 Geo. J. Leg. Ethics 205 (Winter 1999), a preliminary version of that piece that appeared in the 1998 Symposium Issue of *The Professional Lawyer* entitled "Regulation of Unethical Billing Practices: Progress and Prospects," and *Teaching Moral Perception and Judgment in Legal Ethics Courses: A Dialogue About Goals*, 39 Wm. & Mary L. Rev. 457 (1998), in addition to the piece on the Fairchilds cited in the body of the Readings.

5. William G. Ross' article, *The Ethics of Hourly Billing*, 44 Rutgers L. Rev. 1 (1991), is perhaps the first significant article dealing with a modern analysis of lawyers' billing practices. It includes the lawyers survey mentioned in Goldhaber's article, in which Ross found, among other matters, that the vast majority of lawyers believed that their colleagues padded their bills, and 50% acknowledged that they had billed two clients for the same amount of time. Ross authored the book *The Honest Hour: The Ethics of Time-Based Billing by Attorneys* (1997), and summarized it in the 1998 *Professional Lawyer* symposium issue. He has also written on the insurance auditing controversy, *An Ironic and Unnecessary Controversy: Ethical Restrictions on Billing Guidelines and Submission of Insurance Defense Bills to Outside Auditors,* 14 N.D. J. L. Ethics & Pub. Policy 527 (2000).

6. Two other law professors who have written extensively on billing issues are Carl T. Bogus, whose article *The Death of an Honorable Profession*, 71 Ind. L. J. 911 (1996), is an excellent contribution to the discussion about the effect of money on the practice of law; and Susan Saab Fortney, whose *An Emperical Study of Associate Satisfaction, Law firm Culture and the Effects of Billable Hour Requirements*, 64 Tex. Bar J. 1060 (2001), is an effective summary of associate unhappiness.

7. Darlene Ricker, a lawyer and *Los Angeles Times* editor, has written several interesting articles on billing abuses, including "Greed, Ignorance and Overbilling," *ABA Journal* (August 1994).

8. Dennis Curtis & Judith Resnik, in *Teaching Billing: Metrics of Value in Law Firms and Law Schools*, 54 Stan. L. Rev. 1409 (2002), review Deborah Rhode's book, *In the Interests of Justice: Reforming the Legal Profession* and argue that "law schools ought to join in the conversation about the role of hourly billing in shaping concepts of professionalization."

PROBLEM 28

Racial, cultural, and gender bias are facts of life in our society. Some biases are overt; others come in more subtle forms. They affect the practice of law every bit as much as they do other walks of life. Some might argue that countering such biases in the form of ethical requirements is using ethics in an effort to be "politically correct." Others contend that the fundamental inequalities of our society, some of which are described in the readings below, warrant the conclusion that the ethical lawyer is the lawyer who does what is possible to understand, deal with, and affirmatively counteract such biases.

Of course, all decisions to *not* hire, or promote, women or minority attorneys don't automatically signal bias, either overt or subtle. But vigilance is required to ensure that such biases do not determine the issue. Take the case of Sharon Chau.

Is There a Glass Ceiling as Lawyers Climb the Law Firm Ladder?

Sharon Chau is an attractive, ambitious, Asian attorney at Donovan, Kemper, Newcomb & Yates, an Ocean City law firm with 20 partners and 35 associates. She has been working there for eight years. During this time, she has had a few opportunities to try her own cases, and has developed a reputation as a skillful and aggressive trial lawyer. She has even attracted a few small and modest-sized new clients to DKNY.

Chau, however, makes an effort to leave the office by 5 p.m. and is not frequently seen by the partners "grinding out the hours" at work. In the last three years, she has averaged about 150 fewer billable hours per year than the average senior associate.

At DKNY, the third Friday of the month has traditionally been reserved by the litigation unit for after work socializing over drinks at the Olympian Club. Chau, however, rarely joins the group. Except for one or two close friends, she does not often see her colleagues outside the office. Moreover, she is not often available to socialize with clients during evening hours. Rather, Chau goes home to take care of her two children, Jessica, 5, and Matthew, 9. After Jessica was born, Chau took one year of maternity leave from DKNY. She is now a single parent. She often prepares for trial at home, after the kids are in bed.

Next month Chau will be reviewed by the DKNY partners to determine whether she should be offered partnership. If it is offered, she would be the first female minority partner of the firm. The DKNY partners currently include two white females, both married without children, one Spanish-surnamed male whose family has resided in suburban La Vista for three generations, and one older Japanese-American male who heads the international trade department and also maintains an office in Japan. The remainder of the partners are Caucasian men.

Two weeks before the partnership meeting, Chau is approached by partner James Taylor. They have been cordial in the past, but she only knows him professionally. Taylor tells Chau that he would like to take her to dinner to discuss her future at DKNY, and if things go as he anticipates, he can almost guarantee her partnership at the firm.

QUESTIONS

1. You are a voting member of the partnership committee. Discuss the pros and cons of inviting Chau to become a partner at DKNY. Which factors are appropriate to consider?

2. Suppose the partnership committee votes no partnership, telling Chau that their decision is based on her time constraints and billable hours. Are these valid reasons?

3. Just prior to the partnership meeting, one male and one female partner ask Chau numerous questions regarding her family life and responsibilities. Chau asks the other female partner whether she was subjected to the same questions, and she replies "no." Is there a legitimate basis for such questioning?

4. Before the partnership meeting, while completing an assignment for Newcomb, Chau overhears him saying to Yates, "I can't believe that Chinese company stole that trademark right from under us. You've got to watch them, you know, they're always sneaky and quiet until they want something, and then they'll do anything . . . ."

Chau is extremely upset when she hears this, but she is also concerned about her job. What actions, if any, should Chau take? Should she discuss the matter with other members of the firm?

5. Is Taylor's dinner invitation proper? Should she accept? What if she believes that Taylor's vote could determine the outcome? Would it matter if Taylor is one of the two partners who supervises Chau's work?

READINGS

1. Women in the Legal Workplace. Women now form a substantial segment of most law school populations. Thus, law firms should have no problem finding academically qualified women candidates to employ. Once inside the firm, however, problems can arise for the woman associate. Two of them are the "me-not-me" dilemma (to be a good lawyer you must "be like a man"), and the "mommy track" problem (when, if ever, and at what price can women lawyers have children).

The "me-not-me" syndrome occurs most clearly in the courtroom; the image of the good advocate is one who is aggressive and forceful, and "plays the game" by rules that have traditionally been masculine. "Being like a man" in the courtroom may give rise to accusations of being overly "aggressive" or "insensitive," while acting more feminine may bring accusations about ineffectiveness. It is a fine line to have to walk.

These and other problems faced by women lawyers in the law firm setting are addressed by the following article, which describes the thin tightrope to success which women lawyers must walk. Although written in 1990, the issues continue today.

MONA D. MILLER, BREAKING THROUGH THE
GLASS CEILING
California Lawyer (August 1990)[1]

In 1977, when I graduated from law school, I thought if I worked very hard and did my best, I could eventually become a partner at the medium-sized Los Angeles law firm I was about to join. And I did, although by that time the firm had grown and I was less naive about the ways in which women associates are expected to conform to a predominantly male culture. A hopeful, headlong plunge into the law and the determination to do an enormous amount of work are helpful, but they simply aren't enough. . . .

While probably no more sexist than the world at large, law firms, caught in a mire of cut-throat competition, rising overhead and the shifting loyalties of clients and partners, are hardly oases of egalitarianism. Women associates must deal with latent and open sexism, a dearth of role models and minority status. Though women now make up 50 percent of many law school classes, the ratio of women partners is increasing by only 1 percent a year. A study of Harvard Law School graduates in private practice 10 years out of law school showed that while 59 percent of the men had made partner, only 23 percent of the women had. And more than 80 percent of the respondents in a recent [California] State Bar survey reported a subtle but pervasive sense of gender bias.

. . . .

To become a partner, a woman must . . . present herself in a way that conforms to the firm's perception of its requirements. Different firms value different qualities, and they may not in fact value what they say they value.

. . . .

Whether sexist or just used to the comfort of the familiar, men often have difficulty acknowledging competence in a woman. Some can hardly believe they've encountered it. I'll never forget a juror telling me after a long trial that a young male partner and I had won, "You weren't as bad as I thought you'd be."

Thus a female associate must not only have ability, her "style"— her personality and way of communicating, her attitudes and expression — must instill confidence in her superiors. She needs to be able to present herself as a highly competent lawyer and inevitable future partner without seeming threatening, overpowering, abrasive, abusive, self-righteous, or (at the other end of the spectrum) defensive, overanxious, insecure, hysterical, rigid, or, God forbid, humorless. (A sense of humor is essential for survival in this profession.) Women need to select and maintain a professional demeanor that does not offend yet does not leave room for warmth or friendliness to be mistaken for a sexual overture.

A woman in a big firm cannot afford to be so different that the men feel uncomfortable with her. And the range of behaviors male partners tolerate from women associates is, in my experience, both narrower and different from what they tolerate in a man. One night, for example, a male associate in my

---

[1] Copyright © 1990. Reprinted by permission.

firm, apparently irritated at the intense ribbing he was taking about an unusual tie, "mooned" a group of lawyers chatting and drinking in a conference room. The incident was much remembered, with chuckles, but I never heard any of the partners present say his behavior was unprofessional. I cannot imagine a woman ever getting away with anything like that without having her credibility as a professional destroyed.

Even a woman's physical appearance is more closely examined. I have heard male partners complain about female associates' excessive weight, makeup or lack of makeup, strong perfume or wrinkled suits while overlooking the creases or badly fitting suits, untucked shirt tails, scuffed shoes or bloodstained shirts on some of their male colleagues.

Motherhood is another area where the gap between a firm's self-image and what really goes on within its walls is apparent. Maternity-leave policies are driven by economic realities. Some partners view a firm's maternity-leave policy as a generous gift, not something to which the associate is entitled. A senior associate I knew who might otherwise have received a handsome discretionary bonus for long hours found her bonus reduced pro rata for the time she took off for maternity leave. I question whether the same thing would have happened to a male associate temporarily disabled by a back or leg injury for the same period of time.

Though a firm may claim to be pro-family, women who defer partnership to have children make some partners very uneasy. The women's commitment is questioned because they may not be available for work at night or on weekends, or because they are not treating partnership as the be-all-and-end-all of existence. Some partners are simply uncomfortable hearing about infants. One attorney mother I know says she avoids the "B" word with certain partners.

Too much talk about one's child may seem unprofessional, but focusing exclusively on work may bring a woman criticism to which a man would not be subject. Older partners may be offended by a new mother's "premature" return to work. On the other hand, a woman who works fewer hours with reduced compensation may cause amazing resentment. . . .

At some point you have to ask yourself how much compromise is too much. Where do you draw the line in conforming to male-dominated institutional values? You'll know when something inside you rebels. I didn't have to draw that line; it started drawing itself.

. . . .

I drew the line . . . early in my career, when I was the "grunt" worker on a huge antitrust team and had the opportunity to meet a manager of the corporate client and review some records in Fresno. I had worked very hard on the case and looked forward to getting out of the library to see our client's plant, but there was no reason the trip had to take place immediately. I was anticipating with great pleasure a visit from a sister I saw only once or twice a year. When the senior partner announced he was sending me to Fresno for a week, I said something like "Oh, no, that's the week my sister's coming to L.A."

The more senior (and male) associate advised me privately that I'd made a big mistake. I should have expressed how thrilled and happy I — a nobody who'd been slaving away on this case 10 hours a day for months — was at being sent on a wonderful and exciting business trip. A sister's visit was a totally unacceptable reason not to want to go, calling my entire level of commitment into question. Apparently months of well-executed work could be erased by a spontaneous remark.

I later apologized to the partner in charge [but] the trip was rescheduled to a better time for me. Undoubtedly, I had foolishly communicated my feeling that making the trip just then was not essential; no superior ever wants his decisions criticized, especially by a woman . . . .

Since that time I have supervised many associates and I now have more sympathy for the senior partner than I did in 1978. People who are inflexible about their personal schedules make life harder for the rest of us. But the prevalent myth among some lawyers that no life outside the firm should ever intrude into office discussions strikes me as sick and inherently sexist in a world where working mothers usually bear more child-rearing responsibilities than their husbands, and wives deal more than husbands with the physical and emotional maintenance of the home. . . . I don't think emphasis on a more balanced approach to work, leaving time for family and community, should be treated as a sign of inexcusable weakness.

. . . .

I did have help from many male colleagues. These men assumed I would be able to deal with whatever came my way, which forced me to learn a great deal and to develop a thicker skin. At the same time, some of them recognized the power they had to control the tone of various encounters. Their willingness to step in and deflect sexist comments eliminated the need for me to respond and face being branded as "defensive" or "humorless."

Nevertheless, while useful mentors and allies may be found along the way, the person who engineers a woman's arrival into the partnership is the woman.

NOTES

Some have argued that the issues raised by the Miller piece are "quality of life" rather than gender issues. Is Miller correct that these issues affect women much more strongly than men? Should these issues be treated as sex-neutral, or is legitimate to understand that they affect women more?

Appearance is an issue easy to trivialize or stereotype, but it is still a part of what women face. Recall the "controversy" in the O.J. Simpson case, when chief prosecutor Marcia Clark's angel pin, red suit, and even her skirt length drew more comments than her lawyering skills.[2] Can you imagine a similar emphasis on Johnnie Cochran's ties?

2. The "Mommy Track" and Caretakers. Mona Miller eventually resigned her partnership after the birth of her daughter and returned to practice

---

[2] *See, e.g.*, Harriet Chiang, *Why Marcia Clark's Clothing Matters*, SAN FRANCISCO CHRONICLE, Feb. 9, 1995, at 1.

with another firm on a part-time basis. Should the "mommy track" force women to resign their partnerships? Can there be a part-time partner at a firm? On one hand, many feel the bias against women with kids has continued unabated. When Southwestern law professor Judy Sloan role-plays with her students divided into law firms deciding on female candidates, the "pregnant woman" rarely gets the job. On the other, in the decade since Miller's article, more firms are looking at these possibilities, in an effort to keep lawyers, mostly but not exclusively women, who have other personal priorities but who want to continue with the "serious" practice of law. One report, a 1997 law placement survey, found that over 90 percent of the 500 firms surveyed claimed to offer part-time employment for their attorneys.

But that doesn't necessarily make it easier. In June 1998, Florida attorney Alice Hector, a partner and senior trial lawyer at a large Miami law firm, lost a custody battle with her ex-husband because, with an iffy employment record, he was adjudged more available as a parent to their children. The ruling, *Young v. Hector*, 740 So. 2d 1153 (Fla. App. 1998), shocked the legal world. In an unusual proceeding, the Florida appeals court agreed to rehear the case *en banc* and a year later changed its decision, using the same original citation to wipe the previous opinion off the books. Many women found the original *Hector* opinion outrageous, but many also reported having succeeded in merging partnership careers with lives as parents. Almost all those who succeeded cited unusually supportive spouses, nannies who were "like a member of the family," and the reality of working two full-time jobs.

One surprising "mommy track" stumbling block, according to some younger woman attorneys, is that older women who have "made it," while they may be mentors and role models, are sometimes of little help in encouraging changes such as part-time partnership tracks. Indeed, some claim that some older women lawyers are often among those most resistant. "I'm not going to make exceptions for anybody in my court," a woman judge said at a recent bias seminar. "I dealt with my child care problems; attorneys appearing in my court will simply have to deal with theirs." This is an understandable point of view, but is it reasonable?

We invite anyone with doubts about whether women routinely face subtle forms of "mommy track" bias to try this test. Lawyer X attends an afternoon judicial conference, such as a pretrial settlement conference. After waiting their turn on the calendar, the lawyers go into chambers, where X tells the judge the following: 'Your Honor, I really need to be out of here by 4:30. You know, I'm a single parent, and I have to pick up my little girl at day care by 5:15." If X is a man, the likely response from the bench — be the judge man or woman — is sympathy and understanding, even a positive reaction ("Gee, what a caring Dad.") But if X is a woman, the likely response is anger at her request for "special favors," and a negative reaction ("Having kids is fine, but she's not taking her law practice seriously enough.") Try this test empirically; unfortunately, the results have been borne out by the similar experiences of many lawyers.

The following article describes one poignant real-life experience.

STUART HANLON, GETTING IT
California Lawyer (April 2000)[3]

I recently was forced to withdraw from the case of *People v. Sara Jane Olson aka Kathleen Soliah*, for personal but very simple reasons: I am a single father of two young boys, ages eight and twelve, and my wife, attorney Kathleen Ryan, died more than two years ago of leukemia. When I agreed to be one of Sara's lawyers I thought it would be a six-to-eight-week trial involving the charges that she and others supposedly connected to the Symbionese Liberation Army (SLA) planted bombs under two Los Angeles police cars in 1975. My commitment to live in Los Angeles four or five nights a week for the period of time seemed workable during the school year because I had family lined up to help take care of my sons. The prosecution . . . decided to expand the scope of the trial to include other evidence [of SLA activity including] the kidnapping of Patricia Hearst. The court agreed . . . and a likely two-month trial suddenly because a six-to-eight-month trial.

Within hours, I came to the conclusion that I could not leave my kids for that long a period, and shortly thereafter I asked to withdraw as counsel. This was an extremely difficult decision to make because I was committed to represent Sara. I strongly believe in her innocence. . . . I knew that leaving the case would put both Sara and [my co-counsel] Susan Jordan in a difficult situation. Whenever a lawyer leaves a case, especially a massive one like this, there is a void. . . . However, the decision was clear: My children's needs were more important than any professional considerations.

I was surprised by the positive publicity surrounding my withdrawal. I was portrayed as sacrificing a high-profile case for the sake of my children and taking the moral high road. It was not only embarrassing but strange. After all, I was just a lawyer quitting a case. Then I realized that I was receiving all this attention because it was so unusual for a man to give up anything in his professional life for the sake of his family. If I had been a female attorney in the same situation, there would have been nothing heroic about quitting to care for my children. It would have been expected. . . . [I]n fact, if I had been a woman and had *not* left the case, I probably would have been criticized for being cold and uncaring. . . .

I have had to think a lot about sexual stereotypes since the death of my wife. . . . Sexism is nothing new in our society or in the law. Most female attorneys reading this will probably think, *Duh! Didn't you get this before?* And the answer would be, no I didn't. If Kathy were still alive, I would have gone off to Los Angeles for six months without much of a thought and left her to not only care for our two children but also her very demanding domestic law practice. . . .

I hope the publicity surrounding my withdrawal and my personal situation helps some of us men in the legal profession understand the difficult and painful choices that are faced every day by lawyers, prosecutors, and judges who also happen to be women and mothers. No articles are written about how terrific they are or how difficult their professional choices are.

There is one very big difference between those women and myself: I was forced into this situation by the death of a wonderful person, lawyer, and mother, yet I receive credit for my choices because I am awkward in my new role, and it is uncommon for men to have to make such decisions. Kathleen and many other professional women embrace their roles as mothers and manage the balance between their professional and family lives with grace and ease. I, for one, have learned how difficult their choices are.

NOTES

In modern America, women are often called upon to take primary care responsibility for their children and even the care of or arrangements for aging parents. The following *New York Times* article looks at how one New York prosecutor's office is dealing with the mommy track and what happens when employees are discriminated against because they have caretaking responsibilities.

LISA BELKIN, FAMILY NEEDS IN THE LEGAL BALANCE
The New York Times (July 30, 2006)[4]

Twp unrelated but linked bits of news have been heating up . . . in recent weeks. The first is an announcement by Kathleen M. Rice, the new district attorney in Nassau County, N.Y., that she will not allow part-time work in her office. The dozen prosecutors — mostly women, mostly working a reduced schedule to spend more time with their children — were told they had to ramp up to full time or leave.

The second is the release of a study by the Center for WorkLife Law at the University of California Hastings College of Law in San Francisco, which discovers, in effect, a new category of discrimination suit being brought and being won. Mary C. Still, a faculty fellow at the center and author of the report, has named the subgroup "family responsibilities discrimination," or F.R.D. (You can call it Fred.) The plaintiffs are mostly parents and mostly women, but about 10 percent are men, and some are caring for spouses or parents, not children. All are claiming discrimination at work because they are giving care at home.

Like so many evolving subsets in law, F.R.D. does not exist in any statute. . . . "Discrimination based on caregiving is not an expressed category," said Joan C. Williams, executive director of the center. "It's a reflection of the creativity of lawyers who have set up a new subcategory of litigation within existing workplace discrimination laws."

And they are doing so with increasing frequency. The first case that could be considered F.R.D. was brought in 1971. There were eight such cases in the 1970s. From 1996 to 2005, in contrast, there were 481, which in turn was a 400 percent increase over the total brought during the decade before. Strikingly, all this came at a time when total antidiscrimination cases in general decreased 23 percent.

---

[4] Copyright © 2006 by the New York Times Company. Reprinted by permission.

This is gratifying to Ms. Williams because she helped start the trend. In her book "Unbending Gender: Why Family and Work Conflict and What to Do About It" Ms. Williams refuted the prevailing argument of the time, one she sums up as "You can't sue for work-family conflict; that's a woman's choice." She argued that discrimination suits were justified when limits or penalties were placed on employees simply because of their role as givers of care.

And sue they have in the years since Ms. Williams first made her case. A school psychologist's right to sue was upheld when she accused her district of denying her tenure after telling her it was "not possible to be a good mother and have this job." A sales representative for a mattress company was granted $1.1 million . . . when she was denied a promotion because she had children and her supervisor "did not think she'd want to relocate her family." A woman who was being paid less per hour because of a part-time schedule was awarded $500,000.

It is a trend that has "confounded observers," Ms. Williams says, because these decisions are being upheld by both liberal and conservative judges. Recently the Supreme Court ruled unanimously in favor of a man fired for taking time off to care for his extremely ill wife and, also unanimously, confirmed a lower-court ruling in favor of a woman whose hours were changed, preventing her from caring for her son, who has Down syndrome.

. . . .

Which takes us back to the Nassau County district attorney. It would be simple to paint her as an uncaring throwback, a woman without children and no sympathy for those who do. But, as she explained in an op-ed response in Newsday this month, it is more complicated. "By county mandate," she writes, "the district attorney's office is limited in the number of prosecutors it can have at any one time. Each part-time employee takes up one position as though he or she were a full-time prosecutor."

But there have to be other ways. Changing the staffing formula comes to mind, so that part-time workers count as, well, part-time workers. As Ms. Williams points out, that might not merely be the right thing to do, it might also be the best legal route — because, I am told, at least one of the lawyers about to lose her part-time schedule has already contacted a lawyer.

3. Women as "Rainmakers," and "Networking." "Rainmaking," creating business, becoming a business center, is what many of the most successful lawyers are all about. But rainmaking means being able to "network," the traditional way lawyers obtain clients. And there can be de facto gender and racial barriers to effective networking: the woman lawyer who has difficulty inviting the male client out to dinner. As Jean MacLean Snyder, a successful rainmaking woman lawyer put it some years ago, "Men take clients out. They take their wives, and the clients — almost always men — take their wives. Women have to renegotiate all of that, right from picking up the phone to say, 'Would you like to go out to dinner?' Or maybe, 'Could I take you out to dinner?' . . . Is the woman going to bring her husband with her? Does the client bring his wife?"[5]

---

[5] Jean MacLean Snder, Oral remarks at 1990 ABA litigation symposium, reprinted in *Woman As Rainmakers*, LITIGATION (Spring 1991).

Networking also suffers significantly because of female, black, or latino lawyers who are not allowed into all-male or all-white clubs. While this problem has decreased considerably in the last decade, it has not disappeared.

And, as Snyder notes, there's still male bonding over sports, "a great source of business for men . . . . Every October several men in our firm get their guns and their permits and go hunting. I can't imagine anything worse. They don't invite me, and I don't want to be invited. But this kind of traditional activity has gone on and still goes on, and women don't have an equal activity . . . ."

Even those women who successfully "learn the rules of the man's world" may find it still does not completely level the playing field. For example, a male lawyer of our acquaintance works primarily with other lawyers advising them on their own attorney practice issues. He has three or four close colleagues to whom he refers cases when he is unable to undertake them himself. He tells us that when he refers a lawyer to one of his male colleagues, his referral is simply accepted. But when he suggests a woman colleague, he is still frequently questioned on her background and experience, even, upon occasion, her age and whether she may look too youthful. "Clearly," he reports, "the lawyers who consult me react very differently when I refer them to a woman lawyer, no matter how well qualified." The implication of inequality seems apparent.

4. Minority Law Students, Minority Attorneys. If the road is tougher for women than men, it may be even more difficult for members of minorities, especially, according to the statistical and anecdotal evidence, African-Americans. Read the following article about the struggles in California after passage of Proposition 209, barring all state-supported affirmative action.

DENNIS PFAFF & MICHAEL UEDA, DESPITE EFFORTS FOR EQUALITY, MINORITY NUMBERS STILL LAG; EXPERTS DEBATE WHY
The Daily Journal (February 11, 1998)[6]

Eric Brooks may represent the enduring image of this country's latest struggle over race, education and the law. Brooks is the sole black student enrolled at Boalt Hall School of Law last year. He found himself in what he called that "unique and unenviable" position after 14 other black Boalt admittees declined to attend in the wake of the University of California's decision to dismantle affirmative action.

It wasn't supposed to end that way. A system born of the civil rights struggles in the 1950s and 1960s to correct past injustices, affirmative action had fallen victim to a widespread perception that it is itself an instrument of unfairness. That backlash culminated in the 1996 passage of California's Proposition 209, which outlawed race-and-sex-based preferences in all state programs and sparked a similar assault nationwide.

Almost lost in the debate, however, is the fact that more than 30 years after . . . the landmark Civil Rights Act of 1964 and the next year's Voting Rights

---

Act . . . there are but a few areas where racial balance has been fully realized. And for the legal profession, affirmative action efforts have failed miserably, many experts on both sides of the debate agree.

For example, in California, a state that is nearly half nonwhite, a State Bar survey in 1993 showed fewer than one lawyer in 10 was a racial minority. The supply of new minority lawyers is not increasing quickly.

There is wide disagreement over why most minorities have failed to make greater gains in the legal profession. "I won't say it's based solely on race," said Randy Jones, a San Diego lawyer who is president of the National Bar Association, the country's main organization of black lawyers. "There are other factors but a lot of them have to do with discrimination." . . .

Brooks' situation confirms the worst fears of critics of "race-blind" admissions. They see what is happening in California and around the country as destroying a crucial bridge between underprivileged minorities and a career in the law.

Among those who successfully made that trip was Gary Lafayette. A black native of South Central Los Angeles, Lafayette unabashedly rode affirmative action to stellar educations at Dartmouth University and Boalt Hall. There is no doubt, he says, that what are now attacked as unfair preferences helped him succeed.

"Without [affirmative action], I would probably be a postman," said Lafayette, a name partner at [his own firm].

But more than three decades after affirmative action became a matter of federal policy, people like Lafayette remain the rarest of the rare — not only a black lawyer but a black law-firm partner.

"There has been very little total progress made in terms of sheer overall numbers," said Raymond Marshall, a black partner at San Francisco's Mc-Cutchen, Doyle, Brown & Enersen.

. . . .

"Many firms tell us that they would like to diversify and have more minorities to reflect the changing society's needs," said Los Angeles legal recruiter Sandy Lechtick, president of Esquire, Inc. Despite that apparent self-interest, however, many discount the efforts firms are making to colorize their rosters.

"Almost every major law firm is giving lip service to affirmative action, and none are achieving it," is the assessment of Robert Gnaizda, general counsel for [San Francisco's] Greenlining Institute, [which has studied the issue.]

. . . .

. . . .

Further fueling the debate are statistics showing that minorities fare much worse than their white counterparts on the bar exam, the last major hurdle before entering the legal profession. With passage rates for some minorities about half that of whites, critics contend schools have been far more interested in boosting their enrollment figures than in the quality of student they have been recruiting.

Affirmative actions proponents, however, argue that such statistics should result in a redoubling of efforts, not the end of them. Scrapping the programs because they have not achieved all their promise, they say, is like firing all the police because crime has not stopped.

Many also argue that over reliance on tests such at the State Bar exam and the Law School Admissions Test is part of the problem. Some even advocate doing away with the bar exam altogether . . . . "Why are we using this arcane and strange device as a measure of merit?" said Neil Gotanda, a professor at Western State University College of Law who has extensively studied affirmative action. "We know it has a disparate impact on minorities."

. . . .

"Why are we using this arcane and strange device as a measure of merit?" said Neil Gotanda, a professor at Western State University College of Law who has extensively studied affirmative action. "We know it has a disparate impact on minorities."

. . . .

Although not all UC schools have suffered such drastic declines in minority enrollment as Boalt — . . . the vision of a solitary Eric Brooks remains compelling to many. . . . Some conservative critics of affirmative action, however, argue that such stories are overblown, and that nationwide minorities will be able to gain admission — if not to Boalt Hall, then to some other law school.

"In fact, there are lots of seats available in law school," said [Gail] Heriot, the University of San Diego law professor who was active in the campaign for Proposition 209. "The issue is, should people of certain races be assured place in the better law schools? I think that's inappropriate."

But the top law firms remain, either by inertia, snobbery or competitive pressures, stuck on recruiting from the "elite" schools such as Boalt, some authorities note . . . . "In California, there is no future for a law school designed solely for the use of Caucasians," said James Brosnahan, a Morrison & Foerster partner.

. . . .

"You hear employers say all the time, 'We can't find qualified people,'" said Jones, the San Diego lawyer. "I think that is a lot of bull."

NOTES

The question of finding minority, and especially black, law students is, of course, not just a California problem. In 2000, the University of Texas admitted only 10 African-Americans. At about the same time, the ABA advised Texas Southern's Thurgood Marshall School of Law to improve its students' low bar passage rates. The law school — largely black — was created as a result of a 1946 suit by an African-American denied admission to UT because of his race.

And in *The Good Black: A True Story of Race in America* (1999), author Paul M. Barrett describes, at page 55, one white partner's view of affirmative action: "There are lots of minorities, African-Americans in particular, who are running around with Harvard and Yale degrees and who are not qualified in any sense" to practice law with his firm.

Read the following article, which seems, unfortunately, to affirm the prevalence of this attitude.

LEONARD M. BAYNES, FALLING THROUGH THE CRACKS: RACE AND CORPORATE LAW FIRMS
77 St. John's Law Review 785 (2002)[7]

[S]ome lawyers of color who work in corporate law firms still have remarkably different experiences than their white counterparts. For instance, in the 1990s, Cleary, Gottlieb, Steen & Hamilton established a "critical mass" of minority associates: thirty African Americans, fourteen Latinos, and twenty-four Asian Americans. Most of the African American associates hired during this period, however, left the firm. Unfortunately, this problem is not confined to Cleary. By the third year, most associates of color leave corporate law firms; whereas, forty percent of associates in general leave during the same time frame. . . .

Evan Davis, a Cleary partner, blamed the departure of many of the African American associates on "the prejudice of low expectations," the type of "subconscious prejudice [that] affects people of color." Former Cleary attorney Roslyn Powell described the problem this way: "Senior associates felt that their views were ignored. You get lousy work assignments, then they say that everything you do is wrong [or they say that] you can't write." . . . Another former black Cleary associate stated that "[Cleary] assume[s] blacks are interested in pro bono, but not corporate transactions. There's this view that we're not really interested in corporate work."

Others focused on Cleary's management structure as the problem. It had "no formal departments" but instead was "organized around informal groups of partners and associates who focus on specific areas of practice such as mergers and acquisitions, tax, intellectual property, or litigation." . . . Some reported that the informality resulted in the formation of racial cliques that kept African American associates from receiving good work assignments. For most of the African American associates, the coup de grace was Cleary's failure to invite senior African American associate Lynn Dummett into the partnership ranks. After the partnership meeting deciding Ms. Dummett's fate, rumors spread that racist comments were made at the meeting. [Many saw this] as a signal that the firm was uninterested in diversifying its partnership ranks.

. . . .

Two very important discrimination cases [have] caused corporate heads to spin. In the first case, Andargachew Zelleke, a cum laude graduate of Harvard Law School, who was of Ethiopian ancestry, alleged that while working at White & Case, senior associate Donald Ries made racially derogatory comments against him. At the time of the suit, White & Case had three Latino partners but no African American partners, [and] only eight African American associates but sixteen Latino ones. [Reis's alleged] comments were . . . (1) Mr. Zelleke was only admitted to Harvard because of affirmative action; (2) Mr. Zelleke was a "black prince"; and (3) Mr. Zelleke "is so stupid because he is half-black." Mr. Ries denied making the derogatory statements; however, other associates allegedly confirmed the charges . . . .

Given Mr. Zelleke's biracial background, White & Case attorneys allegedly were confused over his racial identity. The executive partner of the Los Angeles office wrote: "In the first place, Andy Zelleke's skin is not black . . . . We hire Mexican lawyers. Are they black? I don't know whether they're black or not. Some of them have very dark skin. Do I care? I don't care." This confusion over Mr. Zelleke's racial identity seems disingenuous and misses the point. First, Mr. Zelleke requested that the law firm list him as black in its EEO records. Second, . . . despite how he described himself or appeared, he apparently faced discrimination because of his black identity. Ultimately, White & Case and Mr. Zelleke agreed to a $505,000 negotiated judgment to resolve the lawsuit. It was reputedly "the first race-discrimination lawsuit by an attorney to result in a formal judgment against a major firm."

   . . . .

In the second case, Lawrence Mungin, an African American, Harvard-educated bankruptcy associate, sued his former law firm, Katten Muchin & Zavis, alleging that they racially discriminated against him. The jury awarded Mr. Mungin $2.5 million in damages, including punitive damages of $1.5 million. The Washington Post reported that the award was the largest discrimination judgment against a law firm.

At the time of Mr. Mungin's employment, the firm had only four African American attorneys out of 350 attorneys nationwide, and Mr. Mungin was the only African American attorney in the Washington, D.C. office. Mr. Mungin alleged that the law firm discriminated against him by paying him less than other lawyers in his entering class, by failing to provide him with quality assignments, and by failing to consider him for partner. As several of the department's partners left the firm, Mr. Mungin's status became more precarious. The law firm told him that "he had to handle first-year associate work," even though he was a seventh-year associate. Additionally, the firm lowered his billing rate from $185 to $125 per hour. In his seventh year, the firm failed to officially review his performance. One partner, however, did evaluate him, stating:

"Much of Larry's time is consumed by routine tasks, such as drafting status letters to our client. Occasionally we receive a challenging assignment from AIG [a large client], which Larry accomplishes with great skill. AIG is a very difficult client and Larry's ongoing efforts to coordinate with me have made a potentially troublesome situation, relatively easy. I do not believe that, for the most part, AIG offers challenging work to Larry. Larry nonetheless accomplishes the tasks for AIG with a helpful attitude and a willingness to tackle the unique problems this client presents."

Katten's head partner found this evaluation lauded Mr. Mungin's "affability," not his technical expertise and discounted the evaluation because he did not respect the partner who wrote it. Mr. Mungin was humiliated by the evaluation, and when asked to read it from the witness stand, he cried . . . .

In a highly unusual decision, the D.C. Circuit reversed and remanded the jury verdict. At the hearing, although Mr. Mungin's qualification were not challenged by defense counsel at the lower court or on appeal, Judge Randolph, sua sponte, asked about Mr. Mungin's grades at Harvard and whether he had been fired from his previous law firms. It seems that Judge Randolph engaged in the same stereotypes about African American attorneys that some of the partners in Katten Muchin had. So it should come as no surprise that the D.C. Circuit, by a 2-1 vote, found that no reasonable jury could find for Mr. Mungin and reversed the jury verdict. . . .

5. The San Francisco Experience. In 1989, the Bar Association of San Francisco began a concerted effort to increase the percentages of minority associates and partners in its member law firms. Specific goals were targeted: 15% minority associates or junior counsel and 5% minority partners or senior counsel by the end of 1995; and 25% and 10%, respectively, by the end of the year 2000. San Francisco, a West Coast legal center with a widely diverse population that includes large numbers of African-Americans, Latinos, and Asian-Americans, was perhaps the ideal locus for such a plan.

When it issued its interim report in December 1993, the Bar Association noted a substantial increase in the numbers of minority attorneys, an increase that applied across-the-board to large, mid-sized, and small firms, and corporate law departments. During this period the Association itself had its first minority presidents, a Chinese-American and an African-American, McCutcheon's Marshall, quoted in Pfaff-Ueda article above. The positive result was clearly due in significant part to a system-wide approach, led by the bar association, which made law firm diversity the right road to take, and used this form of "peer pressure" to counter and begin to change deep-seated cultural attitudes. Nevertheless, many firms fell well short of the targeted goals.

Perhaps a more significant problem, however, was that to some observers, while minority hiring had increased, the corporate world's willingness to spread business to minority attorneys lagged far behind. At the annual dinner of the California Minority Counsel Program, then-bar president Marshall threw down the gauntlet, stating that the program "had not helped increase professional opportunities" for "partners of color."[8]

By 1998, while the program's progress had continued for associates, it had slowed substantially for minority partners, especially those who were not Asian. A *Daily Journal* survey found that in California's 20 largest firms, most of them based in the Bay Area, only 38 of the over 3,000 partners were African-American, and 11 of the 20 firms had either one or *no* black partners. Periodic reports in 1999 and 2004 showed that firms remained close to on track for minority associates, but had continued to fall well short of their partnership goal. The bar's own report showed that in the largest firms that were the focus of the study, only 6% of partners were minorities. Worse, in San Francisco's "large mid-sized firms" minority partners comprised 2.6%, a rate the 1999 report described as "dismal." Significantly, the report also found that law firms with affirmative programs to encourage diversity did far better than those that adopted a "color blind" approach.

---

[8] Michael J. Hall, *BASF Leader Calls Minority Plan Weak*, L.A. & S.F. DAILY J., Oct. 24, 1994.

The disappointing numbers reported in 2004 caused the Bar's leadership to redouble their efforts, by including members of the minority bar counsel program on its board of directors, increasing the number of minority law student scholarships, and, perhaps most significantly, raising the visibility of the issue once again.

6. Minority Partners. The following article demonstrates that even when minority members make partner, the struggle may be just beginning. Harvard professor David Wilkins has long examined and written about the experience of black lawyers in large corporate law firms, focusing increasingly on the high attrition rate of African-American lawyers who have already become partners. By doing research among Chicago's population of black partners and conducting interviews with over 150 law firm partners or former partners, Wilkins has developed a clear-eyed look at the causes of black partner attrition.

DAVID B. WILKINS, PARTNERS WITHOUT POWER? A PRELIMINARY LOOK AT BLACK PARTNERS IN CORPORATE LAW FIRMS
2 [Hofstra] Journal of the Institute for the Study of Legal Ethics 15 (1999)[9]

Discussions about law firm diversity tend to treat increasing the number of minority partners as both the ultimate goal and the end of the analysis. The emphasis that diversity advocates place on partnership statistics is understandable.

Nevertheless, . . . just because a minority lawyer becomes a partner does not mean that he or she will stay a partner. In today's competitive environment, partnership is no longer the equivalent of tenure. . . . [A]lthough the term "partner" invokes reassuring connotations of equality, it is now painfully clear that some law firm partners are substantially more equal than others. . . . Partners who make the biggest contribution to the bottom line also tend to have significant influence over firm management. . . .

[M]inority partners are located at the bottom end of the partnership pecking order. . . . Because they have less seniority and clout than their white peers, minority partners are more likely to look for other employment opportunities. . . . At the same time, minority partners live in constant fear of the kind of demotion or even outright expulsion that happens to partners who have neither the financial nor the political resources to protect their interests inside the firm.

[Wilkins then discusses "the vanishing black partner," described his anecdotal evidence, gathered by scores of interviews of African-American partners in Chicago's large firms, and what statistics are available, all which show great attrition among black partners.]

---

9 Copyright © 1999 by Hofstra University School of Law. Reprinted by permission. Professor Wilkins has written several articles about the African-American legal experience, focusing especially on black partners, that he plans to culminate in a book.

The Markets of Power

Partners . . . compete in three distinct markets: the *external* market for clients, the *internal* market for referrals, and the market for *labor*. Each of these markets utilizes a different form of currency.

As many have noted, the currency that brings success in the external market is *connections*. . . . The internal market operates on a different currency . . . *reciprocity*. Partners are more likely to refer business from their existing clients to those who can both do the work well . . . and who can return the favor by sending work back. . . .

Finally, the currency in the labor market is *clout*. Although partners have formal power over associates, [many senior associates can] select the partners for whom they will, and more important, *will not*, work. In a world in which all partners are not created equal, savvy senior associates understand that their best strategy for maximizing their chances of winning the [partnership] tournament lie in developing working relationships with powerful partners whose views will carry weight at partnership time. . . .

Partners with power are, therefore, those partners with significant reservoirs of connections, reciprocity, and clout. Black partners, unfortunately, face significant barriers to obtaining each of these three forms of capital.

Why the Last Typically Remain Last

. . . . Racism . . . cannot provide the full explanation for why black lawyers remain partners without power in many firms. By almost every account, overt racism is on the decline, particularly among highly educated and economically successful whites. Moreover, in recent years many elite firms have instituted programs to try to improve the representation of blacks and other minorities among both partners and associates . . . .

Acknowledging that black professionals are subject to the same forces that affect their white coworkers does not mean, as some conservative commentators have suggested, that black professionals have "transcended" race. . . . When placed in the context of the natural predisposition of human beings to favor those who are most like themselves, it is clear that the simple credo of "class not race" fails accurately to account for the role that race plays in the lives of middle class blacks . . . .

[B]lack lawyers who become partners have had to overcome obstacles that, although not different in kind from those encountered by their white peers, are nevertheless rendered more difficult because of race. Chief among these obstacles is the problem of finding mentors. . . . Black lawyers consistently report that they have difficulty finding partners who are willing to enter into these crucial relationships.

The blacks who make partner have found a way to surmount this challenge. Some have done so by having superior academic credentials, for example, graduating from an elite law school. . . . Thus, seventy-seven percent of all of the black partners listed in the Minority Partners Handbook in 1995 graduated from one of the eleven elite schools from which corporate firms typically recruit, with fully 47% attending either Harvard or Yale law school. . . . Contrary to the skeptic's assertion, therefore, with respect to educational credentials, the average black partner is *better* qualified than his or her white peers.

. . . .

If neither racism nor their own lack of ability dooms the careers of black partners, then why are these lawyers, nevertheless, disproportionately represented among the partners without power? The answer to this question lies in the complex intersection among the institutional dynamics of elite firms, race, and the strategies for becoming a partner with power; strategies that are quite different from those that lead to success as an associate . . . . Moreover, unlike their peers, black partners must also negotiate these pressures in an environment in which they still face negative stereotypes and preconceptions because of their race.

. . . .

A. *The Politics of Rain*

Connections are the currency of the external market for new clients. Given this reality, it should come as no surprise that black partners are at a disadvantage in this market. As one prominent black partner ruefully notes:

> We don't sit in the corporate boardrooms, and our mothers and fathers don't sit in the corporate boardrooms. We're not members of the $40,000-a-head country club and neither are our mothers and our fathers. We're just not naturally networked — because of the history of our country, quite frankly — into the kinds of business opportunities or avenues that our white counterparts are networked into.[10]

To be sure, there are many white partners whose mothers and fathers don't sit on corporate boards either. Unlike the so-called "golden age," elite firm lawyers are no longer chosen primarily on the basis of their social pedigree. Nevertheless, it remains true that blacks are less likely than whites to have the kind of contacts from which important business relationships are developed.

. . . .

There is, however, one area where many black partners have the kind of contacts that produce lucrative business. One of the salient developments in the post civil rights era has been the rise in black political power . . . . Predictably, many black partners have made cultivating black political contacts a major part of their rainmaking strategy.

This political strategy, however, is a double edge sword. The example of the city of Chicago is illustrative. On the positive side, many black lawyers in Chicago's large firms saw their fortunes rise considerably when Harold Washington was elected Mayor in 1983. . . . Washington made it clear that any firm wishing to do business with the city of Chicago would have to demonstrate its commitment to diversity. . . . Several of the black lawyers

---

[10] Chicago partner Frederick H. Bates, quoted in Steven Keeva, *Unequal Partners*, ABA J., Feb. 1993. *See* the Supplemental Readings for a further description of this article.

I interviewed benefitted directly . . . . This reality became bitterly apparent to many black partners in Chicago when Harold Washington died unexpectedly shortly after his reelection in 1987 [and was replaced] by Richard M. Daly (who is white). . . . The repercussions of this new state of affairs for the careers of several black partners in Chicago were both swift and severe. In one particularly graphic example, the day after Washington died, the managing partner of a large Chicago firm called in the firm's only two black partners, both of whom had brought in significant city work, and asked them how they intended to support themselves now that Washington was dead.

B. Getting the Franchise — and Keeping It

. . . . Law firms distribute partner work for existing clients in three ways: inheritance, referrals, and cross marketing. Black partners appear to face significant obstacles in each of these arenas.

1. Inheritance — Although few like to admit it, many of today's senior partners acquired their most important clients the old fashioned way: they inherited them. The process is as familiar as it is rarely discussed. Senior partners with important client relationships bequeath them to favored junior colleagues. As the term implies, this process is traditionally done when the senior partner is about to retire. . . .

The black partners in my study have had little success in the inheritance market. In one of my first interviews, a black partner in a major firm in Chicago challenged me to find one example of a black partner who had either assumed a leading role for one of the firm's important institutional clients or was being groomed to do so in the future. After more than sixty interviews with black lawyers who are either senior associates or partners in Chicago, I have yet to find a single example. . . .

2. Referrals — One of the primary benefits of working in a law firm, as opposed to being a solo practitioner, is the potential for internal referrals. Clients frequently call a lawyer with whom they have a close relationship about a problem outside of that lawyer's areas of expertise. . . . The question remains, however, which of his partners the lawyer will call. . . .

Once again, black lawyers are less likely than their peers to get all or part of the franchise in a given area. . . . To the extent that black lawyers have had fewer mentors as associates, and tend to be more isolated as partners, they are less likely to have the kind of cross-cutting relationships throughout the firm that generate significant referral business. . . .

Finally, to the extent that referring partners seek return business, the barriers black partners face in the external and inheritance markets are likely to impede their chances for referrals as well. . . .

3. Cross Marketing — The final mechanism for generating and allocating business from existing clients is cross marketing . . . . The essence of cross marketing is simply taking a proactive stance towards referrals. Rather than waiting for the client to call with a new kind of problem, law firms are increasingly approaching existing clients about the possibility of doing work for them in other areas. . . .

Several black partners . . . felt that they were excluded from these marketing initiatives for the same reasons that they were largely left out of the inheritance and referral markets. Rarely are black partners considered by their peers to be the "best" lawyers to convince a client to send additional business to the firm. . . .

When they are invited, black partners frequently complain that they are only there for show, perhaps because the client is concerned about diversity, and are rarely given credit for any work that subsequently comes in. . . . Finally, even if a black lawyer learns about the new matter and is asked to participate, successfully convincing firm leaders that he or she deserves significant credit for producing the business depends upon having a substantial amount of institutional clout — exactly what most black partners do not have.

. . . .

And so the circle continues. Black partners have a harder time getting clients from the outside, which in turn undermines their participation in the internal referral market, which in turn stymies their efforts to secure the services of senior associates, which in turn places added burdens on their efforts to recruit clients and solicit referrals. Given this reality, it is no wonder that many black partners have decided to seek their fortunes in arenas other than the large law firm.

NOTES

Suzanne Baer, a New York bar association diversity consultant, reinforces Wilkins' view. Baer was quoted in Steven Keeva's *ABA Journal* article about a fundamental difference between the way white and black Americans see the world: "When you grow up never having to deal with racism, always seeing positive portrayals of people like yourself in the mass media, it creates an adult who has the ability to access wealth and do client development with some confidence, because that person knows that the door he or she is knocking on is going to have a white person behind it. This compensates for the fact that he or she doesn't have family connections. It's very hard for people to understand this automatic benefit . . . even if you're wealthier than the white boy who sat next to you in school."

The paucity of minority general counsel also bears out Wilkins' thesis about "franchise" and "markets." According to an October 1999 *National Law Journal* survey, only 10 of the Fortune 500 companies had minority general counsel — and only one of those was a woman.[11]

7. Facing Dual Discrimination. African-American as well as other minority women lawyers can face dual discrimination.[12] If anything, the road to large firm partnership is even steeper. In 1988, one black woman judge from Atlanta estimated the number of black women lawyers in partnership track positions as *one*. In 1998, a minority placement study showed that while

---

[11] Darryl Van Duch, *Minority GCs Are Few, Far Between*, NATIONAL LAW J., Oct. 18, 1999.

[12] Among other sources, these paragraphs draw from the Hayes and Burleigh *ABA Journal* articles more fully described in the Supplemental Readings.

minority members accounted for only 3% of law firm partners, women were a mere 14% of that small segment.

Government and public service work is much more a part of the minority woman's legal world. A 1998 survey showed 2% of white lawyers — and 2% of male minority attorneys — took public interest jobs after law school. The percentage for minority women was three times higher. Ten years earlier, the *ABA Journal* found that 48% of black women lawyers eventually went into government or public interest law. For all women, this may be one of the indirect effects of the "mommy track." But it is also possibly due to self-selection — a personal commitment to be in a more public service-oriented part of the profession.

Role models undoubtedly play a part as well. NAACP Legal Defense Fund lawyer Gail J. Wright acknowledged that she had been heavily influenced by black women judges, especially New York's Constance Baker Motley, the daughter of a Yale Law School cook and the nation's first black woman federal judge, who "give me a sense of direction and a sense of strength.. They had obstacles so much greater than mine, and they were able to overcome them."

But the obstacles continue. The next article, from an *ABA Journal*, tells the story of "why women of color are vanishing from large law firms."

JILL SCHACHNER CHANEN, EARLY EXITS
A.B.A. Journal (August 2006)[13]

From her office in a curved-glass building in downtown Chicago, Tina Tchen has all the trappings of success: a view, positions in national bar associations and a partnership at one of the country's most prestigious law firms — Skadden, Arps, Slate, Meagher & Flom. To those who know her, Tchen's success is no surprise. A graduate of a top law school, she's worked hard to earn her reputation as a bet-the-company trial lawyer.

What is surprising, though, is that Tchen decided to stick it out at a law firm at all. According to a new study by the ABA's Commission on Women in the Profession, few women of color ever get the kinds of equal opportunities that Tchen received to put them on the road to partnership. As a result, most choose to leave their firms rather than stay and fight for equality.

The study, *Visible Invisibility: Women of Color in Law Firms,* explores the experiences of these women. And what it shows is not pretty.

According to the study, women of color are leaving large law firm practices in droves because they are the victims of an uninterrupted cycle of institutional discrimination.

. . . .

Women of color say race and gender still carry a lot of baggage in the workplace. And nowhere is that baggage more of a burden for them than in large law firms where the good-old-boy network of white male leadership still predominates.

---

[13] Copyright © 2006 by ABA Journal. ABA Journal and ABA Journal eReport are published by the American Bar Association. Reprinted by permission.

The issue has taken on heightened importance for law firms of late as corporate clients are starting to demand diversity — not just in the composition of their legal teams, but also in entire firms. But many women of color report that law firms in general continue to be unresponsive. Though most law firms are making efforts to diversify through recruiting, it seems few pay attention to what happens once women of color actually start working full time at the firm.

Behind the Findings

The commission's study is not the first to spotlight this situation. Study after study show that minority female lawyers have exceptional attrition rates in large law firms, defined as 25 attorneys or more. By some measures, nearly 100 percent of these women leave law firms within eight years. Other studies put the number closer to 66 percent within five years . . . .

"There are very few women of color in law firms. We are basically invisible," says Paulette Brown, a lawyer . . . in Short Hills, N.J., who co-chaired the study for the women's commission.

Brown, who notes that she is one of just three African American women partners in large law firms in the entire state of New Jersey, says that law firm leaders have been ignoring this problem for far too long . . . .

The women's commission enlisted the National Opinion Research Center at the University of Chicago to explore the unique experience of female lawyers of color. Using data obtained from self-administered questionnaires and from focus groups, the study has produced one-of-a-kind qualitative and quantitative data highlighting the differences in the hiring, development and advancement of women of color when compared to their male and nonminority counterparts in law firms, says Arin Reeves, a Chicago lawyer and diversity consultant who served as a co-chair of the study for the commission.

. . . .

Reeves says she sees women of color slipping through the cracks of law firms. Others, she says, are pushed out, while still more read the tea leaves and jump. "We are losing incredible talent from our profession because we have not been able to value, integrate and respect women of color," she says.

"The attrition has different points of origination, but, I think for a lot of law firms, . . . even if you decide to jump; you are not making the decision to jump in an ideal world.where you have the some opportunities," Reeves adds.

Skirting the Periphery

While many law firms have diversity initiatives that focus on either gender or race, few — if any — pay attention to the overlap of these factors known as "intersectionality," says Reeves. And that's where many of the problems lie. "Women of color often are twice removed," she explains. As a result, she says, they tend to feel isolated and operate on the periphery in law firms.

[M]any of these women of color working in large law firms are recruited from top law schools and often are at the top of their class, [but] 43.5 percent of the women of color surveyed reported missing out on desirable assignments because of race or gender . . . compared to 25 percent of men of color, 38.6 percent of white women and 1.9 percent of white men. And 42.6 percent said they did not have access to client development and client relationship opportunities due to their race or gender . . . .

Like others, Tehen suspects that minority women are inadvertently overlooked when work assignments are made. It likely happens because of individuals' comfort zones. "The people handing out the work are more comfortable with others like themselves, and since the majority of the people handing out the work are white men it is just perpetuating itself."

. . . .

Seattle lawyer Jacqueline Parker, now first vice president and counsel of Washington Mutual Bank, came to work at a large law firm with several years of experience in banking and finance and still found herself being denied opportunities. "I wanted to do financial services work, and if the partners and senior associates were not willing to give it to me, that is when I knew that it was time to find another opportunity," she says.

It was not until Parker approached a black partner at her firm and asked why she was not being given the opportunities she wanted that she was introduced to a senior white lawyer with substantial business in her preferred practice area.

Parker says the relationship she developed with these two lawyers helped her not only at the firm, but also in her law career. "I got absolutely invaluable feedback about what I did right and wrong," she says. But she wonders what would have happened without the support of these lawyers who took her under their wings.

Indeed, Parker's experience points to another issue raised by the surveyed women of color: the lack of mentoring . . . .

Finding a mentor is difficult enough, but it's tougher for minority women lawyers because there are so few senior women of color in law firms to whom they can relate.

. . . .

Reports of Overt Racism

Perhaps the most noteworthy finding of the women's commission study, however, was that nearly half of minority women lawyers reported that they are experiencing frequent and blatantly racist behavior in the workplace. According to the study, some 49 percent of the women of color surveyed reported experiencing demeaning comments or other types of harassment.

. . . .

The [anonymous] Am Law 100 associate says many women she knows have found that, no matter how well-educated they are, they cannot endure the treatment they suffered at these law firms because of racism. "It breaks my heart because their spirits were broken here," she says. This lawyer says she does not know why she has put up with the discrimination she personally has experienced, but she now is enjoying seeing senior lawyers be solicitous to her after she developed a substantial book of business. "I've learned that black does not matter; green does."

NOTES

As we have noted before, in many respects, overt racism is relatively easy to deal with — the enemy you know. The more insidious indirect issues — doing a lot to recruit but very little to mentor, or not understanding why women of color "jump" from the firm — are more difficult to address. The solution, as the last lawyer quoted notes, is developing one's own book of business. But developing that business is where the latent racial issues provide among the biggest hurdles.

8. Is Bias an Ethical Issue? The answer to this question is, increasingly, "yes." In the past few years, many states have passed disciplinary rules prohibiting discrimination by lawyers. Unlike most rules, whose development begins on a national level through the ABA, individual states, often motivated by local lobbying, have taken the lead in developing bias rules. As a result, and because these rules have little in the way of precedent to guide their direction, the substance of the rules varies widely from state to state.

By 1995, over half the states had anti-bias rules. In about 10 states, bias misconduct must be connected to the practice of law, and does not cover such issues as discrimination in employment. Other jurisdictions — including three of the nation's largest, New York, California, and the District of Columbia — have barred employment discrimination as well.

Nevertheless, the enforcement impact of rules prohibiting employment discrimination is likely to be slight. In Vermont, for example, according to *Texas Lawyer*, a female Burlington attorney filed an employment discrimination complaint only to be told that the bar did not have the resources to investigate it. D.C.'s rule has generated very few complaints. And in New York and California, prohibited conduct may not result in discipline unless there is first a civil adjudication that the lawyer's conduct was wrong, a precondition that severely limits the rule's impact.

Since 1995, some of the focus has shifted from discrimination against women and minorities to bias encountered by gays and lesbians and those with disabilities. The National Association for Law Placement (NALP) began tracking lawyers by sexual preference in 1996. Everyone involved with the process admits this is harder to do than to track the progress of minorities and women, as sexual preference is not physically apparent, and because — at least in some parts of the country — sexual preference is not a characteristic lawyers always openly acknowledge. Whether it is because of increased hiring or increased self-reporting, the numbers of gay and lesbian attorneys hired at law firms seem to have risen significantly.

Disabled lawyers face a far more difficult mountain to climb. A 1996 NALP survey showed that only 54% of disabled lawyers found full-time law jobs, and less than half of those jobs were in private practice. And courts may serve, as one continuing education video put it, as "obstacle courts" for those with disabilities.

Are anti-discrimination rules effective? These rules, Washington, D.C. lawyer David Isbell told the *National Law Journal*, are "likely to serve mainly a hortatory purpose" rather than be a "major disciplinary tool." But if Isbell, who served as chair of the ABA ethics committee that considered such a rule, is correct, are anti-bias rules justified? Yes, says Isbell, because they "set a useful standard" that lawyers should try to meet. Still, one must wonder how deep the commitment to anti-bias rules runs among state regulatory agencies if regulations are drafted without enough teeth to make them truly enforceable. Should a civil adjudication of discrimination be necessary when, for example, a criminal adjudication of theft is not required to discipline lawyers who steal money from their client trustee accounts?

9. Bias in the Courts. Bias in the legal profession is not limited to the words and actions of lawyers. Indeed, if anything our courts are slower to change than the rest of the profession. One problem that has gotten widespread publicity in recent years is the lack of minority clerks working at the United States Supreme Court. In the late 1990s, *USA Today* and *Legal Times*, the Washington D.C. law daily, reported that only seven of the 394 clerks hired by the nine sitting justices were African-American, and only four were Latino. Tony Mauro, longtime Supreme Court reporter for *American Lawyer* and its affiliates, reported that civil rights and minority bar groups attempted to sit down with then-Chief Justice Rehnquist in 1998 to discuss the situation, but he refused to meet with them.[14]

The nation's highest court hasn't fared much better when it comes to women clerks. Indeed, for the Fall 2006 Supreme Court term, only seven of the 37 law clerkships went to women, half the number for previous year, according to Pulitzer-prize-winning Supreme Court reporter Linda Greenhouse in the *New York Times*.[15] The *Times* reports that from 2000 to 2006 only 7% of Justice Scalia's clerks were women, and only 11% of Justice Kennedy's. While on the appeals court, both new justices, Roberts and Alito, had a ratio of male to female clerks of greater than 4:1.

The high court does not stand alone. A September 1998 report found that of 66 research attorneys at the California Supreme Court (these are permanent staff positions, not law clerks who cycle through the courts), there were two Asian-Americans, one African-American, and no Latinos. The only minority member of the First District Court of Appeals' 52-lawyer research staff was a single Latino lawyer.[16]

Lack of minority research attorneys is just the tip of the iceberg. Judges' power means that their behavior often is not subject to the same checks found in most law firms. In 1990 a California commission found widespread sex discrimination among the state's judges. The commission's report cited "openly hostile" attitudes, demeaning remarks, inappropriate sexual advances, even telling dirty jokes on the bench. "Across the board," said the report, "we see

---

[14] Tony Mauro, *Supreme Court Doors Opening Slightly*, LEGAL TIMES & AM. LAW. MEDIA, March 6, 2000. This article discusses a conference at Howard University that focused on this issue.

[15] Linda Greenhouse, *Women Suddenly Scarce Among Justices' Clerks*, N.Y. TIMES, Aug. 30, 2006.

[16] *See* Greg Mitchell, *No Place at the Table*, THE RECORDER (San Francisco), Sept. 18, 1999.

one common thread — and that is the lack of credibility that women receive, whether they are lawyers or other participants in the process."

In the decade since, sex discrimination on the bench has abated but hardly ceased. We invite anyone with doubts about whether women routinely face subtle forms of bias from the bench to try the test we discuss in Section 2 above about the disparate reactions to the male and female lawyers needing to care for their children.

Occasionally, overt incidents of sexism or racism continue to occur. In two 1999 cases, one Arizona judge, among numerous other offenses, e-mailed raunchy sexual material to his staff, while a Syracuse, New York judge — among other charges — commiserated with a prosecutor by describing an elderly murder victim as "just some old nigger bitch." The Arizona judge resigned and the New York judge was removed.

As most of the authors in these readings have pointed out, bias is usually not a matter of prejudice this overt, but rather subtle and almost unstated forms of unequal treatment. This unequal treatment is often due to people's expectations of the situation, expectations that have developed over many years by a society dominated by white males — the traditionally predominant group from which judges are selected.

10. Making Diversity Work in the Law Firm. The writer of this last piece is not a lawyer, but someone who works often with law firms. As a management consultant dedicated to "creative cultural changes," Jacob Herring sees firsthand the problems of dealing with diversity issues. In this hard-hitting article, he suggests that the negative messages minority members get from law firms originate from cultural assumptions about people of color. His many thoughtful and provocative ideas about bias in the workplace, its causes and its remedies, make this an excellent close to our discussion.

JACOB H. HERRING, DIVERSITY IN THE WORKPLACE
San Francisco Attorney (October/November 1992)[17]

If you're looking for resistant hold-outs regarding workforce diversity, look no farther than most U.S. law firms.

For over 15 years I have worked with Fortune 100 companies and government agencies in . . . managing and valuing racial and gender diversity, and my experience tells me that diversity, at its best, thrives in an environment where it receives the support of the organization. Corporations that made the transition to the diverse workplace in the early-to-mid '70s are now working on issues of true corporate culture change: they know that minority men and white women have different experiences, and they are striving to reduce barriers to allow *all* their employees to achieve in their organizations.

This is rarely the case with law firms, which by nature represent the conservative tendencies to maintain the status quo. . . . Combining a lack of awareness with a determination to reinforce comfortable "norms," law firms have barriers to achieving, much less encouraging, workforce diversity. The partners, by-and-large, are not trained in management skills and concepts,

---

[17] Copyright © 1992 by Jacob N. Herring. Reprinted by permission.

and many approach human issues as legal problems to be litigated rather than issues directly related to how people respond to each other.

The vast majority of American companies and law firms were built for, by, and about able, married, apparently straight white men. . . . Thus, women, people of color, gays and lesbians, and people of varied physical and learning abilities get left out of the overall culture of their respective [organizations].

Almost all of the firms with which I work perceive themselves to be liberal on issues of race and gender; in their own perception, they are more liberal than the next individual or firm, and their deep, genuine *feelings* about diversity sometimes remain unrecognized and unexamined.

I assume that when individuals in an outwardly sincere attempt to embrace and foster diversity send messages that convey racist or sexist attitudes, they are genuinely not conscious of the impact of such messages. (. . . [M]ost organizations' internal systems limit the effectiveness of individuals who are consciously bigoted. . . .)

[A]ll of us, to varying degrees, have been programmed to see each other not as we in fact are — as unique individuals — but as the culture would have us see each other.

Our culture programs us to think about and see each "other" in particular ways.

For example, cultural assumptions about white men are that they are generally insensitive, racist, sexist, power-hungry, ruthless . . . .

Blacks are considered lazy, irresponsible, violent and dumb.

Hispanics are considered possessors of many of the same dubious "characteristics" as blacks, with "hot-blooded" and "hot headed" thrown in for good measure.

Asians are assumed to be hard workers, not very assertive, and usually submissive.

And women — assumed to be someone else's possessions, sex objects, and nurturers — are further limited through some religious groups' influence that dictate "woman's place."

This cultural assumptions programming is provided by parents, schools, churches, the media — via messages that are reinforced until one believes them. Once the cultural assumptions are believed or accepted without examination, they become institutionalized. After awhile, one accepts them as valid because the cultural assumptions are most of what one has heard about the "other" group.

Cultural assumptions are so powerful that they can alter the way we see individuals with whom we interact daily and in intimate relationships, such as marriage. But cultural assumptions are absolutely devastating and most limiting when applied to groups with which we have very little interaction, leaving no opportunity to dispel myths.

Thus, the black male partner who is seen on-site after hours is assumed to be "up to something"; the physically attractive female associate "invites" flirting; the hispanic associate lives for a "good time."

Another reason that women, minorities, and "others" (read: not straight while males) get negative messages in and from law firms is due to certain innate characteristics of communication.

Communication is composed of two major elements: digital communication and analog communication. Digital communication consists of words put together in a grammatical and syntactical fashion. It has the advantage of being precise and elegant, but can also mislead and, in fact, lie. Analog communication is everything else beyond digital communication, such as the context in which something is said. Voice volume, pitch, and rhythm, body language, gestures, etc. . . .

In face-to-face interactions, 65% or more of what is communicated is analog communication. It is the ambiguity of analog communication that presents the problem. While people may use digital communication to say things that are socially acceptable, their analog communication sends negative messages — leaving individuals or full departments off memo rotations, not informing people about meetings, etc. . . .

Sometimes people send negative messages that do not represent their true intent, like the male partner who lauds a female associate for "finally learning to think like a man," or the sincere associate who mentions to his new-found colleague over drinks that "I don't even think of you as being black anymore!"

Minorities and white women are predisposed to make or give negative interpretations of dominant group behavior (read: white in general or white men in particular), because their cultures and their experience in and out of work over a lifetime tell them that negative interpretations are more often valid than not, and are the least risky approach to workplace survival. While white men are ignorant of the cultural assumptions made about them, they unknowingly play those cultural assumptions out, not realizing that they are being scrutinized. . . .

White men are unique in that they are the only group in our society that truly perceives themselves as individuals, with little or no *group* identity. So, one white male observing another behaving in a way that reinforces the negative cultural assumptions about white men does not usually speak up to check the offensive behavior of his colleague. And, in fact, does not usually *feel the need* to do so.

Minorities, white women, and disabled people at least *feel* that they want to check the offending behavior of others in their groups, and a lot of their behavior is governed by how it reflects not only on them as individuals, but also on them as a group. They do this because they know that negative behavior on their part or on the part of their same-group peers will result in each member of the group receiving negative image reinforcement.

. . . .

Those who are not white males, then, get small, ambiguous, subtle messages — "micro-gressions" — that make them feel bad. A significant number of people of color and white women are predisposed to interpret such messages negatively, resulting in feelings of alienation, anger, and rage. Such feelings get in the way of bonding with the firm's partners and other associates. . . .

In order to change this, the partners must examine their own organizations' cultures and . . . be willing to change those elements that interfere with diversity, because the behavior of employees is more determined by the corporate or organizational culture and structure than by anything else. . . .

Profit motives aside, partners who are dead serious about encouraging diversity in their law firms and client bases see it from a moral and creative perspective, and they see how it's going to help them and achieve their higher goals. They already know *why* they want to embrace diversity; they just want to know *how* to make it happen. . . . Some law firms attempt to embrace diversity because they have to — clients, partners, the Bar, and other influences are pressuring them. They often are not resistant so much as indifferent, and indifference still creates roadblocks to bringing about effective change and true diversity. Those who adamantly resist, choosing to act at their own pace or not at all, find in time that their inaction may be quite detrimental when valuable associates "vote with their feet" by leaving. . . .

While preparing for the global marketplace of the future, *all* American corporate environments, in order to maintain their positions, to stimulate growth from within, and to "do the right thing," need to address issues of workplace diversity, and law firms should become the pioneers in managing it. After all, it is the interpretation of law that not only governs, but defines what we as a society should be and do.

NOTES

Note that while Herring begins by saying law firms are behind other businesses in dealing with diversity issues, he ends by holding out hope that they can lead the way in the future. Is he being overly optimistic? Or are law firms, schooled in the law and focused on what society should be and should do, the best place to look for progressive change?

SUPPLEMENTAL READINGS

1. Rand Jack & Dana Crowley Jack, *Moral Vision and Professional Decisions: The Changing Values of Women and Men Lawyers* (1989). Chapter 5 of this book is excerpted in 57 Fordham L. Rev. 933 (1989). This study, by an attorney and a developmental psychologist, while done some time ago, is a thorough and interesting look at the different roles played by men and women in the law firm setting, and the ways in which women must "pattern" themselves to adapt to this setting.

2. Cynthia Grant Bowman, *Women and the Legal Profession*, 7 Am. U. J. Gender Soc. Pol'y & L. (1998), is an interesting article that reaffirms the slower progress of women up the law firm ladder but also argues that the subtle forms of discrimination against women in litigation have become more overt in recent years.

3. Lisa Brennan, "Women Having It All," *National Law Journal*, August 17, 1998, p. 1, reports on a group of women making it in the legal world as law firm partners and in their personal lives as parents, with a lot of support at both ends of their lives.

4. Stanford ethics professor Deborah Rhode has written several important and cogent academic pieces on women and the law, including *Perspectives on Professional Women*, 40 Stan. L. Rev. 1163 (1988), *Myths of Meritocracy*, 65 Fordham L. Rev. 585 (Nov. 1996) and *Lesbians in the Law: Sex-Based Discrimination: Common Legacies and Common Challenges*, 5 S. Cal. Rev. L. & Women's Stud. 11 (Fall 1995).

5. Several valuable more recent articles are: Christine Alice Corcos, *We Don't Want Advantqages: The Woman Lawyer Hero and Her Quest for Power in Popular Culture*, 53 Syracuse L. Rev. 1225 (2003), which explains popular culture's impact on images of women attorneys — and the disadvantage they face because of the lack of woman iconic heroes; Patricia Hatamyar & Kevin M. Simmons, *Are Women More Ethical Lawyers? An Emperical Study,* 31 Fla. St. U. L. Rev. 785 (2004), an interesting project showing that woman are significantly less likely to be disciplined by the bar than men; and Judith L. Maute, *Writings Concerning Women in the Legal Profession*, 1982-2002, 38 Tulsa L. Rev. 167 (2002), a thorough review of the literature on this subject.

6. Reed Abelson, "A Push From the Top Shatters a Glass Ceiling," *New York Times* (August 22, 1999), is not about law firms, but the story of how Hewlett-Packard's board chairman developed an appreciation for the value of women in the workplace and later fought for a woman to succeed him as CEO of the company.

7. *Hishon v. King & Spalding*, 467 U.S. 69, 104 S. Ct. 2229 (1984), held that a woman lawyer who was denied an invitation to become a partner could state a cognizable claim of sex discrimination under Title VII of the 1964 Civil Rights Act.

8. Steven Keeva, "Unequal Partners," *ABA Journal* (Feb. 1993), which we excerpted in our first edition, is an important and thorough article about the dissatisfaction and high attrition rates of black partners, that particularly in Chicago. Keeva has long been a staff writer and editor for the *ABA Journal*. Like Professor Wilkins, he interviewed many African-American partners, and gained substantial insight into the difficult road black partners face even after partnership.

9. In addition to the more recent effort excerpted above, *The ABA Journal* has produced two important articles about black women in the law: Nina Burleigh, "Black Women Lawyers — Coping With Dual Discrimination," (June 1, 1988), and Arthur S. Hayes, "Color-Coded Hurdle" (February 1999). The latter article came from a particularly valuable February 1999 issue of the *ABA Journal* magazine featuring 16 different articles on race and the law.

Chapter 11

MENTAL HEALTH, SUBSTANCE ABUSE, AND THE REALITIES OF MODERN PRACTICE

PROBLEM 29

Lawyers work high stress jobs in a high stress world. The rewards of the profession can be great, but so are the pressures. Lawyers' work can impaired by mental illness, all sorts of addictions and two increasingly prevalent problems, gambling, given the instant availability of the Internet and the addictive nature of the problem, and dementia, related to the growing aged population of lawyers who do not retire, some of whom exhibit signs of Alzheimer's and other serious impairments. The incidence of lawyer drug abuse — all drugs, but most particularly alcohol, is high: Higher than for other professions. And when a lawyer loses control to addiction, be it to alcohol, drugs, or something else, the lawyer's colleagues — and clients — often suffer as well. Here, our problem focuses on alcoholism, but the same issues would apply in similar ways to these other circumstances.

A Lawyer in Trouble and His Friends on the Spot

Bill "Rabbit" Worthington is partner at the firm of Dill, Straight & Smith, one of the oldest and most prestigious law firms in town. Worthington has been with the firm for over 30 years. His colleagues call him "Rabbit" because of his creativity in facing and solving new legal problems. They used to say at Dill, Straight that he could take an impossible case and pull a rabbit out of his hat to win it, hence his nickname.

I. Recently, things have changed for Worthington. At first he seemed simply less efficient and energetic. Everyone thought he was just going through a "lazy spell." But there began to be other telltale signs. He seemed to get little done after lunch, and those who ate with him noted that his lunchtime "glass" of wine had become three or four. "Rabbit" had long had an "open door" policy, encouraging late afternoon "schmoozing" with young associates who wanted the benefit of his counsel; his office had been dubbed "the Rabbit warren" because of all the traffic and activity centered there. In the past several months, though, Rabbit's door has stayed closed most afternoons, and he often doesn't emerge at all until he heads for home.

Chuck Chenier is the firm's managing partner, and a friend of Rabbit's since law school. He has begun noticing a strong smell of alcohol on Rabbit's breath in the afternoons. He has also observed that Worthington just doesn't seem like "the old Rabbit." What, if anything, should he do about this?

II. Another year has gone by. Chuck Chenier talked to Rabbit, who promised to "get myself under control," but otherwise Chuck has taken no action. In the past several months, the associates who work with Rabbit have noticed problems with his work. He lost one client's original documents, only to find them months later in another client's file. One late afternoon, as the deadline for filing neared, his draft memo of a key motion was nowhere to be found, and no one knew where Rabbit was either. His secretary rummaged through his briefcase until she found a tape and retranscribed it. He now loses paperwork so often that his secretary has begun to open his mail and keep a copy of everything in a cabinet known as "Rabbit's file."

Jane Diaz is a second year associate at the firm. She was originally thrilled that one of the partners she was assigned to work with was Worthington. Jane had heard of him, and at first found him to be just like she imagined, but she increasingly became aware of Rabbit's work sloppiness and found herself having to "cover" for him more and more. Last week, she and Worthington were with a major client who was being deposed by opposing counsel. It was Jane's first "big" case, and she was excited. Rabbit "defended" the deposition, but to Jane just didn't seem to be paying attention. He failed to object several times to questions which Jane thought were obviously irrelevant and prejudicial. His breath smelled like alcohol, though Jane wasn't sure anyone else could detect it.

QUESTIONS

1. What should Jane do? Should she discuss the matter with Chuck Chenier? Should she talk directly to Worthington? Or is the matter simply not something she should tackle herself?

2. What, if anything, should Chenier do?

3. What, if anything, should be done about Rabbit's clients? Should they be told anything, and if so, what should they be told?

III. Think about what you would do if you discovered that a good friend and colleague, your fellow law student or associate, had developed a mental health, substance abuse, or gambling problem. Is there anything that you feel you *must* do?

READINGS

1. Current Statistics on Lawyers and Depression. As this first article explains, lawyers have the dubious distinction of having the highest rate of depression of any profession. And studies show a clear correlation between depression and drug and alcohol abuse as people attempt to self-medicate.

JOAN E. MOUNTEER, DEPRESSION AMONG LAWYERS
33 Colorado Lawyer 35 (2004)[1]

Everyone experiences the occasional "blue day" or a period of feeling "down." It also is normal to feel sadness or grief after a loss. Sadness is a part of life. But chronic feelings of sadness are not a normal part of life. Depression, a serious medical disorder, differs vastly from the transitory state of feeling "down in the dumps."

---

[1] Copyright © 2004 by the Colorado Lawyer and Colorado Bar Association. Reprinted by permission.

Depression produces a profound low mood and influences a person's thoughts, feelings, health, and behavior. It is an illness, just like heart disease and cancer are illnesses. At one time or another, depression will afflict more than 25 percent of the population. It strikes all ages, all races, all economic groups, and both sexes . . . . Fortunately, depression can be successfully treated in approximately 80 percent of cases.

Depression is not something to be ashamed of. It is not a character flaw or a sign of personality weakness. Moreover, it is not a "mood" that a person can "snap out of," any more than a person can "snap out of" diabetes. Depression strikes the legal profession more often than any other profession . . . .

Symptoms of Depression and Contributing Factors

According to Dr. Amiram Elwork, a clinical psychologist and director of the Law & Psychology Training Program at Widener University in Minnesota, the symptoms of depression come in clusters and include the following:

- Persistent sad, anxious, "empty" mood
- Feelings of hopelessness, pessimism
- Feelings of guilt, worthlessness, helplessness
- Loss of interest or pleasure in ordinary activities, including sex
- Withdrawal from family and friends
- Sleep disturbances (insomnia, early morning waking, or oversleeping)
- Eating disturbances (either loss or gain of appetite and weight)
- Decreased energy, fatigue, being "slowed down"
- Thoughts of death or suicide, suicide attempts
- Restlessness or irritability
- Increased alcohol consumption (self-medication)
- Difficulty concentrating, remembering, making decisions
- Physical symptoms (such as headaches, digestive disorders, and chronic pain) that do not respond to treatment.

Depression in the Legal Profession

In a study of more than 100 occupations, lawyers had the highest rate of depression. In fact, lawyers are almost four times more likely to experience depression than the general population. Aside from depression, one in four lawyers also experience feelings of inadequacy and inferiority in personal relationships, as well as anxiety or social alienation, at much higher rates than the population at large.

Especially among lawyers, depression can be life-threatening . . . . A disproportionate number of lawyers commit suicide, unfortunately during middle age, when they would be most productive. Some attribute this to the depressed lawyer's typical retreat into isolation, which greatly enhances the risk of acting on suicidal thoughts . . . .

Why is depression such a problem in the profession? First, the increase in the number of lawyers likely has led to increased competition and diminishing personal relationships with other lawyers. Second, new technology creates an unrelenting and faster work pace. Also, the law is overwhelmingly complex today. Changing legal standards make it difficult to know how to advise clients, and courts render so many decisions that it is not easy to understand what the law actually is. The only certainty is that whatever the causes, lawyers suffer increased rates of burnout, disillusionment, and dissatisfaction, which can lead to attorney neglect of files, anxiety, depression, substance abuse, or suicide.

Because depression impacts productivity in the workplace, lawyers toiling under its burdens can cause irreparable damage to clients, law firms or offices, and the legal profession, as well as to their own health. A major hurdle for depressed lawyers is to realize they are, in fact, depressed. Depression is insidious. Often, those who suffer from depression do not recognize it as such. This may be because those who have lived with suffering for so long are used to feeling depressed or are out of touch with their feelings — being depressed can have a numbing effect.

Empirical research suggests that lawyers have personality characteristics that distinguish them from the general population . . . . Lawyers are trained to be rational and objective. This training, combined with the devaluation of emotional concerns and feelings, can become obstacles to seeking help. Due to their unique personality traits, lawyers may not recognize their own problem until the disciplinary committee comes knocking on the door.

NOTES

Not every lawyer suffers from depression, any more than all lawyers are alcoholics. But since many lawyers have personalities that make it *difficult to recognize symptoms*, being aware of this fact should help increase our awareness and watchfulness — in our friends and in ourselves.

2. A Case History of a Lawyer in Trouble. What happens when a lawyer uses drugs or alcohol to excess? When no one intervenes to prevent such behavior, the consequences can be a swift slide down a slope towards legal oblivion. At first, the consequences may be personal to the attorney, but over time, the clients of that lawyer and the lawyer's firm will likely begin to feel the effects. Read what happened to one fallen lawyer and how his misfortune affected his life, both negatively and positively.

BARBARA MAHAN, DISBARRED
California Lawyer (July 1992)[2]

Most lawyers expect a lot from their careers. They endure three rough years of law school, a grueling bar exam and the long hours necessary to establish a practice. In return they hope for such benefits as a high salary, respected status and the satisfaction of helping clients.

---

[2] Copyright © 1992 by Barbara Mahan. Reprinted by permission.

Sometimes it works out that way; sometimes it doesn't. . . . Lawyers become disenchanted with what they do, or how they do it, or what it brings them. They make mistakes — little ones at first, then bigger and bigger ones. The system they swore to uphold doesn't seem worth the effort anymore. They violate the standards of the profession or the law itself. Stories about these lawyers we hear only in whispers, or read in the stilted prose of a State Bar disciplinary report.

The accounts below come from five former lawyers who were either disbarred or resigned because they were certain they would be disbarred. Banished from the profession, they testify here from the legal underground. They agreed to be interviewed . . . [because] they believed either that telling their stories would help others or that it would help them face and accept their pasts. . . .

Two of the former lawyers who speak here . . . abused alcohol or drugs. That is not a coincidence. The State Bar estimates that 30 to 50 percent of discipline cases are related to substance abuse.

From their vantage outside the profession, these men touch on several common themes. One is the economic and social cost of being forced from their work. Disbarred lawyers not only lose their ticket to practice law; they lose their financial security. Many go bankrupt. Their marriages or relationships fail, their friends drift away, their colleagues don't call, their health begins to falter.

Another theme is the depth of their personal loss. Cast from legal society, they question their identities and self-worth. They agonize at failing their fathers and their own children. Some wonder if there is any point in going on; they contemplate escape or suicide.

A third is the difficulty of starting over. Educated for the law, former practitioners can't or don't want to find a new career. Many become paralegals, doing much of the same work they performed as lawyers at substantially less pay. Those who attempt new kinds of work usually struggle for a period after making the switch.

A final, unexpected theme is a growing sense of social responsibility. Two lawyers who once were consumed by addictions now help others stop abusing drugs and alcohol. . . .

After they resigned or were disbarred, some of these men became better fathers, sons, husbands and friends. They saw clearly some things that had been clouded or hidden. Their failures, in varying degrees, appear to have led to redemption. Deprived of their profession, they gave more of themselves to other people than they ever had before.

In reviewing their stories, one cannot help wondering whether these former lawyers would have achieved the same advances in self-awareness and social commitment had they not suffered the loss of their profession . . . .

David K. Demergian

By his second year out of law school, David Demergian had reached a level of success that many young lawyers dream of. He had established his own practice in San Diego, landed some top real estate clients and was making well into six figures a year. He had an expensive home, a pretty wife, a Mercedes and a baby daughter. But for Demergian, it wasn't enough.

In 1983 he started pulling this dream life apart. He fell in love with his secretary and left his wife and child. Single for the first time in years, he threw himself into a fast lane of parties and women. He began representing topless and bottomless clubs, dancers and drug defendants. It made him feel good to walk into exotic bars and be treated like a big shot.

In late 1984 his secretary introduced him to freebase cocaine, and within a short time he was hooked. His addiction, which lasted only seven months, cost him his profession, his financial solvency and his self-respect. He believes it also cost him his father's life.

Demergian, 39, has turned his life around since his disbarment. Once concerned chiefly with the power, prestige and trappings of the law, he now works as a law clerk, drafting documents to which he cannot sign his name. He has married again, has another daughter and spends a lot of time with his girls. . . .

In his spare time Demergian works with lawyers and judges who are alcoholics and addicts. A consultant for The Other Bar [a rehabilitation program sponsored by the California State Bar], Demergian gets up to 40 calls a month for help, from people in trouble and from their families, colleagues and friends. He tells them his story of catastrophe and hope, and attempts to offer others what he wishes he could have found: a way off the path toward self-destruction before everything was lost.

Until I got hooked on freebase cocaine around December 1984, my law practice had been exemplary. But by January or February 1985, I no longer went into the office. I stayed home every day, calling in for trials, saying I was sick. All day long I smoked cocaine. The high ends quickly, and the crash is lower than anything you can imagine. So every 10 or 15 minutes I would take another hit. Then I would clean my place. I had all this energy. I arranged my shirts in my closet alphabetically by color. I recorded oldies from the radio, 20 cassettes of them, and cross-indexed the songs. I only went to the office late at night to use the computer for my oldies index and to pick up any money that came in.

In seven months I went through $80,000. Unfortunately, only $60,000 of it was mine. In April or May 1985 I took $20,000 from a client trust fund, the proceeds of the sale of a client's house in a divorce settlement. I had run out of money. . . . I told myself I would pay it back. The denial involved in my addiction was frightening and extreme. . . .

On Father's Day 1985 around 3 a.m. my doorbell rang. I had been up all night having a party, and there were half-naked girls and drugs all around. I opened the door and there on the doorstep was my father, who was a doctor. He had flown out from Wisconsin because Stephanie, the woman who is now my wife, called him and said, "Your son is killing himself with drugs." My father and I had always been close. But I wouldn't let him in. The tears were streaming down his face when I slammed the door.

My father and Stephanie began conspiring to get me into treatment. I went into a drug treatment center, but I was not committed to it and I left. Over the next three days I went through a lot of cocaine. At the end I was as pitiful and incomprehensibly demoralized as a human being can be. . . . An old friend showed up at my place and stayed with me until he found a hospital that would take me. I went back into treatment June 28, 1985, and I have been clean ever since.

In the program I learned rigorous honesty. After I was in the hospital three days, I borrowed the money from my parents and paid back my client. When I got out, I called all my clients and told them everything. They all stayed with me except the drug dealers.

Ironically, after I got well . . . I got a notice of my interim suspension from the State Bar effective January 1987.

The stress of helping me get into treatment killed my father. He had a stoke a year and half after I recovered and passed away about the time I was sending out the . . . notices to close out my practice. He was only 57. He got me through as much as he could and then he died.

After my suspension, I got a job as a law clerk for a small firm, starting out at $800 a month. Then the State Bar hearings began. No one except me thought it would result in disbarment, because I had no prior discipline [record] and I had more than 70 letters of support from lawyers and judges. But deep in my heart I knew I should be disbarred.

About a year after my sobriety I got involved with The Other Bar. At first I thought it would look good for my discipline case. Then it became something I really believed in. As it started to get inside me, I thought maybe I could help other people avoid what happened to me. In the last three years I have helped maybe 100 people. It's one of the things that lets me sleep at night. I lie there and see dozens of faces of lawyers who are still practicing and alive because of me.

I make $4,600 a month as a law clerk doing general civil litigation research and writing. . . . I was eligible to apply for reinstatement in January 1992, but I was not sure I would do it right away. It's real important to me to get my license back because they took it away. But being a lawyer isn't so important anymore. I used to care about the power, the prestige, the money. Now I want to preserve the happiness I have. . . .

NOTES

The effect on the clients of a lawyer who abuses drugs or alcohol is not always as graphic as in the case history described above. But the abilities of lawyers to perform their fiduciary duties to their clients — to put the causes and needs of their clients first — often become seriously impaired when lawyers are more concerned with their substance addictions. Deadlines are missed, responses are not filed, and more subtle lapses — some of which the client may not be able to discover — occur with increasing regularity.

Psychologists, management consultants, and other experts in the field offer a great deal of advice about how to deal with the problem attorney. But most experts would tell us that the most important advice they can give is the following: Don't ignore the problem, or even worse, participate in the cover-up. Take action, because inaction will be viewed as tacit acceptance of the situation. The more difficult it is to take action, because of friendship or close long-term business relationships with your colleague, the more important taking action becomes.

And as for David Demergian? Almost four years to the day after he was disbarred, he was readmitted to active practice. He has had an unblemished record since.

3. Identifying the Problem and Doing Something About It. The following article discusses how addictions are currently treated by lawyer disciplinary agencies around the country — there has been little change in this regard since this article was published — and the extent to which such addictions should be considered "mitigating" factors.

MICHAEL A. BLOOM & CAROL LYNN WALLINGER, LAWYERS AND ALCOHOLISM: IS IT TIME FOR A NEW APPROACH?
61 Temple Law Review 1409 (1988)[3]

Oregon's Professional Liability Fund has determined that more than one-half the attorneys admitted to its alcoholism treatment program already have been sued for malpractice. Surveys taken in New York and in California reveal that as many as fifty to seventy percent of all disciplinary cases involve alcoholism.

The syndrome of alcoholism results from the prolonged overuse of alcohol. It typically is characterized by a "high risk" individual who develops self-perpetuating behaviors. This combination leads to an addiction. Genetic, social and psychological predisposing factors exist which contribute to a susceptibility to alcoholism and create a high risk individual. Alcoholics (and other substance abusers as well) also tend to have a certain psychological profile. Whether this profile is a cause or effect of addiction is not clear.

. . . .

The process of healing oneself begins when the person admits to being an addict. This is the most crucial part in recovery of an addict because denial is the cornerstone of addiction. Breaking through this denial is the most important step in the recovery process and often is the most difficult task if treatment is to be successful.

An excellent example of denial is the reluctance of most lawyers to report incompetent or impaired work. Although technically obligated to do so under the Model Code and the Model Rules, this "conspiracy of silence" has been cited as the "greatest obstacle to better regulation of the legal profession.". . .

This is a classic example of the psychological concept of "enabling," whereby we consciously or "unconsciously help alcoholics block their perception of their illness." There often are signals, other than obvious drunkenness, that point to a potential drinking problem. Some of these signals include long weekends

---

[3] Reproduced with the permission of Temple Law Review. Copyright © 1988 by Temple University of the Commonwealth System of Higher Education.

and/or frequent late arrivals and early departures from work; failure to file court papers; forgetting to show up for scheduled court appearances and appointments; neglecting correspondence and phone messages; "borrowing" from client trust funds; and often missing deadlines. As the disease progresses, the alcoholic increasingly requires the help of others to cover his or her decreasingly effective performance of life's daily responsibilities. Colleagues in the legal community (secretaries, associates, partners, even judges) often are recruited, to participate in the "cover-up." When colleagues allow this behavior to continue unchecked, the alcoholic lawyer is enabled to progress deeper and deeper into alcoholism. The resulting harm to clients is not something from which these colleagues should hold themselves (or be permitted to hold themselves) entirely blameless. Nor should they be permitted to escape liability to clients for a risk they knew existed, but took no steps to prevent.

. . . .

Effect of Alcoholism on Disciplinary Proceedings

The model of alcoholism as a disease views the alcoholic as a person with an illness which is outside his or her control, or involuntary. Although the behavior of drinking is involuntary, it is often difficult to determine what other behaviors of the alcoholic also are involuntary. The issue of voluntariness must be addressed when designing any policy concerning alcoholism. The complexity of defining what is "voluntary" action by an alcoholic lawyer involved in disciplinary proceedings is demonstrated by the following cases, where the courts of New Jersey and Washington, D.C. struggled with terms such as "intent" and "but for," while attempting to balance protection of the public interest with appropriate disciplinary sanctions for attorney misconduct.

A. Non-Mitigating Factor Approach

New Jersey has steadfastly resisted consideration of alcoholism as a mitigating factor in determining attorney discipline. Disbarment always is the result when the lawyer's conduct involves misappropriation of client funds. Maintenance of public confidence in the bar is viewed as controlling in these cases; rarely will mitigating factors be considered. Two recent cases illustrate the view of the New Jersey Supreme Court on this issue.

. . . .

In re Crowley [105 N.J. 89, 519 A.2d 361 (1987)] concerned an attorney who was admitted to the bar in 1957 and maintained a solo practice concentrating in real estate, matrimonial, and estate matters. In 1978, his alcohol consumption and dependence began to increase and his practice began to decline. Crowley began taking extended lunches and not returning phone calls. In 1981, he undertook a real estate closing on behalf of a client, but failed to satisfy an outstanding mortgage of $11,500 from the closing proceeds. A complaint was filed and eventually it was conceded that Crowley had diverted, for payment of his own office expenses, a total of $17,684 from five different clients.

In this case, the DRB [Disciplinary Review Board] had the benefit of a report from the Alcohol Advisory Committee, which determined that alcoholism was a contributing factor in Crowley's behavior, and that he was now a recovering alcoholic. The DRB recommended indefinite suspension until recovery was demonstrated, and also required restitution of losses.

The New Jersey Supreme Court rejected the recommendations of the DRB and voted 7-0 for disbarment. The court noted . . . the probable direct relationship between Crowley's unethical behavior and his alcoholism. The court, however, was not impressed with this connection, and observed that the same causal relationship could occur from severe financial reversals or other family hardships. Declining to use this case to create a new exception, the court instead elected to continue its ironclad policy of disbarring attorneys who misappropriate client funds.

B. Mitigating Factor Approach

In *In re Kersey*, [520 A.2d 321 (D.C. 1987)] the District of Columbia Board of Professional Responsibility found Kersey guilty of twenty-four Code violations and concluded that Kersey's "pattern of dishonesty and deceit was so pervasive that disbarment was the only appropriate sanction."

Facing disbarment, Kersey, whose drinking problems had begun in high school, reluctantly entered and completed an alcohol detoxification program. Together with the D.C. Bar Special Committee on Alcohol Abuse, Kersey then petitioned the District of Columbia Court of Appeals to stay his disbarment, and asked for reconsideration of his discipline in light of his alcoholism and his prognosis for recovery.

The court acknowledged that alcoholism is treated as a mitigating factor by many jurisdictions in determining lawyer discipline and held that the "but for" standard "must be met in order to prove causation in disciplinary cases involving alcoholism." The court stated its belief that but for Kersey's alcoholism, his misconduct would not have occurred.

In discussing the appropriate discipline to be imposed, the court considered the likely result that due to the "pre-treatment alcoholic's persistent and virtually unshakable denial of his alcoholism," other alcoholic attorneys would fail to make any connection between Kersey's case and their own situations. Reasoning that suspending Kersey would not alter the behavior of other alcoholic attorneys, the court ordered that Kersey be placed on probation for five years, under supervision of a sobriety monitor, a practice monitor, and a financial monitor.

These two jurisdictions could not be more inconsistent. . . . [O]bvious from these cases is that neither of these approaches protects the public from impaired lawyers before harm to clients occurs. Given a choice between the two approaches, it is not hard to imagine which result the general public endorses. The public has no choice but to see the results in Kersey's case as a "protection of one's own" and to view the New Jersey approach as "rough justice" at work. Viewed in context, is this the message that the legal profession wishes to send?

4. Defining the Ethical Requirements, and Two ABA Opinions on Impairment. The requirement under the Model Rules that incompetence or "impaired work" be reported[4] is more often ignored than acted on. Rules describing the responsibilities of supervising and subordinate lawyers are largely silent on the issue of what to do about an impaired colleague. Even in Illinois, where *Himmel*[5] gives lawyers an "absolute duty" to report, rates of reporting lawyer impairment have hardly skyrocketed.

This reality raises many questions. What actions should be taken? Should an impaired lawyer be removed from a case? Reported to a firm committee? Reported to a board of professional discipline? Fired? What should clients be told? What, then, do the rules of ethics require? Where the client is being hurt, does another law firm member have an obligation to protect that client's interests? If the lawyer's individual fiduciary duty is imputed to each member of the law firm, is "whistleblowing" to the client necessary? Must other firm members step in and act to protect client interests? Even if an ethics complaint doesn't follow for the impaired lawyer, could a law firm be liable for malpractice and breach of fiduciary duty if a client later learns that the firm failed to advise about a partner's impairment? Finally, how else other than "whistle-blowing" might the goal of client protection be accomplished?

In 2003, the American Bar Association published two separate ethics opinions dealing with the impaired lawyer.

Formal Opinion 03-429 (2003) addresses impaired attorneys within their law firms while Formal Opinion 03-431 (2003) focuses on the responsibility of other attorneys who observe impairment in a lawyer from another firm. On the one hand, it is laudable that the ABA has directly addressed this important issue, not once but twice. On the other, some see the opinions as begging more questions than they answer. On the one hand, the focus of the opinions is where it should be — on the client. On the other, the opinions are relatively narrow and do little to directly help the impaired lawyer or the lawyer's firm, nor do they fully solve client protection issues.

Opinion 429's focus is on whether the lawyer is so impaired that his or her ability to represent clients with the "legal knowledge, skill thoroughness and preparation reasonably necessary for the representation" has been materially affected. In other words, does the lawyer remain "competent, diligent, and effective." The opinion notes that it is important to distinguish "erratic" behavior that doesn't impair competence[6]

Opinion 429 requires the law firm to create "measures giving reasonable assurance that all lawyers in the firm conform to the Rules of Professional Conduct." To that end, firms should develop policies specifically for impaired lawyers. The opinion does not explain how small firms and sole practitioners — still a clear majority of the American bar — can develop such policies, particularly in light of the difficulties lawyers — indeed, anyone — have in recognizing their own impairment.

---

[4] *See* MR 8.3; DR 1-103(A).

[5] 112 Ill. 2d 531, 533 N.E.2d 790 (1988). *See* discussion in Problem 26.

[6] The opinion uses the example of Tourette's Syndrome, although if not carefully treated that condition could lead to impairment due to the involuntary tics and verbalizations it includes.

The opinion is less than definitive on the question of disclosure. While there "may" be an obligation to disclose the situation to the client so that the client can "make informed decisions regarding the representation," the trigger for disclosure is unclear, and the disclosure made in a way that "to the extent possible, should be conscious of the privacy rights of the impaired lawyer." When it comes to reporting he lawyer for disciplinary purposes, the opinion again warns about jumping to conclusions, and indicates that no reporting is necessary if no client was harmed.

On disclosure, Formal Opinion 429 and Formal Opinion 431 both pay careful attention to client confidentiality, Whether reporting one's own colleague or a lawyer from another firm, the reporting lawyer must be careful not to violate client confidentiality, which, as we have learned, is quite broad and includes more than a client's communications. Opinion 431 strongly urges lawyers to get the client's informed consent before reporting and also admonishes that the reporting lawyer must be confident that the condition of the other lawyer rises to the level of "material impairment." But as we have seen, triggering the reporting standards of "honesty, trustworthiness or fitness as a lawyer" differs substantially from state to state. This limits the opinion's utility.

5. Intervention. Intervention programs such as Chicago's Lawyer Assistance Program have become an increasingly common way to deal with addiction issues. Such intervention programs often have the same message conveyed by psychologists — the need to be tough, especially with those with whom we are close. But some discipline counsel feel that treating alcoholism as a disease may be letting lawyers off the disciplinary hook. How would you balance these considerations in the case of "Rabbit" Worthington?

TRIPP BALTZ, PRESENTING THE HARD FACTS OF A LIQUID HABIT TO IMPAIRED LAWYERS
Chicago Lawyer (December 1991)[7]

She glares across the circle of people at her sister, the alcoholic lawyer, and begins.

"For as long as I remember, you've been tearing up every family gathering and ruining every holiday," she says, her voice quaking.

"At my house you get drunk and pass out," she continues. "We could go to your house; you get drunk and pass out. At a restaurant, you get drunk and embarrass everybody. You throw up in the bathroom, and you fall down . . . ."

Cook County Circuit Judge Warren D. Wolfson breaks in. "Lemme stop it at this point," he says. "This would not happen."

Lawyer's Assistance Program interventions are no place for emotional outbursts, Wolfson explains. Participants must stick to retelling specific events of what they have seen and heard and how they felt about it. Things like always tearing up family gatherings "are throw-aways. You can't have it," he says.

Wolfson and other LAP intervention veterans were conducting a training session for about 40 lawyers and judges who volunteered to be intervenors

---

[7] Copyright © 1991 by Chicago Lawyer. Reprinted by permission.

— people who confront attorneys with substance abuse problems in hopes of creating change. Intervenors also inform people about alcoholism and act as resources within firms.

. . . .

Through LAP, intervenors confront lawyers or judges addicted to alcohol or other drugs with their problem to try to breach the impaired attorney's denial and encourage him or her to seek treatment. Intervenors work in teams of three, including a judge and at least one recovering alcoholic.

Intervenors surround alcoholics with reality, [Former LAP President Michael J.] Howlett explained prior to the training session. They encourage family, friends and co-workers — the witnesses and victims of the chaos of alcoholism — to present hard facts of drinking to the impaired attorney.

LAP intervenors . . . come from all parts of the legal community [and include] three sitting judges, one retired judge and a smattering of solo practitioners, corporate counsel and government agency attorneys.

The group is a mix of women and men, jackets and suits, tight-knotted ties and open collars, thin gray hairs and long curly locks.

. . . .

Based on intervention services, LAP is not a disciplinary organization, a temperance society or a recovery program.

"We don't shake tambourines and beat drums," Wolfson says. "We treat alcoholism as a treatable disease. We share the common conviction that we care about chemical abuse victims and their families, friends, co-workers, partners and associates. We try to get all parts of the person's life."

The relationship between trained intervenors and the judges and attorneys who receive assistance through LAP is privileged under Rule 1.6 of the Illinois Supreme Court's Code of Professional Conduct, Howlett says.

"What is said at an intervention never goes out," he says. To retain the LAP privilege and the right to participate in an intervention, one has to stay for the entire training program, he says. During the next four hours, no one will leave . . . .

Wolfson describes how a team prepares for an intervention. The team interviews the addicted lawyer's family, friends and co-workers who are willing to participate as if they were preparing witnesses. Some of those interviewed will accompany the LAP team when it confronts the addicted person.

Intervenors plumb for solid evidence and specific events.

"We're lawyers," Wolfson says. "We know how to ask the question; we know how to get the information. We need information that will stand up. It can't be hearsay. It can't be gossip or rumor.

"It has to be specific, and you will need to lay the same kind of foundation you would need to get a conversation into evidence: who was there, when was it, what happened."

Intervenors advise participants to write down on yellow legal pads the facts and incidents that will be useful later, Wolfson says.

. . . .

"If the alcoholic senses a weak point, he'll go after it like a dog after a rabbit," he says.

So if a participant falters or loses heart, Howlett says, the intervention team is there to gently nudge him or her back to the purpose by reminding them of something they wrote down.

"If a partner talks in terms of, 'Well, I'm not so sure that George has a problem,' then an associate can remind him, 'Well, we did find him walking down the center of the L tracks twice. And we know that he's talked his way out of the last three DUI tickets.'

"Or the last time we entertained a client, he put his face in the salad," Howlett says. "We engage in what I call the duck school of diagnosis. Walks like a duck, talks like a duck, hangs around with ducks, acts like a duck — it's a drunk . . . ."

"It's an equal opportunity disease: men and women, all races, makes no difference. We take the position that this is a disease that doesn't recognize any barriers," he says.

Throughout the session, the trainers used the term "alcoholic" to refer to any person impaired by substance abuse or addiction.

. . . .

Wolfson . . . explains the importance of setting limits: Having a person deliver the message that the lawyer's job is in peril if they fail to seek treatment.

"There is no more powerful motivator" than the prospect of losing your job, Wolfson says. "The limit-setter will often be the last person to speak at an intervention, designated as the clean-up hitter," he says.

Murphy adds, "You gotta make sure they mean it, and you make sure they're gonna say it." Partners sometimes back down. "It's like impeachment," he groans . . . .

"We had a head of public office say they were going to fire this person if they didn't get help," he continues. When we got to the point where the hammer was supposed to fall, and we turned to the supervisor and said, 'Is there anything you want to say to him now?' he said, 'Get help, or I'm going to be disappointed.'

"You have nothing further to say? 'Get help or I'm really going to be disappointed.' Wasn't there something you wanted to say about his job? 'Yeah, if he doesn't get help, he's not going to be very good at his job.'"

Howlett, like an entertainer on stage, relates the ironic humor of the story. But he follows through with its seriousness: "It was sad because it takes a lot of courage to do what we ask these people to do. You have to prepare them well enough and give them the support that will carry them through it."

The alcoholic cannot argue with the participants' feelings, Murphy says.

"We're going to hit them with facts, but we're going to tell them how that made you feel," he says. "And we want them to know that the feeling hurts that person."

"The alcoholic can do all kinds of bad things, and he thinks he's only hurting himself. We want to now let him know he's hurting these people. We want to get all these people to give them that message."

. . . .

When everyone is prepared, the judge on the team calls the subject and invites him to a meeting in the judge's chambers, saying there are a number of people concerned about him, Howlett says. The alcoholic usually knows the reason for the call, he says.

. . . .

Howlett instructs Wolfson to start the mock intervention. Trainees playing the concerned people in the alcoholic lawyer's life sit in a circle in Wolfson's chambers. The judge greets Sue, who takes her seat at the center of the circle. After Sue's sister has spoken, an associate tells her story.

"First of all, I'm glad I can work for you," she says. "You were the prime reason I joined this firm. You have an excellent reputation, and I have learned a lot. Over the last couple of years, though, things have gone downhill . . . ."

Howlett interrupts. "Get to the drink," he says.

Wolfson backs him up: "Here again, it's much too general. . . . You can't just say her work's getting worse.

"You have to say, 'Last Tuesday, there was a client waiting in the office, a Mr. Jones; and when you didn't come back from work, I had to meet with him. When you came back later that day, you smelled of alcohol and I had to lie to a partner about where you were.'"

. . . .

A recovering alcoholic rises to describe the role he plays at an intervention. "You won't find this on my resume," he begins. . . .

"One of the big things I always say to them is that the other people in this room talk about how hard it is and how difficult it is for them to be here and for you to be here.

"They don't know how difficult it is. There are only two people in the room who know how difficult it is for you to be here." Now only his voice and the low rattle of the air conditioning can be heard in the room.

"I've been there," he continues. "I sat in that chair; I walked down the same road as you. I sat in the same bars. I ruined my life. I, too, had a drinking problem."

. . . .

The intervention should last less than an hour, Wolfson says.

. . . .

[B]efore the intervention, a member of the team will have arranged for a bed for the subject at a treatment facility, most likely Parkside.

Treatment usually starts with the alcoholic entering an in-patient program that lasts 28 days and exposes him to the medical and academic side of the disease, Howlett says. But it also begins his relationship with Alcoholics

Anonymous, Howlett says, one he will most likely continue for the rest of his life as long as he stays in recovery.

"I welcome you to all this," Howlett says as the session comes to an end. "I have found that it is, next to what I do as a husband and a father, the most significant thing I do with my time."

. . . .

Wolfson: "When a 6-or 7-year-old child turns to her father and says, 'I want my daddy back, please get help,' there isn't a dry eye in the room."

NOTES

Note the idea of setting clear limits and sticking with them. The emphasis on not "changing the finish line" by giving second chances again and again is central to the intervention's success. Other pre-emptive approaches are being proposed as ways to address a lawyer's substance abuse problem *before* it leads to severe discipline. See Rick Allan's proposals in the following article.

After discussing the problem of alcoholism and substance abuse among lawyers, Allan, director of the Nebraska Lawyer Assistance Program, describes the travails of the unfortunate lawyer in a Nebraska case,[8] who was disbarred after relapsing with alcohol while on probation for earlier disciplinary violations. He then comes up with a series of recommendations, which form the brief excerpt below.

RICK B. ALLAN, ALCOHOLISM, DRUG ABUSE AND LAWYERS: ARE WE READY TO ADDRESS THE DENIAL?
31 Creighton Law Review 265 (1997)[9]

The saga of this alcoholic lawyer in Nebraska raises two issues. First, if probation is appropriate in a disciplinary proceeding, how can the bar better serve the Nebraska Court and Counsel for Discipline in an effort to promote compliance by the lawyer placed on probation? Second, whether alcoholism is accepted or not as mitigation in a lawyer disciplinary proceeding, neither approach protects the public from alcoholic lawyers. The obvious reason is that no formal action will be sanctioned against the alcoholic lawyer until the harm has occurred.

. . . .

Recommendations: Monitoring and Diversion

The most important factor in successful treatment of alcoholism is early detection. Lawyer Assistance Programs are in part designed to protect the public from lawyer misconduct. Protection of the public is accomplished by assisting alcoholic lawyers in their recovery and providing education concerning recognition of the problem and the treatment options available. The Nebraska State Bar Association has acknowledged the problem of the alcoholic

---

[8] *Nebraska ex rel. Nebraska State Bar Assoc. v. Barnett*, 248 Neb. 601, 537 N.W.2d 633 (1995).

[9] Reprinted with permission. Copyright © 1997 by Creighton University.

lawyer and has taken positive steps in the creation of the [Nebraska Lawyers Assistance Program].

In addition to starting Lawyers Assistance Programs, other states have instituted monitoring and diversion programs in response to the problems of chemical dependency in the profession. . . . Monitoring programs have been shown to be highly effective in satisfying the dual goals of protection of the public and rehabilitation of the impaired practitioner. . . .

Monitoring programs are really in their infancy and vary from state to state. Highly trained probation monitors may be assigned in disciplinary cases when disbarment is not mandated, but public protection must be insured. Disciplined lawyers are assigned highly skilled probation monitors who evaluate their law practices, finances, and sobriety, filing regular reports as may be required.

While disciplinary-probation monitoring generally follows serious misconduct, diversion programs are designed to "divert" the impaired lawyer before serious disciplinary violations have occurred. Lawyers in need of help are referred to professionals, groups or agencies for treatment and education in order to address the problems that lead to misconduct.

NOTES

One of the major aspects of diversion programs is that because they are implemented before official disciplinary charges are filed against the lawyer, the information given to the regulating agency is considered confidential. If the lawyer successfully completes the diversionary program, no one besides the law firm, the lawyer, the program, and the lawyer's immediate family need know about the lawyer's participation in the program or any of the information that resulted in his participation.

Public knowledge can deter lawyers from coming forth and admitting that they have a problem; therefore, confidential diversion programs are a way to encourage lawyers to obtain early treatment before the disease leads to publicly-announced misconduct. But what of the public's right to know of a lawyer's addiction? Is the trade-off of preemptive treatment worth keeping the public in the dark? The answer may lie in how successfully these diversion monitoring programs provide long-term success.

6. Stress, Dissatisfaction, and Wellness. If there were better ways to avoid stress in the first place, perhaps fewer people would get to the point of needing intervention. From time to time, various surveys have attempted to measure lawyers' stress. What have you done to prepare yourself to meet and deal with this stress? The best time to put a workable plan in place is now, before the reality of the daily practice of law has begun to take its toll.

In 1999, a group of forward-thinking law professors led by Larry Krieger of Florida State University began an on-line discussion group on "humanizing" legal education. By 2001, the group had put on workshops and a conference that focused, as one of the group's coordinators, Capital University law professor Susan Daicoff put it, on "ways of practicing law and resolving legal disputes that are positive, healing, and humanistic." In addition to more traditional views, the group looked well beyond the legal profession itself, examined holistic solutions, and made a conscious effort to begin searching for better ways of protecting the health of the minds and bodies of lawyers and law students alike. In the last few years, the group has coalesced more formally around the concept of "humanizing legal education." An increasing number of professors have written on wellness and personal satisfaction and how to get it. They include Professor Krieger, whose prescription for wellness — actually written to assist law professors in teaching humanizing values — is excerpted here.

LAWRENCE S. KRIEGER, THE INSEPARABILITY OF PROFESSIONALISM AND PERSONAL SATISFACTION: PERSPECTIVES ON VALUES, INTEGRITY AND HAPPINESS
11 Clinical Law Review 425 (2005)[10]

There is a lot of talk about "professionalism" in law schools and the legal profession today, with little evidence of positive impact . . . . One crucial reason that our rhetoric fails is that it is contradicted by the competitive, outcome-oriented institutional values one typically finds dominating law schools and the highly visible and commercialized segments of the profession. It is reasonable that law students and young lawyers "tune out" the noble but dissonant messages about professionalism, but the regrettable result is that many of them fail to really comprehend the foundations of their future working life.

Professionalism training typically amounts to telling law students and lawyers that they should act in certain ways, for generally noble reasons including the high calling of our profession; and that they'd better do so, for more coercive reasons including the potential for bar discipline. Neither of these motives — guilt or fear — is likely to be effective in producing the desired result. Rarely, if ever, is one's actual life experience — including one's happiness and career satisfaction — raised as part of the professionalism discussion. This fact further enables students to distance themselves from a discussion they perceive as theoretical rather than personal.

I will argue (1) that satisfaction and professional behavior are inseparable manifestations of a well-integrated and well-motivated person; and (2) that depression and unprofessional behavior among law students and lawyers typically proceed from a loss of integrity — a disconnection from intrinsic values and motivations, personal and cultural beliefs, conscience, or other defining parts of their personality and humanity . . . .

Values and Personal Satisfaction as a Perspective for Teaching Professionalism

I begin with a strong dose of the truth for my students. This is something too rarely done at our schools . . . . I tell students the truth about the dismal results of surveys on attorney mental health and career satisfaction, and I tell them the truth about the egregiously low standard of behavior often encountered among attorneys and judges in the real world they are preparing

---

10 Copyright © 2005 by Clinical Law Review. Reprinted by permission.

to enter . . . . Not surprisingly, students are often taken aback when they see data summaries showing lawyers to have the highest incidence of depression of any occupation in the United States, or to suffer other forms of emotional distress up to 15 times more frequently than the general population.

I transition to the positive side of our topics by focusing on the values and motivations common to most people . . . . First, it is no coincidence that there is a perception among the public, scholars, and bar leaders alike that values like money, power, and an uncompromising drive to win are displacing values like integrity, decency, and mutuality among many lawyers. The second reason for this focus makes the discussion most relevant to students and lawyers: Those values and motivations that promote or attend professionalism have been empirically shown to correlate with well being and life satisfaction, while those that undermine or discourage professionalism empirically correlate with distress and dissatisfaction. These conclusions are supported by both recent empirical studies and classical humanistic theory describing psychological health and maturity.

Professionalism and Satisfaction as Dual Expressions of Psychological Maturity

I present professionalism to law students as a combination of developed legal skills and various personal virtues that we typically seek in lawyers: broad vision/wisdom, integrity and honesty, compassion, respect for others and for differences, unselfishness, the desire to serve others and one's community, self-confidence, individualism, and a real commitment to justice . . . .

Modern psychology classifies both values and motivation as either intrinsic or extrinsic. A person is intrinsically motivated when he chooses a self-directed action which he genuinely enjoys or which furthers a fundamental life purpose, while extrinsically motivated choices are directed towards external rewards (i.e. money, grades, honors), avoidance of guilt or fear, or pleasing/impressing others . . . .

Attorneys who are deeply committed to their own values are less likely to pursue the values or desires of their clients with unethical or abusive tactics. And a lawyer who chose her career path for the most fundamental intrinsic reason — because she genuinely enjoys the work — will generate a better work product and be consistently happy at work, thereby creating a positive effect on her clients, adverse counsel, court personnel. The converse is also true — an attorney who does the work primarily for the money or to bolster his image will be more frustrated with the process, less effective, and much less pleasant to work with (or against).

Understanding Integrity As Physical And Psychological Health

One more principle that illuminates the relationship between personal satisfaction and professionalism is integrity. Integrity is clearly a foundation of professionalism, but its effect on personal well-being is perhaps even more direct. In fact, integrity is conceptually synonymous with health. Although we may commonly think of "health" in terms of the body and "integrity" in terms of the personality or character, the essence of each is the same — a condition of wholeness or integrated functioning within one's self. Furthermore, the functioning of the personality and of the physiology are closely interrelated: a person's level of personal integrity affects his physical health and well-being directly. For example . . . lying or deceptive behavior, which clearly manifests a loss of character integrity, is often attended by the experience of psychological anxiety and physical stress (increased heart rate, damp palms, etc.) . . . .

We may certainly discourage lying, deception, manipulation of fact or law, or abuse of people or process because such behavior is "unprofessional." But the impact will be multiplied if we also explain that such behavior erodes integrity by separating the lawyer from key parts of her self — her conscience, sense of decency and/or intrinsic values. The results are likely to include loss of her professional reputation along with physical and emotional stress that will ultimately undermine her health.

NOTES

Does this correlation between integrity and health make sense to you? Or is Prof. Krieger just trying to "sell" law students on putting morality ahead of winning, money, and the other traditional trappings of success? His article is supported by ample empirical evidence, but is that determinative? Might this "humanizing" group be naïve, or have they understood a basic truth? Finally, and most importantly, is the path Prof. Krieger suggests one worth taking? Recall David Dermagian's words: "I used to care about the power, the prestige, the money. Now I want to preserve the happiness I have."

7. Stress, Drugs, and the Rock 'n' Roll of Law Practice. Even if you adopt Prof. Krieger's wellness standards, it would be simplistic to ignore the reality of a law firm practice, and both the peer pressure and professional pressure it creates. The peer pressure to go out drinking, for example, can be substantial at certain firms, where it can become a way of life for most of the lawyers who practice there. Young associates who do not carefully consider these issues can get swept up into a lifestyle they did not affirmatively choose. It is always difficult to resist the expectations of one's own law firm. Retreats at some firms can turn into late night parties, where it is hard to "just say no" without standing out among your friends and colleagues, or, perhaps worse, your superiors. Many associates report that partners expect them to go out drinking with clients, reminding them that "wining and dining" is what the client wants and expects. Thus, doing this becomes a matter of economic survival rather than strictly a matter of choice.

It would also be simplistic to say that merely working out at the local athletic club, jogging or mountain biking on weekends or reading a good book every night at bedtime will protect all of us from using — and sometimes abusing — drugs or alcohol. First, many lawyers, particularly young associates faced with seemingly insurmountable billable hours requirements, may be too tired, too overworked, or too burned out to always keep their stress-reduction programs in place. Second, many lawyers *like* to have a drink or two when they socialize, and feel, correctly, that it never negatively affects their performance.

Where should the line be drawn? Should it be only when the clients of the lawyer are actually adversely affected? What about when it appears that those clients' rights may be seriously endangered? Should any lawyer who uses illegal drugs or gets obviously drunk be subject to discipline, or at least brought to a bar intervention program? Or would this be legislating morality? Indeed, *should* lawyers be imposing such moral values on others? Neither these nor other questions are completely clear. What is clear is the need to give serious consideration to these issues which affect so many of today's practicing lawyers. And, of course, for each of us to consider our own behavior in terms of our own well-being.

8. How Should We Treat the Mentally Ill Lawyer? We close with the same subject that opened this problem — mental illness. The Supplemental Readings note several readings on "character and fitness" — the issue of whether one should gain initial admission to the bar due the prospective lawyer's mental condition. To date, perhaps due to legal requirements, few lawyers have been denied admission on the grounds of lack of mental health. Such a standard would have been unlikely to screen out Robert Rowe, as what he did was hardly predictable by anyone. Sometimes, as in Rowe's case, the stress of life manifests itself in something even worse than alcoholism or drug addiction. Robert Rowe came back from the abyss — almost literally back from the dead — and tried to regain a place in his former profession, as this next article describes.

DAVID MARGOLICK, AT THE BAR: 15 YEARS LATER, DISBARRED LAWYER CAN'T ERASE HORROR'S STIGMA
The New York Times (May 15, 1993)[11]

One winter morning 15 years ago, a 48-year-old lawyer named Robert T. Rowe simply snapped. As his eldest son lay sleeping, Mr. Rowe killed him with a baseball bat. Then he killed his daughter, and then his second son, in the same grisly way. When his wife returned from work, he bludgeoned her to death as well.

Unable to turn the bat on himself, Mr. Rowe instead turned on the gas stove at his home in Mill Basin, Brooklyn. He was saved from suicide only when neighbors smelled the fumes and called the police.

For Mr. Rowe, a veteran of the Korean War and a graduate of St. John's University Law School, the carnage culminated years of psychological turmoil, brought on primarily by the strain of caring for one son who was deaf and blind and another who suffered from asthma, a congenital hip disease, and other ailments. Having lost his job with an insurance company, failed as a cabdriver and seen his wife reduced to working 16 hours a day, he apparently saw the killings as an act of love, a way to spare his family the humiliation of poverty.

Society first pronounced Mr. Rowe blameless in the killings; in the language of the law, not guilty by reason of mental disease or effect. Then, after

---

[11] Copyright © 1993 by The New York Times Company. Reprinted by permission.

institutionalizing him for two years and providing him psychotherapy for eight more, it pronounced him cured. But despite an eight-year legal struggle by Mr. Rowe, it will not let him practice law again, as he did for 22 years before what he calls "the incident" or "the tragedy" occurred.

For those who can get past its horrific facts, Mr. Rowe's case raises profound questions about mental illness, punishment and the legal profession. How high a price must someone pay for conduct for which he is found not culpable? When psychiatrists vouch for a patient's recovery, does anyone really believe it? And should public perceptions of insanity — and the courts' fear of those perceptions — govern who is deemed fit to practice law?

In 1978, three months after he was institutionalized, the Appellate Division of the State Supreme Court in Brooklyn suspended Mr. Rowe's law license "for an indefinite period." Twelve years later, a psychiatrist appointed by the same court to examine Mr. Rowe concluded that he made a "complete recovery" and that any risk of recurrence was minor.

"Mr. Rowe is, from the psychiatric point of view, fully able to practice his profession," the psychiatrist, Dr. Henry Pinsker, concluded in 1990.

But when Mr. Rowe tried to retrieve his license, the Appellate Division disbarred him instead. "We have taken into consideration the mitigating circumstances advanced by the respondent," it ruled in January 1992, referring to Mr. Rowe. "Nevertheless, the respondent is guilty of serious professional misconduct. Accordingly, the respondent is disbarred forthwith."

Mr. Rowe then took his case to the New York Court of Appeals, the state's highest. Between hearing arguments in the case in October 1992 and deciding it the following month, its own Chief Judge, Sol Wachtler, suffered a mental breakdown of his own and resigned. Still, the court upheld Mr. Rowe's disbarment. Though Mr. Rowe's conduct was not criminal, it held, what mattered was whether it "tended to undermine public confidence" in the bar . . . .

Mr. Rowe, who remarried in 1989, has spent the past 13 years mostly doing volunteer work, teaching children and illiterate adults, working at a hospice in Queens, and studying history and Asian studies at St. John's University. As he recuperates from heart surgery, he paints and earns pocket money doing investigations for lawyers.

Practicing law again, Mr. Rowe said, would mean more than another chance to do what he does best. It would allow him to add another, happier last chapter to his life, to ease things for his 2-year-old daughter when she learns of his past. It would afford him an opportunity to help people in the mental health system, something he has come to appreciate from the inside.

A Blow Against Ignorance

More than anything else, he said, it would strike a blow against what he considers the nation's ignorance — and the bar's hypocrisy — on the subject of mental illness. Mr. Rowe, who has heretofore declined to speak with reporters and still refuses to be photographed, said the legal establishment was unable to acknowledge mental illness in its midst, and was sacrificing him to protect its own battered reputation.

"I had been a lawyer in good standing before the tragedy, and it seemed terribly logical to me that if you become unmentally ill, you'd be reinstated," he said. "But instead of pointing to me, and saying, 'One of our own came back,' they went after me as though I were a criminal."

"What is the matter with me?" he said. "What is the matter with me? This thing happened 15 years ago. You can live three lifetimes in 15 years."

. . . .

Mr. Rowe recounts his story matter-of-factly until the topic turned to the killings. "I'm going to start bawling," he said quietly. "Let's not even talk about it. That's four people who aren't here."

Were he reinstated, he said, he would represent clients in the mental health system. "I've been inside some very strange places," he said. "I'd tell them, 'I was there and you can come out of it.'"

"I don't know what I'd be taking away from the profession," he said. "The reputation of lawyers is already at the bottom of the pile."

NOTES

If we allow alcoholism to be used as a mitigating circumstance, should we not be more lenient in readmitting an attorney who acted through a mental illness of which he has now been effectively cured? Or is the horror of the act, coupled with the need for the organized bar to maintain the public's trust, sufficient to cause this lawyer's lifetime expulsion?

Some courts have concluded that bipolar (manic depressive) disorder is *not* a mitigating factor warranting relief from disbarment, even though it is a recognized disability under the Americans With Disabilities Act. (See, for example, *Florida Bar v. Peter Charles Clement*, 662 So. 2d 690 (Fla. 1995).) The *Clement* court reached its decision in part on the fact that no doctor could guarantee that Clement wouldn't suffer a relapse.

SUPPLEMENTAL READINGS

1. Patricia Sue Heil, *Tending the Bar in Texas: Alcoholism as a Mitigating Factor in Attorney Discipline*, 24 St. Mary's L.J. 1263 (1993), is an extensive evaluation of how and in what ways alcoholism is or is not accepted as a mitigating factor in bar disciplinary proceedings.

2. Nathaniel S. Currall, *Cirrhosis of the Legal Profession — Alcoholism as an Ethical Violation or Disease Within the Profession*, 12 Geo. J. Leg. Ethics 739 (1999). This excellent law student note argues strongly for treating alcoholism as a disease — and allowing it to be considered a mitigating factor in discipline.

3. *Willner v. Thornburgh*, 738 F. Supp. 1 (D.D.C. 1990). Willner, an attorney who had been offered a job in the Antitrust Division of the Justice Department, objected to the department policy of requiring a drug test for each new employee. The federal district court agreed, and barred the testing.

4. George Edward Bailey, "Impairment, the Profession and Your Law Partner," 11 *The* [ABA] *Professional Lawyer*, 2 (Fall 1999), presents an excellent overview of the subject, discussing impairment, discipline, mitigation, and the *Kersey* case, the New Jersey no-mitigation rule, and — at some length — how to cope with the impaired lawyer in the law firm setting. Another good article on a similar subject is Maureen Hynd, "A Friend in Need May be a Malpractice Claim Waiting to Happen," in the January 2004 issue of *W. Va. Lawyer* (2004), which focuses on the malpractice consequences of the conduct of impaired lawyers.

5. Carol M. Langford, *Depression, Substance Abuse, and Intellectual Property Lawyers*, 53 Kans. L. Rev. 875 (2005). This article is adopted from a report done for the ABA Intellectual Property Section Ethics Committee that surveyed intellectual property lawyers nationwide on these issues. It includes emperical information on the prevalence of alcoholism and drug addiction in lawyers in general as well as a review of state disciplinary case law on these subjects.

6. Does a lawyer have an obligation to help a *client* who is suffering from a drug or alcohol problem? Two practicing attorneys came to opposite conclusions in two 1992 articles. John A. Wasowicz, in the January 1992 *Virginia Lawyer*, writes that "a lawyer has done a less than adequate job . . . if the problem of addiction is not addressed in the context of the attorney-client relationship." Francis D. Doucette evaluates Wasowicz's reasoning and respectfully disagrees in his article in the May 4, 1992 *Massachusetts Lawyers Weekly*, "Advocacy, Ethics and the Addicted Client."

7. There is an excellent site on humanizing legal education, managed by Prof. Larry Krieger: http://www.law.fsu.edu/academic_programs/humanizing_lawschool/humanizing_lawschool.html.

8. Len Klingen, *The Mentally Ill Attorney,* 27 Nova L. Rev. 157 (2002). This straightforward article examines what lawyers should do to prevent and mitigate the harm to their clients caused by their mental illness, what clients can do to mitigate their own damages, and what the lawyer's partners and the Bar should do to limit damages when a lawyer is mentally ill. He notes that lawyers are not subject to discipline for being mentally ill, but rather for the behaviors that follow if their illness goes undetected and untreated. He gives examples of the types of mental illnesses lawyers may suffer from and specific protections a client, lawyer, and law firm can provide.

9. Among articles addressing the "character and fitness" portion of the bar admissions process are these: Tricia S. Heil, *From Gatekeeping to Disbarment and Back Again: Chemical Dependency and Mental Health Issues in Licensing and Discipline,* 64 Tex. B.J. 158 (2001), explains how the character and fitness process works. Jon Bauer's piece, *The Character of the Questions and the Fitness of the Process: Mental Health, Bar Admissions and the Americans With Disabilities Act*, 49 UCLA L. Rev. 93 (2001), is more pointed. It examines Bar admissions agencies' increased focus on mental health issues and its legality — which he disputes — under the Americans With Disabilities Act.

Chapter 12

THE ECONOMICS OF LAWYERING

PROBLEM 30

Among the images of lawyers most readily available to the public on a daily basis are those left by their advertisements and other efforts to solicit business. This marks a complete departure from a quarter-century ago, when there simply was *no* advertising, and ethical rules required that even law firm letterheads and business cards meet strict standards of dignity and decorum. The majority of America's lawyers may long to return to those times, and the past few years have seen increased efforts to re-regulate what once was totally forbidden. But the First Amendment, as interpreted by the United States Supreme Court, has assured that lawyer advertising is here to stay.

Counselors in Action Go for the Gold

The law firm of Garcia, Weir and Lesh decides to open a chain of legal clinics called "Counselors In Action" (C.I.A.) that charge lower fees for most routine services. G, W & L believe that if they can capture market volume, they will be able to make more profit than if they operated as a more conventional law firm. In order to achieve this, they must pay their attorneys less than most firms. While most of C.I.A.'s staff attorneys are from local law schools, Garcia and Weir attended Harvard, while Lesh attended Stanford. Garcia, Weir and Lesh all have had considerable success as trial lawyers over the years. The C.I.A. staff attorneys, however, are largely inexperienced.

I. C.I.A. decides to advertise. It hires an advertising and public relations firm to help promote business. The agency proposes the following ad copy:

> a. "Counselors In Action employs among the most qualified lawyers in town. Many of our lawyers attended the most prestigious law schools and have won many large trials and settlements. You can count on Counselors In Action to win."

> b. "Here's what Counselors In Action's senior trial lawyers have accomplished: *Garcia* has won his last twelve trials; *Weir* is a past recipient of the Trial Lawyer Network's 'Advocate of the Year' award; and each of *Lesh*'s last six jury successes has gone for six figures."

> c. "Your simple divorce will cost you $750, your simple will only $450. On personal injury cases, you pay *nothing* except a portion of the award *you* recover. No recovery means no fee. And you will get the personal, professional service you should expect."

Are these advertisements appropriate? Do they meet ethical requirements?

II. The ad agency suggests that G, W & L hire television actor Chad Murray Michael and singer Kelly Clark Sun to portray the typical C.I.A. attorney in a series of TV spots. Ethical? Appropriate?

III. The partners realize that C.I.A.'s chances of success will be maximized if they emphasize personal injury claims. The agency suggests a direct mail approach to anyone in the greater metropolitan area whose injury accident is reported over the police band radio. They suggest that the mailing be a personalized letter introducing the firm and a brochure emphasizing C.I.A.'s personal injury experience. They also suggest that one of the partners follow up the letter with a phone call. Ethical? Appropriate?

IV. In a further effort to spur business, Garcia hires a web site designer to prepare a website for C.I.A. Garcia proposes not only to list the names and backgrounds of the three named partners, but also to provide "tips" to potential plaintiffs looking for attorneys to take their cases. These tips do little more than regurgitate applicable professional rules regulating contingent fee contracts and suggested questions for clients to ask lawyers they are contemplating hiring. The site would also encourage clients to contact the firm by e-mail with any questions.

Is this ethical? Does a potential client's e-mail create an attorney-client relationship? Are there certain problems with advertising on the Internet that do not exist in other media?

V. Despite all these efforts, business has not picked up, and C.I.A. is forced to lay off several associates. Weir takes charge of C.I.A. in order to develop a referral business. C.I.A. sends out glossy brochures advertising its new referral service, which state, "C.I.A. can find you a lawyer of any kind. We guarantee to find you one of the best lawyers in the business . . . and it's all free to consumers." Once a client is referred, C.I.A. requires the attorney to pay C.I.A. 25% of all attorney fees collected, as a "professional courtesy."

Is this ethical? Suppose G, W & L forms a side practice on its own, yet retains its ties to C.I.A. May Weir refer cases to the G, W & L practice?

READINGS

1. Before *Bates*. The way it used to be, lawyers simply didn't advertise. Outside of "dignified" business cards and letterheads and a listing in a directory for attorneys such as Martindale-Hubbell, lawyers were not supposed to promote their services. Solicitation of business — at least in the usual commercial sense — was simply forbidden. Canon 27 of the ABA's 1908 Canons put it this way: "The most worthy and effective advertisement possible . . . is the establishment of a well-merited reputation for professional capacity and fidelity to trust. This cannot be forced, but must be the outcome of character and conduct . . . ." Much of this sentiment remains expressed in Canon 2 of the Model Code, especially in DRs 2-101 through 2-104, even though these rules are anachronisms largely unenforceable in light of the Supreme Court's constitutional requirements.

Of course, it was not entirely true that lawyers never solicited business, but rather that they did so outside of public scrutiny, in boardrooms, at business luncheons, and at country clubs. As the practice of law became more diverse a generation ago, younger lawyers searched for new avenues of attracting business. As Justice Blackmun implied in the seminal *Bates* case excerpted below, it was no longer possible for lawyers to hold themselves above other trades with the idea that the law must be an especially "dignified" profession. The traditional ban on lawyer advertising, said Blackmun, was more a rule of etiquette than ethics. And, one might add, a rule for the far less diverse profession of 30 years ago.

2. *Bates v. State Bar*. Let us look, then, at the *Bates* opinion. Two Arizona lawyers opened a legal clinic and advertised their services with the newspaper ad, included in the appendix to the court's opinion, which we reproduce on page 795. Justice Blackmun evaluated each of the Arizona Bar's reasons for banning advertising, rejected each in turn, and reversed the lawyers' discipline.

BATES v. STATE BAR OF ARIZONA
33 U.S. 350, 97 S. Ct. 2691 (1977)

The issue presently before us is a narrow one. First, we need not address the peculiar problems associated with advertising claims relating to the *quality* of legal services. Such claims probably are not susceptible of precise measurement or verification and, under some circumstances, might well be deceptive or misleading to the public, or even false. Appellee does not suggest, nor do we perceive, that appellants' advertisement contained claims, extravagant or otherwise, as to the quality of services. Accordingly, we leave that issue for another day. . . .

The heart of the dispute before us today is whether lawyers . . . may constitutionally advertise the *prices* at which certain routine services will be performed. Numerous justifications are proffered for the restriction of such price advertising. We consider each in turn:

1. *The Adverse Effect on Professionalism*. . . . It is claimed that price advertising will bring about commercialization, which will undermine the attorney's sense of dignity and self-worth. . . . Advertising is also said to erode the client's trust in his attorney: Once the client perceives that the lawyer is motivated by profit, his confidence that the attorney is acting out of a commitment to the client's welfare is jeopardized. . . .

[W]e find the postulated connection between advertising and the erosion of true professionalism to be severely strained. At its core, the argument presumes that attorneys must conceal from themselves and from their clients the real-life fact that lawyers earn their livelihood at the bar. . . .

The absence of advertising may be seen to reflect the profession's failure to reach out and serve the community: Studies reveal that many persons do not obtain counsel even when they perceive a need because of the feared price of services or because of an inability to locate a competent attorney . . . .

It appears that the ban on advertising originated as a rule of etiquette and not as a rule of ethics. . . . Since the belief that lawyers are somehow "above" trade has become an anachronism, the historical foundation for the advertising restraint has crumbled.

2. *The Inherently Misleading Nature of Attorney Advertising*. It is argued that advertising of legal services inevitably will be misleading (a) because such services are so individualized with regard to content and quality as to prevent informed comparison on the basis of an advertisement, (b) because the

consumer of legal services is unable to determine in advance just what services he needs, and (c) because advertising by attorneys will highlight irrelevant factors and fail to show the relevant factor of skill.

We are not persuaded that restrained professional advertising by lawyers inevitably will be misleading . . . . The only services that lend themselves to advertising are the routine ones: the uncontested divorce, the simple adoption, the uncontested personal bankruptcy, the change of name, and the like — the very services advertised by appellants. Although the precise service demanded in each task may vary slightly, and although legal services are not fungible, these facts do not make advertising misleading so long as the attorney does the necessary work at the advertised price.

. . . .

The third component is not without merit: Advertising does not provide a complete foundation on which to select an attorney. But it seems peculiar to deny the consumer, on the ground that the information is incomplete, at least some of the relevant information needed to reach an informed decision. The alternative — the prohibition of advertising — serves only to restrict the information that flows to consumers. Moreover, the argument assumes that the public is not sophisticated enough to realize the limitations of advertising, and that the public is better kept in ignorance than trusted with correct but incomplete information. We suspect the argument rests on an underestimation of the public. . . .

3. *The Adverse Effect on the Administration of Justice.* Advertising is said to have the undesirable effect of stirring up litigation. . . . Advertising, it is argued, serves to encourage the assertion of legal rights in the courts, thereby undesirably unsettling societal repose. There is even a suggestion of barratry.

But advertising by attorneys is not an unmitigated source of harm to the administration of justice. It may offer great benefits. Although advertising might increase the use of the judicial machinery, we cannot accept the notion that it is always better for a person to suffer a wrong silently than to redress it by legal action. As the bar acknowledges, "the middle 70% of our population is not being reached or served adequately by the legal profession." . . .

4. *The Undesirable Economic Effects of Advertising.* It is claimed that advertising will increase the overhead costs of the profession, and that these costs then will be passed along to consumers in the form of increased fees

. . . .

These two arguments seem dubious at best. Neither . . . appears relevant to the First Amendment. . . .

5. *The Adverse Effect of Advertising on the Quality of Service.* It is argued that the attorney may advertise a given "package" of service at a set price, and will be inclined to provide, by indiscriminate use, the standard package regardless of whether it fits the client's needs.

Restraints on advertising, however, are an ineffective way of deterring shoddy work. An attorney who is inclined to cut quality will do so regardless of the rule on advertising. . . . Even if advertising leads to the creation of "legal clinics" like that of appellants' — clinics that emphasize standardized

procedures for routine problems — it is possible that such clinics will improve service by reducing the likelihood of error.

6. *The Difficulties of Enforcement.* Finally, it is argued that the wholesale restriction is justified by the problems of enforcement if any other course is taken. Because the public lacks sophistication in legal matters, it may be particularly susceptible to misleading or deceptive advertising by lawyers. . . .

We suspect that, with advertising, most lawyers will behave as they always have: They will abide by their solemn oaths to uphold the integrity and honor of their profession and of the legal system. For every attorney who overreaches through advertising, there will be thousands of others who will be candid and honest and straightforward. . . .

 . . . .

In holding that advertising by attorneys may not be subjected to blanket suppression, and that the advertisement at issue is protected, we, of course, do not hold that advertising by attorneys may not be regulated in any way. We mention some of the clearly permissible limitations on advertising not foreclosed by our holding.

Advertising that is false, deceptive, or misleading of course is subject to restraint . . . . For example, advertising claims as to the quality of services — a matter we do not address today — are not susceptible of measurement or verification; accordingly, such claims may be so likely to be misleading as to warrant restriction. Similar objections might justify restraints on in-person solicitation. We do not foreclose the possibility that some limited supplementation, by way of warning or disclaimer or the like, might be required of even an advertisement of the kind ruled upon today so as to assure that the consumer is not misled . . . .

As with other varieties of speech, it follows as well that there may be reasonable restrictions on the time, place, and manner of advertising. . . .

The constitutional issue in this case is only whether the State may prevent the publication in a newspaper of appellants' truthful advertising concerning the availability and terms of routine legal services. We rule simply that the flow of such information may not be restrained, and we therefore hold the present application of the disciplinary rule against appellants to be violative of the First Amendment.

NOTES

Was *Bates* a decision whose time had come, a case which simply reflected the changing needs of society? It is interesting to read Justice Blackmun's analysis of the Arizona Bar's arguments from the perspective of time passed and new cases decided. Which of the Bar's arguments seem anachronistic and exclusionary by today's standards? Which of Justice Blackmun's points seem strong and which weak? How do you feel about Blackmun's argument that enforcement will not be a problem because only a very few in the profession will overreach and distort? Has this proved to be correct? Blackmun makes it clear that the *Bates* opinion is limited to its facts. His conclusion specifically states that many other forms of advertising and solicitation are not to be deemed acceptable by virtue of the *Bates* decision. Has it worked out this way? Or did *Bates* open Pandora's box, letting all manner and means of undignified and unpleasant legal advertising escape?

3. Have the Walls Come Tumbling Down? How far have lawyers gone in promoting their services in the years since *Bates*? Anyone familiar with the legal marketplace knows some of the ways. Telephone yellow pages are now saturated with print ads containing assurances, approvals and certifications, and pictures of the stars of the show — the lawyers who make those assurances. Ads proliferate on radio and late night television. "Targeted" mailings are sent to people with particularized legal problems. Some plaintiffs' lawyers practicing in the area of toxic and occupational torts went even further, as the following article describes.

TRACY SCHROTH, "AMBULANCE DRIVING"; MEDICAL SCREENING FOR CLIENTS STIRS CONTROVERSY
New Jersey Law Journal (March 12, 1990)[1]

Some asbestos plaintiffs lawyers don't round up business by ambulance chasing exactly. Sometimes, it's more like ambulance driving.

Last summer, an East Brunswick, N.J., firm offered free chest X-rays to factory workers exposed to asbestos — potential clients all.

A Philadelphia lawyer who sits on the board of a hospital has picked up several hundred cases through a free medical screening program at the hospital, which he helped coordinate.

And one California attorney went so far as to operate medical screening vans, known as "examobiles," that traveled from coast to coast screening tire factory workers for asbestos exposure.

The scramble for personal-injury clients — especially in the areas of product liability and toxic tort — has propelled lawyers closer and closer to the line that separates what is proper from what is not.

But that line is blurred, and fierce competition is prompting lawyers to press the limits.

Many in the legal profession say they see nothing wrong with the aggressive pursuit of clients, as long as that pursuit does not technically breach ethics. In the field of occupational disease, they contend, marketing by lawyers often provides a public service.

"There is a school of thought that says lawyers should be aggressive in searching out potential clients and advising them of their rights," says Stephen Gillers, a professor at New York University School of Law and an ethics expert.

"Inhibition mainly benefits the defendant class, who are sued less if lawyers are stymied more," he notes. . . .

Dial 1-800-8-SILICA

The issue of marketing and solicitation is especially sensitive when it concerns occupational diseases, such as asbestosis, where potential clients are considered vulnerable and unsophisticated. As the race for business intensifies and firms turn to unconventional methods, even some of the participants are uncomfortable with their tactics.

Two New Jersey firms, for example, have run newspaper advertisements notifying workers exposed to silica — a finely particled mineral used in the manufacture of iron, steel, and concrete — that they may have a right to compensation.

The inhalation of silica leads to silicosis, a progressive lung disease similar to asbestosis. Potential claimants were instructed to call "1-800-8-SILICA for a free consultation."

The ads caused a stir in the legal community, and now some lawyers from the firms that ran the ads are expressing regrets.

. . . .

Discerning Fine Lines

Meanwhile, some of the methods employed by plaintiffs attorneys are drawing the ire of ethics officials.

East Brunswick's Garruto, Galex & Cantor halted its offering of free medical screening last July when the New Jersey Supreme Court's Advisory Committee on Professional Ethics stated that the practice ran afoul of the Rules of Professional Conduct. . . .

The ethics panel, which is authorized not to take disciplinary action but only to issue opinions, said that the free-screening offer violated a rule that lawyers cannot "provide financial assistance to a client in connection with pending or contemplated litigation."

. . . .

"I have trouble differentiating between what is permissible and what is not," says Daniel Jones, director of administration for Princeton, N.J.'s Pellettieri, Rabstein & Altman, which represents asbestos plaintiffs.

"It's a very fine line. If someone has a valid claim and can't afford to get a doctor's test done, then that man's claim is no longer valid," Jones points out.

. . . .

"Tacky" Promotion

Gillers notes that even the operation of medical screening vans is not necessarily unethical.

"The defense would be that people are walking around with claims of which they are unaware. The statute of limitations may be running out or they may be dying, and the lawyer is helping the person learn," he says.

In 1986 and 1987, Gordon Stemple, a partner in Los Angeles' Stemple & Boyajian, directed medical vans that traveled to tire factories across the country to screen workers for asbestos exposure. Stemple, who also set up a non-profit group known as the National Tire Workers Litigation Project, has been sued by Raymark Industries, Inc., an asbestos manufacturer, on charges that he violated Racketeer Influenced and Corrupt Organizations laws and falsified test results. The suit is pending in U.S. District Court in Kansas.

Though unorthodox, so-called ambulance chasing, or ambulance driving, is becoming an accepted practice.

"Ambulance chasing is not a precise term. The extent to which we have allowed lawyers to be aggressive has changed over time," says Gillers.

"It may be tacky," Gillers concludes, "but it is not self-evident that it would result in more injustice."

4. Some Inventive Methods of Promotion. The activities described in the previous article are by no means the only inventive promotional techniques which lawyers have used in the past decade. Here are just a few others:

The 800 Number Hot Line. Law firms, and consortiums of law firms, have set up 800 number "hotlines" to answer simple questions, and to generate cases in the event the simple question can't be answered on the phone. Some lawyers have also tried 900 numbers, where the customer who calls must pay a per-minute fee. After costs, the profits from 900 numbers are shared between the phone company and the information provider (in this case, the lawyer or law firm).

Seminars are offered in areas of law which are either lucrative or of particular concern to specific groups, such as the elderly. Those that attend the seminars may be encouraged to engage the services of the lawyers conducting the program.

Endorsements and Testimonials are used in television ads to encourage prospective clients to call. In one series of frequently shown California TV spots, famous baseball personalities were used to encourage callers in both English and Spanish to hire a particular group of lawyers.

Private Referral Services. Many bar associations run nonprofit referral services which qualify lawyers by experience and refer potential clients to those lawyers. The past several years have seen the development of private referral services, many emphasizing personal injury referrals. Lawyers typically pay such services an initial fee plus a monthly charge — ranging anywhere from a few hundred dollars to several thousand dollars per month — and in return are rewarded with cases referred to them by the service. These services proliferate for several reasons. First, consumers have long sought out referral services, on the assumption they provide trustworthy information about lawyers from an objective source. Second, referral services have sometimes been afforded advantageous placement ahead of lawyers in the yellow pages, allowing such services to "get a jump" on the competition. Third, lawyers and non-lawyers alike see them as potential profit centers, especially since neither referral services nor those who run them (who need not be lawyers) are subject to regulation in most states.[2]

Sexually Suggestive Advertising. One female attorney, frustrated by the "old boy network" of attorneys who had cornered the market on mortgage closings, placed a series of provocative ads in the *New York Mortgage Press* to bolster her business. One had her posed alluringly on a motorcycle, clad in leather, over the inscription: "We will ride anything . . . to get to your closing on time." Her business increased 800%. Although she was threatened with discipline, the New York Supreme Court's Grievance Committee backed down. She claims that other women attorneys should use their sexual assets as weapons to manipulate men to advance their careers. In response, one male competitor appeared shirtless in an ad advertising, "I do good loans."

Advertising on the Internet. We discussed the use of Internet websites in Problem 6. When it comes to advertising, one problem that is peculiar to the Internet is the issue of lawyers broadcasting their messages far beyond the boundaries of their state of practice. May a lawyer place ads on the Internet knowing that they are accessible nation-or world-wide?

Most state bars have concluded that a lawyer may advertise on the Internet as long as the lawyer is licensed to practice in the state where the ad is initially placed. *See, e.g.*, New York State Bar Association, Committee on Professional Ethics, Opinion No. 55-97 (September 16, 1998). However, it is usually required that such ads specify the jurisdictions in which the lawyer is admitted to practice. Otherwise, as long as the ad is not false, deceptive, or misleading, Internet advertising remains an increasingly popular choice for lawyers to get out their message.

5. Websites, Solicitation, and Confidentiality. Lawyers increasingly do their advertising on the Internet, and even sole practitioners can get good, professional-looking websites to help market their services. As we discussed in Problem 6, we are still at the beginning of the Internet learning stage. Our level of understanding of websites and their relationship to solicitation and advertising will increase over time, but some issues are already emerging. David Hricik, the computer ethics expert who we last visited in Problem 6, has some thoughtful ideas about lawyers' receipt of e-mails from their websites, and the effect this has on confidentiality.

DAVID HRICIK, TO WHOM IT MAY CONCERN: USING DISCLAIMERS TO AVOID DISQUALIFICATION BY RECEIPT OF UNSOLICITED E-MAIL FROM PROSPECTIVE CLIENTS
16 (ABA) Professional Lawyer No. 3 (2005)[3]

Not too long ago, a person who wanted to hire a lawyer had to call him on the phone or stop by to see him. In that initial interview, the lawyer had to

---

[2] While the ABA Model Code and Model Rules contain provisions making it difficult for profit-making services to operate, these sections did not withstand constitutional free speech scrutiny where tested in individual states. A few states, including Texas, Florida, and California, devised regulatory schemes for these services in the late 1980s. *See, e.g.*, California Bus. & Prof. Code § 6155. In 1993, the ABA approved model standards which regulate both private and public referral services, but which have not yet been adopted in most states.

[3] Copyright © 2005 by the American Bar Association. Reprinted by permission.

make sure that undertaking the representation would not create a conflict of interest with an existing or former client. Many states hold that a person who discloses confidential information to a law firm in a good faith effort to hire it can disqualify that firm to the same extent as if it had retained it.

To avoid disqualification, the lawyer in the initial interview must control disclosure of information by the prospective client so that the lawyer learns only that information from the prospective client necessary to check conflicts. A lawyer who is *talking* to a prospective client can control the disclosure: . . . the lawyer can ask the prospective client who the adverse party will be, inquire as to the general nature of the matter, and perform a conflicts check.

In the digital age, there is less control over receipt of confidences, and greater opportunity for them to be received by firms. A web page listing lawyer e-mail addresses allows a putative client to send an e-mail to a lawyer that discloses important confidential information that could lead to disqualification of the firm. For example, a person could read a law firm web site and conclude that the firm would be an excellent choice to represent her. She could then send the firm an e-mail explaining the case, and discussing its potential strengths and weaknesses, and asking for a meeting . . . .

As one commentator posited:

> Suppose an online visitor submits an inquiry to an attorney along with the requisite information, and, before responding, the attorney determines that a partner or other member of the firm already represents the opposing party. The attorney is now in receipt of information that could create an impermissible conflict such that the online visitor making the inquiry can attempt to force a withdrawal of representation of the opposing party.

A visit to most law firms' websites reveals that lawyers are posting many different kinds . . . "disclaimers" . . . that state, essentially, that any information sent by e-mail before the firm agrees to represent the transmitting party will not be held to be confidential by the firm. Others say that no attorney-client relationship will be formed by submitting the information. These website disclaimers appear designed to avoid disqualification by receipt of information from prospective clients . . . .

For practical reasons, existence of a law firm web site increases the need for disclaimers. Having a website gives any person connected to the Internet the easy means to transmit unsolicited information to law firms, which can be done unilaterally and even contrary to the intent of the lawyer. A lawyer who receives an unsolicited telephone call can simply stop the prospective client from disclosing additional information as soon as the lawyer recognizes a conflict exists. However, an e-mail is sent instantaneously, and opened in full at once.

. . . [H]as a lawyer who merely opens an unsolicited e-mail done something to indicate to its sender that the lawyer desires to represent that person? Should an e-mail sent unilaterally by a prospective client through a law firm website be treated any differently than a phone call placed to a lawyer, or a meeting held between lawyer and prospective client? The Arizona Bar Association concluded that a lawyer who did not have a website, but had an e-mail address, did not implicitly invite submission of information by prospective clients. According to the committee, such lawyers owed no duty of confidentiality to prospective clients, since the absence of a website indicated no willingness to accept clients by e-mail.

On the other hand, the Arizona opinion reasoned that "if the attorney maintains a website without any express limitations on forming an attorney-client relation, or disclaimers explaining that information provided or received by would-be clients will not be held confidential," then the lawyer has implicitly agreed to consider forming an attorney-client relationship with those who transmit e-mail.

[Prof. Hricik then discusses a California ethics opinion that was in draft form when his article was published, which became California Formal Opinion 168-2005, and a 2005 Ninth Circuit case, *Barton v. Smith-Kline Beecham*, 410 F.3d 1104 (9th Cir. 2005).]

The California opinion dealt with possible disqualification of the law firm. The use of law firm website disclaimers may also impact the attorney-client privilege. In a recent case, the Ninth Circuit held that a plaintiff could claim privilege over information it submitted through a law firm site even though when it submitted the information it acknowledged it was not creating an attorney-client relationship. It held the information could still be claimed as privileged because the client had never agreed the information would not be held confidential and the privilege does apply to preliminary consultations.

The California opinion holds that it is not enough to avoid disqualification if a firm received information with only a "no attorney-client relationship" disclaimer. But, if the firm uses a "no confidentiality" approach, then it likely cannot claim privilege if the prospective client becomes an actual client of the firm. Thus, "no attorney-client relationship" disclaimers fail to avoid disqualification, and "no confidences" disclaimers deny prospective clients the ability to claim privilege if the firm later represents the prospective client.

In my view, neither disclaimer is the right one. The approach of Model Rule 1.18 is instructive. It does not state that there is no attorney-client relationship, or that the information will not be held in confidence. Instead, it provides that receipt of the information by the firm will not preclude it from representing another party in the matter. The principle endorsed by the rule is important. It allows firms to continue [to] represent a client in a matter adverse to a prospective client, but does not permit the firm to misuse confidential information submitted to the firm in good faith. Objections to that approach have less force than objections to an approach that ostensibly lets the firm disclose to its client critical information that had been disclosed by a prospective client who had in good faith submitted it to the firm.

NOTES

The *Barton* case referred to in the Hricik article involved a claim of attorney-client privilege in which the client and lawyer joined. That is, both argued theat the unsolicited e-mail *should* be confidential. That fact might change its application. As other state ethics committees begin examining this issue it remains to be seen where the ultimate line will be drawn.

6. The Supreme Court's Post-*Bates* Perspective. The Supreme Court has revisited the issues of lawyer advertising and solicitation several times in the years since *Bates*. With one single exception, every decision by the Court favored permitting the lawyer's activity. We briefly review each decision in turn.

● *Ohralik v. Ohio State Bar Association*, 436 U.S. 447, 98 S. Ct. 1912 (1978), and *In re Primus*, 436 U.S. 412, 98 S. Ct. 1893 (1978). These two cases were the first opportunity after *Bates* for the Court to revisit the issue of commercial speech for lawyers. They were decided on the same day, and represent opposite extremes on the issue of direct, case-specific solicitation.

In *Ohralik*, attorney Ohralik learned that two teenage girls had been injured in an automobile accident. He visited the parents of one, whom he knew slightly, and then went to the hospital, where he asked the girl, in traction, to sign a one-third contingency fee agreement. Two days later, he went back to the hospital and she signed.

Ohralik visited the second girl at her home the day after she was released from the hospital. He carried a concealed tape recorder. He told her he represented the first girl and asked if she wanted him to represent her as well. At first, she seemed confused, but ultimately said "O.K." After she changed her mind the next day, Ohralik, who had captured their conversation on tape, insisted that the girl had entered into a binding agreement, and attempted to obtain about $2,500 in fees from her. Eventually, the first girl fired Ohralik, who sued for breach of contract. Both girls complained to the bar, and the Ohio Supreme Court handed Ohralik an indefinite suspension.

The Supreme Court distinguished *Bates*, and concluded that Ohralik's overt, "overreaching" in-person solicitation of clients was not commercial free speech protected under the First Amendment. Justice Powell's opinion emphasized the danger of in-person solicitation:

> Although it is argued that personal solicitation is valuable because it may apprise a victim of misfortune of his legal rights, the very plight of that person not only makes him more vulnerable to influence but also may make advice all the more intrusive. Thus, under these adverse conditions the overtures of an uninvited lawyer may distress the solicited individual simply because of their obtrusiveness and the invasion of the individual's privacy, even when no other harm materializes. . . .

> Unlike the advertising in *Bates*, in-person solicitation is not visible or otherwise open to public scrutiny. Often there is no witness other than the lawyer and the lay person whom he has solicited, rendering it difficult or impossible to obtain reliable proof of what actually took place.

Powell concluded by emphasizing the circumstances of the Ohralik solicitations: the youth of the two girls; their vulnerability, one still in the hospital, the other seen on her first day home; the lack of opportunity for either girl to think objectively about her decision; Ohralik's emphasis on "what sounded like a cost-free and therefore irresistible offer." "The facts of this case," concluded Powell, "present a striking example of the potential for overreaching that is inherent in a lawyer's in-person solicitation."

Primus concerned the actions of attorney Primus, a private lawyer who also served as a local ACLU officer and cooperating attorney, and as a consultant to the South Carolina Council on Human Relations. On behalf of the Council, Primus met with a group of women who contended they had been sterilized as a condition of receiving Medicaid, and discussed with the women their legal rights. Later, after the ACLU agreed to provide representation in a law suit against a particular doctor, Primus wrote a letter to a woman who had attended the meeting and who had been sterilized by that doctor. She informed the woman that the ACLU would provide free legal counsel, and that "we" would come see her to "explain what is involved." The woman showed the letter to the doctor and then called Primus to decline the offer.

Again, Justice Powell wrote for the Court, but this time he found the lawyer's actions protected, and distinguished Primus' conduct from that of Ohralik:

> Unlike the situation in *Ohralik*, however, appellant's act of solicitation took the form of a letter to a woman with whom appellant had discussed the possibility of seeking redress for an allegedly unconstitutional sterilization. This was not in-person solicitation for pecuniary gain. Appellant was communicating an offer of free assistance by attorneys associated with the ACLU, not an offer predicated on entitlement to a share of any monetary recovery.

The Court relied heavily on *NAACP v. Button*, 371 U.S. 415, 83 S. Ct. 328 (1963), in determining that Primus' actions were protected by the First Amendment. Applying *Button* to the case before him, Powell concluded that "solicitation . . . for the purpose of furthering the civil-rights objectives of the organization and its members" is a protected association "for the advancement of beliefs and ideas."

Ohralik and *Primus*, though they were decided together and both deal with solicitation, are clearly distinguishable. Primus' conduct seems positively pristine in light of Ohralik's behavior, and her solicitation was by mail only, while his was in person and unusually obtrusive.

• *In re R.M.J.*, 455 U.S. 191, 102 S. Ct. 929 (1982). In this case, Missouri limited advertising to very specific categories of information. Attorney R.M.J. circulated a professional announcement which said that he was admitted in both Missouri and Illinois, that he practiced "personal injury" and "real estate" law (rather than the approved terms "tort law" and "property law"), and that he was admitted to practice before the United States Supreme Court. Justice Powell again spoke for the Court. In agreeing with *R.M.J.*, Powell drew a distinction between truthful and misleading advertising:

> Truthful advertising related to lawful activities is entitled to the protections of the First Amendment. But when the particular content or method of the advertising suggests that it is inherently misleading or when experience has proved that in fact such advertising is subject to abuse, the States may impose appropriate restrictions. Misleading advertising may be prohibited entirely. But the States may not place

an absolute prohibition on certain types of potentially misleading information, e.g., a listing of areas of practice, if the information also may be presented in a way that is not deceptive. . . .

Although the potential for deception and confusion is particularly strong in the context of advertising professional services, restrictions upon such advertising may be no broader than reasonably necessary to prevent the deception.

• *Zauderer v. Office of Disciplinary Counsel*, 471 U.S. 626, 105 S. Ct. 2265 (1985). This case concerned attorney Zauderer's "targeted" advertisement, placed in 36 newspapers throughout the state, asking women, "Did you use this IUD?" and providing information about the dangers of the Dalkon Shield. The Supreme Court reversed the reprimand imposed by Ohio, and explored why Zauderer's case was materially different from Ohralik's. Wrote Justice White:

> Because appellant's statements regarding the Dalkon Shield were not false or deceptive, our decisions impose on the State the burden of establishing that prohibiting the use of such statements to solicit or obtain legal business directly advances a substantial governmental interest.
>
> . . . . Although some sensitive souls may have found appellant's advertisement in poor taste, it can hardly be said to have invaded the privacy of those who read it. More significantly, appellant's advertisement — and print advertising generally — poses much less risk of overreaching or undue influence. Print advertising may convey information and ideas more or less effectively, but in most cases, it will lack the coercive force of the personal presence of a trained advocate [and] is not likely to involve pressure on the potential client for an immediate yes-or-no answer to the offer of representation. . . . Accordingly, the substantial interests that justified the ban on in-person solicitation upheld in *Ohralik* cannot justify the discipline imposed on appellant for the content of his advertisement.

White also directly addressed the issue of "dignity," which for so long had operated to govern attorney conduct:

> [A]lthough the State undoubtedly has a substantial interest in ensuring that its attorneys behave with dignity and decorum in the courtroom, we are unsure that [this] is an interest substantial enough to justify the abridgment of their First Amendment rights. . . . [T]he mere possibility that some members of the population might find advertising embarrassing or offensive cannot justify suppressing it.

• *Shapero v. Kentucky Bar Ass'n*, 486 U.S. 466, 108 S. Ct. 1916 (1988). Attorney Shapero took "targeted" advertising one giant step beyond *Zauderer*. He asked the state advertising commission for permission to send a letter directly to "potential clients who have had a foreclosure suit filed against them." Shapero did not know these people, only that they were facing foreclosure. The mailing, which could hardly qualify as "dignified," is worth reproducing here:

> It has come to my attention that your home is being foreclosed on. If this is true, you may be about to lose your home. Federal law may

allow you to keep your home by ORDERING your creditor [sic] to STOP and give you more time to pay them.

You may call my office anytime from 8:30 a.m. to 5:00 p.m. for FREE information on how you can keep your home. Call NOW, don't wait. It may surprise you what I may be able to do for you. Just call and tell me that you got this letter. Remember it is FREE, there is NO charge for calling.

Justice Brennan, speaking for the Court, found Shapero's conduct closer to that of Zauderer than Ohralik, reasoning as follows:

Of course, a particular potential client will feel equally "overwhelmed" by his legal troubles and will have the same "impaired capacity for good judgment" regardless of whether a lawyer mails him an untargeted letter or exposes him to a newspaper advertisement — concededly constitutionally protected activities — or instead mails a targeted letter. The relevant inquiry is not whether there exist potential clients whose "condition" makes them susceptible to undue influence, but whether the mode of communication poses a serious danger that lawyers will exploit any such susceptibility.

While the Brennan opinion upheld Shapero's right to send his letter, the Court was much more fundamentally divided in the 4-2-3 *Shapero* decision than at any time since the 5-4 decision in *Bates*. Justice O'Connor's dissent called for the reconsideration of the expansion of advertising since *Bates*, claiming the cases following *Bates* were based on "defective premises and flawed reasoning."

● *Peel v. Attorney Registration & Disciplinary Comm'n*, 496 U.S. 91, 110 S. Ct. 2281 (1990). Attorney Peel put on his letterhead that he was certified by the National Board of Trial Advocacy. The Court, despite the noises about retrenching heard in the *Shapero* dissent, supported Peel, holding the letterhead was neither actually nor inherently misleading.

● *Ibanez v. Florida Board of Accountancy*, 512 U.S. 136, 114 S. Ct. 2084 (1994). Ibanez was an attorney who also was a CPA and a certified financial planner (CFP). Her plans to use these designations on her letterhead and business cards, as well as in her yellow pages advertising, ran afoul of the Florida Board of Accountancy (but not the State Bar). The Accountancy Board reprimanded her for "false, deceptive and misleading advertising." The Supreme Court reversed, finding Florida's position "entirely insubstantial." In dissent, Chief Justice Rehnquist and Justice O'Connor complained that the designated initials, particularly the little-known "CFP," might be inherently misleading.

● *Florida Bar v. Went For It, Inc.*, 515 U.S. 618, 115 S. Ct. 2371 (1995). If the above cases left the state of the law and the extent to which advertising and solicitation may be ethical in flux, nothing prepared lawyers for the Supreme Court's decision in *The Florida Bar v. Went For It, Inc.* There, Justice O'Connor, who had shown an increasing discomfort with the extent of lawyer advertising, wrote for a 5-4 majority that upheld a Florida ban on written communications with accident victims within 30 days of the accident. Her opinion contrasted sharply with the dissent by Justice Kennedy.

O'Connor justified the Florida regulation by agreeing with the Florida Bar that "it has a substantial interest in protecting the privacy and tranquility of personal injury victims and their loved ones against intrusive, unsolicited contact by lawyers." She relied in part on a lengthy Bar summary and study containing "both statistical and anecdotal [information] supporting the Bar's contentions that the Florida public views direct-mail solicitations in the immediate wake of accidents as an intrusion on privacy that reflects poorly upon the profession." O'Connor distinguished *Shapero* by noting that the Kentucky regulation was "a broad ban on all direct-mail solicitations, whatever the time frame and whoever the recipient." She also noted that "the State in *Shapero* assembled no evidence attempting to demonstrate any actual harm."

Justice Kennedy's blistering dissent asserted that "[a]ttorneys who communicate their willingness to assist potential clients are engaged in speech protected by the First and Fourteenth Amendments," a principle "understood since *Bates*." Kennedy found it "uncontroverted that when an accident results in death or injury, it is often urgent at once to investigate the occurrence, identify witnesses, and preserve evidence. Vital interests in speech and expression are, therefore, at stake . . . ."

As for restricting speech on privacy grounds, Kennedy wrote that "we do not allow restrictions on speech to be justified on the ground that the expression might offend the listener," and thus the First Amendment must prevail. The fact that the advertising might be "offensive" or "undignified" was of no import, Kennedy noted, pointing to the opinions of the previous Supreme Court cases on commercial free speech.

Then, in unusually strong language, he wrote that "the State is doing nothing more [than engaging in] censorship pure and simple; and censorship is antithetical to the first principles of free expression. The majority describes [the Florida Bar's] anecdotal matter as 'noteworthy for its breadth and detail,'" Kennedy continued, "but when examined, it is noteworthy for its incompetence." He ended his dissent by remarking: "If public respect for the profession erodes because solicitation distorts the idea of the law as most lawyers see it, it must be remembered that real progress begins with more rational speech, not less."

7. Is Increased Regulation Either Desirable or Possible? Justice Kennedy seemed to see the entire purpose of lawyer commercial-free-speech cases screeching to a halt in *Went For It*. His arguments have resonance, particularly that the majority chose to protect lawyers' public image over free speech, and that "opposing parties" may step in during the 30-day ban.

But despite the dire predictions from those who agree with this view, thus far there have been relatively few judicial repercussions. Most court decisions that followed *Went For It* continued to uphold a lawyer's right to advertise and solicit. Some distinguished *Went For It* on the basis that Florida had a substantial body of evidence to bolster that state's claim that such contacts were invasive and caused suffering, while subsequent cases have not had such evidentiary support. Rather, it was the state bar regulators who took the lead after *Went For It*, adopting more stringent controls on both advertising and solicitation.

But state bars can wield great power when the Supreme Court is not speaking. First, read what happened in Kentucky in the aftermath of *Shapero*. Then, read how other more recent cases have been decided as many states try to beef up their regulations while still meeting the Supreme Court's constitutional requirements.

ANDREW WOLFSON, LAWYERS WHO SOLICIT CLIENTS BY MAIL PROMPT COMPLAINTS
The Courier-Journal (Louisville) (February 24, 1991)[4]

Nearly three years after Louisville lawyer Richard Shapero won America's attorneys the right to drum up business through the mail, as many as a dozen Kentucky lawyers are plastering accident victims, accused drunken drivers and other potential customers with mail solicitations.

In Jefferson County, motorists involved in wrecks — even those who suffer no apparent injuries — can expect letters from up to a half-dozen lawyers who routinely glean victims' names and addresses from police accident reports. The reports are considered public under the Kentucky Open Records Act.

Attorneys who use "targeted direct mail" say they provide a service by apprising victims and defendants of their legal rights. Louisville lawyer David Kaplan, who sends 60 to 90 such letters a week, said people who don't like them "can treat them like any other junk mail and throw them away."

But since Shapero won his case, *Shapero v. Kentucky Bar Association*, at the U.S. Supreme Court in June 1988, targeted direct mail has prompted more than 25 complaints, said Bruce Davis, KBA executive director. Davis said some complaints have come from lawyers concerned that others were trying to steal their clients.

Several motorists involved in accidents during the last two months, and who received mailings, told *The Courier-Journal* they found the solicitations annoying and unseemly.

When F.L. Ryan's car was rear-ended New Year's Day, he didn't think the accident had the makings of a court case: There were no injuries and little damage to his car.

Yet that didn't stop lawyer Sidney Hanish from rushing him a flier offering a "free first appointment" to discuss a potential personal-injury claim. To Ryan, a retired insurance adjuster, the mailing seemed like an "underhanded way to solicit business" and spur a "pseudo-injury claim." . . .

In Florida the use of targeted mail was authorized the year before the Shapero decision, and now 600 lawyers send out several hundred thousand letters annually. [But] in a June 1988 survey of 400 Floridians who received letters, 11 percent said they were so convinced that lawyers were trying to drum up phony litigation that they couldn't sit as impartial jurors if called to hear a civil case . . . . In Florida, attorneys must [now] wait 30 days before corresponding with the family of a person who has died in an accident.

. . . .

---

[4] Copyright © 1991 by Courier-Journal & Louisville Times Co. Reprinted by permission.

Louisville attorney Don Cox, who argued Shapero's case at the Supreme Court, said lawyers who oppose targeted letters are really trying to protect their traditional sources of business, not the public.

He defended the right of lawyers to immediately write to the families of deceased accident victims, noting that it is important to preserve evidence quickly in cases in which "your best witness is gone."

Cox, who doesn't use targeted mail, also defended local lawyers who send letters to motorists who have no injuries apparent at the time of their accidents.

Ironically, Shapero said that while the case made him nationally famous, targeted direct mail has been a big disappointment for him. Although his firm continues to send letters to debtors slapped with federal tax liens and to car accident victims, he said the returns have not matched the $60,000 in legal fees he spent to defeat the KBA.

NOTES

The Florida rule referred to at the end of the last article is the one that was challenged, and ultimately upheld, in the *Went For It* case.

As for "aspirational" advertising rules, how effective will they be in limiting the "hucksterism" and lack of dignity objected to by so many lawyers? And how effective will new state regulations be in light of constitutional requirements? Typical of these increased regulations is the series of advertising "standards" promulgated by the State Bar of California. These standards are quite specific in nature, including, for example, requirements for notices on both targeted and untargeted direct mail, and disclaimers for endorsements and testimonials. In contrast, the ethics rule itself ambiguously states that no solicitation of new clients is permitted "unless the solicitation is protected from abridgment by the Constitution . . . ." Does this provision imply that the new standards themselves may be overbroad? Putting these two provisions together gives the practitioner little guidance in determining what solicitations may constitutionally be regulated.

Florida approved more restrictive rules on lawyer advertising in addition to those upheld in *Went For It*. These include prohibitions on using celebrity voices, dramatizations, testimonials, and background sounds other than instrumental music, and requiring television and other visual ads to carry a legend that warns: "The hiring of a lawyer . . . should not be based solely on advertisements." These rules were challenged in *Jacobs v. Florida Bar*, 50 F.3d 901 (11th Cir. 1995). There the court reversed a grant of summary judgment in favor of the bar, and instead directed the trial court to determine if the bar could prove that the harms complained of were real and that the restrictions actually would materially alleviate the harms. And in *Mason v. Florida Bar*, 208 F.3d 953 (11th Cir. 2000), the court allowed a lawyer to use his Martindale-Hubbell "AV" rating — the organization's highest — without having to use the disclaiming language the bar wanted to require.

On the other hand, other states have allowed broader advertising and solicitation limits. Indiana, with several relatively restrictive court opinions, is one such state. In *In re Keller*, 792 N.E.2d (Ind. Sup. Ct. 2003), a law firm's television commercial, complete with a celebrity voice, had a script that called for the "insurance defense lawyer," upon learning that the Keller firm was opposing counsel, to say "Let's settle this one." No, let's not, said the state Supreme Court, which issued a public reprimand. New Jersey, another state with a history of restrictive regulation, held in 2006 that the phrase "Super Lawyer" was an impermissible and misleading marketing vehicle.[5]

Ultimately, however, history of advertising and solicitation regulations has been that they take a back seat to the Supreme Court's interpretation of the First Amendment, which has led the way in this area. State disciplinary agencies can only fill in the gaps as best they can, subject to eventual constitutional interpretation. But since the high court has not issued an opinion in over a decade, in the meantime, those state regulations fill the void, and are enforceable at the peril of the lawyers the rules cover.

8. Insurance Companies, Insurance Lawyers, and Advertising. One of the most common complaints from plaintiffs' lawyers about bans on soliciting accident victims is that posited by Justice Kennedy's dissent in *Went For It*: The bans don't apply to insurance companies, allowing them to quickly contact the victims first and encourage them to settle their claims for far less than what they are worth. In effect, some insurance companies mount "anti-lawyer" campaigns designed to dissuade or distract potential claimants from hiring lawyers to pursue their claims.

Insurance companies know that the more they can avoid having claims go to court, the more money they will save. We referenced in Problem 11's Supplemental Readings the actions of Allstate Insurance Company. Allstate was sued by injured persons after they received a company pamphlet entitled, "Do I Need an Attorney?" Some criticized the pamphlet as a thinly veiled attempt to dissuade the injured parties from hiring attorneys to pursue their claims. Both a Washington trial court and the West Virginia State Bar have agreed with this.

The rules that regulate attorney advertising and solicitation do not apply to these contacts by the insurance company and its attorneys, because the contacts are not being made for the purpose of obtaining clients. However, the fact that such contacts are permitted does not always carry much weight when limitations on solicitations by plaintiffs' attorneys are considered.

There are other examples of insurance company efforts to reach early (and low) settlements with claimants. In one California case, a claims adjuster and an insurance company lawyer manipulated a couple whose baby was badly burned while in a relative's care into believing that they were acting with the couple's and their daughter's interests in mind. The lawyer involved said he had gone to court "on behalf" of insureds "dozens and dozens of times."[6]

As we learned in Problem 11, some insurance companies use their own attorney employees to represent their insureds against third party claims,

---

[5] Opinion 39, N.J. Committee on Advertising (2006).

[6] *See Settle v. Civil Service Employees' Ins., Harper, et al.*, Alameda Co. (Calif.) Super. Ct. No. 754597-3. This case is reported in ZITRIN & LANGFORD, THE MORAL COMPASS OF THE AMERICAN LAWYER 132-33 (1999).

though a minority of jurisdictions disallow this practice. Should these in-house insurance attorneys be required to indicate on their letterhead, business cards, or websites their actual relationship with the carrier? Does failure to make these disclosures mislead the insureds into thinking that their lawyers are independent of the insurers? (Some attorneys argue that placing the affiliation on stationery or business cards will mislead the insureds into thinking that the attorneys will *not* represent their best interests.)

The Nassau County (New York) Bar Association concluded that any rule, one way or the other, was too inflexible; rather, the insured should be apprised of the lawyer's true status and then consent to the representation.[7] California State Bar Formal Opinion 1987-91 reached a different result: Anything on the letterhead other than "Law Division" would be misleading and therefore unethical.

SUPPLEMENTAL READINGS

1. Geoffrey C. Hazard, Jr., Russell Pearce, & Jeffrey W. Stempel, *Why Lawyers Should Be Allowed to Advertise: A Market Analysis of Legal Services*, 58 N.Y.U. L. Rev. 1084 (1983). A fascinating article describing in great depth the need for advertising of certain types of legal services as a way to generate demand and economies of scale. At the same time, the authors feel advertising is, at best, useless in the delivery of certain types of legal services.

2. *In re Anis*, 126 N.J. 448, 599 A.2d 1265 (1992). A well-written opinion by the New Jersey Supreme Court discussing the uncharted waters of ethical decency, after a law firm contacted the parents of one of the victims of the air disaster over Lockerbie, Scotland, the day after the body of their son had been identified.

3. Nina Keilin, *Client Outreach 101: Solicitation of Elderly Clients by Seminar Under the Model Rules of Professional Conduct*, 62 Fordham L. Rev. 1547 (March 1994). This article describes the practice of using "educational seminars" on wills, trusts, and senior entitlements to attract elderly potential clients, and the vulnerability of the elderly to the pressures which can be exerted by lawyer "salespeople."

4. *Bishop v. Iowa Comm. on Prof. Ethics & Conduct,* 521 F. Supp. 1219 (S.D. Iowa 1981), *vacated as moot*, 686 F.2d 1278 (8th Cir. 1982). This case upholds the use of "verifiable, truthful" assertions in a lawyer's advertisement, including that the associate of the lawyer who advertised was black. The court pointed out that this was a fact which some citizens in the community would want to know in choosing their attorney.

5. Several articles on Internet solicitation in addition to David Hricik's have begun to appear in academic journals. One of the more useful is Cyrus D. Mehta & Elizabeth T. Reichard, "The Ethics of Practicing Law on the Internet: Advertising, Client Confidentiality and Avoiding the Unauthorized Practice of Law," 145 PLI/NY 351 (2004), which provides a brief outline of guidelines for advertising on the Internet, including a discussion of the risks of engaging in the unauthorized practice of law, and a section on how Internet technologies

---

[7] *See* Nassau Bar Ethics Opinion 95-5 (1995).

such as e-mail affect formation and confidentiality issues relating to the attorney-client relationship The article focuses on New York, one of the few states thus far with an opinion on the issue — Opinion 2001-1 of the Association of the Bar of the City of New York (March 1, 2001).

6. *Ficker v. Curran*, 119 F.3d 1150 (4th Cir. 1997). Despite the Supreme Court's holding in *Florida Bar v. Went For It*, the Fourth Circuit held that an attorney is permitted to send written solicitations to criminal defendants within 30 days of their arrest. The court distinguished between civil cases, where the potential clients would be the ones to bring the lawsuits and had ample time beyond the 30 days to decide what to do, and criminal cases, where the client is charged against his will, cases come to trial quickly, and an attorney is needed from the outset.

7. Frederick C. Moss, *The Ethics of Law Practice Marketing*, 61 Notre Dame L. Rev. 601 (1986). A survey of lawyer advertising issues, this article is particularly helpful on the issues of intra-lawyer referral and absconding with the clients of another firm.

8. Steven A. Delchin & Sean P. Costello, *Show Me Your Wares: The Use of Sexually Provocative Ads to Attract Clients*, 30 Seton Hall L. Rev. 64 (1999). This is the article that details and explains the ramifications of Rosalie Osias' ad campaign for mortgage clients described earlier in the readings. It uses Osias' ads as a basis for analyzing the law-as-profession/law-as-business debate. What seems to astound everyone is the success of Ms. Osias' campaign.

9. Amy Busa & Carl G. Sussman, *Expanding the Market for Justice: Arguments for Extending In-Person Client Solicitation*, 34 Harv. C.R.-C.L. L. Rev. 487 (Summer 1997). The authors argue that legal services attorneys and others who provide services to low income persons should be able to solicit them in person. They argue that the state's interest in seeing that such persons have access to the courts outweighs any countervailing dangers of solicitation.

PROBLEM 31

Early in recorded history, lawyers — or their precursors — worked without compensation, except for the occasional "gratuities" they received. Today, of course, things are much different. But every lawyer is exhorted by aspirational ethical guidelines to help represent the poor and disadvantaged, the people who can't otherwise afford the services of an attorney. Despite this, legal aid lawyers, whose job it is to work with poor people, are continually overworked and overwhelmed, not to mention underpaid. How do legal aid agencies deal with the needs of the people they serve? And what should be the responsibility of *all* lawyers to assist in providing needed legal services?

The Economics of Legal Services for Indigent Clients

I. You have just been hired to head the Gold County Legal Aid Office. This is the only office in the entire county serving indigent and fixed income clients on a no fee basis. The local bar association has a pro bono panel, but it doesn't come close to meeting all the needs of the poor. The only other services offered for free are those of the public defender in criminal cases.

You find that the resources of the legal aid office are severely limited. Your staff is working as hard as can be expected but is not nearly able to handle all the routine problems that come in. After some time to assess the situation, you realize you face a number of important decisions.

1. A number of clients come to you complaining that Len Lord, one of the big rental property owners in the county, has raised rents each year by 10% or more despite a county ordinance limiting rent raises to the rate of inflation or 3.0%, whichever is less. You have handled a few individual cases, but you realize that the best approach would be a multi-party "private attorney-general" or public interest lawsuit designed to force Lord to stop his practice as to all tenants, many (but not all) of whom would qualify for legal aid services. On the other hand, you know that such litigation will be costly and very time consuming for your staff.

Should the legal aid office undertake the suit? May you refuse it when you know that many renters will get no relief otherwise?

2. After six months, the time/cost studies you have instituted show that child custody and visitation cases take up a disproportionately large amount of staff time. In addition, your clients have been able to prevail in just 18% of the cases. Many have come to you with requests for custody where you believe they stand little or no chance of success. You also find that bankruptcy cases take too much staff time, especially since the bankruptcy court is located 80 miles away.

(a) May you decide to refuse to handle all child custody and visitation proceedings? May you screen these cases and take only the ones you or your staff believe are truly meritorious? Or that you think you will actually win?

(b) May the legal aid office refuse all bankruptcy matters if you arrange instead to have a volunteer lawyer give a do-it-yourself seminar once a month to explain how people can handle their own bankruptcy filings? May you refuse these cases even if you don't give this seminar?

3. You recently sent out a survey in which your clientele voiced its opinions about the issues it found most important. The three issues at the top of the list were housing, homelessness, and basic and emergency health care. May you make these three areas your highest priority? What if you discover that the fourth most important issue in your survey was social security, but that a very high percentage of seniors who responded listed this concern number one? May you ignore this, and thus ignore the seniors' greatest need on the theory of "the greatest good for the greatest number"? Or must you take social security cases?

II. Now put yourself in the position of a first-or second-year associate in a large downtown firm. You want to do pro bono public work, but the firm has a requirement of 2,150 billable hours, which of course takes a tremendous commitment of your time. Besides, your firm does not have a substantial pro bono commitment. You haven't been able to find a partner who will serve as a pro bono mentor or support your desire to do this work. And the firm has told you that any pro bono work you do will not be credited towards your billable hours.

What can you do? What should you do? Finally, what are your thoughts about *law students* being required to perform pro bono?

READINGS

1. Life as a Legal Aid Lawyer. What is life like in the legal aid fast lane? Read this article about dedicated young attorney Robert Doggett.

RICHARD ZITRIN, FIVE WHO GOT IT RIGHT
13 Widener Law Journal 209 (2003)[1]

THE TRUE BELIEVER — Robert Doggett, Texas Rural Legal Aid, Austin, Texas.

In the 1970s, many legal aid offices had federal funding, and young, idealistic law graduates could get fellowships that gave them the opportunity to spend a few years representing poor people. Some stayed on as staff lawyers. But the days when the needs of the poor were a high funding priority are long gone. Many legal services agencies have closed, and financial woes are a constant strain for those that remain.

Today's legal aid lawyers must accept personal costs if they want to represent the poor. They will be grossly underpaid. They will be overwhelmed with work. Far more people will need their services than even the best of them can possibly handle. Yet, some still seek this work. Those few who, like Robert Doggett, decide to make a career of representing poor people make a long-term commitment to personal sacrifice. [Here in his own words is Robert Doggett's story.]

---

[1] Copyright © 2003 by Richard Zitrin. Used with permission of the author and the Widener Law Journal. All rights reserved.

* * * * *

My clients are poor people. They have problems they don't deserve and didn't cause. Most aren't well educated and have little power. They're the least likely to complain or have the resources to change their situation. But they're the ones who need help the most. My job is to help as best as I can.

When I got out of law school, I went to work for the Dallas Tenants Association. Part of my job was to try and keep people from being homeless, and we were very effective at that. In court I'd see people representing themselves and getting evicted in about ten seconds. So I'd jump in and say "Excuse me, judge; just a moment." I'd walk up to the person and say, "It seems like you need some help; I'm free and I'd be happy to help you." The judges just hated that! It would slow down their docket and the eviction process. But when I got involved, they would actually have to hear evidence on the issues. I still did some of those cases long after my job changed because I just couldn't stop — I hear such horrible stories.

Now, a lot of people tell me they're against what I'm doing. But if you tell people the facts of a particular case, then they say, "Of course, that's different." Once I worked on a tenant's action where the people in a housing complex lost their utilities and air conditioning for two months. It was a hot Texas summer, and the landlord was doing nothing. He even threatened to call the cops on us. It was so bad we got some good TV coverage.

Anyway, it's getting extremely ugly when I get a call at home at 8:00 on a Saturday morning from the landlord's lawyer. He says "It's fixed, I promise, it's all fixed. So I want you to call off Monday's hearing." We call to check with the tenants and it's true: after 63 days, the problems are fixed! So my co-counsel and I get back on the phone with the landlord's lawyer, and he says "I want to put somebody on the line named Dorothy and I want you to do me a favor. Just confirm the truth." Then he says "Now, Dorothy, can you hear? I have the tenants' lawyers on the line."

It turns out Dorothy is the owner's mother-in-law. It seems she saw the stories on TV, realized it was one of her son-in-law's complexes, and felt shamed. The attorney told me that at Shabbas dinner — they're Jewish — she blew a gasket and said to fix the problems, no matter what the cost. So the lawyer wanted me to confirm that everything was fixed. It's funny, we like to think that we're the saviors, that it's our great legal work that fixes things, when this time it was the defendant's mother-in-law.

I worked four years at the Tenants Association. I was their only attorney. My first year, I worked for $25,000 and then they raised me to $30,000. My student loans? I never really liked to add them up back then, but they were in the $50,000 zone. It wasn't real good; I just couldn't afford to pay them. But I was lucky. My rent was low and my wife's law school had a loan forgiveness program for public service. Last year I paid the loans off. It only took twelve years!

When I started law school, I was on the standard career track. If somebody had said "You're going to be doing Legal Aid work," I'd have said "No way." But I quickly realized that there were things happening out in the real world that I had never been exposed to before. A friend invited me to help him interview applicants for a free legal clinic.

Maybe it was meeting these people and understanding what they had been through. They'd tell me their whole life story hoping I'd help. We had to tell a lot of people that we couldn't help them, and that was very disturbing to me. They poured their guts out and nothing was going to come of it just because there weren't enough volunteer attorneys.

So I got involved with the law student *pro bono* committee at Southern Methodist. I pulled just about every trick in the book to get students to do volunteer work. One time I wrote an article for the school newspaper called "This Has Nothing to Do with Sex." It didn't! It was about *pro bono* work. I know, it's a cheap trick.

I interviewed with the big firms. I ate at all the fancy places in town my last year. I had one offer from a good firm. But I knew fighting for an insurance company or a big bank wouldn't really get me going, and if I don't get excited about what I'm doing, I'm not going to do as good a job. Besides, living from vacation to vacation was not my idea of life . . . .

So when I turned down the offer from the firm, I had no job. That was the most difficult part. My father wasn't thrilled when I told him.

My parents were both puzzled. They knew I had a lot of student loans. I got a birthday card a few years ago saying something like, "We are proud of what you are doing. We are still not really sure why." For years, my mom wondered why I do what I do. She would like to feel she doesn't have to worry about me anymore. When I worked in Dallas, every once in a while when she wanted to do me a favor my Mom would have my dry cleaning done. She'd pick up my suits and shirts, have them cleaned, and bring them back, just to save me a little money.

* * * * *

I finally did get to work for Legal Services of North Texas. In one of my first cases there, I represented some low income folks on a hazardous waste problem, something legal services traditionally hasn't done. But the environment is an issue that affects poor people more than most. They have a hazardous waste blender in West Dallas that is an extreme danger to the community right across the street, and the State agency had the audacity to say that we didn't have the right to be heard in the permit process. All we were after was the same level of protection as anyone else.

The homes across from the plant are owned by the residents. They're all Hispanic. Most of them speak broken English at best and they generally don't get involved in lawsuits, but the stench coming from the plant was so bad they couldn't go outside. They were afraid for their kids. We had testimony about the stench, but the agency still said "Sorry, it doesn't prove the odors come from the plant." We finally got a court opinion saying it's absurd for a state agency to deny us the right to be heard.

Poverty work comes down to benefits, family issues and housing and consumer issues. At this point, I am not scared of any issue. Just get me up to speed on it, let's find the problem and go after it.

Usually, though, Rule No. 1 is "Don't file a lawsuit." You have to break Rule No. 1 once in a while, but it's a rule you start with. Lawyers are trained to be technicians, to look to the law to solve problems. But I was trained to think of more creative ways. If we sue and lose, the other side will claim that everything they were doing was fine, even if that's not what the judge said. I walk into a room full of people and say "How many of you think a judge is going to solve your problems today? I am dying to file a lawsuit." Nobody raises their hand . . . .

* * * * *

Bill Bridge, my evidence professor and a very good listener, taught me something. I said "Hey, I'll just get one of these regular jobs and do *pro bono* work on the side, and I can pay off my student loans in a couple of years." He looked at me and said "You know what's going to happen if you do that? You'll work your butt off, come home at 9:00 at night and there is no way you're going to have time to do *pro bono* work. Don't fool yourself."

I went from a small country town to Plano, a nice suburb, but hardly a cultural melting pot, graduated from Texas A&M, then to SMU law school, and I turned out like this! After ten years of practice in two legal aid jobs, I was 33 and living in the same apartment I had when I was in law school. I lived there for 13 years. The price was right!

My parents were both conservative Republicans, but we were always taught "do unto others." Until my dad died a few years ago, he worked for a refrigeration company. I remember going with him to people's houses at 3:00 a.m. holding a flashlight while he repaired a busted refrigerator. He was always willing to help people no matter when, day or night.

Personal life? Frankly it's hard to have time for one. But I finally found someone who lived in Austin. Raman moved to Dallas to start at the Public Defender's office. She and I got married a few years ago. We're compatible because we're both very intolerant of intolerance.

Raman never much liked Dallas, so we eventually went to Austin. She works part-time for the Texas Innocence Project and part-time for Texas Appleseed. We both love what we do. A family? Let's say we don't have kids yet but we're in intense negotiations.

[And] regardless of where I live or exactly what I'm doing, I don't have any intention of stopping this work, ever.

* * * * *

Robert Doggett is a long way from the novice attorney straight out of law school who began his career with only his student pro bono experience as training. He's now a recognized expert in housing and environmental issues involving poor people. In late 1999, he took a break from his legal aid service to serve a stint working with the Dallas City Attorney. His job was to teach staff attorneys the techniques he had developed to successfully sue slumlords. Having completed this task, he returned to legal aid. His job in Austin is his third as a legal aid lawyer, he considers himself a "lifer."

2. Making Choices About Which Cases to Take. We will reconsider the advisability of mandatory pro bono later in these readings. But before we do, let's take a closer look at one legal aid office confronted by problems similar to those faced in Gold County: underfunding, understaffing, and far too many cases to choose from.

RALPH JIMENEZ, VETO WILL AFFECT LEGAL ASSISTANCE FOR STATE'S POOR
The Boston Globe (June 12, 1994)[2]

Every week, the Manchester office of New Hampshire Legal Assistance receives several hundred pleas for help from people who are losing their homes, facing utility shutoffs or being denied pension, health care or welfare benefits.

On Thursdays, the office staff rides a trembling shower stall of an elevator up to the dingy Elm Street rooms where they meet to decide whose case they can afford to take and who will get a pamphlet explaining their rights and an apology. Next year, because of a gubernatorial veto, more people will get an apology instead of their day in court, the nonprofit organization's lawyers said.

"It's an agonizing, triage decision," Elliott Berry, a legal assistance lawyer since 1976, said of the Thursday meetings. "We decide who is likely to make it without our help and who is likely to lose no matter what we do. Then we try to concentrate on who we can do the most for. But it really is like playing God and it's by far the worst part of the job. I can't remember our resources ever being thinner than they are now."

New Hampshire is one of seven states that spends no money to provide legal help to poor people who are not accused of a crime serious enough to land them in jail. On Wednesday, Gov. Stephen E. Merrill vetoed a bill that would have raised $240,000 for Legal Assistance by adding a $5 surcharge to the court fees paid by those who file civil lawsuits.

State Sen. Susan McLane, prime sponsor of the funding bill, thinks Legal Assistance supporters have the votes to pull off the first override of a Merrill veto. The bill has the support of former Sen. Warren Rudman, a national champion of legal services for the poor, and like Merrill, a former attorney general.

"It is clear to me that this organization plays a pivotal role in making sure our justice system works for everyone, regardless of income. Federal funding for legal assistance has never been sufficient and private contributions cannot make up the difference," Rudman said in a letter supporting the bill.

In issuing his seventh veto of the session, the governor faulted Legal Assistance for suing the state in the past and said he does not intend to provide money to an organization that intends to haul the state into court in the future. . . .

"I am not trying to do away with Legal Assistance. I think as they were originally intended to be, which is an organization to help the poor and needy, they did a good job and continue to do a good job," Merrill said. "But I don't

---

[2] Reprinted courtesy of The Boston Globe.

want to encourage them to become a cause-oriented organization that continues to spend too much of its time lobbying and too much of its time bringing litigation against the state in matters that, in my opinion, are not related to poverty."

. . . .

[Both Legal Assistance Director Robert] Gross and Berry, however, say class action suits by Legal Assistance were a major force behind reforms that have made New Hampshire's mental health and penal systems a model for the nation. And such suits are filed only when other means have failed to solve a problem shared by many people, Gross said. . . .

Legal Assistance gets the bulk of its $1.7 million budget from two sources, the federal Legal Services Corp. and a program that captures the interest earned on temporary bank accounts held in trust briefly by lawyers for clients. Federal funds are off because New Hampshire's poor were last officially counted in 1989 — before recession swelled their numbers, Gross said. And low bank interest rates have cost the agency $200,000 a year.

With 18 lawyers to cover the state and more than 24,000 calls for help — 10,000 to the Manchester office alone — a low-income resident's odds of securing a lawyer are less than one in seven. Last week's veto, unless it is overridden later this month, will mean Legal Assistance's staff will shrink by two or three more people, Gross said.

"It's going to mean that 4,000 to 5,000 people that we might have helped through one means or another will not receive help," Gross said. "In the last three years, we've cut our program by 20 percent."

NOTES

Is Governor Merrill right that New Hampshire Legal Assistance did not sufficiently steer clear of politics? Or can class actions be a necessary part of the work of representing the poor? And what effect should threats to funding have on a legal aid group's decision to take on class actions or declaratory relief cases?

3. Tough Lawyers Making Tough Choices. In the years since the previous article was written, legal assistance has taken more hits, including a 25% decrease in federal funding between 1996 and 2000, and a 1996 Congressional act prohibiting federally-funded legal services organizations from engaging in class actions.[3] This means a lot of tough decisions for legal aid lawyers everywhere. Compounding the problem is the fact that even if funding isn't *legally* tied to not suing the state or other powerful entities, practicalities often limit a program's available scope. Robert Doggett ran into just that problem when the associates he recruited from Dallas' Akin, Gump found themselves in court opposing a landlord who was a good friend of several of the firm's partners. More overt conflicts of interest, of course, can knock potential pro bono volunteers right off a case.

---

[3] Though in *Legal Services Corp. v. Velazquez*, 531 U.S. 533, 121 S. Ct. 1043 (2001), the Supreme Court, citing First Amendment grounds, prohibited Congress' ability to limit funds to Legal Services Corporation organizations that challenged existing welfare laws.

Sometimes, the tough choices made by well-meaning but understaffed and financially strapped public service attorneys arouse the ire of the very communities they are trying to serve. In early 1994, the Legal Assistance Foundation of Chicago realized it too was only serving a small percentage of those in need. But when the foundation chose to close an office in a largely Latino area, the closing resulted in distress and outrage in both the Spanish-speaking community and the leadership of the Spanish-speaking bar.

Meanwhile, more states declined to pick up their share of the funding burden. IOLTA (client trust account) monies for legal aid organizations have long been insufficient and diminish enormously when interest rates are low. IOLTA accounts have been under attack by parties who are claiming to have financial losses and in the past few years, several cases have made it to the United States Supreme Court. After you read this case, consider whether you think IOLTA accounts are an appropriate source of funding for legal services to the poor. Who or what should bear the financial burden of providing legal services to those who cannot afford them?

BROWN v. LEGAL FOUNDATION OF WASHINGTON
538 U.S. 216, 123 S. Ct. 1406 (2003)

JUSTICE STEVENS delivered the opinion of the Court.

The State of Washington, like every other State in the Union, uses interest on lawyers' trust accounts (IOLTA) to pay for legal services provided to the needy. Some IOLTA programs were created by statute, but in Washington, as in most other States, the IOLTA program was established by the State Supreme Court pursuant to its authority to regulate the practice of law. In *Phillips v. Washington Legal Foundation,* 524 U.S. 156, 118 S.Ct. 1925, 141 L.Ed.2d 174 (1998), a case involving the Texas IOLTA program, we held "that the interest income generated by funds held in IOLTA accounts is the 'private property' of the owner of the principal." We did not, however, express any opinion on the question whether the income had been "taken" by the State or "as to the amount of 'just compensation,' if any, due respondents." We now confront those questions.

I

As we explained in *Phillips,* in the course of their legal practice, attorneys are frequently required to hold clients' funds for various lengths of time . . . . Before 1980 client funds were typically held in non-interest-bearing federally insured checking accounts. Because federal banking regulations in effect since the Great Depression prohibited banks from paying interest on checking accounts, the value of the use of the clients' money in such accounts inured to the banking institutions.

In 1980, Congress authorized federally insured banks to pay interest on a limited category of demand deposits referred to as "NOW accounts." In response to the change in federal law, Florida adopted the first IOLTA program in 1981 authorizing the use of NOW accounts for the deposit of client funds, and providing that all of the interest on such accounts be used for charitable purposes. Every State in the Nation and the District of Columbia have followed Florida's lead and adopted an IOLTA program, either through their legislatures or their highest courts. The result is that . . . today, because of the adoption of IOLTA programs, [t]he aggregate value of those contributions in 2001 apparently exceeded $200 million.

. . . .

A state law that requires client funds that could not otherwise generate net earnings for the client to be deposited in an IOLTA account is not a "regulatory taking." A law that requires that the interest on those funds be transferred to a different owner for a legitimate public use, however, could be a *per se* taking requiring the payment of "just compensation" to the client. Because that compensation is measured by the owner's pecuniary loss — which is zero whenever the Washington law is obeyed — there has been no violation of the Just Compensation Clause of the Fifth Amendment in this case.

NOTES

There is one additional ray of sunshine on this otherwise bleak landscape: the efforts on the part of a number of law schools to offer full or substantial payment of student loans for any graduate working in low-paying public interest law jobs. New York University, a school long committed to extensive programs in the public interest, led the way with a proposal that for every year a graduate remained in a public service job, the law school would repay one-tenth of that lawyer's student loans, up to a 100% payment after 10 years. The purpose was clear: encourage new lawyers to go into public interest fields by substantially reducing their concern about repaying loans. "If [students] want a career in public service," the executive director of N.Y.U.'s Public Interest Law Center told the *New York Times*, "we can tell them . . . nothing will stand in your way. The choice is yours."[4] But public interest jobs, among the most sought-after by law students, are themselves limited by the funding problems such programs face. Does your law school have a loan forgiveness program? Do you think this is an acceptable way of encouraging people to do public interest work? How should we define "public interest work"?

4. Walking the Walk: Accomplishing Pro Bono Work. It is clear from the circumstances we've described that the legal needs of all Americans cannot be met by legal aid alone. Much has been said and much more written about the need for pro bono work to bridge the gap.

What can a young associate bring to the table? Robert Doggett recalls having to cover two courts and searching for a body, any body with a bar card, to stand before one judge alongside a client in need. Whether a young lawyer has that opportunity will depend in large part on the law firm.

Many of the nation's largest and most prestigious firms have come to consider pro bono as an important part of their practice. Some, like New York's Cravath, Swaine, have taken on impact litigation to preserve important rights for people who could not otherwise afford representation. Others send their attorneys to legal aid clinics, or to assist lawyers like Robert Doggett in handling their overwhelming caseloads. A few, like Morgan, Lewis & Bockius, not

---

[4] *See* N.Y. TIMES, Nov. 9, 1994.

only count all pro bono hours towards the billable hour requirement, but don't limit those hours once a case is accepted. Washington, D.C.'s Hogan & Hartson has created a separate community services department within the firm with the specific task of handling pro bono cases. The department is peopled by one partner, rotated every three or four years, and three associates.

D.C.'s Crowell & Moring hired a full-time lawyer to coordinate pro bono work. She gets to do everything from deciding what kinds of cases to take, to exhorting her colleagues to do the work and matching them with the most appropriate cases, to overseeing the work and providing training, backup, guidance, and quality control.

In many localities, bar associations have taken the lead by making pro bono work by its member law firms a high priority item. Partly because it gives its pro bono participants a high profile, the Bar Association of San Francisco has helped persuade hundreds of attorneys from scores of firms both to take on cases in the bar's own extensive pro bono projects and to undertake pro bono matters on their own.

Though they lag behind the most productive law firms, many corporate law departments also provide significant pro bono services. Companies like Aetna and Xerox have long encouraged their lawyers to participate in pro bono, and have organized pro bono committees within their law departments.

We have heard from countless lawyers, many of them former students, that their pro bono work was the most gratifying work they were doing. Here is an example, from a young tax attorney at a large New York firm.

VICTOR E. FLEISCHER, NEEDLEWORK AND SOAP OPERAS ON DEATH ROW
law.com (May 7, 2001)[5]

This is how you find out you are next: an execution order that you — the condemned — must sign. No reassuring words like habeas corpus or executive clemency. No phone call from your lawyer, because you do not have one. "I, Larry L. Jenkins Jr., shall be executed by the Department of Corrections at such penal institution and on such a date and time within the aforementioned time period as may be designated by said Department . . . ."

You sign the order. You do what you are told. Certainly you don't know the law. What do you know? Georgia still has the electric chair. You've heard about Old Sparky, the chair used in Florida. You've seen the pictures. You wonder if next month it will be a picture of you . . . .

What you need is a lawyer. You need a lawyer to explain that the execution order is just a legal chess move — the attorney general's procedural gambit to force a habeas petition to be filed quickly. You need a lawyer to take a second look at the trial that landed you on death row.

I am writing this article to encourage other big-firm associates to get involved with death penalty work. . . .

Larry Jenkins became a client of Davis Polk & Wardwell shortly before his execution order went into effect. In hopes of taking a death penalty case, our

---

[5] Copyright © Victor E. Fleischer. Reprinted by permission of the author and law.com.

firm had been in contact with Terri Piazza, a member of the tireless staff of the nonprofit Georgia Resource Center in Atlanta . . . . [I]n March 1999, I signed my very first court paper as a lawyer: Motion for Stay of Execution. An unusual court paper for anyone to file, let alone a junior associate in the tax department at a large firm in New York City.

A few weeks later I visited our new client on death row at the Diagnostic and Classification Center in Jackson, Ga. Many things I learned that day were trivial, yet I will never forget them. I learned that mentally retarded persons, like Larry Jenkins, usually look "normal." I learned that Larry spends 23 hours a day in his cell, mostly watching television. I learned that crocheting is the new hobby on death row. (Who knew? Apparently the prison gives the inmates plastic needles and yarn, and the inmates can send away for patterns.)

Larry had crocheted a picture of Jesus to give to Terri. . . . Larry and I talked about his favorite soap operas, "General Hospital" and "All My Children." Larry explained that he does his needlework during the commercials, because he has to pay full attention during the soaps. I learned that Larry was in ninth grade when he was arrested for murder. Finally we talked about basketball, which at least is something I know a little about. Larry confirmed that every hoops fan outside New York, including those on Georgia's death row, hates the Knicks.

I also learned on that day that I had a client who needed me. I have spent much of my three years in the practice of law feeling a bit daunted by the often surreal nature of my work — facing abstruse questions like whether the tax-straddle rules apply to prepaid forward contracts. Not exactly the cliff-hanger material of "Law and Order" or "The Practice." On Larry's case we argue about whether the jury would have sentenced this young man to death if he had received a fair trial. That's a prime-time question.

And the human connection to my client is more real than anything I've personally felt on a conference call. My billable work has been stimulating, challenging and rewarding . . . . But the one time in my short legal career I have not harbored any doubts about what I was doing was that afternoon when I walked out of that prison, thinking about needlework, soap operas, and Larry Jenkins. If I am ever asked what I accomplished before I turned 30, I will speak with pride about my work for Larry Jenkins. It is the one thing I have done so far with my J.D. that I will someday tell my grandchildren about.

      . . . .

Many of the best and brightest law school graduates each year come to New York to work for big firms. We all have been fortunate enough to receive outstanding legal educations. Some of us have spent a year or two clerking for the federal courts and working on death penalty cases. We have a responsibility to put that training to use.

I urge you to speak up. Write a quick e-mail to the pro bono coordinator, or the recruiting coordinator, or a partner, at your firm. . . . Visit www.probono.net to get an idea of the resources that are available. Talk to the dedicated lawyers at local organizations . . . who stand ready to guide volunteer lawyers through the process. Talk to lawyers at other firms who have been involved with a case. The clients are waiting, and they need you.

NOTES

Victor Fleischer continues his work as a valued member of the New York City bar's capital punishment committee. There are several obvious points to be learned from this article. We mention two: First, the lawyer got as much out of the experience as the client, a most common experience. Second, while Fleischer calls out for representation of those on death row without counsel, the call could be for many other indigent clients in many other situations. Only the names — and the legal issues — are different. The stories, though, are no less compelling.

5. A Pervasive and Increasing Need for Assistance. Clearly, many lawyers dedicate themselves devotedly to pro bono work. Significantly, however, despite the participation of these attorneys in big firms and small — and the joy they get from their experience — there are far more in need of legal services than those receiving help. Worse, the evidence is that the gulf is growing wider.

Participation in pro bono programs by lawyers and law students alike is uneven at best, with many, perhaps most, giving *no* time to such efforts. For example, while some corporate law departments are strongly committed to pro bono, a 1990 ABA survey showed that over three-fourths of large corporate counsel departments had no formal pro bono program.

While many private law firms do extensive pro bono work, some averaging as much as 100 hours or more per lawyer per year, others do little or none. "I do pro bono work myself and started a firm pro bono committee, but frankly, the committee consists mostly of me," complains one lawyer of our acquaintance, a partner in a 200-lawyer firm. "I get no support from my partners. Most of them think I'm wasting time — time I could turn into billable hours. So the associates I try to encourage are instead discouraged from helping me." Even in firms which extol the virtues of pro bono and emphasize their commitment, pro bono may not be accorded an equal status. Thus, while Crowell & Moring's hiring of a full-time pro bono coordinating lawyer is laudable, the attorney occupies a non-partnership track position.

The recent upturn in big firm salaries, and the subsequent economic downturn, have only made matters worse, as the following article describes.

GREG WINTER, LEGAL FIRMS CUTTING BACK ON FREE SERVICES FOR POOR
The New York Times (August 17, 2000)[6]

Many of the nation's biggest law firms — inundated with more business than they can often handle and pressing lawyers to raise their billable hours to pay escalating salaries — have cut back on pro bono work so sharply that they fall far below professional guidelines for representing people who cannot afford to pay.

---

[6] Copyright © 2000 by The New York Times Company. Reprinted by permission.

The roughly 50,000 lawyers at the nation's 100 highest-grossing firms spent an average of just eight minutes a day on pro bono cases in 1999. . . . That comes out to about 36 hours a year, down significantly from 56 hours in 1992. . . . Yet with the economy booming, firms are enjoying record profits, the survey also found. . . .

"When there is more work than lawyers to do it, and there are not enough new lawyers out there to hire, the pro bono gets shelved," [said Jack] Londen, [a partner at San Francisco's Morrison & Foerster.]

. . . .

"What we're seeing is a sea change, rather than just a rogue wave," said Eugene R. Fidell, head of an advisory committee of the Federal District Court in Washington [D.C.];

Since many large firms raised starting pay for new associates by as much as $25,000 this year, hoping to dissuade them from flocking to Internet start-ups, many worry that the ebb in pro bono work will only accelerate.

"We're under pressure to work hard to pay for these rising salaries," said John Payton, a partner at Wilmer, Cutler & Pickering and president-elect of the Bar Association of Washington.

Susan Hoffman, the partner in charge of pro bono assignments at Crowell & Moring, has taken to cornering lawyers in hallways at the big Washington firm. Her e-mail pleas go unanswered, memos no longer work and phone calls leave her colleagues unmoved. . . .

The drop-off in pro bono work comes when the legal community can least afford it, many public interest groups say. Since 1996, the Legal Services Corporation, a major source of representation for low-income people in noncriminal cases, has lost a quarter of its financing from the federal government. . . .

Vera E. Kennedy, 55, is also frustrated by the lack of free legal representation. Ms. Kennedy's apartment is one of about 270 units at Hunter's View, a San Francisco public housing development that the city wants to demolish and rebuild.

When similar buildings were torn down a few years ago, prominent firms made sure residents had adequate interim housing and would be allowed to move back when work was finished. Local public interest lawyers have been scrambling unsuccessfully for months to find a firm to do the same for Ms. Kennedy and the other tenants. "There are mothers with young children here," she said. "They need the protection of having a place to live."

. . . . A 1993 study by the American Bar Association showed that less than 30 percent of low-income people who needed a lawyer for a civil matter actually got one — proof that, even at its best, volunteerism may not solve the legal difficulties of the poor.

"But a problem that was bad in 1993 is only going to be exacerbated by the fact that you have fewer lawyers doing pro bono," said Deputy Attorney General Eric H. Holder Jr., who has been directed by President Clinton to monitor and promote pro bono work in minority communities.

. . . .

Most firms say it is not their commitment that has waned, just their ability to take on as many cases as in the past. While lawyers typically billed 1,700 hours annually just a few years ago, today they routinely bill 2,200 to 2,300 hours, said Esther F. Lardent, director of the Pro Bono Institute at the Georgetown University Law Center.

. . . .

To pay for rising salaries, most firms have raised the minimum number of hours lawyers are expected to bill clients, yet often do not count pro bono work in the totals.

"We didn't want to be in a position where the associates would decide between doing their fee-paying work or not," said R. Bruce McLean, chairman of Akin, Gump, Strauss, Hauer & Field in Washington. Last year, the firm decided not to credit pro bono time until lawyers billed at least 2,000 hours in a given year.

. . . .

But even when volunteer hours, are, in theory, given equal weight, some associates feel that their careers will be better served by concentrating on paying clients and steering new business to the firm.

NOTES

Note that the same Crowell & Moring that created a pro bono coordinator now finds that coordinator struggling to get lawyers to participate. If pro bono is in such trouble in firms that are favorably disposed to public service, like Crowell and San Francisco's Morrison, what is the likely story at those firms without such a strong tradition? The evidence points to pro bono work being grossly inadequate to meet needs. Yet, with approximately 1.2 million lawyers in the country, if even half did the ABA-recommended 50 hours a year, that would mean 30 *million* lawyer-hours a year devoted to those in need.

6. A Call for Mandatory Pro Bono. Should every lawyer be *required* to perform pro bono service? The issue has been debated in the last 30 years among legal services lawyers, bar association officials, and other representatives of both the profession and public interest groups. But little consensus has been reached.

One of the most compelling and widely discussed and reproduced statements favoring mandatory pro bono was the testimony of Orville H. Schell, then president of the Association of the Bar of the City of New York, before a U.S. Senate Judiciary subcommittee over a quarter of a century ago. Schell concluded not only that pro bono was "one of profession's principal obligations," but that there was "a longstanding general lack of commitment by lawyers" to do this work. Most controversial was his view that pro bono service should be mandatory: "Not to have it enforceable will leave the providing of these services right where it is now, on the shoulders of a few lawyers of good will while the great majority go merrily on their way." Moreover, Schell took the position that lawyers could neither buy themselves out of doing pro bono, nor fulfill it by doing good works — such as for churches or schools — that were not legal services.

Schell's reasoning did not rest on the frequently advanced theory that lawyers hold a monopoly on legal work through their licensing; he pointed out that "plumbers and TV repairmen" were also licensed. Instead he cited lawyers' role in the administration of justice.

"I am now convinced, as a philosophical matter," Schell stated, "that lawyers, unlike groups such as plumbers, manufacturers of can openers, oil barons (unhappily), undertake an obligation to the public when they enter the bar. That obligation is to devote some portion of their professional life to the delivery of legal services at non-compensatory rates, or no fees at all."

"Believing, then, that the profession does have such an obligation, I submit that, one way or the other, it must be made an enforceable obligation."[7]

Schell's remarks, given much play at the time, were immediately controversial. Some argued that "mandatory pro bono" was indentured servitude, others that it was an oxymoron — after all, how could anything done pro bono be "mandatory"? Nothing much came of his pronouncement, but it set the stage for future debate. Moreover, in addition to raising the fundamental question of whether pro bono work should be required at all, Schell's statement contained many of the elements of what has become a long-running continuing debate on mandatory pro bono. Among them are these:

(1) Should lawyers be entitled to buy themselves out of participation in pro bono by paying a fee, or by allowing more junior lawyers in their firm to do the work for them, or must everyone participate, as Schell believes? (2) Should doing non-legal community service suffice, or is the very nature of pro bono work legal? (3) Should the pro bono work necessarily be on behalf of poor people, or should work "on behalf of the legal system or legal profession" also be allowed? (4) Should those in public interest work or in the public sector also be required to do pro bono? (5) What about sole practitioners who claim they struggle to make it as it is, and who see many potential clients whom they consider "pro bono" because they provide these people uncompensated advice without it resulting in a case? And, always, (6) How will pro bono projects be funded?

Let us add one other question: Should "pro bono" include work which, if successful, might result in a substantial attorneys' fee award to the law firm? We know of several firms that have appeared to base their selection of pro bono "impact" cases on the likelihood of being awarded fees down the road.

7. Should — and Can — Mandatory Pro Bono Be Legislated? Interestingly, some of those most strongly in favor of mandatory pro bono have been attorneys from larger, well-established firms who, like Orville Schell, see a clear professional obligation. These lawyers also understand that associates who wish to do pro bono in a law firm with little pro bono history are likely to encounter enormous resistance unless they are fulfilling a requirement of the profession.

Just as interesting is the fact that some of the strongest opponents of mandatory pro bono are legal services attorneys themselves, who feel that forcing a lawyer to do pro bono may provide their programs with "volunteer" attorneys

---

[7] Testimony from the U.S. Subcommittee on Judiciary subcommittee, Feb. 3, 1974.

who are neither ready nor willing to do the job, nor motivated to learn. Many public service lawyers would rather see the money which would be spent for mandatory pro bono reporting systems going to enhance their own programs' limited budgets.

The debate over defining what constitutes pro bono has also caused controversy. In January 1980, the ABA proposed a rule requiring "unpaid public interest legal service," but allowing that a lawyer could "discharge this responsibility by service in activities for improving the law, the legal system, or the legal profession" as well as by representing the poor. To some attorneys, this was a reasonable way to get every lawyer's participation. To others, including many involved in legal services for the poor, this was simply too broad a definition of pro bono. The proposal was never approved.

By the early 1990s, the movement toward mandatory pro bono, while it had hardly been a groundswell, started to pick up steam again. Some proponents felt that the prevalence and acceptance, though sometimes begrudging, of mandatory continuing legal education showed that lawyers would eventually accept mandatory pro bono if they had to. But by the end of the decade there had been little change. The following article describes what happened when a Colorado advisory committee recommended a minimal mandatory pro bono scheme.

DEBRA BAKER, MANDATING GOOD WORKS
ABA *Journal* (March 1999)[8]

The subject of pro bono service seldom makes for lively conversation, but in Colorado it is almost all lawyers are talking about.

A proposal that would make Colorado the first state to force its lawyers to provide free legal service to the needy is arousing heated debate among the state's 25,000 lawyers, most of whom oppose the idea.

The concept came out of an 18-month study by a committee of the state's Judicial Advisory Council . . . .

Last June, the committee released its recommendations, one of which was mandatory pro bono service. . . .

"It is the best way to increase the level of services," says Ed Kahn, co-chair of the council's legal services committee. "It won't solve the problem, but if we increase the level of services, it will be a substantial step in the right direction."

Under the proposal, lawyers would be required to provide 25 hours of pro bono service a year. At least half the service must be in the form of free legal work to the needy. The other half may be fulfilled by other charitable activities, such as service in bar organizations or work on nonprofit boards. A "buyout provision" would allow lawyers to avoid service altogether by paying $ 1,000 — 25 hours at the court-appointed rate of $ 40 an hour. The money would go to legal aid agencies.

. . . .

---

[8] Copyright © 1999 by The American Bar Association. Reprinted by permission.

Although a straw vote of the full council last June indicated support for the plan, intense opposition from almost every bar organization around the state may influence the final outcome. A survey by the Denver Bar Association showed 90 percent of its members opposed the idea. . . .

Denver attorney Barbara Kelley, a member of the legal services committee who opposes the plan, says the issue comes down to whether it is the legal profession's responsibility to address a societal problem. . . . Even if the full council supports the recommendation, it ultimately will be up to the supreme court to decide whether to implement the plan.

NOTES

By June 1999, not only was this proposal disapproved by the Colorado Supreme Court, but the court also refused to implement a reporting requirement similar to that instituted in Florida in 1993. In rejecting even the reporting concept, Colorado Supreme Court Chief Justice Mary Mallarkey said that "we view the mandatory reporting as a step toward the imposition of mandatory pro bono requirements. Since we are unwilling to arrive at that destination, we are also unwilling to take the first step."[9]

But things in Colorado have changed, at least a little. In January 2005, Colorado Rule of Civil Procdure 260.8 went into effect. This rule, like similar rules in a few other states, among them Delaware, New York, Tennessee, Washington, and Wyoming, permits lawyers who provide pro bono representation — or who mentor law students or other lawyers — to receive one hour of continuing legal education credit for every five otherwise-billable hours of pro bono, to a maximum of nine credits for each three-year compliance period. Work for a bar association or "access to justice" organization may count towards CLE.

This plan met with little resistance, and had the co-sponsorship of many of Colorado's major bars. But at nine credit hours every three years, lawyers will "max out" at 45 billable hours, or only 15 hours a year. Thus, this new rule is hardly ambitious, especially compared to the previous proposal.

8. Mandatory Reporting of Pro Bono. Several states now require that lawyers must report how many pro bono hours they've done. Read the following article to get a better idea of the purpose of this reporting.

MARGARET C. BENSON, NEED FOR PRO BONO, UNFORTUNATELY, IS CLEAR
Chicago Lawyer 16 (April 2005)[10]

The recently published [Illinois] Legal Needs Study II found that although nearly half of all low-income Illinoisans faced legal problems in 2003, only one-sixth got help. More than one million legal needs of the poor went unresolved.

---

[9] *See, e.g.*, Sue Lindsay, *Lawyers Won't Be Forced Into Free Work*, ROCKY MOUNTAIN NEWS, June 3, 1999.

[10] Copyright © 2005 by Margaret C. Benson, Executive Director, Chicago Volunteer Legal Services Foundation. Reprinted by permission.

. . . .

The study recommends that the Illinois Supreme Court adopt a comprehensive plan to increase pro bono participation, based on models adopted in Florida, Maryland and Nevada. The plan should include the following elements: amended court rules to make explicit an attorney's professional responsibility to perform voluntary pro bono; annual reporting on voluntary pro bono activities or a financial contribution to legal aid; and judicially appointed planning groups to find appropriate means, based on local conditions, to increase attorney volunteerism . . . .

Notice what is not recommended? Mandatory pro bono. In fact, the study modeled its conclusions on those made in 2003 by the Illinois Supreme Court's Special Committee on Pro Bono Public Legal Service, which categorically rejected mandating pro bono.

It is important to emphasize that the study's call for attorneys to annually report their pro bono is not a requirement to actually perform it. Legal authorities across the state agree that attorneys should not be forced to donate their services. Reporting voluntary contributions is quite different.

The idea that reporting pro bono could improve legal services makes sense for two reasons. One, reporting would help unearth underground pro bono that we know exists. Attorneys do a lot of freebies for friends of friends and relatives, etc. These cases are not counted; they should be. Second, reporting pro bono work once a year would force every attorney to think about the subject at least that often. Pro bono is something that most attorneys want to do, but never get around to actually doing. The annual reporting requirement might prompt a few attorneys to take the next step.

We know the devil is in the details. In the case of mandatory reporting, that devil has yet to be exorcised. However, make no mistake — mandatory pro bono is not, and will not be, on the table.

NOTES

When the Florida Supreme Court approved a plan that would require every lawyer in the state to report each year the amount of free services that lawyer provided to the poor, it was the first of its kind in the country. As the previous article notes, this plan does not amount to mandatory pro bono. It is only a reporting requirement; actually doing the work is *not* required. Those who report that they have not done pro bono work can expect to have their names publicized by the bar. But this was enough to have one lawyer who heads a group emphasizing "lawyers' rights" to compare the reporting and disclosure tactics to McCarthyism. Indeed, the plan was challenged on due process and equal protection grounds, but upheld by the Eleventh Circuit in *Schwartz v. Kogan*, 132 F.3d 1387 (11th Cir. 1998).

The Florida plan makes several concessions. One exempts judges and many government attorneys, while another allows law firms to "collectively discharge" their obligation by having a few in the firm do pro bono work not only for themselves but on behalf of their colleagues as well. The rule also contains a provision allowing lawyers to buy out of the requirement for a $350 per year donation to legal aid, an idea that troubled Chief Justice Rosemary Barkett enough to cause her to voice her objections in a concurring opinion.

Finally, the Florida plan reached an interesting balancing test on the significant issue of defining pro bono. The court held that the work must involve "legal services to the poor" and the "working poor." But the court also said that working with charitable, civic, religious, or educational organizations might qualify if the work is done "in matters predominantly designed to address the needs of poor persons."

The Florida plan did require work for "the poor." If the Illinois plan as implemented actually counts "freebies for friends of friends," as the writer recommends, that would seem to be inconsistent with the most common definition of pro bono, which includes providing services to the poor or at least those with significant economic need.

As for Florida, the plan remains a work in progress. The Florida Bar has reported that the plan had materially increased pro bono participation among the state's attorneys. But many lawyers who have long pro bono histories boycotted the reporting requirements, at least in the rule's early years, on the grounds that it was both offensive and too little. Other bars have adopted *voluntary* reporting requirements.

Does Florida have the right approach? What other alternatives or avenues might be available short of mandatory pro bono? Is either mandatory pro bono or a Florida-style system the best way of solving the problem of the gross legal services shortage?

9. Pro Bono From All Lawyers — Top to Bottom? Northwestern University Law Professor Steven Lubet argues that representing the poor is not a political issue, but one of professionalism, with service as the professional ideal, to be undertaken by all. We excerpt the portion of his law review article that focuses on the "real world" practice of law — here, on the eleventh floor of a courthouse in Chicago.

STEVEN LUBET, PROFESSIONALISM REVISITED
42 Emory Law Journal 197 (1993)[11]

[P]ro bono obligations [are] personal . . . . I call [it] the Eleventh Floor Principle, and it is best explained through a vignette from my own early days in practice.

For two years after I graduated from law school, I worked in a legal services office on Chicago's west side. From my first day on the job I became our office's "consumer law expert," which required me to spend considerable time in the courtrooms on the eleventh floor of the civic center. . . .

In the early 1970s the eleventh floor was a no-man's land for poor people. It housed the landlord-tenant and collection courts, and therefore saw an endless stream of hapless individuals come before the bench to be processed. The all but inevitable outcome of every case was either an eviction or a wage garnishment . . . . The defendants were almost always unrepresented. If they had defenses, they had no way of recognizing or raising them. The best result

---

[11] Copyright © 1993 by Emory Law Journal. Reprinted by permission.

that a defendant could hope for, whether liable or not, was usually a few extra days in his or her apartment or a few extra months to pay a debt.

The worst feature of the eleventh floor, however, was not the judgments that were entered [but] the way that the defendants were treated. The judges were nasty and peremptory. They rushed through the cases without allowing the defendants to talk, and they ridiculed defendants who attempted to say a few words in their own behalves. The clerks and bailiffs were worse, refusing to answer questions or to give explanations. The only advice they would give was "sit down and wait until your case is called." . . .

Every courtroom on the eleventh floor seemed to operate in continual bedlam. The plaintiffs' attorneys were always huddled and talking to each other. The clerks were always shouting orders to the ill-fated defendants. The judges were also barking out their judgments — seven days to move, thirty days to pay, add on the attorney's fees, and do not ask any questions. To me, the noise represented the character of the entire place; I thought of it as the din of injustice.

Legal services lawyers were seen as interlopers, people who wanted to ruin everyone else's easy time. We were tolerated, but just barely. I think that the judges considered us to occupy a position about half a step higher than the indigent defendants. These were courtrooms badly in need of reform.[12]

Then one day, when I was sitting in one of the worst courtrooms waiting for my daily portion of judicial abuse, it happened. A pinstriped, downtown lawyer walked up to the bench and said, "Your Honor, I would like to present Mr. Albert Jenner." In 1975, the late Albert Jenner was probably the most well known and widely respected lawyer in Chicago. A named partner in Jenner & Block, he was most famous as the Republican counsel to the Senate Watergate Committee. Many believed that Mr. Jenner was the man most responsible for the eventual committee vote to impeach President Nixon. His visage — stern countenance, ramrod posture, piercing eyes, and signature bow tie — was well known to every Chicagoan who owned a television set. Albert Jenner was a man of unrivaled prominence, integrity, and power, and he had apparently come to the eleventh floor as a favor to a friend or employee.

Once Mr. Jenner's presence was announced, the entire courtroom suddenly metamorphosed. The muttering plaintiffs' bar fell silent. Clerks began answering inquiries from unrepresented defendants. The judge actually asked questions about the facts and the law. It was as though we were now in a real courtroom where justice, and people, mattered . . . .

More than anything else imaginable, the unexpected presence of an important lawyer recast procedures on the eleventh floor. The judges and court personnel began to worry about how they appeared. Instead of facing only disinterested regulars and perceived no-accounts, they now had to be concerned about the well-to-do and powerful. For the rest of that day it was possible to practice law on the eleventh floor as though we were in a real

---

[12] [28] I am not suggesting that defaulting tenants should not be evicted or that deadbeats should not be compelled to pay their debts. I am not arguing for "politically biased" outcomes. Rather, my point is that the process was bad. . . . Respect for the law was diminished and neutral justice suffered. . . .

courtroom. By the next week, unfortunately, the residual effects of Mr. Jenner's visit had worn off . . . . There is a lesson in this digression. The presence of a prominent lawyer can have a transformative effect on a courtroom. And there are many courtrooms that are in serious need of transformation. While the eleventh floor of the 1970s might have been unique in its combination of clerical squall and juridic torpor, there are numerous others today that differ only as a matter of degree.

. . . .

Again, it is not "politically biased" to say that justice is best done in the sunlight . . . . Eleventh floor type courts are essentially lawless in that they operate without reference to the norms, rules, and procedures that are intended to govern our judicial system. The required presence of important lawyers at all levels of the judicial system would provide a robust corrective against this hazard.

Note that the effect of the Eleventh Floor Principle would go far beyond Terrell's and Wildman's proposed lawyer tax.[13] While taxation of attorneys might raise sufficient funds to fulfill a collective obligation to provide legal services, it would not place influential lawyers in courtrooms generally occupied only by the powerless. . . . No matter how many cases they handle, "do-gooders" will always be regarded as marginal by bureaucrats and case processors. It is "establishment" lawyers who are esteemed, respected, and accommodated.

The point of the Eleventh Floor Principle is not only, or even chiefly, to provide a certain level of legal services. Rather, its objective is to heighten respect for the law within the courts themselves. This is a function that only lawyers can perform. This goal cannot be achieved through the dispensation of funds. . . . It is the presence of lawyers that would achieve the necessary results. Nothing else will do.

NOTES

What is Prof. Lubet's point? Is it that when *every* lawyer, no matter how great or "important," participates, not only the poor but the entire system benefits? Is it that Jenner dignified both the courts and the poor people who appeared there?

Finally, what if the potential pro bono attorney we're talking about is *you*, not Albert Jenner? Do you agree that it will be *your* responsibility as a lawyer to do pro bono work? If so, should we legislate such an obligation to make it part of the privilege of practicing law? Is Orville Schell correct to distinguish lawyers from plumbers, the manufacturers of can openers, and oil barons? If he is, does that make lawyers' obligations to the needs of society different as well?

---

[13] [30] Terrell and Wildman believe that lawyers have no individual responsibility to provide pro bono services, and that the profession's collective responsibility could be met through a "special tax or fee" used to subsidize legal services. [Timothy Terrell & James Wildman, *Rethinking "Professionalism,"* 41 Emory L.J. 403 (1992).]

10. How About Our Law Schools? Should the Buck Start Here? What about law students? Increasingly, law schools are participating in pro bono, both through clinical programs that represent people too poor to otherwise afford a lawyer, and with stand-alone pro bono programs, often largely student-run. To date, most law schools have not regularized their pro bono commitments, though the number that have is on the rise. While many schools now encourage pro bono and provide an increasing number of clinical opportunities to work with poor people, few have defined what their own, or their students', pro bono commitments should be.

Some observers feel that clinical programs, while extremely valuable, are not pure pro bono, since students receive credits toward their law school degrees for participating. Others think the more important issue is whether law schools should make pro bono participation a requirement for graduation. They point out that in law students, pro bono programs not only have a "captive audience," but also one which is more dedicated to learning and more open to assisting the disadvantaged members of our society than most lawyers. Part of the training of law school could be developing the pro bono habits of a lifetime.

Left on their own, with only the spirit of volunteerism to guide them, how many law students will step forward to participate in pro bono service? Robert Doggett did, but found it was a hard sell when he tried to enlist others.

Nevertheless, the number of law schools requiring pro bono continues to increase. According to a 2005 article in the Miami Business Review the Charleston School of Law recently added its name to the roster of law schools requiring pro bono work. This commitment was notable given that the law school had just been founded the previous year, and had not yet obtained ABA accreditation.[14]

As of 2006, there were approximately 20 law schools that required pro bono. While the ABA's general accreditation standards state that all law schools should provide students an opportunity to participate in pro bono work, a study by the Center for Postgraduate Research at the University of Indiana, as reported in the Miami article, showed that a majority of law students did no pro bono work at all.

What do you see as an appropriate pro bono requirement for law students? SHould it be mandatory for all? If so, is 30 hours before getting a degree enough? Dean Gershon told the Miami reporter that he expected that many students would give more time. What do you think of his assertion? Should faculty members' participation be required, just voluntary, or irrelevant? Should clinics not be counted as pro bono because students are "getting" something, including credits towards their degree?

Interestingly, many of our nation's high schools, mostly but not exclusively private schools, have instituted a "public service" requirement for graduation. School administrators see this as Victor Fleischer does — a "win-win" situation for both the student (or lawyer) and the person in need who is being helped.

---

[14] Leigh Jones, *Want to Graduate? Brush Up on Your Pro Bono*, 79 MIAMI DAILY BUS. REV., May 13, 2005.

NOTES

What do you see as an appropriate pro bono requirement for law students? Should it be mandatory for all? If so, is 30 hours before getting a degree enough? What do you think of Dean Gershon's "expectation" that many students will give more time? Should faculty members' participation be required, just voluntary, or irrelevant? Should clinics not be counted as pro bono because students are "getting" something, including credits towards their degree?

Interestingly, many of our nation's high schools, mostly but not exclusively private schools, have instituted a "public service" requirement for graduation. School administrators see this as Victor Fleischer does — a "win-win" situation for both the student (or lawyer) and the person in need who is being helped.

SUPPLEMENTAL READINGS

1. Michael Milleman, *Mandatory Pro Bono in Civil Cases: A Partial Answer to the Right Question*, 49 Md. L. Rev. 18 (1990). An excellent comprehensive survey of the history of pro bono in the Anglo-American tradition of jurisprudence.

2. *The Law Firm and the Public Good*, (Robert A. Katzmann, ed., 1995), especially Chapter 5, Donald W. Hoagland, "Community Service Makes Better Lawyers," a persuasive argument about the mutual benefits to client and lawyer — including the improvement of the lawyer's skills — of pro bono work in a world where "as much as 85 percent of the legitimate legal needs of the poor go unmet."

3. Reed Elizabeth Loder, *Tending the Generous Heart: Mandatory Pro Bono and Moral Development*, 14 Geo. J. Leg. Ethics 459 (2001), looks at pro bono from the perspective of moral theory. Prof. Loder argues that while one can't teach morality by insisting on pro bono, doing this work often enhances lawyers' moral development.

4. Caryn Tamber, "Linking Needs to Pro Bono Attorneys: New Organization Coordinates Transactional Legal Services," *Legal Intelligencer*, February 4, 2003, emphasizes the underappreciated importance of pro bono work in a transactional setting.

5. Abner J. Mikva, "Casualties of the Salary War," law.com, American Law Media and *The Recorder* [San Francisco], May 3, 2000, gives us the perspective of this former chief judge of the D.C. circuit, member of Congress, and chief White House counsel about the dearth of pro bono in light of today's salaries and hourly demands.

6. Deborah L. Rhode, professor of law and director of Stanford's legal ethics center, has written extensively about the need for lawyers' pro bono commitment. *Cultures of Commitment: Pro Bono for Lawyers and Law Students*, 67 Fordham L. Rev. 2415 (1999), discusses the meaning of pro bono and the various ways it can be implemented in a law school setting, and reviews what has been done to date. Her recent book, *Pro Bono in Principle and in Practice*

(2006), includes an extensive empirical study that demonstrates how little pro bono work the average lawyer does and how much is thus left undone.

7. Mary Coombs, *Your Money or Your Life: A Modest Proposal for Mandatory Pro Bono Services*, 3 B.U. Pub. Int. L.J. 215 (1993). With a self-describing title, this article discusses the "Florida Plan," and suggests other alternatives.

8. Lawrence J. Fox, *Should We Mandate Doing Well By Doing Good?*, 33 Fordham Urban L. J. 249 (2005) is an article by a noted ethics guru *and* recent recipient of the ABA's Pro Bono Publico Award. Fox announces his recent conversion to the belief that pro bono work should be mandatory and explains his reasoning in thoughtful and clear terms, including the monopoly lawyers continue to have on legal services.

9. Jonathan R. Macey, *Mandatory Pro Bono: Comfort for the Poor or Welfare for the Rich?*, 77 Cornell L. Rev. 1115 (1992). This Cornell professor takes issue with the recent views favoring mandatory pro bono, attacking the concept by pointing out that pro bono advocates often are too quick to decide both what constitutes pro bono, and what is meant by "the interests of society."

PART FOUR
OTHER ATTORNEY PRACTICE ISSUES

Chapter 13
ADMISSIONS, DISCIPLINE, AND SOME OTHER RULES OF LAWYERING

A. ADMISSION TO THE BAR

Though the image of lawyers has suffered in the recent past, becoming a lawyer not only remains a popular goal for American students, but continues to demand more rigorous requirements than in any other Western country, with the possible exception of Canada. The three principal requirements are extensive education, passing a comprehensive bar examination, and the determination of good moral character. America's federal system, and the fact that both procedural and substantive law vary widely from state to state, means that lawyers are only admitted to the bars of their respective states. We first look briefly at the educational and examination requirements, then evaluate what is meant by "good moral character," and finally take a look at how the modern practice of law is affected by our federal system.[1]

Preliminarily, according to data found on the American Bar Association webpage,[2] the legal profession looks like this:

NUMBER OF LICENSED LAWYERS — 2006
1,116,967*

*Source: ABA Market Research Department, 6/2006.

GENDER

	1980**	1991**	2000**
Male	92%	80%	73%
Female	8%	20%	27%

**Sources: *The Lawyer Statistical Report*, American Bar Foundation, 1985, 1994, 2004 editions.

---

[1] Requirements for obtaining a license to practice law are available online from the American Bar Association Section of Legal Education and Admissions to the Bar and the National Conference of Bar Examiners (NCBE) at www.abanet.org/legaled/bar.html.

[2] http://www.abanet.org/marketresearch/resource.html#Demographics.

AGE

	1980*	1991*	2000*
29 yrs. or less	15%	10%	7%
30-34	21%	16%	12%
35-39	15%	18%	14%
40-44	9%	18%	15%
45-54	16%	18%	28%
55-64	12%	10%	13%
65+	13%	10%	12%
Median age	39	41	45

*Sources: *The Lawyer Statistical Report*, American Bar Foundation, 1985, 1994, 2004 editions.

RACE / ETHNICITY

	1990**	2000**
White, not Hispanic	92.6%	88.8%
Black, not Hispanic	3.3%	4.2%
Hispanic	2.5%	3.4%
Asian Pacific American, not Hispanic	1.4%	2.2%
American Indian, not Hispanic	0.2%	0.2%
Native Hawaiian or Pacific Islander, not Hispanic	—	.04%
2+ races	—	1.2%

**Source: 1990, 2000 U.S. Census, Bureau of the Census.

NOTE: U.S. Census considers Hispanic an ethnicity, not a race. Persons of Hispanic origin can be of any race.

1. Educational Requirements and the Bar Exam. Admission to practice is granted by the courts of each state and by the various federal courts. Generally, local federal rules automatically admit an attorney to practice in the federal district courts within a state once that lawyer has been admitted to practice in that state's courts. Though there still are a few states — such as California — which allow a would-be lawyer to "read the law" (i.e., to sit for the bar examination without having to attend law school), almost all would-be lawyers in America must first complete seven years of higher education: four years in an accredited college plus an additional three years of law school. Although it may seem that law students proliferate in enormous quantity, they actually make up less than 3% of the total higher education population in America. For the most part, they attend one of the American Bar Association accredited law schools. The ABA has set up a rigorous accreditation scheme which, among other things, requires a complete periodic on-site audit of the school's operations and programs.

Gaining entrance into an ABA-accredited school is no small matter. Some states also have a network of unaccredited law schools which have a statewide accreditation or acceptance. Graduation from these schools will permit the student to sit for the bar in that particular state, but generally not in other states. Wisconsin has "diploma privileges" which mean graduates of Wisconsin law schools are admitted to practice in Wisconsin without taking a bar exam.

Whether a law student eventually becomes a lawyer may have a lot to do with where that student takes the bar exam. Some have argued that the bar exam is a superficial hurdle and passage has little to do with a person's ability to practice law, while others argue it is an important measure of minimal competence that protects the public. In most states, however, not only must every prospective lawyer take an exam, but he or she must take one of considerable difficulty. California and New York routinely fail between 40% and 55% of those taking their exams. New Jersey's bar exam, which seeks to make it challenging for neighbors from New York or Pennsylvania to pass it, is particularly difficult. Illinois, on the other hand, passes 90% to 95%. Many of these exams include one day devoted to the short answer Multistate Bar Examination, administered uniformly in many states. Most states also require that students pass the Multistate Professional Responsibility Examination.

Attacks on bar examinations by those claiming they violate constitutional or antitrust protections have consistently failed. So have attacks which argue the lack of uniformity in standards, including the widely disparate standards from one state to another. The right of states to limit the number of times someone may take an exam has also been consistently upheld.[3]

However, in recent years data have emerged to support the argument that the bar exam is creates an unnecessary barrier to admission to practice and may be culturally biased. For example, an ABA report evaluating California's bar exam found that for "the July 2004 exam, 74.6% of white takers passed, while only 48.2% of African-Americans, 53.4% of Hispanics, and 65.5% of Asians (grouped together here) succeeded.[4]

This issue has been raised in several law suits that have argued, among other things, that essay questions tend to favor whites who communicate in a particular cultural style, and that lower passage rates for minority members show the exams' biases. These challenges, too, have been uniformly turned down. For example, in *Pettit v. Ginerich*, 582 F.2d 869 (4th Cir. 1978), the court heard a class action brought by African-American plaintiffs who had failed the Maryland exam and were thus denied admission to practice. Maryland is a state which historically discriminated against blacks, where Supreme Court Justice Thurgood Marshall was once denied access to higher education. But the court upheld the validity of an essay type examination as having a rational relationship to the practice of law, and held that it was reasonable to require that an applicant receive a score of at least 70%.[5]

---

[3] *See, e.g., Younger v. Colorado State Bd. of Law Exm'rs*, 625 F.2d 372 (10th Cir. 1980); *Poats v. Givan*, 651 F.2d 495 (7th Cir. 1981).

[4] ABA, at http://www.abanet.org/minorities/publications/g9/v11n1/mountains.html. There is also interesting emperical data, developed primarily by Marjorie Schultz, a law professor at Berkeley, and her colleague Sheldon Zedeck, a psychology professor, that demonstrate a racial bias in the LSAT exam.

[5] See also *Delgado v. McTighe*, 522 F. Supp. 886 (E.D. Pa. 1981), which denied a challenge to the Pennsylvania bar exam based on disparate passing rates.

Under the Americans With Disabilities Act, 42 U.S.C. § 12101-12213, persons with learning disabilities are entitled to reasonable accommodations when taking the bar exam. The disability must be one which substantially affects a major life activity. Thus the court in *Bartlett v. New York State Board of Law Examiners*, 2 F. Supp. 2d 388 (S.D.N.Y. 1997), allowed a woman with reading speed and comprehension problems several accommodations including: "double time" to take the exam; the use of a computer to answer essay questions; permission to circle multiple choice answers in the examination booklet as opposed to being required to draw in circles on an answer sheet; and a large-print version of the exam.

2. Comparing Educational Processes: The Making of a Lawyer in America and Europe. In both England and continental Europe, the study of law is part and parcel of one's undergraduate university education. This education consists of from three to five years dedicated primarily to the study of law. This results in a considerably narrower educational focus than that required of most American students, who first go through an ordinary college curriculum. The end result is that, at least nominally, American lawyers are more educated than, say, British solicitors. But someone seeking to become a barrister — a trial lawyer — must spend an additional year attending lectures and dining at the Inns of Court, participating in practical exercises and passing a bar exam, and then spend an additional year as an unpaid apprentice with an experienced barrister. Thus, an English trial attorney is probably more prepared than an American one at the outset of his or her career.

Most of Western Europe follows a procedure where students go directly from secondary school education to the study of law. In France, the study of law takes four years, after which the candidate receives a Masters of Law. As in most of the rest of Europe, the organized bar has little or no influence on the French legal curriculum. All the schools are run by the government; half of the curriculum is dictated by the Ministry of Education and half by the school, with electives chosen by the student body. The French law curriculum includes the teaching of economics. Joint degrees are common, but by and large, clinical training is nonexistent. The French law graduate is thus more of a theoretician than a practitioner upon graduation into actual practice.

In Germany, a legal education begins with two years of theoretical study followed by 18 months of practical internship at a court, administrative agency, or prosecutor's office or with a private practitioner. Students must then pass two statewide exams. German lawyers are arguably better trained in law than their American counterparts because of their extensive clinical experience, which includes broad exposure to different areas of practice.

In most of Western Europe, tuition is free to most law students. In many countries, including both France and Germany, students are admitted based on their achievements on their technical trade (high school) exams. Thus, admissions in Europe can be just as selective as in America, if not more. The attrition rate in some systems, such as in France, is as high as 50% during the first two years. And with the sole exceptions of the Scandinavian countries and the Netherlands, little, if any, official attention is paid to ethnic and racial diversity in the profession. Thus, a European law student body can be even less representative of its society than in America, perpetuating a palpable elitism in the law profession.

3. What Should Race Have to Do With Law School Admission? The number of women at law schools continue to rise. Some minority groups also show substantial increases in law student population. But at least one recent survey shows that the percentage of African-American law students has *decreased* substantially in the ten years between 1994 and 2004.[6]

At the University of California's Boalt Hall law school, the focal point of the Supreme Court's famed *Bakke* decision on affirmative action almost 30 years ago,[7] there was a year after the passage of the anti-affirmative-action Proposition 209 in which only one African-American joined the entering class.

Douglas Laycock, Professor of Law at the University of Texas, has worked on affirmative action issues for legal teams representing both the University of Texas[8] and the American Law Deans Association as amicus curiae in *Grutter v. Bollinger*, defending affirmative action at the University of Michigan law school. In this excerpt from his article about affirmative action cases, he explains the underlying rationale for affirmative action in *Bakke* and *Grutter* and the current state of the law on "diversity" in the admissions process.

DOUGLAS LAYCOCK, THE BROADER CASE FOR AFFIRMATIVE ACTION, DESEGREGATION, ACADEMIC EXCELLENCE, AND FUTURE LEADERSHIP
78 Tulane Law Review 1767 (2004)[9]

"Diversity" is the Supreme Court's chosen ground for upholding race-based affirmative action in admissions to higher education.[10] "Diversity" has multiple meanings, and the United States Supreme Court's opinion in *Grutter v. Bollinger* substantially expanded those meanings and shifted their base. But however defined, diversity is not the only reason for affirmative action, and perhaps not the best label for what diversity has grown to include.

. . . .

Affirmative action has been the most effective method, and generally the only effective method, of desegregating schools with highly selective admission standards. Perhaps least understood of all the reasons for affirmative action, directly considering race preserves selective admission standards and thus protects academic excellence. Affirmative action is needed to create a leadership class for a diverse American future, including the rapidly approaching time when some states will be led by their minority populations. Affirmative action is a partial remedy for the effects of past and present discrimination

---

[6] John Nussbaumer, *Misuse of the Law School Admissions Test, Racial Distrimination, and the De Facto Quota System for Restricting African-American Access to the Legal Profession*, 80 ST. JOHN'S L. REV. 167 (2006).

[7] *Regents of Univ. of Cal. v. Bakke*, 438 U.S. 265, 98 S. Ct. 2733 (1978), which held that race and ethnicity may be taken into account in admissions, but only if done flexibly, and where race is not the sole factor considered for admission.

[8] *Hopwood v. Texas*, 78 F.3d 932 (5th Cir. 1996).

[9] Copyright © 2004 by the Tulane Law Review. Reprinted by permission.

[10] [1] *Grutter v. Bollinger*, 539 U.S. 306, 328 (2003).

in public elementary and secondary education. And no race-neutral means work nearly as well . . . .

In his controlling opinion in *Regents of the University of California v. Bakke*, Justice Powell chose diversity as the ground for upholding race-based affirmative action in university admissions. In a system based on precedent, his solo choice created powerful incentives a quarter-century later for the lawyers representing the University of Michigan in *Grutter v. Bollinger* and *Gratz v. Bollinger*, and a prominent path of least resistance for justices inclined to uphold affirmative action in those cases . . . . And so the law is that affirmative action in university admissions is permissible because diversity in higher education is a compelling governmental interest.

For Justice Powell, diversity meant diversity of background and experience within the classroom, for the purpose of improving the educational experience in that classroom. This was explicitly a First Amendment interest in the "robust exchange of ideas." His brief discussion contained just a passing hint about improved race relations; combining thoughts from the first and last sentences of a paragraph suggests that studying with racially diverse medical students might help future doctors "serve a heterogeneous population . . . with understanding."

For the majority in *Grutter*, diversity starts with Justice Powell's opinion and includes Justice Powell's meaning. But diversity in *Grutter* is a much broader concept, anchored more in racial justice and the values of the Equal Protection Clause than in the First Amendment. In the longer and more elaborated discussion in *Grutter*, diversity is about promoting racial tolerance and understanding; developing workers, citizens, and leaders for a racially diverse society; and preserving the legitimacy of American government. Diversity in Justice Powell's sense is a plausible reason for affirmative action in admissions; diversity in *Grutter*'s sense is a much better reason.

 . . . . Diversity is emphatically not confined to racial and ethnic diversity. If a university's admissions process considers race, it must also "meaningfully" consider "all factors that may contribute to student body diversity." But the Court twice pointed out that the university need not give equal weight to all diversity factors, and it upheld a Michigan program that gave special weight to "one particular type of diversity, that is, racial and ethnic diversity with special reference to the inclusion of students from groups which have been historically discriminated against, like African-Americans, Hispanics and Native Americans, who without this commitment might not be represented in our student body in meaningful numbers."

4. In Search of a Uniform Definition of Good Moral Character. The last big hurdle in gaining admission to the bar is the determination of good moral character, now a prerequisite for membership in every state. To date, definitions of "good moral character" are anything but uniform. Courts and state bars have done better establishing what good moral character is not; there are well over 100 cases in which courts have examined applicants' moral fitness to practice law.

There is no question that this negative definition has evolved over time, revealing a connection between "good moral character" and contemporary politics. Today, for instance, the issue of sexual orientation would be unlikely to defeat one's effort to gain bar membership, but as recently as 20 years ago, acknowledged homosexuality, or even "cohabitation," could well have resulted in a negative "character" finding in many states.

The history of the "good moral character" requirement is permeated with politics and subjective judgments. In colonial times, Massachusetts required the approval of one's moral qualifications by three sitting judges. Given the strict Puritanical politics of the time, it is likely that the requirement also served as something of a political and religious loyalty test. Until the early part of this century, moral character was almost always determined colloquially through one's reputation and acquaintances. Those seeking to become lawyers usually belonged to families with ties to the legal profession. Few women, blacks, or Jews were admitted. In the South, until Reconstruction, membership was limited to those who could gain entrance to the state's Inns of Court, literally an "old boys" club open to very few.

Beginning in the 1890s and continuing into the 1930s, states began to adopt less casual and more systematic forms of background screening. Undoubtedly, the growing complexity and diversity of society had much to do with this. So did the growing immigration of Jews and eastern Europeans. Also of importance was the emergence of large workers', populist and radical movements in parts of the country such as the Dakotas, the Upper Midwest, and the Rocky Mountains, as well as the Northeast, which focused attention on the efforts to exclude political "undesirables" from the bar.[11] Still, quite a few made it in. For instance, the National Lawyers Guild was formed by mostly Jewish radical lawyers employed by the federal Works Products Administration in New York City. One of its first campaigns was to send a brigade of volunteer lawyers to fight with the "Abraham Lincoln brigade" on the loyalist side in the Spanish Civil War.

In the years after World War II, the issue, not surprisingly, was communism. In 1957, the Supreme Court addressed the issue in two cases decided on the same day. In *Schware v. Board of Bar Examiners of New Mexico*,[12] the Court held that the New Mexico Bar could not exclude applicant Schware, a former Communist party member who had used aliases and had been arrested at numerous demonstrations, since those activities were 15 years old or more and Schware had no current negative comments about his character. The Court found that qualifications for bar admission "must have a rational connection with the applicant's fitness or capacity to practice law." In the second case, *Konigsberg v. State Bar of Calfornia*, the Court used the same "rational connection" standard in evaluating the propriety of asking an applicant about past Communist party participation.[13]

---

[11] *See* JEROLD S. AUERBACH, UNEQUAL JUSTICE: LAWYERS AND SOCIAL CHANGE IN MODERN AMERICA (1976).

[12] 353 U.S. 232, 77 S. Ct. 752 (1957).

[13] 353 U.S. 252, 77 S. Ct. 722 (1957). Other cases have qualified this rule in various ways. See particularly, two cases decided together, *In re Anastaplo*, 366 U.S. 82, 81 S. Ct. 978 (1961), and *Konigsberg v. State Bar of Cal.*, 366 U.S. 36, 81 S. Ct. 997 (1961), known colloquially as *Konigsberg II*; see also *Baird v. State of Arizona*, 401 U.S. 1, 91 S. Ct. 702 (1971), and *Law Students Civ. Rights Research Council, Inc. v. Wadmond*, 401 U.S. 154, 91 S. Ct. 720 (1971).

Because a lawyer's duty is ultimately to the public, any significant doubts about a Bar applicant's character have been traditionally resolved in favor of protecting the public by denying admission to the applicant.[14]

To help clarify what is meant by "good moral character," the American Bar Association has issued a comprehensive list of relevant conduct that might warrant further inquiry before examiners decide whether the applicant is fit to practice law. The list includes:

- unlawful conduct
- academic misconduct
- making of false statements, including omissions
- misconduct in employment
- acts involving dishonesty, fraud, deceit, or misrepresentation
- abuse of legal process
- neglect of financial responsibilities
- violation of an order of a court
- evidence of mental or emotional instability
- evidence of drug or alcohol dependency
- denial of admission to the Bar in another jurisdiction on character and fitness grounds
- disciplinary action by a lawyer disciplinary agency or other professional disciplinary agency of any jurisdiction.[15]

The requirement of good moral character is ostensibly used as a forecast of how one might act as a lawyer. But there are no large-scale studies showing that character determinations are accurate. All disbarred or disciplined attorneys were once deemed of good moral character. Whether the estimated 0.2% denied admission nationwide based on character issues turn out any better — or any worse — than nonlawyers is not known. Some argue that the fact most lawyers don't "get into trouble" proves the value of the requirement. Prior bad acts are often seen as indicative of future bad acts. But clearly, there will continue to be constitutional limits on the use of "character" as a litmus test.

Yet bar associations may inquire into conduct that is arguably protected by the First Amendment. For example, Paul Converse was denied admission by the Nebraska State Bar Commission for being what his own lawyer described as a "pain in the neck." He had demonstrated hostile, abusive, and disruptive behavior throughout his law school career, including threatening frivolous litigation, contacting the press when he felt slighted by his law school, and creating and marketing shirts featuring the law school dean in a compromising position. He argued that he could not be denied admission

---

[14] Deborah L. Rhode, *Professional in Perspective: Alternative Approaches to Nonlawyer Practice*, 1 J. Inst. Stud. Legal Ethics 197, 199 (1998).

[15] A.B.A. Section on Legal Education & Admissions, A Review of Legal Education in the United States: Law Schools and Bar Admission Requirements (Fall 1990). (The Code of Recommended Standards for Bar Examiners: Moral Character and Fitness).

based solely on his inappropriate behavior. The Supreme Court of Nebraska, however, affirmed the denial.[16]

5. The Matthew Hale File. Matthew Hale is a self-proclaimed racist and leader of a "church" that advocates the deportation of African-Americans, Jews, and other "mud races," and "RAHOWA," or racial holy war. In late 1998, an "inquiry panel" of the Character and Fitness Committee of the Illinois Supreme Court found by a 2-1 vote that Hale did not have the moral character requisite for bar admission. The following June, a full hearing panel unanimously agreed. Hale's requests for hearing before the Illinois and United States Supreme Courts were both summarily denied.[17] Although Hale was later found to have had a history of arrests and even a felony conviction (albeit one that was reversed on appeal) that he had failed to disclose on his bar application,[18] he initially provoked a heated national debate among legal scholars on whether being an avowed racist, standing alone, was sufficient grounds for rejecting his bar membership.

Mr. Hale's church had as one of its major tenets the hatred of minorities and the admiration of Adolph Hitler, yet he unhesitatingly declared that he would have no trouble taking the lawyers' oath to support the United States and Illinois constitutions. He likened his situation to that of a juror whose duty is to follow the law, even though they may disagree with it. Indeed, he had worked, albeit briefly, as a law clerk for a law firm where he dealt with minority clients without engaging in acts of racism. But the reviewing authorities remained unconvinced.

We first excerpt part of the inquiry panel's opinion, then the brief filed in Hale's support while the matter was under submission to the subsequent five-member hearing panel, and finally the hearing panel's opinion.

IN THE MATTER OF THE APPLICATION FOR ADMISSION TO THE BAR OF MATTHEW F. HALE, DECISION OF INQUIRY PANEL
(December 18, 1998)

In declining to certify the applicant and thereby causing the matter to be referred to a Hearing Panel, we are setting forth our reasons for this decision in some detail.

Rule 4.1 of the Rules of Procedure places the burden on the applicant to prove by clear and convincing evidence that he has the requisite character and fitness for admission to the practice of law. Nonetheless, the denial of a request for admission results in serious adverse consequences for the applicant, as noted by the United States Supreme Court in *Konigsberg v. State Bar of California*, 353 U.S. 252, 257-258 (1957).

. . . .

---

[16] *In Re Converse*, 602 N.W.2d 500 (Neb. 1990).

[17] *In re Matthew F. Hale*, M.R. 16075, Order of November 12, 1999; *Hale v. The Committee on Character and Fitness of the Illinois Bar*, 530 U.S. 1261 (2000).

[18] See, e.g., the thorough review by Bob Van Voris, *More Than Hale's Views Might Be in Question*, NATIONAL LAW J., Feb. 11, 2000, which describes Hale's "string of run-ins with the law."

[T]he reasons for our decision relate to the applicant's active advocacy of his core beliefs. When an issue of that type is injected into the reasons for denial of certification, "a heavy burden lies" upon the State to demonstrate that "a legitimate state interest" is sought to be protected. *Baird v. Arizona*, 401 U.S. 1, 6-7 (1971).

. . . .

Mr. Hale is currently the head of an organization called the World Church of the Creator which is claimed to be a religious organization. His title as head of this church is Pontifex Maximum (Supreme Leader). . . . This religion . . . has as one of its major tenets the hatred of Jews, blacks and other colored people.

. . . .

The Inquiry Panel's interview with Mr. Hale occurred November 25, 1998. At that time, Mr. Hale was extremely polite and answered all questions quite candidly. He is intelligent and articulate. He stated that after becoming a lawyer he would continue his activities as leader of his church, including his distribution of racist literature. He also plans to be active on the Internet to promote his church's racist views.

On the issue of moral character, he argued that his frank and open admission of the advocacy of racism shows greater moral character than do lawyers and others who are in fact racist but who utter such thoughts only in privacy.

Mr. Hale was asked whether or not he could take the oath to support the United States Constitution and the Constitution of the State of Illinois in good conscience. He unhesitatingly answered that he would have no difficulty. . . .

. . . .

Additionally, Rule 8.4(a)(5) of the Rules of Professional Conduct for lawyers was brought to his attention. Mr. Hale was asked if he could abide by that rule if admitted to the Bar. The rule, in part, states that a lawyer shall not engage in conduct that is prejudicial to the administration of justice. In relation thereto, a lawyer shall not engage in adverse discriminatory treatment of litigants, jurors, witnesses, lawyers, and others, based on race, sex, religion, or national origin. Again, Mr. Hale stated that he would have no problem with following this rule, reaffirming his statements that he would follow the law until such time as he could have it changed by peaceful means. . . .

As indicated, Mr. Hale's life mission is to bring about peaceable change in the United States in order to deny the equal protection of the laws to all Americans except perhaps those that his church determines to be of the "white race." Under any civilized standards of decency, the incitement of racial hatred for the ultimate purpose of depriving selected groups of their legal rights shows a gross deficiency in moral character, particularly for lawyers who have a special responsibility to uphold the rule of law for all persons.

However, even if the Illinois standards for considering moral character and general fitness to practice law allows the Committee to make a determination in this manner, the question remains as to whether or not denying certification for admission to the Bar is constitutional on that basis.

. . . .

[T]he Membership Manual for his church, which is on the Internet, describes 15 attributes of a church member under a heading entitled, "The Essence of a Creator." The number 1 essence listed is that "A CREATOR puts loyalty towards his own race above every other loyalty." (http://www.rahowa.com/manual.htm.) A reasonable question for the applicant is what happens when that loyalty conflicts with his oath to support the United States and Illinois Constitutions?

Additionally, even though Mr. Hale claimed to be able to abide by the Rules of Professional Conduct relating to non-discriminatory treatment, his activities in this regard arguably cast doubt on these representations. For example, in 1995, only a few weeks before he started law school, he wrote a letter to a woman who apparently had made comments in the *Peoria Journal Star* on racial issues that were contrary to his. In this letter he referred to "the nigger race" as "*inferior* in intellectual capacity" and condemned the "misbegotten equality myth" as "garbage" that was "destroying" "our whole country." (Emphasis in original.) He also suggested that this woman's rape or murder by a "nigger beast" might enlighten her.

With the applicant capable of such outrageous and intemperate conduct, one might have concluded that he was insincere when he said he could comply with the Rules of Professional Conduct and conscientiously take the oath. However, later cases of the United States Supreme Court suggest that these very real questions about the applicant might be a frail reed upon which to deny certification. . . .

The easiest resolution of Mr. Hale's application would be to certify him. This would be in accord with the view that [the] First Amendment is virtually absolute. Nonetheless, on balance, a majority of the Inquiry Panel has concluded that the constitutional issues involving a case precisely like this one are open, and that the Illinois requirement for moral character and general fitness to practice law precludes the applicant from being certified.

The latest United States Supreme Court decisions relating to bar admissions located by the Inquiry Panel are over 25 years old. In 1971, the year of its most recent cases on this subject, the Court characterized its earlier opinions as containing "confusing formulas, refined reasonings, and puzzling holdings." *Baird v. Arizona*, 401 U.S. 1, 4 (1971).

In that case, the Court, in a 5 to 4 split decision, held that "a State may not inquire about a man's views or associations solely for the purpose of withholding a right or benefit because of what he believes." 401 U.S. 1 at 7. The Court also said in that case:

"The First Amendment's protection of association prohibits a state from excluding a person from a profession or punishing him *solely* because he is a member of a particular political organization or because he holds certain beliefs." (Emphasis added.) 401 U.S. 1, at 6. A similar result in another 5 to 4 decision was reached on the same day in 1971 in the case of [*In*] *Re Stolar*, 401 U.S. 23, 31 (1971).

Neither of those decisions involved individuals who were actively involved in inciting racial hatred and who had dedicated their lives to destroying equal rights under law that all Americans currently enjoy. On the contrary, the applicants in those cases refused to reveal their views.

But in this case Matthew Hale has no interest in keeping his views a secret.

. . . .

While Matthew Hale has not yet threatened to exterminate anyone, history tells us that extermination is sometimes not far behind when governmental power is held by persons of his racial views. The Bar of Illinois cannot certify someone as having good moral character and general fitness to practice law who has dedicated his life to inciting racial hatred for the purpose of implementing those views.

MR. HALE'S BRIEF BEFORE THE COMMITTEE ON CHARACTER AND FITNESS FOR THE THIRD APPELLATE DISTRICT OF THE SUPREME COURT OF ILLINOIS
(April 1999)

The great majority of the hearing was directed at adducing Mr. Hale's views, both as they were understood by his character witnesses and as they were stated by Mr. Hale directly. Mr. Hale apparently holds views in opposition to those held dear by members of the panel. . . . Yet it is precisely this diversity of views that provides the foundation for freedom of intellectual thought in this country to which the First Amendment so eloquently speaks. "Government censorship can no more be reconciled with our national constitutional standard of freedom of speech and press when done in the guise of determining 'moral character' than if it should be attempted directly." *Konigsberg v. State Bar of California*, 77 S.Ct. 722, 731 (1957). . . .

Attorneys are often called upon to represent clients with whom they have personal, moral or philosophical differences. Law-abiding criminal defense lawyers represent clients accused of the most heinous crimes, Jewish lawyers represent Nazis, and African-American lawyers represent the Ku Klux Klan. Recusal is always an option. Neither lawyers nor judges are required to accept a case in which they have philosophical, religious or ethical reservations. As Judge Lustfeld acknowledged at the hearing, a judge with strong pro-life views would not be required to sit in judgment of the rights of an abortionist.

The testimony of Mr. McPheeters, Mr. Hale's former employer, amply demonstrated that Mr. Hale's personal views on race did not interfere with his providing competent, professional and courteous legal services to minority clients. Nor did Mr. Hale's beliefs interfere with his professional relationship with the secretary assigned to him by the law firm, even though that secretary was known to have borne a biracial child during an interracial marriage; a notion anathema to Mr. Hale.

. . . .

Konigsberg holds that while a state bar can require good moral character, the term good moral character cannot be defined to equate "unorthodox political beliefs or membership in lawful political parties with bad moral character."

. . . .

Mr. Hale has the right to practice law despite holding views that will undoubtedly be uncomfortable to the members of the legal community he will come into contact with, as well as the general citizenry. There is no competent evidence demonstrating anything other than Mr. Hale's good moral character as it is defined by the relevant United States and Illinois Supreme Court cases. The most noble action that we can take as lawyers is to protect, defend and preserve the rights of those with whom we may personally disagree. Let that noble action start here by certifying Mr. Hale for admission to the Illinois Bar.

IN THE MATTER OF THE APPLICATION FOR ADMISSION TO THE BAR OF MATTHEW F. HALE, DECISION OF HEARING PANEL
(Hearing April 10, 1999; Decision June 30, 1999)

This case is not about Mr. Hale's First Amendment rights. He is certainly entitled to his own beliefs, and the free expression thereof. The issue here is whether Mr. Hale possesses the requisite character and fitness for admission to the practice of law. The applicant has the burden of proving [this] by clear and convincing evidence. . . .

Having considered all the evidence, and having observed the witness' testimony, including that of the applicant, it is the unanimous decision of this panel that the applicant has not met his burden of proof, and that he should not be recommended for certification. While relying on the entire record in support of its decision, the panel specifically notes the following:

1. The applicant expressed no difficulty in taking the necessary oath to become an attorney. However, a willingness to take the oath does not end our inquiry. . . . [H]aving observed Mr. Hale's testimony, the panel finds that he has failed to show that he will abide by the Rules of Professional Conduct.

In the first instance, Mr. Hale has an incorrect view as to the application of the Rules to his behavior. The substance of his testimony was that he believed these rules only applied to him when he was actually working as a lawyer, and not at any other time. The view is, of course, incorrect. The Rules of Professional Conduct govern the conduct of lawyers in all their actions. Many attorneys have been disciplined over the years for actions outside of traditional legal activities. Even more troubling to the panel is Mr. Hale's belief that . . . the Rules of Professional Conduct (specifically Rule 8.4(a)5 which forbids adverse discriminatory treatment of others) did not apply to his "private behavior in the exercise of his religion." . . . Mr. Hale's own words lead to the conclusion that he intends to follow the Rules only when he feels like it, and feels free to disregard them at any time, as he deems necessary.

. . . . One document [from his church] that Mr. Hale believes in is entitled "The Sixteen Commandments of Creativity." . . . Commandment 4 states: "The guiding principle of all your actions shall be: What is best for the White Race?" . . . Commandment 7 states: "Show preferential treatment in business dealings with members of your own race. Phase out all dealing with Jews as soon as possible. Do not employ niggers or other coloreds." . . .

Mr. Hale's long standing and strongly held beliefs are in absolute contradiction to the letter and spirit of Rule 8.4(a)5. He is absolutely entitled to hold these beliefs, but at the same time the public and the bar are entitled to be treated fairly and decently by attorneys. . . .

2. The panel is also concerned about a letter that Mr. Hale sent to a Ms. Roberson on July 22, 1995. At that time, Mr. Hale was a 24 year old college graduate, about to enter law school that fall. The letter was in response to Ms. Roberson's published comments in support of Affirmative Action programs. The actual letter [quoted by the Inquiry Panel] is part of the record herein. To say that the letter is insulting and totally inappropriate, is to put it mildly. To suggest, as the applicant did in his brief, that the letter does not contain "fighting words" and is therefore protected from our scrutiny by the First Amendment is simply erroneous.

Mr. Hale was questioned about the letter by the panel. He had the chance to clearly and positively repudiate it, to attribute it to youth, or poor judgment — he did not do so. In fact, he stated that this letter, referring to Ms. Roberson's rape or murder at the hands of a "nigger beast" was not beyond the pale of a letter a lawyer would write. . . . Mr. Hale also testified that he did not feel that the reference to a rape or murder by a "nigger beast" was insulting.

This statement shows a monumental lack of sound judgment. This lack of judgment will surely set the applicant, if admitted to the bar, on a collision course with the Rules of Professional Conduct.

NOTES

The two disciplinary panels' decisions and Hale's brief (written, interestingly, by his Jewish attorneys) rarely intersect. What may underlie the panels' decisions without being clearly stated is what Donald Lundberg of the Indiana Supreme Court Disciplinary Commission later described as Hale's "ability to perform the functions of a lawyer in a responsible manner."[19] It is a necessary part of legal practice that lawyers, no matter where they practice, deal on a daily basis with men and women, and Jewish-, African-, Asian- and Hispanic-Americans as opposing counsel, court personnel, or members of the bench. Asked Lundberg, "Can an individual who has expressed such hateful attitudes towards non-white people, indeed one who has founded a 'church' dedicated to the very notion of white superiority and non-white inferiority, be trusted to work within a system that relies upon functional working relationships with opposing counsel and respect towards the bench? I think not."

Hale's legal woes did not end with his denial of admission. He was later sued by two men injured by Benjamin Smith, a member of Mr. Hale's church who, allegedly motivated by news of Hale's denial of bar admission, went on a murder spree across two states in 1999, targeting blacks, Jews, and Asian-Americans. After Smith committed suicide in the face of imminent capture by the police, Hale stated "As far as we're concerned, the loss is one white man." By 2006, Hale was in prison for acts not related to his abortive attempt to practice law.

---

[19] On-line discussion; remarks used with permission.

6. Other "Character" Grounds for Denying Admission. We now look briefly at some of the other grounds that courts and bars have cited in making findings that an applicant is not of good moral character.

Lack of Candor. One of the most frequently cited reasons for denial of admission is the failure to answer truthfully while applying for membership. False, misleading, or evasive answers on bar applications may, in and of themselves, be sufficient grounds for finding a lack of fitness to practice. For example, in the case of *In re Greenberg*, 126 Ariz. 290 (1980), the Arizona Supreme Court held that falsely testifying before the bar's committee was enough of a breach of the duty of candor to deny admission based on lack of good moral character. The rules on this issue vary materially from state to state.

Conviction of a Crime. Felony convictions usually stack the cards against the applicant, although the passage of time after the completion of a sentence, coupled with clear rehabilitation, may result in leniency about admission in some states. This lenient attitude is by no means guaranteed and is applied unevenly. Admission is more likely after commission of a misdemeanor, but criteria are applied as unevenly as with felonies.

Drug Use. Drug use has often been excused when accompanied by strong evidence of rehabilitation and a substantial passage of time. Conviction for possession of a small quantity of marijuana has been held insufficient in several states to disqualify an applicant. The New Jersey Supreme Court has recognized that drug addiction is a treatable disease.[20] A prior criminal record, where all of the offenses were related to drug addiction begun as a teenager, and where 12 years had passed since such offenses and 13 since the last drug use, was held not to be grounds for denying admission in Maryland.[21]

Mental Health. The mental health of applicants is something that traditionally has been of concern to state bar boards. "The purpose is not to thin the herd of people admitted to practice, but to ascertain whether they're able to function," Erica Moeser, then president of the National Conference of Bar Examiners, told the *ABA Journal* in 2000. In Colorado, two law school graduates sued their state's bar examiners over a requirement to include all information about mental health for a period of five years prior to their applications.[22] They argued that the inquiries should focus on conduct, a more accurate gauge of a person's fitness.

In Virginia, a request for information about "any mental, emotional or nervous disorders" was deemed too broad; the question was rewritten to include only treatment over the last five years for illnesses that significantly impair "behavior, judgment, understanding, capacity to recognize reality, or ability to function in school, work, or other important life activities." *Texas State Board of Law Examiners v. Malloy*, 793 S.W.2d 753 (Tex. 1990), considered the applicant's having been in counseling as a teenager to be relevant. In *In re Ronwin*, 113 Ariz. 357 (1976), the admissions board's finding of a

---

[20] *In re Strait*, 577 A.2d 149 (N.J. 1990).

[21] *Application of A.T.*, 286 Md. 507 (1979).

[22] *Doe v. Colorado Supreme Court*, No. 99-M-967.

"personality disorder" which it believed would impair the applicant's performance was upheld by the Arizona Supreme Court.

Several bars have been sued or threatened with suit under the Americans With Disabilities Act and state privacy laws for prying too closely or without cause into these issues. Alcohol abuse has also resulted in inconsistent findings of fitness. In at least one case, alcoholism was found to be grounds for denial of admission.[23] It is unclear whether alcoholism itself would today be held sufficient grounds for exclusion.

Financial Problems. While the Supremacy Clause prevents a state from denying admission to the bar solely because of an applicant's filing for bankruptcy, money problems have nevertheless been held relevant in determining admission to the practice of law in New York,[24] Minnesota and Oregon,[25] as well as other states. Some states have cases going both ways on this issue. Thus, in Florida, the mere fact that debts are incurred beyond a debtor's present ability to repay is not sufficient to warrant denial of admission.[26] But where a precipitous bankruptcy was filed before even the first installment of a debt was due, that constituted grounds for denial of admission based on financial irresponsibility.[27]

Personal Lifestyles. The past 20 years have seen a material liberalization of how the courts look at applicants' private lives. Even in relatively conservative states, such as in the South, courts have held that an applicant who is living with someone of the opposite sex outside of marriage would not today be denied admission,[28] and that it is not appropriate to ask an applicant about the commission of homosexual acts, since to do so would violate the *Schware/ Konigsberg* "rational connection" standard.[29]

7. Some Problems of Multiple Jurisdictions. It is generally recognized that New Jersey tries to be tough on bar admissions to discourage lawyers from New York and Pennsylvania, both bigger neighbors with large legal centers, from invading their courts en masse. Most states participate to some extent in a system of "reciprocity," which gives experienced counsel the opportunity to gain admission in another state based on that experience, a series of personal references, and sometimes a foreshortened (and much easier) bar examination. New Jersey does not, making it as difficult for experienced lawyers from a neighboring state to gain admission as it is for new law school graduates (maybe more difficult, since the experienced lawyer may be much less prepared or less willing to take a tough bar exam). Of course, anyone from Pennsylvania or New York who is ready and able to take the full New Jersey bar exam and pass it will still be admitted to practice in that state. But what

---

[23] *In re Monaghan*, 167 A.2d 81 (Vt. 1961).

[24] *In re Anonymous*, 74 N.Y.2d 938, 549 N.E.2d 472, 550 N.Y.S.2d 270 (1989), where applicant had displayed an inability to handle finances and suffered a bankruptcy, but the court found the bankruptcy not to be the sole reason for denial.

[25] *Application of Gahan*, 279 N.W.2d 826 (Minn. 1979), and *Application of Taylor*, 293 Or. 285 (1982), where the applicants had failed to repay student loans.

[26] *In re Groot*, 365 So. 2d 164 (Fla. 1978).

[27] *In re G.W.L.*, 364 So. 2d 454 (Fla. 1978).

[28] *Cord v. Gibb*, 219 Va. 1019, 254 S.E.2d 71 (1979).

[29] *In re N.R.S.*, 403 So. 2d 1315 (Fla. 1981).

about the federal courts, which after all are arms of the United States government? May the federal courts in New Jersey still restrict membership to New Jersey bar members? Yes, according to *In re Roberts*, 682 F.2d 105 (3d Cir. 1982), which noted that cases in federal court often rely on state law.

As recently as 1998 the California Supreme Court's ruling in *Birbrower, Montalbano, Condon & Frank v. Superior Court*, 17 Cal. 4th 119 (1998) prohibited a New York law firm from collecting fees from a dissatisfied California client because the firm, in advising the client about settling a pending arbitration matter, had practiced law in California without a license. The *Birbrower* court broadly defined both "the practice of law" and "in California", implying that the latter term might include a "virtual" electronic presence without physically being in the state.

Despite some states' restrictiveness, the modern day practice of law is full of lawyers with national venues, especially those who work for companies that do business throughout the country. Within a few weeks of the *Birbrower* decision, the Hawai'i Supreme Court decided *Fought & Co. v. Steel Engineering & Erection*, 87 Haw. 37, 951 P.2d 487 (1998). The *Fought* court evaluated *Birbrower* both from the perspective of what constitutes the practice of law, with which it largely agreed, and what constituted a lawyer's presence in the state, where it diverged from the California case.

Before the Hawai'i court was the application of the phrase "within the jurisdiction." Fought, an Oregon company, used its longtime Oregon lawyer to advise it on issues relating to Hawai'i litigation over construction of Maui's airport. Fought also had local counsel. The court recognized that it was dealing with a case of first impression, then allowed Fought's lawyer to collect fees owed to Fought in the litigation as the prevailing party. The court noted that the fact that the dispute was litigated in Hawai'i should not in itself cost Fought the use of its trusted longtime counsel, particularly since counsel's advice was general, and was transmitted back in Oregon. Thus, the phrase "within the jurisdiction" was more narrowly construed than was the *Birbrower* court's interpretation of "in California."

If private counsel represent their clients on an ad hoc basis, they can seek admission in the new jurisdiction *pro hac vice*, or for the purposes of the particular litigation. But what if they are in-house counsel? May a lawyer admitted in New York working as deputy general counsel in California advise a Delaware corporation about how to defend a law suit in federal court in Arizona? If some accommodation for this kind of situation is not made, the practical consequences for thousands of businesses and perhaps tens of thousands of lawyers are enormous.

By 1999, 14 states and the District of Columbia had decided to allow non-admitted house counsel to practice. [30] Several other states have tried to solve this problem by setting up two classes of practitioners, including one which would allow in-house counsel to do most of the transactional work required of them without having to pass the bar examination. But in some of these

---

[30] Carol A. Needham, *Permitting Lawyers to Participate in Multidisciplinary Practices: Business as Usual or the End of the Profession as We Know It?*, 84 MINN. L. REV. 1315 (2000).

states, in-house counsel themselves have objected, railing against what they perceive as second-class status.[31]

The principal problem remains individual states' protectionism. For some small states, like New Hampshire, Nevada, and even New Jersey, though it has a much larger bar, this may be perceived as necessary for survival of their bar. For others, like California or New York, the protectionism seems more like purely a desire for control. There has also been a concern raised that reciprocity agreements allow individuals who take simple bar exams in one state to get "credit" when they come to California or New York, where passing the bar is much more difficult.

Nevertheless, almost all in the profession recognize that the practice of law no longer stops at the borders of each state. Large corporations and many individuals find themselves involved in legal matters that are increasingly national — and often international — in scope. Our nation and world continue to get smaller through better technology, quicker communication, and the now-routine use of the Internet. Many in the organized bar have not only begun to grapple head-on with the issue of how to deal with multijurisdictional practice, but have called for substantial change.

In 2000, the American Bar Association formed a commission to study multijurisdictional practice. In California, a Supreme Court advisory task force on multijurisdictional practice published preliminary recommendations in mid-2001 that broke materially from the court's reasoning in *Birbrower*. The task force recommended a "registration" procedure for in-house counsel,[32] and, more significantly, a narrowing of the definition of "the practice of law" to allow out-of-state attorneys to perform more functions traditionally reserved for California-admitted lawyers. This thinking is hardly unique to California. Increasingly, bar groups have begun to recognize the need for a "national" bar, at least in general federal court practice and certain kinds of legal matters, such as the transactional advice given to Fought & Co. by its Oregon counsel on its Hawai'ian case, and for certain kinds of lawyers, such as in-house and public interest attorneys.

The specifics of the future course of multijurisdictional practice remain unknown, and as of this writing the ABA's commission had not spoken. But many see the outcome as inevitable: the walls between the states crumbling, slowly at first for litigation and other matters unique to each state, but crumbling all the same. Discipline of interstate attorneys remains a controversial issue, with the most common suggestion being the submission of out-of-state lawyers to the jurisdiction of the state in which they engage in work for their clients.

---

[31] *See* Richard A. Zitrin, *In-House Outlaws?*, CAL. LAW., Dec. 1990.

[32] Albeit the kind of reform that house counsel had rejected in the 1980s. Zitrin, *In-House Outlaws?*, *supra*.

B. DISCIPLINE OF LAWYERS

1. An Overview of Lawyer Discipline. The highest court of each state, acting under its inherent judicial powers, has the ultimate decision whether to discipline an attorney admitted to practice before it.[33] Where did these courts get these inherent powers? They generally declared them for themselves, reasoning that their state constitutions would not have provided for courts without some inherent ability to regulate those who appear before them. Without exception, courts' inherent powers to review and determine the suitability of lawyers to practice before them have been upheld.

So, too, has been the power of courts to order the creation of an "integrated bar," meaning one which requires all the state's lawyers to be members. These mandatory bars are sometimes set up by statute.[34] The emergence of an integrated bar in most states has given the courts a way to enforce discipline, by using the bar as its investigative arm. While the way this is accomplished varies significantly from state to state, in most states integrated bars serve to investigate instances of discipline, issue complaints, and conduct administrative hearings. In many states, this work rests on the shoulders of volunteer lawyers.

One expert described the top 10 reasons clients file ethics complaints against attorneys as: a failure by the lawyer to communicate with the client; lack of diligence in working on the case; failure to keep client funds in trust; disagreements over fees; improper advocacy; personal behavior outside of their law practice; incompetence; misleading advertising and solicitation; conflicts of interest; and revelation of confidential information.[35]

If the administrative hearing results in a finding that the complaint against a lawyer is valid, a wide variety of sanctions may be imposed, from private or public reprimands to probation, often with conditions such as restitution, participation in counseling, or periodic audits of the practice by a monitor, to suspension and disbarment. Just as with criminal cases, plea bargaining is common in almost every state, with the respondent attorney often agreeing to a probationary period with certain conditions, possibly including an interim suspension, in order to avoid a more serious penalty. An attorney who fights the case through a hearing generally has the right to an adjudication before the state's supreme court. Since the proceedings are "quasi-criminal,"[36] due process safeguards are available to the respondents, albeit with fewer of the constitutional exclusionary defenses available to criminal defendants.

---

[33] It is difficult to provide definitive data comparing how states handle disciplinary complaints because of distinctions in terminology. The ABA Center for Professional Discipline does an annual report, the most recent of which covers 2004. Surveys from 1998-2004 appear on the Center's website: www.abanet.org/cpr/discipline/sold/home.html.

[34] The formation and purposes of mandatory bars have been approved twice by the United States Supreme Court. *See Keller v. State Bar of Cal.*, 496 U.S. 1, 110 S. Ct. 2228 (1990) and *Lathrop v. Donohue*, 367 U.S. 820, 81 S. Ct. 1826 (1961). In *Keller*, however, the Court circumscribed the ability of an integrated bar to take positions on political issues not directly related to the legal profession, since dues-paying members have no choice about their mandatory membership.

[35] Loren Singer, *Preventing Problems in Legal Ethics*, LEGAL INTELLIGENCER, April 26, 1996.

[36] *In Re Ruffalo*, 390 U.S. 544, 88 S. Ct. 1222 (1968).

In *In Re Pressman*, 658 N.E. 2d 156 (Ma. 1995), the court held that a lawyer who had testified before a federal grand jury pursuant to an order that his testimony could not be used against him in a criminal case was not immunized from use of that testimony in disbarment proceedings. The court held that state judges did not have to follow a federal trial judge's grant of immunity in a later bar proceeding involving Pressman's accepting bribes.

Perhaps the most famous lawyer to be pursued by a state bar is President Clinton. On June 7, 2000, Little Rock lawyer Marie-Bernarde Miller was appointed by the Arkansas Supreme Court's Committee on Professional Conduct to pursue its recommendation for Clinton's disbarment. The complaint, filed on June 30, 2000, is based on a finding of contempt in which a judge concluded that the president had misled the court and opposing counsel in deposition testimony about the nature of his relationship with Monica Lewinsky. Previous Arkansas cases involving lying under oath have not resulted in disbarment, but some ethics experts in that state and elsewhere argued that their ethics rules created a higher level of responsibility for lawyers who hold public office.

2. Law Firm Discipline. Discipline is usually an individual matter, even where the attorney claims the questioned conduct was motivated by intrafirm culture or solidarity, following a boss' orders, fear of getting fired, or defending one's client at any cost. Conversely, there is generally no imputed misconduct for the actions of others in the firm. But this may be changing. Thus, while individual attorneys are subject to criminal prosecution for their unlawful acts of misconduct, such as stealing their clients' funds, this criminal liability has recently begun to be applied to law firms. In 1994, a New York trial court held that a law partnership could be indicted for the crime of fraud even though only one partner was actually involved.[37] New Jersey was the first state to impose law firm discipline when it reprimanded Jacoby & Meyers in 1997 for depositing trust account funds out-of-state, rather than in New Jersey banks. The New Jersey court relied heavily on a 1993 report of the New York Committee on Professional Responsibility, which, as we discussed in Problem 26, eventually led to New York becoming the first state to formalize law firm discipline. The New Jersey court, however, stopped short of fining the offending firm, deciding instead to study the issue of whether a fine would be proper. It remains to be seen how widespread law firm discipline will become, and what level of punishment will be permitted.

As we saw in Problem 29, most state bars now have drug and alcohol intervention programs which protect confidentiality for any disclosures made by the attorneys seeking help. Some of these confidentiality "cones of silence" are stronger than the confidentiality required by the attorney-client privilege. While few question the value of these programs, many recognize that they create an inherent conflict with the disciplinary enforcement goals of the bar. To the extent addictions are considered diseases, the bar's programs must serve to treat and protect lawyers seeking help. But often, as we have seen, addictions are accompanied by professional incompetence. To solve this dilemma, some jurisdictions have set up systems where lawyers seeking help

---

[37] *People v. Lessoff & Berger*, 159 Misc. 2d 1096, 608 N.Y.S.2d 54 (1994).

can voluntarily retreat from practice for a period of time to participate in treatment.

3. Should Lawyers Discipline Lawyers? Although discipline is subject to review by a state's highest court, in almost every state, the day-to-day workings of the disciplinary system are conducted in-house by state bars. As the anti-lawyer crescendo continues, many argue that a system which has lawyers policing lawyers is like having the fox guard the henhouse. By contrast, physicians, psychologists, and other mental health professionals are usually disciplined by an independent state agency or an arm of the state's attorney general.

In 1992, an ABA commission reported that while discipline in most states was conducted in a much more professional manner than it had been 20 years before, the mechanisms of lawyer discipline still left many problems unsolved. First among these problems was the continued failure to have a truly independent enforcement scheme. Among the other problems noted by the ABA commission and other observers are these: Too many complaints in too many states still take too long to adjudicate, and those who complain often find the system unresponsive, self-protective and too willing to give wrist-slaps for all but the most egregious conduct. Too much of the disciplinary system continues to occur in secret; understandable efforts to protect falsely accused lawyers can have the effect of shielding for too long dishonorable members of the profession whose guilt has been proved. Certain kinds of matters simply don't get prosecuted. Many state bars expressly refuse to prosecute non-lawyers for engaging in the unauthorized practice of law. And some of the most common complaints, such as fee disputes and negligence, are ignored by some enforcement agencies, even where these complaints also allege fraud or gross incompetence, on the theory that such clients have adequate civil remedies.

Standardizing the penalty for rule violations has proven difficult in many states. But it is open to debate whether inconsistent outcomes are evidence that the discipline system doesn't work. In insisting that the dismissal of disciplinary cases for driving under the influence of alcohol be reviewed, the Michigan Supreme Court concluded that "attorney misconduct cases are fact-sensitive inquiries that turn on the unique circumstances of each case."[38]

In an attempt to minimize exposure to risk, many law firms have committees or designated in-house counsel charged with responsibility to avoid ethics violations, evaluate conflicts of interest, and prevent malpractice. One author has suggested that these internal processes will eventually generate information that law firms can provide to sophisticated prospective clients. Such committees and procedures could serve as selling points; market forces, rather than disciplinary systems, would thus control a law firm's conduct.[39]

It remains to be seen, of course, whether market forces can control large law firms, much less attorney ethics.

---

[38] *Grievance Administrator v. Deutch and Howell*, 455 Mich. 149, 166; 565 N.W.2d 369, 377 (1997).

[39] *See* Elizabeth H. Gorman, *Explaining the Spread of Law Firm In-House Counsel Positions: A Response to Professor Chambliss*, 84 N.C. L. REV. 1577, 1578 (2006).

4. Civil and Other Remedies. Talk of reform continues to be little more than just talk. Clients who want results have increasingly taken their disputes to the civil courts. Most states' courts make it clear that a lawyer's violation of the disciplinary rules does not create a civil cause of action or provide conclusive evidence of a civil wrong. But most of these courts also agree that where the violation of such rules is relevant to the issues alleged in the civil case, that violation may serve as evidence in support of the civil claim.[40] Some states have also held that, as a matter of public policy or to deter lawyers' violations of their fiduciary duties to their clients, unethical conduct may also result in a denial of attorneys' fees.[41]

As we have seen, other remedies for the unethical behavior of lawyers come in the form of sanctions imposed by courts for such matters as the frivolous filing of lawsuits or breaches of discovery requirements. In addition, certain agencies, especially within the federal government, reserve the right to exclude a lawyer from practice before those agencies. Other agencies, such as the Securities and Exchange Commission, the Internal Revenue Service, and the Immigration and Naturalization Service, also monitor the behavior of lawyers appearing before them. Of course, the SEC's new lawyer reporting regulations have garnered by far the most amount of attention, but how actual admission to practice will be affected remains to be seen. And courts, particularly federal courts, continue to reserve the right to exclude from practice before them lawyers they find to be unfit. The federal government has issued proposed rules for immigration practitioners. Among their proposals is the immediate suspension of any practitioner who has been suspended by the bar of any state or federal court, though practitioners are troubled by the possibility of being judged by the very personnel who have been hostile to their clients' claims of asylum.

C. THE UNAUTHORIZED PRACTICE OF LAW AND MULTIDISCIPLINARY PRACTICE

1. A Brief Overview of Unauthorized Practice. The question of what constitutes the unauthorized practice of law is a complex one. Clearly, someone who represents himself or herself to be a lawyer but actually has not gained admission to practice is engaged in the unauthorized practice of law. So, too, is a suspended or disbarred lawyer who continues to represent clients. But what about a lawyer who is a member of one state bar but appears on pleadings in federal district court in another state? Or an attorney admitted in one state who works in another state as in-house counsel, advising the corporate client on transactional matters that relate primarily to federal law?

On the other end of the spectrum are nonlawyers who seek to perform legal or quasi-legal tasks. Whether they call themselves paralegals or legal assistants, they in effect have challenged the essence of the profession itself, by

---

40 *See, e.g., Fishman v. Brooks*, 396 Mass. 643, 487 N.E.2d 1377 (1986); *Mirabito v. Liccardo*, 4 Cal. App. 4th 41, 5 Cal. Rptr. 2d 571 (1992); *Lipton v. Boesky*, 110 Mich. App. 589, 313 N.W.2d 163 (1981).

41 *See, e.g., Goldstein v. Lees*, 46 Cal. App. 3d 614, 120 Cal. Rptr. 253 (1975); *In re Estate of Halas*, 512 N.E.2d 1276 (Ill. 1987).

questioning its ability to maintain a monopoly. Is their involvement in drafting simple documents or giving advice about how to fill in the blanks on legal forms enough to constitute the unauthorized practice of law? Are those who do this work defrauding the public or serving a public need? Does their work provide consumers with a needed choice? We take a brief look below at these issues.

First, however, a word about enforcement. Many states still have statutes making the unauthorized practice of law a misdemeanor, while others regard it as contempt of court. Many state bars, such as those in Texas and Massachusetts, continue to maintain active unauthorized practice of law departments to specifically deal with the issue, while other bars, such as California's, have completely abandoned their "UPL" units. But whether enforcement is left to the state bar, the courts, or traditional law enforcement agencies, prosecution for the unauthorized practice of law has diminished in many states, and all but disappeared in several.

There are many reasons for this. First, the last several years have seen a significant increase in the willingness of courts and regulatory agencies to allow nonlawyer representatives to participate in the legal system, and "unbundled" services for the poor. Second, many states are dissuaded from prosecution both by the costs of prosecuting such cases and the relatively low priority that the cases are given. If prosecution is done by a state bar, unauthorized practice often takes a back seat to the substantive violations of practicing lawyers; if prosecution is turned over to law enforcement, unauthorized practice is considered less important a crime than ordinary criminal offenses. Third, many lawyers now recognize that on certain routine matters, their fees effectively eliminate them from being hired. The practical reality is that more people find themselves in need of legal help without the means of affording a lawyer. This is true both for individuals of modest means and for companies that operate nationally but which need economies of scale and simply can't afford to hire in-house counsel admitted in every state.

2. What Is Meant by "The Practice of Law"? It stands to reason that before one can evaluate the *unauthorized* practice of law, it is necessary to define what constitutes the practice of law. Efforts to create a uniform definition have not met with much success. Here is one court's attempt at a definition. In *Norvell v. Credit Bureau of Albuquerque*, 85 N.M. 521 (1973), the New Mexico Supreme Court listed six factors demonstrating the practice of law: 1) representation of parties before judicial or administrative bodies; 2) preparation of pleadings and other papers incidental to actions and special proceedings; 3) management of such actions and proceedings; 4) giving legal advice and counsel; 5) rendering services that require using legal knowledge and skill; and 6) preparing instruments such as contracts by which rights are secured. This definition may not be perfect — among other things, it gives rise to the need for other definitions, such as what is meant by "legal advice" or "legal knowledge." But it is similar to and probably as good as most efforts in most other states. The District of Columbia amended Rule 49, its unauthorized practice of law rule, in 1998 to attempt to define terms and exceptions that were traditionally left for the courts to decide.

Definitions usually don't help the out-of-state house counsel who is trying to decide on the propriety of advising a national corporation; they most probably are of relatively little assistance and even less comfort.

3. Defining What Nonlawyers May Do. Many states have examined the kinds of services that nonlawyers will and will not be permitted to perform. In some states, courts have become less concerned about the quality of legal assistance and more with providing people at least *some* form of assistance. In several states, some use of nonlawyer legal assistants has been sanctioned by statute.

Below is a brief look at some areas of law, or at least what many still consider "the practice of law," that are now considered by some states permissible territory for nonlawyer assistance. The kinds of relatively routine services described here are typical of those areas in which nonlawyers are being afforded more and more opportunities for work. How much leeway continues to vary greatly from state to state.

Real Estate Transactions. Increased mobility in the last 40 years has resulted in many states relaxing the rules on what real estate brokers and salespersons may do to complete the necessary legal steps required in a real estate transaction, including, in some states, the escrow closing itself. Other states allow title insurance companies wide latitude in drafting documents, and at least one state, Indiana, allows some bank officials to fill out real estate papers. But some states, such as Iowa, still prohibit nonlawyers from doing anything at all.

Landlord-Tenant Matters. Some states, such as Maryland and California, allow registered legal assistants to provide services in eviction cases. Florida allows a variety of nonlawyers to file many of the documents necessary for evictions, default judgments, and uncontested writs of possession.

Administrative Law. The Social Security Administration permits non-lawyers to provide representation in both adversarial and nonadversarial proceedings, as does the U.S. Citizenship and Immigration Services, by regulating (and thus accepting) nonlawyers. Several states allow nonlawyers to appear in administrative hearings and appeals. Other states allow non-lawyers at unemployment hearings. New Jersey courts provide a wide spectrum of avenues available to nonlawyers who want to represent others, explicitly set forth in that state's administrative code.

Tax Law. Accountants, for-profit tax preparation companies, and even unions and, in some parts of the country, notary publics[42] commonly assist people with tax forms, and in effect give tax advice. CPAs, some former Internal Revenue Service agents and specially enrolled nonlawyers who have passed an IRS examination may appear with clients in certain tax forums.

Family Law. While most states hold to a traditional lawyers-only line, a few states like Florida allow nonlawyers to help parties complete domestic relations forms. In Washington, parties to divorces who are not represented

---

[42] In some segments of society, such as much of the Spanish-speaking community, notary publics are regarded as important functionaries, as they are in much of Latin America and the Mediterranean countries of Europe.

by counsel may be assisted by a court-sponsored Family Law Facilitator Program. Similar programs exist in other states.

Wills and Trusts. Many bookstores offer will kits (see below). But helping someone write a will has been found in one state to be the unauthorized practice of law where those providing the help also received a bequest.[43]

Other Areas of Law. An increasing number of states, including California and West Virginia, now allow nonlawyers to represent people before worker's compensation appeals boards. Several states allow nonlawyers to represent individuals before public utilities commissions, planning boards, and appeals boards. Nonadmitted patent lawyers have long engaged in the practice of patent law. Most states allow nonlawyers in labor hearings and arbitrations; indeed, many arbitrators are themselves nonlawyers.

Computer Software and Books. In the late 1990s, the state of Texas launched an attack on both computer software and books, claiming that Nolo Press' popular self-help literature and programs like Quicken Family Lawyer constituted the unauthorized practice of law. The disciplinary authorities eventually backed down in the case of Nolo Press. But the Texas Supreme Court's Unauthorized Practice of Law Committee successfully won a summary judgment motion enjoining the sale in Texas of Quicken Family Lawyer because the software package constituted the unlawful practice of law.[44] "QFL" involves more than "merely instructing someone how to fill in a blank form," said the court. "QFL" conducts an "interview" with the user, customizes documents, and selects certain documents over others. This, the court concluded, all met the definition of practicing law.

The attack on software and books provoked controversy in all quarters and distress in many. After all, neither computer software programs nor books require human interaction of any kind, and self-help, often thought to have constitutional protections, has been part of the legal landscape for over a generation. In the aftermath of the QFL case, Texas amended its unauthorized practice statute to exclude software that conspicuously states it is "not a substitute for the advice of an attorney," after which the injunction against QFL was lifted.

4. Multidisciplinary Practice (MDP): Non-lawyer Practice on a Large Scale. Here, we refer to the increasing efforts, and increasing prevalence, of lawyers working in concert with others, such as accountants, financial advisers, and insurance and real estate brokers, in one organizational entity, sometimes itself called an MDP. In late 1999, for example, a then-"Big 5" accounting giant financed the opening of a new Washington, D.C. law firm, called McKee, Nelson, Ernst & Young. McKee and Nelson, the lawyer components in the firm's name, felt they were able to risk such an open undertaking with Ernst & Young because the District of Columbia features the most liberal interpretation of Rule 5.4 in the country. The D.C. rule allows for lawyers both to share fees and form partnerships with nonlawyers such as accountants.

---

[43] *See Marks v. Estate of Marks*, 957 P. 2d 235 (Wash. App. 1998).

[44] *Unauthorized Practice of Law Committee v. Parsons Technology, Inc.*, 1999 U.S. Dist. Lexis 813 (1999).

But while sharing fees and partnerships may be liberalized in some places, lawyers express abiding concerns over the requirements that attorneys exercise independent professional judgment, avoid conflicts of interest, and maintain confidences. Accounting firms are seen by many as potentially interfering with a lawyer's judgment as a result of partnership and financial pressures. Moreover, accountants operate under different conflicts of interest rules — screening, for example, is common — and instead of requiring relatively strict confidentiality, accountants are often in the position of being required to *disclose* information to various regulatory and oversight agencies.

At the other end of the economic spectrum from high-powered MDPs are so-called "unbundled" legal services, the term used to describe combining lawyers with nonlawyer personnel to solve the problems of poor and modest-means people in need of legal help. The holistic lawyering movement would support lawyers working with psychologists, planners, nurses, social workers, and a myriad of other professions depending on the nature of the work. While these efforts are less dependent on the bottom line, they deal every bit as much with the issue of MDPs as do the large accountancy and financial firms.

Reading Model Rule 5.4 gives the impression that not much has changed in the legal profession's insistence on keeping itself separate from other professionals, primarily to preserve confidentiality but also, perhaps, to maintain a monopoly on services. Some, including the outspoken Professor William Simon, whom we have noted elsewhere in this volume, question the rationale for confidentiality. Simon claims that the isolation of lawyers undermines their accountability to their clients and thus their usefulness.[45] For the moment, at least, he remains in a rather small minority. But a day when his vision of lawyering could take hold may be neither so far off nor so far-fetched.

SUPPLEMENTAL READINGS

1. Timothy T. Clydesdale, *A Forked River Runs Through Law School: Toward Understanding Race, Gender, Age, and Related Gaps in Law School Performance and Bar Passage Rate*, 29 Law & Soc. Inquiry 711, (2004). This well-documented article contains extensive data on admissions and admissions tests, performance in law school, and bar passage rates across different groups. It argues for reducing reliance on the LSAT admissions test, supporting first year students with mentoring and tutorial programs, and increasing the diversity of law school faculty as ways of helping to improve diversity in the profession.

2. M.A. Cunningham, *The Professional Image Standard: An Untold Standard of Admission to the Bar*, 66 Tulane L. Rev. 1015 (1992). This article discusses the political aspects of the term "fitness" to practice law, and its use as it relates to applicants of various racial, economic, gender, and sexual preference backgrounds.

---

[45] *See* William H. Simon, *Introduction: The Post Enron Identity Crisis of the Business Lawyer*, 74 FORDHAM L. REV. 947, 952 (2005). If this topic interests you, you should look at the other articles in this colloquium.

3. Jane Gross, "A Killer in Law School: Admirable or Abominable?," *New York Times*, September 13, 1993, tells the story of James Hamm, convicted of murder in 1974 and attending an Arizona law school 20 years later, and evaluates the question of whether this fully-rehabilitated ex-convict should be admitted to the practice of law. In 2000, Eben Gossage, an admitted former drug addict once convicted of manslaughter for killing his sister, who later became a law student and passed the bar exam in 1993, failed to gain admission to the California bar. The bar examiners cited more recent traffic infractions as heavily as they did the past manslaughter. *See, e.g.*, Kevin Livingston, "Convicted Killer Denied Bar Card," *The Recorder* (San Francisco), August 15, 2000.

4. Thom Weidlich, "Minor Discipline Cases Get 'Diverted' by Bars," *National Law Journal*, March 14, 1994. This article describes how lawyers are generally not disciplined for minor offenses, and why.

5. Emelie E. East, *Note: The Case of Matthew F. Hale: Implications for First Amendment Rights, Social Mores, and the Direction of Bar Examiners in an Era of Intolerance of Hatred*, Geo. J. Legal Ethics, Vol. XIII, No. 4 (Summer 2000). This is a relatively balanced and well-documented review of the Hale case, its pleadings, and its constitutional issues, leaning towards the side of Hale's admission.

6. Carla D. Pratt, *Should Klansmen Be Lawyers? Racism as an Ethical Barrier to the Legal Profession*, 30 Fla. St. U. L. Rev. 857 (2003), takes off from the Hale matter and argues that "in order to possess the requisite moral character to be an . . . attorney, an individual must subscribe to the core value of equal justice that serves as a cornerstone of our entire system of justice."

7. Carol A. Needham, *Splitting Bar Admission Into Federal and State Components: National Admission for Advice on Federal Law*, 45 Kan. L. Rev. 453 (1997). This thoughtful article advocates national admission for practice in federal courts. Her more recent piece, *Permitting Lawyers to Participate in Multidisciplinary Practices: Business as Usual or the End of the Profession as We Know It?*, 84 Minn. L. Rev. 1315 (2000), footnoted above, provides a reality-check discussion about issues regarding multijurisdictional and multidisciplinary practice.

8. The vast majority of states now require Mandatory Continuing Legal Education, or MCLE. The website, http://www.abanet.org/cle/mcleview.html, is an excellent web resource that warehouses information on each state's MCLE requirements.

9. Some, particularly outside the legal profession, feel strongly that lawyers do a poor job of regulating themselves. David B. Wilkins, *Who Should Regulate Lawyers?*, 105 Harv. L. Rev. 801 (1992), is an excellent and thorough analysis of this important issue.

10. Lawrence Fox, *Accountants, the Hawks of the Professional World: They Foul Our Nest and Theirs Too, Plus Other Ruminations on the Issue of MDPs*, 84 Minn. L. Rev. 1097 (2000). With this and a number of other articles, the ever-outspoken Mr. Fox rails eloquently against the attack on lawyers' professional independence that he sees coming from the "Big 5" (now Big 4) accounting firms and other proponents of MDPs.

TABLE OF CASES

[References are to pages; principal cases appear in capital letters.]

[References are to pages; principal cases appear in capital letters.]

[References are to pages; principal cases appear in capital letters.]

[References are to pages; principal cases appear in capital letters.]

[References are to pages; principal cases appear in capital letters.]

[References are to pages; principal cases appear in capital letters.]

[References are to pages; principal cases appear in capital letters.]

TABLE OF RULES AND OPINIONS

[References are to page and note numbers.]

ABA Standards Relating to the Administration of Criminal Justice

State and Municipal Rules, Regulations, and Codes of Ethics

INDEX

[References are to pages.]

A

ABRAHAM LINCOLN
Views of . . . 13

ABUSIVE DISCOVERY
Extremes of . . . 466
Sanctions
    Dismissal of suit . . . 461
    "Issue" sanctions . . . 461
Sources of . . . 454

ADMINISTRATIVE LAW
Unauthorized practice of law . . . 862

ADMISSION TO THE BAR
Generally . . . 839
Bar exams . . . 839
Education of lawyers (See LAW SCHOOL
    EDUCATION)
"Good moral character" requirement
    Generally . . . 844
    Denial of admission, specific grounds for
        . . . 853
    Matthew Hale file . . . 847
Multiple jurisdictions . . . 854

ADVERSE LEGAL AUTHORITY
Disclosure of . . . 444

ADVERTISING AND MARKETING
Generally . . . 791
Bates case
    Generally . . . 793
    Before Bates . . . 792
    Post-Bates . . . 797
    Supreme Court's post-Bates perspective
        . . . 803
Class action notices . . . 318
Insurance companies/lawyers . . . 810
Inventive promotional methods . . . 799
Mail, direct . . . 807
Online solicitation of clients . . . 82; 800
Regulation, increase in . . . 807

ADVISING CLIENTS
Generally . . . 631
Asset protection trusts . . . 652
Corporate clients' mistakes (See CORPORATE
    CLIENTS, subhead: Mistakes, advice as to)
Corporate counsel . . . 643
Cover up, legal advice as . . . 643
"Don't ask, don't tell" . . . 633
Investigate, knowledge and the duty to . . .
    642
Kaye Scholer case and its fallout . . . 651
Tax advice . . . 633

ADVISING CLIENTS—Cont.
Torture, advising on . . . 637

ADVOCACY, DUTY OF
Generally . . . 371
Adversary theorem revisited . . . 374
Cause lawyers . . . 378
Guilty persons, defending (See DEFENDING
    THE GUILTY)
Lying clients . . . 399
Truth, search for truth . . . 375

AFRICAN AMERICANS
(See also MINORITIES)
Trial tactics . . . 512

ALCOHOL ABUSE (See SUBSTANCE ABUSE)

ANTI-SLAPP LEGISLATION
Generally . . . 441

ARBITRATION (See MEDIATION)

ASSET PROTECTION TRUSTS
Advising clients . . . 652

ATTORNEY-CLIENT PRIVILEGE
Generally . . . 159

ATTORNEY-CLIENT RELATIONSHIP
(See also CLIENTS)
Generally . . . 81
Attorneys' rights, government taping a viola-
    tion of . . . 130
Beginning of . . . 81
Business relationships . . . 98
Confidentiality of communications (See CON-
    FIDENTIALITY AND PRIVILEGE)
Conflicts of interest (See CONFLICTS OF
    INTEREST)
Consulting lawyer . . . 145
Consumers versus clients . . . 84
Corporate clients (See CORPORATE CLI-
    ENTS)
Death, question of extension beyond . . 156
Decisionmaking (See DECISIONMAKING BE-
    TWEEN LAWYER AND CLIENT)
Fees (See FEES)
Fiduciary duty to clients . . . 54
Government attorneys . . . 605; 625
Government taping of conversations after 9/11
    . . . 130
Indigent clients
    Generally (See INDIGENT CLIENTS)
    Pro bono cases (See PRO BONO WORK)
Limited utility of ethical rules . . . 61
Loyalty, duty of
    Generally . . . 189

[References are to pages.]

[References are to pages.]

[References are to pages.]

[References are to pages.]

[References are to pages.]

[References are to pages.]

[References are to pages.]

[References are to pages.]

[References are to pages.]

[References are to pages.]

[References are to pages.]